Great Events from History

The Renaissance & Early Modern Era

1454 - 1600

The Renaissance & Early Modern Era

1454 - 1600

Volume 1
1454-1532

Editor
Christina J. Moose

SALEM PRESS

Pasadena, California   Hackensack, New Jersey

Editor in Chief: Dawn P. Dawson
Acquisitions Editor: Mark Rehn
Research Supervisor: Jeffry Jensen
Manuscript Editors: Desiree Dreeuws, Andy Perry
Assistant Editor: Andrea E. Miller

Production Editor: Cynthia Beres
Graphics and Design: James Hutson
Editorial Assistant: Dana Garey
Layout: William Zimmerman
Photograph Editor: Philip Bader

Cover photos: Corbis, PhotoDisc

(Pictured left to right, top to bottom: Ming Dynasty warrior, China; 16th century chateau, Loire Valley, France; Blue Mosque in Istanbul, Turkey; Michelangelo's statue of *David*; African Mask from Namibia; fortified granary, Tunisia)

Some of the essays in this work originally appeared in the following Salem Press sets: *Chronology of European History: 15,000 B.C. to 1997* (1997, edited by John Powell), *Great Events from History: North American Series, Revised Edition* (1997, edited by Frank N. Magill; associate editor, John L. Loos), and *Great Events from History: Modern European Series* (1973, edited by Frank N. Magill; associate editors, Thomas P. Neill and José M. Sánchez).

Library of Congress Cataloging-in-Publication Data

Great events from history. The Renaissance & early modern era, 1454-1600 / editor, Christina J. Moose.
    p. cm.
Some of the essays were previously published in various works.
Includes bibliographical references and index.
ISBN 1-58765-214-5 (set : alk. paper) — ISBN 1-58765-215-3 (vol. 1 : alk. paper) — ISBN 1-58765-216-1 (vol. 2 : alk. paper)
    1. Fifteenth century. 2. Sixteenth century. 3. History, Modern—16th century. I. Title: Renaissance & early modern era, 1454-1600. II. Moose, Christina J., 1952-

D228.G73 2005
909′.5—dc22

2004028878

First Printing

PRINTED IN THE UNITED STATES OF AMERICA

CONTENTS

1450's

1460's

1470's

1480's

1490's

Contents

1500's

1510's

1520's

1530's

PUBLISHER'S NOTE

Great Events from History: The Renaissance & Early Modern Era, 1454-1600 is the third installment in the ongoing *Great Events from History* series, which was initiated in 2004 with the two-volume *Great Events from History: The Ancient World, Prehistory-476*. The series is projected to extend to the present day: In addition to the current volumes covering the Renaissance and early modern period, subsequent volumes will address *The Seventeenth Century, The Eighteenth Century, The Nineteenth Century,* and *The Twentieth Century*.

EXPANDED COVERAGE

Like the rest of the series, the current volumes represent both a revision and a significant expansion of the twelve-volume *Great Events from History* (1972-1980), incorporating essays from the *Chronology of European History: 15,000 B.C. to 1997* (3 vols., 1997), *Great Events from History: North American Series, Revised Edition* (4 vols., 1997), and *Great Events from History: Modern European Series* (3 vols., 1973).

Each installment in the new series is being enlarged with a significant amount of new material—often more than half the original contents. *The Renaissance & Early Modern Era* joins 242 completely new essays—commissioned especially for the new series and appearing for the first time—to 88 previously published core entries. In addition, the new series features a new page design, expanded and updated bibliographies, internal and external cross-references, a section containing maps of the world during the late fifteenth and sixteenth centuries, new appendices and indexes, plus numerous sidebars, maps, and illustrations throughout.

SCOPE OF COVERAGE

The beginning date of 1454 was selected because it follows the end of the Hundred Years' War and the Fall of Constantinople. (Because they fall into this period, a few ongoing events of the 1450's are included as well.) The era is marked by the height of the Renaissance in Europe; the rise of the Ottomans; the Wars of the Roses in Britain; European colonial expansion into Africa, Asia, and the Americas; the unification of Japan; the rise of both indigenous and intrusive trade empires in Africa; and major changes in world economics and demographics in the

wake of early globalization. The next set in the series, which will cover *The Seventeenth Century*, dictates that the current volumes end with 1600, the last year of the sixteenth century.

The events—from the Peace of Lodi (1454) to Queen Elizabeth's chartering of the British East India Company—fall into one or more of the following categories: agriculture, 4; anthropology, 3; architecture, 8; arts, 14; astronomy, 7; biology, 5; colonization, 26; cultural and intellectual history, 38; diplomacy and international relations, 60; economics, 17; education, 4; engineering, 3; environment, 2; exploration, 32; geography, 2; geology, 1; geopolitical expansion and land acquisition, 117; government/politics, 129; health and medicine, 7; inventions, 3; laws/acts, 11; literature, 16; mathematics, 2; music, 6; natural disasters, 3; organizations and institutions, 18; philosophy, 4; physics, 4; religion, 67; science and technology, 23; social reform, 9; theater, 4; trade and commerce, 30; transportation, 2; and wars, uprisings, and civil unrest, 128.

The scope of this set is equally broad geographically, with essays on events associated with one or more of the following countries or regions: Afghanistan, 2; Africa, 24; Albania, 2; the Americas, 38; Arabian peninsula, 4; Austria, 6; the Balkans, 2; the Baltic, 2; modern-day Belgium, 6; Bohemia (now the Czech Republic), 1; Bolivia, 1; Brazil, 1; Burma (now Myanmar), 7; modern-day Cambodia, 2; modern-day Canada, 6; the Caribbean, 4; Central Asia, 8; China, 19; Cyprus, 1; Denmark, 2; Egypt, 5; England, 41; Estonia, 1; Ethiopia, 2; Europe (general), 11; France, 23; modern-day Germany, 14; Greece, 4; the Holy Roman Empire (essentially Germany, Austria, and northern Italy), 2; Hungary, 6; India, 19; modern-day Indonesia, 1; Iran, 7; modern-day Iraq, 3; Ireland, 2; Italy, 46; Japan, 21; modern-day Kazakhstan, 3; Korea, 2; modern-day Laos, 1; Latvia, 1; modern-day Lebanon, 1; Livonia, 1; modern-day Luxembourg, 3; modern-day Malaysia, 1; Malta, 1; modern-day Mexico, 9; Moldavia, 2; the Moluccas, 1; Morocco, 2; the Netherlands, 8; the Ottoman Empire, 25; Palestine, 1; Peru, 5; the Philippines, 1; Poland, 5; Portugal, 6; Prussia, 1; Rhodes, 2; Russia, 12; Scotland, 4; Southeast Asia, 14; Spain, 19; Ceylon (Sri Lanka), 1; Sweden, 2; Switzerland, 5; Syria, 2; Thailand, 5; Tibet, 1; Transoxiana, 2;

Transylvania, 1; Turkey, 19; modern-day Turkmenistan, 2; modern-day Uzbekistan, 3; modern-day Vietnam, 3; and Walachia, 1. In addition, 4 essays cover developments with worldwide impact.

ESSAY LENGTH AND FORMAT

Each essay averages 1,600 words (2-3 pages) in length and follows a standard format. The ready-reference top matter of every essay prominently displays the most precise available information on the following:
- the most precise *date* (or date range)
- the *name of the event*
- a *summary paragraph* that encapsulates the event's significance
- the *locale*, or where the event occurred, including both contemporary and (where different) modern place-names
- the *Categories*, or the type of event covered, from "Architecture" to "Wars, uprisings, and civil unrest"
- *Key Figures*, a list of the major individuals involved in the event, with birth and death dates, a brief descriptor, and reign dates for rulers

The text of each essay follows and is divided into standard sections:
- *Summary of Event*, devoted to a chronological description of the facts of the event
- *Significance*, assessing the event's historical impact
- *Further Reading*, an annotated list of sources for further study
- *See also*, cross-references to other essays within *Great Events*, and
- *Related articles*, which lists essays of interest in Salem's companion publication, *Great Lives from History: The Renaissance & Early Modern Era, 1454-1600* (2 vols., 2005).

SPECIAL FEATURES

A section of historical maps appears in the front matter of both volumes, displaying regions of the Renaissance world for easy reference. Accompanying the essays are sidebars—including quotations from primary source documents—as well as additional maps and approximately 175 illustrations: renderings of artworks, battles, buildings, sculptures, people, and other icons of the period.

A *Keyword List of Contents* appears in the front matter to both volumes and alphabetically lists all essays, permuted by all keywords in the essay's title, to assist students in locating events by name.

In addition, several research aids appear as appendices at the end of Volume 2:
- The *Time Line* lists major events in the late fifteenth and sixteenth centuries; unlike the Chronological List of Entries (see below), the Time Line is a chronological listing of events by subject area and lists both those events covered by the entries and also a substantial number of other events and developments during the period.
- The *Glossary* defines more than 200 terms and concepts.
- The *Bibliography* cites more than 600 major sources on the period.
- *Electronic Resources* provides URLs and descriptions of Internet sites devoted to period studies.
- The *Chronological List of Entries* organizes the contents chronologically in one place for ease of reference. (Because this is the same order in which the contents appear, this is essentially a full table of contents for ease of reference across the two volumes.)

Four indexes round out the set:
- *Geographical Index* lists essays by region or country.
- *Category Index* lists essays by type of event (Agriculture, Architecture, Arts, and so on).
- *Personages Index* lists major personages discussed throughout.
- *Subject Index* lists persons, concepts, terms, events, organizations, artworks, and many other topics of discussion, with cross-references to the Category and Geographical indexes.

USAGE NOTES

The worldwide scope of *Great Events from History* results in the inclusion of many names and words that must be transliterated from languages that do not use the Roman alphabet, and in some cases, more than one system of transliteration exists. In many cases, transliterated words in this set follow the American Library Association and Library of Congress (ALA-LC) transliteration format for that language. However, if another form of a name or word is judged to be more familiar to the general audience, it is used instead. The variants for names of essay subjects are listed in ready-reference top matter and are cross-referenced in the subject and personages indexes. The Pinyin transliteration is used for Chinese topics, with Wade-Giles variants provided for major names and dynasties; in a few cases, a common name that is not Pinyin has been used. Sanskrit and other South Asian names generally follow the ALA-LC transliteration rules, although again, the more familiar form of a word is used when deemed appropriate for the general reader.

Titles of books and other literature appear, upon first mention in the essay, with their full publication and translation data as known: an indication of the first date of publication or appearance, followed by the English title in translation and its first date of appearance in English; if no translation has been published in English, and if the context of the discussion does not make the meaning of the title obvious, a "literal translation" appears in roman type.

In the listing of Key Figures and in parenthetical material within the text, the editors have used these abbreviations: "r." for "reigned," "b." for "born," "d." for "died,"

and "fl." for flourished. Where a date range appears appended to a name without one of these designators, the reader may assume it signifies birth and death dates.

THE CONTRIBUTORS

Salem Press would like to extend its appreciation to the contributors and to all who have been involved in the development and production of this work. The essays were written by academicians who specialize in the area of discussion, and without their expert contribution, a project of this nature would not be possible. A full list of contributors and their affiliations appears in the front matter of this volume.

CONTRIBUTORS

Richard Adler
University of Michigan—Dearborn

Ken Albala
University of the Pacific

Ingrid Alexander-Skipnes
Stavanger University College

Michele Arduengo
Independent Scholar

Sharon L. Arnoult
Midwestern State University

Bryan Aubrey
Independent Scholar

Mario J. Azevedo
*University of North Carolina at
    Charlotte*

James A. Baer
Northern Virginia Community College

Ann Stewart Balakier
University of South Dakota

Renzo Baldasso
Columbia University

Carl L. Bankston III
Tulane University

John W. Barker
University of Wisconsin—Madison

Xavier Baron
University of Wisconsin—Milwaukee

Frederic J. Baumgartner
*Virginia Polytechnic Institute and
    State University*

Douglas Clark Baxter
Ohio University

Milton Berman
University of Rochester

Cynthia A. Bily
Adrian College

Charlene Villaseñor Black
*University of California at
    Los Angeles*

Robert C. Braddock
Saginaw Valley State University

Jean R. Brink
Huntington Library

William S. Brockington, Jr.
University of South Carolina, Aiken

Norbert Brockman
St. Mary's University

Kendall W. Brown
Brigham Young University

Elwira Buszewicz
Jagiellonian University

Joseph P. Byrne
Belmont University

Clare Callaghan
Independent Scholar

Edmund J. Campion
University of Tennessee

Byron Cannon
University of Utah

Peter Carravetta
*City University of New York
    Graduate Center
    Queens College*

Mariano Madrid Castro
Universidad Nacional a Distancia

Douglas Clouatre
Mid Plains Community College

Arnold Victor Coonin
Rhodes College

Daniel A. Crews
Central Missouri State University

LouAnn Faris Culley
Kansas State University

Marsha Daigle-Williamson
Spring Arbor University

Bruce J. DeHart
*University of North Carolina at
    Pembroke*

Rene M. Descartes
*State University of New York at
    Cobleskill*

M. Casey Diana
*University of Illinois at Urbana-
    Champaign*

Paul M. Dover
Georgian Court College

Thomas Drucker
University of Wisconsin—Whitewater

David Allen Duncan
Tennessee Wesleyan College

John P. Dunn
Valdosta State University

William E. Engel
Independent Scholar

Robert F. Erickson
Southern Illinois University

Thomas L. Erskine
Salisbury University

Barbara M. Fahy
Albright College

Randall Fegley
Pennsylvania State University

Mark S. Ferrara
University of Denver

Stephanie Annette Finley-
Croswhite
Old Dominion University

Richard D. Fitzgerald
Onondaga Community College

Charles J. Fleener
Saint Louis University

Luminita Florea
University of California at Berkeley

George J. Flynn
*State University of New York,
Plattsburgh*

James H. Forse
Bowling Green State University

Ronald K. Frank
Pace University

Maia Wellington Gahtan
University of Pennsylvania

Michael J. Galgano
James Madison University

Stephannie S. Gearhart
Lehigh University

Don R. Gerlach
University of Akron

Paul Gleed
*State University of New York,
Buffalo*

Nancy M. Gordon
Independent Scholar

Johnpeter Horst Grill
Mississippi State University

M. Wayne Guillory
Georgia State University

Irwin Halfond
McKendree College

Gavin R. G. Hambly
University of Texas at Dallas

Sheldon Hanft
Appalachian State University

Wells S. Hansen
Milton Academy

Peter B. Heller
Manhattan College

Mark C. Herman
Edison College

John McDonnell Hintermaier
Purdue University

James F. Hitchcock
Saint Louis University

Elisabeth Hodges
Miami University

Hal Holladay
Simon's Rock College

Marian T. Horvat
University of Kansas

Raymond Pierre Hylton
Virginia Union University

Mary Evelyn Jegen
University of Dayton

Bruce E. Johansen
University of Nebraska at Omaha

Jane Anderson Jones
Manatee Community College

Antonín Kalous
Palacký University

Charles L. Kammer III
The College of Wooster

Edward P. Keleher
Purdue University at Calumet

Jordan Kellman
University of Louisiana at Lafayette

Leigh Husband Kimmel
Independent Scholar

Dorothy Kinsella
College of Saint Francis

Grove Koger
Boise Public Library

Paul E. Kuhl
Winston-Salem State University

Julian Kunnie
University of Arizona

Rebecca Kuzins
Independent Scholar

Ralph L. Langenheim, Jr.
*University of Illinois at Urbana-
Champaign*

Lawrence N. Langer
University of Connecticut

Eugene Larson
Los Angeles Pierce College

Ernest H. Latham, Jr.
American Romanian Academy

Donald L. Layton
Indiana State University

Christina H. Lee
San Jose State University

Thomas Tandy Lewis
*Anoka-Ramsey Community
College*

Huping Ling
Truman State University

Pietro Lorenzini
St. Xavier University

R. C. Lutz
CII Group

Michael McCaskey
Georgetown University

Thomas McGeary
Independent Scholar

James Edward McGoldrick
Greenville Presbyterian Theological Seminary

Douglas J. McMillan
East Carolina University

Paul Madden
Hardin-Simmons University

Russell M. Magnaghi
Northern Michigan University

Bill Manikas
Gaston College

Shawn Martin
University of Michigan

Joan E. Meznar
Eastern Connecticut State University

Timothy C. Miller
Millersville University of Pennsylvania

Randall L. Milstein
Oregon State University

Bella Mirabella
New York University

Alice Myers
Simon's Rock College

John Myers
Simon's Rock College

Gary A. Olson
San Bernardino Valley College

Edward J. Olszewski
Case Western Reserve University

Joseph M. Ortiz
Princeton University

William A. Paquette
Tidewater Community College

Michael C. Paul
University of Indianapolis

Zena Pearlstone
California State University, Fullerton

Jan Pendergrass
University of Georgia

Matthew Penney
Independent Scholar

Andy Perry
Independent Scholar

Marilyn Elizabeth Perry
Independent Scholar

Gerhard Petersmann
Universität Salzburg

Monica Piotter
Harvard University

Cosmin Popa-Gorjanu
University of Alba Iulia

Clifton W. Potter, Jr.
Lynchburg College

Tina Powell
Florida State University

Luke Powers
Tennessee State University

Edna B. Quinn
Salisbury University

P. S. Ramsey
Independent Scholar

Avelina Carrera de la Red
University of Valladolid

Kevin B. Reid
Henderson Community College

Rosemary M. Canfield Reisman
Charleston Southern University

Bernd Renner
Brooklyn College

Douglas W. Richmond
University of Texas at Arlington

Edward A. Riedinger
Ohio State University Libraries

Edward J. Rielly
Saint Joseph's College of Maine

Charles W. Rogers
Southwestern Oklahoma State University

Carl F. Rohne
Southern Methodist University

Carl Rollyson
Baruch College of the City University of New York

Susan Rose
University of Surrey Roehampton

John Alan Ross
Eastern Washington University

Rosa M. Salzberg
University of Melbourne

José M. Sánchez
Saint Louis University

Randy P. Schiff
University of California at Santa Barbara

Glenn Schiffman
Independent Scholar

Helmut J. Schmeller
Fort Hays State University

R. J. Schoeck
University of Colorado

William C. Schrader
Tennessee Technological University

Elizabeth L. Scully
University of Texas at Arlington

Rose Secrest
Independent Scholar

R. Baird Shuman
University of Illinois at Urbana-Champaign

Marc Sidwell
Independent Scholar

Narasingha P. Sil
Western Oregon University

Marcello Simonetta
Wesleyan University

Shumet Sishagne
Christopher Newport University

Gary Scott Smith
Grove City College

Richard L. Smith
Ferrum College

Roger Smith
Independent Scholar

Stefan C. A. Halikowski Smith
Brown University

Larry Smolucha
Independent Scholar

Sonia Sorrell
Pepperdine University

Karen R. Sorsby
California State University, Chico

Joseph L. Spradley
Wheaton College

Barbara C. Stanley
Independent Scholar

August W. Staub
University of Georgia

Barry M. Stentiford
Grambling State University

Pamela R. Stern
Independent Scholar

Paul Stewart
Southern Connecticut State University

Fred Strickert
Wartburg College

Taylor Stults
Muskingum College

Charles R. Sullivan
University of Dallas

Glenn L. Swygart
Tennessee Temple University

Robert D. Talbott
University of Northern Iowa

Leslie V. Tischauser
Prairie State College

Brian G. Tobin
Lassen College

A. G. Traver
Southeastern Louisiana University

William L. Urban
Monmouth College

Lisa Urkevich
American University of Kuwait

Sem Vermeersch
Keimyung University

Joseph M. Victor
Syracuse University

William T. Walker
Chestnut Hill College

John R. Wallace
University of California at Berkeley

William E. Watson
Immaculata University

Paul A. Whelan
Air War College, Maxwell AFB

D. Anthony White
Sonoma State University

Michael Witkoski
Independent Scholar

Fatima Wu
Loyola Marymount University

Amanda Wunder
University of New Hampshire

Kristen L. Zacharias
Albright College

Yunqiu Zhang
North Carolina A&T State University

C. K. Zulkosky
Independent Scholar

KEYWORD LIST OF CONTENTS

LIST OF MAPS, TABLES, AND SIDEBARS

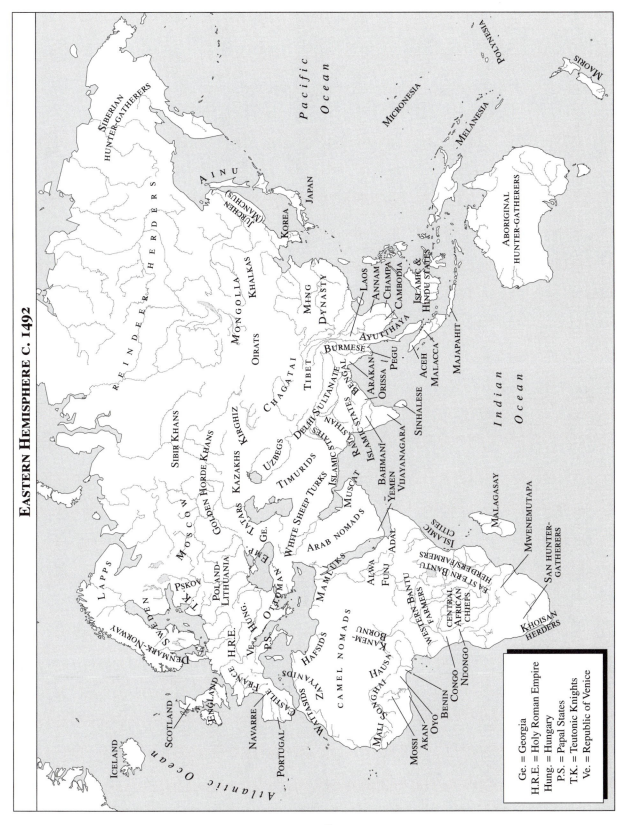

Eastern Hemisphere c. 1492

Ge. = Georgia
H.R.E. = Holy Roman Empire
Hung. = Hungary
P.S. = Papal States
T.K. = Teutonic Knights
Ve. = Republic of Venice

World Exploration in the Sixteenth Century

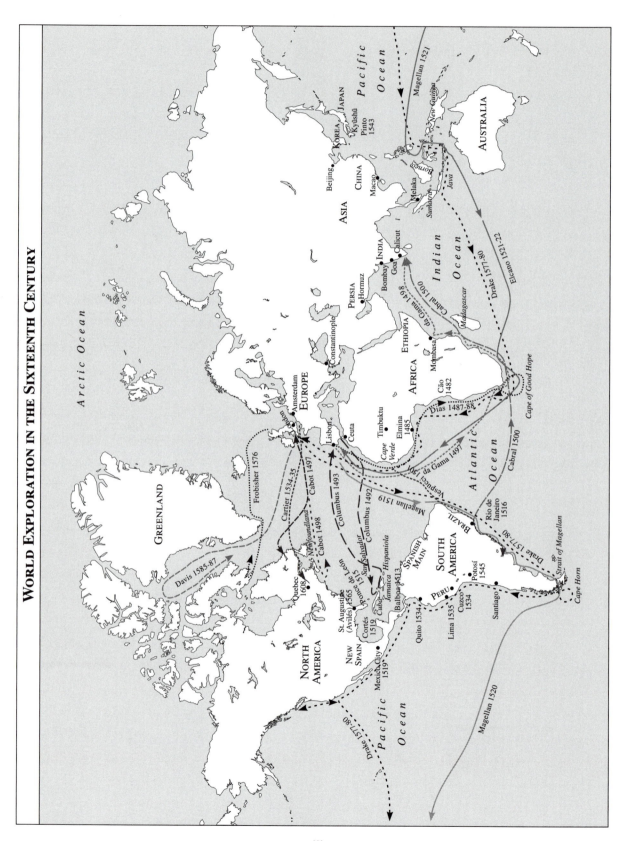

AFRICA C. 1500

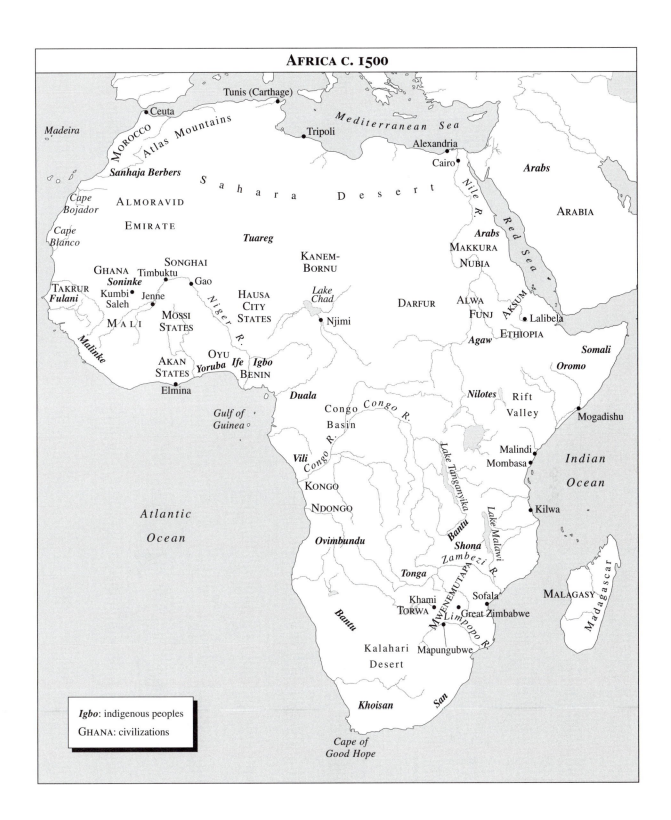

Madeira

Tunis (Carthage)

Ceuta

MOROCCO Atlas Mountains

Mediterranean Sea

Tripoli

Alexandria

Cairo

Arabs

Sanhaja Berbers

S a h a r a   D e s e r t

Nile R.

Red Sea

Cape Bojador

ALMORAVID

EMIRATE

Tuareg

KANEM-BORNU

Arabs

MAKKURA

NUBIA

ARABIA

Cape Blanco

SONGHAI

GHANA

Timbuktu

Gao

Soninke

Lake Chad

DARFUR

ALWA

FUNJ

AKSUM

Lalibela

TAKRUR

Fulani

Kumbi Saleh

Jenne

HAUSA CITY STATES

Njimi

ETHIOPIA

M A L I

MOSSI STATES

Niger R.

Agaw

Somali

Oromo

Malinke

AKAN STATES

OYU

Yoruba

Ife

Igbo

BENIN

Nilotes

Rift Valley

Elmina

Duala

Congo Basin

Congo R.

Mogadishu

Gulf of Guinea

Congo R.

Vili

Lake Tanganyika

Malindi

Mombasa

Indian Ocean

Atlantic Ocean

KONGO

NDONGO

Ovimbundu

Bantu

Shona

Zambezi R.

Lake Malawi

Kilwa

Tonga

Khami

TORWA

MWENEMUTAPA

Sofala

Great Zimbabwe

MALAGASY

Madagascar

Bantu

Limpopo R.

Kalahari Desert

Mapungubwe

San

Khoisan

Cape of Good Hope

Igbo: indigenous peoples

GHANA: civilizations

THE AMERICAS: SIXTEENTH CENTURY EUROPEAN SETTLEMENTS

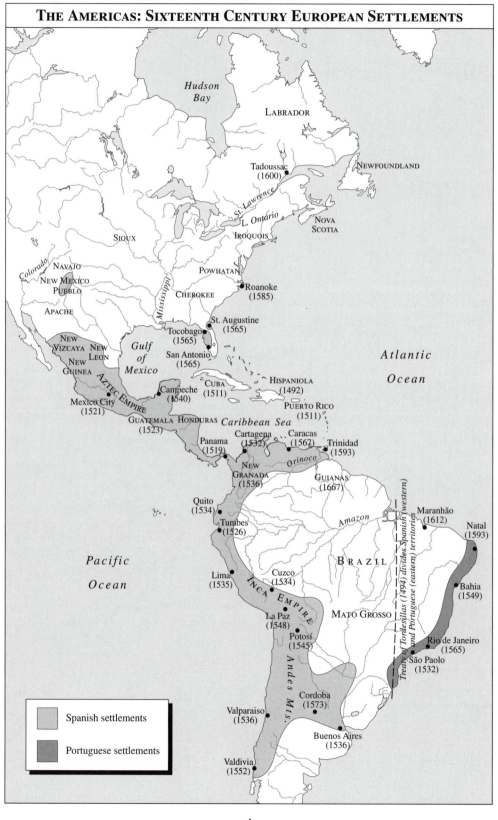

Hudson Bay

LABRADOR

NEWFOUNDLAND

Tadoussac
(1600)

St. Lawrence

L. Ontario

NOVA
SCOTIA

IROQUOIS

SIOUX

Colorado

NAVAJO

NEW MEXICO
PUEBLO

POWHATAN

APACHE

CHEROKEE

Mississippi

Roanoke
(1585)

*Atlantic
Ocean*

NEW
VIZCAYA
NEW
LEON

NEW
GUINEA

*Gulf
of
Mexico*

St. Augustine
(1565)

Tocobago
(1565)

San Antonio
(1565)

AZTEC EMPIRE

Campeche
(1540)

CUBA
(1511)

HISPANIOLA
(1492)

Mexico City
(1521)

GUATEMALA
(1523)

HONDURAS

PUERTO RICO
(1511)

Caribbean Sea

Panama
(1519)

Cartagena
(1532)

Caracas
(1567)

Trinidad
(1593)

NEW
GRANADA
(1536)

Orinoco

GUIANAS
(1667)

Quito
(1534)

Amazon

Maranhão
(1612)

Natal
(1593)

Tumbes
(1526)

B R A Z I L

Bahia
(1549)

*Pacific

Ocean*

Lima
(1535)

Cuzco
(1534)

INCA EMPIRE

La Paz
(1548)

MATO GROSSO

Potosí
(1545)

Rio de Janeiro
(1565)

São Paolo
(1532)

Andes Mts.

Cordoba
(1573)

Valparaiso
(1536)

Buenos Aires
(1536)

Valdivia
(1552)

Treaty of Tordesillas (1494) divides Spanish (western) and Portuguese (eastern) territories

Spanish settlements

Portuguese settlements

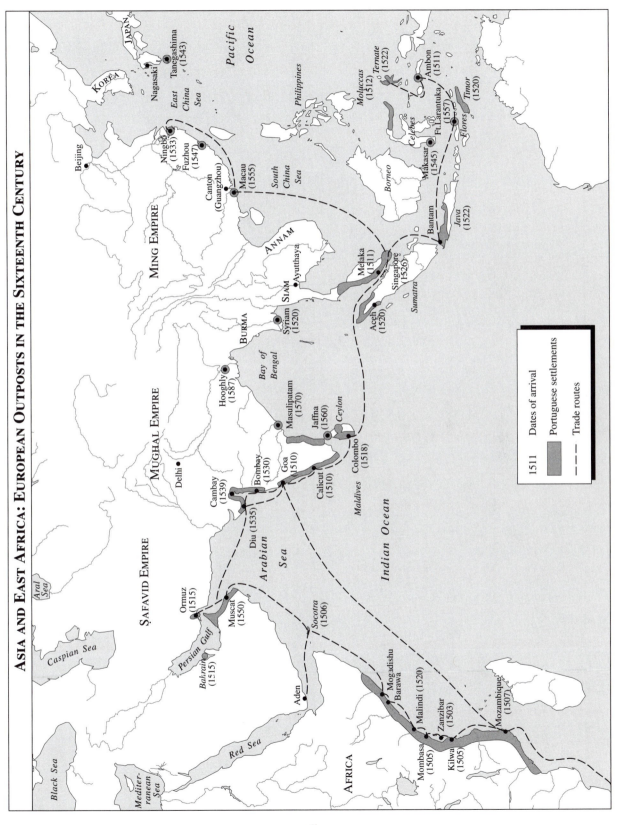

ASIA AND EAST AFRICA: EUROPEAN OUTPOSTS IN THE SIXTEENTH CENTURY

Pacific
Ocean

JAPAN

Tanegashima (1543)

KOREA

Nagasaki

East
China
Sea

Beijing

Philippines

Ningbo (1533)
Fuzhou (1547)

Ternate (1522)

Moluccas (1512)

Ambon (1511)

Fort Larantuka (1557)

Timor (1520)

Flores

MING EMPIRE

Canton (Guangzhou)

Macau (1555)

South
China
Sea

Celebes

Makasar (1545)

ANNAM

Borneo

Bantam

Java (1522)

Melaka (1511)

Ayutthaya

SIAM

Singapore (1526)

Sumatra

BURMA

Syriam (1520)

Aceh (1520)

Bay of
Bengal

MUGHAL EMPIRE

Hooghly (1587)

Masulipatam (1570)

Jaffna (1560)

Ceylon

Delhi

Colombo (1518)

Bombay (1530)

Goa (1510)

Cambay (1539)

Calicut (1510)

Maldives

Diu (1535)

Indian Ocean

Arabian
Sea

SAFAVID EMPIRE

Ormuz (1515)

Muscat (1550)

Socotra (1506)

Aral
Sea

Caspian Sea

Persian Gulf

Bahrain (1515)

Aden

Mogadishu
Barawa

Malindi (1520)

Zanzibar (1503)

Mozambique (1507)

Black Sea

Red Sea

Mediterranean
Sea

AFRICA

Mombasa (1505)

Kilwa (1505)

1511   Dates of arrival

▨   Portuguese settlements

- - -   Trade routes

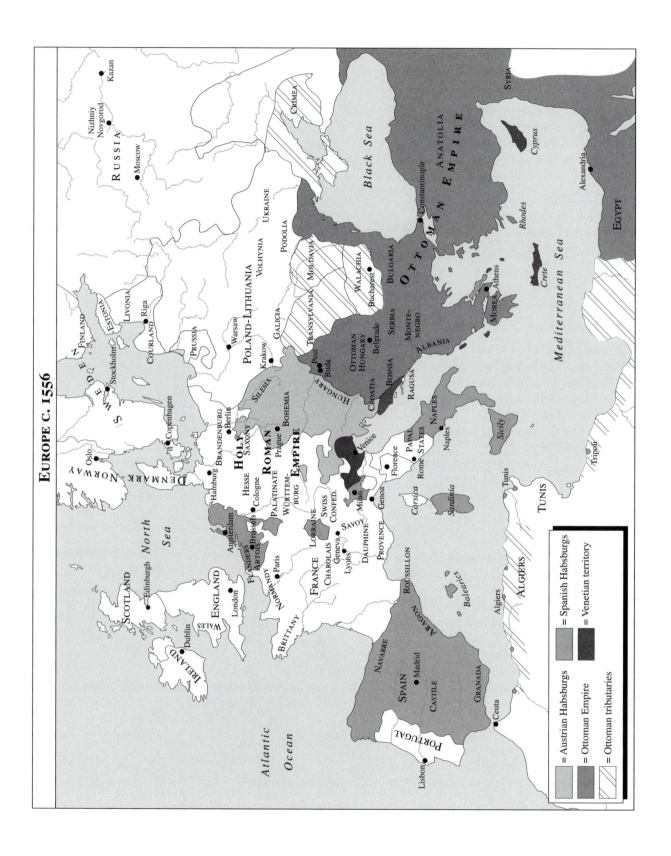

EUROPE C. 1556

Atlantic Ocean

North Sea

IRELAND
Dublin

SCOTLAND
Edinburgh

WALES
ENGLAND
London

FRANCE
Paris
NORMANDY
BRITTANY
LORRAINE
CHAROLAIS
Geneva
Lyons
DAUPHINE
PROVENCE
ROUSSILLON

NAVARRE
ARAGON
SPAIN
Madrid
CASTILE
GRANADA
Ceuta
PORTUGAL
Lisbon

FLANDERS
ARTOIS
Brussels
Amsterdam
Hamburg
Cologne
HESSE
PALATINATE
WÜRTTEM-BURG
SWISS CONFED.
SAVOY

DENMARK-NORWAY
Oslo
Copenhagen

SWEDEN
Stockholm

FINLAND
ESTONIA
LIVONIA
Riga
COURLAND
PRUSSIA

BRANDENBURG
Berlin
SAXONY
HOLY ROMAN EMPIRE
Prague
BOHEMIA
SILESIA

POLAND-LITHUANIA
Warsaw
Krakow
GALICIA
VOLHYNIA
PODOLIA
UKRAINE

RUSSIA
Kazan
Nizhniy Novgorod
Moscow

CRIMEA
Black Sea

MOLDAVIA
TRANSYLVANIA
WALACHIA
Bucharest
BULGARIA
SERBIA
Belgrade
MONTE-NEGRO
ALBANIA
BOSNIA
RAGUSA
CROATIA
Ottoman HUNGARY
Pest
Buda
HUNGARY

OTTOMAN EMPIRE
Constantinople
ANATOLIA

SYRIA
Cyprus
Alexandria
EGYPT

Rhodes
Crete
MOREA
Athens

Mediterranean Sea

Milan
Venice
Genoa
Florence
PAPAL STATES
Rome
NAPLES
Naples
Corsica
Sardinia
Sicily
Balearics
Tripoli
Tunis
TUNIS
Algiers
ALGIERS

= Austrian Habsburgs
= Spanish Habsburgs
= Ottoman Empire
= Venetian territory
= Ottoman tributaries

xlii

Mid-15th century
FOUNDATION OF THE SAUD DYNASTY

Saudi Arabia, the only country named after its ruling family, and one that has thrived into the twenty-first century, was founded after the establishment of the Saud Dynasty, which hails from the harsh desert heartland of the Arabian Peninsula.

LOCALE: Dirʿīyah, central Najd region of the Arabian Peninsula (now Dirʿīyah, Saudi Arabia)

CATEGORIES: Government and politics; religion; expansion and land acquisition

KEY FIGURE

Maniʿ al-Muraydi (fl. mid-fifteenth century), Anazah tribe member and founder of Dirʿīyah settlement

SUMMARY OF EVENT

For the past three thousand years, the Arabian Peninsula has been inhabited by Semitic-speaking people, making the Kingdom of Saudi Arabia a relatively young nation that was not established officially until 1932. This large and diverse country covers 80 percent of the peninsula and comprises almost 1 million square miles, an area approximately one-third the size of the United States.

This vast landscape had been traversed by tribes whose cultures were largely reflective of nomadic Bedouin life and desert conditions. Occasionally, however, tribal members would settle along caravan routes and at oases (like that of Mecca) and develop villages. A tribal leader or family would sometimes establish rule over such settlements, as did the Saud clan in the oasis of Dirʿīyah.

The mercantile and pilgrimage cities of Mecca and Medina, both in the eastern Hejaz region near the Red Sea, were thriving by 622, the year of the Hegira (flight) of the Prophet Muḥammad (c. 570-632). Within a few years after the death of the Prophet, Islam had spread widely, and pilgrimages to Mecca and Medina increased greatly. Islamic political power, which was often accompanied by intellectual vitality, left the region, however. Under the Umayyad Dynasty (661-750), Damascus became the Islamic capital, and under the ʿAbbāsid caliphs, the capital became Baghdad. By 900, the Islamic seat would move even farther from the Arabian Peninsula and, consequently, so did intellectual vigor. Thus, for almost the next one thousand years, Arabia, specifically the core area of what is now Saudi Arabia, was a largely isolated and uncultivated terrain where the way of life changed little from the time of the Prophet Moḥammad.

It was during this time that the Saud emerged.

Little is known of the Saudis before the 1700's. Indeed, they and similar desert dwellers are sometimes referred to as a people without a history. It is known, however, that the Saud family in Arabia can be traced back to the fifteenth century, although their presence predates this. They hail from the harsh Najd Desert of central-north Arabia and have inhabited this extremely arid land, known for its Bedouin camel herders.

Some profess that the Saudis are descendants of the Bani Hanifah tribe, an oasis-dwelling people who lived in Riyadh (the current capital of Saudi Arabia), which was probably settled by the first millennium B.C.E. Many others trace Saudi genealogy to the Anazah, a large and powerful confederation of tribes known for their Arab lineage. The Anazah primarily were located in the central Najd region but also dwelled in parts of the western Hijaz, and members could be found scattered throughout the peninsula. The Anazah were subdivided into several tribes and within each were various powerful families, including the ruling families of what is now Kuwait (the al-Sabah) and what is now Bahrain (the al-Khalifah).

In 1446-1447, according to chroniclers, an ancestor of the Saudis, the Anazah tribesman Maniʿ al-Muraydi, founded the settlement of Dirʿīyah, which was approximately nine miles north of Riyadh. He perhaps came from Qatif, the second largest oasis of the eastern province, and with his son and their respective families began farming the lands around Dirʿīyah. Thus, from the fifteenth century on, it is likely that the Saudis were not Bedouins per se but instead were a sedentary group. Within the next few hundred years, apparently, they established themselves as a landholding merchant class of Najd and acquired cultivated land and wells around the Dirʿīyah settlement. Artisans inhabited the settlement, too.

Palm dates were the main crop of Dirʿīyah in the fifteenth century and throughout most of its history, but livestock was raised, too. Limited trading in the Najd took place usually in the northern and central regions, where routes were marked by pilgrims from Syria and Iraq traveling to Mecca and Medina. By 1300, however, many pilgrims found it easier to go around Najd's inhospitable desert landscape and difficult mountain barrier. Dirʿīyah, in the southern Najd, was not located on a trade or pilgrimage route and thus remained quite isolated. There was, however, some trading between the Dirʿīyah

Saudi village and settlements of eastern Arabia and Kuwait and Bahrain.

There is little doubt that the Saud clan was skilled at warfare. For centuries in Arabia, there had been ongoing tribal invasion, whereby neighboring settlements were raided for their animals and other booty. Counterraids and, at times, tribal feuds, followed. Battles were frequent, fought not only for booty but also to dispel boredom and the abject poverty of brutal desert life. Fighting was small scale, however, and since rules of Arabian chivalry were well respected, few individuals were seriously injured. Indeed, raids and battles were often viewed more as sport than malicious aggression.

As the leaders of Dirʿīyah, the Saud clan certainly would have coordinated supporters and would, in turn, have served as defenders during attacks. It is also likely that the Saud Dynasty spirited their own raids on Bedouins and other settlement people. In any event, they must have been successful at warfare, for leaders of the time had to keep fighting and winning to maintain their positions, and Saudi leaders kept their stronghold for centuries.

In the fifteenth century, the clan was not called "Saud," which is actually a given, or first, name. Surnames were not used in Arabia, but one would be known as "ibn" or "bint" (son of or daughter of), followed by one's father's name. The eponym for the name "Saudi Arabia" is Saud ibn Muḥammad ibn Mughrin (d. 1725), an eighth-generation descendant of Maniʿ al-Muraydi, who became emir of Dirʿīyah in the 1710's. Mughrin was not a significant historical figure, but his son, Muḥammad ibn Saud, who became emir of Dirʿīyah in 1726, combined his power with that of the strict Salafi/Wahhabi Muslim Muḥammad ibn ʿAbd al-Wahhab and established the first Saudi state.

The Saud Dynasty was unable to extend its power beyond the small village of Dirʿīyah, a settlement that may have had about seventy families only, beyond the fifteenth century. When joined with Wahhabi Islam in the early 1700's, however, the Saudis began their extraordinary feat of unifying under their banner the expansive terrain and the diverse tribes of Arabia.

SIGNIFICANCE

The Saud Dynasty, made up of descendants of a powerful Arabian confederation, has survived for hundreds of years in one of the harshest environments of the Middle East, often without adequate sustenance or supplies, and certainly without luxuries. The early twenty-first century sees the Saudis, direct descendants of ancient Arab peoples and their cultures, living in Najd still.

The Saudis also were leaders of their region for generations, a remarkable amount of time in a place where, as a matter of course, loyalty was fleeting. Unlike most Middle Eastern countries, the Saudis of Najd have never been under foreign control and have experienced little, if any, outside cultural influence.

—*Lisa Urkevich*

FURTHER READING

Al-Rasheed, Madawi. *A History of Saudi Arabia*. New York: Cambridge University Press, 2002. An accessible, scholarly history written by a social anthropologist.

Peterson, J. E. *Historical Dictionary of Saudi Arabia* Asian Historical Dictionaries 14. Washington, D.C.: Scarecrow Press, 1993. An excellent dictionary that includes terms, people, regions, and brief histories. Extensive bibliography.

Vassiliev, Alexei. *The History of Saudi Arabia*. London: Saqi Books, 1998. The most comprehensive history of Saudi Arabia to date. Well cited, including many Russian sources.

SEE ALSO: Late 15th cent.: Mombasa, Malindi, and Kilwa Reach Their Height; May, 1485-Apr. 13, 1517: Mamlūk-Ottoman Wars.

1450's-1471
CHAMPA CIVIL WARS

The Kingdom of Champa, unable to maintain a stable royal system, suffered through decades of civil wars, which fatally weakened the kingdom against the Vietnamese. The Vietnamese defeated Champa in a battle that ended Cham power in Southeast Asia.

LOCALE: Central and South Vietnam

CATEGORIES: Wars, uprisings, and civil unrest; government and politics; expansion and land acquisition

KEY FIGURES

Qui Lai (d. 1449), king of Champa, r. 1446-1449, who was installed by the Vietnamese

Qui Do (Bi Do; d. 1458), king of Champa, r. 1449-1458, and younger brother of Qui Lai

Ban La Tra Nguyet (Tra Duyet; d. 1460), king of Champa, r. 1458-1460

Ban La Tra Toan (d. 1471), king of Champa, r. 1460-1471

Le Thanh Tong (1442-1497), emperor of Vietnam, r. 1460-1497

SUMMARY OF EVENT

The Kingdom of Champa suffered from civil wars at a time that was already highly volatile for the state and the region. The Vietnamese had been pressuring Champa from the north, and wars with the Cambodians had alienated Champa from that state. Only a unified kingdom could hope to survive in these circumstances, but unity eluded Champa.

The death of Champa's successful king Jaya Sinhavarman V (r. 1401-1441) ushered in a period of civil strife. From its beginnings in the first and second century B.C.E., Champa had always been a less centrally organized and less ethnically homogeneous state than its neighbors and rivals. The people along the coast were descendants of maritime nomads from Malaysia and Indonesia, for example, while the uphill Cham consisted of mountain tribes such as the Rhade and Jarai. Once an orderly royal succession had been disrupted, the sociopolitical structure of Champa invited prolonged strife. By 1450, Champa was a nation populated by a mix of people whose diversity and rather loose political association worked against, rather than toward, a unified nation.

After Maija Vijaya (r. 1441-1446) won the contest to succeed his uncle, Jaya Sinhavarman, in 1441, Champa's civil unrest continued, and it did not give up its habit of seaborne raids to the north. Cham raiders continued to pillage land contested with the Vietnamese empire, called Dai Viet. These raids had earned the Cham the enmity of the Vietnamese, who had fought each other for more than fourteen hundred years.

After King Maija Vijaya raided the Vietnamese province of Hoa Chau (near modern Quang Tri) for two consecutive years, the Vietnamese struck back in 1446. The civil unrest against Maija Vijaya's rule helped the success of the Vietnamese punitive expedition. In 1446, Vietnamese forces captured Champa's capital of Vijaya, and Vietnam intervened directly in the Champa civil war. Maija Vijaya was captured, deposed, and deported to Vietnam, together with his wives. The Vietnamese made one of his cousins, Qui Lai, the new king of Champa.

Even though Qui Lai was a son of Jaya Sinhavarman, his installment by the Vietnamese angered many Cham, who violently opposed his rule. Despite the reoccupation of the capital, Vijaya, by Champa soon after the Vietnamese departed, the nation did not regain political stability. After just three years, Qui Do succeeded his older brother, Qui Lai, as the new king.

In 1458, Ban La Tra Nguyet killed Qui Do and usurped the throne. In an effort to shore up the nation's position against the Vietnamese, King Tra Nguyet sent his younger brother Ban La Tra Toan to the Ming court in Beijing. Tra Toan's mission was to ask the Chinese emperor for the throne of Vietnam. Nominally, China still considered both the Dai Viet Empire and the Kingdom of Champa as dependent vassal states. In 1407, a Chinese invasion of Vietnam had saved Champa from a Vietnamese onslaught. While China had ruled Vietnam briefly from 1407 until 1428, Champa had been able to recover some land lost to Dai Viet. King Tra Nguyet's strategy was to look to China as a possible ally, but the Ming court declined any intervention in Vietnam, where it had suffered a military defeat and had been expelled. The Vietnamese were made alert by these events, and as civil strife troubled Champa, they launched a few raids there.

Tra Toan became king of Champa in 1460, upon the death of his brother. Yet some Cham still were opposed to his rule, which rested on his family's violent accession. Unfortunately for the fate of Champa, while the country was suffering from civil discord, Vietnam saw the coronation of a strong and energetic emperor, Le Thanh Tong.

From the Vietnamese point of view, the Cham were barbaric pirates who needed to be stopped and defeated if

Dai Viet was to enjoy peace on its southern border. The Cham considered the Vietnamese robbers of their old lands. Yet civil war weakened Champa considerably. In the years leading up to 1470, clashes between the forces and people of Champa and Dai Viet continued. While Le Thanh Tong strengthened his army, Tra Toan still had to fight with rivals to his throne. Diplomatic efforts to resolve the increasing crisis came to no avail.

Even though his hold over his kingdom was not absolute, King Tra Toan allowed another raid into Hoa Chau, in 1469. Emperor Le Thanh Tong accelerated his troop build up and intensified military training. In October of 1470, King Tra Toan invaded Hoa Chau with a huge combined land and naval force. Contemporary Vietnamese accounts show that the force had 100,000 soldiers, but this number may be inflated. Faced with this, Le Thanh Tong readied his empire for war. A Vietnamese diplomatic mission to Beijing in October and November of 1470 ensured Chinese acquiescence.

On November 28, 1470, Le Thanh Tong formally launched his attack. In a speech, he used the Champa civil war as an excuse for his invasion: The Cham people were suffering from the illegitimate rule of Tra Toan, a rule gained after his brother murdered the legitimate king Qui Do, and the Vietnamese were coming as liberators, not invaders. After naming more reasons for war, the Vietnamese army and navy of 150,000 men crossed into Champa.

The Cham of the border province of Quang Nam (a province that includes the modern city of Da Nang) surrendered quickly, enabling Le Thanh Tong to advance south in early 1471. In despair, King Tra Toan ordered his younger brother to attack with soldiers mounted on five thousand elephants. However, Le Thanh Tong learned of the attack and took effective countermeasures. Well prepared, the Vietnamese soldiers struck at the Cham on their elephants and defeated them. Tra Toan's offer for negotiations went unanswered, and Le Thanh Tong advanced on Vijaya (near what is now Qui Nhon).

On March 22, 1471, Vijaya fell to the Vietnamese. The city was completely destroyed, and at least forty thousand, if not sixty thousand, Cham were killed. Thirty thousand other Cham followed their king Tra Toan and his wives into Vietnamese captivity. The Vietnamese cut off the left ear of each of their prisoners of war and enslaved them for life. When Tra Toan died of natural causes on his way to Vietnam, Le Thanh Tong had the head of the Tra Toan's corpse decapitated and displayed on his ship beneath a white flag and a sarcastic inscription.

In April, 1471, the Champa civil wars came to an end.

All of Champa north of the Cu Mong Pass (below what is now An Nhon), including the destroyed city of Vijaya, was annexed to Dai Viet. The rest of Champa to the south was divided into three dukedoms, each too weak to resist the Vietnamese. Champa's civil wars had ended with its defeat at the hands of their enemies.

SIGNIFICANCE

The civil wars that had disrupted Champa also accelerated its fall, preventing the Cham from effectively marshaling national resources to withstand the Vietnamese invasion of 1470. Champa's unwillingness to end its raids into territories wrested from it by the Vietnamese, however, destroyed all chances for a peaceful accommodation of the two peoples.

By 1471, the loss of more than one-third of its territory to Vietnam in the north effectively destroyed Champa as an independent power in Southeast Asia. In the seventeenth and eighteenth centuries, Vietnam would finalize its conquest of the remaining Cham territory.

Since its foundation, Champa had been an Indianized nation culturally, in stark contrast to the Chinese-influenced culture of Vietnam. Champa had remained a Hindu nation well into the fifteenth century, at a time when its neighbor Cambodia had become Buddhist, and represented a cultural link to India.

After its defeat in 1471, the remainder of Champa became quickly Islamized. Historians have set the date of Champa's conversion to Islam at the 1471 defeat, rather than in the early 1400's, as previously believed. Many scholars believe that the massive defeat of the Cham at the hands of the non-Hindu Vietnamese led them to become severely disappointed with their religion, which had failed to save them. In turn, the Cham looked to Islam for salvation. Into the twenty-first century, the vast majority of the approximately sixty thousand ethnic Cham surviving in Vietnam, and their peers in Cambodia and southern China, have remained Muslim.

—*R. C. Lutz*

FURTHER READING

Chapuis, Oscar. *A History of Vietnam*. Westport, Conn.: Greenwood Press, 1995. Discusses the event in detail from both a Cham and a Vietnamese point of view. Very readable. Includes maps, a bibliography, and an index.

Guillon, Emmanuel. *Cham Art*. Translated by Tom White. London: Thames and Hudson, 2001. A richly illustrated work with a valuable chapter on the history of Champa. Includes maps of the region as it appeared at the time of the civil wars.

Maspero, Georges. *The Champa Kingdom: The History of an Extinct Vietnamese Culture.* Translated by Walter E. J. Tips. Bangkok, Thailand: White Lotus Press, 2002. The first English translation of Maspero's classic 1928 history of Champa, from its origins to its decline. Includes illustrations and chronological table of Champa kings.

Phuong, Tran Ky. *Unique Vestiges of Cham Civilization.* Hanoi, Vietnam: The Giio, 2000. An illustrated guidebook to Cham ruins in Vietnam, with a useful survey of Cham history, including its decline.

Thurgood, Graham. *From Ancient Cham to Modern Dialects.* Honolulu: University of Hawaii Press, 1999. Examines primarily the Cham language but also surveys Champa's history using updated historical and anthropological sources.

SEE ALSO: Mar. 18-22, 1471: Battle of Vijaya; 1539: Jiajing Threatens Vietnam.

RELATED ARTICLE in *Great Lives from History: The Renaissance & Early Modern Era, 1454-1600:* Le Thanh Tong.

1450's-1529
THAI WARS

The Thai kingdoms of Chiang Mai, Ayutthaya, and Sukhothai engaged in a series of rotating battles, punctuated with fluid alliances and alternating rivalries and coalitions. The disputes over kingship and a drive for domination of Siam (modern Thailand) started in the fourteenth century.

LOCALE: Thailand, Burma (now Myanmar), Cambodia

CATEGORIES: Wars, uprisings, and civil unrest; government and politics; expansion and land acquisition

KEY FIGURES

Trailok (Borommatrailokanat; 1431-1488), king of Ayutthaya, r. 1448-1488, and archrival of Tilok king Chiang Mai

Sri Sutham Tilok (1411-1487), king of Chiang Mai who engaged in constant war with Ayutthaya

Ramathibodi II (1472-1529), king of Ayutthaya, r. 1491-1529, who strengthened and centralized his kingdom

SUMMARY OF EVENT

The fifteenth century was a period of unrelenting war in the Thai kingdoms. At various times, the kingdoms of Chiang Mai (in the north), Ayutthaya (south-central), and Sukhothai (center) attempted to conquer one another. A series of fluid alliances pitted these states in a dance of alternating rivalry and coalition. The usual cause was succession—on the death of a ruler, two leading sons would dispute the kingship and seek alliances from other Thai kingdoms, which often enough were ruled by members of their extended family. While these

Thai wars are usually identified in histories one by one, in fact they represent rotating episodes in a continuing drive for domination of Siam from the fourteenth century until external threats overrode them.

Throughout this period, Ayutthaya, the strongest of the kingdoms, was also involved in attempts to control the Malay provinces. The consolidation of Islam early in the century had made that faith a rallying point for Malay identity against the Buddhist Thais. Ayutthaya was unable to make the rich trading port of Melaka, or Malacca, a vassal state (the Portuguese did that in 1511), although Ayutthaya did dominate trade in the lower peninsula. The kingdom grew wealthy by shipping grain south and receiving luxury goods and Indian cotton for the lucrative Chinese trade. Trade was a monopoly of the king, who set his own price for anything he purchased before allowing traders to sell what was left.

Ayutthaya amassed a considerable treasury, enabling Ramathibodi to build in 1503 a 50-foot statue of Buddha, encrusted with 378 pounds of gold and the largest such statue in the world at that time. The kings of Ayutthaya also used their wealth to build a strong military and acquire modern military equipment. The expanding wealth of Ayutthaya allowed for social and cultural changes as well. In the fifteenth century, the amalgam of Mon, Tai, and Khmer influences began to coalesce into what became recognized as Siamese culture, adding to tensions between Ayutthaya and the Lan culture of Chiang Mai.

The Thai War of 1387-1390 between Ayutthaya and Chiang Mai marked the start of the long series of conflicts. The Thai War of 1442-1448 started after the king of Chiang Mai was deposed by his sixth son, Sri Sutham

Tilok, who proclaimed himself king. Another son took the deposed king to a vassal town, where the local governor supported him by enlisting the aid of Ayutthaya, which was eager to extend its power northward. Tilok's army, however, met his half brother and the governor on the march, killing them both. Tilok employed Lao spies to infiltrate the Ayutthayan army, where they sabotaged the war elephants by cutting off their tails and stampeding them. In the chaos that followed, Ayutthayan forces were routed. Tilok also led small adventures against petty warlords, taking men and cattle for the impending major conflict, but he hoped also to weaken the smaller states on the fringe between the central plain (usually dominated but not controlled by Ayutthaya) and the mountainous redoubts of Chiang Mai.

Three years later, hostilities broke out again, this time in the Thai War of 1451–1456. Ayutthaya remained an expansive power, and after King Trailok succeeded to the throne in 1448, he strengthened his forces and plotted to take Chiang Mai. Tilok opened the door to invasion when he sided with a 1451 insurrection in Sukhothai, which Ayutthaya has subdued into vassalage. A Sukhothai prince asked Tilok for help in regaining Sukhothai independence. Tilok invaded but was driven back, and Trailok pressed his advantage and occupied Chiang Mai the following year. The Laotians then intervened, forcing Trailok back but also compelling the Chiang Mai to defend their territory. They counterattacked against Ayutthaya, but the indecisive Battle of Kamphaeng Phet (1456) closed the campaign.

Historians believe the next war started in 1461, but in reality, hostilities never ceased. Tilok mounted unsuccessful offensives in 1459 and 1460. The Thai War of 1461–1464 began after a governor, who was an Ayutthaya vassal, defected to Chiang Mai and was named a town headman there. Emboldened, Tilok moved south to Ayutthaya, occupied its vassal state of Sukhothai, and laid siege to Phitsanulok. With his forces drawn south, Tilok was unprepared when China unleashed a surprise attack from the north, so he had to beat a hasty retreat to defend his capital. This marked the first sign that forces outside the region could take advantage of the continuing warfare in Siam. In 1463, Trailok moved the Ayutthayan capital to Phitsanulok to centralize his authority and military control. Nevertheless, Tilok attacked Sukhothai again but was repulsed. At the Battle of Doi Ba (1463), deep in Chiang Mai territory, the Chiang Mai war elephants drove the Ayutthayan infantry into a swamp and brought the war to a close.

The two kingdoms attempted a diplomatic settlement,

but the period after the 1464 cease-fire involved conspiracies and armed clashes. In an odd turn of events, Trailok built himself a monastery and was ordained a monk. His astonished enemies came to the ordination ceremony and provided his robes, which is the highest form of merit for a Thai Buddhist. From his monastery, however, Trailok sent a sorcerer to Chiang Mai. The sorcerer spread dissension in the Chiang Mai court and caused the crown prince to be executed for treason. In 1466, Trailok returned to his throne and sent emissaries to Chiang Mai, but his duplicity was revealed, and the sorcerer-spy was clubbed to death in a sack (the method of execution for a noble or a monk, which kept the executioner's hands from touching the condemned). Trailok's diplomats were assassinated on their return trip.

The Thai War of 1474–1475 began with an Ayutthayan invasion, but Tilok negotiated a cease-fire; also, his death in 1487 brought five years of peace. Then the Thai War of 1492 erupted over the theft of a crystal Buddha statue, stolen from Chiang Mai by an Ayutthayan royal prince who spent some time as a monk. Chiang Mai king Phra Yot invaded and retrieved the statue from Ramathibodi.

Ramathibodi reorganized his army, instituted compulsory military training for all able-bodied males, and modernized the army's command and staff, who also received a new instructional manual on strategy and tactics. Ramathibodi then signed a peace pact with Portugal, which gave Portugal the right of residence in Siam and the freedom to conduct missionary activities. In return, the Portuguese provided military training, guns, and ammunition. By the middle of the next Thai war, Ayutthaya was producing its own artillery pieces and using Portuguese mercenaries in the field.

The Thai War of 1500–1529 was a protracted conflict in which Chiang Mai, threatened by the larger and more powerful Ayutthaya, often took the offensive. King Ratana of Chiang Mai invaded in 1507 and engaged the enemy at Sukhothai, where he was pushed back after an exhausting battle. Ayutthaya pressed its advantage in 1508 and met Ratana at Phrae, where an equally bloody battle forced King Ramathibodi to withdraw. Another Ayutthayan incursion took place in 1510, followed by ongoing skirmishes through the next five years. Ramathibodi took the offensive in 1515, and in the Battle of Lampang, he routed Chiang Mai and seized a sacred Buddha statue. In the battle, Ayutthaya had the advantage of Portuguese military training and artillery. The final decade of the war consisted of mopping-up exercises, and by 1529, the year Ramathibodi died, Sukhothai and Ayutthaya were firmly under Ayutthayan control. The following year, the Chinese Empire recognized Ayutthaya as the legitimate heir of the Kingdom of Sukhothai.

Tilok died in 1487 and was replaced by his grandson; Tilok's only son and heir had been executed. The grandson was then deposed in favor of his own thirteen-year-old son. Even with a cultural and religious revival during this period, Chiang Mai went into protracted decline and engaged in a series of wars against Ayutthaya and incursions by tribal peoples on the northern frontier. After 1526, the kingdom fell into disarray, with kings deposed and murdered, and Chiang Mai slowly disintegrated.

SIGNIFICANCE

The Kingdom of Ayutthaya was consolidated but hardly unified. It declined into a confederation of petty states with self-governing principalities ruled by members of the royal family. Each state had its own army, and each army saw constant fighting with other states. Added to the self-governing states were tributary states of various degrees of loyalty. The king often attempted to maintain a balance among the feuding princes, any one of whom was capable of allying with others to topple him. Trailok tried to stabilize the succession by naming an *uparaja*, or heir, a tricky situation in a polygamous society. He did succeed in forging a tighter and more loyal administrative system, however, and it is this achievement that is his most significant legacy.

—*Norbert Brockman*

FURTHER READING

Heidhues, Mary Somers. *Southeast Asia: A Concise History*. New York: Thames and Hudson, 2000. A comprehensive if concise history of Southeast Asia. Well illustrated.

Osborne, Milton. *Southeast Asia*. 7th ed. Chiang Mai, Thailand: Silkworm Books, 1994. Focuses on peninsular Southeast Asia.

Tarling, Nicholas, ed. *The Cambridge History of Southeast Asia*. New York: Cambridge University Press, 1999. A detailed and scholarly multivolume presentation of the region, with thorough treatment of the peninsular wars.

Wyatt, David. *Thailand: A Short History*. New Haven, Conn.: Yale University Press, 1984. One of the best short histories of Thailand, with good detail on the medieval period and the wars.

SEE ALSO: 1454: China Subdues Burma; 1469-1481: Reign of the Ava King Thihathura; c. 1488-1594: Khmer-Thai Wars; 1505-1515: Portuguese Viceroys Establish Overseas Trade Empire; 1511-c. 1515: Melaka Falls to the Portuguese; 1527-1599: Burmese Civil Wars; 1548-1600: Siamese-Burmese Wars; 1558-1593: Burmese-Laotian Wars; c. 1580-c. 1600: Siamese-Cambodian Wars.

RELATED ARTICLES in *Great Lives from History: The Renaissance & Early Modern Era, 1454-1600*: Afonso de Albuquerque; Tomé Pires; Saint Francis Xavier; Zhengde.

1451-1526
LODI KINGS DOMINATE NORTHERN INDIA

The Lodī Dynasty was the last of several Delhi sultanates. It came to an end when its army failed to win the Battle of Panipat against Mughal emperor Bābur. The fall of the Lodīs marked the beginning of Mughal rule, which became one of India's most illustrious and long-lasting dynasties.

LOCALE: Northern India
CATEGORIES: Government and politics; wars, uprisings, and civil unrest; expansion and land acquisition

KEY FIGURES

Bahlūl Lodī (d. 1489), Delhi sultan, r. 1451-1489
Sikandar Lodī (d. 1517), Delhi sultan, r. 1489-1517
Ibrāhīm Lodī (d. 1526), Delhi sultan, r. 1517-1526

Bābur (Zahīr-ud-Dīn Muḥammad; 1483-1530), first Mughal emperor of India, r. 1526-1530

SUMMARY OF EVENT

The Lodī Dynasty was the last of the Delhi sultanates, which were originally established in 1192-1193 with the victory of military leader Muhammad of Ghor (d. 1206) over the Hindu Rājputs at the Battle of Tarain. Muhammad of Ghor was from Ghazni in modern Afghanistan, and most of the subsequent Delhi sultanate dynasties, including the Lodīs, were of Afghan origin. The sultans, or rulers, of the several sultanates were all Muslims, and conflicts were frequent between Muslim invaders and India's majority Hindu population.

Islam first gained a major presence in India in the late tenth and early eleventh centuries under the military leadership of sultan Maḥmūd of Ghazni (r. 997-1030), who plundered Indian cities and temples. Like Maḥmūd, most of the later Delhi sultanate rulers were from Afghanistan, the gateway into the Indian subcontinent long before the invasions of Alexander the Great in the 320's B.C.E. The Delhi sultans, the last of whom were the Lodīs, ruled much of northern India for more than three centuries but were unable to extend their rule south into the Deccan.

Religious differences were not always paramount, however, and alliances were often made across the sectarian divide, and through the centuries, the fiercest opponents of the Delhi sultans were frequently their fellow Muslims.

Muhammad of Ghor was assassinated in 1206. One of his Turkish generals (Aibak) subsequently established what is called the Slave Dynasty, so named because when freed and given the opportunity, slaves were often both loyal and talented. The Slave Dynasty sultans ruled until 1290, to be followed by the Khaljīs from 1290 to 1320, the Tughluqs from 1320 to 1413, and the Sayyids from 1414 until 1451.

Through the centuries, the Delhi sultanate was challenged not only by rivals from within the Indian subcontinent but also from without, notably the Mongols from Asia. In 1398, Mongol warrior Tamerlane (Timur) sacked Delhi, massacring or enslaving most of the city's Hindu population. Tamerlane abandoned northern India the following year, and the sultanate recovered, although it was smaller and more fragmented by the time the Lodīs assumed power in Delhi by deposing the last of the Sayyids in 1451.

The Lodīs were successful horse breeders, had been ennobled, and had ruled the Punjab, to the west of Delhi, under the Sayyids. The first of the Lodī sultans was Bahlūl Lodī, who reigned over Delhi and the Punjab for nearly four decades. His reputation was that of a just ruler, and during his reign, numerous Muslim herdsmen-peasants from Afghan settled in North India.

Like their Delhi sultanate predecessors, the Lodī kings were Muslims, but during the years of Lodī rule several non-Muslim religious movements achieved considerable significance. From the southern part of the subcontinent, a devotional Hinduism known as bhakti spread north to the Ganges River area, giving Hinduism a new vigor. Kabīr (1440-1518), an illiterate Muslim inspired by the teachings of a Hindu sage, abandoned the sectarianism of both Hinduism and Islam and founded a religious movement focused on simply loving God, which laid the foundation for Sikhism. In the Lodī-ruled Punjab, the Hindu-born Nānak (1469-1539), influenced by the more democratic theology of Islam, abandoned the Hindu concept of caste and became the first guru, or divine teacher, of Sikhism, worshiping a single universal God. By the reign of Sikandar Lodī, Bahlūl's son, India was divided and fragmented both politically and spiritually.

Sikandar Lodī ruled the Delhi sultanate from 1489 until 1517, and was praised by his contemporaries as the greatest of all Delhi sultans, a claim that should be accepted with suitable caution. Following the practice of his father, Sikandar was a patron of artistic and intellectual endeavors and was a poet. His mother was a Hindu, and a first love was a Hindu princess. Although new mystic sects blending Islam and Hindu emerged during his reign, Sikandar, perhaps because of guilt and as a reaction to the religion of his mother and his early love, was an orthodox Muslim. He also was more iconoclastic in his destruction of Hindu temples than his peers.

Sikandar also established a second capital city at Āgra, near Delhi, signifying his ambitions to expand Lodī rule farther south, and although much of Āgra was destroyed by an earthquake in 1505, he immediately ordered its rebuilding. It was during his reign that the Portuguese, led by explorer Vasco da Gama, reached India in 1498, the first Europeans to reach South Asia by sea, an event that went unrecorded in Delhi.

The last of the three Lodī sultans was Ibrāhīm, who ascended the throne with the death of his father in 1517. Ibrāhīm's reign was a troubled one. Because of his aristocratic and indolent ways, he failed to maintain the loyalty of many of those who served Sikandar, and he faced several uprisings, including one by his younger brother, whom Ibrāhīm captured and executed. A rebellion also occurred in Bihar, to the east of Delhi, and another in Lahore in the Punjab, led by his uncle. Rānā Sāngā of Mewar, the raja (chief) of the Hindu Rājput confederacy, headed another uprising against the Lodī sultan, in 1527.

The demise of the Lodī sultans and Ibrāhīm came not from within India, however, but from the Lodī homeland, from Afghanistan, where Bābur, a direct descendant of Tamerlane, had imperial ambitions. Initially, Bābur focused on reestablishing the old Mongol Empire in Central Asia, although he did lead forays into India in 1505 and 1519, but on neither occasion did he try to maintain a foothold in the subcontinent. In 1525, he launched a major invasion.

Because of their expert mastery of horses, Bābur's forces, like all Mughal armies, were both swift and mobile. That mobility gave them an advantage over larger armies, not least in India, where the debilitating climate made it difficult to breed sufficient numbers of horses for war. In addition, Bābur, although a skilled archer, was well acquainted with cannon and matchlock guns, a characteristic similar to what was occurring in the west in the Muslim empires of the Ottomans in modern Turkey and the Ṣafavids in Persia (Iran). There is little evidence to indicate that Ibrāhīm and the Lodīs had gunpowder technology at their disposal.

During Bābur's 1525 invasion, the Hindu Rājputs were still in rebellion and the Lodī family was not united, for it was Ibrāhīm's uncle who urged Bābur to attack the Delhi sultanate. Ibrāhīm's Lodī army met Bābur at Panipat, north and west of Delhi, on April 21, 1526. Even though the Lodī forces outnumbered those of Bābur ten to one, it helped that Bābur was an experienced and successful military leader, much more so than Ibrāhīm. After a standoff of several days, the Lodī army attacked Bābur's impregnable defensive position, and as the battle raged, the larger army became increasingly concentrated and immobilized. It is estimated that fifteen thousand Lodī warriors died at the Battle of Panipat, including Ibrāhīm. The Lodī Dynasty and the Delhi sultanate had come to an end.

SIGNIFICANCE

It is not clear if Ibrāhīm Lodī's failure at the Battle of Panipat was a result of his own inadequacies, or if the loss resulted from the superior military experience of Bābur (or Bābur's mastery of gunpowder). Nevertheless, whatever the cause, the defeat of the Lodī sultans in 1526 proved to be one of the major turning points in the history of India. Bābur established Mughal rule, and his successors, including his son Humāyūn, Akbar, Jahāngīr, Shāh Jahān, and ʿĀlamgīr, made the Mughals one of India's most famous and glorious dynasties.

—Eugene Larson

FURTHER READING

Bakshi, S. R., ed. *Advanced History of Medieval India*. 3 vols. Rev ed. New Delhi, India: Anmol, 2003. Volume 1 covers the period 712-1525, which includes a section on the Lodī Dynasty.

Haig, W., ed. *The Cambridge History of India: Turks and Afghans*. Vol. 3. Cambridge, England: Cambridge University Press, 1922. The third volume of this multivolume history of India includes a discussion of the reigns of the Lodī sultans.

Jayapalan, N. *Medieval History of India*. Delhi, India: Atlantic, 2001. This history of medieval India includes a discussion of the Delhi sultanate and the Lodī kings.

Qureshi, Ishtiaq Husain. *Administration of the Sultanate of Delhi*. 1942. Reprint. New Delhi, India: Oriental Books Reprint, 1996. Qureshi's study remains the foremost analysis of the administrative and political structures of the Delhi sultanate.

Streusand, Douglas E. *The Formation of the Mughal Empire*. New York: Oxford University Press, 1999. Examines Bābur's conquest of the Lodīs and the establishment of India's Mughal Dynasty.

Wolpert, Stanley. *A New History of India*. New York: Oxford University Press, 2000. This widely accessible and well-written work includes a description of the Delhi sultans and Bābur's conquest of India.

SEE ALSO: 1459: Rāo Jodha Founds Jodhpur; Early 16th cent.: Devotional Bhakti Traditions Emerge; 1507: End of the Timurid Dynasty; Dec. 2, 1510: Battle of Merv Establishes the Shaybānīd Dynasty; Apr. 21, 1526: First Battle of Panipat; Mar. 17, 1527: Battle of Khānua; Dec. 30, 1530: Humāyūn Inherits the Throne in India; 1540-1545: Shēr Shāh Sūr Becomes Emperor of Delhi; 1556-1605: Reign of Akbar; 1578: First Dalai Lama Becomes Buddhist Spiritual Leader; Feb., 1586: Annexation of Kashmir; 1598: Astrakhanid Dynasty Is Established.

RELATED ARTICLES in *Great Lives from History: The Renaissance & Early Modern Era, 1454-1600:* Akbar; Bābur; Vasco da Gama; Humāyūn; Ibrāhīm Lodī; Krishnadevaraya.

1454
CHINA SUBDUES BURMA

China and Burma's Kingdom of Ava battled over trade routes, initially resulting in the subjugation of Ava as a Chinese "comforter." Although China secured loyalty from several Burmese states, by the early sixteenth century it lost control as strife among the Burmese states set the stage for a national conciousness.

LOCALE: Upper Burma (now Myanmar)
CATEGORIES: Wars, uprisings, and civil unrest; diplomacy and international relations

KEY FIGURES
Narapati (d. 1469), king of Ava, r. 1443-1469
Thonganbwa (d. 1446), chief of Mohnyin
Thihathura (d. 1481), king of Ava, r. 1469-1481
Wang Ji (Wang Chi; fl. 1440's), president of China's Board of War
Minhkaung (d. 1502), king of Ava, r. 1481-1502

SUMMARY OF EVENT
After conquering Pagan in 1287, the Mongol emperor Kublai Khan controlled large portions of Burma and utilized the region as a major trade route. When Kublai Khan's Yuan Dynasty fell in 1368, China lost control over not only portions of Burma but also its trade route to the west. To reestablish that route, the Ming planned first to take over the Maw (Mao) Shans in northern Burma, then continue into the Irrawaddy Delta, which extended into the Bay of Bengal. The struggle between the Maw Shans and the Chinese lasted from 1438 to 1465 and involved the Burmese kingdom of Ava beginning in 1441.

The Maw Shan chieftain Thonganbwa had planned to revive the Nanchao Empire, a move that would challenge Chinese authority and obstruct trade routes. The Chinese emperor, in an effort to recruit more people willing to fight, offered to give Thonganbwa's land to whoever arrested him. The president of China's Board of War, Wang Ji, was given a strong army in 1441, and he successfully drove Thonganbwa and his Maw Shan army to the province of Mohnyin, a Shan state on the border with China. It was here that Thonganbwa was captured by the Burmese and presented to their king, Narapati, at his coronation.

Wang Ji followed Thonganbwa to Mohnyin, captured the state, and threatened to capture Ava as well if Thonganbwa was not turned over. Narapati refused, so Wang Ji returned to China to gather a stronger army. In 1445, Chinese and Burmese forces clashed near Tagaung, and a Chinese general was killed. In 1446, the

Chinese appeared in even greater numbers at the walls of Ava, still demanding Thonganbwa. Narapati conceded this time, and rather than being taken by the Chinese, Thonganbwa committed suicide. His body and troops were handed over to the Chinese, saving Ava from possible ruin. The Chinese desecrated Thonganbwa's body by drying out his skin and then placing a spit through his corpse. This would be the last time in Ava's history—as the main kingdom of Burma— that it would submit to China. China's grip on Burma would loosen, but, for a short time after, China was still able to control Burma through tributaries, the payment of tributes to China by the recently subjugated Burmese.

Because Narapati conceded to China's request, he had to accept Chinese overlordship and was appointed the title of comforter (pacifier) of Ava in 1451. By 1454, China considered eight states to be comforters. Ava's status as comforter afforded it some protection, and in a show of appreciation, the Chinese gave Narapati a piece of Mohnyin province in 1456. Although relations between China and Ava appeared peaceful, in an incident in 1449, Ava managed to keep the Chinese from its land.

By 1454, the Burmese-Chinese war that began in 1441 was virtually over, and a majority of the conflicts were little more than skirmishes. Ava, for the most part, was left alone by Chinese forces, who were focused instead on keeping the Shan states subdued. Some Shan states were rich in jewels, further encouraging the Chinese to control the area. In 1465, the Momeik state's chieftain, the queen regent Nang-han-lung, sent a ruby tribute to China's frontier eunuch, attempted to ally with Annam (Vietnam), then stole most of the Shan state of Hsenwi. When China sent officials to deal with Nang-han-lung, she offered rubies as gifts to the officials and maintained that Momeik had outgrown Hsenwi. The Chinese officials sympathized, so Momeik remained in China's possession. China was still worried that Momeik would attack Hsenwi, so, in 1488, Mohnyin was ordered to send troops to prevent a battle, but Mohnyin's troops were ill-prepared and beaten back. China pursued no other options, a strong indication that its control was loosening.

Narapati's apparent loyalty to China aided his son Thihathura, who managed to maintain peace with the Chinese Empire for most of his reign and therefore was usually not harassed. One minor incident, however, occurred between Ava and China during Thihathura's reign, again involving Mohnyin. In 1472, Thihathura, wanting to expand his kingdom, demanded the cession of Mohnyin to Ava. Around the same time, though, China was once again having difficulty controlling the Shan states of Upper Burma, so China instead focused its attention on keeping the Shan states divided. The Chinese wanted to keep the Shan states from becoming a strong, unified threat. Allowing Mohnyin to go to Ava would not only allow a Shan state to gain strength but would also obstruct China's trade route into Burma. China denied Thihathura's request, and the Ava king decided against taking Mohnyin by force, which would have enraged the Chinese.

By the time Minhkaung ascended the throne, China's control over the Shan states, and therefore China's trade route, had weakened significantly, allowing the states to grow stronger. Because of this, Minhkaung and his successor had to resort to appeasement with portions of territory to keep the Shans from sacking Ava. In 1520, China became concerned about the situation and moved its base closer to the conflicts, but its presence had little effect. Ava was sacked in 1527, and Thohanbwa, the son of a Mohnyin chief, became ruler of Ava. By this time, Ava was descending into several decades of civil war, which ended with a strong national kingship that united all Burmese.

SIGNIFICANCE

The Burmese-Chinese Wars significantly affected not only Burmese but also Chinese history. To keep its trade route open, China had to keep a firm grip on the Shan states of upper Burma, focusing on separating the states so that no central power could arise. Whereas this separation was detrimental to China, it helped Burma create a national conciousness. The increasingly powerful yet divided Shan states fought with one another and united only after Toungoo became the most powerful state in Burma. When Toungoo's king Bayinnaung (r. 1551-1581) attempted to annex Ava in 1555, the Shans were not strong enough to keep them back, so they became part of the Kingdom of Burma. If the Shans had been able to develop a centralized power, the makeup of the Kingdom of Burma would have been different.

The Burmese-Chinese Wars also affected relations between the two countries, even into modern times. Narapati's recognition of Chinese rights to Burma signified to the emperor that Ava, and eventually Burma, were to be permanent comforters. Because of this recognition, all relations and policies toward Burma after this period

were based on China's belief that Burmese comforters would be always loyal and subordinate to China. Chinese-Burmese relations often deteriorated into war whenever China felt its belief in Burma's subordinate status to be challenged. China still considered Burma to be, even into the eighteenth and nineteenth centuries, a tributary.

China and the British Empire also fought over rights to Burma. It has been postulated that the status as comforter also has marred relations between Communist China and Communist Burma (now Myanmar), affecting trade, politics, and the multiple Indochinese wars of the second half of the twentieth century.

—Tina Powell

FURTHER READING

Aung-Thwin, Michael A. *Myth and History in the Historiography of Early Burma: Paradigms, Primary Sources, and Prejudices.* Monographs in International Studies 102, Southeast Asia Series. Athens: Ohio University Press, 1998. Discusses the historic basis of various myths of the three kingdoms of Pagan, Ava, and Toungoo.

Hall, D. G. E. *A History of Southeast Asia.* 4th ed. New York: St. Martin's Press, 1980. A concise history of the struggles between China and Burma, with a focus on Narapati, Thonganbwa, and Wang Chi.

Phayre, Arthur P. *History of Burma Including Burma Proper, Pegu, Taungu, Tenasserim, and Arakan: From the Earliest Time to the End of the First War with British India.* 1883. Reprint. Bangkok, Thailand: Orchid Press, 1998. A comprehensive history of Burma, with some discussion of the conflicts between China and the Burmese states.

1454-1481
RISE OF THE OTTOMAN EMPIRE

The conquests of Mehmed II established the Ottoman Empire as the greatest military power in southeastern Europe and Asia Minor. After his seizure of Constantinople in 1453, the Ottomans transformed the city, now known as Istanbul, into the vibrant political, commercial, and cultural center of the Western Islamic world.

LOCALE: Southeastern Europe and Asia Minor (now the Balkans, Greece, and Turkey)

CATEGORIES: Wars, uprisings, and civil unrest; expansion and land acquisition; government and politics

KEY FIGURES

Mehmed II (1432-1481), Ottoman sultan, r. 1444-1446 and 1451-1481

Constantine XI Palaeologus (1404-1453), Byzantine emperor, r. 1449-1453

Gennadius II Scholarios (Georgios Scholarios; c. 1405-1473), Orthodox patriarch, 1454-1464

Uzun Ḥasan (1423-1478), ruler of the Ak Kuyunlu, or White Sheep, Empire, r. 1453-1478

SUMMARY OF EVENT

By the mid-fifteenth century, the Ottoman Empire was a significant but not yet dominant power in the Balkans and eastern Mediterranean basin. Because of the military campaigns of Sultan Murad II (r. 1421-1451), the Turks, who formed the core of the Ottoman Empire, came to rule much of northern and western Anatolia directly. The empire had continued its expansion into Europe—known as Rumeli, "the land of the Romans"—but there the sultan exercised only a limited suzerainty over many Muslim and Christian vassals.

The Byzantine Empire had been truncated but not destroyed; Ottoman ambitions in the Balkans still were contested by formidable Venetian fleets and Hungarian armies. To the south, the Egyptian Mamlūk sultanate dominated the western Muslim world in both its military and its cultural achievements. The Ottoman capital of Edirne (Adrianople) in Thrace remained intellectually inferior, outshone by traditional seats of learning in Cairo and Damascus.

Prematurely elevated to the throne by Murad's abdication in 1444, the twelve-year-old Mehmed proved unequal to a rapid succession of threats, which included a renewed Hungarian crusade and a rebellion by elite Janissary troops in Edirne. He was deposed at the instigation of Murad's favorite vizier in 1446.

After his second accession and Murad's death, in 1451, Mehmed immediately prepared, both diplomatically and militarily, to besiege Constantinople and eliminate the Byzantine Empire, which by then controlled little territory beyond the city's walls. Despite the weakness of the Byzantine emperor, Constantine XI (who owed his contested accession to Murad), Mehmed understood that the survival of an Orthodox capital in the heart of his territory presented a ready justification for European intervention and an obstacle to easy military communication between his Rumelian and Anatolian provinces. The siege, involving more than 100,000 troops and nearly five hundred ships, began in April, 1453. On May 29, the city fell to a massive, frenzied land and naval assault, thunderously aided by the most powerful siege cannons in existence.

The conquest of Constantinople was the defining military achievement of Mehmed's reign, winning for him the sobriquet *fatih*, "the conqueror." Almost thirty years of nonstop campaigning in Asia Minor, the Balkans, and Greece followed. These assaults confirmed Ottoman Turkey as the rising Muslim power and the principal threat to Christian Europe. Between 1463 and 1479, Mehmed conducted an exhausting but successful war against a coalition made up of Venice, Hungary, and the Turkmen ruler Uzun Ḥasan. Although he failed in efforts to take Belgrade and Rhodes, campaigns within Europe eventually enabled him to annex or establish Turkish suzerainty over the remaining Byzantine, Genoese, and Venetian possessions in Greece and the Aegean, and also Serbia, Bosnia and Herzegovina, Walachia, and Crimea. Within Anatolia, he added to his domain the last Byzantine "empire" of Trebizond and the Muslim emirates of Karaman (by conquest) and Sinope (through intimidation).

The restoration and repopulation of Constantinople formed a central preoccupation of Mehmed's reign. The young sultan fancied himself the new Alexander (Iskander) of Macedon, and he now possessed a capital whose pedigree matched his dreams of world domination. Although many survivors of the 1453 siege were sold into slavery, the city was rapidly repeopled by forced relocations of entire communities from Mehmed's accumulating conquests. Unchecked epidemics of bubonic plague periodically necessitated new infusions of the unwilling, but by 1480, a diverse and dynamic Istanbul was home to an estimated sixty thousand to seventy thousand permanent residents.

Mehmed encouraged the development of luxury trades by resettling expert craftspeople in Istanbul, which became noted for the production of fine glazed ceramics. Much of the best Ottoman work in this field owed its inspiration to Persian and older Seljuk Turkish influences. Mehmed favored Persian literature and, to the resentment of many able Turkish subjects, often granted important government posts to unqualified Persian literati. Few domestic poets of note emerged during Mehmed's reign, but even the worthy Ahmed Pasha (d. 1496/1497) imitated the Persian style.

The sultan's private interest in Western painting, including "objects of lechery" (*cose de lossuria*), also attracted an unknown number of Italian artists to Istanbul. Portraits by Italian painter Gentile Bellini (1479-1481) and a commemorative medallion by Costanzo de Ferrara (1481) are among the few works known to have survived destruction at the hands of Mehmed's iconoclastic son, Bayezid II (r. 1481-1512).

A private freethinker, Mehmed sternly upheld Sunni orthodoxy in the interest of public order. In 1477, the sultan had the *kanunnames* (secular laws) compiled to augment the Shariʿa (sacred canon law), which was based on the Qurʾān and Ḥadīth (sayings of the Prophet). During the 1470's, Mehmed also endowed eight colleges (*madrasas*) in the vicinity of the only great mosque commissioned during his reign (the Mosque of the Conqueror). These *madrasas* became the elite institutions in a new educational hierarchy that focused on training teachers, judges, and *mufti* (Islamic legal scholars) for an expanding administration. Recognized Muslim scholars, especially Persians, were attracted by the sultan's celebrated patronage and the prospect of lucrative government appointments. Aside from a few theological glosses, however, little original scholarship took place under Mehmed. Curricula here, as elsewhere in the Muslim world, placed a stultifying emphasis on theology and law.

Conquest remained the *raison d'être* of the Ottoman state; Mehmed's subjects, however, especially those outside his capital, derived few benefits from Ottoman conquest and rule. Provincial administrations were organized, and feudalism was introduced in conquered lands to maximize the availability of trained, well-equipped cavalrymen (*sipahis*). The financial demands imposed by constant warfare forced Mehmed to grant innumerable leases and monopolies, make regular use of predatory tax farmers, and frequently debase the silver coinage. Little or no effort was made to proselytize Orthodox populations, for only Christians (*reaya*) paid the crucial head tax; native Turks and converts were exempt.

Christians served another valuable purpose. Every five years, on average, the Turks exacted a tribute of able-bodied Christian males from the Balkans who were between the ages of ten and fifteen (the *devşirme*). Taken to Constantinople and converted to Islam, these youths served in the palace household or the Janissaries, an intensively indoctrinated infantry renowned for its fanatical loyalty to the sultan.

A depiction of the death of Ottoman sultan Mehmed II in 1481. Mehmed's sack and control of Constantinople in 1453 marked the beginning of the Ottoman Empire. (Frederick Ungar Publishing Co.)

Mehmed introduced the law of fratricide, which required new sultans to have all brothers executed to eliminate the discords that had marked many previous imperial successions. Mehmed also understood the dangers that an entrenched Turkish aristocracy could pose, and he relied increasingly on converted scions of Christian noble families to fill the highest posts. Candarli Halil Paşa (executed in 1453) was the last grand vizier of Turkish birth to serve Mehmed but not the last to experience the sultan's vengefulness.

Most striking was Mehmed's decision to preserve Constantinople's Orthodox patriarchate as a means to control the empire's Greek subject nationality (millets). Gennadius II Scholarios, selected after the fall of Constantinople for his known hostility to the Papacy in Rome, initially proved a willing collaborator and was the most effective of Mehmed's choices for this role.

SIGNIFICANCE

Under Mehmed, the Ottoman Empire became the leading military power of the age. Mehmed shaped its internal character for centuries to come, harnessing every aspect of Ottoman government and society to a policy of military aggrandizement. The effectiveness of this system permitted—even necessitated—sustained territorial expansion after Mehmed's death, but the fiscal and staffing demands imposed by incessant warfare compelled Mehmed to initiate exploitive policies that discouraged economic development and precluded national integration.

No province prospered during Mehmed's reign, and all eventually stagnated under his later successors, until patriotism was nonexistent outside the empire's Anatolian heartland. Even at the later height of Ottoman power, subject peoples from Serbia to Arabia retained their distinctive cultures. Once the empire began its irreversible decline, Ottoman subjects outside Anatolia reasserted their national identities and strove for independence.

Restored to glory as the capital and symbol of an expansionist Islam, Istanbul became a center of scholarship that quickly rivaled traditional seats of learning such as Cairo and Damascus. Because of the legal and artistic strictures of Sunni orthodoxy, however, it was not possible to meld Islamic with European culture. The Ottoman Empire under Mehmed and his successors would derive its strength from policies that emphasized the gulf between ruling Muslims (often converts) and subordinate Christians.

—*M. Wayne Guillory*

FURTHER READING

Babinger, Franz. *Mehmed the Conqueror and His Time.* Translated by Ralph Manheim, with a preface by William C. Hickman. Princeton, N.J.: Princeton University Press, 1978. A definitive, detailed narrative describing Mehmed's personality, campaigns, and policies.

Imber, Colin. *The Ottoman Empire, 1300-1650: The Structure of Power.* New York: Palgrave, 2002. Essential to understanding Mehmed within the context of Turkish history, this work uses primary source materials to analyze the dynasty and its administrative, legal, and military policies.

Kafadar, Cemal. *Between Two Worlds: The Construction of the Ottoman State.* Berkeley: University of California Press, 1995. A cultural history that uses medieval and modern sources to reveal how the Ottoman Empire was shaped by competing ethnic, religious, and political forces.

Turnbull, Stephen. *The Ottoman Empire*, 1326-1699. New York: Routledge, 2004. This history of Ottoman rule, imperial expansion, and military tactics focuses especially on the struggle for the Balkans and battles against European powers.

SEE ALSO: 1478-1482: Albanian-Turkish Wars End; 1534-1535: Ottomans Claim Sovereignty over Mesopotamia; 1566-1574: Reign of Selim II; 1574-1595: Reign of Murad III; 1589: Second Janissary Revolt in Constantinople; 1593-1606: Ottoman-Austrian War.

RELATED ARTICLES in *Great Lives from History: The Renaissance & Early Modern Era, 1454-1600:* Bayezid II; İbrahim Paşa; Matthias I Corvinus; Mehmed II; Mehmed III; Süleyman the Magnificent.

April 9, 1454
PEACE OF LODI

The Peace of Lodi ended the war between Venice and Milan and established a renewable mutual defense pact that was later expanded to include Florence, Naples, and the Papacy, bringing peace and modern diplomatic practices to Italy.

LOCALE: Lodi, Duchy of Milan (now in Italy)

CATEGORIES: Diplomacy and international relations; wars, uprisings, and civil unrest

KEY FIGURES

Francesco Sforza (1401-1466), duke of Milan, r. 1450-1456

Francesco Foscari (c. 1373-1457), doge of Venice, r. 1423-1457

Nicholas V (Tommaso Parentucelli; 1397-1455), Roman Catholic pope, 1447-1455

Simonetto da Camerino (fl. mid-fifteenth century), Augustinian friar

Mehmed II (1432-1481), Ottoman sultan, r. 1444-1446, 1451-1481

Cosimo de' Medici (1389-1464), ruler of Florence, r. 1434-1464

Alfonso V (1396-1458), king of Aragon, r. 1416-1458, and king of Naples, r. 1442-1458 as Alfonso I

SUMMARY OF EVENT

The fall of Constantinople to the Ottoman Turks on May 29, 1453, had a profound effect on Italy's internal politics and provided a foundation for increased diplomatic cooperation between the peninsula's five principal states. The victory of Sultan Mehmed II exposed the Balkans and threatened the Venetian commercial empire in the eastern Mediterranean. Italians everywhere feared the imminent advance of Ottoman power toward the Adriatic and their homeland. Compounding the pressures against Venice, the state closest to Turkish expansion, was a dangerous alliance along its western frontier. France had recently joined Milan and Florence in a war against the Venetian Republic over Francesco Sforza's succession to Milan's dukedom.

Before the French entered the conflict, the combatants had been fairly equal in strength, and Venice actually entertained hopes of annexing Milan. The French presence tipped the balance of power in favor of Milan. However, it also encouraged Venice and Milan to search for peace, as neither side welcomed a powerful foreign presence in Italy. Pope Nicholas V invited the combatants

and the lesser Italian states to assemble in Rome to settle their disputes and prepare for the anticipated confrontation with Mehmed's armies. Despite common fears of impending disaster, though, the pope offered little constructive leadership during the extended debates. As a result, the sessions were inconclusive and the congress disbanded in failure by March of 1454.

Both Sforza and Venetian doge Francesco Foscari understood the advantages of peace, however, and, with the assistance of a secret intermediary, the Augustinian friar Simonetto da Camerino, they settled their differences and signed the Peace of Lodi on April 9, 1454. Under the terms of this agreement, Francesco Sforza was acknowledged as the rightful ruler of Milan, Venice retained its territorial gains in northern Italy, and all began to prepare for war against the Turks. Simonetto reported to Francesco Sforza later in the same month that the Venetians were vigorously arming galleys and urged the Milanese to ready themselves as well.

Although the immediate cessation of hostilities was significant and French influence in Italy was successfully restrained for many years, other aspects of the treaty were probably more important. In particular, one clause called for the formation of a defensive military alliance between Venice and Milan. Through the extension and application of this clause, the Peace of Lodi achieved its lasting historical value. Cosimo de' Medici brought Florence into the new alliance on August 30. Naples joined the following January, and Nicholas V sanctioned the treaty a month later. In an official announcement from Rome on March 2, 1455, the five principal Italian powers bound themselves in a defensive league for a quarter of a century. The smaller Italian states soon agreed to follow suit, until all but Genoa and Rimini were members.

Venice, Milan, Florence, the Papacy, and Naples established an Italian League through which they pledged to defend one another in the event of attack from powers outside Italy, especially the anticipated invaders from the East. Venice committed six thousand cavalry and two thousand infantry to assist against foreign aggression, and the others pledged like forces. All signatories accepted existing territorial boundaries, and each vowed to consult the other before altering individual military or diplomatic arrangements that might upset the common peace. Though uneasy at times and not always successful in preventing minor wars between individual Italian

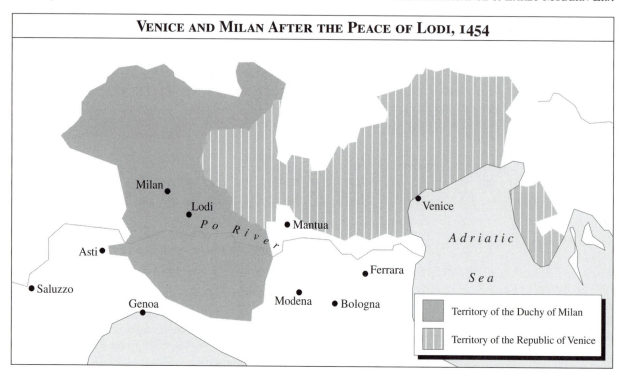

VENICE AND MILAN AFTER THE PEACE OF LODI, 1454

Milan • Lodi • *Po River* • Mantua • Asti • Saluzzo • Genoa • Modena • Bologna • Ferrara • Venice • *Adriatic Sea*

Territory of the Duchy of Milan
Territory of the Republic of Venice

states, the overall peace endured for almost forty years until the French invasion of 1494.

Another critical dimension of the treaty was the establishment of a balance among the several powers of Italy. In the north, Venice, though the strongest individual state in the peninsula, found its might counterbalanced by a union between Milan and Florence. In a like manner, the Papacy checked Naples in the south. Though each state continued to place its own interests first and the balance was not always a comfortable one, it did serve to constrain the aspirations of individual states at the expense of their neighbors and to stabilize Italian affairs for nearly half a century.

SIGNIFICANCE

The Peace of Lodi generally preserved the peace in Italy for nearly forty years. It maintained a balance of power and discouraged any state from appealing to outside force to augment its authority at the expense of a neighboring state. It encouraged military and diplomatic cooperation among the signatories.

Perhaps the most enduring legacy of the Peace of Lodi and its collateral agreements was in the area of diplomacy. By 1460, resident ambassadors became a permanent feature among the principal secular powers of Italy. The exchange of such ambassadors was bilateral from

the outset, except for the Papacy, which received ambassadors but did not send them. Naples was the last secular state to set up resident ambassadors: King Alfonso I sent one to Venice in 1457 and another to Milan the next year. Smaller states and principalities were considerably slower and less consistent in establishing their own ambassadors.

The development of the resident ambassador system resulted from the need for the Italian League's member states to consult about common threats on a regular basis. This system replaced the earlier custom of sending an ambassador or envoy to another state only for a specific purpose and a clearly defined period of time. The practice was quickly imitated across Europe and later became the cornerstone of the global system of diplomacy. Even the Italian word *ambasciatore* came to be universally adopted.

The Italian states entrusted their ambassadors with special authority to negotiate on their behalf and over time created the structures of permanent embassies. During the later half of the fifteenth century, the standard house and personal staff for an embassy came to include ten to twelve men with a complement of six to eight horses. The staff was paid for by the ambassador and responsible to him. In the same period, states began to provide their resident ambassadors with secretaries. The first to adopt this custom were the Venetians and Florentines. Diplomatic secretaries were separately appointed and separately paid. As time passed, they became a bridge between ambassadorial appointments, remaining at their posts when an ambassador resigned, retired, or was recalled, and thereby represented diplomatic continuity, as well as providing informed instruction for new appointees.

The new, resident embassies served, according to Renaissance historian Francesco Guicciardini, as the "eyes and ears" of their governments, gathering daily information, preparing detailed reports, and sending them to their home governments through diplomatic couriers on a steady basis. The Venetians, in particular, excelled in collecting thorough intelligence about all political figures, customs, practices, and physical characteristics of those countries where embassies were received and their *relazioni* became the standard against which all other reports were measured. Rome remained the center of the Italian diplomatic community, receiving ambassadors but not sending any. The city functioned throughout the Renaissance as a place to train future diplomats, because each state was careful to send only its most experienced there to serve. Thus, would-be ambassadors had an opportunity to learn from the very best diplomats of their time.

—*Michael J. Galgano*

FURTHER READING

Crouzet-Pavan, Elisabeth. *Venice Triumphant: The Horizons of a Myth*. Translated by Lydia G. Cochrane. Baltimore, Md.: Johns Hopkins University Press, 2002. A history of Venice from Roman times through the sixteenth century, focusing on the physical environment of the city and the effects of geography and space upon Venetian daily life, politics, and history. Includes photographic plates, illustrations, maps, chronology, glossary, bibliography, and index.

Hale, John. *The Civilization of Europe in the Renaissance*. New York: Atheneum, 1994. A scholarly, readable though traditional survey of the period by a leading English scholar.

Kirschner, Julius, ed. *The Origins of the State in Italy, 1300-1600*. Chicago: University of Chicago Press, 1996. Collection of essays, all originally published in the *Journal of Modern History*, discussing the development, interrelations, culture, and politics of the early modern Italian states. Includes bibliographic references and index.

Mallett, M. E., and J. R. Hale. *The Military Organization of a Renaissance State: Venice, c. 1400 to 1617*. New York: Cambridge University Press, 1984. Examines the relationship between the Venetian government and its mercenary armies; illustrates the development of a standing army.

Mattingly, Garrett. *Renaissance Diplomacy*. Reprint. New York: Dover, 1988. Originally published in 1955, this work is a classic study of diplomacy and the development of diplomatic institutions in Renaissance Italy and Europe.

Nicol, Donald M. *Byzantium and Venice: A Study in Diplomatic and Cultural Relations*. New York: Cambridge University Press, 1988. Surveys relations between the two cultures culminating in the fall of Constantinople.

Pyle, Cynthia M. *Milan and Lombardy in the Renaissance: Essays in Cultural History*. Rome: La Fenice, 1997. Collection of essays on the culture of Renaissance Milan. Includes illustrations, bibliographic references, and index.

Setton, Kenneth M. *The Papacy and the Levant, 1204-1571*. 4 vols. Philadelphia: American Philosophical Society, 1976-1984. Describes military, political, and diplomatic history of Christian Europe and the Ottoman Empire leading to the Battle of Lepanto. Rich in detail.

SEE ALSO: 1454-1481: Rise of the Ottoman Empire; 1463-1479: Ottoman-Venetian War; 1481-1499: Ludovico Sforza Rules Milan; Sept., 1494-Oct., 1495: Charles VIII of France Invades Italy; Apr. 11, 1512: Battle of Ravenna; Sept. 13-14, 1515: Battle of Marignano; Oct. 7, 1571: Battle of Lepanto.

RELATED ARTICLE in *Great Lives from History: The Renaissance & Early Modern Era, 1454-1600:* Mehmed II.

1455-1485
WARS OF THE ROSES

The reign of Henry VI erupted into violent disorder as a contest for the throne of England, named the War of the Roses, developed between the rival families of York and Lancaster. The conflict was finally extinguished when Henry VII became the first Tudor Dynasty king.

LOCALE: England and Wales
CATEGORIES: Wars, uprisings, and civil unrest; government and politics

KEY FIGURES

Henry VI (1421-1471), king of England, r. 1422-1461 and 1470-1471
Margaret of Anjou (1430-1482), wife of Henry VI
Richard, duke of York (1411-1460), third duke of York
Edward of York (1442-1483), king of England as Edward IV, r. 1461-1470 and 1471-1483
Earl of Warwick (Richard Neville; 1428-1471), earl and kingmaker
Richard III (1452-1485), Yorkist king of England, r. 1483-1485
Henry VII (1457-1509), first Tudor king of England, r. 1485-1509

SUMMARY OF EVENT

When Henry V, the hero of the 1415 Battle of Agincourt in France, died of battlefield dysentery in 1422, he left as his heir a child who was just nine months old, Henry VI. However, the war in France was going well, England itself was peaceful and well governed, and the memory of Henry IV's seizure of the throne from Richard II had faded considerably.

By the time Henry VI was old enough to exercise royal authority in the late 1430's, the situation was less

An illustrated scene from William Shakespeare's play Henry VI, *in which roses are chosen to represent the Houses of Lancaster (red) and York (white). The roses stood as symbols for the wars between the two families.* (Hulton|Archive by Getty Images)

favorable. The French were successfully regaining territory from the English. Royal rule at home seemed increasingly weak and uncertain, leading to factions among the nobility and to the eventual emergence of a rival claimant to the throne, Richard, duke of York. His descent from both Lionel, duke of Clarence, and Edmund, duke of York, respectively the second and fourth sons of Edward III, provided a stronger claim to the throne than that of Henry himself, who was descended from John of Gaunt, duke of Lancaster, the third son of Edward III.

Modern scholars have tended to lessen the significance of this dynastic aspect of the conflict, downplaying that there were two hostile groups in the kingdom identified by their respective badges: the red rose of Lancaster and the white rose of York. Rather, most historians consider the conflict to come from both political ineptitude at the center and the effects of a severe economic depression in England in mid-century. By 1450, the loss of nearly all English territory in France (after 1453 only Calais remained) and distrust of the king's close advisers had led to a major rebellion in the southeast. By 1452, Richard, duke of York, had emerged as the leader of those dissatisfied with Henry VI's kingship, but it is also clear that most of the nobility and gentry were very reluctant to move from grumbling to armed rebellion.

At this point, Henry suffered the first of his attacks of severe mental illness, probably a form of catatonic schizophrenia. Richard was appointed protector of the realm, but the situation changed rapidly when Henry recovered in early 1455. He now had a son (born during his illness) and a queen, Margaret of Anjou, who would devote all of her energies to ensuring the future succession of their son.

In May, an indecisive skirmish among the houses and gardens of St. Albans, just north of London, was the first armed conflict. It was now much clearer that Richard and his supporters were hostile to the court if not to the king. By November, in fact, the king had suffered a relapse and Richard was once more protector, until the spring of the following year.

Despite attempts at reconciliation, however, tensions increased between the two groups. The Lancastrians based themselves in The Midlands of central England, where the king and his main supporters had extensive lands. Richard was on the border with Wales, while his main ally, Richard Neville, the earl of Warwick and captain of Calais, developed Calais into his power base. By 1459, open warfare had begun. Early victories for the Lancastrians (by the forces inspired by Margaret) were followed by the crushing defeat of the Lancastrians by Warwick and the Yorkists at Northampton. The crown

seemed to be within Richard of York's grasp, but five months later he was killed with many of his followers at the Battle of Wakefield, and his severed head was impaled on the gates of York.

Warwick's attempt to hold London for the Yorkist cause also failed at the second Battle of St. Albans in 1461. Richard's eldest son, Edward of York, however, did not accept defeat. Having beaten a small Lancastrian force at Mortimer's Cross, he marched on London, proclaimed himself king, and then followed Margaret's retreating forces north. At Towton, near York, a ferocious and bloody battle took place in a snowstorm on March 29. The result was complete victory for the new king, Edward IV.

Some Lancastrian resistance continued, however. Henry VI, Margaret, and their son Edward, prince of Wales, were in exile abroad, but continued to attempt to stir trouble, particularly on the border with Scotland. Edward IV eventually subdued the rebels, and, in 1465, Henry VI fell into his hands as a prisoner. This fortunate turn of events was overshadowed by the growth of new factions at court. Warwick, who believed he was the cause of the young king's success, was angered by the king favoring others, especially the family of the new queen, Elizabeth Woodville. He intrigued with Edward's brother, George, duke of Clarence, and, in 1469, attempted to seize power.

Driven into exile in France by Edward, he vowed allegiance to Margaret and her son, who were in exile in France as well. In September, 1470, Warwick led an invasion fleet to Devon. Edward was surprised, and, in his turn, fled for his life across the North Sea to Bruges in the Low Countries. The pathetic Henry VI was released from his imprisonment in the Tower of London and restored to the throne under Warwick's tutelage.

During the reascension of Henry VI, Edward IV was busy negotiating with Charles the Bold, the duke of Burgundy, for support. In March, 1471, Edward landed at Ravenspur in Yorkshire. Despite an initially hostile reception, he pressed south. By the time he reached London, Edward had regained the support of Clarence and also had a considerable army, which met Warwick's Lancastrian forces at Barnet in a thick fog April 14. Edward crushed his enemies, and Warwick and other leaders were killed. Final victory came at Tewkesbury in the Severn Valley in early May. Margaret and her son had landed at Weymouth on the very day of the Battle of Barnet. Edward moved rapidly to the west to counter this new threat, and he caught the Lancastrians before they could muster more forces in Wales and Cheshire. Edward,

Fighting between the Houses of Lancaster and York known as the Wars of the Roses ended after the marriage of Henry VII and Eliza-beth of York in 1485. Some believe the union helped to stop the wars. (Hulton|Archive by Getty Images)

prince of Wales, was killed; his mother was once more a fugitive and the Lancastrian cause seemed leaderless. Henry VI, sick and old before his time, was probably murdered in the Tower of London shortly after the battle.

Until his death in 1483, Edward IV ruled successfully, although he finally broke with Clarence and ordered Clarence's execution for treason in 1478. The events of the summer of 1483, however, the deaths of the "princes in the Tower" (Edward V and his young brother, Richard, duke of York), and the seizure of the throne by Richard III reignited the hopes of the few remaining Lancastrians. There was no direct descendant of Henry VI alive, but his distant cousin, Henry Tudor, earl of Richmond, was head of the family. With the help of the French, Henry was able to land a small force at Milford Haven in Pembrokeshire, Wales, on August 7, 1485. Richard III gathered his forces near Leicester, and the two armies met at Bosworth on August 22. This battle, too, was hard fought, but Richard

was killed, leaving Henry Tudor the victor to assume the English crown as Henry VII.

To some historians, the Battle of Bosworth marked the end of the Wars of the Roses, with Henry uniting the factions under his leadership by marrying Elizabeth of York, the eldest daughter of Edward IV. Others see the Battle of Stoke-on-Trent in 1487, where Henry defeated a Yorkist pretender, as the last battle of the wars. Opinions are also divided as to the nature of the wars. Some point out that there were only about three months of actual fighting in a thirty-year period. To others, the whole period was marked by lawlessness, with bands of armed men, in the service of lords, terrorizing their neighbors.

SIGNIFICANCE

The Wars of the Roses ushered in a new dynasty, the Tudor line, that would rule England for the next century and a half. William Shakespeare provided a very influential view of the whole series of events, ranging from the deposition of King Richard II in 1399 to the death of King Richard III, in a series of history plays that emphasized the role of Henry VII and the Tudors as saviors of the nation. Many recent writers are most interested not in battles but in what the events reveal about the role of royal government and what was expected of a "good" ruler. All agree, however, that an understanding of fifteenth century England would not be complete without some knowledge of the Wars of the Roses.

—*Susan Rose*

FURTHER READING

Carpenter, Christine. *The Wars of the Roses: Politics and the Constitution in England, c. 1437-1509*. New York: Cambridge University Press, 1997. Provides a thoughtful interpretation of the political aspect of the Wars and subsequent years.

Dockray, Keith. *Henry VI, Margaret of Anjou, and the Wars of the Roses: A Source Book*. Stroud, Sutton, England: 2000. A collection of extracts from primary sources, with helpful introductions.

Haigh, Philip. *The Military Campaigns of the Wars of the Roses*. Stroud, Sutton, England: 1995. Concentrates on the military aspects of the wars, with battle plans and discussion of strategy and tactics.

Hicks, Michael. *Warwick the Kingmaker*. Cambridge, Mass.: Blackwell, 2002. A full scholarly account of the life of this crucial figure.

Webster, Bruce. *The Wars of the Roses*. London: UCL Press, 1998. Gives a clear outline of the politics of the period taking full account of recent writing.

SEE ALSO: Aug. 29, 1475: Peace of Picquigny; 1483-1485: Richard III Rules England; Beginning 1485: The Tudors Rule England; Dec. 1, 1494: Poynings' Law.

RELATED ARTICLES in *Great Lives from History: The Renaissance & Early Modern Era, 1454-1600:* Edward IV; Henry VII; Richard III; Earl of Warwick.

1456
PUBLICATION OF GUTENBERG'S MAZARIN BIBLE

Gutenberg's publication of the first book printed from movable type was a major landmark in the development of Western civilization. Arguably the first step in the creation of a distinctively modern culture, it permanently transformed, in both method and scope, the circulation of information, narratives, and ideas in society.

LOCALE: Mainz (now in Germany)
CATEGORIES: Science and technology; literature; cultural and intellectual history; religion

KEY FIGURES

Johann Gutenberg (1394/1399-1468), German inventor of movable-type printing
Johann Fust (c. 1400-1466), Gutenberg's partner
Peter Schoeffer (1425?-1502), Gutenberg's employee
Laurens Coster (c. 1370-1440?), Dutch wood-block printer believed by some to have invented movable-type printing.

SUMMARY OF EVENT

Johann Gutenberg, a German printer from Mainz, is generally credited with inventing movable type in the fifteenth century. Books printed before Gutenberg's time, such as the *Jin gang jing* (868; *Diamond Sutra*, 1912),

were made by engraving and inking woodblocks, pressing paper over their surface, and lifting off page prints. Hundreds of copies could be produced in a short time using this process, but thousands of copies could be produced in the same amount of time using movable type. This phenomenal increase in the number of books one could produce changed the very nature and function of the book within Western culture.

Prior to wood-block printing, literature had been painstakingly copied onto scrolls for thousands of years. By the early second century, the Romans were using notebooks made of two wooden tablets, tied together, filled with pigmented wax, and written on with a metal stylus. These tablets were later replaced by treated animal skins. By the fifth century, the codex, a manuscript made of several gatherings of parchment stitched together in leaf-book format, had replaced the notebook in the Western world. Codices, popular with early Christians, had the advantage of compactness and easy portability. (The four gospels could be contained in a single codex; 31 feet of scroll were required to contain the Gospel of Luke alone.) During the Middle Ages, monks spent years copying the scriptures. The time required to produce these manuscripts, as well as the cost of parch-

An artist's rendering of Gutenberg looking over pages printed with movable type, which was Gutenberg's innovation. The Mazarin Bible of 1456 was printed using movable type.

ment, made Gutenberg's invention a revolutionary technological breakthrough.

Born to a wealthy family in Mainz in about 1397 and trained as a goldsmith, Gutenberg was implicated in an uprising against the nobility in his hometown. As a result, he relocated to Strasbourg, probably in 1427. Legal documents from 1439 reveal that he entered into a partnership there with three persons to whom he promised to teach the secret art of printing. Some authorities claim that Gutenberg became involved in experimentation with printing in Holland with Laurens Coster, taking Coster's types and printing apparatus after Coster's death. They therefore attribute the invention of printing to Coster. There is no doubt, however, that it was Gutenberg who made movable-type printing practically feasible.

Gutenberg's Strasbourg partnership ended about 1444, and by 1448, he was back in Mainz. There he entered into a partnership with Johann Fust, who advanced the capital to establish and operate a printing business. There is no known description of Gutenberg's shop or printing press, which was probably derived from presses used in papermaking, but it is known that his type was made by striking a hard metal die shaped in the mirror image of a letter against soft metal. The resulting impression, or matrix, was then filled with a molten alloy, which when cooled hardened to form a piece of type. The letters thus formed were set into a plate, locked in, inked, and pressed against paper to make a page of type.

Fust was a skilled goldsmith and engraver, and his former apprentice, Peter Schoeffer, was a skilled penman. Their talents contributed to the exquisite Bible Gutenberg printed sometime between 1450 and 1455. Sample pages of this book—called the Mazarin Bible because the first known copy was found in the library of the French cardinal Mazarin—were exhibited at the Frankfurt trade fair in 1454 and praised by Aeneas Silvius

Piccolomini, the bishop of Sienna and future Pope Pius II. Buyers for all of the approximately 180 copies then in production were soon found.

By the end of 1455, however, Gutenberg and Fust had fallen out with each other. Fust sued Gutenberg and was awarded the printing equipment and materials. Fust and Schoeffer, now his son-in-law, finished production on the Bible and issued a remarkable edition of the Psalter in 1457, the first book to bear the complete imprint of printer, place, and date. The impoverished Gutenberg began afresh in 1459, but he retired in 1465 to accept an appointment to the court of the archbishop of Mainz. He died in 1468.

Meanwhile, in 1462, political disturbances in Mainz brought the printing business to a halt. The original German printers fled to other states, and the art of printing quickly spread throughout Europe. Occurring at the same time as the Renaissance, the invention of movable type ignited an explosion of new information. Within fifty years, the number of books in Europe had increased from thousands to millions. There were at least one thousand different working presses. The literacy rate, less than 2 percent in the Middle Ages, increased dramatically.

The text of the Mazarin Bible was the revised Vulgate translation produced at the University of Paris in the early thirteenth century. Each Bible was printed in the folio format then common for Bibles that were to be used for public readings. Each set of two, sometimes four, pages was made from a single large sheet folded over once. Most pages (twelve hundred in all) had forty-two lines of text arranged in double columns—hence Gutenberg's Bible is also known as the Forty-two-Line Bible. Made to resemble a hand-copied manuscript edition, the Bible has no title page, page numbers, or evidence of the printer's name or place and date of printing. To further disguise the machine-made origins of his letters, Gutenberg made multiple casts of certain letters, casting a total of about 270 Gothic-style letters and 125 symbols of abbreviations. The Gutenberg Bible is the first great work of the printer's art. The purity of the paper, the luster of the ink, and the elegant uniformity and sharpness of the type remain impressive even today.

SIGNIFICANCE

Literature and scholarship flourished in the wake of Gutenberg's invention. Major Latin works, many Greek classics, and more than 250 editions of the Bible or parts of the Bible appeared in publication. In Italy, pocket-sized editions of the classics were published to satisfy an ever-increasing demand. Books were prized for their rich

bindings and artistic decorations, such as woodcut illustrations by artists Albrecht Dürer and Hans Holbein, the Younger. Royalty and wealthy private collectors acquired extensive libraries, many of which later became the basis for national libraries. Presses and eventually large publishing houses became established all over Europe.

Before the sixteenth century, finance, politics, and theology were beyond the scope of even the educated population. After the sixteenth century, especially in England and northern Europe, powerful groups—nobles, judges, and merchants—became avid readers of books and pamphlets dealing with political and religious controversies. As they read more political matter and became more cognizant of contemporary controversies, people began to demand a voice in public affairs as well. Thus, print played a significant role in the rejection of absolutism and the development of populism and democracy.

Pamphlets of the period reveal deep popular resentment against royal tax collectors representing central authority. Although kings and bishops tried to stamp out "subversive" ideas, censorship failed miserably. Books were easily transported across borders, and secret presses were hard to find and destroy. By the 1640's, political upheaval was widespread. States that managed to control the presses (Spain and eastern Europe, for example) could control religious and political thought, but the flood of printed matter in most of northern Europe contributed to the breakdown of traditional institutions and values.

Perhaps the greatest immediate effect of the printing press was its contribution to the Reformation. Following Martin Luther's break with the Roman Church in 1517, Bibles and Protestant writings were printed and sold by the thousands. One of the central ideas of the Protestant Reformation, that Christians should read and understand the Word for themselves rather than have it explained to them by a priest, would have been a ridiculous and literally impossible idea less than one hundred years earlier, when there simply could not be enough Bibles to go around. In a very real sense, then, the invention of print was directly responsible for one portion of the Reformation. By the same token, the Reformation itself provided a crucial impetus for the development and spread of printing. As Bibles proliferated, Christian unity collapsed worldwide, and the stage was set for secularization and the modern age.

—Edna B. Quinn

FURTHER READING

Febvre, Lucien, and Henri-Jean Martin. *The Coming of the Book: The Impact of Printing, 1450-1800.* Translated by David Gerard, edited by Geoffrey Nowell-Smith and David Wooter. London: Foundations of History Library, 1997. Reviews the historical importance of the development of printing against the background of ideological and social upheaval in Western Europe.

Huber, Robert V., ed. *The Bible Through the Ages.* Pleasantville, N.Y.: Reader's Digest General Books, 1996. Useful background for the history of books prior to Gutenberg's invention of printing with movable type.

Kapr, Albert. *Johann Gutenberg: The Man and His Invention.* Translated by Douglas Martin. 1986. 3d ed. Aldershot, Hampshire, England: Scolar Press, 1996. First modern biography of Gutenberg appearing in English. Scholarly account of Gutenberg's life within a broad cultural and historical context. Includes many illustrations and reproductions of original documents and references in eight volumes.

Man, John. *Gutenberg: How One Man Remade the World with Words.* New York: John Wiley and Sons, 2002. Well-written history of the invention of printing, detailing the dramatic political, religious and social consequences.

Thorpe, James. *The Gutenberg Bible: Landmark in Learning.* 2d ed. San Marino, Calif.: Huntington Library Press, 2002. Concise history of printing that includes a discussion of the status of printing today. Ele-

gant book with color reproductions and details, issued by an institution that houses one of the rare extant copies of Gutenberg's Bible.

SEE ALSO: Nov. 1, 1478: Establishment of the Spanish Inquisition; 1486-1487: Pico della Mirandola Writes *Oration on the Dignity of Man*; 1490's: Aldus Manutius Founds the Aldine Press; 1499-1517: Erasmus Advances Humanism in England; 1516: Sir Thomas More Publishes *Utopia*; Oct. 31, 1517: Luther Posts His Ninety-five Theses; 1528: Castiglione's *Book of the Courtier* Is Published; Mar., 1536: Calvin Publishes *Institutes of the Christian Religion*; July 15, 1542-1559: Paul III Establishes the Index of Prohibited Books; 1543: Copernicus Publishes *De Revolutionibus*; 1543: Vesalius Publishes *On the Fabric of the Human Body*; 1550's: Tartaglia Publishes *The New Science*; 1552: Las Casas Publishes *The Tears of the Indians*; Apr. or May, 1560: Publication of the Geneva Bible; 1580-1595: Montaigne Publishes His *Essays*; 1592: Publication of Wu Chengen's *The Journey to the West*.

RELATED ARTICLES in *Great Lives from History: The Renaissance & Early Modern Era, 1454-1600:* Albrecht Dürer; Hans Holbein, the Younger; Martin Luther; Aldus Manutius; Pius II.

1457-1480's
SPREAD OF JŌDO SHINSHŪ BUDDHISM

The Buddhist monk Rennyo established a base for proselytizing in Yoshizaki, in Japan's Echizen Province; as a result of his efforts, the Jōdo Shinshū sect spread through northwestern Honshū.

LOCALE: Honshū, Japan
CATEGORY: Religion

KEY FIGURES
Hōnen (1133-1212), a Japanese Buddhist monk from the monastery on Mount Hiei
Shinran (1173-1262), a disciple of Hōnen and founder of the True Pure Land Buddhist sect in Japan
Rennyo (1415-1499), a descendant of Shinran and leader of Jōdo Shinshū

SUMMARY OF EVENT
The Japanese terms Jōdo Shin and Jōdo Shinshū are usually translated as True Pure Land Buddhism, since *jōdo*

means "pure land," *shin* means "true," and *shū* means "religion" or "faith." The roots of Pure Land Buddhism can be traced to northwestern India in the first century C.E. after the Theravāda and Mahāyāna forms of Buddhism had emerged as the two major approaches to the religion. The Theravāda tradition emphasized the efforts of individual believers to achieve enlightenment, especially through entering monasteries. The Mahāyāna tradition focused more on enlightened beings, or bodhisattvas, who could help ordinary humans achieve enlightenment and salvation. Among the Indian sutras, or sacred writings, several scriptures described the work of an enlightened being, the Bodhisattva Dharmākara (literally, "buddha to be"), who meditated and struggled to establish a perfect realm, or pure land, where faithful followers of Buddhism could be reborn. Dharmākara became the Buddha Amitābha or Amida.

The Pure Land school of Mahāyāna Buddhism did not

establish itself widely in India, but it did spread to China. In China, the idea that expressions of devotion to the ideals of the Amida Buddha could lead to rebirth in the Pure Land became a part of monastic practice in many locations. Chinese lay societies devoted to the Amida Buddha also grew. As Japan adopted Buddhism from China, Pure Land Buddhism began to become part of Japanese religious history. Many other types of Buddhism required extensive periods of time in monasteries and years spent in learning or meditation. Because Pure Land Buddhism concentrated on expressions of faith, it had a special appeal to ordinary people in Japan.

One of the earliest figures in True Pure Land Buddhism was the monk Hōnen, who entered the monastery on Mount Hiei when he was thirteen and emerged to teach Pure Land Buddhism to people of all social classes in 1175. One of Hōnen's disciples, Shinran, who had also been a monk at Mount Hiei before leaving to follow Hōnen, developed a radical version of Pure Land, known as the True Pure Land. According to Shinran, monastic renunciation and meditation were much less important than the simple and sincere recitation of a statement of faith in the Amida Buddha, such as the Nembutsu: "Namu Amida Butsu" ("I put faith in the Amida Buddha").

Ten years after Shinran's death, his daughter built a mausoleum for him at Otani, east of Kyōto. The mausoleum became the site of a temple, which eventually became known as Honganji, or Temple of the Original Vow. The abbots of Honganji were direct descendants of Shinran, passing the office from father to firstborn son.

Rennyo became the eighth abbot of Honganji in 1457. He was the illegitimate son of the previous abbot, Zonnyo, and because of his illegitimacy, his claim to the leadership of the monastery provoked some controversy. As soon as he came into office, he began making contact with various Buddhist groups that had been influenced by Shinran and recruiting new members for Honganji. Some of Rennyo's most effective teaching was in the form of letters to the faithful. He began his efforts in the province of Ōmi, and his first pastoral letter is dated 1461.

Under Rennyo, the doctrines of Shinran spread rapidly. The dominant Tendai sect of Mount Hiei, from which Shinran had split, became alarmed at the challenge of Rennyo's teachings. In 1465, the monastery of Mount Hiei sent an army to attack and destroy Honganji. Rennyo moved farther north, to Yoshizaki in Echizen Province along the road of the Hokuriku seaboard. There, after several years of moving from place to place

with an image of Shinran, he established himself in 1471. In the meantime, the Ōnin War had begun in 1467, inaugurating an era of Japanese history that would come to be known as the Sengoku Jidai, or Warring States period. With warfare and social disorder throughout the country, the people were ready for new beliefs and new views of life.

In the area of Hokuriku, Rennyo built popular support for Shinran's Pure Land Buddhism by first traveling to villages and temples and preaching his beliefs. After he had established a widespread following, he continued to spread the faith by writing more pastoral letters, most of which were composed after his move to the Hokuriku coast. By 1475, he had a sufficiently widespread following that he could move back to the Kyōto area. Initially, he made his headquarters at Deguchi, near the location of modern Ōsaka. There, he continued to write letters encouraging what he saw as the true religion, condemning improper behavior, and opposing false teachings.

Rennyo and his followers decided on a new site for rebuilding the Honganji temple in 1478. For the next five years, laborers worked on the magnificent temple complex at Yamashina, a suburb of Kyōto. The buildings, with their beautiful gardens, moats, and bridges, lent additional prestige to the faith that Shinran had handed down to Rennyo.

Jōdo Shinshū underwent several changes under Rennyo's direction. An annual ceremony known as the Hoonko, which had long been performed in memory of Shinran, became one of the most important rituals at Honganji. Previously a modest affair dedicated to remembering the work of Shinran, the Hoonko became a large-scale service similar in some respects to a religious revival meeting. Rennyo also gave new emphasis to the hymns and chants authored by Shinran. The recitation of faith had taken a number of forms in sacred inscriptions before Rennyo's time, but Rennyo established the words "Namu Amida Butsu" as the standard form. Perhaps most important, Rennyo created a stable and extensive institutional framework for his religious tradition. Honganji became the top of a pyramid of religious communities, extending down through mid-level temples to various local congregations.

SIGNIFICANCE

Before Rennyo's time, Jōdo Shinshū was a minor sect on the margins of Japanese society. Rennyo transformed it into one of Japan's most influential schools of Buddhism and into an important political and social force. Shinran's True Pure Land Buddhism had split into diverse, often conflicting factions. Through his teaching and constant work of organizing, Rennyo brought these into a single network of religious communities and established the standard forms of devotion for his followers.

Jōdo Shinshū, as it was reorganized and spread by Rennyo, offered a version of Buddhism that could appeal to the masses of people, who were unable to dedicate their lives to meditation and study as monks. This mass appeal made it consistent with the interests of new social groups in Japanese society, such as merchants and nonaristocratic soldiers. Jōdo Shinshū also appealed to villagers in Rennyo's time and after, since central political control of villages in this disorderly period loosened and villages sought some degree of self-governance. With its deep roots in the lives of villages and its great popular following, Honganji itself became a political power in Japan.

Rennyo himself became a popular figure in Japanese tradition and literature. He was the source of popular anecdotes and stories among the common people of Japan. Legends about Rennyo and his teachings have appeared in drama and even in modern literature. The novel *Kuroi ame* (1965; *Black Rain*, 1969), by Ibuse Masuji, for example, includes a scene in which a layperson uses one of Rennyo's letters for a funeral service after the atomic destruction of Hiroshima.

—*Carl L. Bankston III*

FURTHER READING

Amstutz, Galen D. *Interpreting Amida: History and Orientalism in the Study of Pure Land Buddhism.* Albany: State University of New York Press, 1997. Concerned with the ways in which non-Japanese have studied and interpreted Jōdo Shinshū. The first chapter, on the background of the religion, gives a good historical summary of the faith's development.

Dobbins, James C. *Jodo Shinshu: Shin Buddhism in Medieval Japan.* Honolulu: University of Hawaii Press, 2002. A detailed examination of the development, structure, and beliefs of Shin Buddhism that provides the perspectives of both modern scholars and the religion's adherents.

Kitagawa, Joseph. *Religion in Japanese History.* New York: Columbia University Press, 1990. First published in 1966 and reissued in 1990, this is a classic overview of the history of Japanese religion by a University of Chicago professor regarded as one of the world's foremost authorities on the history of religion.

Rogers, Minor, and Ann Rogers. *Rennyo: The Second Founder of Shin Buddhism.* Fremont, Calif.: Asian Humanities Press, 1992. One of the few books to deal exclusively with Rennyo, this volume contains annotated translations of his major pastoral letters.

SEE ALSO: 1467-1477: Ōnin War; 1477-1600: Japan's "Age of the Country at War"; Mar. 5, 1488: Composition of the *Renga* Masterpiece *Minase sangin hyakuin*; Beginning 1513: Kanō School Flourishes; 1532-1536: Temmon Hokke Rebellion; 1549-1552: Father Xavier Introduces Christianity to Japan; 1550's-1567: Japanese Pirates Pillage the Chinese Coast; 1550-1593: Japanese Wars of Unification; Sept., 1553: First Battle of Kawanakajima; June 12, 1560: Battle of Okehazama; 1568: Oda Nobunaga Seizes Kyōto; 1587: Toyotomi Hideyoshi Hosts a Ten-Day Tea Ceremony; 1590: Odawara Campaign; 1592-1599: Japan Invades Korea; 1594-1595: Taikō Kenchi Survey; Oct., 1596-Feb., 1597: *San Felipe* Incident; Oct. 21, 1600: Battle of Sekigahara.

RELATED ARTICLES in *Great Lives from History: The Renaissance & Early Modern Era, 1454-1600:* Hōjō Ujimasa; Hosokawa Gracia; Oda Nobunaga; Ōgimachi; Oichi; Sesshū; Toyotomi Hideyoshi.

February 11, 1457
RESTORATION OF ZHENGTONG

Zhengtong (first reign name) or Tianshun (second reign name), also known by his temple name, Yingzong, was emperor of China twice: After being captured and imprisoned by the Mongols, on his release he was returned to the throne. His second reign was marked by the early rise to power of the eunuch class.

LOCALE: China
CATEGORY: Government and politics

KEY FIGURES

Yingzong (temple name, also Ying-tsung; personal name Zhu Qizhen, Chu Ch'i-chen; posthumous name Ruidi, Jui-ti; first reign name Zhengtong, Cheng-t'ung; second reign name Tianshun, T'ien-shun; 1427-1464), emperor of China, first r. 1436-1449, second r. 1457-1464

Esen Taiji (d. 1455), Mongol leader

Wang Zhen (Wang Chen; fl. fifteenth century), a powerful eunuch in Yingzong's court

Xu Youzhen (Hsü Yu-chen; fl. mid-fifteenth century), supporter of Yingzong and leader of the coup that restored him to power

Jingtai (reign name, also Ching-ta'i; personal name Zhu Qiyu, Chu Ch'i-yü; posthumous name Jingdi, Ching-ti; temple name Daizong, Tai-tsung; 1428-1457), emperor of China, r. 1449-1457

Yu Qian (Yü Ch'ien; fl. mid-fifteenth century), Jingtai's war minister

SUMMARY OF EVENT

The emperor whose temple name was Yingzong was born in 1427 and became emperor at age eight as Zhengtong, during the period in China's history now known as the Ming Dynasty (1368-1644). As a youth, Yingzong was precocious and well educated. Under the regency of his grandmother (the grand empress dowager), three able grand secretaries, and three eunuchs, his people enjoyed good government.

A turning point in Yingzong's life came with the Tumubao (T'u-mu) debacle. In July of 1449, the Mongol leader Esen Taiji invaded China. One of the eunuchs, Wang Zhen, persuaded the emperor, by then in his early twenties, to lead his army personally in a reckless expedition against Esen's forces. Leaving his half brother Zhu Qiyu behind as regent, Yingzong set out on August 4 with an army said to contain half a million men.

The disastrous expedition was ill equipped and ill planned, hindered by heavy rains and disorganized leadership. On August 31, the Chinese army camped at Tumubao instead of seeking refuge in a nearby city. The Mongols surrounded the army and attacked; the Chinese panicked and most of the army, generals, and nobles, as well as Wang Zhen, were massacred; the emperor was captured. The Mongol Esen was so surprised at his sudden and easy victory that instead of marching on to the undefended capital Beijing, he plundered the battlefield and returned north with the Chinese emperor. The Chinese were able to recover firearms and armor from the battlefield, and they returned to their capital.

The news of the emperor's capture at Tumubao threw the capital into confusion. Xu Youzhen advised evacuating southward, but he was opposed by the war minister Yu Qian, who urged the Chinese to keep their government in Beijing and defend it. He said those who advocated retreating were cowards and should be executed. The court decided to remain, and the ministers fortified the capital. The Chinese needed an emperor, and Yingzong's younger brother was put on the throne in his place as emperor. He reigned as Jingtai (reign name, meaning "bright exhalation") from 1449 to 1457.

Esen invaded China again but was beaten back. Realizing that he would not be able to get much treasure from Jingtai as ransom for his brother, he released Yingzong from captivity after a year. In September of 1450, Yingzong returned to China and renounced all claims to the throne. His brother, still reigning as emperor, prohibited any welcome, and the returning former emperor was met with only one sedan chair and two horses. When he returned to the palace, Jingtai treated him coolly and at once escorted him and Yingzong's wife to a compound in the Southern Palace, where they were kept isolated for six and one-half years, guarded by soliders. Even on Yingzong's birthday, officials were forbidden to congratulate him.

Jingtai's reign as emperor was supposed to be temporary, but he stayed firmly in power and declared his own son the heir-apparent. Some palace officials who still spoke on behalf of Yingzong were imprisoned and some were killed—arousing dissatisfaction and opposition to Jingtai, who lost popularity and prestige. As a result, the court split into factions and conspiracies.

When Jingtai fell ill in 1457, Yingzong's supporters, including Xu Youzhen, saw their chance. On February 11, 1457, they gathered up about four hundred imperial

MING DYNASTY, 1368-1644

Ming emperors were generally best known by their reign names. Often these would take the form of "the [reign name] emperor," as in the Hongwu emperor (Zhu Yuanzhang). Sometimes more than one dynasty had emperors by the same reign name, in which case the Ming emperor is often alternatively listed under the temple name preceded by "Ming," as in Ming Taizu for the Hongwu emperor.

Years	Personal Name	Posthumous Name	Temple Name	Reign Name
1368-1398	Zhu Yuanzhang	Gaodi	Taizu	Hongwu
1398-1402	Zhu Yunwen	Huidi	None available	Jianwen
1402-1424	Zhu Di	Wendi	Chengzu or Taizong	Yongle
1424-1425	Zhu Gaozhi	Zhaodi	Renzong	Hongxi
1426-1435	Zhu Zhanji	Zhangdi	Xuanzong	Xuande
1436-49, 1457-64	Zhu Qizhen	Ruidi	Yingzong	Zhengtong (1436-49), Tianshun (1457-64)
1449-1457	Zhu Qiyu	Jingdi	Daizong	Jingtai
1465-1487	Zhu Jianshen	Chundi	Xianzong	Chenghua
1488-1505	Zhu Youtang	Jingdi	Xiaozong	Hongzhi
1505-1521	Zhu Houzhao	Yidi	Wuzong	Zhengde
1522-1567	Zhu Houzong	Sudi	Shizong	Jiajing
1567-1572	Zhu Zaihou	Zhuangdi	Muzong	Longqing
1573-1620	Zhu Yijun	Xiandi	Shenzong	Wanli
1620	Zhu Changluo	Zhengdi	Guangzong	Taichang
1621-1627	Zhu Youjiao	Zhedi	Xizong	Tianqi
1628-1644	Zhu Youjian	Zhuangliemin	Sizong	Chongzhen

bodyguards, stormed the Southern Palace, freed Yingzong, and carried him to the throne room. Yingzong started his second reign as Tianshun (meaning "obedient to heaven"). The night on which this occurred came to be known as *duo men (to-men)*, meaning "the forcing of the palace gate." The deposed emperor died shortly afterward, by some accounts strangled by one of the palace eunuchs. His crowning as Emperor Jingtai while Yingzong was held captive by the Mongols had been considered an act of necessity, because China needed an emperor. The *duo men*, therefore, was a crude grab for power.

After years in confinement, Yingzong was suspicious and eager for revenge. He used the palace eunuchs and the secret police to purge the palace officials of the previous reign. Many were stripped of office, sent to the frontier, or executed. He even killed leaders of the coup who returned him to the throne. Those whom the war minister Yu Qian had accused in 1449 of being cowards because they had wanted to abandon the imperial capital were the ones who had restored Yingzong. In revenge, they falsely accused Yu Qian of treason, and he was executed five days after Yingzong's restoration. These executions made the first year of Yingzong's second reign unpopular; he appointed some popular secretaries, but he still used the police and secret service to suppress criticism and maintain security.

The *duo men* was the result of a successful conspiracy, and Yingzong's supporters expected, and received, offices, titles, and rewards. The result was a flood of greed, corruption, and scandal. The leader of the of the coup, Xu Youzhen, was appointed head of the grand secretariat and minister of war, but he so abused his power that after four months, he was arrested and exiled. Shi Heng (Shih Heng), the leading general, whose extravagant luxuries became a public scandal, was arrested and died in prison. Others guilty of corruption were executed.

Those in the court began to feel threated. Cao Jixiang (Ts'ao Chi-hsiang) and Cao Qin (Ts'ao Ch'in), who controlled all the garrison troops, planned a rebellion in August, 1461. They were betrayed to loyal generals; the rebellion failed, and the two leaders were killed or committed suicide. With the collapse of this coup, all the leaders of the 1457 coup themselves were now dead.

According to contemporary witnesses, Yingzong rose early and attended diligently to affairs of state. He was a man of compassion. Before his death, he decreed that the emperor's concubines no longer had to commit suicide so they could accompany their masters in death. He honored Daoism, and during his reign, the reprinting of many Buddhist and Daoist texts was completed. A great book on ethics, the *Wu-lun shu*, was completed and printed in 1443.

In 1443, he wrote, or had someone write for him, a new preface to a classic work on acupuncture that dated to the Song Dynasty, the *Tongren shuxue zhenjiu tu*, which consisted of a bronze model of the human body, illustrations engraved on stone, and a written text. The new preface reveals that Yingzong had ordered a new stone inscription and new bronze model. He forbade wearing Mongolian dress and speaking the Mongolian language in Beijing; he also ordered that all images of Confucius dressed in Mongolian style (with buttons on the left side) be changed to Chinese style (with buttons on the right).

Finally, during Yingzong's reign, the empire had a monopoly on the manufacture of the fine porcelain now popularly called china. Yingzong forbade the private sale of the precious blue-and-white porcelain, and later this ban was extended to the private sale of all other colors as well. As a result, there is today a great scarcity of porcelain from this period.

SIGNIFICANCE

Revenge and purges were a hallmark of the early part of Yingzong's second reign. At first, he purged the officials of the preceding reign of his brother, installing in their place those who had engineered his coup and return to the throne. When these officials overreached and became corrupt, they in turn were replaced. Thereafter, his government functioned smoothly.

Yingzong's reigns marked a turning point in the period of China's history. Wang Zhen was one of the first eunuchs in a series of these court officials who would gain great influence over the emperors during the Ming Dynasty. They used their power to rule the empire, sell offices, gain vast wealth, run secret police offices, and even depose emperors. Wang Zhen's incompetence and egomania, however, led to great disasters for Yingzong. The disastrous battle at Tumubao marked the end of the Ming emperors' superiority over the Mongols.

—*Thomas McGeary*

FURTHER READING

Dictionary of Ming Biography. 2 vols. New York: Columbia University Press, 1976. Full biographies of emperors and other important figures of the Ming Dynasty.

Hook, Brian, and Denis Twitchett, eds. *The Cambridge Encyclopedia of China.* 2d ed. Cambridge, England: Cambridge University Press, 1991. Brief account of Yingzong, but extensive coverage on the artistic and social culture of the period.

Mote, Frederick W. *Imperial China, 900-1800.* Cambridge, Mass.: Harvard University Press, 1999. Good coverage of Yingzong's reign.

Mote, Frederick W., and Denis Twitchett, eds. *The Ming Dynasty, 1368-1644, Part 1.* Vol. 7 in *The Cambridge History of China.* Cambridge, England: Cambridge University Press, 1988. Thorough and detailed history of the Ming Dynasty; mostly political history.

Paludan, Ann. *Chronicle of the Chinese Emperors: The Reign-by-Reign Record of the Rulers of Imperial China.* London: Thames and Hudson, 1998. As the title suggests, concise accounts of the emperors; lavishly illustrated with maps and photographs, many in color.

SEE ALSO: 1465-1487: Reign of Xianzong; 1474: Great Wall of China Is Built; 1488-1505: Reign of Xiaozong; 16th cent.: China's Population Boom; 16th cent.: Rise of the *Shenshi*; 1505-1521: Reign of Zhengde and Liu Jin.

RELATED ARTICLES in *Great Lives from History: The Renaissance & Early Modern Era, 1454-1600:* Wang Yangming; Xiaozong.

April 14, 1457-July 2, 1504
REIGN OF STEPHEN THE GREAT

Stephen the Great established Moldavian independence, blocked Ottoman expansion in the region, and ensured the necessary prosperity for cultural accomplishments.

LOCALE: Moldavia (now in Romania, Moldova, and Ukraine)

CATEGORY: Government and politics

KEY FIGURES

Stephen the Great (Stephen cel Mare; 1435-1504), prince of Moldavia, r. 1457-1504

Mehmed II (1432-1481), Ottoman sultan, r. 1444-1446, 1451-1481

Bayezid II (1447/1448-1512), Ottoman sultan, r. 1481-1512

Süleyman the Magnificent (1494/1495-1566), Ottoman sultan, r. 1520-1566

Matthias I Corvinus (Mátyás Hunyadi; 1443-1490), king of Hungary, r. 1458-1490

Vlad III the Impaler (Vlad Tepes; 1431-1476), prince of Walachia, r. 1448, 1456-1462, and 1476

Casimir IV (1427-1492), king of Poland, r. 1447-1492

John I Albert (1459-1501), king of Poland, r. 1492-1501

Maria de Mangop (d. 1477), wife of Stephen the Great

SUMMARY OF EVENT

In 1457, Stephen the Great was proclaimed prince of Moldavia, ending the dynastic strife that had weakened the principality since the death of his grandfather in 1432. Having consolidated power by eliminating rivals and nobles of doubtful loyalty, he strengthened the defenses of Suceava, his capital, reinforcing the walls with stone able to withstand increasingly common explosives and artillery. Eventually, he constructed or improved a series of frontier fortifications, including those on vital trade routes through Cetatea Albă, at the mouth of the Dniester River, and Kiliya, near the delta of the Danube.

Recurring invasions and ceaseless diplomacy characterized Stephen's reign. The principal powers allied or at war with Moldavia included Hungary and Poland, both of which wanted Moldavia as a vassal principality, and the Ottoman Empire, which was consolidating its hold on the Balkans and securing its flanks before advancing up the Danube. The Crimean Tatars, intermittently allied with the Ottomans, also threatened Moldavia from the northeast. Finally, the principality of Walachia acted as a buffer zone between Moldavia and the Ottoman Empire, in which both powers jostled for influence. In this con-

test, the Ottomans were the more successful, especially after Vlad III the Impaler was dethroned in 1462; thereafter, Walachians frequently allied with the sultan against Moldavia, despite their common language, culture, and religion.

The challenges facing Stephen divide into three periods. The first began in November, 1467, when King Matthias I Corvinus of Hungary invaded Moldavia to punish Stephen for aiding some disloyal Hungarian nobles the previous summer and to regain the Kiliya fortress that had been captured by Stephen in 1465. The Hungarian army moved eastward, plundering towns and capturing Baia on December 14. Stephen's forces set the town afire. In the confusion, the Hungarians sustained heavy losses and Matthias himself was wounded, thus ending Hungary's last attempt to gain Moldavia as a vassal.

Stephen faced an Ottoman challenge in the second period, dating from 1471, when he refused to pay the sultan's annual tribute. In November, 1473, Stephen replaced the sultan's appointed prince of Walachia, Radu III the Handsome, with his own man, Basarab Laiotă the Old. Thus provoked, Sultan Mehmed II ordered his forces, ironically aided by the traitorous Basarab Laiotă himself, into Moldavia. On January 10, 1475, at Podul Inalt, located south of Vaslui in a foggy marsh surrounded by forests, the Moldavians attacked. Stephen had carefully selected the site to nullify the enemy's numerical superiority and to ensure the overwhelming Moldavian victory that followed. On January 25, Stephen addressed a circular letter to the rulers of Europe, inviting their participation in an anti-Ottoman crusade. This invitation was not accepted, but Pope Sixtus IV increased Stephen's growing fame by calling him "the athlete of Christ."

Mehmed II took revenge in 1476, ordering the Crimean Tatars to cross the Dniester River and attack Suceava. Elements of the Moldavian army rushed north to meet the threat to their capital and thus were unavailable when Ottoman forces entered Moldavia that July. At Razboieni in the Valea Alba, the Turks, commanded by Mehmed II himself, defeated the Moldavians on July 26. The sultan continued his advance and laid siege to Suceava. Thereafter, the detachments sent to confront the Tatars rejoined Stephen, Ottoman supplies ran short, cholera broke out in the Ottoman camp, and the Hungarians advanced eastward, threatening the Turkish lines of supply and retreat. As a result, Mehmed II ordered withdrawal on August 10.

In 1477, Stephen again set about building an anti-Ottoman coalition. When Venice signed a peace treaty with the Turks in January of 1479, Stephen realized that he, too, had to negotiate. That year, he resumed tribute payments to the sultan. Nevertheless, in July of 1484, Sultan Bayezid II captured Kiliya and Cetatea Albă. Seeking Polish support, Stephen reconfirmed the old Moldavian-Polish treaty and swore fealty to King Casimir IV on September 15, 1485. The Ottoman army, however, took advantage of Stephen's absence in Poland: It invaded Moldavia and burned down Suceava on September 19, 1485. A combined Polish-Moldavian army forced the Turks to retreat, but hope of reconquering their lost fortresses disappeared in 1489, when Poland also concluded a treaty with the sultan. Stephen was forced to do the same and resumed the tribute, thus bringing to an end his anti-Ottoman efforts.

The third period of Stephen's reign dates from the death of Matthias I Corvinus in 1490. John Albert, the Jagiellon heir apparent to the Polish crown, advanced claims to Hungary's throne as well. To forestall a Polish-Hungarian union, Stephen invaded Poland, annexing the territory of Pocutia. Complicated diplomatic activity followed for several years between the countries of the area, during which time Casimir IV died and John Albert succeeded his father as king of Poland.

King John I Albert invaded Moldavia in August of 1497 and laid siege to Suceava. Successful negotiations lifted the siege, but the Poles failed to follow the stipulated withdrawal route. Stephen attacked and defeated them at Codrii Cosminului on October 26, 1497. Pressing his advantage, Stephen invaded Poland the following year. Hungarian mediation restored peace on July 12, 1499, and John I Albert abandoned hope of making Moldavia a vassal.

The years immediately before Stephen's death on July 2, 1504, were peaceful. The years thereafter, however, were marked by a succession crisis, revolts by Moldavian nobles, and further conflicts with Walachia and Poland. Weakened and unable to resist the Ottomans, who were led by Süleyman the Magnificent, Moldavia became a Turkish vassal in 1538 and so remained until the nineteenth century.

SIGNIFICANCE

The rapid decline after Stephen's death only underlines his skill in maintaining Moldavian independence for forty-seven years. Because his wars were usually fought in Moldavia, he almost invariably enjoyed better intelligence, superior knowledge of the terrain, and shorter supply lines than his enemies. These advantages were coupled with Stephen's uncanny ability to coax his enemies into pursuit as he retreated behind scorched earth until they were positioned where superior numbers were no advantage and their baggage and artillery a distinct disadvantage. Although his army fought as infantry, it maneuvered on horseback for speed and surprise.

Stephen was an equally skilled diplomat, making and discarding treaties with a sure sense of Moldavia's shifting needs. Although the grand anti-Ottoman coalition of which he dreamed eluded him, he was a master at dividing his enemies and setting them against each other.

Beyond his military and diplomatic successes, however, Stephen's epithet, the Great, derives from his presiding over and generously patronizing one of the richest periods of Romanian culture. The Moldavian ecclesiastical architectural style, combining Byzantine and Gothic with traditional Moldavian elements, was perfected during his reign. The resulting structures reveal balance, proportion, and unexpected unity of design. Best known are the painted monasteries at Voronet and Neamt, whose exterior frescoes were added after Stephen's death. Many churches he endowed were built during the peaceful, prosperous period after the Ottoman invasions. Putna monastery, however, was finished in 1466, and Stephen was buried there with his wife, Maria de Mangop, whose tomb covering is considered a masterpiece of medieval embroidery.

Stephen was a generous patron of many arts. The illuminated manuscripts, icons, frescoes, richly embroidered vestments, gold and silver liturgical vessels, and book bindings that he donated to churches throughout the Romanian area preserved the memory of his reign long after his death, as he doubtless hoped would be the case. Also helpful in preserving his memory was *The Chronicle from the Origins of the Moldavian Land*, which he commissioned and to which he himself contributed some passages concerning his accomplishments.

For his piety, generosity, and determined defense of Christendom, Stephen the Great was canonized by the Romanian Orthodox Church on June 20, 1992.

— *Ernest H. Latham, Jr.*

FURTHER READING

Iorga, Nicolae. *Byzantium After Byzantium*. Translated by Laura Treptow. Portland, Oreg.: Center for Romanian Studies, 2000. A study of Moldavia and other Romanian territories in the years following the 1453 fall of Constantinople. Includes illustrations, bibliographic references, and index.

Panaite, Viorel. *The Ottoman Law of War and Peace: The Ottoman Empire and Tribute Payers*. Boulder, Colo.: East European Monographs, 2000. Discusses Stephen the Great and his attempts to resist the Ottoman demand for tribute. Includes maps, bibliographic references, and index.

Papacostea, Serban. *Stephen the Great: Prince of Moldavia, 1457-1504*. Translated by Sergiu Celac. Reprint. Bucharest: Editura Enciclopedică, 1996. Biographical monograph by a noted Romanian historian with useful bibliography.

Rosetti, R. "Stephen the Great of Moldavia and the Turkish Invasion." *Slavonic Review* 6, no. 16 (June, 1927): 87-103. Romanian military historian's examination of Stephen's army and its organization, tactics, and strategy in the Ottoman wars.

Sadoveanu, Mihail. *The Life of Stephen the Great*. Vol. 3 in *Classics of Romanian Literature*. New York: Columbia University Press, 1991. Romantic narrative by a famous Romanian novelist, underlining the rich legends surrounding Stephen.

Sedlar, Jean W. *East Central Europe in the Middle Ages, 1000-1500*. Vol. 3 in *A History of East Central Europe*. Seattle: University of Washington Press, 1994. A series of essays by a noted medievalist on social, economic, intellectual, and political topics.

Sugar, Peter F. *Southeastern Europe Under Ottoman Rule, 1354-1804*. Vol. 5 in *A History of East Central Europe*. Seattle: University of Washington Press, 1977. Authoritative study of Ottoman penetration and rule in the Balkans with separate chapters on such vassal states as Moldavia.

Treptow, Kurt W. "Stefan cel Mare—Images of a Medieval Hero." *Romanian Civilization* 1, no. 2 (Fall, 1992): 35-41. Contrasts Stephen's image as heroic symbol of Romanian national unity with historical reality.

SEE ALSO: 1454-1481: Rise of the Ottoman Empire; 1458-1490: Hungarian Renaissance; 1463-1479: Ottoman-Venetian War; 1478-1482: Albanian-Turkish Wars End; 1481-1512: Reign of Bayezid II and Ottoman Civil Wars; 1520-1566: Reign of Süleyman.

RELATED ARTICLES in *Great Lives from History: The Renaissance & Early Modern Era, 1454-1600:* Bayezid II; Mattius I Corvinus; Mehmed II; Sixtus IV; Süleyman the Magnificent; Vlad III the Impaler.

1458-1490
HUNGARIAN RENAISSANCE

Matthias I Corvinus expanded the boundaries of Hungary, established an advanced legal code and court system, ushered in enlightened social and judicial policies, and inspired lasting cultural achievements in Hungary.

LOCALE: Hungary

CATEGORIES: Cultural and intellectual history; government and politics

KEY FIGURES

Ladislas V (1440-1457), king of Hungary, r. 1444-1457 and king of Bohemia, r. 1453-1457

Matthias I Corvinus (Mátyás Hunyadi; 1443-1490), king of Hungary, r. 1458-1490, and son of János Hunyadi

János Hunyadi (c. 1407-1456), Hungarian military leader and national hero

János Vitéz (1408-1472), bishop of Nagyvárad until 1465 and archbishop of Esztergom, 1465-1472

Mihály Szilágyi (d. 1461), uncle of Matthias I Corvinus and regent of Hungary

George of Podebrady (Jiří z Poděbrad; 1420-1471), king of Bohemia, r. 1458-1471

Frederick III (1415-1493), Holy Roman Emperor, r. 1440-1493

Casimir IV (1427-1492), king of Poland, r. 1447-1492

Vladislav II (Władysław Jagiełło II; 1456-1516), king of Bohemia, r. 1471-1516, king of Hungary as Ulászló II, r. 1490-1516, and son of Casimir IV

János Pannonius (John Czezmicei; 1434-1472), poet and bishop of Pécs, 1457-1472

SUMMARY OF EVENT

When Ladislas V, king of Hungary, died in Prague without an heir, Matthias Corvinus, the eighteen-year-old second son of the Hungarian national hero, János Hunyadi, became a leading candidate for the crown. Mihály Szilágyi, Matthias's uncle, organized the lesser nobles to support Matthias, and on January 24, 1458, a diet in Buda elected him king. The competing claims of Casimir IV of Poland and Holy Roman Emperor Frederick III, the brother-in-law and uncle of Ladislas, respectively, were rejected. Szilágyi and János Vitéz, Matthias's tutor and mentor, then negotiated the release of the young king from Prague, where he had been imprisoned by Ladislas's scheming uncle Ulrich.

George of Podebrady, king of Bohemia, extracted a substantial ransom for Matthias, but he also betrothed his daughter, Catherine, to Matthias. The diet enacted a law, forbidding the new king from imposing taxes without their consent, which King Matthias I Corvinus pledged to obey in his coronation oath. Nobles also were prohibited from bringing armed retainers to diet meetings, thus bringing peace and calm to such meetings and allowing the king to rule effectively. With the aid of Vitéz, King Matthias quickly repaid his uncle for the ransom payment to George of Podebrady. Matthias also negotiated a settlement with Emperor Frederick III and ransomed the sacred crown of Saint Stephen.

Appointed regent, Szilágyi sought to dominate his nephew but was quickly outmaneuvered with Vitéz's assistance. Matthias took full control and established a strong centralized government, conducting state affairs through his own chancellery and royal council. These bodies were largely composed of younger men, selected by Matthias for their capabilities rather than their familial connections or wealth. In this way, he minimized the influence of the diet and reduced the political power of the magnates.

To pursue an effective foreign policy and maintain his position as king, Matthias reinforced the militia in 1458 by ordering every twenty *jobbagy* (households on the lands of great lords) to supply one mounted soldier. This quota was increased to one soldier per ten households in 1465. More important, beginning in 1462, Matthias organized the "Black Army," a hired standing army of twenty thousand cavalry and ten thousand foot soldiers. This force, an innovation for the time, gave Matthias a reliable standing army independent of the nobles.

To support his army, Matthias reorganized finances under royal administration and greatly increased taxation. He canceled the existing tax exemptions granted by his predecessors for many properties, communes, and districts. A new treasury tax of one-fifth of a gold florin for every town house or peasant homestead was introduced in 1467 and was quintupled in 1468. In addition, Matthias regularly levied special taxes. The actual taxes fell on the *jobbagys*, except in the case of the poorest nobles: Nobles having no *jobbagys* were required to pay the taxes personally. In this way, Matthias more than doubled royal revenues to almost two million gold florins. This increased wealth proved a burden, however, that

King Matthias I Corvinus of Hungary. (Hulton|Archive by Getty Images)

provoked unsuccessful conspiracies against him in 1467 and 1471.

Matthias's legal code, the *Decretum majus*, proclaimed in 1486, protected and defined individual rights. His reformed legal administration speeded legal procedures, which formerly were a function of the periodic meetings of the diet, and it largely prevented bribery. It also curbed the influence of the magnates. Lower courts were organized in each *megye* (county) and met at regular intervals. Courts consisted of a *föispán*, the king's administrative representative in the *megye*, four elected judges from the *megye*, and ten *homini regius*, or king's men. Appeals were first submitted to the *tabula regia judicaria*, presided over by a professional judge known as the *protonotarius*. Above this, the supreme court consisted of the king and assisting members of the royal council.

Matthias also encouraged Hungarian cultural development. János Vitéz, who was one of his principal agents and became archbishop of Esztergom in 1465, had begun his humanistic career under King Sigismund but served the Hunyadis for more than thirty years. Vitéz made his bishopric a center of culture and began accumulating the library that became the Corvina. He employed talented copyists whose works were distributed among distinguished Humanists. His interest in astrology led him to commission a treatise for calculating solar and lunar eclipses. Vitéz also founded the short-lived University at Pozsony (Bratislava). Another outstanding Hungarian Humanist of the time, John Czezmicei, known as János Pannonius, served as bishop of Pécs and was Vitéz's nephew. Pannonius was a prolific and influential poet, but much of his work was written in Italy and is unrelated to Hungarian life. While he served as bishop of Pécs, however, his poetry became more serious and more Hungarian in character.

Matthias's most significant achievement was his magnificent library. Starting in the early 1460's, the Corvina grew rapidly under the management of Taddeo Ugoleto. Buyers, copyists, and illustrators were engaged in Vienna and many Italian towns. A library workshop at Buda employed some thirty men in copying and illustrating. Some early printed works also were acquired and a short-lived press was established at Buda in 1478. The first map of Hungary was also produced in Matthias's court. After Matthias's death, many books were lost, as scholars failed to return volumes borrowed from the Corvina. Finally, the Ottoman Turks captured the library and added its contents to the sultan's library in Istanbul after the fall of Buda in 1541. About 170 of approximately 2,000 volumes contained in the Corvina have survived, and titles of an additional 300 books are known. A significant number of early editions of the classics are based on volumes from the Corvina.

Matthias effectively protected his royal position but in hindsight appears misguided for not having opposed the Ottomans more vigorously. When the newly crowned Matthias returned to Hungary from Prague, he was engaged to the Czech king's daughter and, under pressure from the Hungarian magnates, loyally refused to break the alliance. In 1464, after the death of his first wife, Matthias severed connections with King George of Bohemia, a Hussite, and, in pursuit of his ambition to be elected Holy Roman Emperor, he volunteered to lead a crusade against "heretical" Bohemia. Matthias attacked Moravia, occupied Brno and Olomouc and, with the aid of Catholic lords, was crowned king of Bohemia in 1468, despite the fact that George of Podebrady retained that same title.

Seeking support against King Matthias of Bohemia, King George of Bohemia immediately made Władysław Jagiełło, son of the Polish king Casimir IV, his heir. Upon George's death, Emperor Frederick recognized Jagiełło as King Vladislav II of Bohemia, leaving Matthias to face both the Poles and Bohemians. The war's expense forced Matthias to request a tax increase at the Diet of 1470. Refused, he collected the taxes without consent, thus igniting a conspiracy involving his longtime allies, János Vitéz and János Pannonius, who worked to usurp his throne and replace him with Casimir, the younger son of the Polish king.

Casimir invaded with seventeen thousand men but quickly withdrew when Matthias successfully reenlisted the sympathy of many magnates and proposed remedies for many of the conspirators' complaints at the Diet of 1471. Vitéz reconciled with Matthias but soon died. Pannonius died while fleeing the country, and the diet adjourned itself for two years. The war in Bohemia, however, continued until

---

ANTONIO BONFINI ON THE HUNGARIAN RENAISSANCE

Early in his reign, Matthias I Corvinus transformed Hungary, which was thought to be less than civil, into a nation modeled on the Renaissance culture of Italy. Here, Italian-born contemporary scholar Antonio Bonfini describes initial native-Hungarian resistance to Matthias's attempts to beautify Hungary through various projects, in this case, artistic and practical, and through supporting the life of the mind.

He assiduously sought out from all parts the most pre-eminent men in whatever field and employed them. He held in high esteem astronomers, physicians, mathematicians and lawyers, he did not even abhor magicians and necromancers; he never considered any art as unimportant.

Conversely, the Hungarians, lacking civil refinement and the niceties of life, bore all these things ill. They condemned the senseless expenditure and daily found fault with the sovereign for being wanton with money and for disbursing taxes set up for better uses on things that were worthless and vain.... There were many things with which they reproached him and they submitted to them with an ill grace. But for his part that divine ruler, a father of all the liberal arts, and patron of men of talent, openly condemned the Hungarians for their ways, and publicly reproached them for their Hunnish rusticity and uncultivated life. He utterly abhorred their barbarous customs. Gradually he introduced civil manners and encouraged magnates to adopt a civilized way of life.... And so it was that, chiefly by the king's example, they were all attracted towards all these ideas.

Source: From Ten Books on Hungarian Matters (c. 1496), by Antonio Bonfini. Excerpted in *The Renaissance in Europe: An Anthology*, edited by Peter Elmer, Nick Webb, and Roberta Wood (New Haven, Conn.: Yale University Press, 2000), pp. 207-209.

1478, when the Treaty of Olomouc affirmed Matthias's possession of Moravia, Silesia, and Lausitz and allowed both Matthias and Vladislav the title king of Bohemia. Meanwhile, the Ottoman Turks successfully invaded southern Hungary and constructed a fortress, Sabach, on Hungarian territory. Matthias mounted a campaign against the Ottomans and besieged Sabach, which surrendered in 1476.

Throughout his reign, Matthias was forced to contend with Emperor Frederick's unrelinquished claim to the Hungarian throne. After his Polish-Bohemian war, Matthias fought three campaigns against Frederick between 1477 and 1490 to end Frederick's influence. The first two wars ended on Matthias's terms and gave him all of Bohemia. Frederick did not comply with all the terms, however, and hostilities resumed. In the third war, Matthias captured Vienna in 1485. There, Matthias died on December 6, 1490.

SIGNIFICANCE

Matthias's legacies to his nation and to Eastern Europe were of varying durations. Militarily, his conquests were lost soon after his death, and Hungary was left alone to face the Ottomans. In the legal sphere, Matthias's code and courts were more advanced and more humane than most contemporary systems, and the memory of them as an ideal had a lasting impact on the European juridical imagination. Their immediate practical effects did not long survive following Matthias's reign, however, giving rise to the saying, "Matthias is dead—justice is lost." It was arguably the cultural achievements of Matthias's regime that had the most obvious and lasting effects on early modern history, and it was this development of intellectual and artistic culture that resulted in his reign being designated as the "Hungarian Renaissance."

—*Ralph L. Langenheim, Jr.*

FURTHER READING

Bak, János. "The Late Medieval Period." In *A History of Hungary*, edited by Peter F. Sugar, Peter Hanak, and Frank Tibor. London: I. B. Tauris, 1990. Comprehensive though short account of Matthias's life and times.

Bibliotheca Corviniana, 1490-1990: International Corvina Exhibition on the Five Hundredth Anniversary of the Death of King Matthias, National Széchényi Library, 6 April-6 October, 1990. Budapest, Hungary: The Library, 1990. Catalog of an exhibition of materials from Matthias's library. Includes color illustrations and bibliographic references.

Birnbaum, Marianna D. *Thr [sic] Orb and the Pen: Janus Pannonius, Matthias Corvinus, and the Buda Court*. Budapest, Hungary: Balassi, 1996. Collection of eleven interdisciplinary essays on the Hungarian Renaissance, focusing especially on Pannonius's poetry and Matthias's library. Includes color illustrations, bibliographic references, and index.

Erdei, Ferenc. *Information Hungary*. Vol. 2 in *Countries of the World*, edited by Robert Maxwell. Oxford, England: Pergamon Press, 1968. A Marxist account of Matthias's reign.

Feuer-Tóth, Rózsa. *Art and Humanism in Hungary in the Age of Matthias Corvinus*. Translated by Györgyi Jakobi. Edited by Péter Farbaky. Budapest, Hungary: Akadémiai Kiadó, 1990. A study of Matthias's court, his patronage of the arts, and the spread of Humanism in the Hungarian Renaissance. Includes eight pages of photographic plates, illustrations, bibliographic references, and index.

Klaniczay, Tibor, and József Jankovics, eds. *Matthias Corvinus and the Humanism in Central Europe*. Budapest, Hungary: Balassi Kiadó, 1994. Anthology of essays originally presented at a conference on Matthias I and Humanism in Székesfehérvár, Hungary, in May, 1990. Includes photographic plates, illustrations, bibliographic references, and index.

Macartney, C. A. *Hungary: A Short History*. Chicago: Aldine, 1961. Includes a brief account of Matthias's reign.

Pamlenyi, Erving, ed. *A History of Hungary*. London: Collets, 1975. A detailed history of Hungary that includes discussion of Matthias and his accomplishments.

Sinor, Denis. *History of Hungary*. New York: Frederick A. Praeger, 1959. Reprint. Westport, Conn.: Greenwood Press, 1976. Includes a chapter on Matthias. With maps and index.

SEE ALSO: 1454-1481: Rise of the Ottoman Empire; Apr. 14, 1457-July 2, 1504: Reign of Stephen the Great; June 12, 1477-Aug. 17, 1487: Hungarian War with the Holy Roman Empire; 1514: Hungarian Peasants' Revolt; 1526-1547: Hungarian Civil Wars; Aug. 29, 1526: Battle of Mohács; 1576-1612: Reign of Rudolf II.

RELATED ARTICLES in *Great Lives from History: The Renaissance & Early Modern Era, 1454-1600:* Frederick III; Matthias I Corvinus; Vladislav II.

1459
RĀO JODHA FOUNDS JODHPUR

Rāo Jodha's construction of the massive Meherangarh fortress symbolized the heart of the city of Jodhpur in Rājasthān. Jodhpur would become the center of the Marwar state, which would spread its influence throughout the region.

LOCALE: Jodhpur (now part of the Indian state of Rājasthān)

CATEGORIES: Government and politics; architecture; expansion and land acquisition

KEY FIGURE

Rāo Jodha (d. 1488), Rathor ruler of Marwar, r. 1431-1488

SUMMARY OF EVENT

It is important for modern historians to understand the city of Jodhpur and its rise within the context of the factional strife that characterized much of the early modern period in India, including times of foreign influences, especially Turkish and Muslim. Indeed, far from being a fortress constructed to maintain extensive domination in Rājasthān, the Meherangarh fortress is instead a product of a time of uncertainty and change for the Marwar state.

It is not surprising that the prominence of Jodhpur itself is a product of the protection and importance that the Meherangarh fort brought to the area surrounding it. This fortress city of the Thar Desert became, in time, the capital of Marwar, the largest and most influential of the Rājput states. The imposing fort, which now dominates the western district of the modern city, is the stronghold from which the Rathor clan methodically spread the influence of their state of Marwar (land of the dead, in reference to the inhospitable Thar Desert) over a massive section of Rājasthān. Jodhpur is also the seed from which has grown many popular notions about the martial prowess and chivalry of the Rājput states and peoples.

The period of rising Arab and Turkish interference in northwest India was most challenging for border locales such as Rājasthān, but these times also provided opportunities for the augmentation of the ancient prestige of the various Rājput families. These opportunities came in the form of legendary resistance (Prthviraja III, the Chauhan Rājput, defeated Muhammad of Ghor at Tarain in 1191) and creative political alliances (Raja Surender's service with the Mughal emperor Akbar, including the capture of Gujarat).

Additionally, pressure from external forces seems to have awakened Rājput princes to the need to preserve the prestige of their rulers among the local populations. These factors were especially at play during two periods of occupation: the Delhi sultanate (1206-1526), a time of Turkish domination, and the rise of the Mughal Empire (beginning in 1526). Indian history between the early twelfth century and the early eighteenth century is often framed as a struggle for control between the largely Hindu and Jainist peoples native to the Indian subcontinent and Islamic forces from the northwest. Two factors are important to remember in this regard. First, the invaders were themselves rarely free from harassment by other forces (for example, the Mughals) and, second, the control of Indian states by foreign powers typically was exercised through a combination of conquest and diplomacy; various Indian states entered into a wide variety of relationships with the organizing and imperial forces. Those states, such as Marwar, that would emerge most successfully from this period were those that best understood how to read an increasingly complex and labile political scene.

Despite valiant resistance by Rājput and other Indian constituencies, the scene was set for the emergence of the Delhi sultanate by the end of the thirteenth century. A year after his heroic victory, Prthviraja III was defeated by Muhammad of Ghor (again at Tarain). In the following year (1193), Muhammad of Ghor captured the traditional Rathor stronghold, Kannauj, in north-central India, then under the command of Jai Chand. Chand's descendants, however, were political leaders who soon reestablished Rathor dominance, with their seat of power in Mandore, a fort previously under Pratihara control, and their principal trading center in Pali, just south of the site of Jodhpur. Mandore became the official Marwar capital in 1381 under Rāo Chandra. Rāo Chandra's son and Rāo Jodha's father, Rainmal, was allied closely with his nephew, an heir to the Mewar throne and fortress at Chitor. Sadly, internal feuds between the Mewari and Marwari led to the assassination of Rainmal in 1438 and the establishment of Mewar and Marwar as separate kingdoms.

Rāo Jodha fled Rājasthān temporarily, returning in 1453 to recapture Mandore and establish Marwari dominance over the region. To consolidate his holdings and increase the Marwar state to what would be its largest extent, Rāo Jodha constructed a new capital, naming it

Jodhpur, after himself. From here, the Rathor clan would build the state of Mawar into the largest Rājput state, one covering some 35,000 square miles.

With the rise of the Mughal Empire, Jodhpur initially aligned itself against the emperors and fought under Ganga Singh against Bābur.

At the accession of Akbar, however, Jodhpur changed sides and championed the cause of the emperors. This allowed Jodhpur and its rulers to bring increased stability to the region, maintain the prestige of their local rulers, and open up economic opportunities for the Marwar state and Rājasthān generally. Along with the economic advantages that accrued to Jodhpur from the mid-sixteenth to the mid-seventeenth centuries, especially as a center of trade between Central Asia and the northern Indian coast (Gulf of Cambay), there were also cultural advantages. Jodhpur became a center of culture and arts, adding to its prestige.

Jodhpur's period of cooperation with the Mughal Empire dissolved in 1658 after ʿĀlamgīr deposed his father, Shāh Jahān (r. 1626-1658); Maharaja Jaswant Singh I, then ruling at Jodhpur, had not anticipated that ʿĀlamgīr, who had asserted a claim to his father's throne along with all three of his brothers, would prevail. Although Jodhpur would eventually gain independence from the Mughal Empire, it would fall under British control in 1818. The dominance that Jodhpur had built, starting from the foundation of the Meherangarh fortress, was enough to ensure that even in the British period the Marwari would play a major role in northwestern Indian politics.

SIGNIFICANCE

During years of occupation and internecine struggle, the Rājput princes, especially the Rathores of Marwar, developed a sense of family identity that superseded ties to place, allowing the clan to maintain fierce internal loyalty despite moving their capital and shifting their allegiances. These characteristics opened the way to the foundation of Jodhpur as a new beginning for Marwar.

Jodhpur helped to localize Marwar pride, placing it in a critical position (locally and politically) to become an economic, political, and cultural leader in the region, and the largest of the Rājput states. Even in modern Indian history, successful bankers and traders from northwest India (even those who did not actually come from Marwar) are given the name "Marwari," a name that continues the trading legacy of the great city.

—Wells S. Hansen

FURTHER READING

Alam, Muzaffar, and Sanjay Subrahmanyam, eds. *The Mughal State, 1526-1750*. New York: Oxford University Press, 1998. Groups of four and five essays organized around central themes in Indian medieval history. All are written by experts and bring the time period into clear focus. Especially useful for those interested in the Rājput states is the section on "The Formation and Consolidation of Authority."

Chandra, Satish. *Essays on Medieval Indian History*. New York: Oxford University Press, 2003. Contains some of the most clear recent analysis of Rājput and Mughal relations in this period. This book is best suited to those who have already read some more general volumes on this period of Indian history.

Keay, John. *A History of India*. New York: Atlantic Monthly Press, 2000. The best written concise modern history of India now in print. Authoritative and compellingly written. This one-volume work relates the story of India from prehistory through the present. It includes a wealth of genealogical tables, maps, and full bibliography.

Mehta, J. L. *Advanced Study in the History of Medieval India*. Brill Academic, 1980. Volume 1 of this set is organized around a series of interesting topics, providing insightful analyses of events in Indian history, especially of the Rājputs and of Marwari.

SEE ALSO: 1451-1526: Lodī Kings Dominate Northern India; Mar. 17, 1527: Battle of Khānua; Feb. 23, 1568: Fall of Chitor.

RELATED ARTICLES in *Great Lives from History: The Renaissance & Early Modern Era, 1454-1600*: Akbar; Bābur.

Early 1460's
LABOR SHORTAGES ALTER EUROPE'S SOCIAL STRUCTURE

In the decades following the plague, a labor shortage radically altered the social and economic structures of Europe. Populations dwindled and family sizes decreased, and the economy transformed from one that was primarily agricultural and based on the bartering of services to an economy based on the marketplace and the selling of agricultural and manufactured goods.

LOCALE: Europe

CATEGORIES: Economics; trade and commerce; cultural and intellectual history

KEY FIGURES

Fugger family (1367-1806), dominant merchant banking family in Augsburg, Germany

Henry VIII (1491-1547), king of England, r. 1509-1547

Elizabeth I (1533-1603), queen of England, r. 1558-1603

SUMMARY OF EVENT

The bubonic and pneumonic plagues that terrorized Europe in 1348, and again at irregular intervals in the succeeding century, had a devastating effect on Europe's human capital. Though the exact numbers of deaths will never be known, it is now estimated that about 40 percent of Europe's population died. In comparison, the memorable widespread health disaster of the twentieth century, the influenza epidemic of 1918-1919, killed about 0.5 percent of the U.S. population.

In addition to the ravages of the plague, the endemic warfare of the fourteenth and fifteenth centuries wreaked havoc on the countryside of France and England. Military action, but also the devastation brought about by unpaid mercenaries who pillaged at will, reduced the economies of much of Western Europe tremendously.

By the time the European economy began to recover, from the 1460's onward, population decimation had changed the social structure of the continent in profound ways. Whereas, prior to the plague, population growth had pushed agricultural production to the margins of suitable land, after the plague, the number of people available to carry out the sowing and the reaping was reduced severely. The prior system of agriculture management, the manorial system, had relied on some nine-tenths of

the population to do the hard work in the fields. These field-workers were serfs, bound to the soil and its cultivation.

With a 40 percent reduction in available workers, however, serfs could bargain in ways that had been unavailable to them, for the laws of supply and demand worked then as they do in the twenty-first century. The serfs—the remaining agricultural workers—were able to demand that their obligations to the landlord be fulfilled, not with labor services but with money, and small amounts at that. They were able to demand the right to take over the plots of their neighbors who had died, in many cases becoming landowners themselves. They were able to convert plots that were no longer being cultivated into pasturage, to own that acreage's grazing cattle and sheep, and sell the livestock if they so desired. Also, they had the option, if slight, to relocate to urban areas to look for work.

Sheep-shearing in late fifteenth century Europe. (Frederick Ungar Publishing Co.)

In the century or so after the plagues became infrequent and more localized, the surviving populace looked quite different from the one that had prevailed in the first half of the four-teenth century. Instead of a relatively uniform agricultural labor force, what emerged was one that was highly differentiated. At the top of the labor scale were active landlords, who rented out their land for money or who hired stewards to cultivate it for them and to sell the produce at market. Midway on the scale were agricultural workers who had their own holdings but who sold their labor for money to the large landlords. At the bottom were those without land, or with perhaps no more than a small plot with a cottage and a garden, who supported themselves en-tirely from their wages.

As the agriculture-based system converted to a market-based system, many chose to leave ag-riculture altogether and migrate to the towns. Even though towns were breeding grounds for the plague and other diseases because of their in-adequate sources of water and waste disposal, they had jobs for those who had nothing to sell but their labor. Getting goods, both agricultural and manufactured, to the marketplace required the efforts of many, as the new market-based economy flourished.

Agriculture shifted from crops (grain was needed less and less because of the smaller pop-ulation) to pasturing livestock. The market for sheep's wool, for example, increased because sheep were being raised in areas once dominated by crop lands. When there seemed to be a shortage of land for the market-based production of grain and wool in En-gland, King Henry VIII seized the land-rich monasteries there in 1546 and disbanded them, opening the monastery lands to the cultivation of crops and the raising of sheep.

Before wool could be sold, it had to be spun and wo-ven, so many came to earn their living weaving woollen cloth. Whereas England and Spain exported ever-larger amounts of wool, laborers in the Low Countries and in It-aly spun and wove the wool into cloth. Profits from trade supported a growing urban middle class. Construction in many urban areas grew substantially, and builders pros-pered; their wages doubled between 1350 and 1500.

As many parts of Europe depended more on trade than they did on agriculture, those who had once controlled land shifted their focus. They rented out the land they controlled directly, often to men who made their living

The late fifteenth century European economy transformed from one based on agriculture and the bartering of services to one that sold goods and services. (Frederick Ungar Publishing Co.)

1460's

managing agricultural activity. They converted their cas-tles and manor houses into country residences and lived there only part of the time. Also, they devoted far less of their time to military service and far more to administrat-ing the growing national kingdoms.

Those members of the new middle class who were lucky enough to own land in the major urban centers, such as London or Paris, became rich renting out their properties. They would invest their profits in the innu-merable government loans issued by the new national rulers, becoming, in effect, "rentiers," living off the in-come generated by their assets, both real and financial. The wealthy Fugger family of Augsburg, Germany, con-trolled most of the silver mines in Austria and lent money to the Habsburgs, the ruling family in Germany. Several Italian families, including the Medici, had become rich through trade and became rulers also.

SIGNIFICANCE

The devastating drop in Europe's population between 1348 and 1450 had social consequences that reached beyond the conversion to a market- and, hence, money-based economy: The structure of the family changed. Starting in the late fifteenth century, the population began to recover. Sometime in the sixteenth century, and in some places, the population reached the level that it had achieved two hundred years earlier.

Europeans were still wary, however, about returning to the conditions of that earlier time, so they tended to restrict their family size to one that they knew they could sustain. Modern studies show that by delaying marriage, Europeans would limit the number of children they had depending on anticipated income from land holdings or from the parents' job. Even though many had the chance to emigrate to the newly forming colonies of the New World, this cautious approach to reproduction continued. Not until the nineteenth century did Europeans again begin to create large families, when the Industrial Revolution offered new means of support.

Not all attempts to balance family size and means of support were successful. The late fifteenth and especially the sixteenth century witnessed "sturdy vagabonds," unemployed men roving the countryside. During the reign of England's queen Elizabeth I, vagabonding became such a problem that attempts were made to restrict those needing public assistance. Men would receive that help if they limited their residence to their place of birth. Some of these men could be pressed into military or naval service, but they were generally unwilling soldiers and sailors. Europe began to confront the issue of welfare.

—*Nancy M. Gordon*

FURTHER READING

Braudel, Fernand. *The Structures of Everyday Life.* New York: Harper & Row, 1981. The first volume of Braudel's magisterial account of the rise of capitalism in western Europe, from 1500 to 1800.

Cipolla, Carlo. *The Middle Ages.* Vol. 1 in *The Fontana Economic History of Europe.* New York: Harper & Row, 1976. Contrary to its title, most of this book deals with the transition from the medieval economy to the early modern economy.

Hatcher, John. *Plague, Population, and the English Economy, 1348-1530.* London: Macmillan, 1977. Describes the full effects of the plague on the population and economy of England.

Hoppenbrouwers, Peter, and Jan Luiten van Zanden, eds. *Peasants into Farmers? The Transformation of Rural Economy and Society in the Low Countries (Middle Ages-Nineteenth Century) in Light of the Brenner Debate.* Turnhout, Belgium: Brepols, 2001. A collection that examines the transition from a rural, or agricultural, economy and social structure to a market economy—from feudalism to capitalism—in the Low Countries during the Middle Ages and later.

Huppert, George. *After the Black Death: A Social History of Early Modern Europe.* Bloomington: Indiana University Press, 1998. Describes the social consequences of the plague, especially in rural communities.

Potter, G. R., ed. *The New Cambridge Modern History.* Vol. 1. Cambridge, England: Cambridge University Press, 1957. Chapters examine Europe during the Renaissance.

Toch, Michael. *Peasants and Jews in Medieval Germany: Studies in Cultural, Social, and Economic History.* Burlington, Vt.: Ashgate, 2003. Examines the experience of the German peasantry, especially Jews, during the Middle Ages and through the fifteenth century, with a chapter on "Making Do with Little: Studies in the Economic History of the German Peasantry."

SEE ALSO: 16th cent.: Worldwide Inflation; 1531-1585: Antwerp Becomes the Commercial Capital of Europe; 1549: Kett's Rebellion.

RELATED ARTICLES in *Great Lives from History: The Renaissance & Early Modern Era, 1454-1600:* Elizabeth I; Henry VIII.

1460-1600
RISE OF THE AKAN KINGDOMS

The emergence of kingdoms in Akan began a process of political development in the region that would culminate in the creation of the Asante empire.

LOCALE: Akan region, Ghana (now in Republic of Ghana)

CATEGORIES: Government and politics; anthropology; expansion and land acquisition

SUMMARY OF EVENT

The ancestors of the Akan people migrated to Ghana from various parts of northern Africa as a result of social and political upheavals in the area. For example, communities such as Badu, Seikwa, and Nkorankwagya, found in the northwest of Bono in central Guinea, were the result of the Kulamo people moving into the Akan region. The various northern ethnic groups who came to Akan shared a set of related languages known collectively as Twi. In the fourteenth century, the town of Bighu was founded and subsequently became a major center of commerce. By the end of the fifteenth century, the Akan states had organized themselves into ten major states: Adanse, Akyem, Assin, Denkyira, Asante, Bono-Tekyiman, Banda, Twifo, Fante, and Akwamu. Adanse was considered the most significant state, and it was held to be the place where the founders of the five states originated.

The Akan states gave rise to some of the earliest major urban centers in West Africa. At first, they were principally an agricultural people, cultivating staple food crops like millet and sorghum in the coastal areas and yams, plantains, and rice in the forested interior. Vegetables, legumes, and spices were grown as supplementary crops. Once gold was discovered in the Akan forest region, the society's agricultural endeavors were supplemented by a significant mining industry.

The fifteenth century saw an increasing movement of Mandinke traders known as the Wangara from Mali to the gold-producing fields of the northern Akan kingdoms. The Akan traded in gold with the Wangara and later with European colonial nations, such as the Portuguese in the 1470's. Bono was founded as a consequence of the expansion of the gold trade. Additionally, the tropical forest where the Akan lived held vast plantations of kola nut trees. The kola possessed thirst-quenching properties and contained a stimulant similar to caffeine.

The Wangara, interested in the trade in kola and gold, traveled south to the forest belt. All extractions of gold from the southern tip of the Black Volta goldfields and from goldfields at Bambuk and Bure, west of Akan land, passed through Bighu. Bighu became the transition point for trade highways connecting minor states and towns like Kong and Bobo-Dioulasso to Djenné and Timbuktu in the northwest, to the Hausa states in the northeast, and to Elmina and Accra on the southeastern coast.

In addition to trading in raw materials, Wangara blacksmiths and goldsmiths from such groups as the Bamba, Kamaghatay, Jabaghatay, Timitay, Kurubario, and Gbanic fashioned jewelry and other commodities that gave further impetus to trade and commerce in the region. Oral traditions from Kommenda and Elmina describe the local manufacturing of salt from salt water retrieved from estuaries and boiled dry to leave the salt, as well as the export of roasted fish by merchants (*batafo*) to Fante states and to Adanse, Wassa, and Brong Ahafo. Evidence of a thriving textile industry in the Bighu area has also been found, along with remnants of ivory industries, which attained their peak in the fifteenth and sixteenth centuries, when Akan ivory workers carved finely crafted trumpets.

At the height of their commercial development, the Akan exported gold, kola nuts, ivory, honey, corn, hides and skins, and palm oil. In return, they received cloth, glassware, weapons, copper, glass beads, brocades, dried figs, dates, cowrie shells, pottery, smoking pipes, tobacco, drinks, books, horses, firearms, and cutlery. Their thriving trade network provided the basis for the centralization and consolidation of the Akan kingdoms, which would later facilitate the formation of the powerful Asante Empire of the eighteenth and nineteenth centuries. The Akan also imported enslaved people who had been captured by the Portuguese in Benin along the West African coast. The Akan used these captives as forced labor in the gold mines and the palm and kola nut plantations.

Ghanaian archaeologist James Anquandah notes that iron-extractive industries flourished in Akan towns and villages between 1000 and 1500. Akan farming towns in Adanse constructed iron furnaces and utilized indigenous iron sources called *atwetweboo* in iron smelting. Ironsmiths made agricultural tools, weapons, and other implements.

In the sixteenth century, brass casting developed alongside this iron-smelting tradition, particularly in northern Ghana, and resulted in the manufacture of brass bracelets, amulets, anklets, rings, and other jewelry. Brass casters in Brong Ahafo and Asante were skilled in melting down European metals, and they produced gold weights, brass caskets for storing gold dust, gold dust spoons, and jewel boxes.

There is historical documentation of gold mining and goldsmithing in Ghana dating back to at least 1471, when Portuguese explorer Pedro Escobar recorded the practice. In southern Ghana, gold dust (*sika futuro*) became the principal currency, preceded by iron, brass, and cowries. Since gold was so highly valued, trade involved meticulous measurements of the quantities involved, leading to the development of the Asante system of weights. Gold dust was stored in a ceremonial bowl, the *kuduo*, which was an exquisite and finely engraved brass vessel used during both religious and civic ceremonies.

At its inception, Akan society differed from the other societies in the region in that it was matrilineal. The Akan kingdoms were characterized by a centralized political structure, presided over by a queen mother (the *ohemmaa*) and a king (the *omanhene*). The *oman*, a major settlement with a significant political and administrative apparatus accompanied by smaller neighboring settlements, functioned as the center of the Akan political unit. The central apparatus of the *oman* consisted of a hierarchy of councils that connected the diverse kinship groups. The councils were responsible for passing laws, allocating land for public utility, performing religious rites, declaring war, and settling for peace.

The queen mother and the king sat at the helm of the administrative structure and, though supreme, ruled in conjunction with a council of elders (*ahenfo*). The king and the queen mother each sat on a stool (*nnua*) which signified reverence for royalty and assumed a sacral status within the Akan ruling structure. Female stools were complementary to male stools, and women actively participated within their respective councils in making legislative and judicial decisions affecting the community's well-being.

Denkyira was one of most significant of the Akan kingdoms. At the beginning of the sixteenth century, the Denkyira became vassals of the Twifo and the Adanse of the region. Even though Adanse invaded Denkyira, the onslaught was repelled and Denkyira proclaimed its independence. Denkyira grew over the seventeenth century and prospered from its maritime trade and commercial enterprise, particularly following the capture of Elmina on the coast. The Denkyira were defeated in 1701, however, by the Asante, marking the beginning of the latter's growth into an empire.

SIGNIFICANCE

Francophone West African historians have described the Akan civilization as *la civilization de l'or*, the golden civilization, precisely because of its majesty and monumental success during the period prior to European penetration in West Africa. There is no question that the region the fifteenth and sixteenth centuries witnessed a golden age of Akan creativity, when the Akan were not satisfied with merely producing raw gold, but proceeded to establish manufacturing industries predicated upon that gold. The resulting period of industrialism and commerce paved the way for the emergence of the formidable Asante empire, which developed in the eighteenth and nineteenth centuries. Akan civilization is also noteworthy in that, contrary to popular opinion, it established enduring indigenous social, economic, and political institutions and urban centers without Islamic intervention.

—*Julian Kunnie*

FURTHER READING

Ajayi, J. F. A., and Michael Crowder, eds. *History of West Africa*. 2d ed. Vol. 1. New York: Columbia University Press, 1976. This comprehensive volume contains an informative chapter by Ivor Wilks, a scholar of West African history who has done extensive research on Akan history entitled, "The Mossi and Akan States to 1800."

Anquandah, James. *Rediscovering Ghana's Past*. Harlow, Essex, England: Longman, 1982. Critical work by a Ghanaian archaeologist who has engaged in excavations and studied oral traditions in Ghana meticulously and provides a very detailed exposition of Ghanaian history.

Boahen, Adu, with J. F. Ade Ajayi and Michael Tidy. *Topics in West African History*. 2d ed. London: Longman Group, 1986. Excellent account that spans the breadth of West African history—including illumination of the Sudanese states and empires and the Kingdoms of the Guinea Coast—and provides detailed treatment of West African history from the precolonial era through the late 1970's. Illustrations, map, bibliography.

Chambers, Catherine. *Looking Back: West African States Before Colonialism*. London: Evans Brothers, 1999. Though this book is not an academic treatise, it is nevertheless valuable in that it provides a pre-colonial history of Akan and other West African civilizations, with well-selected educational themes and beautiful photographs.

Falola, T., and A. Adebayo. *A History of West Africa, A.D. 1000-1984*. Lagos, Nigeria: Paico, 1985. Furnishes a concisely detailed chronology of West African history, particularly focusing on West African states over the past millennium, illuminating both medieval civilizations and the colonial period.

Farrar, Tarikhu. *Building Technology and Settlement Planning in a West African Civilization: Precolonial Akan Cities and Towns*. Lewiston, N.Y.: Edwin Mellen Press, 1996. Well-researched academic text that provides an introduction to Akan civilization with focus on origins, political organization, matrilineal clans, economics, and religion, and contains an excellent discussion of the technology of building and complex architectural expertise that the Akan possessed.

Nkansa Kyeremateng, K. *The Akans of Ghana: Their History and Culture*. Accra, Ghana: Sebewie, 1996. Brief monograph on the social customs and history of the Akan. Includes illustrations and maps.

Wilks, Ivor. "Wangara, Akan, and Portuguese in the Fifteenth and Sixteenth Centuries." In *Mines of Silver and Gold in the Americas*, edited by Peter Bakewell. Brookfield, Vt.: Variorum, 1997. An analysis of the Akan gold trade with both the Wangara and the Portuguese. Includes illustrations, maps, bibliographic references, and index.

SEE ALSO: Late 15th cent.: Mombasa, Malindi, and Kilwa Reach Their Height; 1481-1482: Founding of Elmina; c. 1485: Portuguese Establish a Foothold in Africa; 16th century: Trans-Saharan Trade Enriches Akan Kingdoms.

RELATED ARTICLES in *Great Lives from History: The Renaissance & Early Modern Era, 1454-1600:* Amina Sarauniya Zazzua; Askia Daud; Mohammed I Askia.

1462
FOUNDING OF THE PLATONIC ACADEMY

Marsilio Ficino became the leader of an informal group of scholars, artists, and intellectuals known as the Platonic Academy. Through his writings and lectures, Platonic philosophy spread throughout and influenced Florentine society at a time when Florence was the center of Italian Renaissance art and culture.

LOCALE: Florence (now in Italy)
CATEGORIES: Philosophy; organizations and institutions

KEY FIGURES
Marsilio Ficino (1433-1499), leader of the Platonic Academy
Cosimo de' Medici (1389-1464), ruler of Florence, r. 1434-1464
Lorenzo de' Medici (1449-1492), ruler of Florence, r. 1469-1492
George Gemistus Plethon (c. 1355-1450/1455), leading Byzantine Platonist
Giovanni Pico della Mirandola (1463-1494), Italian scholar and philosopher
Sandro Botticelli (Alessandro di Mariano dei Filipepi; c. 1444-1510), Italian painter

SUMMARY OF EVENT
For Renaissance philosophy, as for most major periods in Western philosophy, Greek philosopher Plato (c. 427-347 B.C.E.) was a seminal figure. Plato's works were read and discussed by several major Renaissance thinkers, who also wrote important commentaries on them. The most conspicuous center of Renaissance Platonism was

Marsilio Ficino. (The Granger Collection, New York)

FICINO ON THE SEARCHING SOUL

Marsilio Ficino brought together an informal group of intellectuals and artists to form the Platonic Academy of Florence. In his own work he introduced the philosophy of Plato to Renaissance Europe. In the excerpt here, Ficino tells of the soul's never-ending pursuit of truth, goodness, and God.

We have shown that our soul in all its acts is trying with all its power to attain the first gift of God, that is, the possession of all truth and all goodness. Does it also seek His second attribute? Does not the soul try to become everything just as God is everything? It does so in a wonderful way; for the soul lives the life of a plant when it serves the body in feeding it; the life of an animal, when it flatters the senses; the life of a man, when it deliberates through reason on human affairs; the life of the heroes, when it investigates natural things; the life of the daemons, when it speculates on mathematics; the life of the angels, when inquires into divine mysteries; the life of God, when it does everything for God's sake. Every man's soul experiences all these things in itself in some way, . . . and thus the human species strives to become all things by living the lives of all things.

Source: From *Platonic Theology* (c. 1474), excerpted from *The Portable Renaissance Reader*, edited by James Bruce Ross and Mary Martin McLaughlin (New York: Viking Press, 1968), p. 390.

the Platonic Academy in Florence, which was active under the patronage of the Medici from 1462 until 1494. Its leader was Marsilio Ficino.

The academy was founded in an informal manner. In 1462, Cosimo de' Medici gave to Marsilio Ficino a small villa near the town of Careggi and several manuscripts of Plato to translate. The informal group that gathered around Ficino became known as the Platonic Academy, since Ficino had dedicated himself to a lifelong study of Plato and his commentators.

The academy, though an important indication that interest in Plato was increasing in Renaissance Italy, did not mark the sudden reappearance of Platonism in the West after a long absence. Plato's student and philosophical rival, Aristotle (384-322 B.C.E.), had eclipsed his teacher in importance during the Middle Ages, but Plato's thought was never entirely effaced by the Aristoteleans.

Indeed, the medieval Platonic tradition, which anticipated Renaissance Platonism in many ways, was persistent, inspired as it was by certain writings of Plato then available, by the thought of Augustine, and by other Christian and non-Christian Neoplatonists. Even when Aristotelianism became the dominant philosophical current in the thirteenth century, Augustinianism remained a viable secondary current, especially in the Franciscan Or-

der. Moreover, even such confirmed Aristotelians as Albert the Great and Thomas Aquinas had easily identifiable strands of Platonism through Augustinianism.

In addition to medieval interest in Plato, another important current that contributed to Renaissance Platonism originated in the Renaissance itself. This was Humanism, which started as a literary scholarly movement deeply concerned with the study and imitation of classical antiquity. The interests of the Humanists in Plato's works were purely literary and eclectic. They made no attempt to rethink the basic metaphysical views of Plato or otherwise to contribute to the discipline of philosophy as such. Nonetheless, because of their admiration for antiquity, they promoted the study of Plato in fifteenth century Italy.

The third important current that facilitated Renaissance Platonism came from the Byzantine East, where throughout the Middle Ages Plato had been carefully studied. One of the most important Eastern Platonic scholars was Gemistus Plethon, who had come to Italy in 1438. He made a strong impression on all he met, especially upon Cosimo de' Medici. Twenty-four years later, Cosimo was to establish the Platonic Academy.

It is clear, therefore, that Ficino was not solely responsible for a Renaissance Platonic revival. Ficino's personal influence and prestige did, however, increase the currency of Plato's ideas in Florence and assure them the widest possible audience. Platonic philosophy spread rapidly throughout the educated levels of society, especially among poets such as Cosimo's grandson Lorenzo de' Medici, who was both a member of the Platonic Academy and ruler of Florence. The visual arts also felt the impact of Ficino's Platonism: Many artists encountered Platonic ideas and attempted to incorporate them in their painting. Foremost among these men in Florence was the great painter Sandro Botticelli. In the realm of philosophy, Giovanni Pico della Mirandola, a younger friend of Ficino, helped spread many of the basic ideas of the founder of the academy.

The name "Academy" implies a more formal organization than in fact ever existed at Careggi. Ficino did no regular teaching, nor were any formal courses offered or students enrolled. Ficino did, however, give lectures to large audiences in Florence and hold intimate dinner parties for his guests at Careggi at which Platonic philosophy was discussed.

When one studies Ficino's literary activities as leader of the academy, it becomes apparent that he was a prolific author. Inspired by the thought of Plato as the culmination of the pagan tradition of wisdom, Ficino devoted his first endeavors to translating ancient sources. He next translated the Platonic dialogues, completing the work in 1468. He thereupon elaborated his own philosophy in two important works: the *Theologia Platonica* (1482; *Platonic Theology*, 2001ff.) and *Liber de Christiana religione* (1474; book on the Christian religion). Finally, he resumed his translating activities by translating into Latin both Christian and non-Christian Neoplatonic philosophers.

SIGNIFICANCE

The Platonic Academy gathered together under the direction and inspiration of Ficino the various strands of Plato's philosophy that had been woven into the intellectual life of the Middle Ages and early Renaissance. For these strands, the academy was a semi-institutional yet highly personalized focal point, and through the work and prestige of its leader, it served as the fountain by which Plato's thought flowed first throughout Renaissance Italy and later to the remainder of Europe.

—*Joseph M. Victor*

FURTHER READING

Allen, Michael J. B., Valery Rees, and Martin Davies, eds. *Marsilio Ficino: His Theology, His Philosophy, His Legacy.* Boston: Brill, 2002. Collection of twenty-one essays on Ficino; includes discussions of the Platonic Academy and of the importance of Renaissance Platonism generally. Includes photographic plates, illustrations, bibliographic references, and index.

Celenza, Christopher S. *The Lost Italian Renaissance: Humanists, Historians, and Latin's Legacy.* Baltimore, Md.: Johns Hopkins University Press, 2004. Study of texts of the Italian Renaissance that were neglected by their contemporaries because they were written in Latin rather than vernacular Italian. Includes a chapter on Marsilio Ficino and his importance to intellectual history. With bibliographic references and index.

Ficino, Marsilio. *Platonic Theology.* 4 vols. to date. Translated by Michael J. B. Allen. Edited by James Hankins with William Bowen. Cambridge, Mass.: Harvard University Press, 2001-2004. The first four volumes of a projected six-volume set, this is the first translation into English of one of Ficino's most important works. Includes bibliographic references and index.

Field, Arthur. *The Origins of the Platonic Academy of Florence.* Princeton, N.J.: Princeton University Press, 1988. The only book-length study of the Platonic Academy's founding in English. Includes bibliography and indexes.

Kristeller, Paul Oscar. *The Philosophy of Marsilio Ficino.* New York: Columbia University Press, 1943. Reprint. Gloucester, Mass.: Peter Smith, 1964. Detailed study of the thought and aims of Marsilio Ficino. Traces both his debt to his precursors and his influence on later thinkers.

_____. *Studies in Renaissance Thought and Letters.* Rome, Italy: Edizioni di storia e letteratura, 1956. Excellent collection of studies of Ficino and other Renaissance thinkers.

Robb, Nesca Adeline. *Neoplatonism of the Italian Renaissance.* London: George Allen & Unwin, 1935. Reprint. New York: Octagon Books, 1968. An older account that remains useful.

Shepherd, Michael, ed. *Friend to Mankind: Marsilio Ficino, 1433-1499.* London: Shepheard-Walwyn, 1999. Anthology of essays reevaluating Ficino's influence upon the Florentine Renaissance in the light of new translations of his writings into English. Includes bibliographic references.

Walker, D. P. *Spiritual and Demonic Magic from Ficino to Campanella.* London: Warburg and Courtauld Institute, 1958. Reprint. University Park: Pennsylvania State University Press, 2000. Without refuting or denying any of Kristeller's assertions concerning Ficino's philosophical and theological speculations, Walker traces the magical side of Ficino's career and thus adds a new dimension to this man of many interests.

Yates, Frances Amelia. *Giordano Bruno and the Hermetic Tradition.* Chicago: University of Chicago Press, 1964. Contains a detailed account of Ficino's magical beliefs and practices.

SEE ALSO: 1469-1492: Rule of Lorenzo de' Medici; 1490's: Aldus Manutius Founds the Aldine Press; c. 1500: Revival of Classical Themes in Art.

RELATED ARTICLES in *Great Lives from History: The Renaissance & Early Modern Era, 1454-1600:* Sandro Botticelli; Marsilio Ficino; Lorenzo de' Medici; Giovanni Pico della Mirandola.

1460's

c. 1462
KAZAK EMPIRE IS ESTABLISHED

Kazak clan leaders broke away from the Uzbek khanate and established a rival state of nomadic cattle herders in what is now Kazakhstan. Immigration and further defections swelled the new Kazak khanate, which continued to expand, dividing into three hordes in the sixteenth century.

LOCALE: Kazakhstan
CATEGORIES: Expansion and land acquisition; government and politics

KEY FIGURES
Girei (d. 1474), Kazak khan, r. 1459-1474
Janibeg (d. 1465), Kazak khan, r. 1459-1465
Abū'l-Khayr (d. 1468), Uzbek khan, r. 1429-1468
Kasim (d. 1523), Kazak khan, r. 1511-1523

SUMMARY OF EVENT
Between 1428 and 1456, Khan Abū'l-Khayr established the Turko-Mongol Shaybānīd Uzbek khanate as the major power in the region between the Ural and Irtyah Rivers, directly north of the thriving Timurid domain. He further spread Uzbek hegemony into the Syr Darya River Basin and Khwārizm. Perhaps alarmed at this expansion, eastern Mongols, either Oyrats or Kalmyks or some combination, took over the region of the Middle Syr Darya, forcing out the Uzbeks.

Girei and Janibeg, two of Abū'l-Khayr's most important vassals and the sons of his predecessor, had long resented Abū'l-Khayr's leadership and took advantage of these dislocations. They abandoned the Uzbek horde and migrated out of Shaybānīd territory. It was not a peaceful or amicable secession, and much blood was spilled in its wake.

Girei and Janibeg and their tribes moved eastward into Chagatai territory, eventually being settled by a Chagatai lord along the frontiers of Moghulistan in southeastern Kazakhstan sometime before 1462. As Abū'l-Khayr's Uzbek empire continued to crumble, more and more Uzbeks joined the nascent nomadic state, further weakening Shaybānīd power and swelling the new horde. Finally, in 1468, Abū'l-Khayr attacked Girei, but Girei's warriors soundly defeated and killed him. Bad blood continued into the next genera-

tion, though Uzbek weakness prevented anything greater than skirmishing, and the Kazaks preferred hit-and-run plunder and destruction.

The attraction of the new khanate was its traditionally nomadic lifestyle. Sources and scholars differ on the origin and meaning of the name "Kazak" (also Qazak and Kazakh) and when the Uzbeks first applied it to themselves. It seems to denote "free warrior" or "steppe roamer," though some translate it as "those who left the horde." It was thus an indication of the group's independent and nomadic or seminomadic condition rather than an ethnic label.

Ethnically, the early Kazaks were Turkic or Turko-Mongol, and certainly were the heirs of the steppe traditions. One modern theory shows the Kazaks as descendants from the *ulus* (independent territory) of Orda-Ejen, the eldest son of Jöchi, heir of Mongol conqueror and ruler Genghis Khan (r. 1206-1227). The Kok-Orda provided the core of the original Kazaks. These tribes were at first consigned to the horde of Shaybān, from which they later seceded.

The Kazaks, whose name and perhaps ethnicity is related to the Russian term "cossack," valued their mobility in an age when their cousins, the Uzbeks, were making ever more successful attempts to control urban areas and achieve a settled existence. Little is known or agreed on about this early period because the travelers and chroniclers of the time who recorded events and impressions concentrated on the cities and not the camps of the nomads.

The Kazaks herded cattle, moved with their herds, and recognized no central authority. The khan was elected in

---

THE KAZAKS AND THE NOMADIC WAY OF LIFE

One famous characterization of the Kazaks was recorded by a contemporary chronicler, Mirza Haidar, in a history of the nomadic clans written in 1544-1545, and was supposedly uttered by Girei's grandson Kasim, considered by some to be the first Kazak khan.

We are inhabitants of the steppe; we have no rare or valuable possessions or goods; our most valuable possession is our horses. Meat and skin from it serve as our best food and clothing; our most enjoyable drink is their milk and what we prepare from it. We have no gardens or buildings on our land. Our place of recreation is the cattle pasture and the herding of horses. We go to the herds and take pleasure in the sight of horses.

Mongol fashion by the *quriltay*, or assembly of clan elders and military leaders. With little in the way of urban life or administrative bureaucracy and a populace that was always on the move, there was little room for despotism. The khan stepped forward with an iron fist, however, during periods of armed struggle; then the steppe horsemen appreciated the coordination that well directed cooperation brought.

The Uzbeks gained an upper hand around 1490 when Maḥmūd Khan of Moghulistan granted Turkistan to the Uzbeks under Abū'l-Khayr's grandson, Muḥammad Shaybānī. Muḥammad and Muryndyk Khan (r. 1474-1511), son of Girei, fought for hegemony over the cities of the Syr Darya (Oxus) basin, and Muryndyk gained the city of Yasī as a sort of capital for his people. In 1500, Muḥammad and Muryndyk agreed on a peace settlement that established a loose confederation between the Uzbeks and Kazaks.

In the early sixteenth century, however, the charismatic Kazak khan Kasim abrogated this agreement and reestablished their independence, an act often considered the start of an independent Kazak state. He and Mimash (1518-1523) made life miserable for the Uzbeks in Transoxiana. Their steppe-style raids never were considerable military threats, but they did present the Uzbeks with a second front as they sought to establish a new empire and manage the aggressive Ṣafavids in Iran.

Under Kasim, the Kazak state expanded into the lower Syr Darya and Chu River valleys, gaining control of important trade routes and centers. Mimash's successor, Tahir Khan (r. 1523-1526), tried to weld the Kazak horsemen into a formidable force that could effectively challenge their neighbors, but the fiercely independent tribes balked at his authoritarian methods and many broke away.

Leadership of the Kazaks was soon divided among three men—Boydas (r. 1526-1534) in the east, Togim (r. 1526-1538) in the south, and Uziaq Ahmad (r. 1526-1535) in the north. Aq Nazak Khan (r. 1538-1580) managed to pull the three segments together, and they weathered brutal invasions by the Mongolian Kalmyks and Oyrats from the Kobdo region between 1552 and 1555. Nonetheless, the tribal divisions remained and were recognized in the establishment of the three *zhuzes* of the Great (Elder), Middle, and Lesser Hordes. Tawekel Khan (r. 1586-1598) achieved an effective confederation of the hordes that prevented further disintegration. The dissolution of the Siberian and Nogai hordes under Russian pressure in the later sixteenth century further fed the Kazak population, estimated by some to have been as high as one million around the turn of the century.

SIGNIFICANCE

Discussion of the origins of the Kazaks is hindered by a lack of written records. The outlines, however, are clear. The Kazaks constituted a new community of desert-steppe nomads in Central Asia. They clearly had a self-generated sense of group consciousness and self-reliance through which they identified themselves and their sedentary neighbors. In many ways it was a step backward, away from the kind of city-centered life that the Uzbeks and other early modern remnants of the Turko-Mongol hordes were adopting.

Yet they did not develop into a predatory people that victimized the settled as had the Turks and Mongols before them. They rather coexisted with those they often despised as slaves. Despite a lack of clear common ethnic identity or claims of shared ancestry, Kazaks retained their fierce sense of self-reliance and identity as "steppe roamers" into the twentieth century.

—*Joseph P. Byrne*

FURTHER READING

Grousset, René. *The Empire of the Steppes: A History of Central Asia.* Translated by Naomi Walford. New Brunswick, N.J.: Rutgers University Press, 1970. Deals with the "Kirghiz-Kazaks" largely in terms of their relations with other, usually sedentary peoples.

Haidar, Mirza Muḥammad. *A History of the Moghuls of Central Asia: The Tarikh-i-Rashidi of Mirza Muhammad Haidar, Dughlat.* 2 vols. Translated by E. Denison Ross. Edited by N. Elias. New Delhi, India: ABI, 1998. A contemporary history of the nomadic Mongol clans, the only history of its kind.

Olcott, Martha Brill. *The Kazakhs.* 2d ed. Stanford, Calif.: Hoover Institute, 1995. Though focused on contemporary political situations and implications, Olcott provides a fine introduction to the early emergence of the Kazak people and state.

Paksoy, H. B. *Central Asia Reader: The Rediscovery of History.* Armonk, N.Y.: M. E. Sharpe, 1994. A chapter on the Kazaks provides brief coverage dealing largely with questions of ethnicity.

SEE ALSO: 1507: End of the Timurid Dynasty; Dec. 2, 1510: Battle of Merv Establishes the Shaybānīd Dynasty; Summer, 1556: Ivan the Terrible Annexes Astrakhan; July 21, 1582: Battle of the Tobol River; 1598: Astrakhanid Dynasty Is Established.

RELATED ARTICLES in *Great Lives from History: The Renaissance & Early Modern Era, 1454-1600:* Ivan the Great; Ivan the Terrible.

1460's

1462

REGIOMONTANUS COMPLETES THE *EPITOME* OF PTOLEMY'S *ALMAGEST*

The first Latin translation of Ptolemy's Almagest, *meticulously revised with new observations and data by Regiomontanus, made widely available for the first time the most important astronomical treatise of antiquity and the Middle Ages, sparking a revolution in astronomy and mathematics.*

LOCALE: Rome (now in Italy)
CATEGORIES: Astronomy; mathematics; science and technology

KEY FIGURES

Regiomontanus (Johannes Müller; 1436-1476), Viennese astronomer
Bessarion (1403-1472), Greek Orthodox cardinal and papal legate, philosopher, and patron of science
Georg von Peuerbach (1423-1461), Viennese astronomer
Nicolaus Copernicus (1473-1543), Polish astronomer and first modern proponent of a sun-centered astronomical system
Amerigo Vespucci (1454-1512), Italian navigator and the namesake of the Americas
Christopher Columbus (1451-1506), Italian-born commander of the first Spanish voyages to the New World
Johannes Hamman (1482-1509), Venetian publisher

SUMMARY OF EVENT

Regiomontanus's *Epitome* of Ptolemy's *Almagest* (*Epytoma in almagestum Ptolomaei*; wr. 1462, pb. 1496) brought the Humanist movement to the sciences, changed the course of mathematics, and revolutionized astronomy. Johannes Müller, better known as Regiomontanus (the Latinized name of his hometown, Königsberg), was a prodigy, studying under the astronomer Georg von Peuerbach and receiving his bachelor's degree from the University of Vienna in 1452 at the age of fifteen. By 1457, he was a professor there, working closely with his mentor von Peuerbach.

The inception of the *Epitome* of Ptolemy's *Almagest* came through a fortuitous visit to Vienna in May of 1460 by the Greek cardinal Bessarion, a Byzantine scholar trained in philosophy, and, after the Ottoman invasion of the East, the papal legate to the Holy Roman Empire. Bessarion was an early proponent of the Humanist move-

ment, which sought the revival, translation, printing, distribution, and reexamination of obscure classical texts. Bessarion supported reconciliation between the Eastern Orthodox and Roman Churches, and he campaigned especially to make Greek texts better known in the Latin West. In Vienna, he persuaded von Peuerbach to begin work on a concise Latin edition of the most influential of Greek astronomical texts, Ptolemy's *Mathēmatikē syntaxis* (c. 150). After the twelfth century, it was more commonly known by the title *Almagest* (English translation, 1952), meaning "the greatest," a name given to the work by medieval Arabic readers. *Almagest* was a vast compendium of astronomical observations and tables of calculations based on a geocentric (Earth-centered) model of the cosmos, bringing together the astronomical knowledge of the entire ancient world, from the Babylonians to the Romans. Though he did not know Greek, von Peuerbach had earlier Latin-manuscript translations of the ancient work, and using these he completed *Almagest* through book VI before he died in April of 1461, just under a year after Bessarion's arrival.

Upon von Peuerbach's death, Regiomontanus, his most brilliant student and closest collaborator, inherited the project and began to study Greek under the guidance of Bessarion so that he could read *Almagest* in its original language. The two traveled together to Rome, where they arrived on November 20, 1461, and they stayed there until 1463. Regiomontanus studied full-time Ptolemy's language and astronomy, acquiring fluency in Greek and gaining complete mastery of *Almagest*. He finished the manuscript translation, which he dedicated to Bessarion, at the end of 1462.

At the time of Regiomontanus's translation, Ptolemy's *Almagest* was still considered the most authoritative astronomical reference available. Yet many of the second- and third-generation copies that circulated through Europe were filled with errors. By returning to the original Greek text, and by adding extensive new computations, observations, and commentary, Regiomontanus updated Ptolemy's system, advancing astronomical knowledge and exposing for the first time some of the crucial flaws in Ptolemy's astronomy.

In 1463, Regiomontanus followed Bessarion to Venice, and through his patronage began teaching mathematics at Padua. Here, Regiomontanus began pursuing another problem raised in the *Epitome*. Determining astronomical positions frequently required geometrical calculations comparing angles in spherical triangles. Yet, as Regiomontanus noted in the *Epitome*, no systematic geometry text was available that allowed for the computation of angles for plane or spherical triangles. To remedy this, Regiomontanus composed his treatise *De triangulis omnimodis* (wr. 1464, pb. 1533; *On Triangles*, 1967). It was in this text that Regiomontanus became the first scholar in the Latin West to use the then-new mathematical language developed by medieval Islamic scholars—algebra—to solve a trigonometric problem. It was here that Regiomontanus formulated for the first time the co-

sine law for spherical triangles and created trigonometry as an independent branch of mathematics.

Regiomontanus further developed applied trigonometry in his *Tabulae directionum* (wr. 1467, pb. 1490; tables of directions), introducing a table of tangents in modern form and placing the calculation of celestial positions on a new footing. These innovations influenced astronomers and mathematicians through the next hundred years and spurred the revolution in astronomy that culminated in Isaac Newton's unified physical system of the cosmos.

In 1471, Regiomontanus moved to Nuremberg, where he set up a printing press in his house. From here he printed and disseminated a variety of scientific works, becoming the first to turn the new printing press into an agent of scientific mass communication. His first published works included a version of von Peuerbach's *Theoricae novae planetarum* (1474; English translation, 1987) and the first printed astronomical tables, the *Ephemerides* (1474). Regiomontanus intended to print his *Epitome* at his own press, but he died at age forty, before he could do so. The Venetian publisher Johannes Hamman acquired the manuscript of the *Epitome* and distributed the first printed edition in 1496.

Navigator Amerigo Vespucci was using the tables three years later, comparing the apparent distance between the Moon and Mars to values given in the tables. By calculating the difference between the two values, Vespucci became the first navigator to use lunar distances to determine longitude, among the most reliable methods until the advent of the marine chronometer at the end of the eighteenth century. Christopher Columbus carried a copy of the *Ephemerides* on his last voyage to the New World in 1504, and he used the power of prediction it gave him to forecast a lunar eclipse, astounding the indigenous peoples of Jamaica and allowing him to take possession of the island. In spite of revolutionary advances in both theoretical and observational astronomy, Regiomontanus's celestial almanacs remained the standard ones for three centuries after his death.

Some scholars believe Regiomontanus asserted the motion of the earth and thus indirectly influenced Nicolaus Copernicus's cosmological beliefs. In a letter from the last years of his life, Regiomontanus was reported to have written, "The motion of the stars must vary a tiny bit on account of the motion of the earth." On the basis of this fragment, a tradition emerged that Regiomontanus might have been the originator or inspiration of the Sun-centered (heliocentric) Copernican system. In the *Epitome*, however, and in his other known writings,

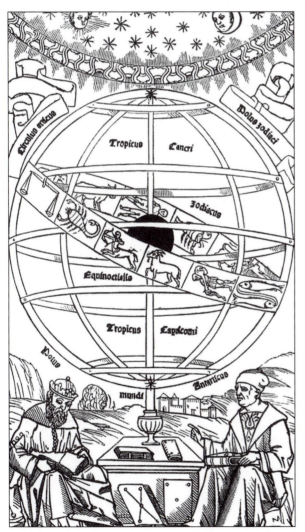

A facsimile page from Regiomontanus's Epitome *of Ptolemy's* Almagest, *first printed in 1496.* (Frederick Ungar Publishing Co.)

Regiomontanus refrained from explicit critiques of the theoretical assumptions of Ptolemy's system, focusing instead on improving its calculations. In so doing, however, he made the text all the more accessible to the scrutiny of other astronomers who had more revolutionary approaches and intentions.

SIGNIFICANCE

As soon as it was published, the *Epitome* of Ptolemy's *Almagest* began to circulate widely among astronomers. At half *Almagest*'s length, it was considerably less intimidating and more useful. Regiomontanus's masterful translations and meticulous editing made it a vastly superior tool to the previous Latin translations and other available corrupted copies.

The *Epitome* revealed technical problems with Ptolemy's theory that became a central focus for astronomers: According to its formulas, the apparent diameter of the Moon should sometimes vary by up to four times its normal size. This prediction, far from observed values, alerted Copernicus to the fallibility of Ptolemy's system and began his search for an alternative to the universally accepted, Earth-centered cosmological model at the heart of *Almagest*.

When the *Epitome* was published in Venice, Copernicus, then a young student at the nearby University of Bologna, avidly read the new translation. These discrepancies started Copernicus on his lifelong preoccupation with the shortcomings of Ptolemaic astronomy, culminating with the 1543 publication of his solution to the problems, his *De revolutionibus orbium coelestium* (1543; *On the Revolutions of the Heavenly Spheres*, 1952; better known as *De revolutionibus*), which argued against Ptolemy's model of a geocentric cosmos and replaced it instead with a heliocentric model, where the earth revolved daily about its axis and orbited the sun once a year.

The *Epitome* fulfilled the Renaissance Humanist dream of reviving the treasures of classical antiquity and making them available for a wide audience. Its prose and organization were unequaled, and it quickly became a model for the new form of scientific communication invented by Regiomontanus himself, the printed scientific book.

—Jordan Kellman

FURTHER READING

Heilbron, John L. *The Sun in the Church: Cathedrals as Solar Observatories*. Cambridge, Mass.: Harvard University Press, 2001. Challenges age-old assumptions about the relationship between the Roman Catholic Church and astronomy, showing the importance of Church sponsorship in the research and publications of astronomers from Regiomontanus to Galileo.

Hellman, C. Doris. *The Comet of 1577: Its Place in the History of Astronomy*. New York: Columbia University Press, 1944. Far broader in scope and interest than its title would suggest, this study explores the observational careers of the great European astronomers of the sixteenth century, placing Regiomontanus in the context of his contemporaries.

Swerdlow, Noel. "Regiomontanus's Concentric-sphere Models for the Sun and Moon." *Journal for the History of Astronomy* 30 (1999): 1-23. A technical treatment that traces Regiomontanus's specific alterations to several of Ptolemy's astronomical models and argues for their importance.

Zinner, Ernst. *Regiomontanus: His Life and Work*. Translated by Ezra Brown. New York: North-Holland, 1990. The definitive study of Regiomontanus, based on a thorough study of the manuscript sources. Followed by a series of essays showing how research since Zinner's classic 1968 study appeared has revised knowledge of Regiomontanus's career.

SEE ALSO: 1490's: Aldus Manutius Founds the Aldine Press; Oct. 12, 1492: Columbus Lands in the Americas; 1543: Copernicus Publishes *De Revolutionibus*; 1572-1574: Tycho Brahe Observes a Supernova; 1580's-1590's: Galileo Conducts His Early Experiments; 1582: Gregory XIII Reforms the Calendar; 1600: William Gilbert Publishes *De Magnete*.

RELATED ARTICLES in *Great Lives from History: The Renaissance & Early Modern Era, 1454-1600:* Tycho Brahe; Giordano Bruno; Gerolamo Cardano; Christopher Columbus; Nicolaus Copernicus; John Dee; William Gilbert; John Napier; Nicholas of Cusa; Georg von Peuerbach; Rheticus; Niccolò Fontana Tartaglia; Amerigo Vespucci.

1463-1479
OTTOMAN-VENETIAN WAR

The war between Venice and the Ottoman Empire established the Ottomans as a naval power and saw Venetian hegemony in the eastern Mediterranean replaced by Ottoman hegemony.

LOCALE: Eastern Mediterranean and the Balkans
CATEGORIES: Wars, uprisings, and civil unrest; diplomacy and international relations; expansion and land acquisition

KEY FIGURES
Mehmed II (1432-1481), Ottoman sultan, r. 1444-1446, 1451-1481
Pietro Mocenigo (1406-1476), Venetian admiral and doge, r. 1474-1476
Giovanni Mocenigo (1408-1485), doge of Venice, r. 1478-1485
Uzun Ḥasan (c. 1420-1478), Ak Koyunlu ruler, r. 1453-1478
Pius II (Aeneas Silvius Piccolomini; 1405-1464), Roman Catholic pope, 1458-1464
János Hunyadi (c. 1407-1456), Hungarian military leader

SUMMARY OF EVENT
Ottoman sultan Mehmed II, nicknamed Fatih (the Conqueror), is primarily remembered for conquering Constantinople (Istanbul) in 1453 and for extinguishing the twelve-hundred-year-old Byzantine Empire. Yet these events occurred very early in the sultan's reign, and it is often forgotten that in the remaining twenty-eight years he engaged in strenuous campaigning and achieved the extensive conquests that he bequeathed to his successors.

In accord with Ottoman tradition, Mehmed saw himself as the quintessential *gazi* (fighter for the faith of Islam), waging *jihad* (holy warfare) against non-Muslims, but after 1453, he also claimed to be the heir to the Byzantine Empire, including all of its former territories. His ambition appears to have been to incorporate into his empire all the Balkan lands south of the Danube. Thus, he seized the islands in the northern Aegean, expelled the Florentine dukes of Athens, overran the Byzantine Despotate of the Morea (Peloponnese, Greece) in 1460, and the principality of Trebizond (Trabzon, Turkey) in 1461. By that time, he had already eliminated the vassal-principality of Serbia, which he converted into an Ottoman province in 1459. However, Belgrade, which the sultan had endeavored to take in 1456, remained in

Christian hands, thanks to the heroic defense mounted by the Hungarian regent, János Hunyadi.

In 1461, the *voyevod* of Walachia, Vlad III (r. 1456-1462 and 1476), nicknamed Tepeş, "the Impaler," and the historical progenitor of the fictional Count Dracula, crossed the Danube, captured Vidin, and raided into Ottoman territory, burning villages and massacring the sultan's subjects. Mehmed retaliated in 1462 and ravaged much of Walachia, causing Vlad to flee to Transylvania, where he was eventually imprisoned by King Matthias I Corvinus of Hungary (r. 1458-1490), János Hunyadi's son. Mehmed installed Vlad's younger brother, Radu, a former hostage at the sultan's court, as *voyevod* (1462-1475) in return for annual tribute. Meanwhile, in the western Balkans, the Ottomans moved into southern and central Bosnia in 1463 and completed the conquest of Albania between 1464 and 1479.

The Venetian Republic, although granted favorable trading privileges by Mehmed in 1454, observed with ever-increasing apprehension the Ottoman encroachment on Bosnia and Albania—traditionally Venetian spheres of influence—and the growing Ottoman presence in the Adriatic. At this time, Venice was the greatest Christian power in the eastern Mediterranean. It commanded the finest navy in the world outside China, maintained a sophisticated diplomacy rooted in excellent intelligence-gathering, and enjoyed great commercial wealth.

Hitherto, Venetian dominance of the Adriatic had gone unchallenged, as had the republic's control of the Ionian and Aegean Seas. Venice ruled numerous ports on the mainland and many islands as well, including Crete, its most valuable possession. Mehmed II's capture of Constantinople and the seemingly inexorable growth in his territorial ambitions were a threat to Venice's survival. Even Italy was attracting his attention: It was said that Mehmed intended to stable his horses in St. Peter's in Rome, and the great fleet he was known to be building rendered this far more than just an idle threat. The republic decided that it must make a preemptive strike. In September, 1463, Venice retook the Morea and several Aegean islands from the Ottomans, asserting its control of the region.

Venice's military actions were preceded by vigorous diplomacy, for the republic had no intention of acting alone. The Muslim threat posed by Mehmed was directed not only at Venice, but at all Christendom, and the Venetians found an enthusiastic champion in Pope Pius

II, who called eloquently, although ineffectively, for a crusade. In Hungary, however, Venice found the ally it sought, and on September 12, 1463, a treaty of mutual aggression against the Ottomans was signed between them. If all went well in the ensuing struggle, Venice would retain the Morea and regain its losses in the Adriatic and the Aegean; Hungary would exercise hegemony over Bosnia, Serbia, Walachia, and Bulgaria; and a Byzantine prince would be restored to Constantinople. In addition, Venice planned to send envoys and firearms to the Ottomans' Muslim foes, the rulers of Karaman in central Anatolia, and the Ak Koyunlu Turkomans in western Iran.

Following its preemptive occupation of the Morea in September, 1463, Venice proceeded to blockade the entrance to the Dardanelles, seizing the adjacent islands of Lesbos and Tenedos. Mehmed was quick to react: Two fortresses were constructed at Çanakkale to bar the entrance to the Dardanelles, while on the Bosporus, opposite Rumeli Hisari, another was constructed on the Anatolian shore. Moreover, the sultan's navy had grown to the point where it would soon rival that of Venice.

As his fleet grew, Mehmed's ability to take the initiative increased. His forces reconquered much of the Morea in 1467. When Iskander Beg, Albanian chieftain and ally of the Venetians, died in January of 1468, the Ottomans were able to annex virtually all of Albania and to advance against the inland Venetian city of Scutari (Shkodër), although a heroic defense compelled the Turks to withdraw in 1474. Meanwhile, exasperated by Venetian raids on the coasts of the Aegean and southern Anatolia, Mehmed, in June, 1470, launched a massive expedition, said to number four hundred ships, against the hapless island of Negroponte (Euboea, Greece), which was the fulcrum of Venetian power in the Aegean. Despite this disaster, the Venetians rejected a peace offer in the following year, anticipating that events in Anatolia would force the sultan to turn eastward.

Mehmed had already campaigned against Karaman in 1468 and 1469. In 1471 and 1472, Ottoman forces again marched into Karaman, bringing them into direct conflict with the Ak Koyunlu. To assist the latter, the Venetian fleet, under its heroic captain-general, Pietro Mocenigo, raided Izmir and Antalya (summer, 1472) and provided firearms, munitions, and some trained personnel for the Ak Koyunlu.

The next year, Ottomans and Ak Koyunlu fought a decisive battle at Başkent on the upper Euphrates (August 11, 1473), forcing the Ak Koyunlu ruler, Uzun Ḥasan, to withdraw permanently into western Iran, allowing

Mehmed to concentrate on crushing his Christian enemies in the west.

Between 1460 and 1476, Mehmed had been embroiled with Stephen the Great, *voyevod* of Moldavia (r. 1457-1504). The threat posed by Moldavia was eventually neutralized, however, by Mehmed's conquest of Genoa's remaining Black Sea colonies and by the submission in 1475 of the khan of the Crimea, who henceforth proved a useful Ottoman auxiliary. In 1476, a feint by King Matthias toward Semendria, east of Belgrade on the Danube, brought Mehmed into Serbia again, where he beat off the Hungarians and raided across the frontier, before turning west again to harass northern Albania, taking Montenegro and Herzegovina, and raiding Croatia and Dalmatia. The Venetians hung on grimly to Scutari, but Ottoman raiding columns now swept through Istria and Friuli, and it was said that the fires of the burning villages could be seen from the top of the campanile of St. Mark's.

The Venetians had no alternative but to sue for peace. The newly elected doge, Giovanni Mocenigo, negotiated a treaty to end the seventeen-year-old war. The treaty was signed in Constantinople on January 25, 1479. Venice was forced to hand over Scutari, although it temporarily retained an enclave around Durazzo (Durrës). The Aegean, its islands and coasts, were now incorporated into the Ottoman Empire, although Venice kept the northern Sporades, the Venetian dukes of Naxos survived in the Cyclades, and Genoa kept Chios. In the Morea, Venice retained its great base in Modon (Methoni) on the southwest coast. In return for these concessions, the Venetians had to pay the sultan an annual tribute of ten thousand ducats, but Venice's trading privileges were restored and a Venetian consular representative (*bailo*) was to reside in Constantinople. The terms might have been harsher.

Mehmed was not finished with Italy, however. In 1479, he occupied the Ionian islands—Ithaca, Cephalonia, Zante, and Leucas—and in 1480, an Ottoman fleet seized Otranto in Apulia, establishing there a base for an advance on Rome. Delays followed as reinforcements were assembled. Finally, the expedition was canceled and Otranto evacuated at the news of Mehmed's death on May 3, 1481.

SIGNIFICANCE

The war of 1463-1479 was neither the first nor the last conflict between Venice and the Ottoman Turks, but for Venice it marked a turning point, although Venetians at the time appear not to have realized it. Thereafter, Venice was no longer, as it had been since 1204, mistress of the eastern Mediterranean. In contrast, for the Ottomans, their new navy allowed them to dominate the Aegean and the Black Sea and began the process whereby, a century later, the Mediterranean would become essentially a Turkish domain.

—Gavin R. G. Hambly

FURTHER READING

Babinger, Franz. *Mehmed the Conqueror and His Time.* Princeton, N.J.: Princeton University Press, 1978. The definitive study of the sultan's reign.

Brummett, Palmira J. *Ottoman Seapower and Levantine Diplomacy in the Age of Discovery.* Albany: State University of New York Press, 1994. An important study of naval strategy, an aspect of Ottoman expansion frequently neglected.

Crouzet-Pavan, Elisabeth. *Venice Triumphant: The Horizons of a Myth.* Translated by Lydia G. Cochrane. Baltimore, Md.: Johns Hopkins University Press, 2002. A history of Venice from Roman times through the sixteenth century, focusing on the physical environment of the city and the effects of geography and space upon Venetian daily life, politics, and history. Includes photographic plates, illustrations, maps, chronology, glossary, bibliography, and index.

Imber, Colin. *The Ottoman Empire, 1300-1650.* New York: Palgrave, 2002. Important survey of the classical phase of Ottoman history.

Inalcik, Halil. *The Ottoman Empire: The Classical Age,* 1300-1600. New York: Praeger, 1973. The best account of the early empire.

Kafadar, C. *Between Two Worlds: The Construction of the Ottoman State.* Berkeley: University of California Press, 1995. An extraordinarily perceptive and informative study of the way in which historiography and ideology came together to shape Ottoman imperialism.

McCarthy, Justin. *The Ottoman Turks: An Introductory History to 1923.* New York: Longman, 1997. The most accessible account of the Ottoman Turks, the formation of their empire, and its decline.

Morris, Jan. *The Venetian Empire.* London: Penguin Books, 1990. A scholarly traveler explores Venice's former colonies.

Norwich, John Julius. *A History of Venice.* New York: Alfred A. Knopf, 1982. A first-rate popular narrative.

SEE ALSO: 1454-1481: Rise of the Ottoman Empire; 1469-1508: Ak Koyunlu Dynasty Controls Iraq and Northern Iran; 1478-1482: Albanian-Turkish Wars End; 16th cent.: Evolution of the Galleon; 1512-1520: Reign of Selim I; 1520-1566: Reign of Süleyman; 1536: Turkish Capitulations Begin; July, 1570-Aug., 1571: Siege of Famagusta and Fall of Cyprus; Oct. 7, 1571: Battle of Lepanto.

RELATED ARTICLES in *Great Lives from History: The Renaissance & Early Modern Era, 1454-1600:* Matthias I Corvinus; Mehmed II; Pius II; Vlad III the Impaler.

---

c. 1464-1591
SONGHAI EMPIRE DOMINATES THE WESTERN SUDAN

Sonni ʿAlī's ascent to power in Songhai signaled the decline of Mali and the subsequent hegemony of a small tributary state that dominated trans-Saharan trade in the fifteenth and sixteenth centuries. The dominance of the Songhai Empire contributed to the spread of Islam in the western Sudan, as well as the expansion of educational centers in Gao, Djenné, and Timbuktu.

LOCALE: Songhai Empire, west-central Sudan (now principally in Mali), West Africa

CATEGORIES: Government and politics; expansion and land acquisition

KEY FIGURES

Sonni ʿAlī (d. 1492), Songhai military leader, r. c. 1464-1492

Mohammed I Askia (c. 1442-1538), Songhai ruler, r. 1493-1528

SUMMARY OF EVENT

Questions still linger among historians as to the exact chronological origins of the Songhai state, which have been attributed to both the Sorko fishermen and the Songhai people. It is clear, however, that by the thirteenth century, Songhai was already a constituted state, albeit tiny, and a tributary to Mali, which had also absorbed the kingdom of Ghana. Moreover, the location of this small state along the middle of the Niger River in West Africa provided it with important resources that gave it the potential to become a viable and important kingdom in its own right. These resources included fertile land, irrigation, fishing, development of a sizable fleet, difficult accessibility to enemies, and a flourishing trans-Saharan trade between West and North Africa, consisting mainly of gold, kola nuts, horses, slaves, cotton, and dried fish.

The Songhai state first developed at settlements at Kukiya, its first capital, and Gao, which by the fifteenth century had become an important commercial entrepôt. The earliest recorded dynasty to install itself in Songhai was the Dia (Dya) family, about which very little is now known. It is known, however, that the Dia became tributary to Ghana early in their history. When Ghana was absorbed by Mali, Songhai began to pay tribute to Mali instead.

The Dia rulers did not pay this tribute gladly, however, and the rebellious nature and advanced economic standing of Songhai caught the attention of Mali emperor Mansa Mūsā the Great (r. 1307-1337). Mūsā, on his return from Mecca in 1325, passed through Gao and took as hostages two princely brothers, Ali Kolon and Sulayman Nar, to ensure that Songhai would not break away from the empire. The princes remained in Mali for more than a decade, but they were treated with honor, and Ali Kolon was even entrusted with military expeditions. When Mūsā died in 1337, the brothers escaped and returned to Songhai. They were never recaptured. They found, however, that the Dia Dynasty had been replaced by the Sonni Dynasty in their absence.

The Dia Dynasty had also been responsible for the introduction of Islam into Songhai. Relatively early in Songhai history (1009), Dia king Kossi of Songhai had accepted Islam as his new religion. While he did not force his subjects to convert, King Kossi did take it on himself to defend Islam within his kingdom. In the face of constant incursions by the Tuareg and Fulani nomads, he split his time between Kukiya and Gao, seeking to make each more secure.

When Mansa Mūsā of Mali conquered Gao in 1325, the prospects for Songhai independence grew grimmer. However, around 1464, following the death of Sonni Sulayman, a new king ascended to the throne of Songhai: Sonni ʿAlī. Sonni ʿAlī transformed Songhai into an empire, first asserting the kingdom's independence from Mali, and subsequently seizing control of much of the western Sudan, including portions of its former "colonizer's" territories.

One historian has noted that, because of his successful military campaigns, Sonni ʿAlī was as famous in West Africa as Charlemagne had been in Western Europe. He successfully pushed back the Mossi in the south as well as the Fulani and Dogon elsewhere, expanding Songhai's

territory and establishing stable borders. In 1468, he captured Timbuktu, which had been under the Tuaregs since 1433. The campaign in Timbuktu was particularly bloody, however, and once he controlled the largely Muslim city, Sonni ʿAlī massacred many of its inhabitants. His actions in Timbuktu caused the nascent emperor to be loathed by Muslims of the region. Around 1466, he began an extended siege of Djenné, 300 miles southwest of Timbuktu. The rich city, which had already become a major educational and trading center, finally succumbed to Sonni ʿAlī in 1473.

Through military persistence, Sonni ʿAlī expanded the empire from the southern fringes of the Sahara Desert in the north to the Mossi states in the south. Moreover, his control of Djenné and Timbuktu, as well as Gao, enabled him to control the trade routes and the "grain-producing region of Niger's inland delta." Throughout Sonni ʿAlī's reign, the military played a prominent role in the empire. Military leaders served as governors in areas deemed susceptible to revolt, although many vassal states and towns were allowed to retain their traditional leaders, so long as they continued to pay tribute and taxes.

Despite allowing self-rule, however, the emperor aroused the ire of his Muslim population, especially the imams and scholars at the Senkore Mosque in Timbuktu. Sonni ʿAlī was called a "tyrant," "ruthless," and "an impious 'Muslim' ruler." The Muslim community simply refused to accept his rule. The emperor was forced to rely on support from his subjects who followed traditional West African religions, and to rule over a religiously divided empire.

Sonni ʿAlī met his death allegedly after falling off a horse and drowning in a stream in 1492, as he returned from a campaign against the Mossi. His son, Sonni Baru, also only nominally a Muslim, succeeded him two months later and faced the same opposition from the Muslim population. He was, for example, accused of not praying five times a day and of carrying on "pagan" practices at court.

There was also a constitutional dispute as to which succession tradition the empire should follow. Muslim tradition dictated that the oldest firstborn son of the deceased emperor should succeed, while traditional Songhai society assigned the task of selecting a new ruler to the Council of Elders, who were free to choose one of the emperor's sons or another worthy candidate as they saw fit. The empire's Muslim subjects also demanded that the empire's barter system give way to a money economy. In the end, the Muslim leadership conspired against the emperor and caused his top general, a converted Muslim, to overthrow him and wrestle power from the Sonni Dynasty. This is how Mohammed Ture came to power as Mohammed I Askia (the "usurper") in 1493.

Mohammed I Askia consolidated royal control of the state, continued the campaigns against the Mossi (1498-1499), and conquered Air to the east and Diara and Baghana to the west, increasing the Songhai Empire to its largest size. He made Songhai the trading, commercial, religious, and educational center of the western Sudan. He ruled until 1528 when, old and blind, he was overthrown by his son, Askia Mūsā. The empire continued for more than sixty years, enjoying intermittent periods of domestic tranquillity, until the sultan of Morocco took advantage of a period of decline to attack Songhai. At the Battle of Tondibi in March, 1591, Moroccan forces, using firearms, defeated a much larger Songhai army that was equipped only with spears, poisoned arrows, and swords. A state of total anarchy reigned in Songhai thereafter, as the Moroccan sultan was unable to keep the country together. Until the 1780's, various Moroccan military adventurers would call themselves rulers of portions of the empire, but for all practical purposes, Songhai disintegrated after 1591, never again to recover as a political entity.

SIGNIFICANCE

Sonni ʿAlī's reign inaugurated the ascendancy of the Songhai Empire and its dominance of the western Sudan. Until the end of the sixteenth century, the Songhai Empire remained the most visible symbol of political power in West Africa. It stood as a model of careful empire building, of successful absorption of ethnic and religious diversity, and of the long-term maintenance of peace and prosperity. Songhai created and enhanced urban centers of commerce such as Timbuktu and Gao, and it supported scholarship, as exemplified by the universities of Senkore at Timbuktu and Djenné. Songhai revolutionized West Africa economically, educationally, and militarily. None of this could have been achieved without the tenacity and political astuteness of Sonni ʿAlī. It was his imperial ambition and practical consolidation of power that made possible the later reign of Mohammed I Askia, at the apex of Songhai's power.

—*Mario J. Azevedo*

FURTHER READING

Batuta, Ibn. *Travels in Asia and Africa*. New York: R. M. McBride, 1928. Reprint. London: Darf, 1983. Another firsthand, primary source written by an Arab scholar that sheds light on the greatness and impact of Songhai.

Falola, Toyn. "Kingdoms of West Africa: Ghana, Mali, Songhay, 1000-1600." In *Key Events in African History*. Wesport, Conn.: Greenwood Press, 2000. A thorough discussion of the origins, rise, and demise of the three sister kingdoms. Sonni ʿAlī's life is well covered.

Hunwick, John. "Songhay, Borno and Hausaland in the Sixteenth Century." In *History of West Africa*, edited by J. F. Ajayi and Michael Crowder. 2d ed. Vol. 1. New York: Columbia University Press, 1976. Succinct historical account of the rise, hegemonic rule, and fall of Songhai as well as the role played by Sonni ʿAlī and Mohammed I Askia in West Africa and beyond.

Leo Africanus. *History and Description of Africa*. 3 vols. London: Hakluyt Society, 1897. Reprint. New York: B. Franklin, [1975?]. Written by an Arab scholar in the early sixteenth century, this is one of the classic primary sources on the western Sudan. It includes insightful observations on the history of Songhai and its society, as well as four fold-out maps of the region.

Ogot, B. A., ed. *Africa from the Sixteenth to the Eighteenth Century*. Vol. 5. Paris: UNESCO, 1992. Comprehensive but succinct coverage of Songhai, placing the empire within the context of the western Sudan.

Stoller, Paul. *Sensuous Scholarship*. Philadelphia: University of Pennsylvania Press, 1997. Notwithstanding its title, this is a scholarly treatise on Songhai's history, religion, and social conditions.

SEE ALSO: 1460-1600: Rise of the Akan Kingdoms; 1481-1482: Founding of Elmina; 1493-1528: Reign of Mohammed I Askia; 16th century: Trans-Saharan Trade Enriches Akan Kingdoms; 1510-1578: Saʿdī Sharifs Come to Power in Morocco; 1591: Fall of the Songhai Empire.

RELATED ARTICLES in *Great Lives from History: The Renaissance & Early Modern Era, 1454-1600:* Mohammed I Askia; Sonni ʿAlī.

1465-1487
REIGN OF XIANZONG

Although he corrected many of the injustices of his father's reign, Xiangzong, like many of the Ming emperors, presided over a court dominated by eunuch officials and his favorite, Lady Wan, against whose power the scholar-officials were ineffective.

LOCALE: China
CATEGORY: Government and politics

KEY FIGURES

Xianzong (temple name, also Hsien-tsung; reign name
    Chenghua, Ch'eng-hua; personal name Zhu
    Jianshen, Chu Chien-shen; posthumous name
    Chundi, Ch'un-ti; 1447-1487), emperor of China,
    r. 1465-1487
Wan Guifei (Wan Kuei-fei, known as Lady Wan; 1430-
    1487), Xianzong's nurse and later concubine
Liang Fang (fl. late sixteenth century), Lady Wan's
    favorite eunuch
Wang Zhi (Wang Chih; fl. late sixteenth century), the
    eunuch chief of police
Huai En (d. 1488), director of eunuchs, 1467-1485 and
    1487-1488

SUMMARY OF EVENT

Xianzong was the eldest son of the Emperor Yingzong and Empress Zhou (Chou). He was only twenty months old when his father undertook his disastrous military campaign against the Mongols in 1449, during which the Chinese army was routed and Yingzong was captured. During the seven years of his father's captivity, Xianzong suffered great hardships; he lived with the deposed empress, not his actual mother. When his father was released and returned to court, the family was kept isolated and secluded in the palace. The deprivations of these years no doubt marked Xianzong's character and contributed to his stuttering.

In 1457, Yingzong was freed from his virtual imprisonment in the palace and assumed the throne for a second reign. Xianzong was nine years old. His personality was weak, passive, and indecisive; he was slow to act and spoke with a stutter. His father is thought to have doubted that Xianzong had the fitness and intelligence to rule, but Yingzong was convinced that it was more important to maintain the proper succession than to replace his line with another ruler.

Xianzong's reign was typical of that of many of the Ming emperors. He allowed himself to be dominated by

his favorite concubine and his eunuch servants. He lacked the vindictiveness of his father, but his open honesty and lack of suspicion of others often made it difficult for his ministers to direct him toward wise policy and actions. As a result, his reign was marked by the abuses of the eunuchs, who exploited their offices and their closeness to the emperor for personal gain.

On the other hand, Xianzong also had dedicated and capable scholar-officials, who sought (not always successfully) to administer wise government and protest the abuses at court. Nevertheless, he shared in the greed and avarice of some of his servants, allowing their corruption and bribery because his own income benefited from their activities. He took back vast land holdings from a eunuch and confiscated other lands; he built up vast imperial estates, which he taxed heavily for his own benefit. Another abuse of his reign was the growing practice of allowing the emperor or court to grant appointments of government offices, ranks, and privileges on the grounds of personal favoritism or even bribery, instead of on the basis of qualifications and the procedures of nomination and approval by the Ministry of Personnel.

Xianzong came to the throne around the age of eighteen. He disdained the infighting and feuding of the court factions of his father's reign. He purged the court of those officials he disliked and appointed a number of scholar-officials. Governance was guided by an enlightened council of twelve regents. They corrected the wrongs of the previous reign, granted justice to those falsely punished, and provided famine relief. They also reformed and enlarged the military. They revived the palace guards, creating twelve divisions of ten thousand men each under the leadership of eunuchs, who had special charge of the weapons. Between 1465 and 1479 the new military had many successes, eliminating foreign threats and enlarging territory. Nearly 3,100 miles of the Great Wall were rebuilt, which strengthened the empire's military defenses in the north. This first part of Xianzong's reign, therefore, is regarded as one of the most enlightened periods of the Ming Dynasty.

At court, young Xianzong's nurse was Wan Guifei, known as Lady Wan, who had been in the service of his grandmother. By the time he became emperor, she was his favorite concubine, even though she was more than twice his age. She was shrewish, with a masculine character and a loud voice. She ruled the court like a dictator. Xianzong's first empress, Wu, had ordered Lady Wan beaten for an offense. For this, she was dethroned after reigning only one month. His second empress, Wang, wisely let Lady Wan have free rein at court. With so many women at court, there were many possible heirs to the throne, accompanied by great jealousy and intrigue.

Lady Wan's own son had died, and out of her jealousy that other concubines might produce heirs and achieve the status of mother of the next emperor, she prevented other concubines from having children or would have sons born of other concubines murdered. Xianzong nonetheless left her in power. When a palace servant became pregnant with Xianzong's son, palace attendants took pity on the child and did not murder the boy; the first empress (no doubt to spite her rival Lady Wan) had the mother and child hidden in a distant part of the palace for five years. When Xianzong expressed to his courtiers regret that he had no heir, the first empress produced the child to the delighted father. The court was notified, and the Imperial City celebrated the joyous and important event. A month later, however, the jealous Lady Wan had the mother poisoned. The weak Xianzong, realizing that his son was in danger, sent him to be raised in the safety of his mother's quarters in the palace. In short order, Xianzong fathered eleven other children with other concubines.

In the second part of his reign, Xianzong kept his distance from Lady Wan and rarely interfered in her activities. With his knowledge, Lady Wan—with the assistance of her favorite eunuch, Liang Fang, and the eunuch chief of police, Wang Zhi (Wang Chih)—began a program of systematic corruption and theft of the wealth of the country to enrich themselves. They sold noble titles as a business. They sent agents out into the country to collect copper, gold, silver, and precious gems. The holding of imperial farmlands increased more than fortyfold. Public morality declined and disintegrated. Monks who produced pornography and love potions for the emperor received noble titles. Court eunuchs and offices were given vast tracts of land. Wang Zhi founded a special police organization, the feared Western Depot, and gathered intelligence about suspicious persons. He intimidated and terrorized those at court and in government, confiscating their wealth and sending many to their deaths. Those who sought to expose him were instead punished by the emperor.

Finally, Xianzong realized how much anger Wang Zhi was arousing and demoted him to the post of stable keeper in Nanjing. Despite the open knowledge of her corruption and abuses, however, Xianzong never attempted to restrain Lady Wan. Rather he often punished those who pointed out her improper dealings, bribery, theft, and extravagancies. In contrast to the evil eunuchs in Xianzong's government was the eunuch Huai En, who directed the entire eunuch bureacracy. He was revered for his moral authority, adherence to principle, and opposition to improper actions, and he refused to take bribes from those wanting his assistance.

Xianzong himself was cultivated and artistic. He enjoyed theater and music, painted well, and was a good calligrapher. He was especially noted as an avid connoisseur of porcelain. He encouraged the porcelain works to make multicolored china and to use marks to indicate the emperor who reigned when the china was produced. The multicolored porcelain produced during his reign is among the finest ever produced.

Lady Wan died suddenly after a seizure in February, 1487. Xianzong proclaimed an extraordinary seven days of mourning for her. The emperor himself fell ill and died in September, at age forty. He was succeeded by his son, who took the reign name Hongzhi.

SIGNIFICANCE

Xianzong's reign witnessed the continued rise to power of eunuchs and rival cliques of officeholders, as well as their greedy struggles for personal power and wealth. Government came to be divided between the bureaucracies of the talented career scholar-officials and those of the corrupt eunuchs, against whose abuses the scholar-officials had little control. The corruption brought about by government by cliques and by eunuch favorites became common in the courts of later Ming emperors and one of the ultimate causes of the downfall of the Ming Dynasty.

Although he reversed the vindictiveness and vengefulness of his father's reign, Xianzong's reign was subject to significant dysfunctions in government. His weak personal character ultimately made him a mediocre ruler. He allowed his concubine Lady Wan to dominate his court, and she and several powerful eunuch favorites were able to plunder the country for their personal benefit. The government's ineffectiveness meant that the northern borders were repeatedly threatened by the Mongols, and rebellions of serious proportions by peoples within the empire were not addressed.

—*Thomas McGeary*

FURTHER READING

Dictionary of Ming Biography. 2 vols. New York: Columbia University Press, 1976. Full biographies of emperors and other important figures.

1460's

Hook, Brian, and Denis Twitchett, eds. *The Cambridge Encyclopedia of China*. 2d ed. Cambridge, England: Cambridge University Press, 1991. No mention of this emperor, but extensive coverage on the artistic and social culture of the Ming Dynasty.

Mote, Frederick W. *Imperial China, 900-1800*. Cambridge, Mass.: Harvard University Press, 1999. Good coverage of the reign of Yingzong, Xianzong's father.

Mote, Frederick W., and Denis Twitchett, eds. *The Ming Dynasty, 1368-1644, Part 1*. Vol. 7 in *The Cambridge History of China*. Cambridge, England: Cambridge University Press, 1988. Thorough and detailed history of the Ming Dynasty; mostly political history.

Paludan, Ann. *Chronicle of the Chinese Emperors: The Reign-by-Reign Record of the Rulers of Imperial China*. London. Thames and Hudson, 1998. As the title suggests, concise accounts of the emperors; lavishly illustrated with maps and photographs, many in color.

SEE ALSO: Feb. 11, 1457: Restoration of Zhengtong; 1474: Great Wall of China Is Built; 1488-1505: Reign of Xiaozong; 16th cent.: China's Population Boom; 16th cent.: Rise of the *Shenshi*; 1505-1521: Reign of Zhengde and Liu Jin.

RELATED ARTICLES in *Great Lives from History: The Renaissance & Early Modern Era, 1454-1600:* Wang Yangming; Xiaozong.

July 16, 1465-April, 1559
FRENCH-BURGUNDIAN AND FRENCH-AUSTRIAN WARS

The rivalry between the French monarchy and the House of Burgundy began a series of almost continuous wars that expanded significantly after the House of Burgundy was joined to the Austrian Habsburgs by marriage in 1477. The wars, which at their height brought France into conflict with both Spain and the Holy Roman Empire under Habsburg emperor Charles V, continued until the Peace of Cateau-Cambrésis was signed in 1559.

LOCALE: Southern and western Europe
CATEGORIES: Wars, uprisings, and civil unrest; diplomacy and international relations; expansion and land acquisition

KEY FIGURES
Charles the Bold (1433-1477), duke of Burgundy, r. 1467-1477
Louis XI (1423-1483), king of France, r. 1461-1483
Mary of Burgundy (1457-1482), daughter of Charles the Bold and duchess of Burgundy, r. 1477-1482
Maximilian I (1459-1519), Holy Roman Emperor, r. 1493-1519
Clement VII (Giulio de' Medici; 1478-1534), Roman Catholic pope, 1523-1534
Francis I (1494-1547), king of France, r. 1515-1547
Charles V (1500-1558), Holy Roman Emperor, r. 1519-1556, and king of Spain as Charles I, r. 1516-1556
Henry VIII (1491-1547), king of England, r. 1509-1547
Louise of Savoy (1476-1531), duchess of Angoulême, regent of France, r. 1515, 1525-1526, and mother of Francis I
Margaret of Austria (1480-1530), duchess of Savoy, regent of the Netherlands, r. 1507-1515, 1519-1530, and aunt and guardian of Charles V
Henry II (1519-1559), king of France, r. 1547-1559
Paul IV (1476-1559), Roman Catholic pope, 1555-1559
Philip II (1527-1598), king of Spain, r. 1556-1598

SUMMARY OF EVENT

In the late Middle Ages, the dukes of Burgundy were among Europe's most powerful rulers. Their lands included the duchy of Burgundy and the counties of Artois and Flanders within the kingdom of France, as well as the Franche-Comté (the free county of Burgundy) and the seventeen provinces of the Low Countries, which were units of the Holy Roman Empire. As members of the ruling Valois family of France, they had a major role in internal French politics. When Louis XI's policies drove a large portion of the French nobility to organize the League of the Public Weal in 1464, Charles the Bold of Burgundy served as its leader.

The league and the king met in an indecisive battle at Montlhéry (July 16, 1465), but the rebels' failure to defeat the king passed the initiative to Louis. Louis's cunning diplomacy drew many of Charles's French allies away from him, and Charles was forced to turn to

France's external enemies, England and Aragon, for support. The English attacked out of Calais, demonstrating the value of holding on to that stronghold after the Hundred Years' War. At the same time, the Aragonese attacked Roussillon, and Charles invaded Picardy. The major event of that war was Charles's siege of Beauvais (1472), but his failure to take the city ultimately allowed Louis to defeat his enemies piecemeal.

Charles the Bold then turned his attention to his larger goal of gaining the title of king for a unified block of land from Burgundy to the Low Countries, which entailed conquering Alsace and Lorraine. That caught the attention of the Swiss, who were further enticed by Louis's offer of huge sums of French gold. The Swiss attacked Charles in 1474, and he was killed in the Battle of Nancy (January 5, 1477). He left as his sole heir a daughter, Mary.

Mary cast about Europe for a prince who would help her defend her inheritance against Louis XI, finally choosing to marry Maximilian of Austria. A member of the House of Habsburg, Maximilian was the son of Holy Roman Emperor Frederick III. Meanwhile, Louis took advantage of his victory and occupied Artois and Burgundy, but he failed to secure Flanders. The disposition of those lands poisoned relations between the Habsburgs and the Valois until 1559.

When his father died, Maximilian I became Holy Roman Emperor. Under his erratic leadership, the House of Habsburg remained largely on the sidelines, as France and Spain engaged in war in Italy for control of the kingdom of Naples and the duchy of Milan (1494, 1499, 1515). Maximilian achieved a major coup, however, when he arranged the marriage of his son Philip to Joan the Mad, heiress to Ferdinand II and Isabella I, the Spanish monarchs. Joan being deemed insane, rule of the Spanish kingdoms passed to her son Charles I when Ferdinand died in 1516. Charles was already the ruler of the Low Countries and the Franche-Comté through his father, who had died in 1506. He became duke of Austria and was elected Holy Roman Emperor as Charles V on Maximilian's death in 1519.

Now that Charles the Bold's great-grandson was king of Spain, Holy Roman Emperor, ruler of the Burgundian inheritance, and claimant to the Burgundian lands lost in 1477, the points of conflict between Charles V and Francis I of France were almost endless. Not the least of them was the fact that Charles controlled lands that completely surrounded France. As emperor, one of his first acts was to demand that Francis surrender Milan, which the French had retaken in 1515, on the grounds that it was

still an imperial fief. Francis refused, and in 1522, an imperial army defeated a French force at Bicocca and seized Milan. Francis personally led another French force into Italy, but at the Battle of Pavia (February 24, 1525), he was defeated and captured by imperial forces. He was held in captivity in Spain until he agreed to a huge ransom; its major point was the return of the duchy of Burgundy to Charles. Francis persuaded Charles that only his presence as king could persuade the French people to accept the terms of the ransom, and Charles allowed the king to return to France in exchange for his two older sons as hostages.

Once back on French soil, Francis repudiated the agreement on the grounds that he had been coerced into it by harsh treatment. Securing alliances with Venice, Henry VIII of England, and Pope Clement VII, Francis returned to war. Charles sent an army toward Rome to frighten Clement into abandoning the alliance, but his soldiers, unpaid since Pavia, mutinied and perpetrated the sack of Rome in 1527-1528. Desultory war continued for another two years, while the two French princes languished in Spain. In 1529, Louise of Savoy, Francis's mother, and Marguerite of Austria, Charles's aunt, negotiated the Peace of Cambrai, called the "Peace of the Ladies." France recognized Charles's sovereignty over Flanders, Milan, and Naples, while Charles abandoned his claim to Burgundy. The peace also required that Francis pay two million crowns to ransom his sons.

The Habsburgs conceded the loss of Burgundy from then on, but the French did not abandon hope of regaining the lands they had surrendered. In 1533, Francis and Pope Clement arranged a marriage between Francis's son Henry and Clement's cousin Catherine de Médicis. The pope then recognized Francis as the rightful duke of Milan, and in 1536, the French made another effort to retake the duchy. Charles's efforts to defend Milan were complicated by the presence of the Lutherans in Germany and the attacks of the Ottoman Turks in the Mediterranean. Although he remained a Catholic, Francis was always willing to ally with the German Protestants and the Muslim Turks against Charles. Despite that disadvantage, the emperor successfully defended Milan and invaded southern France. Consequently, in 1538, the two monarchs met at Nice, where Pope Paul III served as arbitrator.

These negotiations reaffirmed the Peace of Cambrai, but the French still would not accept the loss of the lands conceded in it. In 1542, using the murder of two French diplomats near Milan as cause, Francis was back at war. This time, he allied openly with Ottoman Turks and allowed their fleet to spend the winter in the harbor at Toulon, from which it raided coastal villages. The outrage among Europe's Christians, even among most Frenchmen, was immense, and Francis was forced to abandon such an overt alliance in the future.

In 1544, a French army was victorious at Cerisolles in Savoy. Charles, however, had reestablished his alliance with Henry VIII, and the two struck into France, Henry out of Calais and Charles from the Franche-Comté. Francis was forced to pull his forces out of Italy to meet the threat. The English took the fortress of Boulogne but then refused to march on Paris, while Charles's army came within 100 miles (161 kilometers) of the city but had to halt because winter was approaching. The situation soon led to negotiations, which resulted in the Peace of Crépy, once again reaffirming the status quo.

In 1547, Francis I died, and Henry II assumed the French throne. He had been one of the hostages for his father, and he nursed a grudge against the Habsburgs for what he regarded as mistreatment at their hands. Henry sought to harm the emperor in every way possible, but he was slow to take up arms against Charles V because of the threat that English-held Boulogne now posed to Paris. In 1549, he placed Boulogne under siege, and the English agreed to evacuate it for a large sum of gold. Henry then began building alliances with the German Lutheran princes and the Ottomans.

In 1552, the Lutherans recognized the French right to rule those lands in the empire that spoke French, which referred largely to Lorraine. Henry II led an expedition into Lorraine and succeeded in occupying Metz, Toul, and Verdun, known collectively as the Three Bishoprics of Lorraine. Charles counterattacked by laying siege to Metz, but what was probably the largest army assembled in Europe to that point failed to retake it before winter set in. Meanwhile, the combined French and Turkish fleets landed troops on Corsica and took it away from Charles's ally Genoa.

In 1554, Paul IV was elected pope. As a native of Spanish-ruled Naples, he hated Charles V, and he promised to give Naples and Milan to Henry's younger sons if Henry would provide forces to seize them from Charles. Thus, in 1556, Henry dispatched an army to Italy. By then, Charles, worn out by his wars, had abdicated his titles, and his son Philip II was king of Spain and Naples, duke of Milan, and prince of the Low Countries, while his brother Ferdinand I had become Holy Roman Emperor.

Philip responded to the French adventure in Italy by sending an army from Flanders toward Paris. A French ground force defending Saint-Quentin was routed on August 10, 1557. The way to Paris lay open, but Philip declined to move his army against the city until the fortress of Saint-Quentin itself was taken. By the time it fell, he deemed it too late in the year to attack Paris. Meanwhile, Henry had recalled his forces from Italy, forcing the pope to make peace with Philip, and assembled the last scraps of French manpower to protect Paris. When it became clear in early 1558 that Philip's army would not attack Paris, Henry decided to use the forces he had gathered against Calais. The January attack on the English caught them shorthanded, and the marshes around Calais were frozen, making it difficult for the English to mount sallies against the French siege force. As a result, the French took the city after only a week's siege.

With each side gaining a great victory and suffering a major defeat, it was deemed that God had decreed that they should finally make a lasting peace. Negotiations led to the Treaty of Cateau-Cambrésis (April, 1559). The French again conceded the loss of Milan and Naples and returned Corsica to Genoa, but they retained Calais and their foothold in Lorraine. The treaty also called for the marriage of Henry's daughter Elisabeth to Philip, who had recently been widowed. In June, Spanish officials came to Paris to sign the peace and arrange the wedding. Participating in the tournament he held to celebrate, Henry was fatally injured. His death left the French throne to fifteen-year-old Francis II. Very quickly, civil war, called the French Wars of Religion, broke out, which left France incapable of carrying on war against the Habsburgs for the next forty years.

SIGNIFICANCE

France's wars against the houses of Valois and Habsburg coincided with, and had an impact on, several major developments in European history, including the age of exploration, the Renaissance, and the Reformation. In particular, the wars played an important role in the success of the Protestant Reformation, because they made it impossible for Charles V to use his military might to crush the Lutherans in Germany until they were too well established. The wars also distracted the Habsburgs from their ongoing war with the Ottoman Turks in the Balkans and the Mediterranean. They functioned, as well, as a crucible for major military advances, especially the development of an effective infantry force using firearms. The marriages precipitated by the wars and the marshaling of resources required for them led to the rise of Spain as the major power in Europe until well after 1600.

—Frederic J. Baumgartner

FURTHER READING

Baumgartner, Frederic. *France in the Sixteenth Century.* New York: St. Martin's Press, 1996. Places the wars in the context of French history in the era.

Hall, Bert. *Weapons and Warfare in Renaissance Europe.* Baltimore: Johns Hopkins University Press, 1997. Shows how the wars contributed to military developments in the era.

Kendall, Paul. *Louis XI: The Universal Spider.* New York: Norton, 1971. Highly detailed biography of the French king in whose reign the wars began.

Knecht, Robert. *Renaissance Warrior and Patron: The Reign of Francis I.* Cambridge, England: Cambridge University Press, 1994. Best biography of that French king.

Lockyer, Roger. *Habsburg and Bourbon Europe, 1470-1720.* London: Longman, 1974. Provides the political context for the wars.

Tracy, James. *Emperor Charles V: Impresario of War.* Cambridge, England: Cambridge University Press, 2002. Thorough examination of Charles's policy and strategy in his wars, especially strong on how he financed them.

Vaughan, Richard. *Valois Burgundy.* Hamden, Conn.: Archon Books, 1975. Provides a detailed study of the rivalry between the French kings and the dukes of Burgundy.

SEE ALSO: Aug. 17, 1477: Foundation of the Habsburg Dynasty; Aug. 19, 1493-Jan. 12, 1519: Reign of Maximilian I; Sept., 1494-Oct., 1495: Charles VIII of France Invades Italy; Nov. 26, 1504: Joan the Mad Becomes Queen of Castile; June 28, 1519: Charles V Is Elected Holy Roman Emperor; 1521-1559: Valois-Habsburg Wars; Feb., 1525: Battle of Pavia; May 6, 1527-Feb., 1528: Sack of Rome; 1555-1556: Charles V Abdicates; Jan. 1-8, 1558: France Regains Calais from England; Apr. 3, 1559: Treaty of Cateau-Cambrésis.

RELATED ARTICLES in *Great Lives from History: The Renaissance & Early Modern Era, 1454-1600:* Catherine de Médicis; Charles the Bold; Charles V; Clement VII; Ferdinand II and Isabella I; Francis I; Frederick III; Henry II; Louis XI; Margaret of Austria; Mary of Burgundy; Maximilian I; Paul III; Philip II.

October 19, 1466
SECOND PEACE OF THORN

The Second Peace of Thorn brought an end to the Thirteen Years' War between Poland and the Teutonic Knights of Prussia. Under the terms of the peace, Poland gained new territories, becoming more culturally diverse and acquiring a coastline on the Baltic Sea.

LOCALE: Prussia

CATEGORIES: Wars, uprisings, and civil unrest; diplomacy and international relations; expansion and land acquisition

KEY FIGURES

Władisław II Jagiełło (c. 1351-1434), king of Poland, r. 1386-1434

Casimir IV (1427-1492), king of Poland, r. 1447-1492

Konrad von Erlichshausen (d. 1449), grand master of the Teutonic Knights, 1441-1449

Ludwig von Erlichshausen (d. 1467), grand master of the Teutonic Knights, 1450-1467

Frederick III (1415-1493), king of Germany, r. 1440-1493, and Holy Roman Emperor, r. 1452-1493

Nicholas V (Tommaso Parentucelli; 1397-1455), Roman Catholic pope, 1447-1455

Calixtus III (Alfonso de Borgia; 1378-1458), Roman Catholic pope, 1455-1458

Aeneas Silvius Piccolomini (1405-1464), papal legate and later Roman Catholic pope as Pius II, 1458-1464

Rudolf von Rudesheim (c. 1402-1482), bishop of Levant, 1463-1468

SUMMARY OF EVENT

The Thirteen Years' War was but one period of strife in a region that was often the site of war or the threat of war throughout the late Middle Ages and the early modern period. For example, continual tensions, broken occasionally by overt warfare, characterized the relationship between Poland and the Prussian Teutonic Order from the late thirteenth century until 1343. In that year, the two powers negotiated the Peace of Kalisch, as a condition of which King Casimir the Great of Poland waived all claims to the disputed territories of West Prussia and

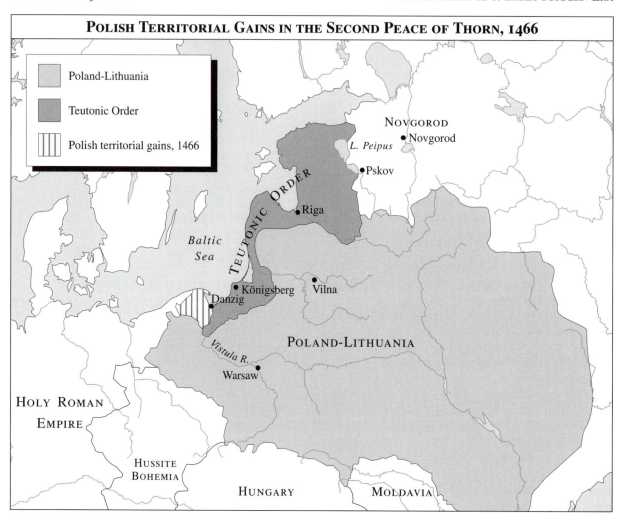

POLISH TERRITORIAL GAINS IN THE SECOND PEACE OF THORN, 1466

Culm. Casimir affirmed that both territories belonged to the Teutonic Order, and Poland and the order then enjoyed a predominantly peaceful relationship for the remainder of the fourteenth century. In the early fifteenth century, however, new crises developed that ultimately led to the famous Battle of Tannenberg in 1410. At Tannenberg, the combined forces of Poland and Lithuania, led by Polish king Władisław II Jagiełło and Lithuanian grand duke Vytautas, crushed the hitherto invincible army of the Teutonic Order.

The surviving members of the Teutonic Order were at first consumed with a desire to avenge their defeat to restore their lost pride and political power. Their already diminished resources, however, were drained a little more every year by the need to maintain a high state of defensive readiness in case King Jagiełło invaded again. Moreover, the order's grand master committed vital re-

sources to assist the Holy Roman Emperor in his crusade against the Hussite rebellion in Bohemia. He hoped in that way to win the emperor's favor and perhaps an alliance against Poland.

The Polish king, for his part, knew how expensive and risky it would be to besiege the massive castles of the Teutonic Knights, and he understood well that his knights and prelates would not be willing to authorize or take part in another campaign in Prussia. Therefore, Jagiełło contented himself with diplomatic efforts at the papal court, at the Council of Constance (1414-1418), and elsewhere, meanwhile allowing the grand masters to imagine that an invasion was imminent.

Thus, for a while, an uneasy stalemate existed between the Teutonic Order and Poland. That stalemate ended when the Bohemian Hussites decided to invade Prussia to strike at the principal supporters of the Holy

Roman Emperor. Poland allowed the Hussite invasion force passage through its territory. The famed discipline of the Teutonic Order broke down. The knights removed one grand master, the convents in Germany refused to recognize his successor, and military defeat dogged their every effort in Prussia, Livonia, and Bohemia.

Konrad von Erlichshausen became grand master of the Teutonic Order in 1441 with a mandate to bring order to their chaotic situation. His solution was to centralize power in his own hands, to raise new taxes, and to demand that the traditionally autonomous Prussian cities contribute more to the Order's political and military ambitions. Konrad was essentially successful in dealing with the Order's own knights, partly because there were fewer of them than ever before and partly because then-current military theory stressed the wisdom of hiring mercenaries when war threatened rather than housing and feeding knights in both war and peace. Konrad's threats, however, provoked only resistance from Prussia's secular knights and burghers, especially those of Danzig. These various knights and burghers formed a loose affiliation called the Prussian League to discuss their mutual interests in resisting Konrad's policies. By the time Konrad died in 1449, the league had been expanded from a mere forum for discussion into a full military alliance.

The Teutonic Order's new grand master, Ludwig von Erlichshausen, petitioned Pope Nicholas V and Holy Roman Emperor Frederick III and obtained rulings from them that the Prussian League was an illegal organization. In 1454, when the Prussian League realized that further negotiations were hopeless, it made a preemptive strike against the Teutonic Order before the grand master could raise a mercenary army. The league quickly captured all but a few castles in West Prussia.

Grand Master Ludwig was taken completely by surprise; little had he realized that the long-standing fear of King Jagiełło had died away in the two decades since that monarch's demise. While the army of the Prussian League besieged the grand master's seemingly invincible residence at Marienburg, the league's diplomats were at the court of King Casimir IV, offering to become Polish subjects in return for his support against Ludwig and the Teutonic Order.

Casimir could not send much help. His activities were restricted by a small number of nobles and prelates who mistrusted any royal action that might increase the king's power. He nevertheless made an armed entry into West Prussia that had all the appearance of a triumphal parade until he reached the fortress of Könitz. There, surprised by the simultaneous arrival of mercenaries from Germany and a sally by the garrison, Casimir's army was cut to pieces. The king fled back to Poland, the grand master recovered his confidence, and the Prussian League prepared for a long struggle—the Thirteen Years' War had begun.

At length, Pope Calixtus III decided that the conflict had lasted long enough. The pope's legates would never be able to organize a crusade against the Turks to recover Constantinople until there was peace in Poland. The pope found himself in a somewhat awkward postion, however. Calixtus had an obligation to protect the Teutonic Order, he had to respect the wishes of the Holy Roman Emperor (who was, like the pope, also the Teutonic Knights' overlord), and he had a moral obligation to uphold the established order and the rule of law. On the other hand, Poland was a powerful land, the Prussian League had valid complaints, and neither side was likely to stop fighting merely because the pope requested it. All that Pope Calixtus could do was to send an agent to look into the matter. He chose Aeneas Silvius Piccolomini, the most prominent Humanist in the Church's service and a master of persuasion.

Piccolomini's efforts proved largely in vain. When he realized that the war would not cease until either one side won a clear-cut military victory or everyone became exhausted, he adopted a policy of patient waiting. Later, when his elevation to the papacy as Pius II allowed him to offer inducements to various participants for cooperation, he would send legates to move the negotiations along. This, too, was to prove ineffective.

In 1457, it briefly appeared that the war was at its end. The grand master's mercenaries, unhappy with not being paid, turned over Marienburg to the Prussian League. Grand Master Ludwig managed to escape to Königsberg, however, and the Prussian League ran out of money to pay its own mercenaries. With neither side able to claim a clear victory, the war resumed. At length, in 1462, Casimir IV sent the league significant reinforcements and a competent general to lead them. The Polish forces won a decisive victory at the Battle of Puck, but it was arguably the League's naval strength that proved the deciding factor. In the fall of 1463, the coalition led by Danzig destroyed the grand master's fleet, and the order was deprived of a vital resource.

With the Teutonic Knights now backed into a corner, the pope sent a new emissary, Rudolf von Rudesheim, to negotiate a peace. The Second Peace of Thorn was formally agreed to on October 19, 1466. West Prussia and Culm (in the southern elbow of the Vistula River) were returned to the king of Poland, the bishopric of Ermland in the center of East Prussia became independent, and the East Prussian districts of Marienburg, Elbing, and Christburg became Polish.

SIGNIFICANCE

The long-term consequences of the Second Peace of Thorn were significant. Most important, Poland's territories now reached to the sea. Its new subjects were largely German-speaking, but the Polish commonwealth was already multilingual and multiconfessional. It was bound together by ties of trade and culture, toleration for diversity, and a high degree of local self-government. In the wake of the peace, "German" nobles adopted Polish customs and spoke Polish; German burghers went about their business, trading with German-speaking merchants clear to the other ends of the Lithuanian grand duchy and the Polish kingdom. All prized their right to govern themselves with minimum interference from the king and his council.

The Teutonic grand master regrouped his resources, trying to make something out of his shrunken state in East Prussia, periodically assisting the Polish king in his wars against the Turks. A new noble class began to establish itself in both East and West Prussia, a class composed of former mercenaries who had accepted fiefs in lieu of payment for their services; this class eventually developed into the famous Junker nobility of Prussia.

The peasantry never recovered completely from the ravages of war. The native Prussian freeholders and knights who had thrived in the service of the Order's armies were now refugees. Dispersed around the countryside, taking refuge in German-speaking towns and villages, within decades they ceased to pass their native language on to their descendants. Some, like many dispossessed German farmers, became serfs.

The Thirteen Years' War, fought to avoid tyranny, taxation, and war with Poland, did at least avoid tyranny for some. The burghers of Danzig and the other large towns profited from the enhanced opportunities for trade and the greater protection that the king could provide against competitors; the nobles enhanced their rights and privileges at the expense of the peasants. The prestige of the Polish crown was greatly enhanced. In fact, if the crown's actual, substantive authority had been equally increased, King Casimir IV would have been powerful indeed. As was the case so often in this era, however,

Casimir's authority in his new lands was dependent on his new subjects' willingness to allow him to exercise it.

—*William L. Urban*

FURTHER READING

Burleigh, Michael. *Prussian Society and the German Order: An Aristocratic Corporation in Crisis, c. 1410-1466*. New York: Cambridge University Press, 1984. Somewhat dour but solid account of fifteenth century Prussian society.

Christiansen, Eric. *The Northern Crusades: The Baltic and the Catholic Frontier, 1100-1525*. Minneapolis: University of Minnesota Press, 1980. Contains a first-class summary of the Peace of Thorn.

Davies, Norman. *God's Playground: A History of Poland in Two Volumes*. New York: Columbia University Press, 1982. Solid on Poland, though holding strong opinions; weak on the Teutonic Order.

Długosz, Jan. *The Annals of Jan Długosz: An English Abridgement*. Translated by Maurice Michael. Edited by Jane Allan. Commentary by Paul Smith. Charlton, West Sussex, England: IM, 1997. An abridgment and translation of one of the most important primary historical sources on medieval and Renaissance Eastern Europe, covering 965 to 1480. Includes illustrations and reproductions of contemporary maps.

Ertman, Thomas. *Birth of the Leviathan: Building States and Regimes in Medieval and Early Modern Europe*. New York: Cambridge University Press, 1997. Compares Prussia's bureaucratic absolutism with Poland's patrimonial constitutionalism. Includes bibliographic references and index.

Jasienica, Pawel. *Jagiellonian Poland*. Translated by Alexander Jordan. Miami, Fla.: American Institute of Polish Culture, 1978. Good on internal Polish politics.

Urban, William. "Renaissance Humanism in Prussia." Parts 1-3. *Journal of Baltic Studies* 22 (Spring-Fall, 1991): 5-72, 95-122, 195-232. A useful series of articles on the cultural consequences of the Thirteen Years' War.

SEE ALSO: 1499-c. 1600: Russo-Polish Wars; c. 1500: Rise of Sarmatism in Poland.

RELATED ARTICLES in *Great Lives from History: The Renaissance & Early Modern Era, 1454-1600:* Frederick III; Pius II.

1467
END OF KING PARĀKRAMABĀHU VI'S REIGN

Parākramabāhu ascended the throne of Kotte, a Sinhalese kingdom forming part of Sri Lanka, in an age of political instability, yet by the end of his reign the kingdom thrived culturally and intellectually, had been stabilized politically, and had re-embraced Buddhism.

LOCALE: Ceylon (now Sri Lanka)
CATEGORY: Government and politics

KEY FIGURES
Parākramabāhu VI (d. 1467), king of Kotte and king of Sri Lanka, r. 1412-1467
Sapumal Kumaraya (d. 1477), king of Kotte as Bhuvanekabāhu VI, r. 1470-1477

SUMMARY OF EVENT
Sri Lanka, an island nation just off the southern tip of India, was without a king after Vīra Alakeṣvara, who had opposed Buddhism in Kotte, was captured by Chinese trader and admiral Zheng He (c. 1371-1435) and taken to China. The political instability that had been brewing since the late thirteenth century increased. Parākramabāhu VI was offered the throne in 1412 and would remedy the instability beyond all expectations. His reign was a landmark period in Sinhalese cultural and political history, as his reign marked the last time that the entire island of Sri Lanka was unified under one Sinhalese sovereign power until modern times.

By the end of his reign in 1467, Parākramabāhu not only had regained control over Kotte but also had brought under his control rival areas of the island, notably Sinhalese Kandy and Tamil Jaffna. Contemporary sources are largely silent about how Parākramabāhu consolidated his power. There is sufficient information, however, to make some assumptions about the directions in which his power traveled. In 1419 and 1420, inscriptions were issued in parts of the island other than Kotte, which referred to Parākramabāhu's sovereignty, including his sovereignty over the Sinhalese kingdom of Kandy. Around the same time, he had repair work done in the Kotte and Kandyan areas, demonstrating that he was responsible for the administration and upkeep of both kingdoms. How he attained power over Kandy is uncertain, and historians do not know if he annexed Kandy peacefully. It is fairly clear, however, that by his fifth regnal year, Parākramabāhu controlled both Kotte and Kandy. While there was a short rebellion by Jotiya Situ

in the Kandyan areas, there were no internal disturbances.

After a difficult struggle, Parākramabāhu forced the Vanni chiefs to submit to his rule. Because they controlled the areas between Kotte and Kandy and the Jaffna Kingdom, it is likely that Parākramabāhu found it necessary to control them to eventually conquer Jaffna. After the Vanni were subjugated, Parākramabāhu dispatched an expedition under the command of Sapumal Kumaraya against Aryachakravarti, the Tamil king of Jaffna. Before attempting to control Jaffna and its ruler, Sapumal pillaged some villages in the Jaffna region, captured prisoners, and brought them to Kotte. It is fairly certain that the Tamil ruler of Jaffna managed to escape to South India. The one source (the seventeenth century chronicle *Rājavaliya*) that suggests he was killed most likely did so to depict Sapumal as a national hero. The conquest of Jaffna led to the total unification of Sri Lanka under one Sinhalese ruler, Parākramabāhu VI. After the areas were conquered, the record appears to show that they had been largely free from internal disturbance and rebellion, which was a relatively unique situation in South Asian history of this period.

Politically unifying and stabilizing Jaffna allowed for a flowering of culture in the age of Parākramabāhu. He was determined, especially in the final years of his reign, to support Buddhism. Even in the early years, chronicles mention that he assembled his viceroys and advisers to discuss how to restore or rebuild the Buddhist monasteries, which had degenerated both tangibly and spiritually. Also, Parākramabāhu kept a number of priests and monks in his specific household employ, built a hall for the monks to perform their ceremonies and rituals, and built an immense shrine for the Tooth Relic called Dalada Maligava, which formed the center of many of the rituals he prescribed. Parākramabāhu also repaired a number of fourteenth century shrines—including Lankatilaka and Gadaladeniya—and temples, such as the Kelaniya temple. He restored places of pilgrimage, such as Samantakuta, where people would worship the footprint of the Buddha. Samantakuta, located on a mountain, received new railings to help pilgrims with the difficult ascent, and a rest house, where pilgrims were offered food and drink.

Parākramabāhu also supported Buddhism as an intellectual enterprise by establishing two educational institutions affiliated with monasteries. Parākramabāhu also patronized existing institutions. The monastery and school at Karagala, Padmavati Pirivena, which was built well before his reign, developed into an outstanding place of learning under Parākramabāhu's patronage. In addition to making land grants and repairing and constructing buildings, Parākramabāhu knew how important books were to the dissemination and retention of Buddhist knowledge. He provided for scribes to copy existing books and assigned officers to make arrangements for the writing of books, largely transcripts of the teachings of contemporary monks.

Also, Parākramabāhu reorganized the Buddhist sangha, the monastic order, which had become corrupt and chaotic prior to his reign. For example, monks who had not been receiving financial support from their monasteries had to make a living somehow, so they took jobs outside the monasteries, a practice believed to have sullied the sangha. Parākramabāhu allocated resources to check the sangha's decline, restore its purity, and ensure its protection. Once it had been stabilized to some degree, Parākramabāhu arranged for annual upasampada festivals, during which novices are ordained as monks.

The political stability and financial support created during Parākramabāhu's reign opened the door for the flowering of many forms of art and literature. Poems paid tribute to Parākramabāhu's patronage of the arts, culture, and religious life. A freedom of expression that was not possible earlier because poetry was bound to strict religious themes allowed for the creation of the sandesha form of poetry in Sinhalese literature. Sandesha (which means message) allowed poets to describe contemporary, everyday life, including the beauties of nature, popular forms of worship, teachers and others of eminence, and similar worldly things. Messages are conveyed in the poems through a living being, often a bird.

The Hansa-Sandeshaya (goose's message) gives an account of the court of Parākramabāhu VI, demonstrating the emphasis on learning and religion that characterized his later reign. The Gira-Sandeshaya is a message sent through a parrot, asking for blessings and protection for Parākramabāhu and for the continued prosperity of Buddhism in Sri Lanka. It serves as an excellent source for the political career of Parākramabāhu, describing, also, his support of monasteries.

SIGNIFICANCE

At the end of Parākramabāhu VI's reign, Sri Lanka became racked with internal turmoil. Instead of political stability and cultural creativity and scholarship, Sri Lanka saw, first, the short-lived reign of Parākramabāhu's grandson Jayabāhu II (r. 1467-1469/1470). Second, two years after Jayabāhu's accession, Sapumal Kumaraya, who had brought victory to Parākramabāhu at Jaffna, marched to Kotte, killed Jayabāhu, and had himself consecrated as Bhuvanekabāhu VI, the new king. Jayabāhu's murder caused the Sri Lankan people to resent the new king, leading to rebellions throughout the once-united, thriving Sinhalese kingdom.

—Monica Piotter

FURTHER READING

Ilanghasinha, H. B. M. *Buddhism in Medieval Sri Lanka.* Delhi, India: Sri Satguru, Indian Books Centre, 1992. A superb study of the Sinhala Buddhist culture of Sri Lanka, which played an absolutely central role in Parākramabāhu's reign. The religious history of Sri Lanka is supported by a great number of sources, including this text.

Enriquez, C. M. *Ceylon: Past and Present.* New Delhi: Asian Educational Services, 1999. A good overview of Sri Lankan history. Reprint of an earlier edition.

Geiger, Wilhelm, trans. *Cūlavamsa: Being the More Recent Part of the Mahāvamsa.* Delhi, India: Motilal Banarsidass, 1996. A Buddhist chronicle that, along with the Mahāvamsa, is a main source for the political and religious history of Sri Lanka, including Parākramabāhu's reign.

SEE ALSO: Early 16th cent.: Devotional Bhakti Traditions Emerge; 1505-1515: Portuguese Viceroys Establish Overseas Trade Empire; 1509-1565: Vijayanagar Wars; 1511-c. 1515: Melaka Falls to the Portuguese; 1549-1552: Father Xavier Introduces Christianity to Japan; 1578: First Dalai Lama Becomes Buddhist Spiritual Leader.

RELATED ARTICLES in *Great Lives from History: The Renaissance & Early Modern Era, 1454-1600:* Afonso de Albuquerque; Nānak; Tomé Pires; Saint Francis Xavier.

1467-1477
ŌNIN WAR

A decade-long conflict fought over the right of succession to the shogunate in the Ashikaga family, this destructive struggle marked the beginning of a century in Japan known as the Sengoku Jidai, or Warring States period, a time marked by a breakdown of central authority and the dominance of local warlords.

LOCALE: Kyōto and environs in central Japan
CATEGORIES: Wars, uprisings, and civil unrest; government and politics

KEY FIGURES
Ashikaga Yoshihisa (1465-1489), shogun, r. 1474-1489
Ashikaga Yoshimasa (1436-1490), shogun, r. 1449-1473
Ashikaga Yoshimi (1439-1491), Yoshimasa's brother
Hino Tomiko (1440-1496), Yoshimasa's wife
Hosokawa Katsumoto (1430-1473), head of the Hosokawa family
Yamana Sōzen (1404-1473), head of the Yamana family
Ōuchi (fl. 1467-1477), a powerful Western warlord

SUMMARY OF EVENT
Beginning in 1338, the Ashikaga shogunate held nominal power over Japan. From its beginnings, however, the system of Ashikaga political control was unable to match the authority held by the previous Kamakura shoguns. Unable to control affairs away from their power base in Kyōto, successive generations of Ashikaga shoguns delegated an increasing number of responsibilities to their regional vassals, known as *shugo daimyō*. By the mid-fifteenth century, several of these lords had come to hold virtually autonomous control over large territories. They also had their own armies. In 1467, a succession conflict within the Ashikaga family caused two powerful *shugo daimyō*—Hosokawa Katsumoto and Yamana Sōzen—to go to war in support of rival claimants. This conflict, which dragged on until 1477, was named the Ōnin War after the Ōnin era (1467-1469) in which it began, and it is considered to be a significant turning point in the history of medieval Japan.

In 1464, Ashikaga Yoshimasa, the eighth Ashikaga ruler, made known his wish to retire from his position as shogun because of his dissatisfaction with the stresses of public life. This practice was not uncommon in Japanese history and Yoshimasa was not considered to be a strong leader, but his intention to retire nevertheless sent ripples of discontent through the shogunal court. Lacking a male heir, Yoshimasa decided to name his brother Yoshimi as his successor. Yoshimi, who had earlier chosen to become a Buddhist monk because high political office was not open to him, was persuaded to quit the priesthood to take up the office of shogun.

Shortly thereafter, however, Yoshimasa's wife, Hino Tomiko, bore him a son who was named Yoshihisa. It was first believed that this would settle the succession issue, but despite the fact that his brother now had a legitimate heir, Yoshimi did not wish to surrender his claim to the office, and Hino, a strong-minded woman experienced in the machinations of life at the shogunal court, decided that she would stop at nothing to see her son named as heir. The situation quickly degenerated when both parties sought outside assistance. Hosokawa Katsumoto, a major political figure and the leader of the powerful Hosokawa family, chose to support Yoshimi, while Yamana Sōzen, a powerful landholder in the west who had built up his power base through ruthless military raiding, backed Hino and her son. Both sides began to move troops, first into the environs of Kyōto and then into the capital itself. War began in earnest in 1467 when a skirmish broke out between the two sides.

The Ōnin War was characterized more by destructive street fighting in and around Kyōto than decisive battles. The result was a costly war of attrition for the rival blocs. From the beginning of the fighting, both the Hosokawa and the Yamana dragged allies into the conflict, worsening the stalemate. Contemporary accounts estimate that each side had approximately eighty thousand men at the beginning of the conflict. Yamana relied heavily on allied forces, so it was believed that Hosokawa, whose troops were thought to be more loyal, had a slight advantage. Nevertheless, numbers were not a decisive factor in the fighting, as neither side could outmaneuver the other. Arson became an important tactic on the urban battlefield, and a large part of the city was razed to the ground as the conflict proceeded. In addition, both sides began to build barricades in the streets, and networks of trenches were dug near the outskirts of the city. There are also reports in contemporary chronicles of improvised catapults being employed in an attempt to introduce a decisive edge to the action. As the war progressed and more areas of the city were reduced to ruins, large-scale military action became possible, but no tactics emerged to break the stalemate.

As the war dragged on, all parties began to become restless. As a result of his role in the fighting, Ashikaga Yoshimi, who had originally held the support of his brother, alienated the shogun, who then chose to support his son, Yoshihisa, as heir in 1469. This proved to be a momentary advantage for Yamana and his men. However, in 1473 both Hosokawa Katsumoto and Yamana Sōzen died of illness. The succession issue, nominally the cause of the conflict in the first place, was also settled in that year, and Yoshihisa became shogun in 1474. By this time, however, the allies of Hosokawa and Yamana were intent on working out their territorial rivalries and sporadic fighting continued. Ōuchi, a powerful Western daimyo (local warlord) who had entered the conflict on the side of the Yamana with twenty thousand men in 1467, chose to pursue a personal vendetta against the daimyō Hatakeyama Masanaga in 1475, and fierce fighting took place in Kyōto and in regions south of the city. In late 1477, Ōuchi complied with a request from the shogun to withdraw his forces from Kyōto, and after a decade that has come to be regarded as one of the most fruitless and destructive in Japanese history, the Ōnin War finally came to a close.

SIGNIFICANCE

The Ōnin War was an important turning point in the history of medieval Japan. When the fighting ended in 1477, the ancient capital Kyōto had been devastated and the military government of the Ashikaga shogunate was in shambles. The Ashikaga shoguns were never able to regain the measure of authority that they had exercised before the beginning of the conflict, and the power of the *shugo daimyō* houses that owed them allegiance also began a swift decline. The undermining of central authority that the Ōnin War represents opened the way for ambitious regional barons known as *sengoku daimyō* to gain power over small areas of the country. These local strongmen fought against one another, and their conflicts ushered in a century-long period of civil strife known as the Sengoku Jidai or Warring States period.

While the Ōnin War did immeasurable damage to Kyōto and its cultural legacies, the political situation that it created brought about many positive developments. Local rulers, in an attempt to consolidate their authority, improved infrastructure and made efforts to increase agricultural production. In addition, they supported craftspeople and the fine arts. The result was cultural and material advancement that culminated in the late six-

teenth century when a series of three military leaders— Oda Nobunaga, Toyotomi Hideyoshi, and Tokugawa Ieyasu—known as the Three Unifiers—brought the Warring States period to an end by once again consolidating central power.

—*Matthew Penney*

FURTHER READING

Sansom, George. *A History of Japan, 1334-1615.* 3 vols. Stanford, Calif.: Stanford University Press, 1961. Despite its age, Sansom's history of premodern Japan is still the most authoritative on the subject in English. Includes a detailed chapter on the Ōnin War.

Sato, Hiroaki. *Legends of the Samurai.* New York: The Overlook Press, 1995. One of the best collections of writing about the wars and culture of the samurai in English.

Turnbull, Stephen. *The Samurai Sourcebook.* London: Arms and Armour Press, 1998. Offers encyclopedic coverage of the important figures in the history of the samurai as well as aspects of their military culture.

Varley, H. Paul. *The Onin War.* New York: Columbia University Press, 1966. The authoritative account of the conflict in English. It contains not only a history of the war itself but also translations from surviving accounts of the fighting and political dealings that surrounded it.

SEE ALSO: 1457-1480's: Spread of Jōdo Shinshū Buddhism; 1477-1600: Japan's "Age of the Country at War"; Mar. 5, 1488: Composition of the *Renga* Masterpiece *Minase sangin hyakuin*; Beginning 1513: Kanō School Flourishes; 1532-1536: Temmon Hokke Rebellion; 1549-1552: Father Xavier Introduces Christianity to Japan; 1550's-1567: Japanese Pirates Pillage the Chinese Coast; 1550-1593: Japanese Wars of Unification; Sept., 1553: First Battle of Kawanakajima; June 12, 1560: Battle of Okehazama; 1568: Oda Nobunaga Seizes Kyōto; 1587: Toyotomi Hideyoshi Hosts a Ten-Day Tea Ceremony; 1590: Odawara Campaign; 1592-1599: Japan Invades Korea; 1594-1595: Taikō Kenchi Survey; Oct., 1596-Feb., 1597: *San Felipe* Incident; Oct. 21, 1600: Battle of Sekigahara.

RELATED ARTICLES in *Great Lives from History: The Renaissance & Early Modern Era, 1454-1600:* Hōjō Ujimasa; Hosokawa Gracia; Oda Nobunaga; Ōgimachi; Oichi; Sesshū; Toyotomi Hideyoshi.

1469-1481
REIGN OF THE AVA KING THIHATHURA

The reign of Thihathura marked a period of peace for the Burmese kingdom of Ava, an increase in the creation of literature and the arts, and a strengthened devotion to Theravāda Buddhism.

LOCALE: Ava, Burma (now central Myanmar)
CATEGORY: Government and politics

KEY FIGURES
Thihathura (d. 1481), king of Ava, r. 1469-1481
Sithukyawhtin (d. 1486), governor of Toungoo
Narapati (d. 1469), king of Ava, r. 1443-1469
Minhkaung (d. 1502), king of Ava, r. 1481-1502

SUMMARY OF EVENT

The Kingdom of Ava (1364-1527) was part of an area now occupied by Myanmar, which lies between modern India to the west, the Bay of Bengal to the southwest, and China, Laos, and Thailand to the northeast and east. The successor of the Kingdom of Pagan (849-1364), Ava was plagued by war about land. The rise of Ava as the new capital of Burma is attributed largely to its control of Kyaukse, a vital rice-growing area, and, therefore, its legitimacy was often contested by various provinces of Burma. Some sought to become the capital, such as Pegu and Toungoo, while others sought independence, such as Prome and Arakan.

In addition to fighting neighboring Burmese provinces, Ava fought the Mongols and, later, the Chinese. China wanted to assert authority over the Burmese provinces to secure its own borders and trade routes, force allegiance to China, and demand tributes from Burma. Despite the atmosphere of conflict surrounding the history of Ava, Thihathura's reign had been relatively unchallenged and peaceful, with most of the conflict occurring at the beginning of his reign.

Narapati, Thihathura's father, disapproved of a love affair between his grandson Minhkaung and Minhkaung's cousin. As a result of this disapproval, Minhkaung stabbed his grandfather in 1468, although the wound was not lethal. The attack forced Narapati to flee to Prome, where he died the following year. Thihathura ascended the throne in 1469 amidst this scandal, and allowed Minhkaung and his cousin to marry. This infuriated the queen dowager (possibly Queen Shinsawbu of Pegu or the queen of Ava), so she convinced Toungoo to revolt.

Eventually, the Mon kingdom of Pegu joined Toungoo. Thihathura suppressed the revolt and turned his at-

tention to Prome, where the ruler, Thihathura's brother, refused to recognize the supremacy of the Ava king. After taking Prome, Thihathura pardoned his brother.

Growing in power, Thihathura demanded in 1472 that China give him control of Mohnyin, a province bordering China that was ethnically Burmese. China was militarily expended because of border skirmishes. Relinquishing Mohnyin to Ava would have allowed an unobstructed trade route from Yunnan to Burma; China considered the idea. Mohnyin's chief, however, had given China's frontier eunuch gifts, including a jeweled girdle, which swayed China's decision in favor of Mohnyin.

In 1475, Thihathura raided Yawnghwe (a Shan state in Burma) with Hsipaw (another Shan state), securing its submission to his rule. Thihathura followed this success by raiding Pegu in 1476, yielding its area of Kawliya to Toungoo governor Sithukyawhtin as reward for his loyalty. Some viewed this as a sign of impending revolt by Toungoo, and to quell those doubts, Thihathura commanded Sithukyawhtin to have himself dragged by his hair to the court of Ava. Sithukyawhtin submitted to express his loyalty.

While Thihathura's reign seems wrought with conflict, Ava nevertheless enjoyed a relative peace. China was busy trying to keep its trade routes open and stable while also facing a rising concern of rebellion in its province that was rich in rubies. In addition, Narapati mistakenly had signaled recognition of Chinese authority when he handed over the body of a Chinese enemy who had committed suicide. Because of this mistake, China turned its attention from Ava. The neighboring provinces of Burma also offered little resistance. Thihathura's brother was the biggest dissident, refusing to acknowledge his inferiority to the king of Ava as the governor of Prome.

This peace allowed Thihathura to improve and strengthen relations with Sri Lanka, then the center of Theravāda Buddhism. Thihathura is considered to be a major figure in the rise of Theravāda Buddhism. His connection with Sri Lanka was so strong that it is possible the Theravāda "capital" had sent relics to temples in Ava. In 1474, Thihathura and his queen had sent a broom made from their hair with a jewel studded handle to the Temple of the Tooth in Sri Lanka. This gift was meant to signify Thihathura's devotion to Theravāda Buddhism, and the broom was meant to sweep the floor of the temple.

Thihathura also strengthened ties with the king of Sri Lanka, sending gifts of Chinese silk.

One documented commemoration tells of a bridge of gilded boats created to connect Ava to the land across the river to celebrate the enshrining of relics received from Sri Lanka. While there is no date for this event, it is believed to have occurred during the late Ava period. It most likely occurred during Thihathura's reign, as Narapati did not reconnect with Sri Lanka until later in his reign, and Minhkaung was constantly at war and had little time for religion.

Thihathura was able to focus his attention on being a Buddhist-Burmese king, taking care of his people and fostering the influence of religion in Burmese life. A Buddhist-Burmese kingship guaranteed an economy where subjects had leisure time to meditate, practice the arts, and take care of the monks. Theravāda monks rely on alms for their food, and keeping the monks well-fed was a sign of the religious dedication of a country and its ruler. Not being able to provide food for the monks because of poor economic conditions reflected poorly on their dedication. Thihathura provided for his people, and because of this, religion and the arts flourished. The genre of Burmese poetry is believed to have been created during this period, and it is still thriving in the twenty-first century.

By the end of his reign, Thihathura had strengthened Ava religiously and culturally, and for a period Ava had a strong military. Ava was the center of political and economic power and Burmese art and literature. Before his death in 1481, Thihathura had sent instructions to his loyal subject Sithukyawhtin. Upon his death, the king's bones were dropped in a river, and per his instructions, Sithukyawhtin aided his son Minhkaung as he ascended the throne.

SIGNIFICANCE

Ava was situated between two great Burmese empires. As it has been considered more of a transitory kingdom than important in its own right, its kings, for the most part, have been forgotten. The fall of Ava is directly connected to the rise of Toungoo, an empire known for its military strength and considered the Second Burmese Empire. By the time Thihathura ascended the throne, Ava was weakening in power, Toungoo was still weak, and China was perched to annex most of Burma. However, because Thihathura was able to keep peace with the Chinese and the various provinces of Burma, Toungoo

was able to gain power. Had China or another Burmese province persisted in attacking Ava, it is likely that Thihathura would have fallen, and Toungoo would not have succeeded Ava as the next Burmese empire. Furthermore, had China decided to go to war with Ava over the demand of Mohnyin, or for any other reason, Burma would have fallen to China and Toungoo might not have taken Kyaukse, the major reason for its succession as the next empire. If this had happened, Myanmar would be a distinctly different country in the twenty-first century, or, possibly, a part of China.

—*Tina Powell*

FURTHER READING

Aung-Thwin, Michael A. *Myth and History in the Historiography of Early Burma: Paradigms, Primary Sources, and Prejudices*. Monographs in International Studies 102, Southeast Asia Series. Athens: Ohio University Press, 1998. Discusses the historic basis of various myths of the three kingdoms of Pagan, Ava, and Toungoo.

Lieberman, Victor. *Integration in the Mainland: Southeast Asia in Global Context, c. 1800*. Volume 1 in *Strange Parallels*. New York: Cambridge University Press, 2003. Examines the reasons for the demise of Pagan and Ava, and Ava's instability.

Phayre, Arthur P. *History of Burma Including Burma Proper, Pegu, Taungu, Tenasserim, and Arakan: From the Earliest Time to the End of the First War with British India*. 1883. Reprint. Bangkok, Thailand: Orchid Press, 1998. A comprehensive history of Burma, with some discussion of conflict between China and the Burmese states.

Sankisyanz, Manuel. *Buddhist Backgrounds of the Burmese Revolution*. The Hague, The Netherlands: M. Nijhoff, 1965. This book examines the role of Buddhist-Burmese kings and how certain activities during a given reign reflected the king's rule.

SEE ALSO: 1450's-1529: Thai Wars; 1454: China Subdues Burma; c. 1488-1594: Khmer-Thai Wars; 1527-1599: Burmese Civil Wars; 1548-1600: Siamese-Burmese Wars; 1558-1593: Burmese-Laotian Wars; 1578: First Dalai Lama Becomes Buddhist Spiritual Leader; c. 1580-c. 1600: Siamese-Cambodian Wars.
RELATED ARTICLES in *Great Lives from History: The Renaissance & Early Modern Era, 1454-1600:* Tomé Pires; Xiaozong; Zhengde.

1469-1492
RULE OF LORENZO DE' MEDICI

Lorenzo de' Medici's court was a cultural hub in which writers, artists, and intellectuals established new standards for European art, philosophy, literature, and architecture. Under his patronage, the Florentine Republic became the center of Renaissance Humanism.

LOCALE: Florence (now in Italy)
CATEGORIES: Government and politics; cultural and intellectual history

KEY FIGURES

Cosimo de' Medici (1389-1464), ruler of Florence, r. 1434-1464, considered the founder of Medici political power
Lorenzo de' Medici (1449-1492), ruler of Florence, r. 1469-1492

Giuliano de' Medici (1453-1478), ruler of Florence, r. 1469-1478
Sixtus IV (Francesco della Rovere; 1414-1484), Roman Catholic pope, 1471-1484
Leonardo da Vinci (1452-1519), Italian architect, artist, inventor, and scientist
Michelangelo (1475-1564), Italian architect, artist, poet, and sculptor
Girolamo Savonarola (1452-1498), Italian church reformer

SUMMARY OF EVENT

Lorenzo de' Medici, called the Magnificent, was the leader of the Republic of Florence during the apex of the Italian Renaissance. Originating from rather humble beginnings in the Tuscan countryside, the Medici family

Florentine ruler Lorenzo de' Medici and his retinue traveling through a forest. (Hulton|Archive by Getty Images)

71

THE MEDICI RULERS OF FLORENCE

1434-1464	Cosimo de' Medici, "the Elder"
1464-1469	Piero di Cosimo de' Medici, "the Gouty"
1469-1492	Lorenzo de' Medici, "the Magnificent"
1469-1478	Giuliano de' Medici (coruler with Lorenzo)
1492-1494	Piero de' Medici, "the Unfortunate"
1512-1513	Giuliano de' Medici, duke of Nemours
1513-1519	Lorenzo de' Medici
1519-1523	Giulio de' Medici (later Pope Clement VII)
1524-1527	Ippolito de' Medici (under the regency of Silvio, Cardinal Passerini)
1530-1537	Alessandro de' Medici (first duke of Florence from 1531)
1537-1574	Cosimo I de' Medici, "the Great" (first grand duke of Tuscany from 1569)
1574-1587	Francesco I de' Medici
1587-1609	Ferdinand I de' Medici

migrated from the Mugello region to Florence in the twelfth century. Once in Florence, family members began to amass significant riches from trade, commerce, and banking, eventually transforming their great wealth into unparalleled political power. The family's first foray into the political life of this Tuscan republic occurred in the thirteenth century, when a member of the family first served in public office.

By the fourteenth century, the Medici family's political fate seemed tied to the common citizenry. In 1378, Salvestro de' Medici led the lower orders in revolt against a Florentine government controlled by the wealthiest elite. When the popular regime Salvestro had inspired fell in 1381, the family seemed to withdraw from political life until the end of the fourteenth century, when Giovanni di Bicci de' Medici (1360-1429) began more openly to use the Medici's vast wealth for political gain.

When Giovanni's son, Cosimo de' Medici (also known as Cosimo il Vecchio, or the Elder), reached adulthood, it was clear that the family's quest for wealth and power was inextricably tied to Florentine politics. The political and cultural influence of Cosimo the Elder was so great that his rule came to be considered the seminal period in the foundation of the Medici both as a political dynasty and as leading patrons of the arts. Cosimo's son, Piero di Cosimo de' Medici (1416-1469), called the Gouty, continued to rule over the family's fortunes until his death in 1469. At Piero's death, his sons Lorenzo de' Medici and Giuliano de' Medici inherited the Medici fortune and the family's political power.

The brothers' unified tyrannical rule was cut down on

April 26, 1478, when political conspirators attempted to end Medici political power by assassination. The assassins' attack, known as the Pazzi Conspiracy, came during Easter mass at the altar of the city's cathedral. Lorenzo managed to take refuge in a sacristy and then escaped from a side door. His brother Giuliano, however, was struck down and killed. Medici retribution was swift. The conspirators were captured and hanged in the city's main square, the Piazza della Signoria. Deeply offended that the archbishop of Pisa was hanged as one of the conspirators, Pope Sixtus IV threatened the Florentine Republic with interdiction and demanded Lorenzo's extradition to Rome.

Acting in a swift and audacious manner, Lorenzo risked personal safety by traveling to Naples to plea with the pope's ally, Ferdinand I, king of Naples. Lorenzo's success in concluding a favorable agreement with this southern Italian kingdom meant that the Papacy was now isolated and, thus, unable to act against Lorenzo and the republic. The course of these unanticipated events ensured that Lorenzo would be the undisputed, if unofficial, leader of the Florentine state for the next fourteen years. During Lorenzo's tenure as Florence's leader, the republic became a central participant in and producer of Italian Renaissance culture.

Following in his grandfather's footsteps, Lorenzo de' Medici exhibited the leadership that established Florence as the cultural capital of Europe. Under Lorenzo's guidance, Florence moved to the forefront of humanistic studies, scientific innovations, artistic achievements, and music and poetry. Seldom has such a stellar era of artistic, literary, and scientific accomplishments been achieved.

Lorenzo engaged in extensive scholarly activities and patronage. He supported the University of Pisa, amassed a significant library of printed works—including ancient texts and translated Greek manuscripts—and funded a book-copying workshop to create and circulate new copies of these texts. His actions helped to spark a resurgent interest in classical literature and philosophy within Italy and later throughout Europe.

The Florentine ruler also made significant contributions to poetry and music that helped nurture both art forms. His poetry, written in the Florentine dialect rather than the traditional Latin, was much admired by his contemporaries. Many members of Italy's educated elite had already come under the influence of Dante's similarly dialect-driven *La divina commedia* (c. 1320; *The Divine Comedy*, 1802), and this influence, combined with the success of Lorenzo's work, helped promote the adoption of the Tuscan dialect as the national language of Italy. Lorenzo's equally committed patronage of music, moreover, eventually led to the development of important new compositions.

Lorenzo's Florentine court also welcomed, nourished, and promoted the artistic talents of such Renaissance masters as Leonardo da Vinci, Michelangelo, Sandro Botticelli, Domenico Ghirlandaio, and Andrea del Verrocchio. Lorenzo treated men of talent and genius with great respect and even friendship. In about 1490, for example, a young Michelangelo's genius was recognized by Lorenzo, and the youthful artist was soon welcomed into the Medici household. He was treated as a member of the family, in addition to receiving academic and artistic instruction. Eventually, Lorenzo's admiration of artists and his support of their labors helped elevate artists from the level of common tradesmen to a new and higher social status established by merit and talent. The elevated

social status enjoyed by artists in modern society results, in no small part, from the new meritocracy of talent and ability that Lorenzo created in Renaissance Florence.

Though often at odds with high clerics of the Roman Catholic Church, Lorenzo allowed Dominican monk Girolamo Savonarola publicly to castigate the church and the Medici for their allegedly sinful actions. From the protection of the pulpit, Savonarola mesmerized the Florentine citizenry with prophetic utterances concerning the divine retribution awaiting evil church and secular rulers. Many thought that the divine retribution of which Savonarola spoke could be seen in the declining health of Lorenzo. According to doubtful popular belief, as Lorenzo's health steadily declined, Savonarola was brought to Lorenzo's death bed, but the popular preacher refused to grant the Florentine ruler final absolution. After Lorenzo's premature death at age forty-three, he was entombed in the Medici family's church, San Lorenzo, in Florence.

SIGNIFICANCE

Lorenzo de' Medici is justly referred to as Lorenzo the Magnificent, as his rule proved a decisive event in Re-

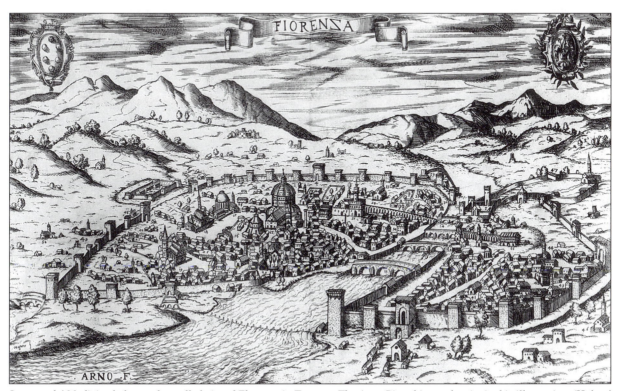

Lorenzo de' Medici ruled over the walled city of Florence in Tuscany. The Arno River bisects the city in this illustration. (Hulton Archive by Getty Images)

OTHER POWERFUL MEDICI

Name	Role
Lorenzo de' Medici, "the Elder"	Banker, patriarch, and brother of Cosimo "the Elder"
Giovanni de' Medici	Pope Leo X, 1513-1521
Giulio de' Medici	Pope Clement VII, 1523-1534
Giovanni dalle Bande Nere	Italian general, killed at the Battle of Mantua (1526)
Lorenzo de' Medici, "Lorenzino"	Playwright and assassin of Duke Alessandro de' Medici
Catherine de Médicis	Queen of France, r. 1547-1559
Alessandro Ottaviano de' Medici	Archbishop of Florence, 1574-1605, later Pope Leo XI, 1605
Marie de Médicis	Queen of France, r. 1600-1610

naissance history. It was during Lorenzo's reign as the de facto ruler of the Republic of Florence that his city came to be the epicenter of artistic production and Humanistic studies. Lorenzo's rule helped bring the European Middle Ages to a final end and, concomitantly, inaugurated a newly emerging meritocratic society where the abilities of the best and brightest were nurtured and their accomplishments were celebrated. Through the implementation of Lorenzo's enlightened policies, those who possessed great talent, such as Leonardo da Vinci and Michelangelo, came to add the product of their genius to the cultural foundations of modern Western civilization. Lorenzo can thus be credited as a harbinger of cultural and social modernity.

In addition, though tyrannical in the governance of Florence, Lorenzo's political leadership marked him as an innovative leader who sought to keep a balance of power between the varied Italian states. For a brief period, Lorenzo's strategy protected Florentine independence, and it also helped ensure that foreign powers would have fewer opportunities to meddle in the political affairs of the Italian peninsula. The political character of Lorenzo's rule and the innumerable advances achieved in humanistic studies and art under his leadership have caused many to conclude that his reign, though tyrannical, was one in which culture flourished and beauty was celebrated.

—Pietro Lorenzini

FURTHER READING

Blessington, Francis. *Lorenzo de' Medici*. Lanham, Md.: Rowman and Littlefield, 1992. The author's fictional work presents an historically accurate picture that, through its mixture of drama and scholarship, sheds light on the conflict between Lorenzo's Renaissance Humanism and the Christian spirituality personified by the Dominican monk, Savonarola.

Greenblatt, Miriam. *Lorenzo de' Medici and Renaissance Italy*. New York: Benchmark Books, 2003. Offers a brief review of the reign of Lorenzo the Magnificent and summarizes the importance of the Medici to the Renaissance.

Hibbert, Christopher. *The House of the Medici: Its Rise and Fall*. New York: Morrow Quill Paperbacks, 1980. This seminal book on the Medici dynasty remains a vital tool for understanding Lorenzo's role in the development of European cultural advancements and for assessing the political machinations of Renaissance Europe.

Martines, Lauro. *April Blood: Florence and the Plot Against the Medici*. New York: Oxford University Press, 2003. This compelling book presents the definitive interpretation of the evolution of Medici power at a critical period, and it also offers a colorful depiction of the complexities of Renaissance politics.

SEE ALSO: Apr. 9, 1454: Peace of Lodi; 1462: Founding of the Platonic Academy; 1477-1482: Work Begins on the Sistine Chapel; c. 1478-1519: Leonardo da Vinci Compiles His Notebooks; Apr. 26, 1478: Pazzi Conspiracy; 1486-1487: Pico della Mirandola Writes *Oration on the Dignity of Man*; 1495-1497: Leonardo da Vinci Paints *The Last Supper*; c. 1500: Revival of Classical Themes in Art; 1508-1520: Raphael Paints His Frescoes; 1508-1512 and 1534-1541: Michelangelo Paints the Sistine Chapel.

RELATED ARTICLES in *Great Lives from History: The Renaissance & Early Modern Era, 1454-1600:* Leonardo da Vinci; Lorenzo de' Medici; Michelangelo; Girolamo Savonarola; Sixtus IV.

1469-1508
AK KOYUNLU DYNASTY CONTROLS IRAQ AND NORTHERN IRAN

The Ak Koyunlu ruled much of present-day eastern Turkey, Iraq, and Iran in the late fifteenth century. They established diplomatic relations with Venice and became an international power whose rulers were recognized for their patronage of architecture, metalwork, and the literary arts.

LOCALE: Diyarbakir (now in Turkey) and Tabrīz (now in Iran)

CATEGORIES: Government and politics; expansion and land acquisition

KEY FIGURES

Kara Osman (1378-1435), founder of the Ak Koyunlu Dynasty, r. 1403-1435

Uzun Ḥasan (c. 1420-1478), Ak Koyunlu ruler, r. 1453-1478

Yaʿqūb (c. 1455-1490), Ak Koyunlu ruler, r. 1478-1490

Mehmed II (1432-1481), Ottoman sultan, r. 1444-1446, 1451-1481

SUMMARY OF EVENT

The Ak Koyunlu (Turkish for "white sheep") were a nomadic Turkoman community named for the white sheep they pastured between the headwaters of the Tigris and Euphrates Rivers in eastern Anatolia. Their banners displayed a white sheep in contrast to the black sheep designating their rivals, the Kara Koyunlu, who came from east of Lake Van.

The first known reference to the Ak Koyunlu mentions a leader named Tur Ali Bey, who in 1340 began attacking the Trebizonds along the Black Sea. The Trebizonds were the heirs to the Christian Byzantine Empire after the Latin crusaders captured Constantinople in 1204. When Tur Ali failed to conquer them, he chose to ally himself with them, establishing important diplomatic relations that continued between these two peoples for more than a century. The Trebizond emperor Alexius III (r. 1349-1390) arranged a marriage between his sister, Maria, and Kutlu, Tur Ali's son. He later married his daughter to Kara Osman, the son of Maria (known as Despina) and Kutlu.

Ruling from 1403 to 1435, Kara Osman is considered the founder of the Ak Koyunlu Dynasty. He joined forces with Tamerlane (also known as Timur) after Tamerlane invaded Mesopotamia. Tamerlane first captured Baghdad and Mosul in 1393 and then set his sights on western Anatolia. When local groups began to revolt, Tamerlane

turned to local chieftains to provide equilibrium. Thus, in 1402, Osman was granted complete control of the city of Diyarbakir at the headwaters of the Tigris River. This control provided Osman with the base of power he needed to consolidate and expand his rule.

Beginning the following year, Osman established the Ak Koyunlu state with numerous neighboring communities joining under its authority. At this time, the Kara Koyunlu, situated east of Lake Van, represented a significant obstacle to Ak Koyunlu expansion. By 1410, this rival group had conquered Baghdad and made it their capital. For nearly three decades, Osman was occupied fighting unsuccessfully against Kara Koyunlu rulers Kara Yusuf and Iskander, keeping them in check until his death in 1435. The Kara Koyunlu seem to have had the superior military of the two, but because of the strong threat from the Timurid empire to the east, the Kara Koyunlu were unable to commit sufficient resources to their western front to advance farther against the Ak Koyunlu. Thus, a stalemate existed between the two groups.

Under Osman's grandson, Uzun Ḥasan, however, the Ak Koyunlu were able to expand to become the major power of the region. In 1466, Uzun Ḥasan enticed the Kara Koyunlu ruler, Jihān Shāh, to leave his capital city of Tabrīz with a large army and to engage him in battle near Lake Van. For eighteen months, Uzun Ḥasan frustrated Jihān with various delays.

On November 11, 1467, when Jihān was retreating with his army to their winter quarters, Uzun Ḥasan made a surprise attack that utterly defeated the Kara Koyunlu army. Jihān was captured and killed, and the Kara Koyunlu Dynasty came to an end. In 1469, Uzun Ḥasan defeated the Timurid ruler, Abū Saʿīd, eliminating the threat to his eastern borders. Within a short time the Ak Koyunlu controlled Mosul, Baghdad, the Persian Gulf, Azerbaijan, and Khorāsān. Uzun Ḥasan moved his capital from Diyarbakir to Tabrīz.

Meanwhile, the situation to the west had been more grim for the Ak Koyunlu. In western Anatolia, the Ottoman sultan Mehmed II conquered Constantinople in 1453. He then expanded eastward toward Ak Koyunlu territory, incorporating various Turkish principalities as he went. Uzun Ḥasan sought diplomatic ties to counter this effort. He renewed the long-standing mutual defense pact with Trebizond, taking the hand in marriage of Katerina, the daughter of Emperor John IV. Uzun Ḥasan sent his army to prevent the Ottomans from attacking

Trebizond but was defeated. Afterward Uzun Ḥasan sent his mother, Sara, to negotiate. In 1461, Mehmed II rejected his offer and attacked Trebizond, bringing that empire to an end. Sara was allowed to return home with the valued jewels of the Trebizonds.

In 1464, Uzun Ḥasan contacted the Venetians, who had been longtime rivals to the growing Ottoman power. Over the next several years, envoys were exchanged, very similar to modern ambassadors. The Venetians promised military aid and provided the confidence needed to keep the Ottomans in check. This led, however, to conflict with the Mamlūks, who defeated the Ak Koyunlu in northern Syria in 1472. From this point on, the Ak Koyunlu did not venture west of the Euphrates River. The Ottomans, however, moved eastward with an army of seventy thousand.

The Ak Koyunlu attempted to resist the Ottoman onslaught. At first, Uzun Ḥasan and his son managed a number of victories, but in the long run they were no match for the massive ammunitions of the Ottomans. Their hope was to hold off the threat until they could be reinforced with Venetian weaponry. Yet, the promised arms never arrived, and Uzun Ḥasan was defeated at Tercan in 1473.

Embarrassed, Uzun Ḥasan returned to Tabrīz, where he continued to rule for another five years. He had already begun construction of the magnificent Nasriyya palace. He gained a reputation as a patron of the arts, including metalworks, calligraphy, miniature painting, and architecture. He also supported writers and scholars, including the court historian Abu Bakr Tihrani-Isfhani and the prominent philosopher and theologian Dawānī, who dedicated many of his works to Uzun Ḥasan. As a ruler, he was also known for enacting laws that protected equally the pasturing rights of competing tribal groups.

The successors of Uzun Ḥasan worked to hold off further Ottoman advance and to hold on to their territory in the east. Yaʿqūb turned his attention inward. In 1484, the Nasriyya mosque and complex were dedicated. Travelers described the complex as an earthly paradise and noted the surrounding schools, hostels, markets, and baths. Poets and writers flocked to Tabrīz. Yet, religious conflict soon became an issue, as religious leaders became increasingly involved in fiscal policy. More and more, the local population showed discontent with the Ak Koyunlu, who were Sunni Muslims and had imposed their form of Islam upon the previously Shīʿite region.

Following the death of Yaʿqūb, leadership among the Ak Koyunlu passed through six different rulers over the next eighteen years. Among them were three brothers, Alwand, Muḥammad, and Murād, who fought among themselves. Eventually, they were replaced by the Shīʿite Safavid Dynasty from Azerbaijan. The most devastating defeat, at Nakhichevan in 1502, came at the hands of Ismāʿīl I, who then declared himself to be shah and established the Safavid Dynasty at Tabrīz.

In response, Alwand began retreating westward and inflicted damage on his own cities of Mardin and Diyarbakir. By 1508, Ismāʿīl's army had conquered Mosul and Baghdad, defeating Murād and bringing the Ak Koyunlu Dynasty to an end. Soon thereafter, the Ottomans, after inflicting a defeat upon Ismāʿīl, were able to wrest control of northern Mesopotamia while the Safavids remained in control of Iran and Azerbaijan.

SIGNIFICANCE

Prior to the domination of the Middle East by the Ottoman Empire, two Turkoman tribal groups controlled the region of eastern Turkey, northern Iraq, and Iran for over a century: the Kara Koyunlu and the Ak Koyunlu. Their names, meaning respectively "black sheep" and "white sheep," derived from the images on the banners they carried into battle.

These two tribal confederations controlled the territory occupied by the Kurds today: the Kara Koyunlu to the east of Lake Van in the region of Azerbaijan, the Ak Koyunlu to the west centered near the headwaters of the Tigris River at Diyarbakir. They remained rivals, with first the Kara Koyunlu (1351-1469), then the Ak Koyunlu (1469-1508), gaining the upper hand.

While both tribal groups were known for their fighting skills, the Ak Koyunlu went beyond their rival in diplomacy, intermarrying with the Christian kingdom of Trebizond in northern Anatolia and making alliances with the Venetians to keep in check the growing Ottoman threat. The Ak Koyunlu also surpassed their rivals in building programs and as supporters of the arts and philosophy.

Eventually, the Ottomans were victorious in Mesopotamia. Like the Ak Koyunlu, they were Sunni Muslims, while the Safavid in Iran adopted the Shīʿite Islam of the Kara Koyunlu. This territorial split between the Shia and the Sunnis would have lasting consequences for the history of the region over the next five hundred years.

—*Fred Strickert*

FURTHER READING

Jackson, Peter. *The Cambridge History of Iran: The Timurid and Safavid Period.* New York: Cambridge University Press, 1993. A compendium of articles concerning trade, economics, religion, art, and architecture, as well as historical surveys of the period.

McDowall, David. *A Modern History of the Kurds.* New York: I. B. Tauris, 1996. The first chapter presents an overview of the early history of the Kurds and various ruling powers. Detailed maps.

O'Kane, Bernard. *Studies in Persian Art and Architecture.* Cairo: The American University Press, 1995. A collection of O'Kane's previously published articles on various aspects of art for this region.

Woods, John E. *The AqKoyunlu: Clan, Confederation, Empire.* Rev. and exp. ed. Salt Lake City: University of Utah Press, 1999. First published in 1976, this has been the standard scholarly resource for a generation. Now updated.

SEE ALSO: 1454-1481: Rise of the Ottoman Empire; 1463-1479: Ottoman-Venetian War; 1481-1512: Reign of Bayezid II and Ottoman Civil Wars; 1512-1520: Reign of Selim I; 1578-1590: The Battle for Tabrīz.

RELATED ARTICLES in *Great Lives from History: The Renaissance & Early Modern Era, 1454-1600:* Bayezid II; Mehmed II.

October 19, 1469
MARRIAGE OF FERDINAND AND ISABELLA

Ferdinand and Isabella's marriage combined the power and prestige of Aragon and Castile, the two largest kingdoms on the Iberian Peninsula, and defined the future Spanish nation.

LOCALE: Valladolid, Castile (now in Spain)
CATEGORIES: Government and politics; expansion and land acquisition

KEY FIGURES
Ferdinand V (1452-1516), king of Castile, r. 1474-1504, and later king of Aragon, r. 1479-1516, as Ferdinand II
Isabella I (1451-1504), queen of Castile, r. 1474-1504
Alfonso Carrillo (c. 1422-1482), archbishop of Toledo
Pedro González de Mendoza (1428-1495), cardinal of Spain
Henry IV of Castile (1425-1474), king of Castile, r. 1454-1474
John II (1397-1479), king of Aragon, r. 1458-1479

SUMMARY OF EVENT
When Ferdinand, crown prince of Aragon, married his cousin, Isabella, disputed heiress of Castile, on October 19, 1469, they seemed pawns of their elders, notably his father. John II had made Ferdinand king of Sicily to strengthen his position in marriage negotiations. Castile dominated the Iberian Peninsula with about half of its land and three-fifths of its population. Internal rebellion under weak Henry IV of Castile had brought intervention by rulers of Iberia's other kingdoms (Aragon, Portugal, Granada, and Navarre). Henry IV preferred that his sister, Isabella, marry a Castilian lord to strengthen his own position or a foreign ally to secure the succession rights of his own daughter, Princess Juana. Also opposed to this marriage, but ready to play a double game, was Juan Pacheco, master of the military Order of Santiago and Henry IV's favorite. Most nobles adopted a wait-and-see attitude.

Supporting Isabella's marriage to Aragon's heir were the Enríquez family (Ferdinand's maternal kinspeople) and Alfonso Carrillo, archbishop of Toledo, who became Isabella's chief protector. Their marriage required considerable derring-do by the principals (who had never seen each other). Ferdinand traveled from Aragon disguised, with a few retainers. Isabella defied her brother and fled to Carrillo's protection. In their haste to present Henry IV with a fait accompli, they married without requisite papal dispensation, which was needed because of their close kinship.

During the first years of their marriage, the young couple asserted their independence against their elders and built their own power base, including an uneasy reconciliation with Henry IV and an alliance with the Mendoza family. In 1472, support came from papal legate Rodrigo Borgia (later Pope Alexander VI), facilitated by Pedro González de Mendoza, who thereby gained a cardinal's hat. A vassal of John II, Borgia provided the needed dispensation in part because of a barrage of slander against Princess Juana. Queen Juana, wife of Henry IV, had recently borne an illegitimate son, and rumors circulated that her (older) daughter was also illegitimate. Beltrán de la Cueva,, the supposed father of Princess Juana (Juana la Beltraneja), was another royal

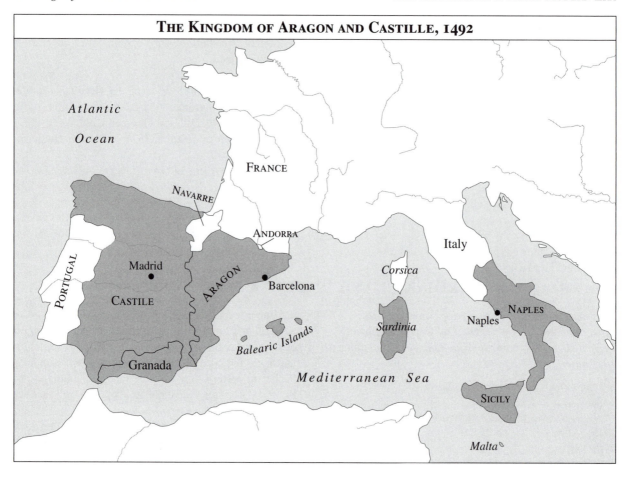

THE KINGDOM OF ARAGON AND CASTILLE, 1492

favorite and a Mendoza in-law. Despite such rumors, many modern historians accept Juana's legitimacy.

The death of Henry IV, about the same time as those of Juan Pacheco and Queen Juana, brought civil war to the peninsula. Aragon backed Isabella; King Afonso V of Portugal, affianced to his niece, Princess Juana, invaded Castile in her interest. Surviving members of the Pacheco family also supported Juana, as did Carrillo, who was upset over the independence of Ferdinand and Isabella and blamed them for his failure to secure a cardinalate. After the couple's five years of marriage, Castilians identified Ferdinand with his wife's cause more than with Aragon; Portugal's king seemed a foreign invader. Isabella played an active political role, whereas the juvenile Juana could not.

Thus, Ferdinand and Isabella gained adherence from most of Castile's nobles and cities. John II supported them unconditionally, although he was harassed by Louis XI of France, who pursued his own interests in Navarre and Aragon, promising much and delivering

nothing to Afonso V. Historians usually consider the 1476 Battle of Toro to have been decisive. Nevertheless, Ferdinand and Isabella did not control Castile until 1479, with the signing of the Treaty of Alcáçovas; by then, John II had died, and the couple also ruled Aragon.

In building control during the civil war, Ferdinand and Isabella shaped the Spanish nation. The Holy Brotherhood, a league of municipalities, had provided mutual assistance and protection to members. In 1476, the monarchs took control and used Brotherhood armies against Juana's supporters. In the period from 1488 to 1495, Ferdinand tried to develop a brotherhood in Aragon. Isabella forced her husband's election as master of the military orders of Santiago in 1477, Calatrave in 1487, and Alcantará in 1494, all of which provided sources of money and military power.

Between 1476 and 1480, the monarchs enacted major reforms through the *cortes* (parliament). Afterward, having received its mandate, Ferdinand and Isabella used the *cortes* infrequently and governed through the bureaucratic royal council, the Brotherhood (for military expenses), and special agents, such as *corregidores*, to handle local problems. The Council of Aragon, established in 1494 and composed of Aragonese personnel, was quite separate, but, meeting in Castile, it demonstrated an osmotic process of national unification. On the other hand, having established royal authority, the monarchs allowed great nobles considerable local autonomy. Similarly, fiscal dependence on the wool trade encouraged Ferdinand and Isabella to allow its guild, the Mesta, great independence. In 1498, no longer needing the Brotherhood, the monarchs allowed it to revert to local control.

In 1478, the pope authorized establishment of Spain's Inquisition, and, from 1483, the same inquisitor general served in both Aragon and Castile. In 1486, the pope granted Ferdinand and Isabella control of church appointments and finances in the Canary Islands and territory conquered from the Muslim kingdom of Granada. This royal patronage extended to the Americas in 1501-1508 and eventually pertained to all of Spain. The Synod of Seville in 1478 witnessed genuine royal concern for

church reform. In 1495, Francisco Jiménez de Cisneros, an ascetic Franciscan friar, succeeded Pedro González de Mendoza as archbishop of Toledo. Royal piety and political acumen combined in rallying Spaniards in the crusade that conquered Granada for Castile (1481-1492). Pope Alexander VI recognized this triumph with the title Catholic Monarchs, also held by subsequent Spanish kings. Edicts in 1492 and 1502 obliged Jews and Muslims to convert to Christianity or leave Spain. Thus, the nation became Europe's most formidable Catholic power.

Control within Spain made possible ambitious projects abroad. After Christopher Columbus returned from the Americas, Castile became a world power; with American treasure, Spain dominated Europe. From 1495, Ferdinand pursued Aragon's rivalry against France in Italian wars in which Castilian Gonzalo Fernández de Córdoba emerged as Europe's greatest commander. Archbishop Jiménez led an army into North Africa serving Aragonese interests. Capping his career, Ferdinand annexed Navarre to Castile in 1512. Ferdinand and Isabella carefully edu-

1460's

The marriage of King Ferdinand II and Queen Isabella I. (F. R. Niglutsch)

cated their children and made strategic marriages for them with two aims: union with Portugal and encirclement of France. Princess Isabella and (after her death in childbirth) her sister Maria were married to Manuel I of Portugal. Their siblings Juan and Joan married Habsburgs of Germany and the Netherlands, and Princess Catherine married King Henry VIII of England. Thus, despite the stipulations in the marriage treaty of Ferdinand and Isabella that Aragon and Castile must remain separate kingdoms, the two kingdoms functioned together in their common interest in foreign and domestic affairs.

Circumstances, however, determined the separation of the two kingdoms. When Queen Isabella died in 1504, the throne of Castile passed to Joan (later known as Juana la Loca, or the mad) and her husband, Philip I, ending the Trastámara Dynasty there. Aragon was ruled separately under Ferdinand. The death of Philip I in 1506 and the mental instability of Joan enabled a restoration of unity under Ferdinand's regency. By then, Ferdinand had married his great-great niece, Germaine de Foix to strengthen his position in that kingdom. Germaine's baby, who might have continued Aragonese separation, died.

SIGNIFICANCE

Ferdinand and Isabella's marriage led to nothing less than the unification of Aragon and Castile, which formed the nation known today as Spain. After Ferdinand's death in 1516, Archbishop Jiménez served as regent for Charles I (later Holy Roman Emperor Charles V), son of Philip I and Joan, who ruled a united Spain. As the heir of Charles and his wife, Isabella of Portugal, Philip II conquered Portugal in 1580. The political union of Spain and Portugal continued until it was dissolved in a war for Portuguese independence (1640-1685).

—Paul Stewart

FURTHER READING

Boruchoff, David A., ed. *Isabel la Católica, Queen of Castile: Critical Essays*. New York: Palgrave Macmillan, 2003. Analyzes the carefully crafted public image of Isabella to gain insight into Isabella's life beyond that image.

Elliott, John H. *Imperial Spain, 1469-1716*. Reprint. New York: Penguin Books, 1990. The classic account of Spain's rise and fall as an imperial power. Emphasizes the barren and humble nature of its beginnings in contrast to the height of its power.

Fernández-Armesto, Felipe. *Ferdinand and Isabella*. New York: Taplinger, 1975. Reliable and filled with humanizing details, this book provides an admirably balanced portrait, giving proper recognition to both husband and wife.

Hillgarth, J. N. *The Spanish Kingdoms, 1250-1516*. Vol. 2. Oxford, England: Clarendon Press, 1978. More detailed than the work of Kamen, this book surpasses earlier standard works on the period.

Kamen, Henry. *Empire: How Spain Became a World Power, 1492-1763*. New York: HarperCollins, 2003. Surveys the roles played by Ferdinand and Isabella in the fashioning of Spain's global empire.

_____. *Spain, 1469-1714: A Society of Conflict*. 2d ed. Reprint. New York: Longman, 1996. A revisionist study that parallels coverage of the period provided by Elliott, who tends more to facts and figures.

Liss, Peggy K. *Isabel the Queen*. New York: Oxford University Press, 1992. Notable for its superior scholarship, Liss's biography provides an in-depth study of Isabella and the full range of her accomplishments.

Rubin, Nancy. *Isabella of Castile: The First Renaissance Queen*. New York: St. Martin's Press, 1992. Issued the same year as the work of Liss, Rubin's biography takes a more popular approach that renders it more accessible for general readers.

Thomas, Hugh. *Rivers of Gold: The Rise of the Spanish Empire*. London: Weidenfeld & Nicolson, 2003. A decidedly conservative and Eurocentric history of Spanish colonialism during Ferdinand and Isabella's rule.

Woodward, Geoffrey. *Spain in the Reigns of Isabella and Ferdinand, 1474-1516*. London: Hodder & Stoughton, 1997. Comprehensive analysis of the social, political, religious, and economic aspects of Ferdinand and Isabella's reign, as well as their foreign policies and relations.

SEE ALSO: 1474-1479: Castilian War of Succession; Aug. 17, 1477: Foundation of the Habsburg Dynasty; Nov. 1, 1478: Establishment of the Spanish Inquisition; 1492: Fall of Granada; 1492: Jews Are Expelled from Spain; Beginning c. 1495: Reform of the Spanish Church; Nov. 26, 1504: Joan the Mad Becomes Queen of Castile; Jan. 23, 1516: Charles I Ascends the Throne of Spain; June 28, 1519: Charles V Is Elected Holy Roman Emperor; 1520-1522: Comunero Revolt; 1555-1556: Charles V Abdicates.

RELATED ARTICLES in *Great Lives from History: The Renaissance & Early Modern Era, 1454-1600:* Boabdil; Christopher Columbus; Ferdinand II and Isabella I; Henry IV of Castile; Francisco Jiménez de Cisneros; Manuel I; Tomás de Torquemada.

1471-1493
REIGN OF TOPA INCA

Topa Inca's conquests added to the extensive and thriving empire conquered by his father, Pachacuti, and solidified Incan control over the empire's subject peoples.

LOCALE: Andes Mountains and west coast of South America (now in Peru)

CATEGORIES: Government and politics; expansion and land acquisition

KEY FIGURES
Pachacuti (c. 1391-1471), ninth king, father of Topa Inca, r. 1438-1471
Topa Inca (d. 1493), tenth king, r. 1471-1493
Huayna Capac (1488?-1525), eleventh king, son of Topa Inca, r. 1493-1525

SUMMARY OF EVENT
In the early 1400's, the Inca controlled the region around Cuzco, Peru, only. Their expansion over much of western South America began with the accession of the ninth king, Pachacuti, in 1438, who led forty thousand inhabitants of the Cuzco region on a spectacular course of conquest. Using superior tactical leadership and recruiting soldiers from conquered groups, Pachacuti built an empire that ultimately included some ten million subjects.

In 1463, he gave control of the army to his younger son, Topa Inca, who continued the northern expansion of Incan territory, while Pachacuti concentrated on organizing the empire more efficiently and rebuilding the capital city of Cuzco. When Topa Inca assumed the throne in 1471, his realm stretched along the Andean highlands from modern Ecuador south to Lake Titicaca on the Chilean border. Topa Inca added to his domain the coastal regions of Peru, the northern half of Chile, and portions of Bolivia and northwest Argentina. Huayna Capac, Topa Inca's son, added jungle territory to the Incan realm.

Rulers were given the title "Inca." The word also designated the inhabitants of the Cuzco valley who claimed descent from the original settlers. The name was extended to neighboring tribes adopted by the Incas, who spoke the same Quechua and were early allies. Loosely applied, the term "Incan" expanded to cover the subject peoples of the Incan state, although they were actually a very diverse collection of more than one hundred tribes and kingdoms, speaking many languages, and considered inferior by the original Incas.

To unite their 1,800-mile-long empire, the Incas built two main highways, one along the coast and the other in the highlands, with many transverse roads. Well-constructed bridges carried the roads over intervening rivers, permitting rapid movement of the army and easy transportation of tribute to Cuzco. The Inca possessed neither the wheel nor draft animals; the roads carried foot traffic and llamas bearing merchandise. Fish could be brought to Cuzco from the coast in two days, arriving fresh enough to eat—after the Spanish conquest, horses and wagons took a week to make the same trip.

The Inca were outstanding engineers and architects. They constructed elaborate road and bridge systems and erected monumental public buildings by fitting together huge stones seamlessly without the use of mortar. Carefully built stone walls testified to the importance of a building and to the high status of its occupants. Many walls demonstrated the skills of their builders by remaining intact more than four hundred years in an earthquake-prone region. The Incas built terraced fields on mountain slopes, supplying water through intricate irrigation canals. Acreage under cultivation and the quantity of food produced increased, easily supporting the Incan army and large governmental and religious organizations.

The Inca had no coinage and no concept of money. Their vestigial trade consisted of bartering surplus goods. Wealth meant controlling the labor of subordinates and possessing land and livestock. Subject people were not taxed, but owed labor service, which might consist of working on roads or public buildings, cultivating state and temple lands, transporting goods, or serving in the army. The Incas claimed all land as property of the king and divided their conquests by reserving one-third for the state, one-third to support the religious establishment, and allotting the rest to the people.

Agriculture was the main economic activity. Depending on altitude and the suitability of the soil, a variety of native plants were grown, including white and sweet potatoes, tomatoes, chili peppers, squash, and many kinds of beans. The major crop, however, was corn, which was used directly and also fermented into corn beer, and consumed with meals and during ritual ceremonies. The main domesticated animals were llamas, valued as pack animals primarily but also sometimes eaten, and alpacas raised for their wool. In addition, ducks and guinea pigs augmented the Incan diet.

Incan society was stratified into rigid hierarchical

1470's

81

lines. At its pinnacle sat the Inca, claiming divine status as a direct descendant of the Sun god. The eldest son did not necessarily inherit the throne; the king designated the son he thought most capable as his successor. Each ruler built palaces for his wives, concubines, and children, endowing the group with extensive fields. The descendants of a deceased king were charged with conserving his mummy, carrying out family rituals, and occasionally showing the mummy to the people while reciting his great deeds. Ranking directly below the royal Incas were the descendants of the first settlers of Cuzco, who were not subject to any labor requirement and were assigned servants from among the conquered people. Next in status were the Incas-by-privilege—inhabitants of areas near Cuzco who were early allies of the Incas. They were exempt from labor requirements and often served with the Incas-by-blood as administrators in the imperial bureaucracy. The Incas recruited promising members from conquered peoples to be leaders of villages and small administrative districts. They formed a lower nobility, a status inherited by their descendants.

Ordinary people of the conquered tribes made up the lowest, but largest, segment of the population. Extended families, consisting of several generations, lived in one-room, rectangular, adobe houses with thatched roofs. Nearby were homes of kinfolk, sometimes arranged within a walled compound. Each family was assigned land to raise its own food; kin groups joined together to carry out required work on state and temple lands. Skilled workers crafted graceful pottery, wove cotton and alpaca wool into cloth, and produced bronze tools and utensils.

The Incas did not possess a written language. To record information concerning their vast empire, the Incas depended on the *quipu*, a set of strings with knots tied at various positions to indicate numbers. The strings hung from a main cord, and their location indicated the object recorded. A skilled group of labor-exempt workers constructed and interpreted the *quipus*. Modern scholars have decoded the numerical *quipus* and shown that they used a decimal system and employed the concept of zero. Incas also recorded the genealogies and life histories of the kings on *quipus*, but no scholar has yet deciphered any literary *quipu*.

The principal deity of the Incas was the Sun god, claimed as the direct ancestor of the royal line. The Incas did not force subject people to abandon their own gods, but insisted they accept the superior position of Incan deities. Incan religious structures were called Houses of the Sun, but they also contained images and altars dedicated to other gods. Important deities included a thunder or weather god, a moon goddess, and a creator god.

The Incas attributed supernatural powers to specific places and objects. A hierarchy of priests and priestesses devoted themselves full-time to temple rituals, supported by produce from one-third of the empire's land. Rituals almost always involved some form of sacrifice. Corn beer might be poured in front of the altar, food or cloth might be burned, guinea pigs or llamas might be slaughtered. Even the poorest Incan inhabitant could participate in such rituals; tearing out an eyelash in honor of the Sun was an acceptable sacrifice. In times of natural catastrophes, famines, and plagues, or when celebrating a king's coronation, human sacrifices were offered—usually children ten to fifteen years old.

SIGNIFICANCE

When Topa Inca died in 1493, he left his son Huayna Capac a powerful and solidly established kingdom whose permanence seemed assured and whose expansion appeared unstoppable. In the short span of fifty-five years, Pachacuti and Topa Inca had created one of history's greatest empires. Wealth poured into Cuzco, providing a magnificent lifestyle for the Incan nobility and supplying the material basis for expectations of endless growth. Although restless subject peoples occasionally rebelled, the Incan armies defeated every insurgency. The Incan system of government molded the Andean Indians into a dominant Incan image. Quechua replaced the many indigenous languages spoken before the Incan arrival. Sacrificing to the Incan gods seemed much more useful than appealing to previously worshiped deities.

With hindsight, one can see that the empire had grown close to its natural limits. Topa Inca had ended his southward drive when the cost of conquering the fiercely resistant Araucanian Indians greatly exceeded any prospective benefit. Huayna Capac pushed into northern and eastern jungle areas, but made slow progress and found material rewards elusive. No one, however, could have foreseen the catastrophic threat to the Incan future posed by the arrival of Christopher Columbus in the Caribbean, one year before Topa Inca died, and the subsequent conquest of the Inca by Francisco Pizarro in 1533.

—*Milton Berman*

FURTHER READING

Julien, Catherine. *Reading Inca History.* Iowa City: University of Iowa Press, 2000. A detailed examination of Inca sources of information, analyzed to determine how much historical reality they contain.

Malpass, Michael A. *Daily Life in the Inca Empire*. Westport, Conn.: Greenwood Press, 1996. Describes the cultural, political, economic, and religious practices of the Incas.

Minelli, Laura Laurencich. *The Inca World: The Development of Pre-Columbian Peru, A.D. 1000-1534*. Norman: University of Oklahoma Press, 1999. Lavishly illustrated examination of the historical, cultural, and material world of the Incas.

Rostworowski de Diez Canseco, María. *History of the Inca Realm*. Translated by Harry B. Iceland. New York: Cambridge University Press, 1999. A premier authority on Inca history and society.

SEE ALSO: 1493-1525: Reign of Huayna Capac; 1525-1532: Huáscar and Atahualpa Share Inca Rule; 1532-1537: Pizarro Conquers the Incas in Peru.

RELATED ARTICLES in *Great Lives from History: The Renaissance & Early Modern Era, 1454-1600:* Atahualpa; Huáscar; Pachacuti; Francisco Pizarro; Hernando de Soto.

March 18-22, 1471
BATTLE OF VIJAYA

The decisive Vietnamese victory over the Kingdom of Champa at the Battle of Vijaya effectively ended Champa's power as a dominant force in Southeast Asia and added much new land to the expanding Vietnamese Empire.

LOCALE: Vijaya (now near Qui Nhon, Vietnam)
CATEGORIES: Wars, uprisings, and civil unrest; expansion and land acquisition

KEY FIGURES
Le Thanh Tong (1442-1497), emperor of Vietnam, r. 1460-1497
Ban La Tra Toan (d. 1471), king of Champa, r. 1460-1471
Bo Tri Tri (d. 1478), duke in Champa, later king of Champa, r. 1471-1478

SUMMARY OF EVENT

The Battle of Vijaya was part of a long history of fighting between the Cham and Vietnamese, which had endured for more than fifteen hundred years. Indeed, from the moment the Cham people entered the historical record at the end of the second century B.C.E., they found themselves in conflict with the Vietnamese to their north, a conflict over the coast of what is now Vietnam.

The Vietnamese considered the Cham fierce barbarians and pirates who raided and plundered the Vietnamese coastal villages and who refused to make peace. No records survive, however, to tell the Cham point of view.

The Cham and Vietnamese were allies in the thirteenth century, but only because Southeast Asia was being threatened by the Mongols from the north. Soon after, however, the Vietnamese and the Cham continued to fight fierce battles, and Vietnam would conquer a large part of Cham territory as the balance between the two warring states shifted in favor of the Vietnamese. Their empire, called Dai Viet, reached south to just beyond Da Nang. Yet the Cham continued to resist. In fighting back, the Cham plundered the Vietnamese capital (what is now Hanoi) and killed a Vietnamese king in 1377 before being expelled.

In 1469, Cham king Ban La Tra Toan raided the Vietnamese province of Hoa Chau (near modern Quang Tri). This convinced the young and energetic Vietnamese emperor, Le Thanh Tong, that war was inevitable. He began to recruit and train fresh soldiers for the Vietnamese army. In October, 1470, King Tra Toan invaded Hoa Chau again, this time with a combined land and sea force. Traditional Vietnamese accounts speak of 100,000 enemy soldiers, but this number may be too high. Le Thanh Tong resolved to fight the invading Cham. A mission to China in October/November of 1470 ensured that China would remain neutral in the coming war, thus Dai Viet's northern border would be protected. Le Thanh Tong declared war on the Kingdom of Champa on November 28, 1470.

The declaration of war began first with an attack on the legitimacy of King Tra Toan. Because Tra Toan's brother had murdered a previous king of Champa, the Vietnamese claimed to be liberators who would restore order. Second, Le Thanh Tong charged Tra Toan with the invasion of Dai Viet and with attempts to inflame China against the Vietnamese. Le Thanh Tong believed his retaliatory attack was fully vindicated.

In early December of 1470, the Vietnamese army and navy of between 100,000 and 150,000 men were ready to cross on foot and aboard 1,700 warships into Cham territory. One anecdote relates that on the day the emperor left for the campaign, fine rain had been falling under soft northern winds, prompting the emperor to compose a poem about the sound of the raindrops softening the steps of the warriors as they embarked their ships.

Personally led by their emperor Le Thanh Tong, who had studied the maps of the enemy territory intensely, the main body of the Vietnamese forces advanced over a pass into Quang Nam province. On December 28, some local Cham rulers submitted to the Vietnamese.

On January 8, 1471, the Vietnamese navy arrived in the waters of Champa. To stop the Vietnamese advance, Tra Toan ordered his younger brother to attack the invaders with elephant cavalry. The Cham planned a surprise, having assembled a force supported by five thousand war elephants near the River Sa Ky (central Vietnam) on February 24, 1471. However, Le Thanh Tong learned of this development. Based on his study of the land, he prepared an effective defense that would prove to be a deadly trap for the Cham. When the Cham attacked on February 26, they were surprised by the vigor and skill of the waiting Vietnamese army. The Cham attack stopped, but when they attempted to leave the field of battle, the Cham discovered that Le Thanh Tong had positioned his troops to block all escape routes. The Vietnamese soldiers struck fiercely, also attacking the elephants. The Cham fled in disorder.

At Vijaya, King Tra Toan heard of his brother's defeat. He sent emissaries to the Vietnamese, asking for peace. However, Le Thanh Tong rejected this offer. Instead, he moved his combined land and sea forces against Vijaya and encircled the capital. On the morning of March 18, 1471, Emperor Le Thanh Tong launched the Battle of Vijaya. The Vietnamese navy captured the capital's harbor, effectively preventing the Cham from escaping by sea. For the next three days, the massive army of the Vietnamese attacked the walls of Vijaya in waves. The Cham defenders put up a fierce fight. Yet, massive catapults, brought from Vietnam, supported the attacking Vietnamese infantry. The catapults hurled stones and incendiary missiles against and over the city walls of Vijaya. On March 22, the Cham defense cracked. The walls of Vijaya were breached, and the Vietnamese flooded the city, killing or capturing the last defenders.

On the order of Emperor Le Thanh Tong, King Tra Toan, his wives, and his children were captured alive and led to him as captives. According to contemporary accounts, between forty thousand and sixty thousand Cham were killed in the Battle of Vijaya. In addition to King Tra Toan, the Vietnamese captured some thirty thousand Cham. Their fate would prove difficult, as they were brought to Vietnam, physically mutilated by having their left ears cut off, and enslaved for life. Their severed ears were deposited in a temple honoring the emperor's ancestors.

Le Thanh Tong deposed King Tra Toan and took him north as prisoner. When Tra Toan died of natural causes while traveling north, Le Thanh Tong performed a symbolic act of cruelty. He ordered Tra Toan's corpse be decapitated and the severed head hung under the bow of the emperor's ship. A white flag attached to it spelled out the name and former title of the dead king of Champa.

SIGNIFICANCE

In April of 1471, Emperor Le Thanh Tong had dictated his terms to the defeated Cham. The empire of Dai Viet annexed a vast stretch of Champa land, along the coast for more than 500 miles to the cape of Hon Lon. This annexation reduced the territory of Champa drastically, by more than one half, even though Vietnamese rule was effectively enforced only up to the Cu Mong Pass, just north of the cape. The conquered territory became the new Vietnamese province of Quang Nam in June/July, 1471, and it provided for a major expansion of Vietnamese land.

The remaining lands of Champa were initially divided into three different duchies. One of the local dukes, Cham general Bo Tri Tri, submitted to Vietnamese rule in exchange for being recognized as a king. He succeeded in rebuilding a small Cham kingdom around the last remaining major cities in what is now South Vietnam. Just before his death in 1478, the Chinese empire also recognized him as king of Champa.

The Battle of Vijaya effectively eliminated Champa as a serious power in Southeast Asia. No longer fearing the Cham, the Vietnamese were quick to settle in their newly gained territory, establishing colonies and enforcing what they believed to be their cultural and military dominance.

With the fall of Vijaya, the backbone of the Cham nation had been broken. During the next 350 years their remaining lands fell to continuing Vietnamese conquests. Some Cham assimilated into Vietnamese culture but others emigrated to Cambodia. By the early twenty-first century, the Cham were a recognized minority of Vietnam.

—*R. C. Lutz*

FURTHER READING

Chapuis, Oscar. *A History of Vietnam*. Westport, Conn.: Greenwood Press, 1995. A well-written, detailed examination of the battle, from both Cham and Vietnamese points of view. Maps, bibliography, index.

Guillon, Emmanuel. *Cham Art.* Translated by Tom White. London: Thames and Hudson, 2001. Provides Cham commentary on the battle. Richly illustrated, with maps of the region.

Hall, Daniel George. *A History of Southeast Asia.* 4th ed. London: Macmillan Press, 1981. Still a standard work on the period. Chapter 8 surveys the history of Champa, chapter 9 explores the history of Vietnam. Illustrations, maps, bibliography, and index.

Heidhues, Mary Somers. *Southeast Asia: A Concise History.* London: Thames and Hudson, 2000. Places Le

Thanh Tong's reign in the context of Vietnam's history. Illustrations, maps, index.

Thurgood, Graham. *From Ancient Cham to Modern Dialects.* Honolulu: University of Hawaii Press, 1999. Although primarily focused on the Cham language, this work also surveys Champa's history using updated historical and anthropological sources.

SEE ALSO: 1450's-1471: Champa Civil Wars; 1539: Jiajing Threatens Vietnam.

RELATED ARTICLE in *Great Lives from History: The Renaissance & Early Modern Era, 1454-1600:* Le Thanh Tong.

---

c. 1473
ASHIKAGA YOSHIMASA BUILDS THE SILVER PAVILION

Ashikaga Yoshimasa, eighth shogun of the Ashikaga Dynasty, established himself as a significant patron of the arts despite his troubled reign, which climaxed in the Ōnin War. His reign is remembered today for the unfinished Silver Pavilion.

LOCALE: Kyōto, Japan

CATEGORIES: Architecture; art; government and politics

KEY FIGURES

Ashikaga Yoshimasa (1436-1490), shogun, r. 1449-1473, reduced by the Ōnin War

Ashikaga Yoshimitsu (1358-1408), the most illustrious of the Ashikaga shoguns, r. 1368-1394

Oda Nobunaga (1534-1582), one of the daimyo who later helped unify Japan, r. 1573-1582

SUMMARY OF EVENT

Ashikaga Yoshimasa was the grandson of the ruler regarded as the most effective and illustrious of the Ashikaga shoguns, the great Yoshimitsu (r. 1368-1394), builder of Kyōto's famous Golden Pavilion (Kinkaku), whose reign dominated the second half of fourteenth century Japan. As the son of the evil-tempered shogun Yoshinori (r. 1429-1441), Yoshimasa assumed the office of shogun in 1449 following the assassination of his notorious father and the subsequent death of an older brother, another child heir named Yoshikatsu (b. 1434), whose brief reign lasted only two years (1442-1443). Such patterns of succession, following close on the murder of an elder lord and the sudden death of one or more

elder brothers, were commonplace during this period of conflict.

Having had the shogunate thrust on him prematurely when he was still a child, Yoshimasa was relegated to the role of a figurehead during his early reign while the actual power of government was exercised by the old governor-general Hatakeyama Mochikuni (1398-1455) and later Hatakeyama's sixteen-year-old successor Hosokawa Katsu (1430-1473), neither of whom possessed the noble character traits or administrative talents needed to deal effectively with the awful complexities of those times. During the rule of Yoshimasa's child predecessor, the Ashikaga clan's control of the eastern territories had already begun to erode as strong local warlords (daimyo) of the Kanto region asserted their autonomy. The arrogant daimyo passed their tax burdens to the already overburdened peasantry, priming them for a large-scale revolt.

It was in this dire situation that young Yoshimasa, at the age of fourteen, assumed his role as shogun. The answers to the virtually insurmountable problems of government that immediately faced him proved elusive. His treasury dwindled while the powerful warlords increasingly defied the court at Kyōto with virtual impunity.

As the years passed, with political conditions degenerating slowly into a stalemate, Yoshimasa retreated into intellectual and spiritual pursuits, including the metaphysical-aesthetic realm of Zen-inspired artforms such as the tea ceremony (*chadō*), of which he became an acknowledged master. Preferring the pleasurable company of renowned artists and the occasional Zen Buddhist monk to that of his quarrelsome court ministers, Yoshimasa distanced himself from governance by leaving the day-to-day administration of his realm in the incapable hands of his indecisive wife, Tomiko, his meddling mother, Shigeko, and his ambitious father-in-law, Ise Sadachika—all of whom took full advantage of the opportunities afforded them and thereby exacerbated the general disorder of Yoshimasa's court. As a result, Yoshimasa fell under the sway of the same powerful daimyo against whom his grandfather had so skillfully maneuvered during the previous century, with predictably disastrous results.

Prior to his retirement at age forty, Yoshimasa undertook construction of a pleasure villa, the so-called Silver Pavilion (Ginkaku-ji), which was intended to stand in glorious counterpoint to the great Golden Pavilion (Kinkaku-ji) built during the reign of his illustrious grandfather. In emulation of the Golden Pavilion, whose outer walls were covered with sheets of hammered gold, mirroring the solar aspect revered in Shintō rites since ancient times, the Silver Pavilion was to have been sheathed in polished silver, representing the subtler light of the lunar aspect. The implicit symbolism of the ethos, or governing spirit, of each man's respective reign is not out of step with historical fact. The Silver Pavilion is smaller, but it aims at a higher state of perfection than its glorious predecessor, mirroring in the subtlety of its comingled Sino-Japanese forms the inward-turning vision of the later Ashikaga shogun.

At the time of the Silver Pavilion's completion, however, Yoshimasa's treasury had become so depleted that it was impossible to complete the building's full architectural program. Therefore, the Silver Pavilion was left to stand, as it does today, an unadorned structure of wood and paper, its two-story frame blackened by the passing of the centuries. It was there, at the foot of the Eastern Hills in the city of Kyōto's Muromachi district, that Yoshimasa spent the last sixteen years of his life after abdicating from the shogunate in 1473. Relieved of the tedium of administrative life and the constant political oppressions of the unruly daimyo—who largely ignored the ineffectual, and sometimes contradictory, proclamations issued from his court at Kyōto—Yoshimasa devoted himself completely to the solitary consolations of the artistic connoisseur. He especially prized his collection of Chinese Song Dynasty painting and pottery, while, outside the gates of his personal sanctuary, a civil war raged.

Perhaps the most far-reaching aspect of Yoshimasa's reign, at least in the political sphere, was the dispute over who was to become his successor. This dispute ignited the disastrous Ōnin War (1467-1477). Yoshimasa had married Tomiko, of the Hino clan, in 1455, but their union did not provide Yoshimasa with a male successor. As was customary in such circumstances, Yoshimasa summoned his younger brother Yoshimi, now a monk, to forsake the monastic life and return to Kyōto to serve as the shogun's successor. Hardly a year had passed since Yoshimi's return, however, when Tomiko gave birth to a boy who would be called Yoshihisa (1465-1489). Tomiko desired that her son Yoshihisa assume the role of shogun instead of Yoshimasa's brother and pressed her cause, supported by the military assistance of Yamana Mochitoyo (1404-1473), an old rival of one of Yoshimasa's former advisers.

In the end Tomiko prevailed. Upon his father's abdication, Yoshihisa became the ninth Ashikaga shogun (r. 1474-1489)—but the matter did not end there. Yoshimasa's brother Yoshimi, the former monk, disputed the succession. Military conflicts erupted, precipitating the bloody and inconclusive conflict of ten years' duration now known as the Ōnin War. This conflict all but decimated the city of Kyōto. After Yoshimasa, the remaining Ashikaga shoguns functioned as little more than royal facades until their shogunate was finally unseated by Oda Nobunaga in the 1570's.

SIGNIFICANCE

Commentators have compared Ashikaga Yoshimasa and his predecessors to the great patrons of Italian Renaissance art Cosimo and Lorenzo de' Medici. Unlike the Medicis, however, Yoshimasa ended his reign in a disastrous civil conflagration, fostered to no small degree by his own indifference and inability. Still, to characterize him merely as an ineffectual ruler would unfairly denigrate the cultural legacy of the Muromachi era in Japanese art and life, to which Yoshimasa contributed significantly. His taste for the austere simplicity of Chinese Song brush-and-ink painting, for example—with its restrained symbolism, extreme economy, and sublime understatement of aesthetic principles—became a template for much of what is valued in later Japanese art and culture.

—*Larry Smolucha*

FURTHER READING

Dolan, Ronald E., and Robert L. Worden, eds. *Japan: A Country Study*. Washington, D.C.: Federal Research Division, Library of Congress, 1992. Especially useful for its concise historical survey, presented in chapter 1, and for additional valuable material in subsequent chapters pertaining to topography, climate, social and cultural trends, and other general information about Japan. Includes regional maps.

Henshall, Kenneth G. *A History of Japan: From Stone Age to Superpower.* New York: St. Martin's Press, 1999. A remarkably readable history of Japan that emphasizes the human dimensions of conflict and historical change. Includes chapter summaries in concise table format for each era's key developments, values, and practices.

Maraini, Fosco. *Meeting with Japan.* New York: Viking Press, 1960. A poignant memoir of the author's visit (as a former prisoner of war) to Japan in the years immediately following World War II. Mingles historical background information with the author's own sympathetic observations on Japanese life and culture.

Turnbull, Stephen. *The Samurai Sourcebook.* London: Cassell, 2000. Treats fully all particulars of the subject through capsulized biographies of the principal samurai and daimyo, detailed data on weaponry, heraldry, strategy and tactics, significant battles, and so on. Well illustrated.

SEE ALSO: 1457-1480's: Spread of Jōdo Shinshū Buddhism; 1467-1477: Ōnin War; 1477-1600: Japan's "Age of the Country at War"; Mar. 5, 1488: Composition of the *Renga* Masterpiece *Minase sangin hyakuin*; Beginning 1513: Kanō School Flourishes; 1532-1536: Temmon Hokke Rebellion; 1550's-1567: Japanese Pirates Pillage the Chinese Coast; 1550-1593: Japanese Wars of Unification; June 12, 1560: Battle of Okehazama; 1568: Oda Nobunaga Seizes Kyōto.

RELATED ARTICLES in *Great Lives from History: The Renaissance & Early Modern Era, 1454-1600:* Oda Nobunaga; Sesshū; Toyotomi Hideyoshi.

1473
JAKOB II FUGGER BECOMES A MERCHANT

Jakob II Fugger bowed to family pressure, abandoned his plans to enter the clergy, and joined his family's business. Under his leadership, the Fuggers became the most important banking family in Renaissance Europe. Their loans placed Charles V on the throne of the Holy Roman Empire, financed many wars and other national ventures, and helped shape the course of early modern capitalism.

LOCALE: Augsburg (now in Germany)
CATEGORIES: Trade and commerce; economics; government and politics

KEY FIGURES

Jakob II Fugger (1459-1525), German merchant and banker
Jakob I Fugger (d. 1469), founder of the main branch of the family, the Fuggers of the Lilies (Fugger von der Gilgen)
Anton Fugger (1493-1560), nephew and heir of Jakob II
Maximilian I (1459-1519), king of Germany, r. 1486-1519, and Holy Roman Emperor, r. 1493-1519
Charles V (1500-1558), Holy Roman Emperor, r. 1519-1556, and king of Spain as Charles I, r. 1516-1556

SUMMARY OF EVENT

In 1367, a weaver and trader named Hans Fugger settled in Augsburg. The Fugger family quickly became valued members of the Augsburg community, and Hans's son Jakob I became the master of the city's weavers' guild. Jakob's brother Andreas became a merchant and banker, founding the branch of the family called the Fugger vom Reh (Fuggers of the Doe, named after their coat of arms). The Fugger vom Reh's firm was not successful; they loaned more money than they could afford, and by 1494, when Andreas's last son died, the firm's debts outweighed its assets.

Jakob I was both a weaver and a trader like his father, and he built up a significant trading company. His branch of the family came to be known as the Fugger von der Lilie (Fuggers of the Lilies). Jakob had seven sons, two of whom died before their father. When Jakob himself died in 1469, five sons remained: Ulrich, George, and Peter, who were meant to run the family business, and Marcus and Jakob II, who were to enter the Church. Peter Fugger died in 1473, however, and Ulrich and George convinced the fourteen-year-old Jakob II to abandon his preparations for a life in the Church and take Peter's place in the Fugger business. Although they could hardly have known it at the time, this decision was to have monumental consequences for world history.

Jakob II Fugger proved to be an economic visionary. He spent a decade learning the merchant trade, apprenticing first in the Fugger family warehouse in Venice and eventually becoming a partner in the firm. Once he had attained this partnership, Jakob began to change the mission and scope of his family's business. He steered the firm away from the commodities that had been its stock in trade: spices, silks, and other textiles. Instead, he began to seek out investments that generated their own income, especially mines, loans, and bills of exchange. The Fugger family had made some investments in such items from the beginning, but it was Jakob II who decisively guided the firm in this direction.

The Fuggers purchased some silver and copper mines outright. They also loaned money to the owners of such mines, accepting the income of the mines as interest and taking complete possession of the mines if the owner defaulted on the loan. In the late 1480's, for example, the firm loaned money to Archduke Siegmund of Tyrol, and they received in return the entire income produced by the archduke's silver mines. It was through this arrangement that the family first came in contact with future Holy Roman Emperor Maximilian I, who took control of Tyrol in 1490.

Maximilian was often in need of funds merely to run his German kingdom and later the Holy Roman Empire. In times of war, his need became desperate. The Fuggers provided vital funds to support the empire's campaigns in Italy and Switzerland. In return, they came to control much of the Habsburg family's interest in silver and copper. In 1511, the family refused Maximilian's request for 300,000 ducats with which to bribe the college of cardinals into electing him pope. On the other hand, they loaned Albrecht of Brandenburg the money necessary for him to become archbishop of Mainz (papal confirmation of archbishoprics had to be purchased in cash), and they loaned money to many prominent cardinals, as well as the pope himself. These loans were repaid in part with the Church's income from selling indulgences.

Jakob II Fugger's most significant loan, however, was to King Charles I of Spain, who found himself in a bidding war with France's Francis I for the title of Holy Roman Emperor. The empire's electors solicited bribes from both monarchs, waiting to see who would pay the most for the imperial throne. The Fuggers loaned Charles more and more money, ultimately 543,000 florins. Including this loan and other loans from the German Welser family and the Italian cities of Genoa and Florence, Charles incurred a debt of 850,000 florins to become emperor. Once he was elected, moreover, Emperor Charles V continued to incur debts to finance his wars with France.

As a result of the debts incurred by both Maximilian and Charles, the Fuggers came to control several German counties; many silver, quicksilver, and copper mines; numerous other parcels of real estate; and the revenue owed to the Spanish crown by three ecclesiastical orders. They were also major players in the world pepper market, leased the royal mint, continued some trade in silks and other commodities, and held significant investments throughout eastern and western Europe. When Hans Fugger had died in the late fourteenth century, he had left his sons three thousand florins. Around the time of Jakob II's death in 1525, the Fuggers' worth, including all assets, private holdings, and outstanding loans, totaled three million florins.

SIGNIFICANCE

Jakob II Fugger left his business to his nephew Anton. Anton continued his uncle's tradition of supporting the Catholic popes and emperors in their military campaigns, while always demanding adequate security for any loan that he advanced. These loans made possible several Catholic victories over Protestants, especially the defeat of the Schmalkaldic League at the Battle of Mühlberg (1547). They also allowed Anton to increase even further the vast wealth of the Fuggers, which at the end of 1546 totaled more than seven million florins.

The creation of this fortune, however, is less important than the example it set and the uses to which it was put. During the Middle Ages, money was not thought of as the kind of thing that, through its use and investment, increased itself. As Richard Ehrenberg points out, this was both a moral observation and a factual one: Not only did Christians believe that loaning money at interest was a sin, they also believed that making an inanimate thing multiply was unnatural. This "unnatural" phenomenon, though, was a necessary prerequisite for the development of modern nations and military empires. It was inseparable from the political evolution of Europe during the Renaissance, and without banking firms such as the Fuggers', that evolution simply would not have occurred.

The Fuggers are therefore inseparable from many of the most admirable and the most despicable aspects of the early modern period. They made charitable donations that demonstrated the power of the wealthy to engage in philanthropy on a truly culture-altering scale. They also funded many bloody wars and contributed to the trans-Atlantic slave trade. All of these activities were made possible by Jakob II Fugger, who conceived of and executed financial operations that were practically unheard of in the early sixteenth century, and who did so on a scale few at the time could even have imagined.

—*Andy Perry*

FURTHER READING

Ehrenberg, Richard. *Capital and Finance in the Age of the Renaissance: A Study of the Fuggers and Their Connections*. Reprint. Translated by H. M. Lucas. Fairfield, N.J.: A. M. Kelly, 1985. An invaluable text on Renaissance economic history and the Fuggers' place in it. The book is divided into three sections: one on the European economy before the Fuggers, one on the Fuggers, and one on the economic legacy of the family.

Mathew, K. S. *Indo-Portuguese Trade and the Fuggers of Germany, Sixteenth Century*. New Delhi, India: Manohar, 1997. A study of the role of the Fugger firm and investments in shaping trade between Portugal and India in the sixteenth century. Includes bibliographic references and index.

Matthews, George T. *The Fugger Newsletters*. Reprint. New York: Capricorn Books, 1970. The Fuggers sent representatives all over the world, and they gave these agents orders to send back home any news or items of interest about the culture in which they found themselves. This volume collects these various broadsides, letters, rumors, and cultural analyses, constituting one of the most important documents in the cultural history of the Renaissance.

Meadow, Mark A. "Merchants and Marvels: Hans Jacob Fugger and the Origins of the Wunderkammer." In *Merchants and Marvels: Commerce, Science, and Art in Early Modern Europe*, edited by Pamela H. Smith and Paula Findlen. New York: Routledge, 2002. An essay on the last major member of the Fugger family and his role in creating the *Wunderkammer* or cabinet of curiosities, a sixteenth century display case for strange or exotic objects.

SEE ALSO: July 16, 1465-April, 1559: French-Burgundian and French-Austrian Wars; August 17, 1477: Foundation of the Habsburg Dynasty; 1482-1492: Maximilian I Takes Control of the Low Countries; August 19, 1493-January 12, 1519: Reign of Maximilian I; 16th century: Worldwide Inflation; June 28, 1519: Charles V Is Elected Holy Roman Emperor; 1521-1559: Valois-Habsburg Wars; 1531-1585: Antwerp Becomes the Commercial Capital of Europe; February 27, 1531: Formation of the Schmalkaldic League.

RELATED ARTICLES in Great Lives from History: The Renaissance & Early Modern Era, 1454-1600: Charles V; Maximilian I.

1473-1600
WITCH-HUNTS AND WITCH TRIALS

Fifteenth and sixteenth century Europe saw a substantial increase in the number of witch-hunts and witch trials, after papal bulls and a flurry of published secular works and secular laws perpetuated the persecution of alleged witches that had begun centuries earlier in Europe. Witches were condemned as devilish and therefore heretical.

LOCALE: Europe

CATEGORIES: Religion; cultural and intellectual history; laws, acts, and legal history; women's issues

KEY FIGURES

Sixtus IV (Francesco della Rovere; 1414-1484), Roman Catholic pope, 1471-1484

Innocent VIII (Giovanni Battista Cibò; 1432-1492), Roman Catholic pope, 1484-1492

Heinrich Krämer (1430-1506), Dominican inquisitor

Jacob Sprenger (1436-1595), Dominican inquisitor

Peter Binsfeld (1546-1598), general vicar of the archdiocese of Trier, Germany

Nicholas Remy (1530-1612), attorney general of Lorraine

Jean Bodin (1530-1596), French political philosopher

SUMMARY OF EVENT

The second half of the fifteenth century saw a significant increase in the number of individuals, mostly poor and older women, who were hunted, charged, tried, and often executed as witches. The rise in condemnations was propelled in large degree by papal bulls, the first in 1473, issued by Pope Sixtus IV, which attacked and condemned sorcery, thought to be practiced by witches. Popes of the first half of the fifteenth century issued bulls, too, con-

A wood engraving attributed to Renaissance German artist Hans Holbein, the Younger, depicting an "old-maid witch" in a rural setting. Older, poor women often were accused of being witches. (Frederick Ungar Publishing Co.)

demning witchcraft and magic. In 1484, Pope Innocent VIII issued the bull *Summis Desiderantes Affectibus*, which officially sanctioned powers already exercised by the Dominican inquisitors Heinrich Krämer and Jacob Sprenger to deal with witchcraft, heresy, and other crimes. Krämer and Sprenger had alerted the pope of heresy among the rural German populations, of the work of the devil, or demonology.

Krämer (also known as Institoris) and Sprenger (also known as James Sprenger), used Innocent VIII's bull as a preface to their own work, the *Malleus Maleficarum* (c. 1486; English translation, 1928), which became a best-seller and legal companion in its time and still is often read and cited. The work summarized contemporary beliefs about witchcraft, with a particular emphasis on women, as witches, and it indicated that witchcraft was a more serious crime than heresy.

Authors of the time used the printing press to disseminate quickly and widely a definition of "witchcraft" that combined *maleficia* (black magic) with diabolism (devil worship). In 1536, Paulus Grillandus, a judge at several trials near Rome, published *Tractatus de hereticis et sortilegiis*, which developed more fully the concept of the witches' sabbath with the devil. After Johann Weyer (1515-1588), a medical doctor, argued in 1563 that witches were merely deranged women, the French political philosopher Jean Bodin replied with his *De la dé-*

monomanie des sorciers (1580; *On the Demon-Mania of Witches*, 1995), which noted that witches deserved torture because of their adoration of Satan. The most comprehensive summary of sabbath activities, *Daemonolatria*, was published in 1598 by Nicolas Remy, the attorney general of Lorraine, who also was involved in numerous witch trials.

Learned publications on witchcraft were supplemented by laws issued by various European states and political entities, transforming the hunts, trials, and tortures into secular affairs. This led to a substantial increase in witchcraft trials in all regions of western Europe. Beginning in 1580, mass trials were concentrated in the region of the Holy Roman Empire, where the overwhelming majority of the executions of witches in Europe took place.

In 1532, Holy Roman Emperor Charles V's *Lex Carolina* stipulated that black magic, or sorcery, should be handled as a criminal offense, and that witches should be put to death if any person was threatened with harm or was actually harmed through that sorcery. By 1563, laws against witchcraft were adopted in England and Scotland. In England, however, Elizabethan law placed emphasis on *maleficia* rather than diabolism, and torture was allowed only with the permission of the Privy Council. In a similar fashion, Ireland passed a law in 1586 that excluded the charge of diabolism and restricted torture. This might explain why there were relatively fewer executions for witchcraft in England and Ireland than there were in Scotland, where the use of torture produced trial after trial between 1590 and 1592. France was the only European nation that did not issue a law dealing with witchcraft.

Trials before 1430 focused on cases of *maleficia*, but in the fifteenth century, the charge of diabolism first emerged in witch trials. Until 1520 trials were most common in northern Italy, southern France, the Swiss cantons, and in the Rhineland. Between 1520 and 1560, the total number of trials decreased. Mass trials started in 1580, affecting all regions of western Europe, including Scotland. Relying on the use of torture, which had been approved by Pope Paul II in 1468, trials produced confessions and further accusations. Both Protestants and Catholics supported witch trials. Martin Luther in 1539 urged that witches be burned, and witch trials occurred in John

Calvin's Geneva (1547-1560) and in Huldrych Zwingli's Zürich (1500-1539).

In addition to religious passions, macroeconomic problems such as inflation and declining real wages after 1500 helped create an atmosphere of crisis. Often specific economic disasters preceded trials. When hail storms ruined the crop in 1562 in the Lutheran community of Wiesenstein, witch trials followed. In Trier, trials in the 1580's and 1590's coincided with poor grape (wine) and grain harvests. Furthermore, plague, famines, and unstable politics contributed to the climate that unleashed mass trials in the late sixteenth century.

Even though much of western and central Europe experienced witch trials during this period, the overwhelming majority of the trials occurred in the Holy Roman Empire. The numerous small religious and secular territories in the empire had the worst record. In Rothenburg, Germany, 150 people were executed between 1578 and 1609, and in the monastic community of Obermachtal, with a population of 350 adults, 50 witches were burned between 1586 and 1588. Unlike England, there was no strong central power that could intervene. Even the inquisitions in Spain, Portugal, and Rome created safeguards that greatly reduced the number of executions in these countries.

Between 1560 and 1660, the Holy Roman Empire, which contained only 20 percent of Europe's population, accounted for almost 90 percent of the trials. Moreover, 75 percent of the nearly thirty thousand people executed for witchcraft during this period spoke a German dialect. The three archbishoprics of Trier, Cologne, and Mainz were responsible for one-third of the executions in Germany (and one-fourth in Europe) in the century after 1560. In addition, in Luxembourg, which bordered the archbishoprics, 150 individuals were burned between 1580 and 1599. The key official responsible for the events in Trier was Peter Binsfeld, the general vicar of the archdiocese of Trier and the author of *Tractatus de confessionibus maleficorum et sagarum* (1596; treatise on the confession of witches and sorcerers). Binsfeld demanded the death penalty for the practice of magic, and he allowed children to testify against adults.

In Bavaria in southern Germany, a strong ruler was able to control the excesses of witch trials, although several hundred people were burned between 1586 and 1595. Small territories like the bishopric of Dillingen, however, held mass trials. On March 20, 1589, the local judge of Böblingen reported to the bishopric of Dillingen that a fourteen-year-old boy of Böblingen claimed that he flew with his cousins to a sabbath, where they bewitched cattle. The bishopric insisted on an inquisition by Hans of Biberach, a notorious torturer. In the end, forty-five people were accused and twenty-seven were burned to death.

Almost 80 percent of trial victims were old women, usually living in villages. They were poor and often depended on charity, or they attempted to earn a living by practicing healing crafts. Moreover, women were en-

---

INNOCENT VIII'S BULL AGAINST WITCHCRAFT

Innocent VIII issued a papal bull to investigate, correct, and punish the "heretical depravity" of witchcraft and devil worship. The bull responded to accusations by the German Dominican inquisitors Heinrich Krämer and Jacob Sprenger, authors of the notorious Malleus Maleficarum, *or* Hammer of Witches. *The inquisitors accused rural villagers, mostly women, of devilish acts.*

It has indeed lately come to Our ears, not without afflicting Us with bitter sorrow, that in some parts of Northern Germany . . . many persons of both sexes, unmindful of their own salvation and straying from the Catholic Faith, have abandoned themselves to devils, incubi and succubi, and by their incantations, spells, conjurations, and other accursed charms and crafts, enormities and horrid offences, have slain infants yet in the mother's womb, as also the offspring of cattle, have blasted the produce of the earth, the grapes of the vine, the fruits of trees, nay, men and women, beasts of burthen, herd-beasts, as well as animals of other kinds, vineyards, orchards, meadows, pasture-land, corn, wheat, and all other cereals; these wretches furthermore afflict and torment men and women, beasts of burthen, herd-beasts, as well as animals of other kinds, with terrible and piteous pains and sore diseases, both internal and external; they hinder men from performing the sexual act and women from conceiving, whence husbands cannot know their wives nor wives receive their husbands; over and above this, they blasphemously renounce that Faith which is theirs by the Sacrament of Baptism, and at the instigation of the Enemy of Mankind they do not shrink from committing and perpetrating the foulest abominations and filthiest excesses to the deadly peril of their own souls, whereby they outrage the Divine Majesty and are a cause of scandal and danger to very many.

Source: "The Bull of Innocent VIII, 1484," preface to *Malleus Maleficarum*, by Heinrich Krämer and James Sprenger. Translated by Montague Summers (New York: Dover, 1971), p. xliii.

A sixteenth century wood engraving depicting a fantastical image of a witch's sabbath. The most comprehensive summary of sabbath activities, Daemonolatria, *was published in 1598 by Nicolas Remy.* (Frederick Ungar Publishing Co.)

gaged in food preparations, and they served as midwives, two activities whereby it was thought witchcraft could be practiced.

In some areas of Europe, males made up the majority of witch-hunt victims. In Normandy, clerics and shepherds were accused of witchcraft, resulting in the execution of twenty men in 1590. In Finland and Iceland, as well as Bavaria, magic was also primarily a male occupation. One case in the mountain village of Oberstdorf, in the bishopric of Augsburg, involved Chonrad Stoeckhlin, a married horse wrangler who considered himself a healer and witch finder. He was tried, tortured, and burned in 1587. The trial soon expanded into the district of Oberstdorf, which had experienced harvest failures. It consumed the lives of sixty-eight people, representing 10 percent of the population.

SIGNIFICANCE

The witch trials took the lives of a minimum of forty thousand people, mostly women. Three-fourths of all executions of European witches occurred between the late sixteenth century and early seventeenth century. Mass trials were inflamed by religious passions and made more acceptable by the social and economic tensions of the sixteenth century.

In the long run, only central political authority could control the witch-hunts, which had originated at the local level primarily. In the seventeenth century, trials declined in areas with strong rulers or institutions such as Bavaria, England, Spain, and Holland. Trials spread also to the English colony of Massachusetts, in what is now the United States, where, in 1648, the colony executed its first assumed witch. In 1682, King Louis XIV of France ordered an end to the witch trials, as did the rulers of Prussia in 1714 and England in 1736.

Equally important was a change in the intellectual climate produced by the scientific revolution and the growing rationalism of the seventeenth century. Moreover, the bitter Thirty Years' War in Germany between 1618 and 1648 caused a reaction against uncontrolled religious fervor. The term "witch-hunt" has survived, though, but it is now applied to secular rather than religious persecutions.

—*Johnpeter Horst Grill*

FURTHER READING

Ankarloo, Bengt, and Stuart Clark, eds. *Witchcraft and Magic in Europe: The Period of the Witch Trials*. Philadelphia: University of Pennsylvania Press, 2002. Geographic survey of witch trials on the Continent.

Behringer, Wolfgang. *Witchcraft Persecutions in Bavaria: Popular Magic, Religious Zealotry, and Reasons of State in Early Modern Europe*. Translated by J. C. Grayson and David Lederer. New York: Cambridge University Press, 1997. Valuable for its treatment of mass persecutions around 1590 in southeastern Germany.

Kors, Alan Charles, and Edward Peters, eds. *Witchcraft in Europe, 400-1700: A Documentary History*. Philadelphia: University of Pennsylvania Press, 2001. Collection of translated primary sources on witchcraft discourses and trials.

Krämer, Heinrich, and James Sprenger. *Malleus Maleficarum*. Translated by Montague Summers. New York: Dover, 1971. The standard translation. This edition includes helpful introductions to the 1928 and 1948 editions of the translated text and includes discussion of the papal bulls issued before, during, and after the fifteenth and sixteenth centuries.

Levack, Brian P. *The Witch-Hunt in Early Modern Europe*. 2d ed. London: Longman, 1995. Examines multiple causes and describes different types of witchhunts.

Midelfort, H. C. Erick. *Witch Hunting in Southwestern Germany 1562-1684: The Social and Intellectual Foundations*. Stanford, Calif.: Stanford University Press, 1972. Study of numerous small territories that constitute the modern state of Baden-Württemberg in Germany.

Sharpe, James. *Instruments of Darkness: Witchcraft in England, 1550-1750*. London: Hamish Hamilton, 1996. Deals with the sixteenth century to eighteenth century witch trials in England.

SEE ALSO: Nov. 1, 1478: Establishment of the Spanish Inquisition.

RELATED ARTICLES in *Great Lives from History: The Renaissance & Early Modern Era, 1454-1600:* Elizabeth Báthory; John Calvin; Martin Luther; Sixtus IV; Tomás de Torquemada; Huldrych Zwingli.

1474
GREAT WALL OF CHINA IS BUILT

China's Great Wall is a massive defensive structure built during the Ming Dynasty to defend the capital at Beijing and to keep Mongols and other invaders from attacking. Ironically, internal corruption, along with the expense of building and maintaining the wall, would contribute significantly to the dynasty's decline.

LOCALE: China's northern border

CATEGORIES: Architecture; engineering; science and technology; diplomacy and international relations

KEY FIGURES

Hongwu (reign name, also Hung-wu; personal name Zhu Yuanzhang, Chu Yüan-chang; posthumous name Gaodi, Kao-ti; temple name Taizu, T'ai-tsu; 1328-1398), founder of the Ming Dynasty, r. 1368-1398

Li Dongyang (Li Tung-yang; 1447-1516), proponent of an offensive strategy against the Mongols

Weng Wanda (Weng Wan-ta; 1498-1552), proponent of peaceful coexistence with the Mongols

SUMMARY OF EVENT

China's strategic history has always been dominated by the threat of invasion by nomadic tribes who occupied the vast territory north of China. These tensions were the result of a clash of civilizations that brought a highly aggressive, nomadic warrior culture into conflict with a sophisticated and very often extremely "soft," sedentary Chinese state. The vast material wealth generated by the Chinese economy was the constant target of thousands of nomadic warriors from all over Central Asia.

For centuries, Chinese strategists debated how best to

deal with this military threat. Some in the defense establishment believed that China should engage the opposition any time the opportunity presented itself. This theory proved to be very risky, and more often than not the nomadic warriors would inflict severe casualties on the Chinese military. Other strategists believed China's best interests lay in the implementation of a defensive plan based on the construction of walled fortifications that could be used as protective barriers against invasion. Over time, the majority of China's military and civilian leadership gravitated toward the defensive position. Finally, some Chinese diplomats developed a third alternative, urging a policy of peaceful coexistence and accommodation. This theory was based on the belief that China's material wealth could be used to pacify the nomads and thus reduce the threat of invasion. In fact, all three strategic theories would be used in Chinese-Mongolian relations.

The Great Wall of China, which traverses a distance of 4,160 miles and is the largest defensive barrier in the history of humankind, was built to defend against Mongols and other invaders. (Hulton|Archive by Getty Images)

The Mongols were extremely aggressive warrior hunters who trained their fighters from a very early age in the techniques of mobile warfare. Between 1206 and 1234, Mongolian armies conquered most of northern China. Four decades later, they were in control of the southern part of the empire as well. The Mongols remained in control of China until 1368, when Zhu Yuanzhang, a Chinese outlaw turned military leader, defeated the Mongol forces and established the Ming Dynasty, reigning as Hongwu.

Hongwu was unable to destroy the Mongolian military machine completely; they retreated back into Mongolia and Central Asia. Out of reach of China's forces, they were able to regroup, and eventually, they became strong enough to launch raids against Chinese overland trade routes in Central Asia. These attacks posed a great danger to both the Chinese economy and its security.

Ming military philosophy was also driven by the belief that the Mongols were barbarians and that they were incapable of civilized, sophisticated, diplomatic discourse. Most Ming military philosophers accepted the reality that the only way to deal safely with the Mongols was through the correct application of force. In an ideal world, this would mean the development of a first strike capability that would cause vast devastation deep within the Mongolian homeland. The passion for these aggressive preemptive strikes was always tempered with the tactical reality that the deeper an army moved into the enemy's territory, the more likely it was to be counterattacked by opponent's forces. In particular, the Mongolian propensity for retreat and counterattack always haunted Ming military commanders. Again and again throughout the history of the Ming Dynasty, commanders limited their scope of maneuvers so as to take advantage of the safety of walled fortifications.

Chinese military philosophers had to contend with two additional problems. The first focused on the challenges of Chinese geography. All military commanders had to realize that the sheer vastness of the territory they had to defend left them vulnerable to Mongol attacks. This challenge was linked to the second problem, the absence of an effective Chinese cavalry. China's traditional method of warfare concentrated on large formations of infantry. These tactics were extremely vulnerable to the Blitzkrieg-like tactics of the Mongols. Warriors using highly accurate bows could devastate a large Chinese force in only a few hours.

To deal with these negative realities, proponents of an active offense, such as Li Dongyang, created a five-part model. It began with the construction of solid defensive walls that would protect Ming territory against a sudden attack by the Mongols. Thus began the structure that would eventually become known as the Great Wall of China. Li Dongyang also called for the creation of an extensive intelligence network that would keep track of the movements of Mongol forces that could cause problems. The government would also have to supply the forces stationed along the defensive walls with all the military supplies and rations needed to guard the empire's northern border.

Li Dongyang's plan called for increasing the quality of military training received by the troops. The most important aspect of this training was to introduce the forces to the highly maneuverable, lightning-quick tactics of the Mongols. Finally, Li Dongyang also called for the development of a mobile set of "shock troops" who would in turn use hit-and-run tactics against the Mongolian forces. These troops would be stationed along the defensive walls and be moved to areas where the intelligence had found that the Mongols would be most vulnerable.

This philosophy of offense and active defense was most successful during Li Dongyang's lifetime, while the Ming Empire was at its peak. Fifteenth century China was the most powerful nation on earth. The early Ming emperors had introduced important bureaucratic reforms that controlled official corruption and increased the efficiency of all the departments of government. There were also extensive social reforms that increased the size of the peasant class, reduced forced labor, and opened vast new territories to agricultural production. The Ming Empire during this period possessed both the domestic tranquillity and the economic strength that traditional Chinese military philosophers said was needed for successful military campaigns. The empire was able to absorb the costs of the construction of great walled fortifications, along with the ability to create, supply, and maintain an effective fighting force. Ming generals, using walled fortifications as their base of operations, were able to carry out successful military strikes against a number of Mongolian tribes.

The most famous of these defensive structures is the Great Wall of China, which stretches from Chinese Turkestan in the west to Manchuria and the northern Korean Peninsula in the east. This massive structure traverses a distance of 4,160 miles (6,700 kilometers) and is the largest defensive barrier in the history of humankind. Originally the wall connected a series of nine major fortifications. In the west, it began by protecting the Kansu Corridor, a narrow caravan route that connected China and Central Asia. In the east, its primary goal was to defend the Chinese government at Beijing. It continued past the capital to Manchuria and Korea both as a fortification against nomadic warriors and to control the strategic avenues leading to the East China Sea.

Architecturally, the average height of the structure is nearly 33 feet (10 meters), and its average width is more than 16 feet (5 meters). In a few very strategic locations, such as around the capital, the width of the wall is nearly 33 feet. The major military structures are towers, with between five and eight towers per kilometer. Some of the towers were used for defense against Mongol attack, while the others were part of an early warning system in which beacons (fire at night and smoke during the day) were activated to direct troop movement along the pathways on the top of the Great Wall. The Ming Dynasty had to employ large numbers of highly skilled masons and developed an extensive network of stone quarries, brick manufacturers, and roads, first to build and then to repair this massive structure. The financial impact of the construction of the Great Wall was significant and contributed to the dynasty's demise.

By the sixteenth century, the Ming Dynasty was in a state of decline. Years of material excess had corrupted the bureaucracy, and there were governmental failures across the empire. Public works projects such as dams, irrigation systems, canals, and roads fell into a state of disrepair. The social consequence of these failures was a devastating famine, which gave rise to peasant rebellions.

This endemic economic and social collapse caused the Ming to drastically alter their military planning. Instead of using walled fortifications as the base of offensive operations, the Ming now regarded them as a part of a new diplomatic tactic that emphasized peaceful coexistence and accommodation. The most notable proponent of this approach was Weng Wanda (1498-1552). He believed the Ming Dynasty had lost its ability to engage the Mongols in successful military campaigns. He was convinced that the only recourse the empire now had was to use tribute payments and trade to buy time, until the government could once again field an army strong enough to defeat the Mongols.

The Ming military establishment quickly challenged this attempt at containment. Many strategists believed the policy of accommodation was extremely dangerous.

1470's

Mongolian access to Chinese commercial establishments would allow them to gain important intelligence concerning Ming economic, political, and social problems. Military leaders were also concerned that an extensive trade policy would allow the Mongols to obtain materials that could be used against the Ming Empire in future military encounters.

Eventually the Ming military rejected this attempt at accommodation and instead embraced the concept of a static defense. The great walled fortifications that had been constructed as part of an offensive strategy were now linked into one massive defensive barrier, today known as the Great Wall of China, and the empire retreated into another period of isolation.

SIGNIFICANCE

The failure of the Ming Dynasty to strengthen its military eventually allowed another nomadic people, the Manchus, to invade China. This was just another example in Chinese history of a strong, vibrant culture subduing a dynasty in decline, whose magnificent wall of static defense became a symbol of a stagnant culture. In 1645, Manchu forces captured Beijing and began a two-decade-long war to subdue the rest of the empire.

Once in power, the Manchu, or Qing, Dynasty adopted a defensive strategy similar to that of the Ming. This "fortress China" mentality would be no match for the new, powerful European technology; eventually China would become the puppet of the industrialized West. China would remain in this colonial state until the twentieth century, when Communist leader Mao Zedong once again made a commitment to adopt an offensive strategy and drove all foreign influence from the mainland.

—*Richard D. Fitzgerald*

FURTHER READING

Gernet, Jacques. *A History of Chinese Civilization*. New York: Cambridge University Press, 1992. An excellent one-volume history of China.

Graff, David, and Robin Higham. *A Military History of China*. Boulder, Colo.: Westview Press, 2002. The best one-volume Chinese military history available today.

Johnson, Alastair. *Cultural Realism: Strategic Culture and Grand Strategy in Chinese History*. Princeton, N.J.: Princeton University Press, 1995. A valuable and interesting history of Chinese military thought.

Lindsay, William. *The Great Wall*. London: Hi Marketing Press, 1999. An interesting account of one man's journey along the entire length of the Great Wall. The book contains great photographs along with a full historical overview.

Sawyer, Ralph. *The Seven Military Classics of Ancient China*. San Francisco: Westview Press, 1993. Contains all the foundational works of Chinese military philosophy.

Waldron, Arthur. *The Great Wall: From History to Myth*. New York: Cambridge University Press, 1998. One of the best one-volume accounts of the history of the Great Wall of China.

SEE ALSO: Feb. 11, 1457: Restoration of Zhengtong; 1465-1487: Reign of Xianzong; 1488-1505: Reign of Xiaozong; 16th cent.: China's Population Boom; 16th cent.: Rise of the *Shenshi*; 1505-1521: Reign of Zhengde and Liu Jin.

RELATED ARTICLES in *Great Lives from History: The Renaissance & Early Modern Era, 1454-1600:* Wang Yangming; Xiaozong.

1474-1479
Castilian War of Succession

The struggle for the Castilian throne determined the future development of the Iberian Peninsula.

Locale: Castile (now in Spain)
Categories: Wars, uprisings, and civil unrest; government and politics

Key Figures
Henry IV of Castile (1425-1474), king of Castile, r. 1454-1474
Joan (1462-1530), Henry's daughter
Isabella I (1451-1504), queen of Castile, r. 1474-1504, and Henry's half sister
Afonso V (1432-1481), king of Portugal, r. 1438-1481

Summary of Event
King John II of Castile (r. 1406-1454), during a long and disturbed reign, married twice. First, he married Maria of Aragon, who provided the heir to the throne, Henry (the future Henry IV). Then he married Isabella of Portugal, who gave him a second son, Alfonso, and a daughter, Isabella.

Henry, in his turn, married twice. In 1440, he married Bianca of Navarre, but the childless marriage was annulled in 1453 on grounds of impotence. By then, Henry was negotiating a second marriage with Joan of Portugal, sister of the Portuguese king, Afonso V. Because of the couple's consanguinity, Pope Nicholas V granted a papal dispensation at the close of 1453, which again referred to Henry's impotence. Nevertheless, the new queen gave birth to a daughter, also named Joan, in February of 1462. In May, the nobility that were assembled in Madrid swore an oath of allegiance to the baby as Henry's heir, and in July, the Castilian *cortes* (parliament) meeting in Toledo did the same.

To historians, Henry IV is an opaque figure. He had inherited from the previous reign a habitually unruly nobility. Henry sought to diminish the influence of the higher nobility by the promotion of new men of his own choice, among whom was his special favorite (*privado*), a young man named Beltrán de la Cueva. Rivals at court asserted that Beltrán was the real father of Princess Joan, who from her birth was derisively nicknamed "La Beltraneja" (the one from Beltrán). The libelous nickname was included in a manifesto drawn up in 1464, which, among a list of humiliating demands made on the king,

required him to acknowledge his half brother, Alfonso, as his heir. Under duress, Henry agreed, but subsequently reneged.

There followed the extraordinary Farsa de Ávila of 1465, in which a wooden effigy of the king was placed on a throne outside the walls of Ávila, to be insulted and then knocked to the ground, symbolizing Henry's deposition. Thereafter, the rebels proclaimed Alfonso as "Alfonso XIII." Civil war followed, but most of the kingdom remained loyal to the king. Henry's victory over the rebels in August of 1467, followed by Alfonso's death in July of 1468, restored a measure of authority to the king. These events provide the background to the succession struggle that followed Henry's death in 1474.

After the Farsa de Ávila and before the tide had turned for him, Henry, overwhelmed by aristocratic faction-fighting, had turned for support to external allies, King Louis XI of France and Afonso V of Portugal. In September, 1465, Henry met with Afonso, and the latter offered military assistance in return for marrying Henry's half sister, Isabella I, while Afonso's son, John II (r. 1481-1495), would marry Henry's daughter, Joan. Isabella rejected this arrangement, which presumably would have ended her days as a youthful dowager queen, and, following the death of her brother Alfonso XIII, she sought a reconciliation with Henry with the Pact of Los Toros de Guisando (1468), where he recognized her as his heir on condition that she not marry without his permission. Isabella favored marriage with Ferdinand II, son of John II of Aragon (r. 1458-1479), and in March, 1469, a surreptitious betrothal was negotiated at Cervera between the seventeen-year-old Isabella and Ferdinand, a year younger. Ferdinand subsequently made his way to Valladolid, where the couple was privately married (October 19, 1469). Henry, furious at being tricked, then proposed to marry Princess Joan to Afonso of Portugal, who was to bring forces into Castile to assist Henry against Isabella and her supporters, and to occupy the frontier-fortresses of Badajoz and Ciudad Rodrigo.

The following five years saw desultory fighting and much intrigue, with Isabella's supporters dominating eastern and central Castile, while Henry controlled Asturias, Galicia, Extremadura, and parts of the south. Then, in December, Henry died, and sporadic civil strife, a feature of Castilian life for half a century, gave way to out-and-out war over the succession.

The initiative then lay with the Portuguese, and Afonso, rejecting the slur of illegitimacy cast at his future bride, offered himself as a chivalric champion going to the rescue of a young woman in distress—Joan was still only thirteen—and since she was also his niece, he secured a papal dispensation for the marriage from Pope Pius II (1458-1464). He believed that Joan enjoyed widespread support in many cities and that he had an active ally in Louis XI. Isabella, meanwhile, used every kind of diplomatic ploy to delay and deflect the anticipated invasion.

In April, 1475, Afonso invaded Extremadura with a force of five thousand cavalry, fifteen thousand infantry, and a siege train, and rapidly captured Salamanca, Arevalo, Zamora, and Toro. His strategy was to advance on Burgos, where he anticipated joining his French allies and advancing through the Basque country. Meanwhile, Joan had been spirited out of Castile and brought to Trujillo, where she and Afonso were formally betrothed (1475). The two then married at Plasencia, and the next day Afonso proclaimed Joan their rightful queen.

It has been suggested that had Afonso turned south, he might have quickly acquired a substantial part of Castile, but the preoccupation with reaching Burgos proved disastrous, since Ferdinand was able to place a joint Aragonese-Castilian force between Afonso and his objective, and to commence the siege of Burgos, since the expected French troops never materialized. The conflict looked as if it might grind to a stalemate, but with generous contributions from the Castilian church, Isabella was able to send raiders across the Portuguese frontier, leaving Afonso at Toro, unable to advance to Burgos or to defend his own kingdom. Burgos surrendered to Ferdinand in January, 1476, releasing troops to dispatch against Zamora. On March 1, 1476, a decisive Castilian victory at the Battle of Toro led to the fall of Zamora, forcing Afonso and Joan to return to Portugal.

Afonso had not given up, however. Leaving Prince John to rule in Lisbon, he set off for France in an attempt to rally Louis's support. He remained in France from September, 1476, to November, 1478, and returned to Lisbon five days after his son's coronation, only to discover his marriage to Joan had been annulled by Pope Sixtus IV (1471-1484) under pressure from Isabella. John returned the royal title, but Afonso was a mere cipher, dying in 1481 on the eve of abdication.

Isabella was now, indubitably, ruler of Castile, but a formal end to hostilities with Portugal called for long, hard bargaining, ending in the Treaty of Alcáçovas

(1479). The Portuguese had wanted Isabella's first-born son to marry the now-available Joan, but Isabella would have none of it. She still viewed Joan as a threat, for many had recognized her as Henry's eldest child, and whatever her paternity, she was clearly a daughter of the House of Avis. Isabella demanded Joan's close confinement in a nunnery. Joan did, indeed, enter the royal convent of Santa Clara-a-Velha in Coimbra, but her confinement was anything but strict. She came and went between her retreat and the royal court, and continued to style herself queen. Isabella fretted and protested, but both John and Portuguese king Manuel I (r. 1495-1521) were indifferent. Joan lived for nearly seventy years, dying in 1530, outliving her cousin, Manuel, by a decade, and her implacable enemy, Isabella, by nearly thirty years. Posterity, however, retains for her the opprobrious nickname bestowed upon her from birth.

SIGNIFICANCE

Historians consider the years 1474 to 1479 to mark a transition between the anarchy of the early Trastamara period and consolidation under Queen Isabella I and King Ferdinand II. The conflict itself was once described as the most frivolous war in Portugal's history. Had victory gone the other way and Castile and Portugal had been united, rather than Castile and Aragon, the history of the Iberian Peninsula and of much of Western Europe would have been quite different.

—*Gavin R. G. Hambly*

FURTHER READING

Edwards, John. *The Spain of the Catholic Monarchs, 1474-1520.* Malden, Mass.: Blackwell, 2000. This is the definitive monograph in English on the reign of the Catholic monarchs.

Liss, Peggy K. *Isabel the Queen: Life and Times.* New York: Oxford University Press, 1992. This scholarly biography provides a detailed account of Isabel's early life and struggle for the throne.

Miller, Townsend. *Henry IV of Castile, 1425-1474.* Philadelphia: Lippincott, 1972. A popular biography of the enigmatic monarch.

Phillips, W. D. *Enrique IV and the Crisis of Fifteenth Century Castile, 1425-1480.* Cambridge, Mass.: Medieval Academy of America, 1978. A reevaluation of Henry and his reign.

Tate, B. T., ed. *Fernando de Pulgar: Claros Varones de Castilla.* Oxford, England: Clarendon Press, 1971. Tate prefaced his edition of this fifteenth century Castilian author with an introduction discussing the

Castilian nobility, which played so great a part in destabilizing contemporary Castile.

Weissberger, Barbara F. *Isabel Rules: Constructing Queenship, Wielding Power.* Minneapolis: University of Minnesota Press, 2004. A detailed analysis of how Isabel acquired power and retained it throughout her lifetime.

SEE ALSO: Oct. 19, 1469: Marriage of Ferdinand and Isabella; 1580-1581: Spain Annexes Portugal.

RELATED ARTICLES in *Great Lives from History: The Renaissance & Early Modern Era, 1454-1600:* Ferdinand II and Isabella I; Henry IV of Castile; Francisco Jiménez de Cisneros; John II; Louis XI; Manuel I.

Late 15th century
MOMBASA, MALINDI, AND KILWA REACH THEIR HEIGHT

Following Islamic migration from the northwest and the establishment of trading networks across the Indian Ocean, gold, slaves, and ivory from Africa were traded for cloth, beads, metal goods, silks, and porcelain from Asia and Europe. Arabic colonies along the east coast of Africa prospered as they became major centers of trade and culture.

LOCALE: East African coast (now in Kenya and Tanzania)

CATEGORIES: Trade and commerce; expansion and land acquisition

KEY FIGURES
Vasco da Gama (c. 1460-1524), Portuguese explorer
Ibn Baṭṭūṭah (1304-1377), Moroccan traveler

SUMMARY OF EVENT
In the late fifteenth century, the coastal trading towns of eastern Africa were thriving concerns, benefiting from their position between the African interior, rich in raw materials, and merchants the East and Middle East. The east coast of Africa had become an active site, not merely for trade, but for settlement, migration, and conquest as well. Some indigenous African groups moved up or down the coast, while others migrated to the sea from inland.

The strongest long-term influences on the area, however, came from two waves of outsiders who established trade routes up and down the Indian Ocean: Arab Muslim merchants from Turkey, beginning in the eleventh century or perhaps earlier, and explorer-conquerors from Portugal, who arrived at the turn of the sixteenth century. The Muslims were largely responsible for the rise of the coastal towns as commercial centers, while the arrival of the Portuguese brought about their swift downfall.

By the fifteenth century, trading in gold, slaves, mangrove poles, and ivory was concentrated in an area reaching from Malindi, in what is now Kenya, south to Kilwa,

in modern Tanzania. Cities along this stretch of coast were populated by Muslim, Swahili-speaking peoples, who shared some cultural elements but who were in constant competition with each other for trade dominance. Kilwa was located at the farthest point south that a trading ship from the Arabian Peninsula could sail to and still return home the same year. Mombasa, farther north, exploited an unsurpassed natural harbor. Malindi, still farther north, was situated favorably to catch the trade winds that could send ships to all the major cities on the Indian Ocean.

In the early centuries of Arab influence, few foreign traders settled permanently in Africa, but gradually more stayed and created new communities into which local Africans were absorbed, generally into the lower classes. From the eleventh to the early fifteenth centuries, Kilwa was the most prominent trading center in East Africa, drawing much of its wealth from the gold trade. A familial line of sultans ruled the city but never sought to expand its influence. Like the other coastal cities, Kilwa operated independently and in competition with the others rather than entering into alliances.

The Moroccan traveler Ibn Baṭṭūṭa reported after a visit to Kilwa in 1332 that the city had a large mosque and several two- and three-story buildings made of coral blocks and decorated with decorative borders in carved stone. He described the lavish court of the sultan, and the wide variety of meats, fruits, and spices available. A century or two later, the largest homes had glass windows. Wealthy people had carpets on the floors, tapestries on the walls, Ming porcelain, and Indian beads.

Mombasa was a bustling harbor as far back as the twelfth century, recorded in the journals of visiting traders as a city of tall white houses and beautiful women dressed in gold and silk. The central buildings, unlike the smaller grass huts found only a mile inland, were made of whitewashed stone.

Malindi was first settled by the Arabs during the thirteenth century. Its economy was based on fishing, agriculture, salt collection, and Indian Ocean trade. Like most of the coastal cities, it was inhabited by an Arab ruling class and an African majority; many of the Africans lived on farms surrounding the central city. Malindi came to prominence by welcoming foreign trade. In 1414, the king of Malindi made overtures to China, sending the Ming emperor the gift of a giraffe and welcoming the trader Zheng He (Cheng Ho). Malindi at its peak in the fifteenth century was a walled city. The Arabs who lived within the walls had two-story stone houses, designed in the Arab fashion around a central courtyard, with heavily carved doors.

Gedi, located ten miles south of Malindi and a little inland, demonstrates the prosperity enjoyed by these coastal cities at their peak. It was built in the late thirteenth or early fourteenth century and was home to approximately twenty-five hundred people. Most of them, the members of the lower classes, lived in mud huts on the outskirts of the town. A nine-foot-high wall surrounded a city of several buildings made of coral and clay, laid out in a deliberate plan. These buildings were decorated with carved wood and ornamented with blue and white Chinese porcelain bowls set into the ceilings.

Gedi had six small private mosques and a *Jumaa*, or Great Mosque, approached through a courtyard. The Great Mosque included a well, a *mimbar* (pulpit) of three stone steps, pillars, and decorated niches for lamps. Gedi's palace had a main entrance with arches and sunken courtyard, large reception rooms, a platform and bench for judicial hearings, kitchens, storerooms, lavatories, and private apartments. Its walls were hung with tapestries, and niches held lamps and Chinese celadon jars. Smaller homes in Gedi were single-storied, with concrete floors and concrete or tiled roofs. Residents owned goods obtained through trade, including glass beads from Venice and ivory and bronze from inland.

The arrival of the Portuguese explorer Vasco da Gama in Mombasa in 1498 marked the beginning of the end for these fabulous cities. Seeking to spread Christianity and to find new trade routes and partners for Portugal, da Gama was repelled by Mombasa, but he forged an alliance with the king of Malindi and established Malindi as a supply station for Portuguese ships. By 1518, Mozambique had replaced Malindi as Portugal's primary supply station, in part because Malindi lacked a natural harbor.

The competitive nature of the relationships between the cities helped speed their downfall. Kilwa, already in decline, was sacked and occupied by the Portuguese in 1502, but might have resisted if neighbors had come to its aid. The king of Mombasa attempted to enter an alliance with the king of Malindi in 1502, but he was rebuffed, because Malindi saw Mombasa as a greater enemy than the Portuguese.

Mombasa was burned to the ground in 1505, and the Portuguese took away so much treasure that they could not sail away with it all at once. Rebuilt, Mombasa was burned again in 1529 but resisted occupation through most of the century. It finally fell in 1592, to a combined force of Portuguese and Malindi invaders. Malindi declined through the sixteenth century because of shifts in trade routes, and by the time the Portuguese built Fort Jesus in Mombasa in 1593, Malindi's importance to international trade was minor. Gedi was not located on the coast, and so was not important to the Portuguese; it was abandoned in the seventeenth century for reasons still unknown.

SIGNIFICANCE

For some five hundred years, the cities along the East Coast of Africa grew steadily wealthier, providing wealth for traders all around the Indian Ocean and reaching the height of their prosperity in the late 1400's. Their exported gold, ivory, and slaves left their mark on the peoples who received them. The gold trade, in particular, attracted the attention of Portuguese traders and ultimately led to the European domination of Africa that continued well into the twentieth century.

The Swahili cultures that grew out of these cities remained active long after the cities ceased to influence global commerce. They are still active in modern East Africa, especially in the coastal towns of Lamu and Mombasa in Kenya and Dar es Salaam in Tanzania. A blending of Arab and African influences, Swahili people are generally Muslim, generally coastal, but as varied as any ancient group of people in a region where trade and migration have brought different people together. The Swahili language is learned as a second language by many Africans south of the equator and is used as a common tongue in many parts of the continent.

—*Cynthia A. Bily*

FURTHER READING

Kusimba, Chapurukha Makokha. *The Rise and Fall of Swahili States*. Walnut Creek, Calif.: AltaMira Press, 1999. Study of the development of Swahili language, architecture, economy, and religion on the African coast from 100 B.C.E. to the sixteenth century European conquest.

Middleton, John. *African Merchants of the Indian Ocean: Swahili of the East African Coast*. Long Grove, Ill.:

Waveland Press, 2004. Introduction to Swahili culture by a scholar with fifty years of personal contact.

Oliver, Roland, and Anthony Atmore. *The African Middle Ages, 1400-1800*. New York: Cambridge University Press, 1981. This history covers the entire continent, emphasizing African encounters with the outside influences of Islamic migration and of European and Asian trade.

Pearson, Michael N. *Port Cities and Intruders: The Swahili Coast, India, and Portugal in the Early Modern Era*. Baltimore: Johns Hopkins University Press, 1998. A historical analysis of the international influences upon the culture and economy of the Swahili people of the East African Coast.

SEE ALSO: 1460-1600: Rise of the Akan Kingdoms; c. 1464-1591: Songhai Empire Dominates the Western Sudan; 1481-1482: Founding of Elmina; c. 1485: Portuguese Establish a Foothold in Africa; Aug., 1487-Dec., 1488: Dias Rounds the Cape of Good Hope; 1490's: Decline of the Silk Road; Jan., 1498: Portuguese Reach the Swahili Coast; 16th century: Trans-Saharan Trade Enriches Akan Kingdoms; 16th century: Worldwide Inflation; Dec. 31, 1600: Elizabeth I Charters the East India Company.

RELATED ARTICLES in *Great Lives from History: The Renaissance & Early Modern Era, 1454-1600:* Bartolomeu Dias; Vasco da Gama.

August 29, 1475
PEACE OF PICQUIGNY

The Peace of Picquigny between Edward IV of England and Louis XI of France halted Edward's proposed invasion of France, weakened Charles the Bold's coalition against France, and initiated a seven-year truce between the two countries.

LOCALE: Picquigny, France
CATEGORY: Diplomacy and international relations

KEY FIGURES

Edward IV (1442-1483), king of England, r. 1461-1470, 1471-1483
Louis XI (1423-1483), king of France, r. 1461-1483
Charles the Bold (1433-1477), duke of Burgundy, r. 1467-1477
Margaret of Anjou (1430-1482), queen of England, r. 1445-1461, 1470-1471

SUMMARY OF EVENT

England and France had been embroiled in territorial disputes since at least 1066, when William the Conqueror, duke of Normandy, became the king of England. The Hundred Years' War (1337-1453), however, resulted in a temporary halt to those disputes and was also a time when England lost its French territory, except for the northern seaport of Calais. The war ended, but that did not end the traditional enmity between the two countries. A challenge from England to the ownership of various French territories arose once more.

In 1461, new kings began to reign in both England and France. In the midst of the Wars of the Roses in England,

Edward, duke of York, with the help of his chief ally and cousin, Richard Neville, earl of Warwick, defeated the Lancastrian king Henry VI and took the throne as Edward IV. Edward continued to face Lancastrian uprisings, and a growing rift with Warwick over Edward's anti-French foreign policy created new internal hostilities against his rule.

In 1461, Louis XI, the new French king, was dealing with internal unrest as well. Having inherited a country that was divided into rival duchies such as Normandy, Burgundy, and Brittany, Louis's goal was to unite all of France under his rule. The independent nobles of the realm, who as vassals owed loyalty to their suzerain under the feudal system, jointly resisted his efforts at centralized government, but Louis (also known as the spider king) continued to weave elaborate webs of alliances to achieve his goals, shifting his position as needed.

Louis XI's continuing struggle with the French nobles intensified in 1467, when Charles the Bold became the duke of Burgundy. The Burgundian kingdom, which included the Low Countries, Luxembourg, and Franche-Compté, was clearly a rival principality within France. Charles, wishing to expand his kingdom and receive the imperial crown, began to conquer land that separated his various possessions. He had strengthened his alliance with England by his marriage to Margaret of York, Edward IV's sister, in July, 1468. Increasing tensions further, Louis supported Warwick's invasion of England with Margaret of Anjou in 1470 to restore her husband, Henry VI, to the throne. With Charles's support, Edward

French king Louis XI, seen here at a reception for a military order he created, signed a treaty with England's king Edward IV in 1475 that initiated a seven-year truce between the two countries. (Frederick Ungar Publishing Co.)

the truce. A special bridge over the Somme River had been constructed for the meeting, with a trellis whose interstices had space only for a person's arm (to avoid physical danger to either king). The two kings, each with twelve of their nobles, met midway on the bridge and ratified the treaty. Louis was willing to pay a high price to end the potential invasion: 75,000 gold crowns for Edward's withdrawal from France, with the promise of an annual pension of 50,000 crowns to be paid on Easter and Michaelmas (September 29) during a seven-year truce. He also ransomed Margaret of Anjou, the wife of the late Henry VI, who had been living in confinement in England since 1471, for 50,000 crowns, with Edward's stipulation that she renounce her title and all claims to England. The truce included a promise of mutual assistance if either country were attacked, a proposed marriage alliance between Edward's eldest daughter and the dauphin of France, and a commercial treaty between the two countries.

Both kings were pleased with the results. Edward IV saw the diplomatic benefits to England: a bloodless victory, increased trade revenue, the right to hold the title of king of France, and his daughter as the future queen of France. He also saw the personal financial benefits. Edward IV no longer had to rely on Parliament for funding and he could leave his heirs an inheritance. Louis XI also found the truce to his advantage: He avoided a costly war, neutralized any threat from England, inherited Margaret of Anjou's territories (Anjou, Provence, and Lorraine), and could refocus on his primary goal of subduing the French nobles.

Because of the treaty, Edward IV's alliance with France weakened the coalition of nobles against Louis XI. Charles the Bold, in his continuing attempt to expand his Burgundian empire, was killed in 1477 fighting the duke of Lorraine and the Swiss confederation at the Battle of Nancy. His holdings eventually were divided between Louis, who took Burgundy and Picardy, and Charles's daughter, Mary of Burgundy, who kept the Low Countries and Flanders. The demise of the powerful kingdom of Burgundy paved the way for Louis to continue increasing his land holdings and his power.

In 1478, the terms of the Peace of Picquigny were reconfirmed, with a revision prolonging Edward's pension

regained the throne after a few months. Louis's problems with the growing anti-French alliance escalated when Edward and Charles, in the Treaty of London (1474), agreed to divide the kingdom of France between them and to have Edward crowned king of France at Reims.

Edward IV landed in Calais on July 4, 1475, to join the massive English army that had been transported to Calais in June. However, Charles, arriving ten days later, was unprepared to launch a full campaign or to help Edward with supplies because his own troops were engaged in Lorraine. Disappointed but undaunted, Edward marched south. Although there was a minor skirmish at St. Quentin, Louis XI's army made no move to engage in battle.

Always preferring diplomacy to war, Louis XI offered terms of peace to Edward IV. The terms were negotiated by August 23, 1475, at Amiens, where Edward's army was camped. On August 29, the two kings met 8 miles downstream from Amiens, at Picquigny, to solemnize until one year after the demise of whichever king died first; the terms were again reconfirmed in the fall of 1481. In 1482, however, Louis XI repudiated the treaty's provisions by ceasing payment of Edward's pension and by establishing a new marriage alliance for the dauphin with the daughter of the Habsburg rulers. Edward contemplated a new invasion of France but became ill and died. Edward IV and Louis XI, who began their reigns in the same year also died in the same year, 1483. New kings for England and France meant the negotiation of new relations between the two countries, and the force and relevance of the Peace of Picquigny ended.

SIGNIFICANCE

The seven-year truce between England and France allowed both kings to focus on internal affairs and bring stability to their countries. In his last years, Edward IV improved law enforcement, collected manuscripts, and supported William Caxton in his efforts to establish the printing press at Westminster. Edward's daughter, Elizabeth of York, no longer betrothed to the French dauphin, would enter into marriage with Henry VII, which initiated the long-standing Tudor Dynasty for England.

England's withdrawal from France left Louis XI free to intensify his efforts on his program of unifying France. The death of his chief local rival, Charles the Bold, accelerated progress toward his goal, once the Burgundian kingdom ceased to exist as an independent state. Louis's rule gradually became accepted, from the Pyrenees to the Low Countries, as he continued to lay a foundation for the absolute monarchy of future French kings.

The Peace of Picquigny did not end English-French hostilities, which had existed for centuries, but it did avert war between them long enough to afford each country the chance to set the stage for the royal dynasties that would rule in the following century.

—*Marsha Daigle-Williamson*

FURTHER READING

Calmette, Joseph. *The Golden Age of Burgundy.* Translated by Doreen Weightman. New York: W. W. Norton, 1963. Provides several chapters on Charles the Bold and details of the treaty.

Clive, Mary. *The Sun of York: A Biography of Edward IV.* New York: Alfred Knopf, 1974. Includes extensive details of the treaty along with illustrations, maps, genealogies, and an index.

Hallam, Elizabeth, ed. *The Wars of the Roses: From Richard II to the Fall of Richard III at Bosworth Field—Seen Through the Eyes of Their Contemporaries.* Preface by Hugh Trevor-Roper. New York: Weidenfeld & Nicolson, 1988. Useful overview of English-French relations, details of the treaty, and extensive illustrations, maps, index, and a bibliography.

Huizinga, Johan. *The Autumn of the Middle Ages.* Translated by Rodney J. Payton and Ulrich Mammitzsch. Chicago: University of Chicago Press, 1996. A new translation with augmented notes of the 1921 Dutch masterpiece. An interpretive account of the relationship between Edward, Louis, and Charles.

Kendall, Paul Murray. *Louis XI: The Universal Spider.* New York: W. W. Norton, 1971. Emphasis on Louis's cunning diplomacy, details of the treaty, and illustrations, an index, and extensive notes.

Maurer, Helen E. *Margaret of Anjou: Queenship and Power in Late Medieval England.* Rochester, N.Y.: Boydell & Brewer, 2004. Analysis of Margaret's exercise of power and her influence.

SEE ALSO: 1455-1485: Wars of the Roses.
RELATED ARTICLES in *Great Lives from History: The Renaissance & Early Modern Era, 1454-1600:* Charles the Bold; Edward IV; Louis XI; Mary of Burgundy; Earl of Warwick.

1470's

1477-1482
WORK BEGINS ON THE SISTINE CHAPEL

Under Pope Sixtus IV, this Vatican structure was completed within five years, after which many of the great masters of the period were summoned to contribute to its interior decoration.

LOCALE: Rome (now in Italy)
CATEGORIES: Architecture; art

KEY FIGURES

Sixtus IV (Francesco della Rovere; 1414-1484), Roman Catholic pope, 1471-1484
Giovanni dei Dolci (fl. late sixteenth century), believed to have been the chapel's primary architect
Perugino (Pietro Vannuci; c. 1450-1523),
Pinturicchio (Bernardino Betti; c. 1454-1513),
Sandro Botticelli (Alessandro di Mariano dei Filipepi; c. 1444-1510),
Domenico Ghirlandaio (Domenico di Tommaso Bigordi; 1449-1494),
Cosimo Rosselli (1439-1507), and
Luca Signorelli (1445/1450-1523), artists who participated in the early program of decoration

SUMMARY OF EVENT

Around 1477, Pope Sixtus IV inaugurated the construction of the Sistine Chapel, which was meant to celebrate his pontificate. Giorgio Vasari (1511-1574), now famous for his biographies of artists of the period, attributed the design of the building to Baccio Pontelli, though it is unclear whether he was the main architect. The most likely candidate for that task appears to have been Giovanni dei Dolci.

The new chapel had to be built on top of the Capella Magna (Big Chapel), until then used for conclaves and other major official church rites. The rectangular space was three times as long as its width, and it was as tall as half of its length. One of the reasons adduced for the strange vault structure is that it would guarantee bad acoustics, so that the private conversations of cardinals reunited to elect a new pope would be not heard.

Andrea Trapeziuntius, a papal secretary, wrote in May of 1482 that the construction had been rushed because of the Florentine war. The main body of the building was most likely finished by 1479, in the final year of the so-called Pazzi War. To understand the birth of the chapel, it is important to be aware of the political context in which it developed.

In April, 1478, the Pazzi family, which had close ties with the pope, was involved in the attempted coup in which Lorenzo de' Medici, known as the Magnificent, was wounded and his brother Giuliano was stabbed to death. In the riots that followed the conspiracy, many members of the Pazzi clan were killed, along with the archbishop of Pisa, Francesco Salviati. The young cardinal Raffaele Riario, nephew of the pope, was kept hostage for a few weeks until he was released under Roman pressure. The release without ransom did not prevent the threat of excommunication, which was proclaimed in June, 1478. Subsequently, two years of violent fighting pitted the Florentine and Milanese front against the papal and Neapolitan troops, conducted by captains Federico da Montefeltro (who had been part of the Pazzi plot) and Roberto Malatesta. In December, 1479, when the military situation of Florence was desperate, Lorenzo de' Medici decided to go to Naples and plead to King Ferrante of Aragón (Ferdinand II) for a peace treaty, which he eventually obtained. The pope was forced to accept the agreement in December, 1480.

In the summer of 1481, Sixtus IV summoned a group of Florentine painters to decorate the Sistine Chapel, under the direction of the papal painter Pietro Perugino. The resulting contract, for ten frescoes (supposedly the total for the original plan), is dated October 27, 1481. The four masters commissioned to paint them were Sandro Botticelli, Cosimo Rosselli, Domenico Ghirlandaio, and Perugino himself. The estimate for the cost of the first four frescoes is dated January 17, 1482. The contracts were drawn between the painters and the clerk of works, architect Giovanni dei Dolci.

The structure of the two cycles is symmetrical, with the *Life of Moses* on the south wall and the *Life of Christ* on the north wall. The original Latin *tituli* (inscriptions), recovered after the restorations of the 1970's, bear constant reference to the "written law" (the Old Testament in the Moses cycle) and to the "evangelical Law" (the Gospel in the Christ cycle). A total of eight frescoes were originally executed in each cycle. The first two on the altar wall were destroyed by Michelangelo when he painted *The Last Judgment*. The last two on the entrance wall collapsed in 1522 and were later repainted, presumably with some resemblance to the original ones, by Matteo da Lecce (1547-1600).

The scenes selected as subjects from the Bible are a combination of well-known episodes, such as Moses and the burning bush and Moses upon the Sinai, and much less familiar stories, for which the theological erudition of the pope was most likely an inspiration. The first extant fresco is *The Circumcision of the Son of Moses*, attributed to Perugino and Pinturicchio; the latter is also responsible for the elegant decorations around the pictures. The second, *Moses in Egypt*, and the fifth, *The Punishment of Corah*, are attributed to Botticelli. In the latter, the background is an Arch of Constantine on which one reads the warning for the rebels against divine authority. Some historians have thought it to be a reference to the archbishop of Krain, Andrea Zamometić, whose appeal for a general council to depose the pope did in fact follow the completion of the cycles in the summer of 1482. A more plausible hypothesis, however, is that the inscription refers to the recent violent outbreak with the Florentines. It is perhaps not a coincidence that as the painter most involved with the Medici family—who had executed a fresco representing the Pazzi plotters hung to the windows of the Palazzo della Signoria and a posthumous portrait of Giuliano (now at the National Gallery in Washington, D.C.)—Botticelli was chosen for this task.

To Rosselli are attributed *The Crossing of the Red Sea*, *The Punishment of the Idolaters*, *The Sermon of the Mount*, and *The Institution of the Eucharist*, and to Ghirlandaio, *The Calling of the First Apostles*. The last two episodes of the Moses cycle, *The Appointment of Joshua* and *The Archangel Michael Defending the Body of Moses*, were given to Luca Signorelli, the young and promising assistant of Perugino.

Botticelli probably left Rome by May, 1482. He had not been paid. On October 5, Perugino, Ghirlandaio, and Botticelli were commissioned to paint the Sala dei Gigli in the Palazzo Vecchio in Florence—a sort of anti-Sistine project. On December 31, Perugino's commission was revoked and given to Filippo Lippi (1406?-1469) instead. There were rumors that he did not get along with the other Tuscan masters, which may be indirect evidence of the ongoing Florentine feud.

Perugino was the uncontested leader of the enterprise: He painted *The Baptism of Christ* and the thematically most significant fresco of the Christ cycle: *The Charge to St. Peter*. Facing *The Punishment of Corah*, it contains two arches modeled after the Arch of Constantine. They commemorate Sixtus as the builder of the palace chapel. Perugino also painted *The Assump-*

tion on the Altar, with the portrait of Sixtus IV. In 1479, he had decorated the apse of St. Peter's Basilica with a fresco of the Virgin and saints, which also includes the kneeling figure of the pope.

The pontiff—who, more than half a century later, ordered the destruction of the paintings of the altar wall and specifically of the portrait of Sixtus IV—was Clement VII (1478-1534), born Giulio de' Medici, the posthumous son of Giuliano, who had been killed during the Pazzi uprising, in which the role of Pope Sixtus IV had been instrumental. In the light of this event, Michelangelo's *The Last Judgment* also appears, at least indirectly, as a late papal vendetta.

SIGNIFICANCE

The two fresco cycles by the four Italian masters represent a unique achievement in quattrocento Italian painting. The complexity of themes and the variety of styles exhibited by the four masters and the young Signorelli

A sketch of the interior of the Sistine Chapel. (G. P. Putnam's Sons)

are witness to an extraordinary artistic enterprise, to be matched and surpassed only by the singlehanded effort of Michelangelo's ceiling and altar wall a few years later. The political (and possibly polemical) context in which they were executed only adds interest to their layered composition.

—Marcello Simonetta

FURTHER READING

Ettlinger, L. D. *The Sistine Chapel Before Michelangelo. Religious Imagery an Papal Primacy.* Oxford, England: Clarendon Press, 1965. The most extensive study of the topic to date, providing a more theological than historical interpretation of the whole cycle.

Goffen, Rona. "Friar Sixtus IV and the Sistine Chapel." *Renaissance Quarterly* 39, no. 2 (Summer, 1986): 218-262. A theological reading of the cycle in "Franciscan terms," based on the newly discovered *tituli*, the original Latin inscriptions of the frescoes.

King, Ross. *Michelangelo and the Pope's Ceiling.* London: Chatto & Windus, 2002. Extremely detailed narrative of the creation of the Sistine Chapel fresco, from the political intrigues behind Michelangelo's receipt of the commission through its completion. Details both the artist's daily life and rivalries of the period, and the technical details of the creation itself, as well as emphasizing the importance of Michelangelo's work to the history of art. Includes photographic plates, illustrations, maps, bibliographic references, and index.

Monfasani, John. "A Description of the Sistine Chapel Under Pope Sixtus IV." *Artibus and Historiae* 7 (1983): 9-16. Publishes and summarizes a very important document, the description of the decorated Chapel by Andrea Trapeziuntius, dated May, 1482.

Pagliara, Pier Nicola. "La costruzione della cappella sistina." In *Michelangelo: La cappella Sistina.* Novara: Istituto Geografico De Agostini, 1994. Gives an architectural history of the building and confirms the attribution of the plan to Giovanni de' Dolci. In Italian.

Shearman, John. "La storia della cappella Sistina." In *Michelangelo e la Sistina.* Rome: Palombi Editori, 1990. An overview after the Vatican restorations. In Italian.

SEE ALSO: 1469-1492: Rule of Lorenzo de' Medici; c. 1478-1519: Leonardo da Vinci Compiles His Notebooks; Apr. 26, 1478: Pazzi Conspiracy; c. 1500: Netherlandish School of Painting; 1500: Roman Jubilee; 1508-1520: Raphael Paints His Frescoes; 1508-1512 and 1534-1541: Michelangelo Paints the Sistine Chapel; Nov. 3, 1522-Nov. 17, 1530: Correggio Paints the *Assumption of the Virgin*; May 6, 1527-Feb., 1528: Sack of Rome; 1532: Holbein Settles in London; Dec. 23, 1534-1540: Parmigianino Paints *Madonna with the Long Neck*; 1563-1584: Construction of the Escorial; June, 1564: Tintoretto Paints for the Scuola di San Rocco.

RELATED ARTICLE in *Great Lives from History: The Renaissance & Early Modern Era, 1454-1600:* Michelangelo.

1477-1600
JAPAN'S "AGE OF THE COUNTRY AT WAR"

In the last half of the fifteenth century, Japan's imperial power base fragmented into scattered regional strongholds controlled by samurai overlords, each vying for military supremacy.

LOCALE: Kyōto and the outlying Yamashiro Province
CATEGORIES: Wars, uprisings, and civil unrest; government and politics; expansion and land acquisition

KEY FIGURES

Ashikaga Yoshimasa (1436-1490), shogun, r. 1449-1473, who was reduced by the Ōnin Wars
Takeda Shingen (Takeda Harunobu; 1521-1573), samurai chieftain

Uesugi Kenshin (Nagao Kagetora; 1530-1578), celebrated commander and archrival of the Takeda clan

SUMMARY OF EVENT

During the bitter and inconclusive Ōnin War of 1467-1477, fought to resolve a succession dispute among rival factions of the Ashikaga clan, the centralized authority of the military dictator, or shogun, faded to a ghostly shadow of what it had once been. In the last years of the Ōnin conflict, the fighting had spread from the city of Kyōto (especially the area west of the Kamo River) outward to the surrounding countryside. This displacement of the conflict allowed the decimated city of ravaged palaces, burned shops, and improvised battlements to return slowly to life. In Kyōto's Muromachi district (after which the historical era of 1333-1573 takes its name), the figure of the once powerful shogun, Ashikaga Yoshimasa (1435-1490), continued to live on, but in an impoverished, politically impotent condition, his imperial status diminished to the level of a mere figurehead. Nor did circumstances improve for his six successors, the last of whom was finally deposed in 1573.

In the aftermath of the Ōnin War and to fill the resulting political and military voids left by the erosion of the Ashikaga shogunate's power, there arose in Yamashiro Province beyond the gates of Kyōto a class of strong local lords, called daimyo, who exercised absolute control within the limited boundaries of their own regional strongholds. These small "principalities" backed their own favorites, playing at their own power games of grabbing at land and power while ignoring the decisions and proclamations that issued from Kyōto. The regional power of these daimyo effectively brought an end to any semblance of a national authority. Nobles who had once ruled their provinces in abstentia from the effete cultured confines of the imperial court at Kyōto found themselves suddenly dispossessed of their holdings.

Decentralized authority and subsequent power struggles immediately following the Ōnin War (1477) came to be called the Sengoku Jidai, the Warring States period or Age of the Country at War, a name that alludes directly to a similar period in Chinese history. Social organization in Japan during this period was not unlike the nearly contemporary feudal system that evolved in medieval Europe. In Japan, as in the European feudal system, an elaborate network of rights and obligations all revolved around a status hierarchy tied directly to land tenure. Peasant farmers were permitted to inhabit and to work the estate lands of the daimyo and lived under his protection, but in exchange for these privileges, the peasant farmers surrendered a considerable portion of their harvest to the lord and were also expected to take up arms in his service should the need arise.

Notably lacking in this Japanese form of feudalism, however, were two of the romanticized aspects of European medieval knighthood: the cult of the adoration of women and the knightly code of chivalry—both of which were indirectly inspired in Europe by the medieval Church, hence their absence in this context. In stark contrast, daughters of the samurai daimyo were traded like horses to further regional alliances. In place of the code of chivalry, the Japanese warrior was bound by the highly disciplined warrior code of *bushidō*, which emphasized

responsibilities of loyalty, personal duty, and a rigorous code of honor that, if breached, demanded the terrible penalty of *seppuku*, the ritual act of self-disembowelment.

Samurai warriors, already well established as members of the Japanese military caste, held a prominent place in the conflicts of this period. Many of the daimyo arose from the numbers of masterless samurai (*rōnin*), from disinherited or adopted sons, or from disaffected retainers who revolted against their overlords and seized control by force when favorable circumstances presented themselves; indeed, such were the origins of some of the best-known names of the period, among them Takeda Shingen and his great military rival Uesugi Kenshin.

In fact, however, the majority of military forces of this period consisted largely of light infantry, called *ashigaru*, drawn from the peasant farmer class. Given a modicum of training and inexpensively outfitted with long wooden or bamboo-shafted spears resembling European pikes, the *ashigaru* fought in coordinated groups for maximum combat effectiveness. They became so celebrated as a military force that manuals were written concerning their training and battlefield deportment.

In later years, the *ashigaru* were raised to a new rank of distinction, being regarded as the lowest status of samurai (rather than the highest status of peasant). The more battle-hardened samurai often acted as mounted field officers over the *ashigaru*, directing them at the tactical level. In the conflicts of this period, the defeat of a main body of *ashigaru* usually proved catastrophic for the daimyo. At the conclusion of a successful military campaign, the *ashigaru* disbanded, returning to their rice fields until such time as they were, once again, summoned by the overlord. As a result, conflicts tended to be sporadic, of short duration, and self-limiting. Such were the vicissitudes of life during the Sengoku era that many samurai were reduced to becoming part-time farmers, laboring ankle-deep in mud with their spears stuck upright in the dirt windrows, never farther than an arm's reach.

As conflicts between neighboring daimyo dragged on, a new class of rebellious peasant leagues, called *ikki*, gradually emerged to challenge the power of the samurai warlords. In the confused atmosphere of the later Muromachi period, the rural *ikki* directed their aggression against the urban merchants, or *doso* (literally "warehouse keepers"), who, in turn, formed urban *ikki* of their own to protect themselves and their interests. Similar *ikki* leagues arose among sects of Buddhist "warrior monks" who involved themselves in the fierce skirmishes of the rival samurai clans. Such leagues eventually supplanted the individual samurai as the principal military force.

SIGNIFICANCE

Ironically, the fragmentation of power among scattered regional daimyo during the Age of the Country at War did not result in widespread social chaos; in fact, quite the opposite was true. The collection of tribute taxes, for example, was greatly facilitated by the localization of authority in the person of the local chieftain, rather than in some abstract political entity headquartered at several days' traveling distance. As the borders of the individual daimyo estates tended to follow natural geographic boundaries (especially mountain ridges and rivers), their compact size tended to make these lands easier to control.

Over time, power came to be consolidated in fewer, more capable hands. The lesser daimyo were gradually absorbed by more powerful neighbors or succumbed to attacks of encircling rivals. In the unsettled atmosphere of precarious alliances and rapidly shifting military advantage, additional fortified towns and castles were built. To supply the necessary raw materials, mines and quarries were dug, which, in many instances, yielded unanticipated finds of rich metallic ores. Roads were constructed to facilitate more efficient traffic of goods and people. As a consequence, communication between geographic regions improved along with the general economy, stimulated by trade, tariffs, and the formation of merchants' and craftspeople's guilds.

Finally, by the mid-sixteenth century, the first Portuguese explorers had arrived by sea (1543), followed by Saint Francis Xavier and the Jesuits (1549), the Spanish (1587), and the Dutch (1609), bringing the Sengoku and Muromachi periods to a close on or around 1600. Centralized government would reemerge during the Tokugawa period (mid-sixteenth to nineteenth centuries), but only after long and costly struggles.

—Larry Smolucha

FURTHER READING

Dolan, Ronald E., and Robert L. Worden, eds. *Japan: A Country Study*. Washington, D.C.: Federal Research Division, Library of Congress, 1992. Especially useful for its concise historical survey presented in chapter 1, with additional valuable background information in subsequent chapters pertaining to topography, climate, and social and cultural trends. Includes regional maps.

Henshall, Kenneth G. *A History of Japan: From Stone Age to Superpower*. New York: St. Martin's Press, 1999. A remarkably readable history of Japan that emphasizes the human dimension of conflict and historical change. Includes chapter summaries in concise table format for each era's key developments, values, and practices.

Turnbull, Stephen. *The Samurai Sourcebook*. London: Cassel, 2000. Another fine reference work by the author of *Samurai Warriors*, but treats more fully the particulars of the subject through thumbnail biographies of principal samurai and detailed data on weapons, heraldry, strategy and tactics, great battles, and more. Well illustrated.

_____. *Samurai Warriors*. New York: Blandford Press, 1987. An episodic treatment of the samurai tradition. Very well illustrated with both historical and contemporary drawings, paintings, maps, diagrams, and photographs.

SEE ALSO: 1457-1480's: Spread of Jōdo Shinshū Buddhism; 1467-1477: Ōnin War; 1477-1600: Japan's "Age of the Country at War"; Mar. 5, 1488: Composition of the *Renga* Masterpiece *Minase sangin hyakuin*; Beginning 1513: Kanō School Flourishes; 1532-1536: Temmon Hokke Rebellion; 1549-1552: Father Xavier Introduces Christianity to Japan; 1550's-1567: Japanese Pirates Pillage the Chinese Coast; 1550-1593: Japanese Wars of Unification; Sept., 1553: First Battle of Kawanakajima; June 12, 1560: Battle of Okehazama; 1568: Oda Nobunaga Seizes Kyōto; 1587: Toyotomi Hideyoshi Hosts a Ten-Day Tea Ceremony; 1590: Odawara Campaign; 1592-1599: Japan Invades Korea; 1594-1595: Taikō Kenchi Survey; Oct., 1596-Feb., 1597: *San Felipe* Incident; Oct. 21, 1600: Battle of Sekigahara.

RELATED ARTICLES in *Great Lives from History: The Renaissance & Early Modern Era, 1454-1600*: Hōjō Ujimasa; Hosokawa Gracia; Oda Nobunaga; Ōgimachi; Oichi; Sesshū; Toyotomi Hideyoshi.

June 12, 1477-August 17, 1487
HUNGARIAN WAR WITH THE HOLY ROMAN EMPIRE

The war between Matthias I Corvinus of Hungary and Emperor Frederick III for control of the Danube region resulted in the creation of a short-lived Danubian Empire under Hungarian control.

LOCALE: Vienna, Austria; Lower Austria; middle-Danube region

CATEGORIES: Wars, uprisings, and civil unrest; expansion and land acquisition; diplomacy and international relations

KEY FIGURES

Matthias I Corvinus (Mátyás Hunyadi; 1443-1490), king of Hungary, r. 1458-1490

Frederick III (1415-1493), Holy Roman Emperor, r. 1440-1493

Jan Zelený (fl. 1470's-1480's), Hungarian military commander of Czech descent

Vladislav II (Władisław Jagiełło II; 1456-1516), king of Bohemia, r. 1471-1516, king of Hungary as Ulászló II, r. 1490-1516, and son of Casimir IV

Johann Beckensloer (1427-1489), archbishop of Esztergom, 1474-1479

Dobeš of Boskovice and Černá Hora (Dobeš Cernohorsky of Boskovice; d. 1493), Hungarian military commander of Czech descent

SUMMARY OF EVENT

The first war between Matthias I Corvinus, king of Hungary, and Holy Roman Emperor Frederick III started in 1459 as a result of Frederick's desire to enforce his claims to the Hungarian throne. The clash ended with the Treaty of Wiener Neustadt of 1463-1464, which confirmed the Habsburg claims to Hungary in the event that Matthias should die without an heir. Subsequent relations between the two monarchs seemed friendly: Frederick even asked Matthias for help against the heretical Czechs in 1467. The friendship, however, was short-lived. Matthias supported the uprising of Andreas Baumkircher, a nobleman from Styria, against the emperor (1469-1470), while Frederick refused to cede the title of king of Hungary, which he had held since 1459. Frederick and Matthias, then, each believed himself to have legitimate grievances against the other. They broke openly in 1470, at their meeting in Vienna.

Matthias tried to isolate the emperor diplomatically by allying with Charles the Bold, duke of Burgundy, and the Knights of the Teutonic Order, while calling a truce

with Vladislav II, king of Bohemia. The emperor, however, attempted to woo Vladislav to his side. Matthias had a claim to the Bohemian throne, and had even taken the title king of Bohemia. Frederick chose to endorse the claims of Vladislav to the title and formally invested him with the kingdom of Bohemia on June 10, 1477. In addition, Johann Beckensloer, archbishop of Esztergom and adviser to Matthias, had fallen from favor with the king. In 1476, he fled to Austria and was granted asylum by Frederick III. Matthias interpreted these acts of Frederick as deliberate provocations, and on June 12, 1477, the Hungarian king responded by declaring war on the Holy Roman Emperor.

Matthias immediately led his army into Lower Austria, where his troops, under the leadership of the Czech captain Jan Zelený, pillaged and plundered the country up to Vienna. They took the most important castles, including Bruck an der Leitha, Trautmannsdorf, and Klosterneuburg, as well as several small towns—contemporary sources report that more than one hundred castles and thirty towns were seized. Matthias's army also besieged Vienna, Hainburg, and Krems. By August, Frederick had sued for peace. Matthias demanded compensation of 752,000 florins. This figure was too high for the emperor, and hostilities dragged on for another few months. Ultimately, the monarchs agreed on a figure of 100,000 florins, and the peace treaty was signed on December 1, 1477. Matthias was formally acknowledged king of Bohemia by Frederick on December 13. This second campaign of Matthias in Lower Austria lacked pitched battles; it was fought only through sieges and by capturing towns and castles.

Though it seemed that the peace treaty would solve the problems of King Matthias I Corvinus and Emperor Frederick III, new conflicts emerged quite early and the treaty never came into practical effect. It was Matthias's support of the rebellious bishops of Salzburg and Passau and the emperor's permanent support of Beckensloer that were still ruining the relations between them. There was, however, no open war, since Matthias then had his army in the south fighting the Ottomans.

Mattias's forces were victorious over the Ottomans at the Battle of Kenyérmező (1479). They continued to fight the Turks, traveling next to Bosnia and Serbia (1480-1481) and even to Italy, where they helped to retake Otranto (1481). Frederick took advantage of the Hungarian forces' long absence from home: He attacked

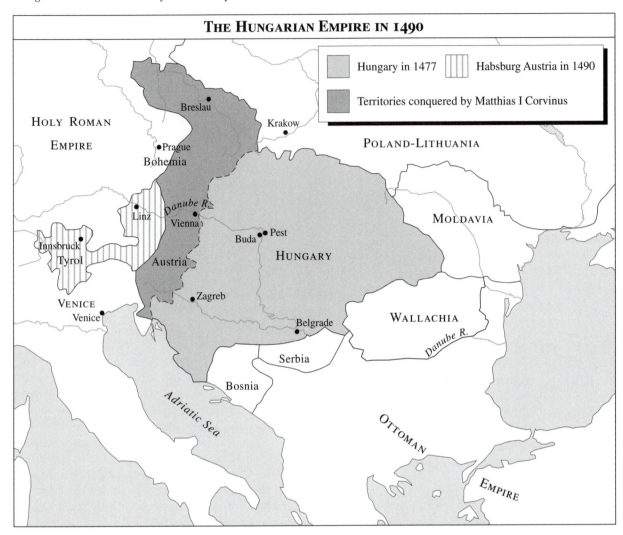

THE HUNGARIAN EMPIRE IN 1490

Hungary in 1477   Habsburg Austria in 1490

Territories conquered by Matthias I Corvinus

HOLY ROMAN EMPIRE

Breslau

Krakow

POLAND-LITHUANIA

Prague

Bohemia

Danube R.

Linz

Vienna

Innsbruck

Tyrol

Buda Pest

HUNGARY

MOLDAVIA

Austria

VENICE

Venice

Zagreb

Belgrade

WALLACHIA

Danube R.

Serbia

Bosnia

OTTOMAN

Adriatic Sea

EMPIRE

Hungary with the very troops designated by the Imperial Diet to help fight the Ottomans, but this campaign was stopped near Győr in January, 1481. A new truce was signed in Vienna that May. However, despite the best diplomatic attempts of third-party mediators, including the dukes of the Holy Roman Empire and even the pope, this truce did not last either.

Matthias launched a third invasion of Lower Austria in March, 1482. Both of the rivals were better prepared for the war than they had been in 1477. Frederick now had five thousand to six thousand mobile troops: He no longer had to rely solely on his strongholds for defense. Matthias, on the other hand, invaded with a diverse and resourceful army of heavy and light cavalry, infantry, and artillery—about eight thousand to ten thousand men in all. Most of the Hungarian forces were mercenaries, led

among others by famous Czech captains Jan Zelený and Dobeš of Boskovice and Černá Hora, as well as the Hungarian István (or Stephen) Zápolya, the later captain of Lower Austria.

The war started with an Austrian attempt to recapture the castle of Merkenstein from the Hungarians in March, 1482. The castle's defenders successfully repelled the attack, and they used the battle as a springboard for their own campaign. Matthias's invasion proceeded similarly to that of 1477, but this time his goal was different. Although before he had sought only to weaken the emperor, he now wanted to conquer and occupy Frederick's lands. Accordingly, his first step was to take the border stronghold of Hainburg, the gateway to Austria. Hainburg, however, was very well protected by the Austrian mobile troops, who attacked the Hungarians attempting to besiege the fortress. Finally, King Matthias himself came in June to lead the siege, and the town surrendered on September 30, 1482. The way was now open to Lower Austria. Further attempts to reconcile the two opponents were made by the pope and by Venice, but Matthias's demands were simply too high for Frederick to accept.

The war continued in 1483 with further attacks on towns and castles. The two sides were fairly evenly matched, however, and Hungary's only significant gain was the capture of Klosterneuburg by Boskovice. The fall of that castle drove the emperor out of Vienna, and in November, 1484, he settled in Linz, the most important Austrian city still in his hands.

All that remained for Matthias to declare victory was to capture Vienna. The Hungarian forces spent nearly a year carefully preparing for this final battle. On March 11, 1484, Hungary destroyed Austria's mobile troops in the decisive Battle of Leitzersdorf, the largest open battle of the war. At first, the battle went against Hungary's forces, under the command of István Dávidházy, but the Austrians' undisciplined celebration in the face of victory left them ill-prepared for a second wave of attack led by Boskovice, and they were soundly defeated.

With its mobile troops gone, Austria no longer had any means of breaking Hungary's sieges. Matthias therefore followed the Battle of Leitzersdorf by laying siege to two key towns supporting Vienna. He took Bruck an der Leitha (March-April, 1484), and, after a siege of eight months, Korneuburg fell in December, 1484. Finally, Vienna lay defenseless before the Hungarians, without its emperor to rally the inhabitants to its defense, without mobile troops to attack besieging forces, and without nearby strongholds to provide either supplies or military support.

The siege of Vienna began on January 29, 1485, and, though the citizens of Vienna were able to make several sorties on the Hungarian army and to communicate with the emperor in Linz, they never received Frederick's military support. They were forced to surrender on June 1, 1485. Matthias immediately proclaimed himself duke of Austria. His proclamation was premature, however: Even with the capital firmly held by the invaders, other Austrian strongholds continued to fight.

The war did not truly come to an end until the capture of Wiener Neustadt, an eminent stronghold of the emperor. It was taken, after a long siege, on August 17, 1487. By then, Matthias had conquered Lower Austria, Styria, and Carinthia. The military campaign was over. What followed were mainly diplomatic meetings and negotiations to discuss the parameters of Frederick's capit-

ulation to Matthias. The emperor, though, was stubborn to the end. No formal peace treaty was ever signed, and the conflict was still not completely resolved at the time of Matthias's sudden and unexpected death in Vienna on April 6, 1490.

SIGNIFICANCE

Due to Matthias's sudden death, Hungary's annexation of Austria was extremely short-lived. The impact of the conquest, however, survived the conquest itself. The lands surrounding the central Danube briefly came under the sovereignty of Matthias I Corvinus. This represented a significant humiliation to Frederick III—the Holy Roman Emperor and the last such emperor to have that title validated with a papal coronation ceremony. It also meant that a new Central European Empire came, however briefly, into being. This ephemeral empire of Matthias I Corvinus, including Hungary, parts of Bohemia, and Austria, was an expression of Matthias's struggle both to legitimize his kingship and to dignify it in relation to the empires of Frederick or the Ottomans.

The result of this drive for legitimacy was a fleeting glimpse of the Austria-Hungary of the future, which, however, quickly split again into separate kingdoms without a strong and motivated monarch to hold it together. For Hungary, the war had significant long-term economic and military consequences. Three separate campaigns in ten years took a significant toll on the nation's coffers, without ultimately producing any compensatory revenue. Militarily, Matthias's war in Austria diverted his resources and attention from the Ottomans to the west, which gave the Ottomans time free from assault to build up and consolidate their own imperial forces. The war thus definitively eliminated any realistic hope of controlling the Ottomans' flow into Central Europe, which was perhaps its single greatest consequence. For Austria and the Habsburgs, the war represented merely one of many episodes that would eventually lead to their final acquisition of power over Hungary in 1526.

—*Antonín Kalous*

FURTHER READING

Bak, János M., and Béla K. Király, eds. *From Hunyadi to Rákóczi: War and Society in Late Medieval and Early Modern Hungary.* Brooklyn, N.Y.: Social Science Monographs, 1982. Collection of articles on Hungarian warfare and its influence on the society. Chapter 7 concentrates on the mercenary army of Matthias.

Engel, Pál. *The Realm of St. Stephen: A History of Medieval Hungary, 895-1526.* New York: I. B. Tauris,

2001. Chapter 18 provides a modern account of the reign of Matthias.

Press, Victor. "The Habsburg Lands: The Holy Roman Empire, 1400-1555." In *Handbook of European History, 1400-1600: Late Middle Ages, Renaissance, and Reformation*, edited by Thomas A. Brady et al. New York: E. J. Brill, 1994. Places Frederick's reign and his territorial sovereignty within the context of dynastic and national rivalries within the empire.

Rázsó, Guyla. *Die Feldzüge des Königs Matthias Corvinus in Niederösterreich 1477-1490*. Wien: Heeresgeschichtlichen Museum, 1977. A detailed overview of the war. In German.

Veszprémy, László, and Béla K. Király, eds. *A Millennium of Hungarian Military History*. Boulder, Colo.: Atlantic Research and Publications, 2002. A fundamental discussion of the development of Hungarian warfare in the fifteenth century appears on pp. 54-82.

SEE ALSO: Apr. 14, 1457-July 2, 1504: Reign of Stephen the Great; 1458-1490: Hungarian Renaissance; 1463-1479: Ottoman-Venetian War; 1478-1482: Albanian-Turkish Wars End; 1499-c. 1600: Russo-Polish Wars; 1526-1547: Hungarian Civil Wars; Aug. 29, 1526: Battle of Mohács; Sept. 27-Oct. 16, 1529: Siege of Vienna; 1576-1612: Reign of Rudolf II.

RELATED ARTICLES in *Great Lives from History: The Renaissance & Early Modern Era, 1454-1600:* Frederick III; Matthias I Corvinus; Vladislav II.

August 17, 1477
FOUNDATION OF THE HABSBURG DYNASTY

The marriage of Maximilian I and Mary of Burgundy led to the creation of the Habsburg Dynasty and restructured European power for nearly 450 years. Ultimately, their descendants developed the first global empire, which remained a significant European power until the twentieth century.

LOCALE: Ghent (now in Belgium)
CATEGORIES: Expansion and land acquisition; government and politics

KEY FIGURES
Maximilian I (1459-1519), Holy Roman Emperor, r. 1493-1519
Mary of Burgundy (1457-1482), duchess of Burgundy, r. 1477-1482
Philip the Fair (1478-1506), sovereign of the Netherlands, r. 1494-1506, and son of Maximilian and Mary
Frederick III (1415-1493), Holy Roman Emperor, r. 1440-1493
Charles V (1500-1558), king of Spain as Charles I, r. 1516-1556, and Holy Roman Emperor, r. 1519-1556

SUMMARY OF EVENT
On the evening of August 16, 1477, Archduke Maximilian entered Ghent, the city in Flanders that housed the ducal palace. Dressed in silver gilt armor, crowned with jewels, decorated with the Burgundy cross, and blond and handsome in appearance, he was an arresting figure, a character out of a medieval romance. His mission was no less chivalric than his appearance: to rescue and marry his betrothed, Mary, the heiress of Burgundy, who had been held captive by townspeople for months in her castle.

That evening, they were briefly introduced, and the next day, August 17, 1477, they married, effectively establishing the Habsburg Dynasty. Even though some believe the two were devoted to each other, others consider the marriage politically expedient.

Maximilian and Mary remained in the Low Countries after marrying, and Maximilian led the defense of the duchy against the attacks of Louis XI, king of France. In June of 1478, Mary gave birth to Philip (later known as Philip the Fair). In 1480, their only daughter, Margaret, was born.

Meanwhile, Louis's attacks grew more serious and the Burgundians were losing more people and territory to him. To settle the conflict, Maximilian and Mary first ceded to Louis much of the duchy of Burgundy and then betrothed their infant daughter Margaret to Louis's heir. The following year, in 1481, Mary gave birth to a second son, who lived only a few days. In March, 1482, while out hunting, Mary fell from her horse and was fatally injured. She died March 27, 1482.

Political realities were held at bay by the unexpectedly successful match between Mary and Maximilian, but politics soon reasserted itself. The people of Flanders made it clear to Maximilian that, though the widower of their duchess, his stay was not welcome. They also made clear their interest in their future leader, the toddler Philip the Fair, so the heir of Burgundy remained in Ghent under the care of Margaret of York.

Their daughter Margaret's betrothal to the French dauphin was eventually dissolved for political reasons, so she was sent from the French court, where she had been raised as part of the betrothal agreement, to the Netherlands. Philip became the ruler of the Netherlands in his own right when he was sixteen years old, close to the time that a treaty with the French restored most of his lands, retaining the portions inside today's French-Belgian border only.

It could be said that Maximilian I and Mary of Burgundy became the founders of the Habsburg Dynasty because their son Philip had married Joan (known as Joan the Mad), third in line for the Spanish throne. Margaret, meanwhile, had married Juan, the Spanish crown prince, but Juan and his elder sister passed away within a few years, however, leaving no children and leaving Joan, Philip's wife, heir to the Spanish crown.

Philip and Joan had six children. Their eldest son became Charles I of Spain and was elected Holy Roman Emperor, becoming Charles V. His election, following on the heels of his inheritance of all his family territories and thrones, formally created the Habsburg Empire of Spain, Austria, the Netherlands, and their associated colonies, and fulfilled the dream of Mary's father.

The marriage of Mary of Burgundy to Maximilian I marked the beginning of the Habsburg Dynasty in Europe, the first global empire and one that remained powerful until the twentieth century. (Frederick Ungar Publishing Co.)

This critical alliance between Maximilian and Mary almost did not occur, however. It was first considered in 1473, when Mary's father, Charles the Bold, was one of the wealthiest and most powerful nobles in Europe. His duchy of Burgundy was anchored in France and extended to the edges of the Netherlands. As her father's only child, Mary was heir to one of the largest fortunes and landholdings in Europe, rivaling the holdings of many of the royal families.

Although Emperor Frederick was impoverished compared with Charles, they spent much time negotiating a marriage contract between their children. The talks continued because Frederick possessed an imperial title, which Charles desperately wanted for himself, or at least

for his heirs. The talks between the two progressed to the point where, in 1473, Frederick and Maximilian traveled to Triers, preparing to complete a betrothal. It is unclear whether the betrothal agreements were finalized at that time. Charles's demands were high and failed to acknowledge the constraints on the title of Holy Roman Emperor. It was an electoral, not hereditary, title at the time, so Frederick could make no guarantees about whether their heirs might possess it, no matter how hard Charles pressed.

Soon after the initial betrothal talks, Charles attempted to achieve an imperial title on his own by conquering lands belonging to Louis XI and thereby restoring the medieval boundaries of Burgundy. This policy was futile, and it led Charles back to discussions with Frederick in 1476. It is unclear if at this time there was a renewal of the 1473 betrothal or whether a first betrothal was established. However, clear marriage terms were accepted by both sides. Then, Charles the Bold died in battle during his return to Ghent, just before he could agree to the wedding date.

Unexpectedly freed of Charles and his intimidations, the people of Ghent rose up against Mary. They barricaded her in the palace and exiled her stepmother, Margaret of York. They planned to ignore the betrothal contract with the Habsburgs and marry Mary to someone else, such as the heir to the French throne, who would be more helpful to them politically. Mary held firm to the betrothal her father had made, which prompted a proxy wedding between Mary and Maximilian. In this ceremony, a Habsburg representative symbolically married Mary on behalf of Maximilian, speaking the vows and lying down, fully dressed, on a bed with her. However, few took the proxy ceremony seriously; as late as June, 1477, Louis XI was still promising favors to the townspeople if they forced Mary to marry his son.

Maximilian finally arrived in August, after leaving Vienna in May. The journey was delayed not only by necessary ceremonial obligations but also by his running out of money. Margaret of York rescued him by sending him cash to make the final stage of the journey. The Habsburg's poverty led to speculation that Maximilian was marrying simply for the sake of money, but the image of a chivalric Maximilian riding into Ghent gave rise also to romantic speculation about their relationship and coincided with popular talk about Maximilian as the last true knight.

SIGNIFICANCE

Mary and Maximilian's marriage could have been nothing more than romantic legend, a pretty story without impact on the map of European history. Their titles were empty, their territories were shrinking, and their treasures and lands were encumbered by debt.

Chivalric legend aside, Mary and Maximilian's marriage established the Habsburgs in the Low Countries, for the first time expanding their territories outside Austria. Their eldest grandson, the son of Philip and Joan, inherited the Spanish and Netherlands crowns and the

Habsburg lands in Austria. The Habsburg Dynasty had been established in full sight but ironically without notice.

—*Clare Callaghan*

FURTHER READING

Bérenger, Jean. *A History of the Habsburg Empire, 1273-1700*. Translated by C. A. Simpson. Vol. 1. New York: Longmans, 1994. Analyzes not only the Habsburgs but also other figures and sociopolitical movements to show how Habsburgs rose to prominence, beginning with the earliest Habsburg Holy Roman Emperor.

Brook-Shepherd, Gordon. *The Austrians: A Thousand Year Odyssey*. New York: Carroll & Graf, 1996. Focuses on the development of an Austrian people from warring medieval tribes, not simply the rise of their rulers.

Fichtner, Paula Sutter. *The Hapsburg Monarchy, 1490-1848: Attributes of Empire*. New York: Palgrave Macmillan, 2003. Although its focus begins at the end of Maximilian I's life, its comprehensive background section begins with the earliest Habsburg who was a Holy Roman Emperor.

McGuigan, Dorothy Guis. *The Habsburgs*. New York: Doubleday, 1966. Colorful, highly readable narrative of the rise of the Habsburgs.

SEE ALSO: Oct. 19, 1469: Marriage of Ferdinand and Isabella; 1482-1492: Maximilian I Takes Control of the Low Countries; Aug. 19, 1493-Jan. 12, 1519: Reign of Maximilian I; Nov. 26, 1504: Joan the Mad Becomes Queen of Castile; Jan. 23, 1516: Charles I Ascends the Throne of Spain; June 28, 1519: Charles V Is Elected Holy Roman Emperor; 1521-1559: Valois-Habsburg Wars; Aug. 29, 1526: Battle of Mohács; 1555-1556: Charles V Abdicates; July 26, 1581: The United Provinces Declare Independence from Spain; 1593-1606: Ottoman-Austrian War; May 2, 1598: Treaty of Vervins.

RELATED ARTICLES in *Great Lives from History: The Renaissance & Early Modern Era, 1454-1600:* Charles the Bold; Charles V; Ferdinand II and Isabella I; Francis I; Frederick III; Louis XII; Mary of Burgundy; Maximilian I.

1478

MUSCOVITE CONQUEST OF NOVGOROD

Moscow absorbed Novgorod, paving the way for the unification of all the Russian principalities under the autocratic rule of the princes of Moscow.

LOCALE: Novgorod and Moscow, Russia
CATEGORIES: Expansion and land acquisition; wars, uprisings, and civil unrest

KEY FIGURES

Vasily II (1415-1462), grand prince of Moscow, r. 1425-1462, and father of Ivan the Great
Ivan the Great (Ivan III; 1440-1505), grand prince of Moscow, r. 1462-1505
Vasily III (1479-1533), grand prince of Moscow, r. 1505-1533
Sophia Palaeologus (c. 1449-1503), niece of Byzantine emperor Constantine XI and wife of Ivan the Great

SUMMARY OF EVENT

Because of its control of a trading empire that extended from the middle of the Volga River to the Ural Mountains, Novgorod was the richest Russian state. By the fifteenth century, it was a republic dominated by a boyar upper class, whose wealth was derived from the fur trade, banking, and managing large estates. During the trying mid-thirteenth century, Novgorod was able to maintain its independence in spite of a major invasion by the Teutonic Knights (which it repelled by force) and the Mongol conquest of most of Russia (which it survived by paying tribute). Two centuries later, Novgorod faced the dual threat of an expanding Lithuanian state and a prince of Moscow ambitious to build a new Russian empire based on Muscovite dominance.

Constantinople (the "Second Rome") had fallen to the Ottoman Turks in 1453. In its wake, Muscovite leaders viewed their principality as the heir apparent of the Eastern Roman (Byzantine) Empire and the center of the "Third Rome." It had been Novgorod's own "hero prince," Saint Alexander Nevsky (r. 1236-1252), who, in 1263, had willed his youngest son, Daniel Aleksandrovich (r. 1276-1303), the then-remote forest principality of Moscow. Although Muscovy consisted only of 500 square miles (1,295 square kilometers) in 1263, it was located at a strategic river and trade route crossroad. Designated as tax collectors for the Mongols, Daniel's successors increased in wealth and power. By the 1400's, Muscovy's territory had grown more than thirty times, encompassing a state of more than 15,000 square miles (38,850 square kilometers).

Unlike Novgorod, which maintained representative institutions shared between boyar committees and the *veche* (council of freemen), Muscovy was governed under autocratic rule. While Novgorod gained prosperity through widespread trade and commerce, Moscow gained its wealth by keeping a portion of the taxes it collected for the Mongols. In relation to political and social systems, Novgorod and Moscow were worlds apart.

By the fifteenth century, the highly diversified Novgorod social system became split between clearly defined upper and lower classes. An increasingly wealthy merchant boyar class tightened its grip on Novgorod's economic activity, politics, and even judicial decisions.

To symbolize the annexation of Novgorod by Moscow in 1478, the great veche bell, representative of Novgorod's traditional liberties, was removed during Ivan the Great's conquest and taken to Moscow. (R. S. Peale and J. A. Hill)

115

Although divided into competing power factions, the boyars were united in their fear of growing Muscovite power. Most boyars looked to Lithuania (which was in the process of uniting with Poland) as a solid ally against further encroachments by Moscow. In contrast, Novgorod's lower classes believed that Moscow could be used to diminish their domination under the boyars. The lower classes were not prone to support sacrifices in money or in life aimed at blocking Muscovite hegemony.

Two events in the mid-fifteenth century brought a Moscow-Novgorod conflict to a head. In 1445, the Mongol Golden Horde separated into four separate khanates. Although the Golden Horde did not completely collapse until 1502, this division was a sign that its power was slipping. It called into question the Hordes's ability to control Rus through Moscow. Moreover, in 1453, Constantinople fell to the Ottoman Turks. The Second Rome was no more, and Muscovy was preparing to be its successor as the Third Rome.

Several months before the fall of Constantinople, Prince Vasily II (the Blind) of Moscow ceased tax payments to the Mongols. Lithuania also positioned itself to take advantage of the lifting of the "Mongol Yoke" by forming closer relations with the Russian appanages. Wanting nothing more than to keep its large trading empire intact in a rapidly changing political landscape, Novgorod geared its foreign policy toward fomenting conflict between Moscow and Lithuania and between Moscow and Tver', Moscow's powerful neighboring principality.

In 1456, fearful of closer Novgorod-Lithuanian ties, Vasily II used military force to impose on Novgorod the Treaty of Iazhelbitsy. This treaty gave Moscow effective control over Novgorod's foreign policy. Violating the spirit, if not the letter of the treaty, Novgorod selected two Lithuanians in succession to serve as their princes. An enraged Vasily II planned for an attack on Novgorod. However, his sudden death in 1462 cut short invasion plans.

Vasily's oldest son, Ivan the Great, was well trained to succeed his father and remained steadfast in his determination to bring the other Russian principalities under Muscovite dominance. In 1470, Novgorod recognized

---

THE BATTLE AT SHELON RIVER

The Chronicle of Novgorod gives a detailed, if slanted, account of the 1471 battle at the Shelon River between Muscovite and Novgorod forces. The final section of the Chronicle *(about the year 1471), was added and then edited by Ivan the Terrible after the Muscovite conquest of Novgorod.*

The *Veliki Knyaz* [grand prince], being informed of the unceasing evil doings of the men of Novgorod, dispatched to Novgorod the Great [the full name of Novgorod] a challenge in writing, exposing the malpractices of the people and their treason, and announcing that he was himself marching with a force against them. . . .

[Meanwhile,] Great Novgorod collected together, forming a fighting body of 30,000 men, being unaware that the sword of God was sharpened against them, and mounting their horses, rode quickly out of the town to fall upon the advance force of the *Veliki Knyaz*. . . .

Early on the morning of July 14 . . . the entire force of the men of Novgorod was ranged on the Shelon river, and the opposing armies faced each other across the river.

When they saw the forces of the men of Novgorod the troops of the *Veliki Knyaz* precipitated themselves into the river on their horses, not one of their horses stumbling in descending the steep bank nor floundering in the water, and closing up they rushed upon the whole body of the men of Novgorod and they joined in battle.

And here was fulfilled what was said by the Prophet: "Like drunken men did they stagger and fall into confusion, and all their understanding was swallowed up"; and again: "As in drowsiness they mounted their horses, terrible art Thou, O Lord; who can stand against Thee?"

Source: The Chronicle of Novgorod, 1016-1471, translated by Robert Michell and Nevill Forbes. Camden Third Series 25 (London: The Camden Society, 1914), pp. 211, 214.

---

the king of Poland as its leader, promising him the same amount of tribute that had formerly been paid to the Golden Horde. Ivan needed no greater excuse to attack. Launching his forces against a piecemeal Novgorod army, he won a decisive battle on the banks of the Shelon River in 1471. Novgorod's access to the Volga River, its main artery for food supplies and trade, was effectively severed. Polish aid never materialized. To make peace, Novgorod was forced to cede part of its lands to Moscow, pay a large indemnity, and take an oath of loyalty to Ivan. A handful of leading boyars were executed for their complicity in the crisis, while others were imprisoned or exiled.

In the aftermath of his victory, Ivan married Sophia Palaeologus (1472), the niece of the last emperor of Byzantium. The marriage elevated his stature and would prove useful in the future casting of Moscow as the Third Rome. In 1475, he visited Novgorod in the role of supreme judge. Several pro-Lithuanian boyars were convicted of attempted treason for their pro-Lithuanian sympathies and sentenced to imprisonment in Moscow. The message to the other boyars was unmistakably clear.

Though defeated and humiliated, Novgorod was still permitted to maintain much of its autonomy. Public opinion after 1475 was sharply divided between accommodation with Moscow and conflict. In spite of dire warnings by the metropolitan (religious leader) of Novgorod, new boyar leaders were able to steer Novgorod into an alliance with Lithuania. Infuriated by what he viewed as treason, Ivan again gathered a large army. In 1478, he besieged Novgorod. Deserted by Lithuania and unable to muster sufficient forces for its defense, Novgorod surrendered without a fight. This surrender marked the end of Novgorod's independence.

Following his bloodless victory, Ivan incorporated Novgorod into the Muscovy state. Scores of pro-Lithuanian boyars were executed, and their family estates were confiscated and turned over to Muscovites. To symbolize the annexation of Novgorod by Moscow, on January 15, 1478, the great veche bell, representative of Novgorod's traditional liberties, was removed and taken to Moscow. What remained was the wealth of Novgorod as the center of Russian trade and craftsmanship. However, this wealth would be heavily taxed to provide Ivan with the financial support he needed to annex the rest of Russia. Even Novgorod peasants were organized into taxing communes, to make annual payments to Moscow more efficient.

SIGNIFICANCE

After the annexation of Novgorod in 1478, not much remained of the independent political traditions stemming from medieval Kievan Rus. Ivan the Great and his successors continued on the path of "gathering" the rest of the Russian principalities, under the pretext of establishing a Third Rome. By 1480, Ivan had succeeded in pressuring all four of his younger brothers to relinquish to him the territories they had inherited from Vasily II. Ivan used as a pretext the instructions in the will that the younger brothers should follow his dictates as they would those of their father. In 1485, Ivan invaded and annexed neighboring Tver' without a major battle. In 1489, Vyatka was similarly annexed to Muscovy.

Ivan the Great died in 1505, leaving his son Vasily III to complete the work of incorporating appanage Russia into the new Muscovy state. Pskov, which shared with Novgorod a strong representative governmental tradition, was annexed in 1510. Smolensk fell under Vasily's

rule in 1514 and Ryazan' in 1521. While Western Europe headed forward toward transformation in its early modern period, the Russian state forged by Muscovy shifted into reverse gear, backing toward feudalism. What continued to the twentieth century, as the princes of Moscow became czars, was continued expansion within an autocratic tradition. The final death knell of old Novgorod came in 1570, when Vasily's successor, Ivan the Terrible, wreaked utter devastation and destroyed the remnants of the Novgorod boyar class.

—Irwin Halfond

FURTHER READING

Almedingen, E. M. *The Land of Muscovy: The History of Early Russia.* New York: Farrar, Straus, and Giroux, 1972. Basic and concise treatment of the expansion of Muscovite power.

Birnbaum, H. *Lord Novgorod the Great: Essays in the History and Culture of a Medieval City State.* Columbus, Ohio: Slavica Publications, 1981. A variety of scholarly essays on Novgorod's political development, economy, and culture.

Crummey, Robert O. *The Formation of Muscovy, 1304-1613.* London: Longman, 1987. A detailed study of Muscovite expansion and its consequences for Novgorod and other Russian principalities.

Grey, Ian. *Ivan III and the Unification of Russia.* New York: Macmillan, 1964. A somewhat jumpy but standard biographical study of the policies of the Machiavellian prince of Moscow who annexed Novgorod.

Martin, Janet L. *Medieval Russia, 980-1584.* New York: Cambridge University Press, 1995. A concise and clear explanation of Russian developments during the medieval period.

Riasanovsky, Nicholas V. *A History of Russia.* 6th ed. New York: Oxford University Press, 1999. Updated and still the standard starting point for themes and major events in Russia's development.

SEE ALSO: 1480-1502: Destruction of the Golden Horde; After 1480: Ivan the Great Organizes the "Third Rome"; 1499-c. 1600: Russo-Polish Wars; Jan. 16, 1547: Coronation of Ivan the Terrible; Summer, 1556: Ivan the Terrible Annexes Astrakhan; 1581-1597: Cossacks Seize Sibir; 1584-1613: Russia's Time of Troubles.

RELATED ARTICLES in *Great Lives from History: The Renaissance & Early Modern Era, 1454-1600:* Ivan the Great; Ivan the Terrible; Sophia Palaeologus; Vasily III.

1470's

1478-1482
ALBANIAN-TURKISH WARS END

After decades of resisting Ottoman attempts to defeat them, the Albanians were forced to capitulate to the Turkish invaders. The decisive end of Albanian independence came in 1482, and Ottoman rule prevailed over Albania for the next four and a half centuries.

LOCALE: Albania

CATEGORIES: Wars, uprisings, and civil unrest; expansion and land acquisition; diplomacy and international relations

KEY FIGURES

Skanderbeg (George Kastrioti; 1405-1468), leader of Albanian resistance

Isa Evrenos Bey (fl. fifteenth century), Ottoman commander of forces that invaded Albania

Mehmed II (1432-1481), Ottoman sultan, r. 1444-1446 and 1451-1481

Moïse Golem (fl. fifteenth century), an Albanian commander who defected in favor of the Ottomans

János Hunyadi (c. 1407-1456), Hungarian patriot leader

Hamza Kastrioti (fl. fifteenth century), governor of Krujë

SUMMARY OF EVENT

In 1453, when the Ottoman Empire prevailed over the Byzantine Empire, seizing the Byzantine capital of Constantinople, the Ottomans also were involved in an ongoing war with Albania that had begun a decade earlier and would last for another quarter century. Traditionally, northern Albania had been Christian and southern Albania had been Islamic.

The Turkish influence was so pervasive in Albania during the fifteenth century that the country was at times essentially subjugated by the Turks, who attempted to establish Albania as an Islamic nation. At this point, Pope Eugenius IV and influential ecclesiastical authorities from Naples and Venice intervened, helping the Albanians to resist the Turks and to scuttle their attempts to establish Islam as Albania's official religion.

Albania's national hero, born George Kastrioti, was given the name Skanderbeg when he served in the sultan's elite Janissary corps. This new name combined the name Skander (Alexander), reminiscent of Alexander the Great, to whom he was frequently compared, with the honorific title "beg," which was reserved for nobles.

When Skanderbeg defected from the Turkish army in 1443 and returned to Albania, he reverted to his earlier faith, Christianity, and thus made it the official religion of his domain. He gave his subjects two options: conversion to Christianity or execution. Through this move, Skanderbeg garnered substantial support, moral and financial, from Pope Eugenius IV as well as from Church leaders and members of the nobility in Naples and Venice. Both groups derived a princely income from their Albanian interests.

Between 1443 and 1461, when Skanderbeg led Albania into an open revolt against the Turks, the Turks launched thirteen major assaults upon Skanderbeg's forces in Albania but were rebuffed in most of them. In 1451, a force led by Sultan Murad II besieged Krujë for five months but could not take the town and retreated after King Alfonso V of Aragon (r. 1416-1458) and Naples (r. 1442-1458) came to Skanderbeg's assistance. After traveling to Naples attempting to gain assistance from his Christian allies, Skanderbeg received some additional help from Alfonso, who provided troops and ammunition to the Albanians in 1453.

More important, Skanderbeg helped to create a military alliance consisting of Albanians, Hungarians, and Serbians, which joined forces to resist the ravages of the invading Ottomans. This alliance gave Skanderbeg the forces he needed to attack the Ottomans, who were now sequestered in Berat. His troops assaulted the city relentlessly until the Ottomans were on the brink of surrender. At that point, however, Moïse Golem, a commander whose traitorous trickery made it possible for forty thousand Ottoman troops to attack Skanderbeg's coalition from the rear, created a situation in which Skanderbeg's forces faced defeat. This setback caused Alfonso to withhold further support from the Albanians.

The tide turned in Skanderbeg's favor in 1456, however, when Golem led an army of fifteen thousand Ottoman cavalrymen into Albania, where they were soundly defeated at Oranik by Skanderbeg's troops. The following year, the Turks made another assault on Albania, sending an estimated eighty thousand troops, led by the Ottoman commander, Isa Evrenos Bey, into lowland coastal Albania. The Ottomans captured most of the lowlands, only to be driven back by Skanderbeg's forces when Evrenos Bey's army approached Krujë, where Hamza Kastrioti had been appointed governor by the Turkish sultan.

In 1461, the warring factions agreed to a decade-long truce, designed to end nearly two decades of unrest and bloodshed. In 1463, however, Skanderbeg violated this truce and once again attacked the Turks, who, in 1466, under the son of Murad II, Sultan Mehmed II, conquered some of Albania but were unable to defeat Skanderbeg's forces at Krujë. Mehmed was determined to exterminate the Albanians, attacking Krujë with an army of 150,000. One month later, he deployed some of these troops elsewhere and put the remaining army under the command of Ballaban Pasha. The Albanians repulsed troops that were sent in April, 1467, to buttress the Ottoman army. Ballaban Pasha was killed. Mehmed, under great pressure to subdue the Albanians, then sent his entire army into Albania and won a devastating battle, after which his forces moved on to Krujë. After three weeks of fighting there, Mehmed's forces retreated, leaving Skanderbeg victorious.

On January 17, 1468, Skanderbeg died of a fever contracted the previous month. By now his forces, which were seriously overextended, had been severely weakened and were drastically underfinanced. His death thwarted his plan to have a meeting of nobles, scheduled for later in 1468 and designed to enlist more extensive aid.

Shortly before Skanderbeg's death, Pope Paul II, who supported a crusade against the Turks, declared him a "Champion of Christendom." His Albanian followers continued to fight the Turks for another decade, but their efforts proved futile because their opponents kept pressing into Albania. In 1478, the Turks conquered Shkodër (present-day Scutari), the last Albanian outpost to submit to them. This surrender essentially marked an end to the Albanian-Turkish Wars, although scattered resistance continued in the lowlands for another year.

In 1479, when Venice pulled its forces out of Albania, the Turks readily snuffed out most of the remaining Albanian resistance. Skanderbeg's son, John, still hoping to defeat the Turks, was driven out in 1482.

SIGNIFICANCE

The history of fifteenth century Albania reflects the remarkable ability of a small country—actually of several small feudal states—to hold off a compelling and well-established force. It is unlikely that Skanderbeg would ever have been able to return from Turkey to Krujë and to mobilize his forces had János Hunyadi, the celebrated Hungarian commander, not drawn Turkish forces into the conflict in the north, where a Turkish-Hungarian war was raging. At this point, the timing was perfect for Skanderbeg to return to Albania, defecting from the Turkish army, in which he fought brilliantly up to and including the Battle of Niš in 1443.

An early Balkan uprising, although unsuccessful, presaged the discontent of the Albanian people against Turkish rule. This discontent festered through much of the following decade, so that when Skanderbeg returned to Krujë late in 1443 to reaffirm his Christianity and to claim leadership in the feudal state that his family had ruled for many decades, the populace very much needed a leader who could free them from the oppression and exploitation of Turkish rule. Skanderbeg was such a leader, but Albania faced overwhelming odds that, in the end, resulted in its capitulation to the powerful Turks, who gained control in 1478 and retained it until the early twentieth century.

Skanderbeg's son, John, still hoping to shake loose from Turkish rule, lingered in Albania until 1482. Fearing assassination, he left Albania and sought safe haven in Italy. His departure quite definitively established that the fight for Albanian independence had been lost.

—*R. Baird Shuman*

FURTHER READING

Chekrezi, Constantine A. *Albania Past and Present*. 1919. Reprint. New York: Arno Press, 1971. Chekrezi offers a brief overview of Skanderbeg's life and achievements.

Giaffo, Lou. *Albania: Eye of the Balkan Vortex*. Princeton, N.J.: Xlibris, 1999. A worthwhile discussion of Skanderbeg and his contributions to Albanian history.

Hutchings, Raymond. *Historical Dictionary of Albania*. Lanham, Md.: Scarecrow Press, 1996. A splendid overall resource with a detailed entry on Skanderbeg and a shorter but valuable entry on Albanian-Turkish relations.

Imber, Colin. *The Ottoman Empire, 1300-1650: The Structure of Power*. New York: Macmillan, 2002. Includes a number of references to the conflicts between the Turks and the Albanians and to the involvement of the Ottoman sultans Mehmed I and Murad II in gaining control of Albania.

Jacques, Edwin E. *The Albanians: An Ethnic History from Prehistoric Times to the Present*. Jefferson, N.C.: McFarland, 1975. The most comprehensive overall history of Albania. Strongly recommended.

Somel, Selcuk Aksin. *Historical Dictionary of the Ottoman Empire*. Lanham, Md.: Scarecrow Press, 2003. Contains a brief but informative entry on Albania. Also provides useful information about the Ottoman sultans who tried to impose Turkish rule on Albania.

1470's

Vickers, Miranda. *The Albanians: A Modern History.* Rev. ed. New York: I. B. Tauris, 1997. Concentrates largely on recent Albanian history, but offers illuminating and accessible background material on the Albanian-Turkish conflicts of the fifteenth century.

SEE ALSO: 1454-1481: Rise of the Ottoman Empire; Apr. 14, 1457-July 2, 1504: Reign of Stephen the Great; 1481-1512: Reign of Bayezid II and Ottoman Civil Wars; June 28, 1522-Dec. 27, 1522: Siege and Fall of Rhodes; 1526-1547: Hungarian Civil Wars; Aug. 29, 1526: Battle of Mohács; 1534-1535: Ottomans Claim Sovereignty over Mesopotamia; 1566-1574: Reign of Selim II; 1593-1606: Ottoman-Austrian War.

RELATED ARTICLES in *Great Lives from History: The Renaissance & Early Modern Era, 1454-1600:* Bayezid II; Mehmed II; Süleyman the Magnificent.

---

c. 1478-1519
LEONARDO DA VINCI COMPILES HIS NOTEBOOKS

Initially trained as an artist, Leonardo also compiled notebooks filled with thousands of pages of his drawings and descriptions of a number of scientific, mechanical, and technical subjects.

LOCALE: Florence, Milan, and Rome (now in Italy)
CATEGORIES: Science and technology; astronomy; cultural and intellectual history; engineering; health and medicine; mathematics; physics

KEY FIGURES
Leonardo da Vinci (1452-1519), Italian artist and inventor
Francesco Melzi (1493-1570), Italian artist who inherited Leonardo's notebooks
Andrea del Verrocchio (1435-1488), Italian painter in whose workshop Leonardo first trained
Ludovico Sforza (Il Moro; 1452-1508), duke of Milan, r. 1481-1499, and patron of Leonardo

SUMMARY OF EVENT
The notebooks of Leonardo da Vinci, never published during his lifetime, filled some thirteen thousand pages. Leonardo had bequeathed the work to his constant companion, artist Francesco Melzi, who, in turn, bequeathed them to his son, Orazio. As Orazio had no interest in the notebooks, he gave many away. *The Literary Works of Leonardo da Vinci*, containing translations of selections from the notebooks, was published in English in 1883.

An estimated seven thousand pages are known to exist, dispersed throughout France, Italy, Spain, England, and in private collections. In 1994, Microsoft Corporation founder and chairman, Bill Gates, bought the most famous collection, the Codex Hammer, restored to its traditional name, the Codex Leicester. The notebooks were fragmentary in nature and were not composed in any systematic manner. Leonardo often returned to a subject, making some passages contradict each other. The notebooks reveal that he mastered the ideas of predecessors, dating to antiquity where relevant. Often he invented new terminology.

Leonardo da Vinci was born on April 15, 1452, the illegitimate son of Piero da Vinci, a notary, and a peasant woman known only as Caterina. Because the Italian middle classes of the fifteenth century ostracized those born out of wedlock, Leonardo could not attend a university or enter a profession such as medicine or law. He demonstrated talent in music and art as a child, so his father in 1465 or 1466 apprenticed him to the famed Florentine artist Andrea del Verrocchio. Upon concluding his artistic apprenticeship in 1478, Leonardo embarked on a lifelong program of self-education. While many classical authors were accessible in Italian translations, Leonardo lacked knowledge of Latin, the language of most scientific works. He taught himself the language in the late 1480's, and though he never fully mastered it, he used it to report his discoveries.

During his early days in Verrocchio's workshop, Leonardo developed an interest in engineering and practical mechanical problems. He became an independent artist in 1478, the approximate date of the first folios of the scientific and mechanical studies collected into the various notebooks.

During his lifetime, Leonardo enjoyed the reputation of both engineer and artist. The earliest notebooks reflected two main interests: military technology and the study of acoustics and design of musical instruments. His early sketches include improvements on musical instruments and their odd combinations. No model or finished instrument exists, however.

Having gained familiarity with bronzecasting in

Verrocchio's studio, Leonardo drew up elaborate technical plans to cast a huge horse for a monument for his patron, Ludovico Sforza in Milan. The early notebooks contain sketches of cannons, an armored tanklike vehicle, automated and labor-saving devices such as a military drum with six automatically controlled sticks, machines to pump water to lay siege to towers, and an underwater breathing apparatus.

During his association with Sforza (between 1483 and 1499), he sketched a parachute, pumps, irrigation systems, and digging machinery. Later, he drew various flying machines, among which was a helicopter-like contraption. Numerous drawings of gears also exist, reflecting his response to one of the greatest problems of contemporary technology: friction and the loss of efficiency due to inadequate construction. He devised clever equipment, including friction banks, conducted experiments, and derived several still-valid principles of friction. His interest in economy and practical efficiency led him to conceive devices that would reduce friction, including worm gears and ball bearings.

The notebooks that were written during the 1490's also reveal the development of a holistic view of nature; Leonardo's study of optics is an example. As an artist, he was interested in vision and light and in shadows and colors, and as a scholar, he was familiar with classical and medieval theories of light and vision, including the traditional explanation that the eye gave off light. He joined an interest in water behavior with light to propose a wave theory of light, analogous to the propagation of transverse waves generated by dropping pebbles in water. He proposed that sound was a wave phenomenon and speculated that waves could also explain smell.

In his earliest anatomical investigations, Leonardo dissected the eye and may have been the first to understand the function of its lens. In turn, he related the eye to the camera obscura and then drew a sketch of a projector.

Whereas a few anatomical drawings date from his earlier notebooks, Leonardo probably had few opportunities to do actual dissections until perhaps the first decade of the sixteenth century. By mid-decade, he claimed to have dissected ten human bodies, and in 1507 he performed a postmortem on a man who had claimed to be one hundred years old. His drawings of humans sometimes included animal parts, such as the cow cotyledons depicted

on the human uterus. His drawing of the fetus is quite accurate, as is his osteology (descriptions of bones) and myology (studies of muscles).

Leonardo approached anatomy from the viewpoint of engineering; the bones were levers and the attached muscles represented the lines of forces acting on them. He analyzed complex motions such as supination and pronation and correctly illustrated them.

Leonardo made some admirable contributions to anatomical method. For example, he devised an ingenious method to study the brain: He filled the ventricles of the brain with wax to preserve their shape. Moreover, he introduced to anatomy the techniques of representing structures from different aspects and of displaying cross-sections. At first, Leonardo accepted Aristotle's physiol-

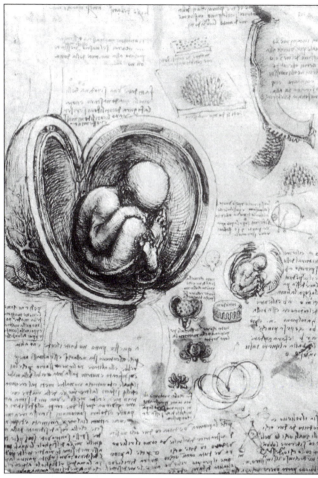

Leonardo da Vinci's notebooks were filled not only with drawings of and commentaries on machines but also sketches of the workings of the human body, including this detail of a womb and fetus. (Royal Library, Windsor Castle)

121

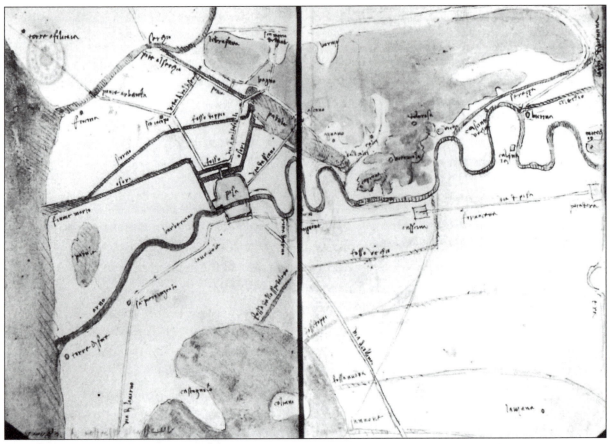

Leonardo sketched a map of the city of Pisa for his grand-scale plan to divert the city's Arno River. (Burndy Library)

ogy, then Galen's, and, at the end of his life, moved beyond the ancient views. Leonardo also did comparative anatomy.

Manuscripts on mechanics reveal that Leonardo had absorbed medieval works on levers. He worked with the bent-lever law and extended it. His mechanical writings included considerations of tensions of weighted cord segments; the problem of the center of gravity of systems of bodies in equilibrium, such as suspended beams with attached weights; and the problem of the determination of the center of gravity of solids. Other topics included hydrostatics and theories of violent and inertial motion based on the medieval concept of impetus. His ideas on motion informed his conception of life, which he defined as a form of motion. He also studied percussion, which along with movement, weight, and force comprised the four powers of nature.

Botany, perspective, physiognomy, and the science of water also received Leonardo's attention. In the science of water, Leonardo was involved in a plan to divert the

Arno River to facilitate communication between Pisa and Florence.

SIGNIFICANCE

As Leonardo did not publish any material from his scientific, mechanical, and technical notebooks, he cannot be said to have exerted a major influence on the development of science. To his credit, however, his notebooks are representative of what could be known during his time. The extensive discussions of technology and the drawings representing his inventions (few of which were ever built) indicate the state of technology during his lifetime and illustrate its theoretical problems and problems of applicability.

Moreover, he represented the growing awareness of the importance of mathematics in understanding the physical world, recalling astronomer Galileo Galilei's much-later dictum—"the book of nature is written in mathematics." Leonardo's ideas still reflected classical and medieval learning, however, as, for example, in his

Leonardo da Vinci Compiles His Notebooks

acceptance of the microcosm-macrocosm analogy. His practice of performing experiments and dissections anticipated the methods employed more systematically in the later successful investigations of Galileo and of the anatomist Andreas Vesalius.

Leonardo's goals reflected the nature of a Renaissance figure who wanted to understand natural causes and effects and to use that knowledge to control nature. In the end, his science is a complicated blend of inherited knowledge, imaginative speculation, intense inquiry and discussion, observation, and experimentation.

—*Kristen L. Zacharias*

FURTHER READING

Ahl, Diane Cole, ed. *Leonardo da Vinci's Sforza Monument Horse: The Art and the Engineering*. Bethlehem: Lehigh University Press and Associated University Presses, 1995. An account of the reciprocal influence of Leonardo's artistic and technical interests as illustrated by plans for a huge equestrian monument, the model of which was greatly admired though never cast.

Farago, Claire, ed. *Leonardo's Science and Technology: Essential Readings for the Non-Scientist*. New York: Garland, 1999. A collection of previously published articles on Leonardo's theory of vision and pictorial perspective, and on his work in physiognomy, anatomy, botany, water science, and technology.

Leonardo da Vinci. *The Notebooks of Leonardo da Vinci*. Edited by Irma Richter. 1939. New ed. New York: Oxford University Press, 1980. The best succinct introduction to the wealth of material contained in Leonardo's notebooks. This text was originally published in 1883 as *The Literary Works of Leonardo da Vinci* and was edited by Jean Paul Richter.

Letze, Otto, and Thomas Buchsteiner, eds. *Leonardo da Vinci: Scientist, Inventor, Artist*. Ostfildern-Rit, Germany: Gerd Hatje, 1997. The catalog for an exhibition on Leonardo da Vinci in Germany with sumptuous copies of painting and pages from the notebooks, along with brief discussions and an outline of his life.

MacCurdy, Edward. *The Notebooks of Leonardo da Vinci*. New York: George Braziller, 1939. A massive translation of the texts of about five thousand folio pages, which includes biographical information about Leonardo and a history of the notebooks.

O'Malley, Charles D., and J. B. de C. M. Saunders. *Leonardo da Vinci on the Human Body: The Anatomical, Physiological, and Embryological Drawings of Leonardo da Vinci*. New York: Henry Schuman, 1952. An extensive presentation of Leonardo's anatomical drawings with translations of the accompanying descriptions.

White, Michael. *Leonardo: The First Scientist*. New York: St. Martin's Press, 2000. A nontechnical biography focusing on Leonardo's scientific and technical notebooks and details of his personal life.

SEE ALSO: 1495-1497: Leonardo da Vinci Paints *The Last Supper*; 1543: Copernicus Publishes *De Revolutionibus*; 1543: Vesalius Publishes *On the Fabric of the Human Body*; 1553: Servetus Describes the Circulatory System; 1572-1574: Tycho Brahe Observes a Supernova; 1580's-1590's: Galileo Conducts His Early Experiments; 1582: Gregory XIII Reforms the Calendar; 1600: William Gilbert Publishes *De Magnete*.

RELATED ARTICLES in *Great Lives from History: The Renaissance & Early Modern Era, 1454-1600*: Andrea del Sarto; Sophie Brahe; Tycho Brahe; Donato Bramante; Giordano Bruno; Nicolaus Copernicus; Correggio; Francis I; William Gilbert; Giorgione; Leonardo da Vinci; Michelangelo; Raphael; Michael Servetus; Ludovico Sforza; Simon Stevin; Giorgio Vasari; Andrea del Verrocchio; Andreas Vesalius.

1470's

April 26, 1478
PAZZI CONSPIRACY

A plot to assassinate both Lorenzo and Giuliano de' Medici in the Florentine cathedral on Easter Sunday led to violent retaliation against the Pazzi family and their coconspirators.

LOCALE: Florence (now in Italy)
CATEGORIES: Terrorism and political assassination; government and politics

KEY FIGURES

Lorenzo de' Medici (1449-1492), ruler of Florence, r. 1469-1492
Giuliano de' Medici (1453-1478), ruler of Florence, r. 1469-1478
Sixtus IV (Francesco della Rovere; 1414-1484), Roman Catholic pope, 1471-1484
Francesco Salviati (1443-1478), archbishop of Pisa, 1474-1478
Girolamo Riario (1443-1488), lord of Imola and Forli', r. 1477-1488
Francesco de' Pazzi (1444-1478), head of the Pazzi bank in Rome
Bernardo Bandini Baroncelli (d. 1478), Pazzi coconspirator

SUMMARY OF EVENT

In the fifteenth century, Florence, along with Milan, Venice, the Papal States, and the Kingdom of Naples, was one of the five centers of power in Italy. Smaller Tuscan city-states such as San Gimignano, Siena, Pisa, and Lucca were essentially controlled by Florence. Although Florence had long been a republic, wealthy families like the Medici ran the government without actually holding political office.

During the fifteenth century, Florence enjoyed great economic growth in trade and finance and became a center of political, economic, educational, and artistic influence. Both Cosimo de' Medici (1389-1464) and his grandson, Lorenzo de' Medici, were Humanists and patrons of the arts. Artists such as Fra Angelico (c. 1400-1455) and Michelangelo (1475-1564) flourished under their patronage. One of the highlights of Florentine Humanism was the founding of the Platonic Academy in 1462 by Marsilio Ficino (1433-1499), supported by both Cosimo and Lorenzo.

After Cosimo's death, the Medici family essentially ran the government of Florence. They did this by carefully balancing their friends and their enemies and by curtailing the power of rival families, like the Pazzi. The Pazzi were a noble Florentine family, older than the Medici. They were well respected and wealthy with banking and merchant holdings all over Europe. Threatened by the potential power of the Pazzi, Lorenzo de' Medici took repeated measures to thwart the family's quest for power.

The Pazzi, frustrated and angry, retaliated financially and politically by courting and winning the favor of Pope Sixtus IV. The pope had his own grudge against the Medici. He would have liked to see Lorenzo out of Florence so that he could elevate his nephew Girolamo Riario to power. Furthermore, Sixtus was angry over Lorenzo's failure to support the pope's purchase of the city of Imola for Riario. Consequently, Sixtus canceled most of the financial arrangements he had with the Medici bank, transferred most of the papal monies to the Pazzi, and bought Imola with a loan from the Pazzi. Sixtus further insulted the Medici by appointing Francesco Salviati to the archbishopric of Pisa in 1474 without the approval of Florence. These events laid the foundation for the murder in the cathedral.

The chief conspirators, Francesco de' Pazzi, Riario, and Salviati, with the tacit approval of Sixtus, persuaded the older Jacopo de' Pazzi to assent to the plot. They planned to kill both Lorenzo and Giuliano de' Medici at lunch in the Medici Palazzo after Sunday Mass on April 26, 1478. When it was learned that Giuliano would not attend, however, the plotters quickly decided that the deed would take place during mass in the great Florentine cathedral.

A new problem arose when Giovan Battista, the count of Montesecco, a mercenary assigned to kill Lorenzo, refused to commit murder in a sacred space. Instead two priests, apparently with fewer scruples, willingly took his place. Another obstacle soon arose and almost thwarted the plot. Giuliano was not in the cathedral; suffering with a bad leg, he had remained at home. Two conspirators, Francesco de' Pazzi and Bernardo Bandini Baroncelli, were sent to convince him to attend. Walking arm and arm with Giuliano along Via Larga, Francesco de' Pazzi used the opportunity to put his arm around Giuliano in friendship and determine that Giuliano was unarmed.

During one of the most sacred moments of the mass, perhaps the elevation of the host, the attack began. Giuliano died quickly, stabbed nineteen times and so frantically by Francesco de' Pazzi that Pazzi suffered a knife wound in his own leg. Lorenzo escaped with only a neck wound. Archbishop Salviati's simultaneous plan to take over the Palazzo Vecchio, the seat of government, failed, in part because of the suspicion and quick response of the *ganfaloniere*, Cesare Petrucci. The Pazzi assumed the citizens of Florence would support them. Instead, when the bells of the city rang, the citizens ran to the Piazza, ignored Jacopo's cry of "People and liberty!" and rallied around the Medici, shouting "palle, palle," referring to the balls emblazoned on the Medici coat of arms.

The retaliation against the conspirators was swift and brutal. Francesco de' Pazzi was ignominiously hanged naked from the Palazzo Vecchio; alongside him hung the archbishop. Throughout the day, people were hanged, either from the Palazzo Vecchio or the Bargello, fortress of the police. The two priests were castrated and then hanged. Many bodies were thrown into the Piazza Signoria or cut down after being hanged and then stripped and hacked. For days, people marched around with body parts. In a macabre incident, the body of Jacopo de' Pazzi was exhumed three weeks after his death and dragged around the city by the very rope with which he had been hanged. His body was eventually thrown into the river Arno. Montesecco, after giving a confession, was allowed to be beheaded rather than suffer the humiliation of being hanged.

By the end of the first day, more than sixty people had been killed, and before the revenge ended, two hundred had been executed. Baroncelli had escaped, but he was tracked down in Constantinople and returned by the sultan to be hanged out of the window of the Bargello. As a reminder of the plot, Lorenzo commissioned the painter Sandro Botticelli to paint the figures of the conspirators as they hung. Lorenzo wrote a versed epitaph to accompany each picture. These were publicly displayed until 1494, when the Medici were exiled from Florence and the paintings were destroyed.

The houses of the Pazzi and Salviati were sacked. The wealth of the Pazzi was seized, and the Medici and the government of Florence passed laws to obliterate the Pazzi family. All remaining Pazzi had to change their names and their coats of arms. All symbols of the Pazzi, such as their sign of the dolphin, were removed from Florence. The Pazzi name was removed from the tax records. Any man who married a Pazzi woman was discredited. Furthermore, the remaining Pazzi men were imprisoned in Volterra.

Lorenzo de' Medici weathered the attack and strengthened his position, particularly by traveling to Naples in 1479. After ten weeks, he negotiated an end to hostilities with the pope and Ferdinand I of Naples, hostilities that had resulted from the failed conspiracy. He was only twenty-nine years old at the time. Lorenzo continued to control Florence until his death in 1492, always surrounded by an armed guard. Eventually, he let the Pazzi women marry. He also released the Pazzi men from prison in Volterra; however, they had to live outside Florentine territory. He worked to maintain peace until he died and had such great influence with Sixtus's successor, Pope Innocent VIII, that some felt he directed the policies of Rome. He continued his Humanist activities and his patronage of the arts and letters, attracting men of learning to Florence, thereby ensuring that the city continued to flourish as a center for the arts.

Two years after Lorenzo's death, his son Piero, unable to hold on to Florence in the face of a threatened invasion by France, fled the city. It was at this moment that the republic was reinstalled, in part encouraged by Girolamo Savonarola (1452-1498), who had originally been in-

---

MACHIAVELLI ON THE INEPT ASSASSINS

Despite striking at him many times, the men charged with killing Lorenzo de' Medici landed only one blow, wounding him lightly in the neck. These failed assassins had been chosen at the last minute to replace a more able man who had experienced a change of heart. In this passage from his Florentine Histories, *contemporary chronicler Niccolò Machiavelli discusses this last-minute substitution.*

Giovan Battista refused to consider [killing Lorenzo de' Medici in the cathedral]; he said he would never have enough spirit to commit such an excess in church and accompany betrayal with sacrilege. This was the beginning of the ruin of [the conspirators'] enterprise, because, since time was pressing, of necessity they had to give this task to Messer Antonio da Volterra and to the priest Stephano, two men who by practice and by nature were very inept for so great an undertaking. For if ever any deed requires a great and firm spirit made resolute in both life and death through much experience, it is necessary to have it in this, where it has been seen very many times that men skilled in arms and soaked in blood have lacked spirit.

Source: From *Florentine Histories*, by Niccolò Machiavelli. Translated by Laura F. Banfield and Harvey C. Mansfield, Jr. (Princeton, N.J.: Princeton University Press, 1988), pp. 322-323.

vited to Florence by Lorenzo in 1489. From his pulpit in the church of San Marco, Savonarola preached against the excesses of Florence and the Medici while also arguing for a republic. With Lorenzo's forceful hold on Florence gone, Savonarola's wishes were realized. He held great sway over the city, but he himself was burned at the stake in 1498 when the Medici once again returned to power.

SIGNIFICANCE

The Pazzi Conspiracy revealed the power that the Medici had over Florence and its territories, most particularly under Cosimo and Lorenzo. The anger that fueled the conspiracy and sparked the Pazzi and their allies to try to overthrow Medici control was shared by many in Italy. However, the aftermath of the conspiracy and the Medici family's return to power in 1498 revealed that the family had the intellectual, political, and financial resources to control Florence for many years to come.

—*Bella Mirabella*

FURTHER READING

Acton, Harold. *The Pazzi Conspiracy: The Plot Against the Medici.* London: Thames and Hudson, 1979. Concise history of the conspiracy including preceding history and aftermath.

Connell, William J. *Society and Individual in Renaissance Florence.* Berkeley: University of California Press, 2000. Collection of essays that considers the role of the individual in the Renaissance, including the merchant elite of Florence.

Hibbert, Christopher. *The House of the Medici: Its Rise and Fall.* New York: William and Morrow, 1974. Thorough history of the Medici family with careful consideration of Lorenzo and the conspiracy.

Machiavelli, Niccolò. *Florentine Histories.* Translated by L. F. Banfield and H. C. Mansfield. Princeton, N.J.: Princeton University Press, 1988. Contemporary narrative of the events, originally published in 1532.

Martines, Lauro. *April Blood: Florence and the Plot Against the Medici.* New York: Oxford University Press, 2003. Thorough history and analysis of the conspiracy with new material.

SEE ALSO: Apr. 9, 1454: Peace of Lodi; 1462: Founding of the Platonic Academy; 1469-1492: Rule of Lorenzo de' Medici; Sept., 1494-Oct., 1495: Charles VIII of France Invades Italy; July-Dec., 1513: Machiavelli Writes *The Prince.*

RELATED ARTICLES in *Great Lives from History: The Renaissance & Early Modern Era, 1454-1600:* Lorenzo de' Medici; Girolamo Savonarola; Sixtus IV.

November 1, 1478
ESTABLISHMENT OF THE SPANISH INQUISITION

The Spanish Inquisition permitted the Catholic Church and its inquisitors to prosecute converted Jews suspected of heresy, but it soon expanded to enforce orthodoxy by pursuing converted Muslims, alleged witches, Protestants, and others within Spain for more than three hundred years.

LOCALE: Castile, Aragon, and other Iberian kingdoms (now Spain)

CATEGORIES: Religion; organizations and institutions; government and politics; laws, acts, and legal history

KEY FIGURES

Tomás de Torquemada (1420-1498), Dominican priest and leading inquisitor

Sixtus IV (Francesco della Rovere; 1414-1484), Roman Catholic pope, 1471-1484

Alonso de Espina (d. 1469), Franciscan priest and anti-Semitic writer

Ferdinand V (1452-1516), king of Castile, r. 1474-1504, and king of Aragon as Ferdinand II, r. 1479-1516

Henry IV of Castile (1425-1474), king of Castile, r. 1454-1474

Isabella I (1451-1504), queen of Castile, r. 1474-1504

SUMMARY OF EVENT

The term "inquisition" denotes the judicial persecution of heretics by special Church courts. The Spanish Inquisition differed from other such tribunals in that it was directly under the authority of the Crown, but it was not the first inquisition to operate in Spain. Although no medieval inquisition was ever organized in the kingdom of Castile, one had been founded in the kingdom of Aragon in 1233 to combat the Catharist religion centered in neighboring France. By the fourteenth century, few traces of heresy remained among Iberian Christians, and since the inquisition had no jurisdiction over unbaptized Jews

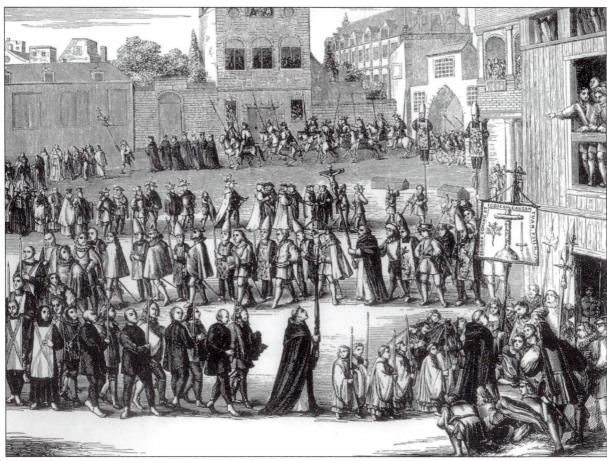

An engraved depiction of an auto-da-fé *procession—a public condemnation of the accused—in Spain.* (Frederick Ungar Publishing Co.)

and Muslims, it almost ceased to function. In its place, Spain's crusading Christians focused on the reconquest (Reconquista) of southern regions still occupied by Muslims.

While Jews were expelled from England in 1290 and from France in 1306, they were allowed limited rights to reside in Spain until 1492. When Jewish communities grew and prospered, however, anti-Semitism became increasingly widespread. After Barcelona and other cities experienced terrible pogroms in 1391, thousands of Jews were forced to convert to Christianity, to be called *conversos* (converts), "New Christians," or *marranos* (pigs). By the middle of the fifteenth century, there were approximately 250,000 *conversos* in Spain, and many succeeded in occupying important positions in government and business, leading to bitter resentment by "Old Christians."

Following their baptisms, *conversos* often continued to adhere to food taboos and other Hebrew traditions alien to Spanish culture, and Old Christians tended to suspect that they were also guilty of secretive Judaizing heresies. The more ethnocentric Spaniards even believed that Jews constituted a separate race, and that their "impure blood" made it impossible for them to become good Christians. In the city of Toledo in 1449, there was a violent anti-*converso* riot, leading to a harsh ordinance, a *Sentencia-Estatuto*, which limited severely the political and economic rights of all *conversos*, whatever their postbaptismal behavior. Although the king of Castile and the pope prevented the ordinance from being enforced, it continued to have widespread support by the public.

In the 1460's, conservative Spanish churchmen, both despising and fearing the *conversos*, agitated to convince King Henry IV of Castile to establish an inquisition for Castile. Alonso de Espina's large treatise, *Fortalitium fidei* (1460), warned of contamination by heresies of all kinds, but concentrated on the *converso* threat with the racist argument.

Alonso de Oropesa, prior of the Order of St. Jerome, also called for an inquisition, but without Espina's racism. Henry was persuaded, and after unsuccessfully appealing to the pope to authorize an inquisition, he organized a panel of bishops in Toledo in 1463 to investigate charges of heresy.

With Henry's death in 1474, Castile's new monarchs, Ferdinand II and Isabella I, were fervent crusaders and nationalists, and they also wished to discredit Henry, who had been considered lax in combating heresy and its evils. Beginning in 1475, one of their first acts was to reactivate the inquisition that was already established in their royal domain of Sicily. During the early years of their reign, they were probably influenced by Isabella's personal confessor, Tomás de Torquemada, a Dominican friar obsessed with the goal of eradicating unorthodox beliefs and practices.

In 1477, the young Queen Isabella visited the city of Seville, where she heard a sermon by another crusading Dominican, Alonso de Hojeda, who claimed to have discovered a circle of Judaizing *conversos*. Isabella appointed investigators, and they confirmed Hojeda's charges. Armed with this new evidence, the "Catholic Monarchs" requested a papal bull to establish an inquisition in Castile. Apparently, the monarchs acted from several motivations: They wanted to save souls from condemnation, to promote religious conformity, to centralize their political control, to appease public prejudices, and also to raise funds.

On November 1, 1478, Pope Sixtus IV issued a bull that authorized the monarchs of "genuine devotion and sound faith" to appoint two or three "God-fearing" priests as inquisitors. At first, Sixtus expected that the Church would exercise its traditional control over the Inquisition, but Ferdinand and Isabella quickly declared that the Holy Tribunal was a royal institution, meaning that confiscated property would be seized by the Crown.

The monarchs permitted a two-year warning period before appointing three Dominicans as inquisitors, but then the tribunals energetically began their work. In 1481, inquisitors claimed to have uncovered a *converso* plot to take up arms in Seville, and trials resulted in the first large public condemnation, known as an *auto-da-fé*, or act of faith. Within a year, more than two hundred *conversos* had been turned over to the secular government to be burned alive, while hundreds more were given severe penalties, including various combinations of imprisonment, public floggings, wearing the *sanbenito* (sackcloth coat), and confiscation of property. Impressed by the popularity of the public punishments, Ferdinand quietly reorganized and reactivated the Inquisition within his kingdom of Aragon.

In 1482, after Pope Sixtus and Ferdinand briefly disagreed about the harsh methods being used against the *conversos*, the pope, recognizing his need for Spanish support, agreed to the appointment of eight more inquisitors, and granted the two monarchs permission to conduct the tribunals as they saw fit. The following year Sixtus accepted appointment of the infamous Torquemada as inquisitor-general of Castile. In 1487, Pope Innocent VIII expanded Torquemada's jurisdiction to include all of Spain.

Within the first decade under Torquemada's direction, Spain's Inquisition gave death penalties to about two thousand people (who were mostly *conversos*). Although these proceedings have often been criticized for their widespread use of torture, undisclosed accusations, secret witnesses, and absence of counsel, such procedures were not essentially different from those used by other ecclesiastical inquisitions or by many secular courts at the time.

A HANDBOOK FOR INQUISITORS

The prisons of the Spanish Inquisition are described in a "handbook" by Inquisitor General Tomás de Torquemada called Compilación de las Instrucciones del Oficio de la S. Inquisición *(wr. late 1400's, pb. 1667), which initially included twenty-eight articles, or directives.*

The prisons of the Inquisition—which, with the instruments of torture, still exist in some cities in Spain, as in Saragossa—were small, dark, damp apartments, often underground. The food of the captives, furnished at their own cost, was both meager and poor; and their only beverage was water. Complaining aloud, crying, or whimpering was rigorously repressed. The punishment inflicted by the Inquisition was imprisonment, either for a stated time or for life, or death by fire. If impenitent the condemned was tied to the stake and burned alive; if penitent he was strangled before being placed on the pile. Flight was considered equivalent to a confession or to a relapse (*relapso*) to Judaism. The property of the fugitive was confiscated, and he himself was burned in effigy.

Source: The Jewish Encyclopedia: A Descriptive Record of the History, Religion, Literature, and Customs of the Jewish People from the Earliest Times to the Present Day, edited by Cyrus Adler et al. (New York: Funk & Wagnalls, 1903-1906), p. 591.

SIGNIFICANCE

Originally founded to find and punish *conversos* who were not truly converted, by the turn of the century the Spanish Inquisition also began to examine the orthodoxy of Moriscos (Muslims who had converted to Christianity). During the sixteenth century, the Inquisition expanded its interests to campaign against Erasmian humanism, Protestantism, witchcraft, unorthodox books, and forbidden practices such as polygamy and homosexuality. While the Spanish Inquisition's influence declined after the seventeenth century, it continued to issue death penalties as late as 1780 and was not abolished until 1834. Throughout this long history, the best evidence indicates that the Inquisition condemned approximately three thousand people to be burned at the stake and also rendered about fifty thousand harsh penalties.

—*Thomas Tandy Lewis*

The Spanish Inquisition was notorious for its brutal torture of the accused, including strapping a person to a rotating wheel with fire below to exact a confession. Monks would stand to the side to record the confession, if it came. (Hulton|Archive by Getty Images)

FURTHER READING

Anderson, James M. *Daily Life During the Spanish Inquisition*. Westport, Conn.: Greenwood Press, 2002. Part of the Daily Life Through History series, this book surveys the effects of the Inquisition on every aspect of mundane existence, from the royal court to rural farming communities, from military life to the daily experience of students. Includes illustrations, bibliographic references, and index.

Baer, Yitzhak. *A History of the Jews in Christian Spain*. Vol. 2. Translated by Louis Schoffman. Philadelphia: Jewish Publishing Society, 1966. Provides a balanced account of how the Inquisition affected the Jewish and *converso* communities.

Edwards, John. *The Spanish Inquisition*. Stroud, Gloucestershire, England: Tempus, 1999. Analysis of the motivations behind the Inquisition, its political and religious functions, and its cost in lives and suffering. Includes photographic plates, illustrations, maps, bibliographic references, and index.

Kamen, Henry. *The Spanish Inquisition: A Historical Revision*. New Haven, Conn.: Yale University Press, 1998. A follow-up to Kamen's previous work. Attempts to argue that the Inquisition was neither as widely accepted nor as cruel as is generally believed. While accepting the judgment that the Inquisition had disastrous and brutal effects upon the Jewish population, Kamen argues that it was not an all-powerful instrument of terror and domination, and that other nations of the time in fact used torture more frequently and malevolently. Includes illustrations, maps, bibliographic references, and index.

Lea, Henry Charles. *The Moriscos of Spain: Their Conversion and Expulsion*. New Delhi, India: Goodword Books, 2002. Analyzes the lives of the converted Muslims (Moriscos) in Spain during the Inquisition, up to the early seventeenth century. Recommended reading.

Liss, Peggy. *Isabel the Queen: Life and Times*. New York: Oxford University Press, 1992. A sympathetic biography with chapter 10 devoted to the queen's role in the Inquisition.

Llorente, Juan Antonio. *A Critical History of the Inquisition in Spain*. Reprint. Williamstown, N.Y.: John Lilburne, 1967. Classic work of 1818, written by a former inquisitor using original archives. Llorente's numbers are now considered inflated.

1470's

Netanyahu, Benzion. *The Origins of the Inquisition in Fifteenth Century Spain*. 2d ed. New York: New York Review Books, 2001. A scholarly, massive, and one-sided concentration on the anti-Semitism of the Inquisition, with the questionable thesis that almost no *conversos* remained loyal to the Jewish faith.

Peters, Edward. *Inquisition*. New York: Free Press, 1988. The best relatively brief history of all major inquisitions from the thirteenth century, with an excellent discussion of sources and interpretations. Highly recommended.

Roth, Norman. *Conversos, Inquisition, and the Expulsion of the Jews from Spain*. Madison: University of Wisconsin Press, 2002. A study of the experience of Jews under the Inquisition, especially those who attempted to convert to Catholicism. Includes bibliographic references and index.

Whitechapel, Simon. *Flesh Inferno: Atrocities of Torquemada and the Spanish Inquisition*. London: Creation, 2003. A somewhat sensational and one-sided but informative portrayal of Torquemada and the horrors of the Inquisition. Includes bibliographic references.

SEE ALSO: Oct. 19, 1469: Marriage of Ferdinand and Isabella; 1473-1600: Witch-Hunts and Witch Trials; 1492: Jews Are Expelled from Spain; Beginning c. 1495: Reform of the Spanish Church; Aug. 15, 1534: Founding of the Jesuit Order.

RELATED ARTICLES in *Great Lives from History: The Renaissance & Early Modern Era, 1454-1600:* Ferdinand II and Isabella I; Henry IV of Castile; Francisco Jiménez de Cisneros; John III; Sixtus IV; Tomás de Torquemada.

1480-1502
DESTRUCTION OF THE GOLDEN HORDE

The destruction of the Golden Horde marked the emergence of Russia as a unified European political entity. Russia's newfound freedom from the dominance of the Mongol khans enabled it to grow in both strength and territory, becoming an important power.

LOCALE: Russia

CATEGORIES: Expansion and land acquisition; wars, uprisings, and civil unrest

KEY FIGURES

Ivan the Great (1440-1505), grand prince of Moscow and czar of Russia, r. 1462-1505

Aḥmad (d. 1481), khan of the Golden Horde, r. c. 1465-1481

Mengli Giray (c. 1440-1515), khan of the Crimean Tatars, r. c. 1468-1515, and ally of Ivan

Dmitry Donskoy (1350-1389), prince of Moscow, r. 1359-1389, and grand duke of Vladimir, r. 1362-1389

SUMMARY OF EVENT

The destruction of the Golden Horde marked the end of nearly two and a half centuries of Mongol rule in Russia. It was brought about by the rise to power of Ivan the Great, who bound several Russian states together into a single powerful political entity, and by the nearly simultaneous weakening of the Golden Horde as its formerly strong central khanate splintered into a loose collection of minor khanates.

The Mongols first appeared in Russia in May of 1223, when a raiding party, pushing northward from Persia, defeated a joint Russian-Polovtsy force at the Kalka River in the steppes north of the Black Sea. In 1237, Mongol khan Batu (d. 1255), the grandson of Genghis Khan, began a systematic campaign to extend the Mongol Empire to the west. In the winter of 1237-1238, Batu's forces sacked the Russian city of Riazan, destroyed the then-small town of Moscow, and devastated Vladimir, the capital city of northern Russia. Batu's army laid waste to Kiev in 1240 and gained control of southern Russia as well. However, domestic problems within the empire caused the Mongols to halt their advance, which had taken them into Poland and Hungary. They pulled back into the Russian lands, where they established the Golden Horde, the westernmost subdivision of the Mongol Empire, with a capital at Sarai, in the lower Volga Valley.

At first, the Golden Horde was an integral part of the great Mongol Empire, but by the beginning of the fourteenth century, it had become an independent state. In general, although the Mongols interfered little in Russian daily life, they maintained an effective control over Russia until the end of the fourteenth century. In 1378, Dmitry Donskoy, prince of Moscow, rebelled against the

Golden Horde and defeated a Mongol force along the Vozh River. Dmitry won an even bigger victory over the Mongols in 1380 at Kulikovo, near the upper reaches of the Don River. In 1382, however, Khan Tokhtamysh mounted a punitive campaign against Dmitry, sacked Moscow, and reestablished Mongol authority.

Internal difficulties began to beset the Golden Horde, however, and its unity began to disintegrate during the reign of Ulugh Muhammad, who first became khan in 1419. In 1430, the Crimean khanate separated itself from the Golden Horde, with Kazan following in 1436 and Astrakhan in 1462. The Golden Horde tried to reassert itself and to bring its Russian vassals back under control. Khan Aḥmad directed three campaigns against Moscow in 1451, 1455, and 1461, but he failed to secure any decisive results.

Moscow's abrogation of the Mongol yoke finally came in 1476, when Ivan the Great renounced all further payment of tribute to the Golden Horde, thus terminating diplomatic relations between Moscow and Sarai. Aḥmad's final attempt to punish Ivan failed in 1480. Early in January, 1481, while making his way southward, Aḥmad was assassinated by a rival.

SIGNIFICANCE

Khan Aḥmad's retreat marked the liberation of Russia from Mongol rule. Despite its shortcomings, Ivan's less than heroic victory over the Mongols added to his prestige in the eyes of his contemporaries and more than facilitated the consolidation of his 1478 conquest of Novgorod and subsequent acquisition of other areas, such as Tver' in 1485. Much of the great Russian heartland began to recognize the new titles that Ivan had bestowed upon himself, namely Czar or Caesar of all Rus, and Autocrat. In 1491, in cooperation with his old ally Mengli Giray, Ivan invaded and virtually crushed the Golden Horde. Eleven years later, in 1502, Mengli's Crimean Tatars delivered the final blow, and the Golden Horde collapsed. A small remnant managed to survive at the mouth of the Volga as part of the khanate of Astrakhan. Ivan the Great left to his grandson Ivan the Terrible the task of annexing the whole of the lower Volga region, which was done by 1556.

—Edward P. Keleher, updated by Donald L. Layton

FURTHER READING

Chambers, James. *The Devil's Horsemen: The Mongol Invasion of Europe*. New York: Atheneum, 1979. A narrative history of the thirteenth century Mongol invasion of Europe and the Near East.

Crummey, Robert O. *The Formation of Muscovy, 1304-1613*. London: Longman, 1987. Work of historical synthesis that covers the history of Muscovite Russia, including an informative account of the achievements and legacy of the Mongols.

Curtin, Jeremiah. *The Mongols in Russia*. Boston: Little, Brown, 1908. Although dated, Curtin's work still provides a useful and inclusive summary of the history of the Mongols in Russia.

Fedorov-Davydov, German A. *The Silk Road and the Cities of the Golden Horde*. Translated by Aleksandr Naymark. Edited by Jeannine Davis-Kimball. Berkeley, Calif.: Zinat Press, 2001. Portrait of the civilization and culture of the Golden Horde, based largely on archaeological studies of their principal cities. Includes illustrations, maps, genealogical tables, catalog of archaeological findings from the Volga River region, bibliographic references, and index.

Halecki, Oscar. *Borderlands of Western Civilization: A History of East Central Europe*. New York: Ronald Press, 1952. A review of the collapse of Mongol power.

Halperin, Charles J. *Russia and the Golden Horde: The Mongols' Impact on Medieval Russian History*. Bloomington: Indiana University Press, 1985. Integrates up-to-date Western and Soviet scholarship about the Mongols, offering a new interpretation of the role and impact of the Mongols on Russian history.

Hartog, Leo de. *Russia and the Mongol Yoke: The History of the Russian Principalities and the Golden Horde, 1221-1502*. New York: British Academic Press, 1996. Thorough survey detailing the entire history of Russian-Mongol strife, from the background of each civilization before the first invasion through the final defeat of the Horde in 1502. Includes maps, genealogical appendix, bibliographic references, and index.

Ostrowski, Donald. *Muscovy and the Mongols: Cross-Cultural Influences on the Steppe Frontier, 1304-1589*. New York: Cambridge University Press, 1998. A history of the development of Muscovy and the Russian state that focuses on its relationship to and interactions with other cultures, especially those of the Mongols. Looks at the extent to which external secular and religious practices were modified and incorporated by Russian religious and political institutions, and the ways in which cross-cultural influence shaped the nation. Includes glossary, chronology, bibliography, and index.

Wren, Melvin C. *The Course of Russian History.* 5th ed. Prospect Heights, Ill.: Waveland Press, 1994. Provides an informative discussion of the lifting of the Mongol yoke in 1480. Includes illustrations, bibliographic references, and index.

SEE ALSO: 1478: Muscovite Conquest of Novgorod; After 1480: Ivan the Great Organizes the "Third Rome";

1499-c. 1600: Russo-Polish Wars; Jan. 16, 1547: Coronation of Ivan the Terrible; Summer, 1556: Ivan the Terrible Annexes Astrakhan; 1581-1597: Cossacks Seize Sibir; 1584-1613: Russia's Time of Troubles.

RELATED ARTICLES in *Great Lives from History: The Renaissance & Early Modern Era, 1454-1600:* Ivan the Great; Ivan the Terrible.

After 1480
IVAN THE GREAT ORGANIZES THE "THIRD ROME"

Ivan the Great organized the "Third Rome," establishing Russia's claim as the center of Orthodox Christianity. Russia's religious power both enhanced and derived from the growth of the Russian monarchy's internal authority, as well as the state's increasing territorial expansion and importance as a world power.

LOCALE: Russia
CATEGORIES: Government and politics; religion

KEY FIGURES
Filofei (Filotheus or Philotheus; fl. sixteenth century), Russian monk who portrayed Moscow as the "Third Rome"
Ivan the Great (1440-1505), grand prince of Moscow, r. 1462-1505
Sophia Palaeologus (c. 1449-1503), niece of the last Byzantine emperor and wife of Ivan
Zosima (fl. 1490-1494), metropolitan of the Russian Orthodox Church, 1490-1494

SUMMARY OF EVENT
In the early sixteenth century, the Russian monk Filofei set forth what is known as the Third Rome doctrine, extolling the preeminence of Moscow as the leader of a universal Christian empire. According to Filofei, the first Rome of classical times had fallen because of its acceptance of heretical doctrine and papal domination, while the second Rome, Constantinople, capital of the Byzantine Empire and Greek Orthodoxy, fell to the Turks in 1453 because of its moral weakness and the rapprochement with the Latin Church.

The third Rome, Moscow, the political and religious successor of Byzantium, would survive forever. Two Romes had fallen to heresy, but the third would stand firm: There would never be a fourth. Filofei based this theoretical enunciation of Russia's preeminence primar-

ily on the expansion of Moscow's power and influence during the reign of Ivan the Great and the city's significance as the center of Orthodox Christianity in Russia. Although the exact date of his statement is disputed by scholars, it clearly reflects the power and authority Ivan had attached to the Russian throne.

For a century and a half prior to Ivan the Great's coming to power, Moscow had been the capital of one of several relatively minor principalities situated in the heart of Russia. These lands had fallen under the ruthless domination of the Golden Horde, which invading Mongols established in the thirteenth century. During the fourteenth and early fifteenth centuries, however, Moscow steadily enlarged the territory under its control at the expense of the Golden Horde.

Muscovite rulers beginning with Ivan I (r. 1328-1341) developed the independence and influence of their provincial state, even while nominally serving their Mongol overlords. As a result, the prestige of the growing urban center of Moscow and the area under its jurisdiction, commonly known as Muscovy, gradually increased. Moreover, in the 1320's, the metropolitan of the Russian Orthodox Church, the highest ecclesiastical official in Russia, moved his administrative headquarters from Vladimir to Moscow, placing Moscow at the center of Russian religious life. A half century later, in 1380, Moscow's grand prince, Dmitry Donskoy, won a battlefield victory over the Mongol army at Kulikovo. Although Kulikovo did not permanently break the power of the Golden Horde, it added to the reputation of the city and its leaders.

In 1462, Ivan the Great ascended the throne of the grand prince of Moscow as Ivan III. He sought to throw off the Mongol yoke completely and to unify all the Russian principalities, both large and small, under Muscovite leadership. Ivan's campaigns met with great success:

The huge state of Novgorod to the north was annexed to Muscovy in 1478. Tver', to the northwest, was acquired in 1485. Ivan absorbed many smaller territories as well, including numerous appanage lands, many of them enclaves of Muscovy, that his father had bequeathed to his other sons and relatives. Ivan also seized significant territories from Lithuania, managing by 1500 to conquer portions of White Russia to the west and Little Russia (another term for the Ukraine) in the south.

Ivan's most spectacular achievement, however, was winning final independence from the authority and jurisdiction of the Golden Horde after 1480 without open warfare. Ivan's liberation of Russia from the Golden Horde's authority facilitated the further consolidation of his power over territorial acquisitions such as Novgorod and Tver'. Moscow's growing prominence understandably increased his prestige in the eyes of contemporary chroniclers, as well as later writers such as Filofei. By 1480, most of Russia was beginning to recognize the new titles that Ivan had bestowed upon himself, namely Autocrat and Czar of all Rus.

Since most of Europe's states sought a historical or religious rationale to bolster their claims to legitimacy and authority, it is not surprising that Ivan's successes prompted him and his contemporaries to advance claims on behalf of Moscow as the political and religious successor to Constantinople, capital of the former Byzantine Empire. Russia was by this time the leading independent state in the Orthodox world. Ivan and his supporters exploited his second marriage in 1472 to Sophia -logus, the orphaned niece of the last Byzantine emperor. They glorified Moscow as the legitimate heir to the empire of the caesars and the champion of Christian Orthodoxy.

Moscow's position as successor to the Eastern Roman Empire was symbolized by adding the Byzantine double-headed eagle to the state crest and seal, and Zosima, metropolitan of the Russian Orthodox Church, referred in 1492 to "the new Emperor Constantine of the new Constantinople—Moscow." Several years later, the monk Filofei from the neighboring principality of Pskov expanded this salutation into the "Third Rome" doctrine.

SIGNIFICANCE

The reign of Ivan the Great marked the birth of the modern Russian nation, both politically and geographically. Ivan's greatness lies in the fact that he took the territorial

Ivan the Great, grand prince of Moscow (standing center right) defies the Tartar khan. (F. R. Niglutsch)

state left him by his father, unified and expanded it, broke Mongol control, and transformed the principality of Moscow into a fully sovereign state encompassing the great Russian heartland. The success of his leadership provided political and religious justification for Moscow's claim to greatness by his marriage into the dynasty of fallen Constantinople.

To solidify control over his domains, Ivan promulgated in 1497 a code of common law, the *Sudebnik*, intended to improve administrative uniformity and increase the centralization of autocratic power. This Russian prince brought political factions and the aristocratic boyar class, groups that historically opposed the national government in previous centuries, under his effective control.

Ivan the Great bequeathed to his successors a compact and well-organized state, a legacy of Moscow's right as symbolized in the double-headed eagle looking both eastward and westward. This was to be the historical mission of the Third Rome. While some scholars interpret the theory as applying solely to Moscow in its narrower religious context, others apply it to the entire Russian nation as justification for territorial expansion. In either case, this sense of a divinely ordained mission did not perish until the last czar gave up his title as well as his life as consequences of violent revolution in 1917.

—Edward P. Keleher, updated by Taylor Stults

FURTHER READING

Anderson, Thornton. *Russian Political Thought: An Introduction*. Ithaca, N.Y.: Cornell University Press, 1967. Includes discussion of the Third Rome theory and provides a substantial passage of the famous Filofei statement justifying this concept.

Crummey, R. O. *The Formation of Muscovy, 1304-1613*. New York: Longman, 1987. Solid account of the emergence of Moscow as the nucleus of the revived Russian state.

Fennell, J. L. I. *Ivan the Great of Moscow*. New York: St. Martin's Press, 1963. Biography of the famous Russian leader, with primary focus on political, diplomatic, and military matters.

Grey, Ian. *Ivan III and the Unification of Russia*. New York: Collier Books, 1967. Brief, readable account of

---

> ### FILOFEI ON THE THIRD ROME
>
> *Russian monk Filofei is credited with the first enunciation of the doctrine of the Third Rome in a letter to Vasily III written c. 1514-1521, excerpted here.*
>
> The Apollinarian heresy caused the downfall of old Rome. The Turks used their axes to shatter the doors of all churches of the Second Rome, the city of Constantinople. Now [in Moscow], the new Third Rome, the Holy Ecumenical Apostolic Church of your sovereign state shines brighter than the sun in the universal Orthodox Christian faith throughout the world. Pious Tsar! Let [people of] your state know that all states of the Orthodox faith have now merged into one, your state. You are the only true Christian ruler under the sky!
>
> *Source:* From "Moscow the Third Rome (excerpts)." University of Durham, England. http://www.dur.ac.uk/~dml0www/3rdrome.html. Linked from the Internet Medieval Sourcebook. http://www.fordham.edu/halsall/sbook.html. Accessed September 16, 2004.

Ivan's life and rule includes a useful assessment of the Third Rome theory.

Hunczak, Taras, ed. *Russian Imperialism from Ivan the Great to the Revolution*. Reprint. Lanham, Md.: University Press of America, 2000. Anthology of essays detailing the rise to power of the modern Russian state and its imperial aspirations from the late fifteenth century to the early twentieth century. Includes maps, bibliographic references, and index.

Kollmann, Nancy Shields. *Kinship and Politics: The Making of the Muscovite Political System, 1345-1547*. Stanford, Calif.: Stanford University Press, 1987. Study of the influence of the Russian aristocracy during the years of growing centralization of power.

Ostrowski, Donald. *Muscovy and the Mongols: Cross-Cultural Influences on the Steppe Frontier, 1304-1589*. New York: Cambridge University Press, 1998. A history of the development of Muscovy and the Russian state that focuses on its relationship to and interactions with other cultures, especially those of the Mongols. Devotes a chapter to the concept of a Third Rome and its role in delimiting the power and authority of the Russian ruler. Includes glossary, chronology, bibliography, and index.

Riasanovsky, Nicholas V. *A History of Russia*. 6th ed. New York: Oxford University Press, 2000. Discusses the importance of the Third Rome doctrine to the development of the Russian state. Includes photographic plates, illustrations, maps, bibliography, and index.

Vernadsky, George. *Russia at the Dawn of the Modern Age*. Vol. 4 in *A History of Russia*. New Haven, Conn.: Yale University Press, 1959. This highly respected study of the fifteenth and sixteenth centuries includes the reign of Ivan III and the Third Rome topic.

Zernov, N. *Moscow: The Third Rome*. Reprint. New York: AMS Press, 1971. Reprint of a brief history of the Orthodox Church in Russia and the place of Moscow as the leader of the faith.

SEE ALSO: 1478: Muscovite Conquest of Novgorod; 1480-1502: Destruction of the Golden Horde; 1499-

c. 1600: Russo-Polish Wars; Jan. 16, 1547: Coronation of Ivan the Terrible; Jan.-May, 1551: The Stoglav Convenes; Summer, 1556: Ivan the Terrible Annexes Astrakhan; 1581-1597: Cossacks Seize Sibir; 1584-1613: Russia's Time of Troubles; 1589: Russian Patriarchate Is Established.

RELATED ARTICLES in *Great Lives from History: The Renaissance & Early Modern Era, 1454-1600:* Ivan the Great; Sophia Palaeologus.

1481-1482
FOUNDING OF ELMINA

Portugal's fortress at Elmina was Europe's first permanent settlement in sub-Saharan Africa. The fortress was intended to protect Portugal's trade in slaves and in gold, spices, and other goods from competition from other European powers.

LOCALE: Elmina, West African Gold Coast (now in Ghana)

CATEGORIES: Colonization; expansion and land acquisition; trade and commerce

KEY FIGURES

Prince Henry the Navigator (1394-1460), Portuguese prince

Afonso V (1432-1481), king of Portugal, r. 1438-1481

John II (1455-1495), king of Portugal, r. 1481-1495

Diogo de Azambuja (1432-1518), Portuguese courtier who oversaw construction of the fortress at Elmina

Fernão Gomes (fl. 1470's), Portuguese explorer

SUMMARY OF EVENT

In 1415, King John I of Portugal invaded Ceuta, a fortified port on the African side of the Strait of Gibraltar. Portugal's seizure of Ceuta blocked Muslim shipping from the Atlantic Ocean, but the cost of the victory made further land attacks prohibitive. The Portuguese discovered, however, that Ceuta was the terminus of a trans-Saharan caravan route bringing gold to the Mediterranean world from Guinea—a region previously unknown to the Europeans. King John's third son, Prince Henry the Navigator, concluded from sketchy information that the gold mines in this new region were accessible to ships, and he persuaded his father to support Portuguese explorations past Cape Bojador down the uncharted western coast of Africa in search of the mines.

From his palace at Sagres on Cape St. Vincent, Prince Henry granted licenses to a succession of captains to go farther south along the African coast. The voyages of exploration were to chart the coastline, tides, currents, and winds and to establish trade relations with whatever societies they encountered. The expeditions turned into seaborne *razzias*, the plundering raids characteristic of the seven centuries of war between the Moors (Muslims) and the Christians on the Iberian Peninsula. Sailors combined purchase with robbery and kidnapping and returned to the port of Lagos with gold, peppers, ostrich eggs, salt, cloth, and slaves.

News of the Portuguese successes prompted French, Flemish, Genoese, and Castilian sea captains to try to establish their own contacts in Africa and to raid Portuguese ships on return voyages. King John I and Prince Henry ordered patrols to intercept and punish the interlopers.

In an effort to stop Christian nations from warring on each other and to encourage them to unite in resistance to the advancing Ottoman Empire, Popes Nicholas V and Calixtus III issued three successive papal bulls that approved what the Portuguese had done in Africa so far, encouraged them to spread Christianity in the continent, and gave Portugal a monopoly on trade in Africa. Even the fall of Constantinople in 1453 and Turkish advances in central Europe did not unite the Christian rulers, and Portugal had to make great efforts to defend its papally mandated monopoly.

When Prince Henry died in 1460, the Portuguese had explored as far as the northern edge of what became known as the Grain Coast, now Sierra Leone and Liberia. King Afonso V focused his energies on consolidating the new discoveries and acquisitions into administrative and military organizations. For a substantial annual payment, King Afonso gave, in 1469, exclusive exploration rights to Fernão Gomes, on the condition that he explore at least 300 miles (483 kilometers) of new coastline each year.

Gomes's captains quickly mapped the Grain Coast and then turned west into tricky waters. From Cape Palmas to Cape Three Points, the Ivory Coast, there were long sandy coasts with no natural harbors and dangerous surf. Farther east, however, the coast was more hospitable. Between Cape Three Points and the mouth of the Volta River, the Portuguese found a gentler coastline and safe harbors. Moreover, in each of the relatively small communities they encountered, the residents had plentiful amounts of gold dust, which they said they had acquired through trade at mines to the north.

Calling this section of the coast A Mina, the Mine, the Portuguese immediately sought sites for a permanent trade center. The most promising place was a rocky promontory jutting a mile past the mouth of the Benya River. At the base of the promontory was a rock quarry, and across the river and inland was a large, deep lagoon that protected anchored ships from storms and pirates. On the little peninsula was a community of about two hundred Akan-speaking villagers. The Portuguese named the village El Mina, possibly a corruption of the Arabic term, *el-Minnah*, meaning the port.

Beyond the Volta River, the Portuguese encountered more inhospitable coastline until they headed south. There the Portuguese could buy slaves to resell to the Akan at El Mina, which became simply Elmina. The Akan took the slaves north to be sold to the Asante for gold. News of A Mina and the great profits the Portuguese were making leaked out of Portugal to the rest of Europe.

Upon Afonso's death in 1481, his successor, King John II, acted swiftly to protect A Mina from his European neighbors. He commissioned Diogo de Azambuja to construct a fortress at Elmina, the best situated of several trade sites. Azambuja arrived in January, 1482, with an armada of ten ships and five hundred soldiers and servants, as well as one hundred stonemasons, carpenters, and craftsmen. The ships carried pre-cut stone from Portugal for the foundations, arches, and windows. The rest of the stone was to come from the nearby quarries.

Azambuja secured permission to build the fortress by pledging to protect the Akan village from its neighbors, the large states of Eguafo and Fetu that both claimed the territory surrounding the Benya lagoon. The fortress resembled a krak, a Middle Eastern crusader castle. It was rectangular with rounded turrets at the corners. Curtain walls were high enough to protect two-story buildings inside that included a chapel, a refectory, living quarters,

and administrative space. Azambuja named the fortress after the soldier-martyr who was the patron saint of Portugal: Castelo de São Jorge da Mina, or St. George's Castle of the Mine.

SIGNIFICANCE

Elmina became the major entrepôt for trade on the Gold Coast. From Portugal came cloth, brass goods, glass beads, spiced wine, knives, swords, hatchets, iron bars, copper rods, trumpets, striped wool, and candles. The Portuguese neither raided for slaves nor purchased slaves from the region to the north. By 1500, every thirty days a ship with 100 to 120 slaves on board would leave the island of São Tomé for Elmina. As the demand for labor in the Americas grew in the sixteenth century, Elmina became a collection point for slaves from the Niger delta and regions south. Slaves not sold for the northbound caravans became destined for the New World empires.

The little community nestled next to the castle quickly grew to be the largest of the Portuguese trade communities. The prosperity of Elmina angered the Eguafo and Fetu rulers. They regarded the Portuguese as trespassers who were strengthening their formerly weak neighbors. The Akan-speaking peoples who gravitated to the fort acted first as an autonomous state and then as a kingship. The already numerous Asante farther north expanded their territory, as new slaves absorbed into their communities made them stronger yet. The Eguafo and Fetu did not recognize the Portuguese claim to a monopoly on African trade with Europe, and they welcomed smugglers as trade partners and allies, especially the Dutch.

In the sixteenth century, Portugal encountered more problems than it could overcome. Diseases in its tropical empire in Africa, Asia, and the Americas decimated soldiers, merchants, missionaries, and bureaucrats who moved there. Portuguese craftspeople could not meet the imperial demand for goods, and the Portuguese became retailers of European goods competing with other nations' merchants. After 1530, French, Dutch, and English pirates took a terrible toll on Portugal's commercial shipping interests along A Mina. The pirates also doubled as smugglers, circumventing Portugal's monopoly by clandestinely importing African commodities back into Europe.

By the end of the century, illegitimate trade surpassed the volume of Portuguese commerce. The Dutch built a fort at Mori, just 10 miles (16 kilometers) east of Elmina. With African allies, the Dutch launched unsuccessful attacks on Elmina in 1596, 1603, 1606, 1615, and 1625. In 1637, the Dutch attacked with an army of eight hundred

Dutch soldiers and fourteen hundred men from the states of Eguafo and Asebu. The Portuguese, with a garrison of only thirty-five officials and soldiers, were forced to surrender. Elmina became the jewel of the Dutch empire in Africa.

—*Paul E. Kuhl*

FURTHER READING

DeCorse, Christopher R. *An Archaeology of Elmina: Africans and Europeans on the Gold Coast, 1400-1900.* Washington, D.C.: Smithsonian Institution Press, 2001. Fascinating blend of document, ethnographic, and artifact sources of Elmina.

Fage, J. D. *A History of Africa.* 4th ed. New York: Routledge, 2001. Devotes three chapters to the expansion of Europeans into Africa and the slave trade.

Thomas, Hugh. *The Slave Trade: The Story of the Atlantic Slave Trade, 1440-1870.* New York: Simon & Schuster, 1997. Careful attention to Portugal's role in the origins of the slave trade by a great student of all things Iberian.

Vogt, John. *Portuguese Rule on the Gold Coast, 1469-1682.* Athens: University of Georgia Press, 1979. Survey of the history of Portugal's colonization and exploitation of the Gold Coast, with particular attention to the role of Elmina. Includes bibliography and index.

SEE ALSO: 1460-1600: Rise of the Akan Kingdoms; Late 15th cent.: Mombasa, Malindi, and Kilwa Reach Their Height; c. 1485: Portuguese Establish a Foothold in Africa; Aug., 1487-Dec., 1488: Dias Rounds the Cape of Good Hope; 1491-1545: Christianity Is Established in the Kingdom of Kongo; Jan., 1498: Portuguese Reach the Swahili Coast; 16th century: Trans-Saharan Trade Enriches Akan Kingdoms; 1502: Beginning of the Transatlantic Slave Trade; 1505-1515: Portuguese Viceroys Establish Overseas Trade Empire.

RELATED ARTICLES in *Great Lives from History: The Renaissance & Early Modern Era, 1454-1600:* Bartolomeu Dias; John II.

1481-1499
LUDOVICO SFORZA RULES MILAN

Ludovico's twenty years of rule over the Duchy of Milan combined skill in administration with patronage of a magnificent court. A practitioner of diplomatic intrigue, Ludovico facilitated the French invasion of Italy in 1494, which led to several decades of European dynastic conflict on the peninsula and the end of Milanese autonomy.

LOCALE: Duchy of Milan (now in Italy)
CATEGORY: Government and politics

KEY FIGURES

Ludovico Sforza (1452-1508), duke of Milan, r. 1481-1499

Gian Galeazzo Sforza (1469-1494), duke of Milan, r. 1476-1481, nephew of Ludovico

Alexander VI (Rodrigo de Borja y Doms; 1431-1503), Roman Catholic pope, 1492-1503

Maximilian I (1459-1519), Holy Roman Emperor, r. 1493-1519

Charles VIII (1470-1498), king of France, r. 1483-1498

Louis XII (1462-1515), king of France, r. 1498-1515

Beatrice d'Este (1475-1497), duchess of Milan, r. 1494-1497

Leonardo da Vinci (1452-1519), painter, sculptor, and architect active in Milan

SUMMARY OF EVENT

Jakob Burckhardt, the nineteenth century scholar and father of Renaissance studies, called Ludovico Sforza "the most perfect type of Renaissance despot" and a man who "disarms our moral judgment." First as the regent of the youthful and feckless Duke Gian Galeazzo Sforza and then as duke himself, Ludovico dominated political and cultural life in the Duchy of Milan. The cunning that Ludovico displayed in consolidating his power in Milan was mirrored in his diplomacy, as he engaged in an increasingly dangerous political game that threatened to upset the balance of power in Italy by inviting French intervention in Italian affairs.

The route to power that Ludovico charted in Milan was as unlikely as it was ruthless and opportunistic. He was born the fourth legitimate son of Francesco Sforza, the first of the Sforza dukes to rule in Milan (r. 1450-1466). Ludovico received a refined Humanist education and was widely admired for his intelligence and charm as a young man. Following his father's death in 1466, he remained in Milan as a faithful follower of Francesco's mercurial heir, Galeazzo Maria Sforza (r. 1466-1476).

Ludovico's political ambition and ruthlessness became evident, however, almost immediately after Galeazzo Maria's assassination on Christmas Eve, 1476. In 1477, along with several associates, he launched a failed bid to seize power from his nephew and was exiled to Pisa. The regency passed to Galeazzo Maria's widow, Bona. Ludovico returned to Milan in the autumn of 1479, and he promptly overthrew Bona and her first secretary, Cicco Simonetta. The departure of Bona meant that Ludovico was soon free to exercise his complete domination over the young duke. Although Gian Galeazzo retained the official title of duke until 1494, Ludovico was the de facto ruler of Milan from 1481.

Observers were under no illusion as to who really controlled the levers of power in Milan, even after Gian Galeazzo reached his majority. Residing largely away from the capital in Pavia, Gian Galeazzo preferred hunting or hawking to the duties of leadership, and he regularly overindulged in drink. Ludovico deliberately encouraged Gian Galeazzo's vices, and the nominal duke remained mentally and physically immature well into his adulthood, utterly dependent on his uncle.

In foreign affairs, Ludovico took full advantage of the sophisticated diplomatic network established by Francesco Sforza to operate in an Italian political arena that placed a premium on shrewd diplomacy. Between 1482 and 1484, Ludovico involved Milan in the War of Ferrara

against Venice and sent aid to the king of Naples when his barons revolted beginning in 1485. This support, however, did not prevent relations with Naples from gradually deteriorating over the ensuing years.

In 1489, Duke Gian Galeazzo married Isabella of Aragon, the daughter of King Ferdinand I of Naples (also known as Ferrante), but Ludovico tightly controlled the couple's movement and access to funds. Ferdinand complained vociferously about the treatment of Isabella and about the pretensions of Ludovico's wife, Beatrice d'Este, whom Ludovico married in a grand ceremony in 1491. Following the suspicious death of Gian Galeazzo in 1494, Ludovico officially assumed the ducal title when he was able to secure the all-important imperial investiture of the Duchy of Milan from Holy Roman Emperor Maximilian I. At last he had legal claim to the power he had wielded illegitimately for fourteen years.

From 1492 to 1494, Ludovico's involvement in diplomatic intrigue had reached its peak. By the 1490's, Ludovico's rivalries with Ferdinand and with Ferdinand's son Ludovico, the duke of Calabria, had become deeply personal. While Gian Galeazzo was alive, Ferdinand repeatedly demanded that the regent officially hand over power to the duke and Isabella, but Ludovico refused. These challenges from Ferdinand prompted Ludovico to form an alliance with the new Borgia pope, Alexander VI (negotiated by Ludovico's brother, Cardinal Ascanio Sforza), and to encourage French king Charles VIII to press the long-standing claim of the House of Anjou to the Kingdom of Naples.

The newly legitimated duke of Milan offered his support to France in the event of an invasion. This was playing with fire, for Ludovico underestimated the determination of Charles to make good on his Italian aspirations. Charles invaded Italy and conquered the Kingdom of Naples without great difficulty, with the tacit cooperation of Milan. The French success, however, only increased the insecurity of Ludovico's position, for there was also an outstanding claim to the Duchy of Milan itself by the French House of Orléans. Therefore, when a coalition of Italian states banded together to drive the French army, already crippled by syphilis, out of the peninsula in 1495, Ludovico joined the anti-French alliance.

In the short-term, Ludovico appeared triumphant: Naples was neutralized, and his usurpation of the Milanese dukedom was solemnized by imperial investiture. He even managed to effect a reconciliation with Charles VIII. Many in France, however, would not forget Ludovico's diplomatic treachery. When the French returned to Italy in 1499, this time under King Louis XII (formerly

---

THE SFORZA DUKES OF MILAN

The Sforza family ruled Milan for most of the period between 1450 and 1535. The family was twice driven from the city by French monarchs: once in 1499 by Louis XII and once in 1515 by Francis I.

1450-1466	Francesco Sforza
1466-1476	Galeazzo Maria Sforza
1476-1481	Gian Galeazzo Sforza (under the regency of Bona Sforza)
1481-1494	Gian Galeazzo Sforza (under the regency of Ludovico Sforza)
1494-1499	Ludovico Sforza
1512-1515	Massimiliano Sforza
1522-1535	Francesco Maria Sforza

the duke of Orléans), it was Milan that was the target of their invasion.

The French forces on this occasion were led by Gian Giacomo Trivulzio, formerly one of Milan's top soldiers and an intimate of Ludovico Sforza. Tivulzio had become the maréchal of France and an implacable foe of the Milanese duke. The duchy succumbed easily to the French armies when Ludovico's Swiss mercenaries abandoned him, and Ludovico himself suffered the indignity of capture and imprisonment in a French jail in Touraine, where he would stay, virtually forgotten, until his death in 1508.

Despite the nearly constant political turmoil of Ludovico's reign, Renaissance Milan reached the height of its cultural output under his rulership. Ludovico himself showed considerable interest in the collection and copying of manuscripts, and he was also an enthusiastic patron of learning inside the duchy, showing particular favor to the University of Pavia. Following the example of his brother Galeazzo Maria, Ludovico spent lavishly on court pomp and ceremony and patronized artists, architects, and musicians liberally.

Among the names associated with Ludovico's court were Donato Bramante and Leonardo da Vinci. Leonardo, who arrived in Milan in the early 1480's, served the Sforza court primarily as a military engineer and architect, but his tenure in Milan also saw the creation some of his finest books and works of art. These include *The Last Supper*, one of the Western world's most famous fresco paintings. The court also engaged musicians from all over Europe, continuing Milan's tradition as a musical center.

Thus, the Milanese court in the final two decades of the fifteenth century became the most splendid in all of Italy. Ludovico's wife, Beatrice, who had a great appetite for clothes, jewels, and other luxuries, played a particularly important role in this courtly splendor. She was the life of the court, hosting dances, concerts, and hunts.

The Sforzas, including Ludovico's father, Francesco, were patrons of the arts, architecture, and charity. The Milan hospital was founded in the mid-1450's by Francesco. (Frederick Ungar Publishing Co.)

SIGNIFICANCE

In addition to his considerable cultural legacy, which can still be appreciated today, Ludovico Sforza's ascendancy in Milan had a lasting impact on the political scene of both Italy and Europe. Ludovico's facilitation of the 1494 French invasion had parlous consequences. Once Charles VIII's armies crossed into Italy to press his claims to Naples, the relative isolation of Italy over the previous fifty years came to an end, and the peninsula became the chief battleground of the dynastic conflict between France and Spain.

Italian independence was soon at an end. By 1500, Milan had surrendered its own political autonomy and the duchy, whose control was contested between the European powers, came to be regarded as the strategic key to Italy. Although two of Ludovico's sons, Massimiliano and Francesco, eventually became dukes of Milan themselves (following the brief restoration of Sforza rule in 1512, 1521, and 1529, around periods of foreign occupation), in the long term, Milan, along with most of the rest of Italy, would fall under the domination of the Habsburg Dynasty.

—*Paul M. Dover*

FURTHER READING

Abulafia, David, ed. *The French Descent into Renaissance Italy, 1494-1495.* Aldershot, Hampshire, England: Variorum, 1995. A collection of essays dealing with the antecedents and effects of the French invasion of 1494, in which Ludovico played a key role.

1480's

Ady, Cecilia. *A History of Milan Under the Sforza*. London: Methuen, 1907. A rather old-fashioned and gossipy, nonetheless useful, narrative of the dynasty by a great historian. Includes two chapters on the reign of Ludovico.

Collison-Morley, Lacy. *The Story of the Sforzas*. New York: E. P. Hutton, 1934. A political and cultural history of the Sforzas in Milan that emphasizes the personalities of the major historical figures, including Ludovico.

Ianziti, Gary. *Humanistic Historiography Under the Sforzas: Politics and Propaganda in Fifteenth-Century Milan*. Oxford, England: Clarendon Press, 1988. An examination of the role of Humanists resident at the Sforza court in constructing a historical ideology of rule for the dynasty. Focuses especially on the reign of Ludovico.

Munro, Cynthia Pyle. *Milan and Lombardy in the Renaissance: Essays in Cultural History*. Rome, Italy: La Fenice, 1997. A wide-ranging collection of essays that examine the cultural climate of Milan before and during the reign of Ludovico. These essays are in English and Italian.

SEE ALSO: Apr. 9, 1454: Peace of Lodi; Sept., 1494-Oct., 1495: Charles VIII of France Invades Italy; 1495-1497: Leonardo da Vinci Paints *The Last Supper*; September 22, 1504: Treaty of Blois; Apr. 11, 1512: Battle of Ravenna; Sept. 13-14, 1515: Battle of Marignano; 1521-1559: Valois-Habsburg Wars; Feb., 1525: Battle of Pavia; May 6, 1527-Feb., 1528: Sack of Rome; Apr. 3, 1559: Treaty of Cateau-Cambrésis.

RELATED ARTICLES in *Great Lives from History: The Renaissance & Early Modern Era, 1454-1600:* Alexander VI; Lucrezia Borgia; Donato Bramante; Charles VIII; Isabella d'Este; Leonardo da Vinci; Louis XII; Maximilian I; Caterina Sforza; Ludovico Sforza.

1481-1512
REIGN OF BAYEZID II AND OTTOMAN CIVIL WARS

Bayezid's reign was marked by feuds over succession, which caused years of civil war. He was, however, successful in setting up the powerful Ottoman navy, which would dominate the Mediterranean region for nearly a century, and for ridding the Ottoman Empire of corruption.

LOCALE: Ottoman Empire, Mamlūk Egypt, Iran, Rhodes, France, and Italy

CATEGORIES: Wars, uprisings, and civil unrest; government and politics

KEY FIGURES

Mehmed II (1432-1481), sultan of the Ottoman Empire, r. 1444-1446 and 1451-1481, and Bayezid's father

Bayezid II (1447/1448-1512), sultan of the Ottoman Empire, r. 1481-1512

Cem (1459-1495), Bayezid's younger brother and a rival claimant to the throne

Selim I (1467-1520), Bayezid's son and his successor as sultan, r. 1512-1520

Ismāʿīl I (1487-1524), shah of Iran and founder of the Ṣafavid Dynasty, r. 1501-1524

Pierre d'Aubusson (1423-1503), fortieth grand master of the Order of the Knights of St. John, 1476-1503

SUMMARY OF EVENT

The future Ottoman sultan, Bayezid II, was the son of Sultan Mehmed II and Mukrime Hatun. Mehmed, however, appears to have favored a younger son, Cem, who, like his father, was very aggressive and an expansionist politically, while Bayezid advocated a more passive policy and less centralized control.

In keeping with Ottoman tradition, Mehmed allowed both sons to administer parts of the empire as governors: Bayezid over Sivas, Amasya, and Tokat (in northeastern Anatolia), and Cem over Konya and Karaman (southern Anatolia). This arrangement virtually guaranteed that civil war over succession to the throne would occur among the siblings on the sultan's death.

When Mehmed II died on May 3, 1481, at issue was which of the princes could establish his claim to the throne in the capital city of Constantinople and, at the same time, command the strongest support. One crucial factor was that Bayezid was the first to receive word of his father's death and thus was able to establish himself as sultan within the month. Elements that were disaffected by Mehmed's strong-handed government and his seemingly unending wars of conquest rallied to Bayezid's cause. Most crucial was the support of the elite Janissary corps (whose loyalty Bayezid further ensured through a generous bribe).

Cem, though outmaneuvered and now considered a pretender, received assistance from other elements and established a rival sultanate at Bursa, offering to divide the Ottoman lands with his brother. Bayezid's rejection of this scheme set off a civil war that would linger until Cem's death in 1495.

Bayezid's leading commander, Gedik Ahmed Pasha, marched on Bursa, leading to a crushing military loss for Cem at the Battle of Yenişehir in June, 1481. Cem then fled to Egypt and lived under the protection of the Mamlūk sultan, Qāytbāy.

Returning to Anatolia in 1482, Cem renewed his struggle to gain power, but again he was thwarted. Bayezid's forces kept Cem from escaping to Egypt, so he was forced to accept the asylum offered him by Pierre d'Aubusson, the grand master of the Order of the Knights of St. John, who had long been fending off Ottoman attacks from their base on the island of Rhodes.

D'Aubusson, however, kept Cem under arrest, using him to prevent Bayezid from attacking Rhodes and other Christian states. D'Aubusson received 45,000 gold ducats per year from Sultan Bayezid, who feared that, without such reward, the grand master would release his brother to begin a new round of fighting. To lessen the chance that a valuable hostage such as Cem could be kidnapped or assassinated, d'Aubusson spirited him away to different castles in France, which were maintained by the order. In 1490, the grand master transferred the custody of the Ottoman prince to Pope Innocent VIII, who promptly awarded d'Aubusson the rank of cardinal in the Catholic Church. The annual payments made to keep Cem under arrest were transferred to the Papacy and remained until 1494, when Pope Alexander VI in turn transferred custody to King Charles VIII of France. Charles VIII had just entered Italy with a powerful military force.

Though Charles spoke of invading the Ottoman Empire and setting Cem in place as sultan, he did not act on his words. Cem's death in Naples on February 25, 1495, put an end to the idea of Cem becoming sultan. Bayezid negotiated to have Cem's body brought to Constantinople to keep pretenders from claiming to be Cem and, thus, reigniting the Ottoman civil wars; Cem's body was brought to Constantinople, but not until 1499.

Bayezid's leadership style differed from Mehmed's in

that the new sultan was more focused on religion and artistic and cultural patronage than he was on military matters, particularly as long as Cem loomed as a threat. Gedik Ahmed Pasha, who had become grand vizier, advocated forcefully a massive campaign to conquer Italy, where the Turks had a foothold in Otranto. Believing this venture to be foolhardy, and fearing that the grand vizier was in correspondence with Cem, Bayezid ordered his death in December of 1482.

Though achieving little during his reign, Bayezid *was* successful in deflecting a series of military threats. From 1484 to 1491, the Ottomans were locked in a bloody, deadlocked conflict with Qāytbāy's Mamlūks, and a war with Venice between 1499 and 1502 did result in modest territorial acquisitions in Greece, but this war, too, was inconclusive. The most daunting threat, however, came from a revival of power in Iran, where the Shīʿite warlord Ismāʿīl became shah. Ismāʿīl would make significant inroads into Ottoman interests in the Middle East, seizing Baghdad in 1504 and successfully campaigning along the eastern Ottoman frontiers; this incited the Turkmen tribes of Anatolia to constant revolt against the sultan's authority.

In 1511, civil war again broke out as Bayezid's three sons, Selim, Ahmed, and Korkut, vied for the succession. Bayezid had favored Ahmed, but support from the Janissaries and other disgruntled groups who had become alarmed at the Ṣafavid threat coming from Iran (including large Anatolian estate owners and Sunni religious leaders) secured Selim's victory. On April 25, 1512, Selim arranged for Bayezid's abdication and became Sultan Selim I (the Grim). Selim successfully presented himself as a champion of strong military action against the Ṣafavid Shīʿites. The deposed Bayezid died one month after he abdicated.

SIGNIFICANCE

Apart from the civil strife of the early and final years, Bayezid's reign was generally one of economic expansion and prosperity. He is credited with having laid the foundations for the Ottoman navy (during the Venetian War) and thus having set the stage for the empire's maritime dominance of the Mediterranean, a dominance that would be pursued during the reigns of the three succeeding sultans and would not be lost until the Battle of Lepanto in 1571.

Bayezid's military expeditions were somewhat productive, too. In 1483, his forces had secured the province of Herzegovina and, in 1498, the province of Moldavia. However, his preference for negotiation and coexistence over war and conquest made him appear to be weak and ineffectual in comparison with his father.

His regime gained a reputation for religious piety, fairness, and efficiency, augmented by a determined campaign to root out corruption, and future generations would refer to him as Bayezid the Just.

—*Raymond Pierre Hylton*

FURTHER READING

Brummett, Palmira J. *Ottoman Seapower and Levantine Diplomacy in the Age of Discovery.* Albany: State University of New York Press, 1994. This work seeks to integrate Ottoman history into European, Asian, and world history by demonstrating the importance of inherited Euro-Asian trade networks to the development and expansion of the Ottoman Empire, as well as the effects of continual commercial struggles between the empire and other world trading powers upon all aspects of imperial and mercantile history.

Goodwin, Jason. *Lords of the Horizon: A History of the Ottoman Empire.* New York: Henry Holt, 1999. Generally sympathetic, this study credits Bayezid's reign as being comparatively humane and innovative. Contains a useful time line.

Imber, Colin. *The Ottoman Empire, 1300-1650: The Structure of Power.* New York: Palgrave Macmillan, 2002. Emphasizes the significance of institutional structure, particularly the almost-absolute power of the sultan and the means by which he could achieve and ensure loyalty among his most powerful supporters.

Inalcik, Halil. *The Ottoman Empire: The Classical Age, 1300-1600.* Translated by Norman Itzkowitz and Colin Imber. New York: Praeger, 1973. Gives a detailed account of Ottoman governance, problems of succession, and the role of the Janissaries. Refutes the idea that Bayezid's reign was one of total weakness and stagnation.

McCarthy, Justin. *The Ottoman Turks: An Introductory History to 1923.* New York: Longman, 1997. Bayezid and his times are portrayed here in some detail. Also argues that his reign marked a prosperous era of peace and renewal.

Vucinich, Wayne S. *The Ottoman Empire: Its Record and Legacy.* Princeton, N.J.: Van Nostrand, 1965. A solid, basic starting point for the reader that outlines the period and its personalities. The author implies that Cem's death was occasioned by foul play.

Wheatcroft, Andrew. *The Ottomans.* New York: Penguin/ Viking, 1993. The author is fairly dismissive of Bayezid as a sultan who was overshadowed by his father and his immediate successors, Selim I and Süleyman the Magnificent.

SEE ALSO: 1454-1481: Rise of the Ottoman Empire; Aug. 29, 1526: Battle of Mohács; 1589: Second Janissary Revolt in Constantinople.

RELATED ARTICLES in *Great Lives from History: The Renaissance & Early Modern Era, 1454-1600:* Alexander VI; Barbarossa; Bayezid II; Charles VIII; Mehmed II; Pius II; Süleyman the Magnificent; Qāytbāy.

1482-1492
MAXIMILIAN I TAKES CONTROL OF THE LOW COUNTRIES

Using heavy taxation and brutal military force to subdue the Netherlands, Habsburg Dynasty ruler Maximilian I recovered his family's earlier territorial losses and built a dynasty that dominated much of Europe for more than four centuries.

LOCALE: Belgium, the Netherlands, and Luxembourg

CATEGORIES: Government and politics; wars, uprisings, and civil unrest; expansion and land acquisition

KEY FIGURES

Maximilian I (1459-1519), Holy Roman Emperor, r. 1493-1519

Frederick III (1415-1493), Holy Roman Emperor, r. 1440-1493

Charles V (1500-1558), Holy Roman Emperor, r. 1519-1556, king of Spain, r. 1516-1556, as Charles I

SUMMARY OF EVENT

Comprising present-day Belgium, the Netherlands (or Holland), and Luxembourg, the Low Countries have been known collectively throughout history as the Netherlands. Though a focus of conflict between France, England, and the Holy Roman Empire, this region prospered as one of medieval Europe's few urban, manufacturing centers. For centuries, French kings tried in vain to annex the wealthy southern provinces of Flanders. Simi-

Maximilian I, Holy Roman Emperor. (Hulton|Archive by Getty Images)

larly, Holy Roman Emperors tried to dominate neighboring Brabant and Luxembourg. Fending off both the French and the emperors, the dukes of Burgundy ruled the area by the mid-1300's. The often rebellious cities of the Netherlands, particularly Bruges, Ghent, and Ypres in Flanders, retained a measure of independence that would end amid intense dynastic rivalries in the late fifteenth century.

To the east, the Habsburg family, who ruled Austria, eliminated the custom of dividing territories among sons, thereby consolidating their power. In 1440, the electors, seven high aristocrats and archbishops who appointed Holy Roman Emperors, chose a Habsburg, Frederick V of Styria, to reign as Frederick III. The last emperor to be crowned by a pope in Rome, he did much to extend Habsburg possessions. He arranged the betrothal of his eldest son, Maximilian I, to Mary of Burgundy, the only child of

Duke Charles the Bold. This highly political tie was intended to counter pressure on the Burgundians to bring together in marriage Mary and the heir to the French throne. The couple wed after Charles the Bold died battling the French at Nancy in 1477. Two years later Louis XI of France unsuccessfully attacked the Burgundian holdings.

Following Mary's tragic death in a hunting accident in 1482, the twenty-three-year-old Maximilian became the target of much hostility directed at his wife's family, who had tripled taxes to pursue their military campaigns and artistic tastes. Unaccustomed to the deeply rooted civic traditions strengthened under his father-in-law's often neglectful rule, Maximilian ignored the wishes of city councils and the states-general, the parliament of the Netherlands. Despite a prenuptial agreement preventing him from inheriting his wife's holdings, Maximilian assumed the regency of their son Philip and the right to rule over Burgundian territories. The cities of Flanders rebelled and were soon joined by Holland's independent-minded nobles. Hoping for the support of disaffected urban areas, the French king offered to restore Ypres's age-old cloth monopoly. In a counter move, Maximilian offered inducements to foreigners settling in Antwerp and other communities along the rivers Scheldt and Dender in Brabant, which in turn strongly supported the young ruler.

On his father's initiative, Maximilian was elected and crowned king of the Romans (emperor-elect) at Aachen in 1486. With their overlord's departure from the Netherlands, Ghent rebelled. Returning to reassert his authority, Maximilian was captured by rebels in Bruges on January 31, 1488, and forced to turn over the regency to local administrators. His supporters from the Scheldt and Dender marched west. Sacking as they went, they were joined by Maximilian's father, Frederick III, whose army arrived at Bruges in May, 1488. Maximilian was freed and then immediately set out to harshly avenge his humiliation. First, the coast was subdued. Holland's rebel fleet was annihilated and its leaders were executed. French involvement ended with a 1489 treaty confirming Maximilian's possession of the Free County of Burgundy (Franche-Comté) and the Netherlands. Without foreign assistance, Bruges capitulated the next year. Ghent and Sluis held until 1492.

Events in the Netherlands spurred Maximilian to maximize his power elsewhere. In 1490, he recovered Austria, which had been occupied by Hungarian king Matthias I Corvinus. Through the 1491 Treaty of Pressburg, he secured the right of succession to the Hungarian and Bohemian thrones. He married Anne of Brittany, daughter of Duke François II, by proxy in 1490 and tried to prevent a French invasion of Brittany. French king Charles VIII, however, occupied the province and forced Anne to marry him in 1491. Meanwhile, in the Netherlands, he abrogated the agreements he had made under duress and subjected its cities to central control with the Peace of Kadzand of July, 1492.

Becoming Holy Roman Emperor on his father's death in 1493, Maximilian drove the Turks from the empire's southeastern borders and accelerated efforts to make his family Europe's dominant royal house. In 1494, he joined the Holy League and invaded Italy to counter French ambitions there. Applying his father's marriage strategies to good effect, he married Bianca, daughter of Duke Galeazzo Maria Sforza of Milan. In 1495, he arranged for his son, Philip, to marry Joan the Mad, heiress

to the thrones of Castile and Aragón, which resulted in two centuries of Habsburg rule in Spain. Following an attempt by the electors to take the imperial administration from the emperor, Maximilian created an imperial council and court of justice in 1500. However, he and later Habsburgs had no intention of uniting the empire around a German identity, in conflict with their own dynastic visions of seizing all of Europe as the heirs of Holy Roman Emperor Charlemagne (r. 800-814). These differences would become more pronounced over the next four centuries.

Maximilian made peace with Louis XII of France in 1504, and four years later, he joined the French against Venice in the League of Cambrai. However, in 1511, he fought the French again in alliance with England, Spain, and the pope. This conflict ended with a victory over the French in the Battle of the Spurs near the Flemish village of Guinegate in 1513. Now firmly under Habsburg control, the Netherlands brought the empire enormous wealth and strategic advantages. Displacing older Flemish ports, Antwerp rose to prominence as Europe's most important trading center. To reduce growing pressures on the empire brought about by treaties between the rulers of France, Poland, Hungary, Bohemia, and Russia, Maximilian met with King Vladislav II of Hungary and Bohemia and King Sigismund I, the Old, of Poland in Vienna in 1515. Marriages arranged as a result brought four centuries of Habsburg rule to Hungary and Bohemia.

Because his only son, Philip, had died in 1506, Maximilian campaigned throughout 1518 to have his Ghent-born grandson Charles elected to succeed him as Holy Roman Emperor. Shortly thereafter, Maximilian died at Wels in Upper Austria. His heir, Charles V, inherited the imperial crown; the wealthy duchies of Milan, Burgundy, and Brabant; the kingdoms of Spain, Naples, and Sicily; and vast tracts of the New World. Remembering his grandfather's difficulties in Flanders, he humiliated Ghent's city fathers, forcing them to parade through the streets wearing nooses, an event still commemorated annually.

During Charles's reign, Martin Luther would emerge to challenge the unity of the Catholic Church, a bastion of Habsburg power. Unable to effectively rule one of history's largest empires, Charles abdicated the Spanish crown, Italian possessions, and Burgundian inheritance to his only son, Philip II, in 1556. He then resigned the imperial crown to ensure its inheritance by his brother Ferdinand, the first Habsburg to combine the crowns of the Holy Roman Empire, Austria, Hungary, and Bohemia.

SIGNIFICANCE

Despite centuries of ineffective rule, the Holy Roman Empire emerged as a major power by the end of the Middle Ages. However, it failed to secure either political unity for its many tiny German-speaking principalities or strong central government as had developed in England, France, and Spain. These successes and failures were both the work largely of the Habsburg family, who dominated early modern Europe and held the imperial crown continuously between 1438 and 1740. Almost completely encircling his French arch-rivals, Emperor Maximilian I added vast lands to his family's traditional Austrian holdings, including the Netherlands and Burgundy by his own marriage; Hungary, Bohemia, and parts of Italy by military pressure and treaty; and Spain and its empire by his son's marriage.

The last Holy Roman Emperor of the Middle Ages, Maximilian set a precedent of coercive rule in the Low Countries that would culminate in the Dutch Wars of Independence and the separation of the Netherlands and Belgium within a half century of his death. A source of both great conflict and high culture, Habsburg rule in the Low Countries ended with the French Revolution, and the dynasty's power in Austria collapsed with its defeat in World War I.

—Randall Fegley

FURTHER READING

Blom, J. C. H., and E. Lamberts, eds. *History of the Low Countries*. Translated by James C. Kennedy. New York: Berghahn Books, 1999. An excellent history of Belgium, the Netherlands, and Luxembourg, with much material on Habsburg rule.

Carson, Patricia. *The Fair Face of Flanders*. Ghent, Belgium: E. Story-Scientia, 1969. An older, well-written survey of Flemish history.

Coxe, William. *History of the House of Austria*. North Stratford, N.H.: Ayer, 1970. A reprint of an insightful early nineteenth century history of the Habsburgs from 1218 to 1792.

Fichtner, Paula Sutter. *The Habsburg Monarchy, 1490-1848: Attributes of Empire*. New York: Palgrave Macmillan, 2003. A work that questions past assumptions about the Habsburgs.

Milton, Joyce, and Caroline Davidson. *The House of Hapsburg*. Boston: Boston Publishing, 1987. A good, short work on Habsburg dynastic politics.

Nicholas, David. *Medieval Flanders*. London: Longman, 1992. Covering Flemish history from late antiquity to the reign of Charles V, Nicholas's work is particularly good on dynastic, governmental, economic, and urban affairs.

Okey, Robin. *The Habsburg Monarchy: From Enlightenment to Eclipse*. New York: St. Martin's Press, 2000. A good look at the Habsburgs at the height of their prominence.

SEE ALSO: Aug. 17, 1477: Foundation of the Habsburg Dynasty; Aug. 19, 1493-Jan. 12, 1519: Reign of Maximilian I; Nov. 26, 1504: Joan the Mad Becomes Queen of Castile; 1508: Formation of the League of Cambrai; 1531-1585: Antwerp Becomes the Commercial Capital of Europe; 1555-1556: Charles V Abdicates; 1568-1648: Dutch Wars of Independence; July 26, 1581: The United Provinces Declare Independence from Spain.

RELATED ARTICLES in *Great Lives from History: The Renaissance & Early Modern Era, 1454-1600:* Anne of Brittany; Charles the Bold; Charles V; Charles VIII; Frederick III; Louis XII; Mary of Burgundy; Matthias I Corvinus; Maximilian I; Philip II; Sigismund I, the Old; Vladislav II.

1480's

1483-1485
RICHARD III RULES ENGLAND

The brief, bloody reign of the usurper king Richard III produced important reforms, but his unpopularity with the English people, including the nobility, began when he evidently had his two young nephews murdered at the Tower of London. This led to his eventual defeat and death at Bosworth Field and to the accession of Henry VII as the first Tudor Dynasty king.

LOCALE: England
CATEGORY: Government and politics

KEY FIGURES

Richard III (1452-1485), duke of Gloucester and king of England, r. 1483-1485
Henry VII (Henry Tudor; 1457-1509), earl of Richmond and king of England, r. 1485-1509
Edward V (1470-1483), succeeded father King Edward IV, r. April to June, 1483
Elizabeth Woodville (1437-1492), wife of Edward IV and queen of England, r. 1464-1483
Henry Stafford (c. 1454-1483), second duke of Buckingham

SUMMARY OF EVENT

After a young, mentally defective king ascended the throne of England in 1422, the country was plunged into near anarchy. By 1455, the king's family, the house of Lancaster, and the rival house of York, both of which were descended from the sons of Edward III (r. 1327-1377), were locked into a conflict later called the Wars of the Roses, which would last thirty years. The Yorkist symbol was reportedly a white rose, the Lancastrian symbol a red rose.

After eliminating the Lancastrian king, the Yorkist king, Edward IV (r. 1461-1470, 1471-1483), managed to hold the throne despite threats both from the Lancastrians and from his own party. When at his death he was succeeded by his twelve-year-old son, however, the Yorkists expected the real power to be wielded by the queen, Elizabeth Woodville, whom they disliked because of her Lancastrian ancestry, her less-than-noble birth, and her habit of seeing that her relatives were preferred at court. Richard, duke of Gloucester, Edward IV's youngest brother and his loyal supporter during his lifetime, was determined to seize the throne. He believed that the queen's unpopularity with the Yorkists would make it much easier for him to succeed.

In the late king's will, Gloucester had been named

protector and regent, so it was easy for him to have Edward V placed in the Tower of London, supposedly until his coronation, and then to convince Elizabeth Woodville that nine-year-old Richard should keep his brother company. Meanwhile, Gloucester argued that he was his father's sole legitimate heir, circulating rumors that his own mother, a woman of unquestioned piety, had been an adulterer. He said also that because of a previous marriage on Edward IV's part, all of Elizabeth Woodville's children were illegitimate. Although few believed these allegations, no one wanted to oppose the usurper. On July 6, 1483, less than three months after Edward IV's death, Richard, the duke of Gloucester, was crowned King Richard III.

In August, the little princes disappeared, and even those historians who are most sympathetic to Richard admit that he almost certainly had them murdered. The king provided for the succession on September 8, 1483, by having his only legitimate son, ten-year-old Edward, made prince of Wales. When the boy died the following April, there were those who whispered of divine judgment.

Henry Stafford, duke of Buckingham, whom the king had made Lord High Constable (commander in chief of England's armed forces), led a rebellion against Richard, probably because he believed that no king as mistrusted as Richard could remain in power for any significant period of time. On October 11, the king learned from his spies that rebellions were imminent throughout the south of England on October 18, followed by attacks by mercenaries and the Welsh. The rebels would be joined by the Lancastrian pretender, Henry Tudor, earl of Richmond, another of Edward III's descendants, who would land on the southwestern coast of England, accompanied by five thousand Breton mercenaries. The plot might well have succeeded, but unseasonable storms halted Buckingham's progress by land and scattered Richmond's fleet. By the time the pretender reached port, Richard's troops were in place, and the pretender returned to the Continent.

After quelling the rebellion, Richard had certain rebels executed, including Buckingham, pardoned others to gain a reputation for generosity, and confiscated estates throughout the south of England. He then infuriated southerners by bestowing these lands and titles upon his friends from the north and also by placing northerners in administrative offices throughout the south.

Richard, however, had many of the qualities of a good administrator. He got along well with his parliament, and he persuaded them to pass some beneficial laws. For example, it was made illegal for a seller of land to conceal secret agreements that would cloud the title to the property and result in expensive lawsuits. Other measures protected Richard's subjects against false accusations, made it easier for them to obtain bail, and safeguarded the property of those who were awaiting trial. Parliament also abolished the notorious "benevolences," or forced loans to the king, that had impoverished some of England's most prosperous individuals during the reign of Edward IV.

Richard also demonstrated his abilities in foreign affairs. He visited Ireland, and by his generosity there won the support of his peers and the Irish people alike. He successfully negotiated peace treaties with Scotland and Brittany, and he was even very close to having the Bretons hand over Henry Tudor, but the pretender was warned in time to make his escape to France.

At home, Richard tried to improve his image by surrounding himself with churchmen and scholars and by issuing pious pronouncements. He even tried to win over the Woodvilles by promising Elizabeth Woodville, the mother of the murdered princes, that he would cherish her daughters and see them married to peers of the realm. Richard had an immediate problem, though: His son was dead, he had no heir, and his queen was evidently barren and also very ill. Callously, Richard began a scandalously bold courtship of the sister of the dead princes, his niece, Elizabeth of York. The court was shocked by this and by his clear desire to see his wife die. His cruelty toward the queen undoubtedly hastened her death; it was even rumored that he had poisoned her. The rumors were so widely circulated that Richard had to deny the allegation publicly. Moreover, he was forced to assert that he had never wanted to marry Elizabeth, and to support his declaration, he sent her away from court.

Meanwhile, Lancastrians and Yorkists were gathering around the pretender. On August 7, 1485, Henry Tudor landed in South Wales with a large contingent of French mercenaries and several hundred English exiles. Though many Welshmen joined him as he marched eastward, he reached Bosworth Field with less than half the men that were under Richard's command. When the battle began

early on the morning of August 22, it seemed certain that Richard would win. Several nobles, however, who had been vacillating as to which side they would support, joined Henry's forces at a crucial time, thus ensuring his success. Though Richard fought bravely, he was killed, his army fled, and the pretender was crowned Henry VII. Richard's corpse was beheaded, stripped, mangled, and carried to Leicester to be displayed and then thrown into a pauper's grave.

SIGNIFICANCE

With the death of Richard III and the subsequent marriage of the new Lancastrian king to the Yorkist princess Elizabeth, the Wars of the Roses ended. However, Richard is still the subject of controversy. In his play *Richard III* (pr. c. 1592-1593), William Shakespeare followed the lead of the earlier writer, Sir Thomas More, who portrayed Richard as a bloodthirsty tyrant. Many later historians have agreed, though others have argued that such an interpretation was Tudor propaganda rather than truth. Fictional works such as Josephine Tey's mystery *The Daughter of Time* (1951) and Sharon Kay Penman's historical novel *The Sunne in Splendour* (1982) convince readers that Richard was a good person and a conscientious king. The Richard III Society, boasting thousands of members, works tirelessly to rally support for their maligned hero. Richard III ruled for two years only and

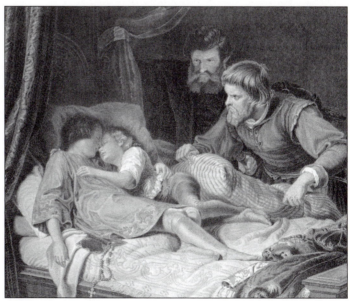

Usurper king Richard III of England had his two nephews murdered. The young Edward V, king of England, and his brother, Richard, were killed while they slept. (Hulton|Archive by Getty Images)

died defeated, but he remains one of the best-known monarchs in British history.

　　　　　　　　　　　　　—Rosemary M. Canfield Reisman

FURTHER READING

Cunningham, Sean. *Richard III: A Royal Enigma*. Kew, England: National Archives, 2003. An objective account of Richard's reign, supported by reproduced extracts from surviving letters and state papers.

Fields, Bertram. *Royal Blood: Richard III and the Mystery of the Princes*. New York: ReganBooks, 2000. A well-known entertainment lawyer applies modern courtroom techniques to his subject.

Gillingham, John, ed. *Richard III: A Medieval Kingship*. New York: St. Martin's Press, 1993. Seven leading fifteenth-century scholars consider how established political and governmental frameworks shaped the reign of Richard III and influenced his subjects' attitude toward him.

Kendall, Paul Murray. *Richard the Third*. London: Allen & Unwin, 1955. Argues that, though flawed, Richard was no monster. One of the most important works written in his defense.

Ross, Charles. *Richard III*. Berkeley: University of California Press, 1981. Another major defense of Richard. Insists that he was intelligent, pious, and a fine administrator.

Seward, Desmond. *Richard III: England's Black Legend*. 1984. Rev. ed. New York: Penguin, 1998. The writer of this superbly written study explains why he believes that Richard was indeed as evil as his long-standing reputation.

SEE ALSO: 1455-1485: Wars of the Roses; Beginning 1485: The Tudors Rule England.

RELATED ARTICLES in *Great Lives from History: The Renaissance & Early Modern Era, 1454-1600:* Henry VII; Richard III; William Shakespeare.

c. 1485
PORTUGUESE ESTABLISH A FOOTHOLD IN AFRICA

Portugal made contact with the kingdom of Benin in West Africa, a civilization just as developed, well organized, and prepared for trade as its own. The two civilizations were able to ally as equals, providing Portugal with an important base and trading partner and providing Benin with increased wealth, resources, and military power.

LOCALE: Kingdom of Benin (now in Nigeria)
CATEGORIES: Diplomacy and international relations; exploration and discovery; trade and commerce

KEY FIGURES

João Alfonso d'Aveiro (fl. c. 1485), believed to be the first Portuguese explorer to reach Benin
Henry the Navigator (1394-1460), prince of Portugal
Ewuare (d. 1473), oba (king) of Benin, r. c. 1440-1473
John II (João II; 1455-1495), king of Portugal, r. 1481-1495
Ozolua (d. 1504), oba of Benin, r. 1481-1504
Esigie (d. 1550), oba of Benin, r. c. 1504-1550

SUMMARY OF EVENT

The Portuguese sailors and merchants who explored the west coast of Africa in the fifteenth century were prompted by several motives. They hoped to outflank their traditional enemies and trading opponents, the Muslims, who occupied North Africa and controlled trade with sub-Saharan Africa and the Far East. They also hoped to spread their Christian faith and to recruit a potential ally against the Muslims—the legendary Prester John, who was thought to rule a Christian kingdom somewhere in Africa. In 1485, these motives brought them into close and extended contact with the kingdom of Benin, an African civilization whose cultural and political achievements matched their own.

Portuguese expansion into Africa had begun in 1415, when, under the command of Prince Henry of Aviz (later known as "the Navigator"), the European country captured the North African port of Ceuta from the Muslims. Further encouraged by Prince Henry, who established a school for navigation at Sagres in southwestern Portugal, the Portuguese then began an intensive period of exploration and discovery. They colonized the island of Madeira, near the coast of Africa, in 1420; rounded the difficult and supposedly impassable Cape Bojador in 1434; and reached the more southerly Cape Blanco in 1441. On a darker note, the captains responsible for this last accomplishment, Antão Gonçalves and Nuno Tristão, transported a dozen African slaves to Portugal from the Cape Blanco region in 1441.

By 1472, Portugal's explorers had reached what would later be identified as the mouth of the Niger. The mighty river emptied into the Bight of Benin, a large, open bay forming the northwestern part of the Gulf of Guinea. Inland lay the city and kingdom of Benin. Located west of the Niger in a humid, heavily forested region of what is now southern Nigeria, the kingdom of Benin (not to be confused with the modern nation of the same name) was originally populated by the Edo people.

Benin began to grow in power and influence in the fifteenth century under Oba (King) Ewuare, who had conquered the territory of the Yoruba people to the west and the Igbo people to the east. Subsequently Ewuare reorganized and rebuilt the capital city of Benin, enclosing his extensive palace complex within a series of moats and ramparts. He employed numerous artists and craftspeople to create works in ivory and bronze to celebrate the burgeoning kingdom. An extensive trade developed, helping to make the kingdom the largest and most powerful state on the Gulf of Guinea.

It is not certain when the Portuguese first reached Benin. The merchants Ruy Sequeira and Fernão Gomes sailed into the Bight of Benin in 1472, although it is unclear how far their voyage took them. It is more likely that João Alfonso d'Aveiro's journey to the court of Benin in 1485 (or possibly 1486), during the reign of Ewuare's son, Oba Ozolua, marked the first Portuguese visit. Subsequently, the explorer informed Portuguese king John II of the great opportunities for trade and proselytizing that awaited them there. The chief of Benin's port city of Gwatto accompanied d'Aveiro as ambassador on his return trip to Portugal, where he was feted and treated as an equal.

For more than a century the Portuguese and the Edo lived, worked, and sometimes worshiped in close harmony. So pervasive did the European country's influence become that Portuguese was spoken at court, startling later visitors. During this period, Portugal had no territorial or military ambitions beyond fortifying its trading stations against attack by its European competitors. Instead of conquering Benin and adding it to its empire, Portugal's soldiers fought for the African nation as mercenaries in Benin's own wars of territorial expansion. Portuguese missionaries built a church in Benin City in 1516, and in the same year Oba Esigie ordered his son and two of his noblemen to become Christians.

Portuguese merchants carried on trade with their counterparts, offering cheap European manufactured goods such as tools and simple weapons, coral and glass beads, and brass and copper *manillas* (bracelets), the latter of which became a form of currency that was in use well into the twentieth century. In return, they received stone beads, ivory, textiles, animal pelts, pepper, and—for a period of time—slaves. Some of these commodities the Portuguese would exchange for gold on what had become known as the Gold Coast to the west, while others (such as pepper) would be transported back to Portugal.

Eventually, however, Portuguese activity in Benin foundered. Private trade in African pepper was prohibited by the Portuguese crown, which had established a monopoly in the spice imported from the East Indies. Benin itself suspended the sale of slaves, forcing the Portuguese to turn elsewhere for their commerce in human beings. In addition, the Portuguese, like other Europeans, found the region unhealthy, succumbing in large numbers to such diseases as malaria and yellow fever. The region's reputation was summed up in a popular saying: "Beware and take heed of the Bight of Benin/ Where few come out though many go in." Finally, the fact that the Edo regarded the oba as divine inhibited the spread of Christianity.

SIGNIFICANCE

Although Portugal would eventually establish several large colonies in Africa, its enterprises on the continent were seldom successful, and its achievements are not highly regarded, particularly given its extensive involvement in the African slave trade. Portugal profited briefly from its trade with Benin, principally from the gold it obtained indirectly, but it remained one of the poorest countries in Europe.

Benin profited more from its association with the European country, and in a greater variety of ways. Portuguese mercenaries (and, later, firearms) helped the kingdom subdue its enemies. Before the appearance of the Portuguese, Benin had imported copper from its eastern neighbors to make the alloy bronze. Thanks to the copper *manillas* the Portuguese offered in trade, the kingdom's craftspeople were able to produce larger statues and bas-reliefs—highly sophisticated works that would influence the course of Western art when introduced into Europe in the twentieth century.

The kingdom of Benin itself declined during the eighteenth and nineteenth centuries. In 1897, the city of Benin was captured by the British, and in 1900, the territory was absorbed by the British protectorate of southern Nigeria.

—Grove Koger

FURTHER READING

Blier, Suzanne Preston. "Imaging Otherness in Ivory: African Portrayals of the Portuguese, ca. 1492." *Art Bulletin* 75, no. 3 (September, 1993): 375-396. Discusses representations from Benin and other regions of West Africa of Portuguese explorers, merchants, and mercenaries. Notes and bibliography.

Bradbury, R. E. "The Kingdom of Benin." In *Benin Studies*. New York: Oxford University Press, 1973. Brief overview of the kingdom's history as well as its social and political institutions. Excellent map.

Falola, Toyin. *The History of Nigeria*. Westport, Conn.: Greenwood Press, 1999. Opening chapters deal with the precolonial period and European penetration. Selected bibliography.

Nigeria: A Country Study. 5th ed. Washington, D.C.: Federal Research Division, Library of Congress, 1992. The study's opening chapter sketches the area's ethnographic makeup and summarizes its history, beginning with early states before 1500. Maps, substantial bibliography.

Roese, Peter M., and D. M. Bondarenko. *A Popular History of Benin: The Rise and Fall of a Mighty Forest Kingdom*. New York: Peter Lang, 2004. A comprehensive history by two specialists in the field. Maps, illustrations, bibliography.

Ryder, A. F. C. "From the Volta to Cameroon." In *Africa from the Twelfth to the Sixteenth Century*, edited by Joseph Ki-Zerbo and Djibril Tamsir Niane. Vol. 4 in *General History of Africa*. Abridged ed. Berkeley: University of California Press, 1997. Surveys the civilizations of the region at the time of their first contact with the Portuguese. Map, black-and-white illustrations.

SEE ALSO: Late 15th cent.: Mombasa, Malindi, and Kilwa Reach Their Height; 1481-1482: Founding of Elmina; Aug., 1487-Dec., 1488: Dias Rounds the Cape of Good Hope; Jan., 1498: Portuguese Reach the Swahili Coast; 1502: Beginning of the Transatlantic Slave Trade; 1505-1515: Portuguese Viceroys Establish Overseas Trade Empire; Aug. 4, 1578: Battle of Ksar el-Kebir.

RELATED ARTICLE in *Great Lives from History: The Renaissance & Early Modern Era, 1454-1600:* John II.

Beginning 1485
THE TUDORS RULE ENGLAND

The Tudor Dynasty, established in England after Henry VII seized the English throne from the Lancastrian king Richard III, had its accomplishments consolidated by Henry VII's son, Henry VIII. The beginning of the dynasty also marked the end of the Wars of the Roses between the houses of Lancaster and York.

LOCALE: England
CATEGORIES: Government and politics

KEY FIGURES

Henry VII (1457-1509), first Tudor king of England, r. 1485-1509

Henry VIII (1491-1547), second Tudor king of England, r. 1509-1547

Catherine of Aragon (1485-1536), first wife of Henry VIII

Richard III (1452-1485), Yorkist king of England, r. 1483-1485

Cardinal Thomas Wolsey (1471/1472-1530), Lord Chancellor of England

Thomas Cromwell (1485?-1540), Wolsey's agent, later vicar-general

Sir Thomas More (1478-1535), Wolsey's successor as Lord Chancellor

SUMMARY OF EVENT

On August 22, 1485, at the battle of Bosworth Field, a rebel army under Henry Tudor, earl of Richmond, defeated the forces of the legitimate Yorkist monarch, Richard III. This victory for Henry—a claimant to the English throne through his mother's family—put an end to the lingering Wars of the Roses between the houses of Lancaster and York, and at least provisionally established a new dynasty, the Tudors, on the English throne. It would be the work of Henry's reign, and that of his son, Henry VIII, to firmly establish the Tudors as the rightful and accepted rulers of England.

Within three months, Parliament had accepted Henry VII's claim and title to the English throne. His immediate concerns were to establish the security and stability of the new Tudor rule. His marriage to Elizabeth of York five months after Bosworth was part of this strategy; through this marriage Henry "united" the red and white roses of the Yorkist and Lancastrian families and so wrote a symbolic ending to the seemingly interminable civil wars of the past three generations. The birth of four children, including two sons, Arthur (b. 1486) and Henry (b. 1491) further secured the position of the new dynasty.

The change in ruling families was immediately important only at the upper strata of English political and social life, and even in those spheres there was considerable continuity. Administrative and bureaucratic reforms begun by the Yorkist king Edward IV and continued by his brother and heir, Richard III, remained in place. In some instances, Henry VII even expanded upon them to consolidate and enlarge royal authority and prerogatives. The restoration of the power of the monarchy, especially in fiscal affairs, which had started under Edward IV, was continued by the Tudors, and often with the same advisers. Henry VII wisely retained a number of Edward's and Richard's chief ministers: Out of forty of Edward IV's councillors who were alive in 1485, twenty-two became councillors to Henry VII. Twenty of the chief councillors who had served Richard III (including some who had also been active in the court of his brother, Edward) were to be found in the service of Henry VII.

Henry VII's domestic and foreign policies were fundamentally conservative. At home, he made relatively few changes; his major innovations were in the greater efficiency and functioning of the royal bureaucracy. As his reign progressed, however, Henry took an increasingly personal role in daily activities, especially fiscal and judicial policy. The delegation of authority that was to become first notable under his son Henry VIII and then routine under his granddaughter Elizabeth I was not part of Henry VII's matured view of royal government. In part, no doubt, this could be attributed to his position as the first member of a new dynasty, as well as someone constitutionally incapable, from long years of exile and plotting, from fully trusting anyone else.

Henry VII's major goal in foreign policy was to reduce England's commitment to potentially dangerous entanglements in Europe, especially those involving France, Burgundy, and the Low Countries. Although he had received help and encouragement from the French during the period of this exile, Henry VII was generally successful in avoiding any lasting commitment on the European

Henry VII, the first monarch of the Tudor Dynasty in England. (Hulton|Archive by Getty Images)

mainland. His generally defensive foreign policy was cemented by the engagement and marriage of Catherine of Aragon, daughter of King Ferdinand II and Queen Isabella I, to his son Prince Arthur. After Arthur's death Catherine was married to Henry VIII.

In general, Henry VII was successful in his efforts. There were few pretenders and no serious rivals to his position as monarch during his reign. He won recognition of his title from Parliament, the Papacy, and the nation in general. Through his careful efforts and diligent service he kept England free of foreign adventures and built up a substantial treasury. On his death in 1509, it was left to his son, Henry VIII, to consolidate Tudor rule in England and to expand England's influence throughout Europe.

Henry VIII became king of England when his father died April 21, 1509, and his immediate—and lasting—desire was to augment royal power and enhance England's position in European political affairs. Internally, he initially sought to increase the flow and regularity of revenues into the Crown's purse; later, he attempted to stamp his version of acceptable religious belief and practices on the kingdom. Externally, Henry sought to establish England as an "empire," the term used during the time for a power of the first rank. To accomplish this, Henry repeatedly engaged in European affairs, including

1480's

151

a series of invasions of France that practically amounted to a renewal of the Hundred Years' War. Although he was ultimately unsuccessful in his attempts, and to a considerable degree emptied the English treasury through his efforts, Henry did make his nation once again a major player in European political affairs.

Through his brilliant minister Cardinal Thomas Wolsey, Henry was much more successful in consolidating and enlarging royal power at home. Wolsey, who took his seat on the king's council in 1510, rose quickly through his abilities as an administrator. From his selection as Lord Chancellor in December of 1515 to his fall from power in 1529, he was commonly acknowledged as practically a second king (*alter rex*, in Latin) in England, whose initiatives and policies were equal to those of Henry VIII himself. Although in many respects highhanded and even dictatorial, Wolsey had a firm belief in administrative and legal fairness and competence; throughout his career he upheld the right of the common people to justice and fairness, and he did much to advance the growth of English administrative law.

Wolsey's fall was bound up with Henry VIII's obsessive desire to secure his divorce from Catherine of Aragon. Having no legitimate male heir, Henry felt the Tudor line seriously threatened, and he convinced himself that by marrying his brother's widow he had seriously transgressed God's law. Wolsey, as his chief minister, was charged with securing a dispensation from the pope; unfortunately for the cardinal, European political conditions made such an accomplishment impossible. In 1529, Henry dismissed Wolsey; the cardinal died the following year while en route to the Tower of London to almost certain execution. Sir Thomas More was named chancellor, but he too felt Henry's displeasure over the "divorce question" and was beheaded in 1535.

In the meantime, Henry had effectively broken with Rome. By 1531, his propaganda machine was using the printing press to advance his case for the divorce and was spreading the theory that the king, rather than the pope, was the Supreme Head of the Church in England. In May of 1532, this theory became fact with the forced submission of the English clergy to Henry's royal power. (It was this that caused More's resignation as chancellor and his eventual execution.) Thomas Cromwell, who had served as Wolsey's deputy, rose to power and brought the full weight of royal power to bear on suppressing English Catholics, dissolving the monasteries and other church establishments and making Henry VIII in fact, as well as name, head of a new, national church called the Church of England.

SIGNIFICANCE

The establishment of the Tudor Dynasty in England can be seen as essentially a two-step process. First, Henry VII seized the throne from the ruling monarch, Richard III, and then established himself and his family by cautious, even conservative policies that left most of English society unaffected by the transformation at the court and that brought a period of relative peace and prosperity to the nation. Then, the more ambitious and public monarchy of his son Henry VIII awakened a sense of national pride and identity that, despite the upheaval of the break with the Roman Catholic Church and subsequent turmoil, left England and the English with a sense of a unique and separate nationhood that was fully and brilliantly exploited by the greatest of the Tudor monarchs, Elizabeth I.

—*Michael Witkoski*

FURTHER READING

Bucholz, Robert, and Newton Key. *Early Modern England, 1485-1714*. Malden, Mass.: Blackwell, 2004. Comprehensive survey and introduction to English history under the Tudors and the Stuarts. Covers both the political history of the monarchs themselves and cultural and social history during their reigns. Includes illustrations, maps, genealogical tables, bibliographic references, and index.

Collinson, Patrick, ed. *The Sixteenth Century, 1485-1603*. New York: Oxford University Press, 2002. Anthology of essays on English and British culture during the Tudor Dynasty. Covers economics, religion, the scope of monarchic power, and foreign relations. Includes illustrations, maps, bibliographic references, and index.

Elton, G. R. *England Under the Tudors*. 3d ed. New York: Routledge, 1991. A general survey that provides a comprehensive review of English life under the dynasty, encompassing political, religious, and economic affairs.

Griffiths, Ralph. *The Making of the Tudor Dynasty*. New York: St. Martin's Press, 1985. Excellent in its review of the background of Henry Tudor and his family, and perceptive in its study of his shrewd, if sometimes unscrupulous, tactics in maneuvering himself into first the pretendership and then the monarchy itself.

Guy, John. *Tudor England*. New York: Oxford University Press, 1988. Detailed, lucid, and learned, this volume provides an excellent introduction to the life of England under the dynasty, with an outstanding discussion of the operations of royal administration. It is perceptive and sympathetic in its treatment of Cardinal Wolsey, one of England's most underrated ministers.

Loades, David. *The Tudor Court*. 3d ed. Oxford, England: Davenant, 2003. Comprehensive account of the courts of the Tudor monarchs. Discusses both the external trappings and the internal politics of the court, and the often labyrinthine nature of the relationship between appearance and political reality. Includes illustrations, bibliographic references, and index.

Morris, Christopher. *The Tudors*. London: Severn House, 1976. A good starting point for the beginning student who needs to understand the worldview of sixteenth century England in a broad context.

Rex, Richard. *The Tudors*. Stroud, Gloucestershire, England: Tempus, 2003. A study of the relationship between the public persona and the private life of each of the Tudors. Emphasizes the common characteristics of the monarchs, especially their mixture of charisma with the threat of violent action. Includes photographic plates, illustrations, bibliographic references, and index.

Ridley, Jasper. *A Brief History of the Tudor Age*. New York: Carroll & Graf, 2002. Brief but comprehensive survey of English culture under the Tudors. The focus on both London and rural England is especially useful, given the tendency of other sources to look primarily at the royal court. Includes photographic plates, illustrations, bibliographic references, and index.

SEE ALSO: 1455-1485: Wars of the Roses; Aug. 29, 1475: Peace of Picquigny; 1483-1485: Richard III Rules England; 1515-1529: Wolsey Serves as Lord Chancellor and Cardinal; July, 1553: Coronation of Mary Tudor; 1558-1603: Reign of Elizabeth I.

RELATED ARTICLES in *Great Lives from History: The Renaissance & Early Modern Era, 1454-1600:* Anne of Cleves; Anne Boleyn; Catherine of Aragon; Thomas Cranmer; Thomas Cromwell; Elizabeth I; Henry VII; Henry VIII; Catherine Howard; Mary I; Sir Thomas More; Catherine Parr; Richard III; Jane Seymour; The Tudor Family; Cardinal Thomas Wolsey.

May, 1485-April 13, 1517
MAMLŪK-OTTOMAN WARS

Mamlūk and Ottoman sultans fought two major wars to dominate Syria. The second war concluded with the destruction of the Mamlūk sultanate and the elevation of the Ottoman Empire to the status of a world power.

LOCALE: Southern Anatolia, Syria, and Egypt

CATEGORIES: Diplomacy and international relations; expansion and land acquisition; wars, uprisings, and civil unrest

KEY FIGURES

Qāytbāy (1414-1496), Mamlūk sultan, r. 1468-1496

Qānṣawh II al-Ghawrī (1441-1516), Mamlūk sultan, r. 1501-1516

Bayezid II (1447/1448-1512), Ottoman sultan, r. 1481-1512

Selim I (1467-1520), Ottoman sultan, r. 1512-1520

Azbak min Tutukh (fl. 1480's), Mamlūk general

SUMMARY OF EVENT

Eccentric in format, yet traditional, indeed hidebound in outlook, the Mamlūk sultanate controlled Egypt, Syria, Palestine, Arabia, and portions of southern Anatolia.

Facing few serious rivals since the 1400-1401 invasion of Syria by Tamerlane (also known as Timur), the so-called slave soldiers who dominated the Mamlūk Empire supported a Middle Eastern status quo. Drastic change, however, was sought by the Anatolia-based Ottoman Empire.

The Ottomans' imperial project seemed to be doomed in the early fifteenth century, when Tamerlane's great victory over them at Angora (1402) nearly destroyed their empire, realigned the balance of power in Anatolia, and allowed many small states to emerge. However, with Tamerlane's death in 1405 and the rapid dissolution of his empire, Ottoman power enjoyed a remarkable resurgence. Moreover, the fifteenth century also saw the conduct of Middle Eastern machinations by Venice, Florence, Genoa, and the Hospitaller Knights of Rhodes, as a result of which Anatolia and Syria were more likely poised for volatile change than a continuation of the status quo.

The Mamlūk sultans, when not focused on the turbulent politics of their power base in Egypt, viewed Syria as a vital interest. They maintained several client states in southern Anatolia as buffers and guardians of the mountain passes that funneled north-south travel in the region. Karaman and Dulkadir (Dhū al-Qadr) were good examples of such crucial client states. Both states were also targets for Ottoman expansion starting in the 1470's.

Ottoman sultan Bayezid II initiated hostilities in 1484, when he sent an army into Dulkadir. His Mamlūk counterpart, Qāytbāy, had spent the previous decade propping up a client government there, and he was unwilling to abandon his interests. The result was the First Mamlūk-Ottoman War (1485-1491). A complex struggle that featured radically different military machines, it included naval operations, sieges, and set-piece battles.

Ottoman armies comprised a mix of professional soldiers—the Kapikulu, which included the famous Janissaries (yeni çeri), heavy cavalry, and artillery—and provincial troops. The latter were mainly cavalry forces and included newly acquired provincials of dubious loyalty. One outstanding feature of Ottoman soldiery was the use of gunpowder weapons. Matchlock muskets were employed in quantity and provided significant firepower. With its strong economic base, the Ottoman state could afford large armies equipped with such weapons.

Mamlūk armies were smaller, elitist, and conservative. All power and prestige went to the cavalry, especially the Julban, the personal guard of the reigning sultan. Armored and trained to employ bows plus a variety of bladed weapons, Mamlūks liked to boast that they were "equal to a thousand other soldiers." Even their enemies agreed that Mamlūks were the best horsemen in the Middle East, but they also noted tremendous internal rivalry and poor discipline caused by the constant struggle for status in the Mamlūk system. Another problem in the Mamlūk army was a complete disdain for infantry. As artillery, and the only effective handguns of the 1400's, were designed for foot soldiers, Mamlūk cavaliers disdained all gunpowder weapons. Finally, as the purchase and training of Mamlūk slave soldiers were tremendously expensive, they were few in number.

Ottoman forces started the war with a rapid occupation of Tarsus, Adana, and key fortresses in the ancient land of Cilicia. The Ottomans' superior resources presented the Mamlūks with a considerable challenge. First, Qāytbāy's treasury was hard pressed to fund a war, so his mobilization was slow, allowing the Ottomans time to rebuild damaged fortresses and prepare a strong defense. Also, Mamlūk politics placed great value on residence at the seat of power, Cairo, so no leader, from the lowest emir up to the sultan, would support a long campaign far from the capital.

Demonstrating his status as the last great Mamlūk sultan, Qāytbāy produced a significant force, one that included more than half of his Julban. Under the command of Azbak min Tutukh (also known as Ozbeg or Uzbek min Tutuh), this army moved north in October, 1485. On February 9, 1486, they attacked a poorly prepared Ottoman force near Adana, scattering these troops, and then laid siege to the city. Mehmed Karagoz Paşa directed an Ottoman relief force but was smashed at the second Battle of Adana on March 15. Several other Mamlūk victories followed.

Having defeated the immediate Ottoman forces, Mamlūk troopers, always a difficult body to discipline, demanded a bonus, plus rapid demobilization. Despite the need to complete several sieges and organize against a possible Ottoman counterattack, Azbak was unable to keep his army on the field, and most Mamlūks returned to Cairo by the end of 1486. Bayezid, meanwhile, organized a new army. He augmented the army by opening peace talks with Hungary, freeing experienced Balkan troops for deployment to Anatolia. During the spring and summer of 1487, commanded by Grand Vizier Davud Paşa, the Ottoman forces smashed Turkoman clans who had traditionally supported Mamlūk authority in the Taurus Mountains.

Spring of 1488 marked the start of a renewed Ottoman offensive into Cilicia. Hadim Ali Paşa commanded the invasion, designed, as Turkish contemporary historian Idris Bidlisi wrote, "to free the entire land of Syria from . . . the vile Circassian people." With the Turkoman crushed a year before and no effective Mamlūk field army, the Ottomans quickly reoccupied key cities, forts, and mountain passes.

Qāytbāy dug deep into his treasury and produced what eyewitness Ibn Iyas described as "the largest army produced by Egypt in a hundred years." About forty thousand strong, again commanded by Azbak, it faced an Ottoman defensive screen that included fortresses, a field army, and a fleet hovering off the Cilician coast.

Azbak benefited from a turn in the weather that sank or drove away the enemy ships and opened up the Bab al-Malik, the sea coast pass for north-south traffic into Cilicia. Deploying his army at Aga-Cayiri, Azbak set up the largest battle of the war. On August 16, 1488, Ottoman forces arrived and fighting began at noon. Although it exacted the heavy price of eight thousand casualties, Aga-Cayiri was a Mamlūk victory. Azbak next took his army to raid Ottoman Anatolia. Bayezid, facing the possibility of renewed conflict in the Balkans, was now willing to end the war. Qāytbāy, nearly bankrupt, was anxious to do the same. A treaty of peace on September 11, 1491, returned the Anatolian frontier to the antebellum status quo.

Mamlūk power declined rapidly after 1491. Internal discord continued, while plagues ravaged the highly urbanized warrior elite. Financial hard times, already evident at the end of Qāytbāy's reign, continued into the 1500's, as Portuguese mariners established themselves in the Indian Ocean, creating a different trade route between Asia and Europe.

When Qānṣawh II al-Ghawrī became sultan in 1501, he inherited a Mamlūk kingdom on the verge of financial and political collapse. Threats in the Balkans and Iraq distracted Ottoman attention until their decisive victory over Shah Ismā'īl I Ṣafavid at Chāldirān in 1514. Having chastised the Iranians, Selim I, called Yavuz ("the Grim"), turned his superb army toward Syria.

Again, control of Dulkadir sparked conflict, but this time Ottoman commanders were competent, their soldiers well trained, and the technological disparity between the two armies even greater. The armies met at Marj Dabiq (August 24, 1516), where twenty thousand Mamlūks faced at least sixty thousand Ottomans. Massed artillery and matchlock fire devastated the Mamlūk cavalry, which broke after Sultan Qānṣawh suffered a fatal stroke. The Ottoman victory was so complete, Selim disdainfully sent a lame clerk to demand the surrender of nearby Aleppo. Several battles followed Marj Dabiq, the most significant being Raydaniyah, near Cairo, on January 22, 1517. All featured Mamlūk defeats, and the war concluded with the incorporation of the Mamlūk sultanate into the Ottoman Empire.

SIGNIFICANCE

Concluding these wars with total victory, the Ottoman Empire became a great world power. Egypt, Syria, Palestine, and Arabia provided not only financial and military assets but also an equally important level of prestige, as these provinces contained the holiest cities of Islam. This combination allowed Selim, and future Ottoman sultans, to stand as leaders of the Muslim world. In addition, eliminating their last Middle Eastern rival made it possible for the Ottomans to extend their power into the Balkans, Central Europe, and the Mediterranean.

Although the Mamlūks continued to play a role in Egyptian affairs until 1811, they never seriously influenced regional politics after 1517. Egypt itself remained under the direct control of the Ottomans until Napoleon Bonaparte's 1798 invasion, and it was considered a part of the Ottoman Empire until 1914. Syria, Arabia, and Palestine were imperial provinces until the empire's demise in 1918.

—*John P. Dunn*

FURTHER READING

Ayalon, David. *Gunpowder and Firearms in the Mamluk Kingdom: A Challenge to Mediaeval Society.* London: F. Cass, 1978. Important work examining why the Mamlūks failed to employ gunpowder technology.

Har-el, Shai. *Struggle for Domination in the Middle East: The Ottoman-Mamluk War, 1485-91.* Boston: E. J. Brill, 1995. The best work in any language, with detailed coverage of diplomatic, economic, political, and military aspects of the first conflict.

Petry, Carl F. *Protectors or Praetorians: The Last Mamlūk Sultans and Egypt's Waning as a Great Power.* Albany: State University of New York Press, 1994. Examines the disintegration of the Mamlūk army, economy, and society in the late 1400's through the end in 1517.

_____. *Twilight of Majesty: The Reigns of the Mamlūk Sultans al-Ashrāf Qāytbāy and Qanṣūh al-Ghawrī in Egypt.* Seattle: University of Washington Press, 1993. A strong biography by a leading scholar, placing Mamlūk leadership from both wars under intense scrutiny.

Petry, Carl F., ed. *Islamic Egypt, 640-1517.* Vol. 1 in *The Cambridge History of Egypt.* New York: Cambridge University Press, 1998. Extensive coverage by experts on all aspects of late Mamlūk Egypt.

1486-1487
PICO DELLA MIRANDOLA WRITES *ORATION ON THE DIGNITY OF MAN*

The Oration on the Dignity of Man, *considered by many the manifesto of Italian Renaissance Humanism, is the most widely read and quoted text of the era. Pico, like Plato and as in the Bible, considered humans to be the center of the world and, thus, makers of their own destinies.*

LOCALE: Rome and Tuscany

CATEGORIES: Philosophy; religion; cultural and intellectual history

KEY FIGURES

Giovanni Pico della Mirandola (1463-1494), Italian philosopher and writer

Marsilio Ficino (1433-1499), philosopher, translator of Plato and Plotinus, and leader of the Platonic Academy in Florence, 1460-1499

Innocent VIII (1432-1492), Roman Catholic pope, 1484-1492, who declared Pico a heretic

Lorenzo de' Medici (Il Magnifico; 1449-1492), Florentine statesman and patron of the arts who supported Pico's scholarly pursuits and protected him politically

SUMMARY OF EVENT

In 1486, Italy was subdivided into five major power blocs centered in Naples, Rome, Florence, Milan, and Venice, amid several smaller ministates. Under the guidance of Lorenzo de' Medici, who managed to keep the peace by appeasing the Papacy and warding off a long-threatened French invasion, a sophisticated urban culture flourished, especially in Florence. There was a strong rebirth of classical learning, inspired by the importation from Byzantine Greece of ancient manuscripts, and centered upon humanity's civic humanism.

Giovanni Pico della Mirandola was a prodigious and ambitious philosopher who, though only twenty-three years old, planned to defend in public a set of nine hundred theses, known as the *Conclusiones* (1496; English translation, 1998), in January of 1487, in Rome. The theses were based on a vast array of sources, some biblical and Christian, some Platonic, but some of exoteric, magical, and mystical origin as well, which expanded on Pico's belief that humans are driven to self-elevation through learning and introspection. The first third of *De hominis dignitate oratio* (wr. 1486-1487; *Oration on the Dignity of Man*, 1956; better known as *Oration*) was supposed to be the preface to the *Conclusiones*, which was

actually printed before the *Oration* in December of 1486 and circulated publicly in light of the coming debate in January. Sensing controversy, Pico had introduced pages about universal peace and about a defense of the faith.

Despite Pico's efforts, Pope Innocent VIII suspended the debate definitively in February because some of its contents were considered unacceptable to the Church. In the spring of 1487, disappointed and furious, Pico wrote a passionate *Apologia* (defense) to his theses (which makes up the second half of the *Oration*) but was nevertheless condemned for heresy by a papal commission; while fleeing Italy he was arrested for a short period. He was later pardoned by another pope, Alexander VI, in 1493.

The full text of the *Oration* became known after his death, in 1496, when his nephew published his complete works. The *Oration* begins with Pico asserting that, according to different sources—Saracen, Hermetic, Persian, biblical—it is agreed that "there is nothing more wonderful than man." He then argues that the supreme architect, having created the divine temple that humans inhabit, in His wisdom had adorned the heavens with intelligences, animated the spheres with immortal souls, and quickened with diverse animals the lower world. God had wished that there would be someone to comprehend and appreciate this great work, one who would love its beauty and wonder at its vastness. As told by Moses and Timaeus, He conceived of humans lastly. However, there were no more archetypes upon which to model such a creature, no treasures left to bestow as inheritance, and no seat from which to judge the universe. God thus decided that the creature to whom nothing specific was given should possess what belonged individually to each and every thing. God takes the human being, a "creature of indeterminate nature" or, in different translations, "a work of indeterminate form," and, having assigned him a place in the middle of the world, says,

> Adam, I have not given you a fixed abode or a specific form or a task specific to your kind in order that you may, according to your desire and your judgment, have the seat, form and role you want. The nature of all other beings is limited and constrained by my laws. But you are not confined by any bounds, your nature will be determined by your own free will, under whose power I entrust you. I have made you neither heavenly nor earthly, neither mortal nor immortal, so that through freedom of choice, judge of your own self, you can shape yourself into whatever you should like to be. You have the power

to degenerate into the brutish lower forms, or you may from your reason elect to be reborn into the higher forms, which are divine.

Pico believed that at birth all seeds are planted and a person may become what he or she wants according to what he or she cultivates. Thus, humans can change; they are like chameleons, Protean figures. Metamorphosis is a fundamental aspect of existence, and though this may strike some as implying that humans have no set identities, or universal, stable essences, as both the Platonists and the Scholastics held, Pico's position is that, in the language of later centuries, existence precedes essence and humans fabricate their values. Individual and social values are, therefore, a function of reason completely, of that divine intellect that distinguishes the human radically from other living beings.

Pico found support for his thesis in the diverse writings of varied traditions. From the ancient Hebrews and the Pythagoreans he learned that a person can be changed into a brute or an angel. From Empedocles he learned that a person can be changed into a plant. From the Persian

Italian philosopher Giovanni Pico della Mirandola. (Hulton Archive by Getty Images)

Euanthes he learned, based on his commentary on Chaldean theology, that "man is a being of varied, manifold and inconstant nature." A strong believer in scholarship, Pico here unfolds a long list of exemplary, authoritative lives, from Saint Paul to Jacob, from Osiris to Job, from the pseudo-Dionysius to Plato. If natural philosophy teaches that struggle is the lot of humans, if the Pythagoreans explain that the end of philosophy is friendship, and if the ancient mysteries hold that God is both philosopher and prophet, then the moral imperative is for humans to attain the wisdom of theology, to seek the ultimate concord, peace, and inner illumination.

Pico's threefold philosophy is thus: moderation, self-knowledge, and elevation. The first implies learning all positions and meditating as much as possible; the second implies that humans ought to see their own inner selves and make choices on the basis of what they feel is right; and the third is for humans to seek the divine, to improve themselves through striving to be as close to God as possible. The second part of the *Oration* is more virulent. Pico attacks those who take money for sharing their knowledge and those who merely follow established dogmas. He believes in public debates because knowledge ought to be evaluated by an entire community. He holds that, properly understood, some forms of magic, of astrology, and of numerology can lead to truth and illumination on the ways of humans and God. Pico also introduces the Kabbala as consistent with Christian theology, for he believed that the Kabbala tradition held the secret to a unity of all doctrines, of all the languages of the godhead. For Pico, the will to choose for oneself meant the will to learn how all fits together.

Throughout his life, Pico struggled to prove that Plato's and Aristotle's philosophies are not reciprocally exclusive. He published, however, the first part of this project only, called *De ente et uno* (1492; *Of Being and Unity*, 1943).

SIGNIFICANCE

Pico altered Marsilio Ficino's basic triad of beauty, love, and appetite after he proposed an ontological triad made up of beauty, intellect, and will. In this way, he broke down the individual's position from the fixed hierarchy in the chain of being, because will allows the individual to no longer be a prisoner of transcendent essences or of nature. Pico brought Neoplatonism down to earth, for he was pursuing civil, moral, and intellectual values, while his theology was bound to incite purists from all religious persuasions.

The *Oration on the Dignity of Man* has been made a

forerunner of philosophies of self-determination, of love of freedom, and of a critical attitude that seeks to find common ground in theories typically considered incompatible. The *Oration* also stimulated Renaissance culture to look beyond the Greek and Latin classical traditions—which were the mainstays of Humanism—and also took seriously the relevance of texts from Middle Eastern cultures.

—Peter Carravetta

FURTHER READING

Carravetta, Peter. "In Pursuit of the Chameleon: The Interpretations of Pico." In *Italiana*, edited by A. Mancini, P. Giordano, and P. R. Baldini. River Forest, Ill.: Rosary College, 1988. A reading of the *Oration on the Dignity of Man* and Pico's contemporary work, the *Commentary on a Poem of Platonic Love*, in a hermeneutic perspective.

Craven, William G. *Giovanni Pico della Mirandola, Symbol of His Age: Modern Interpretations of a Renaissance Philosopher.* Geneva, Switzerland: Librairie Droz, 1981. A detailed analysis of all of Pico's works, which studies the different meanings of the *Oration*.

Farmer, S. A. *Syncretism in the West: Pico's Nine Hundred Theses (1486): The Evolution of Traditional, Religious, and Philosophical Systems.* Tempe, Ariz.: Medieval & Renaissance Texts & Studies, 1998. Presents a translation of Pico's *Oration*, with commentary and introductory essays.

Hankins, James. "Pico della Mirandola, Giovanni." In *Routledge Encyclopedia of Philosophy*. New York: Routledge, 1998. One of the best short introductions to Pico, which places *Oration* in the context of his reformation of Neoplatonism; it touches on the various interpretations given to this emblematic text.

Kibre, Pearl. *The Library of Pico della Mirandola.* New York: Columbia University Press, 1936. For advanced work on the variety of Pico's sources.

Pico della Mirandola, Giovanni. *On the Dignity of Man, On Being and the One, and Heptaplus.* Indianapolis, Ind.: Bobbs-Merrill, 1965. Contains all three major texts by Pico, with a useful introduction by J. W. Miller.

_____. *Oration on the Dignity of Man.* Translated by A. Robert Caponigri. Introduction by Russell Kirk. Chicago: Gateway Editions, 1956. A good translation and introduction, but a work that is difficult to locate.

SEE ALSO: 1462: Founding of the Platonic Academy; 1490's: Aldus Manutius Founds the Aldine Press; 1499-1517: Erasmus Advances Humanism in England; c. 1500: Revival of Classical Themes in Art.

RELATED ARTICLES in *Great Lives from History: The Renaissance and Early Modern Era, 1454-1600:* Desiderius Erasmus; Marsilio Ficino; Francesco Guicciardini; Lorenzo de Medici; Sir Thomas More; Giovanni Pico della Mirandola; Peter Ramus; Girolamo Savonarola.

August, 1487-December, 1488
DIAS ROUNDS THE CAPE OF GOOD HOPE

Dias rounded the Cape of Good Hope and opened up a water route to the Far East, thus eliminating the trade monopoly of Arab and Italian middlemen.

LOCALE: West coast and southern tip of Africa
CATEGORY: Exploration and discovery

KEY FIGURES
Bartolomeu Dias (c. 1450-1500), Portuguese explorer
Prince Henry the Navigator (1394-1460), Portuguese prince
John II (João II; 1455-1495), king of Portugal, r. 1481-1495
Diogo Cão (fl. 1480-1486), Portuguese explorer

SUMMARY OF EVENT

The Dias expedition was the final phase of more than a century of voyages initiated by Prince Henry the Navigator. At his center for study at Sagres in southern Portugal, Henry gathered the finest minds and compiled extensive geographical data. His school studied ancient geographers, medieval maps, and the use of the compass at open sea and directed the design and development of the caravel, the type of ship utilized in the exploration of the African coast.

Motivated by crusading zeal and a desire for wealth, Portuguese expeditions were sent south along the African coast almost annually, beginning in 1418. Henry sought to open communication with the fabled kingdom of Prester John (modern Ethiopia), develop sea trade,

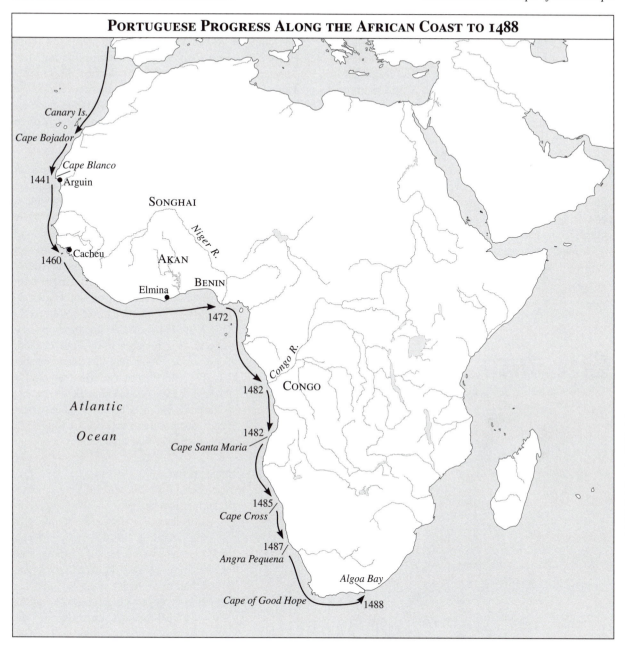

PORTUGUESE PROGRESS ALONG THE AFRICAN COAST TO 1488

Canary Is.

Cape Bojador

Cape Blanco

1441 ● Arguin

SONGHAI

Niger R.

1460 ● Cacheu

AKAN

Elmina ●

BENIN

1472

Atlantic

Ocean

Congo R.

1482 CONGO

1482

Cape Santa Maria

1485
Cape Cross

1487
Angra Pequena

Algoa Bay

Cape of Good Hope 1488

1480's

spread Christianity, and eventually discover a sea route to India. From 1418 to 1460, Portuguese explorers cautiously proceeded southward, discovering and occupying the Madeira, Azores, and Canary Islands, doubling Cape Bojador, and rounding Cape Verde.

Portugal's painstaking African explorations produced immediate benefits, such as an increase in geographical knowledge and the development of trade along the coast of Guinea, of which the infamous African slave trade was

an unfortunate result. For a time, the Portuguese became so involved in commerce and the insidious traffic in African slaves that explorations farther south were curtailed. With the accession of John II in 1481, however, voyages of exploration resumed, and by 1486, Diogo Cão had reached Cape Cross and Cape Negro in southwest Africa.

Bartolomeu Dias was a cavalier of the royal court, superintendent of the royal warehouses, and sailing master

159

of a man-of-war when King John II appointed him head of an expedition around the southern end of Africa. In August, 1487, the expedition set off in the belief "that ships which sailed down the coast of Guinea might be sure to reach the end of land by persisting in a southward direction."

The expedition was made up of three caravels, two armed caravels of fifty tons each and one supply ship to allow the others greater mobility. Most of the officers, including Dias, were veterans of previous African voyages. Besides the Portuguese, there were six Africans on board who had been taken by Cão. They were outfitted in European dress and were to be set ashore at suitable spots to explain to the natives the purpose of the expedition.

Through most of the autumn, the expedition sailed southward, landing at Angra Pequena (modern Lüderitz

A caravel like the one depicted here in a drawing attributed to Christopher Columbus was used by explorers of the African coast and of Asia, including Bartolomeu Dias. (Frederick Ungar Publishing Co.)

Bay) early in December. The store ship anchored in the bay, and the two remaining caravels continued southward. They were soon caught in a storm that lasted for thirteen days and tossed them around the Cape of Good Hope without their knowledge. Their first landfall beyond the cape was at Mossel Bay, South Africa, in February of 1488. As the ships headed in a northeasterly direction, Dias realized that Africa had been rounded and that India lay ahead.

He was unable to continue much farther, however, since the crew, distressed by the length of the voyage, demanded to return. Following the coast, he was able to reach Algoa Bay and then the limit of his exploration, the Great Fish River. There, the two ships turned westward, having traveled 520 miles (837 kilometers) eastward from the Cape. On his return voyage, Dias discovered the cape itself, to which he gave the name Cabo Tormentoso (stormy cape). Only after the importance of the voyage was realized did King John II propose the cape be renamed to Cabo da Boa Esperanza, or Cape of Good Hope. In December of 1488, Dias returned to Lisbon after an absence of sixteen months and seventeen days. He had shown the way to Vasco da Gama, whom he had accompanied in a subordinate position in 1497 as far as the Cape Verde Islands.

SIGNIFICANCE

The return of the Dias expedition roused little enthusiasm in Portugal, where such accounts of discovery were commonplace by 1488. Nevertheless, this discovery provided the Portuguese with a wealth of knowledge. Of primary value was the fact that they believed that an all-water route to India had been discovered, so King John broke off his talks with Christopher Columbus, who was proposing a western route to Asia. The voyage of Dias greatly added to the geographical knowledge of the day, with the Cape of Good Hope appearing soon afterward on an Italian map (c. 1489-1492).

The Portuguese realized that their caravels were too low and frail to survive south Atlantic storms and too small for satisfactory payloads. Vasco da Gama's ships were made larger. Dias himself never set foot in India. While making a second attempt to reach the subcontinent in 1500, Dias commanded a ship in the expedition of Pedro Álvares Cabral. Unfortunately, his vessel was wrecked not far from the Cape of Good Hope, which he had discovered thirteen years before. To quote Antonio Galvano, the Portuguese chronicler: "It may be said that he saw the land of India, but like Moses and the Promised Land, he did not enter it."

—*Russell M. Magnaghi, updated by Marian T. Horvat*

FURTHER READING

Diffie, Bailey, and George D. Winius. *Foundations of the Portuguese Empire, 1415-1580.* Minneapolis: University of Minnesota Press, 1977. Written for student audiences, this simple exposition portrays Portuguese expansion as the result of long-term economic and maritime development, rather than the work of one man.

Hanson, Carl. *Atlantic Emporium: Portugal and the Wider World, 1147-1497.* New Orleans: University Press of the South, 2001. Survey of the Portuguese sphere of influence from the twelfth to fifteenth centuries, covering political, economic, and cultural history. Emphasizes Portugal's contribution to the creation, for the first time, of a global economy, and the importance of Dias's journey in making such an economy possible. Includes illustrations, bibliographic references, and index.

Hart, Henry H. *Sea Road to the Indies: An Account of the Voyages and Exploits of the Portuguese Navigators.* New York: Macmillan, 1950. A scholarly account by an American historian based on original documents.

Knox-Johnston, Robin. *The Cape of Good Hope: A Maritime History.* London: Hodder & Stoughton, 1989. A very technical and up-to-date account of the discoveries, voyages, and captains.

Penrose, Boies. *Travel and Discovery in the Renaissance, 1420-1620.* New York: Atheneum, 1962. Emphasis is on colonial history and settlement, especially the Portuguese explorations. The Dias expedition is discussed as part of a development of mental and physical techniques of conquest.

Prestage, Edgar. *The Portuguese Pioneers.* New York: Barnes & Noble, 1967. A well-documented, romantic work that treats all of the recorded Portuguese voyages to the end of the fifteenth century and the more important ones up to the mid-sixteenth century. The Dias voyage receives treatment of some length.

Russell, P. E., ed. *Portugal, Spain, and the African Atlantic, 1343-1490: Chivalry and Crusade from John of Gaunt to Henry the Navigator.* Brookfield, Vt.: Variorum, 1995. Anthology of essays detailing the expansion of Portugal's exploration and influence across the African Atlantic in search of a route to India. Includes illustrations, maps, bibliographic references, and index.

Winius, George D., ed. *Portugal, the Pathfinder: Journeys from the Medieval Toward the Modern World, 1300-ca. 1600.* Madison, Wis.: Hispanic Seminary of Medieval Studies, 1995. Anthology of essays on Portuguese exploration, including several on the discovery of the sea route to India and Portugal's subsequent activities in South Asia. Includes a bibliographic essay by the editor surveying all major sources pertaining to the fifteenth and sixteenth centuries.

SEE ALSO: 1481-1482: Founding of Elmina; c. 1485: Portuguese Establish a Foothold in Africa; Oct. 12, 1492: Columbus Lands in the Americas; Jan., 1498: Portuguese Reach the Swahili Coast; 1502: Beginning of the Transatlantic Slave Trade; 1505-1515: Portuguese Viceroys Establish Overseas Trade Empire; Sept. 29, 1513: Balboa Reaches the Pacific Ocean; Aug. 4, 1578: Battle of Ksar el-Kebir; Dec. 31, 1600: Elizabeth I Charters the East India Company.

RELATED ARTICLES in *Great Lives from History: The Renaissance & Early Modern Era, 1454-1600:* Afonso de Albuquerque; Christopher Columbus; Pêro da Covilhã; Bartolomeu Dias; Vasco da Gama; John II; Ferdinand Magellan; Manuel I.

1480's

1488-1505
REIGN OF XIAOZONG

During the reign of Xiaozong, the struggle between the scholar-officials of the Hanlin Academy and the emperor's private bureaucracy of eunuchs continued, as did military warfare along the northern frontier. Natural disasters also marked Xiaozong's reign, and these were met with wise leadership that brought general stability.

LOCALE: China
CATEGORY: Government and politics

KEY FIGURES

Xiaozong (temple name, also Hsiao-tsung; personal name Zhu Youtang, Chu Yu-t'ang; posthumous name Jingdi, Ching-ti; reign name Hongzhi, Hung-chih; 1470-1505), emperor of China, r. 1488-1505
Huai En (d. 1488), director of eunuchs, 1467-1485 and 1487-1488
Wang Shu (1416-1508), the celebrated minister of personnel, 1487-1493

SUMMARY OF EVENT

Xiaozong ascended to the throne of Ming China when he was seventeen years old. His father, the emperor Xianzong (temple name Hsien-tsung, given name Zhu Jianshen or Chu Chien-shen, reign motto Zhenghua, Chenghua; r. 1465-1487), allowed unworthy servitors great liberty, and their avarice weakened the state as they sold titles and collected precious metals and stones throughout the empire. Xiaozong acted immediately to dismiss two thousand irregularly secured posts, rid the court of one thousand of his father's Buddhist and Daoist clerics, and slowed the growth of the eunuch bureaucracy. After issuing the dismissals, Xiaozong recalled from retirement the virtuous eunuch Huai En to head the eunuch organization. Huai En quickly selected Wang Shu as minister of personnel, an appointment that later brought many good officials into the bureaucracy.

During the second half of the fifteenth century, the eunuch bureaucracy expanded its civil and military postings and took larger responsibilities in the management of imperial factories, in official building projects, and in the secret police. Three years before Xiaozong took power, an official of the censorate estimated that there were more than ten thousand eunuchs, who represented an increasing financial burden on the state's resources. At the end of the Ming Dynasty in 1644, some estimates put the total number of eunuchs in the capital at seventy

thousand. Many eunuchs grew wealthy, acquired land, and even had retainers. Their rise to prominence angered the scholar-officials, who saw themselves as the moral upholders of society and the eunuchs as inappropriate holders of authority. The opposition to eunuch power grew within their numbers. The eunuchs, of course, had an interest in enlarging the bureaucracy over which they presided, although it functioned in tandem with the civil service bureaucracy.

The Ming Dynasty's founder, Ming Taizu (Zhu Yuanzhang, the Hongwu emperor; r. 1368-1398), had unwittingly helped the eunuchs by insisting that his successors act as their own prime ministers to secure personal control over the three branches of government—the administration, military, and censorate. Realistically, however, imperial authority had to be delegated, since the demands of imperial office were too much for one individual, and so the eunuch bureaucracy continued grow throughout the Ming Dynasty despite many attempts to curtail it. Although emperor Xiaozong attempted to promote only honest individuals, others found fault in his understandable reliance on certain eunuchs charged with dispatching his many duties.

The Mongols remained China's national enemy throughout this period, and the wars with the Mongols were persistent, costly, and dangerous. While Emperor Xianzong had followed his military-minded grandfather and father—the emperors Xuande (r. 1426-1435) and Yingzong (r. 1436-1449, 1457-1464) respectively—Xiaozong, a pacifist Confucian ruler, only reluctantly mounted military campaigns. Instead, he focused largely on defense. The "long walls" (*chang cheng*), known to the West singularly as the Great Wall, were fortified and integrated during his reign. Xiaozong's only notable military expeditions were minor ones to Hami in 1495 to suppress small uprisings. He did, however, face banditry that threatened local order and safety, as well as rebellions that challenged the authority of the state, such as the one on Hainan Island, where the native Li people organized a resistance to villainous prefectural magistrates. These rebels were aided in their fight by the mountainous interior of the island, which afforded them places to hide, but the three-year uprising was finally repressed in 1503 with heavy Han losses.

From the 1490's until the end of the Xiaozong reign in 1505, natural disasters occurred frequently and were severe. In an attempt to reduce flooding and increase trade through the country, the Chinese diverted the Yellow

River from its path in 1495. The river subsequently entered the sea through the channel of the Huai River, thereby extending the Grand Canal from Hangzhou in the south to Beijing in the north. Although confining the Yellow River to artificial channels required expensive maintenance and could not prevent flooding, the canal connected the south of China to the north and allowed easy movement of the tax grains on which the north depended. Floods did cause regular breaks in the dikes of the Yellow River, but the emperor granted relief to the affected population in the form of tax remissions, for Xiaozong adhered to the ancient Confucian belief concerning the correlative interactions between humanity and the cosmos. Unnatural events, such as frequent flooding, required self-criticism on the part of the ruler, as well as other measures, to restore cosmic harmony. Xiaozong took this Confucian ideal to heart. He earnestly strove to correct the weaknesses of this father, and there is evidence that his dedication to imperial duties shortened his life.

The Xiaozong reign saw the compilation of two important works: *Da Ming huidian* (pb. 1509; collection of official Ming Dynasty documents) and *Wenxing tiaoli* (pb. 1500; detailed rules of law), which contained 297 articles supplementing the code of the dynasty. The emperor was also fond of art and sponsored court artists such as Lu Zhi (1496-1576), a painter of landscapes and natural objects. The increased prosperity of wealthy families of the south during this period, particularly in the silk-production center of Suzhou, encouraged the flourishing of the Wu school of artists, including Shen Zhao and Tang Yin.

SIGNIFICANCE

By and large, the reign of Xiaozong marks a period of relative calm during which no great national crises occurred. Emperor Xiaozong generally made sound official appointments, such as that of Huai En, and was legitimately concerned about the welfare of the people. No doubt his punctilious attendance to his duties added stability to his reign. Xiaozong was also remarkable for being the only monogamous emperor in Chinese history. However, he was not without fault. He indulged Empress Zhang and her two brothers Zhang Heling (d. 1537?) and Zhang Yanling (d. 1546). These notorious brothers involved themselves in illegal activities in real estate, the salt trade, and usury, amassing fortunes by oppressive means with only mild reprimands.

Although Xiaozong initiated many reforms, most would be undone with the succession of his son Wuzong (reign name Zhengde; r. 1505-1521), who reacted against his father's Confucianism and embarked on a life of leisure, filling the court with entertainers. Officials even tried unsuccessfully to remove Wuzong from the throne in 1506. Yet, even though the reforms of the ninth Ming emperor proved temporary, his modest, humble, and diligent manner of governing helped reduce the consumption of luxuries by the court, improve the financial basis of the dynasty, and eliminate abuses such as selling appointments and the creation of imperial estates through confiscation.

Xiaozong's reign also saw the increasing development of fine manufactured goods, such as silks from Suzhou, which created a rich upper class who competed with the nobility in the procurement of fine art during a time of relative stability and harmony. Present during Xiaozong's reign, however, were the beginnings of trends that contributed to the political ills of later Ming: the continued expansion of the eunuch bureaucracy, the increasing unrest on the northern borders, and the shift in wealth and culture to the lower Yangzi region, which led to an increase in large estates that displaced the peasant farmers and created a floating urban proletariat.

—*Mark S. Ferrara*

FURTHER READING

Goodrich, L. Carrington, ed. *Dictionary of Ming Biography, 1368-1644*. New York: Columbia University Press, 1976. Contains useful biographies of Xiaozong and other prominent Ming figures.

Mote, Frederick W. *Imperial China, 900-1800*. Cambridge, Mass.: Harvard University Press, 1999. Useful discussion of the mid-Ming period.

Mote, Frederick W., and Denis Twitchett, eds. *The Ming Dynasty, 1368-1644, Part 1*. Vol. 7 in *The Cambridge History of China*. Cambridge, England: Cambridge University Press, 1988. In-depth overview of the reign of the emperor Xiaozong.

Paludan, Ann. *Chronicle of the Chinese Emperors: The Reign-by-Reign Record of the Rulers of China*. London: Thames and Hudson, 1998. Includes a brief discussion of the emperors of the Ming Dynasty that provides historical context.

Tsai, Henry. *The Eunuchs in the Ming Dynasty*. Albany: New York State University Press, 1996. The most complete account of the impact of eunuchs in the Ming Dynasty.

SEE ALSO: Feb. 11, 1457: Restoration of Zhengtong; 1465-1487: Reign of Xianzong; 1474: Great Wall of

China Is Built; 16th cent.: Rise of the *Shenshi*; 16th cent.: Single-Whip Reform; 1505-1521: Reign of Zhengde and Liu Jin; 1514-1598: Portuguese Reach China; 1521-1567: Reign of Jiajing; 1550-1571: Mongols Raid Beijing; Jan. 23, 1556: Earthquake in China Kills Thousands; 1573-1620: Reign of Wanli;

1583-1610: Matteo Ricci Travels to Beijing; 1592: Publication of Wu Chengen's *The Journey to the West*.

RELATED ARTICLES in *Great Lives from History: The Renaissance & Early Modern Era, 1454-1600:* Matteo Ricci; Wang Yangming; Xiaozong; Zhengde.

c. 1488-1594
KHMER-THAI WARS

By the end of the fifteenth century, the Thai people had completed their political integration and their kingdom, Siam, became a great regional power. The Khmer people, who had previously dominated the region, contributed significantly to Thai culture and sought to renew their former dominance. During the late fifteenth century and most of the sixteenth century, the two powers were in constant conflict.

LOCALE: Thailand and Cambodia
CATEGORIES: Wars, uprisings, and civil unrest; diplomacy and international relations; expansion and land acquisition

KEY FIGURES
Borommaracha II (d. 1448), king of Ayutthaya, r. 1431-1448, who conquered Angkor
Trailok (Borommatrailokanat; 1431-1488), king of Ayutthaya, r. 1448-1488, who expanded the kingdom's power and wealth
Naresuan (1555-1605), king of Ayutthaya, r. 1590-1605, who freed Siam from external threat

SUMMARY OF EVENT
From the ninth to the eleventh century, the dominant power in Southeast Asia was the great Khmer Empire, centered on Angkor, the magnificent capital and temple city on the Tonle Sap, a natural floodplain reservoir. The empire controlled much of what is now southern Vietnam, Laos, Thailand, and Cambodia, which was its heartland. (The Khmer are also known as Cambodian.) The Thai chiefs were able to maintain some semblance of autonomy in the far uplands only. Thais were often taken into slavery, and in subsequent centuries, the struggle for Thai identity and independence produced a long-lasting enmity between the Thais and the Khmer. In the fifteenth and sixteenth centuries, this hostility broke out into a series of military conflicts.

The antagonism between the two peoples has colored the historical record, since much of the analysis of the period has been written by Thai scholars and has passed into Thai national consciousness through popular histories written for the schools. This can be attributed to the evolution of a Siamese (Thai) historiography made possible by Thai independence, while Cambodia came under colonial powers. Gradually, the Khmer came to accept the Thai interpretation of their cultural inferiority, even though Thai culture was influenced by Khmer ideas, customs, and art. An influential legend relates that the Siamese took two sacred statues containing scrolls of secret wisdom when they invaded Lovek in 1594, a battle that asserted Thai dominance over Cambodia for the next century. When the Thais smashed the statues, the occult knowledge was revealed and thus denied to the Khmer. The myth holds that the scrolls conferred superior knowledge on the Thais, thus justifying their overlordship. Thai ethnic and cultural prejudice against the Khmer persists into the twenty-first century.

By the fourteenth century, there were Thai kingdoms in the north (Lan Na, also known as Chiang Mai) and in the center at Sukhothai and Ayutthaya. In 1438, Ayutthaya reduced Sukhothai to vassal status, which began a long series of Thai-against-Thai wars that would persist for seventy-five years. Ayutthaya was by this time both prosperous and powerful, its armies swelled with captives and its coffers enriched by trade. Conflict with Angkor had started earlier, with the greatest victory coming under Borommaracha, who seized and looted Angkor. The Khmer heir abandoned Angkor and fled to Phnom Penh. From this small base, later transferred to Lovet (Laweat), Khmer kings mounted a series of attacks and incursions into Ayutthayan territory to bolster their population and strengthen their fragile independence, which owed more to Ayutthaya's concern with larger threats than to Khmer power.

In 1448, Borommaracha left a tightly managed kingdom, with mandatory military service and a levy of labor that required six months each year to be given to the king for public works. By tying the freedmen to the authority of local officials, the traditional patron system of personal allegiances was broken. This gave Ayutthaya both political control and flexibility, which was a large advantage over its rivals.

At the end of King Trailok's long reign in 1488, Ayutthaya was enlarged through trade, and its expansion continued under his son. The coast of the Bay of Bengal and the Malay Peninsula came under Ayutthayan control, with rich mercantile trade in rice and cotton. When Ramathibodi II succeeded to the throne in 1491, he inherited a court that included many Khmer lawyers, scribes, and other professionals, who were recruited from the Angkorian elite of the conquered territories. Khmer royal traditions began to enter Ayutthayan court culture, elevating the king to a mystical, godlike personage, insulated from his subjects by layers of bureaucratic retainers. The Khmer became as the Greeks were to the Roman nobility—advisers, teachers of their sons, and culturally influential. Ramathibodi used his wealth to build major religious monuments and to expand and equip his army. Military power and awe-inspiring royal prestige combined to create a myth of imperial invincibility.

During the same period, the regions east of Ayutthaya coalesced into the kingdoms of Lan Sang, a Lao state centered on Vientiane, and Cambodia, known after its capital as the Kingdom of Lovek. The Khmer kings moved up the Mekong River from Phnom Penh and again occupied (but had not settled) Angkor. They guarded the Mekong Delta, which served as their economic base and transport waterway. While Ayutthaya was occupied with the Thai wars of the fifteenth to sixteenth centuries and harassed by constant threats from Burma, Lovek took advantage of Siamese instability to attack its old enemy and keep it off balance. Unable to conquer Siam, Lovek instead played Siam against other enemies of the Thais and kept them from aggressive action against the remnants of the Khmer kingdom.

One of the Khmer interventions was instigated by the Siamese crisis of 1547, when the death of King Chairacha resulted in a palace conspiracy in which the eleven-year-old successor was poisoned by the queen regent, who installed her lover as king. In reaction, the court nobility assassinated both and brought in a pious prince from his monastery as King Chakrapat (r. 1548-1569). His royal name, referring to the Buddhist wheel of righteousness, means "the wheel-turning king around whom the world revolves." In the ensuing confusion, a major

Burmese force attacked, sweeping through the north to the capital. The Khmer then took the opportunity to raid the easternmost province for loot and military conscripts. This incursion cost them dearly, as Chakrapat first negotiated a settlement with the Burmese and then turned on the hapless Khmer. In 1555-1556, Chakrapat struck Lovek with a large naval force and an army led by war elephants. The Khmer submitted, although they were permitted to keep their independence.

Soon, however, Ayutthaya faced a far more dangerous enemy as the Burmese returned to obliterate the landscape, drive out the population, and destroy the main Siamese cities. For twenty years, the Burmese ruled Siam through puppet king Maha Thammaracha (r. 1569-1590), Chakrapat's son-in-law. The Burmese army garrisoned Ayutthaya and the now-vassal kingdom was left without defenses. The Burmese demolished most of the Thai fortifications, making the frontier districts difficult to defend. The Khmer again took advantage of the situation by striking Siam six times during this period—in 1570, 1575, 1578, twice in 1582, and in 1587. In each case, the Khmer sought to maintain Thai weakness and take captives to populate their own western provinces. Generally, they did not attempt to occupy the raided territories (although in 1582 they took Phetburi) because they did not want to raise the ire of the Burmese overlords. Finally, in 1580, the Thais persuaded the Burmese to allow some measure of self-protection, arguing that their weakened state left the eastern provinces open to pillage and depopulation and threatened rice production. The walls around Ayutthaya were replaced and strengthened.

Thai culture was shattered, but a new identity was forged in the next century, especially under the dynamic leadership of Naresuan. As the son of Maha Thammaracha and his chief queen (a daughter of Chakrapat), he was heir-presumptive to the Ayutthayan throne. He distinguished himself in battle against the Khmer, but as he built up Siamese forces in the 1580's, he came into repeated conflict with the Burmese. On three occasions between 1586 and 1587, he repulsed attempts to capture him and occupy the capital. During the last of these crises, in 1587, the Khmer took up their spoiler role and advanced into Thai territory, but Naresuan repelled them easily. When Burma mounted its last attack of this period in 1593, the Khmer made no attempt at a flanking sortie, and Naresuan defeated the Burmese at Nong Sarai, freeing Siam from serious threat for a century.

Able to turn his attention to other rivals, Naresuan struck Cambodia in several annual campaigns. Ayutsthaya had begun manufacturing arms and cannon, which it exported to China, Japan, and Melaka (Malacca). Now Naresuan turned the full force of an enlarged army on Cambodia. The desperate Khmer turned to the Portuguese for help, but they responded with only a handful of adventurers who were soon captured by Naresuan. With the fall of Lovek in 1594, Khmer king Chetta I (r. 1576-1594) fled to Laos and Cambodia was reduced to a tributary state after its many years of harassing attacks on Siam.

SIGNIFICANCE

The Khmer-Thai Wars set the stage for the formation of modern Southeast Asia. As peace was established, war captives and refugees returned to Siam from Cambodia. Stability allowed for the establishment of new trade routes, and Siam became the dominant regional power. The first Western contacts had been made, but Siam was strong enough after this testing period to keep it from being colonized. Its neighbors, however, who were weakened by the conflicts, came under the influence and eventual control of European powers.

—*Norbert Brockman*

FURTHER READING

Chandler, David. *A History of Cambodia.* 3d ed. Boulder, Colo.: Westview Press, 2000. A standard history of Cambodia and the Khmer people from earliest times, written by a leading Western scholar.

Coedés, George. *The Making of Southeast Asia.* Translated by H. M. Wright. London: Routledge, Kegan & Paul, 1966. A classic introduction to early Southeast Asian history that examines the Siamese-Cambodian wars of the sixteenth century.

Mabbett, Ian, and David Chandler. *The Khmers.* Cambridge, Mass.: Basil Blackwell, 1995. A cultural history, with accounts of the kingdoms and their conflicts.

Wyatt, David. *Thailand: A Short History.* New Haven, Conn.: Yale University Press, 1984. One of the best accounts of the Thai peoples, covering all the kingdoms and their eventual grouping into Siam.

SEE ALSO: 1450's-1529: Thai Wars; 1454: China Subdues Burma; 1469-1481: Reign of the Ava King Thihathura; 1505-1515: Portuguese Viceroys Establish Overseas Trade Empire; 1511-c. 1515: Melaka Falls to the Portuguese; 1527-1599: Burmese Civil Wars; 1548-1600: Siamese-Burmese Wars; 1558-1593: Burmese-Laotian Wars; c. 1580-c. 1600: Siamese-Cambodian Wars.

RELATED ARTICLES in *Great Lives from History: The Renaissance & Early Modern Era, 1454-1600:* Afonso de Albuquerque; Tomé Pires; Saint Francis Xavier.

March 5, 1488
COMPOSITION OF THE *RENGA* MASTERPIECE *MINASE SANGIN HYAKUIN*

The composition of the Minase sangin hyakuin *marked the high point in the development of linked-verse, or* renga, *poetry in Japan.*

LOCALE: Minase, Japan
CATEGORY: Literature

KEY FIGURES

Sōgi (Iio Sōgi or Inō Sōgi; 1421-1502), literary critic and scholar of classics, the leading *renga* poet of his time

Botanka Shōhaku (1443-1527), Sōgi's senior student and a renowned poet

Saiokuken Sōchō (1448-1532), another of Sōgi's students, also renowned as a poet and critic

Go-Toba (1180-1239), Japanese emperor, r. 1183-1198, to whom the *Minase sangin hyakuin* was dedicated

SUMMARY OF EVENT

Linked verse or *renga*—a poetic form created by several or many individuals who assembled to share, by alternating turns, the line-by-line composition of a poem constrained by numerous specific topical rules—emerged in the fifteenth century as Japan's most important form of poetry against a backdrop of social turmoil. The Ōnin War of 1467-1477, which burned the capital and ushered in nearly a century of interstate war, resulted in severe social disarray. Social mobility—unpredictable both upward and downward—was the order of the day, as was increased cultural intercourse between many levels of society. The manner in which linked-verse poems were composed—in gatherings of writers from diverse backgrounds who shared the process of composing a single poem among them—was emblematic of the new social dynamics of the time.

The *Minase sangin hyakuin*, literally "one hundred

lines offered by three poets at Minase" (English translation, 1956), consists, as its title indicates, of one hundred lines of *renga* composed on the twenty-second day of the first month of the second year of Chōkyō (March 5, 1488). It was presented to a shrine in a village west of Kyōto, Minase, after having been composed there or close to there, as a reverent offering to Emperor Go-Toba, who was respected as a patron deity of poetry because of his outstanding contributions to the art during his lifetime. The exact date of composition was chosen in consideration of the anniversary of the emperor's death 250 years earlier. Minase was the location of one of his villas, where he had sponsored numerous poetry banquets.

The three poets who collaborated to compose *Minase sangin hyakuin* were Sōgi, Botanka Shōhaku, and Saiokuken Sōchō. In the year *Minase* was composed, Sōgi was sixty-seven, and though it is generally believed that he was born of humble origins, by this time he was at the peak of his career and firmly established as the premier poet and literary critic of the day, appearing before the shogun, major military leaders, and nobility. He had studied under the great authorities of his time, receiving instruction in the revered classics *Kokin Waka Shū* (wr. c. 905, *Kokinshu*; the first imperially commanded poetry anthology, first full English translation 1984) and Murasaki Shikibu's *Genji monogatari* (c. 1004; *The Tale of Genji*, 1925-1933), the massive eleventh century classic still highly esteemed today. During the most violent years of the Ōnin Wars, he lived in the east of the country, and throughout his life he traveled widely. His travels exposed him to many literary masters and, conversely, extended his own reputation. Sōgi was admired for the verses he composed but above all for his ability to orchestrate verse sequences better than any other living linked-verse poet.

Shōhaku and Sōchō, both some twenty years younger than Sōgi, were his disciples. Shōhaku was a Buddhist monk whose father was a minister with exceptionally high rank. He traveled with Sōgi and helped him with his seminal *Shinsen Tsukuba shū* (1495; the newly selected tsukuba linked-verse collection), a work that redefined the aesthetic standards of *renga*. Sōchō is the better remembered of the two, partly because of his colorful personality, one amply conveyed by the diary he wrote late in his life. More important, however, his reputation stands on the excellence of his work. After Sōgi's death and Shōhaku's retirement, Sōchō became the reigning authority on linked verse.

Because it is a one-hundred-verse sequence written as an "offering by linked verse" (*hōraku renga*), the tone of *Minase sangin hyakuin* is formal and solemn. This is evident in the first movement, or preface (*jo*), of the poem, its first eight lines, which over the centuries have been called perfect by more than one literary critic. The opening lines establish this tone with a grandness of scale and reference to a poem written centuries earlier by the emperor the poets wish to honor:

1: *yuki nagara yama moto kasumu yūbe kana*
   This evening—
   At the base of snow-dotted mountains,
   Spring mist has settled.
                                    —Sōgi

2: *yuku mizu tōku mume niou sato*
   Afar cascades the springmelt;
   At hand, a hamlet glows with the perfume of plums.
                                    —Shōhaku

The scene is expansive, like a Chinese-style screen painting, with the distant mountains and foregrounded village playing off each other to generate a sense of space. The reference to Emperor Go-Toba lies in the phrase "Spring mist has settled," which is a line from the emperor's own poem describing an autumn evening at Minase River.

The special achievement of a linked-verse poem is in how the preconditions of multiple authors and compositional rules establish shifts in scenes and topics as a new verse picks up and alters the line of poetry that preceded it. Such verse-to-verse progressions also work at higher levels to weave overarching patterns of elaborate repetition and diversion. Evolutions of images proceed concurrently at several levels, involving conceptual categories such as transitions between objects near and far, rising and falling, light and dark, one season and another, or, as below, the world of nature and human concerns:

68: *usuhana susuki chiramaku mo oshi*
   What a loss
   Should they be wind-scattered—
   These burnished plumes of pampas.
                                    —Sōchō

69: *uzura naku katayama kurete samuki hi ni*
   A cold day
   Fades on a hill's shoulder
   And cries a quail,
                                    —Sōgi

70: *no to naru sato mo wabitsutsu zo sumu*
　　While I live with my sorrows
　　In a hamlet now a moor.
　　　　　　　　　　　—Shōhaku

71: *kaerikoba machishi omoi o hito ya mimu*
　　Should you ever return
　　Might you see how I waited,
　　Tender in thought?
　　　　　　　　　　　—Sōchō

In this series the predetermined topics are autumn and grass for line 68; autumn, mountains, and birds for line 69; being at home for line 70; and love for line 71. The conceptual flow is from the chill of autumn to the loneliness of living in a desolate location to the very personal question of the state of affairs between two lovers or spouses.

SIGNIFICANCE

Minase sangin hyakuin is widely considered the preeminent achievement of the linked-verse genre. It succeeded in the linked-verse ideal, that is, to offer an ever-changing, fresh reading experience by orchestrating the many poetic images and topics that must be included at specific points in the poem. Sōgi's poetic abilities joined in turns with the talents of the other two poets while his exceptional skill in negotiating the rules of linked-verse composition gave the poem in its entirety a subtly complex structure. In many of this era's arts, aesthetic sensibility took shape around the demanding discipline of formal rules. *Minase sangin hyakuin* is an excellent example of this strict formalism.

On a broader scale, the manner in which linked verses were composed and patronized, cutting across social groups and levels, affords a window into the dynamics of Japan's fifteenth century. The *Minase sangin hyakuin* itself, with its melancholic mood, draws deeply both on the direction of several centuries of poetics that evolved in conjunction with Buddhist reforms and on the more immediate context of a war-torn country. Yet its supreme balance reflects a mastery of the discipline required of the arts as well as the level of sophistication that poetry had achieved from centuries of active critical self-evaluation.

　　　　　　　　　　　—*John R. Wallace*

FURTHER READING

Carter, Steve, trans. *Traditional Japanese Poetry: An Anthology.* Stanford, Calif.: Stanford University Press,

1991. Complete translation with brief introduction and limited notes.

Horton, H. Mack. "Renga Unbound: Performative Aspects of Japanese Linked Verse." *Harvard Journal of Asiatic Studies* 53, no. 2 (December, 1993): 443-512. Discusses the details of the finer points of the rules of linked-verse composition.

_____. *Song in an Age of Discord: The Journal of Sōchō and Poetic Life in Late Medieval Japan.* Stanford, Calif.: Stanford University Press, 2002. A thorough examination of Sōchō's life, with some discussion of the broader historical period.

_____, trans. *The Journal of Sōchō.* Stanford, Calif.: Stanford University Press, 2002. A complete translation of Sōchō's colorful personal diary.

Keene, Donald. *Seeds of the Heart: Japanese Literature from the Earliest Times to the Late Sixteenth Century.* New York: Henry Holt, 1993. Extensive biographical information on all three poets, placing them in the context of Japan's literary history.

Konishi, Jin'ichi. *The High Middle Ages.* Vol. 3 in *A History of Japanese Literature.* Translated by Aileen Gatten and Mark Harbison. Princeton, N.J.: Princeton University Press, 1991. A keen discussion of the *Minase sangin hyakuin* and the history of linked verse. Konishi is one of the few living individuals who has received traditional training in the art.

Konishi, Jin'ichi, Karen Brazell, and Lewis Cook. "The Art of Renga." *Journal of Japanese Studies* 2, no. 1 (Autumn, 1975): 29-31, 33-61. Discusses the details of the rules of linked-verse composition.

Miner, Earl. *Japanese Linked Poetry: An Account with Translations of Renga and Haikai Sequences.* Princeton, N.J.: Princeton University Press, 1979. The most extensive analysis of linked verse in the English language. Includes a complete translation of the *Minase sangin hyakuin* with extensive introductory material and thorough notes.

Yasuda, Kenneth, trans. *Minase Sangin Hyakuin: A Poem of One Hundred Links.* Tokyo: Kogakusha, 1956. The first complete translation into English.

SEE ALSO: 1457-1480's: Spread of Jōdo Shinshū Buddhism; 1467-1477: Ōnin War; 1477-1600: Japan's "Age of the Country at War"; Beginning 1513: Kanō School Flourishes; 1532-1536: Temmon Hokke Rebellion; 1549-1552: Father Xavier Introduces Christianity to Japan; 1550's-1567: Japanese Pirates Pillage the Chinese Coast; 1550-1593: Japanese Wars of Unification; Sept., 1553: First Battle of Kawanakajima;

June 12, 1560: Battle of Okehazama; 1568: Oda Nobunaga Seizes Kyōto; 1587: Toyotomi Hideyoshi Hosts a Ten-Day Tea Ceremony; 1590: Odawara Campaign; 1592-1599: Japan Invades Korea; 1594-1595: Taikō Kenchi Survey; Oct., 1596-Feb., 1597: *San*

Felipe Incident; Oct. 21, 1600: Battle of Sekigahara.

RELATED ARTICLES in *Great Lives from History: The Renaissance & Early Modern Era, 1454-1600:* Hōjō Ujimasa; Hosokawa Gracia; Oda Nobunaga; Ōgimachi; Oichi; Sesshū; Toyotomi Hideyoshi.

1489
ʿĀDIL SHAH DYNASTY FOUNDED

The Muslim 'Ādil Shah Dynasty attained independence from the declining Bahmani Dynasty and flourished despite political infighting and intrigue. The 'Ādil Shah Dynasty won the bloodiest battle in the history of India against its Hindu neighbor, the Vijayanagar Empire, but in doing so opened the door to later Mughal and British invasion.

LOCALE: Bijāpur, India

CATEGORIES: Government and politics; expansion and land acquisition

KEY FIGURES

Yūsuf 'Ādil Khan (d. 1510), founder of independent Bijāpur as Yūsuf 'Ādil Shah, r. 1489-1510

Ismā'īl 'Ādil Shah (1498?-1534), second sultan of Bijāpur, r. 1510-1534

Ibrahim 'Ādil Shah I (d. 1558), third sultan of Bijāpur, r. 1534-1558

'Ali 'Ādil Shah (d. 1580), fourth sultan of Bijāpur, r. 1558-1580

SUMMARY OF EVENT

The Bahmani sultanate in the Deccan declined sharply following the death of Sultan Shams ud-Dīn Muḥammad Shah III in 1482 (r. 1463-1482), but it had begun to disintegrate years before. Yūsuf 'Ādil Khan, founder of the 'Ādil Shah Dynasty, manipulated Sultan Muḥammad Shah to acquiesce to the demands of the nobles for greater power, and Bijāpur was conferred upon Yūsuf. Muḥammad Shah was dependent on Yūsuf and the other governors to defend the kingdom from the might of neighboring Hindu Vijayanagar Empire, and he tolerated their rebellious behavior for fear of a complete revolt.

After Muḥammad's death, the regent and his vizier recognized Yūsuf's status among the nobles and formed a conspiracy to remove him from Bijāpur, hoping that if Bijāpur were in the hands of its allies and its troublesome leader was gone, they would be able to destroy the rest of

the foreign nobles in short order. This plan failed miserably, however. Nearly four thousand lives were lost on both sides until the holy men of Bīdar, the city in which the fighting took place, persuaded Yūsuf to retire and return with his family to Bijāpur. He had the *khutba* read in his name in 1489, announcing that Bijāpur was an independent kingdom, the third to rise out of the remains of the Bahmani Dynasty, which would continue to decline in the following years.

Yūsuf's rivals resented his success. Qāsim Barīd had long been interested in Bijāpur for its rich natural resources and had desired the territory for himself. Because he was one of the head officials of the declining Bahmani Dynasty, he considered Yūsuf a rebel and usurper, and then raised a coalition against him. Hindu Vijayanagar joined for territory and succeeded in controlling Rāichūr and its forts, but Yūsuf's skill in statecraft prevented further damage, as he convinced Vijayanagar to go no further by recognizing that the newly conquered territory was indeed part of the Vijayanagar Empire.

Qāsim Barīd and his allies met Yūsuf's army at Naldurg, but the battle was indecisive because Qāsim fled soon after they engaged. Confused, the allies came to a peaceful settlement with Yūsuf and parted.

Yūsuf prepared to battle with Vijayanagar, and they met at the Tungabhadra River in 1493. Militarily, Bijāpur was no match for the great Vijayanagar Empire, but Yūsuf's craft and deceit allowed him to succeed in regaining Rāichūr and the two forts. Once Yūsuf had proved his independent strength, ironically, the young Bahmani sultan Mahmūd sought his help in calming the officials who had opposed Yūsuf, including Qāsim Barīd. Yūsuf also successfully checked the Portuguese incursion in the west, which would eventually become Goa.

By the time of Yūsuf's death in 1510, he had completed the challenge of creating an independent and strong Bijāpur; however, it was by no means a stable state. Yūsuf attempted to ensure a stable succession by unequivocally naming his son Ismāʿīl as successor, and, since the boy was about twelve years old, named the adviser Kamal Khan as Lord Protector, or regent, until Ismāʿīl came of age. Unfortunately, Kamal Khan began attempts to gradually seize the young king's power. He was not content with a de facto rule that would terminate when Ismāʿīl came of age, but instead wanted to consolidate power in his hands that would terminate only upon Kamal's death. He had enlisted a friend, Amir Barīd, and their plans grew until even the details of Kamal's coronation were organized. Ismāʿīl's mother, Bibiji Khanam, however, an intelligent, well-educated Mārathā woman, upset Kamal's plots by having him assassinated. Kamal's mother attempted to continue, and she encouraged Kamal's son to rally the army that had supported Kamal and march on the royal palace. They did so but were unsuccessful, and this allowed for Ismāʿīl to fare relatively smoothly in the domestic sphere. His foreign dealings were less secure, and attempts to quell problems in Ahmadnagar and Berar by marrying his sisters to the dominions were unsuccessful. Until his death in 1534, however, Bijāpur enjoyed relative peace.

Ismāʿīl's eldest son, Mullu, succeeded him, but after six irresponsible months fraught with problems, even those who had supported Mullu initially realized that his neglect of affairs of state demonstrated that he could be no king of Bijāpur. Bibiji Khanam again intervened to preserve the kingdom, enlisting chief ministers in her plan to remove Mullu from the throne and replace him with Ibrahim, Ismāʿīl's third son.

Ibrahim's reign ushered in a new era for Bijāpur, as he revised the policies of the previous reigns. Especially significant was the replacement of Shīʿite Islam with Sunni Islam and the expulsion of the foreign nobles from the armed forces. Excluding from the military the foreign nobles, who had previously made up much of the strength of both revolutionary and independent Bijāpur, caused them to return to the other successor states of the Bahmani kingdom, strengthening their armies and allowing them to menace Bijāpur.

Ibrahim was a very suspicious ruler, so his ministers were less apt to be loyal and trusting and more prone to rebel, forcing Ibrahim to admit losses to both the Portuguese and Vijayanagar. Ibrahim did have the occasional success, including his victory over the Vijayanagar armies led by Venkatadri. Unlike his father's, Ibrahim's reign was turbulent, and upon his death in 1558, he had not clearly delineated which of his two sons, ʿAli or Ṭah-

masp, would succeed him. ʿAli ʿĀdil Shah was more aggressive, declaring himself the rightful heir. Most of the nobles and important officials, including Kishwar Khan and Zain Khan, commander of the fort of Bijāpur, offered allegiance to him, even though ʿAli had been disliked by his father and had spent the later years of Ibrahim's reign imprisoned. Ibrahim and Ṭahmasp were Sunni Muslims, but ʿAli had followed the Shīʿite tradition. He began to systematically denounce the practice of Sunni Islam, having associated it with his father.

In the foreign sphere, ʿAli ʿĀdil Shah's reign was extremely successful, though very pragmatic and mercenary. Despite relatively good relations with Vijayanagar and extremely valuable help from the empire, ʿAli ʿĀdil Shah decided to attack and destroy Vijayanagar anyway. He convened the other Muslim rulers in the Deccan region and argued that no single power could defeat Vijayanagar, but if allied, they surely could do so. General contempt for Hindu Vijayanagar and desire for its wealth led to success for ʿAli ʿĀdil Shah's call to arms.

The armies of Golconda, Bīdar, Ahmadnagar, and Bijāpur met and began their march to Vijayanagar at the end of 1564. They met the Vijayanagara, and one of the bloodiest battles in Indian history ensued, a battle that came to be known as the Battle of Talikota (1565). Vijayanagar forces were evenly matched against the four allied Muslim rulers, making it particularly damaging to both sides. (It is said that the Krishna River ran red with blood.) Clever maneuvering, however, led to victory for Bijāpur and its allies. They captured and killed the ruler, whose wife had named ʿAli as her son, plundered the city, and utterly decentralized the Vijayanagar Empire. Even after the forces scattered following the murder of their commander, Bijāpur and the other allies pursued them to ensure their victory.

Victory over Vijayanagar inspired arrogance in ʿAli. He attempted with allies to rout the Portuguese but was defeated. In 1580, he was found in his private apartments having died a bloody death. ʿAli's nine-year-old nephew Ibrahim ʿĀdil Shah II succeeded him with a legion of regents and Chand Bibi, the dowager queen. There was great political intrigue and corruption as the various regents and ministers attempted to check the influence of Chand Bibi, and she responded in kind. Additionally, under Emperor Akbar, the Mughals slowly had been moving southward and were becoming a very real threat. When Akbar had subjugated Ahmadnagar, Ibrahim entered into a humiliating alliance in which he paid tribute to Akbar, also giving his daughter.

SIGNIFICANCE

Unwittingly, by destroying Vijayanagar, ʿAli ʿĀdil Shah removed the only real block to Mughal and British expansion into south India. The alliance during Ibrahim II's reign allowed Bijāpur to continue to exist, but its power rapidly declined at the hands of both the Mughals and the Mārathās. Bijāpur was annexed by the Mughal ʿĀlamgīr (r. 1658-1707) in 1686, bringing an end to a dynasty that also left a legacy of great Islamic architecture and patronage of the arts, and a cosmopolitan culture.

—*Monica Piotter*

FURTHER READING

Cousens, Henry. *Bijāpur and Its Architectural Remains.* Columbia, Mo.: South Asia Books, 1996. Explores the structures, monuments, and buildings of Bijāpur.

Eaton, Richard Maxwell. *Sufis of Bijāpur, 1300-1700.* Columbia, Mo.: South Asia Books, 1996. An excellent social history of Sufism and other religions in Bijāpur.

Verma, D. C. *History of Bijāpur.* New Delhi, India: Kumar Brothers, 1974. The best textbook treatment of Bijāpur.

SEE ALSO: c. 1490: Fragmentation of the Bahmani Sultanate; 1509-1565: Vijayanagar Wars; 1552: Struggle for the Strait of Hormuz.

RELATED ARTICLES in *Great Lives from History: The Renaissance & Early Modern Era, 1454-1600:* Akbar; Alfonso de Albuquerque; Krishnadevaraya.

1489
YORKSHIRE REBELLION

Organized resistance to the collection of a tax levied by Henry VII led to the killing of the earl of Northumberland. Although the rebels took York, the earl of Surrey soon quelled the rebellion, and a judicial commission was convened to try the rebels.

LOCALE: Yorkshire, England

CATEGORIES: Wars, uprisings, and civil unrest; government and politics

KEY FIGURES

Henry VII (1457-1509), king of England, r. 1485-1509

Henry Percy (c. 1449-1489), fourth earl of Northumberland, r. 1473-1489

Robert Chamber (d. 1489), leader of the Yorkshire Rebellion

Thomas Howard (1443-1524), earl of Surrey, r. 1483-1485, 1489-1524

Polydore Vergil (c. 1470-1555), Italian historian

SUMMARY OF EVENT

Throughout the 1480's, a decade that featured frequent warfare on the Anglo-Scottish borderlands, the citizens of Yorkshire were pressured to provide supplies and troops for the nearby border conflicts. They were all the more hard hit, then, by a series of taxes initiated in 1487. From 1487 to 1489, Yorkshire county, already depressed by years of military conflict, began to seethe at the collection of nearly one-third of its wealth in taxes and grants. Anger at excessive taxation, as well as resentment at the exemption of the nearby Borders county from a 1489 tax, apparently left numerous Yorkshire citizens ready to resist collection of the latest tax: The seeds were planted for open rebellion.

Although many details of the Yorkshire Rebellion have generally been gleaned from Polydore Vergil's historical account, which was commissioned by Henry VII approximately fifteen years after the rising, full records of the royal commission of oyer and terminer (that is, the order creating and authorizing the court that tried the rebels) also remain. This commission details the indictments against the rebels and has allowed historians to reconstruct much of what actually transpired.

Planning of the armed resistance seems to have begun on April 20, 1489, at a secret assembly convened at Ayton in Cleveland. Although the number of attendees from the nearby area is not clear, records show that the meeting was presided over by Robert Chamber of Ayton, a yeoman who was apparently the initial leader of the uprising. Chamber was assisted by at least two other yeomen and a chaplain. Most probably, the would-be rebels decided to marshal a large body of citizens and march to Thirsk to raise their grievances about excessive taxation with Henry Percy, the earl of Northumberland. Theoretically, commoners and gentry could make their grievances known to the king by communicating their complaints to the most proximate magnate, who would function as the representative of the Crown. Indeed, the earl of Northumberland was not only the most powerful noble in the Yorkshire area but also the key magnate in all of northern England.

The earl of Northumberland evidently gained intelligence of the rebels' plans. On April 24, Northumberland summoned to Thirsk Sir Robert Plumpton and his armed retainers. The two forces met at South Kilvington on April 28, by which time Chamber had put together a force of some seven hundred rebels. Percy's retainers apparently neglected to defend the earl from the rebels, for Northumberland seems to have been the only individual murdered during the Yorkshire Rebellion—a rising that eventually involved huge numbers of armed insurgents. Contemporaries such as the Paston family and the poet John Skelton seem to have been greatly disturbed by the killing of Northumberland, commenting on the violence and chaos created by the Yorkshire rioters.

After the murder of Northumberland, the rebels apparently sensed both that their avenue to legitimate complaint had been closed and that a strong response would come from Henry VII's armies, for they soon began recruiting insurgents for a more widespread uprising. The recruitment of rebels involved some written proclamations but probably relied primarily on oral communication among the largely illiterate commoners who formed the majority of the rebels. The issues motivating the rebels now went beyond those of taxation, expanding to include claimed breaches in the rights of sanctuary and assembly.

Fresh rebels for the rising were recruited both in North Yorkshire and, under the leadership of Sir John Egremont, in nearby East Riding. The rebel contingents convened at Sheriff Hutton and soon marched southward, through Bramham Moor and Ferrybridge, reaching Doncaster by May 13. Hugh Bunting, a York fletcher, provided arrows for the rebel forces, who were joined at Dringham by a throng of York citizens bent on joining the rebel ranks.

On May 15, 1489, the rebel army, numbering some five thousand insurgents and apparently under the command of Sir John Egremont, was apparently welcomed into the city of York by citizens supporting the revolt. The rebels succeeded in seizing the city, which they did not in any way loot. Henry VII, whose fragile regime was only in its fourth year of rule, responded by raising an army under the command of Thomas Howard, earl of Surrey. Surrey succeeded in quickly dispersing the rebel forces. The sheer might of his royally raised army apparently cowed the rebels into surrendering without serious incident.

Beginning on May 27, 1489, and lasting only until June 1, a royal commission of oyer and terminer was established at the York Guildhall, with thirteen peers, six judges, and King Henry VII presiding over the proceedings. Although thousands of rebels were apparently involved in the riots, there were only sixty-six indictments, with only forty-four of these indictments involving rebellion. (The remainder were presumably criminals who took advantage of the chaos surrounding open rebellion to commit various misdeeds.) Jurors were chosen from the surrounding area, with most of these apparently being gentry or otherwise well-to-do individuals.

During the proceedings, it is reported, many commoners debased themselves to plead for mercy from Henry VII. Five rebels were condemned to death by hanging, including the original ringleader, Robert Chamber of Ayton, as well as Christopher Atkinson of Ayton, James Binks of Sowerby (both yeomen), and a cobbler, William Lister. Thomas Wrangwish, the mayor of York, was also condemned to death but was pardoned by Henry VII. Henry also pardoned six others accused of lesser crimes, including Sir John Egremont, one of the leaders in the recruitment of rebels that followed the killing of Northumberland. The legal proceedings appear to have been thorough and relatively fair, as is evidenced by the acquittal of Henry Middlewood and the mitigation of charges against John Slingsby. By June 1, the proceedings were terminated, and the Yorkshire Rebellion was effectively quelled, less than six weeks after it had arisen.

SIGNIFICANCE

While the Yorkshire Rebellion of 1489 had little direct impact on Henry VII's England, it was the first of a series of rebellions against Tudor monarchs that would punctuate that dynasty's reign. The rising itself seems to have led to only a single death and was apparently bloodlessly disbanded by Surrey's army, so it must be seen as both largely nonviolent and fundamentally unsuccessful. Its effects on English history and on the imagination of English subjects, however, are hard to measure.

Historians of the Renaissance have emphasized that Tudor rule was enforced as much by the representation of power as it was by power itself: Counterfeiting currency was a capital offense, because coins were branded with the image of the monarch, an image which must always remain in the monarch's absolute control. Moreover, when the earl of Essex wished to foment rebellion against Elizabeth I in the wake of the Tyrone and Essex Rebellions (1597-1601), he is reputed to have staged a performance of William Shakespeare's *Richard II* (pr. c. 1595-1596). Elizabeth understood very well the significance of a play representing the deposing of an English monarch—any English monarch—and she reacted to it as a direct threat to her authority, asking "Know ye not that I am Richard?"

The Tudors, then, seem to have understood their power to rest on their subjects' belief in that power's utter inviolability. Understood in this context, the consequences of any rebellion against royal authority, no matter how quickly defeated, must be judged as significant.

Robert Chamber's rebellion did not spread beyond Yorkshire, and it appears to have been confined to the southeast and northeast portions of the county. Indeed, Henry VII's decision to hold court proceedings in York itself, the relatively small number of individuals indicted for rioting, and the leniency with which Henry treated those on trial all point to the fact that Henry VII did not feel particularly threatened by the revolt. The rebellion's only obvious effect on the English political landscape was the promotion of the earl of Surrey to the position of "king's lieutenant," which disrupted the traditional Percy domination of the north of England.

The Yorkshire Rebellion did, however, have clear and lasting psychological effects: Contemporaries were clearly shaken by the disturbance, as is evidenced by the Pastons' and the poet John Skelton's condemnation of the rioting, as well as by Polydore Vergil's detailed recounting of a violent and chaotic revolt. The extent to which these men were shaken by a seemingly inconsequential event may indicate that Henry himself underestimated its importance, both for his own reign and for those of his descendants. In retrospect, the rebellion is remembered as the first of a series of anti-Tudor uprisings, including the Cornish Rebellion (1497), the Pilgrimage of Grace (1536-1546), Kett's Rebellion (1549), the Western Rebellion (1549), Wyatt's Rebellion (1554), the Northern Earls' Rebellion (1569), and the Tyrone and Essex Rebellions (1597-1601).

—*Randy P. Schiff*

FURTHER READING

Hicks, M. A. "The Yorkshire Rebellion of 1489 Reconsidered." *Northern History* 22 (1986): 39-62. Offers an exhaustive description of the events surrounding the rebellion, using as evidence detailed analysis of the records of the royal commission investigating the revolt. Argues that the revolt was a "loyal rebellion," largely nonviolent and self-righteous, suggesting that historians have wrongly focused on exaggerated contemporary accounts.

Hicks, Michael. *English Political Culture in the Fifteenth Century.* New York: Routledge, 2002. Broad survey of the background of political activity in late medieval England, valuable for its discussion of peasant perspectives, alongside those of individuals higher up on the social scale. Argues that communities succeeded in remaining stable, despite risings and widespread warfare.

Palliser, David. *Tudor York.* Oxford, England: Oxford University Press, 1979. Broad survey of the history of the region in which the Yorkshire Rebellion occurred, providing details of the rising and a clear context for the players involved.

Skater, Victor, ed. *The Political History of Tudor and Stuart England: A Sourcebook.* New York: Routledge, 2002. Collection of primary sources, edited so as to illustrate the sociopolitical background of a chaotic period of social upheavals, of which the Yorkshire Rebellion is one striking instance.

SEE ALSO: 1455-1485: Wars of the Roses; Beginning 1485: The Tudors Rule England; 1497: Cornish Rebellion; Aug. 22, 1513-July 6, 1560: Anglo-Scottish Wars; Oct., 1536-June, 1537: Pilgrimage of Grace; 1549: Kett's Rebellion; Jan. 25-Feb. 7, 1554: Wyatt's Rebellion; Nov. 9, 1569: Rebellion of the Northern Earls; 1597-Sept., 1601: Tyrone Rebellion.

RELATED ARTICLE in *Great Lives from History: The Renaissance & Early Modern Era, 1454-1600:* Henry VII.

1480's

1490's
ALDUS MANUTIUS FOUNDS THE ALDINE PRESS

Manutius founded a publishing company that became one of the most influential in Europe, printing numerous first editions of important classical and contemporary works, which helped spread the ideas of Humanism to European readers. The Aldine Press also developed the pocket-sized book, which made reading affordable and more accessible.

LOCALE: Venice, Republic of Venice (now in Italy)

CATEGORIES: Organizations and institutions; cultural and intellectual history; art; literature; philosophy; science and technology; communications

KEY FIGURES

Aldus Manutius (c. 1450-1515), Humanist scholar and publisher

Andrea Torresani (1451-1528), Venetian printer who became Aldus's main business partner

Paulus Manutius (1512-1574), Venetian publisher and Aldus's youngest son

Aldus Manutius, the Younger (1547-1597), Venetian publisher and Paulus's eldest son

SUMMARY OF EVENT

By the early 1490's, three decades after the introduction of printing to Italy, Venice was Europe's largest producer of printed books. Around this time, Humanist scholar and former teacher Aldus Manutius settled in Venice and founded what was to become one of the most famous and influential printing firms in European history.

Aldus had been educated in some of the most eminent intellectual circles in Italy and was associated with leading scholars, such as Giovanni Pico della Mirandola, whose nephews, princes Alberto and Leonello Pio of Carpi, he tutored in the 1480's. Aldus was to exploit well these excellent contacts and credentials in his twenty-year printing career, becoming the first true scholar-publisher and producing books that appealed not only to Europe's social and intellectual elite but also to a new, wider readership.

In Venice, Aldus acquired powerful business partners in the form of the established and successful printer Andrea Torresani and the Venetian patrician Pierfrancesco Barbarigo, and set about implementing his printing plans. Aldus's chief goal, as expressed in the elegant dedications and prefatory letters he appended to many of his books, was to print the great works of classical antiquity, particularly Greek antiquity, from the most authoritative manuscript sources he could track down across Europe. Like many Humanists, he believed that the revival of ancient languages and literatures would herald a new golden age, and he considered printing to be the ideal tool for this endeavor.

In this spirit, from the beginning, he laid emphasis on both the stylistic and intellectual virtues of his books. His types were cut in imitation of the most accepted Humanist hands and his books edited with a (generally) unprecedented rigor, even if they do not always live up to today's standards of scholarly editing.

The company's first dated publication was a Greek grammar by Constantine Lascaris called *Erotemata* (1495), and the next few years saw the production of a number of other works in the same vein. These were produced with the help of eminent scholars, some of whom hailed from Venice's large expatriate Greek community. Chief among these publications was a series of Aristotle's works (1495-1498); however, also published were important Latin and vernacular works. These included Pietro Bembo's *De Aetna* (1496), which was printed using a very influential new Roman typeface, and the *Hypnerotomachia polifili* (1499) by Francesco Colonna,

Aldus Manutius. (Hulton|Archive by Getty Images)

a vernacular romance with stunning woodcut illustrations.

Around 1500, probably ceding to the demands of the market (or of his business partners), Aldus changed the focus of his company from predominantly Greek texts to texts that were more likely to sell, those in Latin and Italian. Exemplary of this trend was the series of classics published from 1501, including ancient writers such as Vergil and Horace as well as newer writers such as Petrarch and Dante. For these books, Aldus employed the small octavo format, which had never before been used for these types of works and which was a precursor to the modern paperback, and a newly cut italic font that was the first of its kind. Perfectly suited to the itinerant lifestyle of the scholars, politicians, and diplomats that Aldus saw as his chief audience, these books were a smashing success, and both the format and type were much copied.

Despite the success of his company to this point, the remaining years of Aldus's life did not always run smoothly, and he interrupted printing during two periods (1505-1507 and 1509-1512), on the latter occasion because of Venice's involvement in the war of the League of Cambrai. During these years Aldus also tried to interest a number of eminent patrons in his long-cherished dream of founding a Humanist educational academy, but with no success. Nevertheless, the group of scholars who were attracted at one time or another to the Aldine Press and its founder included distinguished men of letters from all over Europe. The most famous of these was Dutch humanist Desiderius Erasmus, who stayed for a time with Aldus while his *Adagia* was being published (1500). Other significant publications prior to Aldus's death in 1515 included the works of Plato in Greek, which was dedicated to Pope Leo X (1513).

In 1505, Aldus had married Torresani's daughter, Maria, and on his death his father-in-law and brothers-in-law carried on the company. They published a number of works that continued the spirit of the firm's founder, perhaps the most important being the monumental edition of the works of Galen in Greek (1525). In the early 1530's, Aldus's youngest son, Paulus, became involved with the press, and of Aldus's three sons, he followed most faithfully in his fathers' footsteps, as a scholar as well as a publisher.

After successfully battling his Torresani relations for exclusive use of the italic typeface, Paulus remained es-

Aldus Manutius published important scholarly as well as Latin and vernacular works, including the Hypnerotomachia polifili *(1499) by Francesco Colonna, a vernacular romance with stunning woodcut illustrations. This woodcut was made for the 1546 French translation of Colonna's work.* (Harvard College Library)

sentially the head of the Aldine Press until his death, although some members of the Torresani continued to hark back to their famous forebear, employing Aldus's device of the dolphin and anchor in their own publications.

Paulus, with some help from his two brothers, continued a publication program that was neither as productive nor as illustrious as his father's, although in 1542, he published the first-ever anthology of letters in vernacular Italian and was later appointed as a contract printer for the short-lived Accademia Veneziana. He also forged links with two of the most important printers of the sixteenth century, the Frenchman Henri II Estienne and Christophe Plantin of Antwerp. During the 1560's, Paulus worked as an official printer for the Vatican in Rome, before returning to Venice, where he died in 1574. His own son, Aldus Manutius, the Younger, was also something of a scholar and began to assume responsibility at the press while his father was in Rome. Although with less continuity and commitment than either his father or grandfather, he continued to publish until his own death in 1597.

SIGNIFICANCE

At a time when Venice was producing an enormous quantity of printed books, even if not of the highest quality, the press founded by Aldus Manutius was perhaps the first in Europe to achieve great fame and success for combining solid Humanist scholarship with stylistic features that catered perfectly to the tastes of the European intellectual elite. The typefaces that Aldus employed, particularly the roman and italic, set the standard in printing for many centuries, while his use of the octavo format for a series of classic texts, printed in runs of several thousand copies, was an important step in presenting literature to a larger readership.

Although his vast project to print the great works of classical antiquity (and some of his own day) was often hindered by the tumultuous times in which he lived, Aldus's two decades of toil in pursuit of his aim was rewarded with lasting and well-deserved fame. The reputation for excellence that Aldus gained was not forgotten by his heirs from both the Torresani and Manutius families, whose printing efforts to the end of the sixteenth century evoked his memory continually.

—*Rosa M. Salzberg*

FURTHER READING

Davies, Martin. *Aldus Manutius: Printer and Publisher of Renaissance Venice*. Tempe: Arizona Center for Medieval and Renaissance Studies, 1999. A useful, succinct account of Aldus's career.

Fletcher, H. George. *In Praise of Aldus Manutius: A Quincentenary Exhibition*. New York: Pierpont Morgan Library, 1995. A well-illustrated and annotated catalog of a major exhibition of Aldines that includes a helpful overview of the company's progress to the late sixteenth century.

_____. *New Aldine Studies: Documentary Essays on the Life and Work of Aldus Manutius*. San Francisco: Bernard M. Rosenthal, 1988. Draws together the available evidence to fill out the details of Aldus's life.

Lowry, Martin. *The World of Aldus Manutius: Business and Scholarship in Renaissance Venice*. Ithaca, N.Y.: Cornell University Press, 1979. Still the definitive biography of Manutius. Evaluates his work and legacy in the context of the Venetian intellectual and commercial world. Contains tables of his publications and an extensive bibliography.

Zeidberg, David S., ed. *Aldus Manutius and Renaissance Culture: Essays in Memory of Franklin D. Murphy*. Florence, Italy: Leo S. Olschki, 1994. A collection of scholarly studies on many aspects of Aldus's business, with an essay also on Paulus's publishing work in Rome.

SEE ALSO: 1456: Publication of Gutenberg's Mazarin Bible; 1462: Regiomontanus Completes the *Epitome* of Ptolemy's *Almagest*; 1486-1487: Pico della Mirandola Writes *Oration on the Dignity of Man*; 1494: Sebastian Brant Publishes *The Ship of Fools*.

RELATED ARTICLES in *Great Lives from History: The Renaissance & Early Modern Era, 1454-1600:* William Caxton; Miles Coverdale; Desiderius Erasmus; Leonhard Fuchs; Charlotte Guillard; Hans Holbein, the Younger; Leo X; Aldus Manutius; Giovanni Pico della Mirandola.

1490's
DECLINE OF THE SILK ROAD

The establishment of a new sea route to Asia by explorers and traders, particularly the Portuguese, led to the decline of the Asian trade route called the Silk Road. Climatic changes, politics, and religion also played roles in the road's abandonment. The sea route was the prelude to the colonial occupation by European powers of southern Africa and most of the lands bordering the Indian Ocean.

LOCALE: From western Asia through India, Central Asia, and China

CATEGORIES: Trade and commerce; economics; exploration and discovery; transportation

KEY FIGURES

Vasco da Gama (c. 1460-1524), Portuguese explorer
Jorge Alvares (d. 1521), Portuguese envoy to China
Bartolomeu Dias (c. 1450-1500), Portuguese explorer
Prince Henry the Navigator (1394-1460), Prince of Portugal
Tamerlane (1336-1405), Turko-Mongol warrior

SUMMARY OF EVENT

At its greatest extent, the Silk Road stretched some 5,000 miles from Chang'an in central China to the Mediterranean coast ports of Antioch and Tyre (now called Sur). Actually a series of overlapping and sometimes-competing routes, the road acted as a passage not only for commodities such as silk, ivory, and spices but also for ideas, inventions, and even religions.

Activity along the Silk Road was at its height in the seventh, eighth, and ninth centuries, after which the road slowly began to decline. This decline, however, was not caused by one single event. Instead, a number of factors led to the route's decay and gradual abandonment, the development of a new sea route being the most significant. The sea route would supplant the Silk Road.

Climatic change was another factor in the road's decline, taking place over many centuries. Many towns and trading posts along the lengthy desert stretches of the Silk Road relied on water from oases fed by far-off mountain glaciers. As the glaciers gradually shrank, the oases shrank and so did the trading posts and towns. Furthermore, if war or banditry disrupted the maintenance of the watercourses feeding the oases, even briefly, the surrounding sands encroached, soon burying the sites.

Religion was another factor contributing to the road's decline. During the eighth century, the Tang Dynasty of China (618-907) became alarmed over the growth of Buddhism, which had spread along the Silk Road, and began persecuting the religion's adherents and razing their temples. Islam reached Central Asia about the same time, and because Islam prohibits the veneration of images, believing it leads to idolatry, Islamic converts destroyed the great wall paintings and Buddhist statues of China's western province of Sinkiang. These developments marked an end to the religious tolerance that had distinguished the Silk Road for much of its history.

Political developments also contributed to the demise of the route. After a period of gradual decline, the Silk Road experienced a partial rebirth under the Turko-Mongol conqueror Tamerlane in the late fourteenth century. Hoping to force trade to pass through his lands, especially his capital city of Samarqand, Tamerlane simply destroyed the cities along the competing trade routes to the north. Samarqand prospered as a result, but when the warrior died in 1405, his kingdom fell into a number of warring states. Bandits began to prey on traders in greater numbers, and it became difficult to maintain and protect smaller trading centers and outposts, many of which would be reclaimed by the desert until their rediscovery in the late nineteenth and early twentieth centuries.

In a move related to the growing unrest in the region, the Chinese effectively closed the eastern end of the Silk Road to commerce. After an initial period of commercial expansion, particularly by sea, the nationalistic Ming Dynasty (1368-1644) turned its back on the western world and on the trade routes that led there, hoping not only to preserve its cultural identity but also to defend itself against peoples to the northwest.

Active in Central Asia, Muslims eventually came to dominate the western end of the Silk Road, too. Constantinople (now Istanbul, Turkey) in Asia Minor had already been sacked by the Venetians in 1204 during the Fourth Crusade. Its conquest by the Turks in 1453 further weakened its usefulness as a market for the exchange of goods between east and west. By this time, Muslims had almost complete control of the central and western Asian lands through which the road wound and were able to charge exorbitant taxes on the goods passing through them.

Taken together, these events across the Asian continent encouraged European sailors and merchants to search for a sea route to the east, a development that

1490's

would profoundly change the course of modern history. In particular, the Portuguese prince Henry the Navigator fostered exploration by establishing a school for navigation in Sagres on the southeastern tip of Portugal. Explorer Bartolomeu Dias sailed down the Atlantic and rounded the Cape of Good Hope at the southern tip of Africa in 1488, and in 1497-1498 Vasco da Gama extended Portuguese reach across the Indian Ocean to become the first European explorer to reach India by sea.

The voyages of Dias and Gama were preludes to a burst of Portuguese activity in the Indian and western Pacific Oceans. The country's merchants established trading posts on the coast of India, on the island of Ceylon, and in what would become known as the Spice Islands, today's Malay Archipelago. They achieved another milestone in 1514, when Jorge Alvares visited the Pearl River region of China. An employee of the Portuguese trading post in Melaka (in what is today Malaysia), Alvares became the first European to enter China by sea.

SIGNIFICANCE

The opening of the sea route to Asia was not only a result of the Silk Road's decline but also the *cause* of its final demise. Neglected, most routes of the Silk Road disappeared beneath the sands of the desert and were forgotten for centuries. In fact, the road was given its now-familiar name only in 1877 by German explorer Baron Ferdinand von Richthofen. Its true extent was subsequently revealed by such explorers as Sir Aurel Stein of Great Britain and Sven Anders Hedin of Sweden in the late nineteenth and early twentieth centuries.

In the years that followed Vasco da Gama's expedition, trade by sea was found to be safer and less expensive than the cumbersome overland Silk Road, delivering a deathblow to the ancient route. Venice, which had profited from the spice trade at the western end of the Silk Road, was eclipsed by Portugal's capital city of Lisbon. Even though the new route to Asia would prove to be vital, the changes it brought, including colonialism, were severe and long lasting.

Cultural and religious tolerance had for some enlightened periods been a feature of the Silk Road, but such would not be the case along the new route. Pedro Álvares Cabral led a second Portuguese expedition to India in 1500, but his overbearing behavior resulted in an attack in which fifty of his party died. In revenge, Cabral seized ten Muslim ships, confiscated their cargos, and killed their crews. On a subsequent voyage to India in 1502, Gama commanded a large and powerful convoy that raided Muslim trading posts along the east coast of Af-

rica. Capturing the Muslim ship *Meri*, which was carrying several hundred pilgrims on a return trip from the holy city of Mecca, Gama burned and sank it, sending the pilgrims to their death. Such events were a foretaste of the centuries to come.

—Grove Koger

FURTHER READING

Ball, Warwick. "Following the Mythical Road." *Geographical Magazine* 70 (March, 1998): 18-23. Suggests that the Silk Road never existed in the form we imagine, but instead is the romantic creation of later writers and historians.

Cuyvers, Luc. *Into the Rising Sun: Vasco da Gama and the Search for the Sea Route to the East*. New York: TV Books, 1999. A re-creation of the explorer's epic voyage based on the PBS series of the same name. Map, colored illustrations.

Disney, A. R., and Emily Booth, eds. *Vasco da Gama and the Linking of Europe and Asia*. New York: Oxford University Press, 2000. Papers presented at the Vasco da Gama Quincentenary Conference held in Australia in 1997 and addressing the historical, economic, religious, and cultural aspects of Gama's accomplishments. Bibliographies.

Fernandez-Armesto, Felipe. "Times and Tides." *History Today* 47, no. 12 (December, 1997): 7-9. Considers Vasco da Gama's role in the establishment of the sea route to Asia. Color illustrations.

Franck, Irene M., and David M. Brownstone. *The Silk Road: A History*. New York: Facts On File, 1986. Well-illustrated, detailed, and readable history. Maps on endpapers, extensive bibliography.

Subrahmanyam, Sanjay. *The Career and Legend of Vasco da Gama*. New York: Cambridge University Press, 1997. The explorer and the myths surrounding him as seen from an Indian perspective. Maps, illustrations, bibliography.

Winius, George D., ed. *Portugal, the Pathfinder: Journeys from the Medieval Toward the Modern World, 1300-ca. 1600*. Madison, Wis.: Hispanic Seminary of Medieval Studies, 1995. Anthology of essays on Portuguese exploration, including several on the discovery of the sea route to India and Portugal's subsequent activities in South Asia. Includes a bibliographic essay by the editor surveying all major sources pertaining to the fifteenth and sixteenth centuries.

SEE ALSO: 1454: China Subdues Burma; Aug., 1487-Dec., 1488: Dias Rounds the Cape of Good Hope;

1511-c. 1515: Melaka Falls to the Portuguese; 1531-1585: Antwerp Becomes the Commercial Capital of Europe; 1565: Spain Seizes the Philippines; Dec. 31, 1600: Elizabeth I Charters the East India Company.

RELATED ARTICLES in *Great Lives from History: The Renaissance & Early Modern Era, 1454-1600:* Afonso de Albuquerque; Bartolomeu Dias; Vasco da Gama; John II; Manuel I; Tomé Pires.

Beginning 1490

DEVELOPMENT OF THE CAMERA OBSCURA

The camera obscura, or pinhole camera, was the precursor of the modern photographic camera. Its development as an artist's tool in the early modern period shaped the course of both art history and philosophy for centuries thereafter.

LOCALE: Italy and the Netherlands
CATEGORIES: Science and technology; cultural and intellectual history

KEY FIGURES
Giambattista Della Porta (1535-1615), Italian scientist, philosopher, and writer
Leonardo da Vinci (1452-1519), Italian painter, inventor, and writer
Gerolamo Cardano (1501-1576), Italian mathematician, physician, and philosopher
Reiner Gemma Frisius (1508-1555), Dutch astronomer, mathematician, and surveyor
Daniel Barbaro (1514-1570), Italian aristocrat, translator, and writer

SUMMARY OF EVENT

The camera obscura, or pinhole camera, uses the optical effect that occurs when a pinhole is made in the wall or side of a completely darkened room or box. Light rays from outside the camera pass through the hole and produce an inverted image within the chamber of whatever lies without.

The term "camera obscura" is derived from the Latin words for "darkened chamber [room]" and was coined by the astronomer Johannes Kepler in the seventeenth century. However, the basic optical principles were known in ancient times. The fifth century B.C.E. Chinese philosopher Mozi described an inverted image formed by light rays passing through a pinhole into a "locked treasure room." In 330 B.C.E., the Greek philosopher Aristotle noticed a partial solar eclipse projected on the ground through the holes in a sieve and the gaps in tree foliage. The earliest known formal scientific description of the camera obscura was provided by Alhazen

(965-1039), the Arabian physicist and mathematician.

By 1267, the principle of the pinhole camera had reached Europe. In that year, English philosopher and scientist Roger Bacon, who was familiar with the works of Alhazen, described the optical process behind the camera obscura in his *De multiplicatione specierum* (c. 1267; English translation, 1897). He used the camera obscura to observe solar eclipses, and it became a popular tool for astronomical observations in the Middle Ages. During the Renaissance, significant technical developments in the design of the camera obscura brought

Gerolamo Cardano made the first known reference to a pinhole camera with a lens, which increased the sharpness and intensity of the image projected onto a piece of white paper. (University of California Press)

179

THE CAMERA OBSCURA AND MODERN IDENTITY

The camera obscura developed over the course of the early modern period, at the same time that the medieval, feudal form of identity was evolving into a distinctively modern form of identity. People began to understand themselves for the first time as self-contained private individuals whose rational minds formed enclosed personal spaces, utterly separate both from public communal life and from the physical world of bodily senses and emotions. In the passage excerpted below, art historian Jonathan Crary explains why the camera obscura became the most common metaphor used to describe this new form of identity for more than two hundred years.

Beginning in the late 1500's the figure of the camera obscura begins to assume a preeminent importance in delimiting and defining the relations between observer and world.... [T]he camera obscura performs an operation of individuation; that is, it necessarily defines an observer as isolated, enclosed, and autonomous within its dark confines.... Thus, the camera obscura is inseparable from a certain metaphysic of interiority: it is a figure for both the observer who is nominally a free sovereign individual and a privatized subject confined in a quasi-domestic space, cut off from a public exterior world.... At the same time, another related and equally decisive function of the camera was to sunder the act of seeing from the physical body of the observer, to decorporealize vision.

Source: From *Techniques of the Observer: On Vision and Modernity in the Nineteenth Century*, by Jonathan Crary (Cambridge, Mass.: MIT Press, 1990), pp. 38-39.

Da Vinci was experimenting with techniques for creating images in perspective. Using a darkened chamber with one or two pinholes, he noted that because the light rays crossed as they passed through the hole, the projected image was inverted or upside down.

On January 24, 1544, Dutch scientist Reiner Gemma Frisius used a camera obscura to observe a solar eclipse at Louvain. He included a drawing of this event in his book *De radio astronomica et geometrica* (1545). This picture was the first published illustration of a camera obscura. The drawing shows a solar eclipse projected through a pinhole onto the opposite wall in a classical pavilion. Such large, darkened rooms were typical of the first cameras obscuras, which were used by astronomers. Because the image in a pinhole camera was dim, the only practical application of the camera was the safe observation of a bright object, the sun.

However, with the substitution of a lens for the pinhole, new applications and camera designs developed. A lens made possible a larger aperture that could allow much more light than a pinhole and a brighter, more brilliant image, without sacrificing sharpness. It could also be used to turn the image right-side up. In 1550, the first known reference to a pinhole camera with a lens appeared in Gerolamo Cardano's famous scientific encyclopedia, *De subtilitate libri* (partial English translation, 1934). He described placing a double convex lens or glass disc in the window shutter of a darkened room on a sunny day. Use of this lens increased the sharpness and intensity of the image projected onto a piece of white paper.

In 1558, in Naples, Italy, Giambattista Della Porta published his major work, *Magiae naturalis* (*Natural Magick*, 1658) in four volumes, which included the first complete description of a working pinhole camera. A second edition (twenty volumes) was published in 1589. *Natural Magick* was one of the most popular works on science in the sixteenth century, and it was the most comprehensive record of optical projection produced before the eighteenth century. Della Porta described using a double convex lens to improve image quality. He also explained his new idea of using a concave mirror to enlarge and correct camera obscura images, which had previously been small and upside down. He had discovered, in addition, that placing concave mirrors at an oblique angle

it closer to resembling the modern photographic camera. The camera obscura also came to be used as an artist's tool.

The image created by the camera obscura is an image in true perspective, meaning that the image maps the world's three dimensions onto a two-dimensional surface in a mathematically precise fashion. Perspectival images are often described as realistic—especially in their representation of depth—partly because a single human eye also maps the world in true perspective. Since most people have two eyes, however, there is also a significant difference between binocular human vision and the single point perspective created by the camera obscura. Thus, painting in true perspective requires technical skill and training, and the development of the camera obscura made it much easier for artists to practice the technique.

The earliest known diagrams and detailed descriptions of the pinhole camera date from about 1490. They are contained within Leonardo da Vinci's notebooks, *Codex Atlanticus* and *Manuscript D*. These manuscripts were not deciphered and published until 1797, however.

would set objects in the image produced in proper perspective.

Della Porta recommended and explained the use of the camera obscura as an artistic tool or guide to drawing. He suggested that artists trace the outlines and shapes of a projected image and then paint in the colors later. He also suggested that the camera be used for copying paintings and painting portraits, with the sitter positioned at the right distance in front of the aperture. Della Porta's book, which eventually was issued in more than fifty editions in various languages, helped popularize the camera obscura.

In 1568, Venetian nobleman Daniel Barbaro published *La pratica della perspettiva* (the practice of perspective), one of the most important works on perspective at the time. In this book, Barbaro suggested replacing the pinhole with a biconvex lens. He also recommended placing a disk with a small hole in the center (diaphragm) over the lens to restrict the aperture, thus increasing the depth of field of the image. He believed this camera would help artists draw in perspective.

With these significant technical improvements to the camera obscura, it became a practical tool for artists as well as astronomers during the Renaissance. By 1600, the camera obscura was movable and appeared in the form of light wooden tents and sedan chairs.

SIGNIFICANCE

During the seventeenth and eighteenth centuries, the camera obscura continued to be a useful tool for artists, including Antonio Canaletto (1697-1768) in Venice, Johannes Vermeer (1632-1675) in the Netherlands, and Sir Joshua Reynolds (1723-1792) and Paul Sandby (c. 1730-1809) in England.

Canaletto was the greatest view painter of the eighteenth century. By bringing the camera obscura onsite to project scenes onto canvas or paper, he could quickly and accurately draw views of buildings and places. The Correr Museum in Venice has two models of his original camera. Studies of the paintings of Vermeer suggest that he used a camera obscura with a lens to help achieve the special tonal and lighting effects in his work. The celebrated English portrait artist Sir Joshua Reynolds owned and used a type of camera obscura that folded flat into the form of a book when stored. Paul Sandby, the great English landscape painter, engraver, topographical draughtsman, and founding member of the Royal Academy, also utilized the camera.

By the end of the seventeenth century, completely portable, small hand-held box cameras had appeared. In the early nineteenth century, the design of the camera obscura allowed for the insertion of a light-sensitive sheet, and the modern photographic camera was constructed. In 1826, French inventor Joseph-Nicéphore Niepce (1765-1833) placed a metal plate covered with a chemical called bitumen into his camera obscura. He then captured the world's first photograph or permanent image from nature.

—*Alice Myers*

FURTHER READING

Crary, Jonathan. *Techniques of the Observer: On Vision and Modernity in the Nineteenth Century.* Cambridge, Mass.: MIT Press, 1990. The first half of this book details the development and the cultural meaning of the camera obscura from the sixteenth century through the early nineteenth century. Includes illustrations, an extensive bibliography divided between primary sources and contemporary studies, and an index.

Galassi, Peter. *Before Photography: Painting and the Invention of Photography.* New York: Museum of Modern Art, 1981. Catalog of an exhibition of paintings, together with a critical essay, which together explore the reasons photography was not invented earlier than it was. Discusses the fundamental differences between Renaissance conceptions of vision and art and more modern conceptions. Includes illustrations and bibliography.

Gernsheim, Helmut, and Alison Gernsheim. *The History of Photography: From the Camera Obscura to the Beginning of the Modern Era.* London: Thames and Hudson, 1969. This standard book in the field gives a complete history of the camera obscura. Includes illustrations, notes, and an appendix.

Hammond, John H. *The Camera Obscura.* Bristol, Avon, England: Adam Hilger, 1981. This comprehensive history of the camera obscura includes numerous illustrations and an extensive bibliography.

Hockney, David. *Secret Knowledge: Rediscovering the Lost Techniques of the Old Masters.* New York: Viking Studio, 2001. Hockney shows how some of the great artists used lenses and mirrors as painting aids. The "Textual Evidence" section includes excerpts from historical texts about the camera obscura. Includes beautiful illustrations.

Pollack, Peter. *The Picture History of Photography: From the Earliest Beginnings to the Present Day.* New York: H. N. Abrams, 1969. The chapter on the early beginnings of photography discusses the camera

1490's

obscura. This 708-page book includes illustrations and a bibliography.

Steadman, Philip. *Vermeer's Camera: Uncovering the Truth Behind the Masterpieces.* New York: Oxford University Press, 2001. Includes a long chapter on the history of the camera obscura. Contains illustrations, notes, an appendix, and a bibliography.

Wolf, Bryan Jay. *Vermeer and the Invention of Seeing.* Chicago: University of Chicago Press, 2001. The chapter "Inside the Camera Obscura" analyzes the relationship of the device to the art and intellectual history of the seventeenth century. Includes illustrations and extensive bibliographic notes for each chapter.

SEE ALSO: 1456: Publication of Gutenberg's Mazarin Bible; 1462: Regiomontanus Completes the *Epitome* of Ptolemy's *Almagest*; c. 1478-1519: Leonardo da Vinci Compiles His Notebooks; 1495-1497: Leonardo da Vinci Paints *The Last Supper*; c. 1510: Invention of the Watch; Nov. 3, 1522-Nov. 17, 1530: Correggio Paints the *Assumption of the Virgin*; June, 1564: Tintoretto Paints for the Scuola di San Rocco; 1572-1574: Tycho Brahe Observes a Supernova; 1580's-1590's: Galileo Conducts His Early Experiments.

RELATED ARTICLES in *Great Lives from History: The Renaissance & Early Modern Era, 1454-1600:* Gerolamo Cardano; Leonardo da Vinci.

c. 1490
FRAGMENTATION OF THE BAHMANI SULTANATE

The breakup of the Bahmani sultanate of the Deccan, namely because of the empire's losing control over its provincial governors, saw the emergence of five successor sultanates in the region.

LOCALE: Deccan, India

CATEGORIES: Wars, uprisings, and civil unrest; government and politics; expansion and land acquisition

KEY FIGURES

'Alā'-ud-Dīn Bahman Shah (d. 1358), founder of the Bahmani sultanate

Shihāb-ud-Dīn Aḥmad I (fl. 1422-1436), Bahmani sultan, r. 1422-1436

Maḥmūd Gāwān (1411?-1481), Bahmani chief minister, 1466-1481

Qāsim Barīd (d. 1504), founder of the Barīd-Shāh Dynasty

SUMMARY OF EVENT

During the first half of the fourteenth century, the Delhi sultanate, a north Indian power, expanded its frontiers to include the great tableland of the Deccan (traditionally defined as extending from the Narmada River to the Kistna River) and the far south. The expansion was the work of two sultans, 'Alā'-al-Dīn Muḥammad Khaljī (d. 1316) and Ghiyās-ud-Dīn Tughluq (d. 1325). The result was territorial over-extension, which the logistics of the age could not sustain. Around 1347, a breakaway regime independent of Delhi was established in the Deccan by an ambitious military commander, 'Alā'-ud-Dīn Bahman Shah.

Bahman Shah founded the Bahmani Dynasty, which numbered nearly twenty sovereigns, and it survived until 1527. In addition to consolidating his state by almost continuous warfare, he established his capital at Gulbarga, which he adorned with fine buildings, and encouraged the migration from Delhi to the Deccan of charismatic Sufi sheikhs (Muslim mystics) of the Chishti Order, who would leave a distinctive imprint on the religious life of the region.

The Bahmani sultanate reached its apogee under Shihāb-ud-Dīn Aḥmad I, who transferred the capital from Gulbarga to the more-central location of Bīdar in 1429 and who overthrew the Hindu kingdom of Warangal (northern Telingana) in 1425. By then, the sultanate extended from the Narmada to the Kistna, where the Rāichūr Doab, the land between the Kistna and Tungabhadra Rivers, was bitterly contested with the mighty Hindu kingdom of Vijayanagar, whose capital city lay on the south bank of the Tungabhadra River.

Against Vijayanagar, Aḥmad I won a crushing, if temporary, victory. In the west, his realm extended to the Western Ghats and touched the Arabian Sea at Chaul, but the Bahmanis were never able to absorb effectively the narrow coastal plain. Contacts across the Arabian Sea were, however, extremely important to them, bringing recruits (mainly from Persia), cavalry mounts, and close cultural contacts. In the east, the gentle slope of the Eastern Ghats presented no significant barrier to expansion, and Bahmani rule there extended to the Bay of Bengal.

The Bahmani Dynasty was a formidable military power against Warangal, Vijayanagar, and the Muslim sultanates of Malwa and Gujarat, but, nevertheless, the Bahmanis suffered from certain systemic weaknesses. Constant warfare, especially against Vijayanagar, over which it never secured a permanent advantage, drained the material resources of the sultanate, with dire consequences. In the Deccan, the Muslims were a diverse minority, dependent on Hindu acquiescence and given to fierce internecine rivalries. On one hand, there were the Deccanis (mostly the descendants of earlier conquests and local converts), together with Ḥabshī (Abyssinian) *mamlūks* (slave-soldiers) imported from Africa, all of whom were Sunni Muslims. Set against them were the *afaqi* (outsiders), foreign recruits to the sultan's service, who were either Turks, Arabs, or, increasingly over time, Persians. The Persian recruits were Shīʿites, reflecting the growth of Shīʿite tendencies in Persia itself. Thus, sectarian rivalry reinforced cultural differences and fierce competition for office and patronage.

Inevitably, too, a long-lived dynasty produced rulers of mediocre caliber in its later reigns, with harem rivalries, child rulers, and the offspring of competing wives. Ineffective rulers, as was often the case in the history of medieval Islamic dynasties, inaugurated a process whereby the reality of power gravitated into the hands of dominant outside figures, such as chief ministers or army commanders. These trends came to the fore in the middle decades of the fifteenth century, during the long reign of Shams-ud-Dīn Muḥammad Shah III, who ascended the throne at the age of nine. At first, the government was in the hands of a very experienced vizier (administrator), Makhdum Khwaja Jahān, originally a merchant from Khorāsān, who served a succession of fathers and sons: Aḥmad I, Aḥmad II (r. 1436-1458), Humāyūn (r. 1458-1461), Niẓām (r. 1461-1463), and Muḥammad Shah III (r. 1463-1482).

Inevitably, Jahān made enemies, especially with the queen mother, who procured his death. He was succeeded by another Persian, who had served almost as long in the administration, Maḥmūd Gāwān, who also received the title of Khwaja Jahān. One of the greatest figures in Deccani history—a statesman, soldier, and patron of learning and the arts—he too provoked the jealousy of his suspicious master. So in 1481, Muḥammad Shah III had him beheaded. His *madrasa*, or theological college, in Bīdar, remains one of the finest surviving Bahmani monuments and serves as testimony to Persian architectural and decorative influence in the Deccan.

Muḥammad Shah III died a year later and was succeeded by his equally ineffective and long-reigning son, Maḥmūd (r. 1482-1518), the first of five *rois faineants*

(idle kings), who were puppets in the hands of a Turkish noble at the Bīdar court, Qāsim Barīd, and after the latter's death in 1504, of his son, Amir ʿAlī Barīd, who became the effective ruler of the capital Bīdar and the surrounding districts.

When the last Bahmani died in 1527, the Barīd-Shāh Dynasty took over part of the Bahmani sultanate, which it ruled until 1619, when it was annexed by the ʿĀdil Shah Dynasty of Bijāpur.

Meanwhile, during the feeble reign of Maḥmūd, the outlying provinces became separated under local governors bent on independence. Thus, the former Bahmani state, including the Barīd-Shāh regime in Bīdar, disintegrated into five fragments. The first to break away, as early as 1485, was the governor of Berar, Fatḥ Allāh ʿImād-ul-Mulk, whose descendants, the Imad-Shāhis, maintained their independence until 1572, when Berar was annexed by the Niẓām-Shāh Dynasty of Ahmadnagar. The ʿĀdil Shah Dynasty of Bijāpur (1489-1686) descended from a former governor of Bijāpur, Yūsuf ʿĀdil Khan, a Turk, formed a powerful dynasty that came to rule much of the southwest of the peninsula, fiercely resisting Mughal expansion into the Deccan until the sixth Mughal emperor, ʿĀlamgīr (1658-1707), captured Bijāpur in 1686.

In 1491, Malik Aḥmad Niẓām-ul-Mulk, son of a former Bahmani chief minister, proclaimed himself independent, seized Ahmadnagar and Daulātabād, and established a powerful sultanate in the northwest Deccan, with its capital at Ahmadnagar. It was partially conquered by the third Mughal emperor, Akbar (r. 1556-1605), in 1600, but the resilient ruling line survived as a result of the vigorous opposition to Mughal rule offered by an Abyssinian slave-soldier, Malik ʿAmbār (d. 1626). It was formally annexed by Akbar's grandson in 1633.

Finally, a Turkish commander belonging to the powerful Kara Koyunlu tribe of northwest Iran, Sultan Qulī Quṭb Shāh, who had been appointed governor of Telingana by Maḥmūd Gāwān, acquired in 1512 a vast territory in the southeast Deccan, comprising much of the former kingdom of Warangal and the future Hyderābād state. He established his capital at Golconda, although he also founded the nearby city of Hyderābād. The Quṭb-Shāhī sultanate survived until 1687, when Golconda was overrun by the armies of Mughal emperor ʿĀlamgīr (r. 1658-1707).

SIGNIFICANCE

Despite a record of dynastic rivalry and usurpation, the Bahmani sultanate brought to the Deccan a diverse and cosmopolitan florescence of Indo-Islamic culture, which it passed to the successor-states that followed it. Perhaps the most enduring legacy of the Bahmani was the diffusion of Sufi or Muslim mystical thought and practice. At the same time, the later Bahmani displayed a proclivity for Shiism, which was emulated by the Niẓām-Shāh, ʿĀdil Shah, and Quṭb-Shāh Dynasties.

In architecture, decoration, miniature painting, and music, the Deccani sultanates drew upon many elements—Persian, Turkish, and indigenous Hindu—to sustain a rich, syncretistic cultural and linguistic tradition.

—*Gavin R. G. Hambly*

FURTHER READING

Eaton, Richard M. *Sufis of Bijāpur, 1300-1700: Social Roles of Sufis in Medieval India.* Princeton, N.J.: Princeton University Press, 1978. A brilliant and sensitive study of the Islamic religious culture of the Deccan in Bahmani and later times.

Ernst, Carl W. *Eternal Garden: Mysticism, History, and Politics at a South Asian Sufi Center.* Albany: State University of New York Press, 1992. This monograph perfectly complements Eaton's work (above) and provides marvelous insight into Deccani Islam.

Firishta, Muhammad Qāsim Hindushah Astarabad. *Tarikh-i Firishta.* In *History of the Rise of the Mahomedan Power in India.* Translated by John Briggs. 4 vols. 1829. Reprint. Calcutta, India: 1966. Firishta, who died around 1570, served at the Niẓām-Shāh and ʿĀdil Shah courts, writing a comprehensive history of Muslim rule in India, including a highly informative account of the Bahmani sultans.

Goron, Stan, and J. P. Goenha. *Coins of the Indian Sultans.* Delhi, India: Munshiram Manoharlal, 2001. Indispensable for the complicated chronology of the Bahmani Dynasty and its five successors.

Michell, George, and Mark Zebrowski. *Architecture and Arts of the Deccan Sultanates.* New York: Cambridge University Press, 1999. The essential reference work for the visual arts of the region.

Tabatabai, Ali bin Aziz-Allah. "History of the Bahmani Dynasty." *Indian Antiquary* (1899). Translated by J. S. King. A contemporary of Firishta (see above), Tabatabai served the Niẓām-Shāh court. His chronicle complements that of Firishta.

Wolpert, Stanley. *A New History of India.* New York: Oxford University Press, 2000. This widely accessible and well-written work includes a description of the Delhi sultans and Bābur's conquest of India.

SEE ALSO: 1489: ʿĀdil Shah Dynasty Founded; Early 16th cent.: Devotional Bhakti Traditions Emerge.

RELATED ARTICLES in *Great Lives from History: The Renaissance & Early Modern Era, 1454-1600:* Akbar; Krishnadevaraya.

1490-1492
MARTIN BEHAIM BUILDS THE FIRST WORLD GLOBE

Following an extended commercial residence in Portugal and a voyage to Africa, Behaim constructed the earliest known globe of the world, which summarized the geographical knowledge of educated Europeans at the time of Christopher Columbus's first voyage.

LOCALE: Nuremberg (now in Germany) and Portugal

CATEGORIES: Inventions; geography; science and technology

KEY FIGURES

Martin Behaim (1459?-1507), German geographer, navigator, and merchant

Georg Glockendon (d. 1514), German painter, printer, and woodblock cutter

Diogo Cão (fl. 1480-1486), Portuguese navigator

John II (João II; 1455-1495), king of Portugal, r. 1481-1495

Regiomontanus (Johann Müller; 1436-1476), astronomer who was perhaps Behaim's teacher

SUMMARY OF EVENT

The fifteenth century was a time of expanding commercial activity in Europe, and this activity produced tremendous demands for commodities and raw materials from Asia and Africa. Portugal took the leadership role in establishing trading bases along the coast of West Africa. Early in the century, moreover, Portuguese explorers were already sailing several hundred miles westward. In 1445, Portuguese settlers began colonizing the Azores

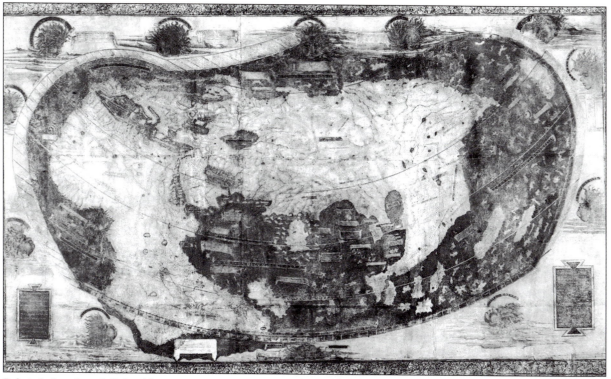

Behaim's "earth-apple," the oldest extant terrestrial globe, was made with a map he possibly owned. This map, however, no longer exists, but it most closely resembles one from 1489—seen here—by Henricus Martellus Germanus. (Hulton|Archive by Getty Images)

(800 miles [1,290 kilometers] west of Portugal), and in 1462, they founded a settlement in the archipelago of Cape Verde. The school for navigators in the Portuguese town of Sagres was one of several centers for the art and science of cartography.

Martin Behaim's career took place within the context of these developments. He was born and raised in a prosperous family of merchants and public officials in the free German city of Frankfurt. His family occupied a large wooden house located at the chief market square of the city. It is not known whether he attended the local parish schools or had a private tutor. Possibly one of his teachers was the celebrated astronomer Regiomontanus, who was a neighbor and friend of the family. Behaim's extant writings, nevertheless, suggest that he never learned to use Latin, even though it was the international language of the time.

At the age of fifteen, Behaim's family sent him to Flanders for professional training in the textile trade, after which he became a successful importer of goods to Frankfurt and other German cities. In 1484, he moved to Portugal to work in the growing spice trade. His business often involved maps and geography. He had every oppor-

tunity to establish connections with prominent cartographers and navigators of the period, and it is known that he possessed maps. Behaim briefly served as a counselor to King John II, who knighted him in 1485. Later that year, he apparently accompanied Diogo Cão on a voyage along the western coast of Africa. In 1486, while at Fayal in the Azores, he married Joanna de Macedo, daughter of the governor of a large Flemish colony in Fayal.

In 1490, Behaim visited Nuremberg for business purposes, and he remained in the city for the next three years. Probably he had been thinking about constructing a globe modeling the earth for some time, and he convinced the leading members of the city council to finance such a project under his direction. It is thought that his motivation was primarily financial, although it is possible that he recognized the educational and publicity value of this visual model of the earth.

To construct the "earth-apple" (*erdapfel* in German), one or more craftspeople made a clay ball twenty-one inches in diameter, which they covered with numerous strips of linen soaked in glue. After drying, the external covering was cut in half to remove the clay. Next, the empty halves were glued together and covered with

1490's

185

leather and additional layers of paper. The sphere was then placed within a wooden ring. Finally, a prominent local artist, Georg Glockendon, painted the surface according to Behaim's instructions.

For the boundaries and place-names that appeared on the globe, Behaim reportedly relied on a large map he owned. Unfortunately, it has not survived. Among surviving maps from the time, Behaim's outline of the earth most closely resembles those produced by Henricus Martellus Germanus of Florence, especially the large Martellus map of 1489 (now at Yale University). In contrast to this map, however, the terms and place-names from Bartolomeu Dias's voyage of 1487-1488 do not appear on the globe. Another difference is that the globe uses German rather than Latin nomenclature, which was very unusual in the late fifteenth century. Behaim's ideas about the earth's size are similar to those of Italian astronomer Paolo Toscanelli dal Pozzo, who influenced Christopher Columbus.

Behaim's globe has no grid of longitudes and latitudes, but it does include the equator, one meridian, the tropics, and the constellations of the zodiac. Some of the details are surprisingly inaccurate when judged by contemporary cartographic knowledge. Even the West African region, which Behaim probably visited, had major mistakes. The unexplored space between Western Europe and Eastern Asia contains several imaginary islands that were most likely based on medieval speculations. The islands of Japan appear to be placed too far to the south (just as Columbus imagined). Some historians think that Behaim's representation of a large island west of the Azores might indicate that he had heard stories about the West Indies or Brazil.

For the fifty drawings and inscriptions on the globe, Behaim incorporated information from a combination of ancient writings and recent explorations. In addition to Ptolemy's *Mathēmatikē syntaxis* (c. 150; *Almagest*, 1948), he made use of the narrative descriptions of Marco Polo, Sir John Mandeville, and Diogo Gomes. Among several mistaken ideas on the globe, one inscription warned that the region south of the equator was dangerously warm, which would prevent compasses from functioning properly.

After Behaim returned to Portugal, King John II entrusted him with a number of official missions. While on a trip to Flanders, he was taken prisoner by the English. He escaped and made his way to the Azores, where he lived for a time. Following John's death in 1495, Behaim was unable to establish a relationship with the new king, Manuel I. The later life of Behaim was one of personal tragedy. He was imprisoned for a time on charges of adultery, and his business failed. He died in obscurity and poverty in Lisbon at about the age of forty-eight.

The beautiful globe Behaim had created remained in the city hall of Nuremberg for more than a century. It was then returned to the Behaim family and almost forgotten. In 1823, it was finally rediscovered. Since 1906, the globe has been on display at the German National Museum in Nuremberg. In 1937, when the family showed interest in selling the globe in the United States, the government of Adolf Hitler purchased it as a patriotic statement.

SIGNIFICANCE

In the case of Behaim, historians have a difficult time separating fact from legend. It is doubtful that he made any significant contribution to astronomy. Most recent historians reject earlier claims that he taught the Portuguese the principles of celestial navigation, the use the cross staff (Jacob's staff), or the astronomical tables of Regiomontanus. The cross staff had been invented a century earlier by Levi ben Gerson, and it was well known on the Iberian Peninsula before Behaim's arrival. The astronomical tables used by Portuguese navigators were apparently different from those developed by Regiomontanus. It is possible that Behaim might have met explorers like Christopher Columbus or Amerigo Vespucci, but there is no evidence of any connection.

Behaim's contribution to geography was to put together a compilation of geographical knowledge existing shortly before Europeans learned about the Western Hemisphere and to record this knowledge in the form of an artistic sphere. Although his is currently the oldest extant terrestrial globe, Behaim was probably not the first person to produce such an object. Less impressive models were naturally less likely to survive the ravages of destructive wars, fires, and neglect. It is doubtful that Behaim ever recognized the great scientific importance of globes as tools in geography. He was a creative entrepreneur who somehow convinced practical city leaders that a large and beautifully constructed model was of commercial value.

Behaim's globe interests many people today, because its existence graphically refutes the myth that educated Europeans in the age of Columbus believed that the earth was flat. An inscription on the globe explicitly asserted that the earth was spherical and therefore it would be possible to travel to any place on the earth's surface. Apparently such an idea did not shock or surprise the people of the Renaissance.

—Thomas Tandy Lewis

FURTHER READING

Gross, John. *Mapmaker's Art: An Illustrated History of Cartography.* Chicago: Rand McNally, 1995. A beautiful, comprehensive guide to three thousand years of maps, showing how they artistically reflected the geographical learning of their times.

Levenson, Jay A. *Circa 1492: Art in the Age of Exploration.* New Haven, Conn.: Yale University Press, 1991. A variety of interesting essays about the period, with interesting accounts of the Portuguese explorations and maps relevant to Behaim's globe.

Ravenstein, Ernst G. *Martin Behaim: His Life and His Globe.* London: George Philip & Sons, 1908. Although out of date in some particulars, this is the only significant book about Behaim in the English language. Students able to read German can find several more recent biographical studies.

Short, John Rennie. *The World Through Maps: A History of Cartography.* Richmond Hill, Ont.: Firefly Books, 2003. The story of mapping from prehistoric times, with interesting material about the great value of sea charts in the fifteenth century.

Thrower, Norman. *Maps and Civilization: Cartography in Culture and Society.* Chicago: University of Chicago Press, 1999. Introductory account about the close links between maps and history from antiquity to the present day.

SEE ALSO: Oct. 12, 1492: Columbus Lands in the Americas; 1519-1522: Magellan Expedition Circumnavigates the Globe; 1569: Mercator Publishes His World Map.

RELATED ARTICLES in *Great Lives from History: The Renaissance & Early Modern Era, 1454-1600:* Christopher Columbus; John II; Ferdinand Magellan; Manuel I; Gerardus Mercator.

1491-1545
CHRISTIANITY IS ESTABLISHED IN THE KINGDOM OF KONGO

In the 1490's, the Kingdom of Kongo embraced Christianity, and under Afonso I, Christianity acquired many African elements. Uniquely African forms of Christian art and religious practice developed. Kongo's new religion allowed it to prosper as a trading partner of Portugal, but the rising slave trade brought conflict and eventually led to the weakening of the kingdom.

LOCALE: Kingdom of Kongo (now in Republic of the Congo, Democratic Republic of the Congo, and Zaire and Cabinda Provinces, Angola)

CATEGORIES: Religion; diplomacy and international relations

KEY FIGURES

João I (Nzinga Nkuwu; d. 1506), manikongo (king) of Kongo, r. to 1506

Afonso I (Nzinga Mbemba; c. late 1450's/early 1460's-1543), king of Kongo, r. 1506-1543

SUMMARY OF EVENT

In the 1440's, Portuguese explorers ventured south along the African coast, and by 1482, Diogo Cão had made the first contact with the Kingdom of Kongo. Kongo then occupied portions of the present-day Congo Republics (Congo and Zaire) and Angola, and it was ruled by Manikongo (king) Nzinga Nkuwu.

Portugal sent a technical delegation, and, impressed by both the West's technology and its faith, Nzinga Nkuwu was baptized as João I in 1491. He was joined by his court officials and his firstborn son, Nzinga Mbemba, who took the name Afonso. The benefits of conversion were immediate: missionaries, teachers, military advisers, and artisans were dispatched from Portugal. Along with them came one of Europe's newest technological marvels, invented only forty years before: a printing press. The soldiers soon proved their worth by leading João's forces in suppressing a local rebellion. João paid for Portugal's cultural and military aid in ivory, copper, and slaves.

As Christianity spread, tensions between the old and new religions increased. The missionaries rejected the assimilation of local religious customs into Christianity, and they destroyed the Kongolese's fetishes. The traditional cult leaders, the *nganga*, fostered dissension by reemphasizing the importance of polygamy, which bound powerful families together. Most of João's sons resented the Christian insistence on monogamy, which they realized would destroy the fragile network of alliances that held Kongo society together. By 1494, the manikongo and most of his sons had abandoned Christianity and returned to traditional religious practice.

At the time of João's death in 1506, the kingdom was

1490's

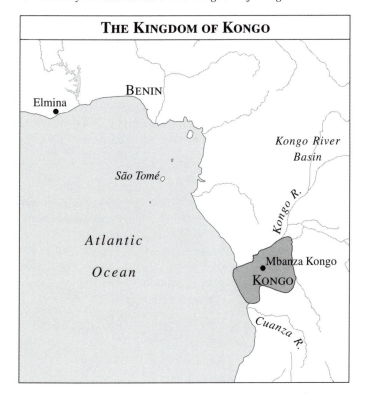

THE KINGDOM OF KONGO

Benin

Elmina

Kongo River Basin

São Tomé

Kongo R.

Atlantic Ocean

Mbanza Kongo

KONGO

Cuanza R.

and, in the case of the Kongo, it was fully embraced in the mythology of Kongolese Christianity.

Once on the throne, Afonso I aggressively used his position to bring the Kongo all the advantages of his Portuguese connections. The Jesuits established a school for the nobility in the capital, while Afonso sent sons and nephews to Lisbon for higher education. One son, Enrique, became the first African bishop since early Christianity (and the last for four hundred years). Afonso feared that Enrique might be poisoned by enemies, however, so he left him little scope for his abilities. These concerns were well founded; several of the king's nephews (and perhaps his sons as well) were taken into slavery, and in 1540, the Portuguese attempted to assassinate Afonso while he attended Easter Sunday Mass.

While remaining a devout Catholic, Afonso spread the faith by incorporating traditional religious practices. He destroyed fetishes but promoted the reverence of relics, and he assigned the high priest of the water cult to be the protector of the holy water in the churches. Afonso practiced monogamy, although his fidelity was questionable—at his death he left three hundred grandsons. In some ways, Christianity became the royal cult, and it took root in the country. Bakongo Catholicism was thoroughly Africanized, with traditional religious categories and cosmology incorporated into the creed and Christian teaching. Christian words for "God" and "priest," for example, were literally taken from the Kikongo language.

In all his efforts, however, Afonso was poorly served by the Portuguese missionaries, many of whom were sent to the Kongo because they had had disciplinary problems at home. He regularly complained to the king of Portugal (and to the pope) about lascivious clergy and their violations of clerical celibacy. The missionaries often baptized large numbers of new converts, but then left them with little or no instruction on the precepts of their new religion.

An important development of Bakongo Christianity was its contribution to African religious art. The Kongo was rich in minerals, especially copper and iron, and Bakongo sculptors proceeded to express their new faith in brass, bronze, and stone carvings. A number of altar crucifixes, statues, wall plaques, and staffs still exist, although most are now held in European museums. The African motifs are striking: several plaques show a seated

extensive and prosperous. The six provinces were governed by appointed chiefs with broad authority. Afonso was governor of Nsundi Province in the northeast, where he fostered the development of his people. After João's death, Afonso, as a baptized chief and potential heir to the throne, became the logical champion of the Christian forces.

To avoid dynastic problems, the Kongolese throne did not pass down to the firstborn of the king's principal spouse but was chosen instead from among the sons of lesser wives. With their European background, however, the Portuguese favored the firstborn. Afonso was challenged by his half brother Mpanzu, whose forces were far superior, although Afonso had Portuguese cannon and cavalry alongside his foot soldiers. Mpanzu, however, prepared the battlefield with poisoned stakes, and as the two forces clashed, Afonso outflanked him and drove him onto his own defenses, where he died.

Soon the legend arose that Santiago (Saint James the Apostle) had appeared in the skies on a white horse to lead the Christian forces. The identical fable is recounted about the Christian victory at Clavijo in 844, which turned back the Moors in Spain, and again about the Spanish victory over the Aztecs at Mexico City. It represents the triumph of Iberian Christianity over paganism,

Father-God with arms outstretched, nude with male genitals. On the crossbars of crucifixes are kneeling attendants, arms folded over their breasts. Grave markers are often carved with a crucified Christ, and there are amusing stone statuettes of missionaries on their donkeys.

One unique statuette, now in a Dutch museum, has an opening in its belly for a reliquary. This sort of statue would be typical in medieval or Renaissance Europe, but around the neck of the figure hangs a collection of amulets and fetishes, a classic example of the blending of Christian and African cultic expressions. The altar crucifixes, perhaps because they were made for the use of foreign priests, are European in style, as are statues of Saint Anthony, a popular native of Portugal. On the other hand, the staffs, which were used by Christian governors and kings, combine African symbols, such as the protective leopard, with the figure of the ruler wearing a cross. The creation of Christian religious art continued in the Kongo for 150 years and was later revived in the colonial missionary period after 1880.

Afonso's prime conflict with his patrons came over slavery. The slave trade proved to be a long-term problem that would eventually contribute to the disintegration of the kingdom. In traditional African society, slaves were either criminals sentenced to a period of servitude or prisoners of war. They might be impressed into service as soldiers, servants, or farmworkers, but they were rarely used in trade. In 1498, however, the first slaves were shipped to the Americas from the Kongo. Portuguese masons, carpenters, and even missionaries soon abandoned those occupations for the lucrative slave trade, over the protests of the manikongo.

Six years after taking power, Afonso was asked to pay for a shipment of military supplies, priests, and artisans by returning the ship filled with slaves. Not having enough prisoners who qualified, Afonso raided a neighboring kingdom and sent six hundred slaves, who were promptly transshipped to Ghana to be exchanged for gold. The demands became more insistent, and when Afonso's protests turned to anger, the pressures became threatening. Afonso was refused permission to build ships for trading and was told that his favored position could easily be transferred to another African ruler. As the manikongo attempted to develop legitimate trade, he found himself increasingly hampered by Portuguese merchants on the island of São Tomé. Impatient with the number of slaves Afonso was willing to produce, they opened their own slave depots on the Kongo mainland and began raiding upriver. Afonso tried to moderate the worst excesses of the slave trade, but to little effect. Most

of the existing twenty-two letters between Afonso and the kings of Portugal concern the slave trade.

SIGNIFICANCE

Events in the Kongo demonstrated that an indigenous African Christianity was possible, though the greed of Western slave traders doomed it to failure. The rise of the slave trade in the Kongo was a foreshadowing of both expanded chattel slavery and colonialism. Later kings continued the Catholic tradition in the Kongo while resisting the Portuguese. Diogo I (r. 1545-1561), the grandson of Afonso I who succeeded him after a dynastic conflict with Afonso's son, continued to evangelize the country. Alvare I (r. 1568-1587), Alvare II (r. 1587-1614), and Alvare III (r. 1614-1622) enlisted the support of the popes. They remonstrated with the Portuguese and supported the Spanish against them, to little avail. By the seventeenth century, however, the new power in the slave trade was the Dutch, and papal appeals fell on deaf ears.

—*Norbert Brockman*

FURTHER READING

Gray, Richard. *Black Christians and White Missionaries.* New Haven, Conn.: Yale University Press, 1992. Details the development of African Christianity.

Hilton, Anne. *The Kingdom of Kongo.* New York: Oxford University Press, 1985. The standard history of the Kongo kingdom.

Thiel, J. F., and Heinz Helf. *Christliche kunst in Afrika.* Berlin: Dietrich Reimer, 1984. An illustrated history of indigenous African Christian art; chapter 3 is on Kongo art of this period. In German.

Thornton, John. *Africa and Africans in the Making of the Atlantic World, 1400-1680.* Cambridge, England: Cambridge University Press, 1992. Details expanding contacts between Africans and the West, leading up to colonialism.

SEE ALSO: Late 15th cent.: Mombasa, Malindi, and Kilwa Reach Their Height; 1481-1482: Founding of Elmina; c. 1485: Portuguese Establish a Foothold in Africa; Jan., 1498: Portuguese Reach the Swahili Coast; 1502: Beginning of the Transatlantic Slave Trade; 1505-1515: Portuguese Viceroys Establish Overseas Trade Empire; 1527-1543: Ethiopia's Early Solomonic Period Ends; Aug. 4, 1578: Battle of Ksar el-Kebir.

RELATED ARTICLE in *Great Lives from History: The Renaissance & Early Modern Era, 1454-1600:* Afonso I.

1492
FALL OF GRANADA

The fall of Granada marked the military conquest of Muslim Spain by the Christian forces of Spanish King Ferdinand II and Queen Isabella I, who retook Granada after nearly 800 years of settlement by the Moors.

LOCALE: Granada, kingdom of Granada (now Granada, Spain)

CATEGORIES: Expansion and land acquisition; religion; wars, uprisings, and civil unrest

KEY FIGURES

Abū al-Ḥasan ʿAlī (d. 1485), emir of Granada, r. 1464-1485

Ferdinand II (1452-1516), king of Aragon, r. 1479-1516

Isabella I (1451-1504), queen of Castile, r. 1474-1504

Boabdil (c. 1464-1527/1538), son of Abū al-Ḥasan ʿAlī and emir of Granada, r. 1482-1492

SUMMARY OF EVENT

Since the early eighth century, the Christians of northern Spain had attempted to repel North African Moorish invaders and settlers from Iberian soil. By the early thirteenth century, their military efforts had been crowned with general success, but one area of Andalusia, Granada, held out.

For more than two centuries, the fertile and fair kingdom of Granada, some 200 miles long and 70 miles wide, remained a bastion of Moorish occupation. The *mudejars* (Muslims) were skilled artisans and workers but could not hope to enter into the more prestigious professions in Christian Spain. Since 1469, when the joint rule of Ferdinand II and Isabella I commenced, a concept of Castilian caste was evolved that discriminated against the Moors as well as the Jews.

Yet the joint rulers of Aragon and Castile generally interacted cordially with the Muslim emirate, sporadic incidents notwithstanding. Christian and Muslim kingdoms enjoyed a sort of workable *convivencia* (coexistence). Once Christian Spain had adopted the Jewish belief of the identity of the state and a single religion, the traditional coexistence was no longer possible. Although it would take a decade of their life to accomplish it, King Ferdinand of Aragon and Queen Isabella of Castile (married since 1469 and joint rulers of Aragon-Castile), determined upon the final Reconquista (reconquest) of Granada.

Slow but relentless Christian advance menaced Málaga and, in 1481, Christian troops on the outskirts of Loja seemed to knock at the gates of Granada. Panicked easily, Granada's emir, Abū al-Ḥasan ʿAlī, rashly struck against the castle of Zahara near Ronda. Although the so-called Catholic Monarchs were not adequately prepared militarily at this time and had limited financial resources, they were not likely to put up with the loss of Zahara. Catholic troops launched a furious and persistent counterattack against the fortress, reoccupying it in 1482, thanks to the valor of Rodrigo Ponce de León, marquis of Cádiz. Thereafter, Christian Spain began to make concerted plans for the overthrow of the emirate. The pope declared a crusade, and Jewish bankers and businesspeople supplied funds.

Ferdinand and Isabella decided to change their strategy. They aimed to strip the Moorish kingdom down to its core city, Granada, by first removing the key defensive positions of Almería and Málaga. The monarchs had also built up a powerful army, complete with supply lines, cavalry and infantry, the most impressive artillery yet collected in Western Europe, and a skilled corps of engineers. This corps of "sappers," as they were called, was to be of decisive importance in the coming campaigns. On one occasion they literally leveled an obstructing mountain, a feat that left the chroniclers in scriptural ecstasy.

In 1484, equipped with this splendid new army financed chiefly through Isabella's remarkable persistence and powers of persuasion, Ferdinand began the siege of the important town of Ronda. His artillery battered Ronda's defenses down, so that Christian victory came on May 15, 1485. The news of the victory electrified Christian Spain. Ferdinand took the town of Loja and then moved on to the great city of Málaga. The city put up such fierce resistance that after months of fighting only the suburbs had been taken. The attack stalled, and the Christian forces were in despair. Ferdinand finally sent for the queen as an omen of good fortune. Isabella's presence outside Málaga worked a miracle in inspiring confidence, and the troops threw themselves into the attack with renewed zeal and determination. At the end, the city capitulated, and its Moorish population was enslaved.

Thus the western portion of Granada had been reduced and only the eastern part remained to be taken. In May of 1489, Ferdinand opened the eastern front by attacking the mountain city of Baza, a campaign described as "the real Calvary of the Spaniards." Nothing went right; the terrain was admirably suited to Moorish guerrilla tactics, the early harsh winter brought despair, roads were washed away, a pestilence broke out, and the Muslims continued fierce sorties. Again, Isabella decided to join her troops, and her presence was again magical. Besides inspiring emotion and enthusiasm, she carried out miracles in organizing supplies. She had roads rebuilt, barracks relocated, and the forces replenished with fresh recruits. After a long and courageous defense the citizens of Baza accepted generous terms from Ferdinand. Málaga's governor, Muḥammad al-Zaghall, who had made his headquarters at Almería, realized the futility of further resistance and sued for peace.

The way to Granada now lay open. Ten years of planning were about to come to fruition. In the spring of 1491, the Spaniards encamped outside the walls and towers of Granada, its Alhambra (the emir's palace) set like a glistening crown on a high hill. The city was crowded with desperate refugees, its supplies were limited, and its leadership was tottering. Abū al-Ḥasan ʿAlī had lost part of his power in 1482, when his son Boabdil staged a partially successful coup. The emirship remained uncertain until 1486, when Boabdil became the unquestioned emir, albeit an emir under siege by Ferdinand. Ferdinand expected the emir to surrender Granada to him. When he refused to do so, a long and costly siege of the city was begun. The siege lasted from April of 1491 to January of 1492.

Finally, Boabdil, the last emir of Granada, consented on October 28, 1491, to surrender the city within sixty days. When news of his treachery reached his nobles and generals, his plight became so desperate that on January 1, 1492, he sent an anguished message to Ferdinand and Isabella offering them the city immediately. The following dawn, the king and queen, followed by the royal choir of Toledo, the archbishop primate of Spain, and the whole Christian host, among others, marched slowly toward the Moorish city. Boabdil, together with his few remaining retainers, descended from the Alhambra and advanced toward the waiting Christians.

With royal dignity seldom displayed during his reign, Boabdil handed the keys of the Alhambra to Ferdinand and kissed his sleeve. Ferdinand in turn gave the keys to Isabella, who held them for a moment, and then passed

Moorish chiefs surrender the keys of a town seized by the Spanish to King Ferdinand II and Queen Isabella I, prior to the 1492 fall of Granada. (Frederick Ungar Publishing Co.)

1490's

them on to the Alhambra's new governor, the count of Tendilla. Boabdil turned slowly away, mounted his horse, and rode off to the mountains. A small detachment of Christians raised the standards over the Alhambra. On the tall Torre de la Vela, the Christian force slowly hoisted the silver cross, which had been kept so long in readiness for the day. Among the hardened Christian soldiers came the cry "Granada! Granada! Granada for Don Ferdinand and Doña Isabel!" The royal choir broke into *Te Deum.*

SIGNIFICANCE

Granada's fall was regarded by contemporary Christians as the most distinguished event in the history of Spain and by the Muslims as one of the most terrible catastrophes to befall Islam. Ferdinand's triumphant message to Rome that the kingdom of Granada, after 780 years of occupation by the infidels, had been finally won "to the glory of God, the exaltation of our Holy Catholic Faith," was acclaimed throughout Europe and brought from the grateful Pope Alexander VI in 1494 the sobriquet of Los Reyes Católicos (the Catholic Monarchs) for the joint rulers of Spain.

—Carl F. Rohne, updated by Narasingha P. Sil

FURTHER READING

Dickie, James. "Granada: A Case Study of Arab Urbanism in Muslim Spain." In *The Legacy of Muslim Spain*, edited by Salma K. Jayyusi. Leiden, the Netherlands: E. J. Brill, 1992. A delightful study of the city and its Islamic people and their culture in the fifteenth century.

Hale, Edwyn Andalus. *Spain Under the Muslims.* London: Robert Hale, 1958. A sound summary of the Arab role in Spanish history.

Harvey, L. P. "The Mudejars." In *The Legacy of Muslim Spain*, edited by Salma K. Jayyusi. Leiden, the Netherlands: E. J. Brill, 1992. Discusses the juridical status of the *mudejars* of the Christian kingdoms of Castile and Aragon and the provinces of Valencia and Navarre in Spain.

Irving, Washington. *The Conquest of Granada.* London: Co-Operative Publication Society, 1829. A picturesque narrative of the fall of Granada that earned the author the praise of his contemporaries. Samuel Taylor Coleridge called the book a masterpiece of literature.

Kamen, Henry. *Empire: How Spain Became a World Power, 1492-1763.* New York: HarperCollins, 2003. Surveys the roles played by Ferdinand and Isabella in the fashioning of Spain's global empire. Includes photographic plates, illustrations, maps, bibliographic references, index.

_____. *Spain, 1469-1714: A Society of Conflict.* 2d ed. Reprint. New York: Longman, 1996. An intelligently written, scholarly, and readable account of the making of the nation state of Spain. The short section titled "The Conquest of Granada" is a marvel of scholarly compression.

Merriman, Roger B. *The Rise of the Spanish Empire in the Old World and in the New.* 4 vols. Reprint. New York: Cooper Square, 1962. Although first published in 1918 and thus quite dated, volume 2, entitled "The Catholic Kings," still constitutes a useful guide to the history of the joint rulers of Aragon and Castile.

Nicolle, David. *Granada, 1492: The Twilight of Moorish Spain.* London: Osprey, 1998. Well-illustrated study of the military campaigns from 1481 to 1491 that led to the conquest of Granada. Includes sketches of leaders and descriptions of opposing armies.

Prescott, W. H. *The Art of War in Spain: The Conquest of Granada, 1481-1492.* Edited by Albert D. McJoynt. London: Greenhill Press, 1995. Classic account of the campaigns that led to Boabdil's defeat and Spain's decisive victory.

Read, Jan. *The Moors in Spain and Portugal.* London: Faber & Faber, 1974. Written from the perspective of the Moors and emphasizing the all-around history of Muslim Spain, this eminently readable book provides an excellent account of the conquest of Granada in chapters 23 and 24.

SEE ALSO: Oct. 19, 1469: Marriage of Ferdinand and Isabella; 1492: Jews Are Expelled from Spain.

RELATED ARTICLES in *Great Lives from History: The Renaissance & Early Modern Era, 1454-1600:* Boabdil; Ferdinand II and Isabella I; Francisco Jiménez de Cisneros.

1492
JEWS ARE EXPELLED FROM SPAIN

The expulsion of Jews from Spain through the edict of King Ferdinand II and Queen Isabella I was launched to achieve religious unity, but it deprived Spain of a most industrious, productive, and intellectual population and helped to account for Spain's decline.

LOCALE: Castile, Aragon, and other Iberian kingdoms (now Spain)

CATEGORIES: Laws, acts, and legal history; religion; government and politics

KEY FIGURES

Tomás de Torquemada (1420-1498), Spanish inquisitor general, 1483-1498

Ferdinand II (1452-1516), king of Aragon, r. 1479-1516, and king of Castile, r. 1474-1504, as Ferdinand V

Isabella I (1451-1504), queen of Castile, r. 1474-1504

Isaac ben Judah Abravanel (1437-1508), Spanish-Jewish scholar and statesman

Abraham Senior (1412-1493), chief rabbi of Castile and principal farmer of taxes

SUMMARY OF EVENT

A people of the Diaspora, Jews have lived through most of their history without a country of their own, a minority group among other peoples. Because the Jewish community in Spain, particularly during the tenth through the twelfth centuries, was especially productive and influential culturally, that period is often called the golden age of Jewish history. During this time, Jews not only produced great works of philosophy, poetry, liturgy, theology, and a general literature for themselves but also served as the vital intellectual link between the Muslim Middle East and Christian Europe.

Countless Jews either were burned alive or expelled from Spain after refusing to convert to Christianity. (Hulton|Archive by Getty Images)

1490's

THE SPANISH EDICT OF EXPULSION

Ferdinand II and Isabella I expelled Jews from the kingdoms of Spain. The edict of 1492 banished an entire population of nonconverted Jews, believed by the Catholic monarchs to be "evil," "wicked," and a danger to the Christian faith.

[W]hereas we have been informed that in these our kingdoms there were some wicked Christians who Judaized and apostatized from our holy Catholic faith, the great cause of which was interaction between the Jews and these Christians, . . . we ordered the separation of the said Jews in all the cities, towns and villages of our kingdoms and lordships and [commanded] that they be given Jewish quarters and separated places where they should live. . . . [G]reat injury has resulted and still results, since the Christians have engaged in and continue to engage in social interaction and communication they have had means and ways they can to subvert and to steal faithful Christians from our holy Catholic faith and to separate them from it, and to draw them to themselves and subvert them to their own wicked belief and conviction, instructing them in the ceremonies and observances of their law. . . .

[B]ecause every day it is found and appears that the said Jews increase in continuing their evil and wicked purpose wherever they live and congregate, and so that there will not be any place where they further offend our holy faith, and corrupt those whom God has until now most desired to preserve, as well as those who had fallen but amended and returned to Holy Mother Church, the which according to the weakness of our humanity and by diabolical astuteness and suggestion that continually wages war against us may easily occur unless the principal cause of it be removed, which is to banish the said Jews from our kingdoms.

Source: "Edict of Expulsion, 1492." From a translation by Edward Peters, 1995. Foundation for the Advancement of Shephardic Studies and Culture. http://www.sephardicstudies.org/decree.html. Accessed September 30, 2004.

The Jewish community in Spain had a long history. While the tradition that has the Jews living there during the time of Solomon is somewhat optimistic, history confirms their residence in the peninsula by the year 300, before the arrival of the Vandals. Although they adjusted as both urban and rural dwellers, they also seemed to have aroused the suspicion of early Christians. The oldest record of Spanish Christianity, included in the canons of the Council of Elvira (early fourth century), already encouraged a separation of Jews and Christians.

The Jews of medieval Spain were the smallest in number and the most vulnerable of the three major religious groups (Islam, Christianity, and Judaism). They were sporadically persecuted by Christians and Muslims but managed to coexist with both and even prosper, achieving distinction in wealth and learning. The Jewish com-

munity reached the zenith of its development during the Muslim domination that began when Ṭāriq ibn-Ziyād invaded Spain from Morocco in 711. Hoping to improve their lot religiously and politically, the Jews welcomed the Arabs. Economically, too, the Muslim conquest was especially attractive to Jews. It opened the markets of North Africa and the entire Muslim world as far away as India. Intellectually, the Arabs had much to offer. They heralded the advance of a dynamic culture in which the legacy of Greece and Rome was wedded to that of Persia and India. Arabic became the international language of a vast caliphate.

Eventually, feuds and dynastic disputes arose among the Muslims; by the eleventh century, Christian states in the north of Spain, even though disunified, were emboldened to undertake a reconquest (Reconquista) of their country. The surrender of Toledo in 1085 meant that the Jews once again had to face the prospect of dealing with a Christian environment. Yet they found Berber conquest even more disconcerting when a new group of Berber conquerors, the Almohads, came to Spain in 1150 and repressed the Jews by forcing them to convert to Islam. Many fled to other Muslim domains in Africa or to other Christian centers in Spain. As the Christian reconquest continued, dynastic disputes within Christian Spain and the general social unrest affected the Jews adversely.

The pent-up fury of the Crusades was often visited on the Jews, and edicts of various Church councils, such as those of the Fourth Lateran Council in 1215, overrode any positive feelings Christian rulers might have had for their Jewish subjects. The introduction of the Inquisition into Spain by papal bull made matters still worse. Mobs killed thousands of alleged heretics. Violence against the Jews climaxed in 1391 when massacres occurred in the ghettos of Seville, Barcelona, Toledo, and other major cities. Thousands accepted or were forced into conversion to Christianity. Some, the so-called crypto-Jews, Marranos, or accursed ones, feigned conversion while maintaining their practice of Judaism in secret. Converted Jews became a large minority and were suspected of insincerity by Christians and distrusted by Jews. As New Christians, they were not subject to the disabilities of Jews and rose to the highest positions in government, the Church, and commerce, further increasing discontent with the Jews.

Conflict between New Christians and Old Christians became bitter. In some cities, New Christians were excluded by statute from holding office. Priests and monks, including Cardinal Mendoza, the archbishop of Seville, and Tomás de Torquemada, denounced the New Christians as Jews.

The marriage of Isabella of Castile and Ferdinand of Aragon in 1469, a union arranged in part by a Jew, Abraham Senior, gave new enthusiasm to the national cause in Spain. Religious fanaticism grew to a high pitch and was chiefly directed against the new Jewish "Christians." The Crown requested the establishment of the Inquisition, and Pope Sixtus IV granted it in 1478. The Inquisition had no authority over unbaptized Christians and could not touch the Jews. It dealt with the orthodoxy of the converts and with Jewish culture within the Church. Civil authorities began to enforce anti-Jewish restrictions rigidly and to banish Jews from municipalities.

Converts, or *conversos*, still practicing Judaism at first suffered confiscation of their property. When Torquemada was appointed inquisitor general of Spain, he was determined to rid Spain of pseudo-Christians entirely. On February 6, 1481, the first *auto-da-fé*, or act of faith, was held, and six men and six women were burned at the stake. Practicing Jews were segregated and forced to wear identifying badges.

Segregated by law and popular prejudice, Jews usually lived in ghettos in the major cities and entered the professions or commerce. The greatest prejudice against the Jews came from their role as financiers and tax collectors for kings, nobles, and the Church. Both Ferdinand and Isabella relied almost exclusively on Jewish financiers.

Ordinary Spaniards resented Jewish merchants for their success in money lending and trade. They were charged with making profits at the expense of the people. The Spanish chronicler Andrés Bernáldez, a parish priest, denounced them for being "merchants, salesmen, tax gatherers, retailers, stewards of nobles, officials, tailors, shoemakers, tanners, weavers, grocers, peddlers, silk-mercers, smiths, jewelers, and other trades; none tilled the earth or became a farmer, carpenter, or builder: all sought after comfortable posts and ways of making profits without much labour."

When Granada, the last Muslim kingdom of Spain, surrendered in November, 1491, and admitted Ferdinand and Isabella on January 2, 1492, the goal of the religious and national forces in Spain was reached. All that remained for complete unification was the subjugation of non-Christians. On March 31, 1492, an edict of expulsion ordered all Jews to leave Spain by the end of July. All who remained had to be baptized under threat of death. Efforts by Abraham Senior, Isaac ben Judah Abravanel, and others to have the edict revoked were in vain. Jews were expelled and went chiefly to North Africa, Italy, and Turkey, harassed by disease and pirates. Perhaps 100,000 went to Portugal but were expelled because of a pending marriage alliance between the king and the daughter of Isabella and Ferdinand. No reliable figures exist for the number of Jews expelled. Probably about 180,000 Jews fled from Castile and Aragon and 50,000 converted.

SIGNIFICANCE

The 1492 edict of expulsion brought about the end of a Jewish community that had lived in Spain for more than a millennium. The expulsion of Jews and Muslims caused Spain to pay a heavy price for its attempts at religious and political unification. The loss of many of Spain's best and most productive citizens brought about a decline in the economy, commerce, literature, arts, sciences, education, professions, and population.

—*Robert D. Talbott*

FURTHER READING

Alpert, Michael. *Crypto-Judaism and the Spanish Inquisition*. New York: Palgrave, 2001. Survey of crypto-Judaism both during and after the Inquisition. Looks at the long-term legacy of the "false" *conversos*. Includes illustrations, map, bibliographic references, and index.

Baer, Yitzhak. *A History of the Jews in Christian Spain*. Translated by Louis Schoffman. 2 vols. Philadelphia: Jewish Publication Society, 1961-1966. This work covers the entire history of Jews in Spain. It is unbiased and complete, and it details the reaction of the Jews.

Kamen, Henry. *Inquisition and Society in Spain in the Sixteenth and Seventeenth Centuries*. Bloomington: Indiana University Press, 1985. Describes the beginnings and procedures of the Inquisition as well as the context in which it developed and operated.

Lindo, Elias Hiam. *The History of the Jews of Spain and Portugal, from the Earliest Times to Their Final Expulsion from Those Kingdoms, and Their Subsequent Dispersion, with Complete Translations of All the Laws Made Respecting Them During Their Long Es-*

1490's

tablishment in the Iberian Peninsula. 1848. Reprint. New York: Burt Franklin, 1970. Includes the beginnings of Jewish migration to Spain and Portugal, their early treatment, and extensive coverage of the expulsion with documents.

Liss, Peggy K. *Isabel the Queen: Life and Times*. New York: Oxford University Press, 1992. Good biography of Isabella, with excellent explanation of the reasons for and influences upon the expulsion.

Netanyahu, Benzion. *The Origins of the Inquisition in Fifteenth Century Spain*. 2d ed. New York: New York Review of Books, 2001. Places the expulsion of the Jews within a history of monumental scope, beginning in 525 B.C.E. Argues that the novelty of fifteenth century Spain's treatment of Jews lay in their focus on race rather than religion, such that even sincere converts (of which the author believes there were many) were not trusted by the inquisitors or the government. Includes photographic plates, illustrations, bibliographic references, and index.

Neuman, Abraham A. *The Jews of Spain*. 2 vols. Philadelphia: Jewish Publication Society, 1942. Excellent social study with a discussion of the Jewish community and its relationship with the king and Christians.

Paris, Erna. *The End of Days: A Story of Tolerance, Tyranny, and the Expulsion of the Jews from Spain*. Amherst, N.Y.: Prometheus Books, 1995. This history of the Inquisition discusses Torquemada's use of the Holy Child of La Guardia trial to motivate the expulsion of Jews. Includes illustrations, maps, bibliographic references, and index.

Roth, Norman. *Conversos, Inquisition, and the Expulsion of the Jews from Spain*. Madison: University of Wisconsin Press, 2002. Study of the experience of Jews under the Inquisition, especially those who attempted to convert to Catholicism. Includes bibliographic references and index.

SEE ALSO: Oct. 19, 1469: Marriage of Ferdinand and Isabella; Nov. 1, 1478: Establishment of the Spanish Inquisition; 1492: Fall of Granada; Beginning c. 1495: Reform of the Spanish Church; Aug. 15, 1534: Founding of the Jesuit Order.

RELATED ARTICLES in *Great Lives from History: The Renaissance & Early Modern Era, 1454-1600:* Isaac ben Judah Abravanel; Ferdinand II and Isabella I; Henry IV of Castile; Francisco Jiménez de Cisneros; John III; Sixtus IV; Tomás de Torquemada.

October 12, 1492

COLUMBUS LANDS IN THE AMERICAS

Columbus's expedition to the Americas brought the Old World to the Western Hemisphere and extended exploration, colonization, migration, and cultural exchange and exploitation to what came to be called the New World. The first recorded transatlantic voyage changed the course of Western history.

LOCALE: San Salvador, Bahama Islands (now Watlings Island or Guanahani)

CATEGORIES: Exploration and discovery; cultural and intellectual history; expansion and land acquisition; colonization

KEY FIGURES

Christopher Columbus (1451-1506), Italian navigator in the service of Spain

Ferdinand II (1452-1516), king of Aragon, r. 1479-1516, who supported Columbus's voyage

Isabella I (1451-1504), queen of Castile, r. 1474-1504, who was patron of the Columbus voyage

Martín Alonso Pinzón (1441-1493), Spanish captain of the *Pinta*

Vicente Yáñez Pinzón (c. 1462-c. 1523), Spanish captain of the *Niña*

Guacanagarí (c. mid-fifteenth century-c. early sixteenth century), Taino tribal leader who befriended Columbus

Rodrigo de Triana (fl. fifteenth century), Spanish lookout who first sighted land in the Caribbean

SUMMARY OF EVENT

At the end of the fifteenth century, the domination of the eastern Mediterranean by the Turks and the obstruction of land routes by the recently triumphant Ottomans at Constantinople had made the old avenues of East-West trade costly and dangerous. The Venetians clung tenaciously to the old routes, while the Genoese and Florentines explored trade links along the west coast of Africa. Their efforts failed.

Portugal, however, under the leadership of King

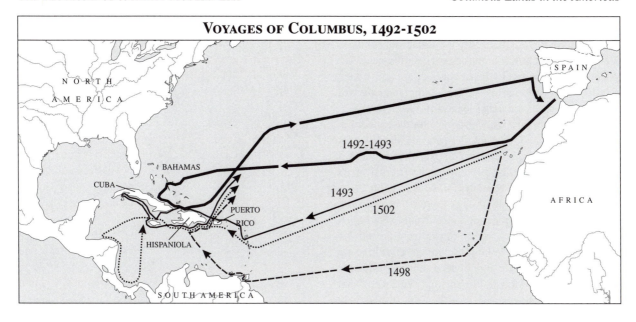

John II and Prince Henry the Navigator, renewed earlier expeditions and found a passage around Africa using their island bases. With papal bulls confirming the Portuguese venture, nothing was left for Spain except the exploration of a western route.

Spanish voyages west trace their origins to the 1470's, when Christopher Columbus came to reside in Portugal and joined trading expeditions to the northwest. He probably visited England and Ireland and learned about ocean navigation and command. Scandinavian mariners had reached Labrador in 986 and 1000 and had brought back tales of an immense continent. During these trade ventures, Columbus may have heard for himself the proud tradition of Leif Eriksson's voyage.

Born in Genoa in 1451 into a Christian weaving and business family, Columbus, following the custom in Genoa, worked at various trades including sailing. When or how he reached Lisbon is unknown, but his sojourn there was critical to his education as a mariner. Columbus married into a sailing family that had served Prince Henry and received from his mother-in-law her late husband's collection of maps and papers.

While the Portuguese were concerned about discovering a sea route to India around Africa, Columbus began to study the feasibility of a voyage west. From fellow sailors and his own trips, he heard of experiences and physical evidence pulled from the sea that suggested lands in that direction. In the 1480's, he proposed to King John II of Portugal that the Crown should equip three vessels for a year of Atlantic exploration. Yet the Portu-

guese were absorbed with the African route, so Columbus, after the death of his wife, moved to Spain, where he had family connections.

In 1486, he presented his scheme to King Ferdinand II and Queen Isabella I at Alcalá using his own world map. While Ferdinand was sufficiently impressed to order a personal copy of Ptolemy's *Geographia*, a special commission studying the proposal concluded it was impractical. They argued, correctly as it turned out, that Asia must be farther west than Columbus supposed. Despite this negative report, Isabella and Ferdinand hinted that they might support a future venture after they had captured Granada. They rewarded the future admiral with a royal pension.

There ensued six years of frustration for Columbus. In 1488, Bartolomeu Dias returned to Lisbon after successfully finding the tip of Africa and a direct sea route to Asia. By 1491, Columbus resolved to leave Spain and submit his project to Charles VIII of France. On January 2, 1492, the seven-century-long Christian reconquest of the Iberian Peninsula was completed with the capture of Granada. To Isabella, it seemed that the achievement of this heroic goal called for the undertaking of another difficult venture.

It was Ferdinand's intervention, however, after a royal council again advised against Columbus's enterprise, that saved the day. The admiral's first report to the sovereigns following the discovery, dated March 4, 1493, suggests that the real reason for supporting his expedition may have been the quest for new revenues to sponsor the liberation of Jerusalem from Islam. In it, Columbus

1490's

197

promised sufficient wealth within seven years to outfit "five thousand cavalry and fifty thousand foot soldiers." Called to Granada, Columbus was given the necessary papers and financing. Included was a diplomatic note to the great khan and an interpreter to communicate with the Indian princes and other leaders in East Asia.

Three vessels were made available for the expedition, the *Santa Maria* and two smaller caravels, the *Niña* and the *Pinta*. Though small, the vessels were handy and well found. They were staffed by sailors and officers from the port of Palos. The *Niña* and the *Pinta* had reliable crews and experienced officers, though the crew of the *Santa Maria* was made up from apprenticed sailors and idlers from the docks of Palos, which in part explains the vessel's subsequent bad sailing. Columbus captained the *Santa Maria*, while two experienced sailors from Palos, brothers Martín Alonso Pinzón and Vicente Yáñez Pinzón, commanded the *Pinta* and the *Niña*, respectively.

On August 3, 1492, the ships sailed with eighty-eight men and provisions for one year. They headed south to the Canary Islands, seeking the winds from the east before they faced west. The expedition had a long stay in Las Palmas, where the *Niña* was altered from a lateen to a square rig similar to the *Pinta*. On September 6, they ventured forth along the twenty-eighth parallel. This course passed along the northern fringe of the northeast trade belt. The trade winds are not always reliable so far north, and September is the hurricane season, so Columbus was fortunate to have had fair winds the whole way out. The weather, as he described it in his log, was "like April in Andalusia, the only thing wanting was to hear nightingales."

On October 12 at 2:00 A.M., under a moon almost full, Rodrigo de Triana, the lookout on the *Niña*, shouted "Land! Land!" He had sighted a small island in the Bahamas, possibly the one known as Watlings Island or Guanahani to its indigenous inhabitants. In 1492, however, Columbus named it San Salvador (Holy Saviour).

On the beach were found Tainos Indians, who received the Europeans courteously. There was no gold on San Salvador, however, so the fleet sailed on, landing in Cuba on October 28. Here, the indigenous people indicated that gold would be found among a more advanced people in the interior called the *Cubanacan*, literally "mid-Cuba." Columbus mistook the name for *El grancan*, the great khan of China. Two Spaniards were sent off with full diplomatic credentials but returned without locating any Asians. They did, however, bring back a report of tobacco, the first time that Europeans had heard of it.

Columbus sailed on to Española (Hispaniola), where

Woodcut from a sketch attributed to Christopher Columbus, showing his landing in Hispaniola in the Caribbean. (Frederick Ungar Publishing Co.)

the *Santa Maria* was grounded on a reef and smashed to pieces on Christmas Eve. Arawak chief Guacanagarí sent his people to help the Spaniards salvage the crew and most of the cargo. Columbus had little choice but to leave part of his crew at the spot to found the settlement of La Navidad. His idea was that the sailor-settlers would be able to explore the island for gold and search out the great khan. Columbus had been eager to return to Spain and report his discoveries. On January 16, 1493, the *Niña* and the *Pinta* began the journey home.

The return voyage was long and miserable because the winds were hostile. After the Azores, storms made the homeward passage difficult. On March 3, Columbus sighted Portugal, and though he realized that he was risking diplomatic complications, requested permission to land and obtain provisions at Lisbon. The *Pinta* had meanwhile sailed on to northwestern Spain, arriving before Columbus finally reached Palos on March 15, 1493.

Columbus was welcomed triumphantly at Barcelona by Ferdinand and Isabella. He received the title "Admiral of the Ocean Sea" and was made "Vice-king and General Governor of the Islands and Terra Firma of Asia and India." It was his finest moment.

SIGNIFICANCE

It has been stated that Columbus would have remained a hero for his generation and for all ages had he retired in 1493. Yet he lived on for thirteen years and made three more voyages to the lands he had discovered, though he would never admit that he had found not Asia but a new continent. In this period, the many flaws of his personality and the limitations of his genius were made obvious through his actions and writings. These imperfections, however, cannot belittle the faith and courage that the "enterprise of the Indies" demanded.

Columbus died in 1506, ignored by his contemporaries and broken in body and heart. Yet his place in history was assured, and his ultimate epitaph could well read, "No man has ever so remade the map of the earth."

—Carl F. Rohne, updated by Michael J. Galgano

FURTHER READING

Axtell, James. "Columbian Encounters: Beyond 1492." *William and Mary Quarterly*, 3d ser. 49 (April, 1992): 335-360.

_____. "Columbian Encounters: 1992-1995." *William and Mary Quarterly*, 3d ser. 52 (October, 1995): 649-696. A comprehensive survey by a leading ethnohistorian. These articles examine the most significant work done on Columbus in the first half of the 1990's.

Columbus, Christopher. *The Diario of Christopher Columbus's First Voyage to America, 1492-1493: Abstracted by Fray Bartolomé de Las Casas.* Translated by Oliver Dunn and James E. Kelley, Jr. Norman: University of Oklahoma Press, 1989. A scholarly translation and edition of Columbus's logbook.

Davidson, Miles H. *Columbus Then and Now: A Life Reexamined.* Norman: University of Oklahoma Press, 1997. A rigorous reconsideration of Columbus's life that surveys and criticizes decades of Columbus biographers for their unreflective accounts and outright errors.

Fernández-Armesto, Felipe. *Columbus.* New York: Oxford University Press, 1992. A fine biography examining Columbus's character, experiences at court, and voyages.

Heat-Moon, William Least. *Columbus in the Americas.* Hoboken, N.J.: John Wiley, 2002. A careful reappraisal of Columbus as explorer, colonizer, and individual, by a best-selling Native American author. Heat-Moon uses many quotations from Columbus's journals to provide insight into the thoughts and motives of the explorer. Includes maps.

Phillips, William D., Jr., and Carla Rahn Phillips. *The Worlds of Christopher Columbus.* New York: Cambridge University Press, 1992. A biography by two leading historians that frames Columbus in the old worlds he drew together to form the modern.

Summerhill, Stephen J., and John Alexander Williams. *Sinking Columbus: Contested History, Cultural Politics, and Mythmaking During the Quincentenary.* Gainesville: University Press of Florida, 2000. A thorough examination of the contemporary legacy of Columbus as seen through the lens of the failure of the planned five hundredth anniversary celebration of his voyage.

Thomas, Hugh. *Rivers of Gold: The Rise of the Spanish Empire.* London: Weidenfeld & Nicolson, 2003. A decidedly conservative and Eurocentric history of Spanish colonialism during Ferdinand and Isabella's rule.

Wilson, Samuel M. *Hispaniola: Caribbean Chiefdoms in the Age of Columbus.* Tuscaloosa: University of Alabama Press, 1990. This archaeological study analyzes Taino life and customs during the first contact with European culture and discusses Guacanagarí.

_____. *The Indigenous People of the Caribbean.* Gainesville: University Press of Florida, 1999. This text offers broader views than does Wilson's volume above.

SEE ALSO: 1462: Regiomontanus Completes the *Epitome* of Ptolemy's *Almagest*; 1493-1521: Ponce de León's Voyages; June 7, 1494: Treaty of Tordesillas; 1495-1510: West Indian Uprisings; 1519-1522: Magellan Expedition Circumnavigates the Globe; 1537: Pope Paul III Declares Rights of New World Peoples; 1542-1543: The New Laws of Spain; 1552: Las Casas Publishes *The Tears of the Indians*; 1565: Spain Seizes the Philippines.

RELATED ARTICLES in *Great Lives from History: The Renaissance & Early Modern Era, 1454-1600:* Charles VIII; Christopher Columbus; Bartolomeu Dias; Ferdinand II and Isabella I; Guacanagarí; John II; Bartolomé de Las Casas; The Pinzón Brothers; Amerigo Vespucci.

1490's

1493-1521
Ponce de León's Voyages

Ponce de León claimed Florida for Spain, founded the Bahama Channel that would serve as a seaway for the Spanish fleet to travel from the Caribbean to the Atlantic, and made the first official contact with indigenous peoples of the North American continent. The Calusa people resisted the incursion and killed Ponce de León before he could settle the land.

Locale: Florida's Gulf coast

Categories: Exploration and discovery; wars, uprisings, and civil unrest; colonization; expansion and land acquisition

Key Figures

Juan Ponce de León (c. 1460-1521), explorer and first governor of Florida, 1513-1521

Chief Carlos (d. 1567), Calusa cacique, executed by the Spanish

Pedro Menéndez de Avilés (1519-1574), Spanish founder of St. Augustine and governor of Florida, 1565-1574

Summary of Event

In 1492, when Christopher Columbus claimed the New World for Spain, the indigenous peoples of Florida numbered at least 100,000, perhaps as many as 925,000, and belonged to seven major tribal groups with numerous subgroups. The major tribal groups were the Apalachee in the panhandle of Florida, the Tocobago near Tampa Bay, the Timucuan on the Atlantic coast, the Ais and the Jeaga in the coastal and Indian River region from Cape Canaveral to the St. Lucie River, the Tequesta from the area of Pompano Beach to Cape Sable, and the Calusa south of Tampa Bay to Cape Sable and inland to the area south of what is now Lake Okeechobee. By 1800, all these tribes were virtually extinct, having fallen to European diseases, conquest, and incursions from the northern Creeks.

Although sometime around 1000, the Norse had made contact with indigenous peoples in what is now southeastern Canada, the Calusas were the first tribe officially to encounter the Europeans on the mainland of North America. It is probable, however, that other Europeans had made landfall in Florida before Juan Ponce de León arrived at the peninsula in 1513. Scholars have asserted that it is nearly certain that Spanish slave hunters came to Florida from Cuba or Mexico prior to Ponce de León's voyages, thus accounting for his hostile reception and reports that he met at least one person who spoke some Spanish.

In 1493, Ponce de León had accompanied Columbus on his second voyage to Hispaniola, sent to plant a permanent settlement in the Caribbean. He found a place in the colonial establishment by commanding a force that put down an indigenous insurrection. After conquering the indigenous population of Borinquén (later Puerto Rico), he was named governor in 1508. Although he built a town, established Spanish authority, and enslaved rebellious indigenous peoples there, he had to cede the governorship of that island to the prior claim of Diego Columbus, Christopher's son.

King Ferdinand II granted Ponce de León a patent on February 2, 1512, to discover and govern the island of Bimini, about which the indigenous had told many tales, including that of the legendary fountain of youth. However, scholars generally agree that the explorer was more interested in claiming land and mineral wealth than in the elusive fountain as he set sail from Puerto Rico on March 3, 1513. On March 27, the expedition sighted land, and on April 2, 1513, the ships reached the Florida coast somewhere between St. Augustine and the St.

Juan Ponce de León started his voyages in 1493 when he accompanied Christopher Columbus on his second voyage to Hispaniola to plant a permanent settlement in the Caribbean. In 1521, Ponce de León founded a colony on the Gulf coast of Florida. (Library of Congress)

Johns River. Ponce de León went ashore, claimed possession of all the contiguous land (in effect, all of North America) in the name of the Spanish crown, and called the land Florida after *pascua florida*, the Easter feast of flowers. He continued his voyage northward to the mouth of the St. Johns River and then turned south; he rounded the Florida Keys (which he named Los Martires, "the Martyrs") and the Dry Tortugas; he then sailed north up the Gulf coast at least to Charlotte Harbor, perhaps to Pensacola Bay.

When Ponce de León sailed into Charlotte Harbor on June 4, 1513, he entered waters controlled by the Calusa, a highly organized tribe of skilled fishermen and warriors headed by a strong, centralized chiefdom. On the pretense of trading with the Spaniards, the Calusa attacked the Spanish ships with twenty canoes filled with warriors. The Spaniards managed to thwart this attack and sent a messenger with two battle prisoners to the Calusa chief to make peace. The cacique promised to come to Ponce de León's ship on the following day; he did—with eighty war canoes whose warriors fought the Spanish from morning until night. The Spaniards retreated and continued on their voyage.

On Ponce de León's return to Puerto Rico in September, 1513, the king made him governor of all he had discovered, commissioning him to colonize the land and to convert the indigenous peoples. However, he was unable to return to Florida until 1521 because he was first sent on a mission to subdue rebellious Caribbean Indians in the Lower Antilles. With two ships, two hundred colonists, fifty horses, livestock, and tools, Ponce de León set off from Puerto Rico to plant a colony on the Gulf coast of Florida, in February, 1521. The party landed on the coast of Charlotte Harbor and began to build shelter. Once again, the Spaniards had to retreat in the face of a fierce attack from the Calusa. Several Spanish were killed in the battle, and Ponce de León received an arrow wound in his leg. The expedition sailed back to Cuba, where Ponce de León died. His body lies buried in Puerto Rico.

SIGNIFICANCE

Numerous ill-fated attempts, including the expeditions of Pánfilo de Narváez in 1528, Hernando de Soto in 1539, and Tristán de Luna y Arellano in 1559, all proved unable to plant a permanent settlement in Florida. It was not until French Huguenots challenged the Spanish dominion of Florida by founding Fort Caroline on the eastern coast that the Spanish finally managed to create a settlement that would set their imprint permanently on Florida soil.

Countering the French challenge, King Philip II appointed Pedro Menéndez de Avilés to drive out the French and to colonize and hold the coast. Subsequent to conquering the French at Fort Caroline and establishing a settlement at St. Augustine in 1565, Menéndez turned his attention to securing the Florida coastlines from pirates and establishing further settlements on the peninsula. When it came to his attention that the Calusa held Spanish captives from shipwrecked vessels and occasionally sacrificed them in religious rituals, he was determined to gain control over the indigenous.

He personally met with Chief Carlos twice in 1566 and 1567, and he established a fort and mission at Calos, the principal village of the Calusa on what is now Key Marcos. Carlos nodded to Menéndez's superior power by an attempt to cement his alliance with the Spanish governor by giving him his sister, later baptized as Antonia, as a wife. Carlos's disappointment in the refusal of the Spanish to help him to defeat his Tocobago enemy and the Calusa's disinterest in Christianity quickly led to renewed strife and tension in their relations with the Spanish.

In his frustration with the Calusa, Menéndez sanctioned the execution of Carlos and later his successor, Felipe. After Felipe's death, the Calusa burnt the village, and the Spanish left in defeat. This and later missions to the Calusa in the seventeenth century resulted in a number of documents about Calusa culture that have been significantly augmented only by archaeological research undertaken since the 1890's.

—*Jane Anderson Jones*

FURTHER READING

Bolton, Herbert E. *The Spanish Borderlands: A Chronicle of Old Florida and the Southwest*. Reprint. Albuquerque: University of New Mexico Press, 1996. Surveys the history of the discovery, exploration, and development of Florida and the Southwest by the Spanish.

Devereux, Anthony Q. *Juan Ponce de León, King Ferdinand, and the Fountain of Youth*. Spartanburg, S.C.: Waccamaw Press, 1993. A biography of the Spanish explorer, with discussion of the quest for the fountain of youth.

Dobyns, Henry F. "The Invasion of Florida: Disease and the Indians of Florida." In *Spanish Pathways in Florida*, edited by Ann L. Henderson and Gary R. Mormino. Sarasota, Fla.: Pineapple Press, 1991. Traces the devastation wrought by European diseases on the indigenous populations of Florida, who were virtually extinct by the first decades of the eighteenth century.

1490's

Dolan, Sean. *Juan Ponce de León.* New York: Chelsea House, 1995. A highly readable biography with vivid illustrations of life in the New World.

Fuson, Robert H. *Juan Ponce de León and the Spanish Discovery of Puerto Rico and Florida.* Blacksburg, Va.: McDonald & Woodward, 2000. Counters the traditional accounts of Ponce de Léon as a naive and ineffective explorer searching for the fountain of youth. Emphasizes his honesty, trustworthiness, basic competence, and relatively humane treatment of indigenous peoples.

Hann, John H., ed. and trans. *Missions to the Calusa.* Gainesville: University of Florida Press and Florida Museum of Natural History, 1991. Historical documents from the sixteenth through the eighteenth centuries, concerning political relations with and missions to the Calusa.

Jones, Jane Anderson, and Maurice O'Sullivan, eds. *Florida in Poetry: A History of the Imagination.* Sarasota, Fla.: Pineapple Press, 1995. Contains bilingual excerpts of poems written by Spanish poets extolling the conquistadores and chronicling their encounters with Florida's inhabitants.

Pérez de Ribas, Andrés. *History of the Triumphs of Our Holy Faith Amongst the Most Barbarous and Fierce Peoples of the New World.* Translated by Daniel T. Reff, Maureen Ahern, and Richard K. Danford. Tucson: University of Arizona Press, 1999. First published in 1645, this history of the Spanish missions in Northern New Spain from 1591 to 1643 begins with an "Approval of Fray Juan Ponce de Léon."

Tebeau, Charlton W. *A History of Florida.* Rev. ed. Coral Gables, Fla.: University of Miami Press, 1980. The first four chapters of this classic Florida history cover the indigenous inhabitants and their initial encounters with the Europeans.

Widmer, Randolph J. *The Evolution of the Calusa: A Nonagricultural Chiefdom of the Southwest Florida Coast.* Tuscaloosa: University of Alabama Press, 1988. An archaeological study of the development of the Calusa, positing that this highly developed hierarchical chiefdom evolved as a result of demographic elements.

SEE ALSO: Oct. 12, 1492: Columbus Lands in the Americas; 1528-1536: Narváez's and Cabeza de Vaca's Expeditions; May 28, 1539-Sept. 10, 1543: De Soto's North American Expedition; Feb. 23, 1540-Oct., 1542: Coronado's Southwest Expedition; 1542-1543: The New Laws of Spain; Sept., 1565: St. Augustine Is Founded; July 4, 1584-1590: Lost Colony of Roanoke; Jan., 1598-Feb., 1599: Oñate's New Mexico Expedition.

RELATED ARTICLES in *Great Lives from History: The Renaissance & Early Modern Era, 1454-1600:* Christopher Columbus; Ferdinand II and Isabella I; Pedro Menéndez de Avilés; Philip II; Juan Ponce de León; Hernando de Soto; Tascalusa.

1493-1525
REIGN OF HUAYNA CAPAC

Huayna Capac weakened the Inca Empire by pushing its boundaries to their greatest extent, which led to rebellions on the empire's fringes. At his death, a bitter struggle for succession further weakened the empire just as the conquering Spaniards arrived.

LOCALE: Inca Empire, Andes Mountains (now in Colombia, Ecuador, Peru, Bolivia, and Chile)

CATEGORIES: Government and politics; expansion and land acquisition

KEY FIGURES

Huayna Capac (1488?-1525), eleventh Inca king, r. 1493-1525

Huáscar (c. 1495-1532), Huayna Capac's son and designated successor, r. 1525-1532

Pachacuti (c. 1391-1471), ninth Inca king, r. 1438-1471, and architect of the grand empire

Topa Inca (d. 1493), tenth Inca king, r. 1471-1493, who greatly increased the size of the empire

Atahualpa (c. 1502-1533), last Inca king, r. 1532-1533

SUMMARY OF EVENT

Under Huayna Capac, the Inca Empire's vast geographical reach strained the resources of the state. Difficult wars on the periphery encouraged large and conquered groups to rebel for independence. The prolonged wars in the north produced a virtual state within a state with its capital in Quito and a substantial number of Incas who no longer regarded Cuzco as their home. The untimely death of Huayna Capac plunged the already weakened state into a war to determine succession just before it was to face its greatest threat for survival: Spanish conqueror Francisco Pizarro.

Tihuantinsuyu, the Inca Empire, exploded from its capital city of Cuzco early in the fifteenth century. Located 11,024 feet above sea level in what is now southern Peru, Cuzco, which means "navel" (signifying the center of the world), was regarded by its rulers as a site chosen by the solar deity to be the center of an empire that would unite the world, hence its name Tihuantinsuyu (four quarters). The rulers claimed descent from the solar deity and called themselves Sapa Incas (divine rulers). The Sapa Incas ruled with the support of their kinsmen, descendants of the founder Manco Capac. One of the greatest of the conquering Sapa Incas was Pachacuti, the ninth king.

At an advanced age and in poor health, Pachacuti called his sons to Cuzco to name a successor, hoping thereby to avoid a struggle for succession at his death. He placed the *borla*, a fringed headband indicating royal authority, on the forehead of one of his sons, Topa Inca, who had been campaigning for three years against the Canaris in the north. Pachacuti asked to see Topa Inca's six-month-old son, and he placed a *borla* on his head, too, named him Huayna Capac, and designated him his father's successor. He announced his decisions to the elite Incas, who pledged their loyalty to Topa Inca, and he retired. Another son, Yamque, assumed duties as domestic ruler, and Topa Inca resumed his northern campaign.

After living two years with his grandfather, Pachacuti, Huayna Capac returned to his birthplace and his father's campaigns. While Huayna Capac was still a teenager, his father became very ill, possibly from poison. Topa Inca assembled the Incas, and in their presence he placed the *borla* on Huayna Capac's forehead. Nevertheless, as soon as Topa Inca died, one of his concubines convinced several Incas that before death Topa Inca had revoked his nomination and chosen her son to succeed him. Huayna Capac was in the care of his uncle, who acted swiftly when he learned of the planned coup. He ordered the concubine's assassination and imprisoned her son. Huayna Capac's marriage to Cusi Rimay, who became the *coya*, official wife, proceeded as scheduled.

For the first years of his reign, Huayna Capac ruled with the assistance of four regents. To cement his rule, Huayna Capac scrupulously observed the funerary and mourning rituals of his father and then made several tours in the vicinity of Cuzco. He gave elaborate gifts to the Inca families and to the *curacas*, heads of communities, to reaffirm mutual loyalties.

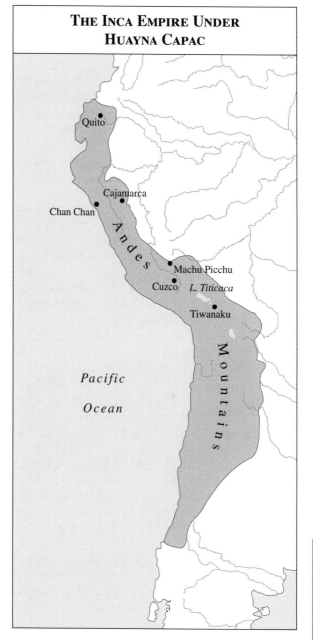

THE INCA EMPIRE UNDER HUAYNA CAPAC

Quito

Cajamarca

Chan Chan

Andes

Machu Picchu

Cuzco   *L. Titicaca*

Tiwanaku

Pacific

Ocean

Mountains

1490's

Similarly, he sent four Inca officials on inspection tours of the realm, one to each of the four major administrative divisions. They, too, were to reestablish loyalties through exchanges of reciprocal gifts and pledges. The inspectors were to hear complaints, settle disputes, ensure that religious ceremonies and sacrifices were practiced as prescribed, and take measures to improve the prosperity of villages. When the regents had confidence that Huayna Capac was mature enough to rule on his own, they resigned. He continued and expanded the range of his inspection tours, still renewing bonds through rituals of reciprocity, initiating construction projects, and encouraging agricultural improvements.

Despite his peaceful initiatives, the fringes of his empire were fraying. He sent his trusted uncle north of Cuzco to modern Colombia as a gesture of peace and cooperation. Likewise, Huayna Capac went south of Cuzco to modern Chile. In these regions, the Incas entered new cultural zones, encountering different language families, different physical environments, and customs that did not include reciprocity rituals and mutual obligations between groups. Huayna Capac had to suppress rebellions, build fortresses, and improve roads to facilitate the movement of armies. In modern Bolivia, and past the easternmost range of the Andes, the Incas moved into the *montaña*, the rain forest. There the Incas met bitter, prolonged resistance. Once defeated, ethnic groups on these extremities complied reluctantly with Inca attempts to restructure their lives and rebelled frequently.

While in the south, Huayna Capac learned that rebellions in the north had been successful, resulting in the deaths of many Inca governors, including his uncle. Huayna Capac returned to Cuzco and raised a large army to punish the rebels and recover lost territory. While roads north were being widened and storehouses filled to supply the army, Huayna Capac assembled the *curacas* from the north and, with ceremonies of reciprocity, settled local quarrels and reaffirmed their loyalty. Despite these promising signs, he had to overcome more rebellions. While preparing for the campaign, he learned that a rebellion in Cuzco itself had been crushed and that five large ethnic groups north of Quito had formed a league to resist Inca expansion.

For the next twelve years, Huayna Capac stayed with his armies in the north. Each campaign resulted in a demand for more soldiers and more Inca officers. Quito became a major administrative and military center. The numbers of Incas in Cuzco diminished because many died in battles and survivors received estates near Quito and Tumibamba that they settled permanently. Huayna Capac became an absentee emperor. He directed and fought in campaigns to the north, to western coasts, and into the *montaña* from his own estate in Tumibamba. He sent rather than led captives to Cuzco for victory processions. While on one of the coastal campaigns, Huayna Capac heard reports of sightings of strange boats. The fishermen and merchants may have spotted the Spaniard Francisco Pizarro's ship along the Ecuadoran coast in late 1524 and early 1525.

In that same year, a strange epidemic spread through Tihuantinsuyu. Because the earliest chroniclers described the victims as having inflammations on the skin, the disease has been often, but not conclusively, associated with smallpox. Huayna Capac, too, became ill. There had been no public announcement of his successor, and Huayna Capac's aides asked him to make his choice. He named Ninan Cuyochi, the only son of Cusi Rimay, to be the first choice and Huáscar the second. Ninan Cuyochi, however, had died of the disease, too.

Another concubine claimed to be the highest-ranking wife and urged that her older son, Huáscar, be designated the next Inca ruler. Huayna Capac died before the aides returned with the news of Ninan Cuyochi's death and before he could confirm the choice of Huáscar. The Incas soon thereafter split into two hostile camps, one supporting Huáscar and the other supporting his half brother, Atahualpa, as Pizarro was outfitting ships for his second voyage down the western coast of South America.

SIGNIFICANCE

A number of factors led to the downfall of the Inca Empire soon after Huayna Capac's reign: traditional uncertainties about the succession of rulers; having one Inca rule; the introduction of devastating diseases from Europe, such as smallpox; a civil war between half brothers Huáscar and Atahualpa, for Inca rule, which decimated the armies and the elite class of the Incas, left the empire without a leader, and opened the door to the empire's demise; and, perhaps most important, the Incas' belief that the Spanish conquerors were gods who could be trusted at a time when leadership was most needed.

—*Paul E. Kuhl*

FURTHER READING

Betanzos, Juan de. *Narrative of the Incas*. Translated and edited by Roland Hamilton and Dana Buchanan. Austin: University of Texas Press, 1996. An account of Inca history and traditions prepared for the viceroy of Peru. Completed in 1557 with assistance from his wife Doña Angelina Yupanqui, niece of Huayna Capac, widow of Atahualpa, and former mistress of Francisco Pizarro.

Cieza de León, Pedro de. *The Discovery and Conquest of Peru: Chronicles of the New World Encounter*. Translated and edited by Alexandra Parma Cook and Noble David Cook. Durham, N.C.: Duke University Press, 1998. One of the earliest chronicles, written by one of Pizarro's soldiers shortly after the events.

Cobo, Bernabé. *History of the Inca Empire: An Account of the Indians' Customs and Their Origin, Together with a Treatise on Inca Legends, History, and Social Institutions.* Translated and edited by Roland Hamilton. Austin: University of Texas Press, 1979. Part of a history of the New World written by a Jesuit priest who lived in Peru. Work based on careful scholarship and completed in 1653.

Davies, Nigel. *The Incas.* Niwot: University of Colorado Press, 1995. A readable and rigorous study of the Inca Empire from its legend-shrouded origins to its catastrophic collapse.

Rostworowski de Diez Canseco, María. *History of the Inca Realm.* Translated by Harry B. Iceland. New York: Cambridge University Press, 1999. A premier authority on Inca history and society.

SEE ALSO: 1471-1493: Reign of Topa Inca; 1525-1532: Huáscar and Atahualpa Share Inca Rule; 1532-1537: Pizarro Conquers the Incas in Peru.

RELATED ARTICLES in *Great Lives from History: The Renaissance & Early Modern Era, 1454-1600:* Atahualpa; Huáscar; Pachacuti; Francisco Pizarro; Hernando de Soto.

1493-1528
REIGN OF MOHAMMED I ASKIA

During Mohammed I Askia's rule, the Songhai Empire reached the height of its political, economic, and military power. Songhai became the most powerful state in the Western Sudan during the late fifteenth and early sixteenth centuries. The overthrow and death of Mohammed presaged the demise of the empire in 1591.

LOCALE: Songhai Empire (now principally in Mali), West Africa

CATEGORIES: Government and politics; expansion and land acquisition

KEY FIGURES
Sonni ʿAlī (d. 1492), Songhai military leader, r. c. 1464-1492
Sonni Baru (fl. 1493), Songhai ruler, r. 1493
Mohammed I Askia (Mohammed Ture; c. 1442-1538), Songhai ruler, r. 1493-1528
Askia Mūsā (d. 1531), Songhai ruler, r. 1528-1531

SUMMARY OF EVENT
Songhai, a state in West Africa that reached its height between the thirteenth and sixteenth centuries, expanded rapidly into an empire in the mid-fifteenth century. This rapid expansion was accompanied by economic prosperity, military coups, palace and dynastic assassinations, civil wars, and long as well as short periods of peace. Emperor Mohammed I Askia personified all these imperial phases. Indeed, even his ascent to power was turbulent.

Following the mysterious but allegedly accidental drowning of Songhai ruler Sonni ʿAlī in 1492, ʿAlī's son, Sonni Baru, took the reins of power. However, like his father, Baru, a half-converted Muslim, encountered insur-

mountable problems from the Muslim community, especially urban dwellers. He was accused, as his father had been, of mistreating Muslims and of still following "pagan" customs. For example, there were allegations that he never prayed five times a day, instead cramming all five rites into the evening prayer.

Baru was weakened by a dispute regarding the rules of succession to the Songhai throne. While the Muslim tradition insisted that the oldest son ought to succeed, traditional Songhai practice required that the Council of Elders determine who, among the sons of the deceased king, should ascend to the throne. Furthermore, a clash existed in the empire regarding financial practices. Whereas most of the people still preferred the barter system, the Muslims had introduced a money economy and insisted that this should be the empire's mode of purchase and trade.

When Baru refused to accede to Muslim demands for better treatment and resisted the introduction of the Sharia (Islamic law) into the empire, Muslim leaders asked Sonni ʿAlī's top general and prime minister, Mohammed Ture, to overthrow the emperor. A civil war ensued in 1492, resulting in Ture's victory and his ascent to power in 1493. Known by birth as Mohammed Ture, the new emperor took the name of Mohammed I Askia and founded the Askia Dynasty. Askia meant "the usurper," and the name was meant to emphasize the fact that he had taken the government by force.

Once in power, the general took upon himself the task of reforming the entire empire. To improve the country's administrative efficiency and guarantee maintenance of his power, Mohammed I Askia divided Songhai into five vice-royalties, each under a vice-royal, or regional commissioner, he appointed. Each vice-royalty was subdivided into provinces entrusted to appointed governors, most often members of the emperor's family or his closest friends.

Mohammed then took steps to further centralize power by making Gao his capital. He expanded the size of the council of ministers by including the commander in chief of the army (the *balama*); a minister of finance or chief tax collector (*farimundya*); a chief of the navy (*hikoy*) for the Niger fleet; a minister of rivers, lakes, and fisheries (*hari-farma*); and a foreign minister. The latter office had become necessary now that foreigners were constantly entering the country as official visitors, traders, scholars, tourists, and religious preachers. For financial and economic uniformity, Mohammed also unified weights and measurements throughout the empire.

Mohammed appointed and fired judges and tax collectors (who were scattered in the towns and markets of the empire) at will and carefully selected envoys to neighboring states. Realizing the prestige and the higher status attributed to Islam, he began to demonstrate religious fervor as a true Muslim. To the Muslim community, Mohammed claimed that his overthrow of Sonni 'Alī was designed to fulfill Allah's will toward the purification of Islam.

Mohammed I Askia's newly acquired devotion was followed in 1496 by one of history's most celebrated pilgrimages to Mecca. The emperor reportedly traveled with an entourage of 1,000 infantrymen and 500 horsemen and carried 300,500 mithkals of goods. The *hajj* lasted two years. While in transit through Egypt, Mohammed had an audience with the sharif, the spiritual leader of the Muslims there, who appointed him his caliph (lieutenant) throughout the Songhai Empire and the Sudan.

Just as Mansa Mūsā of Mali had done 250 years earlier, Mohammed made sure his trip would be memorable by demonstrating extraordinary generosity and religious devotion. He budgeted 300,000 pieces of gold for his journey: 100,000 for the trip's expenses, 100,000 for distribution as alms in Mecca and Medina and for the support of pilgrims from the area, and the remaining 100,000 earmarked for miscellaneous expenses. Afraid of the Muslim urban community, Mohammed I Askia on his return introduced the Sharia, even though he allowed traditional (non-Muslim) practices at the palace. Indeed, he surrounded himself with Muslim learned men and had *muezzins* calling for morning prayers throughout the country daily.

Positioned as an enlightened leader and a shrewd politician, Mohammed I Askia patronized scholars, doctors, students, lawyers, musicians, and priests and created the first professional standing army in the empire, with each soldier riding on his own camel, according to Leo Africanus, who visited Songhai in 1510. On the war front, Mohammed's most frequent and almost always successful campaigns were directed against the Mossi (1498-1499), whom he mercilessly killed or captured, bringing Mossi children to Songhai to be raised as Muslims and employed in his army. He also defended the empire against continuous incursions by Tuaregs, who were creating havoc along the northern and eastern borders of the empire.

However, despite the discipline and devastating impact of the professional Songhai army, one Hausa state, Kano, successfully resisted one of Mohammed's sieges for a year. The state was never conquered or made tributary to Songhai. In fact, to guarantee peace with Kano, Mohammed compelled his daughter to marry Kano's king. The failed siege of Kano notwithstanding, tradition has it that Mohammed I Askia was defeated in battle only once in his imperial reign, namely, by the state of Kebbi during King Kanta's rule.

His otherwise successful military forays enabled Mohammed to expand Songhai until it reached the shores of the Atlantic Ocean in the west, Nigeria in the east, and the borders of Algeria in the north. Arab scholars of the time noted that, quite often, mounted on a camel and surrounded by his noblemen, Mohammed I Askia not only traveled through the thriving cities of Timbuktu and Djenné but also visited the countryside, whose routes and paths had been made entirely safe by his ubiquitous army. As a sign of his power and wealth, it is reported that his scepters of gold weighed as much as 1,300 pounds.

Mohammed ruled for almost thirty-five years. In his eighties, he became almost totally blind and was therefore asked to abdicate. However, he refused to relinquish power. As a result, he met with a palace revolt led by one of his own sons, Mūsā. In an attempt to save his throne, he asked for assistance from one of his brothers, Yahia, who, unfortunately, was killed by the insurgents. Mūsā ascended to power in 1528. However, Mūsā was such an ineffective ruler that his brother, Bengam Korei, assassinated the emperor and replaced him as Mohammed II Askia in 1531. Mohammed II's reign was also brief, and he was replaced by another brother, Ismail, in 1537. Ismail rehabilitated his father politically, but Mohammed I Askia died a few months thereafter.

SIGNIFICANCE

Although not the founder of the Songhai Empire, Mohammed I Askia not only preserved the empire but also made it the most powerful of the Western Sudanic states, giving it a national identity and a place on the world map. He enhanced the empire's various educational, commercial, and religious centers, including Gao, Timbuktu, and Djenné, as well as creating new ones. The bases of his power were his control of trans-Saharan trade to and from West Africa, his monopoly over gold and salt (from the Taghaza mine in the Sahara), and his military genius. He used his standing professional army effectively to thwart and conquer his enemies, and he created and maintained a navy, a feat that had eluded other leaders in the region for a long time. After Mohammed, Songhai had only one other great ruler, Askia Daud (r. 1549-1582), who temporarily corrected the empire's decline and presided over a period of peace and prosperity. After Daud's death, however, the empire declined once more and was conquered by Morocco in 1591.

—*Mario J. Azevedo*

FURTHER READING

Appiah, Kwame, and Henry Louis Gates, Jr. "Mali and Songhay." In *Africana: Encyclopedia of African and African American Experience*. New York: Civitas Books, 1999. A succint treatment of Mali and Songhai for anyone interested in Sonni ʿAlī and Mohammed I Askia and the relationship between the two empires.

Brooks, Lester. *Great Civilizations of Ancient Africa*. New York: Four Winds Press, 1971. A most insightful, extensive, and interesting treatment of ancient Africa, including Egypt, Kush, Ethiopia, Ghana, Mali, and Songhai.

Falola, Toyn, ed. *African History Before 1885*. Vol. 1. Durham, N.C.: Carolina Academic Press, 2000. Divided into four sections. Falola's third section is devoted specifically to the Sudanese states and societies and others in sub-Saharan Africa, giving prominence to the powerful Songhai Empire.

Hale, Thomas, trans. *The Epic of Askia Muhammad*. Bloomington: Indiana University Press, 1996. A primary source for much of what has been written about the famous ruler, including the popular myths about him.

Ogot, B. A., ed. *History of Africa from the Sixteenth to the Seventeenth Century*. Vol. 5. Paris: UNESCO, 1992. Commissioned to some of the most renowned African scholars by the United Nations during the late 1980's, this is one of the most extensive, most authoritative, least biased, and most respected historical works on Africa and its people.

SEE ALSO: 1460-1600: Rise of the Akan Kingdoms; c. 1464-1591: Songhai Empire Dominates the Western Sudan; 1481-1482: Founding of Elmina; 16th century: Trans-Saharan Trade Enriches Akan Kingdoms; 1510-1578: Saʿdī Sharifs Come to Power in Morocco; 1591: Fall of the Songhai Empire.

RELATED ARTICLES in *Great Lives from History: The Renaissance & Early Modern Era, 1454-1600:* Askia Daud; Mohammed I Askia; Sonni ʿAlī.

1490's

August 19, 1493-January 12, 1519
REIGN OF MAXIMILIAN I

During the reign of Maximilian I, the House of Habsburg greatly increased its influence and power by vigorously pursuing a policy of dynastic marriages that led to the establishment of Habsburg power in Burgundy, Bohemia, Hungary, and the possessions of the Spanish crown.

LOCALE: Holy Roman Empire (now Germany, Austria, the Czech Republic, Hungary, northern Italy, western France, Luxembourg, the Netherlands, Belgium, Switzerland), and Burgundy (now parts of western France, the Netherlands, and Belgium)

CATEGORIES: Government and politics; expansion and land acquisition

KEY FIGURES

Maximilian I (1459-1519), Holy Roman Emperor, r. 1493-1519

Philip I (1478-1506), duke of Burgundy, r. 1494-1506, and king of Castile, r. 1504-1506

Frederick III (1415-1493), Roman king, r. 1440-1493, and Holy Roman Emperor, r. 1452-1493

Ferdinand I (1503-1564), king of Bohemia and Hungary, r. 1526-1564, Roman king, r. 1531-1564, and Holy Roman Emperor, r. 1558-1564

SUMMARY OF EVENT

After the death of the Holy Roman Emperor Frederick III in 1493, his son and successor Archduke Maximilian continued to pursue policies aimed at strengthening and extending the holdings of the house of Habsburg. His marriage in 1477 to Mary of Burgundy, the daughter and heiress of Duke Charles the Bold (r. 1467-1477), had projected Habsburg interests into the center of European power politics and compelled Maximilian to defend Mary's Burgundian heritage against French claims, resulting in a conflict with France that dragged on for fifteen years. After Mary's death in 1482, Maximilian became embroiled in protracted conflicts with the heads of the provincial estates of the Netherlands, who favored their own regency government over that of his infant son, Philip the Handsome. However, by 1494, the Netherlands had been brought firmly under the control of the young Duke Philip.

Maximilian's obligations and duties as head of the Habsburg Dynasty and as Roman king (the traditional title of German kings) required considerable resources. As de facto emperor, albeit without papal coronation (which would not occur until 1452), it was one of his principal concerns to safeguard imperial interests in Italy. When Maximilian married Bianca Sforza of Milan in 1494, he invested her uncle, Ludovico Sforza, with the dukedom of Milan. The sizable dowry of his new wife was of some help in financing his operations against Charles VIII of France, whose invasion of Italy in 1494 threatened imperial fiefs and the Spanish holdings there. Responding to the French threat, Maximilian allied himself with Spain, Venice, Milan, and the pope in the Holy League of Venice (1495). Fearful of a French domination of Italy, Maximilian agreed to a dynastic marriage alliance proposed by Ferdinand II, king of Aragon. In 1496, Maximilian's daughter, the Archduchess Margarete, married Prince Juan, the son of Ferdinand of Aragon and Isabella of Castile. Of greater significance was the 1497 marriage of their daughter Juana, later known as Juana the Mad, to Maximilian's son, the Archduke Philip of Austria and Burgundy. It was the couple's eldest son Charles who in 1516 would become known as Charles I in Spain and on Maximilian's death would become Emperor Charles V.

While his dynastic marriage alliance provided some check on French ambitions, Maximilian soon faced serious problems in Italy again. After the Swiss gained their independence from Habsburg rule in the Peace of Basel (1499), Maximilian lost a major supporter when, in the following year, the French king Louis XII conquered the Duchy of Milan and took Ludovico Sforza prisoner. Prevented by Venetian and French forces from crossing the Alps and going to Rome for his coronation, Maximilian had himself proclaimed emperor-elect with the consent of Pope Julius II at Trent in 1508. The conflict over control of Italy continued as several leagues and alliances played their parts until Maximilian could at last be persuaded to make peace in 1516 with the new French king, Francis I. Throughout his various campaigns, Maximilian had been unable to obtain any meaningful support from the German princes, instead having had to resort to loans from German merchant-bankers like the Fuggers and the Welsers, to whom he had to turn over the rich silver and copper mining operations in the Tyrol.

Maximilian's plans for the reform of the empire were to a considerable extent guided by his vision of restoring the empire of Charlemagne (r. 800-814) and of leading a crusade against the Turks, as well as by his need for troops and money. While the German princes duly recognized Maximilian as Roman king and Holy Roman Emperor, they opposed his centralizing efforts and refused to support his foreign wars, suspicious that they were designed principally to further his dynastic goals. The various imperial diets supported instead a smaller army to maintain the domestic peace. Maximilian's principal opponent in this prolonged struggle was the archbishop of Mainz, Berthold of Henneberg, chairman of the Electoral College and arch-chancellor of the empire, who proposed an alternative solution to the anarchy in Germany. Whereas Maximilian favored a strong monarchy on the Burgundian model giving him the right to impose taxes,

Maximilian, Mary of Burgundy, and their son Philip, the future king of Castile, in a fifteenth century illustration. (Frederick Ungar Publishing Co.)

to maintain a strong army, and to decide on questions of war and peace, the archbishop envisioned a system in which the great princes would remain autonomous in their own lands while lending their support to the emperor only in pursuit of common goals.

Still, Maximilian's efforts did bear some fruit in the form of a ban on private warfare and in the creation of an imperial tribunal to enforce the ban. By 1505, he enjoyed a brief triumph that reaffirmed his imperial stature. When he became involved in a dispute over a succession within the Bavarian dynasty, he pronounced the ban of the empire against one of the parties and with the help of the Swabian League defeated his opponents decisively. As a result, he could add some strategically important territory in the Tyrol to the Habsburg holdings.

The last of Maximilian's dynastic marriage arrangements, prompted by the need to secure the empire in the East against persistent threats by the Ottoman Turks, involved the crowns of Bohemia and of Hungary. After the Bohemian ruler, the Jagellonian Władisław II (1456-1516), was chosen king of Hungary in 1490 as Vladislav II, Maximilian arranged for a mutual succession in Austria and in Bohemia and Hungary in case either line should die out. At a meeting in 1515 between Maximilian II, Vladislav II, and King Sigismund I of Poland, the parties confirmed a double marriage compact which provided that Maximilian's grandson Archduke Ferdinand would marry the daughter of Vladislav II, Anna, while his granddaughter, the Archduchess Mary of Habsburg, would marry Vladislav II's son Louis. The result of this marriage alliance proved to have far-reaching consequences. Following the disastrous defeat of the Hungarian army by the Ottoman Turks in 1526 and the death of Louis, the diets of Bohemia and Hungary decided to make common cause with the Habsburgs. They conferred both crowns on Archduke Ferdinand, who would henceforth rule the bulk of the Habsburgs' Central European possessions. In 1558, Ferdinand also became Holy Roman Emperor after the abdication of his brother, Charles V.

SIGNIFICANCE

Maximilian was often referred to as "Last Knight," and his vision and lofty goals reflected the universal aspects of the Holy Roman Empire. As head of the Habsburg Dynasty, he laid the foundations upon which his successors could build an empire

1490's

of global dimensions. That many of his undertakings failed resulted from the fact that his ambitions often exceeded his resources.

Maximilian realized his dynastic ambitions through skillful diplomacy and through a policy of dynastic marriages. Thus he was able to set a course that would enable his grandson, the Emperor Charles V, to rule over an empire stretching from the Danubian plains to all the lands claimed by the Spanish crown. After the division of the empire, the European branch of the Habsburgs carried on the imperial tradition and played a major role in the power politics of Central Europe. Here the Habsburgs served as a major stabilizing factor and guided the Danubian region through the turbulent years of nationalism, well into the first decades of the twentieth century.

In contrast to his successful marriage policies, many of Maximilian's reform proposals to shore up the Holy Roman Empire foundered on the narrow and special interests of the German princes. Suspicious of his dynastic ambitions, they had little sympathy for his centralizing efforts or for his foreign military campaigns, needed to protect the integrity of the empire.

—*Helmut J. Schmeller*

FURTHER READING

Benecke, Gerhard. *Maximilian I, 1459-1519: An Analytical Biography.* London: Routledge & Kegan Paul, 1982. A brief and vivid biography of Maximilian and a social and political history of his time.

Berenger, Jean. *A History of the Habsburg Empire, 1273-1700.* Translated by C. A. Simpson. New York: Longman, 1994. Emphasizes how the empire functioned and how it contributed to the European equilibrium. See chapter 10, "The Work of Maximilian."

Fichtner, Paula Sutter. *The Habsburg Monarchy, 1490-1848: Attributes of Empire.* New York: Palgrave Macmillan, 2003. Focuses on the Habsburg rulers, territorial states, and religious institutions. See chapter 1, "The Pattern of Empire."

Hale, J. R. *Renaissance Europe, 1480-1520.* 2d ed. London: Blackwell, 2000. Presents Maximilian within the broader context of the attitudes, beliefs, and culture of the period. See chapter 2, "Political Europe."

Wheatcroft, Andrew. *The Habsburgs: Embodying Empire.* London: Viking Press, 1995. Lively account of Habsburg imperial ambitions. Excellent maps and comprehensive genealogical charts.

SEE ALSO: Aug. 17, 1477: Foundation of the Habsburg Dynasty; 1482-1492: Maximilian I Takes Control of the Low Countries; September 22, 1504: Treaty of Blois; Nov. 26, 1504: Joan the Mad Becomes Queen of Castile; 1508: Formation of the League of Cambrai; Jan. 23, 1516: Charles I Ascends the Throne of Spain; Aug. 18, 1516: Concordat of Bologna; June 28, 1519: Charles V Is Elected Holy Roman Emperor; 1531-1585: Antwerp Becomes the Commercial Capital of Europe.

RELATED ARTICLES in *Great Lives from History: The Renaissance & Early Modern Era, 1454-1600:* Anne of Brittany; Chevalier de Bayard; Charles the Bold; Charles V; Charles VIII; Francis I; Frederick III; Henry VII; James IV; Julius II; Leo X; Louis XI; Niccolò Machiavelli; Margaret of Austria; Margaret of Parma; Mary of Burgundy; Maximilian I; Maximilian II; Philip the Magnanimous; Ludovico Sforza; Vladislav II.

1494
SEBASTIAN BRANT PUBLISHES *THE SHIP OF FOOLS*

The Ship of Fools, *one of German literature's most influential moral satires and its first international literary sensation, exposes human vice and folly prevalent in late medieval European culture. A majority of the renowned woodcut illustrations adorning the text are thought to have been designed by Albrecht Dürer.*

LOCALE: Basel, Switzerland

CATEGORIES: Literature; art; cultural and intellectual history

KEY FIGURES

Sebastian Brant (1457-1521), German Humanist writer
Albrecht Dürer (1471-1528), German artist
Johann Bergmann von Olpe (c. 1455-1532), German printer
Jakob Locher (1471-1528), German Humanist and translator
Alexander Barclay (c. 1476-1552), British poet and translator

SUMMARY OF EVENT

Sebastian Brant, son of a Strasbourg innkeeper, was a lawyer by profession. He obtained a doctorate in civil and canon law from the University of Basel in 1489 and remained there as a professor of law, working also as an editor in local print shops, until shortly before the city joined the Swiss Confederation in 1501. He then returned to his hometown, where he formed associations with Strasbourg printers and occupied the office of town syndic (magistrate) for approximately twenty years.

During the course of his career in law and letters, he published illustrated broadsides, miscellaneous Latin poetry, editions ranging from Aesop's fables to Petrarch's Latin prose, textbooks on civil and canon law, translations, and sundry other works. Today he is remembered almost exclusively as the author of *Das Narrenschiff* (1494; *The Shyp of Folys of the Worlde*, 1509; Latin, *Stultifera nauis*, 1570; better known as *The Ship of Fools*). A masterpiece in the early art of illustrated printing, it helped establish Early Modern German as a cultural language.

The first edition of *The Ship of Fools* was published in Basel by printer Johann Bergmann von Olpe during Shrovetide in 1494, a time when revelers traditionally engaged in the carnivalesque celebrations that preceded Lent. Written in the author's native Alsatian dialect, the work contains 112 independent chapters in doggerel verse, each satirizing one particular variety of Narr (the German expression for fool). Its purpose, stated in a prologue to the work, is to encourage the pursuit of wisdom by exposing human folly. Brant's gallery of transgressions and transgressors embraces, under the banner of folly, all social registers and all professions. Chapter by chapter the vices, foibles, and moral failings of men and women, doctors, lawyers, merchants, besotted lovers, rich and poor, young and old, are all inexorably exposed to public ridicule.

The primary textual sources for Brant's gnomic satire include the Old and New Testaments, Vergil, Ovid, Horace, Juvenal, the writings of the church fathers, canon law, fables, and proverbial wisdom, but he also drew inspiration from the late medieval tradition of clerical satire, the German Shrovetide plays prominent in fifteenth century Nuremberg, and the popular French *soties*, short satirical plays involving fools and their foolish behavior.

Similar in structure to sixteenth century emblems, each chapter is accompanied by a finely executed woodcut illustrating the poem's general theme, its textual metaphors, or moral aphorism. In all, the first edition of *The Ship of Fools* contains 105 original woodcuts, some used more than once, and close to six thousand verses. Recent scholarship attributes somewhere between seventy-three and seventy-six of those woodcuts to the artistry of an anonymous "German master," usually identified for reasons of style and chronology as Albrecht Dürer. The remaining illustrations, likewise anonymous, are believed to be the work of three, perhaps four different artists.

There is indeed good reason to believe that Dürer designed a majority of the work's woodblock prints. There is no doubt he spent time working in Basel prior to publication of *The Ship of Fools*. Leaving Colmar shortly after the death of the German painter and engraver Martin Schongauer, in 1491, he went to Basel and remained there until sometime around August or September of the following year. A Basel edition of Saint Jerome's letters, published on August 8, 1492, contains a woodcut illustration of Saint Jerome verifiably prepared by Dürer.

Other work generally attributed to the young artist during his stay in Basel includes woodcuts for Michael Furter's edition of the fourteenth century *Der Ritter vom Turn* (*The Book of the Knight of the Tower*, 1862), by Geoffroy de La Tour Landry, published in collaboration with Bergmann in 1493, and some 130 blocks for a pro-

A woodcut by Albrecht Dürer in Sebastian Brant's The Ship of Fools. *(Dover Publications)*

jected edition of the Latin comedies of the second century B.C.E. Roman playwright Terence, an edition in which Brant was also involved. The latter, however, was never published. Thomas Wilhelmi, a specialist in early German literature, believes that Dürer's work in Basel was interrupted when a deadly pestilence broke out there, killing more than three thousand of the city's inhabitants between September, 1492, and March, 1493.

Dürer's abrupt departure, reasons Wilhelmi, probably left Brant with an incomplete set of illustrations for *The Ship of Fools* and so delayed its publication until 1494. Not surprisingly, some of the motifs employed in the artwork of *The Ship of Fools* have been traced back to earlier illustrated books published in Augsburg and Ulm during the 1470's and 1480's. Typically, critics of artwork of *The Ship of Fools* praise the German master's style—Dürer's style—for its attention to natural decor, architectural detail, character portrayal, and spatial perspective.

The appeal of *The Ship of Fools* to Brant's contemporary readership cannot be overrated. Within months of its initial publication, unauthorized editions appeared in Reutlingen (1494), Nuremberg (1494), Augsburg (1494, 1495, 1498) and Strasbourg (1494, 1497), prompting Brant to add a final chapter to his third edition in protest of those who would abuse his intellectual property. Brant issued no less than six authorized editions of *The Ship of Fools* in German (1494, 1495, 1499, 1506, 1509, 1512).

Major international recognition came in 1497 when Brant's colleague and former student, Jakob Locher, adapted and translated the work into Latin. Working perhaps in conjunction with Brant, but certainly with his approval, Locher rearranged the order of certain chapters, condensed passages, added scholarly references, and developed the work's underlying allegory of a ship teeming with fools bound for Narragonia, a paradise of folly and fools. For more than one hundred years, Locher's Latin text was the preferred scholarly edition for numerous translations and adaptations.

By 1500, versions of Brant's catalog of folly were available in Latin, German, Low German, French, and Flemish. The British poet Alexander Barclay first adapted it for the English public in 1509 using Chaucerian stanzas and an early edition of Locher's Latin text as his model. Later that year the Englishman Henry Watson published a competing translation in prose based on a French edition. By the middle of the sixteenth century, more than fifty editions of *The Ship of Fools* had been published in various European languages.

SIGNIFICANCE

The influence of *The Ship of Fools* on European culture, although hard to measure with any degree of precision, was certainly immense. It remains one of German literature's major international successes, and it laid foundations for the popular genre of fool's literature that flourished in sixteenth and seventeenth century Germany, France, and England, and in the Low Countries.

Beneath the apparent simplicity of the author's poetic style lay a wealth of commonsense learning that appealed to readers from all walks of life. From the striking irony of its first chapter "On Useless Books" to its closing encomium of "The Wise Man," Brant's ship of fools navigates an uncharted course between the shoals of Humanistic satire and the terra firma of Catholic conservatism. Hence, over the centuries critics confident in their ability to decipher the author's stern humor have branded him now a conservative, now a precursor of radical reform, when in fact he was perhaps neither or both.

In addition to its appeal strictly as a work of literature, the first Basel edition of *The Ship of Fools* stands out as one of the great achievements in the early history of illustrated printing, not only for the artistic quality of its woodcuts but also for its successful integration of text and image. As such, it may be considered a forerunner to the highly popular emblem books published throughout Europe during the sixteenth and seventeenth centuries.

—*Jan Pendergrass*

FURTHER READING

Davidson, Clifford, ed. *Fools and Folly.* Kalamazoo: Michigan Medieval Institute Publications, 1996. The chapter "Forgotten Fools: Alexander Barclay's *Ship of Fools*" examines Barclay's translation in comparison to the German original.

Lettieri, Dan. "Some Sources and Methods for the Illustration of *Narrenschiff.*" *Gutenberg-Jahrbuch* 69 (1994): 95-105. Examines motifs from *The Ship of Fools* and compares them to woodcuts published by Swabian printers during the 1470's and 1480's.

Sagarra, Eda, and Peter Skrine. *A Companion to German Literature, from 1500 to the Present.* Malden, Mass.: Blackwell, 1997. The first chapter of this book situates Brant's *Narrenschiff* within the sociocultural context of sixteenth century German satire.

Van Cleve, John Walter. "Sebastian Brant, 1457?-1521." *Dictionary of Literary Biography* 179, *German Writers of the Renaissance and Reformation, 1280-* 1580, edited by James Hardin and Max Reinhart. Detroit: Gale Research, 1997. Provides an overview of Brant's life and work, with special emphasis on *The Ship of Fools.*

_____. *Sebastian Brant's* The Ship of Fools *in Critical Perspective, 1800-1991.* Columbia, S.C.: Camden House, 1993. Reviews close to two centuries of research on Brant's work.

Wilhelmi, Thomas, ed. *Sebastian Brant: Forschungsbeiträge zu seinem Leben, zum "Narrenschiff" und zum übrigen Werk.* Basel, Switzerland: Schwabe, 2002. German-language publication oriented toward the specialist. Four of this publication's seven chapters concentrate on *The Ship of Fools;* one examines events surrounding Dürer's stay in Basel.

Zeydel, Edwin H. *Sebastian Brant.* New York: Twayne, 1967. The standard English-language reference devoted to Brant's life and work, with special emphasis on *The Ship of Fools.*

SEE ALSO: 1456: Publication of Gutenberg's Mazarin Bible; 1490's: Aldus Manutius Founds the Aldine Press; 1499-1517: Erasmus Advances Humanism in England.

RELATED ARTICLES in *Great Lives from History: The Renaissance & Early Modern Era, 1454-1600:* Albrecht Dürer; Desiderius Erasmus; Charlotte Guillard; Aldus Manutius.

June 7, 1494
TREATY OF TORDESILLAS

The Treaty of Tordesillas gave the Papacy the authority to divide New World discoveries and possessions between Spain and Portugal and in effect sanctioned the conquering, exploitation, and religious conversion of the New World's indigenous inhabitants.

LOCALE: Tordesillas, Spain
CATEGORIES: Diplomacy and international relations; expansion and land acquisition; religion; exploration and discovery

KEY FIGURES

Alexander VI (Rodrigo de Borja y Doms; 1431-1503), Roman Catholic pope, 1492-1503
Christopher Columbus (1451-1506), commander of the first Spanish voyages to the New World

Ferdinand II (1452-1516), king of Aragon, r. 1479-1516, and king of Castile, r. 1474-1504, as Ferdinand V
Isabella I (1451-1504), queen of Castile, r. 1474-1504
John II (1455-1495), king of Portugal, r. 1481-1495

SUMMARY OF EVENT

When Christopher Columbus returned to Europe from his first voyage to the Caribbean, Spain and Portugal began to dispute which nation had jurisdiction over the new lands. King John II of Portugal claimed that earlier papal bulls had donated any discoveries to his domains. Ferdinand and Isabella sought mediation by Pope Alexander VI, who issued a series of bulls favorable to Spain in 1493. When Portugal refused to accept them, the two governments negotiated the Treaty of Tordesillas in

1490's

1494, which gave both nations a sphere of discovery and colonization. More important, the papal bulls and treaty also provided Spain with a religious rationale for its conquest and colonization of the New World.

On March 5, 1493, Columbus arrived at Lisbon on his return voyage, and King John invited the admiral to visit the Portuguese court. Columbus did so on March 9, and described his discoveries. King John raised the possibility that the islands lay within jurisdiction of Guinea, accorded to Portugal by both papal charters and its agreement with Castile in the Treaty of Alcáçovas (1479). These documents gave Portugal dominion over the Azores, Madeira, and discoveries of non-Christian lands south of the Canary Islands in Africa. The papal bull *Inter Caetera* (1456) of Calixtus III (Alexander VI's uncle), for example, confirmed Portuguese rights to lands south of Cape Bojador and Cape Nao and extending to the Indies. In the Treaty of Alcáçovas, negotiated by Castile and Portugal in 1479, Castile recognized its neighbor's African claims in return for Portugal acknowledging Spanish sovereignty over the Canary Islands.

In his conversation with John II, Columbus reported that he had reached the Indies, adding to the Portuguese king's desire to claim the new discoveries. Yet the news speedily reached Ferdinand and Isabella, before the admiral arrived in Spain, and they did not wait for Columbus before asserting their claims before Pope Alexander VI. Meanwhile, Columbus arrived at Palos de la Frontera on March 15 and continued on to Seville, where he arrived two weeks later. There he received orders from Ferdinand and Isabella to meet them in Barcelona and did so in late April. By that time, the monarchs' negotiations with the Papacy were already bearing the desired fruit.

Alexander VI was, in fact, inclined by nationality and geopolitical concerns to favor the Spaniards' cause, since Alexander was a Valencian by birth. Furthermore, Ferdinand's armies helped protect the papal states from attack by the French under King Charles VIII. Alexander could not afford to defy the Spanish king and queen, and he did not. On May 17, a papal bull entitled *Inter Caetera* reached Spain. It was drawn up in mid-April, although it is customarily dated May 3, 1493. Alexander imposed

Pope Alexander VI issued in 1493 a series of bulls favorable to Spanish exploration. When Portugal refused to accept the bulls, the two governments negotiated the Treaty of Tordesillas (1494), which gave both nations a sphere of discovery and colonization and provided a religious rationale for the conquest and colonization of the New World. (Hulton|Archive by Getty Images)

responsibilities on the Spanish monarchs because of their discoveries.

> Your duty, to lead the peoples dwelling in those islands to embrace the Christian profession; nor at any time let dangers or hardships deter you therefrom, with the stout hope and trust in your hearts and Almighty God will further your undertakings.

He then continued to reward them with title to the discovered lands.

> Do by tenor of these presents give, grant, and assign forever to you and your heirs and successors, kings and queens of Castile and Leon, all and singular the aforesaid countries and islands thus unknown and hitherto discovered by your envoys and to be discovered hereafter, provided however they at no time have been in the actual temporal possession of any Christian owner.

The bull also recognized Portugal's African claims.

Alexander VI soon issued three additional bulls, which attempted to clarify his territorial concessions to Ferdinand and Isabella, despite objections by the Portuguese. *Eximiae Devotionis* (May 3, 1493) reiterated the decisions of the first bull and explicitly gave the Spanish crown the same rights over its new discoveries that Portugal enjoyed in Guinea. *Inter Caetera* went further, drawing a line north to south to separate Portuguese and Spanish spheres of exploration and colonization. It decreed that the line of demarcation lay 100 leagues west of the Azores and Cape Verde Islands. Spain received the exclusive right to trade west of the line and to occupy lands there. Only territories occupied by other Christian powers prior to Christmas of 1492 were excepted. Angry at Alexander's favoritism to the Spanish, John II began gathering a fleet for the purpose of taking Columbus's discoveries. Nonetheless, he also tried to negotiate with the Spanish monarchs. They responded by soliciting another bull, *Dudum Siquidem* (September 26, 1493). It confirmed Alexander's previous concessions to the Spaniards and gave them jurisdiction over all western discoveries, even extending to India. The bull denied John's claims to any lands Portugal did not already hold.

Alexander's mediation between the Spanish and Portuguese failed, in large part because of his obvious partiality to the former. Representatives of the monarchs met in Tordesillas and began direct negotiations, which resulted in the Treaty of Tordesillas, signed June 7, 1494. Both parties achieved their aims in part. The Portuguese, for example, believed the line of demarcation lay too close to the Azores and would limit their exploration in the south Atlantic. Their diplomats successfully insisted that it be moved to a point 370 leagues west of the Cape Verde Islands. The Spanish diplomats accepted this proposal, and in compensation the Portuguese recognized Spain's claims to the islands Columbus had discovered. The treaty further stipulated that within ten months the two parties should send ships west from the Cape Verde Islands to establish the precise location of the line.

Neither monarchy immediately sent ships and experts to establish the precise location of the line. Furthermore, to measure from the Cape Verde Islands was too vague, as those islands ran nearly three degrees in longitude. Nor was their agreement among geographers and cartographers as to the circumference of the earth or the length of a degree. In 1500, the Portuguese discovered the "hump" of Brazil, which clearly lay on their side of the line. The Treaty of Tordesillas thus supported Portugal's claim to its only American colony. Two years later, the "Cantino" map based on Portuguese geographic information clearly depicted the line of demarcation. During the next half century, several geographers proposed locations for the line, generally placing it east of the mouth of the Amazon River. Only after Ferdinand Magellan's voyage did Spain and Portugal try to settle the line's location on the opposite side of the globe. A treaty signed at Zaragoza on April 22, 1529, placed the line 297 leagues east of the Moluccas, or Spice Islands. Spain thereby surrendered its claims to the Spice Islands, although it later conquered and colonized the Philippines, which lay on the Portuguese side of the line.

SIGNIFICANCE

Besides mediating territorial tensions between Spain and Portugal, the papal bulls and Treaty of Tordesillas provided Spaniards with what they deemed to be sovereignty over Spanish America and the indigenous inhabitants of those lands. Ferdinand and Isabella clearly assumed that Alexander's donation gave them clear title to the lands and made the indigenous peoples their subjects and vassals. The Laws of Burgos (1512) and the Requirement (1513) based Spanish rule of the Americas on the papal donation. Even Spaniards who championed indigenous rights, such as Bartolomé de Las Casas, believed the title was legitimate.

More controversial, however, was the question of whether sovereignty obligated Spain to spread Christianity to the New World and whether it also conferred upon Spaniards the right to conquer the indigenous peoples, demand tribute and labor from them, or even enslave them. The papal donation and Treaty of Tordesillas unfortunately provided a cover for conquest and exploitation in the Americas.

—Kendall W. Brown

FURTHER READING

Davenport, Frances Gardiner, ed. *European Treaties Bearing on the History of the United States and Its Dependencies*. Vol. 1. Reprint. Gloucester, Mass.: P. Smith, 1967. Contains the papal bulls conceded to Portugal, those made by Alexander VI, and the treaties between Spain and Portugal. All are presented in the original language with English translations.

Dickason, Olive Patricia. "Old World Law, New World Peoples, and Concepts of Sovereignty." In *Essays on the History of North American Discovery and Exploration*. College Station: Texas A&M University Press, 1988. Traces the development of medieval European legal ideas about territorial sovereignty and how those concepts affected conquest and colonization of the New World.

Hanke, Lewis. *The Spanish Struggle for Justice in the Conquest of America*. Boston: Little, Brown, 1965. Studies the debates between Spanish legalists and humanitarians over whether Alexander VI's donation gave Spain power to conquer indigenous peoples and forcibly convert them to Christianity.

Harley, J. B. *Maps and the Columbian Encounter*. Milwaukee: Golda Meir Library of the University of Wisconsin, 1990. Discusses the European understanding of overseas exploration and settlement and examines the "Cantino" map of 1502.

Kamen, Henry. *Empire: How Spain Became a World Power, 1492-1763*. New York: HarperCollins, 2003. Surveys the roles played by Ferdinand and Isabella in the fashioning of Spain's global empire.

Parry, J. H. *The Age of Reconnaissance*. Rev. ed. Berkeley: University of California Press, 1981. A classic survey of European overseas expansion from 1450 to 1650 that places the Treaty of Tordesillas in historical context.

Russell-Wood, A. J. R. *Portuguese Empire, 1415-1808: A World on the Move*. Baltimore: Johns Hopkins University Press, 1998. A history of the expansion of the Portuguese empire, with particular attention to the individuals involved in the voyages that culminated in a Portuguese presence in the four corners of the world.

Thomas, Hugh. *Rivers of Gold: The Rise of the Spanish Empire*. London: Weidenfeld & Nicolson, 2003. A decidedly conservative and Eurocentric history of Spanish colonialism during Ferdinand and Isabella's rule.

SEE ALSO: Oct. 12, 1492: Columbus Lands in the Americas; 1500-1530's: Portugal Begins to Colonize Brazil; 1505-1515: Portuguese Viceroys Establish Overseas Trade Empire; 1537: Pope Paul III Declares Rights of New World Peoples; 1542-1543: The New Laws of Spain; 1552: Las Casas Publishes *The Tears of the Indians*; 1565: Spain Seizes the Philippines.

RELATED ARTICLES in *Great Lives from History: The Renaissance & Early Modern Era, 1454-1600:* Alexander VI; Christopher Columbus; Ferdinand II and Isabella I; John II; Bartolomé de Las Casas.

September, 1494-October, 1495
CHARLES VIII OF FRANCE INVADES ITALY

Charles VIII's invasion of Italy launched a series of wars that brought civil chaos to Italy. The peninsula ultimately became both battlefield and prize in the wars between France and Spain.

LOCALE: Italy

CATEGORIES: Expansion and land acquisition; wars, uprisings, and civil unrest; diplomacy and international relations

KEY FIGURES

Charles VIII (1470-1498), king of France, r. 1483-1498

Alexander VI (Rodrigo de Borja y Doms; 1431-1503), Roman Catholic pope, 1492-1503

Alfonso II (1448-1495), Aragonese ruler of Naples, r. 1494-1495

Ferdinand II (Ferrandino; 1467-1496), son of Alfonso II and ruler of Naples, r. 1495-1496

Ferdinand II (the Catholic; 1452-1516), king of Aragon, r. 1479-1516, king of Sicily, r. 1468-1516, later king of Naples as Ferdinand III, r. 1504-1516

Ludovico Sforza (1452-1508), duke of Milan, r. 1481-1499

Piero de' Medici (1472-1503), ruler of Florence, r. 1492-1494

Girolamo Savonarola (1452-1498), Dominican friar and evangelical preacher in Florence

Philippe de Comines (c. 1447-1511), French ambassador to Venice

SUMMARY OF EVENT

The 1494 invasion of Italy by King Charles VIII of France proved to be as climactic an event for the rest of Europe as it was for Italy. It was the first of many invasions of Italy by foreign powers that drew those powers into the orbit of Italian politics and, simultaneously, launched Italy into the insatiable jaws of expanding European empires. The French returned in 1499 under Louis XII, the Spanish invaded in 1501, and Rome itself was sacked by the Holy Roman Emperor in 1527.

While the French motive for the 1494 invasion appeared to be partly medieval, the invasion was to have implications and effects that would help shape Europe in the modern era. Charles VIII's dynastic claims to Naples, and ultimately to Jerusalem, reflected a medieval worldview. He planned to conquer Naples and then go on to free Jerusalem from Turkish control. Charles saw him-

self as a universal ruler; this fantasy was abetted by prophetic preachers who surrounded the gullible Charles in his French court.

The French king's claim to Naples rested on the award of the crown, in the thirteenth century, to Charles of Anjou, younger brother of Louis IX (Saint Louis). In succeeding generations, the House of Aragon put forth rival claims to the same throne and actually ruled Naples from 1442, after they ousted the Angevins.

Charles VIII's entire reign was directed toward the Italian campaign and the enterprise in the Holy Land. No one could dissuade him from his plans. Thanks to the military reforms of Charles VII, Charles VIII had a standing army of forty thousand to fifty thousand men at his disposal. The Italians were forced to rely on mercenaries and forged alliances. The French enjoyed a definitive military unity that Italy sorely lacked.

Diplomatic inroads provided Charles with the political backing he needed to invade Italy. In 1489, Innocent VIII, who was feuding with Naples, offered the Neapolitan crown to Charles. Girolamo Savonarola, a Dominican evangelical preacher in Florence who sermonized regularly against the reigning Medici family, referred to Charles in prophetic terms. Savonarola would have a deep psychological and spiritual impact upon the French monarch. Above all, Ludovico Sforza, duke of Milan, made the decisive appeal, based on his own fears of a Florentine-Neapolitan alliance that would isolate Milan and leave it threatened once more by the Venetian Republic.

With his huge army, Charles reached Asti on September 9, 1494. The French were welcomed, guardedly, by Sforza and by Ercole d'Este of Ferrara. The impetuous Piero de' Medici of Florence unwisely ceded fortresses to the French and signed a degrading treaty. Consequently, on his return to Florence, Piero and the Medici family were expelled by their fellow citizens. On November 17, 1494, Charles proceeded through the gates of Florence with his lance at rest, the symbol of a conqueror.

After a brief stop at Siena, Charles entered papal territory. Pope Alexander VI had given the French monarch hollow words of encouragement while secretly negotiating with the Aragonese in Naples. The anxious pope had personal concerns about Charles's motives and plans. Savonarola had encouraged Charles to investigate Alexander's improper election as pope. If a church council were to be called, it could lead to the pope's removal. The wily Alexander was able to distract Charles from a course of church reform that would endanger his own position as pope.

Charles arrived in Rome with lance at rest on December 31, 1494, after a triumphant six-hour procession. On January 15, 1495, the pope signed a treaty with Charles and yielded certain Italian territories to the French. Charles left Rome on January 28, 1495, and headed to Naples with no further obstructions. Meanwhile, Alfonso II had abdicated his Neapolitan throne to his inexperienced son, Ferdinand II (Ferrandino in Italian), who subsequently fled Naples after a baronial revolt. Charles entered Naples virtually unopposed on February 22, 1495, and was installed officially as the Angevin successor to the Neapolitan throne. His harsh policies toward the Neapolitan nobles soon soured relationships with his new subjects.

Outside Naples, the Italians seemed to pull together, at least temporarily, under an alliance called the Holy League. Organized by Alexander VI, it included the Papal States, the German empire, the Spanish empire of Ferdinand II the Catholic, and, briefly, Milan under Ludovico Sforza, who immediately withdrew from the league. In a futile attempt to confuse Charles and his astute ambassador, Philippe de Comines, the Holy League represented itself as a defensive alliance for the protection of Italy against the Turks. The French were not fooled, however, and recognized the seriousness of the league's threat to them.

In May of 1495, Charles left Naples with a small portion of his original army to confront the Holy League. He planned to return eventually to fulfill his crusade against the Turks. This was never to take place. Charles's army of a mere ten thousand troops lumbered toward northern Italy and met the Holy League on the Taro River at Fornovo on July 6, 1495. The battle was indecisive, although both sides claimed victory. The Italians left the field in disarray, while the French lost many provisions but few lives. Charles left Italy in September under the umbrage of safe passage. By the end of 1495, the kingdom of Naples had fallen back to Ferrandino.

Although Charles planned another campaign, these plans were never realized, to the relief of the Italians. The king died suddenly after hitting his head on a door jamb at Amboise on May 28, 1498, and his political dreams died with him.

SIGNIFICANCE

The 1494 campaign had significant consequences for Italy. Italy was no longer protected from the grasp of other European powers. The failure of the Holy League at Fornovo bared Italian disunity to the world. On the French side, Charles VIII's ambition and resources demonstrated the centralization of the French state. In addition, there was a growing awareness of the modern concept of "balance of power." The German empire, for example, entered the Holy League alliance in an effort to block French expansion into Italy, rather than to assert its own claims in the area.

ITALY ON THE EVE OF THE FRENCH INVASION

A portrait of Philippe de Comines, French ambassador to Venice, who, with King Charles VIII, was nearly fooled by the Holy League into believing that the league was a defensive alliance for the protection of Italy against the Turks. (Frederick Ungar Publishing Co.)

France's invasion, then, was one sign of the advent of a modern age of sophisticated military expansion accompanied by intricate diplomatic maneuvers. These maneuvers weakened Italy and drew the peninsula more deeply into the web of European ambitions and entanglements.

—*Robert F. Erickson, updated by Barbara M. Fahy*

FURTHER READING

Abulafia, David. *The French Descent into Renaissance Italy, 1494-95: Antecedents and Effects.* Brookfield, Vt.: Ashgate, 1995. Questions whether the French invasion upset a relatively calm Italy and looks into political, military, diplomatic, and technological aspects of the occupation.

Bridge, John S. C. *The Reign of Charles VIII, 1483-1498.* Vol. 2 in *A History of France from the Death of Louis XI.* Oxford, England: Clarendon Press, 1924. Concerned almost entirely with the first phase of the Italian Wars, this volume provides a traditional ac-

count and relies, almost exclusively, upon political, military, and diplomatic history. There is a completeness about the account that not only reveals the direction of French policy but also provides an insight into Italian diplomacy and politics during the late Italian Renaissance.

Gilbert, Felix. *Machiavelli and Guicciardini.* Princeton, N.J.: Princeton University Press, 1965. A careful and comprehensive work that penetrates the crisis thinking of these two writers, expressed in works generated in the wake of the 1494 invasion.

Hays, Denys, and John Law. *Italy in the Age of the Renaissance, 1380-1530.* New York: Longman, 1989. A useful overview that places the states of Italy in their urban and regional context.

Landucci, Luca. "The Entry of Charles VIII, King of France, into Florence." In *Images of Quattrocento Florence: Selected Writings in Literature, History, and Art*, edited by Stefano Ugo Baldassarri and Arielle Saiber. New Haven, Conn.: Yale University Press, 2000. A discussion of the cultural meaning and historical import of Charles's entrance into the defeated Florence. Includes bibliographic references and index.

Martines, Lauro. *Power and Imagination: City-States in Renaissance Italy.* New York: Alfred A. Knopf, 1979. Skillfully weaves the threads of humanism and social history into urban politics. Good for understanding the background of the 1494 invasion.

Mattingly, Garrett. *Renaissance Diplomacy.* Boston: Houghton Mifflin, 1955. A classic text on the origins of modern diplomacy. In treating the Italian Wars, Mattingly emphasizes that Charles VIII's decision to invade Italy was abetted by Italian adventurers, who promoted the invasion because of their own personal ambitions.

Nicolle, David, and Richard Hook. *Fornovo, 1495.* Oxford, England: Osprey, 1996. An excellent volume that provides an in-depth look into the background of the campaign, the fighting, and its consequences.

Weinstein, Donald. *Savonarola and Florence: Prophecy and Patriotism in the Renaissance.* Princeton, N.J.: Princeton University Press, 1970. Weinstein's excellent work outlines the evolution of Savonarola's prophetic character through careful analysis of the monk's fiery sermons and their relationship to his growing conviction that God had chosen him as a special prophet and Florence as a New Jerusalem. Although it is primarily focused on Savonarola, the changing dynamics of Florentine civic politics, and

1490's

the evolution of the city's nature within the prophet's mind, the 1494 invasion by Charles VIII plays a pivotal role in understanding Savonarola's worldview.

SEE ALSO: Apr. 9, 1454: Peace of Lodi; Apr. 26, 1478: Pazzi Conspiracy; 1481-1499: Ludovico Sforza Rules Milan; Apr. 11, 1512: Battle of Ravenna; July-Dec., 1513: Machiavelli Writes *The Prince*; Sept. 13-14, 1515: Battle of Marignano; 1521-1559: Valois-Habsburg Wars; Feb., 1525: Battle of Pavia; May 6, 1527-Feb., 1528: Sack of Rome; Apr. 3, 1559: Treaty of Cateau-Cambrésis.

RELATED ARTICLES in *Great Lives from History: The Renaissance & Early Modern Era, 1454-1600:* Alexander VI; Charles VIII; Girolamo Savonarola; Ludovico Sforza.

December 1, 1494
POYNINGS' LAW

Poynings' law was intended to place the Irish parliament under the close scrutiny and supervision of the English king and his privy council. Henry VII's attempt to minimize the rights of his Irish subjects enjoyed only limited success, and this failure typified Ireland's resiliency both politically and culturally.

LOCALE: Drogheda, Ireland

CATEGORIES: Government and politics; laws, acts, and legal history

KEY FIGURES

Henry VII (1457-1509), first Tudor king of England, r. 1485-1509

Gerald Fitzgerald (Garret Mór, the Great Earl; 1456-1513), eighth earl of Kildare, 1477-1513, and Lord Deputy of Ireland, 1477-1494, 1496-1513

Sir Edward Poynings (1459-1521), English soldier and diplomat, and Lord Deputy of Ireland, 1494-1496

Richard (1411-1460), third duke of York, 1415-1460, Lord Lieutenant of Ireland, 1447-1450, and father of Richard III

Richard III (1452-1485), duke of Gloucester, 1461-1483, and king of England, r. 1483-1485

Lambert Simnel (c. 1475-1534), Yorkist pretender to the English throne in 1487

Perkin Warbeck (1474?-1499), Yorkist pretender to the English throne during the 1490's

SUMMARY OF EVENT

In 1447, Richard, third duke of York, came to Ireland as lord lieutenant, and by the time he returned to England later that same year, he had amassed unprecedented popularity among both the Anglo-Norman and the Gaelic Irish. The duke later formed the Yorkist party and laid claim to the throne of England, going to war against the supporters of the House of Lancaster, who supported the claims of the duke's cousin, King Henry VI. This civil conflict for the royal succession became known as the Wars of the Roses, and Ireland became a hotbed of sympathy and military assistance to the Yorkist cause. Pro-Yorkist feeling became so intense that in 1460 the Irish parliament passed a defiant resolution that only bills passed in Ireland, rather than in England, should have the force of law in Ireland.

The most powerful of the Anglo-Irish nobles who stood by the House of York was Gerald Fitzgerald, eighth earl of Kildare. Fitzgerald—also known as Garret Mór (the Great Gerald) and as the Great Earl—inherited the title of lord deputy of Ireland from his father in 1477. By 1478, he had become the most powerful of the Irish magnates.

In 1485, the last king of the House of York, Richard III, was defeated and killed at the Battle of Bosworth Field by Henry Tudor, earl of Richmond, who ascended the English throne as King Henry VII. This at first seemed to end the Wars of the Roses, but, when Yorkist pretenders appeared, Ireland proved to be a source of continuing trouble for the English crown. In 1487, the pretender Lambert Simnel won the endorsements of Gerald Fitzgerald, the archbishop of Dublin, and most of the Irish aristocracy and was actually crowned as King Edward VI in Dublin's Christchurch Cathedral on May 24, 1487. It was alleged that he was in fact Edward, earl of Warwick, grandson of Richard, duke of York.

Simnel sailed with an army to England, where his forces were defeated at the Battle of Stoke-on-Trent on June 30. The pretender was imprisoned, and his bid for the throne came to an end. Henry VII reacted mildly, pardoning Fitzgerald and most of the Irish Yorkists and even sparing Simnel's life. He employed the pretender as a kitchen skivvy.

Royal clemency notwithstanding, Fitzgerald and

many Irish nobles still harbored Yorkist sympathies, and this was evidenced by their support for a second pretender, Perkin Warbeck, who landed at Cork in November of 1491, claiming to be the lost prince Richard, son of the late King Edward IV. Though Fitzgerald did not openly endorse Warbeck's pretensions, he did not vigorously oppose them either. Warbeck proved to be a far more tenacious adversary than Simnel had been, gaining the support of Maurice Fitzgerald, earl of Desmond. In 1494, he remained at large and posed a substantial threat to the Tudors.

Henry VII was determined to eliminate Ireland as a potential power base for Warbeck and other future Yorkist adventurers and to organize more efficiently Irish financial administrative procedures. He therefore dispatched a military commander, Sir Edward Poynings, to Dublin to take over the post of lord deputy from the Great Earl. The appointment became legally effective on September 12, 1494. Poynings was impeccably loyal to King Henry, having at one time shared exile with him during the reign of Richard III. Suspicious of Fitzgerald's loyalties and motives, Poynings had the earl arrested and sent to England to await King Henry's pleasure in the Tower of London. He then summoned the Irish parliament to the city of Drogheda, where, on December 1, 1494, he had them enact Poynings' law, which in actuality comprised a series of statutes aimed at strengthening the English government's control over Ireland.

England controversial provision of the new laws was the act that specified that all bills considered for debate by the Irish parliament had to originate in England's royal privy council and be approved by the English parliament. In fact, the Irish parliament would not even be permitted to convene in the first place without the king's authorization. Another provision attempted to reemphasize the 1366 statutes of Kilkenny, which had sought to criminalize and thus weaken Gaelic Irish laws and customs (though in a significant concession to pragmatic logistical considerations, the restrictions on the usage of the Irish language were lifted). Other measures were enacted in order more effectively to fortify and distinguish the area around Dublin known as the Pale, which had often marked the only consistently reliable area of British control.

Uprisings flared up throughout Ireland, mainly from resentment over the imprisonment of the earl of Kildare, with the earl's brother James taking a leading role. Then,

---

THE TEXT OF POYNINGS' LAW

Poynings' law, excerpted here, is officially known as 10 Henry VII, meaning the tenth statute passed in Ireland during the reign of Henry VII.

Item, at the request of the commons of the land of Ireland, be it ordained, enacted, and established that . . . no parliament be holden hereafter in the said land, but at such season as the king's lieutenant and council there first do certify [to] the king, under the great seal of that land, the causes and considerations, and all such acts as them seemeth should pass in the same parliament; and [after] such causes, considerations, and acts affirmed by the king and his council to be good and expedient for that land, and his licence thereupon, as well in affirmation of the said causes and acts, as to summon the said parliament under his great seal of England [are] had and obtained . . . , a parliament [is] to be had and holden after the form and effect above rehearsed. And if any parliament be holden in that land hereafter contrary to the form and provision aforesaid, it [shall] be deemed void and of none effect in law.

Source: From *Statutes at Large, Passed in the Parliaments Held in Ireland: From the Third Year of Edward the Second, A.D. 1310, to the Twenty-sixth Year of George the Third, A.D. 1786 Inclusive,* vol. 1 (Dublin: B. Grierson, 1786-1801), p. 44.

---

in July of 1495, Warbeck and Desmond attacked the port city of Waterford. Poynings had trouble repelling the attack. His mission was also beginning to cost a great deal more in revenues than had been expected, and a far greater danger loomed for England in the person of King James IV of Scotland, who was making aggressive statements against Henry's government.

Convinced that Gerald Fitzgerald might be trusted, and was indeed the only individual who could restore Ireland to a semblance of order, the king recalled Poynings early in 1496 and pardoned the earl of Kildare, restoring him as lord deputy (August, 1496). Lord Deputy Fitzgerald proved loyal to the Tudors and served as "all but king of Ireland" until his death in 1513. Warbeck was ultimately apprehended and executed as a traitor in 1499.

SIGNIFICANCE

In the final analysis, two of Poynings' provisions had little effect. The renewed statement of support for the statutes of Kilkenny proved to be a dead letter, as Irish ways and culture proved to be too resilient to be suppressed—this became obvious as early as the 1530's. In addition, the fortifications around the Pale were inadequate without a substantial garrison within the city to support them.

1490's

221

In 1720, it was even considered necessary to supplement Poynings' law with a special Declaratory Act. However, the statute on parliamentary legislation was of more lasting impact and became the subject of recurrent, sometimes bitter, controversy.

On July 27, 1782, Yelverton's Act repealed the Declaratory Act and virtually overturned Poynings' law by allowing the Irish parliament independently to enact its own statutes and to pass them on to the British government, which, however, retained the right of veto. This parliamentary situation lasted until the time of the union of Great Britain and Ireland in 1801.

—*Raymond Pierre Hylton*

FURTHER READING

Cronin, Mike. *A History of Ireland.* New York: Palgrave, 2001. Ascribes great historical significance to the application of Poynings' law in pacifying Ireland and credits the earl of Kildare with making it a truly effective instrument of policy.

Curtis, Edmund. *A History of Ireland from Earliest Time to 1922.* Rev. ed. New York: Routledge, 2002. Does a creditable job of laying out the background for Poynings' law and considers it to be a brilliant political maneuver.

Duffy, Sean. *An Illustrated History of Ireland.* New York: McGraw-Hill, 2002. Surprisingly detailed text for an illustrated book, offering a presentation that truly blends together the scholarly and the popular.

Ellis, Steven C. *Ireland in the Age of the Tudors, 1447-1603.* New York: Longman, 1998. Contains an extensive, highly scholarly treatment of the subject. The author believes that Poynings' law has been misinterpreted, that its provisions were too vague, and that its effect has thus been overrated.

Hollis, Daniel Webster, III. *The History of Ireland.* Westport, Conn.: Greenwood Press, 2001. Succinct and to the point, this work is a good starting reference for placing Poynings' law into its general historical context.

Moody, T. W., and F. X. Martin, eds. *The Course of Irish History.* Cork, County Cork, Ireland: Mercier Press, 1984. Has stood the test of time as the most substantial of the general histories of Ireland. The section detailing the political background to Poynings' law (by Art Cosgrove) is particularly informative.

SEE ALSO: 1455-1485: Wars of the Roses; 1483-1485: Richard III Rules England; Beginning 1485: The Tudors Rule England; 1497: Cornish Rebellion; Aug. 22, 1513-July 6, 1560: Anglo-Scottish Wars; 1536 and 1543: Acts of Union Between England and Wales; Feb. 27, 1545: Battle of Ancrum Moor; July 29, 1567: James VI Becomes King of Scotland; 1597-Sept., 1601: Tyrone Rebellion.

RELATED ARTICLES in *Great Lives from History: The Renaissance & Early Modern Era, 1454-1600:* Henry VII; Richard III.

Beginning c. 1495
REFORM OF THE SPANISH CHURCH

In union with Queen Isabella I, the archbishop Francisco Jiménez de Cisneros undertook sweeping reforms of the Spanish clergy, including the elimination of corruption within the monasteries and convents and a return to a life of simplicity and austerity. The reforms in Spain long preceded the more widespread Counter-Reformation in Europe that began in the mid-sixteenth century.

LOCALE: Aragon and Castile (now in Spain)
CATEGORIES: Religion; organizations and institutions; social reform

KEY FIGURES
Isabella I (1451-1504), queen of Castile, r. 1474-1504
Francisco Jiménez de Cisneros (1436-1517), primate of Spain and archbishop of Toledo, 1495-1517

Ferdinand II (1452-1516), king of Aragon, r. 1479-1516
Pedro González de Mendoza (1428-1495), archbishop of Toledo, 1482-1495, predecessor of Jiménez
Alexander VI (Rodrigo de Borja y Doms; 1431-1503), Roman Catholic pope, 1492-1503, who made Jiménez archbishop of Toledo
Gil Delfini (fl. fifteenth century), general of the Franciscan Order who was sent from Rome to investigate the Spanish Reformation

SUMMARY OF EVENT
Isabella I, queen of Castile, with her husband Ferdinand II, king of Aragon, had welded Spain into a viable political entity by 1492. The grandees of Castile had

been brought to heel, heretics had been dealt with, commerce and prosperity developed and Granada, the hated symbol of Islam within Spain, had been taken.

Yet a great dream from Isabella's childhood spent at the scandalous court of her brother Enrique had not yet come true: the reform of the Spanish clergy. To accomplish this, the queen needed an ally of far greater moral probity and religious persuasion than her militant spouse, Ferdinand. Finally, after years of quiet searching, the queen discovered someone anxious and able to carry out her great plans of reform and revitalization, Francisco Jiménez de Cisneros. A simple pious cleric of great moral energy, he was destined to rule united Spain as regent.

Jiménez compensated for his poor origins by a keen intelligence and an intense moral purpose. He was educated at the famous university of Salamanca and then at Rome itself, where the pope was so impressed with the young Spaniard's promise that he sent him to Toledo with a letter promising him the first vacant benefice there. Unfortunately, the incumbent archbishop of Toledo, Carillo, demanded the first such position available and clapped Jiménez into jail for six years. The future primate wisely regarded this imprisonment as an opportunity for quiet study. A few years later Jiménez took the Franciscan habit, moved to a tiny hut to discipline his body, and honed his mind by studying Chaldean and Hebrew.

In 1482, the new archbishop of Toledo, Pedro González de Mendoza, gave the friar's career a fateful turn by proposing Jiménez as Isabella's confessor.

In his first interview with the queen, Jiménez laid down immediately the conditions under which he would serve. He was not to be forced to meddle, or advise, in affairs of state; he was to be allowed to beg his food as any good Franciscan; and he was to be permitted his rigorous self-abnegation. The queen found him a sympathetic personality and agreed to have him as confessor on his terms. For more than three years, Isabella studied the sexagenarian at close hand, observing his piety, his willpower, and his dedication to clerical reform as provincial of the Franciscans. Finally, on the death of Mendoza, she decided to nominate him for the primacy of Spain.

Jiménez was discomfited when he opened the papal message naming him archbishop-elect. He actually fled from Madrid, so that it required another papal bull to force him to take up the office. Once installed, however, the new archbishop vigorously began to reform his Church. The episcopal palace of the proud Mendoza was divested of its treasures and lackeys; sumptuous banquets gave way to the coarse food of the Franciscans. When the libertine Pope Alexander VI grew impatient with this unheard-of zeal, he ordered some of the former splendor restored; the ascetic Jiménez obeyed, though he continued to wear a hair shirt under his gorgeous robes of state and spent his nights in prayer on the floor rather than in the vast archiepiscopal bed.

Since the Spanish Franciscans had grown especially powerful and corrupt, Jiménez began his task of reforming the Spanish clergy with the especially debased Conventuals. Traveling alone throughout Spain in his coarse brown robe, the gaunt old man and his poor donkey would suddenly appear at the door of a religious house. With piercing eyes he would examine every detail of daily life in the house, including the corporate books. Then, with a sheaf of details, he would call the chapter to assemble and would lay before the monks the unvarnished facts of their own corruption, laziness, and greed. Those who refused to reform, he summarily dismissed. Otherwise a kind man, Jiménez pensioned those unsuited to the religious life.

The queen, too, assisted directly in the reform effort. Sitting in the shade of the convent patio with her embroidery, she would admonish the nuns to higher standards of religious conduct and of piety, but always, to use her own phrase, *con blandura* (with tact).

The protest against Jiménez even reached Rome, so that Gil Delfini, general of the Franciscan Order, was sent to investigate the Spanish prelate's unpopular work. After a spectacular clash with the implacable Isabella, the inspector submitted an unfavorable report. Isabella, however, was not to be blocked in her project, and her own Roman agents successfully defended the aged archbishop. Armed with new powers, Jiménez next whipped into line the other religious orders; Dominicans, Augustinians, and Benedictines soon entered the fold of the reformed.

Finally, it was necessary to complete the great work with a thorough overhaul of the regular clergy. Cathedral clergy were forced to live a more rigid communal life, their two houses were sold, and their mistresses were dismissed. Again, over all objections, Isabella supported the prelate with her determined tact and political acumen.

SIGNIFICANCE

The work of Jiménez and Isabella affected a startling reform of the Spanish clergy long before the Reformation took place in northern Europe. Isabella had given Spain a cleansed faith through the Inquisition; she and her archbishop together gave Spain a clergy more worthy of the

1490's

faith. Their work paved the way for Ignatius of Loyola, John of the Cross, and Teresa of Ávila.

—*Carl F. Rohne*

FURTHER READING

Boruchoff, David A., ed. *Isabel la Católica, Queen of Castile: Critical Essays*. New York: Palgrave Macmillan, 2003. Anthology of essays that seek to penetrate the carefully crafted public image of Isabella to gain insight into her character and life. Includes photographic plates, illustrations, maps, bibliographic references, and index.

Davies, Reginald Trevor. *The Golden Century of Spain, 1507-1621*. 1937. Reprint. Westport, Conn.: Greenwood Press, 1984. A detailed account of the creation of Spain's global empire and its impact on the nation.

Lynch, John. *Spain, 1516-1598: From Nation State to World Empire*. Cambridge, Mass.: Blackwell, 1991. A serious academic treatment of the first century of rule by the house of Austria; an excellent survey of all aspects of Spanish society during the 1500's.

Mariejol, Jean Hippolyte. *The Spain of Ferdinand and Isabella*. Translated and edited by Benjamin Keen. New Brunswick, N.J.: Rutgers University Press, 1961. A reliable and readable account of Spain's birth as a nation.

Merton, Reginald. *Cardinal Ximenes and the Making of Spain*. London: Kegan Paul, Trench, Trübner, 1934. Argues that Jiménez's religiousness colored all other activities of his long and fruitful career as churchman and statesman.

Plunket, Ierne Arthur Lifford. *Isabel of Castile and the Making of the Spanish Nation, 1451-1504*. 1915. Reprint. New York: AMS Press, 1978. An old but still useful work detailing Isabel's role in forging the modern nation of Spain.

Prescott, William Hickling. *History of the Reign of Ferdinand and Isabella the Catholic*. 3d rev. ed. 3 vols. New York: Hooper, Clark, 1841. Reprint. Abridged by C. Harvey Gardiner. Carbondale: Southern Illinois University Press, 1962. A romantic and dramatic study that, despite an abundance of nineteenth century prejudice, opened up a whole new era of scholarship for Americans.

Rawlings, Helen. *Church, Religion, and Society in Early Modern Spain*. New York: Palgrave, 2002. Critical reexamination of Catholicism in early modern Spain, both within the institution of the Church and in the larger Spanish society. Includes maps, bibliographic references, and index.

Rummel, Erika. *Jiménez de Cisneros: On the Threshold of Spain's Golden Age*. Tempe: Arizona Center for Medieval and Renaissance Studies, 1999. Concise survey of Cisneros's life and influence upon the course of the Spanish church and nation, with a final chapter summarizing his posthumous image. Includes genealogical table, two appendices, bibliography of works cited, and index.

Von Hefele, the Rev. Dr. *The Life of Cardinal Ximenes*. Translated by the Rev. Canon Dalton. London: Catholic Publishing and Bookselling, 1860. Ponderous tome that has become the standard English biography of Jiménez. No other work so ably examines the many facets of Jiménez's genius as church reformer, statesman, translator, and productive ecclesiastical author.

SEE ALSO: Oct. 19, 1469: Marriage of Ferdinand and Isabella; Nov. 1, 1478: Establishment of the Spanish Inquisition; 1492: Jews Are Expelled from Spain; Aug., 1523: Franciscan Missionaries Arrive in Mexico.

RELATED ARTICLES in *Great Lives from History: The Renaissance & Early Modern Era, 1454-1600:* Ferdinand II and Isabella I; Francisco Jiménez de Cisneros; Tomás de Torquemada.

1495-1497
Leonardo da Vinci Paints *The Last Supper*

Leonardo's fresco The Last Supper *marks the epitome of High Renaissance Italian painting. The work is renowned for its depiction of religious devotion, although it is said that Leonardo did not intend to paint a religious work primarily.*

Locale: Milan (now in Italy)
Category: Art

Key Figures
Leonardo da Vinci (1452-1519), Renaissance painter
Ludovico Sforza (Il Moro; 1452-1508), duke of Milan,
    r. 1481-1499

Summary of Event
Modern assessment and understanding of Leonardo da Vinci, the towering genius of the Renaissance, may be said to begin no earlier than the late nineteenth century, when scholars had ready access to almost five thousand pages of his notebooks.

Leonardo, born in a small town near Florence, was already eighteen when he was apprenticed to a painter in Florence. He soon surpassed his masters in uniting precision of line with rhythm of movement, and in finding new

ways to show light and shade. At the same time he revealed his passion for scientific knowledge, which was in constant creative tension with his artistic leanings. Although he spent more and more of his energies on scientific observations, theorizing about and planning a multitude of architectural and engineering projects, few were ever completed. In the fine arts, his actual output was also small, and only about twelve paintings are recognized as authentic.

When he was about thirty years old he left Florence to work for the brilliant despot Ludovico Sforza in Milan. In an early letter to the duke seeking his patronage, Leonardo delineates his accomplishments in military engineering, but he does not mention music and mentions his ability as a painter only briefly near the end of his letter.

At Milan, Leonardo planned and executed pageants, made studies for completing the cathedral and modernizing the city, and planned canals and irrigation projects. He spent much time designing a heroic equestrian statue for Sforza, and though even the model was a remarkable accomplishment, the work was not executed in the way he had planned. He also painted his first version of the famous *Madonna of the Rocks* (c. 1485), which now hangs

Leonardo's The Last Supper *(1495-1497).* (The Granger Collection, New York)

in the Louvre in Paris, though his stay in Milan will always be remembered for *The Last Supper*, which he painted there between 1495 and 1497.

The Last Supper was commissioned by Sforza for the refectory of the Dominican monastery of Santa Maria della Grazle. The novelist Matteo Bandello, a contemporary, related that Leonardo sometimes worked without interruption from sunrise to sunset, but at other times quietly contemplated the painting for an hour or two without touching a brush to it. At other times he would interrupt work elsewhere to mount the scaffolding in the monastery and "take up the brush and give one or two touches to one of the figures, and suddenly give up and go away again." Leonardo's notebook has one entry directly related to his *Last Supper*. Its laconic description of proposed models and poses again shows the dynamism and precision with which he conceived his work.

Other sections of his notebook compare painting and music, which he regarded as "sisters." Painting, however, was the higher art because music was more fluid, more dependent upon time, and less durable; similarly the sense of hearing in his opinion was less worthy than that of the eye because "as soon as harmony . . . is born, it dies." Furthermore, he pointed out that music and poetry present their objects sequentially, whereas painting brings the object as a whole to the viewer and is therefore closer to nature.

Some idea of Leonardo's concept of the "subtle possibilities" of painting can be gained by reflecting on his understanding of sight in its relationship to painting. He recognized ten attributes of sight: darkness and brightness, substance and color, form and place, remoteness and nearness, and movement and rest. Painting was concerned with all ten attributes, whereas sculpture was less intellectual because it could utilize only some of them. Page after page describes his attention to perspective, to the grouping of figures, and to anatomical details down to the physical attitude of a person when he is speaking. There are precise directions for copying figures by using a mirror to ensure accuracy. He always insisted on working from live models.

Unfortunately for the subsequent fate of *The Last Supper*, Leonardo experimented with various new paints, and by the latter part of the sixteenth century *The Last Supper* was ruined, although sketches remained. When the art historian Giorgio Vasari visited Milan in 1566, he reported that he found only a faint spot on the wall. In the 1580's, another observer referred to the painting as being "completely ruined." It is indeed fortunate that modern techniques have restored it admirably.

Detail of Christ from Leonardo's The Last Supper. (Hulton Archive by Getty Images)

SIGNIFICANCE

The influence of *The Last Supper* can hardly be exaggerated. The work has become a standard reference for subsequent paintings on a central theme of Christian devotion. For Leonardo, paradoxically, it was not first and foremost a work of religious inspiration, as far as can be judged from his notebooks and from the facts of his career. His fascination was centered on the technical and artistic challenges offered by the commission. To the art historian, the significance of *The Last Supper* lies in its high degree of excellence in the techniques and the spirit of High Renaissance painting.

—*Mary Evelyn Jegen*

FURTHER READING

Atalay, Bülent. *Math and the Mona Lisa: The Art and Science of Leonardo da Vinci*. Washington, D.C.: Smithsonian Books, 2004. This study of the relationships between science, art, mathematics, and nature treats Leonardo as a mathematician working out his ideas in art instead of numbers, or as an artist whose medium is fundamentally scientific. Includes photographic plates, illustrations, bibliographic references, and index.

Brambilla Barcilon, Pinin. *Leonardo: The Last Supper.* Translated by Harlow Tighe. Chicago: University of Chicago Press, 2001. An incredibly detailed photographic documentation of every inch of *The Last Supper*, produced alongside the saga of its decay and restoration and interpretations of its meaning and importance. Includes more than two hundred pages of color illustrations, as well as bibliographic references and an index.

Clark, Kenneth. *Leonardo da Vinci: An Account of His Development as an Artist.* Rev. ed. New York: Penguin Books, 1967. While Clark takes into account the diversity and complexity of his subject's genius, his book focuses specifically on Leonardo as an artist. He judges *The Last Supper* to be "the climax of Leonardo's career as a painter."

Goldscheider, Ludwig. *Leonardo da Vinci.* 7th ed. London: Phaidon Press, 1964. In addition to Goldscheider's analysis of Leonardo's career, this work includes the famous biography of Leonardo by Giorgio Vasari, originally published in 1568.

Marani, Pietro C. *Leonardo da Vinci: The Complete Paintings.* New York: Harry N. Abrams, 2000. A truly remarkable book, this text includes reproductions and scholarly analysis of all known paintings by da Vinci in loving detail, including double foldout reproductions of his frescoes, extreme close-ups of select details, and a host of sketches and works by Leonardo's contemporaries. Also includes checklists of all extant paintings and all known lost paintings, an appendix of all known primary documents that refer directly to the artist's life, extensive bibliography, and index.

Parr, Adrian. *Exploring the Work of Leonardo da Vinci Within the Context of Contemporary Philosophical Thought and Art.* Lewiston, N.Y.: Edwin Mellen Press, 2003. A reinterpretation of da Vinci's aesthetic project from the point of view of modern and postmodern criticism, especially the work of Gilles Deleuze. Looks at the dynamics of identification and the impossibility of pure verisimilitude. Includes illustrations, bibliographic references, and index.

Richter, Irma A., ed. *The Notebooks of Leonardo da Vinci.* New York: Oxford University Press, 1980. The notebooks are an indispensable source for reaching an understanding of Leonardo.

Steinberg, Leo. *Leonardo's Incessant "Last Supper."* New York: Zone Books, 2001. A brilliant and thought-provoking study of *The Last Supper* by a leading scholar in the field, which denies that the painting is meant to freeze a moment in time, and instead shows the many ways in which it can be read in terms of sequence or duration.

Wallace, R., et al., eds. *The World of Leonardo, 1452-1519.* New York: Time-Life Books, 1966. Includes a brief but informative investigation through text and illustrations of the changing conceptions of *The Last Supper* as a subject of art from the sixth through the twentieth centuries.

Zubov, V. P. *Leonardo da Vinci.* Translated by David H. Kraus. Cambridge, Mass.: Harvard University Press, 1968. An interpretive biography by a historian of science particularly concerned with Leonardo's scientific and philosophical ideas.

SEE ALSO: c. 1478-1519: Leonardo da Vinci Compiles His Notebooks; c. 1500: Revival of Classical Themes in Art; 1508-1520: Raphael Paints His Frescoes; 1508-1512 and 1534-1541: Michelangelo Paints the Sistine Chapel.

RELATED ARTICLES in *Great Lives from History: The Renaissance & Early Modern Era, 1454-1600:* Andrea del Sarto; Donato Bramante; Correggio; Giorgione; Leonardo da Vinci; Michelangelo; Raphael; Ludovico Sforza; Giorgio Vasari; Andrea del Verrocchio.

1490's

1495-1510
WEST INDIAN UPRISINGS

The West Indians of the Caribbean Islands rebelled against the Spanish colonial policy of forced indigenous labor, the colonialists' denial of local ruling authority, and the massacres of the indigenous population by the Spanish. All these factors, and the influx of disease, led to the decline of the West Indians and the beginning of the region's importation of African slaves.

LOCALE: Caribbean Islands
CATEGORIES: Wars, uprisings, and civil unrest; colonization

KEY FIGURES
Christopher Columbus (1451-1506), Italian-born explorer who made first European contact with indigenous peoples of the Americas
Caonabo (fl. 1495), rebel leader
Guarionex (fl. 1495), rebel leader
Agüeybana (d. 1510), chief in the Higüey region
Anacaona (fl. late fifteenth century), chieftain in the western provinces and widow of Caonabo
Guarocuya (d. 1509), nephew of Anacaona
Nicolás de Ovando (c. 1451-c. 1511), governor of Hispaniola, 1502-1509
Diego Velázquez de Cuéllar (c. 1465-1524), Ovando's deputy commander
Bartolomé de Las Casas (1474-1566), Dominican priest

SUMMARY OF EVENT
The island of Hispaniola (what is now Haiti and the Dominican Republic) was the key site of the first New World landing by Christopher Columbus in 1492. Historians have not only Columbus's own account of contacts with the indigenous peoples of the Caribbean islands but also a number of descriptions by other explorers and missionaries who soon came to the first outposts in the Western Hemisphere. These accounts tended from the outset to distinguish two West Indian subgroups: Caribs and Arawaks.

This conventional dualistic view gradually was reworked as ethnohistorians came to reserve the ethnolinguistic term "Arawak" for mainland populations, using the term "Taino" to refer to island groupings, including the indigenous population of Hispaniola. The westernmost Tainos on Cuba and Jamaica appear to have been the most peaceful, both in their relations with other

Taino groupings and in their reaction to the first Spaniards. Ciguayan and Borinquen Tainos of Hispaniola and Puerto Rico had a pre-Columbian tradition of warring, mainly against aggressive raids from groupings now known archaeologically as Island Caribs (from the Lesser Antilles, mainly Guadeloupe). They were, however, relatively receptive in the first ten years after 1492 to trying to adapt to Spanish colonial presence.

It was among the eastern Tainos on the Virgin Islands that the Spaniards encountered the first signs of open hostility to their presence. After clashes with otherwise unidentifiable inhabitants on St. Croix, whom Columbus called Caribs, a number of observations began to enter Spanish accounts, including presumed acts of cannibalism and the enslavement of women captives (later identified as a ceremonial bride-capture tradition).

These early violent encounters with eastern Tainos stemmed more from the indigenous peoples' fear of strangers than from a considered reaction against Spanish plans for colonization. By the time Columbus became Hispaniola's first governor, however, a policy had been defined that called for direct methods of colonial control, including the *encomienda* system. The *encomienda* system involved forced attachment of indigenous laborers to Spanish colonial economic ventures, both in agriculture and in mining. By 1495, when the first West Indian revolt against the Spaniards broke out, the long-term movement of all of Hispaniola's Tainos toward extinction had entered its first stage.

Historians have noted that the indigenous population of Hispaniola declined most dramatically by the first decade of the sixteenth century, mainly because of a lack of immunological resistance to diseases brought by the Spaniards. Scores of thousands died from infectious diseases, others from the overwork and undernourishment associated with the notorious *encomienda* system. A surprising number, however, fell victim to violent repression of resistance movements led by their tribal chiefs.

Between 1495 and 1500, there were at least two armed uprisings against Spanish control. Each of these (that of Caonabo, in 1495, and that of Guarionex, in 1498) was headed by an indigenous tribal head, or cacique, who had been able to retain his leadership (in Caonabo's case, as head of a chiefdom west and south of the island's central mountains; in Guarionex's case, local leadership in Magua, near the gold fields north of the mountains) by at first agreeing to cooperate with the main lines of Spanish colonial policy, including the *encomienda*. Especially after the appointment of Governor Nicolás de Ovando in 1502, however, the situation became worse, and Spanish excesses were bound to cause an escalation of violence.

A final royal note to Ovando, dated in September, 1501, authorized Spaniards to take the indigenous peoples into labor service "in order to get gold and do . . . other labors that we order to have done," probably presuming that reasonable wages would be paid for work carried out. In fact, this was the beginning of forced labor that reduced many to the status of slaves.

The excessive actions of Ovando against any sign of the caciques' discontent with Spanish control set a pattern of violent conflict that took a high toll, especially among the indigenous leadership. Much of the discontent after 1502 came from the sudden dramatic increase in the numbers of Spaniards on Hispaniola. Ovando had arrived with a contingent of about twenty-five hundred persons, including not only soldiers, administrators, and

private settlers but also missionaries such as the Dominican priest Bartolomé de Las Casas, the later famous author of the *Historia de las Indias* (wr. 1527-1561, pb. 1875-1876; partial translation, *History of the Indies*, 1971) and also *Brevísima relación de la destruyción de las Indias* (1552; *The Tears of the Indians*, 1656). Ovando's contingent more than tripled the Spanish population of the previous decade. This increased settler population was certain to demand more indigenous forced labor under the *encomienda* system.

The village chiefdom of Higüey, on the eastern tip of Hispaniola, was the first site of what became major clashes between Spanish troops and what seemed to be rebelling elements of the local population. Governor Ovando's decision in 1502 to kill seven hundred Higüey Indians who had reacted violently to the killing of one of their chiefs by a Spanish dog was followed a year later by a wholesale massacre, in the western province of Xaragua (the former territory of Caonabo, the 1495 rebel leader), of some eighty district chiefs. In the 1503 massa-

Carib Indians, with approaching European ships. The indigenous peoples of the West Indies rose up against the Spanish colonial policy of forced labor, the denial of local rule, and the mass killings of Caribs by the Spanish. (Hulton|Archive by Getty Images)

cre, Caonabo's widow, Anacaona, assembled the chiefs to meet Ovando's party. While the Spanish murdered the subchieftains brutally in a mass slaughter, Ovando's "respect" for Anacaona compelled him to end her life by hanging. The future conquistador of Cuba, Diego Velázquez de Cuéllar, at that time Ovando's deputy commander, followed up the massacre by systematic conquest of the entire western half of Hispaniola.

From 1503 forward, it became obvious that no previously offered Spanish promises to recognize the local ruling authority of caciques in any part of Hispaniola would hold. In 1504, some local chieftains, such as Agüeybana in the Higüey region, began trying to organize serious resistance forces before the Spanish dared to carry out added systematic removals or massacres of the remaining caciques. Despite the fact that Agüeybana's revolt was joined by diverse tribal elements, including groups the Spanish called Caribs, from the Lesser Antilles (more likely Eastern Tainos, not the traditional island Carib enemies of Hispaniola's shores), it was brutally repressed. Agüeybana's execution in 1510 impelled any remaining potential leaders to leave Hispaniola, or at least to take refuge in the more remote eastern Taino region.

Five years after the bloody events in the western region of Xaragua, and shortly after the failure of Agüeybana's abortive efforts in the east, Chief Guarocuya, Anacaona's nephew, tried in 1509 to go into hiding in the island's mountain region of Baonuco. When local troops condemned this act as rebellion, the commanding authorities searched for him and then killed him. More out of fear than in active resistance, the neighboring provinces of Guahaba and Hanyguayaba rebelled, and immediately suffered violent repression by the hand of Diego Velázquez de Cuéllar.

SIGNIFICANCE

With such harsh actions, the short and uneasy period of cooperation between the Spanish and the West Indians was over. As the indigenous population died off under the overwhelming odds of disease, the process of importing African slave laborers began. They became the ancestors of most of today's West Indian population—the inevitable consequence of this breakdown of the *encomienda* system.

—*Byron Cannon*

FURTHER READING

Deagan, Kathleen, and José María Cruxent. *Columbus's Outpost Among the Taínos: Spain and America at La Isabella, 1493-1498*. New Haven, Conn.: Yale University Press, 2002. An account of the five-year history of the town established by the Spanish among the Tainos, on the northern coast of the chiefdom of Higüey, the first European settlement in the Americas.

Hulme, Peter. *Colonial Encounters: Europe and the Native Caribbean, 1492-1797*. New York: Methuen, 1986. Focuses on literary and anthropological approaches to understanding the psychological distances separating the colonial and colonized populations of the Caribbean.

Keegan, William F., ed. *Earliest Hispanic/Native American Interactions in the Caribbean*. New York: Garland, 1991. A series of specialized studies of both Spanish and indigenous Indian institutions, including methods of agriculture and local administration, before and during the Ovando governorate.

Las Casas, Bartolomé de. *History of the Indies*. Translated and edited by Andrée Collard. New York: Harper & Row, 1971. A partial translation of the massive work of the Spanish missionary who, after coming to Hispaniola with Governor Ovando, turned critical of Ovando's and Spain's repressive policies against the indigenous peoples of the New World.

Lupher, David A. *Romans in a New World: Classical Models in Sixteenth Century Spanish America*. Ann Arbor: University of Michigan Press, 2003. Study of the influence of Roman models of empire upon the Spanish imperial project in the Americas.

Pané, Ramón. *An Account of the Antiquities of the Indians: Chronicles of the New World Encounter*. Translated by Susan C. Griswold. Edited by José Juan Arrom. Durham, N.C.: Duke University Press, 1999. Modern translation of the writings of the Spanish friar, brought to Hispaniola on Columbus's second voyage, who lived with the Tainos and recorded many aspects of their lives and culture.

Rouse, Irving. *The Tainos: Rise and Decline of the People Who Greeted Columbus*. New Haven, Conn.: Yale University Press, 1992. Contains the most extensive coverage of the distant past of the indigenous West Indian population, with a concluding chapter on their short history of contacts with Europeans.

Tyler, S. Lyman. *Two Worlds: The Indian Encounter with the European, 1492-1509*. Salt Lake City: University of Utah Press, 1988. Provides the most concise history of the circumstances of West Indian revolts and repression in this period.

SEE ALSO: Oct. 12, 1492: Columbus Lands in the Americas; June 7, 1494: Treaty of Tordesillas; Beginning

1519: Smallpox Kills Thousands of Indigenous Americans; 1527-1547: Maya Resist Spanish Incursions in Yucatán; 1528-1536: Narváez's and Cabeza de Vaca's Expeditions; 1537: Pope Paul III Declares Rights of New World Peoples; Feb. 23, 1540-Oct., 1542: Coronado's Southwest Expedition; 1542-1543: The New Laws of Spain; 1552: Las Casas Publishes *The Tears of the Indians*; Sept. 14, 1585-July 27, 1586: Drake's Expedition to the West Indies.

RELATED ARTICLES in *Great Lives from History: The Renaissance & Early Modern Era, 1454-1600:* Christopher Columbus; Sir Francis Drake; Guacanagarí; Bartolomé de Las Casas; Paul III; Juan Ponce de León.

1497
CORNISH REBELLION

The unsuccessful Cornish Rebellion of 1497, also known as the Perkin Warbeck conspiracy, which began as a protest against exorbitant taxation, revealed the existence of widespread popular discontent with Henry VII and even of efforts to replace him on the throne.

LOCALE: England

CATEGORIES: Wars, uprisings, and civil unrest; government and politics

KEY FIGURES

Henry VII (1457-1509), king of England, r. 1485-1509

Michael An Gof (Michael Joseph; d. 1497), Cornish blacksmith and rebel leader

Thomas Flamank (1450-1497), lawyer and rebel adviser

James Touchet (d. 1497), fourth Baron Audley of Wells, Somerset, the only nobleman among the rebels

Perkin Warbeck (c. 1474-1499), impostor and pretender who conspired with the rebels

Giles, Lord Daubney (fl. 1497-1506), leader of royalist forces

SUMMARY OF EVENT

By the end of the fifteenth century, the inhabitants of Cornwall had resented for more than one hundred years the gradual replacement of their language by English, which they saw as a threat to their cultural identity. These feelings may explain their enthusiastic support of the Tudor pretender, who became King Henry VII, against Richard III, for Henry emphasized his Welsh birth and claimed descent from the Celtic king Arthur.

However, in 1476, Henry VII crippled the Cornish economy by suspending the operation of the Western Stannaries, or tin mines, because the miners had rejected his new regulations. He also imposed exorbitant taxes, which in many cases amounted to tripled assessments.

The Yorkists took advantage of the situation by having their own pretender, Perkin Warbeck, issue a statement in September, 1496, urging subjects who were unhappy with the harsh tax policies of Henry VII to rebel and put Warbeck on the throne as Richard IV.

When the Cornish did rebel, however, their uprising began as a purely local matter. In mid-May, 1497, his neighbors in western Cornwall accused a Penryn provost, John Oby, of siphoning off a portion of the taxes they had paid rather than transmitting them to the crown. Soon their attack on Oby flared up into a full-fledged revolt. It was led by Michael An Gof, a blacksmith, with Thomas Flamank, a lawyer, as his second in command. Among the rebels were numerous members of the clergy, who had been especially hard hit by the new tax policy; gentry unhappy about the loans to the Crown they had been forced to make; and an assortment of people from the lower ranks of society. The gathering army marched eastward toward London, where their stated aim was to persuade Henry VII to dismiss two of his advisers, John Morton and Sir Reginald Bray.

As they marched to London, the rebels attempted to drum up support for their cause and to swell their ranks. Although the people of Exeter, in Devonshire, showed little interest, the rebels found many sympathizers in Somerset, including one nobleman, James Touchet, Lord Audley, who joined them at Wells early in June. Lord Audley's motive for disaffection is not clear. Suggestions that he was impoverished are unfounded, for in actuality he was well off. However, it is true that after becoming king, Henry VII seems to have forgotten the fact that the Audleys had been his supporters during his exile. Lord Audley may have been particularly angry when he saw the Audley interests ignored and royal preferment instead going to rivals like John Cheyne.

In any case, Lord Audley's participation in the rebellion supports the theory that its ostensible purpose, to

Perkin Warbeck, impostor and pretender to the English throne, with Margaret, duchess of Burgundy, King Richard III's sister, and Warbeck's impersonation coach. Warbeck conspired with rebels to attempt to depose King Henry VII. (Hulton|Archive by Getty Images)

London. They split their forces, and Michael An Gof led his men southeast to Winchester, then northeast to Farnham and Guildford, approaching London from the southwest. Audley marched north to Wallingford, near Oxford, perhaps intending to draw the king's army in the wrong direction, perhaps planning to cross the Thames and attack London from the north.

The rebellion broke out so suddenly and developed so rapidly that Henry could very well have been overwhelmed before he realized what was happening. Fortunately, during his long and hazardous exile, he had learned how to respond rapidly to a crisis. Hastily Henry called back the troops that were on their way north to invade Scotland. By the second week of June, he had gathered a large force at Woodstock, and soon he was on his way toward Wallingford. Meanwhile, he sent Giles, Lord Daubney, to the south.

At Guildford, some five hundred of Daubney's men attacked the rebels and sent them scurrying into Kent, where they hoped to augment their numbers. However, finding no support there, they turned back north toward London, finally arriving at Deptford, just above Blackheath. Though they were now in sight of London, their professed goal, the rebels were becoming disheartened; some of them even approached Daubney with an offer to surrender their leaders in return for a general pardon. The offer was rejected, and on June 16, the rebel army encamped at Blackheath.

When the sun rose on June 17, according to some accounts the rebel forces had been so lessened by desertions that they now numbered no more than nine thousand. The king had twenty-five thousand men. Significantly, one-fourth of them had been provided by some twenty of his nobles, who had proven their loyalty to Henry by thus responding to his urgent summons.

During the first attack by the royal army, the rebel bowmen acquitted themselves well, according to one report killing three hundred of Henry's men; later on, the Cornishmen managed to capture Daubney, though they released him unharmed. However, the rebels never had a chance of winning the day. Many of them were killed and many more, including the three leaders, were taken prisoner. By two in the afternoon, Henry was back in London giving thanks at St. Paul's. Ten days later, Thomas Flamank and Michael An Gof were hanged and quartered at Tyburn. Lord Audley was arrayed in a ragged

draw the attention of the king to the grievances of his subjects, was at this point no longer the intent of many of the rebels. Evidence has been found that messages were sent from Wells to the pretender, offering to help him take over the throne, though it is unclear whether they reached him before the battle that ended the rebellion.

By now, there were at least fifteen thousand men in the rebel forces, perhaps many more. From Wells, the rebels sent messengers north to Bristol, ordering the town to surrender. It has been suggested that they intended to fortify that coastal town and bring Warbeck there from Scotland, where he had taken refuge. However, when the mayor of Bristol defied the rebels and refused to capitulate, the rebel leaders decided to speed up their march on coat of armor made of paper, then taken from Newgate to Tower Hill, where he was beheaded. Henry pardoned the other prisoners but levied heavy fines on everyone who had been involved in the rebellion.

SIGNIFICANCE

Although the defeat of the rebels at Blackheath halted Scotland's sponsorship of the Yorkist pretender, it did not end the Perkin Warbeck conspiracy. Later in 1497, Warbeck landed in Cornwall, raised a following of eight thousand men, and prepared to face the king's forces. However, during the night he slipped away from his army and fled toward the coast. After he had to surrender, he confessed that he was a fraud. His disillusioned supporters were left to pay the fines that were always the king's preferred method of punishment. Thus, the year 1497 marked the turning point of Henry VII's reign. After twelve years of peril from plots and uprisings, he was firmly established on the throne.

However, Cornwall was not yet reconciled to being assimilated by England. Over the next 150 years, there would be four more major rebellions in Cornwall and four incursions into England. The Cornish clung stubbornly to their culture and their language until finally, in 1648, when the Cornish Royalists were defeated by the Roundheads, Cornwall had to abandon its tradition of cultural independence and become just another county in England.

—Rosemary M. Canfield Reisman

FURTHER READING

Arthurson, Ian. *The Perkin Warbeck Conspiracy, 1491-1499*. 1994. Reprint. Wolfeboro Falls, N.H.: Alan Sutton, 1998. A thorough, well-documented study of the Cornish Rebellion and its historical background. Notes evidence of Warbeck's involvement in the conspiracy and also points out possible reasons for Lord Audley's actions.

Fletcher, Anthony. *Tudor Rebellions*. 4th ed. London: Longmans, 1997. Contains a brief summary. Includes maps.

Gairdner, James. *Henry the Seventh*. 1926. Reprint. New York: AMS Press, 1989. Explains why Cornwall was a hotbed of rebellion, while counties such as Kent refused to become involved.

Mackie, John Duncan. *The Earlier Tudors, 1485-1558*. 1952. Reprint. New York: Oxford University Press, 1994. A short, readable account, containing some details not found in other sources.

Stoyle, Mark. "Cornish Rebellions, 1497-1648." *History Today* 47 (May, 1997): 22-29. Presents convincing evidence that the five Cornish rebellions were not merely protests against specific measures but were actually expressions of cultural nationalism.

Williamson, James A. *The Tudor Age*. 3d ed. Reprint. London: Longman, 1979. The uprising is seen as to some degree a continuation of the struggle between York and Lancaster.

SEE ALSO: 1455-1485: Wars of the Roses; 1483-1485: Richard III Rules England; Beginning 1485: The Tudors Rule England; 1489: Yorkshire Rebellion; Dec. 1, 1494: Poynings' Law; Aug. 22, 1513-July 6, 1560: Anglo-Scottish Wars; 1536 and 1543: Acts of Union Between England and Wales; Oct., 1536-June, 1537: Pilgrimage of Grace; 1549: Kett's Rebellion; Jan. 25-Feb. 7, 1554: Wyatt's Rebellion; Nov. 9, 1569: Rebellion of the Northern Earls; 1597-Sept., 1601: Tyrone Rebellion.

RELATED ARTICLES in *Great Lives from History: The Renaissance & Early Modern Era, 1454-1600:* Henry VII; Richard III.

1490's

Beginning 1497
DANISH-SWEDISH WARS

This series of wars between two Scandinavian kingdoms over control of the Baltic Sea trade and tolls resulted in military exhaustion for both and allowed Prussia and Russia eventually to dominate the Baltic.

LOCALE: Scandinavia and the Baltic Sea region
CATEGORIES: Wars, uprisings, and civil unrest; diplomacy and international relations; expansion and land acquisition

KEY FIGURES
Gustav I Vasa (1496-1560), king of Sweden, r. 1523-1560
Gustav II Adolf (Gustavus Adolphus; 1594-1632), king of Sweden, r. 1611-1632
Christian IV (1577-1648), king of Denmark, r. 1588-1648

SUMMARY OF EVENT
The Union of Kalmar (1397) united the kingdoms of Denmark, Norway, and Sweden under a single monarch. While the nobles still handled local and regional issues, effective control of Scandinavia and of the Baltic Sea was centered in Denmark. Of particular significance was the Danish monarch's control of the Øresund, the narrow strait that separates Sweden and Denmark. Militarily, the Danish navy made it into an effective barrier to hostile powers seeking either to enter or to leave the Baltic. More important, however, was the international trade that passed through the Øresund.

The significance of the Baltic region during the early modern era cannot be underestimated. From the cities and countries around the Baltic came grain, naval stores, semi-precious gems, and furs; to the Baltic areas went wine, fish, oil, and spices. The Hanseatic League had dominated this trade during the medieval period, but Denmark now controlled it, and all ships traversing the Øresund paid a toll. These tolls were critical to Danish monarchal power, for control of the tolls meant revenue for building military power. It was also an attractive reason for others to challenge Danish control. For nearly three centuries, competing factions in Sweden and Denmark sought to control not only this strategic waterway but also the Baltic area in general. Eventually the Scandinavian powers fell victim to larger, more powerful states, but the Danish-Swedish Wars, which lasted well into the eighteenth century, were an integral part of the emergence of the Baltic as a significant region in early modern Europe.

The Kalmar Union itself was seldom effective, as the size of the area and primitive transportation and communication made control by Denmark virtually impossible. More important, Swedish nobles had little desire to be controlled by a Danish king, and frequent clashes between the two groups occurred throughout the fifteenth century. Finally, in 1497, after a Swedish victory in the Swedish-Russian War (1495-1497), Swedish nobles attempted to secede. A Danish force restored the Union, but Danish pacification often consisted of actions such as the Bloodbath of Stockholm (1520), wherein Swedish nobles were rounded up and executed. Under the leadership of Gustav Eriksson Vasa, Danish control of Sweden was ended and he was elected Swedish king (Gustav I) in 1523. During the next forty years, Denmark made Norway into a possession instead of a kingdom, Lutheranism was implemented, and the king of Denmark became an absolute monarch. Danish strength was based more on naval power and control of the Baltic Sea than upon a strong army. In Sweden, the Vasas adopted Lutheranism, created a centralized monarchy, and focused on building a strong army, which was used to extend Swedish power into Poland and Livonia (1557-1571).

SIGNIFICANCE
The wars between Denmark and Sweden in the late fifteenth century were only the beginning of an ongoing series of conflicts that did not end until the eighteenth century and essentially shaped the modern states known today.

For the next 150 years (1563-1720), Swedish and Danish kings confronted each other intermittently for Baltic hegemony. However, the riches of the region assured its being a target for other imperialistic powers of the era: Austria, Prussia, Russia, the Netherlands, and England. The first major confrontation between the two was the Scandinavian Seven Years' War (Den Nordiske Syvårskrig, 1563-1570), which ended with both kingdoms exhausted and having suffered much destruction. Forty more years of relative peace between the two kingdoms followed, but the wars of religion between Roman Catholics and various Protestant sects ensured international instability. In an effort to solidify Danish control of the western Baltic against Austrian Habsburg ambitions in the Holy Roman Empire, Christian IV of Denmark unsuccessfully attempted to force Sweden to rejoin the Union in the Kalmar War (1611-1613). His failure was largely due to the emergence of a Swedish military genius, Gustav II Adolf, the newly crowned, teenaged king of Sweden.

The Thirty Years' War (1618-1648) was a continent-wide series of religious-political wars. Despite their shared religion, Denmark and Sweden were usually hostilely neutral or overtly active against each other during various phases of this war. Following Habsburg victory in the Bohemian phase of the war (1618-1624), Christian IV attempted to repel Habsburg efforts to dominate the Holy Roman Empire by organizing a Protestant coalition against the Catholic emperor. His failure to gain the support of Gustav II Adolf resulted in a series of humiliating defeats by Habsburg forces that forced him to retire almost entirely from the Baltic mainland. By 1628, Habsburg forces under Count Albrecht Wenzel von Wallenstein had extended imperial control to the Baltic Sea, at which point Swedish forces participated actively, but only after displacing Danish forces.

For four years, until his death at the Battle of Lützen in 1632, the Swedish monarch terrorized Habsburg generals as he extended Swedish control from the southern shore of the Baltic to Bavaria. He offered Christian IV a subordinate role in the war, but the Danish monarch chose neutrality instead. In the final stage of the Thirty Years' War, Denmark was attacked by Sweden (1643-1645). In the Treaty of Brömsebro, the Danes ceded much of their possessions on the Swedish peninsula to Sweden and exempted Swedish vessels from tolls. The Treaty of Westphalia (1648) effectively made the Baltic into a Swedish lake, for it gave Sweden control of the mouths of major rivers along the Baltic as well as eliminating the Habsburgs as a threat to northern Germany.

This hegemony did not last for long: The newly emerging powers of Prussia and Russia soon contested Swedish control. When Swedish forces under Charles XI invaded Poland in 1655, a coalition of Russia, Denmark, and Austria then attacked Sweden. Unfortunately for Denmark, a severe winter froze the coastal waters, allowing a Swedish army to march across the ice to take numerous Danish islands. The Peace of Roskilde (1658) cost Denmark part of Norway as well as Scania (the provinces east of the Øresund). The border between the two kingdoms now passed through the center of the Øresund; Denmark had lost perhaps its most valuable holding. In 1659, the Swedes renewed the conflict by attacking the Danish capital of Copenhagen, but failed. Neither the Netherlands nor England wanted Denmark reduced to Swedish vassalage; thus, in 1660, the Roskilde treaty was renewed.

The final wars between the two countries were the Scania War (Skånske Krig, 1675-1679) and the Great Northern War (Store Nordiske Krig, 1700-1721), during which the Danes fought Sweden between 1709 and 1720. While Denmark could claim to have won the wars, the Danes failed to regain Scania—their reason for both wars. The peace at Stockholm in 1720 ended the long series of wars between the two Scandinavian kingdoms and initiated a peaceful coexistence between the two that continues today. In neither war was Denmark a significant factor, as Sweden, under Charles XII, was fighting for its existence at the hands of Russia and Prussia. Those wars resulted in the virtual elimination of Sweden as a power along the southern Baltic shoreline.

The series of wars between the two Scandinavian states of Denmark and Sweden were critical in their evolution as modern states. In each area the wars resulted in a reduction of power for the nobles and for the church. In both cases a strong monarchy dominated the social, political, religious, and economic structures of the respective states. The wealth of the Baltic region, which neither owned outright but which both, at one point or another, controlled through possession of vital trade points, allowed each to develop military power to protect their interests. Although the wars between the two certainly weakened each, in the end neither was capable of defeating the rising economic and military powers of Europe. In a sense their two-hundred-year struggle for control of the Baltic was either a prelude to or a side clash within the conflicts between the Great Powers in the post-1618 era. Indeed, Swedish-Danish wars were often subsumed by the great wars of the period, and by 1720, neither Scandinavian country was considered a significant Baltic power.

—William S. Brockington, Jr.

FURTHER READING

Frost, Robert I. *The Northern Wars: War, State, and Society in Northeastern Europe, 1558-1721.* New York: Addison Wesley Longman, 2000. This survey of the Baltic wars of the period is particularly good on the Livonian Wars from 1558 to 1583 and the emergence of Russia as a Baltic power.

Kirby, David. *Northern Europe in the Early Modern Period: The Baltic World, 1492-1772.* New York: Longman, 1995. Excellent survey of the Baltic wars, particularly useful for understanding the difficulties of waging war in that area.

Kirchner, Walther. *The Rise of the Baltic Question.* Newark: University of Delaware Press, 1954. Although somewhat dated, this monograph provides a sound introduction to the issues and personages involved in the struggles for control of the Baltic in the early modern era.

Oakley, Stewart P. *War and Peace in the Baltic, 1560-1790*. New York: Routledge, 1993. Provides an excellent overview of the struggles for Baltic control and the rise of Russia to preeminence.

SEE ALSO: Oct. 19, 1466: Second Peace of Thorn; 1499-c. 1600: Russo-Polish Wars; Oct. 31, 1517: Luther Posts His Ninety-five Theses; Apr.-May, 1521: Luther Appears Before the Diet of Worms; 1523: Gustav I Vasa Becomes King of Sweden; 1557-1582: Livonian War.

RELATED ARTICLE in *Great Lives from History: The Renaissance & Early Modern Era, 1454-1600:* Gustav I Vasa.

June 24, 1497-May, 1498
CABOT'S VOYAGES

John Cabot claimed Newfoundland for England, laying the foundation for all future English land claims in North America.

LOCALE: Newfoundland coast (now in Canada)
CATEGORIES: Exploration and discovery; expansion and land acquisition

KEY FIGURES
John Cabot (c. 1450-c. 1498), Italian explorer in the service of England
Sebastian Cabot (c. 1474-1557), his son, English explorer and cartographer
Henry VII (1457-1509), king of England, r. 1485-1509

SUMMARY OF EVENT

The late fifteenth century was an age of increasingly intense national rivalry in Europe. When it became known that Christopher Columbus had discovered a hitherto unknown coast on the other side of the Atlantic, the nations fronting that ocean quickly became interested in exploring the New World and laying claim to some of its territories, territories that Spain and Portugal planned to reserve for themselves. England, finally at peace after the Wars of the Roses, and with a strong government headed by the canny monarch Henry VII, had no intention of being left out. Like other monarchs of the era, Henry was willing to use the services of good seamen whenever they were available. He turned to an Italian, John Cabot, to begin his campaign for a piece of the New World.

Very little is known about John Cabot. Several scholars, however, have turned up a few facts. Cabot is believed to have been born Giovanni Caboto in Genoa, nursery of seamen. He may have been born in 1450, a year before Columbus. It is known that in 1484, he was married and living in Venice, where he had resided for the fifteen years required to gain Venetian citizenship. Between 1490 and 1493, a John Cabot, possibly the navigator, resided in Valencia, Spain. In 1495, Cabot was in England trying to interest Henry VII in transatlantic exploration.

It is significant that Cabot, with his wife and three sons, was then living in Bristol. Bristol, with its good harbor on the Avon River, was the second largest port in England. It faced the Atlantic Ocean, carried on a large trade in spices, and was the headquarters of a large fishing fleet. It is little wonder that many of its inhabitants were deeply interested in western exploration.

Cabot's attempt to engage the king's interest was successful. On March 5, 1496, King Henry granted him letters patent to sail east, west, and north with five ships. This royal support was not just the product of enthusiasm for new discoveries. Henry no doubt hoped that Cabot could succeed in the same venture that had originally motivated his Genoese compatriot Columbus: gaining access to the valuable Asian silk and spice trade by sailing westward across the Atlantic. In fact, contemporary documents show that Columbus had earlier tried, unsuccessfully, to obtain the English crown's support for the voyage he eventually carried out under the banner of Spain's Ferdinand II and Isabella I.

Henry's 1496 letters patent merely gave Cabot the right to undertake oceanic explorations in the Crown's name; actual financial support for the project had to come from elsewhere. Cabot's funding came from wealthy Bristol merchants eager to profit from English entry into what was still an Italian-dominated Eastern spice and silk trade. As the king's lieutenant, Cabot was to govern all lands he might find, but the king was to have one-fifth of all profits. Cabot was not to venture south, for Henry wanted no trouble with Spain or Portugal.

In late May, 1497, Cabot set sail from Bristol. Instead of five ships, he had only one, the *Matthew*, a vessel with a burden of fifty tons and a crew of eighteen. It was the equivalent of a fair-sized modern yacht. Going around the south end of Ireland, he last sighted land at Dursey Head. His plan, a favorite with westbound mariners in that age, was to follow a parallel of latitude straight west. Dursey Head is at latitude 51°33′.

At 5:00 A.M. on June 24, Cabot came in sight of land again. He had made the Atlantic crossing in just over a month. The exact spot where he first saw the coast of North America has been greatly disputed, and the dispute has been complicated by local patriotism, with various locales attempting to claim the honor. The famous historian Samuel Eliot Morison, whose account is one of the best, concluded that Cabot sighted Cape Dégrat, on the northeast tip of Newfoundland (latitude 51°37′, only 4′ off the Dursey Head latitude). If that is true, he had performed an impressive feat of navigation, having come almost straight west from the Irish coast. Furthermore, Cape Dégrat was only five miles from where it is believed Leif Eriksson had landed, nearly five hundred years before.

Turning south, Cabot landed briefly, the only landing of his voyage. He formally took possession of the territory in the name of Henry VII. Following this formality, Cabot is said to have performed a symbolic act: He planted the flag of Saint Mark, the patron saint of Venice, his earlier adopted city-state and nationality. At the time of this first landing, Cabot's party found evidence of human inhabitants, but no real contact—certainly nothing comparable to Columbus's active interchange with the West Indian Tainos—took place. Although a few artifacts were found near abandoned campsites, Cabot decided, probably for security reasons, not to seek out their owners.

Continuing his southward course, Cabot skirted the whole east side of the island and rounded its southern tip, making note of various capes, islands, and bays as he went. Eventually he turned about, retraced his course to Cape Dégrat, and on July 20, left for home. After a fast passage of fifteen days, he made landfall at Ushant on the coast of Brittany, headed north, and on August 6 was in Bristol once more. Cabot had not found the way to Japan or China, and he had brought back neither gold nor spices, but he had found a coast teeming with codfish—a most important fact.

Cabot hurried to London to make his report to Henry. The king gave him ten pounds and on the thirteenth of the following December settled on the explorer a pension of twenty pounds per year. That, for Henry VII, was liberality.

On February 3, 1498, Henry issued new letters patent

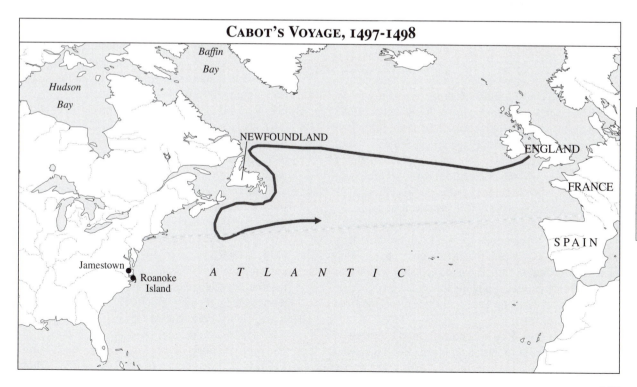

CABOT'S VOYAGE, 1497-1498

1490's

John Cabot's son, Sebastian, with his crew and ship at Labrador along the east Canadian coast. (R. S. Peale and J. A. Hill)

giving Cabot the authority to impress six ships for a second voyage to the New World. Cabot was now to explore more thoroughly the coast he had touched, and when he had reached the source of the spice trade, to set up a trading factory with the intent of funneling that desired commodity to English ports. Cabot succeeded in obtaining five ships, with which he sailed from Bristol at the beginning of May, 1498. In contrast to the *Matthew*, these ships were well stocked, not only with provisions to allow the crews to survive longer on their own if necessary, but also with goods to offer in trade for the Asian products they hoped to find. Bad weather caused damage to one ship soon after Cabot set sail. The damaged ship returned to port on the Irish coast while the others sailed on. After this event, Cabot and the other four ships disappear from the pages of history.

The Cabot story does not end with John's disappearance. Much more is known about his son Sebastian, who may have accompanied his father on the first voyage. He

said that he did, but his statement alone is not particularly good evidence. He also claimed to have made, in 1508, a voyage to discover the fabled Northwest Passage, but as he was a "genial and cheerful liar," this may not be true. He certainly knew how to promote himself. He set himself up as an expert adviser to would-be explorers and was paid by the kings of both England and Spain for his advice. He died in England in 1557. Eventually, John's name was practically forgotten, and historians took Sebastian to be the discoverer of North America.

SIGNIFICANCE

The one voyage of John Cabot, for all the gaps in the story, may seem a small thing in the history of American exploration. However, it had great results, for Cabot's voyage laid the foundation of the British claim to North America. In the short run, Cabot established that there was a bounteous and uncontested source of fish available for the English to exploit. In the long term, Cabot's landfall on the Canadian coast ultimately resulted in England's extensive holdings in North America—holdings that became one of the foundation stones of the British Empire.

—*Don R. Gerlach, updated by Byron Cannon*

FURTHER READING

Beazley, Charles R. *John and Sebastian Cabot: The Discovery of North America*. London: T. F. Unwin, 1898. Reprint. New York: Burt Franklin, 1967. A competent, documented study by an Oxford specialist in historical geography; easier reading than Williamson. Concludes, unlike other modern scholars, that John Cabot returned from his second voyage.

Biddle, Richard. *A Memoir of Sebastian Cabot, with a Review of the History of Maritime Discovery*. Philadelphia: Carey and Lea, 1831. Reprint. Freeport, N.Y.: Books for Libraries Press, 1970. Originally published anonymously, this book was the first attempt to apply serious scholarship to the Cabot story.

Firstbrook, Peter. *The Voyage of the Matthew: John Cabot and the Discovery of North America*. London: BBC Books, 1997. Book chronicling the re-creation of Cabot's 1497 voyage by a modern crew sailing in an exact replica of the *Matthew*. Combines narrative of the first journey with a narrative of the journey commemorating it. Includes bibliographic references and index.

Harrisse, Henry. *John Cabot, the Discoverer of North-America, and Sebastian, His Son: A Chapter of the Maritime History of England Under the Tudors, 1496-1557*. London: B. F. Stevens, 1896. Reprint.

New York: Argosy-Antiquarian, 1968. Written by the then-foremost French expert in the history of American discovery. Attacks the fictions and inflated reputation of Sebastian Cabot.

Lawrence, A. W., and Jean Young, eds. *Narratives of the Discovery of America*. New York: Jonathan Cape and Harrison Smith, 1931. This valuable collection of original documents includes two letters by Italian observers of Cabot's organization for the 1497 voyage to America. One is an official account by the Milanese minister to England, reporting to the duke of Milan.

Parsons, John. *On the Way to Cipango: John Cabot's Voyage of 1498*. St. John's, Nfld.: Creative, 1998. A meticulously researched attempt to reconstruct Cabot's final voyage and determine what really happened to the explorer and his crew. Includes illustrations, maps, bibliography.

Pope, Peter Edward. *The Many Landfalls of John Cabot*. Toronto: University of Toronto Press, 1997. In-depth study of the historical disputes over the exact location of Cabot's landfall in North America. Looks at the various plausible candidates for Cabot's landing point, as well as the competing national traditions that attempt to appropriate Cabot for their own purposes. Includes illustrations, maps, bibliographic references, index.

Quinn, David S. *Sebastian Cabot and the Bristol Exploration*. Bristol, Avon, England: Historical Association (Bristol Branch), 1968. Documents Sebastian Cabot's career, first under his father's guidance, then

Sebastian's attempts to pursue English aims cut short by John Cabot's disappearance, and finally, his switching allegiance to the king of Spain.

Williamson, James A. *The Cabot Voyages and Bristol Discovery Under Henry VII, with the Cartography of the Voyages by R. A. Skelton*. Cambridge, England: Cambridge University Press, 1962. Generally recognized as one of the best books on the Cabots. Thorough research has produced some admittedly tentative conclusions that counter widely accepted views of Cabot's voyages, including the possibility that, as early as 1494, two other Bristol captains had discovered a "New Found Land" in North America.

SEE ALSO: 1455-1485: Wars of the Roses; Beginning 1485: The Tudors Rule England; Oct. 12, 1492: Columbus Lands in the Americas; Early 16th cent.: Rise of the Fur Trade; 1519-1522: Magellan Expedition Circumnavigates the Globe; Apr. 20, 1534-July, 1543: Cartier and Roberval Search for a Northwest Passage; June 7, 1576-July, 1578: Frobisher's Voyages; July 4, 1584-1590: Lost Colony of Roanoke; Sept. 14, 1585-July 27, 1586: Drake's Expedition to the West Indies.

RELATED ARTICLES in *Great Lives from History: The Renaissance & Early Modern Era, 1454-1600:* John Cabot; Sebastian Cabot; Christopher Columbus; Sir Francis Drake; Sir Martin Frobisher; Henry VII; Sir Walter Ralegh.

January, 1498
PORTUGUESE REACH THE SWAHILI COAST

Armed Portuguese merchant ships appeared along the Swahili coast of East Africa, subdued unarmed local traders, and inaugurated a brief period of dominance by Portugal of the trade in spices and luxury products in the Indian Ocean region.

LOCALE: East coast of Africa and western half of the Indian Ocean rim

CATEGORIES: Exploration and discovery; trade and commerce

KEY FIGURES
Bartolomeu Dias (c. 1450-1500), Portuguese explorer
Vasco da Gama (c. 1460-1524), Portuguese explorer
Pedro Álvares Cabral (1467/1468-1520), Portuguese explorer

SUMMARY OF EVENT
Swahili culture developed along the coast of eastern Africa and reached its peak during the early centuries of the second millennium. Along the Swahili coast, there emerged a string of city-states that traded a range of commodities, making the communities interdependent among themselves and with other regions around the Indian Ocean basin. When the Portuguese arrived in 1498, the Swahili social and economic structure had reached its height, extending from the port of Mogadishu, in southern Somaliland just above the equator, to the port of Sofala, on the Mozambique Channel.

The Swahili were tribal Africans from the interior of the continent who had settled along the coast. Progressively, they developed a way of life much different from

1490's

239

their original lifestyle. They elaborated a network of trading patterns with the interior and along the coast from small ports that developed into cities and towns. Their common African root language was Bantu. However, their trading network included Islamic merchants from the north along the coast of the Arabian Peninsula and Islamic and Hindu merchants from the east along the western coast of India. Thus the African coastal Bantu language began to absorb many words of Arabic and some of Hindi.

It was this integrated language, mixing Bantu, Arabic, and Hindi, that came to be known as Swahili or Kiswahili. The culture underlying this language was further solidified and defined at the beginning of the second millennium, as its members converted to Islam. Swahili culture, then, consisted of an Islamized African population settled in port cities along the eastern coast, which supplied materials for prosperous and complex trade relations around the western half of the Indian Ocean.

The monsoon winds over the Indian Ocean formed the maritime basis for Swahili trade. During the summer, these winds blew eastward from Africa to India; during winter, they blew westward from India to Africa. Swahili merchants obtained items for trade from the African hinterland that included gold, ivory, slaves, animal skins and tusks, timber, and minerals. Swahili craftspeople also produced textiles and smelted iron.

The African raw materials were traded to India. In India, their value increased as they were transformed into jewelry, luxury goods, medicinal products, and finely carved woods. Swahili merchants were the middlemen for trade with the African continent, and Arabian merchants were the middlemen for trade between the African coast and India. Arab and some Hindu merchants had representatives in the African cities, adding to the cosmopolitan complexity of the Swahili coast.

Throughout the fifteenth century, the Portuguese steadily advanced down the dangerous and unknown coast of West Africa. By 1488, Bartolomeu Dias had reached the southern tip of the continent. The Portuguese were eager to establish a monopoly trade route to the rich commodities of India and the Far East, especially the spices, in high demand throughout Western Europe, for which the East was the only abundant source. For Europeans, the spice trade occurred only through the Mediterranean Sea, which was dominated by Islamic merchants. The Portuguese believed in a legend holding that beyond the eastern Mediterranean there was a lost Christian kingdom. If they could find it, such an ally would be decisive in defeating Muslim dominance.

In the summer of 1497, a fleet under the command of Vasco da Gama set sail to open a Portuguese route to India. By Christmas, it had reached southern Africa, naming the region Natal. Proceeding slowly northeastward in January, 1498, the fleet came to the mouth of the Zambesi River and the beginning of the Swahili coast. Da Gama encountered hostility at numerous ports, but the Portuguese gradually learned that they were the only traders who sailed on armed ships. All others in the Indian Ocean basin were unarmed and therefore easily overpowered. Uncertain of the winds and currents in the Indian Ocean, da Gama contracted a local Arab pilot to guide him finally to the Indian port of Calcutta, reaching it in May. Many in the region would later consider this pilot a traitor.

The Portuguese intention was to establish a monopoly on oriental trade. With their superior command of force, they intimidated Swahili, Arab, and Hindu competitors. Along the Swahili coast, they built a string of fortifications, establishing strongholds from Mozambique to Mombasa. Bombarding ports, the Portuguese shattered the delicate balance of Swahili markets. They also spent much ultimately futile effort in trying to occupy the interior and thus control the gold mines of the Zambesi Plateau. Portuguese missionaries evangelized in the region, and some Swahili, including rulers, converted. Swahili culture was thus further ruptured.

With superior firepower over unarmed merchant vessels in the Indian Ocean, the Portuguese easily seized control of the trade routes between Swahili Africa and the states of the Indian Ocean basin. Their dominance was ensured when Pedro Álvares Cabral led a second Portuguese voyage to India in 1500. A third voyage, headed by Dias, left behind a patrol of Portuguese boats with orders to prevent any Arabic traders from challenging the Portuguese monopoly on Indian trade.

SIGNIFICANCE

Ultimately, the Portuguese so interrupted the delicate balance of markets and trade along the Swahili coast that they destroyed it. By the middle of the sixteenth century, Swahili cities became shadows of themselves. Moreover, the Portuguese could not maintain a monopoly on trade in the Indian Ocean. During the course of the sixteenth and seventeenth centuries, the Dutch, French, and English all entered and became progressively more powerful in, the area. The Swahili city-states appealed to the advancing power of the Ottoman Turks and eventually came under the control of the Omani Arabs. To manage Omani suzerainty over the Swahili coast, the sultanate shifted its seat in the nineteenth century from its traditional homeland on the southern Arab peninsula to Zanzibar, an island midway along the East African coast.

The lasting consequence of Portugal's entry into the Swahili coast was the establishment of the Portuguese-speaking country of Mozambique and the ruins of a string of fortresses, such as Fort Jesus, which still rises over the harbor of Mombasa, Kenya. Just as the mercantile city-states of Italy could not revive their preeminence after their decline in the sixteenth century, so also the Swahili maritime trading states never recovered their full commercial influence or wealth.

—*Edward A. Riedinger*

FURTHER READING

Freeman-Grenville, G.S.P. *The Swahili Coast, Second to Nineteenth Centuries: Islam, Christianity, and Commerce in Eastern Africa.* London: Variorum Reprints, 1988. Examines the interaction of religion and trade along the east coast of Africa for the past two millennia.

Kusimba, Chapurukha M. *The Rise and Fall of Swahili States.* Walnut Creek, Calif.: AltaMira Press, 1999. Succinct reevaluation of the nature and extent of Swahili culture and history.

Middleton, John. *The World of the Swahili: An African Mercantile Civilization.* New Haven, Conn.: Yale University Press, 1992. Examines the worldview, life cycle, and patterns of Swahili culture over time.

Nurse, Derek, and Thomas Spear. *The Swahili: Reconstructing the History and Language of an African Society, 800-1500.* Philadelphia: University of Pennsylvania Press, 1985. Reassesses the factors in and nature of Swahili linguistic and cultural development during its most vibrant period.

Pearson, Michael M. *Port Cities and Intruders: The Swahili Coast, India, and Portugal in the Early Modern Era.* Baltimore: Johns Hopkins University Press, 1998. Measured reexamination with tables, charts, and maps of Swahili commerce and culture.

SEE ALSO: Late 15th cent.: Mombasa, Malindi, and Kilwa Reach Their Height; 1481-1482: Founding of Elmina; c. 1485: Portuguese Establish a Foothold in Africa; Aug., 1487-Dec., 1488: Dias Rounds the Cape of Good Hope; 1490's: Decline of the Silk Road; 16th century: Worldwide Inflation; 1505-1515: Portuguese Viceroys Establish Overseas Trade Empire; Aug. 4, 1578: Battle of Ksar el-Kebir; Dec. 31, 1600: Elizabeth I Charters the East India Company.

RELATED ARTICLES in *Great Lives from History: The Renaissance & Early Modern Era, 1454-1600:* Bartolomeu Dias; Vasco da Gama.

1499
LOUIS XII OF FRANCE SEIZES MILAN

Shortly after his coronation, Louis XII of France mounted a successful invasion of Italy to press his dynastic claims to the Duchy of Milan. He drove out the ruling duke, Ludovico Sforza, who died in a French prison.

LOCALE: Milan (now in Italy)
CATEGORIES: Wars, uprisings, and civil unrest; expansion and land acquisition; diplomacy and international relations

KEY FIGURES

Louis XII (1462-1515), king of France, r. 1498-1515
Ludovico Sforza (Il Moro; 1452-1508), duke of Milan, r. 1479-1499
Gian Giacomo Trivulzio (1441-1518), Italian mercenary commander of the French army
Galeazzo Sanseverino (1480-1525), son-in-law of Ludovico Sforza and commander of his troops

Alexander VI (Rodrigo de Borja y Doms; 1431-1503), Roman Catholic pope, 1492-1503
Maximilian I (1459-1519), Holy Roman Emperor, r. 1493-1519

SUMMARY OF EVENT

Louis, duke of Orleans, considered himself heir to the Duchy of Milan through his grandmother, Valentina Visconti. When Charles VIII invaded Italy in 1494, Louis expected to seize control of the city and the title from Ludovico Sforza, nicknamed Il Moro, whose family had taken them from the Visconti in 1450. Though he had long acted as duke, Ludovico did not receive the title officially from Holy Roman Emperor Maximilian I until May 26, 1495.

Louis's plans for Milan were thus thwarted, but Charles was soon in no position to challenge the imperial vassal. The French army, in full retreat from Naples, was

1490's

stung badly at Fornovo on July 6, 1495, by the army of the Holy League, which included both Sforza and the emperor. In October, Charles and the Milanese signed the separate Peace of Vercelli, which guaranteed some French rights in Italy, and Charles withdrew completely. In the summer of 1496, Sforza and Emperor Maximilian moved against these French interests in northwestern Italy. This accomplished little except to rile the French, who were preparing a second invasion when Charles died on April 7, 1498.

Duke Louis rapidly succeeded Charles as king, retaining the titles duke of Milan and king of the Two Sicilies (Naples and Sicily). King Louis XII worked tirelessly, both to prepare his own military and diplomatic bases and to undermine Ludovico's. He quickly moved his best general, Gian Giacomo Trivulzio, to the border area of Asti, from which he launched sharp but minor attacks in June. In July, Maximilian, with Milanese financial help, invaded French Burgundy. Though fruitless for Maximilian, the campaign led Louis to make peace with both the emperor and Burgundy's Archduke Philip in August. At the same point Louis signed a nonaggression pact with Ferdinand II of Aragon. He bought off the leaders of Savoy, which lay between France and Milanese territory, gaining free passage and guides for his army and the right to recruit soldiers.

The Swiss Confederation, already angry with Sforza for having supported the emperor in a recent war, allowed the French to recruit Swiss mercenaries in spring of 1499. A French-Venetian alliance was hammered out by April 15, with France guaranteeing Venetian control of eastern Milanese cities in return for fifty-five hundred soldiers. For his part, Pope Alexander VI supported France in return for Louis's provision of Cesare Borgia, the pope's son, with the title duke of the Valentinois and a new wife.

Louis rapidly rebuilt the army Charles had allowed to decompose. He quadrupled the number of heavy cavalry and employed Albanian cavalry as light horse. He also repaired and supplemented the vaunted artillery train, providing it with the eighteen hundred horses it needed. When Trivulzio rode out of Asti, he led some twenty-seven thousand men, including ten thousand cavalry and five thousand Swiss mercenaries, and 130 cast bronze artillery pieces with plenty of iron balls.

Meanwhile, Ludovico Sforza was trying to gather soldiers and funding to stop the French. His Italian allies of 1495 had melted away after his separate peace at Vercelli, or had been bought by Louis. Maximilian dangled promises of support but provided nothing. The duke

of Mantua, a hardy general, might have proven useful, but negotiations between the two lords were impaled on trivial differences. Naples lamely promised support, as did the small states of Bologna and Forlì, both of which, however, were high on Cesare Borgia's list of neighbors to conquer. Many were astounded when word leaked that Ludovico had made an alliance with Turkish sultan Bayezid II, who could be counted on to harry the Venetians, perhaps enough to take pressure off of Milan's border with them. Clearly, he was desperate.

At home, Sforza's fortresses needed repair and supplying, his army needed more men—generally expensive mercenaries—and his treasury needed more money. He taxed heavily, especially Cremona, a border city he expected to lose quickly. Whether he had the loyalty of the Milanese people is an open question, but contemporary chronicler Ambrogio da Paulla wrote in his *Cronaca Milanese* (1476-1515; Milanese chronicle) that "the greater part of the Milanese desired the coming of the king, and they treated secretly with Signor Gian Giacomo [Trivulzio, in Asti] as to the means whereby Il Moro [Sforza] could be destroyed."

Louis's careful plans and arrangements worked superbly. Sforza could put about twenty-three thousand men in the field; most were mercenary Italian cavalry and Swiss infantry. Their commander, Galeazzo Sanseverino, was described as a dashing soldier but a poor general; Il Moro would not be well served. Nonetheless, Ludovico refused a last-ditch offer from Louis, who offered, perhaps cynically, to accept Ludovico's title in return for an annual tribute. Il Moro felt he had time: After all, it was quite late in the year for a French expedition.

On August 10, 1499, Trivulzio led his force from Asti into Savoy. Soon, they reached the first Milanese fortress, Rocca di Arazzo. French artillery took only five hours to pound a hole in the wall, while the massacre that followed—ordered by Louis to intimidate other garrisons—was probably much shorter. A few days later, Annone was treated in the same brutal manner, but three other strongholds surrendered upon the French approach. The terror tactic worked. It was, however, more than merely terror, for these were rebellious subjects of their proper lord, Louis, who deserved death for their treason—or so the French held.

By August 25, the French were surrounding Alessandria, in which city Sanseverino and his army were to make their stand. Three days later, the general and his better troops were sneaking out in the predawn darkness, leaving the townsfolk and army to surrender or flee. Meanwhile, Ludovico slumped ever deeper into illness—

fevers and gout—and palpable despair. From August 19 to August 25, Ludovico prayed and consulted astrologers and fortune-tellers at the convent of Le Grazie, as his army melted away.

Sanseverino conducted what was left of the army to Pavia, the last major city before Milan itself, but the Pavians refused them admittance. As the Venetians raided the duchy's eastern borders and laid siege to Cremona, Trivulzio marched directly on Milan. Ludovico decided to take his family and a few retainers and flee to Como, from which he could continue northward into the Holy Roman Empire if pursued. He felt certain he would return and soon and prepared Milan's fortress for a French siege. September 2 saw the miserable Ludovico depart secretly and Trivulzio enter Milan quite splendidly.

The Citadel surrendered on September 17, and Louis entered Milan in a grand manner on October 6. He came as duke rather than conquering king, but had Trivulzio hand him the city's keys. After Louis departed for France, conditions in the duchy deteriorated and by mid-January Ludovico had gathered an army and entered Como. This time Trivulzio fled, as Sforza reentered Milan on February 5, 1500. By early April, however, Louis's general, Louis de la Trémoille, was reinforcing Trivulzio near Novara on the duchy's western border. Ludovico led his largely Swiss army to Novara, but after the confederation forbade the Swiss from engaging one another in battle, his army disintegrated. Ludovico was captured trying to escape as a departing Swiss pikeman. Milan penitently returned to French control on April 6, 1500. Sforza died in French custody at Loches on May 27, 1508.

SIGNIFICANCE

Louis XII's successes in the north were balanced by disappointment in southern Italy. Ferdinand II of Aragon, who gained nominal control of the Two Sicilies from the pope, was at first supportive of Louis's claims and offered to divide the kingdom between them. This relationship broke down, however, and after French defeats at Garigliano and Cerignola in 1503, Louis recognized the Aragonese claim.

Milan, however, remained in the possession of Louis and his successor until 1535, when it was seized by the Spanish. For three and a half decades, Milan served as a base for French authority and armies in the protracted wars with the Habsburgs that lurched up and down the Italian peninsula. France's staying power ushered in an era of foreign domination in northern Italy unknown since the twelfth century. Italy's states, large and small, would be drawn into the great conflicts, supporting one side or the other and wasting time, talent, and treasure on the seemingly endless wars of the late Italian Renaissance. The French occupation also served, however, to draw the cultural life of that same Renaissance into the courts of France and northern Europe more generally.

—*Joseph P. Byrne*

FURTHER READING

Arnold, Thomas. *The Renaissance at War*. London: Cassell, 2001. Very useful discussion of the context of Louis's campaign, from army organization to weapons and drill. Especially relevant are its discussions of mercenaries and the national armies of France, Spain, and the Holy Roman Empire.

Baumgartner, Frederic J. *Louis XII*. New York: St. Martin's Press, 1994. The first modern biography in English of Louis, with a full chapter devoted to the Milanese campaign.

Guicciardini, Francesco. *The History of Italy*. Princeton, N.J.: Princeton University Press, 1984. This original source details the political life of northern Italy from 1490 to 1534 from the point of view of the educated and worldly Florentine statesman.

Potter, David. *A History of France, 1460-1560: The Emergence of a Nation State*. Basingstoke, Hampshire, England: Macmillan, 1995. Provides broad context for Louis's claims and his campaign of 1499-1500.

SEE ALSO: Apr. 9, 1454: Peace of Lodi; 1481-1499: Ludovico Sforza Rules Milan; Sept., 1494-Oct., 1495: Charles VIII of France Invades Italy; September 22, 1504: Treaty of Blois; Apr. 11, 1512: Battle of Ravenna; Sept. 13-14, 1515: Battle of Marignano; Aug. 18, 1516: Concordat of Bologna; 1521-1559: Valois-Habsburg Wars; Feb., 1525: Battle of Pavia; May 6, 1527-Feb., 1528: Sack of Rome; Apr. 3, 1559: Treaty of Cateau-Cambrésis.

RELATED ARTICLES in *Great Lives from History: The Renaissance & Early Modern Era, 1454-1600:* Alexander VI; Bayezid II; Cesare Borgia; Charles VIII; Ferdinand II and Isabella I; Louis XII; Maximilian I; Ludovico Sforza.

1490's

1499-1517
ERASMUS ADVANCES HUMANISM IN ENGLAND

Erasmus was the leading Christian humanist of the Renaissance, concerned especially with the misinterpretation and misapplication of Christianity's pious and moral principles by sovereigns and by church leadership. He believed in a return to learning, especially of Scripture and the ancient classics.

LOCALE: England and northern Europe

CATEGORIES: Cultural and intellectual history; religion; education; literature

KEY FIGURES

Desiderius Erasmus (1466?-1536), Dutch Humanist scholar

Sir Thomas More (1478-1535), English statesman and scholar

Martin Luther (1483-1546), German leader of the Protestant Reformation, translated the Bible into German

SUMMARY OF EVENT

After about 1500, Desiderius Erasmus was known throughout Europe as the Prince of Humanists. Through his hundreds of writings, by means of his correspondence to several hundred figures around Europe, and by personal example, Erasmus was a powerful influence on education during a period that saw the loosening of scholasticism's hold on university and school curriculums and the introduction of Humanism into educational institutions.

A conspicuous example of Erasmus's influence on education was to be found at Corpus Christi College, Oxford University (founded 1516-1517). Humanism was here understood as the emphasis on classical learning, together with the study of Greek, and in Erasmus and other Christian humanists, it was yoked with a study of Christian Scriptures and theology.

Desiderius Erasmus visited England six times between 1499 and 1517. He stayed six months on his first visit, becoming a friend for life with John Colet and Thomas More and meeting many English scholars. The second visit was from early autumn of 1505 to June of 1506, when he stayed at Cambridge University, thanks to Bishop John Fisher, then chancellor of the university. The third and longest visit was from August, 1509, to August, 1514, a period of active teaching of Greek and theology at Cambridge. Other visits to England were much shorter.

From 1499 until 1517 Erasmus continued to grow as a Humanist, as is manifested in his books. His first book was his *Adagia* (1500; *Proverbs or Adages*, 1622), dedicated to the tutor of King Henry VIII, William Blount, Lord Mountjoy. The *Adagia* provided the core for his later, much enlarged *Adagia* of 1508 and numerous subsequent editions. The work of 1500 provided just 818 adages or proverbs, yet it was a landmark, a rediscovery of Latin and (increasingly) Greek sources. Here, the classical world was for Erasmus an inexhaustible abundance of wisdom. In later editions after 1508, Erasmus increasingly stressed the continuity between the classical world and his own, as he did especially in the *Colloquies familiaria* (1518; *The Colloquies of Erasmus*, 1671), as well as *Moriae encomium* (1511; *The Praise of Folly*, 1549).

Friendship with Thomas More saw its fruition in *The Praise of Folly*, written while Erasmus stayed in More's household; friendship with Colet saw its fruition in the founding of St. Paul's School, with a Humanistic curriculum that stressed Greek; and St. Paul's served as the model for new grammar schools established across England by King Henry VIII.

Guiding these educational reforms and innovations

Desiderius Erasmus. (R. S. Peale and J. A. Hill)

244

was Erasmus's *philosophia Christi*, or philosophy of Christ, which was both a program of learning and of perfecting human nature. There was in Erasmus a basically nonspeculative interest in philosophy and theology, an emphasis on the practical with a strongly moralistic stress on the essential business of living in this world. It vigorously endorsed classical wisdom and learning, and it valued the role of rhetoric in arriving at and in teaching wisdom.

Erasmus's vision was transmitted by the shining example of this Dutch Augustinian's canon, who was in fact the preceptor of all Europe, and whose letters reached every quarter of continental Europe; his writings continued to occupy the center stage of European thought and letters throughout the sixteenth century and beyond, influencing writers such as François Rabelais, Michel de Montaigne, and Francis Bacon.

The Praise of Folly is a satiric masterpiece, for it is a mock expression of praise, an encomium turned upside down: a *declamatio* (declamation) put into the mouth of Folly itself—that is, a praising of folly by the woman Folly. The satire is biting, and leaders of the Church—theologians especially—are revealed as arrogant, self-righteous, and ignorant. In a well-known letter to theologian Martin Dorp that became, in effect, a part of the text of *The Praise of Folly*, Erasmus wrote,

> In the "Folly" I had no other aim than I had in my other writings, but my method was different. In the "Enchiridion" I propounded the character of a Christian life in a straightforward way. . . . And in the "Folly," under the appearance of a joke, my purpose is just the same as in "The Enchiridion." I intended to admonish, not to sting; to help, not to hurt; to promote morality, not to hinder it.

There are several landmarks in the growth of Erasmus's thought and spirituality. The publication of his *Enchiridion militis Christiani* (1503; *The Manual of the Christian Knight*, 1533) marked his coming of age as a Christian humanist and a pastoral theologian.

The full flowering of Erasmian scholarship can be seen in 1516, for that year saw Erasmus's Greek-text edition of the New Testament, which opened the door to a century of scriptural scholarship and translation that culminated in Martin Luther's German Bible and in the King James version of the Bible in 1611. Erasmus's New Testament in Greek did nothing less than spark critical scholarship on the scriptural flaws of ecclesiastical writings. Also among Erasmus's works is *Institutio principis Christiani* (1516; *The Education of a Christian Prince*, 1936) and the completion of years of scholarly work on

ERASMUS PRAISES FOLLY

Desiderius Erasmus, in his The Praise of Folly, *uses comedic wit to express ideas his ideas on the uncertainty of knowing things, on acting as if one knows, and on simply being the fool. For Erasmus, life is a compromise between the possibility of knowing for sure and understanding the limits of knowing.*

[O]ne cannot acquire that widely advertised wisdom, which the wise call the secret of happiness, unless one follows the leadership of Folly. First, everyone admits that all the emotions belong to folly. Indeed, a fool and a wise man are distinguished by the fact that emotions control the former, and reason that latter. Now the Stoics would purge the wise man of all strong emotions, as if they [emotions] were diseases. . . .

If this is the way they [the Stoics] want it, let them keep their wise man. They can love him without any rivals and live with him in Plato's republic or, if they prefer, in the realm of Ideas, or in the gardens of Tantalus. Who would not shudder at such a man and flee from him as from a ghost? . . .

I seem to hear the philosophers disagreeing. This is really unhappiness, they say, this life of folly, error, and ignorance. No, indeed; this is to be human. I cannot see why they should call this unhappiness when it is the common lot of all to be thus born, brought up, and constituted. Nothing can be unhappy if it expresses its true nature. Or do you agree that man is to be pitied because he cannot fly with the birds, and cannot run on four legs with the animals, and is not armed with horns like a bull? It can be argued equally well that the finest horse is not happy because it is not a grammarian and a gourmet. . . .

Source: From *The Praise of Folly*, by Desiderius Erasmus, excerpted in *The Norton Anthology of World Masterpieces*, edited by Maynard Mack, vol. 1 (New York: W. W. Norton, 1980), pp. 1191, 1193.

an edition of Saint Jerome. To that monumental achievement must be added the publication of Thomas More's *Utopia* in 1516, for not only did Erasmus play a major role in the publication of the work in the Low Countries, but the work also embraced the concepts of Erasmus's *The Manual of the Christian Knight* and employed the rhetorical skills of his *The Praise of Folly*.

As well as Erasmus himself and the range of his writings, however, we also must look to several institutions that were inspired by him and embodied his Humanistic values. This was true on the Continent as well as in England, for the Collegium Trilingue in the University of

Louvain (1517) owed an immense debt to the vision of Erasmus and to his guiding hand in the appointment of professors. The role of Erasmus in the conception and planning for St. Paul's School in London is well known, but less known is his role in the planning for and endowment of Corpus Christi College, Oxford University, by Bishop Richard Foxe in 1516. For a college firmly placed within a tradition-rich university there could be no question of abolishing the curricular emphasis on scholasticism; but the introduction of Greek at Corpus Christi had a profound effect for the study of literature and for the study of the Bible and theology. From this small foundation of twenty fellows and twenty students came splendid scholarship. Beginning mid-sixteenth century, there was an unbroken continuity of solid scholarship and deep spirituality, from John Jewel and his defense of English reform mid-century, to his student John Reynolds and his brilliant lectures on the rhetoric of Aristotle (and the concept of a newly revised translation of the Bible into English), to his student Richard Hooker and the magnificent structuring of reason for the foundation of the Anglican Church in his *Of the Lawes of Ecclesiasticall Politie* (1594-1597, 1648, 1662).

The impact of Erasmian ideas for Church (and educational) reform was great on major figures of both the Protestant Reformation and the Counter-Reformation. Within the Roman Catholic Church there were widespread, often bitter, attacks on Erasmus, and, after 1516, much of his energy was spent in replying to Catholic critics; yet the Jesuit *ratio studiorum* drew on Erasmus's educational writings, as did the educational teachings of the Lutheran reformer Philipp Melanchthon (who saw Erasmus as a humanist forerunner of the Reformation). Among the Reformers, however, there was increasing hostility to Erasmus after 1520 because he would not proclaim his support for Martin Luther; instead, in 1524 Erasmus wrote *De libero arbitrio* (*On the Freedom of the Will*, 1961), among other works on faith. Doctrinal differences separated the two, and Luther was turned away by Erasmus's wit and declared that Erasmus was as slippery as an eel. Like many other contemporaries, including a number who remained Roman Catholic, Luther had strongly disapproved of Erasmus's satire in *The Praise of Folly* and *Julius exclusus e coelis* (1513-1514; *The Julius Exclusus*, 1968), even while he approved of the main thrust of Erasmus's call for reform.

SIGNIFICANCE

Erasmus had opened the way for Luther, but Erasmus was never willing, or able, to break with the Church of Rome, as Luther was forced to do after the fateful condemnation of Martin Luther by Pope Leo X in 1520. By 1536, the year of Erasmus's death, the split of Christendom into two camps had unalterably changed not only politics and religion but also Humanism and education.

—*R. J. Schoeck*

FURTHER READING

Akkerman, F., et al., eds. *Northern Humanism in European Context, 1469-1625*. Leiden, the Netherlands: E. J. Brill, 1999. Contains a number of valuable studies.

Erasmus, Desiderius. *Collected Works of Erasmus*. Toronto: University of Toronto Press, 1974-2003. An exhaustive series that offers scholarly translations of all of the works of Erasmus, with meticulous annotation.

McConica, James K., Rev. *English Humanists and Reformation Politics Under Henry VIII and Edward VI*. Oxford, England: Oxford University Press, 1965. A study of the influence of Erasmus upon English politics.

Margolin, Jean-Claude. *Érasme—Précepteur de L'Europe*. Paris: Julliard, 1995. A superb study of Erasmus as teacher, and one which provides a European perspective.

Schoeck, R. J. *Erasmus of Europe*. 2 vols. Edinburgh, Scotland: Edinburgh University Press, 1990-1993. An intellectual biography that discusses individual works and puts them in context.

Trapp, J. B. *Erasmus, Colet, and More: The Early Tudor Humanists and Their Books*. London: British Library, 1991. Detailed catalog and analysis of all books known to be written by, owned, read, printed, or referenced by Colet, More, and Erasmus. Shows not only the specific influences of the humanists but also their general literary milieu.

SEE ALSO: 1486-1487: Pico della Mirandola Writes *Oration on the Dignity of Man*; 1494: Sebastian Brant Publishes *The Ship of Fools*; Oct. 31, 1517: Luther Posts His Ninety-five Theses; 1520-1522: Comunero Revolt; Apr.-May, 1521: Luther Appears Before the Diet of Worms; 1550's-c. 1600: Educational Reforms in Europe; 1580-1595: Montaigne Publishes His *Essays*.

RELATED ARTICLES in *Great Lives from History: The Renaissance & Early Modern Era, 1454-1600:* Francis Bacon; John Calvin; John Colet; Desiderius Erasmus; Jacques Lefèvre d'Étaples; Martin Luther; Philipp Melanchthon; Michel Eyquem de Montaigne; Sir Thomas More; Giovanni Pico della Mirandola; François Rabelais.

1499-c. 1600
Russo-Polish Wars

Having achieved unification under the grand princes of Moscow by the end of the 1400's, the Russian state began expanding westward, bringing it into a long series of wars with Poland and Polish-dominated lands.

Locale: Eastern Europe, between the Baltic Sea and the Black Sea

Categories: Expansion and land acquisition; wars, uprisings, and civil unrest; diplomacy and international relations

Key Figures

Ivan the Great (Ivan III; 1440-1505), grand prince of Moscow, r. 1462-1505

Vasily III (1479-1533), son of Ivan the Great and grand prince of Moscow, r. 1505-1533

Ivan the Terrible (Ivan IV; 1530-1584), son of Vasily III, grand prince of Moscow, r. 1533-1547, and czar of Russia, r. 1547-1584

Fyodor I (1557-1598), son of Ivan the Terrible and czar of Russia, r. 1584-1598

Sigismund II Augustus (1520-1572), coruler with his father of Poland, r. 1530-1548, ruler of the Duchy of Lithuania, r. 1544-1569, king of Poland, r. 1548-1569, king of united Poland and Lithuania, r. 1569-1572

Stephen Báthory (1533-1586), prince of Transylvania, r. 1571-1575, king of Poland-Lithuania, r. 1575-1586

Gregory XIII (Ugo Buoncompagni; 1502-1585), Roman Catholic pope, 1572-1585

Summary of Event

During the 1400's, Russia began to grow in size and power. Under Ivan the Great, the most powerful of many Russian rulers, the diverse Russian regional states were unified into a single nation-state with imperial aspirations. Ivan faced his greatest challenge in the Polish-Lithuanian territories to the west. During the 1300's, the Lithuanians had moved southward and taken control of culturally Russian territories, so that Lithuania stretched all the way from the Baltic Sea in the north to the Black Sea in the South. In 1386, Prince Jagiełło (also spelled Jogaila) of Lithuania married Jadwiga, the queen of Poland. Since the Polish royal house had no surviving male heirs, Jagiełło became king of both countries and took the Polish name Władisław II.

Władisław II also converted from Eastern Orthodoxy to Roman Catholicism, and he required his Lithuanian subjects to become Roman Catholics as well. Although Poland and Lithuania continued to be separate kingdoms until 1569, the two nations were closely linked politically, and Lithuania was culturally influenced by Poland. As the Eastern Orthodox Russians of Moscow, or Muscovy, reached into the western territories, they came into conflict with the Roman Catholic Polish-Lithuanians.

Ivan reached agreements with princes who had been under Lithuanian control, and about 1499, he began preparations for conflict with the Polish-dominated lands to the west. In 1500, with the help of former Lithuanian rulers who had allied themselves with Muscovy, Ivan began a war with the Polish-Lithuanians. He signed a truce in 1503, but by that time he had managed to extend his lands considerably into former Lithuanian territory.

Ivan was succeeded by his son, Vasily III. Vasily continued his father's westward expansionist policies and took the city of Smolensk from the Lithuanians in 1514. In that same year, though, the Lithuanians defeated Vasily at Orsza. Despite this and other reverses, Russian Muscovy became a larger and stronger state under Vasily than it had been when he inherited the throne.

After Vasily's death, his three-year-old son, Ivan IV, became grand prince, at first under the regency of his mother. Later known as Ivan the Terrible, at age sixteen, this ruler became the first to take the title of czar, or emperor, derived from the Roman word "caesar." This title symbolically reinforced the idea that the Russian rulers were the successors of the Byzantine emperors of the Eastern Roman Empire and the foremost protectors of the Eastern Orthodox faith. As he reached young adulthood, Ivan became convinced that his kingdom needed to expand northward, to guarantee access to the Baltic Sea. Ivan therefore invaded Livonia, the site of modern Latvia and Estonia, in 1558.

Czar Ivan IV defeated the forces of the Livonian knights, and Livonia crumbled. However, parts of Livonia appealed to Lithuania for protection. This appeal again brought the Russians into conflict with Lithuania and, therefore, into conflict with Poland, still politically linked to Lithuania. Under the leadership of King Sigismund II Augustus, a descendant of the Lithuanian Jagiełło, Poland resisted Russian expansion. The war also spread to Scandinavia, since the Livonian knights

1490's

<table>
<tbody>
</tbody>
</table>

MAJOR EVENTS OF THE RUSSO-POLISH WARS	
1500	Muscovite Invasion of Lithuania
1512	Muscovite Invasion of Smolensk Province
1514	Fall of Smolensk
1514	Battle of Orsza
1547	Ivan the Terrible is crowned czar of Russia
1563	Fall of Polock
1569	Union of Lublin
1558	Russian Invasion of Livonia
1575	Election of Stephen Báthory
1584	Death of Ivan the Terrible
1586	Death of Stephen Báthory

had handed over pieces of their lands to Sweden and Denmark.

In 1569, under the pressure of the war with Russia, King Sigismund strengthened his position by enacting the Union of Lublin, formally uniting Poland and Lithuania. The union did apparently help Poland-Lithuania in its fight against the Russians. Ivan had enjoyed a number of early successes, but the war began to turn against him. Internal disorders and an invasion of the Tatars from Crimea plagued Russia. Ivan may also have suffered from mental problems in the latter part of his reign, since he began a persecution of his own people and at the very end of his life even murdered his own son and heir to the throne in a fit of rage.

After the death of Sigismund, the nobles of Poland elected Stephen Báthory king in 1575. For two years, Stephen fought to establish his rule in Poland. He then turned his attention to the continuing war with Ivan the Terrible. Stephen pushed into Russian territory. At the same time, Sweden established itself in parts of Livonia. Finally, the Orthodox Russian czar was forced to ask the Catholic Pope Gregory XIII to help negotiate a peace. In 1582, Russia was forced to give back to Poland all of the Lithuanian territory Ivan had conquered, and the Russians had to renounce their claims on Livonia.

With the deaths of Ivan the Terrible, in 1584, and Stephen Báthory, in 1586, Russia and Poland lost two aggressive rulers whose territorial ambitions had contributed to the conflicts of the two states. Still, Poland and Russia continued to be rivals. For the rest of the century, internal troubles made Russia the weaker of the two. When Ivan had lost his temper and hit his oldest son with an iron-tipped stick in 1581, he had deprived his empire

of a competent heir. Another son of Ivan, the feeble-minded Fyodor I, became emperor. Fyodor died in 1598 without an heir of his own, and the ancient Rurik Dynasty of Russian rulers came to an end. This began a period of Russian history known as the Time of Troubles, marked by internal disorder and by intervention and occupation of Russian territory by Polish forces.

SIGNIFICANCE

The Russo-Polish wars of the sixteenth century brought the expanding powers of Poland-Lithuania and Russia into contact and began centuries of conflict between them. When Russia fell into the Time of Troubles after the death of Czar Fyodor I, Poland played a large part in the difficulties of the Eastern Orthodox nation. Fyodor's brother-in-law, Boris Fyodorovich Godunov, became the first Muscovite ruler for centuries not to belong to the Rurik Dynasty.

The half brother of Fyodor, Dmitry, had died earlier, in 1591, but there were popular rumors that Dmitry was still alive and was the legitimate czar. Polish forces supported a pretender to the throne who claimed to be Dmitry and is known to history as the False Dmitry. After Boris Gudonov died in 1605, a mob killed Boris's son and placed the Polish-supported Dmitry on the throne. Dmitry was assassinated soon after, but the Poles helped to support a Second False Dmitry. In the war that resulted, Polish troops invaded Russia and occupied Moscow for a time. The Romanov Dynasty, which ruled Russia until the Revolution of 1917, was established as part of the rallying of the Russians to resist the Polish invaders.

After the rise of the Romanovs, Russo-Polish conflicts cost Poland land and independence. In 1772, Poland lost about one-third of its territory to Russia, Austria, and Prussia, with most of the land going to Russia. In 1793 and 1795, those three nations again divided up Poland, which ceased to exist as a nation. After Poland was reborn following World War I, war with the similarly transformed Soviet Union broke out in the early 1920's.

—*Carl L. Bankston III*

FURTHER READING

Crummey, Robert O. *The Formation of Moscovy, 1304-1613*. New York: Longman, 1987. One of the best books available on the consolidation of Russia under the leadership of Moscow, the conflict with Poland, and the Time of Troubles.

Lukowski, Jerzy, and Hubert Zawadzki. *A Concise History of Poland*. New York: Cambridge University Press, 2001. A useful general history of Poland.

Chapter 2 looks at Jagiellonian Poland during the years 1386-1572. At the end of the book, there are useful charts of Polish rulers, including the sovereigns of the Jagiellonian period and the elective rulers of the Polish-Lithuanian Commonwealth.

Payne, Robert, and Nikita Romanoff. *Ivan the Terrible.* New York: Cooper Square Press, 2002. The definitive biography of Czar Ivan IV and his times.

Riasanovksy, Nicholas V. *A History of Russia.* 6th ed. New York: Oxford University Press, 1999. An updated edition of one the most widely respected and comprehensive histories of Russia, from earliest times to the end of the twentieth century. Chapters 14 and 15 deal with the events of the sixteenth century.

SEE ALSO: Oct. 19, 1466: Second Peace of Thorn; 1478: Muscovite Conquest of Novgorod; 1480-1502: Destruction of the Golden Horde; After 1480: Ivan the Great Organizes the "Third Rome"; c. 1500: Rise of Sarmatism in Poland; Jan. 16, 1547: Coronation of Ivan the Terrible; Summer, 1556: Ivan the Terrible Annexes Astrakhan; 1557-1582: Livonian War; Nov., 1575: Stephen Báthory Becomes King of Poland; 1581-1597: Cossacks Seize Sibir; 1584-1613: Russia's Time of Troubles.

RELATED ARTICLES in *Great Lives from History: The Renaissance & Early Modern Era, 1454-1600:* Gregory XIII; Ivan the Great; Ivan the Terrible; Sigismund II Augustus; Stephen Báthory; Vasily III.

Beginning c. 1500
COFFEE, CACAO, TOBACCO, AND SUGAR ARE SOLD WORLDWIDE

Asian and New World foods were among the first items of global trade. While Europeans treated most new foods with apprehension or grew them as botanical curiosities, coffee, tea, cacao, tobacco and sugar became important plantation crops as colonies were founded and worked by slave labor to satisfy Europeans' desires.

LOCALE: Worldwide

CATEGORIES: Agriculture; economics; trade and commerce; colonization

KEY FIGURES

Vasco da Gama (c. 1460-1524), Portuguese navigator and the first European to reach India by sea

Christopher Columbus (1451-1506), commander of the first Spanish voyages to the New World

Nicolas Monardes (1493-1588), Spanish physician whose books, written in the 1560's and 1570's, were among the first to introduce New World plants to Europe

SUMMARY OF EVENT

The original impetus of European exploration was to find a sea route to Asia to gain direct access to the spice trade. The Portuguese accomplished this at the end of the fifteenth century by rounding the southern tip of Africa in 1488 under Bartolomeu Dias and eventually with the voyage of Vasco da Gama in 1498, which reached India. India became a launching pad for the establishment of numerous trading posts throughout Southeast Asia and ultimately the Spice Islands, or Moluccas, now in Indonesia. In the long run this route circumvented the Venetian spice trade in the Mediterranean via Arab middlemen, increasing the volume of spices reaching Europe, lowering their cost, and thereby making them commodities that enjoyed more widespread consumption.

Hoping to find a westerly route to Asia, Christopher Columbus was commissioned by Isabella, the queen of Castile, in 1492 to venture across the Atlantic and around the globe. Seriously underestimating the circumference of the earth, Columbus believed he had landed somewhere off the coast of Asia when he arrived in the Caribbean. Columbus and his men were the first Europeans to taste the sweet potato, yucca, corn, chilies, and tobacco. These New World products, along with tomatoes, new varieties of beans, squash, turkeys, and eventually cacao from Mexico and potatoes from South America, were soon exported to Europe.

Those foods that readily fit a culinary niche occupied by a similar and familiar food were soon enthusiastically adopted. For example, corn was easy to grow and soon replaced millet and barley in porridges throughout southern Europe. Turkeys were similar to fowl already familiar to Europeans, and New World beans supplemented the varieties already known. None of these, however became major items of world commerce because they could easily adapt to the European climate and were grown at home. In the ensuing decades, chilies were grown in the Middle East and, along with sweet potatoes, found their way to Asia. Tomatoes and potatoes, on the

1500's

other hand, would take several centuries before becoming major parts of the European diet.

A number of crops could be grown only in subtropical climates, and it was these that fueled colonial expansion. The first was sugar, originating in Southeast Asia. During the Middle Ages, Europeans had purchased it through Arab merchants, and it remained a rare and expensive luxury. After experimenting with the crop in the southern Mediterranean and on their island possessions in the Atlantic, Madeira, and the Canaries, Europeans found sugar to be the ideal plantation crop. The Portuguese planted it in Brazil, the Spanish in the Caribbean, and eventually the British on Barbados and Jamaica and the French and Dutch in their Caribbean colonies. To satisfy the European sweet tooth, African slaves were imported to these colonies to supply the cheap labor needed, especially after the Native American populations were decimated by European diseases and warfare. Sugar was used in Europe as a practically universal flavoring, not only in confectionery but also in savory dishes, and increasingly in novel new drinks. As a by-product of sugar manufacturing, molasses and rum distilled from it also became items of commerce.

Cacao was the first of the newly introduced hot drinks, discovered in Mexico among the Aztecs, who drank it flavored with vanilla and chilies. The Europeans added sugar and spices, and cacao became the first New World luxury item to cause a sensation. Physicians proclaimed it a wonderfully nourishing and medicinal food, and Spanish nobles were soon found idly sipping hot chocolate throughout the day. When Nicolas Monardes, a Spanish botanist, first proclaimed its virtues in print, chocolate quickly became a status symbol and a major item of commerce at a time when there were few items available for conspicuous consumption.

Tobacco, another New World product, was similarly hailed as a medicinal herb good to combat coughs and colds. Soon its medicinal reputation was eclipsed by its recreational use, despite the fact that some physicians condemned it, as did the king of England James I in his *Counterblaste to Tobacco*. In the seventeenth century, it would become the crop that sustained the British colony of Virginia, and it led directly to the importation of massive numbers of African slaves into what would become the United States. Other "medicinal" herbs followed a similar fate: After being touted as miracle drugs, they eventually made their way into soft drinks. Sarsaparilla and sassafras (root beer) are prime examples.

Following a more circuitous route, coffee originated in what is now Ethiopia, making its way through Arabia and eventually to the Ottoman Empire, where it was celebrated as a sobering alternative to alcohol, formally forbidden by the Islamic faith. By the seventeenth century, northern European and Protestant countries had enthusiastically embraced coffee as a stimulant that would keep them alert through long hours of work. It also became a vehicle for social and commercial discourse as coffeehouses sprang up and offered a place to quaff the new drink while doing business or discussing politics or the arts. As coffee was grown on a wider scale and became more readily available, it gradually supplanted beer as a typical morning drink, not only for wealthy Europeans but increasingly at every level of society.

Tea had long been an expensive luxury item in Europe and at first lagged behind coffee in popularity. It did not become readily available until the seventeenth century, and it supplanted coffee only in countries such

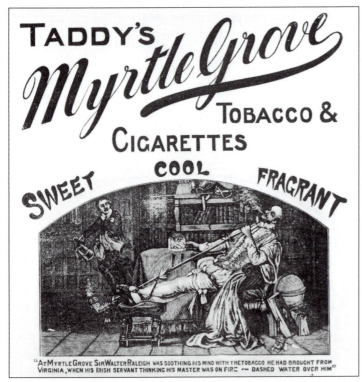

English explorer Sir Walter Ralegh smoking Virginia tobacco, depicted in a late sixteenth century advertisement. (Hulton|Archive by Getty Images)

as Britain after they had established plantations in India and protected the trade of tea throughout their empire. In subsequent centuries, sweetened tea became an indispensable part of the British diet at every level of society, often supplanting more nourishing foods in the average household budget.

SIGNIFICANCE

The introduction of Asian and New World foods not only expanded the global economy in ways that anticipated trade today but also radically transformed the diets of people throughout the world. The Irish came to depend on potatoes for basic sustenance, with disastrous results when this dominant crop was destroyed by blight in the 1840's, followed by famine and migration. Tomatoes and peppers became staples in southern European cooking. The Chinese experienced a population boom

A sixteenth century advertisement for Cope's Tobacco. (Hulton|Archive by Getty Images)

after the introduction of sweet potatoes. Coffee continues to be a major commodity grown and sipped throughout the world, and chocolate, especially in solid edible form, provides one of the principal ingredients for the confectionery industry.

Two commodities that have had perhaps the greatest impact, for different reasons, are tobacco and sugar. Tobacco remains one of the major recreational drugs used throughout the world, with unfortunate consequences for human health, but its successful cultivation fueled the economies of fledgling colonies, notably that of Virginia. Sugar, likewise, became a dominant part of the economies of Caribbean colonies, and its entry into the human diet has had perhaps subtler but widespread implications for human health.

These changes are emblematic of a larger and more important phenomenon: The exchange of plants and animals across the globe, which expanded precipitously after fifteenth and sixteenth century exploration laid the groundwork for seventeenth century colonization. This global exchange dramatically altered the biological makeup and ecology of most places on earth, as native flora and fauna succumbed to the invasions, both intentional and accidental, of plants and animals raised commercially.

The impact of new crops was not only dietary and ecological but also social: To sustain their colonial settlements in Africa, Asia, and the Americas, Europeans— who originally had sought quicker access to trade with the East—were desperate to identify and develop new commodities for export to their mother nations. These commodities would make or break the success the survival of the distant settlements. Over time, resources and particularly labor needed to fuel the success of the new agriculture would lead Europeans to rationalize an increasing dependence on indentured servants and, by the 1620's in the Americas, slavery. This development had radical implications that would both shape and hinder national identities to this day. The legacy of slavery and colonial plantation economies has left transplanted peoples throughout the world and has contributed significantly to grave imbalances in wealth and standards of living across the planet.

—Ken Albala

FURTHER READING

Crosby, Alfred. *Ecological Imperialism.* Cambridge, England: Cambridge University Press, 1986. A study of how the world was biologically transformed by the exchange of plants, animals, humans, and diseases.

Foster, Nelson, and Linda S. Cordell, eds. *Chilies to Chocolate: Foods the Americas Gave to the World.* Tucson: University of Arizona Press, 1992. Detailed articles focus on the introduction of New World products to the rest of the globe.

Mintz, Sidney. *Sweetness and Power.* New York: Pen-

1500's

guin, 1985. The classic treatment of how sugar rose to become a major item of world trade and a major component of the diet.

Salaman, Redcliffe. *The History and Social Influence of the Potato*. Cambridge, England: Cambridge University Press, 1949. The unsurpassed account of how the potato was introduced and became a dietary staple throughout the world.

Schivelbusch, Wolfgang. *Tastes of Paradise*. New York: Vintage Books, 1993. Discusses the allure of exotic new products in the European imagination, arguing that chocolate was an ideal drink for the Spanish, who valued leisure, while coffee and tea, as more potent stimulants, were ideally suited to northern Europe, where the Protestant work ethic held sway.

Sokolov, Raymond. *Why We Eat What We Eat*. New York: Summit Books, 1991. Good basic overview of how the modern diet has been influenced by new foods since the sixteenth century.

SEE ALSO: Early 1460's: Labor Shortages Alter Europe's Social Structure; 1490's: Decline of the Silk Road; Early 16th cent.: Rise of the Fur Trade; 16th cent.: China's Population Boom; 16th century: Worldwide Inflation; 1502: Beginning of the Transatlantic Slave Trade; 1502-1520: Reign of Montezuma II; 1531-1585: Antwerp Becomes the Commercial Capital of Europe; Autumn, 1543: Europeans Begin Trade with Japan; 1545-1548: Silver Is Discovered in Spanish America; Dec. 31, 1600: Elizabeth I Charters the East India Company.
RELATED ARTICLE in *Great Lives from History: The Renaissance & Early Modern Era, 1454-1600:* Christopher Columbus.

c. 1500
NETHERLANDISH SCHOOL OF PAINTING

Netherlandish painters, instrumental in the development of Renaissance art, adopted new advancements in Humanistic thinking while conserving aspects of their strongly spiritual Gothic past.

LOCALE: Low Countries (now Belgium, the Netherlands, and Luxembourg)
CATEGORY: Art

KEY FIGURES
Hugo van der Goes (c. 1440-1482), Netherlandish painter
Hieronymus Bosch (c. 1450-1516), Netherlandish painter
Pieter Bruegel, the Elder (c. 1525-1569), Netherlandish painter
Philip II (1527-1598), king of Spain, r. 1556-1598, and king of Portugal, r. 1580-1598, as Philip I, who collected Netherlandish art

SUMMARY OF EVENT
The year 1500 was a watershed in the cultural history of the Netherlands, as Gothic spiritualism gave way to the new Humanism of the Renaissance. Building more on their Gothic heritage than upon the Greco-Roman past of their Italian counterparts, artists in the Netherlands introduced into painting a new naturalism, an attention to de-

tail, and a rich color palette that influenced even the great Italian Renaissance masters.

Located between France and the Holy Roman Empire (now Germany, Austria, and Switzerland) and with ports along the North Sea, the Netherlands was ideally situated for trade. In addition to providing financial benefits, trade facilitated cultural exchanges across Europe. With the support of wealthy patrons and inspiration from an influx of new ideas, Netherlandish artists developed a unique style that combined the spiritualism of the earlier Gothic era with the new Renaissance emphasis on Humanism.

Contributing to the conservative aspect of Netherlandish art were the guilds, medieval trade organizations that oversaw the training of artists and the production and sale of artworks. In Italy, the influence of the guild system was diluted early in the Renaissance; however, in the north the guilds remained powerfully influential. Young apprentices followed in the tradition of successful older masters, whose Gothic altarpieces held prominent places in churches. The Church itself acted as a conservative force, as it struggled to carry on its traditions by dictating style and content in its commissions.

It was typically through private commissions that artists in the north could experiment with new stylistic concepts. Hugo van der Goes introduced a startling new nat-

Pieter Bruegel, the Elder's, paintings of peasant life, including the Peasant Wedding *(1565), epitomized the focus of many Netherlandish painters on still-life, genre scenes, and landscape.* (Royal Library, Windsor Castle)

uralism into his Portinari altarpiece (c. 1474-1476) with the depiction of three shepherds shown as rustic peasants with weathered faces and calloused hands. Privately commissioned and placed in a family chapel in Florence, the Portinari altarpiece drew the attention of Italian artists, and the theme of the three peasant shepherds was borrowed by the Florentine master Domenico Ghirlandaio (1449-1494). Hugo's masterpiece also was innovative in its new interest in perspective and in the increased volume in some of its figures; both were movements away from the Gothic emphasis on flatness and linearity.

In addition to introducing a new naturalism, the paintings of Hugo and his Netherlandish contemporaries reflected an attention to realistic detail—especially in the depiction of objects such as flowers—details that were to find their way into the works of Italian artists such as Sandro Botticelli (c. 1444-1510). Also of interest to the Italian artists was the Netherlanders' use of oil paint (linseed or walnut oil mixed with pigments), which created an intensely rich color palette and permitted artists to re-

work areas, thereby enabling painters to create nuances of shading and modeling. Various forms of oil paint had been in use for centuries, but it was in the Netherlands that painters developed the medium fully and introduced to the rest of Europe its potential for brilliant color and workability. It was with oil paint that Leonardo da Vinci (1452-1519) and his contemporaries would create subtle shadings in masterpieces such as the *Mona Lisa* (1503).

Another Netherlandish artist who used private commissions to experiment was the enigmatic Hieronymus Bosch. Bosch's most famous work, *The Garden of Earthly Delights* (c. 1505-1510), takes the form of a triptych (three-paneled altarpiece) on which are depicted the *Creation of Eve*, *The Garden of Earthly Delights*, and *Hell*. Bosch's imaginative forms and fantastic creatures create an otherworldly environment and have stimulated much debate as to the painter's intended meaning. Bosch's dream worlds have been variously interpreted as sinister delvings into alchemy to stern morality lessons about the dire consequences of sin.

1500's

253

Two schools of Netherlandish art developed between 1500 and 1530: Mannerism (mannered or artificial) and Romanism (Roman style). Mannerism was centered in the flourishing artistic community of Antwerp, a prosperous harbor city in what is now Belgium. Mostly anonymous, the Antwerp mannerists appealed to the tastes of the clergy by creating compositions with lavish iconography, religious themes, and decorative elaboration. Mannerist works were so popular that an entire industry developed to produce copies of the most popular compositions.

Romanism developed when northern artists returned home from visits to Italy, bringing with them the classical styles of Italian masters such as Michelangelo (1475-1564) and Raphael (1483-1520). Romanist artists used pagan themes to create fanciful classical compositions focusing on decorative architectural elements and undraped figures. One excellent example of Romanist painting is *Neptune and Amphitrite* (1516) by Jan Gossaert (c. 1478-c. 1532).

Following the start of the Protestant Reformation (1517), waves of iconoclasm (the destruction of religious icons or images) spread across Europe and religious commissions grew increasingly scarce, particularly in the northern Protestant provinces of the Netherlands, where artists turned to genre scenes (scenes from everyday life), still-life painting, and landscape painting in an attempt to appeal to a new class of patrons—the wealthy merchants. Even in secular works, Netherlandish artists included allusions to their spiritual beliefs. Quentin Massys (c. 1466-1530) captured the activities of the burgeoning merchant class in his genre scene *The Money Changer and His Wife* (1514), which depicts an industrious couple at work, surrounded by references to both their secular trade and their religious duties. The dual allusions are also included in Pieter Aertsen's (1507/1508-1575) still life *Butcher's Stall* (1551), in which religious scenes are juxtaposed with secular scenes, all incorporated into an ostensibly ordinary still life of meat. In his painting *Landscape with St. Jerome* (c. 1515-1524),

Pieter Aertsen's, still-life The Butcher's Stall *(1551) juxtaposes everyday objects (here, meat) and religious symbolism (the Eucharist).* (Royal Library, Windsor Castle)

Joachim de Patinir (c. 1485-1524) painted a subtle religious scene in which he adopted elements of the fanciful landscapes of his predecessor Bosch and introduced the new interest in naturalism of his own era.

Pieter Bruegel, the Elder, combined the best elements of landscape, still-life, and genre scenes into his depictions of Netherlandish peasant life. Bruegel completed a series of landscape renderings while traveling in Italy. When he returned home, Bruegel translated his interest in general landscapes into a series of paintings depicting monumental landscapes, which serve as settings for a celebration of the daily lives of the ordinary peasant class. Bruegel's interest in seasonal activities probably derived from paintings of seasons found in medieval aristocratic calendars, but in Bruegel's works, the medieval aristocrats were replaced with contemporary country peasants, shown with startling naturalism in unselfconscious poses as they go about their daily lives. Scholars debate whether Bruegel's paintings are literal views of simple peasant activities or are metaphors for a deeper religious significance.

During this period, the Netherlands was under the control of Spain. Recognizing the unique talents of the northern artists, the Spanish became avid collectors of Netherlandish art. The most ardent of these collectors was Philip II, whose acquisitions of Netherlandish paintings included works by Roger van der Weyden (1399/1400-1464), Jan van Eyck (c. 1390-1441), and Joachim de Patinir. Philip took a particular interest in collecting the works of Hieronymus Bosch, whose *Garden of Earthly Delights* still hangs in Philip's palace in Madrid, now known as the Prado Museum, home to one of the world's great collections of Netherlandish paintings.

Rule by a single nation did not create cultural unity across the Netherlands. The northern provinces spoke Dutch and, following the Reformation, adopted Protestantism. The southernmost provinces spoke both Flemish and French and remained Catholic after the Reformation. The northern provinces gained their independence and formed the Dutch Republic after the Dutch Wars of Independence (1568-1648). The southern provinces formed what was to be known as Flanders. From this point, the arts of the Netherlands are referred to as Dutch art and Flemish art respectively.

SIGNIFICANCE

It is commonly believed that Italy was the sole birthplace of Renaissance art, but many critical developments in Renaissance painting came out of the Netherlands. Netherlandish painters contributed to Renaissance art through their understanding of perspective and through their unique depiction of pictorial space and volume, detailed observations of nature, and significant discoveries in the potentials of oil paint.

Netherlandish painters were adept at altering their styles to meet the challenges of frequently changing art markets caused by turbulent political and religious events. True to their Gothic emphasis on spiritualism, Netherlandish painters held firm to their religious convictions even in the harsh light of Renaissance Humanism.

In the end, although split by the Reformation, their Netherlandish religious roots brought forth two new nations—the Dutch Republic and Flanders, inheritors of the great artistic traditions of the Netherlands. The seventeenth century was to become known as the golden age of Dutch and Flemish art.

—Sonia Sorrell

FURTHER READING

Borchert, T.-H., ed. *The Age of Van Eyck: The Mediterranean World and Early Netherlandish Painting, 1430-1530*. Bruges, Belgium: Ludion, 2002. An exhibition catalog that reverses the long-held belief that Renaissance styles originated in Italy and flowed northward, arguing that many northern artistic traits served as models for the Italian Renaissance masters.

Campbell, L. *The Fifteenth Century Netherlandish Schools*. London: National Gallery Publications, 1998. Good overview of Netherlandish painting (1400-1500) using examples from the collection of the National Gallery in London.

Rabb, T. "How Italian Was the Renaissance?" *Journal of Interdisciplinary History* 33, no. 4 (2003): 569-575. Brief but comprehensive overview of the artistic innovations of Netherlandish artists during the Renaissance.

Stechow, W. *Northern Renaissance Art, 1400-1600: Sources and Documents*. Englewood Cliffs, N.J.: Prentice Hall, 1966. Classic compilation of primary sources.

SEE ALSO: c. 1500: Revival of Classical Themes in Art; 1531-1585: Antwerp Becomes the Commercial Capital of Europe.

RELATED ARTICLES in *Great Lives from History: The Renaissance & Early Modern Era, 1454-1600:* Hieronymus Bosch; Sandro Botticelli; Pieter Bruegel, the Elder; Catharina van Hemessen; Margaret of Austria; Philip II.

1500's

c. 1500
REVIVAL OF CLASSICAL THEMES IN ART

Botticelli led the Renaissance revival of classical themes in art and especially painting, which incorporated secular and historical subjects in addition to traditional religious themes.

LOCALE: Italy
CATEGORY: Art

KEY FIGURES

Sandro Botticelli (Alessandro di Mariano dei Filipepi; c. 1444-1510), Italian artist

Michelangelo (1475-1564), Italian artist

Leonardo da Vinci (1452-1519), Italian artist, architect, scientist, and writer

Marsilio Ficino (1433-1499), founder of the Platonic Academy who translated the *Dialogues* of Plato

Giovanni Pico della Mirandola (1463-1494), eminent scholar among Italian Renaissance Humanists

SUMMARY OF EVENT

Two traditions basic to the Western mind, the classical and the Christian, have become so interwoven that to some extent they have always vied for expression in the fine arts. While classical writings embodying the general Hellenic values of antiquity remained an integral part of the medieval heritage, they were kept in a role more formal than inspirational. Christian humanism preferred to find a fresh outlet for itself in a new literature, architecture, painting, and sculpture.

Italian Humanists of the Renaissance period, searching for a secular consciousness in the models of antiquity, branded works of medieval Christian humanism barbaric and Gothic. Consequently, they cultivated a new interest in trying to understand Greek and Roman culture by studying antiquity's belles lettres for their aesthetic merit rather than for their instructional value in technique and form. Art at their hands showed awareness of humanity's

Sandro Botticelli's Primavera, *or* Allegory of Spring *(c. 1478), alludes to classical literature, mythology, religion, paganism, and grace.* (Royal Library, Windsor Castle)

creative powers and breathed a spirit of individualism and secularism that medieval corporatism and spiritualism had all but buried.

A love for the magnificent, stimulated by the affluence of the new rich, provided a spirit of luxury, splendor, and power. A thirst for immortality in the arts inspired creative individuals to initiate daring innovations in form and content. The classical inspiration was all about them. Neoplatonism came to be a sophisticated medium by which values were arbitrated. The old gods of antiquity were reinstated in their places on Mount Olympus as generous euhemeristic figures (deified mortals) responsible for Western civilization; even Protestant reformer Huldrych Zwingli believed that the faithful would see Hercules and Theseus in heaven. It became fashionable for Franks, Scandinavians, Normans, Italians, and Spaniards to associate their history with the noble Trojan cycle. The order of the Golden Fleece was founded in 1430. Popularity of the astrological zodiac helped to keep alive the mythology of the heavens. Even ancient hieroglyphs elicited a lively interest.

In the arts, Christian and pagan themes were irreverently blended. Bas-reliefs dared to display Adam and Hercules in alternate scenes. Pagan heroes, such as Jason, complemented biblical heroes, such as Gideon. Alongside traditional Christian portrayals of the Crucifixion, the Madonna, and the Nativity, painters set classical scenes featuring Jupiter (even as a monk), Apollo, Mercury, Venus, Juno, Diana, Mars, Narcissus, Saturn, Perseus, Bacchus, Vulcan, Cybele, Pan, and Eros, together with centaurs and other appropriate and familiar pagan figures. Allegorical paintings pictured the combat of Ratio and Libido, fitting symbols of the conflict of the Christian and the pagan ways of life.

All these classical themes of the neopagan Renaissance were depicted brilliantly with the aid of new techniques: brighter colors and attention to physical form, space, and perspective. The movement was facilitated by the rise of the affluent and generous patron, particularly conspicuous in the Medici family of Florence, the Athens of the Renaissance.

Typically representative of the painters who helped to revive the classical pagan themes was Alessandro di

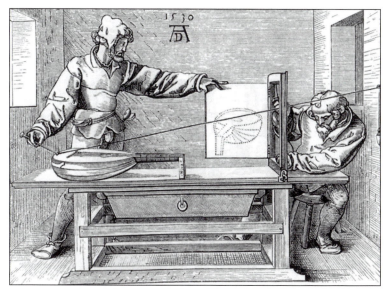

Classical themes in art were depicted with the aid of new techniques, including brighter colors and attention to physical form, space, and, as shown in this illustration, perspective by means of instruments of precision. (Frederick Ungar Publishing Co.)

Mariano dei Filipepi, better known as Sandro Botticelli (little barrel), an artist who was important enough to receive recognition from Leonardo da Vinci in his *Trattato della pittura* (1651; *A Treatise on Painting*, 1721). A pupil of Fra Filippo Lippi, Botticelli lived in a circle of erudite antiquarians who treasured equally the cadences of Vergilian lines and the artistry of Ciceronian periods. Like his contemporaries, he worked to resuscitate ancient masterpieces by seeking inspiration from a Philostatus or a Lucian. In communication with the Neoplatonists Marsilio Ficino, Giovanni Pico della Mirandola, and Politian (Angelo Ambrogini), Botticelli created an art form that aptly expressed the philosophy and sentiment of the Platonic Academy by appealing to religious desires that transcended sect.

While it is true that later in his career, under the influence of Girolamo Savonarola, Botticelli reverted to religious themes, iconographers see in his secular works a tantalizing intertwining of Christian themes with the mythology of antiquity. His works suggested to many the conflict between the pagan ideal, with its vision of earthly beauty, and the Christian ideal of a heavenly, beatific vision. His three Venuses, *Venus and Mars*, the *Birth of Venus*, and the *Primavera* (or *Allegory of Spring*), along with his *Pallas*, conceal equally well allusions to private events in the lives of the Medici and invitations to dwell in ethereal fields of abstraction. His noble, sublime, delicate nudes symbolized to him the "naked truth." A critic of medieval inspirational art questioning the proper artistic role of ethics and religion, he was a bold challenger of methodology and content. In the name of beauty, he felt free to tamper with space and perspective and to mistrust form as a sheer representation of nature. He challenged history as the sole dramatic figuration of human action, seeing antiquity as an ideal rather than a historical period.

SIGNIFICANCE

Through Botticelli, the Hellenic influences of the Renaissance penetrated the depths of Western art, leaving a lasting legacy. Along with Michelangelo and Leonardo da Vinci, Botticelli must be remembered for playing a significant role in the crystallization of the kind of art that is traditional in the West.

—*Dorothy Kinsella, updated by Ann Stewart Balakier*

FURTHER READING

Barkan, Leonard. *Unearthing the Past: Archaeology and Aesthetics in the Making of Renaissance Culture.* New Haven, Conn.: Yale University Press, 1999. Discusses the Renaissance discovery and excavation of buried works of classical art, and the influence of these pagan sculptures on Botticelli and other artists. Includes illustrations, bibliographic references, and index.

Baxandall, Michael. *Painting and Experience in Fifteenth Century Italy: A Primer in the Social History of Pictorial Style.* 2d ed. New York: Oxford University Press, 1988. Baxandall details the manner in which a style grew from the desire to consciously resurrect classical references.

Burckhardt, Jacob C. *The Civilization of the Renaissance in Italy.* Translated by S. B. Middlemore. Introduction by Peter Gay. Reprint. New York: Modern Library, 2002. Burckhardt's work continues to serve as the standard source that traces the change in cultural outlook from the medieval period into the Renaissance.

Ettlinger, Leopold David, and Helen S. Ettlinger. *Botticelli.* London: Thames & Hudson, 1976. This biography provides a still-useful discussion of Botticelli's role in Renaissance painting and the revival of classicism.

Gadol, Joan. "The Unity of the Renaissance: Humanism, Natural Science, and Art." In *From the Renaissance to the Counter-Reformation: Essays in Honor of Garrett*

Mattingly, edited by Charles Carter. New York: Random House, 1965. Gadol's article provides insight into the meaning of Idealism, which permeated the Florentine Academy and the works of artists of the Renaissance.

Hartt, Frederick. *History of Italian Renaissance Art: Painting, Sculpture, Architecture.* 5th ed. New York: H. N. Abrams, 2003. Revised by David G. Wilkins, this work constitutes a comprehensive and widely used survey of the period. Explores the theory and practice of the revival of classical themes.

Kanter, Laurence B., Hilliard T. Goldfarb, and James Hankins. *Botticelli's Witness: Changing Style in a Changing Florence.* Boston: Isabella Stewart Gardner Museum, 1997. An exhibition catalog that contains forty illustrations as well as three essays detailing the relationship of Botticelli's work to Florentine culture. It also surveys the history of Botticelli criticism.

Warburg, Aby. *The Renewal of Pagan Antiquity: Contributions to the Cultural History of the European Renaissance.* Translated by David Britt. Introduction by Kurt W. Forster. Los Angeles: Getty Research Institute for the History of Art and the Humanities, 1999. Collection of essays, originally written between 1893 and 1918, examining the resurgence of classical themes and pagan imagery in Renaissance art. Includes illustrations, maps, bibliographic references, and index.

Zöllner, Frank. *Botticelli: Images of Love and Spring.* Translated by Fiona Elliott. New York: Prestel, 1998. Interpretation of several famous Botticelli paintings, focusing on the artist's intent that they be hung in bridal chambers, as well as the influence of both classical and Renaissance iconography on the works. Includes illustrations and bibliographic references.

SEE ALSO: 1462: Founding of the Platonic Academy; 1469-1492: Rule of Lorenzo de' Medici; 1486-1487: Pico della Mirandola Writes *Oration on the Dignity of Man*; c. 1500: Netherlandish School of Painting.

RELATED ARTICLES in *Great Lives from History: The Renaissance & Early Modern Era, 1454-1600:* Andrea del Sarto; Giovanni Bellini; Sandro Botticelli; Correggio; Marsilio Ficino; Leonardo da Vinci; Cosimi I de' Medici; Lorenzo de' Medici; Michelangelo; Giovanni Pico della Mirandola; Piero della Francesca; Raphael; Sixtus IV.

c. 1500
RISE OF SARMATISM IN POLAND

Sarmatism, an ethno-genetic legend of the national origins of the Polish gentry, rose during the early sixteenth century and helped form the Polish national identity.

LOCALE: Poland and the Polish-Lithuanian Commonwealth (now Poland, Lithuania, Ukraine, Belarus, Latvia, Estonia, and portions of Russia)

CATEGORIES: Cultural and intellectual history; government and politics

KEY FIGURES
Maciej of Miechów (1457?-1523), Polish Renaissance physician, historian, and geographer
Marcin Bielski (1495-1575), Polish poet and chronicler

SUMMARY OF EVENT
Sarmatism began as an ethno-genetic legend about the Polish gentry's descent from the Sarmates, a warrior tribe originating in Asia, who migrated near Danube in the first century B.C.E. The term "Sarmatism" appeared in the linguistic circulation as late as the second half of eighteenth century and was propagated by prominent authors of the Enlightenment to disdain the "Sarmatian" culture of the Polish gentry. This culture, regarded as retrogressive and barbarian, was then decidedly after its heyday and did not go well with the reformist program of Stanisław II Augustus Poniatowski (r. 1764-1795), the last king of Poland. It can be said that Sarmatism may be considered a rich complex of phenomena concerning mentality, ideology, lifestyle, rhetoric, and art, and as such a complex it had previously existed, without being named. Temporal frames of this culture are defined between the late sixteenth and late eighteenth centuries. While some of its reflections survived during later periods, its roots lie in the late fifteenth and early sixteenth centuries.

The term "Sarmatism" originated in the use of the word "Sarmatia," an ancient Roman name for a region northeast of the Black Sea occupied by a people believed to be the ancestors of the Slavs and Poles. It first appeared in the chronicle of a late medieval Polish annalist, Jan Długosz, and was used increasingly after the beginning of the sixteenth century. The reason was certainly the *renovatio antiquorum* (the renaissance or revivification of matters of antiquity), which took ancient traditions, including the geographic nomenclature, very seriously. The term "Sarmatia" had also appeared in Ptolemy's *Geographike hyphegesis* (second century; commonly known as the *Geography*; *The Geography of Ptolemy . . .*, 1732) and Pomponius Mela's *De chorographia* (w. c. 43; *The Worke of Pomponius Mela*, 1585). The latter's work was published and commented upon in the early sixteenth century by Joachim Vadianus (von Watt), who had been to Poland and felt obliged to address the new view of "Sarmatia" in his commentary. Thus, for example, he wrote that despite Mela's information, there were several towns in Sarmatia.

The notion of Sarmatia became widespread owing to Maciej of Miechów, the author of a well-known work, *Tractatus de duabus Sarmatiis, Asiana, et Europiana* (1517; the treatise on both Sarmatias, the European and the Asiatic). Soon the term "Sarmatia" became a synonym for the whole of Sigismund I, the Old's state or simply for the Crown in general and hence for Poland. "Sarmatia" began to appear in maps and was also used in Western European works of cosmography (geography).

Although Maciej of Miechów supposed that the Poles descended from the Vandals, many sixteenth century historians accepted the Sarmatian legend of Polish origins. For instance, Marcin Bielski, the author of *Kronika wszytkiego świata* (1551; the chronicle of the whole world), popularized the Sarmatian legend, pointing to the military virtues of the Sarmates (or Sauromates), who, following a quasi-Greek etymology, would have been a people with "lizard eyes" (*sauros* + *omma*). Confirmed by a later generation of chroniclers and enriched with the connections to the Bible, antiquity, or simply confabulations, the Sarmatian myth became a synonym for national identity of the gentry of the "Commonwealth of Both Nations" (essentially Poland and Lithuania); it was in fact the first national consciousness of this society, a sort of "political nationhood." In this aspect Sarmatism had mainly a political and social function, integrating Poles, Lithuanians, and other groups under one umbrella. Eventually the townspeople also aspired to the ideology and lifestyle connoted by Sarmatia.

The Sarmatian consciousness, then, initially formed on the basis of European traditions and then isolated itself as a special and genuine culture. It was initially conspicuous ideologically and rhetorically, and later expressed itself in garb, lifestyle, and art. The fundamental components of this ideology were religious and political, seeing Poland as the *antemurale christianitatis* (first rampart of Christian religion), the bulwark of Europe against Islam. Although in the sixteenth century the kings of Poland preferred to preserve peace with the Turks, there was much rhetorical evidence of anti-Turkish sentiment, such as Stanisław Orzechowski's Latin speeches (1543-1544), which were immediately translated into Polish and then became very popular.

As Sarmatism developed, its association with the Roman Catholic Church strengthened, connected with a decrease in religious toleration and specific, spectacular forms of piety expressed in weddings, funerals, and celebrations of the anniversaries of battles. The "Polonization" of many saints followed and prepared the background for the Sarmatian messianic tradition.

Poland's "national dress," which took its form during the second half of the sixteenth century, was also an important component of the Sarmatian lifestyle. Persian and Turkish models, mostly by means of the Hungarian ones, were imitated. The zupan (a sort of gown), the kontusz (an upper garment), and the saber suspended on the belt were part of this costume and illustrated the growing Asian influence. Army uniforms and weapons, which were often imported from Turkey and Persia, also reflected this influence. This eastern influence was not contradicted by the rising Polish xenophobia, which was addressed mainly against Western European fashion. Sarmatism, with its ethno-genetic legends, therefore allowed the appropriation of Asian culture.

Sarmatism imposed several personal models as well: the ethos of the knight and citizen, and the ideal of the gentry as landowners (originally the equestrian class, the gentry became an agrarian society during the sixteenth century). Formed for the gentry, Sarmatism emphasized the role of its "golden liberty"; it separated the culture of the gentry from the that of the magnates, establishing a twofold ideological division within the society: that of the "genuine" Sarmatians, the gentry, and that of the "foreign" magnates.

SIGNIFICANCE

The sixteenth century Sarmatian consciousness of the gentry formed the background for the heyday of Sarmatism during the seventeenth century. By then, its most characteristic components had crystallized: the emphasis on the "golden liberty," the defense of Catholicism, ceremonial and spectacular forms of cult and piety, xenophobia, and Asian modes of dress, lifestyle, architecture, and art. Many contradictions appeared soon in this cultural and political formation of the gentry. This class, having commenced with democratic ideals, gradually plunged into anarchy and was easily manipulated by magnate oligarchy.

In Enlightenment thought, the term "Sarmatism" became a synonym for the barbarian and backward mentality of the Polish gentry. By 1791, however, a personal model of the *illuminatus Sarmata* appeared. This attitude propagated respect for genuine tradition and patriotism. In the nineteenth century, the Romantic authors often idealized the Sarmatian lifestyle, regarding Sarmatism as the equivalent of old Polish culture. Because during the nineteenth century the state of Poland practically did not exist in the political sense, Sarmatism kept the image of Poland alive. Even today several Sarmatian ideas are respected among some circles of Polish society, and a Sarmatian nostalgia may be felt among the older generations of Polish emigrants.

—*Elwira Buszewicz*

FURTHER READING

Długosz, Jan. *The Annals*. Translated and abridged by Maurice Michael, with commentary by Paul Smith. Charlton, West Sussex, England: MI, 1997. Reprints material from the best-known late medieval chronicle of Poland (1480), translated from its Latin original. Introduces readers to several basic historical and geographical notions at the dawn of Humanism in Poland and to several ideas of culture and ideology of Polish gentry.

Pasek, Jan Chryzostom. *Memoirs*. Translated by M. Swiecicka-Ziemianek. New York: Kosciuzko Foundation, 1979. The memoirs of Pasek, a seventeenth century Polish noble, are regarded as the best example of the Sarmatian mentality.

Tazbir, Janusz. *Poland: A Rampart of Christian Europe.* Warsaw: Interpress, 1987. Addresses an important element of Sarmatian ideology, the idea of the *antemurale Christianitatis*.

Wasko, Andrzej. "Sarmatism or the Enlightenment: The Dilemma of Polish Culture." *Sarmatian Review* 17, no. 2 (April, 1997). Examines the phenomenon of Sarmatism from a broader temporal, cultural, and political perspective and helps reveal which features of this ideology may be regarded as still valid in contemporary Polish culture.

SEE ALSO: Oct. 19, 1466: Second Peace of Thorn; 1499-c. 1600: Russo-Polish Wars; 1557-1582: Livonian War; Nov., 1575: Stephen Báthory Becomes King of Poland.
RELATED ARTICLES in *Great Lives from History: The Renaissance & Early Modern Era, 1454-1600*: Sigismund I, the Old; Sigismund II Augustus; Stephen Báthory.

1500
ROMAN JUBILEE

A series of brief but eventful pontificates served in combination to strengthen the Papal States politically, administratively, and militarily, but did little to address the problems in the religious institution of the Church that would soon lead to the Protestant Reformation.

LOCALE: Rome (now in Italy)
CATEGORIES: Religion; government and politics; cultural and intellectual history

KEY FIGURES

Alexander VI (Rodrigo de Borja y Doms; 1431-1503), Roman Catholic pope, 1492-1503
Cesare Borgia (1475/1476-1507), Italian military leader and politician, son of Alexander
Lucrezia Borgia (1480-1519), Italian noblewoman, daughter of Alexander
Pius III (Francesco Todeschini Piccolomini; c. 1440-1503), Roman Catholic pope, 1503
Julius II (Giuliano della Rovere; 1443-1513), Roman Catholic pope, 1503-1513
Nicolaus Copernicus (1473-1543), Polish astronomer
Michelangelo (1475-1564), Italian painter and sculptor
Charles VIII (1470-1498), king of France, r. 1483-1498

SUMMARY OF EVENT

On Christmas Eve, 1499, Pope Alexander VI was carried in procession to the old St. Peter's Basilica in Rome. Surrounded by the cardinals and other clergy of Rome, he solemnly opened the holy door, thereby signaling the opening of the Jubilee, or Holy Year, of 1500.

The Jubilee was an institution then two hundred years old. Supposedly celebrated at the beginning of each century, it had in fact been held more frequently and at irregular intervals. The Jubilee was conceived as a public expression of faith and repentance of sin. Christians from all over Europe were encouraged to make a pilgrimage to Rome, visit the four major basilicas of the city, recite certain prayers, and receive as a result a plenary indulgence—that is, the complete forgiveness of all past sins and the removal of all punishments attached to them, including punishments in the afterlife.

Throngs of people visited Rome during 1500, despite the fact that wars were raging in the north of Italy and plague had erupted in several places. Among those who came was astronomer Nicolaus Copernicus, then a young man, who stayed to give lectures for a year. The artist Michelangelo was also present. Large sums of money were collected, partly to finance a crusade against the Turks that never materialized.

Two other persons in Rome during the Jubilee whose presence cast something of a shadow over the proceedings were Cesare and Lucrezia Borgia, children of Pope Alexander, who were famous for their avarice, their ambition, and the intrigues in which their father gave them complete support. Lucrezia was successively the wife of three noblemen, marriages carefully arranged by Alexander; she was later suspected of poisoning her husbands, although the legends are probably untrue.

Cesare was cruel and ruthless; his obsession was the establishment of a Borgia state in northern Italy. He received money and troops from his father and went on several campaigns throughout the Italian peninsula, conquering some minor city-states and threatening the independence of the greater ones. His aggressions ended only with his father's death.

Pope Alexander himself was perhaps the most notorious prelate ever to occupy the papal throne. A Spaniard by birth, Rodrigo de Borja y Doms had decided on a clerical career only after his uncle Alfonso was elected pope as Calixtus III in 1455. Rodrigo became a cardinal the following year at the age of twenty-five, and for the remainder of his life he was intimately involved in the government of the Church at the highest level. He was not ordained a priest until 1468, by which time he had already obtained appointments to a large number of ecclesiastical benefices, including several archbishoprics, and had become enormously wealthy.

Rodrigo's sexual morals were notorious, and on one occasion his scandalous conduct provoked a strong rebuke from Pope Pius II. His permanent mistress was a Roman noblewoman, Vannozza Catanei, who bore him four children, including Cesare and Lucrezia.

Several times Rodrigo was seriously considered for the papacy, and he was finally elected Pope Alexander VI on August 11, 1492. There were accusations of bribery in connection with the election, although the charges have never been proven. Alexander had in fact been an extremely capable and conscientious administrator of papal properties, and his election met with general approval.

Alexander VI continued to administer the possessions of the Church with care and ability, but he also became more deeply involved in Italian politics, partly from a de-

261

sire to provide for his children. Beginning in 1494, Italy was menaced by invasions by the French, the Germans, and Swiss mercenary soldiers, all seeking to carve out empires amid the chaos of the city-states. Alexander skillfully threaded his way among the diplomatic intrigues and military adventures of his pontificate.

In terms of religion, little of note happened during Alexander's pontificate, except for the Jubilee and a few proceedings against heresy. Throughout Europe, there was growing dissatisfaction with the corruptions and abuses of all kinds that afflicted the Church, but Alexander showed little interest in such problems.

He died August 18, 1503, probably of fever, although there were unfounded charges that he had been poisoned. After the brief pontificate of Pius III, the cardinals elected Cardinal Giuliano della Rovere, who had also been a candidate in 1492 and who took the name Julius II. The new pope's career paralleled Alexander's in several respects. He also had entered the Church under the tutelage of an uncle who became pope (Sixtus IV, 1471-

1484). He was made a cardinal at the age of twenty-eight and amassed a large collection of lucrative benefices. He built magnificent palaces, patronized the arts, and fathered three daughters.

Julius's career diverged from Alexander's in that his major interest was not administration or diplomacy but war. When he was a cardinal, he commanded papal armies in battle on a number of occasions, despite prohibitions in canon law against priests bearing arms. He and Alexander had a strong dislike for each other, and della Rovere spent most of Alexander's pontificate on French soil; at one time he managed to persuade King Charles VIII of France to invade Italy with the intention of dethroning Alexander, but a peaceful settlement was arranged.

After the death of Pius III, Julius was elected in the shortest papal conclave on record. He distributed bribes liberally to obtain the papal office, although he later showed some concern about abuses in the Church and issued bulls against bribery.

The Roman Jubilee, or Holy Year, of 1500, began at the old St. Peter's Basilica in Rome after Pope Alexander VI opened its doors. (R. S. Peale and J. A. Hill)

Julius's pontificate is memorable for three occurrences: the laying of the cornerstone of the new St. Peter's Basilica in 1506, the expulsion of the French from Italy with the pope himself commanding the armies, and the summoning of the Fifth Lateran Council in 1512 to deal systematically with abuses in the Church.

Julius died on February 21, 1513, not long after the council had convened. His successor was Cardinal Giovanni de' Medici, then thirty-eight years old, who took the name Leo X. Leo was the son of Lorenzo de' Medici (the Magnificent), ruler of Florence, and had risen to prominence almost entirely through family connections. Unlike Alexander and Julius, he had unimpeachable personal morals and was without scandal. However, he was weak, he loved luxury, and his rule is largely remembered for his patronage of the arts and the beginning of the Reformation. The Fifth Lateran Council continued to meet until 1517, shortly before Martin Luther's posting of the Ninety-five Theses on the church door at Wittenberg, but it accomplished little toward alleviating the many problems that afflicted the Church.

SIGNIFICANCE

The late fifteenth and early sixteenth centuries witnessed, in quick succession, the papacies of Alexander VI, a notoriously immoral man who was nonetheless conscientious and skilled in his administration of the Papal States, and Julius II, a militarily minded and gifted leader who came to be known as the Warrior Pope. These two men were in significant measure responsible both for the fact that the Italian peninsula was opened to foreign conquest in the wake of the French invasion and for the manner in which the Papal States reacted to this event. Julius, in particular, had first encouraged France to invade Italy in a failed bid to place himself on the papal throne and then helped to drive the French forces from the peninsula once he had ascended that throne. Alexander and Julius helped to make Rome both an artistic center of the Renaissance and a political and military power to be reckoned with. They failed, however, to recognize the importance of a pervasive and growing discontent with the corruption of the Catholic Church, a discontent that would soon find a voice in the person of Martin Luther.

—*James F. Hitchcock*

FURTHER READING

Beck, James H. *Three Worlds of Michelangelo*. New York: W. W. Norton, 1999. One of these three interconnected studies of Michelangelo is an analysis of his relationship to Julius II. Includes illustrations, bibliographic references, and index.

Chamberlin, Russell. *The Bad Popes*. Stroud, Gloucestershire, England: Sutton, 2003. Alexander VI is one of seven popes profiled in this study of papal corruption across the six hundred years leading up to the Reformation. Includes photographs, illustrations, genealogical tables, bibliographic references, and index.

Creighton, M. M. *A History of the Papacy from the Great Schism to the Sack of Rome*. Vols. 4-5. New ed. New York: Longmans, Green, 1919. This old work by an Anglican bishop is a balanced appraisal of the Renaissance popes and comes closer than Ferrara's book to the commonly accepted views of modern scholars.

De Roo, Peter. *Material for a History of Pope Alexander VI, His Relatives, and His Time*. 5 vols. New York: Universal Knowledge Foundation, 1924. This work by a Catholic priest is highly favorable to Alexander and has not been generally accepted by modern scholars.

Ferrara, Orestes. *The Borgia Pope: Alexander the Sixth*. New York: Sheed and Ward, 1940. Attempts to salvage Alexander's reputation from the almost universally low esteem in which it has been held by modern scholars.

Mathew, Arnold H. *The Life and Times of Rodrigo Borgia*. London: S. Paul, 1924. This book by an archbishop of a schismatic branch of the Roman Catholic Church is generally unfavorable to Alexander but is scholarly and balanced to some extent.

Pastor, Ludwig. *The History of the Popes from the Close of the Middle Ages*. Translated by Frederick I. Antrobus. Vols. 5-6. Reprint. Wilmington, N.C.: Consortium, 1978. This nineteenth century work by a Catholic scholar is the most thorough history of the modern papacy. Its judgments of Alexander and Julius are balanced and generally unfavorable.

Shaw, Christine. *Julius II: The Warrior Pope*. Cambridge, Mass.: Blackwell, 1996. Primarily a very useful political history of Julius's tenure as pope, this volume also contains a chapter on his patronage of the arts, but it is weak on theological analysis. Includes photographic plates, illustrations, bibliographic references, and index.

Signorotto, Gianvittorio, and Maria Antonietta Visceglia, eds. *Court and Politics in Papal Rome, 1492-1700*. New York: Cambridge University Press, 2002. Collection of essays on the papal court and political structures and intrigues. Places Alexander VI's pa-

1500's

pacy as a turning point in the relative power of pope and cardinals and analyzes the *possesso* ceremony in the sixteenth century. Includes bibliographic references and index.

Stinger, Charles L. *The Renaissance in Rome.* Bloomington: Indiana University Press, 1998. Study of the resurgence of Rome's cultural, religious, and political importance in the Renaissance. Includes maps, illustrations, bibliographic references, and index.

SEE ALSO: 1477-1482: Work Begins on the Sistine Chapel; Sept., 1494-Oct., 1495: Charles VIII of France Invades Italy; 1508-1512 and 1534-1541: Michelan-

gelo Paints the Sistine Chapel; Apr. 11, 1512: Battle of Ravenna; Sept. 13-14, 1515: Battle of Marignano; 1521-1559: Valois-Habsburg Wars; Feb., 1525: Battle of Pavia; May 6, 1527-Feb., 1528: Sack of Rome; July 15, 1542-1559: Paul III Establishes the *Index of Prohibited Books*; Apr. 3, 1559: Treaty of Cateau-Cambrésis; July 22, 1566: Pius V Expels the Prostitutes from Rome; 1567: Palestrina Publishes the *Pope Marcellus Mass.*

RELATED ARTICLES in *Great Lives from History: The Renaissance & Early Modern Era, 1454-1600:* Alexander VI; Cesare Borgia; Lucrezia Borgia; Charles VIII; Nicolaus Copernicus; Julius II; Michelangelo.

1500-1530's
PORTUGAL BEGINS TO COLONIZE BRAZIL

Portugal launched the growth of an overseas Portuguese empire in South America after colonizing what is now called Brazil.

LOCALE: Brazil

CATEGORIES: Colonization; expansion and land acquisition; exploration and discovery

KEY FIGURES

Pedro Álvares Cabral (c. 1467-1520), Portuguese discoverer of Brazil

Martim Afonso de Sousa (c. 1500-1564), commander of the colonizing expedition of 1530

Tomé de Sousa (c. 1515-1573), captain-general of Brazil and leader of the colonizing expedition of 1549

Manuel I (1469-1521), king of Portugal, r. 1495-1521, who asserted Portuguese control of Brazil

John III (1502-1557), king of Portugal, r. 1521-1557, who authorized the *donatário* system of development

SUMMARY OF EVENT

Pedro Álvares Cabral, the commander of the second fleet to India, sailed farther west than previous expeditions and discovered Brazil on May 8, 1500. Cabral founded the port of Cobralia (located 303 miles [488 kilometers] north of what is now Porto Seguro) and left ashore two *degredados*, men who were stranded as punishment, and two boys who hid on shore. After investigating a short time and losing a few men to the indigenous people, he sent Gaspar de Lemos in the supply ship back to Portugal to inform King Manuel I that he had discovered a large is-

land on the Portuguese side of the line of demarcation. The king intended to assert control over the "new discovery" and informed Spain of his intentions.

Whether Cabral was the first to discover Brazil is uncertain. Probably Christopher Columbus, Alonso de Ojeda, and Amerigo Vespucci had touched territory included in the modern boundaries of Brazil. Vespucci did make two voyages to Brazil, the first in 1501 and the second in 1503. The question of previous Portuguese explorations cannot be settled. In 1501, Fernão de Noronha, a wealthy nobleman of Jewish descent, received permission to establish a profitable trade that attracted some New Christians to Brazil.

Portugal was not the only nation showing an interest in the area. The French king encouraged shipmasters from Normandy and Brittany to exploit Brazil. For some time, it appeared that France, and not Portugal, would settle Brazil. The area was so large, however, that both nations could exploit Brazilian wood and other resources without intruding in the territory of the other. England satisfied its interest in the area by occasional trading expeditions.

The Portuguese had to fight with the French and the indigenous peoples. The South American Indians were divided into numerous mutually hostile tribes with differing languages and customs. They fought one another regularly. The Europeans were able to establish friendly relations with some tribes by assisting them in defeating their hereditary enemies. The French were especially effective in winning indigenous allies.

Trade increased and Brazil became more profitable

when the Europeans were able to barter with the indigenous for labor in cutting, dressing, and loading log wood. Although the Europeans wanted to enslave the natives, barter was more reliable. Later labor needs were satisfied by importing African slaves.

Early Portuguese sailors, traders, and *degredados* often took indigenous wives and mistresses; the mixed-blood offspring of these unions were known as mamelukes. As the mameluke population grew, the Portuguese found it easier to settle the coast and establish control.

After coming to the throne in 1521, King John III realized that he needed to devote greater effort to control Brazil. In 1530, he sent a five-ship expedition, with a combined crew of about four hundred men under the command of Martim Afonso de Sousa, to drive out the French and develop a plan of settlement. Sousa established a colony rather than a trading post at São Vicente, not far from the modern city of Santos. He suggested to his sovereign a plan to create a strong colony in Brazil. Conditions seemed to be favorable for Sousa's plan. Overexpansion in India had reduced Portuguese trade opportunities there, and Spain had plans to develop the Río de la Plata area of South America (between what is now Argentina and Uruguay).

The plan was a mixture of feudalism and capitalism. It called for dividing Brazil into fifteen captaincies of varying size extending from the coast west to the papal line of demarcation. Twelve of the captaincies were awarded to wealthy men, called *donatários*, who were to finance the settlement, defense, and development of their captaincies. *Donatários* had the power to rule their captaincies and to subgrant, collect taxes, and administer justice. The Portuguese crown reserved to itself some rights, especially fiscal, and guaranteed some rights to the colonists. The grants were hereditary, and the captaincies could trade with Catholic foreigners.

The captaincy system, however, did not develop as planned. Between 1534 and 1549, six captaincies were established, but only two were successful. The most successful of the *donatários* was Duarte Coelho, who was granted the captaincy of Pernambuco. By 1675, his son was the wealthiest man in Brazil, drawing revenues from quitrents, fifty sugar mills, and many sugar estates. Less profitable was Martim Afonso de Sousa's own São

PORTUGAL'S BRAZILIAN COLONIES

Amazon R.

BRAZIL

Natal

Rio de Janeiro
São Paolo

Parana R.

Asunción

Atlantic

Ocean

Buenos Aires

Spanish settlements

Portuguese settlements

Vicente. Within a dozen years, all but three of the captaincies were bankrupt. The resources of an individual *donatário* were insufficient to sustain a colony.

Colonists complained of abuse at the hands of the *donatários*, the Catholic Church protested the enslavement of the natives, the French were still active in Brazil, and Spanish settlement along the Pacific coast and in the Río de la Plata area surrounded Brazil. Although the *donatário* system was abandoned, the plan was not a

1500's

complete failure. Some settlers went to Brazil, towns were created, and farms and businesses were established.

In 1549, John III sent six ships commanded by Tomé de Sousa, an extremely capable officer, to assume control of the twelve captaincies that had failed or were never started as well as São Vicente and Pernambuco. With him went one thousand colonists, soldiers, and *degredados*. Shortly afterward, the queen sent shiploads of orphan girls to become wives of the settlers. Sousa was ordered to make the colony pay, stop the enslavement of the local people, and keep the French out. For the most part, he was able to accomplish his tasks.

Captain-General Sousa established the capital at Bahia, later known as Salvador. Bahia had a fine natural harbor and was halfway between the rapidly expanding São Paulo and the sugar producing Pernambuco, the two areas that became most populated and wealthy. He was unable to resolve the problem of labor. Although the Crown and the Catholic Church opposed enslavement of the indigenous, the colonists, who would not perform the necessary work themselves, concluded slavery was the only answer, since the indigenous would not work voluntarily.

SIGNIFICANCE

In 1549, Sousa had brought with him six members of the Society of Jesus (the Jesuits), headed by Manuel de Nóbrega. The Jesuits were successful in converting the coastal peoples, settling them in villages, and encouraging them to adopt Western customs. While Father Nóbrega worked successfully in the north, his fellow Jesuit, José de Anchieta, was successful in the south. The indigenous in church settlements were protected by the Jesuits and thus were not available as laborers for the colonists.

Importation of slaves from Africa began in the 1530's and became extensive by the 1570's. Enslavement of Africans provided the labor needed by the colonists and satisfied the moral opposition to enslavement of the indigenous peoples by the Crown and the Church.

Between 1555 and 1567, the captain-general and the Jesuits, leading an indigenous army, expelled the French Huguenot settlement at Rio de Janeiro led by the great French Huguenot leader Admiral Nicholas Durand de Villegaignon.

Between 1631 and 1654, the Dutch West Indies Company occupied some twelve hundred miles of the Brazilian coast between Bahia and Maranhão. The Brazilians rose up against the Dutch and compelled them to evacuate Brazil. Since that time, Brazilians have interpreted their success as an early manifestation of nationalistic feelings.

In spite of the activities of other nations, Portugal was able to retain the colony of Brazil until independence was declared in the early nineteenth century.

—*Robert D. Talbott*

FURTHER READING

Diffie, Bailey W. *A History of Colonial Brazil, 1500-1792*. Malabar, Fla.: Robert E. Krieger, 1987. Written by one of the eminent historians of Brazil. Good coverage of the early period and highly readable.

Graubard, Mark. *English and Irish Settlement on the River Amazon, 1500-1646*. Edited by Joyce Lorimer. London: Hakluyt Society, 1989. A brief account of the activities of the English and Irish in Brazil.

Keen, Benjamin, and Keith Haynes. *A History of Latin America*. 6th ed. Vol. 1. Boston: Houghton Mifflin, 2000. Good survey by a well-known historian of Latin America. Readable, with good illustrations.

Macdonald, N. P. *The Making of Brazil: Portuguese Roots, 1500-1822*. Sussex, England: Book Guild, 1996. History of the precolonization and founding of Brazil, written as a prehistory of the modern state, and emphasizing the contribution of disparate peoples—Portuguese, Brazilian Indians, and Africans—to the complex Brazilian culture that eventually developed. Includes photographic plates, illustrations, maps, bibliographic references, and an index.

Magalháes, Pedro de. *The Histories of Brazil*. Translated by John B. Stetson, Jr. 1922. Reprint. Boston: Longwood Press, 1978. Written in 1576 by a Brazilian colonist, this work includes natural history as well as history of the colony and captaincies.

Marchant, Alexander. *From Barter to Slavery: The Economic Relations of Portugal and Indians in the Settlement of Brazil*. 1942. Reprint. Gloucester, Mass.: P. Smith, 1966. Details the relations between the Portuguese and the South American Indians until black slaves became common.

O'Malley, John W. *The First Jesuits*. Cambridge, Mass.: Harvard University Press, 1993. This outstanding work on the early years of the Society of Jesus provides an excellent account of the role of the Jesuits in Portugal and its territories.

Russell-Wood, A. J. R. *Portuguese Empire, 1415-1808: A World on the Move*. Baltimore: Johns Hopkins University Press, 1998. A history of the expansion of the Portuguese empire, with particular attention to the individuals involved in the voyages that culminated in a Portuguese presence in the four corners of the world.

Schwartz, Stuart B. "Magistracy and Society in Colonial

Brazil." In *Administrators of Empire*, edited by Mark A. Burkholder. Brookfield, Vt.: Ashgate, 1998. Study of the Portuguese colonial administration in Brazil and its effects on the society of both the colonizers and the colonized. Includes illustrations, map, bibliographic references, and index.

Sweet, James H. *Recreating Africa: Culture, Kinship, and Religion in the African-Portuguese World, 1441-1770*. Chapel Hill: University of North Carolina Press, 2003. Study of the African religions, traditions, and other cultural elements that were imported to Brazil by the Portuguese slave trade. Includes illustrations, maps, bibliographic references, and index.

SEE ALSO: Oct. 12, 1492: Columbus Lands in the Americas; June 7, 1494: Treaty of Tordesillas; 1532-1537: Pizarro Conquers the Incas in Peru; 1537: Pope Paul III Declares Rights of New World Peoples; 1552: Las Casas Publishes *The Tears of the Indians*; 1565: Spain Seizes the Philippines; Sept. 14, 1585-July 27, 1586: Drake's Expedition to the West Indies.

RELATED ARTICLES in *Great Lives from History: The Renaissance & Early Modern Era, 1454-1600:* José de Acosta; Sebastian Cabot; Thomas Cavendish; Bartolomeu Dias; Sir Francis Drake; John II; John III; Bartolomé de Las Casas; Manuel I; Francisco Pizarro; Amerigo Vespucci; Saint Francis Xavier.

Early 16th century
ATHAPASKANS ARRIVE IN THE SOUTHWEST

Athapaskan peoples concluded their migratory journey from Western Canada and spread out to occupy much of the American Southwest.

LOCALE: American Southwest
CATEGORIES: Anthropology; expansion and land acquisition

SUMMARY OF EVENT

In the American Southwest today there are seven recognized Southern Athapaskan (Apachean-speaking) groups: Navajo, Chiricahua, Jicarilla, Kiowa-Apache, Lipan, Mescalaro, and Western Apache. The term Apachean includes Navajo and Apache peoples, as opposed to Apache, which excludes the Navajo. The Apacheans now live in parts of eastern Arizona, New Mexico, Colorado, Utah, Oklahoma, Texas, and Mexico. Their southwestern territories may have been more extensive in the past. Scholars agree that these peoples originated from the large group of Athapaskan speakers in the Mackenzie Basin of Canada. These Canadian Athapaskans along with those in Alaska are referred to as the Northern Athapaskans.

Most scholars believe that the Athapaskan migration from Canada concluded in the early 1500's, and that the various Apachean groups began to separate from one another soon thereafter. These groups quickly spread out across the American Southwest and settled in the distinct territories in which European explorers would later encounter them. The Kiowa-Apache branched off from the Lipan and Jicarilla and moved east onto the southern Plains, ending up in Oklahoma. The Western Apache and the Navajo, meanwhile, moved west and south into what is now the "Four Corners" region of Arizona, New Mexico, Colorado, and Utah. By 1600, the Lipan and Jicarilla no longer had contact with the Western Apache or the Navajo. Within the next hundred years, the Lipan and Jicarilla themselves divided. The Lipan moved into central and southern Texas and the Jicarilla into northern New Mexico and southern Colorado. The Chiricahua and Mescalero were probably the last to split from each other. Eventually the Chiricahua moved into southwestern New Mexico, southeastern Arizona, and northern Mexico, while the Mescalero settled farther east, reaching into part of Texas. The Apacheans were in these areas when the Spaniards arrived.

While there is no conclusive proof that Apachean habitation in these territories began in the 1500's, a preponderance of evidence seems to support this belief. This evidence exists, for example, within the surviving oral traditions of the modern tribes, as well as the specific patterns of differentiation between the Apachean languages. The date also seems to accord with what little is known of the historical circumstances of precolonial North America. Moreover, no Apachean archaeological evidence found in the Southwest can be reliably dated to earlier than 1525.

Despite this evidence, however, the theory that the Athapaskans entered the American Southwest in the early sixteenth century is not without controversy. Some scholars argue that the Apacheans were present in the Southwest by 1400 or even earlier. Two scholars have even proposed that the Navajos arrived before 1100 and intermarried with the Anasazi (ancestral Pueblo peoples).

Arguably the best data to use in an attempt to resolve this controversy are linguistic. It is clear that all Athapaskan people, Northern and Southern, have a common ancestral language. All Athapaskan peoples refer to themselves as Diné, "the People." The Navajo speak of their first home in northwestern New Mexico as Dinetah (among the People), compared with Denedah, which carries the same meaning in the languages of the North.

Southern Athapaskan languages diverge from one another much less than the languages of the Northern Athapaskans, and the Northern variations are about equal to those of the Athapaskan language family as a whole. This factor and other linguistic considerations, particularly semantic shift, support the view that the north is the center of dispersal, and that the Southern group spread out and developed different languages considerably later than the beginnings of Athapaskan language diversity.

There is cultural as well as linguistic evidence that the Southern Apacheans have Northern origins. Details of the circumstances of death and burial indicate that all Apacheans are similar in their funerary beliefs and practices, suggesting that they share a similar history. All fear the ghosts of the recently dead, for example, unlike their Pueblo neighbors. Furthermore, the Southern ceremonial emphasis on bodily health and curing has roots in Northern Athapaskan shamanism. The Apache share other practices and beliefs with those in the North, including a concept of power gained from nonhuman helpers, the girls' puberty ceremony, and a belief that disease is caused by contact with certain animals such as the bear, or with lightning.

The cultural similarities among Apachean groups, their range of linguistic diversity, and the fact that the groups all migrated southward from an original northern homeland are about the only things universally agreed on for the Southern Athapaskans. Scholars have differing opinions about the amount of time involved in the move south, the route or routes followed, and whether more than one migration took place.

Most scholars believe that the Southern Apacheans began their southward move about 1000, and that the linguistic evidence indicates that until 1300 the Apacheans were a single group or a number of closely related groups; that is, they did not begin to differentiate themselves linguistically until three hundred years after the start of the move. This linguistic divergence indicates that other aspects of their life also began to change around 1300. The group probably divided and moved in varying directions, absorbing different cultural patterns from their neighbors or developing new ones based on their changing circumstances. Most scholars believe that once the Apacheans reached the Southwest, their linguistic and political differentiation proceeded rather rapidly, and that by the beginning of the eighteenth century they were distinct nations.

Some Apachean languages are more closely related than others. The most closely related are Navajo, Western Apache, Chiricahua, and Mescalero. A few linguists believe that these groups left Western Canada well before the other groups. Other scholars believe that the groups all split from each other sometime within the past thousand years, and that they migrated south by different routes, developing different languages and cultures along the way. Still others, in opposition to the linguistic data noted above, think that the Apacheans arrived in the Southwest as a more or less homogeneous group and then divided once they got there.

There are two differing hypotheses concerning the route that the migrating Athapaskans took south. One group of scholars argues that the Athapaskans came through the mountains by way of today's states of Utah or Colorado and the Great Basin. The second theory states that they moved south through the northwestern and central plains close to the eastern edge of the mountains. It is conceivable that both of these suggestions are correct; if the Apacheans migrated at varying times, it is possible that different groups used different routes. It would be easier to determine the route if the reasons for the migration or migrations were clear, but they are not. One possible explanation for the move is that when bison herds increased, following the severe droughts of the 1400's, the Apacheans followed the animals down through the Great Plains. If this were true, it would speak in favor of a migration route east of the Rocky Mountains.

A resolution to the route question might also be available if there were clear archaeological sites that could be identified as Athapaskan, but because the Apacheans were almost exclusively mobile hunters and gatherers before the coming of Europeans, archaeological evidence is meager. (Some people have argued that the Apacheans were already agriculturalists when they entered the Southwest, but the evidence for this assertion is weak.) Archaeologists have gleaned little information in this regard from sites that are hundreds of years old, even if they can find tipi rings, roasting pits, and buffalo kill sites.

In northwestern New Mexico, there are some sites where remains of dwellings can be reliably ascribed to the Navajo. Archaeologists have located forked-stick hogans with tripod bases (an early house form that the Navajo continued to use after contact). Dendrochronology indicates that these hogans date to the late fifteenth and early sixteenth centuries. Even the remains of hogans, however, do not give clear information after three hundred years. The hogans may not have been the earliest form of Navajo housing, and other Apachean groups may have entered the Southwest before the Navajos. Therefore, the remains of these hogans in no way indicate that their inhabitants were the earliest settlers in the area.

The shared heritage of the Athapaskans did not prevent them from developing new and significantly different beliefs and practices. Major departures from Apachean cultural patterns can generally be explained by interaction with non-Apachean peoples, primarily the Pueblo groups in Arizona and New Mexico. Apacheans almost certainly learned weaving and pottery from their neighbors (possibly on the journey south). Early cloaks, for example, suggest that Navajo women learned weaving from their Pueblo neighbors. It is also likely that the masked dancers of the Navajo and some Apache groups, including "clowns," originated with Pueblo groups. However, it is important to note that none of the Apacheans ever simply imitated Pueblo behaviors. Rather, they adapted these features to conform to their own beliefs and interests.

SIGNIFICANCE

The Southern Athapaskans have played a central role in the history, and changed the character, of the American Southwest. Their relations with older Native American tribes in the area and with Europeans were influenced by their ancestry in the North. The Apache are known for their fierce fighting qualities and, along with the Navajo, they preyed on the Pueblo peoples and later the Spanish. When the United States acquired land from Mexico in the mid-nineteenth century, Apachean lands were in the path of western expansion. Their complex religions, ceremonies, and artworks have added cultural and religious dimensions to Southwestern life. During the 1600's, both Navajo and Apache traded, fought, and intermarried with Pueblo people, and intermarriage between Apacheans and other Indians and Euro-Americans has continued.

—*Zena Pearlstone*

FURTHER READING

Forbes, Jack D. *Apache, Navajo, and Spaniard.* 2d ed. Norman: University of Oklahoma Press, 1994. This history of the Southern Athapascans is based on written documents, and therefore primarily covers the period beginning with their encounters with the Spanish. Goes through 1698. Includes illustrations, maps, bibliographic references, and index.

Foster, Michael K. "Language and the Culture History of North America." In *Languages*, edited by Ives Goddard. Vol. 17 in *Handbook of North American Indians*, edited by William C. Sturtevant. Washington, D.C.: Smithsonian Institution, 1996. Discusses the interrelationship of language and culture.

Haskell, J. Loring. *Southern Athapaskan Migration, A.D. 200-1750.* Tsaile, Ariz.: Navajo Community College Press, 1987. An account of the forebears of the Southern Athapaskans through 1750.

Opler, Morris E. "The Apachean Culture Pattern and Its Origins." In *Southwest*, edited by Alfonso Ortiz. Vol. 10 in *Handbook of North American Indians*, edited by William C. Sturtevant. Washington, D.C.: Smithsonian Institution, 1983. Discusses the origins of the Apacheans and provides highlights of their cultures.

Young, Robert W. "Apachean Languages." In *Southwest*, edited by Alfonso Ortiz. Vol. 10 in *Handbook of North American Indians*, edited by William C. Sturtevant. Washington, D.C.: Smithsonian Institution, 1983. Apachean language origins and development are detailed.

SEE ALSO: 16th cent.: Decline of Moundville; 16th cent.: Iroquois Confederacy Is Established; 1502-1520: Reign of Montezuma II; Beginning 1519: Smallpox Kills Thousands of Indigenous Americans; 1525-1532: Huáscar and Atahualpa Share Inca Rule; 1528-1536: Narváez's and Cabeza de Vaca's Expeditions; 1537: Pope Paul III Declares Rights of New World Peoples; Feb. 23, 1540-Oct., 1542: Coronado's Southwest Expedition; Mid-1570's: Powhatan Confederacy Is Founded; Jan., 1598-Feb., 1599: Oñate's New Mexico Expedition.

RELATED ARTICLES in *Great Lives from History: The Renaissance & Early Modern Era, 1454-1600:* Álvar Núñez Cabeza de Vaca; Francisco Vásquez de Coronado; Hernando de Soto.

1500's

Early 16th century
DEVOTIONAL BHAKTI TRADITIONS EMERGE

Religious teachers used bhakti, a Hindu practice of devotion to the divine, to synthesize Hinduism and Sufi Islam and further develop Sikhism. With vernacular poetry, storytelling, and music they transcended traditional boundaries of creed, caste, and gender and gave voice to marginalized peoples, thereby challenging religious and social convention.

LOCALE: Northern India

CATEGORIES: Religion; cultural and intellectual history; literature; education; organizations and institutions; philosophy

KEY FIGURES

Kabīr (1440-1518),
Nānak (1469-1539),
Ravidās (fl. fifteenth century),
Sūrdās (1483?-1563?), and
Mīrābaī (fl. 1516-1546), northern Indian religious leaders and composers of devotional poetry

SUMMARY OF EVENT

Bhakti, an important component of Hindu practice, is the path of devotion extolled by Krishna in the *Bhagavadgītā* (c. 200 B.C.E.-200 C.E.; *The Bhagavad Gita*, 1785), one of the most sacred of Hindu texts. The expression of this devotion has led to thousands of years of works in literature, music, dance, and painting, reflecting the rich cultural diversity of the peoples of India and extending into all regions and strata of society.

Bhakti is regarded as a form of yoga that strives to unite the individual with the divine. Over time, a large body of literature developed, including the bhakti poetry written in southern India from 6,000 to 1,000 B.C.E., and the twelfth century *Gitagovinda*, a Sanskrit poem written by Jayadeva, which celebrates the love between Krishna and his human consort, Radha, a metaphor for all devotees. Around this time, Muslim Sufis, mystics who also used music and poetry in ecstatic worship, began wandering into parts of northern India, winning converts and entering into dialogues with their Hindu counterparts. In fourteenth century Kashmir, Lal Ded, a Shaivite devotee and practitioner of yoga, began preaching and creating devotional poetry in the Kashmiri language, sharing her knowledge, challenging caste divisions, and earning the respect of her Muslim counterparts.

With the ascendancy of the Mughal Dynasty in India in the sixteenth century came increased Islamic influence and control over a feudal structure that included both Muslim and Hindu provincial rulers. The Mughal emperor of India, Akbar (r. 1556-1605), was fascinated with Hindu literature, arts, and theology, so he established a pattern of court patronage to ensure that material originally inspired by bhakti practice would be cultivated for the enjoyment of the ruling elite.

At the other end of the social spectrum, a continuous evolution of local oral traditions, rituals, and festivals expanded on devotional themes. As Hinduism responded to the impact of Islam in the sixteenth century, several key figures appeared who inspired the population with their emotional intensity and creative use of regional languages in songs and poetry. Some of them were able to draw on insights from both Hinduism and Islam, and all of them offered a dynamic alternative to hierarchical social conventions.

Two of these figures were of humble origin: Kabīr, a Muslim weaver, and Ravidās, a cobbler. Like most of their contemporaries, their lives were described in stories orally, long before being recorded in writing, and both figures were probably illiterate, sharing their ideas through poetry and song. Both of them were inspired by the devotional teachings of Ramananda, a Vaishnavite guru who lived in Benares. Kabīr was very iconoclastic, and he criticized all creeds. Using the metaphor of a diamond that withstands the strokes of a stonecutter, he argued that the truth can withstand scrutiny. His followers included both Hindus and Muslims. Ravidās, said to have been younger than Kabīr, was of even lower social standing. Because they worked with the skins of dead animals, leather workers were regarded as ritually unclean. Ravidās used his occupation as a metaphor for transcendence, explaining that since earthly life is short and full of suffering, one should place more value on one's spiritual development.

The blind poet Sūrdās lived in the Braj region, where Krishna was born. He left an abusive home at a very early age but was fortunate to be taught by the sage Vallabhacharya, from whom he learned Sanskrit literature. Most of his thousands of songs, written in the vernacular Braj, express devotion to Krishna, and he is especially known for his tender descriptions of Krishna's childhood.

In contrast to the other major figures in the bhakti movement, Mīrābaī was born into a high social position, the daughter of a Rajput chieftain, and is sometimes described as a princess of Rajasthan. As a female, however, her life was in some ways just as restricted as those of her poorer male brethren. From an early age, she was an intense devotee of Krishna. After being married to the Rajput prince Bhoj Raj, she refused to submit to the authority of her new family, claiming allegiance to Krishna instead. When her husband died, she refused to be immolated with him as was the custom. Instead, she spent more and more time with wandering mystics and began to dance in front of the image of Krishna, a practice considered improper for a woman of her status. Her husband's family became outraged and then tried to kill her, but she escaped and began her new life as a composer of devotional songs and a leader of devotees.

Nānak, revered as the founder of the Sikh religion, had much in common with most of the other great religious innovators, including his activities as a composer of verse, his use of vernacular language, his incorporation of ideas from both Hinduism and Islam, and his implicit challenge to the power structures of the time. Nānak was born to a Hindu family in the Punjab region, which is now in northwest India and Pakistan, and grew up in a community administered by Muslims. As a child, he learned to read Sanskrit, Arabic, and Persian. Although he showed an early interest in matters of faith, he assumed family and occupational responsibilities, too, when he came of age. After a pivotal experience of enlightenment, he began a series of travels, presenting his ideas by interacting with people of various faiths. He wrote poetry in his native Punjabi, using a very clear and direct language. Like Kabīr, he was an iconoclast, and he asserted the unity of God as transcending sectarian divisions. As time passed, a community of followers developed, and he eventually appointed the first of his nine successors. His religious poetry was written down and is called *Guru Granth Sahib*, the sacred text of the Sikhs.

The main musical-literary genre for most of the bhakti mystics of this time was the *bhajan*, or devotional song. These songs were most commonly in vernacular languages so that they could be completely understood by all individuals, even those who were predominantly illiterate. Painting, sculpture, and dance often were used to convey the deep emotional content and associations of the material, without the symbolic rigidity of spoken language. Bhakti also influenced the development of storytelling, in which the loves and adventures of Krishna, the lives of the saints themselves, and folk wisdom from the various regions of India were narrated. In many cases, parallel written versions of these poems and stories helped to articulate regional languages.

In the courts of the Mughal emperors and their local princes, professional writers, artists, musicians, and dancers set bhakti narratives into forms that reflected the prestige and power of their patrons. In many cases, these were inherited positions, so that generations of specialists developed various schools of technique and interpretation, often being influenced by styles from Persia, Turkey, and the Arabic speaking countries.

In terms of theology and the practice of meditation, there are two major approaches to bhakti, and the figures from the 1500's are usually included in one or another of these categories. Saguna bhakti is based on the attributes of a specific deity, which can be experienced through the senses and immersion in the narrative of the deity, usually through the worship of Krishna or Ram as an incarnation or avatar of Vishnu. Sūrdās and Mīrābaī were poets in the saguna bhakti tradition. While equally passionate, nirguna bhakti is more monotheistic and recognizes the immanence of the Supreme Being in all of reality. Guru Nānak, Kabīr, and Ravidās were part of the nirguna bhakti tradition.

SIGNIFICANCE

Long before the lower castes, women, and other marginalized groups were offered political equality, the bhakti movement gave them a voice, revitalizing Hinduism and helping to provide a social context for the birth of Sikhism. In subsequent years, bhakti influenced the arts and contributed to the formal development of several major Indian languages. Its message of universality and its passionate quest for unity with the divine resonate still.

—*John Myers*

FURTHER READING

Ahmad, Aziz. *Studies in Islamic Culture in the Indian Environment*. New York: Oxford University Press, 1999. A very thorough work that includes chapters on syncretism and the opposition between Hinduism and Islam.

Hay, Stephen. *Sources of Indian Tradition*. 2d ed. New York: Columbia University Press, 1988. A comprehensive compilation of primary literary sources, including introductory historical and analytical material. Includes discussion of the bhakti movement, Guru Nānak, and the emergence of the Sikh tradition.

Jaikishandas, Sadani, trans. *Rosary of Hymns (Selected Poems) of Sūrdās*. New Delhi, India: Wiley Eastern, 1991. English translations of significant poems, with

1500's

an extensive introduction. Includes the Hindi originals, a glossary of terms, and indexes of first lines in both English and Hindi.

Mukta, Parita. *Upholding the Common Life: The Community of Mīrābaī.* New York: Oxford University Press, 1999. Uses the devotional songs of Mīrābaī to reveal developments in popular culture and society.

Singh, Daljeet, and Kharak Singh, eds. *Sikhism: Its Philosophy and History.* Introduction by Choor Singh. Chandigarh, India: Institute of Sikh Studies, 1997.

Comprehensive anthology of essays on all aspects of Sikhism; delves into the history of the religion and the role of Nānak in its founding.

SEE ALSO: c. 1490: Fragmentation of the Bahmani Sultanate; 1556-1605: Reign of Akbar; 1577: Ram Dās Founds Amritsar.

RELATED ARTICLES in *Great Lives from History: The Renaissance & Early Modern Era, 1454-1600:* Akbar; Ibrāhīm Lodī; Nānak.

Early 16th century
FUZULI WRITES POETRY IN THREE LANGUAGES

Fuzuli is considered one of the greatest Turkish poets, whose literary work epitomizes the multicultural achievements of the Ottoman Empire's divan literature. His poetry addressed topics ranging from religion to philosophy and was written in three different languages—Azeri-Turkish, Persian, and Arabic.

LOCALE: Baghdad, Persia (now in Iraq)
CATEGORIES: Literature; religion

KEY FIGURES
Mehmed bin Süleyman Fuzuli (c. 1495-1556), Azeri-Turkish poet
Ismāᶜīl I (1487-1524), Iranian shah, r. 1501-1524, founder of the Ṣafavid Dynasty, and poet
Süleyman the Magnificent (1494/1495-1566), Ottoman sultan, r. 1520-1566

SUMMARY OF EVENT

Fuzuli (also known as Fuduli or Fizuli) was born Mehmed bin Süleyman Fuzuli in central Iraq around 1495. No less than six cities, including Baghdad and Karbala, have claimed him as a native son. He was descended from the Turkomans, and his immediate ancestors migrated to Iraq from what is now Azerbaijan. One tradition claims that his father was a *mufti,* or scholar of Islamic law.

His parents had the means to send their son to a *madrasa* (Islamic religious school) where he was educated not only in Islam, law, and philosophy but also in the classical literatures of Arabic and Persian. Raised as a speaker of Azeri-Turkish, he was effectively trilingual. He seems to have excelled as a student because, in addition to his poetry, he composed prose in Arabic and Per-

sian on a wide variety of subjects relating to Islamic art, philosophy, and science. One legend claims that the young Fuzuli began to write verse after experiencing unrequited love for his teacher's daughter (a story possibly conflated from the ill-starred romance in his *Leylā ve Mecnūn,* published during the seventeenth century and translated into English as *Leylā and Mejnūn* in 1970). While his poetry is imbued with a deep feeling for human suffering and loss, it is guided by a transcendental quest for union with God and reveals his intimate knowledge of the esoteric Islam of mystical Shia and Sufism.

As a young man, Fuzuli moved to Baghdad, the city where he spent most of his life and the place with which he is most commonly identified. While Baghdad remained an important Middle East crossroads during his time, it was no longer the center of the Islamic universe, as it had been under the first caliphs or the fabled court of Caliph Hārūn al-Rashīd (r. 786-809). The city had been ravaged by the Mongols in 1258 and overrun by Tamerlane in 1401.

In Fuzuli's own lifetime, Baghdad changed hands on at least two occasions. In 1508, Ismāᶜīl I, the zealous Shīᶜite founder of the Turko-Persian Ṣafavid Dynasty, took the city in his quest to reestablish a Shīᶜite caliphate. In 1534, Sultan Süleyman the Magnificent, a Sunni Muslim, conquered Baghdad and asserted Ottoman rule, which prevailed until the early twentieth century. While Baghdad remained a prize for the Ottomans, the cultural and political center of their westward-expanding empire had long been Istanbul, which they had taken from the Byzantines, when it was called Constantinople, in 1453.

Fuzuli composed kasidas, or poems of praise, for both the Ṣafavid and Ottoman elite and enjoyed some patronage. For the Ṣafavids, he composed *Bang-u-Badeh*, a poem celebrating the triumphs of Ismāʿīl. He dedicated his major work, *Leylā ad Mejnūn*, among others, to the Ottomans.

Despite his considerable poetic and prose output, he seems to have lived in humble circumstances. While his Shīʿite mysticism was convivial to the court of Ismāʿīl, it probably did little to endear him to the Sunni Ottoman elite who, while generally tolerant, remained wary of heterodoxy within their multicultural empire. Fuzuli died either of plague or cholera during a pilgrimage to the city of Karbala, the holy city of the Shīʿites, where he is buried in the shrine to Imam Hussein, grandson of the Prophet.

The young Fuzuli composed his first divan, or collection of poems, primarily in Azeri-Turkish. (A later divan was composed in Persian and Arabic.) His pen name was a complicated play on words that hinted at the Arabic words for "presumption" and "virtue." While the word "divan" was derived from the Persian for "book," it also had the more general meaning of a "court" or "assembly." Divan poets wrote for and performed in an exclusive court setting, competing for favor with rulers such as Ismāʿīl and Süleyman the Magnificent, who were themselves recognized for versification. Similar to court poets in Europe at the time, a divan poet was a combination entertainer, propagandist, and public-relations specialist. The divan downplayed a lively Turkish oral tradition, which is evident in its harshly syllabic folk song or in its earthy folk literature such as the *Dede korkut* (c. ninth century; *The Book of Dede Korkut*, 1972) for the exoticism and sophistication of the Arab and Persian high literary canon. Indeed, one almost had to have had extensive *madrasa* training to begin to understand the divan poet's breadth of theological and literary allusions and his skillful interweaving of Azeri-Turkish, Arabic, and Persian wordplay.

Just as the Ottoman sultans soon lost their exclusively Turkish identity and bloodlines through intermarriage with the various peoples whom they subjugated, so the divan poets such as Fuzuli promoted an Ottoman culture that was multicultural, polyglot, and elitist.

Fuzuli's three languages were not considered equals. Arabic was the sacred language of Islam, including the

---

FUZULI ON THE PANGS OF LOVE

Fuzuli's version of the storied legends of pre-Islamic Arabic culture, Leylā ve Mecnūn, *is a romantic epic of thwarted love and stands as his major poetic work.*

Yield not the soul to pang of Love, for Love's the soul's fierce glow;
That Love's the torment of the soul doth all the wide world know.
Seek not for gain from fancy wild of pang of Love at all;
For all that comes from fancy wild of Love's pang is grief's throe.
Each curving eyebrow is a blood-stained saber thee to slay;
Each dusky curl, a deadly venomed snake to work thee woe.
Lovely, indeed, the forms of moon-like maidens are to see—
Lovely to see, but ah! the end doth bitter anguish show.
From this I know full well that torment dire in love abides,
That all who lovers are, engrossed with sighs, rove to and fro.
Call not to mind the pupils of the black-eyed damsels bright,
With thought, "I'm man"; be not deceived, 'tis blood they drink, I trow.
E'en if Fuzuli should declare, "In fair ones there is troth,"
Be not deceived—"A poet's words are falsehoods all men know."

Source: From "The Legends & Poetry of the Turks, Selections," Internet Medieval Sourcebook. Middle East & Islamic Studies Collection, Cornell University Library. http://www.library.cornell.edu/colldev/mideast/turkpoet.htm. Accessed September 27, 2004.

Qurʾān and Ḥadīth. Persian was the premier classical language of Fuzuli's day, based upon its literary golden age—the eleventh and thirteenth centuries—which included such works as Firdusi's *Shahnamah* (c. 1010; the book of kings), Rūmī's *Mathnawī-i ma ʿnawī* (late thirteenth century; *The Mathnawi*, 1926-1934), Saʿdi's *Gulistan* (1258; *The Rose Garden*, 1806), and Omar Khayyám's *Rubáiyát* (eleventh century; *The Rubáiyát of Omar Khayyám*, 1879). Both Persian and Arabic had extensive literary traditions with well-established verse forms. The foremost of these were the *masnawi*, a couplet-based form used for long narrative or philosophical works; the *kasida*, or poem of praise; and the *ghazal*, a short poem on the theme of love with an intricate pattern resembling the European sonnet. By Fuzuli's day, a complex literary syncretism was well under way, in which native-speaking Turkish poets adopted the forms and borrowed words and phrases from Arabic and Persian.

This literary syncretism is evident in Fuzuli's magnum opus *Leylā and Mejnūn*, a romantic epic of thwarted love composed in the *masnawi* form but incorporating *ghazals* and other literary forms. This story was based on legends derived from pre-Islamic Arabic culture and centered on Gais, who falls in love with Leylā (or Layla).

1500's

Gais professes his love for Leylā through songs that scandalize the girl's father, who in turn forbids the two to marry. Gais becomes known as Mejnūn, or Majnun (Arabic for "madman") and retreats in despair to the wilderness. After numerous plot twists, the pair are denied an earthly reunion and Majnun falls dead at Leylā's grave.

Fuzuli was not the first poet to put his imprint on the story. Perhaps the best-known version is that of Neẓāmī (1141-1209), called *Leyli o-Mejnūn* (1188; *The Story of Layla and Majnun*, 1966). Neẓāmī fashioned the complete tale in Persian from various Arab legends. While Fuzuli adhered to the narrative established by Neẓāmī, his originality lies both in his literary inventiveness and in the allegorical underpinnings of his version of the tale. Much as British contemporary poet Edmund Spenser refashioned Arthurian legends into the Christian religious allegory of *The Faerie Queene* (1590-1609), so Fuzuli transformed the romantic tale of *Leylā and Mejnūn* into an Islamic allegory about the quest of the soul for mystical union with God. In a final vision, Leylā and Majnun are portrayed as united spiritual forms inhabiting a transcendental Eden.

SIGNIFICANCE

In the centuries since his death, Fuzuli has come to be regarded not only as one of the greatest Turkish poets but also as a great Islamic one, transcending national boundaries. He is considered a national poet of not only Turkey but also Azerbaijan, although he spent his entire life in what is now Iraq.

His literary achievement helps to correct the Western world's bias against the Ottoman Empire as the cultural and political "sick man of Europe"—an image based on the decadent latter days of the empire in the late nineteenth and early twentieth centuries rather than its golden age under Süleyman the Magnificent.

The philosophical and religious depth of Fuzuli's poetry (evident both in his longer works and in his *ghazals*) help to dispel the misconception of Ottoman divan literature as nothing more than the over-sensual and intellectually unsophisticated songs of women and wine.

—*Luke Powers*

FURTHER READING

Andrews, Walter, Najaat Black, and Mehmet Kalpakli. *Ottoman Lyric Poetry: An Anthology.* Austin: University of Texas Press, 1997. Provides a brief overview of Fuzuli's life and work and translations of several of his *ghazals*. The introductory essay examines the misconceptions of Ottoman poetry as sensual and not philosophical.

Gibbs, Elias J. W. *Ottoman Literature: The Poets and Poetry of Turkey.* London: M. W. Dunne, 1901. Provides translations and biographical information on Fuzuli and other Turkish poets. Though dated, this work remains the only complete survey of Ottoman literature in English.

Kunt, I. Metin, Christine Woodhead, and Metin Kunt. *Süleyman the Magnificent and His Age: The Ottoman Empire in the Early Modern World.* Boston: Addison-Wesley, 1995. Cultural history of the golden age of the Ottoman Empire and the court culture in which divan literature flourished.

Lewis, Bernard. *Music of a Distant Drum: Classical Arabic, Persian, Turkish, and Hebrew Poems.* Princeton, N.J.: Princeton University Press, 2001. One of the best-known contemporary scholars of Islamic culture provides an introduction and translations of key poetic texts from rival cultural traditions of the ancient and medieval Middle East.

SEE ALSO: Early 16th cent.: Devotional Bhakti Traditions Emerge; 1501-1524: Reign of Ismāʿīl I; 1512-1520: Reign of Selim I; 1520-1566: Reign of Süleyman.

RELATED ARTICLES in *Great Lives from History: The Renaissance & Early Modern Era, 1454-1600:* Edmund Spenser; Süleyman the Magnificent.

Early 16th century
RISE OF THE FUR TRADE

The development of the fur trade between European explorers and Native Americans created the first commercial industry in North America and had a profound and lasting impact on the Native American population.

LOCALE: Northeastern coast and waterways of North America and Canada

CATEGORIES: Trade and commerce; exploration and discovery; economics

KEY FIGURES

Jacques Cartier (c. 1491-1557), French navigator and explorer

John Cabot (c. 1450-c. 1498), English explorer and navigator

John Davis (c. 1550-1605), English explorer and cartographer

SUMMARY OF EVENT

Throughout the early sixteenth century, European expeditions explored the eastern coast of mainland North America in search of the Northwest Passage to the Orient. What they found instead was an unknown land with a seemingly primitive indigenous population and untapped natural resources. Initially, trading furs with the Native Americans was of secondary importance to explorers, but as the century progressed, beaver fur, sometimes called "soft gold," became a means to finance expeditions. Ultimately, the fur trade would play a vital role in the development of the European colonies and colonial nations in North America throughout the 1500's and the three centuries that followed.

The fur trade and trading in general existed long before the first Europeans reached the North American continent. Native American tribes hunted the indigenous animals for food, and for hides to make clothing. Prior to the arrival of the Europeans, however, the Native Americans had no reason to trap more animals than they could use, and the animal populations remained stable for centuries.

Even before Christopher Columbus reached the New World in 1492, European fishing ships from Portugal, Spain, France, and England were fishing and hunting whales off the coast of what would later become Canada. These fishermen traded with the natives they encountered, both to ensure goodwill and to obtain pelts. The items they traded included iron tools, blankets, clothing, guns, and beads.

As the sixteenth century began, the European beaver had been hunted to near-extinction for its pelt, which was used in making hats. The Russians provided most of the beaver skins in Europe, and the disappearance of the animals from Russia was the reason for that nation's push eastward. As a result, Russian trappers and explorers eventually reached what would become Alaska.

Beaver pelts financed some of the earliest expeditions in search of gold, silver, and the Northwest Passage. They were the perfect cargo and trade commodity—lightweight, easy to transport, and requiring very little investment. There was a preexisting market for furs in Europe, and the Native Americans already knew how to trap beaver.

Most pelts traded were beaver, but otter and deer hides were also utilized. The deer hides were used in making clothing. The soft underbelly fur of the beaver was used to make felt hats, a symbol of wealth in Europe, and the rest of the pelt became part of a winter coat.

At first, trade and exploration were limited to the eastern coastline of North America, but by 1497, John Cabot established the first British claim in the region near Labrador, Newfoundland. As the fur trade become more profitable, the focus of the early expeditions gradually shifted from exploration to exploitation. Lands were claimed in the name of the French and British crowns with no regard for the people who already lived there. At first, the Europeans could trade inexpensive items like cheap knives and beads for furs, but once the novelty of the European goods wore off, trade rates were established.

In 1534, French explorer Jacques Cartier sailed from France with hopes of locating the Northwest Passage to the Orient. He reached the Labrador coast and landed on the Gaspé Peninsula, raised a cross, and claimed the new territory for France. He was unable to find the Northwest Passage, but he did discover the Gulf of St. Lawrence and the St. Lawrence River, claiming those territories for France as well. While Cartier was exploring the region, a large group of Mi'kmac (or Micmac) Indians in forty canoes approached his crew displaying beaver pelts. Unsure of their intentions, Cartier did not approach the Mi'kmac until the following day, when they returned with a smaller party. Despite the language barrier, the two groups managed to work out a trade. The Mi'kmac exchanged their pelts for knives and other items (including a red hat for the chief).

1500's

275

The fur trade relied heavily on Native American labor. Initially, the Native Americans relied on the same methods of trapping they always had. They used nooses, deadfalls, and a variety of traditional cages. Because of the increased demand for pelts, however, Native American trappers gradually shifted from traditional methods of hunting to more efficient European methods, using guns and steel traps obtained from their trading partners. Likewise, manufactured goods from Europe began to replace traditional inter-tribal trade items like corn and dried fish.

Native Americans with European contacts became middlemen between the trappers and the merchants. Not wanting to lose this source of income, they opposed Europeans moving inland to deal with the trappers directly. For their part, the first European traders were in no hurry to make permanent inroads inland or even to establish permanent settlements on the coast. For most of the century, they utilized ad hoc trading camps and temporary settlements along the coastline that would not evolve into permanent trade centers until much later in the 1600's.

The St. Lawrence River and Great Lakes quickly became important trade routes. Early explorers entered the St. Lawrence River between Newfoundland and Nova Scotia and found hundreds of miles of navigable rivers leading into the North American interior. Native American trappers brought furs from the interior to the St. Lawrence River, and the rivers became the first mass-transit systems. Controlling the strategic waterways became vital.

By the last part of the sixteenth century, the French were firmly in control of the fur trade in the New World. In 1577, King Henry III established the first trade monopoly, though it would prove almost impossible to enforce as demand for fur grew and traffic increased in the New World.

At the same time, exploration of the New World continued. English explorer John Davis (sometimes spelled Davys) led three expeditions to find the Northwest Passage in the late 1580's. While he was not successful in that, he did range farther north than anyone had before. Davis mapped huge areas of the region, increasing the territory for fur traders to develop.

SIGNIFICANCE

The arrival of the European explorers forever changed the lives of the Native Americans they encountered, but the full impact of the fur trade would not be measurable until much later. While most of the Native American tribes involved in trade with Europe had already engaged in trade among themselves, the fur trade with the French

and English explorers was their first experience with trade for profit, or capitalism. Trade with the Europeans brought items they never would have owned otherwise: firearms, cooking implements, and liquor. They exchanged raw materials for manufactured goods and for the first time became consumers.

The balance of power shifted between tribes, as those with access to guns were able to defeat their neighbors. Moreover, the opportunity for profit provided a novel motive for tribes to take control of territory and trade routes. Thus, the fur trade gave Native American tribes new reasons to go to war, as well as new weapons to use against their enemies.

As for the Europeans, competition between the English and French for control of the fur trade would become intense over the next century. In 1608, French explorer Samuel de Champlain established a permanent trading post at a site that would become the city of Quebec. King Charles II of England gave his cousin, Prince Rupert, control of the fur trade, resulting in the formation of the Hudson's Bay Company in 1670.

—*P. S. Ramsey*

FURTHER READING

Brown, Jennifer S. H. *Strangers in Blood: Fur Trade Company Families in Indian Country.* Vancouver: Oklahoma Paperbacks, 1996. A scholarly study of the people involved during the centuries following the onset of the fur trade.

Gilman, Carolyn. *Where Two Worlds Meet: The Great Lakes Fur Trade.* St. Paul: Minnesota Historical Society, 1982. A compilation of museum photographs and illustrations of artifacts used by both Native Americans and Europeans during the fur trade, with descriptive essays.

Martin, Calvin. *Keepers of the Game: Indian-Animal Relationships and the Fur Trade.* Berkeley: University of California Press, 1978. Details the relationship between Native Americans and the natural world, both before and after contact with European explorers and traders.

Ray, Arthur J. *Indians in the Fur Trade: Their Role as Trappers, Hunters, and Middlemen in the Lands Southwest of Hudson Bay, 1660-1870.* Buffalo, N.Y.: University of Toronto Press, 1998. Explores the evolution of Native American society and the roles of indigenous trappers and middlemen in the centuries following the initial rise of the fur trade.

Reese, Ted. *Soft Gold: A History of the Fur Trade in the Great Lakes Region and Its Impact on Native Ameri-*

can Culture. Bowie, Md.: Heritage Books, 2001. A specific look at the fur trade of the Great Lakes region and its effect on Native Americans, beginning in the sixteenth century and lasting through the American Revolutionary War.

Van Kirk, Sylvia. *Many Tender Ties: Women in Fur-Trade Society.* Norman: University of Oklahoma Press, 1983. The effects of the fur trade on European and Native American women.

SEE ALSO: Oct. 12, 1492: Columbus Lands in the Americas; June 24, 1497-May, 1498: Cabot's Voyages; 16th century: Worldwide Inflation; Beginning 1519: Smallpox Kills Thousands of Indigenous Americans; Apr. 20, 1534-July, 1543: Cartier and Roberval Search for a Northwest Passage.

RELATED ARTICLES in *Great Lives from History: The Renaissance & Early Modern Era, 1454-1600:* John Cabot; Jacques Cartier; John Davis.

16th century
CHINA'S POPULATION BOOM

An increase in cultivated land, new crops and agricultural technologies, humane policies toward newborns, relative peace, and political stability, as well as nascent industrialization, led to a significant increase of Chinese population in the sixteenth century.

LOCALE: China

CATEGORIES: Cultural and intellectual history; agriculture; economics

KEY FIGURES

Hongwu (reign name, also Hung-wu; personal name Zhu Yuanzhang, Chu Yüan-chang; posthumous name Gaodi, Kao-ti; temple name Taizu, T'ai-tsu; 1328-1398), founder of the Ming Dynasty, r. 1368-1398

Jiajing (reign name, also Chia-ching; personal name Zhu Houzong, Chu Hou-tsung; posthumous name Sudi, Su-ti; temple name Shizong, Shih-tsung; 1507-1567), Ming emperor of China, r. 1522-1567

Wanli (reign name, also Wan-li; personal name Zhu Yijun, Chu I-chün; posthumous name Zhu Yijun, Chu I-chün; temple name Shenzong, Shen-tsung; 1563-1620), the thirteenth Ming emperor, r. 1573-1620, a supporter of the Single-Whip Reform

SUMMARY OF EVENT

In the 1500's, China experienced a remarkable population increase. This came as a direct consequence of the policies of the Hongwu emperor, who founded the Ming Dynasty in 1368. At that time, China's population consisted of approximately 60 million people. By 1600, this number stood as high as 150 million, according to contemporary historians. This tremendous boom was unprecedented in China's history and provided both opportunities and challenges to the nation and the imperial government. Ironically, the Ming emperors of the six-

teenth century themselves believed that their population was dwindling, as their subjects avoided the census to escape from paying taxes.

When the Hongwu emperor came to power in 1368, he immediately implemented measures to reverse the population decline under the previous Yuan Dynasty. He launched an aggressive campaign to resettle northern China, which had been devastated by warfare and neglect. Settlers from the populous south were given start-up aid, tax relief, and free land if they moved north. Thus, more of China's land was put to agrarian use and could sustain a larger population. The introduction of sorghum, a crop that can be dry-farmed, also aided food production in the more arid north.

Throughout his realm, the Hongwu emperor rebuilt irrigation systems such as canals, dykes, reservoirs, and terraced rice paddies. A new variety of rice, which originated in Champa (present-day central Vietnam), was promoted. The new rice took about half the time of Chinese rice to grow and yielded a larger quantity per acre. Even though Champa rice has fewer calories than the Chinese variety, the increase in yield still meant more nutrition was available.

Once irrigation systems were rebuilt, with new pumps or water wheels to aid wet farming, a sophisticated hydraulic agriculture was established. The Ming emperors ordered farmers to plant new crops and to fill the flooded rice paddies with fish. This provided a richer food harvest in two ways: The fish fertilized the soil with their waste, and they also served as a food source.

In the 1500's, the increase of cultivated land, especially in the north, and the continuous introduction of new crops meant that the land could sustain the unfolding and accelerating population boom. The European discovery of America also brought new crops to China by

1500's

way of the Spanish colony of the Philippines. The Ming emperors ordered the peasants to plant these new crops, with positive results. Corn flourished in China and became part of the people's diet. Peanuts and sweet potatoes had the additional benefit that they could be cultivated in drier areas previously left barren. These new crops also allowed for a sophisticated system of crop rotation, because the nitrogen bound in their roots served as a natural fertilizer that refurbished land exhausted by traditional crops. By rotating the plants built on arable land, Chinese farmers increased food production instead of leaving fields to lie fallow, and this increase supported a rapidly growing population. However, the basic conservatism of Ming society precluded the invention of even more high-yielding agricultural machines, and many farming techniques remained unchanged over the centuries.

The conservative approach of Ming rulers like the Jiajing emperor, who reigned until 1567, also found its expression in a humane attitude toward newborns of both genders. The Chinese were exhorted morally to care for their offspring, and infanticide was discouraged. It was considered preferable to sell young girls, even into sexual servitude, rather than kill them as infants. Even though as many as 70,000 eunuchs were in attendance at imperial courts such as that of the Jiajing emperor, the population continued to increase in spite of the number of boys under ten castrated for this purpose. Similarly, the astonishingly high number of death sentences did not negatively impact population growth.

The absence of large-scale warfare during the 1500's in China is considered another major reason for the dynamic population growth of the period. Typically, the Jiajing emperor preferred peace over foreign military expeditions. For example, in 1540, he accepted the formal submission of the Vietnamese emperor, Mac Dang Dung, rather than sending his army into Vietnam. Mongol raiders and pirates were held at bay. In the absence of major conflicts, the Chinese population during the 1500's increased without the typical decimations associated with warfare in this era. When the Wanli emperor defended Korea from the Japanese from 1592 until 1598 (when the Japanese abandoned their invasion), the resulting stress on the Ming economy showed how, in contrast, the previous absence of much warfare had nourished population growth.

The Chinese population boom of the 1500's was aided also by the beginning of industrialization. Based on a stable agricultural sector, industrial enterprises were born and flourished. Among these were the paper, porcelain, and textile industries.

The manufacture of paper, for example, rose in re-sponse to the large state bureaucracy and an increasingly literate population. Paper factories employed and fed thousands of workers who did not depend on tilling the land for their subsistence.

A domestic and international demand for porcelain led to the establishment of industrial-sized kiln combines, sustaining, for example, the one million inhabitants of Jingdezhen. Ironically, the Ming porcelain industry also points at typical limitations hampering further growth that could have sustained an even larger population. For instance, the kilns at Jingdezhen were not perfected further, and profits were often consumed rather than reinvested.

The large-scale cultivation of cotton created a textile industry that rivaled that of the silk industry. At Songjiang, people earned their livelihoods weaving cotton at 100,000 operational looms, while Hangzhou and Suzhou produced their famous silks. Again, however, in these textile industries, further inventions did not materialize that could have matched the pace of industrialization with that of the population growth.

The Wanli emperor did not know it and believed the contrary, but in reality he ruled over an empire with a booming population. Almost three times as many Chinese lived under his reign than under the Hongwu emperor. Increased agricultural production freed people to work in trade and the nascent industries, and even the catastrophic earthquake of 1556, which killed approximately 800,000 people, did not halt the population boom. Relative peace, focus on agricultural production, introduction of new crops from the south and the Americas, and modest application of technological innovations in agriculture and manufacturing gave Ming China a material base for the amazing population boom in the 1500's.

SIGNIFICANCE

The enormous increase in Chinese population in the 1500's created a nation of approximately 150 million inhabitants, nearly tripling the number of people in less than 250 years. For this age, the increase was remarkable. Population increase meant that more people than ever required sustenance. Because their flawed census did not reveal the situation to the emperors, they could neither take advantage of the growing population nor adequately serve its needs and sustain this growth. As a result, hardships developed.

In the north, taxation and a rise of banditry made farming increasingly difficult and prompted people to leave the land. Even in the fertile and prosperous south, food shortages developed because of the imperial government's failure to recognize the needs of the steadily growing population. Industrial profits were often spent on consumption or taxes, leaving insufficient capital to sustain growth. State interference in the economy, as well as an official distaste for nonagrarian production and trade, also began to strangle growth. When the Wanli and other Ming emperors failed to recognize and meet the needs of his people, Chinese emigration to Southeast Asia became one of the consequences.

For all these reasons, and sadly for the Chinese people, the population boom of the late Ming Dynasty proved unsustainable. When the Ming Dynasty fell in 1644, warfare again devastated an already endangered north, and famines spread. Scholars estimate that by 1685 the Chinese population had been decimated by one-third, standing now at only 100 million rather than the estimated height of 150 million during the Ming Dynasty. Nevertheless, the next recovery would take less time than the Ming population expansion, and by 1749 there were 178 million people living in China.

—*R. C. Lutz*

Further Reading

Brook, Timothy. *The Confusions of Pleasure: Commerce and Culture in Ming China.* Berkeley: University of California Press, 1998. Focus on the cultural feeling of the era that brings to life an expanding society and shows the effect of the population boom on Chi-

nese society, particular the upper classes. Bibliography, index.

Huang, Ray. *China: A Macro History.* Armonk, N.Y.: M. E. Sharpe, 1997. Argues that while population boomed during the Ming Dynasty, the conservative political system caused economic and technological stagnation, which left China behind the European level of development. Illustrations, bibliography, index.

Spence, Jonathan. *In Search for Modern China.* New York: Norton, 1990. The first chapter illustrates life during the Ming Dynasty, showing how an expanding population first invigorated and later put pressure on the empire. Still a standard, widely available text. Illustrations, maps, tables.

See also: 16th cent.: Single-Whip Reform; 1505-1521: Reign of Zhengde and Liu Jin; 1514-1598: Portuguese Reach China; 1521-1567: Reign of Jiajing; Spring, 1523: Ōuchi Family Monopolizes Trade with China; 1550-1571: Mongols Raid Beijing; Jan. 23, 1556: Earthquake in China Kills Thousands; 1573-1620: Reign of Wanli; 1592-1599: Japan Invades Korea.

Related articles in *Great Lives from History: The Renaissance & Early Modern Era, 1454-1600:* Wang Yangming; Xiaozong; Zhengde.

16th century
Decline of Moundville

The Mississippian cultural center now called Moundville was built over centuries by prehistoric peoples called Mound Builders and reached its peak during the thirteenth century. The reasons for its decline and eventual collapse over the next two centuries are not fully understood but probably are manifold. Studying this site, however, has provided anthropologists, archaeologists, and historians with insights into one thousand years of human activity in precontact North America.

Locale: Moundville (now in Alabama)
Category: Anthropology

Key Figures

Apafalaya (fl. early sixteenth century), possibly the last of the Moundville chiefs, probably a descendant of the original paramount chief

Hernando de Soto (c. 1496-1542), Spanish explorer whose exploration of the Black River Valley may have facilitated the final abandonment of Moundville

Summary of Event

By around 800, the nomadic lifestyle of the Mississippian Indians had evolved into an agricultural society. Small communities thrived on rich floodplains across southeastern North America. Archaeological evidence paints a picture of a vigorous society following a chiefdom system wherein an elite class governed through inherited or earned positions. Alliances and trade, along with elaborate religious rites, tied the communities together. As their society grew more civilized, their use of mounds became creative and expanded into planned hubs of religion, commerce, and politics.

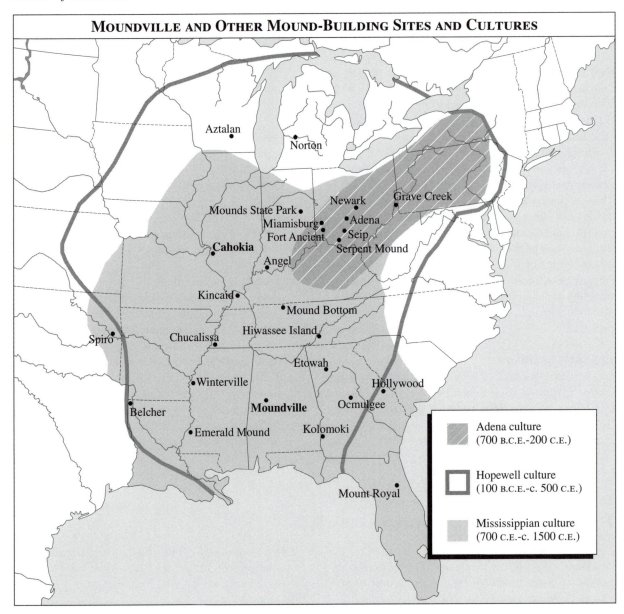

MOUNDVILLE AND OTHER MOUND-BUILDING SITES AND CULTURES

Aztalan

Norton

Grave Creek

Newark

Mounds State Park

Miamisburg
Adena
Fort Ancient
Seip

Cahokia
Serpent Mound

Angel

Kincaid

Mound Bottom

Spiro
Chucalissa
Hiwassee Island

Etowah

Winterville
Hollywood

Ocmulgee
Moundville

Belcher
Kolomoki

Emerald Mound

Mount Royal

Adena culture
(700 B.C.E.-200 C.E.)

Hopewell culture
(100 B.C.E.-c. 500 C.E.)

Mississippian culture
(700 C.E.-c. 1500 C.E.)

Moundville, the second-largest mound site, was built c. 1000-1250 on a high plateau 55 feet (approximately 17 meters) above the Black Warrior River Valley in Alabama. Historians consider it likely that the rise of Moundville marked the ascent of one dominant chief, now referred to as the paramount chief, whose familial dynasty ruled until the center's collapse around 1550.

Twenty-nine mounds were constructed on the Moundville terrace. The largest ceremonial mound—a steep pyramid 58 feet (18 meters) high with two ramps—was centered in a leveled plaza. Fifteen additional mounds of varying sizes were built in an orderly arrangement around the central mound, positioned to define the plaza's rectangular shape. The location of each mound is deliberate, making this one of the first planned communities in North America.

Mound residence or burial was status-related. The largest was erected on a line north of the center mound and is believed to have contained the domicile of the principal chief. On other mounds, workers built homes for the elite or structures for ceremony. Each resident mound had a smaller burial mound nearby.

A palisade with guard towers surrounded the 185-acre (about 75 hectares) site on three sides, with the river bluffs protecting the fourth. Evidence suggests that the bulk of the residents, commoners, lived in settlements within the palisade.

With the rise of Moundville, trade and the arts flourished. Wealthy nobles were buried with finely crafted artifacts made of exotic materials such as copper, mica, greenstone, and marine shell. Farmsteads, spread along 50 to 75 miles (80 to 120 kilometers) of river delta, supported Moundville with tribute, food, labor, and trade. The city was a cultural residential center until about 1300. The population at its peak, estimated at about one thousand, was supported by ten thousand living in outlying farmsteads.

Over the century from 1350 to 1450, Moundville changed. Commoners and low-level nobles left. Activities became ceremonial. Mounds were abandoned, and the tribute of food and labor was reduced. When the Europeans reached the area one hundred years later, the links between Moundville and the people who had created and supported it were irretrievably broken.

Many theories have been postulated to explain why the Mississippians abandoned Moundville. One credits mound building itself as a cause. Since excavation would have created large pits as workers moved soil and almost none of these borrow pits were located inside the palisade, workers might have walked a quarter of a mile or more carrying 60-pound baskets of soil. Mound construction would have taken an army of builders walking from dawn to dusk, carrying baskets of dirt, dumping their burdens and tamping the soil with their feet, then retracing their path to the borrow pit for yet another basketful. Scholars argue that generations lived and died to guarantee the flow of immigrants necessary to expand, maintain, rebuild, and raise the earthworks ever higher. The end of workers and tribute could only result in the collapse of the city.

It is also conceivable that the migration was a conscious decision intended to enhance the sanctity of Moundville's position as the chiefdom's religious and political center. Such a decision may also have been a matter of expedience: Competition for limited resources may have created tensions within tribes and between neighboring tribes. Poor sanitation could have triggered epidemics. Soil and wood depletion may have led to poor crops and famine. Any combination of these factors could have driven people away, and Moundville's nobility evidently did not stop the gradual erosion of the political consolidation that had made Moundville possible.

With the decline of the outlying support, the mound city may have fallen out of favor. Moundville became a home for the elite, a religious center, and a mortuary rather than the cultural and political center it had been earlier.

Another favored theory credits the decline to the restrictive class structure imposed when the paramount ruler consolidated power. Moundville's artificial social structure required a strong leader capable of imposing his will on a rural population. Evidence that this paramount chief existed is found in the very building of Moundville, in the immense amount of labor that had to be mobilized to build the palisade, level the public plaza, and construct the earthworks. Yet that very power, vested as it was in one paramount chief and his kin, depended on strength of will rather than logical social order—leading, some theorize, to the decline.

Yet one more theory considers that people no longer needed the safety of a fortified city. Evidence exists that about the time of the migration away from Moundville, the palisade ceased to be rebuilt, which could indicate a lack of threat in the area. Perhaps related to this theory is the possibility that secondary mound centers, believed to serve and administer to the rural population far from Moundville, drained power from the original center. Eight of these large, flat-topped mounds have been unearthed. Most were supported and survived beyond the decline of Moundville. It is theorized that the support of these centers came at the expense of Moundville, as the populace chose to support only the local center.

Regardless of which of these theories or combinations of causes formed the primary impetus for Moundville's decline, archaeological evidence shows that by about 1500 Moundville was for the most part deserted, with only the chief's mound occupied. Historians disagree about the status of Moundville's chiefdom when European explorer Hernando de Soto arrived in 1540. Evidence exists from de Soto's journals that he encountered Apafalaya, a hereditary Moundville chief, who ruled over a decentralized chiefdom from the now nominal and all but defunct ceremonial center. Apafalaya may have served de Soto as a guide and interpreter, and the European's arrival may have hastened the dispersion of Moundville's remnant population.

Historians do agree, however, that de Soto in no way caused the decline of Moundville. That event was inevitably under way a century before and most likely caused by a combination of the internal stresses mentioned above. Still, it remains possible that European influence, while having no direct consequence, facilitated the final abandonment of Moundville and its periphery mound centers.

1500's

SIGNIFICANCE

Moundville is one of the best examples of the sophistication and organization of Mississippian civilization. Even after centuries of disuse, the mounds remain visible as impressively massive earthen platforms, built with flat tops suitable for elite homes, burial of ancestors, and performance of religious and community rituals. Construction of each mound would have taken crews of workers years to complete, each hauling basket after basket of soil to raise the earthwork to its final dimensions.

The occupational history of Moundville reflects evidence of human activity over centuries: from prehistoric nomads camping on the riverbank, to independent farmsteads growing corn, to small agricultural communities banding together for security, to an impressive planned cultural center, to a declining center suffering from political decentralization, and finally to an abandoned site following an apparent mass exodus from the river valley.

It is important to realize that neither the rise nor the fall of Moundville is completely understood. Scholars have studied Moundville for more than a century, yet much of what is known remains speculation. For all of the mystery and disagreement, however, all agree on one fact: that Moundville was a remarkable achievement for its builders and remains a testimony to their ingenuity and dedication.

— *C. K. Zulkosky*

FURTHER READING

Brown, Ian W., ed. *Bottle Creek: A Pensacola Culture Site in South Alabama*. Tuscaloosa: University of Alabama Press, 2003. Although not directly about Moundville, discusses mound builders and contains useful references to Moundville.

Knight, Vernon James, Jr., ed. *The Moundville Expeditions of Clarence Bloomfield Moore*. Tuscaloosa: University of Alabama Press, 1996. Moore's original reports, complete and unabridged, *Certain Aboriginal Remains of the Black Warrior River* and *Moundville Revisited*, with an excellent introduction by the editor.

Knight, Vernon James, Jr., and Vincas P. Steponatis, eds. *Archaeology of the Moundville Chiefdom*. Washington, D.C.: Smithsonian Institution Press, 1998. Comprehensive and relatively easy to understand, providing summaries of scholarly thinking as well as more detailed papers and presentations of research.

Payne, Mildred Y., and Harry Harrison Kroll. *Mounds in the Mist*. New York: A. S. Barnes, 1969. Although a somewhat romanticized account of the Pinson Indian Mound Complex, still provides good background reading about mound builders, with references to Moundville.

Welch, Paul D. *Moundville's Economy*. Tuscaloosa: University of Alabama Press, 1991. Report of a study of the economic organization of the Moundville chiefdom. Sophisticated and technical.

SEE ALSO: Oct. 12, 1492: Columbus Lands in the Americas; 1493-1521: Ponce de León's Voyages; 1528-1536: Narváez's and Cabeza de Vaca's Expeditions; 1532-1537: Pizarro Conquers the Incas in Peru; May 28, 1539-Sept. 10, 1543: De Soto's North American Expedition.

RELATED ARTICLES in *Great Lives from History: The Renaissance & Early Modern Era, 1454-1600:* Hernando de Soto; Tascalusa.

16th century
EVOLUTION OF THE GALLEON

The seafaring nations of Europe made significant improvements in their oceangoing vessels during the sixteenth century. The galleon evolved in response to the changing political and economic climate, using the best features of the galley, carrack, and caravel, and was suitable for commerce, exploration, and warfare.

LOCALE: Western Europe

CATEGORIES: Transportation; engineering; science and technology; trade and commerce

KEY FIGURES

Matthew Baker (1530-1613), England's principal master shipwright under Elizabeth I

Sir John Hawkins (1532-1595), English admiral, slaver, treasurer of the navy, 1573-1595, and controller of the navy, 1589

Philip II (1527-1598), king of Spain, r. 1556-1598

Elizabeth I (1533-1603), queen of England, r. 1558-1603

SUMMARY OF EVENT

The great sailing ships of Europe transformed dramatically over the course of the sixteenth century, and many vessels of different designs were known as galleons during this period. Most relied solely on sails for power, though some used a combination of oars and sails reminiscent of galleys. Galleons were used as both warships and merchant ships, sometimes serving duty as both at once. It was not until the end of the century that the name "galleon" became associated with the large, multifunctional ships of popular imagery, but even then, the actual design varied between countries and even between shipyards.

At the beginning of the sixteenth century, warships and merchant vessels were of two distinct types. Galleys were used primarily for warfare; these were oared vessels with a single mast that relied on speed to ram their opponents, after which sailors would switch to hand-to-hand combat as they boarded an enemy ship. Galleys were well suited for river, channel, and coastal battles, but they were vulnerable in the open sea, as the oars and rowers on the sides provided easy targets for enemy cannons. As the galleys grew bigger, the expense of food and fresh water for increasingly larger crews grew prohibitive, and the constant need for supplies meant they could not stay at sea for long periods of time.

For merchants, sailing ships were more useful than galleys. Replacing oars with sails meant smaller crews needing fewer supplies and more room for cargo and armament. Eliminating the oars also allowed for a rounded hull, which further increased cargo capacity. Most sailing ships at the beginning of the fifteenth century utilized a single mast. The northern European ships used a large square sail hung from a yardarm that crossed the masthead horizontally. The Mediterranean ships used triangular sails, which the northern sailors called "lateen-rigged," because the "Latins" of southern Europe used them. By the middle of the century, changes in the rigging increased maneuverability under sail. Instead of a single mast with a square mainsail, these "full-rigged" ships had multiple masts using both square and lateen sails.

A sixteenth century galley, forerunner of the galleon, in an engraving by Raphael. (Frederick Ungar Publishing Co.)

283

Between the galley and the galleon, there were several variations on the full-rigged sailing ship. Carracks had the ability to make the long ocean voyages required to reach the New World and carried enough cargo in their rounded hulls to make the trip worthwhile. These ships had raised superstructures at both bow and stern, from which the sailors could defend themselves if the ship was boarded. Because of their bulky design, however, carracks lacked speed and maneuverability. The caravel, which originated in Portugal, was smaller and faster than the carrack and was used to open new trade routes, but it could not carry enough cargo to make distant voyages to established ports profitable.

Shipbuilders realized they needed a vessel with the size and cargo capacity of a carrack but the speed and sailing characteristics of a caravel. Much of what is known about the construction of these sixteenth century vessels comes from Matthew Baker's *Fragments of Ancient Shipwrightry* (c. 1570's). Baker was a draftsman as well as a shipwright, and his drawings are the oldest known examples showing the internal construction of a galleon.

A galleon called a man-of-war, or combatant warship, from the sixteenth century. (Frederick Ungar Publishing Co.)

The first galleons were lower, slimmer ships than the bulky carracks, with the proportion of length to beam to freeboard (the area on the side above the waterline) being 4:3:1, as opposed to the carrack's proportions of 3:2:1. These galleons had multiple masts: the bowsprit, the foremast, the mainmast, and one or more mizzenmasts at the rear of the ship. All but the mizzenmasts usually carried square sails, while the mizzenmasts carried lateen sails. Galleons were built to accommodate the heavy cannons that were becoming increasingly necessary. Their fore and aft superstructures were lowered, making them less unwieldy than carracks, and a beakhead similar to that of the old galleys projected from below the bowsprit or front sail.

These redesigned vessels also had more decks and more braces and supports than a carrack. This made them more difficult to load and unload but made for an ideal gun platform. Rows of cannons were mounted against the rigidly braced hull, for both offense and defense. Initially, cannons were mounted on the main deck and fired through openings in the railings, but as shipbuilders increased the number of cannons and moved them below decks in multiple levels, the ships became top-heavy and were in danger of capsizing. To prevent this, galleon hulls were redesigned to slope inward from the water line, placing the cannons on the upper levels closer to the centerline of the hull.

The word "galleon" is of Spanish origin, and Spain was one of the earliest innovators. Because of their conquests in the New World, the Spanish needed ships capable of transoceanic voyages with both a high capacity for cargo and the ability to defend themselves from pirates and enemy vessels. Spanish galleons combined the best of Mediterranean and European ideas into a single ship. The galleon was the backbone of the famous Spanish Armada, a massive fleet of warships launched against England by King Philip II of Spain in 1588.

England responded with the modified, or "race-built," galleon. Under the leadership of Sir John Hawkins, the English utilized an early example of hydrodynamics: Ships were designed to maximize the flow of water around their hulls. These vessels were built as predators, and one of the early drawings from Matthew Baker's manuscript shows a large fish superimposed on the design of a galleon. Even the rudder was streamlined. Fore and aft superstructures were reduced even further, making the ships more maneuverable and allowing for more weight in the form of cannons. A typical galleon carried 3 percent of its weight in armament, whereas a race-built galleon carried 8-11 percent.

The English vessels were true warships, built for battle and lacking the cargo space for transoceanic voyages. With their increased mobility and long-range cannons, England under Queen Elizabeth I was able to repel the ships of Philip II's Spanish Armada, which still relied on boarding parties and melee battle tactics to capture enemy vessels.

SIGNIFICANCE

The evolution of the great sailing ships had a tremendous impact on the European seafaring nations, both at home and as they attempted to colonize and exploit the newly discovered Americas. Although it is not known for certain, many historians believe that the *Santa María*, Christopher Columbus's flagship, may have been a carrack, as it was slower than his other two ships, the *Niña* and the *Pinta*, which were caravels that had been converted to square sails for the long ocean voyage.

Throughout the next two centuries, galleons continued to evolve in response to increased cannon size. English ships in particular were modified and improved to carry heavier armament. Steering improvements followed in the eighteenth century, as the vertical lever for operating the rudder was replaced by a steering "wheel" mounted on the top deck, a design that is still in use today. Changes in the rigging were continuous, and some galleons became "prestige ships," adding sculpture and ornate decorations to the more functional designs of the earlier centuries.

Because of its superior armament, every European navy used the galleon as a battle ship until the late eighteenth century, when they were gradually replaced by the "ship-of-the-line," essentially a floating gun platform with three decks of cannons.

—*P. S. Ramsey*

FURTHER READING

Guilmartin, John F., Jr. *Galleons and Galleys*. London: Cassell, 2002. An in-depth analysis of the evolution of the galley and galleon from the mid-fourteenth century to the mid-seventeenth century.

_____. *Gunpowder and Galleys: Changing Technology and Mediterranean Warfare at Sea in the Sixteenth Century*. Rev. ed. Annapolis, Md.: United States Naval Institute Press, 2004. A comprehensive account of early sixteenth century naval warfare in the Mediterranean and Arabian peninsula regions.

Lane, Frederic Chapin. *Venetian Ships and Shipbuilders of the Renaissance*. Baltimore: Johns Hopkins University Press, 1992. Reprint of 1934 reference book with a detailed history of the Venetian shipyards.

Phillips, Carla Rahn. *Six Galleons for the King of Spain: Imperial Defense in the Early Seventeenth Century*. Baltimore: Johns Hopkins University Press, 1986. A detailed history of Spanish shipbuilding, including the history of many of the ships that were built during that time period.

Wheatley, Joseph. *Historic Sail: The Glory of the Sailing Ship from the Thirteenth to the Nineteenth Century*. London: Greenhill Books, 2000. A lavishly illustrated book with full-color reproductions of drawings of specific ships built during this period.

SEE ALSO: 1463-1479: Ottoman-Venetian War; Aug., 1487-Dec., 1488: Dias Rounds the Cape of Good Hope; 1490's: Decline of the Silk Road; Oct. 12, 1492: Columbus Lands in the Americas; Beginning c. 1500: Coffee, Cacao, Tobacco, and Sugar Are Sold Worldwide; 1519-1522: Magellan Expedition Circumnavigates the Globe; Sept. 27-28, 1538: Battle of Préveza; July 31-Aug. 8, 1588: Defeat of the Spanish Armada; Dec. 31, 1600: Elizabeth I Charters the East India Company.

RELATED ARTICLES in *Great Lives from History: The Renaissance & Early Modern Era, 1454-1600:* Christopher Columbus; Elizabeth I; Philip II.

16th century
IROQUOIS CONFEDERACY IS ESTABLISHED

*The Iroquois, or Haudenosaunee, are the prime
example of the level of cultural evolution that non-
nomadic North American Indian tribes attained. The
tribes that made up the Iroquois Confederacy
controlled parts of the northeastern United States and
southeastern Canada for nearly three centuries.*

LOCALE: Northeastern North America (now primarily
　New York State and Ontario, Canada)
CATEGORIES: Diplomacy and international relations;
　government and politics

KEY FIGURES
Deganawida (The Peacemaker; c. 1550-c. 1600),
　Huron or Mohawk prophet or holy man
Hiawatha (c. 1525-c. 1575), Mohawk chief
Handsome Lake (Ganeodiyo; c. 1735-1815), Seneca
　visionary prophet
Atotarho (fl. 1500's), Onondaga chief

SUMMARY OF EVENT
Archaeological evidence places the predecessors of the
Iroquois in what is now New York State for one thousand
to fifteen hundred years prior to the emergence of the Iroquois Confederacy. A subsistence culture called Owasco
preceded the Iroquois, and the Owasco were preceded in
turn by the Hopewell culture. Both cultures had traceable
influences on Iroquois culture. By 1400, distinctively
Iroquoian villages existed; by 1600, all the units of the
confederacy were calling the larger group Haudenosaunee, the People of the Longhouse.

The Haudenosaunee lived in fortified, stockade villages, were agrarian and matrilineal (that is, their property passed from mothers to daughters), and banded together through a strong political and religious system, in
which ultimate power was vested in the hands of the oldest "sensible" woman of each clan. The foundation of the
culture was called the fireplace, or hearth. Each hearth—
a mother and her children—was part of a larger extended
family, or *owachira*. Two or more *owachiras* made a
clan; eight clans made a tribe.

The Iroquois Confederacy—also referred to as the
League of the Iroquois or the League of Five Nations—
was established as early as 1500 to unite and pacify the
infighting Iroquois and to gain strength in numbers to resist the implacable opposition of Huron- and Algonquian-
speaking neighbors. (The word *iroquois*, as spelled by
the French, probably comes from the Algonquian enemy

name *iriokiu* or "spitting snake.") The confederacy, if
later dates of its inception are accepted, may have formed
as a response to the fur trade. Before the consolidation of
the confederacy, warfare—primarily the revenge feud—
was constant among the Iroquois, who had no mechanism to bring the strife to an end.

The consolidation of the confederacy was primarily a
result of the efforts of the Mohawk chief Hiawatha and
the Onondaga chief Atotarho. These historical figures
based the religious and political principles of the confederacy on the teachings ascribed to the prophet Deganawida (also known as the Peacemaker), whose historical
authenticity is contested. The political rules and regulations, the cultural model, and the spiritual teachings and
religious model all attributed to Deganawida were later
qualified and codified by Handsome Lake (also known as
Ganeodiyo), a late-eighteenth century Seneca visionary
prophet responding to the pressures of Christianity after
the Revolutionary War.

The League of the Iroquois included the Mohawk,
Oneida, Onondaga, Cayuga, and Seneca (the Five Nations). The league was based on a carefully crafted constitution. The "faithkeeper," or central religious leader,
called a yearly council to recite the constitution and its
laws and to resolve differences. The council retained the
roles of the leaders, which were defined from ancient
times by clan system relationships. Fifty chiefs made up
the council and served for life but could be removed from
office by the clan mothers if they violated moral or ethical codes.

Religious life was organized according to the teachings of the Peacemaker. Three men and three women supervised the keeping of the ceremonies. The cosmology
was well defined, and the origin stories were detailed and
sophisticated. Curing illnesses was a central part of daily
religious life. The Iroquois had a profound sense of the
psychology of the soul and understood dreams and divinations to be communications between one's personality
and one's soul.

At the time of the arrival of the Europeans, the coastal
regions of the Northeast were occupied by Algonquian-
speaking peoples, and the inland waterways were occupied by Iroquoian-speaking peoples. The entire area was
crisscrossed by the trails of a vast trading network that
reached to the Subarctic. Storable foods were traded for
furs, nuts, obsidian, shells, flints, and other items. Wam-
pum belts of shells and, later, beads described symboli-

cally and mnemonically almost all political dealings among and within tribes.

The fur trade and European economics changed the lives of the Iroquois drastically. Acquisition, exploitation, and competition became normal for Northeastern tribes. The confederacy created a combined military force of more than a thousand men that, in the mid-seventeenth century, effectively eliminated the Huron, Erie, Petun, and Illinois tribes as players in the fur trade.

The ever-increasing encroachment of the French and the British presented the Iroquois with three options: compromise; adoption of the ways of the Europeans, including their economics and religion; or use of violence to reject the wave of invaders. The Iroquois drew from all three options: They compromised whenever necessary to keep their neutrality and the peace. They adopted the religions and much of the trade economy (thus becoming dependent on metal items), but not the political and societal structures, of the Europeans. Finally, they chose to fight violently against the French and the tribal allies of the French.

SIGNIFICANCE

The nations of the confederacy had a crucial role in U.S. history. After 1609, when a war party of Mohawks met a group of French and Huron soldiers under Samuel de Champlain and lost six Mohawk warriors to the muskets of the French, the Mohawks carried a dogged hatred of the French forward into their alliances—first with the Dutch, from whom they obtained their firearms, and then with the British, from whom they obtained all forms of trade items and by whom they were converted to the Anglican version of Christianity. Thus, the Hudson and Mohawk River Valleys were simultaneously opened to the British and closed to the French. The subsequent British dominance of the New World was made much easier by Iroquois control of the waterways from the east coast into the interior of the continent.

In 1677, the Five Nations of the Confederacy met in Albany and wrote into history their memorized, mnemonically cued Great Law, best described as a constitution. At the end of the seventeenth century, the Iroquois had mastered the artful politics of their pivotal

position. They played the various European traders one against the other, kept their neutrality with level-headed diplomacy, and maintained their control of the riverine system and the Great Lakes with intimidating success. Their hegemony included the territory from Maine to the Mississippi River, and from the Ottawa River in Canada to Kentucky and the Chesapeake Bay region.

In the eighteenth century, the Iroquois had more power than any other indigenous nation in North America. After 1722, a sixth nation, the Tuscarora, joined the confederacy. Colonial delegates from all the states of the Americas traveled to Albany to learn about governing from the Iroquois. The longhouse sachems urged the colonists to form assemblies and to meet and discuss common interests. In 1754, the first intercolonial conference was held at Albany, and Iroquois delegates were in attendance.

The Iroquois maintained their power in spite of the assault of European culture and religion during the eighteenth century. Until about the end of the French and Indian War (1763), the Iroquois were united in their resolve to stay neutral and not be drawn into the imperial wars between the French and the English. By the time of the American Revolution (1776), however, the league's ability to stay neutral and to influence its members had lessened. During the Revolutionary War, the Seneca, Cayuga, and Mohawk fought with the British; the Onon-

A sixteenth century tribal council-meeting. (Hulton|Archive by Getty Images)

daga tried to remain aloof; and the Oneida and Tuscarora sided with the Americans.

The American Revolution ended the power of the Iroquois. By 1800, only two thousand survived on tiny reservations in western New York. Another six thousand had fled to Canada. Despite the conflicts and contacts with European cultures, the Iroquois have retained their society and many of their cultural practices, including kinship and ceremonial ties.

—Glenn Schiffman

FURTHER READING

Englebrecht, William. *Iroquoia: The Development of a Native World.* Syracuse, N.Y.: Syracuse University Press, 2003. Comprehensive history of the Iroquois peoples, from prehistory to present-day descendants, based on archaeological research, historical documents, oral tradition, and linguistics. Includes illustrations, maps, bibliographic references, and index.

Fenton, William N. *The Great Law and the Longhouse: A Political History of the Iroquois Confederacy.* Norman: University of Oklahoma Press, 1998. Exhaustive sourcebook on the Iroquois Confederacy from its inception to 1794. Chapters 2 through 6 deal with Hiawatha.

Graymont, Barbara. *The Iroquois.* New York: Chelsea House Press, 1988. Graymont is an expert on the Haudenosaunee; this precise, concise text is essential for scholars of the Longhouse culture.

Henry, Thomas R. *Wilderness Messiah: The Story of Hiawatha and the Iroquois.* New York: W. Sloane, 1955. Defines the line between legend and history in the founding of the Iroquois league, and in the stories of Hiawatha, Deganawida, and Atotarho.

Jennings, Francis. *The Founders of America.* New York: W. W. Norton, 1993. An accurate history of special value to high school teachers.

Lyons, Oren, et al. *Exiled in the Land of the Free.* Santa Fe, N. Mex.: Clear Light, 1992. Lyons, faithkeeper of the Six Nations Confederacy, possesses a distinctive understanding of the role of the American Indian in U.S. history.

Mann, Barbara A., and Jerry L. Fields. "A Sign in the Sky: Dating the League of the Haudenosaunee." *American Indian Culture and Research Journal* 21, no. 2 (1997): 105-163. This article makes a case that the Iroquois Confederacy was founded about 1142, not between 1450 and 1550, as most European American scholars believe.

Richter, Daniel K. *Ordeal of the Longhouse: The Peoples of the Iroquois League in the Era of European Colonization.* Chapel Hill: University of North Carolina Press, 1992. A thorough history of the Iroquois people and their confederacy before and after the arrival of the Europeans.

Snow, Dean R. *The Iroquois.* Reprint. Cambridge, Mass.: Blackwell, 1996. Another comprehensive history of the Iroquois employing the "rise and fall" model to discuss the origins, height, and decline of the Five Nations. Includes illustrations, maps, bibliographic references, and index.

Taylor, Colin F., ed. *The Native Americans: The Indigenous People of North America.* New York: Smithmark, 1991. Companion book to a 1990's televised series on Native Americans.

SEE ALSO: Oct. 12, 1492: Columbus Lands in the Americas; June 24, 1497-May, 1498: Cabot's Voyages; Early 16th cent.: Rise of the Fur Trade; 16th cent.: Decline of Moundville; Beginning 1519: Smallpox Kills Thousands of Indigenous Americans; Apr. 20, 1534-July, 1543: Cartier and Roberval Search for a Northwest Passage; Mid-1570's: Powhatan Confederacy Is Founded; June 7, 1576-July, 1578: Frobisher's Voyages.

RELATED ARTICLES in *Great Lives from History: The Renaissance & Early Modern Era, 1454-1600:* Deganawida; Hiawatha.

16th century
PROLIFERATION OF FIREARMS

Firearms and cannons grew easier to use, more powerful, and more important to land-based and naval tactics in Europe, the Ottoman Empire, and Asia, which led to fundamental changes to military organization and warfare.

LOCALE: Worldwide
CATEGORIES: Science and technology; wars, uprisings, and civil unrest

KEY FIGURES

Niccolò Fontana Tartaglia (c. 1500-1557), Italian mathematician known as the father of ballistics
Süleyman the Magnificent (1494/1495-1566), Ottoman sultan, r. 1520-1566, who mastered siege warfare
Gaston de Foix (1489-1512), duke of Nemours, French commander, and innovator in use of artillery and firearms
Oda Nobunaga (1534-1582), Japanese leader who incorporated firearms into battle tactics

SUMMARY OF EVENT

Gunpowder and cannons, almost certainly invented in China, became known to European countries and the Ottoman Empire by the thirteenth century. Firearms light enough to be used by one person, such as the handgun and harquebus, developed in the following two centuries, and armed forces throughout Europe, the Middle East, and Asia incorporated them gradually. The sixteenth century was a period of technological refinement, standardization, and tactical innovation so extensive that it transformed warfare and altered the social hierarchy of military forces.

This expansion was most evident in artillery. Commanders used cannons initially to supplement the trebuchet and catapult in breaching the walls of cities and castles during sieges, but by 1500, cannons were the primary weapons, even though they were unwieldy. These early cannons were cast from bronze or made of iron rods beaten together and girdled by iron belts, strong enough only for small iron cannonballs or large stone shot. Through the cen-

tury, the trend was for more mobile, powerful cannons and a greater role in supporting infantry maneuvers on the battlefield. By 1600, cast-iron cannons had become common. They were capable of using corned gunpowder (granulated gunpowder, which was more powerful) and could shoot large iron cannonballs at greater ranges.

After a profusion of types and sizes in the early part of the century, countries began to standardize artillery to simplify logistics and maintenance. There were three basic types, according to historian John Norris. First was the culverin type, which were field guns designed for long-range firing and weighed from 200 to 7,000 pounds, had bores of up to 6.5 inches, and had effective ranges of 200 to 2,000 yards. The second type, the cannon, was more mobile and designed to fire heavy projectiles over shorter distances. They varied from 2,000 to 12,000 pounds in weight, 4.6 to 10 inches in bore, and 400 to 750 yards in effective range. The third type, including the pedrero and mortar, was designed to loft large cannonballs or explosive shells over walls during sieges. They weighed as little as 1,500 pounds and as much as 10,000 pounds, had bores of 6.3 to 15 inches, and had effective ranges of 300 to 1,000 yards.

The Ottoman sultan Süleyman the Magnificent shocked the Western world by employing cannons in

An engraving that depicts movable, sixteenth century mortars (cannons). (Frederick Ungar Publishing Co.)

successful sieges of Belgrade (1521), Rhodes (1522), and various strongholds in Hungary (1526). Only Vienna withstood assaults by the Ottoman forces, which, had they succeeded, would have exposed Western Europe to invasion. At sea, cannons were regular armaments aboard ships by 1500 but were used only to damage and disable enemy ships in preparation for boarding and capture through hand-to-hand combat. The advent of lighter, more accurate cannons aboard ships strong enough to withstand the recoil shock of a broadside made stand-off battles possible. In 1588, an English fleet met the Spanish Armada in the English Channel. The English relied on their cannons alone to drive off the reportedly superior Spanish force, which unsuccessfully tried to board the English ships. It was the first large naval battle decided by cannons.

Small arms became progressively lighter, more accurate, and varied during the sixteenth century, supplanting the longbow and crossbow as infantry weapons and reducing the role of the pike. In 1500, the harquebus was the primary type. Its firing mechanism was the matchlock; a smoldering length of fuse, the match, was lowered into a priming charge, which ignited the gunpowder in the gun to fire the projectile, usually a lead ball. For military purposes, it was an awkward weapon: It required the shooter to keep a source of fire handy to light the fuse, making it a fair-weather weapon. Early in the sixteenth century, a mechanical firing mechanism was introduced in Europe. Called the wheel lock, it worked on essentially the same principle as the modern cigarette lighter. A piece of iron pyrite was attached to a hammer-like armature powered by a coiled spring. Pulling the trigger released the hammer so that it struck a spinning metal wheel, which threw the resulting sparks into a priming pan and fired the weapon.

The wheel lock musket had several advantages. A smooth bore of about one inch, it was larger than the harquebus and more powerful, capable of propelling a large ball as much as five hundred yards. Unlike the matchlock, the wheel lock mechanism could be wound up in advance and then fired rapidly, making it tactically more flexible. In rate of fire and accuracy, the wheel lock musket was inferior to the longbow, but whereas it took years of practice to master the bow, recruits could effectively handle the musket after a week of instruction, according to historian Kenneth Chase. The wheel lock musket also was easier to load and supply than the crossbow, which had comparable accuracy and somewhat faster rate of fire. The wheel lock required only one hand to fire once it was cocked, so it was adapted as a pistol

An engraving showing the harquebus, an awkward and cumbersome firearm replaced in the early sixteenth century by a mechanical firing mechanism called the wheel lock, which worked on essentially the same principle as the modern cigarette lighter. (Frederick Ungar Publishing Co.)

and used by cavalry troops by about 1540. Furthermore, rifling (spiral groves inside the barrel) was introduced in the mid-sixteenth century; it caused the weapon's projectile to spin, making it more stable and accurate. Rifled muskets, however, were rare.

The increased use of firearms, combined with artillery support on the battlefield, changed tactics. Massed fire ended the role of heavy cavalry as the main offensive force because balls fired from muskets could pierce the armor of mounted knights well before they posed a threat to the infantry. In his Italian campaign of 1512, French commander Gaston de Foix met a superior Spanish army near Ravenna and defeated it in a battle of maneuver, with batteries of cannons supporting infantry units composed of pikemen and musketeers and cavalry used as scouts and harassers. Oda Nobunaga incorporated matchlocks, introduced to Japan by the Portuguese in 1542, into his infantry of skirmishers and snipers; his consequent battlefield successes led to the unification of Japan under his successor, shogun Tokugawa Ieyasu (r. 1603-1605). In the New World in the early sixteenth century, small forces of Spanish conquistadores armed with guns and a few cannons terrified large Aztec armies in Mexico and the Incan armies in the South American Andes.

Significance

The sixteenth century saw the acceleration of an arms race that has yet to stop. In Europe, the Middle East, and Asia, countries devoted increasing portions of their government resources to making more and better firearms and cannons for professional forces. A technological race, the trend entailed new military specialties in artillery, ordnance, logistics, and engineering (particularly in new fortification designs).

Artillery gave impetus to the mathematical study of ballistics, a complex subject that called for specialist artillery officers acquainted with such published studies as Niccolò Fontana Tartaglia's *La nova scientia* (1537; *The New Science*, 1969), considered the first scientific work in ballistics. Moreover, firearms became an export commodity for European countries. China, for instance, had to import muskets because it fell behind in technological expertise. Infantry, cavalry, and artillery tactics changed during the century, culminating in the development of volley fire by the Dutch in the 1590's, and few major changes were seen again until after the Napoleonic Wars two hundred years later.

Because charges by mounted armored knights were foolhardy in the face of firearms, the chivalric military ethos of the Middle Ages became obsolete. A mere peasant with a musket could kill an aristocratic knight from a safe distance. Instead, the noble families of Europe and Asia began contributing officers to command in mixed commoner-aristocrat units, bringing the classes into greater proximity and somewhat blunting social distinc-

tions, at least in warfare. Conservative aristocrats and the Catholic Church condemned firearms as ignoble, diabolical, and injurious to social structure, but the conservative backlash was overwhelmed by the proliferation of gunpowder weaponry.

—*Roger Smith*

Further Reading

Archer, Christon I., John R. Ferris, Holger H. Herwig, and Timothy H. E. Travers. *World History of Warfare*. Lincoln: University of Nebraska Press, 2002. Chapter 6, "The Age of Gunpowder and Sail," summarizes the effects of developing firearm and artillery technology, focused on land and naval conflicts in Europe and the Middle East.

Arnold, Thomas F. *The Renaissance at War*. London: Cassell, 2001. A colorfully illustrated, concise overview of the Renaissance and its armaments that explains the technology of gunpowder weaponry and the changes in tactics they inspired.

Chase, Kenneth. *Firearms: A Global History to 1700*. New York: Cambridge University Press, 2003. Although providing worldwide coverage, Chase focuses primarily on technological and tactical innovations in Europe, the Ottoman Empire, Japan, and China in developing his thesis that firearms developed in regions with both a broad industrial sophistication and wars of massed combatants.

Norris, John. *Artillery: A History*. Gloucestershire, England: Sutton, 2000. This book, which devotes a chapter to the sixteenth century, examines Europe primarily and England in particular. Norris delineates types of artillery, explains their construction and handling, and comments on their influence on battle tactics.

Tartaglia, Niccolò Fontana. *The New Science*. In *Mechanics in Sixteenth-Century Italy*, edited and translated by Stillman Drake and Israel E. Drabkin. Madison: University of Wisconsin Press, 1969. A translation of Tartaglia's work on artillery and ballistics.

See also: June 28, 1522-Dec. 27, 1522: Siege and Fall of Rhodes; Aug. 29, 1526: Battle of Mohács; Mid-16th cent.: Development of the Caracole Maneuver.
Related articles in *Great Lives from History: The Renaissance & Early Modern Era, 1454-1600:* Oda Nobunaga; Süleyman the Magnificent; Niccolò Fontana Tartaglia.

1500's

16th century
RISE OF THE *SHENSHI*

During the sixteenth century, Chinese officials and scholars known as the shenshi, *or gentry, rose through the examination system. The gentry class functioned as the backbone of the governing structure during the rise of imperial China.*

LOCALE: China

CATEGORIES: Organizations and institutions; cultural and intellectual history; education; government and politics

SUMMARY OF EVENT

The Chinese degree holders of all ranks have been known in Chinese as *shenshi*, "officials and scholars." In English, the term "gentry" has been used to refer to this class; sometimes they are also referred to as the Chinese scholar-official class. In the context of Chinese society, however, the meaning of *shenshi* is broader, including both office-degree holders and landlords. The landlords, from which class the degree holders often originated, were entrusted by the government with the responsibilities of maintaining order and peace and functioned as unofficial extensions of the government at the local level. Therefore, both officeholders and landlords were perceived as the privileged class of gentry.

China's examination system and its official gentry class first came into existence during the Tang Dynasty (618-907). The development of a commercial economy and civil service examinations during the Song Dynasty (960-1279) promoted a much broader social bracket of gentry class. By the time of the Ming Dynasty (1368-1644), the gentry class performed administrative responsibilities without official appointment, thus forming the essential and effective governing structure of traditional China.

The Tang continued the government schools and examination system of the previous dynasty. The specialized national schools were established in the capital. The Ministry of Rites held examinations for students from the government schools and for nominees by the local governments. There were two chief academic degrees, one called *xiu cai* (flowering talent) for current political issues, the other called *jin shi* (presented scholar) for letters—the most prestigious degree and the primary passage to officialdom. The Tang examination system helped create a bureaucracy of merit that selected by and large the most talented of the land to run its bureaucratic machine. Furthermore, the examination system fostered an intellectually unified nation, because all who desired the degree and the subsequent imperial appointment would have to acquire the same classical education.

Commercial development during the Song Dynasty brought profound social and cultural changes. It is believed that Song China transformed the highly aristocratic society of the early Tang into a nearly non-aristocratic, more egalitarian society. Unlike the old aristocracy, the new gentry class depended much less on their agricultural land and its production, and their commercial activities became a significant part of the gentry's family economy. A great number of gentry resided in cities and towns, and the high culture of city was at the center of their social life. The economic wealth of the gentry was translated into political power, which they acquired through education and by passage of the civil service examinations that granted them government offices.

Thus, on the surface the gentry class seemed to have obtained political prominence more from their intellectual achievements than from their economic wealth. Consequently, the gentry rose as the reputable social group and the backbone of the bureaucratic governments throughout the Chinese history.

While the Yuan Dynasty (1279-1368) practiced racial discrimination and class oppression, it also tried to soften hostilities toward the Chinese, especially Confucian scholars. Kublai Khan (or Khubilai) gave orders to protect the Confucian temples and restore Confucianism as the official philosophy. He also exempted Confucian scholars from taxation and encouraged them to serve in his court.

The recovery of Chinese rule over China during the Ming Dynasty (1368-1644) reinstituted the civil service examination system. During the Ming, there existed three levels of examinations. The preliminary examinations held at the county level would select and grant to qualified scholars the *xiu cai*, or flowering talent, degree, which honored a scholar's intellectual achievements and included him in the privileged class of gentry who were exempted from labor service and corporal punishments. Holders of the *xiu cai* could enter the second level of examinations, held at the provincial capitals every three years. During these examinations, which lasted several days, the candidates were confined in rows of tiny cells at the examination field to write essays on Confucian classics. Less than 1 percent of the candidates passed the examination and earned the *ju ren*, or "recommended men" degree, to proceed to the third level of triennial metropolitan examinations held at the capital, Beijing. There, successful candidates would obtain the highest academic title, the *jin shi* or "presented scholar" degree, and these metropolitan graduates took the final examination at the court, presided over by the emperor himself. The palace examination then determined the official ranking and government posts of the *jin shi* holders.

The civil service examination system during the Ming Dynasty was strictly regulated to prevent possible defaults and partiality. The names of candidates were concealed, and sometimes the candidates' papers were copied to ensure anonymity. The proctors of the provincial examinations were dispatched from the capital. The examinations were managed by the Ministry of Rites rather than the Ministry of Personnel, which supervised government officials. Overall, officials selected through the examination system had mastered knowledge of the Confucian classics, and this universal training helped to foster a unified government bureaucracy that strengthened the centralization of government. The system of meritocracy also provided hope, though very slim, for millions of Chinese men who otherwise would never have had a chance to climb the ladder to become part of Ming officialdom.

On the other hand, because the civil service examinations centered on the Confucian classics, candidates were encouraged to develop their book knowledge at the expense of practical issues. The lengthy preparation of the Confucian classics also meant that only those with substantial economic resources could afford the long period of study required to do well. The system thus favored the wealthy over the poor.

SIGNIFICANCE

In many ways, and certainly at the local level, the *shenshi* or gentry class formed the backbone of the Chinese Confucian government, performing administrative responsibilities without official appointment. They helped the government to collect taxes and raised funds for local public works such as the building and repairing of dikes and roads. They handled local disputes over property or conflicts resulting from the clash of individual personalities. The gentry also maintained Confucian culture by establishing and sponsoring local Confucian schools and Confucian temples. They organized charitable institutions for orphans, widows, and the disabled, and they provided relief during natural disasters. They even

formed militias to defend their wealth and the local community.

These administrative, cultural, and social activities were mostly encouraged and recognized by the Ming government. This official recognition, together with the gentry's economic privileges, gave them great prestige and power over the bulk of the population, who were made up of small landowners and tenant farmers. While most gentry restrained themselves with Confucian virtues and morale, a great many abused their power and grew into local despots, exploiting the local people. Such corruption among some of the gentry deepened the social conflict between the landlord class and the tenant class, and at times even incited social upheavals.

—*Huping Ling*

FURTHER READING

Huang, Ray. *1587, a Year of No Significance: The Ming Dynasty in Decline*. New Haven, Conn.: Yale University Press, 1981. A prizewinning work by a distinguished scholar, detailing the ritualistic and practical sides of Ming court politics.

Hucker, Charles O. *The Ming Dynasty: Its Origins and Evolving Institutions*. Ann Arbor: Center for Chinese Studies, the University of Michigan, 1978. Initially written in 1970 for inclusion in *The Cambridge History of China*, this monograph presents Ming institutional history with clarity and factual accuracy.

Marks, Robert B. *Tigers, Rice, Silk, and Silt: Environment and Economy in Late Imperial South China*. Cambridge, England: Cambridge University Press, 1998. Offers exhaustive coverage of the economic conditions of South China during the imperial age.

Mote, Frederick W. *Imperial China, 900-1800*. Cambridge, Mass.: Harvard University Press, 1999. A comprehensive and impressive work on imperial China.

Mote, Frederick W., and Denis Twitchett, eds. *The Ming Dynasty, 1368-1644, Part 1*. Vol. 7 in *The Cambridge History of China*. Cambridge, England: Cambridge University Press, 1988. A collection of essays written by eminent scholars on various aspects of Ming history.

Tsai, Shih-shan Henry. *Perpetual Happiness: The Ming Emperor Yongle*. Seattle: University of Washington Press, 2001. Provides a detailed description of the Chinese empire during the Ming Dynasty, including government, economy, and international relations.

SEE ALSO: Feb. 11, 1457: Restoration of Zhengtong; 1465-1487: Reign of Xianzong; 1474: Great Wall of

1500's

China Is Built; 1488-1505: Reign of Xiaozong; 16th cent.: China's Population Boom; 1505-1521: Reign of Zhengde and Liu Jin.

Related articles in *Great Lives from History: The Renaissance & Early Modern Era, 1454-1600:* Wang Yangming; Xiaozong.

16th century
SINGLE-WHIP REFORM

The Single-Whip Reform was the Ming government's attempt to correct abuses in the tax system by combining various land and service taxes into a single cash payment, thus creating the beginning of a modern tax system.

Locale: China
Categories: Agriculture; economics; social reform

KEY FIGURES
Zhang Juzheng (Chang Chü-cheng; 1525-1582), the chief grant secretary and the chief engineer of the Single-Whip Reform
Wanli (reign name, also Wan-li; personal name Zhu Yijun, Chu I-chün; posthumous name Zhu Yijun, Chu I-chün; temple name Shenzong, Shen-tsung; 1563-1620), the thirteenth Ming emperor, r. 1573-1620, a supporter of the Single-Whip Reform

SUMMARY OF EVENT
During the Ming Dynasty, the Chinese empire enjoyed population growth, an increase in tax grain (rice used to pay taxes), and growth in both domestic and international trade. However, the Chinese court also confronted a number of fiscal problems: an inadequate monetary system, excessive military spending, a shrinkage of government salaries, and a tax system that was too complex to administer efficiently. In an attempt to solve the problems, the Ming government underwent a series of fiscal reforms known collectively as the Single-Whip Reform.

Among the fiscal problems the Ming government faced was the inadequacy of the monetary system. To supplement a shortage of the copper coins that were the main currency, the government introduced unminted silver for use in tax transactions. When grains and other commodities that peasants used for taxes were converted to silver, however, peasants were often forced to pay surcharges. In addition to this monetary problem, military expenditures had grown, taking an ever larger portion of the land tax that the government collected as revenue. Finally, inadequate salaries for government officials, of-

ten converted into commodities at a low exchange rate when government funds were low, affected morale and encouraged corruption.

The biggest problem, however, was the confusion and complexity of the tax system and its effect on land and labor. The land tax during the Ming was assessed according to how the land was classified, and the land was reclassified approximately every ten years. This system was maintained by the heads of local wealthy households, which because of their conflict of interest were therefore motivated to avoid their tax responsibilities by falsifying the land records. The falsification of land records was compounded by the complexity of taxes and labor services. For example, the number of male adults in each jurisdiction, on which the tax assessments were in part based, varied according to local need and by decision of the local authorities. As taxation became more corrupt, demands for labor services increasingly added burdens on the local villages. Eventually, the problem of land and labor taxes hit peasants the hardest.

To solve these fiscal problems, the Ming government underwent a series of reforms to simplify the tax structure and to secure the tax collection from 1522 to 1619. Because these reforms combined and simplified many taxes into single monetary payments, they became known as *yi tiao bian,* meaning "many items combined into one." Because *yi tiao bian* sounds also like "a single whip," the movement also became known as the Single-Whip Reform. The Single-Whip Reform was carried out gradually by many provincial officials, first in the southeastern coastal provinces and later throughout the rest of the country, in an attempt to maintain a regular and reliable system of taxation and tax collection. The reforms in the provinces varied in particulars but agreed in essentials. Eventually, with the endorsement of the Ming court, the reform was uniformly implemented.

The first major reform was to simplify the land classification from many different rates to only two or three rates. The second measure combined the land taxes from thirty or forty different taxes into two or three types of taxes. Third, both land and labor taxes were computed into one kind of tax to be paid in silver. Finally, the government established standard tax collection dates to reduce the possibility of tax fraud and evasion.

Although the reforms were initiated at the provincial level, Chief Grant Secretary Zhang Juzheng was recognized as the primary engineer of the reforms. Zhang, one of the great ministers of the dynasty, had risen to power during the first decade of the reign of the exceptionally intelligent Wanli emperor, Zhu Yijun, who came to the throne in 1573 at age nine. Zhang was appointed to tutor the boy emperor, as he had tutored his father ten years earlier. As a surrogate father figure, Zhang was extremely influential, setting the boy's lessons and explaining the classical texts to him. Wanli respected and trusted Zhang in the role of tutor, endured his sermonizing on personal austerity and conscientious governing, and submitted to Zhang's curbs on boyish pleasures but eventually developed a degree of resentment and hostility toward Zhang.

During the reform era, Zhang's major contributions were to recognize the utility of the reform, to conceive the change, to secure its implementation by the central government, and to combat the inertia and countervailing interests that had benefited from the old system. When in power, Zhang tried to increase the land-tax revenue by reinstating the tax for lands that had been exempted. He also tried to curtail the excessive perquisites and privileges of the imperial family and government functionaries.

Zhang died in 1582 after an incapacitating illness at the age of fifty-seven. After Zhang's death, Wanli, approaching twenty and now free of Zhang's supervision, became completely irresponsible, refusing to conduct court business, avoiding meetings with his ministers and foreign emissaries, and squandering imperial revenues. Zhang was richly rewarded with posthumous honors and gifts, but almost immediately his enemies began to attack him with charges of improperly enriching himself, misusing his authority, and mistreating imperial relatives. Wanli had the charges investigated, and some of them appeared to have merit: Zhang was found to have left vast wealth. Wanli, remembering his tutor's constant appeals for frugality in the imperial household and for personal austerity, felt he had been defrauded. Consequently, Wanli took posthumous revenge on Zhang by destroying his family and weeding out his influence.

SIGNIFICANCE

The Single-Whip Reform was a prototype of modern taxation. Its principles—such as computation of taxes by the

government office and payment in cash rather than in commodities—have been incorporated into the tax structures of modern times. The assessment of taxes was based on the budgetary need of the state and therefore assured a reliable tax income to run the government. The tax payment of silver could be used to pay the government officials and hired laborers. The peasants were also freed from the trouble of transporting tax grain to the government granaries; instead, they simply paid tax directly to the government's local tax-collecting agencies.

The Single-Whip Reform was made possible only through China's dependence on foreign silver. The reforms marked the widespread transition from copper to silver coinage in Chinese markets. As a result of the tax reforms, China's silver imports added at least eight times more bullion to its coinage stock than did its domestic mines in the second half of the sixteenth century, and twenty times more in the first half of the seventeenth century.

—*Huping Ling*

FURTHER READING

Huang, Ray. *1587, a Year of No Significance: The Ming Dynasty in Decline*. New Haven, Conn.: Yale University Press, 1981. A prizewinning work by a distinguished scholar, detailing the ritualistic and practical sides of Ming court politics.

Hucker, Charles O. *The Ming Dynasty: Its Origins and Evolving Institutions*. Ann Arbor: Center for Chinese Studies, University of Michigan, 1978. Initially written in 1970 for inclusion in *The Cambridge History of China*, this account possesses factual accuracy and clarity on the Ming institutions.

Marks, Robert B. *Tigers, Rice, Silk, and Silt: Environment and Economy in Late Imperial South China*. Cambridge, England: Cambridge University Press, 1998. Exhaustive coverage of the economic conditions of South China during the imperial age.

Mote, Frederick W. *Imperial China, 900-1800*. Cambridge, Mass.: Harvard University Press, 1999. A comprehensive and impressive work on imperial China.

Mote, Frederick. W., and Denis Twitchett, eds. *The Ming Dynasty, 1368-1644, Part 1*. Vol. 7 in *The Cambridge History of China*. Cambridge, England: Cambridge University Press, 1988. A collection of essays written by eminent scholars on various aspects of Ming history.

Tsai, Shih-shan Henry. *Perpetual Happiness: The Ming Emperor Yongle*. Seattle: University of Washington

1500's

Press, 2001. Provides a detailed description of the Chinese Empire during the Ming Dynasty, including its government, economy, and international relations.

SEE ALSO: 16th cent.: China's Population Boom; 16th century: Worldwide Inflation; 1514-1598: Portuguese Reach China; 1521-1567: Reign of Jiajing; Spring, 1523: Ōuchi Family Monopolizes Trade with China; 1545-1548: Silver Is Discovered in Spanish America; 1550-1571: Mongols Raid Beijing; Jan. 23, 1556: Earthquake in China Kills Thousands; 1567-1572: Reign of Longqing; 1573-1620: Reign of Wanli; 1583-1610: Matteo Ricci Travels to Beijing.

RELATED ARTICLES in *Great Lives from History: The Renaissance & Early Modern Era, 1454-1600:* Tomé Pires; Matteo Ricci; Xiaozong; Zhengde.

16th century
TRANS-SAHARAN TRADE ENRICHES AKAN KINGDOMS

The Akan goldfields were the greatest of West African deposits, and the last to be mined. They were developed by Wangara traders who channeled the gold into a trans-Saharan trading system that was already centuries old. The outflow of gold brought wealth and resources to a region that was just beginning to organize itself into political states.

LOCALE: Akan forest region, Ghana (now in Republic of Ghana)
CATEGORIES: Trade and commerce; economics

SUMMARY OF EVENT

By the time the Akan mines became the major producer of West African gold in the mid- to late fifteenth century, the trans-Saharan trading system was well established. The earliest of the major West African mines, that of Bambuk in the upper Senegal basin, was sending gold north by at least the eighth century and perhaps as early as the fourth. In the eleventh and twelfth centuries, a larger source was opened at Bure on the upper Niger River. A class of Muslim Soninke merchants, who became known as the Wangara (also Dyula), organized the prospecting, mining, collecting, and transporting of gold. They established trade routes laterally across West Africa that connected into the trans-Saharan system in several cities along the southern border of the desert, chief of which was Timbuktu.

The demand for gold was so great that Wangara traders pushed south and east into the last and greatest of the West African goldfields, which lay between the Comoe and Volta Rivers in the modern Republic of Ghana. Contemporary traders referred to the region as Toom. Today, the people there constitute an ethnic group known as the Akan, a term also applied to the rich goldfields that were once scattered over the region. The Wangara traders who developed the mines probably came from the riverain port city of Djenné, which lay on a tributary of the Niger, 250 miles (402 kilometers) upriver of Timbuktu, since the trade routes that took the gold north ran to Djenné. The mines may have been opened for production as early as the eleventh century but became a major supplier only in the fifteenth.

Most Akan gold came in the form of tiny grains, referred to as *tibr*, or gold dust, and the most common means of finding it was through panning the sand and gravel of streams and rivers. Following heavy rainfalls, gold could be gathered by women using calabashes to pan standing water in fields. Nuggets were sometimes found by divers at the bottoms of riverbeds. In other places, vertical shafts were dug wide enough for a person to descend. At the bottom, the miner would gather soil, which was then sent to the top for processing. Strip mining was also used, although this process was laborious. Gold mining was hard work that usually produced little return, at least for the miners themselves.

Gold was exchanged for a variety of products ranging from basic necessities consumed by the miners to luxuries enjoyed by the rulers. From the beginning of Akan production, gold was traded for copper and its alloy, brass, which was more sought after for decoration and ritual purposes than gold itself. One early report has miners buying copper for two-thirds of its weight in gold. A second product in great demand was textiles. Among the Akan, striped cloth from North Africa was much in vogue for making the burnoose-style robes known in Morocco as jalabayas, which were often the official vestments of chiefs. For a while, at least, the Akan also exchanged gold for slaves. Their economy was booming and their society expanding faster than natural population growth could keep pace. A severe labor shortage developed that was partially filled by captives from the north, who were imported and sold as workers by the Wangara.

Over the long run, however, cloth, copper, slaves, and all other products paled in comparison to salt, since no major deposits of rock salt existed in tropical West Africa. Camel caravans transported tons of salt from mines in the central Sahara to cities like Timbuktu, where it was transshipped often numerous times, by donkey, boat, and head porterage, to forestlands including those of the Akan. In the bargaining that accompanied this trade, scales and cast brass weights were used to measure the gold. These weights, based on standards common in the Islamic world, were introduced to the region by the Wangara. Among the Akan, they became a highly developed art form.

To facilitate the gold trade, the Wangara developed cities on the northern edge of the goldfields, the foremost of which was Begho (often referred to in contemporary reports as Bitu). At the same time, the Akan were in the process of forming organized political states. The basis of the Akan economy was changing from hunting and gathering to agriculture just as the impact of the gold trade began to be felt. The growing need for labor to clear forests, plant crops, and gather and mine gold led to the division of Akan society into three classes: organizers of labor, who became the rulers; free settlers; and slaves, who did the hardest work. A system of large estates evolved into a group of small states from which, through warfare and alliance, larger states emerged. According to tradition, five great towns became the centers of five states, each ruled by a king.

The trans-Saharan component of the Akan gold trade never constituted a monopoly, and it faced increasing challenges over time. The Portuguese arrived on the coast south of the Akan region in 1471 and soon built a large trading castle christened São Jorge da Mina. This and other European posts diverted much gold from the trans-Saharan system. Beginning in the mid-sixteenth century, gold began arriving in the Old World from the Americas in amounts far surpassing West African production. Political changes also had an impact. The fall of the empire of Songhai in 1591 led to problems with security in the West African interior in the following centu-

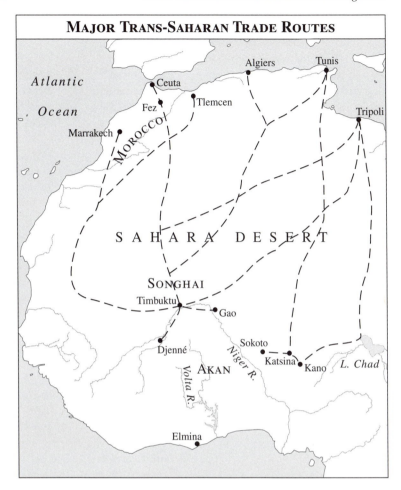

MAJOR TRANS-SAHARAN TRADE ROUTES

ries. In Begho, a dispute between Wangara merchants and the local king led to a civil war, after which the Wangara departed and Begho went into decline.

SIGNIFICANCE

The Akan gold industry had important consequences for West African history. It contributed to both the impetus and the capacity of the region to develop more centralized political structures. Agricultural estates grew into political states as a result of labor divisions fueled by the mining industry. The initial five states competed and eventually engaged in warfare with each other to control the gold trade. By the 1650's, a single state, Denkyira, would defeat its nearest rival, Adanse, and emerge as the paramount power in Akan, controlling much of the region's trade as well as some of the goldfields. The King of Denkyira is said to have ruled from a solid gold stool, by then the symbol of royal power.

In 1701, Denkyira was overwhelmed in turn by a new

1500's

power, the Asante. The Asante dominated all of Akan in the eighteenth century, and with the help of the wealth wrested from the region's goldfields, the Kingdom of Asante became a modern, rich, and powerful state. Although most of the significant gold deposits were mined out by the nineteenth century, Asante remained a viable kingdom through the late nineteenth century, defeating the British in 1824 and successfully resisting colonial occupation until 1896.

Akan's gold also had significant effects upon the larger world economy. In the late fifteenth and early sixteenth centuries, the Akan mines were the largest single supplier of gold to the Mediterranean basin, Europe, and the Middle East. European economies had switched to gold-based currencies beginning in the mid-thirteenth century, but the demand quickly outran the supply. This culminated in the fifteenth century with a precious metal deficit crisis known as the Great Bullion Famine, followed in the succeeding century by a period of chronic inflation, the Great Price Revolution, during which the supply of precious metals could not keep up with the rise in prices. All of this reflected profound demographic and economic changes, culminating in the Atlantic commercial revolution that laid the basis for much of the international trade system of today. Akan gold helped to power this transformation, at least in the decades before the loot of the Americas began to pour in.

—*Richard L. Smith*

FURTHER READING

Austen, Ralph A. "Marginalization, Stagnation, and Growth: The Trans-Saharan Caravan Trade in the Era of European Expansion, 1500-1900." In *The Rise of Merchant Empires: Long Distance Trade in the Early Modern World, 1350-1750*, edited by James D. Tracy. New York: Cambridge University Press, 1990. A good analysis of the transformation of trans-Saharan trade and the importance of gold in it.

Bovill, E.W. *The Golden Trade of the Moors*. 2d rev. ed. New York: Oxford University Press, 1968. Reprint. Princeton, N.J.: Markus Weiner, 1999. A seminal and widely used text, although now dated in important respects.

Fischer, David Hackett. *The Great Wave: Price Revolutions and the Rhythm of History*. New York: Oxford University Press, 1996. Examines the impact of West African gold on early modern Europe and the emerging world economy.

Garrard, Timothy F. *Gold of Africa: Jewelry and Ornaments from Ghana, Côte d'Ivoire, Mali, and Senegal in the Collection of the Barbier-Mueller Museum*. Munich: Prestel-Verlag, 1989. Despite its ponderous subtitle, this work contains an excellent text by a foremost authority with an emphasis on Akan production.

Smith, Richard L. "The Money of Old Timbuktu." *The Numismatist* 115, no. 9 (2002): 1023-1029, 1113-1114. Much Akan gold passed through Djenné and Timbuktu on its way into the trans-Saharan system.

Wilks, Ivor. *Forests of Gold: Essays on the Akan and the Kingdom of Asante*. Athens: Ohio University Press, 1993. This work, by a scholar who is highly regarded as an expert on the Wangara, Akan, Asante, and the impact of the gold trade, brings together ten of his essays, some of which have been extensively reworked.

_____. "Wangara, Akan, and Portuguese in the Fifteenth and Sixteenth Centuries." In *Mines of Silver and Gold in the Americas*, edited by Peter Bakewell. Brookfield, Vt.: Variorum, 1997. An analysis of the Akan gold trade as a precursor to the influx of precious metals from the New World. Includes illustrations, maps, bibliographic references, and index.

SEE ALSO: 1460-1600: Rise of the Akan Kingdoms; c. 1464-1591: Songhai Empire Dominates the Western Sudan; Late 15th cent.: Mombasa, Malindi, and Kilwa Reach Their Height; 1481-1482: Founding of Elmina; c. 1485: Portuguese Establish a Foothold in Africa; 16th century: Worldwide Inflation; 1510-1578: Saʿdī Sharifs Come to Power in Morocco; 1545-1548: Silver Is Discovered in Spanish America; 1591: Fall of the Songhai Empire.

RELATED ARTICLES in *Great Lives from History: The Renaissance & Early Modern Era, 1454-1600*: Amina Sarauniya Zazzua; Askia Daud; Mohammed I Askia.

16th century
WORLDWIDE INFLATION

Prices for goods in Europe in the sixteenth century rose to about four times the level that had prevailed during the preceding three centuries, increasing poverty levels but also raising the profit potential for those who were in a position to exploit an economy that was suddenly based primarily upon money and credit rather than labor and trade.

LOCALE: Europe and its American colonies
CATEGORIES: Economics; trade and commerce

KEY FIGURES

Jean Bodin (1530-1596), French political philosopher
Christopher Columbus (1451-1506), Genoa-born explorer who claimed the Caribbean New World for Spain
Hernán Cortés (1485-1547), Spanish conquistador
Francisco Pizarro (c. 1478-1541), Spanish conquistador
Philip II (1527-1598), king of Spain, r. 1556-1598
William the Silent (1533-1584), stadholder of the Netherlands, r. 1579-1584
Elizabeth I (1533-1603), queen of England, r. 1558-1603

SUMMARY OF EVENT

Prices in Europe, and in European settlements in America, increased at a very rapid rate during the sixteenth century, in comparison to at least the three preceding centuries. Prices of many commodities were, in 1600, about four times what they had been in 1500.

This enormous increase in prices was attributed, as early as 1568, to the huge quantities of gold and silver brought back to Europe by the Spaniards from their conquests in Central and South America, following Christopher Columbus's discovery of America in 1492. Jean Bodin, a French political philosopher, published a pamphlet in 1568 in which he blamed the "debasement" of the coinage of Europe on the very large quantities of bullion imported into Spain, and thence into the rest of Europe.

Initially, the Spanish conquistadors, led by Hernán Cortés, were most attracted to the gold in the numerous ornaments of the conquered Indians and in the mountain streams of Mexico. By the middle of the century, however, their emphasis had shifted to silver, thanks to the conquest, by Francisco Pizarro, of the Andean silver mines at Potosí. Moreover, in the second half of the sixteenth century, a new technology, using an amalgam of mercury, made separating the pure silver from the mined ore substantially quicker, simpler, and more profitable.

Because the kind of detailed statistics common in the twentieth century are lacking for earlier periods of history, analyses of the impact of the American bullion are based only on estimates. However, following some researches done in Spanish archives in the 1930's by American scholar Earl Hamilton, it became possible to arrive at figures for the amount of bullion entering Europe in the sixteenth century from Spain's empire in Central and South America. It is estimated that, during the sixteenth century, some 180 tons of gold reached Europe from America, along with some 15,000 tons of silver.

Since then, the effect of this influx of bullion on the European economy has been played down, as new studies have shown that a good deal of the Spanish silver was not used to create coins but rather was used primarily in payment for the supplies needed by Spanish officials to support their empire, as well as to supply the armies being deployed by Philip II to maintain Spain's political control of its holdings, especially the Netherlands. Spain's dominance of the Netherlands was challenged by the Dutch under William the Silent. At the same time, the empire's dominance of the Atlantic was challenged by the English under Elizabeth I, demonstrated most spectacularly by the English defeat of the Spanish Armada in 1588.

The most widespread impact of sixteenth century inflation was the divergence between the cost of goods and the wages that ordinary people could command. Because the population of Europe was growing at a significant rate—resulting in more people seeking employment than there were jobs available—wages increased far less than the cost of food. Although the great increase in trade that followed the infusion of much new capital into the European economy made many more goods available, ordinary people could not afford to buy these things. Most Europeans of the time lived a subsistence lifestyle, and most of what they bought was food. The price of food skyrocketed, and the result was a widespread descent into poverty. Diets that earlier had included meat instead became almost entirely vegetarian.

Despite the careful controls established by the Spanish government, which ensured that much—though not all—of the bullion coming from America landed in Spain, much of it soon flowed out again. Partly it went to sustain the cost of importing the bullion: About half of each year's imports went to pay for the cost of the next year's voyages. Much of the remainder went to pay for

THE SOCIAL COSTS OF INFLATION

Eighteenth century historian Charles Mathon de La Cour provides a clear example of how an influx of money and wealth into an economy does not necessarily mean a growth in real wages for the working classes. With more currency—more coinage—comes more cost and either frozen or lower wages.

Gold and silver, which are ceaselessly drawn from the bowels of the earth, are spread every year throughout Europe and increase the amount of coin there. Nations do not thereby really become more wealthy, but their wealth becomes more voluminous: the price of foodstuffs and other things necessary to life increases by turn, one has to pay more and more gold and silver to buy a loaf of bread, a house, or a suit of clothes. Wages do not immediately rise to the same extent. Men of feeling observe with sorrow that just when the poor man needs to earn more money to live, this very need sometimes makes wages fall or at any rate serves as a pretext to hold them for a long time at the old rate which no longer corresponds to the wage-earner's expenditure, and thus it is that the gold mines have provided weapons for the egotism of the rich, enabling them more and more to oppress and enslave the industrious classes.

Source: Quoted in *The Wheels of Commerce*, vol. 2 in *Civilization and Capitalism, Fifteenth-Eighteenth Century*, by Fernand Braudel (New York: Harper & Row, 1979), p. 428.

As social relationships came to be determined by economic relationships, the possession of money came to be critical. The aristocracy came to depend on money rents for their land holdings in place of the labor services that had been characteristic of the Middle Ages. Instead of leading a local community, the aristocracy came increasingly to be officeholders of the new national kingdoms that were arising. The rulers of these kingdoms came, moreover, to rely heavily on systems of credit, as they borrowed money to operate their new national governments.

As royal debt became national debt, a new class of "rentiers" arose, those who lived from the income earned by the money they lent both to monarchs and to new commercial enterprises. The commercial enterprises themselves became "international," even "global," in their operations to a far greater extent than in earlier centuries, making use of the large amounts of capital now available. In a sense, this was the first era of "globalization."

the goods needed to sustain the Spanish armies fighting in France and the Netherlands, especially the latter. The supplies for the Spanish armies were bought with funds supplied by Italian financiers, especially from Genoa. The result was a heavy buildup in the Spanish government's debt, which had to be restructured on a number of occasions during the latter half of the sixteenth century.

The growth in population, and the conversion of many social relationships in Europe to ones based on the exchange of money, meant that the trade in agricultural products was of growing importance. Even though an estimated 200,000 Spaniards emigrated to the new Spanish colonies in the New World, the steadily growing population in Europe could no longer be fed by the agricultural products of Western Europe, so that, increasingly, foodstuffs had to be imported. The place these foodstuffs were imported from was Eastern Europe, where the aristocracy converted their estates from self-supporting units into large grain-producing operations. This grain was shipped in ever-increasing amounts to the cities of Western Europe. Not only was an economy based on self-sufficiency gradually being replaced by one based on an exchange of money, but the exchange was no longer local; rather, it embraced the entire continent of Europe.

SIGNIFICANCE

The inflation of the sixteenth century transformed the society of Europe. The gap between prices and wages depressed the living standards of ordinary people, but it enabled those with access to money to increase their assets and their living standards. For those who had money, or who knew how to make money in an inflationary economy, the new conditions made possible a luxurious lifestyle not known since the Roman Empire. Modern capitalism got its start at this time.

—*Nancy M. Gordon*

FURTHER READING

Braudel, Fernand. "Prices in Europe from 1450 to 1750." In *The Cambridge Economic History of Europe*. Vol. 4. Edited by E. E. Rich and C. H. Wilson. Cambridge, England: Cambridge University Press, 1967. Braudel wrote this chapter before his masterwork, *Civilization and Capitalism*, but it concentrates on the issue of inflation.

Elliott, J. H. *Europe Divided, 1559-1598*. Malden, Mass.: Blackwell, 2000. Contains a chapter on the European economy, with a special section dealing with silver and prices.

Fischer, David Hackett. *The Great Wave: Price Revolutions and the Rhythm of History.* New York: Oxford University Press, 1996. Although its conclusions and causal connections have been widely attacked by economists, Fischer's book contains many useful graphs that illustrate what happened to prices over the long haul.

Kamen, Henry. *Spain's Road to Empire: The Making of a World Power, 1492-1763.* London: Allen Lane, 2002. Written by the author of a number of works on sixteenth century Spain, this work portrays Spain's global leadership at that time.

Lynch, John. *Spain, 1516-1598: From Nation State to World Empire.* Malden, Mass.: Blackwell, 1991. A more concentrated treatment than that provided by Kamen, focused on the sixteenth century.

Rich, E. E. "Expansion as a Concern of All Europe." In *The New Cambridge Modern History.* Vol. 1. Edited by G. R. Potter. Cambridge, England: Cambridge University Press, 1957.

SEE ALSO: Early 1460's: Labor Shortages Alter Europe's Social Structure; 1482-1492: Maximilian I Takes Control of the Low Countries; 1490's: Decline of the Silk Road; June 7, 1494: Treaty of Tordesillas; Jan., 1498: Portuguese Reach the Swahili Coast; Beginning c. 1500: Coffee, Cacao, Tobacco, and Sugar Are Sold Worldwide; 1505-1515: Portuguese Viceroys Establish Overseas Trade Empire; 1531-1585: Antwerp Becomes the Commercial Capital of Europe; 1545-1548: Silver Is Discovered in Spanish America; 1558-1603: Reign of Elizabeth I; 1568-1648: Dutch Wars of Independence; 1580-1581: Spain Annexes Portugal; July 26, 1581: The United Provinces Declare Independence from Spain; Dec. 31, 1600: Elizabeth I Charters the East India Company.

RELATED ARTICLES in *Great Lives from History: The Renaissance & Early Modern Era, 1454-1600:* Christopher Columbus; Hernán Cortés; Elizabeth I; Francisco Pizarro; William the Silent.

1501-1524
REIGN OF ISMĀʿĪL I

The young and charismatic Ismāʿīl founded the Ṣafavid Dynasty in Iran and established, through subjugation and annexation, Shīʿite Islam as the state's religion, in effect unifying the country's diverse peoples.

LOCALE: Persia (now Iran)
CATEGORIES: Government and politics; expansion and land acquisition

KEY FIGURES

Ismāʿīl I (1487-1524), Iranian shah, r. 1501-1524, founder of the Ṣafavid Dynasty
Selim I (1467-1520), Ottoman sultan, r. 1512-1520, who defeated Ismāʿīl at Chāldirān
Ṭahmāsp I (1514-1576), Iranian shah, r. 1524-1576, son of Ismāʿīl I, and his successor
Bayezid II (1447/1448-1512), Ottoman sultan, r. 1481-1512, father of Selim I

SUMMARY OF EVENT

Ismāʿīl I was born in Azerbaijan on July 17, 1487, son of Shayleh Ḥaydar, an Iranian, and ʿAlamshāh Begum, a Turkoman, whose marriage was sanctioned by ʿAlamshāh's father, Uzun Ḥasan. This mixed marriage posed no significant problem until after Uzun Ḥasan's death in 1478, when Ḥasan's sons, first Khalil and then Yaʿqūb, acceded to the throne. Ḥaydar, charismatic and a born leader, had attracted enthusiastic followings among Turkomans from Azerbaijan and eastern Anatolia. Yaʿqūb found this sufficiently disquieting, so he had Ḥaydar killed.

After Ḥaydar's murder, Yaʿqūb imprisoned Ḥaydar's three sons, including Ismāʿīl, not quite two years old. The boys were confined almost 1,000 miles south in Istakhr. Yaʿqūb died in 1493, which led to the release of Ḥaydar's sons. Yaʿqūb's successor, Rustam, had one of the sons, ʿAlī, executed, so that the seven-year-old Ismāʿīl then became spiritual leader of the Sufis of Ardabīl.

Ismāʿīl possessed a great deal of his father's charisma. Unusually intelligent, he matured into a handsome youth. The year after Ismāʿīl's release from prison, the Ak Koyunlu Turkomans made a concerted effort to find him in Ardabīl, but his supporters hid him before spiriting him away to Karkiya Mīrzā ʿAlī, a devoted Shīʿite and governor of Lahijan on the Caspian Sea, where Ismāʿīl and his Sufi followers were granted sanctuary.

The boy, realizing that his life was in great peril, remained in Lahijan until 1499. During his five years there, Ismāʿīl received an excellent education, studying the

Qurʾān and gaining proficiency in the Arabic and Persian languages. He also spoke and wrote in Azeri Turkish and, under the pseudonym Khatai, produced poetry to inspire his followers.

By 1499, twelve-year-old Ismāʿīl left Lehijan for Ardabīl, after which he proceeded north to the province of Talish on the Caspian Sea, spending the winter in small villages. Rumors were rife among the Sufis that Ismāʿīl, their proclaimed spiritual leader, would soon be ready to meet with them in Erzincan, far to the west of Talish. The meeting took place in Erzincan in August, 1500, before an assembly of seven thousand followers known as the Kizilbash, or "red heads," because of the distinctive twelvefold red hats they wore to show support for the founders of the Ṣafavid Dynasty. The Kizilbash were eager to participate in transforming the Ṣafavids from a religious into a political group bent on avenging the deaths of Ismāʿīl's father and brother.

There ensued a series of military campaigns that Ismāʿīl led between ages thirteen and twenty-five without experiencing a single defeat. He had the ability to invoke people's loyalty and to lead them. So remarkable was his string of victories, often against substantial odds, that his followers considered him almost a deity.

Ismāʿīl first led his army east to Shamakha near the Caspian Sea, taking, later, Baku; his army then moved toward Tabrīz, where it met the Ak Koyunlu army 20 miles north of that city. Ismāʿīl's army won decisively, also killing the sultan of Ak Koyunlu.

By the end of 1501, at age fourteen, Ismāʿīl was crowned in Tabrīz after having gained control of Azerbaijan. He proclaimed himself *shah*, a title that had not been used in Iran for nine centuries. In their Friday prayers, the twelve imams, Iran's most revered religious leaders, declared him the rightful monarch. In 1508, he charged into Baghdad, driving out the governor and helping the city become a cultural center.

The Ṣafavids, having conquered Iran, began to establish Shia Islam as its state religion. Ḥaydar, Ismāʿīl's father, was a Shīʿite. During Ismāʿīl's internment in Lahijan with the Shīʿite governor, Karkiya Mīrzā ʿAlī, as his protector, he became wholly committed to Shia Islam.

With Iran under control by 1510, Ismāʿīl turned his attention to the Uzbeks in the east and the Ottomans in the west. Fighting on two fronts presented a difficult military challenge. Traditionally, an army was considered part of its leader's household. It was expected to move with him as he moved. The larger the territory to be defended, the more difficult it was to retain any sense of unity among one's troops.

Ismāʿīl's tactics in fighting the Uzbeks at Merv were inspired. The Uzbek leader Muḥammad Shaybānī and his followers sequestered themselves in Merv's citadel, impervious to the continued assaults of the Ṣafavids. Ismāʿīl broke the deadlock by pretending to retreat. Muḥammad Shaybānī and his troops finally emerged from the fortress and headed west. Then, Ismāʿīl's forces engaged them in a deadly battle 12 miles west of Merv, a battle that killed Muḥammad Shaybānī.

After engaging the Uzbeks, Ismāʿīl deployed his forces to the west, but not before losing a battle to the Uzbeks in Ghujduvan, far to the east, in November, 1512. Earlier this same year, the Ottoman sultan, Bayezid II, left his sultancy voluntarily, relinquishing the post to his son, Selim I. Ismāʿīl refused to acknowledge Selim as the legitimate sultan, recognizing instead Bayezid's rightful successor, Ahmad Bayezid. Selim came under considerable pressure as hordes of Turkomans fled from Ottoman territory to align themselves with the Ṣafavids. Greatly threatened by such desertions, Selim I, with an army of 100,000, attacked Iran on March 20, 1514.

By this time, Ismāʿīl had racked up so many military victories that he considered himself unconquerable. He made at minimum two errors in judgment before the battle. First, he refused to use gunpowder in the fight, even though his force of forty thousand was less than half the size of Selim's army and his opponents used considerable artillery against his army. Second, he chose to fight the battle on the vulnerable Chāldirān plain rather than in the mountains, which would have offered his troops greater protection.

A massacre ensued, in which the Ṣafavids lost most of their military leadership and thousands of foot soldiers and cavalry. Ismāʿīl escaped with a handful of his supporters. His opponents returned to Constantinople with five hundred loads of treasure confiscated from the Ṣafavids. They gained control of Diyarbakīr to the southwest in Mesopotamia, which disturbed the tenuous balance of power and pushed Ismāʿīl and his supporters to the east, away from Asia Minor and central Iran.

After his loss at Chāldirān, Ismāʿīl suffered through deep depression and reportedly never again led his forces into battle. His government was now centered in Tabrīz, and his eldest son, Ṭahmāsp, succeeded him in 1524.

SIGNIFICANCE

Ismāʿīl's early life was so extraordinary that it was inevitable that it could not be sustained indefinitely. Becoming an active leader of military forces before the age of fourteen, and being installed as shah of Iran soon thereafter, was remarkable by any standards. His uninterrupted, fourteen-year string of military victories was rare from a military standpoint. That many of these victories were achieved when he was a teenager makes Ismāʿīl comparable to Alexander the Great.

—*R. Baird Shuman*

FURTHER READING

Canby, Sheila R. *The Golden Age of Persian Art: 1501-172.* New York: Harry N. Abrams, 2000. Canby presents one of the best overviews in print of the life and work of Ismāʿīl.

Imber, Colin. *The Ottoman Empire, 1300-1650.* New York: Macmillan, 2002. Although Imber touches only briefly on the career of Ismāʿīl, he still offers useful insights.

Jackson, Peter, ed. *The Timurid and Ṣafavid Periods.* Vol. 6 in *The Cambridge History of Iran.* New York: Cambridge University Press, 1986. Presents the broad picture of the Timurid civilization and discusses its fall, especially from the perspective of the Ṣafavids.

Roemer, H. R. "The Ṣafavid Period." *Cambridge History of Iran.* Vol. 6. New York: Cambridge University Press, 1986. A brief but useful look at the period in which Ismāʿīl flourished.

Somel, Selcuk Aksin. *Historical Dictionary of the Ottoman Empire.* Lanham, Md.: Scarecrow Press, 2003. Although Ismāʿīl is not discussed per se, ancillary discussions of Selim II are pertinent.

SEE ALSO: 1481-1512: Reign of Bayezid II and Ottoman Civil Wars; Early 16th cent.: Fuzuli Writes Poetry in Three Languages; Dec. 2, 1510: Battle of Merv Establishes the Shaybānīd Dynasty; 1512-1520: Reign of Selim I; 1578-1590: The Battle for Tabrīz.

RELATED ARTICLES in *Great Lives from History: The Renaissance & Early Modern Era, 1454-1600:* Bābur; Bayezid II; Humāyūn; Süleyman the Magnificent.

1502
BEGINNING OF THE TRANSATLANTIC SLAVE TRADE

In 1502, the first African slaves were taken to the New World, and eight years later, Spanish king Ferdinand II approved the shipment of 250 additional slaves. The numbers continued to grow until they reached about 10,000 per year by the end of the 1530's.

LOCALE: The Atlantic coasts of Africa and the Americas

CATEGORIES: Economics; colonization; trade and commerce

KEY FIGURES

Isabella I (1451-1504), queen of Castile, r. 1474-1504

Ferdinand II (1452-1516), king of Castile as Ferdinand V, r. 1474-1504, and king of Aragon, r. 1479-1516

Charles V (1500-1558), king of Spain as Charles I, r. 1516-1556, and Holy Roman Emperor, r. 1519-1556

Juan de Córdoba (fl. early sixteenth century), the first European known to take an African slave to America

Juan Rodríguez de Fonseca (1451-1524), head of the Spanish department of Indian affairs, 1493-1524, and chaplain and adviser to Isabella and Ferdinand

Nicolás de Ovando (c. 1451-c. 1511), governor of Spain's American possessions, 1502-1509, and founder of the *encomienda* system

Bartolomé de Las Casas (1474-1566), Spanish priest and advocate of American Indian rights

John III (1502-1557), king of Portugal, r. 1521-1557

SUMMARY OF EVENT

The transatlantic slave trade developed as a logical extension of earlier practices. Since the ninth century, Arab caravans had transported slaves across the Sahara for sale in Mediterranean markets. In 1444, Portuguese ships transported 235 black slaves from the Gulf of Guinea to southern Europe, where most of them were sold as domestic servants. Beginning in the 1470's, Portuguese merchants operated a large slaving base on the fortified island of São Tomé. By the end of the century, more than thirty thousand African slaves had been shipped to Europe, and an additional seven or eight thousand had been taken to Portuguese plantations in the Cape Verde Islands, Madeira, and the Azores.

After Spain annexed the Canary Islands in 1479, Spanish planters also used slave labor on their sugar plantations. By 1500, the planters had imported about a thousand slaves from the African continent. Since ex-

TRANSATLANTIC SLAVE TRADE ROUTES

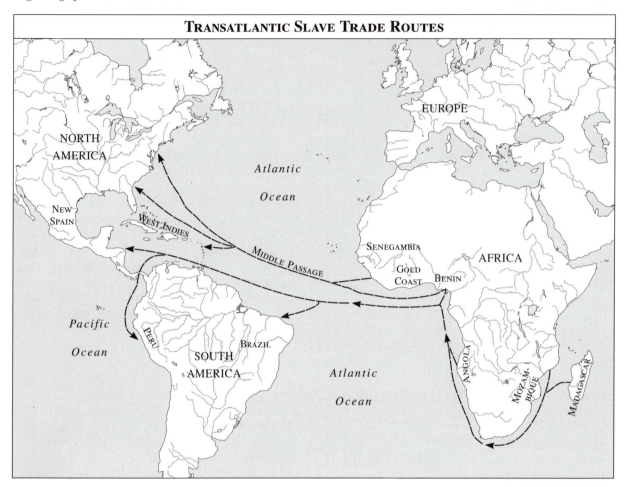

plorer Christopher Columbus looked to the Portuguese and Spanish colonies of the eastern Atlantic as a model, he envisioned the use of slave labor in the colonies he hoped to establish in the western Atlantic. When he landed on the Caribbean islands in 1492, Columbus enthusiastically wrote to the Spanish monarchs that the Indies could provide as many slaves as might be needed. Three years later, he sent about five hundred Caribbean Indian slaves to Europe, the first west-to-east transatlantic slave shipment. Despite Queen Isabella I's scruples about using as slaves people she saw as her vassals, she approved the enslavement of cannibals and any American Indians captured in "just wars," which included wars aimed at converting pagans to Christianity.

In 1501, Isabella prohibited the transportation of outside slaves to the Indies for work in plantations and mines. Her government, however, permitted a few individuals to import privately owned house servants. In 1502, Juan de Córdoba, a Seville merchant and friend of

Columbus, took an African slave to live and work on the island of Hispaniola (now Haiti and the Dominican Republic). Córdoba's slave was the first known to have been transported across the Atlantic Ocean to labor in the New World. Later that year, the governor-general of the island, Nicolás de Ovando, also imported three or four African slaves. Soon after Isabella's death in 1504, the ban on importing slaves ended, and at least seventeen were taken to Hispaniola in 1505.

As Spanish settlers organized mines and large sugar plantations in the Indies, they quickly discovered that the slave labor of the indigenous people was less productive than that of Africans, who were more resistant to European diseases, more accustomed to working with horses, and less likely to escape. In 1509, Governor Diego Columbus, son of the explorer, wrote to King Ferdinand II complaining of a labor shortage and requesting black slaves.

Ferdinand, who was praised by Niccolò Machiavelli,

was a pragmatic politician determined to expand his empire, and he saw no moral or legal reasons to oppose the expansion of slavery. His major adviser for imperial affairs, the bishop of Palencia, Juan Rodríguez de Fonseca, strongly supported Governor Columbus's request. On January 22, 1510, the king instructed the Casa de Contratación, which managed Spanish maritime affairs, to allow 250 slaves (mostly Africans) to be transported to Hispaniola, with a hefty tax to be charged for each new slave.

For the next few years, about fifty slaves a year were sent to the Americas. Meanwhile, the Indian population in the Spanish colonies was rapidly declining because of disease and brutal working conditions. When Charles I became king of Spain in 1516, settlers were clamoring for additional black slaves. Even the humanitarian priest and historian Bartolomé de Las Casas endorsed an increase, for at this time he believed that the importation of Africans would mitigate the cruel treatment of the indigenous population.

On August 18, 1518, Charles issued an *asiento* (royal contract) authorizing a Flemish courtier, Lorenzo de Gorrevod, to import up to four thousand black slaves from Europe to the American colonies. Gorrevod sold the *asiento* to several Genoese merchants, and they, in turn, subcontracted with Portuguese middlemen. Charles continued to grant additional *asientos* for black slaves, who were becoming the majority of laborers on sugar plantations and mills. By 1530, the island of Puerto Rico had about three thousand slaves, ten times the number of Spanish settlers living there.

An important change took place in 1530, when the ship *Nuestra Señora de Begoña* departed São Tomé with three hundred slaves and sailed directly to Hispaniola. Before this date, business records indicate that almost all slaves had been shipped from Africa to Europe and from there to the Americas. Portugal's King John III was happy to give permission to merchants to take the direct route. By reducing transportation costs, the change greatly facilitated the growth of transatlantic trade. In the New World, the slaves sold for more than twice the cost of purchasing them in Af-

rica. The transatlantic traffic in slaves had already grown into one of the major sources of profit for private businessmen as well as for the crowns of Spain and Portugal.

In 1532, the Portuguese began importing a tiny number of African slaves into their recently founded settlements in Brazil. Like the Spanish, Portuguese planters soon recognized that the culture of African slaves made them more desirable than Brazilian Indian slaves. Within fifty years, Brazil would develop into one of the major destinations for ships carrying human cargo.

SIGNIFICANCE

Historians estimate that by 1600, between 200,000 and 500,000 Africans had been carried to the Americas to work on plantations, in mines, or as house servants. Until then, Portugal and Spain largely dominated the Atlantic slave trade, although other European nations did their best to get a share of the spoils. In 1611, the Dutch built a fort on the Gold Coast. In 1619, English settlers in Jamestown obtained their first slaves from a Dutch priva-

---

THE SLAVE TRADE'S MIDDLE PASSAGE

The transatlantic slave trade involved a dehumanizing and dangerous voyage between Europe, the African continent, and the New World, in which 15 to 20 percent of the African slaves died. The Middle Passage, the longest leg of the journey, was marked by slave rebellions, sickness, hunger, torture and humiliation, concubinage, and death (of captives and crew).

During this time most slaves were kept below deck, naked or only partially clothed with a loincloth, shackled in pairs. . . . Cooks prepared meals of fish, beans, or yams in large copper vats below deck. Surgeons sometimes assisted in the preparation and distribution of food. Slaves were given food at mid-morning and late afternoon in small bowls (or "pannikins"). . . . Officers, usually boatswains, mates, and surgeons, were armed with whips such as cat-o'-nine-tails and forced the African captives to dance. The crew's power was enforced through such torture devices as thumbscrews and iron collars. There were several tubs in each compartment below deck in which slaves could relieve themselves, though hindered by being shackled in pairs. . . . To counteract the stench, which was thought to promote sickness, slave vessels were fumigated with vinegars, berries, limes, tars, and turpentines.

By any measurement, mortality rates of both slaves and crew were extraordinarily high on the Atlantic crossing. The crowded, unsanitary conditions below deck were an ideal disease environment for outbreaks of dysentery, the disease from which many slaves died. . . .

Source: Excerpted from "Transatlantic Slave Trade," by Stephen Behrendt. In *Africana: The Encyclopedia of the African and African American Experience*, edited by Kwame Anthony Appiah and Henry Louis Gates (New York: Basic Civitas Books, 1999), pp. 1872-1874.

1500'S

teer. Although a few English ships had made slave voyages as early as the 1560's, it was not until the 1630's that the English emerged as major participants in the Atlantic slave trade. The French became actively involved in the trade during the next decade as well.

The transatlantic slave trade was unquestionably one of the largest and most profitable maritime and commercial ventures in all history. By the time the slave trade finally ended in the 1870's, it is estimated that a total of between eleven million and fourteen million enslaved Africans had been transported across the ocean. About half of these slaves were taken to Brazil, while the area that is now the United States received less than 7 percent of the total migration. The large-scale presence of persons of African ancestry in the Americas is a direct consequence of the transatlantic trade. The injustices and violence of slavery left behind a legacy of poverty, prejudice, and resentment that continues to make racial harmony difficult to achieve.

Most historians think that the slave trade also had a devastating effect on Africa. The economic incentives for tribes to capture and sell slaves promoted an atmosphere of violence and lawlessness. Continuing depopulation and fears of captivity made agricultural and economic development almost impossible. A large percentage of the captives were young men and women who were at the prime age for having children and beginning families. Those left behind were disproportionately elderly, disabled, or otherwise dependent. Some historians argue that the slave trade contributed to the conditions that encouraged European imperialism in Africa during the late nineteenth century.

—*Thomas Tandy Lewis*

FURTHER READING

Blackburn, Robin. *The Making of New World Slavery: From the Baroque to the Modern, 1492-1800.* London: Verso, 1997. A well-written account by a leading New Left historian, arguing that independent traders and businessmen were more responsible than governments for the cruelties of the slave system.

Donnan, Elizabeth. *Documents Illustrative of the Atlantic Slave Trade.* 6 vols. New York: Octagon Books, 1968. In addition to original documents, the introduction to volume 1 includes a detailed factual account of the early history of the trade.

Klein, Herbert S. *The Atlantic Slave Trade.* New York: Cambridge University Press, 1999. A relatively short work that examines the four hundred years of the slave trade from a comparative perspective, outlining both common global features and local differences in the trade.

Northrup, David. *Africa's Discovery of Europe, 1450-1550.* New York: Oxford University Press, 2002. An interesting book written from an Afrocentric perspective, attempting to view history through African eyes and presenting Africans as active participants rather than simply as passive victims.

Thomas, Hugh. *The Slave Trade: The Story of the Atlantic Slave Trade, 1440-1870.* New York: Simon & Schuster, 1997. A comprehensive, scholarly, and balanced narrative that is filled with colorful anecdotes and interesting information about political leaders and businessmen who were involved in the trade.

Thompson, Vincent B. *The Making of the African Diaspora in the Americas, 1441-1900.* New York: Longman, 1987. An interesting synthesis, asserting that there is no evidence of slavery in Africa before the Portuguese arrived and emphasizing that the slave trade was an integral part of the European quest for wealth and power.

SEE ALSO: Oct. 19, 1469: Marriage of Ferdinand and Isabella; 1481-1482: Founding of Elmina; Oct. 12, 1492: Columbus Lands in the Americas; June 7, 1494: Treaty of Tordesillas; Beginning c. 1500: Coffee, Cacao, Tobacco, and Sugar Are Sold Worldwide; 1500-1530's: Portugal Begins to Colonize Brazil; 16th century: Worldwide Inflation; Jan. 23, 1516: Charles I Ascends the Throne of Spain; Beginning 1519: Smallpox Kills Thousands of Indigenous Americans.

RELATED ARTICLES in *Great Lives from History: The Renaissance & Early Modern Era, 1454-1600:* Charles V; Christopher Columbus; Ferdinand II and Isabella I; John III; Bartolomé de Las Casas.

1502-1520
REIGN OF MONTEZUMA II

The reign of the last preconquest Aztec emperor, Montezuma II, witnessed the culmination of imperial control over the Central Mexican Plateau. The urban capital of Tenochtitlán boasted a dense, socially diverse population, sustained through a unique productive economy and raised-plot agriculture and augmented by tribute from conquered peoples, before it fell to the Spanish.

LOCALE: Tenochtitlán, Aztec Empire (now Mexico City, Mexico)

CATEGORIES: Government and politics; colonization

KEY FIGURES

Montezuma II (1467-1520), Aztec emperor, r. 1502-1520

Ahuitzotl (d. 1503), Aztec emperor, r. 1486-1502, and uncle of Montezuma II

Hernán Cortés (1485-1547), Spanish conquistador and conqueror of the Aztecs

SUMMARY OF EVENT

Montezuma II was the ninth emperor of the Mexica, or Aztec, a militaristic culture that had resided in the Valley of Mexico since the early fourteenth century. Montezuma II inherited the territorial acquisitions, diplomatic alliances, and economic institutions that had evolved under his predecessors.

The populations of the Valley of Mexico maintained an uneasy relationship with one another. Political alliances were constructed through marriages and trade networks and functioned to maintain stability. Warfare in earlier centuries was common, as it was under Montezuma II, as individual states attempted to absorb one another.

The Aztecs, from their capital city of Tenochtitlán on Lake Texcoco, united in 1428 with the Texcocans and the Tacubans to form the Triple Alliance, a political-military union designed to conquer and extract tribute. When Montezuma II ascended the throne in 1502 the empire was at its zenith. The previous ruler, Ahuitzotl, Montezuma II's uncle, was an aggressive warrior whose reign was noteworthy for territorial expansion and public works projects.

Ahuitzotl's campaigns included expeditions to the Gulf Coast, the Valley of Oaxaca, and south to the region of the modern Guatemalan border. Most of the Central Mexican Plateau was subdued by 1500. Policy focused on indirect rule, local chiefs being responsible for carrying out Aztec directives. In 1487, the great temple complex was completed, and it would serve as the center of the Aztec world through the reign of Ahuitzotl's ill-fated nephew. The chronicles suggest that more than eighty thousand persons were sacrificed to commemorate the completion of the temple: most likely only a fraction of these sacrifices were realized.

Population growth during the fifteenth century spurred the need to intensify productive agriculture. Fresh water for agriculture and other purposes was directed into Tenochtitlán by an aqueduct, built during Ahuitzotl's reign with a large conscript labor force.

The empire under Montezuma II extended south to the Guatemalan border, northwest to the modern Mexican state of Michoacán on the Pacific coast, and due east to Veracruz on the Gulf of Mexico. This vast region of about 77,000 square miles (200,000 square kilometers) contained eleven million people.

Population estimates for Tenochtitlán range from 200,000 to 300,000 individuals. Tribute flowing into the city included foodstuffs, a wide range of luxury goods

Montezuma II, Rex ultimus Mexicanorum *(Last King of the Aztecs).* (R. S. Peale and J. A. Hill)

such as animal skins and feathers, and sacrificial victims. Records from the reign of Montezuma II indicate that 7,000 tons of maize (6,363 metric tons) and 4,000 tons of beans (3,636 metric tons) and other consumables were transported annually into the capital. Endemic warfare ensured a flow of sacrificial victims destined as offerings to the Aztec divinities.

The Aztec pantheon consisted of more than two hundred gods and goddesses. In Tenochtitlán, a great temple complex was dedicated to Tlaloc, the god of rain and water, and to the war god, Huitzilopochtli, a divinity that symbolized the sun. As a powerful celestial force, Huitzilopochtli required consistent sacrifices to ensure his daily movement across the sky. For an agricultural economy, lacking both the benefits of scientific prediction and advanced technology, the appeasement of these divinities was a perennial preoccupation. Plainly, the religious complex and the ways in which it was integrated with the productive economy meshed with the spectrum of Aztec social institutions. For example, young warriors could elevate their status and earn prestige in the military hierarchy by capturing potential sacrificial victims, rather than annihilating them, on the battlefield.

Intensive cultivation was essential, along with tribute, to provision the great numbers of priests, warriors, and artisans. Nutritional needs were satisfied in part through the chinampa system, which provided four or five crops

annually. Chinampas were raised plots of drained land in the lake, filled with vegetation and mud and defined around their perimeters with stakes and trees. The rich soil was easily tilled with hand tools. Supplementing chinampa technology were terraces and irrigation works, all of which functioned to produce maize, squash, varieties of beans, and chili peppers.

At the apex of society was the emperor, or *Tlatoani*, who was elected from the aristocracy on the death of the previous ruler. The ruler and nobility enjoyed privileges withheld from the great mass of commoners: increased land control and the use for their children of the *Calmécac*, a prestigious, strict, religious school. The ruler was advised by a royal council consisting of four aristocrats. Priests and warriors were organized into powerful and prestigious groups. The free commoners, or *macehuales*, while serving important economic functions for society, were denied access to the benefits enjoyed by the groups superimposed above them. For example, dress codes were enforced, as were regulations pertaining to the consumption of certain foods. Beneath the commoners were the serfs who were tied to the lands of the nobility. The *mayeques*, or slaves used in transportation, were positioned beneath the serfs, and this group resulted from bad fortune or warfare.

A select group enjoying substantial prestige was the *pochteca*, or long-distance merchants. Their travels to different lands provided the imperial sector with luxury items and information that could influence military strategy and diplomacy.

The basic unit of Aztec culture was the *calpulli*, a corporate kinship-linked land-holding group. It functioned in religious rituals and provided warriors for imperial aggression. The *calpulli*, of which there were about twenty in Tenochtitlán, provided a patronage system in which wealthy members provided less fortunate kinsmen with economic opportunities. Repayment of benefits was usually in labor and tribute.

Aztec norms, mores, and values reflected a rigid religious and militaristic society. Parents inculcated children with the value of subordination to all in institutions of society: the family, the religious culture, and the state. Formal education either in the *Calmécac* or in the school for commoners, called the

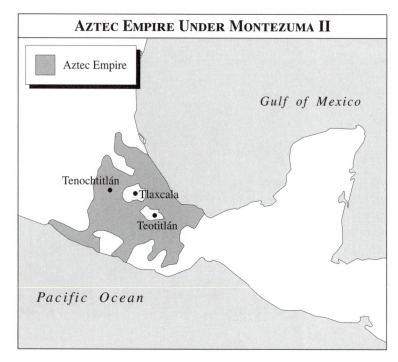

AZTEC EMPIRE UNDER MONTEZUMA II

Aztec Empire

Gulf of Mexico

Tenochtitlán

Tlaxcala

Teotitlán

Pacific Ocean

telpochcalli, emphasized discipline and religious codes, and in the *Calmécac*, leadership skills. The values of respect, reverence for traditions, and self-restraint were taught to children through a range of devices. Punishments varied in intensity. Drunkenness, for example, usually carried a death penalty. The issues of social chaos and disrespect would appear to underlie this penalty. Generosity, in the forms of gifts and food, was exhibited at all levels of Aztec society. An emphasis on natural beauty permeated Aztec culture, exemplified in flowers. Oratorical skills, poetics, and stone sculpture were appreciated and highly sophisticated.

The death knell of traditional Aztec culture sounded on November 8, 1519, when Hernán Cortés, a Spanish conquistador, and five hundred soldiers marched into Tenochtitlán. Montezuma II's indecisiveness and his policy of ingratiating the Spaniards facilitated the conquest. During street fighting in June, 1520, Montezuma II was injured, apparently by his own people, and subsequently died. In the end, he had lost the respect and confidence of his people.

Multiple causes led to the collapse of Aztec civilization: diseases to which the Aztec lacked immunity, Spanish persistence and superior organizational skills, steel weapons and cannons, and the invaluable aid of an indigenous interpreter and adviser, Doña Marina. The Aztec practice of indirectly controlling subjugated peoples maintained a loose empire. These dissatisfied peoples became allied with the Spanish and contributed 100,000 warriors in the final assault on Tenochtitlán on August 13, 1521.

A page with Aztec symbols from a syllabary (table or list of syllables), with marginal notes by a Spanish scribe. (Hulton|Archive by Getty Images)

SIGNIFICANCE

The Aztec Empire was the largest and most complex of the Mesoamerican civilizations. Spanish accounts, in addition to Aztec books, or codexes, detail the growth, expansion, and florescence of an urban society that lacked the technological benefits of early Old World agrarian states: sophisticated metallurgy, draft animals for power and traction, and the wheel, which was important in warfare and agriculture. Discipline grounded in religious principles, as well as conformity to norms that elevated the needs of society over those of the individual, allowed the Aztecs to transform from a wandering tribe to a military state in a brief two-hundred-year period.

—*Rene M. Descartes*

FURTHER READING

Berdan, Frances F., et al. *Aztec Imperial Strategies*. Washington, D.C.: Dumbarton Oaks, 1996. A description of Aztec culture that relies upon textual and artifactual sources.

Davies, Nigel. *The Aztecs*. Norman: University of Oklahoma Press, 1980. A general discussion of Aztec political evolution by an ethnohistorian.

Díaz del Castillo, Bernal. *The Discovery and Conquest of Mexico*. Translated by A. P. Maudslay. Introduction by Hugh Thomas. New York: Da Capo Press, 1996. Written in the 1560's and first published in 1632. Díaz del Castillo wrote his vivid memories of the conquest of Mexico and his observations of the Aztecs and of Montezuma II.

1500's

Longhena, Maria. *Ancient Mexico: The History and Culture of the Maya, Aztecs, and Other Pre-Columbian Peoples.* New York: Stewart, Tabori & Chang, 1998. An examination of Aztec history and culture, alongside the cultures of the Maya, the Olmecs, and other ancient civilizations, emphasizing the importance of religion in every aspect of indigenous people's behavior and experience.

Smith, Michael E. *The Aztecs.* 2d ed. Malden, Mass.: Blackwell, 2003. A well-illustrated discussion of the evolution of the Aztec state, based primarily on archaeological research of the late twentieth century.

Townsend, Richard F. *The Aztecs.* Rev. ed. New York: Thames and Hudson, 2000. An overview of Aztec

culture, incorporating illustrations of Aztec art and their environment.

SEE ALSO: Apr., 1519-Aug., 1521: Cortés Conquers Aztecs in Mexico; Aug., 1523: Franciscan Missionaries Arrive in Mexico; 1527-1547: Maya Resist Spanish Incursions in Yucatán; Feb. 23, 1540-Oct., 1542: Coronado's Southwest Expedition; 1542-1543: The New Laws of Spain; 1552: Las Casas Publishes *The Tears of the Indians.*

RELATED ARTICLES in *Great Lives from History: The Renaissance & Early Modern Era, 1454-1600:* Pedro de Alvarado; Hernán Cortés; Cuauhtémoc; Doña Marina; Montezuma II; Nezahualcóyotl.

Beginning 1504
DECLINE OF THE ḤAFṢID DYNASTY

After enjoying several centuries of autonomy, the Ḥafṣid state of Tunis found itself drawn unavoidably into the conflict between Christian Europe and the Islamic forces of the Ottomans and the Barbary corsairs. Caught between the two sides, Tunis changed hands and allegiances and was eventually conquered by the Ottoman Empire.

LOCALE: Ifriqiya, North Africa (now in Tunisia and eastern Algeria)

CATEGORIES: Government and politics; diplomacy and international relations; wars, uprisings, and civil unrest; expansion and land acquisition

KEY FIGURES

Süleyman the Magnificent (1494/1495-1566), Ottoman sultan, r. 1520-1566

Charles V (1500-1558), Holy Roman Emperor, r. 1519-1556, and king of Spain as Charles I, r. 1516-1556

Barbarossa (Khayr al-Dīn; d. 1546), admiral of the Ottoman fleet, 1533-1546

SUMMARY OF EVENT

The name taken by the Ḥafṣid Dynasty derives not from the founder of the independent Barbary state of Tunis, but from a Tunisian governor's father, Abū Ḥafṣ ʿUmar. In fact, this area of the Barbary Coast had enjoyed many periods of autonomy from the presumed central Islamic authority of the Caliph. During the period of the ʿAbbāsid

Caliphate in Baghdad, several very important semi-independent dynasties, including the Aghlabids (800-909) and the Fāṭimids (909-1171), had left their mark on the region. These dynasties did not govern from the northern city of Tunis but either remained in the traditional inland Islamic capital of al-Qayrawān (Kairouan) or, in the case of the Fāṭimids, founded a new coastal capital, Mahdia. The rise of the city of Tunis began when the entire region of Tunis came under the control of the Islamic reformist Almohad Dynasty of Morocco in the twelfth and thirteenth centuries.

Just as control of Ifriqiya from the Middle East had proved unworkable, control from the Almohad capital at Marrakech was ineffective. Therefore, in the first years of the thirteenth century, the Almohads appointed Abdul Wahid, son of Abū Ḥafṣ ʿUmar, a member of the Almohad inner circle, to serve as governor of Ifriqiya. Upon his death in 1221, local supporters of Abdul Wahid tried to designate his son as successor. After a period of confusion, another appointee arrived from Marrakech in 1228. During his long reign (1228-1249), Abū Zakariyyāʾ Yaḥyā laid the foundations of an autonomous state. His choice of the name Ḥafṣid shows that he recognized at least the symbolic importance of ties to his Almohad origins.

In this early period, there still were a number of Muslim entities in Spain struggling against the advancing Reconquista. The Muslim Naṣrid Dynasty in Granada turned to Abū Zakariyyāʾ for possible military support against Christian advances. He did help the Muslim enclave of Valencia by sending ships, but when Aragon's Christians took the coastal city, Ḥafṣid aid was removed.

During the reign of Abū Zakarīyyā''s son Al Mustanṣir (r. 1249-1277), a number of trade agreements were signed with the Italian city-states of Venice, Pisa, and Genoa, and an increasingly contradictory situation began to take form. Even while subjects of the Christian city-states were taking advantage of good trade relations with the Ḥafṣids, Pope Innocent I was urging Christian forces to mount a formal crusade in North Africa. To complicate matters further, Rome discovered that the Ḥafṣid state had recruited a number of Catalonian and Aragonese soldiers to serve Tunis's Muslim ruler.

It is difficult to say just when Ḥafṣid success in managing the administration of Ifriqiya's traditional hinterland and coastal provinces (including rich oasis areas like Gafsa and Gabès, both important as termini for trans-Saharan caravan trade) combined with Mediterranean trade to enable the Ḥafṣids to claim material and cultural leadership of the central coast area of North Africa. One accomplishment that raised Ifriqiya's stature in the eyes of less developed areas was the regime's maintenance of regional communication systems. Roads between the capital and key towns like Sousse, Monastir, and Sfax were more secure than they had been for many generations.

In stages, Tunis began to supplant al-Qayrawān as the center of Islamic learning in Ifriqiya, especially in matters connected with the Malikite branch of Islamic law. One factor contributing to Tunis's importance as a cosmopolitan center was the arrival, after the fall of Naṣrid Granada in 1492, of Andalusian immigrants from key areas of Spain. In particular, the growth of the Zaytuna mosque and madrasa (Islamic school) complex drew scholars from throughout the Islamic world to what was quickly becoming a rich cultural forum under Ḥafṣid sponsorship. Not only religious scholars but also charitable social institutions, including a major hospital complex, found fertile ground offered to them by the Ḥafṣid rulers. Although some of the Ḥafṣids' main accomplishments in the material sphere would not survive into the post-Ḥafṣid period of the late sixteenth century, these social and scholarly symbols of the cultural ascendancy of Tunis did survive into the modern era.

The Ḥafṣids came to play a pronounced role as political intermediaries between the expanding Islamic Ottoman Empire and Christian Europe in the sixteenth century. The Ottomans' 1517 expansion into the new Arabic-speaking provinces of Syria, Egypt, and the Hijaz

under Sultan Selim I was mainly the result of Selim's eastern campaign against his Islamic rivals, such as the Mamlūk sultanate in Cairo. Selim did not emphasize either the need to defeat Christianity or the political and economic desirability of expansion into the western basin of the Mediterranean. It was Selim's successor, Süleyman the Magnificent, who embraced both those goals.

Even before Süleyman mounted the Ottoman throne in 1520, the activities of renegade Muslim privateers, known among Westerners as Barbary corsairs, were having an impact on North Africa's coasts and on the Ḥafṣid area in particular. Step by step, major corsairs like Barbarossa and his brother ʿArūj gained military strength and even territory along the Barbary coast. Barbarossa first approached the Ḥafṣids around 1504, successfully negotiating permission to use Tunis's port of La Goulette as a base of operations. It was arguably this agreement that signaled the beginning of the Ḥafṣids' decline, since it led both Christian Spain and the Muslim Turks to take notice of the vital strategic importance of Ifriqiya. The corsairs' success eventually attracted Süleyman's attention and caused Istanbul to focus on the Ḥafṣid realm as a potential key to rich acquisitions in southern Italy and even further to the west, along the coasts of France and Spain.

The Ḥafṣids could not predict the Ottoman reaction to their agreement with Barbarossa and ʿArūj. However, the Ḥafṣid sultan soon came to fear the European repercussions of corsair attacks being launched from a Ḥafṣid port. Tunis stood not only to suffer militarily from Christian counterstrikes on its ports, but also to lose the valued European trade relations it had built up over many generations. Perhaps it was these possible consequences that prompted Sultan Muḥammad ibn al-Ḥasan in 1510 to grant a different safe haven to Barbarossa on the island of Jerba, much farther south, in the direction of Tripolitania. The corsairs only redoubled their anti-Christian activities, however, menacing Spanish enclaves as far away as the port of Bejaïa in 1513.

After ascending the thrones of Spain (1516) and the Holy Roman Empire (1519), Charles V began to respond to these attacks by the Barbary corsairs. The Ḥafṣids became even more concerned at the seeming inevitability with which they saw themselves being dragged into a war with Spain, and they took drastic measures to prevent such a war. The Muslim Ḥafṣid Dynasty not only gave up its tacit support of the corsairs' activities but also entered into an alliance with the Christian forces of the Holy Roman Emperor.

It was this politically expedient but ideologically indefensible alliance that brought about the final stages of Ḥafṣid rule in Tunis. As Süleyman's Ottoman forces advanced toward the western basin of the Mediterranean, the presence of what was essentially a Muslim protégé of the Christian enemy at the narrowest point between Africa and Europe was bound to become intolerable. Süleyman formalized the alliance between himself and Barbarossa, making the latter an admiral, absorbing his corsair fleet into the Ottoman navy, and giving Barbarossa joint command of the Ottoman and corsair ships. In 1534, Barbarossa led a successful attack against the Ḥafṣids, driving them from power and taking control of Tunis. Charles struck back the following year, however: He retook Tunis and restored the Ḥafṣid sultan to power.

Just at the end of Süleyman's rule, in 1565, the Turks made a bid to occupy the strategic island of Malta but failed, arguably because no help was forthcoming from Tunis. Thus, after Süleyman's death in 1566, his successor, Selim II (who lost the Battle of Lepanto in 1571), determined that the Ḥafṣids would have to be dethroned. This was accomplished without any significant struggle, perhaps because the Christian powers of the time realized that their Ḥafṣid alliance had become more of a liability than an advantage.

SIGNIFICANCE

The Ḥafṣid phenomenon illustrates the particular role played throughout Islamic history by the relatively rich agricultural region and culturally active subzone of North Africa known as Ifriqiya. Less than 100 miles (160 kilometers) from Sicily, the region controlled by the Ḥafṣids was seen by Europe and the Ottomans alike as too important to leave in the hands of a self-interested and unpredictable dynasty.

Although its strategic location ultimately made it the target of much larger imperial rivals in the sixteenth century, the dynasty is remembered less for its political or military importance than for the flourishing of architecture, arts, and letters under local dynastic sponsorship.

— *Byron Cannon*

FURTHER READING

Abun-Nasr, Jamil. *A History of the Maghrib*. New York: Cambridge University Press, 1987. This general history places the Ḥafṣids in the larger framework of North African events well before the sixteenth century.

Clancy-Smith, Julia. *North Africa, Islam, and the Mediterranean*. London: Cass, 2001. This study covers not only North African political history but also broader cultural issues in the entire Mediterranean region.

Goodwin, Jason. *Lords of the Horizons: The Ottomans*. New York: Holt, 1999. Deals with the growth of Ottoman power and formation of Balkan Christian, Middle Eastern, and North African Islamic provinces.

SEE ALSO: 1463-1479: Ottoman-Venetian War; May, 1485-Apr. 13, 1517: Mamlūk-Ottoman Wars; 16th century: Trans-Saharan Trade Enriches Akan Kingdoms; 1512-1520: Reign of Selim I; Jan. 23, 1516: Charles I Ascends the Throne of Spain; June 28, 1519: Charles V Is Elected Holy Roman Emperor; 1520-1566: Reign of Süleyman; June 28, 1522-Dec. 27, 1522: Siege and Fall of Rhodes; 1529-1574: North Africa Recognizes Ottoman Suzerainty; Sept. 27-28, 1538: Battle of Préveza; Oct. 20-27, 1541: Holy Roman Empire Attacks Ottomans in Algiers; 1566-1574: Reign of Selim II; Oct. 7, 1571: Battle of Lepanto.

RELATED ARTICLES in *Great Lives from History: The Renaissance & Early Modern Era, 1454-1600:* Barbarossa; Charles V; Süleyman the Magnificent.

September 22, 1504
TREATY OF BLOIS

The Treaty of Blois divided much of Italy between France and Spain. Spain gained control of Naples and Sicily, while France temporarily obtained Milan and Genoa. The treaty represented a significant step in the process whereby Italy's city-states were reduced to mere pawns in the power struggles of the larger Renaissance empires.

LOCALE: Naples, Sicily, Milan, and Genoa (now in Italy)

CATEGORIES: Diplomacy and international relations; wars, uprisings, and civil unrest; expansion and land acquisition

KEY FIGURES

Louis XII (1462-1515), king of France, r. 1498-1515

Ferdinand II (1452-1516), king of Aragon, r. 1479-1516, king of Castile, r. 1474-1504, king of Sicily, r. 1468-1516, and king of Naples as Ferdinand III, r. 1504-1516

Charles VIII (1470-1498), king of France, r. 1483-1498

Maximilian I (1459-1519), Holy Roman Emperor, r. 1493-1519

Gonzalo Fernández de Córdoba (1453-1515), leading Spanish general and first governor general of Naples, 1504-1507

Alexander VI (Rodrigo de Borja y Doms; 1431-1503), Roman Catholic pope, 1492-1503

Charles (1500-1558), Burgundian prince and grandson of Maximilian I, later king of Spain as Charles I, r. 1516-1556, and Holy Roman Emperor, r. 1519-1556

SUMMARY OF EVENT

Incessant quarrels between Renaissance Italian city-states often involved mercenary forces from Germany, Switzerland, or smaller city-states in Italy. However, by the sixteenth century, city-state conflicts began to attract powerful kings of newly centralized nation-states. Spain and France, in particular, took advantage of opportunities for dominating and exploiting the wealthy Italian states. Conflicts were waged on a much larger scale than before and had dire consequences for the continued development of Italy.

In September, 1494, King Charles VIII of France invaded Italy, setting off a cataclysmic series of wars that ravaged Italy over the next forty years. After taking Flor-ence, Charles advanced on Rome and then, meeting little resistance, entered Naples on February 22, 1495. Three months later, Charles returned to France, leaving behind forces to garrison Naples. Keeping control of Naples, however, was not as easy as seizing it. Moreover, Charles's claim of Angevin rights to Naples by inheritance through René of Anjou (following the death of his nephew Charles of Maine in 1486), was regarded as of dubious legitimacy. French actions forged a rapid alliance of Milan, Venice, the Holy Roman Emperor Maximilian I, Pope Alexander VI, and Ferdinand II of Aragon. By 1497, the Spanish fleet cut off French supply routes to Naples, and Charles was forced to negotiate an armistice.

During the armistice, Charles died and was succeeded by his son Louis XII. Supported by Venice, which was promised possession of Cremona, Louis invaded Italy in 1499. He quickly occupied both Milan and Genoa. As for Naples, Ferdinand and Louis were able to reach an agreement (the Treaty of Granada) in 1500, sanctioned by Pope Alexander VI, for the partition of Naples between France and Spain. France was to control the north of Naples (Abruzzi and Compania), while Spain was to receive the south (Calabria and Puglia). However, disagreement over the terms of the partition led to a resumption of war between France and Spain in 1502.

In this war, France was supported by the northern Italian states of Florence, Bologna, Mantua, and Ferrara. In 1503, French forces faced armies commanded by Spain's capable commander, Gonzalo Fernández de Córdoba, and suffered serious defeats at the Battle of Cerignola (April 16) and at the Garigliano River (December 29). Poorly provisioned and badly demoralized French forces fled to the fortified city of Gaeta, where they intended to make a stand. They found, however, that Gaeta had insufficient supplies to support them all through an extended siege or conflict. On New Year's Day, 1504, French forces in Italy surrendered at Gaeta. While not fatal for his cause, because France still had significant forces massed in Milan, these defeats increased Louis's receptivity to a compromise settlement with Spain. Negotiations resulted in the signing of the Treaty of Blois on September 22, 1504.

By signing the treaty, Louis renounced his claim to Naples in favor of his niece, Germaine de Foix, who was betrothed to the newly widowed Ferdinand II. Thus the Spanish gained control of Naples and Sicily without openly humiliating France. If no heir was produced by the marriage, the treaty provided for Naples to revert back to Louis's control. In the north of Italy, Emperor Maximilian recognized French control of Milan. However, the treaty specified that after Louis's death, Milan as well as Burgundy should go to Louis XII's daughter, Claude of France, who was to marry Maximilian's grandson (the future Charles V).

While the stipulated marriage of Claude and Charles could be rescinded only if Louis had a son, the French king, under pressure from the Estates General, found another way out of the marriage provision. Claude broke her engagement to Charles, becoming engaged instead to Louis's intended heir, Francis of Angoulême. This action violated the spirit, if not the letter, of the treaty and set the stage for future conflict. Treaty negotiations also led to a promise that no retribution would be taken against the southern Italian barons who had supported France. This promise was kept.

The Treaty of Blois contained a secret provision for France and Spain to launch a future attack on Venice. This attack was ultimately launched in December, 1510, precipitating a long series of wars and Machiavellian alliance changes. The wars involved not only the signatories to the treaty but also the Holy Roman Empire, Swiss and German mercenary forces, the Papal States, and other Italian states. The use of pikes, muskets, cannon, and moving squares (phalanxes) in battle formation resulted in extremely high mortality rates. These wars ravaged Italy, leading to, among other human-made catastrophes, the sack of Rome in 1527-1528. By 1550, conditions had so deteriorated in Italy that historians have long designated this date as the end of the Italian Renaissance. Most of Italy was under the rule of Charles V, who, as Holy Roman Emperor, king of Spain, and master of an ever-increasing empire in the New World, was one of the most powerful individuals on the planet.

SIGNIFICANCE

The takeover of Naples and Sicily facilitated by the Treaty of Blois led to Spanish exploitation of southern Italy for the following two centuries. Heavy taxation, conducted by a series of increasingly corrupt Spanish governors general, impoverished the peasantry. Fernández de Córdoba, called the Great Captain for his ability to command, became the first of these governors general (1504-1507). He used Naples as a base from which to extend Spanish hegemony in Italy. Milan, long considered to be the gateway into Italy, was taken by Spain in 1535.

Hence, the gate by which France could again invade Italy remained shut. By the reign of Philip II, king of Spain (r. 1556-1598), most of Italy was supervised from Madrid by the Council of Italy. Control of Italy shifted from Spain to the Holy Roman Emperor in 1715, leading to policies being set in Vienna instead of Madrid. It would take another 150 years before foreign control was ended by a series of wars and nationalist uprisings.

Italians blame Charles VIII's invasion of Italy in 1494, and the resulting Treaty of Blois ten years later, for starting the process that led to the end of the prosperity of the Italian Renaissance and initiated a four-century-long period of foreign control and exploitation. Perhaps the process of Italian economic decline was already at work during the first half of the sixteenth century as a result of the shift in trade from the Mediterranean Sea to the Atlantic Ocean. Eventual political decline was probably inevitable because of the Italian maintenance of the city-state structure at a time when the nation-state structure was emerging under the "new centralized monarchies." However, it is clear that the signing of the Treaty of Blois was both a symptom of the continuing decline of Italy and a cause of its rapid further disintegration.

—Irwin Halfond

FURTHER READING

Abulafia, David, ed. *The French Descent into Renaissance Italy, 1494-5: Antecedents and Effects.* Brookfield, Vt.: Ashgate, 1995. An excellent collection of scholarly articles about the politics and military encounters of the Italian conflict, including Milan's role in the wars. Several articles end their analyses in mid-sixteenth century.

Baumgartner, Frederic J. *Louis XII.* New York: St. Martin's Press, 1994. A highly readable biography with much attention to the invasion of Italy and diplomatic problems with Milan, which are viewed as a disastrous part of an otherwise productive reign.

Kamen, Henry A. *Spain's Road to Empire: The Making of a World Power, 1492-1763.* London: Allen Lane, 2002. Contains solid analyses of Spain's takeover of Southern Italy. Contains index and bibliography.

Mack Smith, Denis. *Medieval Sicily, 800-1713.* Vol. 1 in *A History of Sicily.* New York: Dorset Press, 1988. The best single account of the Spanish takeover of Sicily and its effects on Sicilian development.

Pettegree, Andrew. *Europe in the Sixteenth Century.* Malden, Mass.: Blackwell, 2002. A good starting point for general background. Chapter 3 is devoted to "The Struggle for Italy."

SEE ALSO: Apr. 9, 1454: Peace of Lodi; Sept., 1494-Oct., 1495: Charles VIII of France Invades Italy; Apr. 11, 1512: Battle of Ravenna; Sept. 13-14, 1515: Battle of Marignano; Jan. 23, 1516: Charles I Ascends the Throne of Spain; June 28, 1519: Charles V Is Elected Holy Roman Emperor; 1521-1559: Valois-Habsburg Wars; Feb., 1525: Battle of Pavia; May 6, 1527-Feb., 1528: Sack of Rome; Apr. 3, 1559: Treaty of Cateau-Cambrésis.

RELATED ARTICLES in *Great Lives from History: The Renaissance & Early Modern Era, 1454-1600:* Alexander VI; Charles V; Charles VIII; Ferdinand II and Isabella I; Louis XII; Maximilian I.

November 26, 1504

JOAN THE MAD BECOMES QUEEN OF CASTILE

Joan the Mad's reign and Ferdinand II's concurrent regency showed combined powers that secured the unity of the Castilian-Aragonese crown and paved the way for a new royal dynasty in Spain, the House of Habsburg.

LOCALE: Castile (now in Spain)
CATEGORY: Government and politics

KEY FIGURES

Joan the Mad (1479-1555), queen of Castile, r. 1504-1516

Ferdinand II (1452-1516), king of Aragon, r. 1479-1516, king of Castile, r. 1474-1504, and regent of Castile, r. 1504-1516

Isabella I (1451-1504), queen of Castile, r. 1474-1504

Philip I (1478-1506), archduke of Austria, sovereign of the Spanish Netherlands, and king consort of Castile, r. 1504-1506

SUMMARY OF EVENT

Joan the Mad was the third child of Queen Isabella I and King Ferdinand II, the Catholic Monarchs. Joan became heir to the throne of Castile on the death of her brother, John, her elder sister Isabella, and Isabella's son, Michael. In 1496, she married Philip I, archduke of Austria, ruler of the Spanish Netherlands, and son of the Holy Roman Emperor Maximilian I. Their marriage was problematic.

First, the princess was vulnerable emotionally, and she fell into fits of understandable jealousy because of Philip's infidelities. It is possible that her mental disability was inherited, although her madness is disputed by historians. Second, the Catholic Monarchs were vexed at Philip's political alliance with France, which was then at war with Spain. All of this, however, did not prevent the *cortes*, or parliament, of Castile—assembled in Toledo on May 22, 1502—from conferring on Philip and Joan the title of prince and princess, respectively, of As-

turias, and thus confirming them as heirs apparent to the throne.

Joan and her husband had arrived in Castile early that year, but in January, 1503, Philip chose to return to Flanders, where he was serving as ruler of the Spanish Netherlands, leaving Joan behind. Joan became very depressed, particularly after she gave birth to her son Ferdinand on March 10, 1503. Joan's obsession with returning to her husband led to a series of notorious episodes of rebelliousness that increased everyone's fears about her mental health. In the light of these events, the *cortes*—assembled in Madrid and Alcalá de Henares—voiced its doubts about Joan's ability to rule, urging Isabella to appoint a regent who would prevent Philip from taking power in Castile. With her mother's strong opposition, Joan traveled to Flanders in May of 1504. In the Flemish court, her personal situation got worse. News reached Castile that her fits of jealousy were increasing in number and that Philip was contemptuous, even cruel, toward her. The clash between husband and wife was complete.

On October 12, 1504, Isabella I dictated her will, which stipulated that Joan, being the universal heir to all of Isabella's territories, would be crowned queen of Castile, with Philip, her husband, as king consort; Isabella's husband and Joan's father, Ferdinand II, would have absolute power as regent of the kingdom until Charles I, Joan and Philip's son, reached the age of twenty. Isabella had finally recognized her daughter's unfitness for rule.

On November 26, 1504, Isabella died in Medina del Campo. The town's main square was witness that same day to Ferdinand relinquishing his royal duties in Castile, transferring them to his daughter and son-in-law, who were at the time in Flanders, but keeping the title of regent for himself.

The queen's will was not to Philip's liking, however; he wanted to be king and not simply king consort, something that Ferdinand would never allow. On January 23, 1505, the *cortes* of Castile, worried by Joan's evident mental instability, assembled in Toro to declare Ferdinand administrator and governor of her realm, in agreement with Isabella's will. Later that year, Philip and Ferdinand signed the Agreement of Salamanca (November, 1505) which stipulated that Ferdinand would have complete power until the royal couple returned to Spain.

In the meantime, Philip was subtly approaching from Flanders the Castilian nobility and high clergy so as to win them for his cause, which he said was also that of Joan, the heir apparent to the throne. The Castilians, for their part, were deeply disappointed with Ferdinand's alliance with King Louis XII of France and with Ferdinand's marriage to Germaine de Foix.

On April 25, 1506, Joan and Philip disembarked in La Coruña from Flanders. Upon their arrival, Philip prevented Joan from meeting her father, while he negotiated with Ferdinand the government of Castile. The two were trying to declare the queen's unfitness to rule, but both men knew well that to govern they needed Joan's consent. Ferdinand, without much support, signed the Villafáfila Agreement (1506), which left all power in Philip's hands. Two weeks later, the *procuradores*, or town clerks, sitting at the *cortes* of Valladolid, swore loyalty to Joan and Philip, and declared Charles—Joan's firstborn and heir—the queen's legitimate successor. Ferdinand, hurt by the treason of the Castilians, left Castile and retired to Aragon.

Philip I, however, died soon afterward in Burgos, a victim of fever. Scholar-official Francisco Jiménez de Cisneros, who had assumed control of the interim government, wrote to Ferdinand, begging him to return to Castile. In July, 1507, Ferdinand disembarked in Valencia and began traveling to the north. By then, Joan had been trying to fulfill her husband's last will: to be buried in Granada beside Isabella's grave. From Burgos in December of 1506, she set off with his coffin in a funeral procession that traveled by night only, surrounded by hundreds of torches, resting during the day in monasteries but never in nunneries. They stopped in January, 1507, in Torquemada, where Joan gave birth to her fifth child, Catherine, but four months later the nightly processions resumed. On August 29, Joan and Ferdinand finally met, and she gave her father unlimited power as long as she was granted complete authority over her husband's remains. The funeral cortege started again and stopped only when it reached Arcos, early in 1509.

Joan's father wanted her in Tordesillas, and she agreed to his wish in February, 1509, on condition that she could take Philip's body with her. Her husband's coffin was laid in the monastery of Santa Clara, where she could see it from a window of her palace. From that time forward, she took little part in the government's affairs. Ferdinand was granted until his death the governments of Castile, Leon, and Granada in a treaty he signed in December, 1509, with Maximilian I of Austria and, nominally, with Charles I (later Charles V) and Joan. Charles would reign when he came of age. The *cortes* of Castile and Leon confirmed Ferdinand as administrator and legitimate governor in his daughter's stead. They also confirmed Charles as Queen Joan's successor. Joan's authority became virtually insignificant.

On January 22, 1516, Ferdinand dictated his will. It confirmed Joan's rights as universal heir to all his territories; it also appointed regents until sixteen-year-old Charles could occupy the throne. The following day, Ferdinand I died. In Brussels, Charles soon proclaimed himself king of Castile and Aragon, ignoring pleas from the Royal Council of Castile for him not to adopt the title of king while his mother was alive. The fact that official documents would include his mother's title in front of his own shows that Joan's son was confirming her right to govern but limiting that right to her presence in the royal signature "Doña Juana, Reina de Castilla" (Joan I, queen of Castile). The people and history would favor her other title, Joan the Mad.

SIGNIFICANCE

The reign of Joan the Mad of Castile was a period marked by the consolidation of some of the projects of territorial expansion and pacification initiated by King Ferdinand and Queen Isabella, including the annexation of Navarre to the kingdom of Castile and the increased presence of Castile in North Africa.

Joan's reign also prepared for the future unity of the Spanish territories under the new dynasty of the Habsburgs. While Joan kept the title of queen in name, Ferdinand's regency preserved the unity of the Crowns of Castile and Aragon that had begun with the marriage of the Catholic Monarchs. The way was paved for the most important dynastic transition in the history of the Spanish monarchy: the arrival in Castile of the House of Habsburg with Charles, Joan's son, the future Holy Roman Emperor Charles V.

—Avelina Carrera de la Red

FURTHER READING

Aram, Bethany. "Juana 'the Mad's' Signature: The Problem of Invoking Royal Authority, 1505-1507." *Six-*

teenth Century Journal 29, no. 2 (1998): 331-358. Analyzes the political motivations that could help reinterpret Joan's madness, an analysis based on a famous letter written by Joan.

_____. "Juana 'the Mad,' the Clares, and the Carthusians: Revising a Necrophilic Legend in Early Habsburg Spain." *Archiv für Reformationsgeschichte* 93 (2002): 172-191. This article attempts to present a new vision of the shifting, and often competing, devotional and dynastic commitments of Joan of Castile.

Dennis, Amarie. *Seek the Darkness: The Story of Juana la Loca.* 5th ed. Madrid: Impresores Sucesores de Rivadeneyra, 1969. A biography of Joan of Castile colored with a taint of romanticism.

Miller, Townsend. *The Castles and the Crown: Spain,* *1451-1555.* London: Victor Gollancz, 1963. An excellent approach to the crossed lives of Isabella, Ferdinand, Joan, and Philip, with a special focus on Joan and Isabella.

SEE ALSO: Oct. 19, 1469: Marriage of Ferdinand and Isabella; Aug. 17, 1477: Foundation of the Habsburg Dynasty; 1482-1492: Maximilian I Takes Control of the Low Countries; Jan. 23, 1516: Charles I Ascends the Throne of Spain; 1520-1522: Comunero Revolt; 1576-1612: Reign of Rudolf II.

RELATED ARTICLES in *Great Lives from History: The Renaissance & Early Modern Era, 1454-1600:* Charles V; Ferdinand II and Isabella I; Mary of Burgundy; Maximilian I; Philip I; Rudolf II.

1505-1515
PORTUGUESE VICEROYS ESTABLISH OVERSEAS TRADE EMPIRE

Portugal's commercial and imperial development forged economic, political, and cultural links between the West and East that eventually led to European world domination.

LOCALE: Indian Ocean, South and Southeast Asia, and the Spice Islands (now the Moluccas)

CATEGORIES: Trade and commerce; expansion and land acquisition; colonization; exploration and discovery; economics

KEY FIGURES

Bartolomeu Dias (c. 1450-1500), Portuguese explorer

Vasco da Gama (c. 1460-1524), Portuguese explorer

Francisco de Almeida (c. 1450-1510), viceroy of Portuguese India, 1505-1509

Afonso de Albuquerque (1453-1515), governor of Portuguese India, 1509-1515

John II (1455-1495), king of Portugal, r. 1481-1495

Manuel I (1469-1521), king of Portugal, r. 1495-1521

SUMMARY OF EVENT

The decade between Bartolomeu Dias's discovery of the Cape of Good Hope (1488) and Vasco da Gama's voyage of 1497-1499—in which he rounded the cape and made contact with India—was a time of preparation. John II of Portugal sent an exploratory party up the Congo River (then considered a branch of the Nile), and he sent Pêro de Covilhã, disguised as a Muslim merchant, through Egypt to learn the Indian Ocean's wind and trading patterns. Other Portuguese explored the Atlantic Ocean and designed ships for the longer voyage; later admirals avoided the tortuous route taken by Dias along Africa's west coast and sailed out into the Atlantic to catch favorable winds and currents. The return of Christopher Columbus, who claimed "the Indies" for Spain, required the formal establishment of zones of influence, as articulated in the Treaty of Tordesillas of 1494. Finally, war in Morocco (1487-1488) renewed arguments in Portugal's royal council against overextending the nation's limited resources.

Manuel I "the Fortunate" succeeded to the throne of Portugal in 1495, and it was under his auspices that Vasco da Gama sailed. Upon reaching Africa's east coast, da Gama found a Muslim pilot to guide his fleet across the Indian Ocean to Calicut, which was reputed to be India's principal trading center for goods from the Far East. Calicut merchants despised Portugal's trading goods, however, and before da Gama sailed home, his fleet exchanged shots with the city's Hindu ruler, the Samorin.

Da Gama established the standard route to India and mapped out the whole shape of Portugal's imperial experience there. The horrendous voyage of twelve thousand miles—six to eight months each way, compared with the six to eight weeks needed to reach Spanish America—regularly cost one-third of an armada's crew and half its ships. Although some individuals in the East stood ready to assist Europeans, ultimately the trading of European goods and gold for Asian luxuries—spices, silks, and

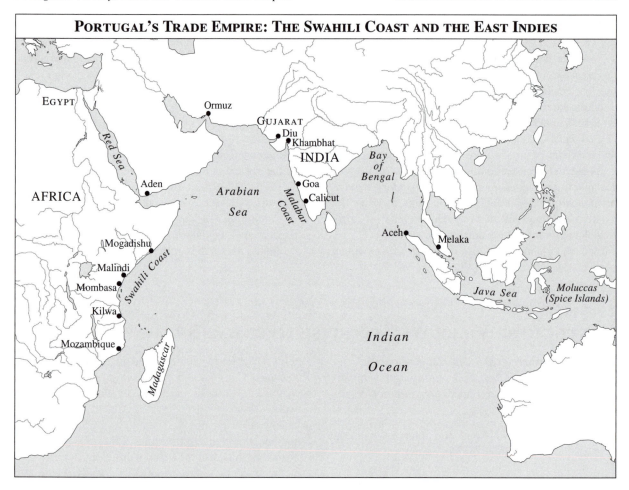

PORTUGAL'S TRADE EMPIRE: THE SWAHILI COAST AND THE EAST INDIES

jewels—depended on politics and war. The Portuguese believed that fabulous riches justified any risk, and five months after da Gama's return, another fleet sailed under the command of Pedro Álvares Cabral. Cabral's fleet discovered Brazil on its outward voyage. Annual armadas followed.

By the time Francisco de Almeida sailed in 1505, Portugal's activities in India had resulted in an alliance being formed against it. The sultan of Egypt, Arab traders, their Indian allies, and Venetian merchants all depended on established trade routes through the Red Sea and Persian Gulf to the Mediterranean, and they would do anything to frustrate the Portuguese newcomers. Periodic forays into the East would be insufficient to contest the resources of so many allied powers. Thus, Portugal needed to establish a continuous presence in India capable of defending its position.

Almeida sailed as viceroy of India, with a three-year term of office and a fleet of twenty-two ships and fifteen hundred warriors to support him. Following royal instructions, he fortified the island city of Kilwa off the coast of east Africa and replaced its king with a Muslim who swore allegiance to King Manuel. The city of Mombasa remained uncooperative, so Almeida destroyed it.

Upon arriving at Angediva Island in India, Almeida loaded half of his ships—"the pepper fleet"—for a return voyage to Portugal. His men paid local harbor dues, but Almeida responded to Indian resistance with fierce brutality. The cooperative cities of Cochin and Cannanore became the chief Portuguese trading ports in India, while the Samorin of Calicut remained Portugal's greatest enemy. Cannanore was besieged from March to August of 1507. The siege was relieved only by the arrival of the annual pepper fleet, and it made clear the dependence of Portugal's position upon control of the seas. Almeida argued against sustaining numerous forts to hold the land, seeing them as an unnecessary drain on limited human resources. He also implemented local shipyards to maintain Portugal's Indian fleet.

Almeida learned that Khambhat (Cambay), not Calicut, was actually India's greatest entrepôt. Khambhat was located in the Gujarat Plains, and Malik Ayaz, the Gujarati sultan, typical of Indian princes, was occupied at the time in defending his land frontiers against attack. The sultan had assigned command of his navy to a Russian renegade.

Ayaz played a double game in the decisive confrontation that established Portuguese control of India for a century. Almeida's fleet of nineteen ships sailed up the coast from Cannanore with the Samorin's fleet close behind. Ahead of Almeida, a fleet of twelve Egyptian ships, four ships under Malik Ayaz, and other ships of lesser princes waited in the Gujarati harbor of Diu. An eyewitness account speaks of three hundred ships; evidently merchantmen and small boats crowded the harbor.

On February 2, 1509, a few ships emerged from the harbor, engaged Almeida's fleet, and returned to safety. Although Indian cannon equaled European cannon, local ships always proved more vulnerable in battle, held together as they were by ropes rather than corrosion-prone iron nails. A great chain across Diu's harbor entrance limited access to a narrow channel protected by cannon. The next day, however, Almeida's fleet sailed boldly through and began to bombard the allied fleet. Apparently, harbor cannon hesitated to fire lest they destroy their own ships in the crowd. It is certain that early in the battle, Malik Ayaz betrayed his allies. Relentless hand-to-hand fighting began at nine o'clock in the morning. By nightfall, the allied fleet was annihilated and the Samorin's ships had fled.

In assembling Portugal's entire Indian Ocean fleet at Diu, Almeida thwarted the distrustful King Manuel's efforts to limit viceregal authority by establishing independent commanders. Jorge de Aguiar was assigned control from the Cape of Good Hope to Khambhat; Diogo Lopes de Sequeira was assigned control east of Cape Comorin at India's tip. Almeida, however, confirmed his authority over these commanders.

Ironically, however, Almeida's authority had already been officially superseded. Manuel had sent Afonso de Albuquerque to India in 1508 to replace Almeida (as governor, rather than viceroy). Albuquerque was ordered to establish bases to control access to the Red Sea and the Persian Gulf. Subordinate captains staged a revolt against the imperious Albuquerque, and the sultan of Ormuz (who controlled the strait at the entrance to the Persian Gulf) opened negotiations with Almeida to ac-

cept Portuguese suzerainty. Facing a showdown at Diu, Almeida arrested Albuquerque but yielded authority when his successor's confirmation arrived. Almeida died on his homeward voyage while fighting natives near the Cape of Good Hope.

Without rejecting Almeida's theory of empire, Albuquerque followed royal instructions to establish key fortified trading posts, located at Goa, Melaka (Malacca), and Ormuz. Perhaps only his failure to control the Red Sea prevented Portugal from exercising complete hegemony over trade in the Indian Ocean. Goa, the best harbor along the Malabar Coast, remained Portugal's central post in India until 1961. In taking this city, Albuquerque had support from local Hindu subjects against their Muslim ruler.

The capture of Goa on November 25, 1510, brought Portugal new respect; even the Samorin and the king of Gujarat sent ambassadors. While engaged taking Goa, Albuquerque had commanded the fleet assigned to Diogo Mendes de Vasconcelos to conquer Melaka; afterward, he took Melaka himself. The following year, in a series of engagements between July 25 and August 24, Albuquerque's nine hundred men overcame a garrison of at least twenty thousand soldiers, again with the assistance of a non-Muslim population ruled by an unpopular sultan.

Frustrated by fortifications at Aden in April, 1513, Albuquerque reconnoitered the Red Sea for another base. He wrote to King Manuel, projecting the destruction of Egypt's Red Sea fleet. Portugal would exercise control of the Red Sea from Jidda, just as it controlled the Indian Ocean from Goa. Soon after receiving reports of the Aden failure, however, the king sent orders for Albuquerque's replacement as governor.

One last triumph remained for Albuquerque, at Ormuz. In February, 1515, after thirteen months spent organizing Goa's government, Albuquerque sailed in command of his most massive fleet: twenty-seven ships and three thousand men. The armada's size and a political coup won the day. Albuquerque surprised and killed a hostile prime minister in front of the boy sultan and the Persian ambassador, who was jockeying for control of Ormuz. While fortifying Ormuz, however, Albuquerque contracted dysentery. He died after reaching Goa.

Before his death, Albuquerque also made contact with Java and Siam, and, in 1511, he sent an armada to the Spice Islands (Moluccas), sources of cloves and nutmeg. Francisco Serrão, a captain in this armada who was shipwrecked while returning to India, returned to the Moluccas instead. There, he joined the service of the sul-

1500's

tan of Ternate (one of the islands). He proved useful when the next Portuguese fleet arrived in 1514. Serrão also suggested to Ferdinand Magellan, his comrade in Albuquerque's Melaka expedition, that he approach the Moluccas from the Americas; thus, Serrão influenced the world's first circumnavigation. Magellan's voyage of 1519-1522 under the Spanish flag raised problems about the ownership of the Moluccas, a dispute that was settled in Portugal's favor by the Treaty of Zaragoza in 1529. Almeida's son had visited Ceylon in 1506; in 1518, Albuquerque's successor, Lopo Soares de Albergaria, established a port there to control its cinnamon trade.

SIGNIFICANCE

With his House of India effectively enjoying a monopoly on the spice trade, Manuel I became Europe's richest monarch. For a few years, Lisbon was Europe's richest port. Even Venetian merchants bought pepper in Lisbon, and from 1508, transshipment of Lisbon's spices made Antwerp the prime European trading center. Europeans had an insatiable appetite for pepper to flavor rancid meat, and Lisbon had the lowest prices. In 1505, a hundredweight of pepper sold for 30 ducats in Lisbon and 192 ducats in Alexandria—the highest prices for a century as a result of Portugal's Indian monopoly and the onslaught of Ottoman Turks attacking Egypt's ruling Mamlūk Turks. The fall of the Mamlūks in 1517 permanently disoriented Mediterranean trade, providing Portugal with even greater control of the spice market.

—*Paul Stewart*

FURTHER READING

Albuquerque, Afonso de. *The Commentaries of the Great Afonso Dalboquerque, Second Viceroy of India.* Edited and translated by Walter de Gray Birch. 4 vols. New Delhi: Asian Educational Services, 2000. Originally published by the Hakluyt Society between 1875 and 1884, this work demonstrates the genius of the Portuguese empire's chief architect.

Diffie, Bailey W., and George D. Winius. *Foundations of the Portuguese Empire, 1415-1580.* Minneapolis: University of Minnesota Press, 1977. A comprehensive, balanced account written by specialists, this book includes a useful annotated bibliography.

Hanson, Carl. *Atlantic Emporium: Portugal and the Wider World, 1147-1497.* New Orleans: University Press of the South, 2001. Survey of the Portuguese sphere of influence from the twelfth to fifteenth centuries, covering political, economic, and cultural history. Emphasizes Portugal's contribution to the cre-

ation, for the first time, of a global economy. Includes illustrations, bibliographic references, and index.

Lach, Donald. *Asia in the Making of Europe.* 3 vols. Chicago: University of Chicago Press, 1965-1993. With three additional volumes projected, this work has unprecedented depth and overwhelming detail.

Pearson, M. N. *The Portuguese in India.* Vol. 1 in *The New Cambridge History of India*, edited by Gordon Johnson. New York: Cambridge University Press, 1987. A scholarly, revisionist book, claiming that Portugal little changed India or commerce in the Indian Ocean.

Russell-Wood, A. J. R. *The Portuguese Empire, 1415-1808: A World on the Move.* Baltimore, Md.: Johns Hopkins University Press, 1998. This thematically organized account of Portuguese colonial expansion seeks to provide insights into the nature of the empire that have been obscured by strictly chronological studies. Illustrations, maps, bibliographic references, and index.

Sanceau, Elaine. *The Reign of Manuel: The Fortunate King.* Hamden, Conn.: Archon Books, 1970. A readable biography of the Portuguese monarch based on contemporary chronicles.

Shastry, B. S. *Goa-Kanara Portuguese Relations, 1498-1763.* Edited by Charles J. Borges. New Delhi: Concept, 2000. History of Portuguese trade and colonization of India beginning with their arrival in 1498. Includes bibliographic references and index.

Subrahmanyam, Sanjay, ed. *Sinners and Saints: The Successors of Vasco da Gama.* New York: Oxford University Press, 1998. Anthology of essays by international scholars detailing the history of Portuguese trade and missionary work in India from the beginning of the sixteenth century. Includes illustrations, map, bibliographic references.

SEE ALSO: c. 1485: Portuguese Establish a Foothold in Africa; Aug., 1487-Dec., 1488: Dias Rounds the Cape of Good Hope; June 7, 1494: Treaty of Tordesillas; Beginning c. 1500: Coffee, Cacao, Tobacco, and Sugar Are Sold Worldwide; 1500-1530's: Portugal Begins to Colonize Brazil; 16th century: Worldwide Inflation; Sept. 29, 1513: Balboa Reaches the Pacific Ocean; 1519-1522: Magellan Expedition Circumnavigates the Globe.

RELATED ARTICLES in *Great Lives from History: The Renaissance & Early Modern Era, 1454-1600:* Afonso de Albuquerque; Bartolomeu Dias; Vasco da Gama; John II; Ferdinand Magellan; Manuel I.

1505-1521
REIGN OF ZHENGDE AND LIU JIN

The reign of Ming emperor Zhengde, during which the eunuch Liu Jin held power, marked a period of great conflict between the eunuchs and the Ming bureaucracy.

LOCALE: China
CATEGORY: Government and politics

KEY FIGURES

Zhengde (reign name, also Cheng-te; given name Zhu Houzhao, Chu Hou-chao; temple name Wuzong, Wu-tsung; 1491-1521), emperor of China, r. 1505-1521

Liu Jin (Liu Chin; 1452-1510), a eunuch who attempted to gain control of China's bureaucracy

Han Wen (1441-1526), minister of finance during the reign of Zhengde

Jiao Fang (Chiao Fang; 1436-1517), an important member of Liu Jin's intelligence network

Zhang Yong (Chang Yung; 1463-1529), a eunuch who led a successful action to remove Liu Jin from power

SUMMARY OF EVENT

Eunuchs played a significant role in government and the military during the Ming Dynasty. In the early fourteenth century, when China was ravaged by civil war, military detachments of eunuchs were given the duty of protecting the royal family. Their military skill was so impressive that the emperor, Yonglo (r. 1402-1424), began to send these excellent fighters to the most dangerous parts of the empire. Companies of eunuchs had considerable success in battles against the Mongols on China's northern borders, while other groups successfully controlled the problem of marauding pirates along China's seacoasts.

By 1411, great numbers of eunuchs had become a significant part of China's military establishment. They also played an important role in the development of China's new military technology. The use of gunpowder as a weapon became very important during the Ming Dynasty. Many eunuchs were placed in charge of research and development as well as production in China's military-industrial complex. When a detachment of eunuchs was given the duty to establish a defensive perimeter around the Ming capital of Beijing, they placed highly accurate cannons in the elevated areas around the capital city. These weapons made Beijing virtually impregnable.

For most of the fifteenth century, the political power of the eunuchs was contained by a series of strong emperors and a powerful Confucian bureaucracy of scholar-officials. This was especially true during the reign of Xiaozong (Zhu Youcheng, Zhu Yutang, Chu Yu-t'ang, reign motto Hongzhi; r. 1488-1505). An excellent ruler, he was trained in the neo-Confucian philosophy that emphasized the characteristics of duty, honor, and commitment to the well-being of the empire.

The unexpected death of Xiaozong in 1505 set in motion a chain of events that would lead to one of the worst periods of political abuse in Chinese history. Xiaozong was succeeded by his thirteen-year-old son, who took the reign name Zhengde. At first the new emperor seemed to be the mirror image of his father, and many people believed that the transition of power signaled the same focus on the Confucian ideals in government. In fact, Zhengde had superior credentials. He was an excellent student who had always been the perfect example of someone who aspired to acting as the ideal Confucian philosopher-king.

Unfortunately, the new emperor inherited three major political problems that would be the foundation of the unrest and abuse that eventually brought down his regime. Like his father and many of the emperors before him, Zhengde faced the traditional problem of nomadic warrior tribes along China's northern borders. Chief among these were the Mongols, who were able to move at will, inflicting heavy casualties on Chinese forces. China's walled fortifications, which also acted as the base of military operations, were always short on supplies. The security of the empire would be placed in great jeopardy if a solution were not found to this problem. Second, there was widespread dissent within the upper levels of the Ming bureaucracy. Finally and perhaps most pressing, the new emperor also faced a growing financial crisis that was placing a tremendous strain on the empire's treasury.

The source of the scholar-officials' discontent was a struggle between the growing influence of a very powerful group of eunuchs known as the Eight Tigers, led by Liu Jin and senior advisers to the new emperor. The most powerful part of this advisory group were four powerful administrators known as the Grand Secretaries. There was a significant generation gap between the young emperor and these advisers, and Zhengde sought confidants closer to his own age.

It was also at this time that the young emperor began

1500's

321

to reject his Confucian upbringing and embrace an extremely worldly attitude toward life. Additionally, Zhengde began a close relationship with Liu Jin and the Eight Tigers. The young emperor soon developed a reputation as a drunkard and carouser. Liu Jin ingratiated himself with Zhengde by helping to provide the young emperor with opportunities to indulge his vices. Zhengde eventually became so corrupt that he completely neglected his duties. His mismanagement was depleting the treasury at such a rapid rate that the empire was on the verge of financial collapse. Zhengde eventually had a meeting with his minister of finance, Han Wen. Han Wen informed the emperor that his government was spending money at approximately four times the rate of his father's regime. Han Wen was a minister of the highest reputation, and he knew that the only way to obtain control of the financial situation was to have Zhengde reduce his spending. When the emperor suggested that the government raise taxes, Han Wen refused on the basis that new taxes would place a large burden on the peasantry, which would eventually cause rebellion and political chaos.

Zhengde responded by placing Liu Jin in charge of increasing the amount of money flowing into the government treasury. Liu Jin immediately began an investigation to attack the traditional bureaucracy and enhance his own power. He also used this investigation as a pretext to gain control of the Ming secret police. This powerful organization, known as the Dongchung, had been established under the emperor Yonglo (r. 1402-1424) in an attempt to prevent subversive activities that could undermine the peace and security of the empire. Over time it penetrated every part of the bureaucracy, and its informants provided the agency with information on thousands of bureaucrats. By the time Liu Jin gained control of the Dongchung, it was the most hated government institution in China. Liu Jin expanded the reach of the Dongchung by adding two spy agencies at the Ming court.

Once he had firmly established his power, Liu Jin initiated a reign of terror in which he attempted to "purge" every government agency of its most senior personnel. He charged many of these powerful bureaucrats with official misconduct and corruption, and he subsequently had them imprisoned and executed. In this manner, Liu Jin was able to disrupt the power base within the Chinese bureaucracy. Many of the senior, established eunuchs viewed these actions as a direct attack on their own security. They created a plan that would outline all of Lui Jin's abuses. They would then take this information to the emperor and ask for his execution.

One of Liu Jin's most trusted intelligence agents, Jiao Fang, discovered the plan and warned Liu Jin that he was in grave danger. Liu Jin took the initiative and asked for an audience with the emperor. He convinced Zhengde that the charges were untrue and constituted an attempt by corrupt bureaucrats to maintain their own power.

On learning that the plan had been exposed, the leaders resigned from their positions in the bureaucracy, and Liu Jin rewarded Jiao Fang with a position as a major court adviser. One of Jiao Fang's first assignments was to carry out a series of assignations against the bureaucrats who had called for Liu Jin's execution. These assassinations began another reign of terror, whose object was to give Liu Jin complete control of the bureaucracy.

This nationwide attack did not go uncontested, and this time the opposition was led by a trusted and highly respected eunuch, Zhang Yong. He was a decorated general officer who had made his reputation as a brave fighter on China's northern boarders. His great skill and success had made him a favorite of the emperor, and he used this connection to bring charges against Liu Jin. Zhang Yong delivered a petition to Zhengde listing the crimes Liu Jin had committed, including a plan to assassinate the emperor. This time the emperor was convinced, and he had Liu Jin executed. Zhengde's regime never recovered from this political chaos, however, and the emperor eventually died from complications from alcoholism.

SIGNIFICANCE

The Ming Dynasty entered into a period of decline in the 1500's, largely the result of a significant lack of imperial leadership and widespread corruption within the state bureaucracy. As time went on, the emperors found it increasingly difficult to trust their administrators and ministers. It became evident that the Ming royal family could not function without the loyalty and obedience of the eunuchs. By the end of the Ming Dynasty, eunuchs occupied important positions in the empire's military establishment, as well as powerful positions as commanders of the Palace Guard. They also held important posts in the Ming military-industrial complex. Not unlike Liu Jin, many eunuchs used their positions to increase their own power, and this led to more widespread corruption.

Political chaos continued to undermine the power of the emperor, and by the middle of the seventeenth century China was torn apart by famine and rebellion. In 1644, the Manchus, a nomadic tribe from the north, captured the capital of Beijing and brought an end to the Ming Dynasty.

—Richard D. Fitzgerald

FURTHER READING

Gernet, Jacques. *A History of Chinese Civilization*. New York: Cambridge University Press, 1990. Excellent account of Chinese cultural history. Maps, index, bibliography.

Graff, David A., and Robin Higham. *A Military History of China*. Cambridge, Mass.: Westview Press, 2002. The best Chinese military history on the market. Maps, index, and bibliography.

Tsai, Henry. *The Eunuchs in the Ming Dynasty*. Albany: New York State University Press, 1996. The most complete account of the impact of eunuchs in the Ming Dynasty.

SEE ALSO: Feb. 11, 1457: Restoration of Zhengtong; 1465-1487: Reign of Xianozong; 1474: Great Wall of China Is Built; 1488-1505: Reign of Xiaozong; 16th cent.: Rise of the *Shenshi*; 16th cent.: Single-Whip Reform; 1514-1598: Portuguese Reach China; 1521-1567: Reign of Jiajing; 1550-1571: Mongols Raid Beijing; Jan. 23, 1556: Earthquake in China Kills Thousands; 1573-1620: Reign of Wanli; 1583-1610: Matteo Ricci Travels to Beijing; 1592: Publication of Wu Chengen's *The Journey to the West*.

RELATED ARTICLES in *Great Lives from History: The Renaissance & Early Modern Era, 1454-1600:* Matteo Ricci; Wang Yangming; Xiaozong; Zhengde.

1507

END OF THE TIMURID DYNASTY

The rise of the Shaybānīd Uzbeks and political infighting among the Turkic Timurids combined to bring about the first Mughal ruler of India, the end of the Timurid Dynasty, more battles for power and control throughout Central Asia, and the end to the patronage of the Timurid court, which created a diaspora of scholars, artists, and writers.

LOCALE: Uzbekistan and Afghanistan

CATEGORIES: Government and politics; expansion and land acquisition; wars, uprisings, and civil unrest

KEY FIGURES

Bābur (Zahīr-ud-Dīn Muḥammad; 1483-1530), sultan of Fergana, r. 1494-1503, and first Mughal ruler in India, r. 1526-1530

Muḥammad Shaybānī (1451-1510), Uzbek ruler, r. 1496-1510

Ḥusayn Bayqarah (Husain-i Baikara; d. 1506), Timurid sultan of Khorāsān, r. 1469-1506

SUMMARY OF EVENT

Shaybānī, for whom the Turko-Mongol Shaybānīd Uzbeks are named, was a grandson of the great Mongol khan, Genghis Khan, and brother of Orda and Batu, founders of the White Horde and Golden Horde, respectively. After the death of Genghis Khan in 1227, Shaybānī gained control of the region east and southeast of the Ural River in the former Kipchak (Turkic) realm.

By the early fifteenth century, the Uzbeks found themselves wedged between the disintegrating Golden Horde to the north and the Timurid Empire to the south. The loose tribal structure was forged into a khanate under Khan Abū'l-Khayr (1429-1468), with its center located between the Ural and Irtyah Rivers. The Kyrgyz-Kazak Uzbeks disputed Abū'l-Khayr's ascension and seceded under their khans Janibeg and Girei. They then settled in southeast of what is now Kazakhstan.

Abū'l-Khayr developed the Uzbek state until 1457, when the Oyrat (Kalmyk) Mongols assaulted his territories from the east and settled in the middle Syr Darya region. Janibeg and Girei took advantage of the situation and began a long, violent struggle against the Uzbeks that lasted until 1500 and all but destroyed the Uzbek state. Abū'l-Khayr's grandson, Muḥammad Shaybānī, a vassal of Maḥmūd Khan, the Jagataite khan of West Moghulstan, received Turkestan as a fief sometime around 1490. This provided him with a firm base of operations. Muḥammad was no nomadic chieftain, but a leader of refined culture and many skills. He was well read in Islamic literature and spoke Turkish, Persian, Arabic, and his native dialect. He was a patron of artists and writers and sought to re-create a Mongol Empire reminiscent of that of Genghis Khan. He would start by helping himself to the rapidly crumbling Timurid Empire to his south.

Timur's (also known as Tamerlane; 1336-1405) empire stretched from east of the Indus River to central Anatolia, and from the Aral Sea to the Arabian Sea. At his death, the empire was divided between two of his sons, Mirān Shāh (d. 1407), who received all but Khorāsān, and Shāh Rokh (1405-1447). Shāh Rokh re-

1500's

323

united the patrimony forcibly and initiated a golden age of culture that contrasted dramatically with his father's brutal rule.

Herāt in Khorāsān (now northwestern Afghanistan) replaced Samarqand as the center of power. After Shāh Rokh's death, internal struggles for power invited Uzbek interference and rebellion. For more than two decades, Timurid ruler Abū Saʿīd (1451-1469) fought with confederations of the Turkic Kara Koyunlu and Ak Koyunlu tribes, managing to keep the aggressive steppe warriors at bay. After his death at the Battle of Karabakh, however, the west fell to the Ak Koyunlu, reducing Timurid power to Khorāsān.

Internal disputes continued in this rump state during the reign of the last major Timurid ruler, Ḥusayn Bayqarah, who rebuilt much of what had been lost. He took Samarqand from Khoja Ahrar, son of Abū Saʿīd, as well as Merv, Khiva, and Herāt, which served as his capital.

The arts continued to flower under Ḥusayn, including poetry, illustration, and the work of the famous painter and calligrapher Naqqāsh and the literature of Mir ʿAlī Shīr Navāʾi, a close friend of Ḥusayn, who has been called the Turkic Chaucer. In Central Asian terms, Herāt was another Renaissance Florence, a true center of culture. The lack of an effective administrative structure, however, made ruling this state difficult, and internal problems continued. One of the main weaknesses of the Timurids was their failure to integrate the sedentary peoples of their realm with the nomadic ones: The steppes and the cities remained distinct.

The Timurid-approved ruler of Transoxiana, Sultan Ahmad, died in 1494. In 1499, Muhammad took advantage of dynastic squabbling and began occupying the region. The following year he made peace with Girei's son, Burunduq, khan of the Kazaks to the north, and quickly seized Bukhara and then confronted Samarqand. The local Timurid ruler, ʿAlī, left the city to negotiate with the Uzbeks, but was brutally killed. After taking the city, Muhammad declared the end of the dynasty and himself ruler of Transoxiana. He quickly lost Bukhara to a counterstroke by Bābur, the Timurid sultan of Fergana (now in Uzbekistan). Muhammad just as quickly retrieved Bukhara and then turned on Khwārizm, which was a vassal state of the Timurids. For ten months in 1505-1506, he laid siege to its main city, Khiva, which was defended by its governor, Ḥusayn, unsuccessfully.

The Uzbeks then proceeded on to Khorāsān and its capital of Herāt. Ḥusayn had just died, and leadership fell

on the new sultan, the last Iranian Timurid, Badīʿ-az-Zāmān, who was unfit to meet the coming challenges. Balkh was attacked during the winter of 1506-1507 and surrendered in the spring. The defense of Herāt by Badīʿ lasted just three days that May; the capital capitulated on May 27, but the struggle for dominance in the region was by no means settled: Muhammad faced a renewed Kazak conflict farther north, which weakened his ability to suppress encroachments from remaining Timurids (Bābur, especially), Mongol Dervishes, and Ṣafavid Iranians. In 1503, Bābur tried again—unsuccessfully—to recapture Timur's old capital city. He lost his home state in addition to the battle.

Late in the decade, Ṣafavid Iranian shah Ismāʿīl threatened to bring his Shīʿite Islam army on a pilgrimage to the sacred city of Mashhad, which was deep in Khorāsān. Allying himself with the Sunni Bābur, he struck when the Kyrgyz attacked the Uzbeks from the northeast, taking Mashhad and Merv and killing Muhammad at the Battle of Merv on December 2, 1510. The nomadic light cavalry proved no match for the shah's field artillery.

Ismāʿīl visited a touch of nomadic barbarity on the defeated Uzbeks by turning their dead leader's skull into a drinking cup. He went on to take Herāt and Balkh, while Bābur seized the opportunity to reestablish his kingdom in Afghanistan, centered in Kabul (which he had ruled from 1504 to 1509), and grabbing Samarqand (October, 1511) and Bukhara from the reeling Uzbeks, who retreated into Tashkent. Within a year, however, the Uzbeks returned and crushed a combined force at Ghajdavan (Ghajawan) on December 12, 1512. This reestablished Uzbek control in Transoxiana, and soon they had retaken Samarqand from Bābur (1514). Bābur, the last Timurid, became the first Mughal ruler in India when he decided to shift the axis of his power from Afghanistan to northern India, having conquered the region by 1526.

SIGNIFICANCE

The Timurids had established a court at Herāt unequaled in its cultural brilliance. Its destruction by the Uzbeks scattered poets, artists, scholars, and works of art and literature across the Central Asian landscape. Even if Ḥusayn Bayqarah and his kin had not mastered the art of integrating steppe culture with sedentary urban culture, they chose to privilege that of the civilized world, a move that proved enormously fruitful in the Islamic Mughal culture that Bābur planted in India.

—*Joseph P. Byrne*

FURTHER READING

Adshead, Samuel A. M. *Central Asia in World History.* New York: Palgrave Macmillan, 1993. Discusses the politics and campaigns involved in the Timurids' fall and places it in the context of the region's broader political situation.

Jackson, Peter, ed. *The Timurid and Ṣafavid Periods.* Vol. 6 in *The Cambridge History of Iran.* New York: Cambridge University Press, 1986. Presents the broad picture of the Timurid civilization and discusses its fall, especially from the Ṣafavid perspective.

Nicolle, David. *The Age of Tamerlane.* New York: Osprey, 1990. A well-illustrated study of warfare in the region to the early sixteenth century.

Thackston, M. W. *A Century of Princes: Sources on Timurid History and Art.* Cambridge, Mass.: Harvard University Press, 1989. A useful collection of materials, especially for the period leading up to the dynasty's fall.

Thackston, W. M., ed. *The Baburnama: Memoirs of Bābur, Prince and Emperor.* New York: Modern Library, 2002. An autobiographical account of Bābur's life.

SEE ALSO: c. 1462: Kazak Empire Is Established; 1469-1508: Ak Koyunlu Dynasty Controls Iraq and Northern Iran; Dec. 2, 1510: Battle of Merv Establishes the Shaybānīd Dynasty; Apr. 21, 1526: First Battle of Panipat; 1598: Astrakhanid Dynasty Is Established.

RELATED ARTICLES in *Great Lives from History: The Renaissance & Early Modern Era, 1454-1600:* Bābur; Ibrāhīm Lodī.

1508
FORMATION OF THE LEAGUE OF CAMBRAI

Julius II formed the League of Cambrai to help restore Italian political stability and to allow the league's members to reclaim lands taken from them by Venice. The league was short-lived, however, because it served inadvertently to upset the balance of power in the region in favor of the French.

LOCALE: Cambrai, in northern France
CATEGORIES: Diplomacy and international relations; expansion and land acquisition

KEY FIGURES

Louis XII (1462-1515), king of France. r. 1498-1515
Maximilian I (1459-1519), Holy Roman Emperor, r. 1493-1519
Ferdinand II (1452-1516), king of Aragon, r. 1479-1516, king of Castile, r. 1474-1504, king of Sicily, r. 1468-1516, king of Naples as Ferdinand III, r. 1504-1516
Julius II (Giuliano della Rovere; 1443-1513), Roman Catholic pope, 1503-1513
Margaret of Austria (1480-1530), regent of the Netherlands, r. 1507-1530
Cardinal Georges d'Amboise (1460-1510), chief minister of France, 1498-1510

SUMMARY OF EVENT

In 1508, the Italian political landscape enjoyed a rare moment of relative stability. Beginning with the French king Charles VIII's invasion of Italy in 1494, the peninsula had been plunged into a state of chaos, as various governments both within and without Italy strove to seize control of as many of the Italian states as possible. The chaos abated somewhat at various times during the first half of the sixteenth century, but the overall political situation would not fully stabilize until the 1559 Treaty of Cateau-Cambrésis.

The temporary stability of 1508 was the result of recent military successes enjoyed by Spain and the papal forces led by Pope Julius II. Spanish forces had defeated the French and had occupied southern Italy, while the French remained in control of Milan, the strategic key to northern Italy. Julius II had brought Bologna, Perugia, and other states under direct papal governance, and he sought to recover cities in northern Romagna that had been taken by the Republic of Venice. Venice had taken advantage of the confusion resulting from the French invasions to occupy not only papal territory but also areas on the mainland of Italy that were claimed by other states. The states that had been disenfranchised by Venice's actions consequently drew together in a plot to retake their lands and to divide between themselves all the mainland possessions of the Venetian Republic.

The League of Cambrai was undoubtedly assembled by more than one diplomat, but Julius II was its guiding voice. In the summer of 1507, he sent a papal legate to Germany to persuade Holy Roman Emperor Maximilian I not to proceed with his projected invasion of Italy but to consider instead the formation of a general league against the Turks and a special league against Venice. In 1508, overtures were also made to the French, and soon a truce was announced between France and the empire, enabling conversations about the pope's proposals to begin in earnest.

In November, 1508, a delegation from King Louis XII of France headed by Cardinal Georges d'Amboise, his chief minister, met a delegation from the emperor at Cambrai, on the Flanders frontier. The imperial delegation was led by Margaret of Austria, a woman whose significant role in history has not always been acknowledged. Within one month, the details for the League of Cambrai had been negotiated, including an open treaty and a secret one. The former established peace and an alliance between France and the Holy Roman Empire and provided as well for a confederation against the Turks and all other enemies of Christendom. This confederation included the pope and the kings of England, Hungary, and Aragon.

The secret treaty, signed the same day, formed a league against the Venetian Republic, stating that its purpose was to put an end to the aggressions of Venice and to restore captured territories to their rightful owners. The principal signatories to the secret treaty were King Louis XII, Pope Julius II, and the Emperor Maximilian, but the kings of Aragon and Hungary were invited to participate with the promise of territorial compensation for their involvement.

The members of the league were required to prepare for war the following April. They were to aid one another in recovering their "rightful" lands, and none was to make a separate peace. One potential difficulty, the fact of Maximilian's alliance with Venice, was surmounted by the device of having the pope call on the emperor, as protector of the Church, to aid in the recovery of papal lands. For his share, Maximilian would achieve the restoration of imperial control of such Italian cities as Goriza, Trieste, and Flume. Louis XII joined the league, not only because of disputes with Venice concerning the division of northern Italy but also because he was strongly influenced by both the pope and the emperor.

The fourth member of the coalition, Ferdinand II, king of Aragon and Naples, demanded the return of the Apulian ports of Brindisi and Otranto, which had been taken from the Kingdom of Naples by the Venetians in 1495. He also feared that failure to participate in the league would leave him politically isolated in Europe. There is no doubt that Ferdinand expected that most of the effort against Venice would be made by the emperor, the pope, and the king of France.

SIGNIFICANCE

The League of Cambrai was an instrument fashioned by Julius II, through which he intended to divide the Republic of Venice to the advantage of the papacy and the major European states. The league actually lasted less than two years, however. The French won a significant victory against Venice at Agnadello in 1509, but the victory had the effect of dividing the league, because it left France too powerful in northern Italy. As a result, Julius II came to an agreement with Venice in 1510 and proceeded to form a new league, the second Holy League, whose avowed purpose was to drive the French out of Italy. The League of Cambrai, then, actually served to disrupt the balance it was meant to capitalize on and to strengthen. Rather than create a stable apportionment of power and territory on the Italian peninsula that could lead to a suspension of military activities if not outright peace, the league ultimately served only to perpetuate the bloody warfare of the period.

—*Robert F. Erickson*

FURTHER READING

Bridge, John S. C. *Reign of Louis XII, 1508-1514*. Vol. 4 in *A History of France from the Death of Louis XI*. Reprint. New York: Octagon Books, 1978. The League of Cambrai is prominently featured in this book on French political and diplomatic history.

Gilbert, Felix. *The Pope, His Banker, and Venice*. Cambridge, Mass.: Harvard University Press, 1980. A detailed examination of Julius's involvement in the League of Cambrai and his war against the Republic of Venice. Stresses the financial arrangements made by both the pope and the Venetian Republic to carry out the extended conflict. An excellent insight into the diplomatic and financial policies at work in the papacy and the importance of finances for the conduct of Renaissance warfare and diplomacy.

Okey, Thomas. *Venice and Its Story*. 4th ed. New York: E. P. Dutton, 1930. History of the Venetian Republic based on chronicles, general histories, and monographs of the nineteenth century. Argues that Venice was already in a state of decline by the mid-fifteenth century.

Ragg, Laura M. *Crises in Venetian History*. London: Methuen, 1928. Studies the history of Venice's foreign relations from the earliest times to World War I.

Shaw, Christine. *Julius II: The Warrior Pope*. Cambridge, Mass.: Blackwell, 1996. Biography of Julius II combined with political history of the Papal States and Italy during the Renaissance. Includes photographic plates, illustrations, bibliographic references, and index.

Stinger, Charles L. *The Renaissance in Rome*. Bloomington: Indiana University Press, 1998. Julius II figures prominently in this study of the resurgence of Rome's cultural, religious, and political importance in the Renaissance. Includes maps, illustrations, bibliographic references, and index.

Zorsi, Alvise. *Venice, 697-1797: A City, a Republic, an Empire*. Rev. English ed. Woodstock, N.Y.: Overlook Press, 2001. Traces the development of Venice from a small fishing village into one of the Renaissance's

great republics. Includes illustrations, maps, bibliographic references, and index.

SEE ALSO: Apr. 9, 1454: Peace of Lodi; Sept., 1494-Oct., 1495: Charles VIII of France Invades Italy; 1499: Louis XII of France Seizes Milan; 1500: Roman Jubilee; 1504: Treaty of Blois; Apr. 11, 1512: Battle of Ravenna; Sept. 13-14, 1515: Battle of Marignano; 1521-1559: Valois-Habsburg Wars; Feb., 1525: Battle of Pavia; May 6, 1527-Feb., 1528: Sack of Rome; Apr. 3, 1559: Treaty of Cateau-Cambrésis.

RELATED ARTICLES in *Great Lives from History: The Renaissance & Early Modern Era, 1454-1600:* Ferdinand II and Isabella I; Julius II; Louis XII; Margaret of Austria; Maximilian I.

1508-1520
RAPHAEL PAINTS HIS FRESCOES

Raphael's frescoes in the Vatican established a high standard of Renaissance pictorial eloquence that influenced later artists. The paintings—covering four rooms—also provided a visual record of Church authority and papal ambitions, as well as the artistic programs of Julius II and Leo X.

LOCALE: Rome, Papal States (now in Italy)
CATEGORY: Art

KEY FIGURES
Raphael (1483-1520), Italian artist born in Urbino
Julius II (Giuliano della Rovere; 1443-1513), Roman Catholic pope, 1503-1513
Leo X (Giovanni de' Medici; 1475-1521), Roman Catholic pope, 1513-1521
Giulio Romano (c. 1499-1546), Raphael's pupil and heir
Donato Bramante (1444-1514), Italian architect and relative of Raphael

SUMMARY OF EVENT
In the autumn of 1508, Raphael was summoned to Rome from Florence by Pope Julius II. The artist may have been recommended to the pope by the architect Donato Bramante, a distant relative of Raphael. Julius II was one of the most powerful and ambitious popes of the Renaissance. Intent on matching the imperial splendor of ancient Rome, Julius II embarked on vigorous building campaigns and called on prominent artists to help fulfill his cultural ambitions.

His strong dislike for his predecessor, Pope Alexander VI, prompted Julius to move from the Borgia Apartments to the floor below and to design rooms of his own. The pope commissioned the young Raphael to decorate several of the rooms in the Vatican papal apartments. The record of preparatory drawings for the rooms, known as Raphael's Stanze, points to a complex scheme for the fresco cycles. Raphael's first commission involved painting frescoes on the walls of the Stanza della Segnatura.

This room, probably intended as the pope's personal library, had a ceiling decoration that consisted of large circular frescoes, or *tondi*, depicting four female figures that correspond to the disciplines painted on the walls below: Theology, Philosophy, Poetry, and Jurisprudence. The entire room evokes Humanist areas of learning. The first scene to be painted, the *Disputa*, representing Theology, focuses on the Trinity represented on a central tiered axis of the painting. God the Father appears above the figure of Christ the Son and the Dove of the Holy Spirit. The Virgin Mary and Saint John the Baptist flank the figure of Christ and are accompanied by a semicircular ring of martyrs and prophets. Below, a group of Church figures are engaged in animated discussion around the eucharistic Host.

Raphael's artistic genius is revealed in the room's most famous fresco, the *School of Athens*, representing Philosophy, painted between 1510 and 1511. Complementing the spatial treatment in the *Disputa* on the oppo-

Raphael's artistic genius is revealed in the fresco School of Athens *(1510-1511), with Plato and Aristotle placed in the center of the painting.* (Royal Library, Windsor Castle)

site wall, if not surpassing it, the *School of Athens* presents Plato and Aristotle, identified by the titles on the books they carry, *Timaeus* and *Ethics*, on a large concourse accompanied by ancient philosophers and scientists as well as contemporary Renaissance figures. Plato points toward heaven to indicate the realm from which his ideas are inspired. Aristotle points earthward to denote that observation of the natural world is key to his philosophical ideas.

The fresco is dominated by the two central philosophers, who seem to walk gracefully into a space filled with groups of figures who interact with each other in a multitude of poses and gestures. A remarkable clarity of tones pervades the painting, and the massive space is structured by a strict and unifying linear perspective. The entire narrative is ordered under a grand architectural setting inspired by Bramante's design for the new St. Peter's Basilica.

On the room's two shorter walls, Raphael painted *Parnassus* and *Jurisprudence*. According to classical mythology, Parnassus was the dwelling place of Apollo and the Muses. Representing Poetry, in *Parnassus* Raphael painted an assembly of great poets of the past and the Muses who are being enchanted by the music of Apollo. On the other short wall, where the artist adopted a circular and rhythmic solution for the shape of the space, *Jurisprudence* is personified by three female virtues: Fortitude, Prudence, and Temperance. These are joined, farther below on the wall, by figures of Pope Gregory IX approving the Decretals and the Byzantine Emperor Justinian I receiving the Pandects. Thus, civic law and ecclesiastical law are represented. The remaining virtue, Justice, is painted in one of the ceiling vaults.

In 1512, Raphael began work on the Stanza d'Eliodoro, which he completed around 1514. Decorated with scenes from legendary and historical events related to Church history, the room may have been used as an audience chamber. The principal motifs are the *Mass at Bolsena*, the *Expulsion of Heliodorus*, the *Deliverance of St. Peter from Prison*, and the *Repulse of Attila*.

The figures depicted in the Stanza d'Eliodoro have achieved a greater heroic dynamism, and the compositions are filled with a greater intensity of feeling and colored in a more dramatic way, than those in the Stanza della Segnatura. In the *Deliverance of St. Peter from Prison*, Raphael adopted an extraordinary range of nocturnal lighting in the semicircular space. From the crescent moonlight in the sky on the left to the dazzling divine light that encircles the angel at the center and on the right, the scenes are no longer constructed around a strict symmetrical balance but rather place their focal points off center.

The *Expulsion of Heliodorus* and the *Mass at Bolsena*, with its miraculous story of the bleeding of the eucharistic Host, must have appealed particularly to Julius II, as his portrait is included in both episodes. Raphael's work on the room continued after Julius's death in 1513. In the Stanza della Segnatura and the Stanza d'Eliodoro, Raphael realized in paint Julius's ideas on the role of the Church.

The decoration of the papal apartments continued under the pontificate of Leo X, when, in 1514, the pope commissioned Raphael to decorate the Stanza dell'Incendio. The room, finished in 1517, takes its name from Raphael's *Fire in the Borgo*, which chronicles a miraculous event in which a fire raging in a district just outside St. Peter's Basilica was extinguished in 847 by Pope Leo IV. The other scenes depicted in the room are the *Oath of Leo III*, the *Coronation of Charlemagne*, and the *Battle of Ostia*. As other artistic projects demanded greater attention, Raphael turned over work on the room to members of his workshop. The increase in figural pro-

Raphael's fresco, the Disputa, *reflects the ideals of Theology and focuses on the Trinity, which is represented at the center of the painting. God the Father appears above the figure of Christ the Son and the Dove of the Holy Spirit.* (G. P. Putnam's Sons)

portions, strained poses, and the dramatic color scheme all stem from the work of assistants, led by Giulio Romano.

Assistants played an even greater role in the Sala di Costantino, the most spacious of the four rooms. Raphael and his students began work on this room in the first part of 1519 under the continued patronage of Leo X. The room had primarily a ceremonial function. At the time of his death in 1520, Raphael was still working on the Sala di Costantino. Giulio Romano and Gianfrancesco Penni (called il Fattore) inherited their master's workshop and continued to work on this room. Thus, a strong mannerist style can be seen in the figures and spatial treatment of the Sala di Costantino's later frescoes. Eight figures of enthroned popes, arranged chronologically from St. Peter to Gregory the Great, decorate the room's corners. The walls are painted with narratives from the life of Constantine. The paintings reflect the Church's earthly power combined with events from the life of the first Christian emperor.

SIGNIFICANCE

Raphael spent the last twelve years of his life in Rome and made an extraordinary contribution to one of the most productive artistic periods in the city. While Raphael painted his Vatican frescoes, Michelangelo was painting the Sistine ceiling and Bramante was building the new St. Peter's. Raphael's Vatican frescoes set a high standard for Humanist art of the period that sought to follow the classical ideals of beauty, and it helped establish the stylistic language of the High Renaissance. He combined nobility, clarity, and grace into a perfect harmony that expressed both Christian and classical thought.

Raphael's frescoes also provide insight into papal intellectual and artistic interests, as well as the decorative projects the popes were engaged in during the early sixteenth century. In the early documents, Raphael is cited as the artist who exhibited perfect coloring, moderation, and figural variation, and he is praised as a master of narrative style. Through his collaboration with the engraver Marcantonio Raimondi, his art was known by many people who were unable to enter the papal apartments and see it firsthand.

Raphael's later work, including the frescoes, also represented a transition from the style of the High Renaissance to the mannerist movement. Mannerism, which was practiced by Giulio Romano and other students of Raphael, represented a rejection of classical ideals of formal beauty and an embrace instead of techniques designed to convey subjective impressions. The famous elongated figures of mannerism, for example—already beginning to appear in Raphael's work—were preferred over figures in perfect proportion because they were more expressive than such figures. Mannerists attempted to portray the ineffable and intangible aspects of life: They created infinite and undefined spaces as opposed to the carefully ordered space of the High Renaissance, they attempted to represent motion at the expense of well-defined static figures, and they sought ways to represent intense spiritual and miraculous experience that transcended the scientific perspective of Renaissance realism.

These later mannerist trends were present in nascent form in Raphael's work. After his death, members of Raphael's workshop emphasized the artist's proto-mannerist aspects when they disseminated their version of his style throughout Rome and beyond. His later style was modified and adapted to the aesthetic requirements of mature mannerism. Raphael's reputation may have been associated somewhat unfavorably with academic art, but he has always been recognized for his genius, innovative method of coloring, and an inventiveness that influenced definitively the development of Renaissance art.

—*Ingrid Alexander-Skipnes*

FURTHER READING

Beck, James. *Raphael*. Rev. ed. New York: Harry N. Abrams, 1998. Concise discussion of the Stanza della Segnatura and the Stanza d'Eliodoro.

Hall, Marcia, ed. *Raphael's "School of Athens."* New York: Cambridge University Press, 1997. A collection of essays that examines in detail aspects of the most famous fresco in the papal apartments, including earlier scholarship and Raphael's use of color, together with past and new interpretations.

Jones, Roger, and Nicholas Penny. *Raphael*. New Haven, Conn.: Yale University Press, 1983. Presents a chronology of Raphael's artistic production with a well-illustrated discussion of the Vatican frescoes.

Joost-Gaugier, Christiane L. *Raphael's Stanza della Segnatura: Meaning and Invention*. New York: Cambridge University Press, 2002. Examines in detail the symbolic content of Raphael's first Vatican project.

Partridge, Loren. *The Art of Renaissance Rome, 1400-1600*. New York: Harry N. Abrams, 1996. A study of the impact of papal artistic patronage and a useful discussion of the Stanza d'Eliodoro and the Sala di Costantino.

Rowland, Ingrid D. *The Culture of the High Renaissance: Ancients and Moderns in Sixteenth Century*

Rome. New York: Cambridge University Press, 1998. Examines how and why the High Renaissance came about by exploring the cultural, political, and intellectual forces behind it.

1508-1512 and 1534-1541
MICHELANGELO PAINTS THE SISTINE CHAPEL

In the Sistine Chapel, Michelangelo painted works considered among the most important achievements of Western art. His unprecedented use of both space and the human form transformed artists' understanding of both, and his treatment of his subject matter provided some of the most powerful, widespread, and iconic images of the most monumental biblical events.

LOCALE: Rome, Papal States (now in Italy)
CATEGORIES: Art; religion

KEY FIGURES
Michelangelo (1475-1564), Italian artist
Sixtus IV (Francesco della Rovere; 1414-1484), Roman Catholic pope, 1471-1484
Julius II (Giuliano della Rovere; 1443-1513), Roman Catholic pope, 1503-1513
Clement VII (Giulio de' Medici; 1478-1534), Roman Catholic pope, 1523-1534
Paul III (Alessandro Farnese; 1468-1549), Roman Catholic pope, 1534-1549

SUMMARY OF EVENT
In 1508, Pope Julius II summoned Michelangelo to Rome to paint the ceiling of the Sistine Chapel. It was a task the artist had no interest in accepting. Michelangelo considered himself first and foremost a sculptor and had little desire to take on a large-scale painting project. Inevitably, however, Michelangelo acquiesced to the pope's wishes, and what emerged is considered one of the greatest masterpieces of Western art.

Upon ascending to the papacy, Julius II had begun a series of ambitious political, religious, and artistic initiatives. In the visual arts, he assembled in Rome the greatest artists living in Italy and essentially initiated the High Renaissance. The architect Donato Bramante was given the task of rebuilding the church of Saint Peter's, Raphael was commissioned to paint the Vatican apartments (Stanze), and Michelangelo was assigned the ambitious project of sculpting the pope's tomb. Though Michelangelo began this enormous monument in 1505, he was destined never to complete it to his own satisfaction, and by 1508, Julius forced Michelangelo to divert his attention to painting the Sistine Chapel ceiling.

The Sistine Chapel was built during the reign of Julius's uncle, Pope Sixtus IV, for whom the structure is named. Located between the church of Saint Peter and the papal apartments, it is a relatively small space that is used for papal ceremonies and continues to host the conclave to elect a new pope. The side walls of the chapel, decorated with stories of Moses and Christ, were painted from 1481 to 1483 by such artists as Pietro Perugino, Sandro Botticelli, Domenico Ghirlandaio, and Luca Signorelli.

Michelangelo's assignment from Julius was to paint the chapel's ceiling vault. The resulting work presented a wondrous but complex iconography whose significance is still debated. Nine rectangular panels make up the center of the vault. In the first three images, God creates the universe. These are followed by three scenes of Adam and Eve and three episodes from the life of Noah. Interspersed among these panels are twenty male nudes (called *ignudi*).

Surrounding this center section, scenes from the biblical stories of David, Judith, Ester, and Moses occupy the four corners of the vault, respectively, while the sides of the vault are decorated with images of biblical prophets, classical sibyls (female prophets), and the ancestors of Christ. In its totality, the ceiling offers a compel-

1500's

Detail of Michelangelo's Creation of Adam *(1508-1512), painted on the ceiling of the Sistine Chapel. The painting is a canonical image of humankind's quest in reaching toward God.* (G. P. Putnam's Sons)

ling if esoteric vision of the times before Christ and a prayer for the redemption that will come with the messianic age.

While the choice and order of subject matter still remain puzzling, Michelangelo's stylistic achievement is staggering. From the moment of its unveiling, the ceiling was recognized as a supreme accomplishment of artistic invention. Over the course of his work on the chapel, Michelangelo himself underwent a remarkable stylistic evolution in his ability to render illusionistic space and dramatic form, especially while painting the nine central scenes (which were painted in reverse of their chronological order in the Bible). Most profoundly, he established the primacy of the human form as the essential conduit of meaning in his art.

The expressive power of the images is most famously recognized in the *Creation of Adam* scene, in which God has just given his supreme creation the divine spark of life. Adam slowly awakes and reaches toward God in a languid classical pose. The small void between his fin-

gers and the outstretched hand of God suggests a profound metaphor for the human condition.

A long-standing myth holds that Michelangelo worked in solitude, lying on his back while painting the ceiling. Recent discoveries prove, however, that Michelangelo had designed an ingenious scaffolding—a bridge anchored to the walls rather than the floor—which allowed him to work standing upright. He also employed assistants for more menial chores. Nevertheless, this monumental undertaking took Michelangelo four years of painstaking work and upon its unveiling was an immediate sensation due to its evident artistic brilliance.

Two decades later, Michelangelo returned to work in the Sistine Chapel. In 1533, Pope Clement VII commissioned Michelangelo to paint the altar wall at the western end of the chapel. The chosen subject was the Last Judgment. Again Michelangelo hesitated, since he was still working on the tomb of Julius II. He eventually accepted the commission, but he tried to abandon the project when Clement died the following year. However, Clement's successor, Pope Paul III, was equally insistent on Michelangelo's employment, and by 1541, the artist had finished the altar wall, having created another tour de force of artistic invention.

Michelangelo reinterprets the traditional theme of the Last Judgment in a new and provocative way. He presents an unusually wrathful but ultimately merciful Christ, and the entire scene is depicted with greater power and more terrifying imagery than had ever been seen before. Christ, physically imposing and bursting with energy, stands as judge, surrounded by a heavenly consort of saints and angels. He raises his right hand to pass judgment, and this gesture creates a cosmic swirl of frenetic activity.

The elect rise to Heaven on the viewer's left (Christ's right), while the damned are condemned to Hell in the lower right corner of the wall. In a pose that mimics that of Christ above, Charon, the mythical oarsman, ferries the damned across the river Styx to the fire-strewn underworld below. This frightening image of Hell is partially based on Dante's *La divina commedia* (c. 1320; *The Divine Comedy*, 1802), a work on which Michelangelo was a recognized expert.

Through this fresco, Michelangelo contrasts the hope of salvation with the threat of damnation. In a telling detail near Christ, Saint Bartholomew holds his own flayed skin, the face of which has been identified as a self-portrait of Michelangelo. The artist was famously plagued by self-doubt, and thus his portrait dangles on the side of the damned, serving as a personal petition or prayer.

Upon its unveiling in 1541, Michelangelo's *The Last Judgment* caused a sensation. It became a school of anatomy for artists to study the nude figure in its various exaggerated poses and contortions. It also provided a new essay in the use of color and light in monumental wall painting. These permutations moved Michelangelo's art further away from the more traditional forms of the High Renaissance toward a style commonly known as mannerist, which would increasingly typify the art of the later sixteenth century.

Detail of Michelangelo's The Last Judgment *(completed in 1541), painted on the ceiling of the Sistine Chapel. The work became a school of anatomy for artists to study the nude figure in its various exaggerated poses and contortions.* (Royal Library, Windsor Castle)

SIGNIFICANCE

The ramifications of Michelangelo's work in the Sistine Chapel are immense. Through the ceiling images, Michelangelo single-handedly transformed the nature of this type of mural painting. He offered new possibilities in the creation of illusionistic space and provided a wealth of provocative ideas on the use of the human body in art and its ability to convey content and metaphorical meaning. Never before had the public witnessed such a comprehensive display of the expressive power of the human form combined with such dramatic coloring and narrative intensity. Moreover, the *Creation of Adam* has become a canonical image of humankind's quest in reaching toward God. On the ceiling's unveiling, Giorgio Vasari, Michelangelo's friend and colleague, claimed that the whole world came to see the work and stood speechless with astonishment before it.

Thirty years later, *The Last Judgment* elicited both admiration for Michelangelo's style and controversy over his work's content, especially due to the positioning and sheer number of nudes. Shortly after Michelangelo's death, one of his principal assistants was ordered to paint loincloths over many of these figures, which earned the artist, Daniele da Volterra, the epithet *il braghettone* or the "breeches-maker."

The technique used by Michelangelo throughout the chapel is fresco, whereby paint is applied over wet plaster and becomes permanently fixed to the wall surface. The frescoes have been cleaned or retouched several times since their creation. In 1994, after a fourteen-year restoration project, the newly cleaned works displayed a remarkable clarity, legibility, and vividness of color, allowing modern viewers a glimpse of their original glory.

—Arnold Victor Coonin

FURTHER READING

Hall, Marcia. *Michelangelo: The Frescoes of the Sistine Chapel.* New York: Abrams, 2002. This fine book by a recognized expert contains an authoritative text complemented by beautiful and abundant color images of both the ceiling and wall frescoes.

Hughes, Anthony. *Michelangelo.* London: Phaidon Press, 1997. Any easy to read and engaging volume in the Art and Ideas series. Includes photographs of key locations in the artist's life, commissioned specifically for this book.

Pietrangeli, Carlo, ed. *The Sistine Chapel: A Glorious Restoration.* New York: Abrams, 1994. Essays by leading scholars on different aspects of the chapel in the light of recent restorations.

Tolnay, Charles de. *Michelangelo.* 5 vols. Princeton, N.J.: Princeton University Press, 1943-1960. A comprehensive study of Michelangelo's works, somewhat dated but still an excellent reference.

Vasari, Giorgio. *Lives of the Artists.* Translated by George Bull. Baltimore: Penguin Books, 1965. Contains a contemporary biography of Michelangelo written by his friend and colleague.

Wallace, William E. *Michelangelo: Selected Scholarship in English.* 5 vols. New York: Garland, 1995. These convenient volumes collect many of the most important scholarly essays on Michelangelo written in English. Volume 2, on the Sistine Chapel, and volume 4, covering the Tomb of Julius, are particularly useful.

SEE ALSO: 1462: Founding of the Platonic Academy; 1469-1492: Rule of Lorenzo de' Medici; 1477-1482: Work Begins on the Sistine Chapel; 1495-1497: Leonardo da Vinci Paints *The Last Supper*; c. 1500: Revival of Classical Themes in Art; 1500: Roman Jubilee; 1508-1520: Raphael Paints His Frescoes; Nov. 3, 1522-Nov. 17, 1530: Correggio Paints the *Assumption of the Virgin*; Dec. 23, 1534-1540: Parmigianino Paints *Madonna with the Long Neck*; June, 1564: Tintoretto Paints for the Scuola di San Rocco.

RELATED ARTICLES in *Great Lives from History: The Renaissance & Early Modern Era, 1454-1600:* Donato Bramante; Clement VII; Julius II; Michelangelo; Paul III; Raphael; Sixtus IV.

1509-1565
VIJAYANAGAR WARS

The Hindu Vijayanagar Empire made many territorial advances through military cleverness, but civil war, internal corruption, and a united Muslim enemy brought the once-great empire to an end at the Battle of Talikota in 1565.

LOCALE: South India (in an area now called Andhra Pradesh)

CATEGORIES: Wars, uprisings, and civil unrest; expansion and land acquisition; government and politics

KEY FIGURES

Krishnadevaraya (d. 1529), king of Vijayanagar, r. 1509-1529

Achyutaraya (d. 1542), Vijayanagar puppet king, r. 1529-1542

Rama Raja (d. 1565), Vijayanagar chief minister

SUMMARY OF EVENT

In 1509, Krishnadevaraya ascended to the throne of the great South Asian Vijayanagar Empire. Around the same time, Portuguese explorers and tradesmen had begun to establish a settlement in Goa, along the west coast of India. Krishnadevaraya took advantage of the unrest caused by the Portuguese to invade most of his neighbors and acquire territory for Vijayanagar. He entered into a contract with the Portuguese for horses for his wars against Yūsuf ʿĀdil Khan (who ruled as Yūsuf ʿĀdil Shah), the sultan of Bijāpur. The Portuguese agreed to supply Krishnadevaraya with mounts for his cavalry.

Krishnadevaraya came to realize that the Portuguese could be a valuable supply ally, so, in 1514, Krishnadevaraya offered the governor of Goa, Afonso de Albuquerque, a substantial sum of money for the exclusive rights to trade in horses. The Portuguese were interested not in South Asian politics, but in business, and the governor did not see exclusivity as being very lucrative. The sultan of Bijāpur heard of Krishnadevaraya's attempts and sent his own envoy to Goa. The governor of Goa wrote to Krishnadevaraya that he would agree to the exclusive supply of horses if he would pay an exorbitant sum of money per year and send his own servants to Goa to fetch the animals. The Portuguese also offered the option of aiding Krishnadevaraya in the war against the sultan if Krishnadevaraya would pay for the troops. The governor made a conflicting agreement with the sultan, but no trouble arose because the governor died soon thereafter.

After defeating a disorganized invasion of Bahmani sultanate forces and capturing the Rāichūr Doab, a region between the Tungabhadra and Kistna Rivers, Krishnadevaraya began his military and diplomatic work. He noticed a quarrel between Bijāpur and the new Bahmani ruler and used it to restore the imprisoned Bahmani sultan to his throne in 1512, earning Krishnadevaraya a staunch ally. Simultaneously, he waged a campaign to subdue the Ummatur to the south and created a new province from the conquest of the Ummatur.

In 1514, Krishnadevaraya marched against Udayagiri, a hill fortress in the domains of the Gajapati king of Orissa, and again succeeded. Krishnadevaraya captured an aunt of the royal family of Orissa, taking her to Vijayanagar as prisoner. Among the spoils was a statue of Krishna, which he set up at Vijayanagar, commemorating Krishna's blessing on the battle with a long inscription. Krishnadevaraya built great temples with the wealth acquired from his victories.

After Udayagiri, Krishnadevaraya proceeded to take another hill fortress in the possession of the king of Orissa. The king recognized the seriousness of his opponent and met Krishnadevaraya there. The king's presence did little, however; Krishnadevaraya defeated the Orissa armies again, capturing the citadel after two months. He then appointed a governor of the conquered provinces and continued northward, triumphing again, this time at Meduru. At Kondapale, the siege took three months, but Krishnadevaraya was ultimately victorious. As at Udayagiri, he captured members of the royal family, taking a wife and son of the imprisoned king. The king of Orissa realized that he was no defensive match for Krishnadevaraya and worked to form a peace, marrying a daughter to Krishnadevaraya to establish their treaty. Krishnadevaraya returned to Orissa some of the territory he had conquered north of the Krishna River.

While Krishnadevaraya was in Orissa, Ismāʿīl ʿĀdil Shah, his Bijāpuri rival, had retaken Raichūr. Krishnadevaraya called in his Portuguese allies and trounced Ismāʿīl and his troops, recapturing Rāichūr in 1520. This victory alone was not enough, however, because he wanted his victory to be memorable and significant. He captured more forts and acquired territory in 1523 in Bijāpur, destroyed Gulbarga, and, once he recognized that the Bahmani sultanate was again in political trouble, restored the territory to a son of Maḥmūd Shah II. Through these actions, Krishnadevaraya's military campaigns ensured immense power for Vijayanagar and greater political stability for South India.

A number of factors contributed to Krishnadevaraya's victories: Well-educated Brahmans served as commanders, Portuguese and Muslim mercenaries made up his garrisons, he recruited foot soldiers from forest tribes, and, to keep his vassals under control, he created subordinate chiefs, or poligars (*pālegāgadu*).

After Krishnadevaraya's death in 1529, Vijayanagar began to decline. Politically, the administration was not clever enough to keep its enemies from uniting. Immediately on Krishnadevaraya's death, Bijāpur, Golconda, and Orissa attacked Vijayanagar. The successor ruler, Achyutaraya, was competent enough to fend off the first wave of attacks, even with the internal difficulties that accompanied a revolt led by the chief minister. The southern chiefs of Ummatur and Tiruvadi also rebelled but were defeated quickly.

Unfortunately, in the later 1530's, Achyutaraya made a fatal mistake. He had entered a power-sharing relationship with his new chief minister, Rama Raja, who in turn decided that sharing was not enough, so he rebelled and then imprisoned Achyutaraya. Some nobles remained loyal, and another revolt by the southern chieftains led to Achyutaraya's release. This caused a civil war in Vijayanagar. The new ruler of Bijāpur, Ibrahim ʿĀdil Shah I, realized that a civil war in the most powerful state in South India would destabilize his own empire. He agreed to moderate a settlement between Achyutaraya and Rama Raja, in which Achyutaraya relinquished all power to Rama Raja but retaining nominal and ceremonial kingship.

At this point, the external boundaries of Vijayanagar had reverted to what they were in 1529. The civil war and internal revolts, however, weakened the imperial hold over some of the provinces, especially those in the south. Rama Raja rectified this problem in 1542 and 1543, after Achyutaraya's death. He crowned Achyutaraya's nephew in 1542 to ensure Vijayanagar would still have a ceremonial king. This king would remain a figurehead, leaving Rama Raja and his brothers to rule Vijayanagar.

Rama Raja subdued the nobles in the east and south and made a treaty with the Portuguese in 1546 to prevent their expansion into India, which would threaten Vijayanagar. When the treaty was broken in 1558, Rama Raja demanded and received compensation from the Portuguese for vandalizing Vijayanagar temples.

The Muslim rivals in Bijāpur realized that Vijayanagar was weakened, so they attacked in 1543, but Rama Raja was still able to defend and repel the attack, sur-

prising the Bijāpur forces. Rama Raja aided Ahmadnagar in a campaign in 1548 but allied with Bijāpur in 1557 against Ahmadnagar and Golconda. The final war led to a collective treaty among the four sultanates—Vijayanagar, Bijāpur, Ahmadnagar, and Golconda—proscribing unjust attacks on one another. If a sultanate was attacked, however, it could call on the other two to stop the aggressor. Ahmadnagar attacked Bijāpur in 1560, and Vijayanagar and Golconda responded, subduing Ahmadnagar. Later, Golconda and Ahmadnagar attacked Bijāpur together but were vanquished by a united Bijāpur and Vijayanagar front, proving that the four partners were not equal.

Significance

Regardless of individual strength and a succession of successful battles, though, Rama Raja's defeat was certain after multiple strong states allied against him. In 1565, Rama Raja led the sultanate into the fateful battle against the ʿĀdil Shah Dynasty at Rakasa-Tangadi, best known as the Battle of Talikota. The combined forces of the Muslim states managed not only to demolish Rama Raja's army and destroy the city of Vijayanagar but also to capture and kill him.

Rama Raja's brother Tirumala made an attempt to establish a new capital at Penukonda to keep the empire intact, but the attempt ultimately was fruitless because most of the provinces had formed into independent sultanates. His Aravidu Dynasty continued to decline into the early seventeenth century.

Telegu houses and the Muslim states decreased their support and reverence of Vijayanagar, and the sieges on Penukonda were increasingly successful.

The government had to relocate to Chandragiri, and more nobles continued to secede. Further decentralization was prevented, yet control over chieftains and nobles remained tenuous; the empire also was degraded by European imperialism.

Internal rebellions and external machinations caused the Vijayanagar Empire to finally collapse to a mere provincial power around 1614. Krishnadevaraya reigned over an empire that, through successful military campaigns, saw great wealth and brought honor. His administrative skills were emulated by the states that formed after the 1565 battle.

—*Monica Piotter*

Further Reading
Karashima, Noboru. *Towards a New Formation: South Indian Society Under Vijayanagar Rule*. New York:

Oxford University Press, 1997. Karashima describes the social history of Vijayanagar, including the provinces, exploring the lives of the people who were conquered by the wars.

Sastri, K. A. Kilakanta, and N. Venkataramanayya. *Further Sources in Vijayanagara History*. Madras: University of Madras Press, 1946. This multivolume set affords translations of texts from and relating to Vijayanagar history, especially between 1509 and 1565.

Sewell, Robert. *Vijayanagar: As Seen by Domingos Paes and Fernao Nuniz (Sixteenth Century Portuguese Chroniclers) and Others*. Edited with introduction and notes by Vasundhara Filliozat. New Delhi, India: National Book Trust, 1999. Documents the accounts of Domingo Paes and Fernao Nuniz, Portuguese explorers who visited Vijayanagar during Krishnadevaraya's reign.

Stein, Burton. *Vijayanagara*. Vol. 1 in *The New Cambridge History of India*. New York: Cambridge University Press, 1989. An excellent source for an introduction to Vijayanagar, which considers the empire's rise and fall and offers an extremely valuable account of the Krishnadevaraya years and Rama Raja's corruption.

SEE ALSO: 1489: ʿĀdil Shah Dynasty Founded; c. 1490: Fragmentation of the Bahmani Sultanate; 1552: Struggle for the Strait of Hormuz.

RELATED ARTICLES in *Great Lives from History: The Renaissance & Early Modern Era, 1454-1600*: Akbar; Afonso de Albuquerque; Bābur; Luís de Camões; Pêro da Covilhã; Humāyūn; Krishnadevaraya; Nānak.

c. 1510
INVENTION OF THE WATCH

The invention of the first watch, a miniature spring-driven clock, revolutionized timekeeping and forever changed how individuals think about and relate to time. Peter Henlein of Nuremberg is the first named maker of an early spherical type of watch, later referred to as the Nuremberg Egg.

LOCALE: Nuremberg (now in Germany)

CATEGORIES: Inventions; cultural and intellectual history; science and technology

KEY FIGURES

Peter Henlein (c. 1485-1542), Nuremberg locksmith and watchmaker

Johannes Cochlaeus (1479-1552), Nuremberg scholar and author

Philipp Melanchthon (1497-1560), religious reformer and owner of the earliest dated watch

Filippo Brunelleschi (1377-1446), sculptor, architect, and engineer

Leonardo da Vinci (1452-1519), Florentine artist and inventor

SUMMARY OF EVENT

The miniaturization of the mechanical clock to the size and portability of a watch was a gradual process that involved many unknown individuals and spanned more than two hundred years.

Invented probably in the thirteenth century to help regulate monastic life, the first clocks were large iron machines possessing a striking mechanism and powered by weights attached to a long, heavy cord. To function, the clocks had to be placed high above ground so that gravity could pull their weights down gradually. By the early fourteenth century, such clocks were placed in municipal towers and served as sources of civic pride.

Later in the century, the wheelworks were reduced just enough (without losing much accuracy) so that clocks could be placed on walls and pedestals and even transported. The clocks could not function while in transit, however, and had to be reset by an expert at their destination. Such portable clocks were expensive rarities, possessed by monarchs and popes only.

The early fifteenth century saw a major breakthrough in the portability of clocks. A new source of power—the spring—was invented to replace the cumbersome weights. Springs had the advantage over gravity-pulled weights because they required no pedestal and could function in any position—even in transit. Because springs do not release their energy in a uniform manner, a cone with spiral winding groves (a fusee) compensated for the spring's ever-decreasing force.

The earliest known example of a spring-drive clock with fusee is the Burgundy clock, housed in the Germanisches Nationalmuseum in Nuremberg and dated around 1430. The first literary reference to the use of springs occurs in Antonio Manetti's biography (wr. c. 1480's) of the Florentine architect and engineer, Filippo Brunelleschi, who is most famous for designing and building the dome of the cathedral of Florence, Santa Maria del Fiore (1417-1436). Brunelleschi most likely tinkered with clock springs in his youth.

Although no name can be attached to the invention of the weight-driven mechanical clock or its adaptation to spring power, tradition gives credit for the invention of the watch, or miniature spring-driven clock, to the Nuremberg watchmaker and locksmith, Peter Henlein. Born probably around 1480 in Nuremberg, Henlein (sometimes referred to as Hele, a Nuremberger dialectical corruption of Henlein) became a master in the Nuremberg guild of locksmiths (which included clock makers who similarly made fine mechanisms in iron) in 1509. Writing about important Germans in his short description of Germany (*Brevis Germaniae descriptio*, 1512), scholar Johannes Cochlaeus noted,

> Each day more subtle things are invented. Thus Peter Hele, still quite a young man, makes works which even very learned mathematicians [cosmographers] admire, for from a little bit of iron he makes clocks composed of many wheels, which, however wound, will run without weights and show the time for forty hours, and which may be carried on the person or in a purse.

This is the first known record concerning a watchmaker. Cochlaeus did not name Peter Henlein as the inventor of watches, but he does suggest wonder at this new art. The fact that Henlein's watches ran for forty hours raises the possibility that he used—and possibly invented—the stackfreed (a curved metal spring brake) to regulate the power of the spring, rather than a fusee. The stackfreed makes for less accuracy but for a longer running time. It also allows for the manufacture of thinner watches, though this does not appear to be the type produced by Henlein.

In his 1547 treatise on Nuremberg artists and artisans, Johann Neudoerfer stated that an "Andreas Henlein" was "nearly the first" to make clocks small enough to fit into little musk boxes (Bisam Koepf). Moreover, the Nuremberg archives record payments to an "H. Henlein" for watches commissioned as gifts of state, one of which was housed inside a "Bisam-äpfel" (musk apple). Sixteenth century musk boxes were sometimes called musk apples because of their spherical shape. Carried around the neck on a chain, musk apple watches were likely to have been the earliest watches because their height would have al-

A French egg-shaped timepiece, likely modeled on the watch design of the Nuremberg Egg, was essentially a miniaturized spring-driven clock. (Hulton|Archive by Getty Images)

lowed ample space for the conical fusee, though it cannot be ruled out that tiny drum clocks with attached metal loops might have predated the use of musk containers. The watches' spherical shape—which developed into an oval by the next century—encouraged a misreading and mistranslation of German satirist Johann Fischart's phrase "Noernbergischen lebendigen Aeurlein" (lovely little clocks of Nuremberg) as Nuremberger "Eierlein" (little eggs).

From these sixteenth century references, it would seem that there existed a family of Henleins (Andreas, Peter, and "H" standing for Hermann, Peter's brother) who worked in the miniature clock or watch business, possibly the first to make watches their specialty. Also, Nuremberg probably was the first city to treat the watch as a state symbol. Peter Henlein is not described as the inventor of watches until 1891 in a pamphlet that generated considerable critical controversy. Henlein's role as inventor of the Nuremberg Egg appears to have received particular emphasis in fascist Germany when a film called "Das unsterbliche Herz" (1939; the immortal heart) and a postage stamp (1942) were produced in his honor.

Few spherical watches exist today, and none can be linked to Henlein or even securely associated with the city of Nuremberg. Only one bears a date of 1530, making it the earliest dated watch, and it belonged to the Protestant reformer, Philipp Melanchthon. It might have been given to him as a gift for his work on the Augsburg Confession, which also was completed in 1530. It was produced in southern Germany, probably in Nuremberg.

Although Nuremberg and Augsburg are likely to have been the first centers of watch production and the Henleins one of the first families to specialize in this art, it is possible that the very first watches were made elsewhere. For example, there is a report by Jacopo Trotti addressed to the duke of Ferrara from 1488 that Ludovico Sforza in Milan was having three fancy jackets made, each with a tiny chiming clock attached. Since Leonardo da Vinci was working for Sforza in those years (1482-1500) and since there are drawings of watch escapements with springs and fusees in his notebooks, it is possible to hypothesize that these early watches were Leonardo's invention.

SIGNIFICANCE

The invention of ever-smaller clocks is of great significance to the history of time, time consciousness, and technology. It appears that the clock was developed to satisfy the needs of the population, since the desire for portability existed before the manufacture of truly portable clocks. Once the clock was given a spring instead of weights, it was just a small step to the most portable timepiece of all: the watch.

First available in the home and then made portable, mechanical timepieces in turn affected the way people related to the passage of time. The presence of timepieces divided the day into twenty-four equal hours, a process initiated by larger public clocks. While the hand and bell of the public tower clock are but distant and intermittent reminders of the passage of the hours, a readily available watch encouraged the internalization and personal management of time segments.

Time—to use the words of the fifteenth century Italian humanist, Leon Battista Alberti—became a third human component, after the soul and the body. Ever present and able to be monitored, time also became more precious. Its loss or wasting came to be that much more devastating.

—*Maia Wellington Gahtan*

FURTHER READING

Abeler, Jürgen. *In Sachen Peter Henlein*. Wuppertal, Germany: Selbstverlage, 1980. The most recent scholarly treatment of Peter Henlein's historical role as clock and watchmaker, with references to all earlier literature. In German.

Dohrn-van Rossum, Gerhard. *History of the Hour: Clocks and Modern Temporal Orders*. Translated by Thomas Dunlap. Chicago: University of Chicago Press, 1996. A concise and intelligent discussion of the miniaturization of the clock set (including a short discussion of Henlein and Nuremberg) within a broader analysis of how clocks and watches function in society.

Gahtan, Maia Wellington, and George Thomas. "GOTT ALLEIN DIE EHRE, engraved on Philipp Melanchthon's Watch of 1530." *Lutheran Quarterly* 15 (2001): 249-272. A description and historical analysis of the earliest dated watch.

Klaus, Maurice. *Die deutsche Räderuhr: Zur Kunst und Technik des mechanischen Zeitmessers im deutschen Sprachraum*. 2 vols. Munich: C. H. Beck, 1976. Offers the most comprehensive survey of early German clock and watch making. In German.

Landes, David. *Revolution in Time: Clocks and the Making of the Modern World*. Cambridge, Mass.: Harvard University Press, 1983. The chapter "My Time Is My Time" is especially relevant. A lively discussion of the impact of the mechanical clock on Western civilization.

Morpurgo, Enrico. *L'origine dell'orologio tascabile*. Rome: Edizioni La Clessidra, 1954. Examines the theory that the watch was invented in Italy. In Italian.

SEE ALSO: c. 1478-1519: Leonardo da Vinci Compiles His Notebooks; c. 1560's: Invention of the "Lead" Pencil; 1582: Gregory XIII Reforms the Calendar.

RELATED ARTICLES in *Great Lives from History: The Renaissance & Early Modern Era, 1454-1600:* Leonardo da Vinci; Philipp Melanchthon.

1510-1578
SAʿDĪ SHARIFS COME TO POWER IN MOROCCO

The Saʿdīs rose from relative obscurity during a period of turmoil to become the rulers of Morocco. Under this dynasty, the development of the Moroccan state advanced, and Morocco became a significant power in the western Mediterranean.

LOCALE: Morocco
CATEGORIES: Government and politics; wars, uprisings, and civil unrest

KEY FIGURES
Muhammad al-Qāʾim (Muḥammad bin Muḥammad al-Ḥasanī; d. 1517), patriarch of the Saʿdīan clan and founder of the dynasty, r. 1510-1517
Aḥmad al-Aʿraj (d. 1557), founder of the first Saʿdīan state in southern Morocco, r. 1517-1544
Muhammad I al-Shaykh (d. 1557), Saʿdī ruler, r. 1544-1557, who secured control over all of Morocco for his dynasty
Abdallah al-Ghālib (d. 1574), sultan of Morocco, r. 1557-1574

SUMMARY OF EVENT
The Saʿdīs were said to have been sharifs (that is, descendants of the Prophet Muḥammad). The family had originated in Yanbo, Arabia, perhaps in the twelfth century, and it settled in the Darʿa Valley. In Morocco, sharifs were held in esteem and considered specialists in religious knowledge. They also inherited the gift of *baraka*, a mystical, spiritual power, which could bring benefits to those in contact with the possessor. Not everyone accepted Saʿdīan claims to be sharifs, however. In fact, the very name Saʿdī was an attempt to cast aspersions on the dynasty and was not allowed to be used during the period when the dynasty was in power. The family preferred the name Hashimi from the Prophet's clan, the Banu Hashim, whereas Saʿdī comes from the Banu Saʿd Hawayin, the tribe of Muḥammad's wet nurse.

For several centuries after arriving in Morocco, the Saʿdīs lived a quiet life, serving their local community in the traditional holy man role. Conditions, however, were changing in Morocco. During the fifteenth century, the Portuguese captured much of the Moroccan coastline. The central government in Fez under the Wattasid Dynasty was in decline, unable to dislodge the invaders and steadily losing power in the rural areas of southern Morocco. In the first decade of the sixteenth century, the Saʿdīan patriarch, Muḥammad al-Qāʾim, stepped into

this power vacuum along with his two sons, Aḥmad al-Aʿraj and Muḥammad al-Shaykh.

Al-Qāʾim was invited to the neighboring Sus valley, which had slipped into a state of near anarchy, to bring order and organize the local war effort against the Portuguese. There, he began laying the foundations for a small state. When Al-Qāʾim died in 1517, he was succeeded by Aḥmad al-Aʿraj, with Muḥammad al-Shaykh as second-in-command. Seven years later, the brothers took the city of Marrakech, either by storming its walls or by poisoning its emir during a peaceful visit (sources conflict). The emir had been a vassal of the Wattasid sultans, and the Saʿdīs subsequently refused to pay taxes to the government in Fez, which led to war in 1527. The Saʿdīs and Wattasids fought each other on and off until 1554, when the last of the Wattasids was killed and the capital of Morocco officially moved to Marrakech.

In the meantime, Saʿdīan forces enjoyed one great victory against the Portuguese, taking the stronghold of Santa Cruz at Agadir in 1542, which forced the Portuguese to evacuate most of their other forts. In the wake of the victory, however, the brothers fell out, resulting in a civil war in which musketeers loyal to Muḥammad al-Shaykh defeated al-Aʿraj's larger force of traditional cavalry. The new sultan, Muḥammad I al-Shaykh, firmly established Saʿdīan control over Morocco, which included the imposition of a tax system that led to many revolts.

Saʿdīan power became based on a reorganized army, the core of which was equipped with artillery and matchlock harquebuses and used tactics similar to those of contemporary European and Turkish armies. Most of the musketeers were Andalusians, refugee Spanish Muslims who had been forced into exile after the fall of Granada. The Andalusians were a productive people, bringing skills and new technology into Morocco. The Saʿdīan rulers came to depend on their support against Berber and Arab tribesmen, who often resented the centralizing policies that emanated from Marrakech.

During the later stages of the long war between the rival dynasties, the Wattasids appealed to the Ottoman Empire for support. The Turkish presence in North Africa dated from the early sixteenth century, when the Ottomans absorbed much of modern Algeria, Tunisia, and Libya into their empire. This brought the Turks into conflict with the Spanish. Sandwiched between these two superpowers was Morocco. By religion and sentiment, the Moroccans should have supported the Ottoman Empire against Spain, which was also an ally of Morocco's enemy, Portugal. However, for the Ottomans, Morocco represented the last step in the conquest of North Africa and an opening on the Atlantic. Early in his career, Muḥammad al-Shaykh came to the conclusion that his real enemy was the Ottoman Empire.

Conflict between Morocco and the Ottoman Empire began in 1550 as another sporadic struggle that lasted several decades. The issues were ideological as well as political and territorial, with Muḥammad I al-Shaykh proclaiming himself caliph, that is, the head of all Muslims, and *mahdi*, the redeemer sent to prepare the faithful for the end of the world. By contrast, as the Saʿdīs were quick to point out, the Ottomans were not even Arabs. To the Ottomans, who controlled the greatest Muslim state in the world, Saʿdīan claims were presumptuous and offered North African Muslims a dangerous alternative to their own rule.

Mutual antagonism against the Turks drew the Moroccans and Spanish into an unofficial alliance from time to time. To balance the Spanish influence in the region, the Saʿdīs cultivated close commercial and political contacts with the English and French. Ottoman frustration with these policies finally led to the assassination of Muḥammad al-Shaykh by Turkish agents in 1557.

Muḥammad al-Shaykh was succeeded by his son, Abdallah al-Ghālib. Al-Ghālib's reign, which lasted until 1574, is seen as the great period of consolidation for the Saʿdī Dynasty. He is remembered as one of Morocco's great building sultans and in particular for his various projects in Marrakech. In foreign relations, he maintained an uneasy, informal tie with Spain, but this was a relatively peaceful period, at least compared to the reign of Muḥammad al-Shaykh. Morocco became prosperous with a booming sugar industry and a revived trans-Saharan trade, principally in gold. Between al-Ghālib and the most famous scion of the dynasty, Aḥmad al-Manṣūr, two brief reigns occurred, those of al-Ghālib's son, Muḥammad al-Mutawakkil (r. 1574-1576), and his brother, ʿAbd al-Malik (r. 1576-1578), accompanied by dynastic contention. When al-Manṣūr came to power in 1578, he reestablished peace and brought a long period (to 1603) of stability and prosperity to the country.

SIGNIFICANCE

Muḥammad I al-Shaykh, along with his father, brother, and sons, brought Morocco out of a period of decline and established the country as an important force on the international scene. Their military and diplomatic activities resulted in the expulsion of the Portuguese from most of the coast, while, at the same time, they kept the Ottoman Empire from absorbing Morocco. The early Saʿdīs laid the foundation for Aḥmad al-Manṣūr's reign, often considered the most brilliant period in post-medieval Moroccan history. Saʿdīan expeditions dispatched into the African interior had a profound, if not generally positive, impact on the peoples of the Sahara and later the western Sudan. European rulers, including Elizabeth I of England and Philip II of Spain, generally treated their Saʿdīan counterparts as equals. Although the Saʿdīan Dynasty did not survive past the mid-seventeenth century, it left Moroccans with the belief that political legitimacy could be vested only in an heir of the Prophet's house, as it is today in the ʿAlawite Dynasty.

—*Richard L. Smith*

FURTHER READING

Abun-Nasr, Jamil M. *A History of the Maghrib in the Islamic Period*. New York: Cambridge University Press, 1987. Standard version of the rise of the Saʿdīs and their place in the larger context of North African history.

Bennison, Amira K. "Liminal States: Morocco and the Iberian Frontier, Between the Twelfth and Nineteenth Centuries." In *North Africa, Islam, and the Mediterranean World: From the Almoravids to the Algerian War*, edited by Julia Clancy-Smith. London: Frank Cass, 2001. Historically Muslim Morocco and Christian Spain were enemies; this article examines the problems inherent in the rapprochement between them.

Cook, Westin F. *The Hundred Years War for Morocco: Gunpowder and the Military Revolution in the Early Modern Muslim World*. Boulder, Colo.: Westview Press, 1994. Thorough account of the Portuguese-Moroccan wars and the development of the Moroccan state under the Wattasids and Saʿdīs.

Hess, Andrew C. *The Forgotten Frontier: A History of the Sixteenth-Century Ibero-African Frontier*. Chicago: University of Chicago Press, 1978. The intricacies of diplomacy and war and Morocco's unique and dangerous position in the geopolitical world of the western Mediterranean are examined.

Yahia, Dahiru. "The Ideological Framework of Saʿdī Foreign Policy." In *Le Maroc et l'Afrique Subsaharienne aux débuts de temps modernes: Les Saʿdiens et l'Empire Songhay*. Rabat, Morocco: Institut des Études Africaines, Université Mohammed V, 1995. The Saʿdīs often had difficulties reconciling their official ideology (millennialist and jihadist) with the realities of state building.

SEE ALSO: c. 1464-1591: Songhai Empire Dominates the Western Sudan; May, 1485-Apr. 13, 1517: Mamlūk-Ottoman Wars; 1493-1528: Reign of Mo-

hammed I Askia; Jan., 1498: Portuguese Reach the Swahili Coast; 1525-1600: Ottoman-Ruled Egypt Sends Expeditions South and East; 1529-1574: North Africa Recognizes Ottoman Suzerainty; Aug. 4, 1578: Battle of Ksar el-Kebir; 1591: Fall of the Songhai Empire.

December 2, 1510
BATTLE OF MERV ESTABLISHES THE SHAYBĀNĪD DYNASTY

The Turko-Mongol Uzbeks established the Shaybānīd Dynasty after battles with the Iranian Ṣafavids in the early 1500's, confirming their control of a vast Central Asian region. They ruled the area until the end of the century, when the dynasty was lost to the rising Astrakhanid Dynasty, kin of the Shaybānīds.

LOCALE: Transoxiana (now in Uzbekistan and Turkmenistan)
CATEGORIES: Wars, uprisings, and civil unrest; government and politics; expansion and land acquisition

KEY FIGURES
Muḥammad Shaybānī (1451-1510), Uzbek khan, r. 1496-1510
ʿUbayd Allāh Shaybānī (d. 1539), Uzbek khan, r. 1512-1539
ʿAbd Allāh II ibn Iskandar Shaybānī (1532/1533-1598), Uzbek khan, r. 1557-1598

SUMMARY OF EVENT
Shaybānī was the fifth grandson of the thirteenth century Mongol conqueror and ruler Genghis Khan (r. 1206-1227). Shaybānī's elder brothers gained control of the White Horde and the Golden Horde, ruled by descendants of Genghis Khan's grandson Batu Khan (d. 1255). The hordes had adopted Islam earlier than any other Mongol Dynasty.

Shaybānī's descendants and their followers remained loosely confederated with the larger Mongol states, evolving socially into the Turko-Mongol Uzbek people. Their rise to power as an independent entity paralleled the more or less separate Kazaks, Kyrgyz, and Oyrats, who shared similar origins. As steppe nomads, they jostled one another in the interstices between larger surrounding powers, especially the Golden Horde and the Timurid Empire that stretched from Afghanistan to Anatolia. As both of these states disintegrated during the

fifteenth century, the fortunes of the Shaybānīd Uzbeks rose and fell.

Around 1490, Muḥammad Shaybānī became governor of Yasī on behalf of Maḥmūd Khan, the Jagataite khan of West Moghulstan (Tashkent). The city was a major regional trading center and the revered site of the tomb of the twelfth century Muslim Sufi Ahmad Yasawī. This became the core of a secular state that he would rule as khan from 1496 until his death in 1510. His Uzbek horde became a military and political arm of the Yasawiyya branch of Sunni Islam, and served as mercenaries for the Turko-Mongol Mughals, who sought to conquer what was left of the Timurid Empire. In June, 1503, however, he turned on Maḥmūd at the Battle of Akhsi in Fergana and brought it and Tashkent under Uzbek control. He further expanded his state, beginning with his incursion into Transoxiana, at the Timurids' expense, in 1499 and 1500. This expansion led to the Shaybānī-Timurid war (1501-1507), which brought the Timurid Empire to a close, with Bābur, the last of the line, shifting the axis of his rule into India in the 1520's.

Beginning in 1501, the Uzbeks took, lost, and then retook Samarqand, Tamerlane's resting place. In 1505-1506, Muḥammad seized Khiva, Bukhara, and Herāt in Khorāsān from Ḥusayn Bayqarah and his vassals. These victories brought him into conflict with Shāh Ismāʿīl of the recently ensconced Ṣafavid Dynasty in Iran, with Bābur, with the Mughals. When the Kyrgyz threatened to overrun his northern borders, Ismāʿīl struck. On December 2, 1510, the Iranian army—equipped with Turkish field artillery—confronted the light horsemen of Muḥammad's horde near Merv and decimated it. Muḥammad was killed, and the vanquished Uzbeks eventually retreated into Tashkent. Khorāsān, including Balkh and Herāt up to the Firoz Kohi ridge, went to the Ṣafavids, and in 1511 with Ismāʿīl's blessing, Bābur grabbed Central Asia, in particular Samarqand and Bukhara.

The Sunni Bābur's dealings with the Persian Shīʿites

angered many in his new territories, and the Uzbeks sensed blood in the water. With Muḥammad's nephew ʿUbayd Allāh in command, the Uzbeks reestablished themselves in Transoxiana at the Battle of Ghazdivan on December 12, 1512. Bābur's forces, and the Iranians, under Najm Sānī—who died in the battle—were soundly defeated. Bābur retained part of Afghanistan, centered on Kabul, and thereafter generally made common cause with the Sunni Muslim Uzbeks against the Shīʿite Iranians, now separated by the Amu Darya (Oxus) River.

Samarqand and Bukhara served as dual capitals of this new khanate, which was initially ruled from Samarqand by Köchkünju Khan, Muḥammad Shaybānī's uncle, until 1531, and by ʿUbayd Allāh from Bukhara, until 1539. This resulted in squabbling, weakened the fabric of the state, and ended in the unification of administration from Bukhara in 1539 under ʿAbd Allāh I Shaybānī. Administration was split again in 1557, but effectively united when ʿAbd Allāh II, ruling in Bukhara, placed his father, Iskandar, on the throne in Samarqand.

ʿAbd Allāh II ruled independently as khan from 1583, having been elected in traditional fashion. The election was ratified by four leaders of the Sunni Muslim dervish (Sufi) sect of the Naqshbandīyah, including the powerful Shaykh Kwaja Saʿd al-Dīn Jūybārī. This sect had gained a powerful position in urban Uzbek society during ʿAbd Allāh's reign. As Muḥammad Shaybānī unified his by using the Yasawiyya sect of Sufis (and they using him), so ʿAbd Allāh II worked with the Naqshbandīyah, which had been founded by Baha al-Din Naqshband (d. 1398). This holy man lived in Bukhara and was buried nearby, his tomb a site of pilgrimage.

True to their steppe roots, the Shaybānīds ruled with a light hand, more as leaders of a confederacy than of an empire, leaving effective administration at the tribal *tumen* level. Resentment against taxes and instability in border areas, both caused by incessant wars with the Ṣafavids and Mughals, undermined Shaybānīd control. Generally allied with the Sunni Muslim Ottoman Turks against the Shīʿite Ṣafavids, the Uzbeks were by turns defending their borders and seeking to expand them. ʿAbd Allāh's conquest of the Persian Herāt, Sabzavar, Isfarain, Tebes, and Mashhad, however, restored Uzbek confidence. In the Shīʿite towns, especially Mashhad, the site of a holy shrine, the Sunni Muslims carried out fierce destruction and killings. This served to restore Uzbek confidence, which was newly shattered only with ʿAbd Allāh's defeat by the Ṣafavids and death in 1598.

Bukhara had long been a major center of trade, and the Shaybānīds, in shifting their power base there from Samarqand, did a great deal to enhance the cityscape. As one might expect, both religious and commercial buildings were erected, under the patronage of Uzbek nobles, religious brotherhoods and the khan. ʿUbayd Allāh rebuilt much of the city, including its 10-meter (33-foot) high and 5-meter (16.5-foot) wide fortified wall. Wide arterial roads facilitated the movement of caravans through the city, which provided newly constructed quarters—caravanserais—for men, beasts, and burden. Domed or arched marketplaces served the needs of inhabitants and visitors. Great bazaars sold luxury goods from three continents.

Numerous places of worship provided for the Muslims' spiritual needs, and many religious schools, or *madrasas*, were built to educate the young and the old. One *madrasa*, with more than one hundred large student cells, was built in the 1530's and is still being used today. In other cities as well, the Shaybānīds paid great attention to commercially useful public works such as bazaars, caravanserais, bridges, and underground reservoirs.

In the later 1590's, the Ṣafavid shah ʿAbbās the Great defeated the Uzbeks in battle near Herāt and thereby regained much of Khorāsān, including Herāt and sacred Mashhad. In 1598, ʿAbd Allāh II died and was replaced by Pir Muḥammad II, who was soon murdered by Bāqī Muḥammad Bahādur, first in the line of Astrakhanid rulers in Bukhara. Bāqī was descended from Genghis Khan through Orda, Shaybānī's older brother, and was related to ʿAbd Allāh by marriage. The new dynasty is sometimes called the Janid, for Bāqī's father, Jani.

SIGNIFICANCE

The Shaybānīd rise to power led to the end of the Timurid Empire, which had gone far in integrating the cultures of steppe and city. The resulting diaspora of intellectuals and artists enriched the Ṣafavid and Ottoman courts, but the Uzbeks proved less worthy patrons. Nonetheless, Bukhara and Samarqand were centers of Turko-Mongol culture and trade during the Shaybānīd period.

Events on the larger stage, however, forced these cities into the background of interregional commerce and activity. During this time European ships were contacting China directly, and caravan routes were shifting away from Transoxiana. Khiva and Qoqand (Kokand) became major rivals for trade between the Muslim world and the expanding Russian state, whose very rise served to isolate the Uzbeks further. The rise of the Shīʿite Ṣafavids and the Uzbeks' intense rivalry with them effectively cut the Uzbeks from the Muslim world beyond Central Asia.

—Joseph P. Byrne

FURTHER READING

Blair, Sheila A. S., and Jonathan Bloom. *The Art and Architecture of Islam, 1250-1800.* New Haven, Conn.: Yale University Press, 1994. Contains easily accessible material on the fine arts in Bukhara during the Shaybānīd period.

Grousset, René. *The Empire of the Steppes: A History of Central Asia.* Translated by Naomi Walford. New Brunswick, N.J.: Rutgers University Press, 1970. Well-organized and comprehensive work that covers the region's history to the eighteenth century. Chapter 13, "The Shaybānīds," is especially helpful.

McCauley, Martin. *Afghanistan and Central Asia: A Short History.* Boston: Pearson Longman, 2002. Brief overview that introduces the main outlines of the conflict between the Shaybānīds and the Ṣafavids.

Soucek, Svat. *The History of Inner Asia.* New York: Cambridge University Press, 2000. Chapter 11, "The Shaybānīds," provides a useful overview of the events and issues of the dynasty's rule.

SEE ALSO: 1451-1526: Lodī Kings Dominate Northern India; c. 1462: Kazak Empire Is Established; 1507: End of the Timurid Dynasty; 1512-1520: Reign of Selim I; Apr. 21, 1526: First Battle of Panipat; July 21, 1582: Battle of the Tobol River; 1587-1629: Reign of ʿAbbās the Great; 1598: Astrakhanid Dynasty Is Established.

RELATED ARTICLES in *Great Lives from History: The Renaissance & Early Modern Era, 1454-1600:* Ivan the Great; Ivan the Terrible.

1511-c. 1515
MELAKA FALLS TO THE PORTUGUESE

Melaka, a thriving trade center on the Malay Peninsula, was captured by the Portuguese, marking the first incursion of a European power into the profitable spice trade of southeast Asia. European powers controlled the area for the next four hundred fifty years.

LOCALE: Melaka, Malay Peninsula (now Malacca, Malaysia)

CATEGORIES: Expansion and land acquisition; wars, uprisings, and civil unrest; colonization; trade and commerce

KEY FIGURES

Afonso de Albuquerque (1453-1515), Portuguese conqueror of Goa and of Melaka and viceroy of the Portuguese Indies

Maḥmūd Shah (d. 1528), Melaka sultan, r. 1488-1511

SUMMARY OF EVENT

When explorer Afonso de Albuquerque claimed Melaka for the Portuguese in August, 1511, the strategically placed city was slightly more than one century old. Paramesvara, a Hindu prince from Sumatra, founded the city on the southwestern tip of the Malay Peninsula in about 1400. Situated on the Strait of Melaka, the new city grew quickly into an important trading center that enriched itself dramatically with the tolls it charged vessels to pass through the strait on their way to and from the Spice Islands.

Afonso de Albuquerque explored southeast Asia extensively for the Portuguese government, charged with establishing fruitful commercial ties with Asian outposts. The king of Portugal hoped to wrest the highly profitable spice trade from the Muslims, who had a monopoly on it, and to open a new route around the Cape of Good Hope in South Africa for transporting valuable cloves, mace, and nutmeg, along with precious jewels and gold, to markets in Europe. In the king's eyes, a collateral benefit in doing so would be the conversion of Muslims to Christianity.

As part of the king's scheme, Afonso had captured Goa on India's west coast in 1510, an initial step in dominating the Muslim spice network. The next objective, to capture Melaka, was achieved the following year when Afonso, in 1511, using Goa as a base, launched an assault on the city with a force of only nine hundred Portuguese and two hundred Indian mercenaries.

Even though Afonso's troops were outnumbered significantly, they were able to take advantage of the political chaos in Melaka at the time and use it to their advantage. Maḥmūd Shah's despotic rule was crumbling rapidly. In 1509, Melaka's prime minister had plotted to assassinate Maḥmūd, who in turn had the prime minister and his immediate family executed. This caused so much political instability that Maḥmūd had to flee, leaving his son to succeed him temporarily.

Melaka at this time was Asia's major trading city.

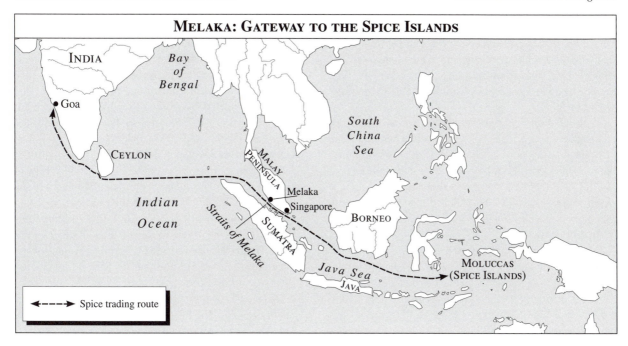

Afonso did not have the weaponry the Melakans possessed. Nevertheless, Melaka's sultan waited so long to address the threat from Afonso's paltry band that by the time he took action, it was too late. Afonso used sheer showmanship to establish his superiority, which was, in all practical terms, nonexistent. He sailed his vessels into Melaka's harbor, flags flying, artillery blasting noisily, to the consternation of Melaka's inhabitants. He set afire some ships in the harbor and four buildings on the waterfront. The sultan, possibly to buy time, released about twenty Portuguese prisoners the Melakans had captured during another Portuguese assault on the city in 1509. This gesture convinced Afonso that the sultan was vulnerable, so he plotted ways to take advantage of the situation.

Melaka was divided geographically into approximately equal halves by the Melaka River, with cramped dwellings and warehouses on both sides. Afonso realized that his best chance for success lay in gaining control of the bridge that connected the two parts of the city and in attacking its crowded parts to assess what resistance he would encounter there. The bridge was easily accessible to landing craft and also provided easy egress should a retreat be required. On July 25, Afonso's forces landed on each side of the river and charged the bridge.

A violent battle ensued, with the Melakans using both artillery and poisoned arrows against the invaders. Nevertheless, shortly past midday, the Portuguese prevailed and the bridge was taken. Afonso waited, expecting some message from the sultan. When such a message had not come by sunset, however, Afonso withdrew. The sultan, not eager for further confrontation, nevertheless was assessing his resources for repelling the Portuguese.

Meanwhile, Afonso filled a Chinese junk with his men and with guns and barrels of sand, and floated it up the river to the bridge at high tide. The next day, the Portuguese landed. Before day's end, they attacked the hastily constructed barricades designed to protect the city. Pushing these barricades aside, the Portuguese unloaded their firearms and invaded the city, capturing a mosque after a pitched battle. The Portuguese pursued fleeing defenders through the open streets.

At that point, the sultan played his trump card: He released a large herd of elephants that raged through the streets to the astonishment of the Portuguese. One of Afonso's men jabbed with his lance the lead elephant's eye. As the wounded animal retreated, howling in pain, its attacker plunged his lance into other tender parts of its body. Seeing the effectiveness of this defense, Afonso's men all began to use similar tactics on the other elephants. The result was that the animals went wild and retreated into the ranks of elephants behind them and into hordes of Melakan defenders. The sultan himself was knocked to the ground.

There came a weeklong lull in the battle, in which twenty-eight Portuguese lost their lives immediately and many more faced lingering deaths from the poisoned arrows. Afonso waited in vain to receive some word from the sultan. Finally, he acceded to requests for protection from many Melakan merchants. Such merchants were issued flags to display outside their establishments with the understanding that no establishment so marked would be looted.

Hearing nothing from the sultan, Afonso again attacked the city, only to learn that the sultan had fled. The Portuguese were now given permission to loot the city but with the stern admonition that any establishment flying the flag against looting would be spared. Melaka's riches were substantial, but Afonso's restraint assured that most of the city's wealth would remain the property of its original owners.

After Afonso returned to Goa in January, 1513, the Javanese warrior Patih Unus attacked Melaka with five thousand troops and more than one hundred vessels. The Portuguese, however, remained in control. Sultan Maḥmūd made two more attacks on Melaka (1518 and 1523), but neither was successful. In 1523, after the second coup, Maḥmūd escaped to Buitang, south of Singapore. The Portuguese remained in control of Melaka for the next 130 years.

SIGNIFICANCE

At the time of its early explorations into southeast Asia, Portugal was not among Europe's most flourishing nations. Certainly it was not the equal of Italy, France, Germany, or the Netherlands. With its conquests of Goa and Melaka, however, it emerged as one of Europe's mighty global powers.

Of special significance is the question of how a thriving city such as Melaka, so advantageously placed, could fall to forces that it outnumbered substantially. The Portuguese did not have the war-waging equipment the Melakans possessed, but the once-proud, well-run government that had brought Melaka to its enviable position in the fifteenth century had given way to the perfidious rule of a despotic sultan.

—*R. Baird Shuman*

FURTHER READING

Albuquerque, Afonso de. *The Commentaries of the Great Afonso Dalboquerque, Second Viceroy of India.* Translated and edited by Walter de Gray Birch. 4 vols. New Delhi: Asian Educational Services, 2000. This work includes Albuquerque's reports and letters compiled originally by his son Brás. It was first published by the Lisbon Academy of Sciences in 1576.

Andaya, Barbara Watson, and Leonard Y. *A History of Malaysia.* 2d ed. Honolulu: University of Hawaii Press, 2001. The chapter entitled "Melaka and Its Heirs" is particularly relevant. It is clearly written and makes a worthwhile starting point for those unfamiliar with the history of southeast Asia.

Diffie, Bailey W., and George D. Winius. *Foundations of the Portuguese Empire, 1415-1580.* Minneapolis: University of Minnesota Press, 1977. The most relevant chapter in this study is Chapter 16, "The Shape of Empire: The Nucleus, 1509-1515," which presents details about Afonso de Albuquerque as governor of the Indian holdings of the Portuguese and, to some degree, about the conquest of Melaka.

Hoyt, Sarnia Hayes. *Old Malacca.* New York: Oxford University Press, 1993. This compact, well-written, and richly illustrated volume discusses the Portuguese conquest of Melaka in Chapter 4, "The Portuguese Prize."

Winius, George D. *Studies on Portuguese Asia, 1495-1689.* Burlington, Vt.: Ashgate, 2001. This excellent study outlines the beginnings of the Portuguese presence in southeast Asia. Contains useful maps.

SEE ALSO: 1490's: Decline of the Silk Road; 1565: Spain Seizes the Philippines; Dec. 31, 1600: Elizabeth I Charters the East India Company.

RELATED ARTICLES in *Great Lives from History: The Renaissance & Early Modern Era, 1454-1600:* Afonso de Albuquerque; Bartolomeu Dias; Vasco da Gama; John II; Manuel I; Tomé Pires.

1512-1520
REIGN OF SELIM I

With support from the elite Janissary corps, Selim ruled an aggressive and expansionist Ottoman Empire that doubled in size during his reign. Also, he sought to eliminate what he believed to be the corruption of Islam by Shīʿites.

LOCALE: Eastern Anatolia and Persia (now Iran), the Levant (Syria, Lebanon, Palestine), Egypt, western Arabia

CATEGORIES: Government and politics; expansion and land acquisition

KEY FIGURES

Selim I (1466-1520), Ottoman sultan, r. 1512-1520
Ismāʿīl I (1487-1524), Persian shah and founder of the Ṣafavid Dynasty, r. 1501-1524
Qānṣawh II al-Ghawrī (1441-1516), Mamlūk sultan of Egypt, r. 1501-1516
Ṭūmān Bay II (Al-Malik al-Ashraf Tumanbai; 1474/ 1475-1517), last Mamlūk sultan, r. 1516-1517

SUMMARY OF EVENT

Driven by religious fanaticism, Selim I, the ninth Ottoman sultan, tried to eliminate Shīʿite resistance in eastern Anatolia beginning in 1513. He had some forty thousand heretics liquidated in the process, many of them partisans, envoys, or agents of the Persian ruler. Thereafter, Selim was engaged in a holy war against Persia's shah Ismāʿīl I, who had made Shiism the official form of Islam in his land east of the Ottoman borders. Ismāʿīl, also, had sided with Selim's brother, Ahmed, in their initial contest for power and given refuge to Ahmed's son, Murad.

Selim was a brutal, cruel—some say evil—uncompromising autocrat. Even the heads of his closest friends and associates were not safe. During his eight-year rule, he had seven of his grand viziers (chief ministers) decapitated for protesting, opposing, or complaining about the sultan's policies.

Selim also was a skillful administrator and a great warrior, hence his wide support in the army, though on two occasions his ambitions to do further battle outstripped his troops' willingness to follow. His anti-Shīʿite crusade, though accompanied by much bloodshed, earned him the nickname of "the Just." Selim fought corruption mercilessly, too.

Yet he also was devoted to culture, the literary arts, and theology. He also directed the architect of the empire to build noteworthy structures, projects that were contin-

ued by his progeny. Selim wrote poetry in Persian, the language of the cultivated and also penned insulting letters to Ismāʿīl I, in Persian, to provoke him into battle. Unlike other sultans, Selim had little interest in the harem or "worldly" pleasures. His possible addiction to opium may have occurred during his terminal sickness.

The Ottoman victory at the Battle of Chāldirān on August 23, 1514, against Ismāʿīl and the Ṣafavids was decisive but inconclusive, even though Selim captured the Persian capital of Tabrīz for a time, a feat involving a march of more than 1,000 miles. While the Ottoman Janissaries and field guns overcame the Persian cavalry, Selim did not integrate the defeated Persian Empire into his own, deciding instead to isolate it by mandating an economic embargo, especially on its silk trade. Silk was Persia's major export and main source of gold and silver revenue.

Ismāʿīl not only survived his battlefield injuries, he and his Ṣafavid Dynasty continued to rule Persia and outlive Selim. One important consequence of the Ottoman victory, however, was the Turkish conquest of all of the shah's possessions in eastern Asia Minor, down to the southeast at Diyarbakir and north up to Kurdistan.

Selim then turned his attention to defeating the non-Arab, originally Circassian, Mamlūk slave dynasty that had been ruling the Levant, Egypt, and western Arabia, including the holy cities of Mecca and Medina. Earlier, at the Mamlūks' request, Selim had helped the latter in their naval buildup to confront the growing Portuguese presence in the Indian Ocean and the Red Sea. The buildup had threatened the Islamic holy places in western Arabia as well as Mamlūk and Ottoman trade in the east. Thereafter, though, Ottoman and Mamlūk rivalry over territory—the headwaters of the Euphrates River in eastern Anatolia—vitiated their previously friendly relations.

With few firearms, which the Mamlūk leaders had despised, Mamlūk lancers, swordsmen, and bowmen were easily outclassed by the musket-armed infantry and state-of-the-art artillery of the Ottomans. After the Ottoman victory near Aleppo in Syria, where Mamlūk sultan Qānṣawh II al-Ghawrī (also known as Qansawh al-Ghawry or Kansuh al-Ghuri) was killed on August 24, 1516, Selim reached Damascus in October and occupied Palestine as far as Gaza.

Selim then crossed the Sinai Desert with thousands of camels carrying water, riflemen, field artillery, and supplies. Benefiting from a rift over succession among the Mamlūks and the treasonable behavior of some of their leaders, Selim again defeated them north of Cairo, on January 23, 1517. He ordered the execution of eight hundred Mamlūks, including the ruling sultan Ṭūmān Bay II, who had succeeded Qānṣawh II al-Ghawrī. Eventually, the whole of Egypt and much of western Arabia was under Ottoman sovereignty.

Having captured the last puppet caliph under Mamlūk control, Ṭūmān Bay, the title "protector of the holy places" was conferred on Selim. With the title, Selim became the leader of the Muslim community. The Mamlūks were left to rule Egypt under Ottoman suzerainty, unlike Syria (including Lebanon and Palestine), which Selim reorganized as regular Ottoman provinces under the direct rule of Ottoman governors.

While Selim was conquering Syria and Egypt, the Barbarossa brothers—Khiḍr and ʿArūj, under the sultan's overlordship—in exchange for aid and official appointment, exercised power in the Mediterranean. Their ships raided the coasts of Spain and maintained constant pressure on Holy Roman Emperor Charles V, who was also the Spanish monarch.

After a two-year absence in Syria on his way back from Egypt, Selim returned to Constantinople. The sultan spent his last two years in Asia Minor (Anatolia) and Europe (Rumelia), trying to straighten out the affairs of state, especially its accounts, even though the conquest of Syria and Egypt brought the Ottoman treasury enough revenue to meet the deficit of these provinces. Indeed, the Mamlūk lands, in addition to being granaries, were now paying an annual tribute to Constantinople. However, Selim was struck with cancer in the spring of 1520 and died that autumn at age fifty-three.

He bequeathed to Süleyman I, later dubbed "the Magnificent," control of a territory to which Selim had added eastern and southeastern Anatolia, the Arab lands south, and enclaves in northwestern Africa. It was left to his successors, however, to expand Ottoman territory in Europe, since Selim was preoccupied with the east and south. For that reason, he was mindful of maintaining peaceful relations with such powers as Venice and, especially, Hungary during his brief reign. In contrast to Selim's rise to power amid civil war, Süleyman, his only son, had an uneventful accession because Selim eliminated all potential rivals to the throne.

SIGNIFICANCE

Selim's short reign had doubled the size of the Ottoman Empire after he added Ṣafavid and Mamlūk territories.

He also captured Tunis and Algiers in North Africa. Selim's acquisitions helped to fund the impressive expansion of the Ottoman navy during his reign, adequate for an attack on Rhodes in 1522, a strategically located, eastern Mediterranean island. The island's Christian Knights Hospitallers had earlier obstructed the sultan from aiding the Mamlūks in their attempts to prevent the Portuguese from taking lands in the east.

Selim's capture of the last ʿAbbāsid caliph, and the subsequent transfer (or usurpation) of his title to the Turkish ruler, gave the Ottoman sultan primacy among Islamic monarchs and bolstered his claim as the champion of Muslim orthodoxy against Shīʿite heresy. For all that, renewed religious insurrection in central Anatolia shortly before his death was a reminder that the struggle between Ottomans and Persians, between Sunni Muslim orthodoxy and Shīʿite radicalism, was to continue.

—Peter B. Heller

FURTHER READING

Brummett, Palmira J. *Ottoman Seapower and Levantine Diplomacy in the Age of Discovery*. Albany: State University of New York Press, 1994. Examines Ottoman diplomatic, economic, and trade matters and discusses Selim's attention to naval power. Glossary, bibliography, illustrations, index.

Goodwin, Godfrey. *The Janissaries*. London: Saqi Books, 1997. Examines the role of the elite infantry corps recruited mostly among Christian boys in the Balkans. Genealogy, glossary, bibliography, illustrations, index.

Goodwin, Jason. *Lords of the Horizons: A History of the Ottoman Empire*. New York: Henry Holt, 1998. A topical, lively, and often-anecdotal account of the Ottomans. Map, glossaries, chronology, bibliography, index.

Imber, Colin. *The Ottoman Empire, 1300-1650: The Structure of Power*. New York: Palgrave-Macmillan, 2002. A topical approach that highlights Selim's contribution to the apogee of the empire. Maps, glossary, bibliography, index.

Kinross, Lord John P. D. B. *The Ottoman Centuries: The Rise and Fall of the Turkish Empire*. New York: William Morrow, 1977. A chronological narrative of the empire by a renowned British scholar. Maps, select bibliography, illustrations, index.

SEE ALSO: 1454-1481: Rise of the Ottoman Empire; Early 16th cent.: Fuzuli Writes Poetry in Three Languages; Dec. 2, 1510: Battle of Merv Establishes the Shaybānīd Dynasty; June 28, 1522-Dec. 27, 1522: Siege and Fall of Rhodes; 1534-1535: Ottomans Claim Sovereignty over Mesopotamia; 1566-1574: Reign of Selim II; 1578-1590: The Battle for Tabrīz;

1587-1629: Reign of ʿAbbās the Great; 1589: Second Janissary Revolt in Constantinople.

Related articles in *Great Lives from History: The Renaissance & Early Modern Era, 1454-1600:* Barbarossa; Mehmed II; Süleyman the Magnificent.

April 11, 1512
Battle of Ravenna

French and Spanish/papal forces engaged in a major battle at Ravenna during the second French invasion of Italy. Ravenna marked the first effective use of cannon as field artillery. The French were victorious, but they suffered heavy casualties and soon were forced to withdraw from Italy.

Locale: Ravenna (now in Italy)
Categories: Wars, uprisings, and civil unrest; expansion and land acquisition

Key Figures
Gaston de Foix (1489-1512), nephew to King Louis XII and commander of the French army
Ramon de Cardona (d. 1522), commander of the Spanish/papal army
Pedro Navarro (c. 1460-1528), count of Olivetto, 1504-1526, military engineer for the Spanish/papal army
Julius II (Giuliano della Rovere; 1443-1513), Roman Catholic pope, 1503-1513
Louis XII (1462-1515), king of France, r. 1498-1515
Ferdinand II (1452-1516), king of Aragon, r. 1479-1516, regent of Castile, r. 1504-1516, king of Sicily, r. 1468-1516, and king of Naples as Ferdinand III, r. 1504-1516

Summary of Event
The Battle of Ravenna was a major episode in the French invasions of Italy, which began in 1494 when Charles VIII occupied the Italian kingdom of Naples. Spain's Ferdinand II intervened, joining Pope Alexander VI's Holy League alongside Germany and Milan. Louis XII, Charles's successor, made good his claim to the duchy of Milan during the second French invasion in 1499. However, the election of Pope Julius II in 1503 brought to power someone determined to rid Italy of foreign powers, beginning with the French, whom he regarded as the most dangerous. Through patient diplomacy, Julius reestablished the Holy League in 1510. The league's second

incarnation consisted of Spain, England, and Venice, as well as a group of Swiss mercenary troops.

Fighting began when Julius's army occupied several towns in the duchy of Ferrara, a French ally. The French response to this provocation was limited, until Louis XII appointed his nephew, Gaston de Foix, the duke of Nemours, as commander of the French army in Italy. Gaston had just turned twenty-two years old when he arrived in Italy to take command in December, 1511. His youthful energy electrified the French forces, and he immediately took the offensive against the enemy. Disregarding the tradition that battles were fought only in summer, he marched his men through the snows of January to relieve French-occupied Bologna, under siege by a Spanish/papal army, and then double-timed his own army to surprise and defeat Venetian forces at Brescia on February 19, 1512.

Aware that reinforcements were on their way to him, Ramon de Cardona, the Spanish commander of the Holy League's forces, retreated southward. De Foix, eager to engage the league before their reinforcements arrived, quickly besieged Ravenna, a major city in the Papal States. Cardona had no choice but to attempt to break the siege with his existing forces. His army consisted of some sixteen thousand men—fourteen thousand foot soldiers and two thousand men-at-arms (knights). Seven thousand of his soldiers came from the papal army; the rest were Spaniards.

Employing tactics that had been successful for the Spanish since 1495, Cardona established a defensive position with his left flank on the Ronco River and surrounded his position with entrenchments designed by the noted military engineer, Pedro Navarro. He had about thirty heavy cannon, which were distributed across the front of his army. Navarro also had two hundred small artillery pieces mounted on carts, which could be moved wherever they were needed during the battle. Cardona then waited for the French to attack, knowing that the lack of supplies would force de Foix either to retreat or come to him to fight.

De Foix's response demonstrated that medieval values still had a hold over fighting men of the early sixteenth century. He sent a formal invitation to battle to Cardona, who accepted it with equal formality. On Easter Sunday, April 11, 1512, de Foix, leaving two thousand men in the siege lines around Ravenna to prevent its garrison from aiding Cardona, moved the rest of his army to give battle. It consisted of about twenty-one thousand men. His infantry forces included seven thousand Frenchmen, seventy-five hundred German mercenaries, and five thousand Italians. His fifteen hundred cavalrymen were mostly French men-at-arms, still regarded as the best fighting men in Europe. The French had fifty-five cannon.

Arriving before the Spanish/papal lines, de Foix placed his men in a large semicircular formation, with the cavalry forming the wings on either end and the infantry in the center. He kept six hundred men-at-arms in reserve behind the center. Cardona made no effort to impede their march, although they had to cross a bridge a short distance from his lines. His experience in several battles with the French since 1495 convinced him that they would move immediately to the attack against even entrenched positions: The élan of the French noblemen required them to attack the enemy without hesitation, regardless of how well entrenched he was. Cardona, therefore, preferred to keep his men in their positions and wait for the French to attack. His battle plan was based on the assumption that they would.

Although de Foix had no experience in fighting Spanish forces, he instinctively recognized that little good could come from assaulting Cardona's well-defended lines. Despite grumbling from his men, who regarded it as a point of honor to attack immediately, he had high enough standing with his troops to keep them in check. By 10:00 A.M. the French had approached to within 200 yards of the enemy trenches. De Foix moved the infantry in his center forward a few paces to simulate an attack, which drew fire from Cardona's guns. Much to Cardona's surprise, the French infantry halted well short of his trenches, and no other forces pressed forward. Instead, the French artillery opened fire.

For about two hours, the cannon exchanged fire directed largely toward the large blocks of infantrymen in both armies. It was the first sustained cannonade in history. The mobile gun carts also scored heavily on the French. Casualties on both sides mounted rapidly. Especially hard hit were the captains of the infantry companies, who stood resplendent in bright clothes in front of their men. Two captains, drinking a toast to their men, were killed with one cannonball.

It was unheard of before this battle for soldiers to take fire for so long a period of time without charging or retreating, a situation much more characteristic of eighteenth century battles than those of the Renaissance. Thus, neither captain achieved the outcome that each both desired and expected: Cardona wanted de Foix's forces to charge the entrenched Spanish lines, and de Foix wanted Cardona's to leave their trenches and charge the French. The stalemate continued until a French officer, perhaps de Foix himself, conceived of a brilliant tactical maneuver: Several cannon were brought around to the flank of the Holy League's lines and began to fire diagonally into them. This enfilading fire soon inflicted severe casualties, and, realizing that his men would not remain in place much longer, Cardona ordered them to charge the French lines. The bitter hand-to-hand fighting that ensued was going to Cardona's advantage, when the French cavalry, which had driven off its counterpart in the league's army, charged into the rear of the league's infantry and forced it to collapse in disorder.

Late in the battle, de Foix was killed. One report had it that he was killed while rallying the French infantry to hold its position. Another report, widely accepted largely because it came from the highly respected Sieur de Bayard, "the knight without reproach," claimed de Foix was killed by a company of Spanish infantrymen while leading a band of cavalrymen in pursuit of the defeated enemy. Bayard claimed that the Spaniards shouted at de Foix to let them retreat unharmed, since the French had already won the day, but he persisted in pursuing them and was killed.

Regardless of which version of de Foix's death is true, the loss of their young commander proved to be a blow to the French that outweighed any advantage their victory gained them. They had been badly battered and had suffered heavy casualties, perhaps as many as forty-five hundred dead, although the league's forces lost at least twice that number. Jacques de La Palise, de Foix's replacement, was not the sort of person to risk marching to Rome and arresting Julius II as a false pope, as Louis XII had ordered de Foix to do. Instead, he moved his battered army back to Milan, pursued by the reinvigorated league army, and then retreated to France.

Most of the places controlled by the French fell into enemy hands by the end of 1512. Milan surrendered to the Swiss. Julius II, who frantically had been preparing to flee Rome when he heard of the league's defeat at

Ravenna, emerged more powerful than ever. He excommunicated Louis XII and encouraged Henry VIII of England, Ferdinand of Aragon, and the Swiss to invade France. Julius's death in February, 1513, took the glue out of the Holy League, however, and Louis made peace with his foes with no further loss of territory.

SIGNIFICANCE

Besides serving as an excellent example of a pyrrhic victory, the Battle of Ravenna was an important step in the development of gunpowder artillery as a field weapon. The potential of cannon as a field weapon was well demonstrated by the French success in using cannon to force Ramon de Cardona's forces to abandon their entrenched lines and make an unsuccessful charge at the French. The death of Gaston de Foix prevented the French from deposing Pope Julius II, which, had it happened, might have dramatically changed the religious history of the era, perhaps even preventing the Reformation from occurring. The French withdrawal from Italy after Ravenna caused them to lose Milan, which in turn led to the third French invasion of Italy and the Battle of Marignano in 1515.

—Frederic J. Baumgartner

FURTHER READING

Baumgartner, Frederic. *Louis XII.* New York: St. Martin's Press, 1994. Places the battle in the context of the reign of the French king.

Bridge, John. *History of France from the Death of Louis XI.* Vol. 4. Reprint. New York: Octagon Books, 1978. A detailed account of the events leading to the battle, the battle itself, and its consequences.

Hall, Bert. *Weapons and Warfare in Renaissance Europe.* Baltimore: Johns Hopkins University Press, 1997. Stresses the innovative character of the battle.

Holt, Mack. *Renaissance and Reformation France.* New York: Oxford University Press, 2002. Provides a discussion of the impact of the battle on French politics and culture.

Oman, Charles. *A History of the Art of War in the Sixteenth Century.* New York: E. P. Dutton, 1937. The most complete description of the battle from a tactical point of view.

Shaw, Christine. *Julius II: The Warrior Pope.* London: Blackwell, 1997. Places the battle in the context of the pope's life.

Taylor, Frederick. *The Art of War in Italy, 1494-1529.* Westport, Conn.: Greenwood Press, 1973. Places the battle in the context of Italian military practice during the Renaissance.

SEE ALSO: Apr. 9, 1454: Peace of Lodi; 1481-1499: Ludovico Sforza Rules Milan; Sept., 1494-Oct., 1495: Charles VIII of France Invades Italy; 1499: Louis XII of France Seizes Milan; 1500: Roman Jubilee; Sept. 13-14, 1515: Battle of Marignano; Aug. 18, 1516: Concordat of Bologna; 1521-1559: Valois-Habsburg Wars; Feb., 1525: Battle of Pavia; May 6, 1527-Feb., 1528: Sack of Rome; Apr. 3, 1559: Treaty of Cateau-Cambrésis.

RELATED ARTICLES in *Great Lives from History: The Renaissance & Early Modern Era, 1454-1600:* Charles VIII; Ferdinand II and Isabella I; Julius II; Louis XII.

Beginning 1513
KANŌ SCHOOL FLOURISHES

In 1513, Kanō Motonobu painted his masterpieces at the Daisen-in Temple in Kyōto, "Patriarchs of Zen Buddhism" and "Birds and Flowers." These represented a new style of painting that came to be known as the Kanō school, which flourished for centuries as the official and dominant painting academy.

LOCALE: Kyōto and Edo (now Tokyo), Japan
CATEGORY: Art

KEY FIGURES

Kanō Motonobu (1476-1559), artist and garden designer who laid the foundation for the Kanō school's success

Kanō Masanobu (1434-1530), Motonobu's father, the first Kanō artist, official painter to the shogunate during the Muromachi period

Kanō Eitoku (1543-1590), Motonobu's grandson and leader of the Kanō school during the Momoyama period

SUMMARY OF EVENT

From about 1192 in the Kamakura period (1185-1333) until the Meiji Restoration (1868-1869), hereditary military dictators called shoguns governed Japan. The emperors were rulers in theory only. During the Muromachi period (1333-1573), the Ashikaga family shogunate (*bakufu*) officially governed from its residence at Muromachi in Kyōto. Chinese-style ink painting and Zen Buddhism flourished, centered in the Zen monasteries. The Ashikaga shoguns promoted the Chinese-style of painting, which produced monochromatic ink paintings depicting Chinese landscapes and subjects. Many Zen monks were outstanding painters, and the shoguns were patrons of artists such as the Zen monk Tenshō Shubūn (fl. 1418-1463), whose expressionistic ink-monochrome landscapes were in the *kanga* style of the Song (960-1279) and Yuan (1279-1368) Dynasties of China. Another Zen monk and one of the foremost artists of Japan was Sesshū (1420-1506). He had actually traveled to China, and his work was inspired by Chinese landscape paintings.

In the latter part of the Muromachi period, a new and truly Japanese style of ink painting developed outside the Zen community. The founder of this new school was a layperson, Kanō Masanobu, who was from a warrior family of Kanō village in eastern Japan. He moved to

Kyōto, became the official artist in the court of the shogun Yoshimasa (r. 1449-1473), and eventually became the first lay artist to paint in the ink-wash medium. His paintings of birds, landscapes, and people were popular with the military class. Masanobu's art retained Chinese themes and style but incorporated occasional touches of pale tints, which were a deviation from the prevailing monochromatic or black Chinese ink-painting technique.

However, it was his son, Kanō Motonobu, who firmly established the Kanō school of painters and defined the Kanō stye of painting. Like his father, Motonobu was the official painter for the Ashikaga shogunate. In 1513, he painted *shoheki-ga*, or sliding-door panel paintings, for the new Daisen-in subtemple of the Daitokuji monastery in Kyōto. These *shoheki-ga* clearly established the fundamental characteristics of the new Kanō style. Although retaining the Chinese subjects or themes of the established style of ink painting, they integrated the qualities of the traditional, classic Japanese style or *yamato-e* (Japanese pictures). Motonobu's paintings showed a decorative style: balanced compositions with large flat areas, vivid colors, and sharply defined line work. The *shoheki-ga* included two of Motonobu's masterpieces: *The Patriarchs of Zen Buddhism* and *Birds and Flowers of the Four Seasons*.

Originally six sliding-door panels composing a single scene, *The Patriarchs of Zen Buddhism* has been remounted and survives as six hanging scrolls in the Tokyo National Museum collection. The Tokyo Imperial Museum (which became the Tokyo National Museum) had acquired them during the Meiji era (1868-1912), and they were designated as "important cultural property." The painting portrays Zen patriarchs in various activities. There are two figures in a rowboat, another drawing a bow and arrow, a patriarch in front of a great waterfall looking across the water, a group of three figures on large rocks, and two figures in conversation. A famous section from this set is the scene titled "Zen Patriarch Xiangyen Zhixian [Hsiang-yen] Sweeping with a Broom."

Originally eight sliding-door panels depicting a single scene, Motonobu's other great work, *Birds and Flowers of the Four Seasons*, has been remounted as eight hanging scrolls in the collection of the Kyōto National Museum and has also been designated an "important cultural property." The highly decorative composition revolves around a large pine tree and a waterfall.

Richly colored birds of various types and sizes swim, fly, or rest. Many varieties of flowers are also painted in bright colors.

With these *shoheki-ga*, Motonobu began the art of large-scale mural composition and laid the foundation for the future prosperity and popularity of the Kanō school. In 1543, he completed another impressive set of *shoheki-ga* in the Reiun-in temple in the Myōshinji monastery at Kyōto. These decorative paintings depict landscapes, flowers, birds, and landscapes with figures.

With a genius for organization, he arranged for large groups consisting of family members and followers to complete commissions from monasteries, merchants, and court nobles. Appealing to every sector of society was a practical necessity, for Motonobu lived in turbulent times. The Ashikaga shogunate had never been a strong central administration. During this period, hundreds of autonomous daimyo (feudal warlords and their families) controlled independent territories, protected by samurai (the warrior class). Throughout the Ashikaga period, there was bitter fighting between the various daimyo.

In 1573, the last Ashikaga shogun, Yoshiaki (r. 1568-1573), was driven out of Kyōto by the warlord Oda Nobunaga, who began the process of unifying Japan. His successor, the warlord Toyotomi Hideyoshi, continued the unification efforts. The era camed to be called the Momoyama period (1573-1603), after the place near Kyōto where Hideyoshi built one of his castles.

Throughout this period, the Kanō school continued to be the official painting school. Both Nobunaga and Hideyoshi became patrons of Motonobu's grandson and designated successor, Kanō Eitoku. Eitoku created elegant screen, wall, sliding door, and ceiling paintings for his patrons' palaces and castles.

SIGNIFICANCE

The Kanō school continued until the end of the Edo period (1603-1863), when Western art became popular. During this period, it split into many branches over time but nevertheless remained the official academy. The most inspired of the later Kanō artists were Kanō Tanyu (1602-1674) and his brother Kanō Naonobu (1607-1650). Numerous schools of painting coexisted during this period. A notable example is the classic genre of woodblock prints called *ukiyo-e* (pictures of the floating world), many of which depicted scenes from places such as restaurants, teahouses, and theaters.

What is most important about the Kanō School is that it was Japan's first truly professional secular school of artists. The largest of its kind, this hereditary line of

painters found patrons from among the wealthy merchant class, court nobility, and Zen monasteries, as well as the military. Motonobu's panel paintings at the Daisen-in subtemple initiated the art of large-scale mural composition in architectural formats, such as the immense wall surfaces of monasteries and palaces. Motonobu established a high standard for successfully soliciting commissions, and his system of group workmanship continued with later generations of Kanō painters. He thus laid the foundation for a prosperous painting academy.

Motonobu also created a new style of painting, the Kanō style, a synthesis of Zen-inspired Chinese ink painting and themes with traditional Japanese (*yamato-e*) lyricism, painting techniques, and decorative arrangement. The Kanō style influenced landscape painting for centuries. The bold compositions, large flat areas, and rich colors would later appear in the popular *ukiyo-e* or classic woodblock print genre depicting landscapes or everyday life during the Edo period. Numerous *ukiyo-e* artists were originally trained in the Kanō academy.

—Alice Myers

FURTHER READING

Doi, Tsugiyoshi. *Momoyama Decorative Painting*. New York: Weatherhill, 1977. Includes the history of the Kanō school painters and their role in the development of decorative painting on screens and sliding partitions. Inlcudes illustrations on almost every page.

Jordan, Brenda, and Victoria Weston, ed. *Copying the Master and Stealing His Secrets*. Honolulu: University of Hawaii Press, 2003. Focuses on the transmission of painting traditions from one generation to the next in the prestigious Kanō painting academy, which shaped the structure of painting pedagogy in premodern Japan. Includes illustrations and bibliography.

Morse, Anne Nishimura. *Japanese Art in the Museum of Fine Arts, Boston*. Boston: Museum of Fine Arts, 1998. Includes numerous examples of early Kanō school painting.

Takeda, Tsuneo. *Kanō Eitoku*. Tokyo: Kodansha International, 1977. This was the first critical work on the Kanō school to appear in English. Includes illustrations, index, and glossary.

Yamane, Yuzo. *Momoyama Genre Painting*. New York: Weatherhill, 1973. Describes the significant impact of the Kanō school on the development of true genre painting. Includes illustrations on almost every page.

July-December, 1513
MACHIAVELLI WRITES *THE PRINCE*

Machiavelli's The Prince *presented a radical political theory, arguing that a ruler's primary responsibility was to stay in power and that morality could play no part in the ruler's attempts to achieve that aim.*

LOCALE: Albergaccio, near Florence (now in Italy)
CATEGORIES: Cultural and intellectual history; government and politics

KEY FIGURES
Niccolò Machiavelli (1469-1527), exiled Florentine diplomat
Lorenzo de' Medici (1492-1519), Florentine ruler, r. 1512-1519, later duke of Urbino, r. 1516-1519
Cesare Borgia (1475/1476-1507), Italian warlord

SUMMARY OF EVENT
In 1512, the Medici family returned to power in Florence after an exile of several years, during which the old republican form of government had been restored in the city. The Medici purged those who had been disloyal, and among those who went into exile was a forty-three-year-old diplomat, Niccolò Machiavelli, who had occupied a subordinate government post under the republic.

Machiavelli withdrew to his villa outside the city and began a major political work, the *Discourses*. In the summer of 1513, however, he turned his attention abruptly to a shorter and somewhat different kind of work, which he probably completed before the end of the year. This shorter work laid down the requisite principles and ethics necessary for the unification of Italy by force. To do so would require a strong man, a description which Machiavelli presumably meant to suggest members of the Medici family. This new work, *Il principe* (pb. 1532; *The Prince*, 1640), had little immediate impact in Italy, although it soon became legendary throughout Europe, and its major ideas have become familiar even to people who have never read the book.

Machiavelli dedicated his treatise to Lorenzo de' Medici, the grandson of Lorenzo il Magnifico, in the hope of regaining favor. Lorenzo is said to have read the work in manuscript and to have dismissed it contemptuously as too theoretical. Later, Machiavelli was given minor diplomatic assignments by the Medici and was

Niccolò Machiavelli. (Hulton|Archive by Getty Images)

commissioned to write a history of Florence. He died in 1527, and *The Prince* was published posthumously in 1532.

During the later twentieth century, some interpreters attempted to rescue Machiavelli from charges of ruthlessness and amorality. Those who have read *The Prince* through the centuries have been impressed, or shocked, by its calm and uncompromising analysis of techniques and methods that the successful ruler must use to gain power and keep it. It is written in the form of advice to the ruler. Machiavelli tells the prince where his best interests lie and how to attain them; he warns him against mistakes, especially against being too lenient.

According to Machiavelli, the prince is a ruler who conquers hostile territory or who comes to power by force or revolution, the normal means of obtaining power among the numerous small city-states of Renaissance Italy. In this situation, Machiavelli counsels the prince to imitate both the lion and the fox: He must appear to be bold and fearless, but he must also use cunning and deception to gain his ends.

Machiavelli believes that events are controlled half by fortune and half by human will, as exemplified by virtue, but he describes fortune as "a woman who will yield herself to force, especially to someone who is young and bold." Machiavelli then concludes that virtue is a bulwark against the whims of fortune. It is the essential quality of a prince, combining courage, talent, strength of character and will, and above all, intelligence. Intelligence is required to take advantage of any opportunity that comes along.

Machiavelli goes on to state that private morality has no place in politics; even if a man deserves praise in private, if he hesitates to act for the good of the state, he must be condemned as a wicked and inept ruler. Furthermore, the reverse must also be true: Even if a man is unworthy of praise privately, if he has acted for the welfare of the state, any actions are justifiable and to be applauded.

Most critics believe that the prince whom Machiavelli praised most unstintingly in *The Prince* was Cesare Borgia, duke of Valentinois and son of Pope Alexander VI. Borgia had recently led military campaigns through central Italy to carve out a new state for himself. On his

---

MACHIAVELLI URGES THE MEDICI TO FREE ITALY

Niccolò Machiavelli's The Prince, *in addition to being a general manual of leadership, is a work of Italian nationalism. It includes analysis of the condition of Italy's major city-states in the 1510's, and it concludes with the following exhortation to Lorenzo de' Medici to act to liberate the peninsula from its occupying foreign powers.*

At the moment, there is nowhere Italy can turn in her search for someone to redeem her with more chance of success than to your own illustrious family [the Medici], which is fortunate and resourceful, is favored by God and by the church (indeed the church is now at its command). . . . God has already shown his hand: The sea has been divided; a cloud has escorted you on your journey; water has flowed out of the rock; manna has fallen from on high. Everything has conspired to make you great. The rest you must do for yourselves.

Source: From *The Prince*, by Niccolò Machiavelli. Translated and edited by David Wootton (Indianapolis, Ind.: Hackett, 1995), pp. 77-78.

---

father's death, he had lost his territories, but Machiavelli regarded him with great admiration as the quintessential prince whose methods and determination were ideally suited to his political ambitions.

Machiavelli contends that, by studying history and exploiting the knowledge gained, one is able to predict future political developments. This view has garnered the criticism that Machiavelli is dogmatic in his thinking and unwilling to acknowledge the uniqueness and complexities of changing political situations. The aspect of Machiavelli's thought that has been most widely condemned, though, is his dictum that in pursuing political aims the ends justify the means. He advises the prince that only one consideration should govern his decisions: the effectiveness of a particular course of action, irrespective of its ethical character. Nothing is superior to the state, and no other factors need be considered.

As a general rule, Machiavelli asserts that the prince should seek to be both feared and loved. If both are not possible, however, it is better to be feared than loved, for people are fickle, and their love can be quickly dissipated. Above all, the prince should not be hated, because hatred may drive men to blind fury and rebellion.

Machiavelli falls short of advocating total ruthlessness and duplicity, because they are ultimately self-defeating. The prince should ordinarily refrain from seizing property or misusing women, since such actions create lasting enmity, but he should deal with rebels without mercy as examples to others. He should avoid lying whenever possible so that his words will be generally believed, but he should not hesitate to lie or break a given treaty as reason dictates. Cruelty may be necessary to conquer a state, but afterward it should be lessened to give the appearance of being merciful and just. Whenever practical, the people of a conquered state should be allowed to keep their old laws and institutions, because these can be effective instruments of the prince's control. Above all, he must weaken newly conquered territory by creating dissension among the people, winning over hostile subjects, and never reducing any subjects to submission by means of fortresses.

Machiavelli states that the prince should refuse the cloak of neutrality; rather, he should boldly declare himself either friend or foe. Through such strong positions in foreign policy, the prince may gain esteem from his peers, just as a strong domestic policy may win the favor of his subjects.

The view of human nature expressed in *The Prince* is negative and pessimistic. Machiavelli claims that self-interest is the dominant motive for human conduct; the prince can feel justified in breaking a treaty, for example, because the other parties to the treaty should also be expected to break it when expedient. Human selfishness is, however, so short-sighted that men are usually taken in by appearances, and the prince must therefore strive to appear mighty, just, and honorable, whatever his real character may be.

The prince must not allow any person or group in the state to maintain power or influence independent of his own. Religion, for example, should be encouraged to inculcate morality and docility in the people, but the prince himself cannot afford to be truly religious; he must require priests to become his spokespeople and the Church an arm of his government.

Machiavelli counseled that the prince's sole area of formal study should be the art of war. Military power is the foundation and the strength of the state. A strong native military implies a solid foundation in the principality of good laws. The most tragic mistake a prince can make is to rely on the services of foreign mercenary soldiers, who can be bribed to desert their employer and who have no incentive to fight boldly or risk their lives. A secure state reposes on the services of a citizens' militia, whose members are devoted to the state and are willing to fight to defend their homes.

SIGNIFICANCE

The Prince is a work of immense and lasting intellectual significance, because it is the first treatise to affirm a new science of statesmanship, the "autonomy of politics." This science defines a new political system, which has its own laws and methods, and which is unable to exist in a subordinate role to ethics or religion. Scholars have disagreed for centuries over the relationship between *The Prince* and Machiavelli's own beliefs and values. Was it an expression of his actual beliefs, or was it simply an attempt to tell the Medici what they wanted to hear in the hope that they would end Machiavelli's exile? Whatever the truth may be, the term "Machiavellian" has come to signify utter ruthlessness and amorality in public life.

—*James F. Hitchcock, updated by Elizabeth L. Scully*

FURTHER READING

Butterfield, Herbert. *The Statecraft of Machiavelli.* New York: Macmillan, 1956. Reprint. New York: Collier Books, 1962. Highly critical of Machiavelli's purposes and goals, but excellent for providing insights into the subtlety of his work.

De Alvarez, Leo Paul S. *The Machiavellian Enterprise.* Dekalb: Northern Illinois University Press, 1999. Extended reading of *The Prince* by one of its modern translators. Argues that the book puts forward a unified, coherent argument in favor of creating a secular, egalitarian civil state. Includes bibliographic references and index.

Jensen, De Lamar, ed. *Machiavelli: Cynic, Patriot, or Political Scientist?* Boston: D. C. Heath, 1960. Reflects a spectrum of interpretations in a collection of interpretive essays.

Kahn, Victoria A. *Machiavellian Rhetoric: From the Counter-Reformation to Milton.* Princeton, N.J.: Princeton University Press, 1994. Criticism and interpretations of Machiavelli's social and political contributions.

Kocis, Robert A. *Machiavelli Redeemed: Retrieving His Humanist Perspectives on Equality, Power, and Glory.* Bethelhem, Pa.: Lehigh University Press, 1998. An attempt to reposition Machiavelli as a Humanist to rescue him from his pervasive portrayal as an amoral advocate of anti-Humanist political practices. Includes illustrations, bibliographic references, index.

Parel, Anthony. *The Machiavellian Cosmos.* New Haven, Conn.: Yale University Press, 1992. Examines Machiavelli's influence upon modern political science.

Pocock, J. G. A. *The Machiavellian Moment: Florentine Political Thought and the Atlantic Republican Tradition.* 2d ed. Princeton, N.J.: Princeton University Press, 2003. Classic study of Machiavelli's conception of a republic and its need to preserve itself, followed by an extended discussion of Machiavelli's influence upon English republicanism and the American Revo-

lution. Includes bibliographic references and index.

Skinner, Quentin. *Machiavelli: A Very Short Introduction*. Rev. ed. New York: Oxford University Press, 2000. Summary of Machiavelli's life and of his thought as revealed in *The Prince*, the *Discourses*, and the *History of Florence*. Includes illustrations, bibliographic references, and index.

Subtleties, Federico. *Machiavelli and the Renaissance*. Translated by David Moore. Cambridge, Mass.: Harvard University Press, 1960. Collection of four essays regarding Machiavelli written during over a period of thirty years.

Viroli, Maurizio. *Machiavelli*. New York: Oxford University Press, 1998. A wide-ranging survey and reexamination of Machiavelli's philosophy, covering his

political and social theories and his thoughts on love, women, religion, humanity, and the good life. Includes bibliographic references and index.

SEE ALSO: Apr. 9, 1454: Peace of Lodi; 1462: Founding of the Platonic Academy; 1469-1492: Rule of Lorenzo de' Medici; Apr. 26, 1478: Pazzi Conspiracy; 1486-1487: Pico della Mirandola Writes *Oration on the Dignity of Man*; 1490's: Aldus Manutius Founds the Aldine Press; Sept., 1494-Oct., 1495: Charles VIII of France Invades Italy; Apr. 11, 1512: Battle of Ravenna.

RELATED ARTICLES in *Great Lives from History: The Renaissance & Early Modern Era, 1454-1600:* Cesare Borgia; Niccolò Machiavelli.

August 22, 1513-July 6, 1560
ANGLO-SCOTTISH WARS

Beginning with the English rout of Scots forces at Flodden in 1513, the sixteenth century witnessed a ferocious period of Anglo-Scottish warfare, the latter part of which was marked by English attempts to force Scotland to marry Mary, Queen of Scots, to Edward, the English heir to Henry VIII.

LOCALE: Northern England and southern Scotland

CATEGORIES: Wars, uprisings, and civil unrest; diplomacy and international relations; government and politics

KEY FIGURES

Henry VIII (1491-1547), king of England, r. 1509-1547

Edward Seymour (c. 1500/1506-1552), earl of Hertford, 1537-1552, duke of Somerset, 1547-1552, lord protector of England, 1547-1550

James IV (1473-1513), king of Scotland, r. 1488-1513

James V (1512-1542), king of Scotland, r. 1513-1542

Mary Stuart (1542-1587), queen of Scotland, r. 1542-1567

Edward VI (1537-1553), king of England, r. 1547-1553

James Hamilton (1515?-1575), second earl of Arran, 1529-1575, duke of Châtelherault, 1548-1575, governor and regent of Scotland, r. 1542-1554

Mary of Guise (1515-1560), queen regent of Scotland, r. 1554-1560

Thomas Howard (1443-1524), earl of Surrey, 1483-1485, 1488-1524, second duke of Norfolk and earl marshal of England, 1513-1524

Thomas Howard (1473-1554), lord high admiral of England, 1513, lord lieutenant of Ireland, 1520-1521, third duke of Norfolk, earl of Surrey, and earl marshal of England, 1524-1554

John Knox (c. 1514-1572), Scottish church reformer

SUMMARY OF EVENT

For much of the first half of the sixteenth century, Anglo-Scottish conflict seemed to increase in cost and intensity, without respite. Scotland made several attempts to strengthen its position by cultivating its traditional alliance with France, England's bitter enemy during the period. This in turn forced England to act aggressively to counter the resulting threat to its northern border. Although events late in this phase of the perennial wars between England and Scotland centered upon the marriage of Mary, Queen of Scots, England's attempts to deal with a Scotland ever ready to ally itself to France were at the heart of the period's many and bitter wars.

Efforts to create a lasting peace between the perennially hostile realms of Scotland and England had resulted, in 1503, in the marriage of James IV, king of Scotland, to Margaret Tudor, the eldest daughter of the English king Henry VII (r. 1485-1509). Hostilities reopened, however, in 1512, when James supported France, which was soon to be the target of an English invasion. After reviving the Franco-Scottish alliance, James prepared to ease the pressure on France by invading England's northern borderlands. He crossed the border on August 22, 1513.

KEY BATTLES OF THE ANGLO-SCOTTISH WARS

Date	Battle	Result
September 7-9, 1513	Flodden	English rout of Scots
November 24, 1542	Solway Moss	English rout of Scots
February 27, 1545	Ancrum Moor	Scottish rout of the English
September 10, 1547	Pinkie	English rout of Scots

After taking Norham Castle, James positioned his army of some thirty thousand troops at Flodden Field, in Northumberland. An English force of about half that number was led by Thomas Howard the elder, earl of Surrey. Howard's son, also named Thomas, led the vanguard. After an initial defeat at the hands of James's larger and better-armed forces, Surrey's troops took advantage of the Scots' decision to give up their elevated position and attack downhill. The Scots soon suffered a humiliating and almost total defeat, with King James IV and numerous other Scottish nobles among the estimated five thousand Scots killed in the battle. James IV was succeeded by his infant son, James V.

In 1542, James V's realm was beset by belligerent acts performed by the English king Henry VIII, who chafed at James's refusal to renounce his support of the French king Francis I (r. 1515-1547). Henry decided to take aggressive action to neutralize the Scottish threat to the north of England, sending, in September, 1542, the third duke of Norfolk on a largely unsuccessful invasion of southern Scotland. James V responded by gathering an army at Lauder, which disbanded after a brief and ineffective campaign of marauding in the borderlands. Another army was soon mustered to invade the West March. On November 24, 1542, the Scottish army was soundly defeated at Solway Moss by English forces under the command of Thomas Wharton, the warden of the West March.

James V died on December 14, 1542, leaving the infant Mary, Queen of Scots, as his sole heir. Mary's marital status initiated a new phase in the Anglo-Scottish conflict, often described as the "Rough Wooing," which involved Henry VIII's efforts to force Mary's marriage to his son, Prince Edward (the future Edward VI). In the spring of 1544, English forces under the command of Edward Seymour, the earl of Hertford, took Leith through a naval invasion aimed at forcing the Scots to accept Henry's demands concerning Mary. Hertford's army ravaged the Scottish Lowlands, sacking Holyrood and Jedburgh.

On February 27, 1545, the Scots routed the English at Ancrum Moor, emboldening those who sought French assistance to lead a retaliatory invasion into England. In September, 1547, Hertford, now the duke of Somerset and the Lord Protector in the new regime of Edward VI, continuing the policy of "Rough Wooing," launched an invasion of Scotland. Somerset's forces, numbering some sixteen thousand troops, met a much larger Scots army under the command of James Hamilton, the earl of Arran, at Pinkie, near Edinburgh. The English routed the Scots army, leaving an estimated ten thousand Scots dead and more than one thousand captured.

The defeat of the Scots at Pinkie did not deal a decisive blow to Scotland's independence, however, and Anglo-Scottish conflict continued through the rest of the 1540's. In 1548, Mary of Guise, James V's widow, convinced the Scottish parliament to nullify the marriage of Mary to Edward, which had been negotiated by Arran in his capacity as Scotland's regent. She also exacerbated Anglo-Scottish conflict by winning acceptance, on July 7, of the Treaty of Haddington, in which the French king Henry II (r. 1547-1559) guaranteed French military support as Scotland's "protector." Anglo-Scottish skirmishes increased in intensity, as French troops, imported by Mary, fought on Scottish and northern English soil. In 1557, the English ranged throughout Scotland, battling their Scots and French enemies in campaigns in the Firth of Forth, as well as through sieges at Aberlady, Boughty Crag, and Haddington.

In 1557, England began openly to support the Lords of the Congregation, a Protestant group led by John Knox that had initiated a civil war to overthrow Mary of Guise, now the queen regent. Although Mary gained support in the civil war from French forces, the reformers, empowered by English support, prevailed, successfully deposing Mary in 1559. Before her death in 1560, Mary of Guise convinced the competing Scottish factions to unite in loyalty to Mary, Queen of Scots. After Mary of Guise's death, England and France agreed to the Treaty of Edinburgh, which entailed the recognition of the sovereignty of Mary, Queen of Scots, and her first husband, Francis II, while also insisting on the legitimacy of Elizabeth I. The treaty was signed on July 6, 1560.

SIGNIFICANCE

Although the conflict between England and Scotland proved to be costly for both sides, the Scots clearly suffered greater losses in troops and prestige than their English counterparts. However, despite such resounding victories as the Battles of Flodden, Solway Moss, and Pinkie, the English failed to deal a decisive blow either to Scotland's independence or to its alliance with England's enemy, France. The death of James IV at Flodden, and James V's death shortly after Solway Moss, dealt serious blows to Scotland, each time plunging the country into the political instability of a realm without a ruler of age. The policy of the "Rough Wooing" of Mary, Queen of Scots, while it indeed led to numerous English victories, proved to be a very costly affair for the English, who needed to mobilize massive resources to supply invading armies and maintain numerous garrisons. England's obsessive attempt to secure Mary's marriage to Edward also led to a strengthening of the Franco-Scottish alliance, ensuring that England's actions against France would always be shadowed by the fear of threats coming from its own northern border.

Perhaps it was the rising tide of Reformation that offered England its best opportunity for decisive defeat of the Scots, insofar as it was only when England intervened in Knox's civil war against Mary of Guise that the English were able to overthrow an entire Scottish administration and gain a strong hand in future negotiations. The Treaty of Edinburgh of 1560, which accorded legitimacy both to Mary, Queen of Scots, and to Elizabeth I, perhaps had the most long-lasting impact, insofar as it was Mary's heir, James VI of Scotland, who would eventually bring about the union of the crowns of Scotland and England that had eluded English aggressors ever since Edward I's first attempts to add Scotland to England's imperial possessions.

—*Randy P. Schiff*

FURTHER READING

Barrell, A. D. M. *Medieval Scotland.* Cambridge, England: Cambridge University Press, 2000. Broad survey of the history of medieval Scotland, covering events up to the Reformation. Includes detailed discussion of the sixteenth century Anglo-Scottish conflict. Features maps and dynastic tables.

Fissel, Mark Charles. *English Warfare, 1511-1642.* New York: Routledge, 2001. A survey of English military history, featuring numerous maps and illustrative plates. Includes detailed treatment of Anglo-Scottish wars, placing military strategies in the broader context of England's other military campaigns.

Phillips, Gervase. *The Anglo-Scots Wars, 1513-1550: A Military History.* Rochester, N.Y.: Boydell Press, 1999. A survey of the armed conflicts opened up by the English victory at Flodden, focusing on technical matters of warfare. Features plates and maps.

Schama, Simon. *A History of Britain: At the Edge of the World?, 3000 B.C.-A.D. 1603.* New York: Hyperion, 2000. A broad survey of British history through the sixteenth century, featuring numerous color plates, maps, and genealogical tables. Includes detailed discussion of the underlying causes of Anglo-Scottish conflict.

SEE ALSO: Beginning 1485: The Tudors Rule England; Dec. 1, 1494: Poynings' Law; 1497: Cornish Rebellion; 1536 and 1543: Acts of Union Between England and Wales; 1544-1628: Anglo-French Wars; Feb. 27, 1545: Battle of Ancrum Moor; Jan. 28, 1547-July 6, 1553: Reign of Edward VI; 1558-1603: Reign of Elizabeth I; May, 1559-Aug., 1561: Scottish Reformation; Jan. 20, 1564: Peace of Troyes; July 29, 1567: James VI.

RELATED ARTICLES in *Great Lives from History: The Renaissance & Early Modern Era, 1454-1600:* Edward VI; Elizabeth I; Henry VIII; Catherine Howard; James IV; James V; Mary, Queen of Scots; Mary of Guise; Jane Seymour.

September 29, 1513
BALBOA REACHES THE PACIFIC OCEAN

Vasco Núñez de Balboa crossed the isthmus of Panama with 190 conquistadores and 600 Indians, and on September 29, 1513, he reached the coast of the Pacific Ocean, never before seen by a European. He named the newly discovered ocean Mar del Sur.

LOCALE: Panama, Darién Province, and the Pacific Ocean

CATEGORY: Exploration and discovery

KEY FIGURE

Vasco Núñez de Balboa (1475-1519), Spanish conquistador

SUMMARY OF EVENT

In 1501, nine years after Christopher Columbus had arrived at the Caribbean islands of Cuba and Hispaniola, the Spanish conquistador Rodrigo de Bastidas was the first to sail along the coasts of present-day Colombia and Panama as far as the Gulf of Darién. As the voyage clearly indicated that they were traveling along the extremities of a new continent, they called Panama *tierra firme* (literally "solid ground" or "continental country"). One of Rodrigo's companions was Vasco Núñez de Balboa, who after this voyage settled in Hispaniola.

In 1510, financial problems forced him to leave again. He joined a group of soldiers to go to Colombia, where another Spanish discoverer, Alonso de Ojeda, was experiencing serious problems with the Indians. After finding only forty-one survivors in San Sebastián (Colombia), Balboa went to the south of Panama, a region called Darién by the Indians, where he founded the first permanent European settlement, Santa Maria de l'Antigua, on the bay of Urabá in the border area of Colombia and Panama. There he proclaimed himself *adelantado* (governor) under the auspices of the Spanish crown, although two other representatives of the Spanish government were already present in Panama.

Contemporary historians note his tolerance, especially toward the Indians, one of whom informed Balboa of a region rich in gold, situated to the west beyond the jungles and mountains and forming the coastline of another ocean. Always on the lookout for gold and fearful in his own political circumstances, Balboa gathered 190 Spanish soldiers and about 600 Indians to find the "other ocean" to which others had referred.

In late August or early September of 1513, Balboa set out from the western point of the Gulf of Darién, the bay of Urabá, and marched for days on end through jungle and swamps, over the hills and mountains of the Cordilleras. On the way he had to fight off hostile native tribes and lost many soldiers and Indians—not only in attacks by the native population but also through disease.

Balboa's expedition had not started out from the narrowest part of the isthmus, which today lies between the two exit points of the Panama Canal. Instead, he went westward from the southern bay of Urabá along the delta of the Atrato River and then through jungles and swamps and over mountains. The length of the isthmus from Darién to the Pacific is about 50 to 60 miles (80 to 100 kilometers).

Several sixteenth century historians reported on Balboa's expedition. The best accounts are by Spanish chronicler Gonzalo Fernández de Oviedo y Valdés (who was in Hispaniola at the time as a trade inspector for Spain) in volume 3 of his *Historia general y natural de las Indias occidentales* (1535), and by the Italian historian Pietro Martire d'Anghiera (Petrus Martyr Anglerius) in his *De orbe novo* (1530). In Anghiera's history of the New World, the story of Balboa is related, in Latin, in the first book of the third decade. Minor differences occur in these accounts, but in general there is agreement on the main events, which are treated as one of the great achievements of humankind.

It took Balboa and his men nearly a full month (September, 1513) to march across the isthmus. Balboa's descent to the ocean took four days. The aforementioned historians report that he reached the Pacific on September 29, 1513, after having fought off Indians at the coast. When amicable relations were subsequently established, these Indians assisted him in exploring the sea gulf and coastal region.

On Tuesday, September 25, Balboa had faced the last hills and mountains before reaching the ocean. Informed by one of the Indians that there would be no further obstacles ahead, Balboa halted his column, mounted the hill alone, and from its summit, at ten o'clock in the morning, became the first European to see the jungles sweeping down to the seacoast. In the morning sun, he gazed on the glittering waters of a "new" ocean, which Europeans had known before only through rumored reports. Balboa called his men to come up, and they praised God; believing that the waters of the new ocean extended as far as India and China, he named it Mar del Sur (literally, "sea of the south").

Anghiera reports in *De orbe novo* that Balboa, standing on the hilltop, addressed his companions after their terrible journey through the wild jungles; their pride in surveying the vast expanse of new ocean is duly emphasized. In one passage, Anghiera compares Balboa with the Carthaginian Hannibal as related in the third decade, book 21, of Livy's *Ab urbe condita libri* (c. 26 B.C.E.; *The History of Rome*, 1600), where the Carthaginian commander stands on an Alpine crag and points out to his Punic troops, exhausted and utterly demoralized after their long march over the Alps, the Italian plains extending below.

In January of 1514, Balboa returned to Darién on the Atlantic coast of Panama. He had taken another route and used as guides local Indians from the friendly tribes of the Pacific coast. On his return to Santa Maria de l'Antigua, he sent dispatches to the Spanish king reporting his discovery of the Mar del Sur. However, these reports reached Spain too late: The king had already sent Pedro Arias d'Ávila as the new governor of Panama and Darién. The latter reached Panama and the settlement of Santa Maria de l'Antigua with a large fleet and new soldiers in the summer of 1514. At first, he made Balboa his deputy, but shortly afterward, he had the illustrious discoverer of the Mar del Sur apprehended. The officer who carried out the arrest on orders from d'Ávila was Francisco Pizarro, who later would conquer Peru.

Balboa was accused of high treason, found guilty, and beheaded with four of his officers in January, 1519. D'Ávila left the settlement of Santa Maria de l'Antigua, founded by Balboa, because his new Spanish contingent encountered severe difficulties with the climate. In addition, a virulent disease, perhaps beriberi, decimated the European inhabitants. D'Ávila crossed the isthmus and founded a new settlement on the Pacific coast near modern Panama City. With the subsequent establishment of a new port, Nombre de Dios, on the Caribbean coast, a new route had been found to reach the Pacific Ocean—the same way used some four hundred years later for the Panama Canal.

The settlement of Nombre de Dios was at that time the most important Atlantic port on the Pacific. A road was constructed, and its pavements still survive. During the sixteenth and seventeenth centuries, small vessels traveling westward from the end of this road could navigate some rivers, thereafter transporting their cargoes by mule to Old Panama on the Pacific.

SIGNIFICANCE

Among the early achievements of the Spanish and Portuguese explorers, the discovery in 1513 of the Mar del Sur contributed to a more accurate understanding of the earth as a globe, of continents, and of oceans. In 1500, Pedro Álvares Cabral, Amerigo Vespucci, and others could show that there was a southern continent connected to a continent in the north. Balboa's discovery of the "other ocean" demonstrated that two continents were joined by a small and narrow strip of land. No one at the time knew whether it was possible to sail by ship from one ocean to the other.

Seven years after Balboa's discovery, the Portuguese

Balboa and his crew appear overjoyed at reaching the Pacific Ocean near the isthmus of Panama, the first time the eastern coast of this ocean had been spotted by Europeans. (R. S. Peale and J. A. Hill)

explorer Ferdinand Magellan sailed through the *estrecho*, now known as the Strait of Magellan, the waterway leading round from the tip of Argentina to Chile, from the Atlantic Ocean to the Mar del Sur. The peaceful sea at the end of the passage he called the Mare Pacificum, or Pacific Ocean, the name still used today for the same ocean Balboa had dubbed the Mar del Sur.

—*Gerhard Petersmann*

FURTHER READING

Anderson, Charles L. G. *Life and Letters of Vasco Núñez de Balboa*. Westport, Conn.: Greenwood Press, 1941. Represents sources on the life of Balboa and gives both text and interpretations of his letters.

Romoli, Kathleen. *Balboa of Darién: Discoverer of the Pacific*. Garden City, N.Y.: Doubleday, 1953. The standard biography in English.

Zweig, Stefan. *The Tide of Fortune: Twelve Historical Miniatures*. 1929. Translated by P. Eden and P. Cedar. New York: Viking Press, 1940. The first of Zweig's

miniatures is dedicated to the great moment when Balboa discovered the Pacific Ocean.

SEE ALSO: Oct. 12, 1492: Columbus Lands in the Americas; 1493-1521: Ponce de León's Voyages; 1502-1520: Reign of Montezuma II; 1519-1522: Magellan Expedition Circumnavigates the Globe; Apr., 1519-Aug., 1521: Cortés Conquers Aztecs in Mexico; Aug., 1523: Franciscan Missionaries Arrive in Mexico; 1527-1547: Maya Resist Spanish Incursions in Yucatán; 1528-1536: Narváez's and Cabeza de Vaca's Expeditions; May 28, 1539-Sept. 10, 1543: De Soto's North American Expedition; Feb. 23, 1540-Oct., 1542: Coronado's Southwest Expedition; 1542-1543: The New Laws of Spain; 1545-1548: Silver Is Discovered in Spanish America; 1552: Las Casas Publishes *The Tears of the Indians*.

RELATED ARTICLE in *Great Lives from History: The Renaissance & Early Modern Era, 1454-1600:* Vasco Núñez de Balboa.

1514
HUNGARIAN PEASANTS' REVOLT

High taxes and intense labor, among other reasons, led to the Hungarian Peasants' Revolt, which in turn triggered centuries of political repression and internal weaknesses, making Hungary vulnerable to foreign invasion and exploitation.

LOCALE: Hungary

CATEGORIES: Wars, uprisings, and civil unrest; social reform; government and politics

KEY FIGURES

György Dózsa (György Szekely; 1470-1514), leader of the peasant revolt

Tamas Bakócz (1442-1521), archbishop of Hungary

John Zápolya (1487-1540), Hungarian magnate and later king of Hungary as John I, r. 1526-1540

Vladislav II (Władisław Jagiełło II; 1456-1516), king of Bohemia, r. 1471-1516, and king of Hungary, r. 1490-1516

István Werbőczi (1458-1541), Hungarian lawyer

SUMMARY OF EVENT

The Peasants' Revolt of 1514 is considered the most violent rural uprising in Hungarian history. Desperate peasants, laboring under avaricious landlords intent on profit-

ing from the rising food prices in European markets, found what little freedom they had harshly restricted. They could keep very little of the foodstuffs they produced; in addition, they were highly taxed. The traditional right to change landlords was revoked, so that virtually all freedom of movement became prohibited.

Peasants who had done well and had moved to market towns suspected that any further financial or political gains would be nullified. Indeed, the better-off class of peasants, those who had emancipated themselves from the worse feudal conditions and were able to settle on an annual basis the dues owed to their landlords, suddenly found themselves coerced to a lower and more regimented level. Peasants, no matter what their plight, could expect little help or attention from King Vladislav II, their dispirited king, known for his melancholy and indecisiveness.

The peasants seemed motivated by what might almost be called a holy war against the landlords. In the spring of 1514, Archbishop Tamas Bakócz returned from Rome as papal legate for eastern Europe to raise an army of fighters for a crusade against the Ottoman Turks. He enlisted the popular Franciscan friars in his mission at the very time that the peasants were gathering to attack the landlords. The crusader army, estimated at twenty thousand, confronting the threat of a peasants' revolt, was disbanded by royal decree. The king and the nobility feared that the crusader army (made up largely of peasants) would turn against them. Landlords also resisted the call for a crusader army, angry that a crusade meant the absence of the peasants from their fields. To many peasants, however, the landlords were viewed as treacherous and unfaithful—unwilling to defend their religion or their country. In this respect, the landlords were considered worse than the Ottomans, against whom the crusade had been launched.

The crusading peasants refused to disband their army when ordered to do so by the king. In both the market towns and the provinces, they united instead under a leader named Dózsa, a soldier and petty nobleman, and attacked the lords. The peasants continued to stipulate their loyalty to the king and to the archbishop, who had gone on recruiting peasants in spite of the royal cancellation of the crusade. This peasant movement was supported by leaders in the agricultural towns, including priests loyal to the archbishop. Those unwilling to join the peasant crusade were punished as traitors. In the spring of 1514, masses of peasants attacked and defeated an army raised by the landlords and the nobility. For two months, peasants plundered and burned manor houses and castles, committing fearful atrocities against the nobility and their families. The well-organized revolt spread from the provinces to an area near the capital, Buda, in northern and northeastern Hungary, and around Varad, in the south.

An alarmed King Vladislav joined the nobility in seeking aid from John Zápolya, a powerful magnate in Transylvania, who later became king of Hungary as John I. Zápolya ruthlessly put down the revolt. By July of 1514, some seventy thousand peasants had been killed. A deliberate policy of extermination was practiced, with one in every ten peasants marked for murder. Dózsa and his followers were captured and executed. Accused of an attempt to usurp King Vladislav's crown, Dózsa was "enthroned" on a stake, and his starving retinue was compelled to bite into his burning flesh. Dózsa's body was then quartered and displayed on the gates of towns across Hungary. Although Hungary has seen much violence, scholars of Hungarian history consider Dózsa's fate a particularly gruesome and horrible event.

In the wake of their hysteria over the power shown by the peasantry, the nobility took steps to consolidate their victory by promulgating the doctrine of a Hungarian lawyer, István Werbőczi. This doctrine identified the one and indivisible nobility, *una eademque nobilitas*, with the Hungarian nation. A nobleman, rich or poor, whether or not a native speaker of Hungarian, became a master of the Hungarian people. The nobleman constituted the only category of free person and citizen. Everyone else was deemed plebeian, "part of the wretched tax-paying mass." By definition, the serfs were tied to the land, and though the harshest interpretations of this doctrine were abandoned by the 1550's, it was nevertheless true that all forms of government and the legal justice system were controlled by the aristocracy.

The ascendancy of the nobility also meant that the king's power had been limited, and he could not—even if he wished to do so—act on behalf of the peasantry. Vladislav II, a weak king, merely abetted the nobility's power grab. From the point of view of the nobility, they had no choice, since the king's government was riddled with corruption, and by the 1490's, he had allowed the Turks to occupy the Hungarian province of Bosnia. Many Hungarian officials were then forced to adopt Islam as their religion to preserve their lives and properties. Long after Vladislav's death, Hungary was vulnerable to Turkish invasion and to the loss of its territory.

SIGNIFICANCE

The revolt resulted in a meeting of the Hungarian Diet in the fall of 1514, enacting laws that enforced the subservience of Hungarian peasants for more than three hundred years. The peasants were deprived of the right to bear arms, and they were required to pay considerable damages for the consequences of their revolt. These laws were not executed uniformly; at times, the most onerous of the prohibitions were suspended, especially when the peasants were needed to deter the Ottomans from encroaching on Hungarian territory. In periods of robust economic development, however, the laws were reinstituted, and the exploitation of the peasantry continued until well into the nineteenth century.

Quite aside from the catastrophic aftermath for the peasants, the 1514 revolt was one of the events that "swept Hungary away from the midstream of European development," as historian Paul Ignotus put it. After 1526, the country split into three parts. In the west and north, the Habsburgs ruled; the Turks occupied a significant part of the country's geographical center; and Transylvania in the east became a fairly independent principality. Such divisions, however, were loosely observed and often a territory might be under the rule of competing powers.

Hungary was deprived of almost all economic mobility and political development because of its crude division into two rigid social classes. As a result, Hungary was unable to compete with its more dynamic European neighbors. Indeed, historian Ivan Volgyes argued that the rift in classes and the split between rural and urban areas remain factors in contemporary Hungary.

—Carl Rollyson

FURTHER READING

Engel, Pál. *The Realm of St. Stephen: A History of Medieval Hungary, 895-1526.* Translated by Tamás Pálosfalvi. Edited by Andrew Ayton. New York: I. B. Tauris, 2001. Places the peasant revolt in the context of the development of the Hungarian state in the Middle Ages. Discusses the role played by the Franciscans in the rebellion.

Evans, R. J. W. *The Making of the Habsburg Monarchy, 1550-1700.* Oxford, England: Clarendon Press, 1979. Chapter 6, "Hungary: Limited Rejection," picks up the fate of Hungary a full generation after the peasants' revolt, but the overview provided of the country's historic role within the Habsburg empire provides a context for assessing the consequences of the 1514 revolt.

Housley, Norman. "Crusading as Social Revolt: The Hungarian Peasant Uprising of 1514." In *Crusading and Warfare in Medieval and Renaissance Europe.* Burlington, Vt.: Ashgate/Variorum, 2001. Investigates the role of the crusades and the crusader army in the uprising.

Ignotus, Paul. *Hungary.* New York: Praeger, 1972. Chapter 1, "The Foundation of European Hungary," gives a sharply analytical and succinct account of the revolt and its consequences.

Josika-Herczeg, Imre. *Hungary After a Thousand Years.* New York: American Hungarian Daily, 1934. Chapter 3, "From the Hunyadis to the Habsburgs," provides a finely etched picture of King Vladislav II and a precise explanation of the corruption and injustice that provoked the peasants' revolt.

Kosary, Dominic. *A History of Hungary.* New York: Benjamin Franklin Bibliophile Society, 1941. Reprint. New York: Arno Press, 1971. Chapter 4, "The Renaissance Power and Its Decline, 1458-1526," presents clear portraits of major figures, such as Bakócz, Zápolya, and Werbőczi.

Rady, Martyn. *Nobility, Land, and Service in Medieval Hungary.* New York: Palgrave, 2000. A study of the medieval Hungarian system of landholding and nobility that led to the peasants' revolt.

Sugar, Peter F., Peter Hanak, and Tibor Frank, eds. *A History of Hungary.* Bloomington: Indiana University Press, 1990. Chapter 7, "The Late Medieval Period, 1382-1562" by János Bak, gives a short but detailed account of the events leading up to and following the revolt, including an analysis of the import of Werbőczi's legal doctrine.

Volgyes, Ivan. *Hungary: A Nation of Contradictions.* Boulder, Colo.: Westview Press, 1982. Chapter 1, "The Magyars: From Roots to Realism," gives a vivid sense of how disastrous the 1514 revolt was, not only for the peasants but also for the entire Hungarian nation.

SEE ALSO: 1458-1490: Hungarian Renaissance; June, 1524-July, 1526: German Peasants' War; 1526-1547: Hungarian Civil Wars; Aug. 29, 1526: Battle of Mohács; 1593-1606: Ottoman-Austrian War.

RELATED ARTICLES in *Great Lives from History: The Renaissance & Early Modern Era, 1454-1600:* Bayezid II; Matthias I Corvinus; Rudolf II; Sigismund I, the Old; Süleyman the Magnificent; Vladislav II.

1514-1598
PORTUGUESE REACH CHINA

The arrival of the Portuguese in China heralded the beginning of European influence in East Asia, although for the first three centuries that influence had minimal impact on China.

LOCALE: Southeast Asia, Macao, southeast China
CATEGORIES: Diplomacy and international relations; exploration and discovery; trade and commerce

KEY FIGURES

Tomé Pires (c. 1468-c. 1540), author, merchant, and diplomat who led Portugal's first delegation to China
Matteo Ricci (Li Madou, Li Ma-tou; 1552-1610), Jesuit scholar and missionary
Alessandro Valignano (1539-1606), Jesuit missionary whose school at Macao influenced generations of Jesuits working in Asia
Xu Guangqi (Hsü Kuang-ch'i; 1562-1633), the first translator of European scientific works into Chinese

SUMMARY OF EVENT

The Portuguese, from the western extreme of Europe, became the first Europeans to sail around the Cape of Good Hope when Vasco da Gama sailed around it in 1497 (Bartolomeu Dias had only reached it in 1487-1488). They quickly established themselves as the dominant naval power in the Indian Ocean and later the Far East, displacing Arab, Indian, and Chinese merchants. By 1510, the Portuguese had solidified their control of Goa on the coast of India and were moving on to Sri Lanka and pushing into the Far East. In 1511, they took control of the strategic island of Melaka from the Arabs, in the straits between the peninsula of Malay and the island of Sumatra.

In 1514, the first contact between the Portuguese and China occurred when a commercial expedition from Melaka reached China. Local Chinese officials forbade the Portuguese from selling their wares on shore, but Chinese merchants with vessels bought the goods ship side, making this early commercial contact very successful for the Portuguese. China's Ming officials, however, were angered by the unauthorized and unwelcome commerce with these new "ocean devils," as they called the Portuguese. The Portuguese built a fort on Lintin island, at the delta of the Zhu Jiang, or Pearl, River (also called the Canton and sometimes called the West or Xi River), 70 miles (113 kilometers) from the city of Guangzhou (Canton, also called Yangcheng), further enraging Ming officials.

The Portuguese sensed that their greatest success depended on the cooperation of the Ming government, and with this goal in mind, Tomé Pires in 1517 led the first official mission to China. At first the mission went well, with the city of Guangzhou welcoming Pires and allowing the establishment of a trading post. However, Ming officials were not disposed to allow the post to remain, and Chinese troops destroyed it. Pires was imprisoned and died in Jiangsu around 1540. However, the commercial success of the post led to a new post being established almost immediately afterward.

The entrance of the Portuguese into China was a slow process fraught with mutual misunderstanding. The Chinese saw the Portuguese as "sea barbarians," at first little different from other "barbarian" peoples outside the Chinese empire. However, the Portuguese quickly established themselves as different, winning a grudging respect for their naval skills and military might. Nevertheless, the Chinese still considered them to be barbarians; official Chinese histories mention that the Portuguese ate Chinese children, a product of the confusion that occurred when Portuguese bought children for use as slaves.

Although China tried to keep the Portuguese out, Western naval superiority prevented the Chinese from dislodging them. In 1557, the Portuguese were permitted to settle on Macao at the Zhu Jiang delta in return for an annual payment. In Macao, situated on a spit of land separated by a wall, the Portuguese exercised some of the trappings of sovereignty, although formal annexation did not occur until 1887. The Portuguese settlement in Macao allowed the Chinese to limit contact between Westerners and Chinese and gave the Portuguese a secure base for further commercial and missionary penetration.

The Portuguese never involved themselves directly in the control of land for the purpose of extraction. Instead, those places they did control, such as Melaka and Macao, were strategically situated ports that allowed them to dominate sea lanes. The Portuguese were predominantly traders, not colonizers, planters, or manufacturers. They showed no inclination to dominate territory beyond these ports and their immediate environs. They had little to offer in exchange for the spices and other goods much desired in Europe, and so they established themselves as the major shippers of goods between various Asian nations. Profits from this trade allowed the Portuguese to purchase spices and other goods for shipment to Europe at even greater profit.

Still, trade was not the only reason for Portuguese interest in the Far East. The Portuguese also used Macao as a base to penetrate other areas of the Far East for missionary work. From Macao, Alessandro Valignano undertook three trips to Japan (1579-1582, 1590-1592, and 1598-1603), where he urged his fellow Jesuits to adapt to Japanese culture and to learn their language. The prospect of new converts to Christianity inspired Portuguese involvement in the largest prize of all, China. The most successful of the early Europeans in China, Matteo Ricci, was a product of Valignano's training center on Macao.

Ricci was an Italian Jesuit thoroughly educated in theology, the humanities, and science. He reached Macao in 1582 and began almost immediately to immerse himself in learning the dominant spoken Chinese language, what would be called "Mandarin" by the Portuguese. He also diligently studied written Chinese. After a year in Macao, he was allowed to enter China proper. There he helped found four Christian missions. Part of his success as a missionary stemmed from his ability to adapt his Western Christianity to Chinese sensibilities. Some of this adaption was superficial, as when he adopted the dress and manners of a Confucian scholar. Also, his curly beard fit the Chinese image of a wise man. However, his knowledge of science and geography, and more important, his skill at presenting his knowledge to the Chinese, earned for him a respect few foreigners would ever attain in China. In 1601, he was granted permission to reside in Beijing, with a stipend from the imperial court. His knowledge of astronomy was perhaps most appreciated by his Chinese hosts, but his skills at mathematics, physics, and cartography also brought him great advantage. He produced a map of the known world for the Chinese, diplomatically placing China at the center, which greatly increased the Chinese understanding of the world beyond the Far East.

Despite Ricci's great learning in the sciences, his real talent was theological, as shown when he adapted Christianity to Chinese Confucian ideals. He downplayed many of the tenets of the Christian religion, such as the nature of God, the Crucifixion, and the spiritual equality of humans before God. Instead he presented Christianity as more of an ethical system quite compatible with Confucianism. Some Chinese scholars did convert. The most important of the early converts was Xu Guangqi, who translated into Chinese many European works on mathe-

matics, astronomy, hydraulics, and geography, thereby making much European learning available to the Chinese for the first time. The later rejection of much of Ricci's theology, after a great controversy within the Catholic Church during the seventeenth and eighteenth centuries, caused tension with the emperors of the Qing Dynasty and created much confusion in official China as to the nature of Christianity.

SIGNIFICANCE

Although the Portuguese soon lost their dominant position in the Far East to the Dutch and later the British, their pioneering work had lasting results. European influence in the East Asia would continue until it was replaced by European domination in the late nineteenth century, which in turn lasted until after World War II. Portuguese efforts to convert the Chinese to Christianity proved less successful, as Confucianism, Buddhism, and ancestor worship proved resistant to the teachings of Christian missionaries, and the Chinese government's official opposition further limited Christian inroads.

In other ways, Portuguese influence continued. Despite the relative decline of Portugal as a world power after the fifteenth century, Portugal kept many of its territorial possessions—not only Macao and East Timor in the Indonesian archipelago but also many small colonies in South Asia and Africa, which would provide convenient stops and later coaling stations for centuries. Although few Portuguese came to settle the kingdom's possessions, merchants and soldiers had a long tradition of intermarrying with local women, creating a population of Catholic, Portuguese-speaking Portuguese subjects of mostly Far East extraction.

—*Barry M. Stentiford*

FURTHER READING

Boxer, C. R. *The Portuguese Seaborne Empire, 1415-1825.* New York: Knopf, 1969. A solid introduction to the Portuguese commercial empire, from its inception to its stagnation and later eclipse by other European empires.

Criveller, Gianni. *Preaching Christ in Late Ming China: Jesuits' Presentation of Christ from Matteo Ricci to Giulio Aleni.* Taipei: Taipei Ricci Institute, 1997. A history of early Christian missionary work in China, with emphasis on the missionaries' success in presenting some of the moral aspects of Christianity and a mixed reaction to other aspects of Christianity.

Kim, Sangkeun. *Strange Names of God: The Missionary Translation of the Divine Name and the Chinese Re-*

sponse to Matteo Ricci's "Shangi" in Late Ming China, 1583-1644. New York: Peter Lang, 2004. Explores the difficulty of translating the Western concept of an all-powerful, all-knowing monotheistic god into something understandable by and agreeable to the Chinese.

Moran J. F. *The Japanese and the Jesuits: Alessandro Valignano in the Sixteenth Century.* New York: Routledge, 1993. Shows the relative success of Valignano in Japan, based on some values of the Japanese nobility and clergy that they shared with the Jesuits. However, other, incompatible values limited that success.

Spence, Jonathan D. *The Memory Palace of Matteo Ricci.* New York: Viking, 1984. A comparative history with emphasis on the problems of presenting Christianity to a Confucian society.

Subrahmanyan, S. *The Portuguese Empire in Asia.* London: Oxford University Press, 1993. Focuses on the establishment of the Portuguese trade empire.

SEE ALSO: 1481-1482: Founding of Elmina; c. 1485: Portuguese Establish a Foothold in Africa; 1491-1545: Christianity Is Established in the Kingdom of Kongo; Jan., 1498: Portuguese Reach the Swahili Coast; 1500-1530's: Portugal Begins to Colonize Brazil; 1505-1515: Portuguese Viceroys Establish Overseas Trade Empire; 1511-c. 1515: Melaka Falls to the Portuguese; Autumn, 1543: Europeans Begin Trade with Japan; 1552: Struggle for the Strait of Hormuz; 1580-1581: Spain Annexes Portugal; 1583-1610: Matteo Ricci Travels to Beijing.

RELATED ARTICLES in *Great Lives from History: The Renaissance & Early Modern Era, 1454-1600:* Gregory XIII; Tomé Pires; Matteo Ricci.

1515-1529
WOLSEY SERVES AS LORD CHANCELLOR AND CARDINAL

Wolsey helped England become a European power, transformed the legal system in England so that the rule of law applied to all, except the king, and, after failing to use his position as cardinal to secure an annulment of the king's marriage to Catherine of Aragon, set in motion the king's rejection of the pope's authority and the establishment of Protestantism as England's primary religion.

LOCALE: England
CATEGORIES: Government and politics; religion

KEY FIGURES

Cardinal Thomas Wolsey (1471/1472-1530), lord
    chancellor of England and cardinal, 1515-1529
Henry VIII (1491-1547), king of England, r. 1509-1547
Catherine of Aragon (1485-1536), first wife of Henry
    VIII
Anne Boleyn (c. 1500/1501-1536), second wife of
    Henry VIII
Charles V (1500-1558), Holy Roman Emperor,
    r. 1519-1556, and king of Spain, r. 1516-1556, as
    Charles I
Clement VII (Giulio de' Medici; 1478-1534), Roman
    Catholic pope, 1523-1534
Leo X (Giovanni de' Medici; 1475-1521), Roman
    Catholic pope, 1513-1521
Francis I (1494-1547), king of France, r. 1515-1547

SUMMARY OF EVENT

Next to King Henry VIII, Thomas Wolsey was the most influential man in England for a period of approximately twenty years. At the time that Henry succeeded to the throne on the death of his father, Henry VII, in 1509, Wolsey, ordained a priest in 1498, already had achieved national prominence. After serving as a chaplain to Henry Dean, archbishop of Canterbury, Wolsey became Henry VII's personal chaplain in 1507. The new king was well aware of Wolsey's abilities and wasted no time in securing his services, appointing him royal almoner (distributor of alms, or charity) in 1509.

Wolsey's rise to both ecclesiastical and secular power was rapid. In 1514, he was consecrated bishop of Lincoln and archbishop of York and, in 1515, was made both a cardinal by Pope Leo X and lord chancellor of England by King Henry.

As lord chancellor and the king's top adviser, Wolsey formulated a complex foreign policy designed to make England the chief power broker of Europe. Skilled in utilizing a combination of diplomacy and military force, Wolsey attempted to play against each other the two main European challengers for supremacy, France and the Holy Roman Empire, to the benefit of his own nation.

Wolsey had demonstrated his acumen in geopolitics in 1513 by organizing the king's successful victory over the French in what is known as the Battle of the Spurs.

Cardinal Thomas Wolsey. (Hulton|Archive by Getty Images)

With the almost simultaneous triumph against the Scots at Flodden Field, England was secure at home and a power to be reckoned with on the Continent.

With Wolsey heavily influential in shaping national and international policy, England shifted steadily between alliances with France, led by King Francis I, and the Holy Roman Empire under Charles V of the Habsburg royal family. Wolsey organized consecutive meetings for Henry with the two continental rulers in 1520, including an opulent three-week session with Francis, known to history as the Field of Cloth of Gold. The meetings resulted in a treaty of friendship with France, a treaty with the Holy Roman Emperor a month later, and Charles and Henry agreeing to forsake any treaties with France for two years.

Neither European power could take England for granted. For example, after initially maintaining neutrality in the war that began in 1521, England entered against France in 1523. Yet, with Wolsey continuing to provide diplomatic and military guidance, by 1528 England was supporting France against the Holy Roman Empire.

Wolsey's international efforts on behalf of Henry required considerable revenue, and the lord chancellor had mixed results finding the necessary money. He suc-

ceeded in acquiring from Parliament a continuing subsidy in 1513 and engineered a major administrative success in 1522 with a new assessment of the nation's wealth, which produced an additional 255,000 pounds. Wolsey's efforts in 1523 to raise money for the war with France elicited a substantial sum, though less than Wolsey had urged. One of his largest failures in securing funding occurred when he sought an "amicable loan" from the nobility in 1525 to further the nation's military effort against France, a reaction at least partly attributable to the nobility's resentment of Wolsey.

As lord chancellor, Wolsey was the most influential member of the king's Privy Council. In that role, he sought to further the king's welfare, not that of the nobles. One of his most significant and far reaching domestic efforts was to transform the judicial system, extending the authority of the star chamber (the king's council functioning as a court) over the nobility. When the star chamber was faced with a flood of cases, Wolsey delegated the handling of many cases to local courts staffed with Wolsey's appointees, thus bringing the nobles throughout England more firmly under royal control. Another Wolsey innovation was the court of requests, which was charged with handling suits involving the poor.

Cardinal Wolsey also was the leader of the church in England. His appointment in 1518 as papal legate *a latere*, that is, the pope's personal representative, established his preeminence over the archbishop of Canterbury as well. Of special interest to both Henry and Wolsey was England's monastic system, which Henry viewed as too independent financially and politically. Anticipating the later, large-scale dissolution of the monasteries, Wolsey suppressed close to thirty monasteries, using their revenue to create two new colleges—one at Ipswich, which did not long survive its founder's own fall, and another, Cardinal's College at Oxford, which did survive, although as Christ Church College.

Wolsey's ecclesiastical stature led him to entertain some hope of being elected pope on the deaths of Leo X in 1521 and Adrian VI in 1523. In each case, the anticipated and necessary support from Charles V did not materialize. Had Wolsey been elected pope, he almost surely would have granted Henry his desired annulment from his first wife, Catherine of Aragon.

Wolsey's downfall was the result of his inability to obtain a papal annulment of Henry and Catherine's marriage. Henry's reasons for seeking the annulment included Catherine's failure to produce a son who would survive to prevent future dynastic conflict, growing fear that God was thus punishing Henry for marrying his brother's widow, and the king's passion for Anne Boleyn.

By 1527, Charles V had extended military control over Rome and, therefore, over Pope Clement VII. The fact that Charles was the nephew of Queen Catherine, along with periodic military conflicts between Henry and Charles, ensured that the pope would have little freedom to decide in Henry's favor.

Wolsey convened a secret ecclesiastical hearing on May 17, 1527, to address what became known as the "King's Great Matter." Failing to resolve the issue, Wolsey turned to Rome, but Pope Clement sent Cardinal Lorenzo Campeggio, the bishop of Salisbury, to try the case with Wolsey. However, the pope withdrew Campeggio in July, 1529, suggesting alternatives unacceptable to Henry, such as merely taking Anne Boleyn as a mistress with the pope's promise to legitimize any children from the union or having the king's illegitimate son, Henry Fitzroy, duke of Richmond, wed Henry and Catherine's daughter, Mary.

Within three months of Campeggio's departure, Wolsey was charged, because of his status as papal legate, with violating the ancient Statute of Praemunire, which outlawed direct papal jurisdiction. His real crime, of course, was his failure to secure the annulment. He was stripped of most of his positions and possessions, with the exception of the archbishopric of York. However, the king did not keep Wolsey long in Yorkshire. The fallen statesman was arrested on November 4, 1530, the victim of Anne Boleyn's campaigning against him, and accusations (generally believed based on faked evidence) of treasonably conspiring with Francis I. Falling ill on his journey to the Tower of London, Wolsey died en route at Leicester Abbey on November 29, 1530, where he was buried.

SIGNIFICANCE

Cardinal Wolsey is often viewed, as in Samuel Johnson's poem "The Vanity of Human Wishes: The Tenth Satire of Juvenal Imitated" (1749), as an exemplar of how far and fast mortals can fall when they put their hopes in earthly power and success. Moralists like to quote Wolsey's supposed deathbed admission that had he served God as well as he served Henry, he would not have died in lonely disgrace. In reality, Wolsey's significance far transcends such moral stereotypes.

Wolsey helped to make England a major international power. The path that he helped to steer would be firmly secured in the next generation with the long and successful reign of Elizabeth I, daughter of Henry VIII and Anne Boleyn. Wolsey also helped to unify the nation under royal rule by diminishing the legal and political independence of the nobility. He also helped to set in motion the suppression of English monasteries that would accelerate after his death.

Finally, Wolsey's failure to secure Henry's desired annulment played a decisive role in the king's decision to reject the authority of the pope and establish himself as head of the Church of England, thus extending the Protestant Reformation from the continent to England and permanently changing the nation's main religion.

—*Edward J. Rielly*

FURTHER READING

Belloc, Hilaire. *Wolsey*. Philadelphia: J. B. Lippincott, 1930. A classic account of Wolsey intended to establish character and motives rather than present exhaustive details.

Cavendish, George. *The Life and Death of Cardinal Wolsey: Two Early Tudor Lives*. Edited by Richard S. Sylvester and Davis P. Harding. New Haven, Conn.: Yale University Press, 1962. Valuable for the first-hand knowledge Cavendish had as a personal attendant on Wolsey.

Ridley, Jasper. *Statesman and Saint: Cardinal Wolsey, Sir Thomas More, and the Politics of Henry VIII*. New York: Viking Press, 1983. A reexamination of two consecutive lords chancellor within the context of the king's political demands.

Weir, Alison. *Six Wives of Henry VIII*. 1992. Reprint. New York: Grove Press, 2000. A detailed study of Henry's wives, including Catherine of Aragon and Anne Boleyn, which draws heavily on primary sources.

Wilson, Derek A. *In the Lion's Court: Power, Ambition, and Sudden Death in the Reign of Henry VIII*. New York: St. Martin's Press, 2002. Considers six key men in the political world of Henry's England, including Wolsey.

SEE ALSO: Beginning 1485: The Tudors Rule England; June 5-24, 1520: Field of Cloth of Gold; Dec. 18, 1534: Act of Supremacy; 1558-1603: Reign of Elizabeth I.

RELATED ARTICLES in *Great Lives from History: The Renaissance & Early Modern Era, 1454-1600:* Anne Boleyn; Catherine of Aragon; Charles V; Clement VII; Thomas Cromwell; Francis I; Henry VIII; Leo X; Sir Thomas More; Cardinal Thomas Wolsey.

September 13-14, 1515
BATTLE OF MARIGNANO

A battle between French and Swiss forces during the third French invasion of Italy, Marignano is noteworthy as the first significant defeat for the Swiss in two hundred years. The defeated Swiss withdrew permanently from Italy, beginning the tradition of Swiss neutrality.

LOCALE: Marignano (now Melegnano, Italy)
CATEGORY: Wars, uprisings, and civil unrest; expansion and land acquisition

KEY FIGURES

Francis I (1494-1547), king of France, r. 1515-1547
Leo X (Giovanni de' Medici; 1475-1521), Roman Catholic pope, 1513-1521
Massimiliano Sforza (1493-1530), duke of Milan, r. 1512-1515
Ferdinand II (1452-1516), king of Aragon, r. 1479-1516, king of Castile, r. 1474-1504, king of Sicily, r. 1468-1516, and king of Naples as Ferdinand III, r. 1504-1516
Bartolomeo d'Alviano (1455-1515), Venetian commander
Matthäus Schiner (c. 1465-1522), Catholic cardinal and Swiss statesman
Huldrych Zwingli (1484-1531), Swiss theologian and church reformer

SUMMARY OF EVENT

Following the Battle of Ravenna in April of 1512, the French, though victorious, were forced to withdraw from Italy to regroup and recover from their losses. As a result, France was unable to retain much of the territory it had won in its second invasion of Italy. By the end of 1512, little of Italy remained in French hands. The Swiss, a papal ally, occupied Milan and restored the former ducal dynasty in the person of Massimiliano Sforza. Meanwhile, the Holy League, which had resisted French aggression until it was defeated at Ravenna, fell apart completely the following year as a result of the death of Pope Julius II, who had been instrumental in the league's creation. France's Louis XII also died on the first day of January, 1515, and Francis I became king of France.

When Francis ascended the French throne, he was determined to recover Milan, restore French honor, and win glory for himself. Because Louis had already been preparing for a new expedition into Italy when he died, it took little time for Francis to ready the French army. The monarch's ability to raise infantry in France itself was handicapped, however, by the medieval prejudice against arming peasants, so the native infantrymen in his army numbered only about eight thousand. Moreover, since the Swiss, the usual source of mercenaries for the French, were now the enemy, Francis had to recruit twenty-three thousand German *Landsknechts* instead. The German mercenaries fought in the same style as the Swiss, and they cost less, but they were also less disciplined. Considered the heart of the French army was its cavalry, especially its twenty-five hundred men-at-arms, who still fought in the traditional style of the knight. The best element, however, was the French artillery. The seventy-two heavy guns that made up the artillery train were the best in Europe.

After securing an alliance with Venice, Francis joined his army in late July, 1515, to begin the trek to Milan. An alliance of Pope Leo X, Ferdinand II, Massimiliano Sforza, and the Swiss prepared to defend Milan. The Swiss were expected to provide most of the troops for that purpose, but Pope Leo dispatched eight hundred papal cavalrymen, since the Swiss had no cavalry of their own. Some nineteen thousand Swiss infantrymen assembled in Milan.

For the previous two hundred years, the Swiss infantry system had been all but invincible in battle, even when outnumbered. Combining the pike, an eighteen-foot-long pole with an iron point, with the halberd, a heavy ax on an eight-foot pole, they had proven their mettle in numerous battles against armored men-at-arms—the mainstay of armies prior to 1500. Handguns had replaced the few crossbows previously present in Swiss armies, but the Swiss relied little on firepower. They brought only eight small artillery pieces to the coming battle.

Arriving in northern Italy in late August, the French army quickly defeated the papal cavalry units, leaving the Swiss virtually without cavalry support. Bartolomeo d'Alviano, the commander of the Venetian army, persuaded Francis to bring his army around Milan to join forces with him and attack the city from the east. As the French army passed south of Milan, the king sought to negotiate the surrender of the city. The Swiss were offered a huge sum in gold, and Sforza was offered the French duchy of Nemours, in exchange for giving up Milan. The captains of several cantons accepted the offer and headed home with about four thousand men. The majority, around fifteen thousand men, were persuaded by Cardinal Matthäus Schiner, the papal representative in Milan, to stay and fight. After a council of war that ended about noon on September 13, they swarmed out of the city, accompanied by three hundred cavalrymen commanded by Schiner. Huldrych Zwingli, then a young priest, marched with them as a chaplain. They silenced their drums in hope of catching the French by surprise, but scouts kept Francis informed of their progress.

The French army had made camp the previous night near Marignano, about 10 miles (16 kilometers) southeast of Milan. Expecting that the Swiss would attack the next day, Francis kept his army there and prepared for battle. He set up his men in the traditional divisions of vanguard, center, and rearguard. The vanguard included nearly all the native French infantry, most of Francis's handgunners, and all his artillery, which was set behind a trench. The center was composed of most of the *Landsknechts* and the men-at-arms, and the rearguard was made up mostly of Francis's remaining cavalry.

The Swiss advanced in their usual formation of three wide columns of about equal size with the second and third some distance behind the first; they marched already in battle formation. As soon as the lead column arrived before the French line at about 4:00 P.M., it moved into battle. The lead Swiss took heavy casualties from the French artillery and handgunners but kept their momentum and broke through the first line of French infantry. Before they could reach the artillery to silence it, however, the French center's *Landsknechts* moved forward, and the cavalry led by the king drove into the flanks of the Swiss column to halt their advance. The arrival of the second and then the third Swiss column failed to turn the tide of battle, while casualties mounted rapidly on both sides.

With a bright moon out, fighting continued until nearly midnight. Both sides disengaged and spent the night only a few yards apart, separated by a ditch. In the morning, the battle resumed with both armies now forming up into a solid long line. The Swiss again charged, but their advance was again slowed by heavy cannon fire and attacks by the French cavalry. Their right wing was making hard-fought progress against the French left—which if it had continued would probably have resulted in the collapse of the entire French line—when the forward units of Alviano's Venetian army arrived in the nick of time.

Encouraged by the arriving help, the French redoubled their efforts, while the Swiss were badly disheart-ened by the unexpected development. The Swiss made a systematic withdrawal, picking up their wounded and re-treating home. The city of Milan immediately capitulated to Francis, who gave Sforza a minor French title and a pension to live in France.

The local gravediggers submitted bills for burying 16,500 bodies, although one can assume they exaggerated the number to increase their pay. That number did not include more than one hundred French nobles, whose bodies were put in barrels of vinegar and returned to France for burial. The number of the casualties in each army is unknown, but those suffered by the Swiss were the greater, largely because of the effective artillery fire that they endured. The French victory demonstrated how the tactical coordination of artillery and cavalry in support of the infantry could defeat the vaunted Swiss heavy infantry, but it held no true lessons for the future, because the Swiss were almost entirely lacking in firepower. In future battles against forces strong in firepower, this French tactic would prove far less successful.

SIGNIFICANCE

Francis I was quick to offer a generous peace treaty to the Swiss, because he wanted them on his side. Ten cantons agreed to his terms, which allowed the French king to have first call on recruiting Swiss mercenaries, and they served in large numbers in the French army until 1600. Marignano was, however, the last time that a Swiss national army fought outside Switzerland's borders. The battle thus marked the beginning of Swiss neutrality. Their defeat did not yet cause the Swiss to lose confidence in their traditional fighting style, but when they suffered another bloody defeat while fighting for the French in 1522 at La Bicocca. the Swiss reliance on traditional tactics came to an end. Chaplain Zwingli, repulsed by the horrendous bloodshed at Marignano, blamed the pope for it, setting him on a path toward becoming the leader of the Swiss Protestants.

Pope Leo, terrified that Francis would march on Rome, rushed northward to meet with the victorious king. Their meeting at Bologna led to an agreement that gave the French king unprecedented control over the Catholic Church in France. This agreement lasted until the French Revolution. Francis had himself installed as the duke of Milan, but his control over the duchy lasted only seven years, as Holy Roman Emperor Charles V declared he had illegally seized the duchy and ousted Francis in 1522.

—*Frederic J. Baumgartner*

FURTHER READING

Hall, Bert. *Weapons and Warfare in Renaissance Europe.* Baltimore: Johns Hopkins University Press, 1997. Stresses the medieval character of the battle in the use of heavy cavalry.

Holt, Mack. *Renaissance and Reformation France.* New York: Oxford University Press, 2002. Provides a discussion of the impact of the battle on French politics and culture.

Knecht, Robert. *Renaissance Warrior and Patron: The Reign of Francis I.* New York: Cambridge University Press, 1994. Best biography of the French king but limited on the battle.

Oman, Charles. *A History of the Art of War in the Sixteenth Century.* New York: E. P. Dutton, 1937. The most complete description of the battle from a tactical point of view.

Seward, Desmond. *Prince of the Renaissance.* New York: Macmillan, 1973. A lively account of the battle in the context of the French king's life.

Snyder, Arnold. "Zollikon Anabaptism and the Sword." *Mennonite Quarterly Review* 69, no. 2 (1995): 205-225. Examines the tradition of pacifism that developed among many Swiss because of the bloodshed of the battle.

Taylor, Frederick. *The Art of War in Italy, 1494-1529.* Westport, Conn.: Greenwood Press, 1973. Places the battle in the context of military practice during the Renaissance.

SEE ALSO: Apr. 9, 1454: Peace of Lodi; July 16, 1465-Apr., 1559: French-Burgundian and French-Austrian Wars; 1481-1499: Ludovico Sforza Rules Milan; Sept., 1494-Oct., 1495: Charles VIII of France Invades Italy; 1499: Louis XII of France Seizes Milan; September 22, 1504: Treaty of Blois; 1508: Formation of the League of Cambrai; Apr. 11, 1512: Battle of Ravenna; Aug. 18, 1516: Concordat of Bologna; 1521-1559: Valois-Habsburg Wars; Feb., 1525: Battle of Pavia; May 6, 1527-Feb., 1528: Sack of Rome; Apr. 3, 1559: Treaty of Cateau-Cambrésis.

RELATED ARTICLES in *Great Lives from History: The Renaissance & Early Modern Era, 1454-1600:* Charles V; Ferdinand II and Isabella I; Francis I; Leo X; Huldrych Zwingli.

1516

SIR THOMAS MORE PUBLISHES *UTOPIA*

Sir Thomas More's Utopia, *which describes a mythical egalitarian society, launched a new literary genre popular through the late nineteenth century.*

LOCALE: Louvain, the Netherlands
CATEGORY: Literature

KEY FIGURES

Sir Thomas More (1478-1535), undersheriff of London, prominent lawyer, and later lord chancellor of England

Desiderius Erasmus (1466?-1536), More's friend, Dutch Humanist scholar

Christopher Columbus (1451-1506), Genoa-born navigator and explorer

Henry VIII (1491-1547), king of England, r. 1509-1547

SUMMARY OF EVENT

"Utopianism" was unknown until 1516 when Sir Thomas More, a prominent London lawyer and Humanist, published *Utopia* in Latin. Destined to become one of the great works of political theory, it was printed in the Netherlands because the English printing industry was still in its infancy. It was quickly exported to England, however, where it was widely read. No less a scholar than Desiderius Erasmus of Rotterdam, More's good friend and proponent of Humanism, oversaw the book's printing.

Utopia (Greek for "no place") was written in two parts. Book 1 is a discussion involving prominent public figures, including More himself, and Raphael (Ralph) Hythloday, a fictitious sailor whom More claims to have met while on diplomatic business in the Netherlands and whose name means "disseminator of nonsense."

The burden of the discussion in the first book concerns the social and economic state of western Europe, which Hythloday constantly compares unfavorably to the mythical land of Utopia, which he is supposed to have visited recently. In particular, he criticizes the warmongering of princes and the greed of the wealthy, who close off common land and tear down peasant villages to facilitate sheep raising.

Hythloday also laments the low state of political life in Europe. Kings are beset by flatterers and do not re-

A woodcut from Sir Thomas More's Utopia, *depicting a lush island—Utopia—with castles, churches, and ships off shore.* (Hulton|Archive by Getty Images)

ficials. All men are eligible for office. All members of the community are required to work regularly at useful occupations, and they spend much of their leisure time in educational and cultural pursuits. The best-educated people are generally given the more important posts. Private property is totally nonexistent. Each family receives what it needs for an adequate but frugal existence. Cities readily share with one another what they have in abundance.

The Utopians go to war only to defend their country, to aid its citizens abroad, or to protect weak nations in distress. They colonize only unoccupied territories. They prefer to use mercenary soldiers to spare their own citizens. They never permit war to break out in their own land, and they pride themselves on using rational, human skills such as diplomacy and trickery to overcome their enemies, rather than using force, which is bestial. They are a strongly religious people and tolerate all religions that do not disturb the commonwealth. Although atheists are not molested, they are excluded from public life because Utopians consider them to be without moral sense.

Much attention is given to philosophy, especially the study of ethics, and the Utopians believe that pleasure, both spiritual and sensual, is the aim of human existence. Only the "higher" pleasures fall into this category, however. Utopians reject low-grade, "apparent" pleasures.

The death penalty is never inflicted. Hardened criminals are enslaved and made to work for the commonwealth, but no one else undergoes such punishment. Suicide is permitted to the chronically ill but to no one else. Adultery and other forms of sexual laxity are severely punished.

The rulers of the state are high-minded and self-sacrificing. They are forbidden to discuss public business outside the council chamber, to avoid attracting popular followings and fomenting rebellion. Magistrates can be removed from office on mere suspicion of tyranny.

Hythloday concludes his narration by saying that in contrast to Utopia, all commonwealths with which he is familiar seem like "conspiracies of rich men." More admits that he cannot accept all the practices of the Utopians, but wishes that many of them would be adopted into English society.

More's account of Utopia owed as much to published reports of the New World as it did to his observations of the Old World. When More wrote *Utopia* in 1515 and

ceive good advice. They do not perceive that the welfare of their subjects lies in prosperity and peace.

Near the end of the first book, Raphael suggests that private property and the drive to accumulate it are at the root of all these abuses and should be abolished. When More questions this idea, Hythloday embarks on a lengthy description of the system existing in Utopia. This material composes book 2.

The ideal state of Utopia is situated on an island no broader than two hundred miles at any point. It comprises fifty-four fair cities and numerous prosperous farms, with the citizens alternating between urban and rural life. The government of the whole island is republican. Each family may cast a vote for the lowest magistrates (the philarchs), who in turn nominate and elect the higher of-

1516, the voyages of discovery of Italian explorer Christopher Columbus were still within living memory, as were the accounts of Amerigo Vespucci and Pietro Martire d'Anghiera. More was familiar with these travel narratives when he wrote his own tale of meeting the sailor-philosopher Hythloday, and he fashioned his novel to mimic the form of such narratives. It was partly for this reason that Renaissance scholar Bruce Burton described *Utopia* as "the first explicit literary example, rooted in the New World, of a political alternative to Europe's tyrannies."

Beyond this formal resemblance, moreover, the content of More's work owes a similar debt to early travel narratives. Indeed, many specific details of More's invented nation are arguably derived from explorers' accounts of the New World. It was a society without lawyers, judges, or debtors' prisons, a place that sounds in some respects amazingly similar to the Native American

societies that would be recalled by Jean-Jacques Rousseau, Benjamin Franklin, Thomas Jefferson, Thomas Paine, and Friedrich Engels, among others. More made of "primitive" societies a mirror of social criticism for "civilized" Europe.

Utopia was not invented wholly of American observation, of course. More's citizens read books and attended lectures, used cattle and horses, and required passports for travel outside their home cities. Utopians also practiced a form of slavery reserved for criminals who worked off their sentences at menial tasks, wrapped in gold chains, a badge of dishonor.

The Latin text was read by the learned throughout Europe until an English translation appeared in 1551. Although it was greatly admired, there is no evidence that it had any profound impact on either contemporary politics or intellectual life. Its meaning was considered somewhat obscure, as it still is.

Shortly after publication of the book, More entered the service of King Henry VIII and rose to the highest post in the realm, that of lord chancellor. In 1532, he resigned rather than support Henry's decision to divorce Catherine of Aragon through a breach with Rome. In 1535, he was beheaded for treason for refusing to take the Oath of Supremacy recognizing Henry as "Supreme Head" of the Church in England. He is regarded as the greatest intellectual figure of the early English Renaissance, and has been declared a saint of the Roman Catholic Church.

SIGNIFICANCE

Columbus's discovery of America was followed closely by the flowering of a literary genre to which Thomas More's *Utopia* gave its name. More's work was only one of many books that used the discovery of vast unmapped regions of the globe to provide readers with imaginative settings for egalitarian fantasies. It was one of the most widely read and discussed examples of the genre, however. Utopian fiction continued to be written for four centuries, until the last frontiers closed on a fully mapped world around 1900. Amid the social and political upheavals of the twentieth century, the genre was pessimistically revived in the form of dystopian novels such as Aldous Huxley's *Brave New World* (1932) and George Orwell's *Nineteen Eighty-Four* (1949).

—*James F. Hitchcock,*
updated by Bruce E. Johansen

MONEY AND POWER IN UTOPIA

In Thomas More's Utopia, *More claims to transcribe a traveler's description of an actual island nation whose citizens have extremely different beliefs, customs, and values from those of the English. In this passage, More's speaker describes the opinions of the Utopians (who do not use money) about the relationship between wealth and power in other parts of the world.*

They [the Utopians] are surprised that gold, a useless commodity in itself, is everywhere valued so highly that man himself, who for his own purposes conferred this value on it, is far less valuable. They do not understand why a dunderhead with no more brains than a post, and who is about as crooked as he is foolish, should command a great many wise and good people, simply because he happens to have a great pile of gold. Yet if this booby should lose his money to the lowest rascal in his household (as can happen by chance, or through some legal trick—for the law can produce reversals as violent as luck itself), he would promptly become one of the fellow's scullions, as if he were personally attached to the coin, and a mere appendage to it. Even more than this, the Utopians are appalled at those people who practically worship a rich man, though they neither owe him anything, nor are obligated to him in any way. What impresses them is simply that the man is rich. Yet all the while they know he is so mean and grasping that as long as he lives not a single penny out of that great mound of money will ever come their way.

Source: From Utopia, *by Sir Thomas More. Translated and edited by Robert M. Adams (New York: W. W. Norton, 1975), p. 53.*

Sir Thomas More, center, with his family at home in London, in an engraving after a painting by Hans Holbein, the Younger. (Hulton|Archive by Getty Images)

FURTHER READING

Ames, Russell. *Citizen Thomas More and His "Utopia."* Princeton, N.J.: Princeton University Press, 1949. *Utopia* in the context of More's life and times.

Baker, David Weil. *Divulging "Utopia": Radical Humanism in Sixteenth-Century England.* Amherst: University of Massachusetts Press, 1999. Close study of the contemporary reception of *Utopia* and its relationship to the Humanist movement. Includes bibliographic references and index.

Baker-Smith, Dominic. *More's "Utopia."* Toronto: University of Toronto Press, 2000. Places More's *Utopia* in its cultural context, explaining its connections to Humanism and Christian political theory. Argues for its treatment as a literary reflection on the nature of political idealism, rather than as an example of such idealism. Includes bibliographic references and index.

Chambers, Raymond Wilson. *Thomas More.* New York: Harcourt, Brace, 1935. Reprint. London: J. Cape, 1962. Wide-ranging biography which is largely sympathetic to More.

Grinde, Donald A., Jr., and Bruce E. Johansen. *Exemplar of Liberty: Native America and the Evolution of Democracy.* Los Angeles: UCLA American Indian Studies Center, 1991. Treats *Utopia* as an example of an early travel narrative.

Guy, John. *Thomas More.* New York: Oxford University Press, 2000. Both a biography of More and a survey of the various other biographical portrayals that have emerged over the centuries. Attempts to adjudicate between the different versions of More, and uses newly discovered evidence to explain what he really believed and the real reasons for his execution. Includes genealogical table, bibliographic references, and index.

Logan, George M., and Robert M. Adams. *Thomas More: "Utopia."* Cambridge, England: Cambridge University Press, 1975. Critical biography of More.

More, Sir Thomas. *Utopia: A Revised Translation, Backgrounds, Criticism.* Translated and edited by Robert M. Adams. 2d ed. New York: Norton, 1992. An authoritative translation of More's novel. Includes background texts by Saint Benedict and Tasso and the set of letters written by major Humanists, among them Erasmus, as well as modern day critical essays, a bibliography, and illustrations.

Olin, John C., ed. *Interpreting Thomas More's "Utopia."* New York: Fordham University Press, 1989. Brief collection of five essays expressing divergent perspectives on More, originally presented at a conference on the author. Includes illustrations and bibliographic references.

SEE ALSO: 1456: Publication of Gutenberg's Mazarin Bible; Beginning 1485: The Tudors Rule England; 1490's: Aldus Manutius Founds the Aldine Press; Oct. 12, 1492: Columbus Lands in the Americas; 1499-1517: Erasmus Advances Humanism in England; July-Dec., 1513: Machiavelli Writes *The Prince*.

RELATED ARTICLES in *Great Lives from History: The Renaissance & Early Modern Era, 1454-1600:* Christopher Columbus; Desiderius Erasmus; Henry VIII; Sir Thomas More.

January 23, 1516
CHARLES I ASCENDS THE THRONE OF SPAIN

Charles I became the first king of a united Spain and its first Habsburg Dynasty ruler, which concerned those who feared Habsburg domination of Spain. Charles's reign, however, also led to the expanding worldwide influence of Spain and Habsburg Austria.

LOCALE: Spain
CATEGORY: Government and politics

KEY FIGURES
Charles I (1500-1558), king of Spain, r. 1516-1556, and Holy Roman Emperor as Charles V, r. 1519-1556

Adrian of Utrecht (Adrian Florensz Boeyens; 1459-1523), tutor and special agent of Charles, later Pope Adrian VI

Guillaume de Croy (1458-1521), sieur de Chièvres, served as principal adviser and grand chamberlain to Charles

Francisco Jiménez de Cisneros (1436-1517), archbishop of Toledo and regent of Spain, 1516-1517

Ferdinand II (1452-1516), king of Aragon, r. 1479-1516, king of Castile, r. 1474-1504, and later regent of Castile, 1504-1516

Isabella I (1451-1504), queen of Castile, r. 1474-1504

Ferdinand of Aragon (1503-1564), younger brother of Charles, later archduke of Austria, and successor to Charles as Holy Roman Emperor Ferdinand I, r. 1558-1564

Joan the Mad (1479-1555), daughter of Ferdinand II and Isabella I, mother of Charles V, queen of Castile, r. 1504-1555, and queen of Aragon, r. 1516-1555

Philip I (1478-1506), husband of Joan the Mad, duke of Burgundy, r. 1482-1506, and later king of Castile, r. 1504-1506

SUMMARY OF EVENT
The accession of Charles I to the throne of Spain was the climax of a bitter dispute over the succession that had its origins in the unusual nature of the marriage contract between his maternal grandparents, Ferdinand of Aragon and Isabella of Castile. Both had been confirmed sovereign in their own kingdoms, but there was nothing in their marriage contract about their successors. According to Spanish law, however, their heir would inherit both kingdoms.

Isabella of Castile died in 1504. Her legitimate successor was her daughter Joan the Mad, who was married to Philip of Habsburg, son of Holy Roman Emperor Maximilian I. Ferdinand and Isabella had arranged the marriage to provide a family alliance with the Habsburgs and thus encircle their common enemy—France. Joan and Philip were proclaimed queen and king of Castile in 1504.

Ferdinand, Isabella's widower and king of Aragon, found this succession unsatisfactory. He disliked having a foreign prince on a Spanish throne, but his eldest son and original heir, Juan (or John), died after Joan's marriage to Philip, thereby making Joan heir to the throne of Aragon as well. Furthermore, bouts of mental illness plagued Joan, clearly limiting any control she might have over her husband.

The political ramifications of a Habsburg succession were even more disturbing. The restless nobility of Castile openly supported Philip because they hoped to find in him a monarch who would rule in accord with their interests, countering Ferdinand and Isabella's efforts to curb the power of the nobles for more than two decades. The only immediate step Ferdinand could take was to have himself proclaimed regent of Castile until Joan and Philip could arrive from Flanders to take possession of their throne.

Shortly after the couple arrived in Spain in 1506, Philip suddenly died. The sudden death of her husband, with whom she had been deeply in love, strained Joan's fragile grasp on sanity and rendered her unable to rule Castile. The right of succession fell upon her eldest son, Charles, who was only six years old at the time. Joan retired to a castle in Tordesillas, where she lived until her death in 1555.

Ferdinand continued to serve as regent of Castile while Charles was reared in Brussels and received tutoring from Adrian of Utrecht in the ways of the Flemish. As he grew, Charles was advised by Guillaume de Croy, sieur de Chièvres, in Habsburg policies. The prospect of having Charles succeed to the thrones of Castile and Aragon disturbed Ferdinand. Because Charles was heir to his paternal grandparents' lands in Burgundy and the Holy Roman Empire, Ferdinand believed that Spain would be subordinated to Habsburg needs if Charles succeeded him. In an effort to circumvent Charles, Ferdinand brought to Spain his namesake, Charles's younger brother, who was trained in Spanish ways and policies. The younger Ferdinand was even named as heir to the throne in a will made by his grandfather.

The Castilian nobility rallied to support Charles, again hoping to have a foreign monarch whom they could dominate. Chièvres sent Adrian to Spain in 1515 to persuade Ferdinand to change his will. Absorbed with foreign policy problems and plagued by the unruly behavior of the Spanish nobility, Ferdinand rescinded his will and named Charles as his heir. When Ferdinand died in 1516, Charles became king of Castile and Aragon, the first monarch of a united Spain.

Until Charles arrived in Spain, the aging Cardinal Francisco Jiménez de Cisneros, archbishop of Toledo, acted as regent of Castile. The Castilian nobility soon rallied to the cause of Charles's brother Ferdinand when they observed the ambitions of Charles's Flemish advisers. Nevertheless, Cisneros was able to block the nobility's attempts at domination. Charles arrived in Spain in 1517, preceded by Chièvres, who dismissed Cisneros as regent.

Charles faced severe difficulties in claiming his Spanish crown. Arriving in Spain on September 18, 1517, after winds buffeted his small fleet, Charles faced his first challenge from the suspicious Castilian *cortes*, or parliament, which recognized him formally as king of Castile on March 21, 1518. The Castilians preferred Charles's brother, Ferdinand; therefore Charles sent him to Germany. More discussions followed with the cantankerous *cortes* of Aragon. Just as Charles was negotiating with the Catalonian *cortes*, his paternal grandfather, Emperor Maximilian I, died. The German electors chose Charles unanimously to succeed Maximilian as Holy Roman Emperor. The Spanish kingdoms thus became part of a continental empire.

As the new emperor prepared to receive money from the Castilians for his journey to the Netherlands, a severe revolt broke out in Castile. The installation of Flemish and other non-Spanish advisers and the assessment of higher taxes angered many native Spaniards, particularly the grandees (nobles). The Castilian cities sought to reverse the encroachment of the nobility upon offices traditionally reserved for the artisan guilds and merchants. A massive Jacquerie attack (a peasant's revolt) on bailiffs and noble properties developed into rural violence that motivated the aristocracy to defend their land if not the king. In the aftermath of the Comunero Revolt (1520-1522), Charles was forced to return and engineer a reform of political administration in Spain. He arranged a compromise whereby Spain provided resources for his imperial ventures while the local nobility gained economic and social rank within Spain.

SIGNIFICANCE

Charles I had inherited not only the Spanish throne but also a vast empire that reached the New World, a region of which he encouraged exploration. His rule extended also to Spain's territories in Italy, the Low Countries, and central Europe's Habsburg lands. His reign set the stage for Spain's golden age, which lasted into the seventeenth century. Finally, Charles was the last Holy Roman Emperor to control European affairs.

—*José M. Sánchez, updated by Douglas W. Richmond*

FURTHER READING

Blockmans, Wim. *Emperor Charles V, 1500-1558*. Translated by Isola van den Hoven-Vardon. London: Arnold, 2002. Blockmans attempts to survey the scope of the vast territory and diverse culture of the Holy Roman Empire by analyzing the relationship between Charles as an individual and the complex, rigid yet unstable power structures within which he governed. Includes illustrations, maps, bibliographic references, index.

Davies, R. Trevor. *The Golden Century of Spain, 1501-1621*. Reprint. Westport, Conn.: Greenwood Press, 1984. Originally published in 1937, this well-written survey covers all aspects of Charles's reign

Elliott, John H. *Imperial Spain, 1469-1719*. New York: St. Martin's Press, 1964. Elliott concentrates on the effects of Charles's imperial policies on Spain.

Fichtner, Paula Sutter. *The Hapsburg Monarchy, 1490-1848: Attributes of Empire*. New York & Hampshire: Palgrave MacMillan, 2003. A comprehensive discussion of the Habsburg Dynasty and its rulers.

Kamen, Henry. *Spain, 1469-1714: A Society of Conflict*. 2d ed. Reprint. New York: Longman, 1996. An excellent survey of early modern Spain. Kamen contends that imperial Spain was never fully equipped to control empires in Europe and the Americas simultaneously.

Lovett, A. W. *Early Hapsburg Spain, 1517-1598*. New York: Oxford University Press, 1986. A lively narrative that incorporates modern advances in Spanish historiography.

Lynch, John. *Spain, 1516-1598: From Nation State to World Empire*. Cambridge, Mass.: Blackwell, 1991. A concentrated, detailed, and immensely valuable study of sixteenth century Spain.

Maltby, William. *The Reign of Charles V*. New York: Palgrave, 2002. A monograph that balances biography of Charles with broad analysis of his foreign and domestic policies and their historical consequences. Includes maps, bibliographic references, index.

Miller, Townsend. *The Castles and the Crown*. New York: Coward-McCann, 1963. An older biographical study, Miller's work remains one of the best accounts of the dispute over the succession and provides perceptive insights into the personalities of Ferdinand, Joan, and Philip.

Richardson, Glenn. *Renaissance Monarchy: The Reigns of Henry VIII, Francis I, and Charles V*. New York: Oxford University Press, 2002. A comparison of Charles to two other monarchs who helped define Renaissance government and culture. Focuses on their careers as warriors, governors, and patrons. Includes maps, bibliographic references, and index.

Tracy, James D. *Emperor Charles V, Impresario of War: Campaign Strategy, International Finance, and Domestic Politics*. New York: Cambridge University Press, 2002. Examination of the financial and political consequences of Charles V's military campaigns. Discusses Charles as a field commander of his armies, as well as the international financial community that loaned Charles the money to pay for battles and thereby gained control over parts of his lands. Also discusses the local governments within the empire that learned to exploit Charles's need for money.

SEE ALSO: Oct. 19, 1469: Marriage of Ferdinand and Isabella; Aug. 17, 1477: Foundation of the Habsburg Dynasty; 1482-1492: Maximilian I Takes Control of the Low Countries; June 28, 1519: Charles V Is Elected Holy Roman Emperor; 1555-1556: Charles V Abdicates; July 26, 1581: The United Provinces Declare Independence from Spain.

RELATED ARTICLES in *Great Lives from History: The Renaissance & Early Modern Era, 1454-1600:* Duke of Alva; Catherine of Aragon; Charles V; Clement VII; Hernán Cortés; Desiderius Erasmus; Ferdinand II and Isabella I; Francis I; Henry II; Saint Ignatius of Loyola; Martin Luther; Margaret of Austria; Margaret of Parma; Mary of Hungary; Mary I; Maximilian I; Mehmed II; Mehmed III; Paul III; Philip II; Francisco Pizarro; Süleyman the Magnificent; Andreas Vesalius; William the Silent.

August 18, 1516
CONCORDAT OF BOLOGNA

In the Concordat of Bologna, France and the Papal States made peace with one another and agreed to a set of political and religious concessions. The concordat influenced the distribution of power in Italy, as well as determining the relationship between monarchal and papal authority within France.

LOCALE: Bologna and Rome, Papal States (now in Italy) and Paris, France

CATEGORIES: Diplomacy and international relations; religion; wars, uprisings, and civil unrest

KEY FIGURES

Julius II (Giuliano della Rovere; 1443-1513), Roman Catholic pope, 1503-1513

Leo X (Giovanni de' Medici; 1475-1521), Roman Catholic pope, 1513-1521

Louis XII (1462-1515), king of France, r. 1498-1515

Francis I (1494-1547), king of France, r. 1515-1547

Maximilian I (1459-1519), Holy Roman Emperor, r. 1493-1519

Lorenzo de' Medici (1492-1519), Florentine ruler, r. 1512-1519, duke of Urbino, r. 1516-1519

SUMMARY OF EVENT

Beginning with Charles VIII in 1494, the French kings fought a series of wars in northern Italy, ostensibly justified by a dubious claim to the Duchy of Milan. During the pontificate of Alexander VI, an alliance between the papacy and France cemented French gains in Milan and extended them southward into the kingdom of Naples. However, with the death of Alexander in 1503 and the election of the previously pro-French Pope Julius II, the alliance was severed, and the Spanish drove the French out of Naples. In 1511, Julius formed the Holy League to drive the French out of Italy entirely, and in 1512, he was successful.

However, the situation changed drastically at that point. Julius died early in 1513 and was succeeded by the peaceful Pope Leo X. Louis XII, king of France, died the following year and was succeeded by his cousin, Francis I, who was determined to regain the lost French territories. At Marignano on September 13-14, 1515, the French armies, reinforced by Swiss mercenaries, defeated Swiss mercenaries in the service of Milan. This battle again established French hegemony in Italy; Milan once more became a French possession.

Leo X, although he had maintained his neutrality dur-

ing Francis's invasion, was terrified at the news, and despite his natural leanings toward Spain, he hastened to make peace with France. His alarm was intensified by the fact that he was a member of the Medici family, the ruling house of Florence, and he feared that France might also conquer Florence.

Francis I was anxious to avoid having the pope as an enemy and so agreed to relatively generous terms. Papal troops were to be withdrawn from certain towns formerly belonging to Milan, but French assistance was promised to the Medici in Florence and certain revenues were bestowed on the pope. Francis asked for a conference with the pope, and Leo promised to meet him at Bologna, on the northern edge of the Papal States. Accord was reached on October 13, 1515, but subsequently Leo temporized about the meeting, fearing a strong Spanish reaction.

However, by November 30, the pope had reached his former home in Florence, where he was given a lavish reception. Early in December, he entered Bologna, which had always resented papal rule, and there he was greeted coldly, with little ceremony. On December 11, Francis entered the city and was met by the pope and cardinals. During the public ceremonies, Francis and his nobles acknowledged having borne arms against Julius II, and Leo absolved them from this offense. However, Francis used the incident to comment dryly on Julius's great military exploits and to assert that he would have been a better general than pope.

In private sessions over the next few days, Francis sought Leo's support for a renewed invasion of Naples, which was still held by Spain. Leo refused, although he did not oppose the plan. Francis insisted that Leo abandon all claims to any territories formerly held by Milan, but by way of compensation he agreed to allow the pope to claim the Duchy of Urbino.

During the negotiations, Francis also asked Leo to confirm the Pragmatic Sanction of Bourges, a document of 1438 by which Charles VII of France had accepted the decrees of the Council of Basel, which had met without papal authority and which endorsed the theories of the Conciliar Movement that general councils were superior to papal authority. By the Pragmatic Sanction, Charles had also abolished papal taxation in France and reserved for himself the right to intervene in Church affairs in his kingdom. The fifteenth century popes had refused to recognize the sanction, which was never fully enforced.

Leo X also refused to affirm the document, which he regarded as a form of blackmail. However, he agreed to negotiate a concordat in which objectionable features of the Pragmatic Sanction would be eliminated and its acceptable features would be confirmed.

Details of subsequent negotiations between the king and the pope are not known, but before leaving Bologna, they had probably agreed on the essentials of the concordat. Ambassadors were left behind by both parties, and after arduous negotiations, the details were worked out by February, 1516. The document was formally ratified on August 18.

Meanwhile, in March, Holy Roman Emperor Maximilian I had attacked Milan; Leo sent no assistance to the French despite his alliance, but Maximilian was repulsed, and in May the papal troops conquered the Duchy of Urbino. Lorenzo de' Medici, Leo's nephew, was installed as duke.

Although the decree was generally favorable to France, Francis immediately encountered opposition to it in his own kingdom. He overrode the opposition and proceeded to publish the treaty. The cardinals also strongly opposed the concordat as inimical to the freedom of the Church, and the six-month delay in signing it was caused by lengthy negotiations between the royal ambassadors and the cardinals. The cardinals were reluctant to accept the document, but on December 19, the Fifth Lateran Council, meeting in Rome, formally approved the concordat with only a few dissenting voices.

Meanwhile, opposition in France, which had been temporarily quelled, erupted again. Various French parlements (judicial bodies with a limited right to accept or reject new laws) refused to register the treaty, despite royal commands. The clergy, the universities, and the parlements all protested strongly against what they considered to be the surrender of the liberties of the French Church embodied in the Pragmatic Sanction. Not until April, 1518, did the parlements register the concordat, and then only under protest and threat of royal action. Several members of the University of Paris were arrested for their opposition, and Leo X solemnly condemned the university for its stand in the affair.

SIGNIFICANCE

The Concordat of Bologna defined and regulated the relation between church and state in France for 275 years. Under the terms of the concordat, the Pragmatic Sanction was officially abolished, reestablishing papal authority in France. However, the French king received the right to nominate all bishops and abbots in France, subject to papal approval. The collection of papal taxes and appeals to papal courts were restricted, but not abolished. In return, the king promised to cooperate in reforming the French Church.

Over all, the concordat confirmed in principle the pope's authority within France, thereby strengthening the Papacy, while it simultaneously provided the French Crown with ample concrete power in religious affairs, so that the power of the Papacy did not threaten the authority of the French monarch. This balance of power arguably influenced the attitude of the Crown toward Protestantism, since France's rulers did not feel weakened by the Catholic power structure after 1516, and they therefore had no direct motive to support the Reformation.

—*James F. Hitchcock*

FURTHER READING

Batiffol, Louis. *The Century of the Renaissance.* New York: G. P. Putnam's Sons, 1916. Reprint. New York: AMS Press, 1967. A brief survey of sixteenth century France.

Bridge, John S. C. *Reign of Louis XII, 1508-1514.* Vol. 4 in *A History of France from the Death of Louis XI.* Reprint. New York: Octagon Books, 1978. Discusses the conflict between Louis XII and Julius II in preparing for the concordat.

Chamberlin, E. R. *The Bad Popes.* Stroud, Gloucestershire, England: Sutton, 2003. Leo's failings are detailed in this study of papal corruption across the six hundred years leading up to the Reformation. Includes photographs, illustrations, genealogical tables, bibliographic references, and index.

Creighton, M. M. *A History of the Papacy from the Great Schism to the Sack of Rome.* Vol. 5. New ed. New York: Longmans, Green, 1919. Unlike Pastor, Creighton does not see the meeting at Bologna as an unquestioned diplomatic victory for Francis. He believes that both the king and the pope came away dissatisfied.

Grant, A. J. *The French Monarchy, 1483-1789.* Reprint. 2 vols. New York: H. Fertig, 1970. A brief but authoritative survey of the concordat. Includes maps and bibliography.

Hackett, Francis. *Francis the First.* Reprint. Garden City, N.Y.: Doubleday, 1968. A highly readable, romantic popular biography, but dated and not always judicious in its conclusions. Hackett's enthusiasm for psychoanalyzing Francis and other figures unfortunately entailed the construction of great edifices of interpretation on flimsy foundations of fact. No notes or bibliography.

Knecht, R. J. *French Renaissance Monarchy: Francis I and Henry II.* 2d ed. New York: Longman, 1996. A detailed survey of the first half of the sixteenth century by the leading English language scholar of Francis I. Includes map, bibliographic references, and index.

Pastor, Ludwig. *Leo X, 1513-1521.* Vol. 8 in *The History of the Popes from the Close of the Middle Ages.* Reprint. Wilmington, N.C.: Consortium, 1978. Argues that although the Concordat of Bologna carried with it some advantages for the Papacy, it was on the whole a diplomatic victory for Francis I, who was a more crafty diplomat than Leo. Calls the treaty the greatest concession ever wrung from the Papacy by a secular ruler.

Richardson, Glenn. *Renaissance Monarchy: The Reigns of Henry VIII, Francis I, and Charles V.* New York: Oxford University Press, 2002. Comparison of Francis I to two other monarchs who helped define Renaissance government and culture. Focuses on their careers as warriors, governors, and patrons. Includes maps, bibliographic references, and index.

Stinger, Charles L. *The Renaissance in Rome.* Bloomington: Indiana University Press, 1998. Leo is a central figure in this study of the resurgence of Rome's cultural, religious, and political importance in the Renaissance. Includes maps, illustrations, bibliographic references, and index.

SEE ALSO: 1469-1492: Rule of Lorenzo de' Medici; 1481-1499: Ludovico Sforza Rules Milan; Sept., 1494-Oct., 1495: Charles VIII of France Invades Italy; 1499: Louis XII of France Seizes Milan; Apr. 11, 1512: Battle of Ravenna; Sept. 13-14, 1515: Battle of Marignano; 1521-1559: Valois-Habsburg Wars; Feb., 1525: Battle of Pavia; May 6, 1527-Feb., 1528: Sack of Rome; Apr. 3, 1559: Treaty of Cateau-Cambrésis; Mar., 1562-May 2, 1598: French Wars of Religion.

RELATED ARTICLES in *Great Lives from History: The Renaissance & Early Modern Era, 1454-1600:* Francis I; Julius II; Leo X; Louis XII; Maximilian I.

1517

FRACASTORO DEVELOPS HIS THEORY OF FOSSILS

Fracastoro, through scientific observation, was one of the first to theorize that fossils are the remains of once-living organisms, the remnants and traces of the history of life on earth.

LOCALE: Italy

CATEGORIES: Geology; biology; science and technology

KEY FIGURES

Girolamo Fracastoro (c. 1478-1553), Italian physician, geologist, and poet

Leonardo da Vinci (1452-1519), Italian artist and inventor

SUMMARY OF EVENT

Prior to the speculations of Girolamo Fracastoro, fossils were viewed as inorganic products of the mineral kingdom formed in situ. During the Middle Ages, definitions of fossils were based on assumptions made by Aristotle, who believed fossils resulted from the petrified and then sedimented remains of an abundance of organisms that came to life through spontaneous generation. Fossils, believed to be formed by many different forces, were classified as oddities of nature, carved stones, or mineral concretions that were by-products of the motions of the stars, seminal vapors, or unidentified petrifying or plastic forces. To further compound the confusion, religious dogma of the time designated all fossils to be relics of Noah's ark and the great flood.

By the early sixteenth century, three questions came to dominate discussions about fossil origins: Are fossils inorganic? Are they relics of Noah's ark? Are fossils the product of a long history of past life on Earth? Fracastoro and his contemporary, Leonardo da Vinci, favored the theory that fossils represented a record of a long history of life on Earth.

Da Vinci's notebooks contain many acute and accurate observations of living mollusks and their ecology and notes on the process of sedimentation. Da Vinci recognized that similarities between living marine life and fossils were so exacting that a causal explanation was necessary to account for a fossil's existence. Da Vinci noted fossils were preserved in various stages of growth and exhibited markings of a life history on their surfaces such as bore holes and parasites. He further speculated that fossils were embedded in stratified rock and were consolidated from "drying out."

Fracastoro was the sixth of seven sons born to a patrician Veronese family. As an adolescent, he was sent to Padua, Italy, for formal education. Fracastoro studied literature, mathematics, philosophy, astronomy, and medicine. After graduating in 1502, he became an instructor of logic at the University of Padua. In 1508, he left the university and returned to Verona to establish residency and dedicate himself to his studies and the practice of medicine.

Fracastoro maintained a villa in Incaffi, on the slopes of Monte Baldo, a location that became a gathering place for philosophical and scientific meetings attended by many leading religious, scientific, and philosophical thinkers of the time. These gatherings expanded Fracastoro's cultural interests into philosophy, the liberal arts, and the natural sciences. It was probably during his stays at Monte Baldo that Fracastoro became familiar with fossils and the significant scientific and philosophical questions that their existence brings to light.

In 1517, Fracastoro observed fossil mollusks and crabs that had been discovered in the foundations of buildings in Verona. He believed they were the remains of once-living shellfish buried after the landscape changed over time, and he argued against suggestions that they were embedded because of a biblical flood or because of a molding force from within the Earth. Fracastoro's interpretation of fossils as organic remains embedded during the continual process of geological and geographical change was clearly secular. He suggested that the existence of fossils could be explained completely in terms of natural law. It is important to note, though, that Fracastoro was an Aristotelian thinker and that it was acceptable to define fossils also as spontaneously generated. Fracastoro referred to the process of spontaneous generation to explain some of the more difficult fossil samples he observed.

SIGNIFICANCE

Because Leonardo da Vinci recorded his theories regarding the marine origin of fossils into his famous coded private notebooks, his ideas had little to no influence on later researchers of fossils. Fracastoro's theories of fossils reflected a similar viewpoint—fossils that looked like modern marine life represented past marine life—and his ideas, made public, would inspire Conrad Gesner's *De rerum fossilium, lapidum, et gemmarum maximè, figuris et similitudinibus liber* (1565; on the shapes and resemblances of fossils, stones, and gems); Andrea Chiocco's *Musaeum Francisci Calceolari Veronensis* (1622), which quotes Fracastoro; and Nicolaus Steno's pivotal work *De solido intra solidum naturaliter*

contento dissertationis prodromus (1669; *The Prodromus to a Dissertation Concerning Solids Naturally Contained Within Solids*, 1671). Though Steno does not quote Fracastoro in his publication, most scholars believe he was familiar with and influenced by Fracastoro's ideas.

Steno's work, considered the founding text of modern geological science, examines the general question of how one solid (fossil) could be contained within another solid (rock strata). It also contests the biblical Noachian deluge explanation of fossils. Steno believed that strata were formed by the deposition of sediments in water; what looked like organic remains found within stratified rock must represent once-living organisms that existed in water at the time the sediments were deposited. Through direct observation, Steno also theorized that the process of sedimentation takes place at a slow rate over long periods of time. This was a revolutionary proposal not only for the formation of fossils but also for the formation of rock strata.

Fracastoro's contribution to the beginnings of modern geological and paleontological thought are indeed significant, but his greatest contributions to the scientific revolution came from two major works in the field of medicine, specifically epidemic diseases. Fracastoro is credited with publishing the first insights into the spread of contagious disease by personal contact and through inhaling airborne contagions and by indirect contact through items such as clothing. In 1530, Fracastoro published a thirteen-hundred-verse poem entitled *Syphilis sive morbus Gallicus* (*Syphilis: Or, A Poetical History of the French Disease*, 1686; better known as *Syphilis*), a mythical tale discussing the possible causes and diffusion of the sexually transmitted disease syphilis; by 1547, he had published a formal treatise on the subject entitled *De contagionibus et contagiosis morbis et eorum curatione libri tres* (1546; *De contagione et contagiosis morbis et eorum curatione*, 1930). The publication of this work assured Fracastoro a lasting place in the history of epidemiology. In the book, he provides detailed descriptions of numerous contagious diseases and speculates on how each is spread. Fracastoro further speculates diseases are spread by "seeds." The idea of "seeds" causing disease would become the basis for modern germ theory some three hundred fifty years later.

—*Randall L. Milstein*

FURTHER READING

Gould, Stephen Jay. "Pathways of Discovery: Deconstructing the 'Science Wars' by Reconstructing an Old

Mold." *Science* 287 (January 14, 2000). A brief discourse on the history of interpreting fossils and the paths of logic required in making the connections between empirical observation and logical conclusions to their origins.

Harrington, J. W. *Dance of the Continents:* New York: V. P. Tarher, 1983. A fine, general geology book including passages on the lives and philosophies of early geological thinkers and innovators.

Lederberg, Joshua. "Pathways to Discovery: Infectious History." *Science* 288 (April 14, 2000). A history and descriptive outline of the early interpretation of infectious diseases, including the pivotal role played by Girolamo Fracastoro.

Rudwick, M. J. S. *The Meaning of Fossils.* New York: Elsevier, 1972. A good, general reference on the history of paleontology and the roles played by early scientists in the field.

See also: 1546: Fracastoro Discovers That Contagion Spreads Disease; c. 1560's: Invention of the "Lead" Pencil.

Related articles in *Great Lives from History: The Renaissance & Early Modern Era, 1454-1600:* Georgius Agricola; Pierre Belon; Andrea Cesalpino; Girolamo Fracastoro; Leonhard Fuchs; Conrad Gesner; Leonardo da Vinci.

October 31, 1517
LUTHER POSTS HIS NINETY-FIVE THESES

Luther's Ninety-five Theses, which expressed his deep concerns with the practices of the Papacy and the Catholic Church, launched the first salvo in the Protestant Reformation, leading to the formation of hundreds of Christian denominations and sects and initiating a fervor for German nationalism.

Locale: Wittenberg, Germany

Categories: Religion; cultural and intellectual history; social reform

Key Figures

Martin Luther (1483-1546), monk and religious reformer

Johann Tetzel (c. 1465-1519), Dominican friar

Cajetan (Tommaso de Vio; 1469-1534), head of the Dominican order, 1508-1518, and papal legate to Germany

Charles V (1500-1558), Holy Roman Emperor, r. 1519-1556

Johann Eck (1486-1543), Dominican friar

Frederick the Wise (1463-1525), elector of Saxony, 1486-1525, and protector of Luther

Leo X (Giovanni de' Medici; 1475-1521), Roman Catholic pope, 1513-1521

Johann von Staupitz (c. 1468-1524), Luther's superior in the Augustinian order

Summary of Event

On the eve of All Saints' Day, 1517, an Augustinian monk named Martin Luther, professor of biblical exegesis at the University of Wittenberg, posted on the door of All Saints Church a list of ninety-five theological propositions he offered to debate with any member of the university.

The Ninety-five Theses were written in Latin and intended as an academic challenge, but they also expressed deep dissatisfaction that Luther, then thirty-three years old, had come to feel about the Church.

The idea for the theses was ignited after the preaching and, in effect, selling of an indulgence by a Dominican friar, Johann Tetzel, in the area bordering electoral Saxony. An indulgence was a declaration by the Church that individual punishments for past sins were wiped out or reduced both in this life and also in purgatory. The indulgence could be applied to the souls of men already in purgatory but was intended to be offered to those who confessed their sins and had received an actual penance. While an indulgence was not an assurance that the sin would be forgiven, it replaced the penance and could lessen one's punishment in purgatory. These indulgences were not to be sold but granted by a priest. Monetary offerings by the sinner were considered to be contributions. Yet Tetzel, commissioned by Pope Leo X, offered the indulgence to all who would contribute money for the rebuilding of St. Peter's Basilica in Rome, although some of the money had been secretly promised to a German bishop who was in financial trouble.

In his Ninety-five Theses, Luther denied that the pope could remove any penalties imposed on a person by God, attacked the sale of indulgences as superstitious, and

LUTHER'S THESES ON CHURCH REFORM

Martin Luther presented ninety-five theses on the question of reforming the abuses of the Catholic Church and the Papacy. Here, several essential theses are excerpted.

1. Our Lord and Master Jesus Christ in saying "Repent ye" (*poenitentium agite*), intended that the whole life of believers should be penitence (*poenitentia*).
2. This word (*poenitentia*) cannot be understood as sacramental penance, that is, the confession and satisfaction which are performed under the ministry of priests. . . .
5. The pope has neither the will nor the power to remit any penalties except those which he has imposed by his own authority, or by that of the canons. . . .
21. [T]hose preachers of indulgences are in error who say that by the indulgences of the pope a man is freed and saved from all punishment. . . .
27. They preach man (rather than God) who say that the soul flies out of purgatory as soon as the money rattles in the chest. . . .
43. Christians should be taught that he who gives to a poor man, or lends to a needy man, does better than if he bought pardons.
44. Because by works of charity, charity increases and the man becomes better, while by means of pardons he does not become better, but only freer from punishment. . . .
56. The treasures of the Church, whence the pope grants indulgences, are neither sufficiently discussed nor understood among the people of Christ. . . .
62. The true treasure of the Church is the holy gospel of the glory and grace of God. . . .

Source: From *The Great Documents of Western Civilization*, edited by Milton Viorst (New York: Bantam Books, Matrix Editions, 1967), pp. 80-81.

---

questioned the existence of purgatory as a state of the soul after death. He emphasized the necessity of inner sorrow for sins and questioned the necessity of external acts of piety. The display of Luther's discontent was not new for the monk, for he had shown his distaste for the practice three years prior to the posting when he lectured before his students in the university.

Although Luther refrained from attacking the power of the pope and basic Catholic doctrines, within two weeks his theses had been translated into German and had spread throughout Germany. His document was soon published so widely that Tetzel and other Dominicans denounced Luther to Rome. Luther also appealed to Pope Leo X, whom he regarded as an enlightened ruler unaware of the excesses of the indulgence sellers. The criticisms that Luther had voiced were the concerned expressions of many. Luther's theses heightened tensions that were already in existence and from there the rift widened.

With the support of his immediate religious superior, Johann von Staupitz, and the somewhat reluctant support of his secular lord, Frederick III, the Wise, founder of the University of Wittenberg, Luther persevered in his position. A year after the posting of the theses, he appeared at Augsburg before the papal legate, Cardinal Cajetan, who first attempted to win him over with kindness but subsequently condemned him. Luther appealed to a general council of the whole Church to hear his case, a respectable tactic after the conciliar movement of the previous century.

Luther's own ideas became more radical and, in a debate with the Dominican Johann Eck at Leipzig in July of 1519, he proposed several radical theories: that the pope was not supreme in the Church, that papal authority was a human invention, that general councils were capable of error, and that the Bible alone was an infallible authority in religious matters. He declared his obedience to the teachings of Jan Hus, who had been declared a heretic in the previous century.

By this time, Luther had become famous throughout Europe, and fierce arguments raged for and against him. For a time, he received the support of the most renowned humanist thinker of the day, Dutch scholar Desiderius Erasmus. Luther continued to publish theological treatises in which he denied the theory of the seven sacraments as the Church conceived them, asserted the individual's total depravity and lack of free will, and proposed that salvation was possible only by complete faith in God, which humans could not achieve by their own efforts but through God's free gift alone. Luther continued to hope that the Church would be reformed from within by the pope along the lines that Luther had suggested; he desired no break with Rome and continued to live as a monk.

In 1520, he published three important pamphlets: *An den christlichen Adel deutscher Nation* (address to the Christian nobility of the German nation), *Von der Freiheit eines Christenmenschen* (the freedom of the

Christian person), and *De captivitate Babylonica ecclesiae praeludium* (the Babylonian captivity of the Church). In these treatises, Luther strongly attacked abuses in the Roman Catholic Church. While calling for papal reform, he blamed the Papacy, and he urged secular rulers to reform the Catholic Church by force if the pope and bishops failed to do so. Leo X, who had shown little interest in Luther's case at first, officially condemned him as a heretic in the papal bull *Exsurge Domine*, which Luther subsequently burned in a public ceremony. In January of 1521, Luther was excommunicated from the Church.

The Diet of the empire was sharply split between princes friendly to Luther and those opposed to him. When Luther appeared before the Diet held at Worms in April, 1521, Holy Roman Emperor Charles V tried to persuade him to recant, but Luther made his famous appeal of the primacy of conscience and then went into hiding. The emperor managed to obtain condemnation of Luther for heresy at a subsequent rump session. Luther was then banished as an outlaw of the empire, and his civil rights in the country were terminated. It was too late, however, to stop those who endorsed Luther's ideas, for he had appealed to all classes of people and had increasingly gained a following of supporters.

Remaining in seclusion within Warburg Castle, Luther prepared a new translation of the Bible into German, which revealed his extraordinary literary ability. The invention of the printing press made the text more readily available, and the translation of the Bible into German enabled many more people to read the Scriptures. Emerging a year later, Luther came to be regarded as the patriarch of the new movement for Protestantism. Until his death in 1546, he sought to curb what he regarded as the excesses of his followers.

SIGNIFICANCE

The northern half of Germany had answered his trumpet call to break with Rome under the secular leadership of princes. A nationalist movement ensued, and Luther's contributions of his written word and open defiance became part of German culture and fueled the activism of both nationalism and religious reform. Hundreds of priests and nuns renounced their vows and embraced the new theology that claimed to reform the Church along biblical lines. Many married, as Luther had in 1525.

Lutheranism soon gained wide acceptance in Germany and Scandinavia. The evolution of Protestantism in Switzerland and the Netherlands followed different paths, but the whole movement was indebted to Luther

for hammering in the revolution when he posted his Ninety-five Theses on the door of the Castle Church at Wittenberg.

*—James F. Hitchcock,
updated by Marilyn Elizabeth Perry*

FURTHER READING

Dillenberger, John, ed. *Martin Luther: Selections from His Writings*. New York: Anchor Books, 1961. Contains the complete text of the Ninety-five Theses.

Erikson, Erik H. *Young Man Luther*. New York: W. W. Norton, 1962. A psychoanalyst looks at Luther's formative years. One of the classic psychoanalytic biographies.

McKim, Donald K., ed. *The Cambridge Companion to Martin Luther*. New York: Cambridge University Press, 2003. Anthology of essays by noted scholars covering Luther's theology, moral thought, skill with words, direct effects, and lasting legacy, among other topics. Includes bibliographic references and index.

Marty, Martin. *Martin Luther*. New York: Viking Penguin, 2004. Subtle and balanced portrayal of Luther's theology and its cultural context, explaining the importance of the debates in which he intervened as well as tracing the ultimate results of that intervention. Luther's character receives an equally nuanced treatment. Includes maps and bibliographic references.

Oberman, Heiko A. *Luther: Man Between God and the Devil*. Translated by Eileen Walliser-Schwarzbart. New Haven, Conn.: Yale University Press, 1989. A biography written by one of the foremost Reformation scholars of the twentieth century. Delves into Luther's mind and places his thoughts and theories within the context of the sixteenth century.

_____. *The Two Reformations: The Journey from the Last Days to the New World*. Edited by Donald Weinstein. New Haven, Conn.: Yale University Press, 2003. Posthumous collection of essays revisiting debates on Luther's anti-Semitism and arguing that medieval religious thought was essential to both Calvin's and Luther's understandings of Christianity. Includes bibliographic references and index.

Ozment, Steven. *Protestants: The Birth of a Revolution*. New York: Doubleday, 1992. This work traces the origins of the Protestant movement and ties it to values found in Western culture.

Pelikan, Jaroslav. *Obedient Rebels*. New York: Harper & Row, 1964. An American Lutheran scholar argues that Luther was faithful to Catholic tradition in his Reformation.

Wengert, Timothy J., ed. *Harvesting Martin Luther's Reflections on Theology, Ethics, and the Church.* Grand Rapids, Mich.: W. B. Eerdmans, 2004. Anthology of essays focused on the practical value of Luther's teachings for daily life. Discusses a range of issues, both doctrinal and secular, to give a full portrayal of Luther's thought and its applications. Includes illustrations, bibliographic references, index.

SEE ALSO: 1456: Publication of Gutenberg's Mazarin Bible; 1499-1517: Erasmus Advances Humanism in England; Apr.-May, 1521: Luther Appears Before the Diet of Worms; 1523: Gustav I Vasa Becomes King of Sweden; June, 1524-July, 1526: German Peasants' War; Feb. 27, 1531: Formation of the Schmalkaldic League; Mar., 1536: Calvin Publishes *Institutes of the Christian Religion*; 1545-1563: Council of Trent; Sept. 25, 1555: Peace of Augsburg; Apr. or May, 1560: Publication of the Geneva Bible; Feb. 25, 1570: Pius V Excommunicates Elizabeth I.

RELATED ARTICLES in *Great Lives from History: The Renaissance & Early Modern Era, 1454-1600:* Martin Bucer; John Calvin; William Caxton; Charles V; Miles Coverdale; Lucas Cranach, the Elder; Elizabeth I; Desiderius Erasmus; Saint John Fisher; Henry VIII; Balthasar Hubmaier; Saint Ignatius of Loyola; John Knox; Leo X; Martin Luther; Marguerite de Navarre; Maximilian II; Philipp Melanchthon; Menno Simons; Philip the Magnanimous; Pius V; Huldrych Zwingli.

Beginning 1519
SMALLPOX KILLS THOUSANDS OF INDIGENOUS AMERICANS

The devastation wrought upon the Aztec Empire and other American Indian cultures left them unable to defend themselves against the Europeans. The resulting defeat and subjugation of the Aztec Empire by Hernán Cortés opened the way to Spanish domination of Mexico and much of western North America.

LOCALE: Tenochtitlán and its environs (now Mexico City, Mexico)
CATEGORIES: Health and medicine; colonization; natural disasters

KEY FIGURES
Hernán Cortés (1485-1547), Spanish conquistador
Montezuma II (1467-1520), last official emperor of the Aztecs, r. 1502-1520
Cuitláhuac (d. 1520), brother and successor of Montezuma II, r. 1520
Cuauhtémoc (c. 1495-1525), last ruler of the Aztecs, r. 1520-1521
Pedro de Alvarado (1485-1541), Spanish conquistador under Cortés
Diego Velázquez (1465-1524), Spanish soldier and governor of Cuba, 1511-1524
Pánfilo de Narváez (c. 1480-1528), Spanish conquistador under Velásquez

SUMMARY OF EVENT
On April 21, 1519, eleven Spanish ships under the command of the Spanish adventurer Hernán Cortés weighed anchor on the east coast of what would become Mexico. On the ships were some 550 soldiers and sailors. The goal of the expedition was to establish a Spanish presence in the area and discover gold or other treasures for their king, Charles I (Holy Roman Emperor Charles V). In addition, the Spanish hoped to convert the Central American Indians to Christianity, the dominant religion of Spain. Meeting Cortés were representatives of the Totonacs. The land was claimed on behalf of the Spanish king, and Cortés prepared to travel inland.

For Europe, the early sixteenth century was a time of discovery in the New World, with Spain and Portugal in the forefront of European exploration. During the second decade of the century, several Spanish explorers had already probed the gulf coast region in the area of the Yucatán Peninsula, with limited success. The 1519 expedition led by Cortés represented only the newest attempt to establish a Spanish presence on the mainland.

Cortés's landing came as no surprise to Montezuma II, the ruler of the Aztec (Mexica) Empire. Runners had brought word to the capital of the Spanish landing. Legend suggests that the Aztecs mistook Cortés for Quetzalcóatl, a light-skinned god who it was believed would appear in the east, and who would ultimately rule over the empire. The reality of the situation is less clear. Montezuma had been selected as ruler in 1502 by a council of nobles. He was a youthful and brilliant warrior, dominating his enemies in a large region around the capital. He was, as well, an enlightened ruler, and, as a student of Aztec theology, was certainly aware of the Quetzalcóatl legend.

There exists little evidence, however, that Montezuma subscribed to the legend of Quetzalcóatl, and in all likelihood, the story was a myth developed by Franciscans for their own theological purposes. The reaction of the Aztecs to the Spaniards was directed more toward the latter's weaponry and the horses they were riding, neither of which the Aztecs had ever encountered before. It is clear, however, that Montezuma initially welcomed Cortés, allowing the Spanish to enter the capital of Tenochtitlán as well as the royal palace. In response, Cortés took Montezuma captive.

The origin of the smallpox epidemic is obscure. Given the disease's relatively short incubation period (one to two weeks), it is unlikely that Cortés brought the virus with him on the ships. Furthermore, no written record from the conquest provides any evidence that Cortés's crew carried the virus. However, the endemic nature of the disease in Spain would probably have resulted in immunity among the crew by this time.

Historian William Prescott has suggested another possible source for the virus: a slave belonging to Diego Velázquez de Cuéllar, the Spanish governor of Cuba. If true, this theory reveals an irony to Cortés's eventual conquest. Velázquez was resentful of Cortés's success in the initial stages of his invasion of the Americas and was particularly jealous of the treasures Cortés had obtained. As a result, Velázquez decided to assert his own authority and arranged for a naval force consisting of some eighteen ships, nine hundred soldiers, and approximately one thousand slaves and local natives under the authority of Pánfilo de Narváez. Their objective was to occupy Mexico in place of Cortés. Cortés, however, became aware of the Velázquez expedition and moved against him first. Leaving the Tenochtitlán garrison under the command of Pedro de Alvarado and extracting a promise of neutrality from the captive Montezuma, Cortés overran the enemy camp and captured Narváez. Cortés ensured the loyalty of Narváez's men by bribing them with the Aztec gold.

The source of the smallpox virus in all likelihood was the invasion force under Narváez. Among the enslaved members of that force may have been a person with smallpox, then endemic in Cuba. The first outbreak among the indigenous population occurred at the landing area of Cempoalla. In response to the high fever symptomatic of the disease, the Indians would bathe in cold water, a practice that served only to exacerbate the illness. The smallpox epidemic spread over the entire area,

reaching the capital of Tenochtitlán later that year. Among its later victims was Cuitláhuac, Montezuma's successor as ruler.

In Cortés's absence, de Alvarado mistook a religious celebration by the Aztecs for a rebellion, and his response resulted in the slaughter of thousands of Aztecs, which transformed their uprising from an imagined revolt into a real one. Montezuma, attempting to calm his subjects, was seriously injured by a rock thrown at his head, and he died several days later. He was succeeded by his brother Cuitláhuac.

There is significant disagreement over the precise population of the Aztec Empire in 1519, but the most reliable figures suggest it was approximately 5 million. The population of the capital, Tenochtitlán, appears to have been approximately 300,000. Following his defeat of the expedition under Narváez, Cortés and some five hundred soldiers returned to Tenochtitlán. His forces were supplemented by around twenty-five thousand to fifty thousand warriors, principally from native tribes previously subjugated by the Aztecs. After building a causeway to allow access by his ships carrying supplies and ammunition, Cortés set siege to the capital.

Somehow, smallpox entered the city. It had spread from the coast, through the countryside of Tlascala, and into the capital. Among its first victims was Cuitláhuac. From Tenochtitlán, the epidemic spread to the Pacific coast and south through Central and South America. In its path, unknown numbers died; the estimate among the Franciscans was that millions ultimately perished. Within a generation, the population of much of the Americas had been reduced by 90 percent.

When Cortés entered the city, the streets were described as being so filled with the dying and dead that the "men could walk over nothing but bodies." The Aztecs, now under the leadership of Cuauhtémoc, continued to resist the Spanish. Even with European weapons and native allies, there is legitimate question as to whether Cortés could ultimately have been successful in the absence of the disease. Smallpox had so ravaged the Aztec population, however, that both the means and the will to resist had disappeared. On August 13, 1521, Cuauhtémoc surrendered to Cortés.

SIGNIFICANCE

The introduction of smallpox in 1519 during the conquest by Cortés decimated the indigenous population, enabling the Spanish to conquer the North American Indians by 1521 and to establish colonies in what would become the southwestern United States and Mexico. This would not be the only time the pestilence would be introduced into parts of the Americas from Europe, and the staggering effects of disease on a population lacking any previous exposure would be repeated through numerous epidemics covering the next three centuries.

The population of the Aztecs at the time of the Cortés expedition is unknown, but it probably numbered in the millions. The deaths en masse of the natives produced two significant effects, one practical and the other psychological. First, Cortés accomplished his mission of conquering the native peoples with a relative handful of men. Even given the presence of weapons viewed as devastating by the natives, the ability of such small numbers to be victorious required additional factors. There is no question that elimination of most of the opposition through disease opened the way for Spanish conquest. In addition, the rapid decimation appeared to some of the natives as an indication the gods were on the side of the conquerors. Psychologically, the Aztecs were forced to conclude that Cortés could not be resisted.

—*Richard Adler*

FURTHER READING

Crosby, Alfred. *Ecological Imperialism: The Biological Expansion of Europe, 900-1900*. New York: Cambridge University Press, 1993. Explores the role of disease in the conquest of lands by European powers. Included are descriptions of the effects on the Aztec population of the Americas.

Díaz del Castillo, Bernal. *The Discovery and Conquest of Mexico*. Translated by A. P. Maudslay and edited by Genaro García. New York: DaCapo Press, 2004. Account of Cortés's conquest of Mexico by a conquistador who accompanied him.

Fenn, Elizabeth. *Pox Americana*. New York: Hill and Wang, 2001. A description of the smallpox epidemics that devastated populations, both native and newly arrived, in the Americas during the late eighteenth century.

Fenner, Frank. *Smallpox and Its Eradication*. Geneva: World Health Organization, 1988. Primarily a history of the disease. The author does address the effects of smallpox on populations that had no natural immunity.

Prescott, William H. *History of the Conquest of Peru*. London: Phoenix Press, 2002. Part of Prescott's classic series on the conquest of the Americas by Spain.

_____. *The World of the Aztecs*. Barcelona, Spain: Industria Grafica, 1974. Reprint of Prescott's classic account (1843) of the defeat of the Aztecs. Prescott, grandson of the American commander at Bunker Hill, became a noted Spanish historian.

Restall, Matthew. *Seven Myths of the Spanish Conquest*. New York: Oxford University Press, 2003. The author provides a new perspective on the Spanish conquest of the Americas. Argues, for example, that the native perception of the conquest was that of a civil war, rather than a foreign invasion.

SEE ALSO: Oct. 12, 1492: Columbus Lands in the Americas; 1493-1521: Ponce de León's Voyages; 1500-1530's: Portugal Begins to Colonize Brazil; 1502-1520: Reign of Montezuma II; Apr., 1519-Aug., 1521: Cortés Conquers Aztecs in Mexico; Aug., 1523: Franciscan Missionaries Arrive in Mexico; 1527-1547: Maya Resist Spanish Incursions in Yucatán; 1528-1536: Narváez's and Cabeza de Vaca's Expeditions; 1532-1537: Pizarro Conquers the Incas in Peru; 1545-1548: Silver Is Discovered in Spanish America; 1552: Las Casas Publishes *The Tears of the Indians*.

RELATED ARTICLES in *Great Lives from History: The Renaissance & Early Modern Era, 1454-1600:* Pedro de Alvarado; Charles V; Hernán Cortés; Cuauhtémoc; Montezuma II.

1519-1522
MAGELLAN EXPEDITION CIRCUMNAVIGATES THE GLOBE

The Magellan expedition's circumnavigation of the globe opened the westward passage to the Spice Islands. The voyage explored and named the Pacific Ocean, demonstrated that the earth is round, and proved the existence of a New World distinct from Asia.

LOCALE: Worldwide
CATEGORY: Exploration and discovery

KEY FIGURES

Charles V (1500-1558), king of Spain as Charles I, r. 1516-1556, and Holy Roman Emperor, r. 1519-1556, patron of the Magellan venture
Ferdinand Magellan (Fernão de Magalhães; c. 1480-1521), Portuguese navigator and explorer in the service of Spain
Antonio Pigafetta (1491-c. 1534), Venetian naturalist, ethnographer, and illuminator of manuscripts who chronicled Magellan's voyage

Juan Rodríguez de Fonseca (1451-1524), Spanish prelate and bishop, later head of department of affairs of the Indias
Andrés San Martín (d. 1521), Spanish scholar who served as Magellan's astronomer-pilot
Juan Sebastián de Elcano (c. 1487-1526), Basque seaman and master of the *Concepción* who commanded the *Victoria* to Spain after Magellan's death

SUMMARY OF EVENT

Ferdinand Magellan was born of an aristocratic family in north Portugal around 1480 and was reared as a page in the royal household, where he learned navigation, astronomy, algebra, and geometry. At age fifteen, he enlisted as a volunteer to sail to India, where he served with distinction and was wounded in the Portuguese siege of Melaka in 1506. In 1508, he returned to India, where he was again wounded at the Battle of Diu the following

Magellan and his expedition at the Strait of Magellan—later named in his honor—connecting the South Atlantic with the South Pacific as it winds 350 miles (563 kilometers) through southern Argentina and southern Chile. (R. S. Peale and J. A. Hill)

year, and in 1510, he was rewarded with a captaincy for his numerous services and bravery. After seven years abroad, Magellan returned to Portugal in 1512 to enlist in a campaign against the Moors in Africa, where he was again severely wounded. Following this venture, Magellan unfortunately found himself unemployed and passed over for further service, as he was out of favor with the court of King Manuel I, being humiliated by accusations of financial irregularities and trading with the Moors. Though the charge was later dropped, Magellan apparently could see no future for his skills in Portugal. He denounced his nationality and emigrated to Spain in 1518. His biographers have described Magellan as an imaginative, resourceful, and energetic man, but one of quiet dignity who apparently felt thwarted at home by continual intrigue.

These personal intrigues were only a small component in global politics designed to seize as much territory as possible in the New World. According to the revised papal donation of Alexander VI, Portugal had been granted all the new lands of the east up to longitude 46° west. The Peninsular statesmen, however, were not sure what islands and areas in Asia fell east and west of longitude 134° east, the continuation of the line of demarcation on the opposite side of the globe. Meanwhile, the Spaniards, in the second decade of the sixteenth century, had established a strong footing on the new continent. After Vasco Núñez de Balboa's discovery of the South Sea in 1513, explorers looked westward, feeling that they had an opportunity to extend their influence to the wealthy lands of Asia. As it turned out, they were mistaken. Longitude 134° east, while placing most of Japan, Australia, and New Guinea in the Spanish sphere, passed far to the east of the Spice Islands (Moluccas). Yet, in 1519, neither Magellan nor his new employers were aware of this.

In the winter of 1518, Magellan visited the imperial court of Charles V at Valladolid and convinced Charles, as king of Castile and Holy Roman Emperor, to authorize a major voyage westward to explore a route to the Spice Islands. Magellan's task of persuasion was easier than that of Christopher Columbus had been, for Magellan had the discoveries of the previous two decades to support his arguments. Armed with the royal commission, Magellan moved to Seville, where he spent more than a year outfitting his fleet.

The five ships granted to Magellan were not completely seaworthy. They were old, were ill-maintained, and had repeatedly been subject to accidents and repair. This somewhat decrepit fleet comprised the *San Antonio*

(120 tons), the *Trinidad* (110 tons), the *Concepción* (90 tons), the *Victoria* (85 tons), and the *Santiago* (75 tons). Unfortunately, only the 85-ton *Victoria* was destined to complete the voyage, which would ultimately cover 45,000 miles (72,420 kilometers), and it would arrive with only 18 survivors from the original complement of 237 men.

Magellan experienced considerable difficulty enlisting crews, particularly since sea travel paid low wages and presented high risks to seamen. Also, the population of Castile was drastically reduced by the bubonic plague. Consequently, the company was composed of sailors from Portugal and all over Europe, as well as Levantines and Africans. Not only were language and ethnic differences a disadvantage, but conditions of health and morale were also such that they would later result in general discontent and even several mutinies. Magellan's enterprise was further jeopardized by having inexperienced, court-appointed Castillian ships' officers, many of whom were arrogant, pompous landlubbers, unqualified as either leaders or seamen. Finally, Magellan's situation was complicated during the voyage by several plots to have him killed by enlisted assassins.

The fleet, replete with all these difficulties, set sail from San Lúcar on September 20, 1519. In addition to the sailors Magellan had managed to enlist, he carried with him noted Venetian naturalist Antonio Pigafetta, who kept records of the voyage; Andrés San Martín, Spanish scholar and Magellan's ill-fated pilot; and Juan Rodríguez de Fonseca, a Spanish bishop interested in the conversion and exploitation of the New World. The fleet made an Atlantic run of more than two months, which landed them in Brazil. From there, they held closely to the coast of South America, being always on the lookout for a strait that would take them to the South Sea. When summer ended in the Southern Hemisphere in 1520, Magellan decided to go into winter quarters in southern Patagonia. In this dreary region, the expedition remained from March to August, 1520, but its stay was not uneventful; mutiny broke out, the *San Antonio* was deserted, and the tiny *Santiago* was smashed to pieces on a reef while exploring and charting the coast.

Finally, in August, Magellan recommenced his long voyage westward, eventually discovering and entering, on October 21, the strait—Strait of Magellan—that now bears his name. Thirty-eight days were spent traversing the 320 miles (515 kilometers) between the Atlantic and Pacific Oceans. This was a relatively slow passage, but Magellan was fortunate with favorable climatic conditions. Finally, on November 28, 1520, seven years after

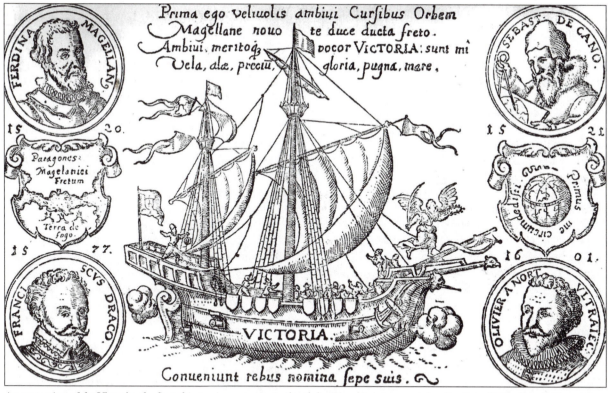

An engraving of the Victoria, *the first ship to circumnavigate the globe. The ship's two captains, Ferdinand Magellan (left) and Juan Sebastián de Elcano, are shown at the top of the image.* (Hulton|Archive by Getty Images)

Balboa had first sighted the South Sea, Magellan, with a fleet reduced to three ships, entered the waters of the Pacific, thereby solving the riddle of the westward passage.

What followed was a great contest of endurance. The seemingly interminable crossing of the Pacific reduced the ships' companies to a diet of rats, weevil-infested hardtack, sawdust, and leather. His crew probably suffered more severely from scurvy than any other trans-Pacific exploration. Not until they reached Guam in the Ladrone Islands on March 6, 1521, did the ships drop anchor. After replenishing their food and water, they then set sail for the Philippines, arriving at Cebu on April 7. There Magellan formed an unfortunate alliance with the local ruler, which later involved him and his crew in a small war that resulted in the death of Magellan and forty of his men.

Following Magellan's death, the expedition disintegrated. For lack of a crew, the *Concepción* was burned. The *Trinidad* attempted to sail to Panama but was eventually captured by the Portuguese. It remained for the *Victoria*, under Basque navigator Juan Sebastián de Elcano, to complete the circumnavigation alone. He steered the

ship through the Spice Islands and across the Indian Ocean for South Africa, deliberately avoiding normal shipping lanes, beset with scurvy, starvation, and Portuguese harassment. With only eighteen Europeans and four Malays, scarcely enough to staff the ship, the resourceful de Elcano sailed into San Lúcar on September 6, 1522, and arrived at Seville on September 8, 1522, three years less twelve days after his departure.

SIGNIFICANCE

After the tragedy of the captain's death, the completion of the voyage was left to his few remaining crewmen. Magellan's goal had arguably been achieved, however, once he had reached Asia by sailing west from Europe. In fact, Magellan's westward journey had probably passed beyond any eastward points that he had touched during his Portuguese service in 1513-1514. Consequently, some historians claim that Magellan in person had indeed been around the world. Though his ill fortune did not allow him to make a single circumnavigation from Spain back to Spain, he had discovered a westward route to the Spice Islands, thereby succeeding where Columbus had failed. Moreover, Magellan proved definitively the roundness of the earth by linking west Europe with east Asia, revolutionized perceptions of relative land mass in comparison to large bodies of water, and demonstrated the existence of a New World of the Americas separate and distinct from Asia.

—*Charles J. Fleener, updated by John Alan Ross*

FURTHER READING

Bergreen, Laurence. *Over the Edge of the World: Magellan's Terrifying Circumnavigation of the Globe.* New York: William Morrow, 2003. Engaging and dramatic narrative of Magellan's voyage, which is portrayed day by day according to ship's logs and the journals of crew members. Includes photographic plates, illustrations, maps, bibliographic references, and index.

Joyner, Tim. *Magellan.* Camden, N.J.: International Marine, 1992. One of the most thorough and well-researched accounts of Magellan, his voyage, and his crew, dealing with the various phases of Portuguese political intrigue.

Morison, Samuel Eliot. *The European Discovery of America: The Southern Voyages.* New York: Oxford University Press, 1974. Written by a noted historian, this work contains a well-researched and annotated chapter on Magellan.

Nowall, Charles E., ed. *Magellan's Voyage Around the World.* Evanston, Ill.: Northwestern University Press, 1962. A useful compendium of historical accounts, particularly the ethnographic accounts and descriptions of flora and fauna encountered by Antonio Pigafetta, as well as the records of Maximilian of Transylvania, who, as secretary to Charles V, debriefed the Magellan expedition survivors.

Oliveira, Fernando. *Another Report About Magellan's Circumnavigation of the World: The Story of Fernando Oliveira.* Translated by Pedro Sastre. Edited by Karl-Heinz Wionzek. Manila, Philippines: National Historical Institute, 2000. Firsthand account of Magellan's voyage, written by a member of his crew. Includes illustrations, maps, and bibliographic references.

Parr, Charles McKew. *Ferdinand Magellan: Circumnavigator.* New York: Thomas Y. Crowell, 1964. Originally published under the title *So Noble a Captain* in 1953, this work provides a comprehensive survey of secondary Portuguese and Spanish archival sources. It explains the sociopolitical intrigue to extend national influence and to break the new spice trade monopoly held by Portugal.

Parry, J. H. *Europe and the Wider World, 1415-1715.* London: Hutchinson, 1949. This older work emphasizes the rivalries within sixteenth century Europe and the subsequent political and socioeconomic impact upon Magellan's voyage.

Penrose, Boies. *Travel and Discovery in the Renaissance, 1420-1620.* Reprint. Cambridge, Mass.: Harvard University Press, 1967. Provides an appraisal and recognition of the importance of Magellan's circumnavigational voyage in chapter 10. Includes illustrations, maps, bibliography, and index.

Pigafetta, Antonio. *Magellan's Voyage: A Narrative Account of the First Circumnavigation.* Translated by R. A. Skelton. New Haven, Conn.: Yale University Press, 1969. Reprint. Mineola, N.Y.: Dover, 1994. English translation from a French text of Pigafetta's Italian journal. Full of detailed descriptions of the events of the voyage, the lands discovered, and the habits, customs, and tales of the indigenous peoples encountered, as well as examples of their vocabulary.

SEE ALSO: Aug., 1487-Dec., 1488: Dias Rounds the Cape of Good Hope; Oct. 12, 1492: Columbus Lands in the Americas; 1500-1530's: Portugal Begins to Colonize Brazil; 1502: Beginning of the Transatlantic Slave Trade; 1511-c. 1515: Melaka Falls to the Portuguese; Sept. 29, 1513: Balboa Reaches the Pacific Ocean; 1514-1598: Portuguese Reach China; Jan. 23, 1516: Charles I Ascends the Throne of Spain; Apr. 20, 1534-July, 1543: Cartier and Roberval Search for a Northwest Passage; 1565: Spain Seizes the Philippines; Dec. 31, 1600: Elizabeth I Charters the East India Company.

RELATED ARTICLES in *Great Lives from History: The Renaissance & Early Modern Era, 1454-1600:* Charles V; Christopher Columbus; Juan Sebastián de Elcano; Ferdinand II and Isabella I; Ferdinand Magellan.

April, 1519-August, 1521
CORTÉS CONQUERS AZTECS IN MEXICO

Cortés conquered the Aztecs of Mexico, giving Spain control over the region and launching a long-term Spanish conquest that would encompass most of the Americas.

LOCALE: Tenochtitlán, Aztec Empire (now Mexico City, Mexico)

CATEGORIES: Expansion and land acquisition; colonization; exploration and discovery; wars, uprisings, and civil unrest

KEY FIGURES

Hernán Cortés (1485-1547), Spanish conqueror

Montezuma II (1467-1520), emperor of the Aztec Empire, r. 1502-1520, when Cortés came to Mexico

Doña Marina (La Malinche; c. 1502-1527/1528), indigenous Mexican translator who became the Spaniards' interpreter and guide

Cuauhtémoc (c. 1495-1525), last of the Aztec emperors, r. 1520-1521

Diego Velázquez de Cuéllar (c. 1465-1524), Spanish governor of Cuba

Pedro de Alvarado (1485-1541), Spanish conquistador

SUMMARY OF EVENT

There is little dispute about the role of Hernán Cortés and the importance of the Spanish conquest of Mexico. Nevertheless, the meaning of these events and the place of Cortés in the history of Mexico have undergone a profound transformation. For centuries, Cortés was seen as a bold adventurer who seized the initiative from a hesitant Montezuma and, with only a small number of Spanish, conquered a vast empire.

Since the Mexican Revolution of 1910-1917, however, many have come to regard Cortés as a greedy mur-

An engraved depiction of Montezuma's and Cortés's first meeting in Tenochtitlán. The Spaniards would later sack the Aztec capital. (Hulton|Archive by Getty Images)

derer, who repaid courtesy with treachery and destroyed an entire nation. The conqueror and the conquest, regardless of the interpretation, have merged into one epic saga.

Following the discovery of Hispaniola and other islands in the Caribbean, the Spanish began a systematic conquest of the Antilles and explored westward toward the mainland. Francisco Hernandez de Córdoba discovered the Yucatán in 1517, and Juan de Grijalva in 1518 found evidence of great wealth to the west. In 1519, Governor Diego Velázquez de Cuéllar of Cuba chose Hernán Cortés to lead a third expedition to the mainland to trade with indigenous peoples. Cortés put on such airs at his appointment that Velázquez attempted to replace Cortés, who sailed before new orders were received. He had eleven ships, six hundred men, and sixteen horses, along with some cannon.

Cortés repeatedly encountered good luck in this enterprise. He also demonstrated capable leadership, resourcefulness, and tenacity in the face of sometimes overwhelming obstacles. Off the coast of the Yucatán, Cortés

heard that stranded Spanish sailors were living with the Maya. One of these was rescued and, knowing the indigenous peoples' language, provided Cortés with a trusted translator from the very beginning. Later, after Cortés and his men defeated an attack and made peace with an indigenous tribe, they were offered twenty indigenous women. One, whom the Spanish called Doña Marina when she became Christian, but known to the Mexicans as La Malinche, spoke several indigenous languages and served Cortés as a spy as well as an interpreter.

In April of 1519, Cortés reached the region controlled by the Aztec Empire. To enhance his authority and justify disobeying the orders of the Cuban governor to trade and return, Cortés constructed a town he called Veracruz and had his men elect him as the king's direct representative. Thus established, Cortés burned his boats, claiming they were unseaworthy, and initiated his march to the capital of the great Aztec Empire, Tenochtitlán.

The Aztec emperor, Montezuma II, ruled an enormous area that encompassed most of central Mexico and contained between twenty-five million and thirty million inhabitants. Spain, with only eight million people, was smaller in both size and population. The Aztecs, however, were not prepared to face Europeans who came with strange beasts and weapons, and who acted so differently. An old myth that predated the Aztecs told of a great god, Quetzalcóatl, the feathered serpent, who had once ruled in Mexico but had been driven out. He sailed eastward, claiming that one day he would return to claim his kingdom. Montezuma, remembering this story, fell victim to Cortés's cunning, when the Spaniard, displaying cannons, mastiffs, and horses that terrified Montezuma's envoys, claimed to be that deity. Torn between fear of the god's wrath and the suspicion that Cortés was only a human enemy, Montezuma alternately plotted to ambush Cortés, offered him presents of gold, pleaded with him to go away, and demanded that his shamans destroy the Spaniard with a curse.

Meanwhile, Cortés was slowly marching his men up into the mountains toward the capital. After being attacked and nearly destroyed by a fierce tribe that detested the Aztecs, Cortés explained that he had come to free the people from their hated enemy,

---

OMENS TELLING OF THE ARRIVAL OF THE SPANIARDS IN MEXICO

According to indigenous accounts, a series of omens foretold the arrival of the Spaniards in Mexico, including conquistador Hernán Cortés before his siege of Tenochtitlán in 1521. The omens presented here come from the firsthand accounts of informants of Spanish missionary and historian Bernardino de Sahagún (Cortés's contemporary), originally written in the Náhuatl language and translated into the Latin alphabet by Sahagún and his informants.

1. Ten years before the Spaniards first came here, a bad omen appeared in the sky. It was like a flaming ear of corn, or a fiery signal, or the blaze of daybreak; it seemed to bleed fire, drop by drop, like a wound in the sky.
2. The temple of Huitzilopochtli burst into flames.
3. A temple was damaged by a lightning-bolt. . . . no thunder was heard. Therefore the lightning-bolt was taken as an omen. The people said: "The temple was struck by a blow from the sun."
4. Fire streamed through the sky while the sun was still shining.
5. The wind lashed the water until it boiled. It was as if it were boiling with rage, as if it were shattering itself in its frenzy.
6. The people heard a weeping woman night after night.
7. A strange creature was captured in the nets. The men who fish the lakes caught a bird the color of ashes, a bird resembling a crane.
8. Monstrous beings appeared in the streets of the city.

Source: Excerpted from "The Omens as Described by Sahagún's Informants," in *The Broken Spears: The Aztec Account of the Conquest of Mexico*, edited by Miguel Leon-Portilla (Boston: Beacon Press, 1970), pp. 4-6.

Cortés's troops ended an indigenous rebellion in Cholula just prior to the Spaniards' sacking of Tenochtitlán and the fall of the Aztecs. (R. S. Peale and J. A. Hill)

and he received them as allies. When Cortés heard from La Malinche that the people of the town of Cholula were preparing a trap for him and his men, Cortés massacred the leaders and allowed his indigenous allies to sack the city. Montezuma remained frozen with fear yet shocked at the Spanish invaders' blatant disregard for Aztec rules of warfare.

On November 8, 1519, Montezuma finally met Cortés and invited him and his men into Tenochtitlán. One of Cortés's soldiers, Bernal Díaz del Castillo, wrote that this fabulous city was grander than most in Europe and bigger than anything he had ever seen in Spain. It was an enormous city of more than 150,000 people, with great palaces and neighborhoods divided by grand canals. Cortés and his men had simply walked in and made themselves masters of the city.

Cortés's control was tenuous, however, and he decided to seize Montezuma on the pretext that some of the

men he had left behind at Veracruz had been killed. Montezuma was horrified when he was taken by the Spanish, who had betrayed his hospitality. In a dignified manner, the Aztec emperor explained to his people that he was not a prisoner, and he was permitted a degree of freedom. Nevertheless, many of the Aztec leaders were upset with Montezuma's meekness and, when Cortés suddenly had to return to Veracruz to face a shipload of men sent by Cuba's angry governor, his second in command, Pedro de Alvarado, feared an uprising. After giving the Aztec aristocrats permission to perform a religious ceremony, Alvarado thought they would use it as an excuse to attack, so he directed the Spanish to massacre the unarmed dancers. This led to a general uprising against the Spanish, in which Montezuma was killed.

When Cortés returned, he could only help his men fight their way out of the capital. On July 1, 1520, *La noche triste*, or the night of sorrows, as the Spanish called it, Cortés and his men were nearly destroyed. They barely escaped with the assistance of their indigenous allies and spent nearly half a year recovering, planning, and building a fleet of boats to attack the Aztec capital from the waters of Lake Texcoco, which surrounded the city.

SIGNIFICANCE

While the Spanish were recovering from their rout, the Aztecs were struck by smallpox, probably from a wounded soldier they had captured to sacrifice. The pestilence decimated the population of the city and left the Aztecs weakened. In spite of their debility, and the death by smallpox of Montezuma's brother and emperor, Cuitláhuac, who had replaced Montezuma, the Aztecs fought bravely and effectively against the Spanish and their indigenous allies.

Under the leadership of Cuauhtémoc, the unrelenting Spanish attacks were pushed back, until Cortés ordered that the entire city be leveled. As ships surrounded the city and Spanish troops cut the water supply, the Aztecs courageously defended their city and their civilization.

Finally, on August 13, 1521, the last Aztec warriors were defeated and, with the city demolished, Emperor Cuauhtémoc was brought before Cortés. The young Aztec emperor begged to be killed, but Cortés refused and treated him with respect. He wanted to use this last symbol of authority to end Aztec control throughout Mexico. One empire had fallen, and another was about to be constructed on its ruins.

—*James A. Baer*

FURTHER READING

Collis, Maurice. *Cortés and Montezuma.* New York: New Directions, 1999. Extensively researched, detailed, and highly accessible account of the meeting between Cortés and Montezuma. Includes illustrations, map, and index.

Cortés, Hernán. *Letters from Mexico.* Edited and translated by Anthony Pagden. Rev. ed. New Haven, Conn.: Yale Nota Bene, 2001. Cortés wrote many letters to his king, Charles V, chronicling his deeds and forever proclaiming his loyal service. Provides the reader with an opportunity to see Cortés's own description of his actions.

Díaz del Castillo, Bernal. *The Discovery and Conquest of Mexico, 1517-1521.* Edited by Genaro García. Translated by A. P. Maudslay. Reprint. New York: Da Capo Press, 1996. An account by a foot soldier under Cortés of the events of the conquest. Although written many

years later, it manages to recapture the emotions of the Spanish conquistadores.

Kandell, Jonathan. *La Capital: The Biography of Mexico City.* New York: Henry Holt, 1988. A lengthy and well-written story of the capital city of Mexico, from Tenochtitlán to Mexico City. Chapter 3 discusses Montezuma and chapter 5 examines the conquest.

Leon-Portilla, Miguel, ed. *The Broken Spears: The Aztec Account of the Conquest of Mexico.* Translated by Lysander Kemp. New ed. Boston: Beacon Press, 1992. Presents the Aztec interpretation of the coming of the Europeans and the conquest. Gives insights into the Aztec mentality and provides critical perceptions of the Spanish.

Meyer, Michael C., William L. Sherman, and Susan M. Deeds. *The Course of Mexican History.* 7th ed. New York: Oxford University Press, 2003. Chapters 6 and 7 detail Cortés's invasion and the fall of the Aztec Empire.

Prescott, William H. *History of the Conquest of Mexico.* Reprint. New York: Modern Library, 2001. Written in the 1840's, this is one of the first truly scholarly works on the history of Mexico in English. Prescott combines sometimes overwhelming detail with a sense of the dramatic.

Thomas, Hugh. *Conquest: Montezuma, Cortés, and the Fall of Old Mexico.* New York: Touchstone, 1995. Thomas's well-researched book focuses on the personal conflict between these two leaders and their widely disparate civilizations.

White, Jon Manchip. *Cortés and the Downfall of the Aztec Empire.* 2d ed. New York: Carroll & Graf, 1996. A psychological and analytical portrait of Cortés and Montezuma that places both leaders in their religious and cultural milieus.

SEE ALSO: 1502-1520: Reign of Montezuma II; Beginning 1519: Smallpox Kills Thousands of Indigenous Americans; Aug., 1523: Franciscan Missionaries Arrive in Mexico; 1527-1547: Maya Resist Spanish Incursions in Yucatán; Feb. 23, 1540-Oct., 1542: Coronado's Southwest Expedition; 1542-1543: The New Laws of Spain; 1545-1548: Silver Is Discovered in Spanish America; 1552: Las Casas Publishes *The Tears of the Indians.*

RELATED ARTICLES in *Great Lives from History: The Renaissance & Early Modern Era, 1454-1600:* José de Acosta; Pedro de Alvarado; Hernán Cortés; Cuauhtémoc; Doña Marina; Montezuma II; Nezahualcóyotl.

June 28, 1519
CHARLES V IS ELECTED HOLY ROMAN EMPEROR

Charles V's election as Holy Roman Emperor consolidated Spain's supremacy within Europe, created the largest empire since the days of the Romans, and launched a century-long rivalry between Spain and France overseas.

LOCALE: Frankfurt (now in Germany)

CATEGORIES: Government and politics; expansion and land acquisition

KEY FIGURES

Maximilian I (1459-1519), Holy Roman Emperor, r. 1493-1519

Charles V (1500-1558), king of Spain as Charles I, r. 1516-1556, Holy Roman Emperor, r. 1519-1556, and grandson of Emperor Maximilian I

Ferdinand of Aragon (1503-1564), brother of Charles, who appointed him regent in Germany in 1521, and also Holy Roman Emperor as Ferdinand I, r. 1558-1564

Francis I (1494-1547), king of France, r. 1515-1547

Leo X (Giovanni de' Medici; 1475-1521), Roman Catholic pope, 1513-1521

SUMMARY OF EVENT

On January 12, 1519, Holy Roman Emperor Maximilian I died at Augsburg, Germany. He was the second Habsburg in succession to occupy the imperial throne. Maximilian's son, Philip the Handsome, married Joan of Spain, and Charles was their eldest son. When Philip died in 1506, Maximilian chose Charles as his heir. For several years before his death, Maximilian had been working for the election of his grandson as his successor to the office of emperor.

The office of the Holy Roman Emperor was the only major secular monarchy in Europe that was elective at the close of the Middle Ages. The right to choose a new emperor was vested in seven electors: the margrave of Brandenburg, the count of the Rhenish Palatinate, the elector of Saxony, the king of Bohemia, and the archbishops of Trier (Trèves), Mainz, and Cologne.

Before his death, Maximilian advised Charles to bestow lavish gifts on the electors to secure their votes, and Charles proceeded to do so. He borrowed immense sums from the Fugger banking house at Augsburg and bribed all the electors except two, the young heir of Bohemia who had been adopted by Maximilian, and the margrave of Brandenburg who was committed to vote for King

Francis I of France. Many German princes opposed the election of Charles because they feared the growing power of the Habsburgs. Charles was not as popular as his grandfather, who posed less of a threat.

The French king was Charles's major rival for the office. Because Charles's election would make him, at least theoretically, the ruler of all the lands bordering France, Francis sought desperately to prevent another Habsburg from succeeding to the office. He also distributed bribes to the electors.

Pope Leo X also fought against the election of Charles. Because the Habsburgs already had extensive holdings in Italy, Leo feared the encirclement of the Papal States. At first, he gave his support to Francis, but when it became clear that the electors would not choose a Frenchman, he tried to persuade the elector of Saxony, Frederick III, to seek the imperial throne. Frederick, who was the protector of Martin Luther and one with growing Protestant sympathies, refused because he was aging and unwell. Frederick knew that he possessed neither the stamina nor the power base to serve as emperor. Instead, he gave his support to Charles, who then became the unanimous but less than enthusiastic choice of all the prince electors. King Henry VIII of England also announced that he was a candidate, but he was never taken seriously.

On June 28, 1519, the electors, meeting at Frankfurt, unanimously nominated Charles as emperor. The margrave of Brandenburg later claimed to have been intimidated, because an army in the pay of Charles was then in the vicinity of the city. On October 22, the new emperor was crowned at Aachen, Charlemagne's ancient capital. Pope Leo reluctantly confirmed the election, as was customary, and some years later Charles was solemnly crowned again at Rome.

A contemporary poem rejoiced that "Others shall wage war. Thou, O happy Austria, shall marry." It was through judicious marriage alliances aided by fortuitous accidents that the huge Habsburg Empire came into existence. Maximilian himself had married Mary of Burgundy, the heiress of the Netherlands. His son Philip married the daughter of Ferdinand and Isabella of Spain, and Charles was born of this union. The death of Philip made Charles the scion of the Habsburg family, and he unexpectedly became heir to the Spanish throne when an older cousin died. The election of Charles as Holy Roman Emperor, together with his inheritances from the

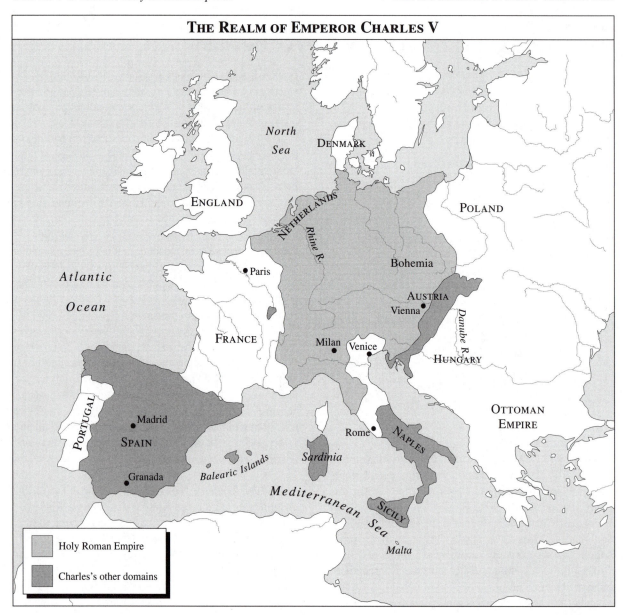

THE REALM OF EMPEROR CHARLES V

houses of Burgundy, Spain, Luxembourg, and Habsburg, made Charles ruler, as he himself said, "over an empire on which the sun never set."

At the time of his election, Charles, who had been born and reared in the Low Countries, was on his first visit to Germany. He could not yet speak the language, although over the next thirty-five years he became thoroughly familiar with German affairs. Charles V had become king of Spain three years before his election as emperor. By birth and as ruler of extensive territories outside Germany, Charles could never be a German king pri-

marily. He was first and last a Habsburg ruler. Year after year, Charles had to make decisions from alternatives that often seemed equally disastrous. His German and Spanish subjects often criticized Charles for subordinating the interests of their countries to those of other areas of the Habsburg Empire.

After his coronation, Charles embarked on state visits to England and France. In 1521, he returned to Germany and summoned the Diet of Worms, his first attempt to deal with the Lutheran movement that was splitting the empire. He also began complicated diplomatic negotiations which in time brought about marriage alliances with every kingdom of Europe. In 1522, he returned to Spain, leaving his brother Ferdinand to act as regent in Germany.

In 1523, the first of several major wars with France broke out in northern Italy. At the Battle of Pavia in 1525, King Francis was captured and imprisoned in Madrid. By the Treaty of Madrid in 1526, Francis was forced to make extensive concessions, including the French duchy of Burgundy, to which Maximilian had laid claim through marriage, and the renunciation of all claims in northern Italy. After his release, Francis repudiated these concessions, and the prolonged Habsburg-Valois rivalry continued for more than a century, everything else in European politics being subordinated to this struggle.

SIGNIFICANCE

The election of Charles was of momentous consequences for the history of Europe during the next century and a half, for it created overnight a vast empire larger than any since the days of the Romans. As king of Spain, Charles already ruled most of the Iberian Peninsula, southern Italy and Sicily, Central and South America (except Brazil), and parts of North Africa; he also had vague claims in Asia and the Pacific. He had inherited most of the Netherlands as well as extensive German lands in Austria with claims in Bohemia and Hungary. As emperor, he became overlord of Germany, Switzerland, and certain territories in northern Italy that Maximilian had conquered.

—*James F. Hitchcock, updated by Robert D. Talbott*

FURTHER READING

Blockmans, Wim. *Emperor Charles V, 1500-1558.* Translated by Isola van den Hoven-Vardon. London: Arnold, 2002. Attempts to survey the vast territory and diverse culture of the Holy Roman Empire by analyzing the relationship between Charles as an individual and the complex, rigid yet unstable power structures within which he governed. Includes illustrations, maps, bibliographic references, index.

Brandi, Karl. *The Emperor Charles V: The Growth and Destiny of a Man and of a World-Empire.* Translated by C. V. Wedgwood. London: Jonathan Cape, 1968. Written by a foremost authority on Charles V, this biography is still the standard account. Brandi states that Charles developed the dynastic theory of the Habsburgs.

Detwiler, Donald S. *Germany: A Short History.* Carbondale: Southern Illinois University Press, 1976. A readable, concise overview of German history with maps, a bibliography of English-language works, and a brief chronology.

Heer, Friedrich. *The Holy Roman Empire.* New York: Frederick A. Praeger, 1968. Heer describes the origins and development of the Holy Roman Empire. His work provides fine coverage of Charles V and is lavishly illustrated, but its bibliography is made up of mostly works in German.

Hughes, Michael. *Early Modern Germany, 1477-1806.* Philadelphia: University of Pennsylvania Press, 1992. A good, concise description of Germany and the changes that took place on the eve of the Protestant Reformation. Includes maps and an extensive bibliography of works in English.

Kamen, Henry. *Spain, 1469-1714: A Society of Conflict.* 2d ed. Reprint. New York: Longman, 1996. An excellent survey of early modern Spain. Kamen contends that imperial Spain was never fully equipped to control empires in Europe and the Americas simultaneously.

Lynch, John. *Spain, 1516-1598: From Nation-State to World Empire.* Cambridge, Mass.: Blackwell, 1991. An internationally recognized scholar of Spanish history, Lynch emphasizes the political difficulties facing Spain and Charles V. His work includes a brief but useful bibliography and tables of economic facts.

Maltby, William. *The Reign of Charles V.* New York: Palgrave, 2002. Monograph balances a biography of Charles with broad analysis of his foreign and domestic policies and their historical consequences. Includes maps, bibliographic references, index.

Richardson, Glenn. *Renaissance Monarchy: The Reigns of Henry VIII, Francis I, and Charles V.* New York: Oxford University Press, 2002. Comparison of Charles to two other monarchs who helped define Renaissance government and culture. Focuses on their careers as warriors, governors, and patrons. Includes maps, bibliographic references, and index.

Tracy, James D. *Emperor Charles V, Impresario of War: Campaign Strategy, International Finance, and Domestic Politics.* New York: Cambridge University Press, 2002. Examination of the financial and political consequences of Charles V's military campaigns. Discusses Charles as a field commander of his armies, and the international financial community that loaned Charles the money to pay for battles and thereby gained control over parts of his lands. Also discusses the local governments within the empire that learned to exploit Charles's need for money. Includes illustrations, maps, bibliographic references, index.

SEE ALSO: Oct. 19, 1469: Marriage of Ferdinand and Isabella; Aug. 17, 1477: Foundation of the Habsburg Dynasty; 1482-1492: Maximilian I Takes Control of the Low Countries; Jan. 23, 1516: Charles I Ascends the Throne of Spain; 1520-1522: Comunero Revolt; 1521-1559: Valois-Habsburg Wars; Apr.-May, 1521: Luther Appears Before the Diet of Worms; Feb., 1525: Battle of Pavia; Oct. 20-27, 1541: Holy Roman Empire Attacks Ottomans in Algiers; 1555-1556: Charles V Abdicates; July 26, 1581: The United Provinces Declare Independence from Spain.

RELATED ARTICLES in *Great Lives from History: The Renaissance & Early Modern Era, 1454-1600:* Charles V; Ferdinand II and Isabella I; Francis I; Martin Luther; Maximilian I.

1520-1522
COMUNERO REVOLT

The Comunero Revolt by the cities of central Castile was sparked by a disputed monarchical succession and evolved into social revolution that called for the right of the Castilian parliament to assemble and discuss, without royal summons, matters pertaining to the realm's welfare.

LOCALE: Central Castile, Spain

CATEGORIES: Social reform; wars, uprisings, and civil unrest; trade and commerce; government and politics; organizations and institutions

KEY FIGURES

Antonio de Acuña (fl. sixteenth century), bishop of Zamora and Comunero general

Charles V (1500-1558), Habsburg king of Spain as Charles I, r. 1516-1556, and Holy Roman Emperor, r. 1519-1556

Juan de Padilla (c. 1490-1521), Toledo city councilman

María de Pacheco Padilla (d. 1531), wife of Juan de Padilla

Joan the Mad (1479-1555), mother of Charles and rallying point of the Comuneros

Adrian of Utrecht (Adrian Florensz Boeyens; 1459-1523), governor of Spain during the revolt and, later, Pope Adrian VI, 1522-1523

SUMMARY OF EVENT

The traditional interpretation has characterized the Comunero Revolt as a xenophobic response to a foreign monarch who threatened feudal rights and privileges. Castilian cities and grandees, the landed nobility, despised Charles I's greedy Burgundian court and opposed his election as Holy Roman Emperor in 1519. The grandees soon abandoned the cities and joined forces with the royalists to crush the revolt, thereby ending medieval urban liberties and ushering in an era of monarchical absolutism.

Modern scholars have challenged the predominantly political and military analysis of the revolt by stressing the social and economic trends that established the preconditions for a modern revolution. During the reign of Ferdinand II and Isabella I, a growing fissure developed between the economic interests of central Castile and the periphery. In the late Middle Ages, central Castile emerged as the most dynamic region of Spain because of its thriving textile industry. The demand for Spanish wool in the industrial centers of Burgundy led to the rise of the Mesta, a sheep owners' guild. Each year a merchant guild in Burgos contracted the raw wool for shipment north. By forcing up the price of local wool and limiting land available for grain, the Burgos trade struck at the economic interests of interior textile centers such as Toledo, the ancient Visigothic capital, and Medina del Campo, the region's trade nexus and site of medieval fairs. The dramatic rise of Seville as an international trade emporium for the American trade also threatened the heartland by introducing greater foreign competition and by causing fluctuations in the price of grain and bread.

Ferdinand and Isabella tamed a rebellious aristocracy by removing them from the councils of government while granting them economic rewards. Following the death of Isabella in 1504, however, Castile endured a series of succession crises that repoliticized the aristocracy and renewed old rivalries. Weary of Ferdinand of Aragon's influence in Castile, a faction of Castilian grandees formed in support of the first Habsburg succession, Philip the Handsome, son of Emperor Maximilian I. Isabella's daughter and heir, Joan, was deemed mentally unfit to govern, so her husband, Philip, assumed the regency of Castile in her name. His sudden death in 1506 further exacerbated Joan's illness and led to Ferdinand's assumption of the regency with the support of anti-Habsburg grandees.

Between the death of Isabella and the arrival of Charles in Castile in 1517, there were four weak regency governments dependent on the support of rival factions of grandees. At the local level, this meant that lawsuits brought by towns against grandees for usurping their grain lands went unheard in royal courts. The aristocratic offensive created an urban-noble conflict that, combined with royal favor of the periphery, created a revolutionary environment in central Castile.

In 1517, Charles arrived in Spain with a court from his native Burgundy intent on exploiting Spanish wealth. Objections quickly arose in the *cortes*, the Castilian parliament, which had the power of voting taxes, the *servicio*. At Charles's first *cortes* in 1518, city representatives complained that he should stop appointing foreigners to office, avoid any increase in taxation, forbid shipment of gold or silver from Spain, and reform the royal law courts to process suits more quickly. Afterward, Charles evaded the *cortes* by naturalizing Burgundians as Spaniards before granting offices and by negotiating huge loans in Germany with Spanish resources as collateral. Following the death of Maximilian I, Charles used these loans to bribe the imperial electors to elect him Holy Roman Emperor in 1519. His plan for an opulent trip to Germany forced him to request an additional *servicio*, though the old one had not expired.

Charles convened the *cortes* in remote Galicia, so he could leave Spain more quickly, and demanded that the *servicio* be voted prior to his hearing grievances. After several large bribes, eight of the eighteen cities in the *cortes* finally passed Charles's *servicio*. Further insulting the *cortes*, Charles appointed his old Burgundian tutor, Adrian of Utrecht, rather than a Spanish grandee, as governor in his absence. Before Charles set sail on May 20, 1520, Toledo was in open revolt under the leadership of city councilman Juan de Padilla.

Few cities heeded Toledo's call to revolt until Adrian sought to punish Segovians for the public murder of a *cortes* delegate who had taken a bribe. After Padilla led a force north to help defend the city, the royalists sought artillery in Medina del Campo. In the ensuing melee, half of the ancient trading center was burned to the ground on August 21, 1520. By October of 1520, fourteen of the *cortes* cities had joined in a revolutionary government in Tordesillas (the *sancta junta*) where they sought legitimacy by professing loyalty to Charles's mother Joan, who they proclaimed the legitimate ruler of Castile. While expressing sympathy with their grievances, Joan shrewdly refused to sign any documents.

Despite the junta's drafting of a broad program of national reform, most cities and grandees focused their attention on using revolution as an excuse to settle local feuds. As individual cities launched assaults against individual grandees, a general anti-señorial movement evolved, which the Comunero junta eventually endorsed. The demagogic champion of the anti-señorial movement was the sixty-five-year-old bishop of Zamora, Antonio de Acuña, who assured his followers that God was on the side of the poor and against the grandees.

As class antagonisms divided the junta, Adrian asked Charles to appoint two Spanish grandees as cogovernors, thereby winning back most grandees. Without the grandees, the armies of Padilla and Zamora lacked cavalry, which proved decisive when Padilla met the royalists on the field of Villalar on April 23, 1521. Padilla and two other Comunero leaders were executed the next day.

Henceforth, the revolution centered on Toledo, where Acuña joined Padilla's widow, María de Pacheco Padilla, in continuing the struggle. Maria appealed to her powerful uncle, Diego Lopez de Pacheco, marquis de Villena, to negotiate a settlement with the Crown. The French invasion of Navarre in northern Spain, along with Villena's warning of the governors that he would not allow them to besiege Toledo, led to protracted negotiations, which were finalized in February, 1522. María went into exile in Portugal, where she died in 1531. Acuña was captured after sneaking out of Toledo to join the French and, after murdering a guard, was later executed. Apart from a few leaders, Charles exercised extreme clemency in punishing former rebels. The general pardon of May, 1521, exempted only 293 individuals, some 150 of whom either bought amnesty or were pardoned.

The traditional image of the loss of urban liberty on the field of Villalar has undergone significant alteration since the 1960's. After the revolt, Charles instituted most of the Comunero junta's demands. He reformed the royal courts and again removed grandees from the high governing councils. He stopped granting Spanish offices to foreigners and Spaniards quickly came to dominate his imperial bureaucracy. The *cortes* met every three years and gained more control over collection of the *servicio*. If adjusted for inflation, the *servicio* actually decreased over the course of Charles's reign.

SIGNIFICANCE

There were, however, negative consequences outside the political arena. Unable to stop rapidly growing foreign competition or to slow the export of Spanish wool, the Castilian textile industry collapsed in the 1540's. Sensing an underlying affinity between the Comuneros and Lutheran rebels in Germany, Charles expanded the authority of the Spanish Inquisition to ferret out any heterodox thought: Lutherans, mystics, even Christian humanists. Increased inquisitorial censorship was the most enduring legacy of the Comunero Revolt.

—*Daniel A. Crews*

FURTHER READING

Crews, Daniel A. "Juan de Valdés and the Comunero Revolt: An Essay on Spanish Civic Humanism." *Sixteenth Century Journal* 22, no. 2 (Summer, 1991): 233-252. Analysis of Fernando de Valdés's role in the revolt and its relation to the political thought of his son Juan de Valdés, the famous Humanist.

Elliott, John H. *Imperial Spain, 1469-1716.* Reprint. New York: Penguin, 1990. Considers the revolt a reactionary, xenophobic response to Charles's imperialism. Its defeat opened Spain to foreign influence, particularly that of Christian Humanist Desiderius Erasmus.

Haliczer, Steven. *The Comuneros of Castile: The Forging of a Revolution, 1485-1521.* Madison: University of Wisconsin Press, 1981. Fine synthesis of European scholarship on the social and economic factors underlying the revolt.

Lynch, John. *Spain, 1516-1598: From Nation State to World Empire.* Cambridge, Mass.: Blackwell, 1991. Brief summary that views the Comunero Revolt as a true revolution but concludes with the traditional argument that it was an unqualified victory for absolutism.

Ruiz, Teofilo F. *Spanish Society, 1400-1600.* New York: Longman, 2001. A detailed and diverse look at all aspects of Spanish cultural history in the fifteenth and sixteenth centuries. Discusses the Comunero Revolt and places it in the context of other Renaissance Spanish rebellions of the poor against the elite.

Seaver, Henry L. *The Great Revolt in Castile: A Study of the Comunero Movement of 1520-1521.* 1928. Reprint. New York: Octagon Books, 1966. Seaver argues that the revolt was a struggle for constitutional monarchy that turned into class war and anarchy. Based on published Spanish sources, especially the six-volume *Historia crítica y documentada de los comunidades de Castilla*, edited by Manuel Danvila (1897-1899).

Tracy, James D. *Emperor Charles V, Impresario of War: Campaign Strategy, International Finance, and Domestic Politics.* New York: Cambridge University Press, 2002. Examination of the financial and political consequences of Charles V's military campaigns. Discusses Charles's relationship to local governments within the empire, especially those that learned to exploit Charles's need for money.

SEE ALSO: Oct. 19, 1469: Marriage of Ferdinand and Isabella; 1499-1517: Erasmus Advances Humanism in England; June 28, 1519: Charles V Is Elected Holy Roman Emperor.

RELATED ARTICLES in *Great Lives from History: The Renaissance & Early Modern Era, 1454-1600:* Adrian VI; Charles V; Ferdinand II and Isabella I.

1520-1566
REIGN OF SÜLEYMAN

Sultan Süleyman's rule marked the zenith of the Ottoman Empire as a major world power because of its territorial and population expansion on subjugated lands, a sophisticated military and other institutional organization, trade and economic growth, and impressive cultural and artistic activity.

LOCALE: Ottoman Empire (now Turkey)
CATEGORY: Government and politics; expansion and land acquisition

KEY FIGURES

Süleyman the Magnificent (1494/1495-1566), Ottoman sultan, r. 1520-1566
Charles V (1500-1558), Austrian Habsburg emperor of the Holy Roman Empire, r. 1519-1556, and, as Charles I, king of Spain, r. 1516-1556
Francis I (1494-1547), king of France, r. 1515-1547
John Zápolya (1487-1540), prince of Transylvania, r. 1511-1526, and king of Hungary as John I, r. 1526-1540

SUMMARY OF EVENT

Süleyman the Magnificent was the son and successor of Selim I "the Grim" and the tenth in his ruling dynasty. He ascended the throne on September 30, 1520, at age twenty-five after attending the palace schools and serving six years as provincial governor. After crushing the Mamlūks of Egypt in 1521 (and again in 1524), Süley-

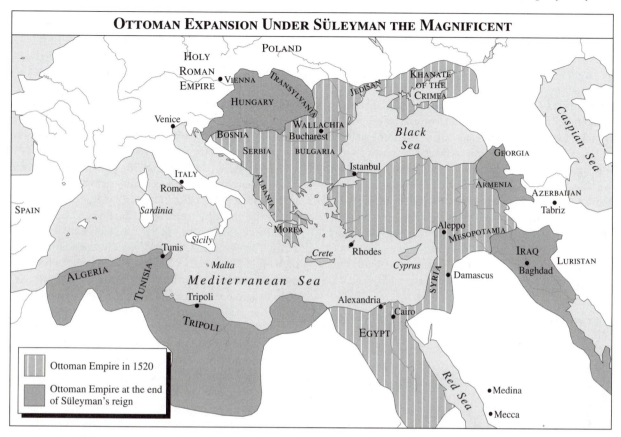

OTTOMAN EXPANSION UNDER SÜLEYMAN THE MAGNIFICENT

Ottoman Empire in 1520

Ottoman Empire at the end of Süleyman's reign

man continued his father's conquests in the Balkans and the Mediterranean, taking Belgrade, Rhodes, much of Hungary, and Crimea. The sultan pressed on with his wars against the Persians, taking Tabrīz (in northwestern Iran) as well as Mosul, Baghdad, and Basra (in modern Iraq), Armenia, Azerbaijan, much of North Africa, and an undefined extent of hinterland inhabited by Arabs. Süleyman's forces captured numerous Aegean islands as well.

His successes in Hungary and Austria were incomplete, however. For example, in 1529, Süleyman failed to take Vienna, and he embarked on another abortive campaign in Austria in 1532, also unsuccessful because of constraints of time and distance, weather, lack of supplies, the weariness of his troops, and the resistance of the Christian forces. Too, he failed to capture Corfu in 1537 or Malta in 1565. He died during a punitive expedition in Hungary on September 6, 1566. For although the death of John Zápolya (John I) in 1540 and his succession by his son, John Sigismund (John, r. 1540-1571) , had provided Süleyman with pretexts for annexing what is now Hungary (except Transylvania), there were con-

stant challenges to Ottoman power in that land. Indeed, while Süleyman had personally commanded thirteen campaigns in his reign, seven of them were in Hungary. Title to that country was sought not only by the native Hungarians themselves but also by Austria's Charles V, the sultan's perennial enemy, and later, following Charles's abdication in 1556, by his younger brother, Ferdinand I.

Süleyman had two of his sons—Mustafa and Bayezid (not to be confused with Bayezid II, the Ottoman sultan who reigned from 1481 to 1512)—eliminated. Thus, his other son, Selim—whose mother was also Roxelana, "the Russian woman" (Hürrem Sultana), the daughter of a Christian Orthodox priest, at first Süleyman's concubine and then his favorite wife (1541-1558)—became Selim II "the Sot" (also known as "the Drunk" or "the Sallow") at Süleyman's death. The empire in general and the sultanate in particular would begin a significant decline under Selim's rule.

Besides being famous for expanding the empire, east and west, by both land and sea (with a fleet of more than a hundred well-armed galleys), Süleyman improved the machinery of government necessary to rule such a vast multiethnic empire. Among others, he added a fifth "millet" (community, nation) to the original four: the Catholic "millet." It followed the conclusion of Süleyman's capitulations agreement with his ally, France's King Francis I. These "chapters" consisted of trading concessions embodying reciprocal extraterritorial privileges for French and Ottoman merchants. These, then, enjoyed tax and customs concessions and could use their own courts, applying the laws of their own lands, administered by the latter's appointed representatives. Initially, in Süleyman's time, the capitulations evidenced Ottoman power, but eventually they proved to be a wedge for Western penetration and exploitation, marginalizing Ottomans from the commercial life of their own empire.

Süleyman's transfer of the harem, the exclusive women's quarters, to the palace compound hastened the

Sultan Süleyman the Magnificent. (Hulton|Archive by Getty Images)

eventual decline of the empire. The concubines and wives in the harem—a few hundred of them in Süleyman's time—came to engage in political maneuvering and intrigues in such state matters as appointments to high office and succession to the throne. Süleyman himself was not above allowing favoritism to trump merit. He also began failing to attend meetings of the Divan, the council of ministers, relegating the job of presiding over it to his grand vizier, the chief minister.

Accordingly, while under Süleyman, the Ottoman Empire reached its zenith as a conquering state in terms of power, wealth, and cultural brilliance, several conditions were already portending its decline and were accelerated under Süleyman's mostly unexceptional and often vice-afflicted successors. Additionally, the restriction of high office to formerly Christian slaves with supposedly unblemished loyalty to the sultan, along with the increasing role of the harem and Janissaries in political life, had begun to spell doom for the Ottomans.

Nevertheless, Süleyman is remembered not only for his military exploits and conquests but also for his interest in justice and legal reform, which resulted in the codification of the common law as the Qanunname, earning him the sobriquet "the Lawgiver" (Qanuni). Indeed, Süleyman felt compelled to abrogate or amplify much of the legislation of his illustrious great-grandfather, Mehmed II (the Conqueror). Süleyman was also a patron of the arts, of literature (a poet in his own right), and of architecture, responsible for the embelishment of Constantinople (modern Istanbul) and Adrianople (Edirne) with mosques, palaces, and public facilities.

SIGNIFICANCE

The accepted wisdom is that Süleyman's military successes and public policy acts far outweighed his political failures and human foibles. During his forty-six-year reign, Süleyman raised the Ottoman Empire to the level of a world state that stretched from the border of Austria to the Persian Gulf, from the Black Sea to North Africa. He focused the sultanate-caliphate as the center of the Islamic empire and synthesized his multiethnic empire over three continents into a nearly organic unit by skillful use of the government, military, judicial, religious, and administrative institutions (notably the "millets"). The orchestration of these institutions and fear of his absolute power ensured domestic tranquillity.

Despite instances of gratuitous brutality—such as having his own grand vizier Ibrāhīm Paşa executed in 1536, his eldest son Mustafa murdered at his orders in 1553, and his son Bayezid executed in 1561—Süleyman was known for his rectitude and morality and for his use of such able chief ministers as Ibrāhīm, Rustem, and Mehmed Sokollu. Süleyman encouraged poets such as Baki and architects such as Sinan (1489-1588; born Christodoulos, of Greek origin). Accordingly, Süleyman the Magnificent—also known as "the Lawgiver," "the Sublime Porte," and "the Grand Turk"—is remembered as one who tempered severity with justice and warlike endeavors with a love of culture.

—Peter B. Heller

FURTHER READING

Bridge, Antony. *Suleiman the Magnificent, Scourge of Heaven*. New York: Franklin Watts, 1983. Highlights Süleyman's military history. Good chronology, select bibliography, and index.

Clot, André. *Suleiman the Magnificent*. Translated by Matthew J. Reisz. 1989. Reprint. New York: New Amsterdam Books, 1992. Divided between "The Sultan of Sultans" and "The Empire of Empires," this masterly work includes sixteen appendixes, a genealogy, a glossary, a chronology, a bibliography, maps, and an index.

Kunt, Metin, and Christine Woodhead, eds. *Süleyman the Magnificent and His Age: The Ottoman Empire in the Early Modern World*. New York: Longman, 1995. Several British and Turkish scholars examine the problems and policies in the sultan's multiethnic empire as well as Ottoman statecraft. Glossaries, bibliographical guide, maps, and index.

Lamb, Harold. *Suleiman the Magnificent: Sultan of the East*. 1951. Reprint. Garden City, N.Y.: Doubleday, 1978. Together with the works of Lybyer and Merriman, one of the classic but revisionist biographies of Süleyman, who is seen as a great man justifying his many wars as a means of survival and progress. Bibliographical references.

Lybyer, Albert H. *The Government of the Ottoman Empire in the Time of Suleiman the Magnificent*. Cambridge, Mass.: Harvard University Press, 1913. An American political scientist describes in great detail the political and military organizations of Süleyman's empire.

Merriman, Roger B. *Suleiman the Magnificent, 1520-1566*. 1944. Reprint. Cambridge, Mass.: Harvard University Press, 1966. The first authoritative work by an American scholar of the life and times of the great sultan. Bibliographical notes, illustrations, and index.

SEE ALSO: Apr. 14, 1457-July 2, 1504: Reign of Stephen the Great; Early 16th cent.: Fuzuli Writes Poetry in Three Languages; 16th cent.: Proliferation of Firearms; Beginning 1504: Decline of the Ḥafṣid Dynasty; June 28, 1522-Dec. 27, 1522: Siege and Fall of Rhodes; 1525-1600: Ottoman-Ruled Egypt Sends Expeditions South and East; 1526-1547: Hungarian Civil Wars; Aug. 29, 1526: Battle of Mohács; 1529-1574: North Africa Recognizes Ottoman Suzerainty; Sept. 27-Oct. 16, 1529: Siege of Vienna; 1534-1535: Ottomans Claim Sovereignty Over Mesopotamia; 1536: Turkish Capitulations Begin; Sept. 27-28, 1538: Battle of Préveza; 1559-1561: Süleyman's Sons Wage Civil War; May 18-Sept. 8, 1565: Siege of Malta; 1566-1574: Reign of Selim II; 1574-1595: Reign of Murad III.

RELATED ARTICLES in *Great Lives from History: The Renaissance & Early Modern Era, 1454-1600:* Barbarossa; Bayezid II; Mehmed II; Mehmed III; Pius II; Süleyman the Magnificent.

1520's

June 5-24, 1520
FIELD OF CLOTH OF GOLD

The Field of Cloth of Gold was a high point in the history of chivalry and the colorful pageantry of the Renaissance. It proved to be a failure, however, as an effort to achieve peace between England and France.

LOCALE: Northwestern France

CATEGORIES: Diplomacy and international relations; cultural and intellectual history; government and politics

KEY FIGURES

Henry VIII (1491-1547), king of England, r. 1509-1547

Cardinal Thomas Wolsey (1471/1472-1530), English cardinal, chief adviser of Henry VIII, and Lord Chancellor of England, 1515-1529

Francis I (1494-1547), king of France, r. 1515-1547

Charles V (1500-1558), Holy Roman Emperor, r. 1519-1556

Margaret of Austria (1480-1530), regent and governor of the Netherlands, r. 1507-1530, and aunt of Charles V

Sir Thomas More (1478-1535), English statesman, scholar, and author

John Rastell (c. 1475-1536), English printer, lawyer, dramatist, and brother-in-law and posthumous publisher of Sir Thomas More

Desiderius Erasmus (1466?-1536), Dutch Humanist scholar

Guillaume Budé (1467-1540), French Humanist scholar and royal librarian of France

SUMMARY OF EVENT

The Field of Cloth of Gold is the popular name for the meeting, in June of 1520, between Henry VIII of England and Francis I of France. The idea of this meeting had been discussed since the Anglo-French treaty of 1514, and it reemerged during the negotiations for the Treaty of London in 1518 (a treaty confirmed by Pope Leo X and ratified by Spain and Venice). Planning for the historic meeting had begun in 1519, and by January, 1520, both Henry and Francis had charged Cardinal Thomas Wolsey with making preparations for it.

Wolsey drew on the best talent and experience in England for the planning and execution of the pageant. By January, 1520, however, the cardinal was confronting serious problems of protocol and logistics, and the erection of the great hall at Guisnes (near Calais) was entrusted to Sir Edward Belknap and Sir Nicholas Vaux. In the spring of 1520, three thousand workmen spent four months constructing the buildings to house the meeting, and some of the finest Tudor master craftspeople and makers of pageants were engaged.

On April 10, Vaux wrote to Wolsey, begging the cardinal to send Alexander Barclay, the Benedictine poet and translator of Sebastian Brant's *Das Narrenschiff* (1494; *The Shyp of Folys of the Worlde*, 1509, better known as *The Ship of Fools*), "to devise histories for the banquet house and other buildings." The many-talented John Rastell—lawyer, playwright, printer, and celebrated deviser of pageants—was called on to design, make, and garnish the roofs of the banquet hall. He succeeded so brilliantly that Edward Hall, the Tudor chronicler, exclaimed especially over the splendors of the roofs and declared that they "were covered with cloth of silke, of the most faire and quicke invention that before that time was seen."

Wolsey's organizational skills were challenged by the sheer scope of the event he had planned. He gathered hundreds of tents and pavilions and tons of plate, cutlery, and glass. Six thousand masons, carpenters, and other builders set to work to render Guisnes Castle suitably magnificent. A contemporary painting of the Field of Cloth of Gold (attributed to Vincenzo Volpe and now in Hampton Court Palace) details the sweep of the tents in the camp located between Guisnes and Ardres, in northwestern France. The foreground depicts one of the elaborate buildings (a replica of an idealized Tudor palace) constructed for the occasion. This single temporary palace built for Henry covered an area of nearly 12,000 square yards (10,034 square meters), and it was decorated sumptuously. Beyond the temporary palace and chapel were fields in which twenty-eight hundred tents were erected for less distinguished visitors. Francis spent an immense sum on the field, and Henry's expenditures were even greater, for Francis was content to stay in a lavish series of tents or pavilions, while Henry had created more expensive *trompe l'oeil* constructions of wood and plaster, painted to look like brick.

The two monarchs and their retinues met on June 5 and continued to meet until June 24, spending the days in jousting and tilting and much feasting. The level of consumption of the monarchs and their courts was almost beyond description. In less than one month's time, the English alone consumed two thousand sheep and all kinds of other provisions: hundreds of barrels of wine and beer, rabbits, storks, eels, quails, and cheese, together with sufficient fuel for the kitchens. When tilting was not possible because of high winds, there was wrestling and dancing, activities in which Henry took the greatest pleasure—until Francis threw him at wrestling.

On the penultimate day of the pageant, Saturday, June 23, an open-air altar was erected, and Wolsey sang a Solemn High Mass before the two kings and numerous ambassadors. The cardinal then delivered a sermon on peace. On the final day, June 24, there was one final banquet and the exchanging of expensive gifts and elaborate farewells.

It is likely that the well-known chapel-master for France's Queen Anne of Brittany, Jean Mouton, was involved in the French preparations for the field. Mouton was a celebrated composer of motets as well as masses and was in the service of Francis. He was also a favorite composer of Leo X, and he added much to the French presentations in the rivaling of chapels at elaborate services. One of his English counterparts was William Cornysh, master of the children of the Chapel Royal, whose play describing the negotiations of Henry and Charles V following the field was performed at court in 1522.

Days before the Field of Cloth of Gold, Henry had met with the Emperor Charles V, and the two had decided to meet again immediately following the field. They rendezvoused at Gravelines (a seaport town near Dunkerque) for two days. Charles V and his aunt, Margaret of Austria, made a return visit to Calais, where a splendid banqueting hall within the palace had been specially constructed, although it was damaged by wind. The emperor left on July 14, and Henry returned to England without further delay. To meet first with Francis and then Charles was not thought contrary to the spirit of the treaty of 1518, and it may well be seen as embodying Wolsey's (and Henry's) intentions to carry further the spirit of that treaty. The French, however, were suspicious.

The reaction of contemporary Humanists to the meeting at the Field of Cloth of Gold was mixed. Some praised the very idea of a meeting of the two monarchs; others expressed their doubts and reservations because of the extravagance involved. Whatever their specific judgment, though, there is no doubt that the event made a significant impression upon observers of the time. Several prominent intellectuals attended the field, including Englishmen Sir Thomas More and John Rastell and celebrated French Humanist Guillaume Budé. At the field, Budé and More, who had been corresponding since 1518, were finally able to meet in person. Afterward Budé traveled with the French court to Amboise and Blois; More went with Henry to meet Charles V at

King Henry VIII of England and King Francis I of France meet at the Field of Cloth of Gold in 1520, a spectacular Renaissance pageantry that celebrated chivalry and attempted but failed to achieve peace between the two nations. (Hulton|Archive by Getty Images)

Calais. There More met with Desiderius Erasmus, although somewhat briefly, owing to the attendance required of each Humanist. Saint John Fisher, the bishop of Rochester, preached against the excessive costs of the Field of Cloth of Gold, as he had preached to censure the clergy at the legatine synod of 1517 for greed, desire for gain, and love of display.

"It is easy to dismiss the Field of Cloth of Gold as vain posturing, as a huge, expensive game, as a Renaissance folly," twentieth century historian J. J. Scarisbrick has written. It was all that: fiercely and proudly extravagant, and in the end productive of little that was to prove permanent, but it was more than a folly. For Wolsey, it was part of a brilliant and seemingly flawlessly executed program to put England on the path of peace with France, but within two years the two were at war again.

SIGNIFICANCE

The Field of Cloth of Gold was spectacular Renaissance pageantry; it celebrated chivalry and the apparent achievement of peace through the personal agreement of two great princes. Whether the planning of the field is attributed solely to Wolsey or credit is given largely to Henry's self-portrayal as the peacemaker of the period, an effort was made during the month of the Field of Cloth of Gold to strengthen and cement the 1518 Treaty of London. In the long run, Henry's confidence in Wolsey was shaken, England's role as the mediator of Europe was tried to the breaking point, and the ancient enmity between France and England proved too deep and too strong to be patched over by a glittering show.

The field was in part a staggeringly expensive game, and the stakes for all the principals were high. None of the principals, neither Wolsey, Henry, Francis, Charles, nor the Pope, can be said to have won. The year 1520 was also the year of the excommunication of a then-obscure Augustinian priest in Germany named Martin Luther, who would shortly take his place on the stage of the Reformation. In retrospect, the field was viewed by most as a vain posturing.

—*R. J. Schoeck*

FURTHER READING

Anglo, Sidney. *Spectacle, Pageantry, and Early Tudor Policy.* 2d ed. New York: Oxford University Press, 1997. Admirable scholarly study by the renowned authority on Renaissance pageants.

Bamforth, Stephen. "Un Poème de Sylvius sur l'entrevue du Camp du Drap d'Or." *Bibliothèque d'Humanisme et Renaissance* 52 (1990): 635-641. A scholarly analysis of a poem viewing the field from a French perspective.

Bietenholz, P. G., et al. *Contemporaries of Erasmus.* 3 vols. Toronto: University of Toronto Press, 1985-1987. Provides biographies of leading figures in the Renaissance and Reformation. Published to accompany, and help explain the context of, a 1974 edition of the works of Erasmus. Includes illustrations and bibliographies.

Richardson, Glenn. "Field of the Cloth of Gold." In *Tudor England*, edited by Arthur Kinney and D. W. Swain. New York: Garland, 2001. Brief but informative essay in an encyclopedia of Tudor England.

Russell, Jocelyn G. *The Field of Cloth of Gold.* New York: Barnes & Noble, 1969. Still the best monograph on the field.

Scarisbrick, J. J. *Henry VIII.* Berkeley: University of California Press, 1968. Recommended for its judicious dealing with highly controversial problems of Henry VIII, the field among them.

SEE ALSO: Aug. 29, 1475: Peace of Picquigny; Beginning 1485: The Tudors Rule England; 1494: Sebastian Brant Publishes *The Ship of Fools*; 1515-1529: Wolsey Serves as Lord Chancellor and Cardinal; Dec. 18, 1534: Act of Supremacy; 1544-1628: Anglo-French Wars; Jan. 1-8, 1558: France Regains Calais from England; Jan. 20, 1564: Peace of Troyes.

RELATED ARTICLES in *Great Lives from History: The Renaissance & Early Modern Era, 1454-1600:* Charles V; Desiderius Erasmus; Francis I; Henry VIII; Martin Luther; Margaret of Austria; Sir Thomas More; Cardinal Thomas Wolsey.

1521-1559
VALOIS-HABSBURG WARS

The contest between the Valois kings of France and the Habsburg kings of Spain for political supremacy in Western Europe erupted into warfare in Burgundy, Picardy, and the Italian peninsula. By 1559, both sides were exhausted, but the Habsburgs emerged as the marginal victors, becoming the dominant power in Italy.

LOCALE: Western Europe

CATEGORIES: Wars, uprisings, and civil unrest; diplomacy and international relations; expansion and land acquisition

KEY FIGURES

Francis I (1494-1547), king of France, r. 1515-1547

Charles V (1500-1558), king of Spain, r. 1516-1556, Holy Roman Emperor, r. 1519-1556

Henry II (1519-1559), king of France, r. 1547-1559

Philip II (1527-1598), king of Spain, r. 1556-1598

Clement VII (Giulio de' Medici; 1478-1534), Roman Catholic pope, 1523-1534

Süleyman the Magnificent (1494/1495-1566), sultan of the Ottoman Empire, r. 1520-1566

Henry VIII (1491-1547), king of England, r. 1509-1547

SUMMARY OF EVENT

The rivalry between the Spanish branch of the Habsburg Dynasty and France's Valois Dynasty dominated the political scene of Renaissance Europe beginning around the turn of the sixteenth century. After 1521, these dynastic conflicts should be considered against the backdrop of the conflicts between Christian Europe and the Ottoman Turks and the religious wars ignited by the Protestant Reformation. In fact, the Habsburgs found themselves engaged in all three conflicts, sometimes simultaneously. This prolonged political and religious strife exerted great demands on the resources and logistical capacity of Habsburg Holy Roman Emperor Charles V, who regarded himself as the guardian of the one true faith against the threat of Muslim infidels and the depredations of the Lutheran movement.

A full sixteen years of Charles V's reign was consumed with war against France, and the central issue of this contest was control of the Duchy of Milan, which the French king, Francis I, had conquered in 1515. Open war between the two monarchs was initiated by Francis. Following the election that made Charles emperor and expanded his realm of influence from Spain to the entirety

of the Holy Roman Empire, Francis found himself practically encircled by Habsburg territory. Fearing for the security of his kingdom, in 1521, he launched a series of preemptive strikes against Charles in Navarre, in the Netherlands, and in Luxembourg. All three of these gambits failed, and the emperor responded by seizing control of Milan. A subsequent attempt by the French army to take back the city ended in a bloody defeat at Bicocca in April, 1522.

Francis himself returned to Italy at the head of an army in 1524. He again managed to take Milan but his siege of an imperial holdout at the Battle of Pavia (February, 1525) ended in a catastrophic defeat. Francis himself was captured and ignominiously transferred back to Madrid, where he and Charles had their first face-to-face meeting. Francis was eventually forced to sign the harsh Treaty of Madrid in January, 1526, whereby he pledged to abandon all his claims in Italy and relinquish control of Burgundy to the Habsburgs.

Ultimately, however, Charles gained very little from his decisive victory at Pavia. He was soon confronted with an alliance of France, the pope, and several Italian states (the League of Cognac), which sought to drive the Habsburgs from Italy. Charles responded by fomenting a rebellion against the Francophile pope Clement VII inside his territories and then, in 1527, by sending an army to Rome under Charles de Bourbon. When Bourbon was killed outside the city, the underpaid and underfed imperial force sacked the Holy City in an orgy of violence that killed thousands and came to be known as the sack of Rome. Clement sought refuge in his Castello Sant'Angelo, becoming a virtual prisoner of the Holy Roman Empire for the next nine months.

MAJOR BATTLES OF THE VALOIS-HABSBURG WARS	
April, 1522	Battle of Bicocca
February 24, 1525	Battle of Pavia
1527	Sack of Rome
1544	Battle of Boulogne
April 14, 1544	Battle of Cerisolles
August, 1557	Battle of Saint-Quentin
January, 1558	Battle of Calais
July 13, 1558	Battle of Gavelines

The sensation of a Christian army sacking Rome did not stop the war in Italy. Francis invaded Milan in the same year. With his ally, the Genoese admiral Andrea Doria, blockading the city's port, it also appeared certain that Naples would fall to the French. At that crucial point, however, Doria decided not to renew his alliance with the French and defected to the imperial side instead. Within months, the French army, weakened by disease, had been forced out of Italy altogether.

The Peace of Cambrai (1529), also known as the Ladies' Peace, reflected the desire for peace on both sides. Both had seen their resources seriously depleted, and Charles watched with alarm as the Ottomans advanced toward Vienna. According to the terms of the peace, Francis again agreed to abandon his claims in Italy and the Netherlands, but this time Charles renounced his long-standing claim to Burgundy. Charles was crowned emperor by the pope at Bologna in 1530, the last emperor so to be honored. Most of Italy was now firmly under

Charles's control. At this point, the contest between empire and papacy seemed to have been decisively settled in favor of the emperor. The appearance of victory for Charles was largely illusory, however, for the twin financial burden of fighting wars both in Italy and against the Ottoman Turks had taken a serious toll on the empire.

In many ways, Cambrai ushered in a new stage in the dynastic contest. Both France and the empire were affected by the increased financial burden of the new military tactics they had adopted. Primarily mobile wars that allowed for rapid changes in fortune with relatively little expense had become a thing of the past. Instead, most military engagements were now long, costly sieges of citadels and cities fortified in the style of the artillery fortress. While one side or the other might win a decisive victory at a particular battle, the great costs of these sieges, in time, in money, and in manpower, helped produce an overall, gradually widening stalemate in the war as a whole. This stalemate was primarily the conse-

The Habsburg Holy Roman Emperor Charles V and Pope Clement VII, who had been in battle earlier over Italy and over religion, ride in solemn procession after Charles's victory over the pope and the authority of the Catholic Church.

quence of money shortages on both sides—just when a breakthrough seemed possible for one side, it ran out of capital and had to suspend operations until more could be found.

Milan remained the apple of Francis's eye. He invaded Italy twice more in his reign with this target in mind, in 1536 and 1543. In both instances, initial French successes proved to be ephemeral. In 1536, Francis was able to overrun Turin and most of Piedmont, but he was soon faced with an answering invasion of Provence by Charles. The two sides agreed to a truce in 1538. Following this truce, in 1539, Charles toured the length of the French kingdom as the king's guest, against the wishes of most of the imperial advisers.

The 1538 truce was as short-lived as the previous ones, and hostilities had recommenced by 1542. On this occasion, Francis took the extraordinary step of allying openly with the Ottomans, going as far as to allow Sultan Süleyman the Magnificent's fleet to winter at Toulon.

Francis launched yet another invasion of Italy and the French defeated an imperial army decisively in a bloody battle in Piedmont at Cerisolles in April, 1544. Despite the victory, Francis was again unable to achieve his true goal, the conquest of Milan. The French king found himself faced not only with an invading imperial army in Champagne but also with a landing by English troops on the Channel coast—Henry VIII of England had allied with the Emperor. These conflicts were ended at the Peace of Crépy (1544), where Francis gained only Savoy and a sliver of Piedmont, ceding Milan once more to Charles. The Italian phase of the Valois-Habsburg conflict was now largely at an end. The Habsburgs dominated the peninsula.

After ascending the French throne, Francis's son and successor, Henry II, waited five years before renewing the conflict with the Habsburgs. Henry allied with Lutheran princes inside the empire itself and, in the spring of 1552, seized the imperial cities of Metz, Toul, and

Clement acknowledged Charles as emperor, and, in 1530, he crowned Charles, the last Roman emperor to be crowned by a pope. (Frederick Ungar Publishing Co.)

Verdun. Charles responded with a lengthy, bloody, and ultimately unsuccessful siege of Metz. Indeed. the war that followed largely consisted of a series of desultory sieges along France's northern border with few significant breakthroughs.

In 1555-1556, an exhausted and disillusioned Charles abdicated his throne, dividing the imperial territories between his brother, Ferdinand, and his son, Philip II, who took the title of king of Spain. The Habsburg-Valois struggle now continued largely in the form of a Franco-Spanish contest. In 1557, Henry II made one last attempt to take Naples, which ended, like the others before it, in French defeat. Subsequent defeats at Saint-Quentin and Gravelines prompted a sickly Henry to negotiate a peace. Luckily his desire for peace was mirrored in Madrid—it appeared that both sides finally wanted a real, lasting peace. This was finally achieved at Cateau-Cambrésis in April, 1559.

SIGNIFICANCE

Virtually no part of Western Europe remained untouched by the Valois-Habsburg Wars. Financially, economically, and politically, the wars had wide-ranging effects. The direct, physical ravages of war hit some regions, especially Italy and northwestern Europe, repeatedly. As in the Cold War, states were forced to align themselves with one side or the other in the contest. Despite the great expenditures they were forced to make in men and money, the Habsburgs emerged from the conflict as the strongest dynasty in Europe. The Spanish branch of the family, under Philip II, enjoyed political dominance over Italy and was enriched by an influx of treasure from the New World. For the next three generations, a primary concern for European statesmen would be the prospect of Habsburg hegemony in Europe.

France, for its part, was afforded very little time to enjoy the coming of peace. At a jousting tournament held to celebrate Cateau-Cambrésis four months after its signing, Henry II received a freak mortal wound when a lance penetrated the eye-slit of his helm. Just as France marked the end of a long chapter of its history filled with conflict

with the Habsburgs, the death of Henry opened a bitter and vicious new chapter marked by several decades of civil war.

—Paul M. Dover

FURTHER READING

Arnold, Thomas. *The Renaissance at War.* London: Cassell, 2001. Military history focused on the sixteenth century with plenty of coverage of the Habsburg-Valois conflict. Beautifully illustrated.

Mackenney, Richard. *Sixteenth-Century Europe.* New York: St. Martin's Press, 1993. Survey written in an entertaining, jaunty style. Brings together very well the multifaceted religious, dynastic, and political factors that drove the conflicts of the era.

Maltby, William. *The Reign of Charles V.* New York: Palgrave, 2002. A comprehensive examination of imperial rule under Charles. Especially useful for understanding how Charles's domestic concerns affected his foreign policy.

Parker, Geoffrey. "The Political World of Charles V." In *Charles V, 1500-1558, and His Time*, edited by Hugo Soly. Antwerp: Mercatorfonds, 1999. A lengthy article in a richly illustrated coffee-table book that deals largely with Charles's grand strategy in facing his manifold foreign policy challenges. By the foremost historian of international relations in the sixteenth and seventeenth centuries.

1521-1567
REIGN OF JIAJING

The reign of Jiajing marks the return of despotic rule to the Ming Dynasty and saw the enactment of controversial revisions to court ritual. Although raids by the Mongols on the northern border increased dramatically during this period, a general avoidance of military confrontation left the problem to future emperors.

LOCALE: China
CATEGORY: Government and politics

KEY FIGURES

Jiajing (reign name, also Chia-ching; personal name Zhu Houzong, Chu Hou-tsung; posthumous name Sudi, Su-ti; temple name Shizong, Shih-tsung; 1507-1567), Ming emperor of China, r. 1522-1567

Yang Tinghe (Yang T'ing-ho; 1459-1529), chief grand secretary

Altan (1507-1582), Mongol khan, r. 1543-1582

Yen Song (Yen Sung; 1480-1565), grand secretary, 1542-1562

Shao Yuanjie (Shao Yüan-chieh; 1459-1539), patriarch of Daoism of the state and minister of rites

Tao Zhongwen (T'ao Chung-wen; c. 1481-1560), a Daoist priest

SUMMARY OF EVENT

In 1522, the Ming Dynasty's chief grand secretary, Yang Tinghe, placed Zhu Houzong, a highly intelligent and classically trained man, on the imperial throne, thereby severing the formal line of succession. Taking the reign name Jiajing, he inherited a state neglected by the heirless tenth Ming emperor Zhengde (Cheng-te, temple name Wuzong or Wu-tsung; r. 1505-1521), whose lust for pleasure led to increased control of government by the powerful eunuch class of bureaucrats.

Perhaps trouble was not expected from Jiajing, but his stubborn insistence on having his own parents recognized officially and given their rightful due soon drew loud protests from many officials, who feared formalizing this broken line of succession. Jiajing had 134 of these officials flogged and jailed, and he ordered the compilation of the history of what became known as the Ta-li affair in 1525. Above all, Jiajing wanted bestowed posthumously on his father honors similar to those accorded the previous emperor. Jiajing also insisted that his mother be received by the court as a dowager empress rather than a princess. His demands, which challenged

the ritual foundations of imperial legitimacy, had the effect of altering the manner in which emperors acknowledged their predecessors.

Jiajing's reign is known to history as one of fiscal crisis and population growth. Between 1522 and 1524, while Yang Tinghe was chief grand secretary, the main imperial granaries held only a three-year reserve, and demand continued to exceed supply year after year. Palace financial reserves were sometimes exhausted during the following decade. Jiajing was forced to cease additional palace and temple construction to slow the depletion of funds, but in May of 1557, the main audience halls and southern ceremonial gates were destroyed by fire and cost more than 730,000 ounces of silver to rebuild. While this project was being undertaken, another fire, started when a lamp tipped over after a night during which the court had indulged in heavy drinking, claimed the emperor's palace in the western garden of the Forbidden City.

Faced with constant deficits, the emperor approved fiscal reorganization, but widespread drought and famine, combined with mounting defense expenditures, continued to deplete imperial funds. On January 23, 1556, a massive earthquake hit the provinces of Shaanxi, Shanxi, and Henan. Buildings and city walls collapsed, giant crevices opened in the earth, and the aftershocks lasted for days. It has been estimated that as many as 830,000 people perished in the subsequent flooding. The financial demands of meeting this disaster was combined with the need to provision increasing numbers of imperial clansmen with stipends, the disappearance of taxable land, and the failure to register newly cultivated land. Legal overseas trade with Japan quickly degenerated into piracy and its concomitant violence, which spiraled out of control by 1556. Imperial finances would not begin to improve until the 1570's.

Potential sources of revenues such as trade with the Mongols went untapped. Jiajing despised the Mongols and refused to grant their petitions for trade. This intransigence had dire consequences. The Mongols prized items such as silk, tea, metalwares, and pottery, and the procurement of these items became inextricably intertwined with power. The Mongol khan Altan conducted major raids deep into Ming territory in search of scarce supplies after his petitions for trade with China were rejected. Though Jiajing committed precious funds to building new defensive walls, the underling causes of the raids were not addressed. The Mongols were emboldened after defeating the imperial army in 1548, and by March of 1550, no rain or snow had fallen for more than 150 days. The Mongols prepared to attack again. On October 1, they besieged Beijing and looted the suburbs successfully. When an imperial army could not be raised to drive off the invaders, they retreated several days later—booty intact. The Mongols continued their raids from 1550 to 1556, and the Ming armies won only a single significant victory during this period. Not surprisingly, between 1550 and 1560, payments for garrisons doubled while revenues remained constant.

Although the first years of Jiajing's reign saw genuine changes that included the dismissal of hundreds of eunuchs and unqualified persons and the seizure of their property by the state, this zeal for office did not continue. As Jiajing's health declined in the 1530's, he ceased attending to the routine details of government and left such tasks to the likes of Yen Song, the grand secretary from 1542 to 1562. Jiajing had stopped officiating at the Sacrifice to Earth and Heaven altogether by 1553.

Relieved of the most onerous duties of office, Jiajing pursued an ardent interest in the magical arts of Daoism and was encouraged in this pursuit first by a priest named Shao Yuanjie and later by Tao Zhongwen. This obsession began with an interest in increasing fertility, for the emperor remained childless the first ten years of his reign. Soon, however, Jiajing began relying on divinations in matters of state and increasingly ingested aphrodisiacs. His quest for longevity and immortality led to his addiction to the stimulants found in these aphrodisiacs, which were made largely from red lead and white arsenic. Ironically, these elixirs caused mood swings, diminished his mental capacity, and eventually led to his early death. Jiajing's interest in attaining immortality may even have contributed to an assassination attempt by concubines who dreaded his visits. On November 27, 1542, eighteen palace girls tried to strangle him while he was in a drunken stupor. It seems that some of the elixirs of immortality pursued by Jiajing required intercourse with fourteen-year-old virgins at their first instance of menses. Tao Zhongwen once selected eight hundred girls between the ages of eight and fourteen for use in refining the elixir.

Jiajing's obsession with Daoism had political implications as well. He turned against the Hanlin Academy, the bastion of Confucianism in imperial China. He demoted and reassigned many Hanlin officials to provincial posts and replaced them with individuals who had no previous affiliation with the academy. Late in 1530, he

changed the sacrifices and titles for Confucius (who had been deemed a prince since 738) and did away with all titles of nobility conferred on Confucius and his followers. Images were even ordered abolished from Confucian temples, though this decree was not widely enforced. As Daoist activities increased on the palace grounds, officials able to write well in the poetic Daoist literary form, known as *Qing ci*, received high favor. Attempts were made to suppress Buddhism as well during this period. In 1536, the Buddhist temple on the palace grounds was ordered dismantled, and 169 of its gold and silver images were melted down.

SIGNIFICANCE

During Jiajing's reign, the wealth of the Ming Dynasty began to decline, though economic activity increased, driven by growth in agricultural technology and the development of the cloth and handicraft industries. Part of the reason for this economic decline amid increased production was the disappearance of existing taxable land and the failure to register new land properly. The increase in population, a series of building projects and natural disasters, and the mounting defense expenditures also contributed to the fiscal crisis. Mongol invasions from the north increased and were met defensively; consequently, the Mongols were not driven from the frontier. Raids by Japanese and other pirates began in the 1520's and reached a peak by the mid-1550's, when they threatened the canal cities of Hangzhou, Suzhou, and Nanjing. Though the emperor refused to change his position, his ban on maritime trade (and trade with the Mongols) proved ineffective. All of these problems remained unsolved into the seventeenth century and contributed to the demise of the Ming Dynasty in 1644, less than a century after Jiajing's death in 1567.

—*Mark S. Ferrara*

FURTHER READING

Goodrich, L. Carrington, ed. *Dictionary of Ming Biography 1368-1644*. New York: Columbia University Press, 1976. Contains useful biographies of Jiajing and other prominent Ming figures.

Mote, Fredrick W. *Imperial China, 900-1800*. Cambridge, Mass.: Harvard University Press, 1999. Useful discussion of the mid-Ming period.

Mote, Fredrick W., and Denis Twitchett, ed. *The Ming Dynasty, 1368-1644, Part 1*. Vol. 7 in *The Cambridge History of China*. Cambridge, England: Cambridge University Press, 1988. In-depth overview of the reign of Jiajing.

Paludan, Ann. *Chronicle of the Chinese Emperors: The Reign by Reign Record of the Rulers of China*. London: Thames and Hudson, 1998. Includes a brief discussion of the emperors of the Ming Dynasty and provides historical context.

SEE ALSO: 16th cent.: China's Population Boom; 16th cent.: Single-Whip Reform; 1505-1521: Reign of Zhengde and Liu Jin; 1514-1598: Portuguese Reach China; 1550's-1567: Japanese Pirates Pillage the Chinese Coast; 1550-1571: Mongols Raid Beijing; Jan. 23, 1556: Earthquake in China Kills Thousands; 1567-1572: Reign of Longqing; 1573-1620: Reign of Wanli; 1592-1599: Japan Invades Korea.

RELATED ARTICLES in *Great Lives from History: The Renaissance & Early Modern Era, 1454-1600:* Tomé Pires; Matteo Ricci; Wang Yangming; Xiaozong; Zhengde.

April-May, 1521
LUTHER APPEARS BEFORE THE DIET OF WORMS

Martin Luther refused to recant his Protestant Reformist views at the Diet of Worms, which led to his subsequent condemnation by the Catholic Church and the eventual rise of Protestantism.

LOCALE: Worms (now in Germany)
CATEGORIES: Religion; government and politics

KEY FIGURES
Martin Luther (1483-1546), university professor and former Catholic monk whose views were examined at the diet
Charles V (1500-1558), Holy Roman Emperor, r. 1519-1556, and king of Spain as Charles I, r. 1516-1556, who convened the diet
Desiderius Erasmus (1466?-1536), a leading humanist Catholic scholar who worked to achieve reconciliation between Luther and the Catholic Church
Frederick the Wise (1463-1525), elector of Saxony who defended Luther's right to a trial in Germany
Jerome Alexander (1480-1542), papal representative who helped lead the opposition to Luther at the Diet

SUMMARY OF EVENT
The Catholic Church's condemnation of Martin Luther's teachings at the Diet of Worms was a pivotal event in the Protestant Reformation, intensifying the dispute within the Church over theology, polity, and worship and helping produce a permanent division.

The Reformation's roots lie in political, educational, technological, social, and religious developments between 1450 and 1517. Growing nationalism and the desire of European countries for greater independence from Rome contributed to the rise of Protestantism. So did Johannes Gutenberg's invention of the printing press, which enabled Luther's attacks on the Catholic Church to be widely disseminated, and the expansion of universities, many of which supported the teachings of the Reformers. The revival of trade, growth of cities, and development of a middle class also played a role. The Reformation, however, was primarily a protest against religious abuses, especially the tremendous financial power and alleged doctrinal errors of the Church, the corruption of the Papacy, and the ignorance and moral laxity of priests.

Martin Luther was declared a heretic at the Diet of Worms (1521) for his teachings against the Church. (R. S. Peale and J. A. Hill)

In 1516, Luther, an Augustinian monk and professor at the University of Wittenberg, experienced a religious awakening that led him to attack many of the Church's teachings. The next year, he posted Ninety-five Theses that he wished to debate publicly with other Catholic scholars. These theses challenged the Church's political and economic power and its monopoly over spiritual matters. Guided by his belief that justification was by grace through faith alone, Luther rejected the Church's long-standing practice of selling indulgences as a means of granting forgiveness of sin and insisted instead that only heart-felt confession brought such remission.

During the next few years, Luther continued to denounce major Church doctrines through a series of very popular pamphlets. He contended that God had established only two sacraments—baptism and communion—rather than seven, argued that all Christians should read and interpret the Bible themselves, and urged laypeople to reform the Church.

In response, Pope Leo X issued a bull in June of 1520, condemning Luther's teachings and excommunicating him from the Church. When the papal edict reached Luther, he protested that it offered no scriptural proof to refute any of his charges against the Church. In response to the burning of his books by Catholic authorities in Rome, Cologne, and other cities, Luther, on December 10, sur-rounded by a crowd of onlookers, threw the papal edict and the papal constitutions and the canon law into a bonfire.

Frustrated by the failure of his appeals to the pope to call a council to reform the Church, Luther had written in August, 1520, to twenty-year-old Charles V, who was soon to be crowned king of Spain and officially given the title of Holy Roman Emperor by the pope, asking for a hearing. After the Church's condemnation of Luther, Frederick the Wise, elector of the German province of Saxony, urged Charles V to hold a public trial in Germany to examine Luther's views. Some Germans opposed this action. They reasoned that since the Church had already condemned Luther, the state should simply execute the Church's edict against the heretic. The papal representative at the trial, Jerome Alexander, sought to convince Charles V to settle the case by himself without even consulting the German nobles who were divided in their opinions of Luther. This was not politically expedient, however, because Luther's supporters in Germany were numerous, powerful, and outspoken.

A middle party, led by Desiderius Erasmus of Rotterdam, strove to mediate between these opposing groups and proposed creating an impartial tribunal to decide the case against Luther. In November of 1520, Charles V invited Luther to attend a hearing to present his views. The next month, after Luther's burning of the papal bull, Charles V rescinded the invitation. Asked to endorse the imperial edict proclaiming Luther a heretic and a revolutionary, the German nobles protested that his teachings were so popular among the German people that condemning him without a hearing might provoke an insurrection. As a result, Luther was invited in the name of both Charles V and the German nobles to a council at Worms to examine his views.

Originally called to deal with issues relating to the administration of the empire, foreign policy, economics, and public peace, the diet had already been meeting for more than two months when Luther arrived on April 16 in Worms to a warm welcome by two thousand supporters. The next day Luther was summoned before the emperor, the German electors, and other civic leaders and was

---

THE DIET OF WORMS CONDEMNS MARTIN LUTHER

The Diet of Worms, in May of 1521, issued an edict that called for the condemnation of Protestant reformer Martin Luther for his heresies and blasphemies against the Roman Catholic Church. The following excerpt from the edict focuses on Luther's character and his public teachings and preachings.

For he teaches a loose, self-willed life, severed from all laws and wholly brutish; and he is a loose, self-willed man, who condemns and rejects all laws; for he has shown no fear or shame in burning publicly the decretals and canon law. And had he feared the secular sword no more than the ban and penalties of the pope, he would have committed much worse offenses against the civil law. . . .

This fellow appears to be not so much a man as the wicked demon in the form of a man and under a monk's cowl. He has collected many heresies of the worst heretics, long since condemned and forgotten, together with some newly invented ones, in one stinking pool, under pretext of preaching *faith*, which he extols with so great industry in order that he may ruin the true and genuine faith, and under the name and appearance of evangelical doctrine overturn and destroy all evangelical peace and love, as well as all righteous order and the most excellent hierarchy of the Church. . . .

Source: Excerpted in *Readings in European History,* by James Harvey Robinson, abridged ed. (Boston: Athenaeum Press, 1906), p. 277.

Martin Luther facing the Diet of Worms (1521) for his teachings against the Church. (Hulton|Archive by Getty Images)

asked whether he had authored certain books. Some of those present hoped he would repudiate his vehement denunciation of the sacraments and instead rally the German people in an attack against the financial and political power of the Papacy and help them gain the same concessions that England, Spain, and France already enjoyed. Much to their disappointment, Luther acknowledged his authorship of the books. When asked if he defended all of them, Luther, perhaps awed by the gravity of the situation, begged for time to think over his answer.

Granted a twenty-four-hour reprieve, Luther was summoned on April 18 to a much larger, very crowded hall. In a ringing voice, he declared that all the books were his, but they were of different kinds. Some were simple explanations of Christian faith and life that even his enemies did not dispute. Appealing to German nationalism, he insisted that others of his books explained the "incredible tyranny" of the Papacy that was devouring his country. A third group of books attacked private individuals, but he would not renounce them either unless he was "convicted of error from the prophets and the Gospel." Luther's accusers replied that he simply renewed the errors of earlier Reformers John Wyclif and

Jan Hus. They chastised Luther for putting his own judgment above that of "many famous men," for having the audacity to "question the most holy orthodox faith." In oft-quoted words, Luther responded,

> Unless I am convinced by Scripture and plain reason—I do not accept the authority of popes and councils, for they have contradicted each other—my conscience is captive to the Word of God. I cannot and will not recant anything, for to go against conscience is neither right nor safe.

Following this public meeting, commissioners representing the German estates met with Luther for several days of private conversation but failed to reach a compromise on the disputed issues. As a result, the diet on May 6, after several days of deliberation, approved the Edict of Worms. It accused Luther of sullying marriage, disparaging confession, misunderstanding communion, and promoting "rebellion, division, war, murder, . . . and the collapse of Christendom." Labeling Luther "an obstinate schismatic and a manifest heretic," Charles V commanded Germans to refuse Luther hospitality, lodging, food or drink, take him prisoner if they saw him, and prohibited them from reading his books. Although the edict was published, it was not enforced because Luther's popularity was too great in Germany. This, coupled with the protection provided by Frederick the Wise, saved Luther's life and allowed him to continue to lead the Reformation.

Significance

One of the most striking facts about the Diet of Worms was simply that it occurred, that the emperor did not execute the condemned Luther in private without a public hearing. That a single professor was granted a trial to assess his questions about the central doctrines of the Christian faith indicated that centuries of tradition were under assault. Luther's attack on the Catholic Church not only challenged long-held doctrines but also shook the foundations on which Europe rested. The failure to achieve a compromise between Luther and the Church led to the Protestant Reformation, the division of Christendom, religious wars, and the fracturing of Europe's cultural base.

—*Gary Scott Smith*

Further Reading

Bainton, Roland. *Here I Stand: A Life of Martin Luther.* Rev. ed. New York: New American Library, 1977. A highly acclaimed account of the life, work, and impact of Luther. Includes illustrations, bibliography, and index.

Boehmer, Heinrich. *Road to Reformation: Martin Luther to the Year 1521.* Translated by John W. Doberstein and Theodore G. Tappert. Philadelphia: Muhlenberg Press, 1946. Based thoroughly on primary sources, the book provides exceptional detail and insight into Luther's life and thinking to the conclusion of the Diet of Worms. Lucid and well written, this work is considered by many Luther scholars to be a classic in the field. Includes an index.

Brecht, Martin. *Luther: His Road to the Reformation, 1483-1521.* Translated by James L. Schaff. Philadelphia: Fortress Press, 1985. A judicious analysis of the events leading to the diet, especially Luther's conversion and his critique of the Catholic Church.

Fife, Robert H. *The Revolt of Martin Luther.* New York: Columbia University Press, 1957. A very thorough and balanced biography of Luther that includes a detailed description of the diet.

McGrath, Alister E. *The Intellectual Origins of the European Reformation.* 2d ed. Malden, Mass.: Blackwell, 2004. Traces the influence of medieval theology and Humanism upon Luther and the Reformation. Includes bibliographic references and index.

McKim, Donald K., ed. *The Cambridge Companion to Martin Luther.* New York: Cambridge University Press, 2003. An anthology of essays by noted scholars covering Luther's theology, moral thought, skill with words, direct effects, and lasting legacy, among other topics. Includes bibliographic references and index.

Marty, Martin. *Martin Luther.* New York: Viking Penguin, 2004. Subtle and balanced portrayal of Luther's theology and its cultural context, explaining the importance of the debates in which he intervened and tracing the ultimate results of that intervention. Luther's character receives an equally nuanced treatment. Includes maps and bibliographic references.

Oberman, Heiko A. *Luther: Man Between God and the Devil.* Translated by Eileen Walliser-Shwarzbart. New Haven, Conn.: Yale University Press, 1989. A lively and unconventional account of Luther's development as a person, a theologian, and a Christian, by a renowned scholar.

_____. *The Two Reformations: The Journey from the Last Days to the New World.* Edited by Donald Weinstein. New Haven, Conn.: Yale University Press, 2003. A posthumous collection of essays by one of the foremost Reformation scholars of the twentieth century. Revisits debates on Luther's anti-Semitism. Argues that medieval religious thought was essential to both John Calvin's and Luther's understandings of Christianity. Includes bibliographic references and index.

Von Schwarzenfeld, Gertrude. *Charles V: Father of Europe.* Translated by Ruth M. Bethell. London: Hollis and Carter, 1957. A life of Charles V that explains his participation in and perspective on the Diet.

See also: 1499-1517: Erasmus Advances Humanism in England; Oct. 31, 1517: Luther Posts His Ninety-five Theses; June 28, 1519: Charles V Is Elected Holy Roman Emperor; May 6, 1527-Feb., 1528: Sack of Rome; Mar., 1536: Calvin Publishes *Institutes of the Christian Religion*; Feb. 25, 1570: Pius V Excommunicates Elizabeth I.

Related articles in *Great Lives from History: The Renaissance & Early Modern Era, 1454-1600:* Martin Bucer; John Calvin; Charles V; Desiderius Erasmus; Saint John Fisher; Henry VIII; Balthasar Hubmaier; Saint Ignatius of Loyola; John Knox; Leo X; Martin Luther; Philipp Melanchthon; Menno Simons; Philip the Magnanimous; Pius V; Huldrych Zwingli.

June 28, 1522-December 27, 1522
SIEGE AND FALL OF RHODES

Süleyman the Magnificent's army seized the island of Rhodes in a land-and-sea battle that was part of the Turkish wars of expansion into Europe. Christian knights surrendered and the Ottomans gained control of the eastern Mediterranean.

LOCALE: Rhodes, island in the Aegean Sea (now part of Greece near the southwest coast of Turkey)

CATEGORIES: Expansion and land acquisition; wars, uprisings, and civil unrest

KEY FIGURES

Süleyman the Magnificent (1494/1495-1566), sultan of the Ottoman Empire, r. 1520-1566

Philippe Villiers de l'Isle-Adam (1464-1534), grand master of the Knights Hospitaller

Gabriele Tadino da Martinengo (1480-1543), mercenary engineering officer in service to the Knights Hospitaller

Pierre d'Aubusson (1423-1503), grand master of the Knights Hospitaller during the first attempted siege of Rhodes in 1480

SUMMARY OF EVENT

The crusading Order of Knights of St. John of Jerusalem (Hospitallers) was one of the elite fighting forces of the Middle Ages. Founded in 1110 as a military monastic order of the Catholic Church to guard pilgrims visiting Jerusalem's holy sites, the Hospitallers were generally more disciplined, better trained, and more fanatical in combat than most of their opponents. Their rules of engagement mandated standing their ground in the face of superior opposition. At the Fall of Acre to the Mamlūks in 1291, the remnant Crusader colony relocated to Cyprus, an island that had been controlled by Crusaders since its conquest by Richard I during the Third Crusade (1189-1192).

The order relocated there, also, but from 1306 to 1310, the order helped capture the island of Rhodes along with Genoese forces, who had commercial colonies and interests throughout the Aegean Sea. The largest and one of the most fertile of the Dodecanese group of islands, Rhodes is 540 square miles. In the early fourteenth century, the island contained about ten thousand Byzantine Greeks, and it had a good number of Crusader colonists soon after 1309. The order relocated its headquarters to a defensible spot positioned on the high point within the city of Rhodes, overlooking Mandraki Harbor, where the Colossus of Rhodes once stood in antiquity.

When the Templars (a fellow crusading order) was disbanded in Europe in 1312, the Hospitallers were one of the primary recipients of Templar assets. Much of the assets paid for the defense of the island. The order's citadel was a formidable square building measuring 240 feet by 225 feet, constructed upon an old seventh century Byzantine fort. Hospitaller engineers erected several substantial towers and expanded the city's protective walls. Subterranean chambers were used for storage and for protection from bombardment in the event of a siege. Many of the citadel's defensive engineering marvels were constructed during the tenure of Grand Master Pierre d'Aubusson, who transformed the island into one of the most well-fortified locations anywhere.

Several expansionist Islamic states had emerged in the eastern Mediterranean, including the Mamlūks in Egypt (who destroyed Outremer in 1291) and the Ottomans in Asia Minor (who captured Constantinople in 1453), both of which were implacably hostile to the order. After the defeat of Crusader forces at Hattin in 1187, Egyptian and Syrian sultan Saladin executed captive Hospitallers rather than ransom them. The Mamlūks attempted to capture the island twice—in 1440 and 1444—and were beaten back by the knights each time. D'Aubusson presided over the defense against Turkish forces in 1480. In 1482, Ottoman prince Cem fled to Rhodes for protection from his older brother, Sultan Bayezid II. The order handed him over to the Papacy, which hoped to use him to threaten the stability of Bayezid's regime. He died in captivity in 1495.

The knights used their fleet of seven war galleys to hinder Muslim shipping in the eastern Mediterranean. For a time, they held the island of Cos and the city of Smyrna on Asia Minor. The Turks did not view them as a strategic threat necessarily—there were about five hundred knights total—but the existence of a Crusader state in the middle of the ever-expanding *dar al-Islam* (house of Islam) was considered an outrage. Sultan Selim I had planned an invasion of Rhodes in 1520, but his death precluded an immediate attack. Nevertheless, the knights anticipated an imminent attack from Selim's son, Süleyman the Magnificent, and prepared accordingly.

Grand Master Philippe Villiers de l'Isle-Adam began taking measures similar to those of d'Aubusson some years earlier. Villiers had commanded a portion of the

Hospitaller forces in a successful naval battle at Laiazzo in 1510, and was elected grand master in 1521. He began collecting supplies and bolstering the island's fortifications to deter a new Ottoman assault. He had about five hundred brother knights and fifteen hundred mercenaries at his disposal, and a talented mercenary engineering officer named Gabriele Tadino da Martinengo. Most importantly, his forces had the precise measurements of distances from the citadel to any spot within cannon shot of their artillery.

The expected Ottoman invasion force appeared on June 25, 1522, as 700 ships carrying 20,000 Turkish troops arrived off shore. During the course of the campaign, the Turks brought in more than 140,000 reinforcements. The knights and Christian mercenaries in the citadel were vastly outnumbered, but their ranks included many artillerymen and harquebusiers, who used a weapon called a harquebus, which was fired by lowering a slow-burning match into a gunpowder-filled pan. The defenders did not challenge the Turkish landings, but instead tried to prevent Bosnian and Walachian sappers, who would attempt to undermine or bore through walls, from getting close enough to begin a Turkish bombardment. The siege started on July 28. Defending Hospitaller counterfire, however, was much more effective, given the accurate measurements the order had taken of all surrounding terrain.

Tadino's countermeasures stopped attempts by the

Turks to undermine the order's fixed positions through the late summer. In early September, a large Turkish assault on the Hospitallers' English bastion came close to succeeding after a mine exploded. The Turks then began a huge three-week bombardment of the citadel as a prelude to a new assault. The assault came on September 24 and converged on a large part of the citadel—the Aragonese, English, Italian, and Provençal bastions. Turkish Janissaries managed to take the Aragonese bastion, but again were pushed back.

The bombardment, mining, and sapping continued, however, probing for weaknesses in the citadel. In October, two events harmed the defenders' morale. First, Tadino was seriously injured, and then a spy was discovered in the Hospitaller ranks; he said he was working with Andrea d'Amaral, the order's grand chancellor (and a bitter rival of Villiers). D'Amaral was tortured but refused to confess, so was executed.

By November, the order's supply of gunpowder was beginning to get dangerously low. Sultan Süleyman was determined to acquire the island, and he continued to press the assault week after week, despite losses approaching fifty thousand men. Süleyman had an inexhaustible supply of expendable manpower. Some eighty-five thousand rounds of ammunition (both iron and stone shot) had been fired by the Turks. The defenders had sustained a high proportion of casualties by November, when the weather began to deteriorate, but they could expect no reinforce-

Detail of a plan of the island of Rhodes, before the siege in 1522. (Frederick Ungar Publishing Co.)

The ruins of the barracks of the Order of Knights of St. John of Jerusalem, also called Knights Hospitallers, on the island of Rhodes, in a sketch made three hundred years after the siege. (Frederick Ungar Publishing Co.)

ments. The knights were hard-pressed to repair gaps in their defenses caused by the constant bombardment.

Representatives of the island's Greek population (which had supported the knights' efforts to hold out) informed the order that they were going to surrender en masse to the Turks if the knights did not soon negotiate their own surrender to the sultan. Villiers wished to hold out to the last man, but most of the remaining knights argued against what they considered a suicidal final option.

Negotiations opened on December 1 and lasted until the December 15, when they broke down. Hostilities resumed on December 16, and the Turks managed for the first time to break into the city the following day. A determined counterattack by the knights drove the Turks back on December 18. Negotiations resumed two days later, and the Turks pulled back to a point one mile from the city. On Christmas Eve, the negotiated terms were presented to the knights, and on December 27, Villiers surrendered.

Süleyman was magnanimous in victory, allowing the surviving 180 knights and 1,500 retainers and mercenary survivors to leave with honor, keeping their arms. He allowed their sculpted noble escutcheons to remain intact in the citadel. Among the evacuees was the order's future grand master, Jean Parisot de La Valette. The Hospitallers sailed away from Rhodes on January 1, 1523, to Viterbo, then Nice. Villiers went from court to court trying to secure a new base of operations for the order. Holy Roman Emperor Charles V finally granted the knights the island of Malta in 1530, on condition that they also garrison Tripoli. Villiers died in 1534, and his successors managed to beat back an equally large Turkish assault on Malta in 1565.

SIGNIFICANCE

The Turkish victory at Rhodes solidified the Ottoman hold on the eastern Mediterranean, but the favorable terms of surrender negotiated by Grand Master Philippe Villiers de l'Isle-Adam preserved the order's existence.

The siege was one of the earliest examples of modern warfare in a new era of gunpowder weaponry. It saw heavy artillery bombard a fixed position as the prelude to a heavy infantry assault, and it saw the techniques of sapping and mining to undermine enemy fixed positions. The knights' heroic, six-month defense of the island remains an outstanding example of modern defensive military tactics.

—William E. Watson

FURTHER READING

Brockman, Eric. *The Two Sieges of Rhodes, 1480-1522.* London: J. Murray, 1969. Another accessible yet accurate study of the 1522-1523 siege, which also focuses on the unsuccessful siege of 1480.

Luttrell, Anthony T. *The Hospitaller State on Rhodes and Its Western Provinces, 1306-1462.* Aldershot, Hampshire, England: Ashgate, 1999. Luttrell is perhaps the greatest living scholar of the Hospitallers on Rhodes.

_____. *The Hospitallers in Cyprus, Rhodes, Greece, and the West (1291-1440).* London: Variorum, 1978. Another examination of the Hospitallers.

Seward, Desmond. *The Monks of War: The Military Religious Orders.* 2d ed. London: Penguin Books, 1995. A popular and reliable study of the Hospitallers that employs good source material on the siege of Rhodes.

SEE ALSO: 1454-1481: Rise of the Ottoman Empire; Apr. 14, 1457-July 2, 1504: Reign of Stephen the Great; 1478-1482: Albanian-Turkish Wars End; 1481-1512: Reign of Bayezid II and Ottoman Civil Wars; 1512-1520: Reign of Selim I; 1520-1566: Reign of Süleyman; 1534-1535: Ottomans Claim Sovereignty over Mesopotamia; 1536: Turkish Capitulations Begin; Oct. 20-27, 1541: Holy Roman Empire Attacks Ottomans in Algiers; Mid-16th cent.: Development of the Caracole Maneuver; 1552: Struggle for the Strait of Hormuz; May 18-Sept. 8, 1565: Siege of Malta; July, 1570-Aug., 1571: Siege of Famagusta and Fall of Cyprus; Oct. 7, 1571: Battle of Lepanto.

RELATED ARTICLES in *Great Lives from History: The Renaissance & Early Modern Era, 1454-1600:* Adrian VI; Bayezid II; Charles V; Süleyman the Magnificent.

November 3, 1522-November 17, 1530
CORREGGIO PAINTS THE *ASSUMPTION OF THE VIRGIN*

Correggio painted the dome interior of the major cathedral in Parma which, in subsequent centuries, drew foreign visitors and artists to the city to witness his brilliant illusion of recessive space, and his assertion of the importance of Marian imagery for Roman Catholic dogma in an age of Reformation.

LOCALE: Parma, Italy
CATEGORY: Art; religion

KEY FIGURES

Correggio (Antonio Allegri; c. 1489-1534), Italian painter
Clement VII (Giulio de' Medici; 1478-1534), Roman Catholic pope, 1523-1534
Martin Luther (1483-1546), Protestant reformer

SUMMARY OF EVENT

In November of 1522, a commission for the decoration of the Cathedral of Parma was awarded to the Italian painter Correggio. He was to provide fresco decorations of the apse, octagonal dome, and choir, and although he was able to complete only the cupola, and not until 1530, the results were monumental. The subject of the dome fresco was the *Assumption of the Virgin,* who was one of the major patron saints of the city. The subject was also an important assertion of Marian imagery at a time when the

Catholic Church had suffered attacks by Martin Luther (in 1517) and other Protestant reformers.

Before Correggio had completed his fresco, during the unfortunate papacy of Clement VII, Rome itself would suffer the sack of 1527 by renegade Swiss, German, and Spanish troops of the Holy Roman Emperor Charles V. Shortly after Correggio finished his *Assumption of the Virgin,* Henry VIII would be excommunicated by Clement VII for his divorce of Catherine of Aragon just days before the pope's death. Although these events were unforeseen, they accentuated the cupola fresco as a grand, visible assertion of Catholic dogma against Protestant reformers.

Eight ocular windows at the base of the octagonal dome illuminate the fresco. Decorative aspects were delegated to assistants who included the young Parmigianino. The Virgin, borne physically to paradise by a maelstrom of angels, is almost lost in the billowing clouds and swarm of figures. Correggio places her in the lower portion of the cupola opposite the nave and closest to the apse at the east end.

The center of the dome is open to a divine brilliance outlined by ascending, circling angels. Its base is defined by an illusionistic cornice (which a century later fooled Queen Christina, who wished to ascend to it). This base is supported by four squinches, each of which contains

Detail from Correggio's Assumption of the Virgin *(1522-1530).* (The Granger Collection, New York)

1520's

one of the patron saints of Parma (John the Baptist, Joseph, Hilary of Poitiers, and Bernard degli Uberti) as ecstatic figures on billowing clouds in shell niches (added after March 19, 1528). The city seal of Parma showed the Virgin flanked by Saints John the Baptist and Hilary. Torch-bearing youths along the rim of the cupola are reminiscent of Michelangelo's nudes in the Sistine ceiling, and other poses are permutations of the Hellenistic *Laocoön* sculpture as a prototype.

The topmost circle of figures includes Old and New Testament worthies, and slightly lower is the Virgin accompanied by almost fifty gleeful angels. The figures diminish in size as they ascend, reinforcing the illusion of recession in the dome. Below, at the level of the circular windows, are eleven gigantic apostles who were witnesses to Mary's ascent, two of whom in a gesture of *epiphania* shield their eyes against her divine radiance. They may have been inspired by their counterparts in

Titian's altarpiece of the same subject in Venice (Santa Maria dei Frari, 1516-1519). The Virgin melds with the clouds and angelic host, with only her dangling bare feet, open hands, and foreshortened face visible. Three studies in Dresden and London (British Museum) reveal the contortions Correggio gave her pose in his studies, Michelangelo's *Jonah* in the Sistine ceiling as his inspiration.

Correggio calls attention to Mary through the strongly illuminated rolling cloud and back of the angel below her, and her rose-colored robe and blue cloak, the traditional hues symbolizing her humanitiy and divine protection. Her open gesture with upturned palms alludes to the *orans* mode of prayer recorded in the Old Testament and in catacomb paintings in early Church history. The antiphon of the Mass for the feast of the Assumption carries the pledge of Mary's intercession for the citizens of Parma: "The doors to paradise are open for us through you, who today triumph in glory with the angels."

423

The unparalleled sense of celebration in the angels had not been seen since Donatello (1386-1466) graced the choir loft of Florence cathedral with his coursing putti. The angels' *raison d'être*, according to the sixteenth century Catechism, is to praise, honor, and glorify God, which they do here by conducting Mary to the opening vault of heaven bathed in divine brilliance. Many of the angels hold musical instruments as if in response to Psalm 150, to

> Praise the Lord in His sanctuary; . . . Praise Him with trumpet sound; . . . with lute and harp! . . . with timbrel and dance; . . . with strings and pipe! . . . with sounding cymbals,

and to the *Legenda aurea* (c. 1260, pb. 1470; *The Golden Legend*, 1483), by the Dominican friar Jacopo de Voragine (c. 1228-1298), which describes the angelic orders in musical jubilation.

The dome represented a brilliant visual statement by Correggio for its scale, its creation of a credible illusionistic space, and its fusion of tumbling figures, many in exaggeratedly foreshortened and in varied poses encyclopedic in scope. The brilliant light, soft tangible forms, compelling sentiment, and palpabale figures in convincing flight were some of the qualities that attracted northern European artists to Parma and Correggio's frescoes during the Baroque period.

Correggio's contract for the cupola as dictated to the anonymous canons of the cathedral required 1,000 gold *scudi* plus lime, scaffolding, and a closed storage room. Correggio most likely studied wax and clay models suspended from strings for his levitating angels, a practice later followed by Tintoretto (1518-1594). A single such figure could serve as a model for many poses when viewed from different angles.

Luther and the other Protestant reformers had argued against the efficacy of the Sacraments and the need for a priesthood, stressing faith alone as necessary for salvation. The Church countered by asserting its legitimacy through the continuity of the Scriptures and holy tradition. Correggio's fresco was part of that tradition in its incorporation of saints from the Old and New Testaments, based on an iconography that derived from sacred scriptures.

SIGNIFICANCE

Correggio's *Assumption of the Virgin* led to no further grand commissions for the artist, and it is reported to have received a mixed reception, one critic apparently calling it "a stew of frog's legs." However, later painters admired the fresco, and Correggio's contemporaries ranked the artist with Raphael (1483-1520), Michelangelo (1475-1564), and Titian (c. 1490-1576).

The fresco's completion was accompanied by the Treaty of Cambrai (1529), when French king Francis I renounced French claims to Italy and papal fortunes began to take a turn for the better with Clement's successor to the papacy, Paul III. Paul would inaugurate the Counter-Reformation in following decades with the approval of the Jesuit order in 1540, founded by Ignatius of Loyola, and the establishment of the Council of Trent five years later. In subsequent decades, Ignatius's Jesuits would reclaim Poland from the Calvanists

Correggio's The Holy Night *(c. 1530), also called* Nativity, *is considered the first monumental nocturnal scene in European painting.* (Royal Library, Windsor Castle)

and extend the faith to India, China, and Japan in the wake of Portuguese merchant fleets. The conquest of the Aztec and Inca empires in the 1520's prepared the Church for the bloodletting of its own martyrs, and the introduction of gunpowder into sixteenth century warfare added particular resonance to Correggio's illuminated clouds.

In the seventeenth century, art historians Giovanni Pietro Bellori and Filippo Baldinucci extolled Correggio's virtues as a painter. In the eighteenth century, painters Antoine Watteau, Sir Joshua Reynolds, and Anton Raphael Mengs studied his paintings for models. Although in the nineteenth century art critic John Ruskin and historian Jacob Burckhardt, in his *Der Cicerone* of 1855, lamented the moral tone of Correggio's dome frescoes, they admitted their compelling visual force. Parma continued to be a pilgrimage site during the Grand Tour: In 1846, novelist Charles Dickens in *Pictures from Italy* lamented the physical condition of Correggio's *Assumption of the Virgin* but acknowledged that connoisseurs still fell into raptures over it, marveling himself at the dome's labyrinth of figures and the artist's imaginative entanglement of limbs.

—*Edward J. Olszewski*

FURTHER READING

Bambach, Carmen, Hugo Chapman, Martin Clayton, and George Goldner. *Correggio and Parmigianino: Master Draftsmen of the Renaissance*, London: British Museum Press, 2000. Catalog of an impressive exhibition of Parmigianino's drawings, with two samples of studies for the Parma Cathedral's *Assumption*.

DeGrazia, Diane. *Correggio and His Legacy.* Washington, D.C.: National Gallery of Art, 1984. Catalog for an exhibition of drawings by Correggio and his followers, including color reproductions and two studies for the Parma Cathedral dome.

Ekserdjian, David. *Correggio.* New Haven, Conn.: Yale University Press, 1997. A comprehensive study of the artistic career of the painter.

Gould, Cecil. *The Paintings of Correggio.* Ithaca, N.Y.: Cornell University Press, 1976. A monographic study of the artist's corpus of paintings.

Manca, Joseph. "Stylistic Intentions in Correggio's *Assunta.*" *Notes in the History of Art* 7 (1987): 14-20. The author argues that the intended view of the dome is from the nave. where the figures and gestures have greatest clarity, and not from the presbytery, where Correggio's illusionism fails.

Shearman, John. *Only Connect . . . : Art and the Spectator in the Italian Renaissance.* Princeton, N.J.: Princeton University Press, 1992. The author contends that in the fresco, Christ awaits Mary, who ascends from her tomb in the space below the illusionistic balustrade occupied by the spectator.

Smyth, Carolyn. *Correggio Frescoes in Parma Cathedral.* Princeton, N.J.: Princeton University Press, 1997. A historiography with a viewing of the fresco from various vantage points in the nave of the cathedral.

SEE ALSO: 1469-1492: Rule of Lorenzo de' Medici; 1477-1482: Work Begins on the Sistine Chapel; c. 1478-1519: Leonardo da Vinci Compiles His Notebooks; 1495-1497: Leonardo da Vinci Paints *The Last Supper*; c. 1500: Netherlandish School of Painting; c. 1500: Revival of Classical Themes in Art; 1508-1520: Raphael Paints His Frescoes; 1508-1512 and 1534-1541: Michelangelo Paints the Sistine Chapel; 1532: Holbein Settles in London; Dec. 23, 1534-1540: Parmigianino Paints *Madonna with the Long Neck*; 1563-1584: Construction of the Escorial; June, 1564: Tintoretto Paints for the Scuola di San Rocco.

RELATED ARTICLES in *Great Lives from History: The Renaissance & Early Modern Era, 1454-1600:* The Carracci Family; Correggio; Lavinia Fontana; Giorgione; Isabella d'Este.

1523
GUSTAV I VASA BECOMES KING OF SWEDEN

Gustav's election signaled the beginning of a reign that transformed Sweden from a Danish province to a secondary power in Northern Europe. He recast the administration of Sweden under a nearly absolutist native monarch, created the Lutheran-type reformed Swedish Church, successfully put down several internal rebellions, and fine-tuned Sweden's alliances with foreign states.

LOCALE: Sweden
CATEGORY: Government and politics

KEY FIGURES

Gustav I Vasa (1496-1560), king of Sweden, r. 1523-1560
Konrad von Pyhy (d. 1553), German adventurer and Swedish chancellor, 1538-1543
Georg Norman (d. 1552), super attendant of the Swedish Church and chief minister, 1543-1552
Olaus Petri (1493-1552), Gustav's administrator of religious texts

SUMMARY OF EVENT

The death-knell of the Kalmar Union, which had united Denmark, Norway, and Sweden since 1389, began on November 8, 1520. The previous January, King Christian II of Denmark had defeated a Swedish army fighting for its independence, and in November his supporters executed eighty-two leading nobles in what has been called the Bloodbath of Stockholm.

Gustav I Vasa, a major landowner, became leader of the rebel party (protector), directed a peasant army that swept the Danes from most of Sweden, and was declared regent by the Estates in August of 1521. Aid from the German city of Lübeck allowed the insurgents to drive out some of the remaining Danes in the course of 1523. In March, 1523, the Danish nobles and Church leaders deposed Christian, replacing him with Frederick of Holstein-Gottorp (reigned as Frederick I). The Swedish Estates refused to recognize Frederick as the new monarch and elected Gustav by acclamation on June 6, 1523. His formal coronation was postponed until January 12, 1528, but he acted as monarch from the time of his election.

Gustav's reign of nearly forty years established Sweden as a major power in northern European political life. Under Danish crown control, the roughly 800,000 Swedes had managed their political lives with three tra-

ditional institutions: the annual *landsting*, the local or regional assembly or county council of free landowners and nobles; the Estates meeting in the National Assembly, the Riksdag, which represented the nobles and towns—in theory the Swedish people—at the national level; and the *råd*, a kind of privy council, which advised the monarch on Swedish national affairs. Gustav could not afford to eliminate any of these institutions, but he worked to limit the ability of each to interfere with the exercise of his will.

Local affairs came to be managed by Crown-appointed bailiffs. These men proved key in Gustav's programs of church resource confiscation and in reporting or tempering local dissent. Gustav diluted the power of the Estates, first, by simply not calling them for fifteen years (1529-1544) and, second, by opening them to the clergy in 1544. He did, however, seek their legitimizing approval on truly major national policy matters, such as introducing church reform (the Diet of Våsterås, 1527, and Riksdag of 1544) and replacing royal elections with the dynastic principle (the *arvförening*, or succession pact, of January, 1544). The *råd*, made up of high clerics and selected noblemen, continued to advise the king, but, increasingly, he looked for assistance to two foreign-born men, Konrad von Pyhy and Georg Norman.

Pyhy, a knight, doctor of laws, and diplomat from Augsburg, became Gustav's chancellor in 1538. He quickly replaced the few literate royal servants with a skeletal salaried bureaucracy, and he added a nonfeudal council of government to handle routine administrative decisions. Pyhy fell from favor in the summer of 1543 and died in prison in 1553. Many of his reforms disintegrated, but he left Sweden with a rationalized administrative foundation. His place was taken, in effect, by Georg Norman, who had been directing the latter stages of the Swedish Reformation.

In Gustav's Sweden, an independent Church was a rival for the kind of sweeping power and authority that he sought. It was the single largest landholder (about one-fifth of arable land), was untaxable, had a claim to steady revenue, and had accumulated great wealth in gold and silver vessels and decorations, from the urban cathedrals to the parish churches. Its reliance on and loyalty to papal Rome also rankled the king-elect. Though popular anti-clericalism existed in Sweden prior to the Reformation, the introduction of Lutheran-type reforms beginning in 1523 was almost purely an exercise of Gustav's will.

His reliance on German merchants and German merchant states such as Lübeck led him to Lutheranism, though for reasons of state rather than conscience. He readily accepted Luther's emphases on obedience to secular authorities and his definition of the church as the gathering of God's people, not a supranational organization. He introduced Lutheran ministers in the larger cities, where Germans tended to live, and began imposing vernacular liturgies. He harnessed all Swedish printing presses to the cause of Lutheran literature and propaganda. Wittenberg-trained churchman Olaus Petri (Olof Petersson) developed most of the Lutheran texts in Sweden, including a handbook of the Swedish Church called *Een handbock påå Swensko* (1529; *The Manual of Olavus Petri*, 1529, 1953) and the *Lilla katekes* (1536), from the "small catechism" of Martin Luther. He also had printed the first Swedish New Testament (1541).

Like Henry VIII in England, Gustav dispossessed the church of most of its landed property (appropriating much of it as his own), revenues, and even church plate (six and a half tons of silver alone), and declared himself Supreme Defender of the reformed church. Nevertheless, he failed to adopt any official statement of ecclesiastical reorganization, or Church Ordinance. Rather, he left the relationship of church and state officially ambiguous, allowing for himself as much flexibility as possible.

By 1560, the entire beneficed clergy of Sweden was evangelical. Resistance by most bishops was light, as they feared for their positions, but several uprisings seeking Gustav's overthrow signaled widespread popular discontent. He crushed these uprisings brutally as a warning to others.

Between 1525 and 1534, Sweden saw five major popular rebellions. In the early days, the issue was that of high taxation, primarily, but dissatisfaction with religious policy fuelled later uprisings. The most serious revolt was the Dacke Rebellion in Småland (1542). Several small northern European states supported this rebellion, forcing Gustav to negotiate with its leader, Nils Dacke, in December. Gustav defeated the rebels on March 20, 1543, and Dacke was slain a short time later. The rebellion, although not a complete success, nevertheless caused Gustav to rethink his harsh ruling style, which he modified for the remainder of his reign.

Internationally, Sweden was a minor player, lacking developed industries and markets; what did exist was largely in German hands in the 1520's. Lübeck's defeat by Denmark and Sweden (1534-1536) loosened the German grip on the Swedish economy and extinguished Sweden's debt to the Hanseatic city. Denied a place in the Protestant Schmalkaldic League, Sweden navigated carefully during the Habsburg and Valois struggles.

In September of 1541, Sweden signed the Treaty of Brömsebro, a fifty-year defensive pact with Denmark, and in the following July arranged an alliance with France. Gustav also created Sweden's first navy and Europe's first standing national army, as a hedge against rebellion and foreign attack. He sought to monopolize the movement of Russian goods westward by waging war in 1554, but the attempt failed. He did, however, bolster Sweden's economy by acting as its biggest capitalist, investing in bar-iron forges, steel production, arms manufacturing, and cloth making.

SIGNIFICANCE

Sweden had experienced periods of independence (1448-1457, 1464-1465, and 1467-1470), but the establishment of the Vasa Dynasty ensured Swedish autonomy. Gustav himself was a complex figure who ruled Sweden as an absolutist who brooked no opposition. He was a Machiavellian king who ruled like a stern father, dictating all aspects of national life from church to commerce to court manners.

His dim view of his subjects prompted much of his interference, but it also directed his state-building in a way that ensured national autonomy under a powerful monarch with no major sources of internal dissent or opposition.

His alignment with the Lutheran movement kept him on the winning side of northern European political struggles and gave him legitimate control over the Swedish Church. His reign, however controversial, was vital for establishing and maintaining Swedish independence and power in the sixteenth century and beyond.

—*Joseph P. Byrne*

FURTHER READING

Kirby, David. *Northern Europe in the Early Modern Period: The Baltic World, 1492-1772.* New York: Longman, 1990. A concise source that places Swedish history under the Vasas in the context of the history of the Baltic region.

Moberg, Vilhelm. *A History of the Swedish People: From Renaissance to Revolution.* Translated by Paul Britten Austin. New York: Dorset Press, 1989. In his chapter on Gustav "the tyrant," Moberg emphasizes the absolutist tendencies of Gustav's reign and their adverse impact on common Swedes.

Ozment, Stephen B. *Protestants: The Birth of a Revolution.* New York: Doubleday, 1992. The best up-to-date interpretation of the Reformation and the religious wars of the period.

Petri, Olavus. *The Manual of Olavus Petri, 1529*. Edited by Eric E. Yelverton. London: S. P. C. K., for the Church Historical Society, 1953. A translation of Petri's handbook of the Swedish Church.

Roberts, Michael. *The Early Vasas: A History of Sweden, 1523-1611*. New York: Cambridge University Press, 1986. Presents a detailed, balanced, scholarly, and altogether positive view of Gustav's reign.

SEE ALSO: Oct. 31, 1517: Luther Posts His Ninety-five Theses; Feb. 27, 1531: Formation of the Schmalkaldic League; Mar., 1536: Calvin Publishes *Institutes of the Christian Religion*; Sept. 25, 1555: Peace of Augsburg.

RELATED ARTICLES in *Great Lives from History: The Renaissance & Early Modern Era, 1454-1600:* John Calvin; Charles V; Martin Luther.

Spring, 1523
ŌUCHI FAMILY MONOPOLIZES TRADE WITH CHINA

In the spring of 1523, Hakata merchants, backed by the Ōuchi family, reached the Chinese port of Ningbo, followed shortly by rival Ōsaka traders, connected with the Hosokawa family. Conflict ensued, and the Hakata merchants prevailed. China-Japan trade was interrupted, but the Ōuchi family eventually gained a monopoly on it.

LOCALE: Ningbo, China

CATEGORIES: Trade and commerce; diplomacy and international relations

KEY FIGURES

Ashikaga Yoshitane (1466-1523), the tenth Ashikaga shogun, r. 1490-1493, 1508-1521

Hosokawa Takakuni (1484-1531), who led the efforts of the Hosokawas to dominate trade with China

Ōuchi Yoshioki (1477-1528), head of another powerful trading family

Wang Jin (Wang Chin; fl. sixteenth century), a senior Chinese official in Ningbo

Song Suqing (Sung Su-ching; fl. sixteenth century), a Chinese interpreter and go-between for the Hosokawa traders

SUMMARY OF EVENT

During the early years of the Ming Dynasty, a great expansion of Chinese maritime exploration took place. From 1405 until his death in 1433, Chinese admiral Zheng He took ships as far as the Persian Gulf and the eastern coast of Africa. After Zheng's death in the mid-1430's, however, the Ming government ended its maritime activities on the grounds that naval voyages had not yielded any significant material benefits. There followed a decline in Chinese maritime commerce, since merchant ships had no protection on the sea.

The vacuum left was filled by small fleets belonging to lords of Japanese coastal regions in western Honshū and on the western coast of Kyūshū. Under the leadership of the Ashikaga shogunate, these lords helped control piracy, and in exchange for this the Ming government gave concessions for authorized Japanese vessels to trade in Chinese ports. For public relations purposes in China, these Japanese trading voyages were ostensibly to bring tributary goods from the shogun to the Ming emperor. The Chinese cargo taken back to Japan was portrayed as return gifts to the shogun from the Chinese ruler.

To assure that the only arriving Japanese vessels were those authorized by the shogunate, the Ming government established a system of tallies, with annotated impressions made from imperial seals divided in two parts. One set of parts was sent to Japan to be issued to official Japanese trading vessels, while another was kept in the Chinese port of entry, Ningbo, for verification. When the Ming ruler changed, fresh tallies were made, with the reign name of the new sovereign.

Controlling the western Honshū coastline, the port of Shimonoseki (which commanded the Kanmon Strait), and the southern coast leading into the Inland Sea, the Ōuchi family was able to dominate sea traffic between Japan and the Asian mainland. As a result, the shogunate awarded the China trade concession to the Ōuchi family, and the family maintained this priority over the years, interrupted only by occasional breaches with the shogunate. Maritime traders from Hakata, in the Fukuoka area of Kyūshū, were allied with the family and conducted the actual voyages to China.

Under the leadership of Ōuchi Yoshioki, the family greatly strengthened ties with the shogunate, after its troops helped expel hostile forces from Kyōto and restored Ashikaga Yoshitane as shogun in 1508. Yoshitane then officially confirmed the virtual Ōuchi monopoly over officially authorized China trade. Yoshioki remained in the capital protecting the shogun until 1518, when he moved back to his own domain.

In 1521, Hosokawa Takakuni, who controlled the capital after Yoshioki's departure, deposed Shogun Yoshitane, who died in exile in 1523. The next shogun was a pawn of Takakuni, whose Hosokawa family was in total control of the government. The Ōuchi family lost shogunate backing for its control of the China trade, as the Hosokawa family planned to assume control of this trade. The Hosokawas formed an alliance with sea traders from the port of Sakai in the Ōsaka region, reinforcing them with Hosokawa guards and giving them a tally authorization from the shogunate files.

In the spring of 1523, three Hakata merchant ships backed by the Ōuchi family reached the Chinese port of Ningbo. They had a tally authorization to trade, issued during the reign of the Jiajing emperor (r. 1522-1567). A ship belonging to rival Sakai traders arrived afterward but obtained priority clearance from the Chinese port officials. The angry Hakata merchants received no satisfactory explanation for this special treatment, and they later discovered that the latecomers' tally authorization was from the reign of the previous emperor, Zhengde, who had died in 1521. The Hakata merchants claimed that this Zhengde tally had expired and that they should have been cleared for trade, although it is unclear exactly how they obtained their own more recent tally.

Enraged by the indifference of Chinese officials toward their claims and assuming that these officials had been bribed, the Hakata merchants and their Ōuchi guards attacked the Sakai trading party, killing many of them and burning their ship. They failed, however, to catch Song Suqing, the Chinese interpreter who had accompanied the Hosokawa traders to Ningbo; it was he who, the Hakata merchants believed, had arranged the bribes. The Hakata traders pursued Song for nearly 100 miles (approximately 160 kilometers) before giving up and returning to Ningbo. They captured Wang Jin, the senior Chinese official in Ningbo, and set sail for Japan. Pursued by some Ming coast-guard ships, they fought them off and escaped.

This incident severely strained Sino-Japanese relations, and official trade was interrupted for some time. After protracted negotiations between the Chinese and Japanese governments, using merchants in the Okinawa area as intermediaries, Wang Jin was returned, the Hakata ringleader of the Ningbo incident was remanded to the Ming authorities, and all the Japanese cargo left behind at Ningbo was confiscated by the Chinese.

The Ming authorities never actually banned trade with Japan; rather, it had excluded the Portuguese because of port violence. Hosokawa Takakuni, who had backed the rival Sakai merchants, lost power after 1525 and was killed as the result of a coup in the capital in 1531. The violence at Ningbo, regardless of its immediate consequences, intimidated potential maritime rivals and assured the Ōuchi family of a monopoly on official trade with China, which lasted until Yoshioki's heir, Yoshitaka, died during an uprising in 1551, and Ōuchi power was completely destroyed.

SIGNIFICANCE

The Ōuchi family's virtual control of maritime trade routes in northeast Asian waters filled the vacuum left after the Ming government scrapped its navy to concentrate on coastal defenses after 1433. The Chinese government created an official and exclusive trade relation with Japan at Ningbo in exchange for maritime security. This arrangement also helped make it possible for Chinese and Korean merchant vessels to conduct peaceful trade in various other ports.

The other forces operating in northeast Asian waters were Portuguese vessels and vessels of the *wakō*, a loosely allied group of mostly Japanese pirates. While the Portuguese were primarily interested in trade, they also sometimes clashed with the Chinese. After several violent clashes, the Chinese authorities banned all Portuguese ships from Chinese ports after 1521. In 1545, after Portuguese ships began to return, Chinese forces destroyed a Portuguese trading post at Ningbo and killed all the Portuguese there as well.

The *wakō* also attempted to trade at times, but the Ming authorities regarded them as pirates and viewed their trade as simply another form of criminal activity. The tally arrangement was in fact largely aimed at excluding *wakō* who might pose as legitimate Japanese merchants. Unlike the Portuguese sailors, who were involved in some violent incidents, these Japanese pirates deliberately raided Chinese ports, looting, killing, and in general menacing the Chinese coast.

After the Ōuchi family lost power in the middle of the sixteenth century, neither the Chinese nor the Japanese had enough naval strength to control the Japanese pirates. The Portuguese, regarded as the lesser of two evils, were tacitly allowed to replace the Ōuchi family's maritime forces. The Portuguese did help protect Chinese, Japanese, and Korean merchant ships in some cases, but they became a growing colonial power, establishing a permanent Chinese trading base at Macao in 1556 and developing an official trading relationship with Japan at Nagasaki as of 1570.

—*Michael McCaskey*

FURTHER READING

Arnesen, Peter Judd. *The Medieval Japanese Daimyo: The Ōuchi Family's Rule of Suo and Nagato.* New Haven, Conn.: Yale University Press, 1979. A history of the Ōuchi family in its heyday.

Brook, Timothy. *The Confusions of Pleasure: Commerce and Culture in Ming China.* Berkeley: University of California Press, 1998. Describes how a prosperous trading culture developed during the Ming Dynasty.

Fogel, Joshua A. *Sagacious Monks and Bloodthirsty Warriors: Chinese Views of Japan in the Ming-Qing Period.* Norwalk, Conn.: East Bridge, 2002. Presents contradictory images of the Japanese in Ming-Qing Chinese public opinion.

Levathes, Louise. *When China Ruled the Seas: The Treasure Fleet of the Dragon Throne.* New York: Oxford University Press, 1996. A history of the rise and fall of Chinese naval power and maritime trade during the Ming Dynasty.

So, Kwan-wai. *Japanese Piracy in Ming China During the Sixteenth Century.* East Lansing: Michigan State University Press, 1975. The impact of Japanese piracy on Sino-Japanese relations during the time of the tally trade.

Verschuer, Charlotte von. *Across the Perilous Sea: Japanese Trade with China and Korea from the Seventh to the Sixteenth Century.* Ithaca, N.Y.: Cornell University Press, 2004. Study by an expert on Sino-Japanese maritime trade from earliest times through the sixteenth century.

SEE ALSO: 16th cent.: China's Population Boom; 16th cent.: Single-Whip Reform; 1505-1521: Reign of Zhengde and Liu Jin; 1514-1598: Portuguese Reach China; 1521-1567: Reign of Jiajing; 1550's-1567: Japanese Pirates Pillage the Chinese Coast; 1550-1571: Mongols Raid Beijing; Jan. 23, 1556: Earthquake in China Kills Thousands; 1573-1620: Reign of Wanli; 1592-1599: Japan Invades Korea.

RELATED ARTICLES in *Great Lives from History: The Renaissance & Early Modern Era, 1454-1600:* Tomé Pires; Matteo Ricci; Wang Yangming; Xiaozong; Zhengde.

August, 1523

FRANCISCAN MISSIONARIES ARRIVE IN MEXICO

Franciscans extended the Spanish conquest of the Americas by launching missions to educate and convert to Christianity the indigenous peoples of what is now Mexico.

LOCALE: Mexico
CATEGORY: Religion; colonization

KEY FIGURES

Toribio de Benevente Motolinía (d. 1568), Franciscan father revered by the indigenous peoples

Bernardino de Sahagún (1499-1590), Franciscan father who devoted a lifetime to studying and writing about indigenous culture

Hernán Cortés (1485-1547), Spanish military officer who led the conquest of Mexico

Pedro de Gante (1486?-1572), Franciscan lay brother who pioneered work among the Mexican Indians

Martín of Valencia (d. 1534), leader of the twelve Franciscans who arrived in Mexico in 1524

Juan de Zumárraga (1468-1548), Franciscan father appointed the first bishop of Mexico in 1527

SUMMARY OF EVENT

Immediately after Hernán Cortés's conquest of Mexico (1519-1521), the Spanish began the conversion of the indigenous peoples to Catholicism. This was in keeping with the militant Catholicism that had evolved in medieval Spain, during the Christians' reconquest of the Iberian Peninsula from Muslim control.

Cortés urged the monarchy to send friars to Mexico, and in 1523-1524, a few Franciscans arrived. They were the first wave of missionaries who carried out what historian Robert Ricard called "the spiritual conquest." The friars baptized millions of Mexican Indians, making them at least nominally Christians, and established among them the institutional bases of Roman Catholicism.

The Franciscans were the first regular clergy to accept the challenge, the Dominicans and Augustinians arriving later (1526-1533). Two Flemish Franciscans reached Vera Cruz in 1523, accompanied by a lay brother, Pedro de Gante (allegedly the illegitimate half brother of Charles V). The two ordained friars soon died on Cortés's expedition to Honduras, but Pedro de Gante stayed in Mexico until his death in 1572, a pioneer in virtually every Franciscan endeavor among the indigenous.

Twelve more Franciscans arrived in 1524, called the "Twelve Apostles," led by Father Martín of Valencia. Among the twelve was Toribio de Benevente Motolinía, who was lame, ascetic, and became universally revered as Motolinía, "the poor little one." A papal bull endowed them with remarkable power, including that of administering all the sacraments, and it also freed them from interference by other ecclesiastical authorities.

Early Franciscan missionaries came filled with millenialist fervor. Queen Isabella and her Franciscan confessor, Francisco Jiménez de Cisneros, had reformed the order into the Observant Franciscans only a few years before, emphasizing, among other things, a rededication to the ideal of poverty. Providing their own interpretation of the mystical predictions of Joachim de Fiore, a medieval Calabrian visionary, many Franciscans arrived in Mexico convinced that Christopher Columbus's discovery and Cortés's conquest had set the stage for the final task before the millennium: the conversion of the simple, poor, innocent indigenous peoples.

Believing their labors would bring the end of time, the Franciscans set about learning Nahua (the vernacular language), preparing catechisms, teaching the rudiments of Catholicism, and carrying out mass baptisms. Between 1525 and 1572, the friars established a network of chapels and monasteries across Puebla, Mexico City, Hidalgo, and Michoacán. The Dominicans and Augustinians who came later found the Franciscans occupying most of the important cities in central Mexico. They organized the countryside into *doctrinas* or indigenous parishes, with a main town (*cabecera*), where the Franciscan resided and the church was built; and the surrounding villages (*visitas*), which the friar toured on his ecclesiastical rounds.

They also set up schools and tried to teach Hispanic culture and religious doctrine. Pedro de Gante's school in Tenochtitlán was the forerunner, while the Colegio de Santa Cruz in Tlatelolco Tenochtitlán (established 1536) taught Latin, writing, philosophy, and logic to boys from the indigenous elite (nuns eventually arrived to educate girls). At the Hospital of Santa Fe, Franciscans patterned a community on Thomas More's *Utopia* (1516; English translation, 1551), hoping to re-create primitive Christianity. To assist their missionary labors, they compiled ethnographic information. Two invaluable sources on Aztec culture are Motolinía's *Historia de los indios de la Nueva España* (wr. 1541, pb. 1858; *History of the Indians of New Spain*, 1950) and Bernardino de Sahagún's *Historia general de las cosas de Nueva España* (compiled 1576-1577, pb. 1829, 1831; *General History of the Things of New Spain: Florentine Codex*, 1950-1982).

The task of conversion posed a series of opportunities and challenges. Determined that conversion be an individual, informed decision, the friars insisted that the indigenous be taught the basic beliefs and prayers before baptism. Often they used the children to indoctrinate their parents. The nuances of Nahua linguistics and religious culture were difficult to master, and Nahua contained no equivalent terms for many Christian theological concepts. Communication between the missionaries and the indigenous was less precise and more confusing than the friars admitted or perhaps even realized. Despite these problems, the missionaries pushed ahead with baptism following rudimentary instruction about Catholic beliefs.

Although some of the indigenous, especially adult males, refused this overt sign of conversion, the Franciscans claimed to have baptized four million indigenous by 1537. According to Motolinía, they, along with their Augustinian and Dominican brothers, had baptized nine million by 1540. These were astounding results, achieved by a mere handful of friars. By 1559 in Mexico, there were only 380 Franciscans, 212 Augustinians, and 210 Dominicans.

The conquest itself had discredited the power of indigenous deities, and the Spanish sword blocked the continued open practice of Aztec religion, particularly its frequent human sacrifice and military campaigns to capture sacrificial victims. Nevertheless, indigenous religion permeated the culture that the friars confronted. Fearful the indigenous might revert to their old ways, the friars destroyed idols and temples, burned manuscripts, and persecuted Aztec priests. In their efforts, they found an able ally in Father Juan de Zumárraga, who as first bishop of Mexico (1528-1548) was also a Franciscan. They also criticized the increasingly popular cult of Guadalupe, rejecting claims that the Virgin had appeared in 1531 to a native Indian, Juan Diego, on a hill previously associated with worship of Tonantzín, an indigenous goddess. Nor did they leave it up to the baptized native Indian as to whether he or she attended mass and participated in Catholic religious life. The friars sent out assistants to gather the reluctant and indifferent for services. They whipped or otherwise punished those who refused to comply.

SIGNIFICANCE

Most of the indigenous of central Mexico were baptized within two decades following the military conquest, and Motolinía claimed the missionaries had cleansed Mexico of indigenous idolatry by 1540. Yet it is by no means clear that the indigenous were fully converted to Catholicism. Some of the indigenous undoubtedly became Christian in the full sense of conversion, possessing a clear understanding and commitment to Catholic theology. Others, perhaps most often in rural areas, clung to the ancient ways.

The vast majority probably fell somewhere in the middle, their superficial Catholicism colored to a greater or lesser extent by pre-Hispanic beliefs and practices. Some believed themselves Catholics but did not understand the Church's doctrines. Many participated in Catholic public ritual while privately continuing indigenous practices. Often this reflected religious syncretism; sometimes it was *nepantlism* (a state of confusion about, or an indifference to, both religious traditions).

—*Kendall W. Brown*

FURTHER READING

Browne, Walden. *Sahagún and the Transition to Modernity.* Norman: University of Oklahoma Press, 2000. Study of Sahagún's work with the Mexican Indians, arguing that the father, far from being a precursor of modernity, was caught up in the disintegration of medieval forms of knowledge amid the difficult transition to modern thought and modern forms of knowledge.

Burkhart, Louise M. *Before Guadalupe: The Virgin Mary in Early Colonial Nahuatl Literature.* Albany, N.Y.: University of Texas Press, 2001. Study of the introduction of Marianism into Nahua culture together with a collection of sixteenth and seventeenth century Nahua texts discussing the Virgin Mary.

_____. *The Slippery Earth: Nahua-Christian Moral Dialogue in Sixteenth Century Mexico.* Tucson: University of Arizona Press, 1989. Analysis, by an anthropologist, of the linguistic and conceptual difficulties encountered as friars attempted to translate Catholic moral teachings into Nahua.

Gibson, Charles. *The Aztecs Under Spanish Rule: A History of the Indians of the Valley of Mexico, 1519-1810.* Stanford, Calif.: Stanford University Press, 1964. A masterful summation of Spanish colonialism's effects on indigenous Mexico. Chapter five focuses on religion, including Franciscan conversions, territorial organization, land ownership, and church building.

Lockhart, James. *The Nahuas After the Conquest: A Social and Cultural History of the Indians of Central Mexico, Sixteenth Through Eighteenth Centuries.* Stanford, Calif.: Stanford University Press, 1992. Based on post-Conquest documents written in Nahua, Lockhart assesses the extent to which indigenous culture survived or was modified by colonialism. Chapter 6 deals with "Religious Life."

Molina, Alonso de. *Nahua Confraternities in Early Colonial Mexico: The 1552 Nahuatl Ordinances of Fray Alonso de Molina, OFM.* Translated and edited by Barry D. Sell. Berkeley, Calif.: Academy of American Franciscan History, 2002. Reproduction of and commentary upon the religious ordinances set forth by a Franciscan missionary to the Nahua in the mid-sixteenth century.

Motolinía (Toribio de Benevente). *History of the Indians of New Spain.* Washington, D.C.: Academy of American Franciscan History, 1951. One of the most important sixteenth century Franciscans recounts, with some optimistic exaggeration, the friars' efforts. Also includes ethnographic observations about indigenous peoples.

Phelan, John L. *The Millennial Kingdom of the Franciscans in the New World.* 2d ed. 1970. Reprint. Millwood, N.Y.: Kraus Reprint, 1980. Examines the mysticism and millennial fire of the Franciscans, especially as expressed through the writings of Jeronimo de Mendieta, the sixteenth century missionary author of *Historia eclesiástica indiana.*

Ricard, Robert. *The Spiritual Conquest of Mexico: An Essay on the Apostolate and the Evangelizing Methods of the Mendicant Orders in New Spain, 1523-1572.* Berkeley: University of California Press, 1966. The classic study of Mendicant efforts in Mexico, it is especially strong on the friars' methods but too optimistic in its evaluation of their results.

Sahagún, Bernardino de. *General History of the Things of New Spain: Florentine Codex.* 13 vols. Santa Fe, N.M.: School of American Research, 1950-1982. A great ethnographic treasure, partly derived from information obtained through interviews with the Mexican Indians who lived prior to or during the conquest.

SEE ALSO: Beginning c. 1495: Reform of the Spanish Church; 1502-1520: Reign of Montezuma II; Beginning 1519: Smallpox Kills Thousands of Indigenous Americans; Apr., 1519-Aug., 1521: Cortés Conquers Aztecs in Mexico; 1527-1547: Maya Resist Spanish Incursions in Yucatán; Feb. 23, 1540-Oct., 1542: Coronado's Southwest Expedition; 1542-1543: The New Laws of Spain; 1552: Las Casas Publishes *The Tears of the Indians*; Jan., 1598-Feb., 1599: Oñate's New Mexico Expedition.

RELATED ARTICLES in *Great Lives from History: The Renaissance & Early Modern Era, 1454-1600:* Hernán Cortés; Ferdinand II and Isabella I; Francisco Jiménez de Cisneros.

June, 1524-July, 1526
GERMAN PEASANTS' WAR

The German Peasants' War—caused by a number of factors, including economic, political, and religious—marked the last major and most widespread of a series of peasant revolts throughout Europe, precursors to the later democratic revolutions that ended feudal rule in Europe.

LOCALE: Austria and southwestern Germany

CATEGORIES: Social reform; wars, uprisings, and civil unrest; religion; government and politics

KEY FIGURES

Hans Müller (fl. late fifteenth-early sixteenth century), peasant leader

Michael Gaismair (1490-1532), peasant leader

Andreas Carlstadt (c. 1480-1541), radical preacher

Thomas Münzer (c. 1490-1525), radical preacher

Charles V (1500-1558), Holy Roman Emperor, r. 1519-1556

Philip the Magnanimous (1504-1567), leading Lutheran prince of the Holy Roman Empire

Georg Truchsess von Waldburg (1488-1531), commander of imperial armies in Germany

Martin Luther (1483-1546), German Protestant leader

Götz von Berlichingen (1480-1562), nobleman who became a peasant leader

Florian Geyer (1490-1525), nobleman who became a leader in the peasant movement

Ferdinand I (1503-1564), archduke of Austria and regent of the Holy Roman Empire while Charles was in Italy

Ulrich (1487-1550), duke of Württemberg and German aristocrat exiled by imperial order

SUMMARY OF EVENT

Discontent among the peasantry, common in most parts of Europe throughout the Middle Ages, expressed itself in violence on many occasions, notably the Great English Peasants' Revolt of 1381. The greatest and most prolonged of these revolts was the German Peasants' War of 1524-1526, which involved hundreds of thousands of peasants.

While it was the last of the late, great medieval peasant revolts, the goals, themes, and organization of the revolt make it, in some respects, the first of the modern popular revolutions. While the war consisted of a number of regional uprisings, peasant groups of various princes and lords banded together in a common revolt. The peasants also made alliances with various towns and often were able to enlist the support of some clergy and nobility.

The first outbreak occurred at Stühlingen in the Black Forest in June of 1524, when the peasants were required to labor on a holy day. Hans Müller, a knight, led a force of twelve hundred men to the neighboring town of Waldshut, where an evangelical brotherhood was established.

A small army of the Swabian League, a union of princes and towns, was sent into the district under George Truchsess von Waldburg. Because he was not sure of his strength, he attempted to quiet the peasants with negotiations, pending the arrival of more troops. By early 1525, however, the revolt had broken out in other regions as well, notably near Lake Constance, the duchy of Württemberg, and Swabia. In Württemberg, the rebels were encouraged by the exiled Duke Ulrich, who had been deprived of his duchy by imperial order after a family quarrel.

In February, Truchsess reversed his conciliatory policy, which had held violence to a minimum, and armed rebellion erupted in many places. By the spring, there were three main centers: the Ried district near the city of Ulm, the Black Forest, and Lake Constance. Each district had its own organized forces loosely united as "the Christian Brotherhood."

The leaders of the three divisions met in late February or early March at the town of Memmingen and probably on that occasion drew up the Twelve Articles of the Peasants of Swabia, compiled by laypreacher Sebastian Lötzer. The articles outlined some three hundred grievances as told by the region's peasants, becoming not only the model manifesto for the rebellions throughout Germany but also the classic statements of the peasants' demands.

The twelve articles were prefaced by the assertion that the Bible counseled peace and patience, and that the demands were meant to secure such virtues for the whole people. The first article provided for the popular election of pastors, with the stipulation that they should preach the "pure Gospel alone," a Lutheran idea. The peasants refused to be serfs, "because Christ has purchased us with His blood." Other demands were primarily economic: the mitigation of church tithes, free access to woods and water for game and fish, the abolition of excessive feudal dues, and protection against arbitrary punishment. The twelfth article promised the withdrawal of any of the others that could be proven contrary to Scripture.

Following adoption of the articles, peasant armies began sieges in the diocese of Bamberg and Würtzburg in Germany, and in the duchy of the Tyrol and the diocese of Salzburg in Austria. In all places where local revolts broke out, authorities found themselves without adequate troops because the majority of the armed forces were with Holy Roman Emperor Charles V fighting in Italy.

The demands of the rebels in the Elsass district of Germany were more far-reaching than those of Memmingen. They had nationalistic and democratic overtones, insisting on the deposition of all unpopular officials with full allegiance being promised only to the emperor. All princely power was to be abolished and local government reformed along democratic lines.

The leader of the Tyrolean revolt, Michael Gaismair, put forth the most radical demands for reform. Gaismair advocated a return to simple community living for everyone, with only the authority of the emperor limiting personal freedom. All towns and castles were to be destroyed, individuals were to live in villages on the basis of equality, trade was considered profiteering, and people were to engage in agriculture on a scientific basis.

A moving, if exaggerated, rendering of a "scene" from the German Peasants' War of 1524-1526. (R. S. Peale and J. A. Hill)

In Germany, the rebellion, which already had religious overtones, came to be associated closely with two radical former followers of Martin Luther: Andreas Carlstadt and Thomas Münzer. Carlstadt, a former rector of Wittenberg University, had been forced out of Wittenberg because of his radicalism. He became a leader of revolt in the town of Rothenburg. When the town fell again to the princes in 1525, he fled to Basel, where he ended his days as a professor.

Münzer played an important, if somewhat vague, role in the uprising, chiefly by preaching a democratic, communistic, millenarian Christianity that urged the peasants to murder their enemies, who were regarded as the enemies of true religion. He made a tour of the strife-torn regions of south Germany in 1524-1525, preaching the equalizing effects of Christ's redemption. He settled in the town of Muhlhausen, where a revolt subsequently occurred. In May of 1525, the armies of the Muhlhausen rebels were defeated at Frankenhausen by Philip the Magnanimous, the leading Lutheran prince of the Holy Roman Empire. Münzer was tortured and killed, after he had repudiated his earlier beliefs and actions.

Fighting went on throughout the spring of 1525. Certain areas were controlled by the peasants, who attacked castles and forced nobles and clergy to flee. The peasants sacked many monasteries, which were generally wealthy and strict in dealing with peasants. Many of the peasant bands displayed strong anticlerical and anti-Catholic overtones, although wholesale bloodshed was avoided. The successful peasant leaders were those who, like Müller, came from the middle class or the lower strata of the nobility. Two knights, Florian Geyer and Götz von Berlichingen (who was forced to serve against his will), were the most successful leaders, together with a number of Protestant and Catholic clergy who associated themselves with the uprisings.

The victories of the emperor in Italy brought a steady flow of soldiers back into Germany, and the Swabian League under Truchsess and other princely armies began to subdue the peasants when they began to show signs of disorganization and a lack of morale. The victory of Philip at Frankenhausen began a swift decline in the rebels' fortunes.

In April of 1525, Luther had issued his *Exhortation to Peace on the Twelve Articles*, which urged the peasants to

---

A PEASANTS' MANIFESTO

Laypreacher Sebastian Lötzer compiled the Twelve Articles of the Peasants of Swabia (1524) in response to the mistreatment of peasants by their lords, the increased economic gap between rich and poor, and, consequently, the growing poverty of the peasantry. The Third Article, excerpted here, argues against this mistreatment by direct authority of the gospels.

The Third Article. It has been the custom hitherto for men to hold us as their own property, which is pitiable enough, considering that Christ has delivered and redeemed us all, without exception, by the shedding of his precious blood, the lowly as well as the great. Accordingly it is consistent with Scripture that we should be set free and should wish to be so. . . . He [God] has not commanded us not to obey the authorities, but rather that we should be humble, not only towards those in authority, but towards everyone. We are thus ready to yield obedience according to God's law to our elected and regular authorities in all proper things becoming to a Christian. We therefore take it for granted that you will release us from serfdom as true Christians, unless it should be shown us from the gospel that we are serfs.

Source: From *The Great Documents of Western Civilization*, edited by Milton Viorst (New York: Bantam Books, Matrix Editions, 1967), pp. 90-91.

---

obey their lords, but also blamed the nobility for most of the problems and castigated them strongly for greed and tyranny. The following month, however, he published *Against the Robbing and Murdering Horde of Peasants*, in which he violently condemned the rebels and urged the princes to kill them without mercy.

One by one the peasant armies were subdued and their leaders killed. Götz deserted the peasants and was later pardoned by the emperor. Geyer was defeated in battle, but escaped and was later murdered. Müller was burned at the stake. The princely commanders became more successful and grew increasingly ferocious. As the rebellions were put down, thousands of peasants were slaughtered, towns were burned, and women and children were forced into exile. In the last days of the war, the peasants amassed their largest force of twenty-three thousand at Algäu, but through treachery, they were defeated by Truchsess.

Only in a few districts near Lake Constance were the peasants able to gain substantial concessions from their lords, chiefly because the people of Basel intervened on their side. In parts of Austria, however, Gaismair was able to keep the war going until 1526, while Archduke Ferdinand I, the emperor's brother and regent in his absence, vainly sought a settlement by granting concessions. Finally, in July, Gaismair was defeated. He fled to Venice, where he later became a Venetian diplomat and almost succeeded in negotiating an anti-imperial league to aid the peasants. His return to Austria was eagerly awaited for some time, but he was murdered in 1532, probably on Austrian instigation.

SIGNIFICANCE

A number of factors—economic, political, and religious—caused the rebellions. Population growth in some regions, and tax rates and church tithes on peasant agricultural production approaching 40 percent, led to economic hardship and poverty among peasant groups. Peasants resented the increasing disparity in wealth between themselves and the nobility.

Additionally, religious reform instituted by Luther and the Lutheran reformation and the even more radical Anabaptist movement undermined the religious legitimation of feudalism. The new Protestant movements declared the equality of all persons, articulated in Luther's doctrine of the "priesthood of all believers." Pastors were placed at the call of the people and church hierarchy was replaced by more democratic forms. These ideas challenged the notion of the feudal political hierarchy as well. Additionally, the Protestant claim that all law is to be based in the Word of God allowed the peasants to challenge feudal law and show its contradiction to principles of biblical justice.

In articulating a belief in the equality of persons and demanding more political control and economic justice, the peasants used religious language to articulate many of the themes that were to emerge as the center of modern democratic revolutions.

—James F. Hitchcock,
updated by Charles L. Kammer III

FURTHER READING

Blickle, Peter. *From the Communal Reformation to the Revolution of the Common Man.* Translated by Beat Kümin. Boston: Brill, 1998. Study of the relationship between the communal lives of residents of German towns and villages and the mass movement that spawned the Peasants' War.

Edwards, Mark U. *Printing, Propaganda, and Martin Luther.* Berkeley: University of California Press, 1994. Discusses the role of new technologies of mass printing in the interpretation and spread of the Peasants' War.

Engels, Friedrich. *The Peasant War in Germany.* 3d ed. New York: International, 2000. A Marxist analysis of the economic roots of the Peasants' War by Karl Marx's collaborator.

Greengrass, Mark. *The Longman Companion to the European Reformation, c. 1500-1618.* New York: Longman, 1998. Discusses the Peasants' War alongside the German urban imperial leagues and compares the German and Swiss Reformations.

Hillerbrand, Hans. J., ed. *Radical Tendencies in the Reformation: Divergent Perspectives.* Princeton, N.J.: Sixteenth Century Essays, 1988. A collection of essays documenting the effect of radical religious perspectives on popular unrest in Germany during the time of the Peasants' War.

Scott, Tom, and Bob Scribner, eds. *The German Peasants' War: A History in Documents.* Atlantic Highlands, N.J.: Humanities Press International, 1991. An extensive collection of original documents from various participants and spectators of the Peasants' War.

Scribner, Bob, and Gerhard Benecke. *The German Peasant War of 1525: New Viewpoints.* London: Allen & Unwin, 1979. A collection of essays that analyze the various political, economic, and religious factors that contributed to the social unrest.

Stayer, James M. *The German Peasants' War and Anabaptist Community of Goods.* Montreal, Canada: McGill-Queen's University Press, 1991. A discussion of the role of the Anabaptist theory of communitarianism and its critique of privilege in the Peasants' War.

_____. "The German Peasants' War and the Rural Reformation." In *The Reformation World,* edited by Andrew Pettegree. New York: Routledge, 2000. Discussion of the war in terms of the distinctively rural character of the Reformation in Germany.

SEE ALSO: 1514: Hungarian Peasants' Revolt; Oct. 31, 1517: Luther Posts His Ninety-five Theses; Feb. 27, 1531: Formation of the Schmalkaldic League.

RELATED ARTICLES in *Great Lives from History: The Renaissance & Early Modern Era, 1454-1600:* Martin Bucer; John Calvin; Charles V; Balthasar Hubmaier; Martin Luther; Philipp Melanchthon; Menno Simons; Philip the Magnanimous; Huldrych Zwingli.

1525-1532
HUÁSCAR AND ATAHUALPA SHARE INCA RULE

The death of Inca ruler Huayna Capac created a succession crisis that resulted in a war between two half brothers. The civil war decimated the elite Inca class, left the empire leaderless, and signaled the end of the Inca Empire.

LOCALE: Tumibamba (Cuenca, Ecuador), Cuzco, and Cajamarca, Peru

CATEGORIES: Government and politics; wars, uprisings, and civil unrest

KEY FIGURES

Huayna Capac (1488?-1525), eleventh Inca king, r. 1493-1525

Huáscar (c. 1495-1532), Huayna Capac's son and successor, r. 1525-1532

Atahualpa (c. 1502-1533), Huayna Capac's son, last Inca king, r. 1532-1533

Francisco Pizarro (c. 1478-1541), Spanish conquistador

SUMMARY OF EVENT

When the Spaniards arrived in the Western Hemisphere, an empire called Tihuantinsuyu (four quarters), almost the size of the former Roman, spread across most of the Pacific coastline of South America. The eleventh Sapa Inca (divine ruler) was Huayna Capac, who ruled with the support of his kinsmen (called Incas). The Incas had been pushing their boundaries northward in 1525.

When an epidemic sweeping through Tihuantinsuyu struck Huayna Capac in Quito, there was an immediate need for him to name a successor. The Inca state had no laws of succession, but customarily the Sapa Inca would announce his successor. He placed the *borla*, a tasseled headband, on the forehead of one of his sons of the *coya*, his official wife. The Sapa Inca could choose the most able or the most beloved of those sons. The Inca nobles then ratified the choice and made a public announcement. The designated heir then married a woman from his kinship group, who then became his official wife. The heir-designate also began exercising administrative or military tasks as a coregent. At the Sapa Inca's death, full powers of office passed to the coregent.

Huayna Capac lacked a coregent, and there were other complications in his family situation. His *coya*, Cusi Rimay, had died shortly after giving birth to her only child, Ninan Cuyochi. Hoping to prevent a succession crisis, Huayna Capac married Chimbo Ocllo, but she had given birth to daughters only. Huayna Capac had many

sons by secondary wives, and their kinsmen would champion them as candidates for the *borla*. To prevent intrigue, assassinations, and civil war, a delegation visited the ailing Inca and asked whom he named as successor. Huayna Capac identified Ninan Cuyochi as his principal heir and Huáscar as secondary choice. The nobles quickly went to Ninan Cuyochi but discovered that he had already died of the epidemic, a disease often, but not conclusively, identified as smallpox. They returned to verify that Huáscar was his choice, but Huayna Capac too had died.

The nobles planned to carry Huayna Capac's mummy to Cuzco for proper burial. In Cuzco, where Huáscar was a regional governor, they would invest him with authority, marry him to a suitable *coya*, and announce Huayna Capac's death. However, before the mummification process was completed, messengers, probably from Huáscar's mother, Rahua Ocllo, went to Cuzco and told Huáscar to prepare himself to become the Sapa Inca.

News leaked out to other Inca families, too, and several conflicting rumors about the succession swirled through the empire. One rumor related that Huayna Capac chose Huáscar years before his death, and this choice had been ratified. A second claimed that the principal choice had been another son, Atahualpa. Another rumor said that Huayna Capac's choices of Ninan Cuyochi and Huáscar had been conditioned on good auguries, and the oracle of the Sun reported that neither should wear the *borla*.

Rahua Ocllo had been campaigning with the Inca nobles in Cuzco on Huáscar's behalf. She stressed her descent from a sister of Topa Inca and possibly charged that Atahualpa's mother was a Quiteña princess and not descended from a sister of another Inca ruler, Pachacuti, as had been claimed.

When the procession, which had become openly funereal in character, left Quito, Atahualpa stayed behind. Just outside Quito, three events angered Huáscar and aroused his suspicions of Atahualpa. Huáscar loyalists uncovered a plot to murder Huáscar and make Cusi Atauchi, another half brother, the Inca. Cusi Atauchi and the conspirators were caught and executed.

When the procession neared Cuzco, Huáscar met a delegation of nobles. Having been earlier blamed for not inviting Atahualpa to his father's funeral and to the accession rituals, Huáscar demanded the nobles explain Atahualpa's absence. When they replied that Atahualpa

The Inca of Peru were ingenious in devising methods for crossing the often torrential rivers of the Andes. Three bridges are shown in this drawing: a rope-bridge for crossing on foot, a rope system to transport animals, and a rope system to cross in a basket. (Hulton|Archive by Getty Images)

cepted them. He openly rebelled against the rule of Huáscar.

The Cañaris rebelled against Atahualpa, imprisoned him, and held him for Huáscar, but he escaped to Quito and returned with his army, destroying the city and its population. Huáscar raised an army to send north, and Atahualpa rallied support in the north and punished towns and provinces loyal to Huáscar.

Huáscar alienated many of his Inca supporters in Cuzco shortly after establishing his government. He took office and formed an army without hosting the traditional festivals that established a bond between the ruler and his subjects. He further insulted the generals by dismissing the traditional palace guard led by Inca nobles from the upper moiety and replaced it with troops from the northern provinces of Cañari and Chachapoya and led by nobles from the lower moiety. Furthermore, he threatened to abandon the upper moiety to which he and Atahualpa belonged because of Atahualpa's rebellion. Most of Huáscar's supporters were also from the upper moiety and feared that they had fallen under suspicion because of kinship ties to Atahualpa. Before the first battle between the armies of the two brothers, Huáscar's generals and captains began changing their loyalties.

Huáscar's army defeated Atahualpa in the war's first battle near Tumibamba, but reinforcements from Quito forced a quick second battle that resulted in the death of Huáscar's general and a retreat to the south. Atahualpa organized an investiture ceremony in Tumibamba and accepted the *borla* and the title Sapa Inca. The new Inca's army pressed Huáscar's army to Cotabamba near Cuzco. There, Huáscar planned to trap and destroy Atahualpa's army, but a combination of espionage and subterfuge resulted in Huáscar's own defeat and capture.

Atahualpa was far to the north in Huamachuco when he heard the news. He ordered his generals to advance to Cuzco and kill all of Huáscar's active supporters, including wives, children, and servants. He assumed that all of the sons and daughters of his father Huayna Capac remaining in Cuzco had been his opponents, and he sentenced them, and their households, to death.

Finally, he condemned to death all members of the

stayed with the army to defend Huáscar's realm against rebellion from troublesome groups in the north, he charged the nobles with treason and had them tortured and killed. Finally, Ullco Colla, the *curaca* of Tumibamba, informed Huáscar by messenger that Atahualpa was in reality building a fortress, not a northern palace for Huáscar, in Tumibamba in preparation for an uprising.

When gifts and pledges of fealty arrived in Cuzco from Atahualpa, Huáscar flew into a rage. He killed the messengers and sent messengers of his own to Atahualpa, demanding that he come to Cuzco to display his respect for his father and for him in person. In reciprocation for the gifts Atahualpa had sent, Huáscar sent women's clothing, cosmetics, and jewelry. When Inca generals in the north learned of Huáscar's insult, they knew that it would be followed soon by arrest; so, they offered their loyalty and services to Atahualpa, who ac-

Topa Inca kinship group, to which Huáscar belonged through his mother. Topa Inca, although already dead, was also condemned. His mummy was taken from its shrine and burned to ashes. Atahualpa ordered that Huáscar and his mother be sent as captives to him in Cajamarca, where he hoped to meet the strangers who had arrived by ships on the nearby coast. Atahualpa's victory was complete.

SIGNIFICANCE

Atahualpa's triumph signaled the end of Tihuantinsuyu. The nearly constant wars of expansion of his father and grandfather had been interspersed with rebellions for independence. These wars drained the empire of manpower and resources without establishing a sense of identity of the conquered groups within the empire. When Atahualpa turned his back on Cuzco and headed north to satisfy his curiosity about the strangers, he virtually released his subjects from any claims of loyalty he thought his victory might command.

On November, 1532, Francisco Pizarro captured Atahualpa in a surprise attack. Fearing that Pizarro would reinstate Huáscar, Atahualpa ordered Huáscar killed, and fearing that Atahualpa was secretly amassing an army to rescue him, Pizarro condemned Atahualpa to death. Inca supporters then helped Pizarro suppress the armies that remained loyal to the shattered idea of Inca greatness.

—*Paul E. Kuhl*

FURTHER READING

Betanzos, Juan de. *Narrative of the Incas*. Translated and edited by Roland Hamilton and Dana Buchanan. Austin: University of Texas Press, 1996. An account of Inca history and traditions completed in 1557.

Cieza de León, Pedro de. *The Discovery and Conquest of Peru: Chronicles of the New World Encounter*. Translated and edited by Alexandra Parma Cook and Noble David Cook. Durham, N.C.: Duke University Press, 1998. One of the earliest chronicles, written by one of Pizarro's soldiers shortly after the events.

Davies, Nigel. *The Incas*. Niwot: University of Colorado Press, 1995. A readable and rigorous study of the Inca Empire from its legend-shrouded origins to its catastrophic collapse.

Rostworowski de Diez Canseco, María. *History of the Inca Realm*. Translated by Harry B. Iceland. New York: Cambridge University Press, 1999. Premier authority on Inca history and society.

SEE ALSO: 1471-1493: Reign of Topa Inca; 1493-1525: Reign of Huayna Capac; 1532-1537: Pizarro Conquers the Incas in Peru.

RELATED ARTICLES in *Great Lives from History: The Renaissance & Early Modern Era, 1454-1600:* Atahualpa; Huáscar; Pachacuti; Francisco Pizarro; Hernando de Soto.

1525-1600
OTTOMAN-RULED EGYPT SENDS EXPEDITIONS SOUTH AND EAST

Using Egypt as a base, numerous expeditions, most notably those of Süleyman Paşa in the Indian Ocean and Özdemir Paşa in the Horn of Africa, expanded Ottoman Turkish influence eastward and southward in the 1500's.

LOCALE: Northeast Africa and the Indian Ocean
CATEGORIES: Diplomacy and international relations; expansion and land acquisition; exploration and discovery; wars, uprisings, and civil unrest

KEY FIGURES

Bahādur (d. 1537), sultan of Gujarat, r. 1526-1535, 1536-1537
Barbaros Hayrettin Paşa (1466-1546), Ottoman governor of Algiers and admiral in chief of the Ottoman navy, 1534-1546

Özdemir Paşa (d. 1559), Ottoman governor of Habash
Süleyman the Magnificent (1494/1495-1566), sultan of the Ottoman Empire, r. 1520-1566
Süleyman Paşa (d. 1548), Ottoman governor of Egypt

SUMMARY OF EVENT

In the mid-1510's, the Mamlūk-Ottoman Wars drew to a dramatic and definitive end. The last Mamlūk sultan, Qānṣawh II al-Ghawrī, suffered a fatal stroke during the Battle of Marj Dabiq on August 24, 1516. The Mamlūks were defeated, and by 1517, the Ottoman Empire was firmly in control of Egypt, Syria, Palestine, and Arabia. The greatest of the Ottoman sultans, Süleyman the Magnificent, came to power three years later. Süleyman spent much of his sultanate systematically consolidating and expanding the empire's territories. Within approxi-

439

mately thirty years, the Ottoman Empire had laid claim to the entire North African coast east of Morocco, including Algiers, Tripoli, and Tunis (although the latter would elude the Ottomans' grasp until 1574). The empire continued to grow. Led by Ottoman governor of Algiers Barbaros Hayrettin, Turkish navies raided Italy, France, and Spain's Balearic Islands. Despite the considerable power of Habsburg emperor Charles V, Ottoman armies occupied Hungary and lunged toward Vienna. Süleyman's Iraqi campaign of 1534-1535 captured Basra.

Arguably the farthest-reaching of all the Ottomans' military ventures, however, were launched from Egypt. From bases on the Red Sea and in Upper Egypt, the sultan's hand-picked governor, Süleyman Paşa, oversaw the empire's expansion over distant territories in Africa and Asia. After former Mamlūk naval officer Selman Reis opened the Sea of Oman in 1525, Ottoman fleets roamed the western Indian Ocean.

South of Egypt, the Horn of Africa was in turmoil. Urging Muslims to stop paying tribute to Ethiopia's Christian emperor, warlord Aḥmad Grāñ (Aḥmad ibn Ibrāhim al-Ghāzī) defeated Emperor Lebna Dengel's armies at ad-Dir in 1527 and again at Shimbra-Kure in 1529 before invading the Abyssinian highlands. Just before his death, Lebna Dengel requested Portuguese assistance. In February, 1541, four hundred musketeers led by Christóvão da Gama arrived in Massawa. Although half were killed in their first engagement, the remainder managed to join the forces of the new emperor, Galawdewos. The outnumbered Ethiopians and Portuguese killed Aḥmad Grāñ in battle in February, 1543. With the loss of their leader, Aḥmad's followers fled. Exhausted by years of warfare and slave raiding, however, neither the Ethiopians nor their Muslim enemies were able to gain regional hegemony, and the area became ripe for Ottoman expansion.

Meanwhile, in India, the Portuguese trading empire was making significant gains. Goa became the capital of Portuguese India in 1530. Following a series of attacks beginning in 1529, Daman was acquired from the sultan of Gujarat by treaty in 1559. At one point in this conflict, the commander of Daman was an Ethiopian seconded by the Ottomans to Gujarat. The Portuguese tried to capture the important trading base of Diu in 1531 but were thwarted by Sultan Bahādur of Gujarat with the assistance of the Turkish navy.

In 1534, Bahādur and Mughal emperor Humāyūn quarreled when a Mughal army invaded Gujarat in pursuit of Mirza Zamal, who had made an attempt on Humāyūn's life. Not wanting to fight on two fronts, the sultan ceded Diu to Portugal in return for the loan of five hundred infantrymen. In 1538, though advanced in age, Süleyman Paşa led an expedition to help fellow Muslim Bahādur contest this agreement. However, Bahādur died while Süleyman Paşa was en route. An Ottoman force, led by Selman Reis's nephew Mustafa Bey, seized control of Aden on the way to India. This alienated the Gujaratis, who refused to resupply the Turks, forcing them to return to Egypt.

The gateway to the Red Sea, Aden's strategic location and commercial importance made it a coveted prize. Turkish commander Abdurrahman Bey defeated the Portuguese on the open seas near Aden in October, 1544. The Ottomans lost the vital harbor to the Portuguese but recaptured it in 1548. Their control of Zebid (Yemen) spread inland, culminating in the capture of Sanʿa in 1547. However, the native Zaydis continued to resist Istanbul's rule in the mountainous interior. Ottoman admiral Pırı Reis conquered Masqat, in what is now Oman, in 1552.

Meanwhile, Özdemir Paşa, a former Mamlūk commander in the Ottoman sultan's service, accomplished great conquests in Habash (Abyssinia) to secure pilgrim routes to Mecca and control of the Indian Ocean spice trade, now constantly disrupted by the Portuguese. Leading an army through Nubia (northern Sudan), he captured the southern reaches of the Red Sea. In 1557, Özdemir defeated the Portuguese army at Massawa, where he established a garrison and expanded inland into modern-day Eritrea, southward to Harer in Ethiopia, and westward to Kassala in Sudan. From 1555 to 1562, he served as governor of Habash, which included Djidda on the Arabian Peninsula. Instituting a Turkish passion for coffee, he introduced the drink from Yemen to the court of Süleyman the Magnificent.

Turkish movement in Sudan was limited by the rise of the sultanate of the Funj, based at Sennar, some 180 miles (290 kilometers) south of modern Khartoum. Known as the Black Sultans, they extended their control over Arab and Nubian tribes along the Nile as far north as the Third Cataract. The Ottoman sultan claimed the rest of Nubia, but the extent of actual Turkish control in the region remains unclear. Istanbul also assumed control of remaining Ethiopian vassal states on the Red Sea coast. Massawa was integrated into the empire, and a local family appointed by the sultan served as viceroys (*naibs*), a status they were to retain well into the 1800's. In 1559, Özdemir Paşa died in Bundiya, where he had built several mosques. His son, Osman Paşa, removed his remains to a shrine in Massawa. Following in his father's footsteps as governor, Osman accomplished further conquests in the region. By the end of the sixteenth century, military expeditions, led by ʿAlī Bey, expanded Turkish domination south of the equator, along the coasts of present day Kenya, Tanzania, and Mozambique.

Significance

Built in 1528, the Süleyman Paşa Mosque in Cairo's Citadel is a magnificent reminder of the Ottoman governor's imperial service. The Ottoman architecture of Massawa and Suakin still serve as reminders of their distinctive heritage. Despite the eventual decline of Turkish power, the Ottoman Khedive of Egypt, Mohammed ʿAlī Paşa, would seize almost all of present-day Sudan in the 1830's. Indeed, as with much of the empire's holdings in Africa, the sixteenth century Ottoman conquest of the region shaped the fate of Nubia and the Sudan both during the heyday of the sultanate and after its decline. The British captured Aden in 1839. Thirty years later, the construction of the Suez Canal brought the Yemeni port added strategic significance. In 1846, the Ottoman sultan leased control of Massawa and its hinterland to the Khedive, whose realm was subsequently dominated by the British. Colonial administrators in Sudan replaced Suakin, the Ottoman base used to conquer Yemen and Eritrea, with a new harbor at Port Sudan. In 1885, Italy acquired Massawa and the rest of Eritrea, which it held until World War II. Goa, Daman, and Diu continued to be ruled by Portugal until their incorporation into India in 1961.

—*Randall Fegley*

Further Reading

Glubb, J. *Soldiers of Fortune*. New York: Dorset, 1973. An authoritative survey of Mamlūk history.

Holt, P. M., and M. W. Daly. *A History of the Sudan*. London: Longman, 1988. This history recounts Turkish influence in the Sudan.

King, G. *Imperial Outpost, Aden: Its Place in British Strategic Policy*. New York: Oxford University Press, 1964. An account of Aden's strategic importance.

Lord Kinross. *The Ottoman Centuries*. New York: Quill, 1977. A thorough and excellent work on the rise and fall of the Ottoman Turks.

Pankhurst, R. *The Ethiopians: A History*. Malden, Mass.: Blackwell, 2001. This survey documents Muslim influence in Ethiopia.

See also: c. 1485: Portuguese Establish a Foothold in Africa; May, 1485-Apr. 13, 1517: Mamlūk-Ottoman Wars; Jan., 1498: Portuguese Reach the Swahili Coast; 1505-1515: Portuguese Viceroys Establish Overseas Trade Empire; 1520-1566: Reign of Süleyman; 1527-1543: Ethiopia's Early Solomonic Period Ends; 1529-1574: North Africa Recognizes Ottoman Suzerainty; Mar. 7, 1529: Battle of Shimbra-Kure; Oct. 20-27, 1541: Holy Roman Empire Attacks Ottomans in Algiers; 1552: Struggle for the Strait of Hormuz; 1566-1574: Reign of Selim II; 1574-1595: Reign of Murad III; 1578-1590: The Battle for Tabrīz.

Related article in *Great Lives from History: The Renaissance & Early Modern Era, 1454-1600:* Süleyman the Magnificent.

1520's

February, 1525
Battle of Pavia

The Battle of Pavia marked a decisive and humiliating defeat for the French during the Valois-Habsburg Wars. Although the resulting treaty was soon violated and hostilities quickly resumed, France never again had the upper hand, and Spain effectively achieved hegemony over Italy.

Locale: Milan (now in Italy)

Categories: Wars, uprisings, and civil unrest; expansion and land acquisition

Key Figures

Francis I (1494-1547), king of France, r. 1515-1547

Charles V (1500-1558), Holy Roman Emperor, r. 1519-1556

Marquis of Pescara (Fernando Francesco de Ávalos; 1490-1525), commander of the Spanish forces in Italy, 1512-1525

Antonio de Leyva (1480-1536), governor of Pavia

Charles de Lannoy (1487-1527), viceroy of Naples

Charles (1490-1527), duke of Bourbon, 1503-1527, and imperial soldier, 1523-1527

Summary of Event

The Battle of Pavia was a major battle in the wars between the House of Valois of France and the Habsburg rulers of the Holy Roman Empire, a struggle to control the Italian peninsula. The first phase of the Italian wars had ended in 1498 with the death of King Charles VIII of

France. The second phase began during the reign of his successor, Louis XII. Pavia took place four years after hostilities between France and the empire resumed yet again under King Francis I.

At the beginning of his reign, Francis formed an alliance with England and Venice against the Holy Roman Empire, Spain, and some Italian states. His initial military efforts met with success. After his great victory at Marignano in 1515, he was able to conclude satisfactory peace terms with all his opponents by the end of 1516. However, the period of peace was brief, and by 1521 the French were once more at war with the empire. The imperial forces were now led by Charles V, who held the great inheritances of both the Spanish and the Austrian Habsburgs. Allied with Charles were the Papal States and England.

At first the new war went badly for the French, who were driven from their bases in Milan, Genoa, and elsewhere in northern Italy. However, in October, 1524, Francis crossed the Alps with a new army consisting of thirty thousand French, Italian, Swiss, and German soldiers. Milan, weakened by the plague, was speedily recaptured, and the victorious army marched on Pavia, a strongly fortified town on the banks of the Ticino River about 22 miles (35 kilometers) south of Milan.

It was apparent later that the march on Pavia was a mistake, for it gave the imperial army at Lodi an opportunity to reorganize and bring in additional troops from Germany. Had Francis marched first on Lodi, he might well have destroyed the last imperial force in northern Italy. However, expecting that Pavia could be taken by assault, he was convinced that the superior artillery of the French would make the operation relatively simple.

By the end of October, the city was completely surrounded, and a long artillery bombardment began during the first week of November. The artillery was followed by two costly infantry assaults that failed because of the skill and toughness of Pavia's defenders. The governor, Antonio de Leyva, not only had strengthened the fortifications of the city, but also had organized all the able-bodied men into a well-trained militia. Combined with his regular force of six thousand men, they were sufficient to withstand all the French attacks.

The French settled down to siege, believing that famine, disease, and the rigors of winter would defeat the city for them. As the weeks passed, it appeared that the

The Battle of Pavia between forces of French king Francis I and Holy Roman Emperor Charles V. (R. S. Peale and J. A. Hill)

Fighters used hand firearms for the first time in battle during the Battle of Pavia. (Hulton|Archive by Getty Images)

French estimate would be correct. The winter was unusually severe, and the defenders suffered not only from a shortage of food but also from a lack of fuel. Finally, it became necessary to demolish churches and houses within the city to keep the army alive. The French, on the outside, possessed everything in abundance, and their camp has been described as an immense market in which a pleasure fair was constantly in progress.

While the siege continued, the emperor, assisted by French expatriot Charles, duke of Bourbon, patiently collected the money and men necessary to rebuild the imperial forces. By the end of January, the Holy Roman Empire's army consisted of more than twenty thousand men. The army left Lodi to raise the siege of Pavia. Commanded by the duke of Bourbon, by Charles de Lannoy, and by the marquis of Pescara, it reached the outskirts of Pavia early in February. Francis welcomed the sight of a new imperial army, because he believed in his own strength and knew that the defeat of Bourbon's forces would leave him in control of the whole of Italy north of Rome.

The battle began with an imperial attack on February 24, an attack swiftly thrown into confusion by the superior artillery fire of the French. Then, however, Francis, in his eagerness to engage the enemy, led a charge that blocked the line of fire of his own guns, and disaster resulted. The French cavalry, pursuing a Spanish infantry force equipped with hand firearms, was suddenly met with a hail of fire and almost annihilated. A fresh sortie from the garrison threw the French into complete disarray, and they withdrew from the field, leaving thousands of dead and wounded, including large numbers of knights. Francis, wounded several times, was taken prisoner toward the end of the battle.

The fate of Italy was now sealed: The Italian principalities had no choice but to acknowledge that they were at the mercy of Emperor Charles. Milan reverted to him, as did several other Italian city-states, and Pope Clement VII abandoned his former French alliance in favor of the emperor.

Francis, sent to Madrid by order of the emperor, was required to sign the Treaty of Madrid in 1526. By its terms, he abandoned all claims to Italy, gave up Burgundy, and renounced all rights in Navarre and Artois. He was permitted to return to France in March, 1526, leaving his two oldest sons in Madrid as hostages. In a short time, however, he renounced the treaty and reopened the Habsburg-Valois wars.

SIGNIFICANCE

It might seem at first glance that the Battle of Pavia settled nothing and that it was merely another bloody event in a long century of bloodshed. However, Pavia was a milestone in military history, for it was on that field that the superiority of hand firearms to the infantry lance and pike was established. Thus, the battle helped to change decisively the way that modern warfare was conducted. From the standpoint of military history, it was a major step in the transition from medieval to modern tactics. In addition, on the political front, the battle reduced France to a secondary position in European affairs. The French nation found itself relegated to a place of inferiority in Europe that would not be overcome for another century.

—*Robert F. Erickson*

FURTHER READING

Brandi, Karl. *The Emperor Charles V: The Growth and Destiny of a Man and of a World-Empire*. Translated by C. V. Wedgwood. Reprint. London: Jonathan Cape, 1968. Translation of a classic work by the great modern authority on Charles V.

Chudoba, Bohdan. *Spain and the Empire, 1519-1643*. Reprint. New York: Octagon Books, 1969. Contains useful information on the diplomatic results of the Battle of Pavia.

Cuneo, Pia F. *Art and Politics in Early Modern Germany: Jörg Breu the Elder and the Fashioning of Political Identity, ca. 1475-1536*. Boston: Brill, 1998. Discusses the representation of the Battle of Pavia by Breu, the political importance of the battle, and the importance of Breu's painting in Germany. Includes thirteen pages of plates, illustrations, bibliographic references, and index.

Durant, Will. *The Reformation: A History of European Civilization from Wyclif to Calvin, 1300-1564*. Vol. 6 in *The Story of Civilization*. Reprint. New York: MJF Books, 1992. A comprehensive and colorful account of the period. Includes illustrations, maps, and a bibliographic guide.

Hackett, Francis. *Francis the First*. Reprint. Garden City, N.Y.: Doubleday, 1968. Hackett's account of the siege of Pavia is lively reading, and he describes the holiday atmosphere in the French camp as contrasted with the grim situation of the defenders within the city. Suggests that Francis was defeated because of faulty tactics by the French and superior tactics by the Spanish infantry.

Hare, Christopher. *Charles de Bourbon: High Constable of France*. New York: John Lane, 1911. Biography of the duke of Bourbon written from source materials such as collections of letters, contemporary diaries, and historical documents. Describes in detail the political and military situations in which he played a significant role, including the siege of Pavia.

Richardson, Glenn. *Renaissance Monarchy: The Reigns of Henry VIII, Francis I, and Charles V*. New York: Oxford University Press, 2002. The reigns of both Francis I and Charles V are examined in this study of monarchs who helped define Renaissance government and culture. Focuses on their careers as warriors, governors, and patrons. Includes maps, bibliographic references, and index.

Salvatorelli, Luigi. *A Concise History of Italy*. Translated by Bernard Miall. New York: Oxford University Press, 1940. Reprint. New York AMS Press, 1977. A standard work, translated from the Italian, containing considerable material on the diplomacy of the Renaissance.

Taylor, F. L. *The Art of War in Italy, 1494-1529*. 1921. Reprint. London: Greenhill Books, 1993. An excellent short analysis, including descriptions of some of the battles that took place during this period.

Wilson, Timothy, ed. *The Battle of Pavia*. Oxford, England: Ashmolean Museum, 2003. In 1683, the Ashmolean was presented with a painting, of unknown origin, of the Battle of Pavia. This short text describes the battle and its major participants in detail. It looks at the representation of the battle in the painting and seeks to ascertain when it was painted, concluding that the painting probably dates from between 1525 and 1528. Includes illustrations and bibliographic references.

SEE ALSO: Apr. 9, 1454: Peace of Lodi; Aug. 17, 1477: Foundation of the Habsburg Dynasty; Sept., 1494-Oct., 1495: Charles VIII of France Invades Italy; Apr. 11, 1512: Battle of Ravenna; Sept. 13-14, 1515: Battle of Marignano; Aug. 18, 1516: Concordat of Bologna; 1521-1559: Valois-Habsburg Wars; May 6, 1527-Feb., 1528: Sack of Rome; Apr. 3, 1559: Treaty of Cateau-Cambrésis.

RELATED ARTICLES in *Great Lives from History: The Renaissance & Early Modern Era, 1454-1600:* Charles V; Charles VIII; Clement VII; Francis I; Louis XII.

1526-1547
HUNGARIAN CIVIL WARS

The unity of Hungary was torn by a violent phase of invasion, partition, and civil strife at a time when the country was embedded between the Habsburg Dynasty and the ever-expanding Ottoman Empire. Domestically, nobles increased their power and gained absolute control over the peasantry, and decreased tax revenues led to an ineffective military and a vulnerable nation.

LOCALE: Hungary

CATEGORIES: Wars, uprisings, and civil unrest; government and politics; expansion and land acquisition

KEY FIGURES

Louis II (Lajos II; 1506-1526), king of Hungary, r. 1516-1526

Süleyman the Magnificent (1494/1495-1566), sultan of the Ottoman Empire, r. 1520-1566

John I (John Zápolya; 1487-1540), governor of Transylvania, king of Hungary, r. 1526-1540

John (John Sigismund; 1540-1571), king of Hungary, r. 1540-1571

Ferdinand I (1503-1564), archduke of Austria, r. 1526-1555, and Holy Roman Emperor, r. 1558-1564

Charles V (1500-1558), king of Spain, r. 1516-1556, and Holy Roman Emperor, r. 1519-1556

György Martinuzzi (1482- 1551), treasurer of Hungary, 1534-1551

SUMMARY OF EVENT

From the fourteenth through the fifteenth centuries, the Hungarian polity evolved from a feudal to an Estates system, that is, a protocapitalist society of the Renaissance model. The Hungarian region included the Carpathian Basin in east-central Europe, which was encircled by Poland and Bohemia in the north, Austria in the west, Russia in the east, and Bosnia, Romania, and Serbia in the south.

Under the two warlords of the Hunyadi Dynasty, from the Vlach noble family of Rumania—János Hunyadi (c. 1407-1456) and Matthias I Corvinus (r. 1458-1490)—Hungary emerged as a strong and cultivated Renaissance state of Eastern Europe.

Hungary's development was retarded, however, by two major events in the first half of the sixteenth century: the abortive but violent Hungarian Peasants' Revolt, led by György Dózsa (c. 1470-1514) in 1514 (during the reign of Vladislav II) and the invasion of the Ottoman

Turks, culminating in the Battle of Mohács in August of 1526 (during the reign of Louis II). The peasants' rebellion occasioned the infamous legislation called the Tripartitum, which entrenched the privileges of the nobility, rendering the kingdom of Hungary a virtual republic of nobles, and condemned the peasantry to servitude.

Hungary's domestic instability began with the accession of the ten-year-old Louis when the government was entrusted to Cardinal Tamas Bakócz (1442-1521). Following his death, the government was vitiated by rivalries between the palatine Stephen Báthory and the eminent jurist and orator, István Werbőczi—both unscrupulous place-seekers—and the country stood defenseless as the frontier garrisons remained unpaid; even the king's personal *banderium* was disbanded because of a lack of funds.

Taking advantage of the minority of the monarch, the holders of the royal domains refused to surrender them. Revenues diminished drastically as tax collection became increasingly difficult. As Hungary began to languish in corruption and weakness, the Turks began their advance toward Europe.

The first blow fell on August 29, 1521, when Sultan Süleyman the Magnificent occupied the southern fortress of Šabac and Belgrade. Hungary, still reeling under the effects of the great Peasants' Revolt of 1514 and rent by factions, was saved for the time being, as the Turks' attention was diverted toward Egypt and the Island of Rhodes.

Meanwhile, the Hungarian government sought military help from the Holy Roman Empire, Rome, and other regions of Western Europe, though to little effect. A former court favorite, Archbishop Pál Tomori, was recalled to take over the southern command. Even the royal *banderia* was reactivated. Yet the Hungarian army proved no match for the Ottoman force, which renewed its advance in 1526. Louis set out from Buda with thirty-three hundred men, and by the time he confronted the Turkish army, his force had swollen to twenty-five thousand men. However, detachments from Transylvania and Croatia had not arrived. Without waiting for reinforcements, Louis attacked the Ottoman force of between seventy thousand and eighty thousand soldiers. On August 29, at the Danubian market town of Mohács, the sultan's army routed the Hungarian host, and King Louis fell in the battle, most probably murdered by one of his enraged men.

After this disastrous battle, the Turks occupied Buda on September 12 but returned soon after to concentrate on their Persian frontiers, carrying with them more than one hundred thousand captives to be sold as slaves in the markets of the east.

On October 14, John Zápolya, *vojevod* (governor) of Transylvania, was elected king of Hungary at the Diet of Tokai, representing the towns and the counties, and was crowned the following month at a second diet held at Hungary's historical capital, Székesfehérvár. His forces occupied most of the country vacated by the Turks. Archduke Ferdinand I of Austria, however, claimed the Hungarian crown by right of inheritance in the name of his wife, Anna, sister of Louis II, and was elected in December at Pozsony by a diet of deputies from Croatia and the towns of Pressburg and Sopron. The two kings engaged in a civil war.

In May, 1527, King John I was driven out of Buda by Ferdinand's faction. The royal fugitive retreated into Transylvania and, subsequently, in 1528, sought shelter in Poland and military support from Sultan Süleyman. The sultan preferred supporting a rival to the Austrian archduke so that he could transform Hungary into a vassal state; but he recognized John's claim. By treaty in 1528, the Turks recognized his claim, and he became the sultan's vassal.

In May, 1529, Buda was reconquered by the Turks, who had also laid siege to Vienna on September 28 and mounted a direct assault on October 14, failing, however, to conquer the city. The Turks tried to attack Vienna once more in June, 1532, and failed again. Süleyman was forced to enter into a treaty with Austria on June 22, 1534. The treaty's terms stipulated that John should remain king of Hungary but Ferdinand was to keep the third of the country he had been occupying.

The existence of two rival kings of Hungary and the political volatility that resulted gave fortune hunters and desperadoes the chance to plunder the properties of the landowners and to oppress the peasants and workers as self-proclaimed representatives of the contending monarchs. Not wishing to partition the country, the Hungarian Estates arrived at a solution to these serious problems but could not reach a final decision because of powerful external influences: the Habsburgs and the Ottomans.

Because the civil war continued, a war in which only the Turks profited, Ferdinand and John were forced to come to terms. Ultimately at the insistence of Ferdinand, Hungary was divided between the two kings through the secret Peace of Nagyvárad on February 24, 1538. The archduke would control the mountainous northwest, which had the Slovak mining towns, and the five western counties partly settled by Germans. John would retain the remaining two-thirds of the royal title and have his court at Buda. Around the same time, Ferdinand was formally acknowledged as John's successor, even if John had a male heir.

During the final six years of John's reign (1534-1540), his kingdom, under the able guidance of the new treasurer, György Martinuzzi, bishop of Nagyvárad, grew stable and maintained a balance between Vienna and Istanbul. However, Martinuzzi refused to hand over the country to Ferdinand when John died. Instead, Martinuzzi had the infant son of the late king John I, John Sigismund (r. 1540-1571), elected monarch and had the election confirmed by the Ottomans. Ferdinand asserted his rights by force of arms and attacked Buda in May, 1541, but his less-than-adequate army failed to occupy the town.

In August, 1541, Süleyman invaded Hungary and occupied Buda on the thirtieth of the same month. During the following six years, several cities were conquered by the Turks. Buda became an Ottoman *eyalet* (province) and, in fact, the center of Ottoman Hungary. Hungary was divided into three parts: The west would be held by Ferdinand, the center would be a Turkish province, and the east—the principality of Transylvania—would be an Ottoman vassal state.

SIGNIFICANCE

In 1547, the Turks were importuned by the Persian wars, and Süleyman was persuaded to enter into a five-year armistice with Charles V, the Holy Roman Emperor and Ferdinand's elder brother. According to the Peace of Edirne (1547), Ferdinand agreed to pay 30,000 gold florins (or ducats) annually to the Porte, the Ottoman government, as taxes for the thirty-five counties occupied by the Habsburgs, including Croatia and Slavonia, while the rest of the land, comprising most of the central counties, was annexed to the Ottoman Empire. John II would retain Transylvania and sixteen adjacent counties and have the title of prince.

The tripartite division of Hungary and the resulting Habsburg threat in the west and the Ottoman threat in the east made the land of the Magyars a focal point for the foreign policies of these two powerful monarchies. The twin threat to Hungary's national identity and integrity inspired a sense of protonationalism among the emerging "gallant men" or "gentlemen," a specific social class placed between the nobles and the serfs.

—*Narasingha P. Sil*

FURTHER READING

Ignotus, Paul. *Hungary*. London: Ernest Benn, 1972. A straightforward, clear, and useful narrative account of Hungary.

Kafadar, Cemal. *Between Two Worlds: The Construction of the Ottoman State*. Berkeley: University of California Press, 1995. An extraordinarily perceptive and informative study of the way in which historiography and ideology came together to shape Ottoman imperialism.

_____. "The Ottomans and Europe." In Vol. 1 of *Handbook of European History, 1400-1600*, edited by Thomas A. Brady, Jr., Heiko A. Oberman, and James D. Tracy, 2 vols. Grand Rapids, Mich.: William B. Eerdmans, 1994. An excellent examination of the Ottomans in and around Europe, including Hungary.

Kubinyi, Andras. "The Battle of Szavaszentdemeter-Nagyolaszi, 1523: Ottoman Advance and Hungarian Defence on the Eve of Mohács." In *Ottomans, Hungarians, and Habsburgs in Central Europe: The Military Confines in the Era of Ottoman Conquest*, edited by Géza Dávid and Pál Fodor. Boston: Brill, 2000. A study of a significant precursor battle to Mohács, analyzing the military strategies employed and compar-

ing them to those of the decisive conflict that would occur three years later.

Steed, H. Wickham, Walter A. Phillips, and David Hannay. *A Short History of Austria-Hungary and Poland*. London: Encyclopedia Britannica, 1914. Though quite dated, chapter 27 is still extremely useful.

Szakály, Ferenc. "The Early Ottoman Period, Including Royal Hungary, 1526-1606." In *A History of Hungary*, edited by Peter F. Sugar, Péter Hanák, and Tibor Frank. Bloomington: Indiana University Press, 1994. A clear, concise, and authoritative study of the Ottomans in Hungary.

SEE ALSO: 1458-1490: Hungarian Renaissance; 1463-1479: Ottoman-Venetian War; Aug. 17, 1477: Foundation of the Habsburg Dynasty; Aug. 19, 1493-Jan. 12, 1519: Reign of Maximilian I; 1514: Hungarian Peasants' Revolt; 1555-1556: Charles V Abdicates; 1594-1600: King Michael's Uprising.

RELATED ARTICLES in *Great Lives from History: The Renaissance & Early Modern Era, 1454-1600:* Stephen Báthory; Bayezid II; Charles V; John II; Matthias I Corvinus; Rudolf II; Sigismund I, the Old; Süleyman the Magnificent; Vladislav II.

1520's

April 21, 1526
FIRST BATTLE OF PANIPAT

Bābur defeated the Delhi sultan at the Battle of Panipat in 1526, leading to the establishment of the Mughal Dynasty in India, which ruled for more than three hundred years.

LOCALE: North of Delhi (now in India)

CATEGORY: Wars, uprisings, and civil unrest; government and politics; expansion and land acquisition

KEY FIGURES

Bābur (Ẓahīr-ud-Dīn Muḥammad; 1483-1530), king of Kabul and first Mughal emperor, r. 1526-1530

Ibrāhīm Lodī (d. 1526), sultan of Delhi, r. 1517-1526

Humāyūn (1508-1556), son of Bābur and Mughal emperor, r. 1530-1540, 1555-1556

Vikramāditya (d. 1526), raja of Gwalior, r. 1519-1526

Rānā Sāngā (1482-1527), raja of Mewār, r. 1509-1527

SUMMARY OF EVENT

Bābur, the king of Kabul (now in Afghanistan), defeated Ibrāhīm Lodī, the ruler of the Delhi sultanate, at the Battle of Panipat in 1526. With his victory, Bābur, nicknamed "the Tiger," established the Mughal Empire, one of the longest lived and most glorious of India's dynasties, comparable to the Mauryan and Gupta dynasties of the 300's B.C.E. and the 300's C.E., respectively. The Mughal rule initiated by Bābur survived for more than three hundred years.

The Indian subcontinent rarely was unified, in large part because of its varied geography. The Ganges River and its surrounding plain dominated northern India, from south of the Himalayan Mountains, and throughout its long history, India has suffered periodic invasions from the northwest. The Aryans had traveled the Ganges plain around 1500 B.C.E., as did Alexander the Great in the 300's B.C.E. and the Huns in the 400's and 500's C.E. In the late tenth and early eleventh centuries, the Muslim sultan Maḥmūd of Ghazna (r. 997-1030) invaded India, the birthplace of Hinduism and Buddhism. Known as "the Sword of Islam," Maḥmūd's conquests were fueled in part by his religious convictions.

By the early thirteenth century, a Muslim dynasty had established itself in the Ganges valley. Known as the Delhi sultanate, it endured through several different dynasties until the sixteenth century. The sultanate regime, however, did not go unchallenged. There were other Muslim rulers in North India and several Hindu kingdoms and states in the south. Outsiders were also a constant threat. In 1398, Tamerlane (Timur) captured and sacked Delhi, slaughtering much of the city's Hindu population. However, the Delhi sultanate recovered, and by the latter part of the fifteenth century, the Lodīs, an Afghan clan, had become the sultans.

Bābur, born in central Asia in 1483, was a direct descendant of Tamerlane, and on his mother's side he was also descended from the great Mongol ruler, Genghis Khan. A Mongolian by inheritance, Bābur's language was Turkic and his religion was Islam. His initial military ambitions centered on Tamerlane's old capital of Samarqand, but even though he was able to seize the city on two occasions, he was unable to keep it. Failing at least temporarily in central Asia, in 1504 Bābur captured Kabul, becoming its king. Except for one brief raid into northern India in 1505, Bābur spent the next decade solidifying his rule in Afghanistan. In 1519, he again turned to India, but it was not until 1525 that he launched a major invasion of the subcontinent.

Because Mongol armies relied on and had an expert mastery of horses, they were fast moving and extremely mobile, giving them a significant advantage even against much larger armies. In addition, Bābur used gunpowder, as did the other so-called "gunpowder empires" of the time (the Ottoman Turks and the Persian Ṣafavids). In India, Bābur and his army were equipped with both cannon and matchlock guns. There is little evidence, however, that the Lodī sultans had either at their disposal. A second disadvantage, which the Lodīs would face in any conflict with Bābur and his forces, was that the Lodīs were not united. The reigning sultan, Ibrāhīm Lodī, had defeated his brother and alienated many important figures. Ibrāhīm also faced opposition from Rajput Hindu rulers, such as Rānā Sāngā of Mewar.

Bābur crossed into the Punjab with an army of twelve thousand warriors. After capturing Lahore (now in Pakistan), he continued his advance into north India toward Delhi. Bābur later claimed that by the time his army had reached the vicinity of Delhi, his force was somewhat smaller than the initial twelve thousand troops because of attrition. When the two armies met at Panipat in April, 1526, Ibrāhīm Lodī's sultanate forces are estimated to have outnumbered those of Bābur by about ten to one. Bābur was an experienced and successful military leader, however, whereas Ibrāhīm lacked those skills. It is reported that Bābur had little but contempt for Ibrāhīm on the eve of battle.

With his much larger army, it was expected that Ibrāhīm would take the offensive and attack Bābur's smaller forces. Ibrāhīm was reluctant to act, however, and a standoff of several days occurred before the Lodī army began their assault. Bābur, reacting defensively, had placed his army in a strong position, flanked on one side by the walls of the city of Panipat and by thick brush on the other. Several hundred carts had been confiscated and placed in front of Bābur's forces, giving shelter to the matchlock gunners but also spaced to allow Bābur's cavalry to take the offensive when possible. When Ibrāhīm did launch his expected assaults, his forces were unable to break through Bābur's carts and gunners. Repeated attacks by the Lodī soldiers not only failed in the frontal assault but also resulted in the sultan's army being compacted into a smaller and smaller area. Bābur's cavalry units attacked the now-concentrated and largely immobile Lodī warriors on the flanks and from the rear. Within half a day, Ibrāhīm's army was destroyed. It is estimated that fifteen thousand Lodī troops died at the Battle of Panipat on that April day, including Ibrāhīm.

After his victory at Panipat, Bābur seized the city of Delhi, fifty miles to the south, while his son and heir, Humāyūn, captured the nearby city of Agra, Ibrāhīm's capital, which contained the regime's treasury. At Agra, Humāyūn was presented with a large diamond, which had been obtained by the raja of Gwalior, Vikramāditya, who had been allied with Ibrāhīm at Panipat. The diamond, estimated at 186 carats, first became known as "Bābur's diamond" and later as Koh-I-Nur, "the mountain of light."

SIGNIFICANCE

Bābur's consolidation of his rule in India faced three major obstacles. First, many of his own warriors saw the campaign mainly as an invasion for loot and glory. That obtained, they expected to return to Afghanistan. Bābur, however, convinced most of them to remain in India, promising them land, wealth, and subjects in the newly conquered regions. His success in keeping his warriors allied with him in India determined that the invasion became a conquest and not just an incursion or raid. Second, Afghan nobles allied to the Lodīs were potential threats to Bābur's rule, but he convinced most of them also to accept his regime.

Third, Bābur had to contend with the ambitions of various Hindu rulers, notably Rānā Sāngā of Mewar and his fellow Rajputs. In February, 1527, Rānā Sāngā and the Rajputs confronted Bābur at Khānua, fifty miles south of Agra. Bābur rallied his troops by appealing to their Islamic religious faith against the Hindu Rajputs, with Bābur signaling his own commitment by abandoning alcohol, which he usually consumed with gusto. Like Panipat, the Battle of Khānua also was a victory for Bābur and his Mughal contingent.

Although Bābur continued to wage other campaigns until his death in 1530, the Battle of Panipat against the Lodī Delhi sultanate in 1526 followed by the Battle of Khānua the following year gave Bābur firm control of northern India. Subsequent emperors would extend Mongol rule over much of the subcontinent.

—*Eugene Larson*

FURTHER READING

Bābur. *The Baburnama*. Edited and translated by Wheeler M. Thackston. Introduction by Salman Rushdie. New York: Modern Library, 2002. An exciting and revealing firsthand history of Bābur's life and times in his own words.

Erskine, William. *A History of India Under the Two First Sovereigns of the House of Taimur, Baber, and Humāyūn*. New York: Barnes and Nobles Books, 1972. A reprint of the classic work by one of India's early historians, first published in 1854.

Foltz, Richard C. *Mughal India and Central Asia*. New York: Oxford University Press, 2001. A study of the legacy of Bābur's conquests; the author argues that the background of the Mughals and their origins in Central Asia are crucial to understanding their culture in India. Discusses the nostalgia of Indian Mongol rulers for their former Central Asian homeland.

Keay, John. *India: A History*. New York: Atlantic Monthly Press, 2000. This well-written history of India includes an excellent description of the Battle of Panipat.

Wolpert, Stanley. *A New History of India*. New York: Oxford University Press, 2000. This widely accessible and well-written text includes a discussion of Bābur and his era.

Ziad, Zeenut, ed. *The Magnificent Mughals*. New York: Oxford University Press, 2002. Authoritative anthology of essays by top scholars, each summarizing the history of a different aspect of Mughal culture, including economics, religion, and the arts, as well as the contributions of women to Mughal society.

SEE ALSO: 1451-1526: Lodī Kings Dominate Northern India; 1507: End of the Timurid Dynasty; Dec. 2, 1510: Battle of Merv Establishes the Shaybānīd Dynasty; Mar. 17, 1527: Battle of Khānua; Dec. 30, 1530: Humāyūn Inherits the Throne in India; 1540-1545: Shēr Shāh Sūr Becomes Emperor of Delhi; 1578: First Dalai Lama Becomes Buddhist Spiritual Leader; Feb., 1586: Annexation of Kashmir; 1598: Astrakhanid Dynasty Is Established.

RELATED ARTICLES in *Great Lives from History: The Renaissance & Early Modern Era, 1454-1600:* Akbar; Bābur; Humāyūn; Ibrāhīm Lodī.

1520's

August 29, 1526
BATTLE OF MOHÁCS

The Battle of Mohács destroyed the unified Hungarian nation, helped to establish the Ottomans as a major power in Europe, and opened Hungary to Habsburg and Ottoman domination.

LOCALE: Hungary

CATEGORIES: Wars, uprisings, and civil unrest; expansion and land acquisition

KEY FIGURES

Süleyman the Magnificent (1494/1495-1566), Ottoman sultan, r. 1520-1566

John Zápolya (1487-1540), governor of Transylvania, king of Hungary as John I, r. 1526-1540

Ferdinand I (1503-1564), archduke of Austria and king of Bohemia and Hungary, r. 1526-1564, Holy Roman Emperor, r. 1558-1564

Louis II (1506-1526), king of Hungary, r. 1516-1526

Charles V (1500-1558), Holy Roman Emperor, r. 1519-1556, and king of Spain as Charles I, r. 1516-1556

SUMMARY OF EVENT

On April 23, 1526, Süleyman the Magnificent began marching westward from Belgrade to invade Hungary with almost 100,000 men. Professional soldiers—Janissaries (infantry) and *sipahis* (cavalry)—made up about half of his total force. The remainder consisted of irregular infantry (*azabs*) and cavalry (*akinjis*) to be recompensed by the spoils of war. Artillery consisted of between 150 and 200 guns. He was well prepared, having constructed bridges across the Danubian tributaries Sava and Drava in advance.

In contrast, the Hungarian border fortresses were inadequately staffed and in a poor state of maintenance. The king's professional army had been disbanded and many of the king's vassals had allowed their forces to decline. As a consequence, the border fortresses and troops were unable to effectively delay Ottoman advance until the king's men, feudal levies, and allies could be fully mobilized. Furthermore, King Louis II did not command the wholehearted support of his people. He was married to Archduke Ferdinand's sister, Maria, and he and his nobles made up a Catholic party supporting the Holy Roman Emperor, Charles V. Charles, however, was embroiled in Protestant-Catholic conflict within the empire and with French opposition and gave little support to the Hungarians in spite of their repeated pleas for help.

John Zápolya, governor and effective ruler of Transylvania, represented Calvinist interests and the interests of the lower nobles. Finally, the peasantry had been disarmed and held in strict serfdom following the uprising of 1514 (the Hungarian Peasants' Revolt). As a consequence, many peasants viewed the Ottomans as liberators.

Louis moved south from Buda leading an army of only four thousand men to a rallying point at the plain of Mohács on the right bank of the Danube River. Here he was joined by reinforcements, including some Germans, Poles, and Bohemians, bringing his total force to about twenty-five thousand men with about eighty-five artillery pieces. The imperial Diet at Speyar, in the face of Protestant reluctance to support the Catholic emperor, voted too late to send reinforcements.

At Mohács, Archbishop Pál Tomori, governor in charge of the southern border, and most of the magnates, principal Hungarian nobles, advised Louis to withdraw northward to the fortress of Buda. There he could expect to join forces with Zápolya and his army, which was then a few days' march north on the left bank of the Danube and advancing to reinforce Louis. In addition, a contingent of Bohemians had just entered northern Hungary on their way to join Louis. A slow withdrawal also would lengthen Ottoman supply lines, exposing them to flank attack. The more rash nobles, motivated by antagonism to Zápolya, however, advised an immediate attack, so about twenty-five thousand Hungarians led by Louis launched a heavy cavalry charge against the center of the far larger Ottoman army.

The Ottoman center, monitored by *azabs* and *akinjis*, was crushed, but they inflicted substantial casualties during their retreat toward the concealed main line of Ottoman defense. In this way, the Hungarian cavalry was drawn away from supporting Hungarian infantry and artillery and found themselves confronted with massed Ottoman artillery backed by the Janissary corps. Heavy artillery fire decimated the Hungarian cavalry. At this point, the Ottoman flanks advanced to surround the Hungarians, and Süleyman's *sipahis* overran the Hungarian foot soldiers and artillery. The Hungarian army was essentially annihilated, suffering twenty-four thousand casualties, including Louis, who fell under his horse and was drowned attempting to flee.

The Ottomans also slaughtered two thousand prisoners and sent many women and children to Constantinople as slaves. Twenty-eight principal barons, five hundred other nobles, and seven bishops, almost the entire royal governing leadership, also were killed, leaving only Zápolya's Protestant party and army to maintain the Hungarian state. Mohács was burned and the *akinjis* were unloosed to pillage the countryside.

Zápolya and his army arrived at the Danube the day after the battle, but, informed of the results of the battle, withdrew. The advancing Bohemian reinforcements also turned back, and organized resistance ceased. Süleyman continued to Buda, arriving September 10, where he destroyed the city, except the royal palace, where he took temporary residence. The great Corvinus Library, the royal treasury, and the two trophy cannons, taken from Sultan Mehmed II when he was thrown back at Belgrade, all were removed to Constantinople.

After considering the condition of his army and his probable inability to control the countryside during the oncoming winter, Süleyman decided to withdraw rather than to occupy the country. He bridged the Danube, crossed to Pesth, burned the city, and returned home, laying waste to the left bank of the river.

Louis's death left the throne of Hungary vacant because he was the last of his line. Archduke Ferdinand, brother of Emperor Charles V, claimed the Crown on the strength of an agreement with Louis, which made him heir to the throne in the event that Louis died without a male heir. This agreement, however, violated a law requiring the king to be a Hungarian. Thus, a diet composed of Hungarian nobles belonging to the nationalist faction elected Zápolya king, and he entered Budapest to be crowned King John I.

A few weeks later, another, smaller diet of pro-Habsburg magnates rallied around the widowed Queen Mary and elected Archduke Ferdinand as king. Ferdinand's troops defeated John in the ensuing civil war, driving him into exile in Poland. From exile, John sought Ottoman aid. Süleyman then recognized John in 1528, and promised military assistance without requiring tribute. Ottoman troops reentered Hungary in 1529, quickly defeated Ferdinand's troops, and again occupied Buda. Thereafter, an Ottoman detachment remained in Buda, and John became an Ottoman vassal. Ferdinand, however, managed to retain the western margin of Hungary, "Royal Hungary," where he also ruled as king of Hungary. After John's death in 1540, however, Süleyman annexed his part of Hungary, placing a pasha at Buda, but left Transylvania as a vassal state.

SIGNIFICANCE

The Battle of Mohács led to the tripartite subdivision of Hungary into Royal Hungary on the west, the pashalik of Buda in the core of the country, and the principality of Transylvania (later annexed to the Ottoman Empire). The divisions persisted, with many modifications, until the Treaty of Karlowitz in 1699, when Hungary came under the control of the Habsburgs.

—*Ralph L. Langenheim, Jr.*

FURTHER READING

Ahmed, S. Z. *The Zenith of an Empire: The Glory of Suleiman the Magnificent and the Law Giver.* Trumbull, Conn.: Weatherhill, 2001. Biography of Süleyman, emphasizing the creative and dynamic aspects of his rule and his empire.

Fregosi, Paul. *Jihad in the West: Muslim Conquests from the Seventh to the Twenty-First Centuries.* Amherst, N.Y.: Prometheus Books, 1998. The Battle of Mohács is discussed in this study of Islamic wars in the West.

Goffman, Daniel. *The Ottoman Empire and Early Modern Europe.* New York: Cambridge University Press, 2002. A reconsideration of the Ottoman Empire, arguing that it should be understood as part of Renaissance Europe rather than as a "world apart," isolated and exotic.

Kinross, Lord. *The Ottoman Centuries: The Rise and Fall of the Turkish Empire.* New York: William Morrow, 1977. Includes an account of the Battle of Mohács, its antecedents, and its consequences, within a comprehensive history of the Ottoman Empire.

Kubinyi, Andras. "The Battle of Szavaszentdemeter-Nagyolaszi, 1523: Ottoman Advance and Hungarian Defence on the Eve of Mohacs." In *Ottomans, Hungarians, and Habsburgs in Central Europe: The Military Confines in the Era of Ottoman Conquest*, edited by Géza Dávid and Pál Fodor. Boston: Brill, 2000. A study of a significant precursor battle to Mohács, analyzing the military strategies employed and comparing them to those of the decisive conflict that would occur three years later.

Kunt, Metin, and Christine Woodhead, eds. *Süleyman the Magnificent and His Age: The Ottoman Empire in the Early Modern World.* New York: Longman, 1995. Anthology covering the genesis of the Ottoman Empire, the policies and problems faced by the empire in the sixteenth century, and Süleyman's reign in the context of those problems.

Lukinch, Imre. *A History of Hungary in Biographical Sketches.* Translated by Catherine Dallas. Freeport,

1520's

N.Y.: Books for Libraries, 1937. Includes an account of the politics surrounding the Battle of Mohács.

Pamlényi, Ervin, ed. *A History of Hungary.* Translated by Lálszló Bores, Isván Farkas, Gyula Gulayás, and Eva Róna. Revised by Margaret Morris and Richard Alton. London: Collet's, 1975. Discusses the political and economic context of Mohács from a communist point of view.

Sugar, Peter F., Péter Hának, and Frank Tibor, eds. *A History of Hungary.* Bloomington: Indiana University Press, 1990. Includes essays on events leading to the Battle of Mohács and on the partition of Hungary into Royal Hungary, Ottoman Hungary, and the principality of Transylvania.

Wheatcraft, Andrew. *The Ottomans.* New York: Viking,

1993. Includes a fairly detailed account of the Battle of Mohács.

SEE ALSO: 1454-1481: Rise of the Ottoman Empire; Aug. 17, 1477: Foundation of the Habsburg Dynasty; 1478-1482: Albanian-Turkish Wars End; 1481-1512: Reign of Bayezid II and Ottoman Civil Wars; 16th cent.: Proliferation of Firearms; 1514: Hungarian Peasants' Revolt; 1555-1556: Charles V Abdicates; 1589: Second Janissary Revolt in Constantinople.

RELATED ARTICLES in *Great Lives from History: The Renaissance & Early Modern Era, 1454-1600:* Stephen Báthory; Bayezid II; Charles V; John II; Mary of Hungary; Matthias I Corvinus; Rudolf II; Sigismund I, the Old; Süleyman the Magnificent; Vladislav II.

1527-1543
ETHIOPIA'S EARLY SOLOMONIC PERIOD ENDS

The decline of the Solomonic Dynasty and the rise of a powerful Muslim movement threw the Christian kingdom of Ethiopia into a period of severe crisis that threatened the very existence of the Ethiopian state.

LOCALE: Ethiopian Empire (now in southern Egypt, Republic of the Sudan, and Ethiopia)
CATEGORIES: Government and politics; wars, uprisings, and civil unrest

KEY FIGURES

Zara Yacob (1399-1468), Ethiopian emperor whose reign marked the high point of Christian power, r. 1434-1468
Baeda Mariam (d. 1478), Zara Yacob's son and Ethiopian emperor, r. 1468-1478
Naod (d. 1508), Ethiopian emperor, r. 1494-1508
Lebna Dengel (d. 1540), Ethiopian emperor, r. 1508-1540
Aḥmad Grāñ (Aḥmad ibn Ibrāhim al-Ghāzī; c. 1506-1543), leader of a militant Muslim movement in Adal, r. 1529-1543
Christóvão da Gama (d. 1542), commander of Portuguese troops sent to aid Christian forces in Ethiopia
Galawdewos (d. 1559), Ethiopian emperor, r. 1540-1559

SUMMARY OF EVENT

The Solomonic rulers who assumed the Ethiopian throne in the thirteenth century, claiming descent from the bibli-

cal king Solomon and the mythical Ethiopian queen Sheba, ushered in an era of territorial expansion, state building, and a remarkable revival of Christian culture. However, by the early sixteenth century, the Solomonic Dynasty no longer enjoyed its original level of political and military dynamism. The later kings not only failed to maintain the momentum generated by the early Solomonic rulers but also proved incapable of neutralizing the gathering political storm that was soon to overwhelm the country and to test the continued viability of the Christian kingdom.

A number of internal and external factors contributed to the downward spiral of Solomonic power. In a way, the Solomonic rulers were victims of their own success. The spectacular expansion that began in the fourteenth century had dangerously overextended the Christian empire. The process of cultural assimilation and political integration of the diverse linguistic, ethnic, and religious communities within the empire remained incomplete. Outside the core area that constituted the predominantly Christian population of the northern and central highlands, the remaining vast regions to the west, the south, and the east were only marginally affected by the cultural and political traditions of the center.

Loyalty to the Christian monarch at the center of the empire did not extend beyond nominal submission, expressed through the payment of annual tributes. While in theory the Solomonic emperor had absolute power over political and military affairs throughout the empire, in practice, local hereditary families were often left in power in each community, especially in newly incorporated regions. Only the presence of strong imperial garrisons and fear of the wrath of the powerful Solomonic kings kept the periphery of the empire loyal to its center. Weakness in the center almost invariably resulted in unrest at the periphery.

The viability of the medieval Ethiopian state rested heavily on the person of its Solomonic rulers. The extraordinary political and military exploits of a succession of capable kings, combined with a skillful propaganda apparatus that linked the dynasty with the House of David, had invested the monarchy with an aura of invincibility. Powerful emperors like Zara Yacob not only reigned supreme over affairs of state but forged a much tighter union with the Ethiopian Orthodox Church as well. The Solomonic system suffered from a fatal flaw, however, that eventually proved its undoing: It lacked an orderly system of succession. The death of a monarch was often followed by political strife. The problem was complicated by the polygamous customs of Ethiopian emperors. The institution of a royal prison at Mount Gishen, where all male members of the Solomonic Dynasty except the reigning monarch and his own sons were detained, was only partially successful in ensuring an orderly transfer of power.

The succession problem grew far worse after the death of Zara Yacob, the last effective medieval emperor. His son, Baeda Mariam, reversed Zara Yacob's centralizing policy and created conditions that encouraged the proliferation of powerful factions within the empire. On the death of Baeda Mariam, civil war broke out between rival supporters of his two minor sons. Rivalries and internal division among the officials of the royal courts greatly undermined the unity of the Christian polity that was so essential for the defense and administration of the extensive Ethiopian Empire.

The political strife in the capital distracted the Christian kingdom from focusing on the management of its frontier areas, thereby allowing the opposition at the periphery to grow unchecked. The predominantly Muslim region in the east was a particular source of resistance, beginning from the early years of the sixteenth century. While in the past Ethiopia had dealt effectively with

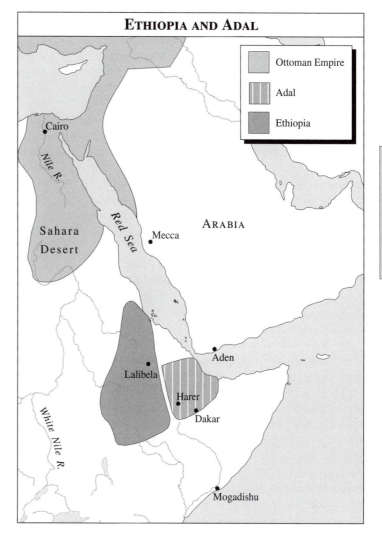

ETHIOPIA AND ADAL

Ottoman Empire
Adal
Ethiopia

1520's

Muslim resistance to the east of its borders, it had not yet been challenged by such a unified and highly organized Muslim force. The new Islamic movement was centered at Adal, a Muslim principality located around present-day Harer, far from the immediate reach of the emperors. Adal provided the focal point for widespread Muslim insurgency against Christian hegemony. Muslims in the frontier provinces of Yifat, Dawaro, Fatagar, and Bali were inspired to follow Adal's example and leadership. The limited military successes of emperors Naod and Lebna Dengel were insufficient to reverse the insurgency. Naod himself was killed in battle with the eastern Muslims in 1508.

The expansion of Ottoman power over the Red Sea area in the second decade of the sixteenth century provided an additional moral boost and material support to the Muslims of Adal. The fighting strength of the Muslim forces was greatly increased, moreover, by the introduction of firearms and the arrival of Turkish and Arab matchlock men to swell their ranks.

A crucial factor in the rise of a formidable Muslim power in Adal was the leadership of Aḥmad ibn Ibrāhīm al-Ghāzī, popularly known to Ethiopians as Grāñ (the left handed). A charismatic imam who preached a fiery brand of Islam, Aḥmad Grāñ imbued the Muslim movement with a new sense of mission and coherence. He first carried out a series of expeditions against his own fellow Afar and the Somali tribes to impose discipline and unity upon the unruly desert warriors. He followed this campaign by declaring a *jihad* against the Christian kingdom of Ethiopia in 1527.

Religious fervor and the prospect of plunder galvanized the pastoral Muslims rallying behind the imam. Ethiopia's defenses crumbled in the face of the superior leadership, firearms, and new tactics of the Muslim army. Most of the border provinces fell within the first two years of the offensive. The traumatized Christian army evacuated one post after another, allowing Aḥmad's army deep into the Christian highlands.

The most important battle took place at Shimbra-Kure on the central Shewan plateau on March 7, 1529. Here, the army of Emperor Lebna Dengel was decisively defeated by Aḥmad Grāñ. Although the emperor escaped with his life, a good portion of the military and political leadership of the empire died on the battlefield. Aḥmad pressed his victory by rapidly advancing toward the empire's core, destroying churches and laying waste to Christian villages. Christian resistance was reduced to local guerrilla warfare.

Emperor Lebna Dengel spent the next decade retreating from one mountain fortress to another. In desperation, he appealed to the Portuguese king for military assistance, but he died in 1540, a few months before a contingent of four hundred Portuguese troops arrived at the coast to aid the embattled Christian forces. About half of this small Portuguese force, including its commander Christóvão da Gama, the son of the famous explorer Vasco da Gama, were killed in their first engagement with Aḥmad Grāñ at Tigray. The surviving Portuguese soldiers managed to join forces with the new Emperor Galawdewos. Galawdewos had some success in reviving Christian morale, and on February 22, 1543, he fought and killed Aḥmad Grāñ at the Battle of Woina Dega. The overstretched Muslim army had been held together by the sheer force of the personality of the imam, and it fell apart soon after his death.

SIGNIFICANCE

The decline of the Solomonic Dynasty and the rise of a powerful Muslim movement in the eastern part of the country threw Ethiopia into profound convulsion that threatened both the social order of the Christian community and the very existence of the state. Although the state survived, its power was greatly diminished, and it lost a significant portion of its southern territories as a result. Moreover, the wars of the sixteenth century caused enormous material and cultural destruction within the empire and impeded the development of Ethiopian culture for centuries.

—*Shumet Sishagne*

FURTHER READING

Crummey, Donald. *Land and Society in the Christian Kingdom of Ethiopia, from the Thirteenth to the Twentieth Century.* Urbana-Champaign: University of Illinois Press, 2000. An excellent work on the political and social history of Ethiopia, particularly useful in underlining the economic basis of political domination.

Marcus, Harold. *History of Ethiopia.* Berkeley: University of California Press, 1994. A general survey of Ethiopian history from ancient times to the present.

Shihab ad-Din Ahmad bin Abd al-Qader bin Salem bin Utman. *Futuh al-Habasha/The Conquest of Abyssinia.* Translated by Paul Lester Stenhouse. Hollywood, Calif.: Tsehai, 2003. An eyewitness account of the Muslim conquest of the Christian kingdom of Ethiopia by a Yemeni writer who accompanied Aḥmad Grāñ.

Tadesse Tamrat. *Church and State in Ethiopia, 1270-1527.* Oxford, England: Clarendon Press, 1972. One of the most respected works on the history of medieval Ethiopia, especially useful for understanding the background to the decline of the Solomonic Dynasty.

_____. "The Horn of Africa: The Solomonids in Ethiopia and the States of the Horn of Africa." In *Africa from the Twelfth to the Sixteenth Century.* Vol. 4 in *General History of Africa.* Berkeley: University of California, 1984. A succinct account of the political conditions in the Horn of Africa in the fifteenth and sixteenth centuries.

Trimingham, J. S. *Islam in Ethiopia.* New York: Clarendon Press, 1952. A valuable work on the history of Muslim-Christian interaction in Ethiopia.

SEE ALSO: 1460-1600: Rise of the Akan Kingdoms; c. 1464-1591: Songhai Empire Dominates the Western

Sudan; Late 15th cent.: Mombasa, Malindi, and Kilwa Reach Their Height; May, 1485-Apr. 13, 1517: Mamlūk-Ottoman Wars; 1491-1545: Christianity Is Established in the Kingdom of Kongo; Jan., 1498: Portuguese Reach the Swahili Coast; 1510-1578: Saʿdī Sharifs Come to Power in Morocco; 1525-1600: Ottoman-Ruled Egypt Sends Expeditions South and East; 1529-1574: North Africa Recognizes Ottoman Suzerainty; Mar. 7, 1529: Battle of Shimbra-Kure; 1591: Fall of the Songhai Empire.

RELATED ARTICLE in *Great Lives from History: The Renaissance & Early Modern Era, 1454-1600:* Vasco da Gama.

1527-1547
MAYA RESIST SPANISH INCURSIONS IN YUCATÁN

After Hernán Cortés conquered the Aztecs, Spaniards turned their attention to the Maya of Yucatán, hoping to extend the conquest and to amass further wealth. Unlike the Aztecs, however, who succumbed to the Spaniards and their indigenous allies within two years, the Maya successfully resisted the conquistadores for twenty years.

LOCALE: Yucatán (now in Mexico)
CATEGORIES: Wars, uprisings, and civil unrest; colonization; diplomacy and international relations; expansion and land acquisition

KEY FIGURES
Francisco de Montego the Elder (1479-1553), Spanish conquistador
Francisco de Montego the Younger (1508-1565), Spanish conquistador
Nachi Cocom (d. 1560/1561), Maya ruler who led resistance against the Spaniards
Gonzalo Guerrero (d. 1535?), shipwrecked Spaniard who aided the Maya in their struggle against the Spaniards
Charles V (1500-1558), Holy Roman Emperor, r. 1519-1556, and king of Spain as Charles I, r. 1516-1556
Hernán Cortés (1485-1547), Spanish conqueror of Mexico

SUMMARY OF EVENT
Following the conquest of Mexico (1519-1521), Spanish adventurers sought to replicate in Yucatán the exploits of Hernán Cortés. Although the first royally sanctioned Spanish landings on the coast of Yucatán had occurred in 1517 and 1518, interest in the region diminished when Spaniards, led by Cortés, reached the fabulous Aztec Empire of Montezuma II in 1519.

After the spoils from the Mexican campaign had been divided, however, Spanish soldiers again turned their attention to the south. By the sixteenth century, however, the Maya no longer boasted the large ceremonial centers that had characterized classic Maya culture. They lived in small, dispersed villages and showed little evidence of possessing gold or other treasures of interest to Spaniards. Their persistent resistance to Spanish encroachments in the 1520's, coupled with the difficulties of performing military maneuvers in the harsh Yucatán terrain, encouraged Europeans to seek fortune elsewhere.

In the early 1530's, the wealth of Peru lured Spanish adventurers from Yucatán to South America. Only after the treasures of Peru had also been divided did they return to Yucatán, this time to stay. Maya resistance was fierce, culminating in the rebellion of 1546-1547. After quashing the uprising, the Spaniards established themselves in Yucatán permanently.

The Yucatán peninsula, jutting out into the Caribbean Sea not far from the island of Cuba, provided a logical stopping point for Spaniards sailing from Cuba to the mainland in the early years of the sixteenth century. In 1511, a Spanish vessel shipwrecked off the coast of Yucatán. Although most of the Europeans on board perished, two survived and lived among the Maya. One joined the Spanish expedition to Mexico, serving as interpreter, after he was found by Hernán Cortés in 1519. The other, Gonzalo Guerrero, allied with the Maya and instructed them on how best to resist Spanish incursions. Thus the people of Yucatán had an important resource the Aztecs did not have: someone to instruct them in European military strategy to be used against the Spanish conquistadores.

Spanish interest in Yucatán waned as Cortés and his men marched into Mexico. When the fabulous Aztec treasure reached Spain, however, European adventurers flocked to the New World seeking their fortune. Cortés, knowing that the Mexican spoils had been divided by 1524, encouraged these newcomers to explore farther to

A Mayan palace, in ruins, in the Yucatán. (R. S. Peale and J. A. Hill)

the south. Some who had participated in the conquest of Mexico also embarked on the new campaigns. Francisco de Montego the Elder, who had fought with Cortés in Mexico, was given the royal grant to conquer Yucatán. Unlike Mexico, however, Yucatán was not overseen by a single powerful leader.

Montejo found it difficult to exploit indigenous rivalries as the Maya fiercely resisted the Europeans. The Maya shot at them with deadly arrows, and they dug holes in forest trails and covered them with branches so that they could capture both horses and their riders at the same time. Disgruntled by the paucity of wealth, Montejo and his followers were eager to head farther south once they learned of Francisco Pizarro's success against the Inca in South America. They questioned why they should waste their time in desolate and dangerous Yucatán when fame and fortune awaited them in Peru. To the relief of the Maya, the Spaniards abandoned Yucatán in 1535. That year also, the Spaniards found the body of a heavily tattooed European man among the casualties of a scrimmage between Maya soldiers and Europeans in Honduras; Gonzalo Guerrero was dead.

As had happened in Mexico, many European adventurers were sorely disappointed when they did not share in the rewards from the conquest of Peru. In 1540, Francisco de Montejo the Elder's son (Francisco de Montejo the Younger) returned to Yucatán with a group determined to settle the region. For the next six years, they struggled again with the Maya. This time, knowing that there was no gold to be had as reward, they expected only to receive *encomiendas*, allotments of indigenous peoples as slave laborers who would pay them the equivalent of feudal rents in either labor or tribute.

By 1540, voices had already been raised against the Spanish practice of *encomienda*. Bartolomé de Las Casas, who had participated in the early conquest of the Caribbean and for that was himself rewarded with an *encomienda*, had turned against the practice, claiming that the virtual enslavement of the indigenous encouraged disregard for their lives and resulted in horrible abuses against them. He became a Dominican friar who spent years between America and Spain, persuading Charles V that the practice of *encomienda* must stop. This set the stage for a division within Spanish ranks in the Yucatán. While conquistadores and settlers coveted the rewards of indigenous service, priests who sought to bring Maya souls to Christ saw themselves as protectors of exploited indigenous peoples.

By the time the Spaniards returned to Yucatán in 1540, Maya communities had become much weaker than they had been in the 1520's. Earlier Spanish raids had taken their toll; and even with the foreigners gone, Maya communities continued to suffer disruptions. Although battles with Europeans had stopped, the diseases brought by the foreign soldiers raged on. As droughts and ensuing famine also punished the region, more and more of the Maya died. In these new and troubled times, old rivalries between Maya groups resurfaced. Nachi Cocom, an Itza leader from Sotuta, availed himself of the opportunity to punish the Xiu of Mani for past treacheries. Civil wars broke out. Thus, the Europeans dominated not because a stronger group of Spaniards could finally conquer the peninsula but because they were determined to stay at a time when the Maya were no longer able to marshal enough force to push them out.

In the 1540's, Franciscan friars came with the conquistadores to Yucatán. They assured the Maya that they would protect them from abuses by *encomenderos*. Yet when the practice of *encomienda* did not stop, the Maya turned against the priests. In 1546, they organized a large-scale rebellion to expel all Spaniards from their land. Although many of the Spanish died, the revolt was finally suppressed in 1547. The Europeans settled permanently in the Yucatán, bringing with them a new style of government and a new religion, yet they could not be fully certain that the Maya had accepted their control. The dire consequences of indigenous unrest haunted Spanish settlers in the centuries to come, as periodic deadly revolts confirmed their worst fears.

SIGNIFICANCE

Spanish attempts to control Yucatán revealed the fierce determination of Maya Indians to maintain their own authority. Despite the superiority of Spanish weapons and the devastation of disease, the Maya were extraordinarily effective in their struggle against the Spaniards.

Even though Spanish government came to Yucatán after almost two decades of warfare, the Maya did not give up. They adopted Spanish ways, but in ways that suited them, guarding their own religion and culture carefully. Throughout the colonial period, Maya uprisings shocked those Spaniards who had tried to convince themselves

that, at last, the Maya had been subdued. As late as the nineteenth century, a major Maya rebellion occurred in Yucatán. In what came to be known as the Caste War, the Maya killed thousands of Spanish-speakers and established their own government, which lasted from the 1850's to the first decade of the twentieth century.

—*Joan E. Meznar*

FURTHER READING

Chamberlain, Robert S. *The Conquest and Colonization of Yucatán, 1517-1550*. Washington, D.C.: Washington Carnegie Institute, 1948. A still-useful, classic study of the Spanish conquest of the Yucatán Maya.

Clendinnen, Inga. *Ambivalent Conquests: Maya and Spaniard in Yucatán, 1517-1570*. 2d ed. New York: Cambridge University Press, 2003. An excellent reconstruction of the cultural misunderstandings between the Maya and Spaniards in the sixteenth century.

Farriss, Nancy M. *Maya Society Under Colonial Rule: The Collective Enterprise of Survival*. Princeton, N.J.: Princeton University Press, 1984. A thorough discussion of the many ways in which the Maya resisted Spanish control in Yucatán.

_____. "Persistent Maya Resistance and Cultural Retention in Yucatán." In *The Indian in Latin American History: Resistance, Resilience, and Acculturation*, edited by John E. Kicza. Rev. ed. Wilmington, Del.: Scholarly Resources, 2000. Focuses on the significance of Maya religion in resisting Spanish dominance.

1527-1599
BURMESE CIVIL WARS

The Burmese Civil Wars, rather than create an era of instability, allowed the Toungoo Dynasty to unify the various states and ethnic tribes under the kingdom of Burma.

LOCALE: Burma (Myanmar)
CATEGORIES: Wars, uprisings, and civil unrest; government and politics

KEY FIGURES
Minkyinyo (d. 1531), king of Toungoo, r. 1486-1531
Tabinshwehti (d. 1550), king of Toungoo, r. 1531-1546, king of Burma, r. 1546-1550
Takayutpi (d. 1539?), king of Pegu, r. 1526-1539
Bayinnaung (d. 1581), king of Burma, r. 1551-1581
Nanda Bayin (d. 1599), king of Burma, r. 1581-1599

SUMMARY OF EVENT
The area now occupied by Myanmar (also known as Burma) lies between modern India to the west, the Bay of Bengal to the southwest, and China, Laos, and Thailand to the northeast and east. It began to form its own political powers in the ninth century, when the Burman people of Bagan (modern Pegu), a city on the Irrawaddy River, were able to fill a power vacuum left when the people of Nanzhao (southwestern China) overcame another major people of Burma, the Pyu. As a result, the Burmans were able to dominate the country, incorporating the Mon kingdom and their Theravāda Buddhist influence (1057), until the Mongols overpowered them in the late thirteenth century and left the area to conflicts between the Mon and the Burmans that lasted for the next two centuries. The Mon would ultimately fall to the Burmans of the Toungoo Dynasty, founded by King Minkyinyo in 1486. This dynasty would eventually overrun the city-states of several other peoples in the area, forming the basis for modern Burma.

As Minkyinyo took the throne at Toungoo, situated on the Sittang River north of the Irrawaddy Delta region, the state of Ava (near modern Mandalay) was increasingly declining in power. Ava was Toungoo's strongest rival for dominance in Burma, and Minkyinyo took the opportunity to seize Kyauske, a vital rice area belonging to Ava. Following this, Minkyinyo expanded his territory. In 1527, the Shan people (from northern Burma) sacked Ava, placing their own king, Thonganbwa, on the throne. Not wanting to submit to Shan rule, Burmese chiefs fled Ava and pledged loyalty to Minkyinyo. At Minkyinyo's death, Toungoo was the premier state in Burma.

Tabinshwehti ascended the throne after Minkyinyo, intending to expand his territory and rule all of Burma. By 1535, he had completely overrun the Irrawaddy Delta. He then turned his sites on Pegu, the Mon capital, presumably for its riches. At the beginning of the siege, Bassein and Myanugmya fell. Ava assisted Pegu, and in 1539 after four years of fighting, Pegu fell. The Mon chiefs pledged loyalty to Tabinshwehti, and the Mon king, Takayutpi, fled to Prome. He was followed by Tabinshwehti and Bayinnaung, Tabinshwehti's brother-in-law.

Tabinshwehti's first attack on Prome was unsuccessful. He was thwarted by a flotilla of soldiers from Ava, so he retreated. He focused on Martaban and its coastal areas, enlisting the help of Portuguese gunners and Mon mercenaries to supplement his army. In 1541, Martaban fell, and Tabinshwehti annexed the Tenasserim coast down to Tavoy on the border with Siam (modern Thailand). Previously, Tabinshwehti had been careful to respect the people, customs, and cultures of those he conquered, which allowed him to gain their acceptance. However, the army that sacked Martaban was full of Mon and Portuguese mercenaries, and there was pillaging and massacre for three days. While this was not Tabinshwehti's way, it did benefit his military campaigns. The Mons were so frightened by the savagery at Martaban that the Mon state of Moulmein submitted without conflict.

Tabinshwehti returned to Prome, and this time not only Ava but also Arakan (on the coast northeast of the Bay of Bengal) came to help Prome. After a five-month siege, the people of Prome were starving; their city fell in 1542. Shortly after, the site of Pagan, Burma's ancient empire, was taken. In 1544, the Shan states united, and Ava, Hsenwi, Bhamo, Mohnyin, Momeik, Mone, and Yawnghwe, attacked Prome in an effort to reclaim it. They were unsuccessful, and Tabinshwehti's Portuguese gunners were able to resist the Shans. By now Tabinshwehti controlled a large portion of Burma, and in 1546, he was crowned king of Burma at Pagan and moved his capital to Pegu. In 1544 and 1546-1547, Tabinshwehti attacked Arakan unsuccessfully. The Arakanese capital, Mrohaung, was well defended and Tabinshwehti had to call a halt to that campaign.

Now that he had conquered most of Burma, Tabinshwehti focused on expanding his borders into Siam, which was threatening Tavoy. His attacks failed, and consequently he lost control of his kingdom. The Mons rebelled, Pegu fell to a member of the Mon royal family, and in 1550, Tabinshwehti was assassinated, possibly because people believed he was corrupted by his Portuguese associations. Prome and Toungoo declared independence, and the era of warring states was about to return. The allegiance of the Mons was divided, but a majority of Mons and Burmese agreed that a national kingship was better than separated states, a legacy of Minkyinyo and Tabinshwehti. Bayinnaung, with the help of a Portuguese leader, Diogo Soarez de Mello, captured Toungoo and became Tabinshwehti's successor.

Bayinnaung, referred to as the "Napoleon of Burma," immediately began to reestablish the kingdom of Burma. He retook Pegu from Mon rebels in 1551. From 1554 to 1555, he captured the Shan states Ava and Shwebo in bloodless battles. By 1562, he had forced allegiance of most of the Shan states. He captured the Siamese capital of Chiang Mai in 1564, lost it to rebellion, and recaptured it again. This angered the Burmese, and Bayinnaung was faced with quenching rebellions. The same thing occurred when he tried to take Laos, and he therefore had to abandon his desire to expand Burma into foreign lands. In 1581, Arakan again became a target, but Bayinnaung and the campaign ended. The constant wars had impoverished the Burmese, the Portuguese mercenaries that he befriended tended to defy the king, and famine occurred in 1567. These conditions created an atmosphere of revolt.

Bayinnaung's son, Nanda Bayin, ascended the throne as king of Burma, but the country was quickly descending into rebellion. At first, Nanda Bayin was able to suppress each revolt. A Venetian writer, Gasparo Balbi, described a 1583 execution of suspected rebels and their families, specifically involving a revolt led by Nanda Bayin's uncle, the viceroy of Ava.

Siam soon realized that Burma was weakening and began a series of attacks to reclaim its territory and parts of Lower Burma. Nanda Bayin's eldest son was killed by the Siamese in 1593. The Mons felt the brunt of the Siamese attacks, as their land was torn by war and the people were forced into labor and military service. The Mons began to rebel but met with savage results. This treatment forced the Mons to migrate to Siam, and in 1595 thousands fled with the Siamese army.

Prome, Toungoo, and Chiang Mai also revolted. Toungoo and Prome, both ruled by Nanda Bayin's brothers, also fought one another. As the kingdom shattered, Siam launched another attack on Burma, and Arakan seized Syriam (in the Rangoon Delta region) and joined Toungoo in an attack on Pegu. Nanda Bayin surrendered and was taken to Toungoo, where he was murdered. Pegu was destroyed. Various forces, such as the Portuguese, Siamese, and Arakenese, began to carve out pieces of Burma for themselves, and the kingdom was no longer unified.

SIGNIFICANCE

The Burmese Civil Wars had two important effects on Burma, both historically and culturally, which reverberated into modern Myanmar. Despite the constant fighting, Burma was relatively stable as a result of Tabinshwehti's and Bayinnaung's reigns. The two kings united the Mons, Shans, the Burmese and their respective states under the kingdom of Burma, and despite their tribal allegiances, they all became Burmese. This marked the first time that all the states of Burma, except Arakan, were united politically and created a national consciousness that allowed the tribes to retain their customs and traditions. The people of modern Myanmar retain this identity to this day. Had the kings failed to unify the kingdom, a sense of national unity would possibly never have risen, and Burma's constituent tribes might have broken off and created their own countries.

While Tabinshwehti and Bayinnaung united Burma, Nanda Bayin completely divided it, and the Mons, Shans, and Burmese returned to their tribal loyalties. However, Nanda Bayin shattered the country so much that he not only splintered that country's unity but also undermined the invasion and occupation of foreign forces. Siam took portions of Burma and a large population of Mons migrated to Siam. The Portuguese, whose role in the civil wars was mainly mercenary, carved out their own portion of coastal Burma.

The demise of a national kingship therefore had two effects: It reduced Burma's importance as an overseas trade partner, and it opened the way for European colonization. The end of the first Toungoo Dynasty created tribal strife, and when the second Toungoo Dynasty appeared soon afterward, the Mons and Shans viewed each other as inferior, which made the idea of Burmese unity impossible. Although the Toungoo Dynasty survived until the mid-eighteenth century, it was weakened, and the national disintegration allowed the Portuguese to gain more land and power, paving the way for inroads by English as well. Nevertheless, the brief period of unity during the first Tonguoo Dynasty created the beginnings of a modern state.

—*Tina Powell*

FURTHER READING

Aung-Thwin, Michael A. *Myth and History in the Historiography of Early Burma: Paradigms, Primary Sources, and Prejudices*. Number 102 in the Monographs in International Studies, Southeast Asia Series. Athens: Ohio University Press, 1998. Discusses the historic basis of various myths of the three kingdoms of Pagan, Ava, and Toungoo.

Gommans, Jos, and Jacques Leider, eds. *The Maritime Frontier of Burma: Exploring Political, Cultural and Commercial Interaction in the Indian World, 1200-1800*. Chicago: University of Chicago Press, 2004. Discusses mainly the importance of overseas trade to the kingdom of Burma and how politics and the civil wars affected it.

Phayre, Arthur P. *History of Burma: From the Earliest Time to the End of the First War with British India*. Bangkok, Thailand: Orchid Press, 1998. Gives a brief breakdown of the important events of each Burmese king's reign.

Tarling, Nicholas. *The Cambridge History of Southeast Asia: From c. 1500 to c. 1800*. Vol. 2. Cambridge, England: Cambridge University Press, 2000. Discusses the Toungoo Dynasty and its various wars between other Burmese states.

SEE ALSO: 1450's-1471: Champa Civil Wars; 1450's-1529: Thai Wars; 1454: China Subdues Burma; 1469-1481: Reign of the Ava King Thihathura; c. 1488-1594: Khmer-Thai Wars; 1548-1600: Siamese-Burmese Wars; 1558-1593: Burmese-Laotian Wars; c. 1580-c. 1600: Siamese-Cambodian Wars.

March 17, 1527
BATTLE OF KHĀNUA

Mughal emperor Bābur, a Muslim, was victorious over the Hindu Rājputs at the Battle of Khānua, a victory that completed his conquest of northern India and helped lay the foundation for centuries of Mughal rule.

LOCALE: Rājasthān, India
CATEGORIES: Wars, uprisings, and civil unrest; expansion and land acquisition

KEY FIGURES

Bābur (1483-1530), first Mughal emperor, r. 1526-1530
Rānā Sāngā (1482-1527), raja of Mewar, r. 1509-1527

SUMMARY OF EVENT

The sultanate of Delhi, which had dominated much of northern and central India during the thirteenth and fourteenth centuries, collapsed following the sack of Delhi by Tamerlane (Timur) in 1398-1399. Thereafter, throughout the fifteenth and early sixteenth centuries, the Indian subcontinent was divided mainly among regional sultanates, such as those of Bengal, Malwa, and Gujarat.

Also characteristic of this period was the intense rivalry between two competing groups: Afghans from beyond the Indus River, established in Punjab and much of the Gangetic plain; and Rājputs, centered in Rājasthān and Malwa. The origins of the Rājputs remain obscure, but by the fifteenth century, they were fully integrated into the Hindu caste system as *kshatriyas* (the second highest warrior caste). Their premier chieftain was the ruler of Mewar, Rānā Sāngā, who had long dreamed of establishing a Rājput hegemony, which would replace that of the hated *mlecchas* (non-Hindus), the Muslims.

In 1526, however, one event shattered whatever equilibrium existed on the north Indian political scene. Bābur, who was a descendant of Tamerlane and, through his mother, a descendant of Mongol conqueror and leader Genghis Khan (r. 1206-1227), assembled an army and invaded Punjab. Between 1504 and 1526, Bābur had been ruler of the Kabul valley and its environs, and he had been on the lookout for opportunities to enlarge his territories. So, informed of the ineffectiveness of the Afghan sultan of Delhi, Ibrāhīm Lodī (r. 1517-1526), he took the road to Delhi and was confronted by Ibrāhīm's far-larger army at Panipat, 55 miles from Delhi. Bābur enjoyed the innovative advantage of firearms, at that time little known in northern India, and he secured a decisive victory. Ibrāhīm perished sword in hand.

Bābur then advanced unopposed to Delhi and Āgra, intending to move eastward, down the Gangetic plain, to mop up further Afghan resistance. He learned that Rānā Sāngā of Mewar was marching north with an enormous army, intent upon intercepting him before he grew in power. Rānā Sāngā had succeeded to the throne of Mewar around 1509 and had established a reputation as an indefatigable fighter in the traditional Rājput heroic mold. A statesman and a warrior, he had made Mewar supreme in a Rājput confederation. He believed the Rājput should sweep away the moribund Delhi sultanate, and those of Malwa and Gujarat, with which he had long wrestled. Shrewd and farsighted as he was, he could not have failed to appreciate that Bābur's victory at Panipat had introduced a new and ominous element into the north Indian equation. There could be no room for both a Rājput and a Mughal dominion.

Meanwhile, Bābur's troops were skirmishing beyond Āgra, but they became increasingly demoralized because of the Rājputs' fearful reputation as fighters. Bābur's memoirs show clearly that he, too, was apprehensive. Soon, he concentrated his forces at the village of Sikri, 25 miles south of Āgra, where he fortified his encampment by surrounding it with a laager, a defensive position with wagons bound together by ropes of raw hide. This was the first time Bābur and his men found themselves fighting non-Muslims. Bābur, not usually thought of as a Muslim fanatic, would present himself to the army as a devout believer in *jihad*.

Bābur, who had been a habitual drinker (ignoring the Islamic prohibition), rallied his troops by publicly swearing off drinking. He had his gold and silver cups smashed before their eyes and the proceeds distributed to the poor. He harangued the men with stirring rhetoric, calling their foes infidels, polytheists, and idolators. The appeal worked, and his listeners swore on the Qur'ān that they would not give up.

The confrontation came on March 17, 1527, at a place known as Khānua (Kanua), 50 miles west of Āgra. Rānā Sāngā had prepared for the battle carefully. He was said to have commanded a force of 800,000 men and 500 war elephants. The exact size of Bābur's force is unknown, but it was substantially smaller. Because of the difference between the sizes of the two armies, Bābur's plan was to maintain as long as possible a defensive stance, hoping to wear down the Rājputs. Thus, at the opening of the engagement, he presented the enemy with a long line of roped-together wagons, interspersed with cannon, mortars, and men with matchlocks, with the wings of the line shielded by cavalry. The bulk of the cavalry, however, remained behind the center of the line of wagons, commanded by Bābur. Because of the Rājputs' numbers, there could be no question of Bābur employing the enveloping pincer movement known as the *taulgama*, favored by commanders like Genghis Khan and Tamerlane.

The battle began in the morning, after Rānā Sāngā, in typical Rājput fashion, impetuously hurled division after division against the Mughal line. His warriors and their horses and elephants, however, were confused by their first encounter with gunpowder, and much of the fiercest

fighting shifted toward the wings. The Rājput left thrust at the Mughal right, where Bābur's eldest son, Humāyūn, needed help, and Bābur sent reinforcements from the center, which drove the Rājputs back into their own lines. Meanwhile, Bābur's left wing came under intense pressure, with both sides sending reinforcements, which, in Bābur's case, threatened to weaken his center. Eventually, though, the Mughals were able to press the advantage as far as the Rājput camp, only to be forced back once again.

The conflict had now raged for about three hours: The Mughal line had held firm and the Rājput assaults had lost some of their bravura. Until past noon, Bābur held back his crack troops, but then ordered them to advance down two corridors, which opened up through the line of wagons, cannon, and matchlock men, falling upon the exhausted Rājput center. This ferocious melée, after hours of hand-to-hand fighting, marked the beginning of the end.

Rānā Sāngā was struck by an arrow or a bullet and was hurried from the field. He died within the year, possibly of the wounds he received at Khānua. The surviving Rājputs broke ranks, pursued by the victorious Mughals. Having plundered the Rājput camp, Bābur did not immediately dare to pursue the enemy into the bare, arid Rājput homeland, where securing provisions and fodder presented insuperable problems. The baking Indian summer, hateful to Bābur's Central Asian followers, would soon engulf them. Instead of striking into the Rājasthān heartland, he turned southeast to take Chanderi, which Rānā Sāngā had given to one of his principal lieutenants.

In December, 1527, Bābur advanced down the Yamuna River to its confluence with the Chambal River, detaching part of his army toward Bihar. He reached the vicinity of Chanderi on January 21, 1528, after hard marching through near-impenetrable jungle. His principal lieutenant withdrew behind his walls. Preliminary attempts at a negotiated surrender broke down, city and citadel were closely invested, and eventually the Mughals broke into the latter in the face of exceptionally fierce resistance from the garrison of five thousand. The struggle ended with the Rājput ritual of *jauhar*, in which, having immolated their women and children in the inner fort, the surviving Rājput warriors dispensed with their armor to speed a suicidal death by hurling themselves on the weapons of their Mughal foes.

In a well-established tradition, Bābur then ordered the building of a tower of dead-enemy skulls. Even while besieging Chanderi, he had received the news that his army in the east had been defeated. It was essential for him to

461

rejoin his retreating troops. Bābur never crossed swords with the Rājputs again. On December 26, 1530, Bābur died in Āgra.

SIGNIFICANCE

The Battle of Khānua confirmed Bābur's hold over northwestern India in a way in which the victory at Panipat had not: Panipat might have been the climax to a brilliant but possibly inconsequential raid, such as Tamerlane's had been a century and a half before.

The victory at Khānua also ended the possibility of Rājput hegemony. More importantly, Khānua demonstrated to the first generation of Mughals the extraordinary martial qualities of the Rājputs. Little more than thirty years later, Bābur's grandson Akbar established a Mughal-Rājput partnership that consolidated Mughal rule, a partnership that continued to work effectively until Mughal emperor ʿĀlamgīr (r. 1658-1707), who, in a spirit of religious intolerance, alienated the great Rājput feudatories of the empire, thereby contributing substantially to its disintegration.

—*Gavin R. G. Hambly*

FURTHER READING

Gommans, Jos. *Mughal Warfare: Indian Frontiers and High Roads to Empire, 1500-1700*. New York: Routledge, 2002. A study of Mughal weaponry, logistics, tactics, strategy, and ideology.

Richards, John F. *The Mughal Empire*. New York: Cambridge University Press, 1993. An excellent single-volume account of the Mughal Empire, which contextualizes Bābur's contribution within its overall development.

Thackston, Wheeler M., trans. *The Baburnama: Memoirs of Bābur, Prince and Emperor*. New York: Oxford University Press, 1996. A translation of Bābur's autobiography, constituting a principal source for the period.

Tod, James. *The Annals and Antiquities of Rājasthān*. 2 vols. 1829-1832. Reprint. London: Routledge & Kegan Paul, 1950. Based upon traditional Rājput bardic literature, this is the classic account of Rājput history and legend.

SEE ALSO: 1451-1526: Lodī Kings Dominate Northern India; 1459: Rāo Jodha Founds Jodhpur; Early 16th cent.: Devotional Bhakti Traditions Emerge; 1507: End of the Timurid Dynasty; Apr. 21, 1526: First Battle of Panipat; Dec. 30, 1530: Humāyūn Inherits the Throne in India; 1540-1545: Shēr Shāh Sūr Becomes Emperor of Delhi; 1556-1605: Reign of Akbar; Feb. 23, 1568: Fall of Chitor.

RELATED ARTICLES in *Great Lives from History: The Renaissance & Early Modern Era, 1454-1600:* Akbar; Bābur; Humāyūn; Ibrāhīm Lodī; Krishnadevaraya.

May 6, 1527-February, 1528
SACK OF ROME

Troops of Holy Roman Emperor Charles V sacked Rome, directly challenging the power of the Catholic Church and helping to advance Protestantism in Europe. The siege also marked the virtual end of the Italian Renaissance and, in the eyes of some historians, the end of the High Renaissance.

LOCALE: Rome and Florence (now in Italy)
CATEGORIES: Cultural and intellectual history; wars, uprisings, and civil unrest

KEY FIGURES

Charles V (1500-1558), Holy Roman Emperor, r. 1519-1556
Clement VII (Giulio de' Medici; 1478-1534), Roman Catholic pope, 1523-1534

Charles III (1490-1527), eighth duke of Bourbon and governor of Milan
Francis I (1494-1547), king of France, r. 1515-1547
Leo X (Giovanni de' Medici; 1475-1521), Roman Catholic pope, 1513-1521, and son of Lorenzo de' Medici
Lorenzo de' Medici (1449-1492), influential Italian merchant prince

SUMMARY OF EVENT

The sack of Rome began on May 6, 1527 when an army of Spanish Catholics and Lutherans beholden to Charles V and led by Charles III marched rebelliously into Rome, a city the troops held in a state of siege for nine months. When marauding, unpaid troops entered the city, they plundered, looted, and pillaged ceaselessly for eight days, inflicting harsh treatment upon those who were directly associated with the Roman Catholic Church, most notably priests, monks, and nuns.

The rampaging invaders raped nuns as well as other female residents of Rome. They destroyed many of the city's most valued and beautiful frescoes and smashed priceless statuary. This was clearly a battle that largely resulted from the growing ascendancy of Protestantism in northern Europe.

Pope Clement VII, protected by his cadre of Swiss Guards, fled the Vatican just one step ahead of the invaders, taking refuge in the castle of Sant' Angelo. Many of Clement's guards were killed. The invaders from the north charged through the streets, humiliating the Romans in every possible way. They mocked them by dressing their leader in papal garb and leading him around the streets of the Vatican on a donkey. They ravaged the sacred tomb of Saint Peter and stole its riches. One soldier plundered the head of the lance that was supposed to have punctured Christ's side as he hung dying on the cross. The soldier then attached the lance head to his own weapon.

Pope Clement VII, the illegitimate son of Giuliano de' Medici, was orphaned at an early age. He was raised in the household of Lorenzo de' Medici, whose son, Leo X, was the boy's cousin. When Leo became pope in 1513, overlooking his cousin's illegitimacy, he named Clement archbishop of Florence and made him a cardinal. In this capacity, Clement was regarded as one of the most effective personages in the papal court. He served through Leo's papacy, which ended with Leo's death in 1521. He continued to serve through the papacy of Adrian VI, who was an unpopular pontiff and served less than two years before his death in 1523.

When Clement was elected pope on November 19, 1523, Italy was immersed in a struggle between Francis I, king of France, and Charles V, king of Spain and Holy Roman Emperor. Clement attempted to appease Charles V, but he had to make a choice eventually. Clement was forced to take sides, casting his lot with Francis and joining the League of Cognac with him in 1526, thereby infuriating Charles V. Francis was a strong Catholic, whereas Charles V clearly veered toward the Protestantism that was sweeping through northern Europe.

Clement fully expected Francis to provide troops to help protect the Vatican. This, however, did not happen. Francis, deeply in debt, could not afford to deploy troops to Italy when they were most needed to defend the Vatican in 1527.

From the time Clement became pope to the spring of 1527, wars racked Italy and destroyed much of the country. The troops of Charles V gathered in Milan. Charles III, governor of Milan and a close ally of Charles V, was their leader. Francis I was unwilling and unable to assist the pope, who was seeking a truce with Charles V, but this was impossible because Charles's troops were becoming rebellious; they had not been paid for several months. Hungry for plunder, they marched south toward Rome and arrived there May 6, 1527. The sack of Rome ensued.

The carnage was considerable. During the occupation of the city, more than two thousand bodies were disposed of in the Tiber River and another ten thousand were buried in Rome and its environs. The losses on both sides were substantial. Many of the invaders succumbed to the plague that swept through Rome in the summer of 1527. The occupation continued until the following February.

Pope Clement surrendered shortly after the invasion began and was a prisoner of the invaders until December 6, 1527. Upon his release, which was negotiated by paying Charles 400,000 ducats and surrendering several cities to him, Clement fled to Orvieto and then to Viterbo, staying in these cities for most of the next two years, essentially evicted from the Holy See. Clement eventually reached an accord with Charles V and acknowledged him as the Holy Roman Emperor, making official in the eyes of the Church the title that Charles had been granted through inheritance in 1519. Charles returned many of the spoils of the invasion, said to have a combined value of more than 4,000,000 ducats, to the Vatican.

SIGNIFICANCE

The sack of Rome marked the end of Rome's distinction as the unofficial capital of the Renaissance world, although the city recovered with remarkable speed from the northern invasion. Some historians think that the sack of Rome marked the end of the Renaissance altogether. Certainly, the age of Leonardo da Vinci and Michelangelo had passed, but the sixteenth century advanced in art and music nonetheless. One could say that the sack of Rome marked the end of the *High* Renaissance.

More significantly, Charles V's invasion challenged the authority of the Roman Catholic Church and marked a considerable advance for Protestantism. In 1533, Clement had to make the delicate decision about whether to grant King Henry VIII of England an annulment of his marriage to Catherine of Aragon in a manner the Church could sanction. His decision was as significant in the annals of Protestant advancement as was the sack of Rome.

Keenly aware that Catherine was the aunt of Charles V, who had a decided interest in Henry's petition, Clement denied the request, which caused Henry to withdraw from the Roman Catholic Church. The Church soon excommunicated him, leading to the formation of the Protestant Church of England. Without the sack of Rome and without Clement finding it necessary to consider how Charles V would react to his decision about the annulment, the pope might well have acceded to Henry's request, which would have had a profound effect on the course of European history.

—*R. Baird Shuman*

FURTHER READING

Connell, William J., ed. *Society and Individual in Renaissance Florence.* Berkeley: University of California Press, 2002. Chapter 16 by Paul Flemer, "Clement VII and the Crisis of the Sack of Rome," offers a succinct, well-written account of the sack of Rome and its aftermath. This essay is extensively documented and provides considerable information about Clement's growing up in Lorenzo de' Medici's intriguing household. In twenty-five well-considered pages, the author captures the essence of Clement's conflicts as pope.

Gouwens, Kenneth, ed. *The Italian Renaissance.* Malden, Mass.: Blackwell, 2004. Part V, "The Power of Knowledge," which contains a translation of the text of Pietro Alcionio's oration concerning the sack of Rome, is the most relevant section of this highly significant text.

_____. *Remembering the Renaissance: Humanist Narratives of the Sack of Rome.* Boston: Brill, 1998. Gouwens's consideration of the sack of Rome as a demonstration of cultural discontinuity is original and intelligent. His presentation of materials by and about such papal advisers as Pietro Alcionio, Pietro Corsi, and Jacopo Sadoleto provides unique insights into the pressures under which Pope Clement was placed by Charles V and his armies.

Guicciardini, Luigi. *The Sack of Rome.* Translated, edited, and introduced by James H. McGregor. New York: Italica Press, 1993. A translation of a contemporary account of the siege of Rome, especially useful for students. This historical work is also useful for its examination of sixteenth century Italian politics. McGregor provides an excellent introduction and notes to the text.

Hook, Judith. *The Sack of Rome: 1527.* 2d ed. New York: Palgrave Macmillan, 2003. Originally published in 1957, this work presents a classic narrative history of the siege, one of the first histories of the sack written in English.

Stinger, Charles L. *The Renaissance in Rome.* Bloomington: Indiana University Press, 1985. This volume's epilogue, "The Sack and Its Aftermath," is valuable for its discussion of the attack on Rome and its aftermath. Stinger demonstrates how important a role the attack played in the spread of Protestantism in northern Europe and in England. He draws interesting parallels between the sack of Rome and the ancient destruction of Jerusalem, showing how other writers have drawn such a parallel.

Zimmermann, T. C. Price. *Paolo Giovio: The Historian and the Crisis of Sixteenth Century Italy.* Princeton, N.J.: Princeton University Press, 1995. Chapter 6, "Clement VII and the Sack of Rome," provides a comprehensive overview of the attack. In about twenty-five pages, it captures vividly much of the atmosphere of the era.

1528
CASTIGLIONE'S *BOOK OF THE COURTIER* IS PUBLISHED

A detailed description of Italian aristocratic mores and manners in the sixteenth century, Castiglione's The Book of the Courtier *established for the first time the Renaissance ideal of the courtier and court lady. The book was imitated and translated into several European languages, and it influenced William Shakespeare, Philip Sidney, Thomas Elyot, and John Donne.*

LOCALE: Venice, Republic of Venice (now in Italy)
CATEGORY: Literature

KEY FIGURES

Baldassare Castiglione (1478-1529), Italian courtier, diplomat, and writer
Aldus Manutius (c. 1450-1515), Italian scholar, printer, and publisher
Guidobaldo da Montefeltro (1472-1508), duke of Urbino, r. 1482-1502, 1503-1508, and Castiglione's protector
Giuliano de' Medici (1471-1516), son of Lorenzo de' Medici the Magnificent and brother of Pope Leo X
Count Ludovico da Canossa (1476-1532), a friend of Castiglione and designated speaker in Book I
Pietro Bembo (1470-1547), cardinal, scholar, secretary to Pope Leo X, and the prime mover behind the Petrarchan revival

SUMMARY OF EVENT

Baldassare Castiglione's *Il libro del cortegiano* (1528; *The Book of the Courtier*, 1561) was written at the urging of Alfonso Ariosto (1475-1525), a cousin of the poet Ludovico Ariosto (1474-1533), and was originally dedicated to Alfonso, whom Castiglione described as "an affable youth, prudent, abounding in the gentlest manners, and apt in everything befitting a man who lives at court." Castiglione's purpose was to depict the profile of the perfect courtier, one who would have the ability to serve his prince to perfection and to win, through this ability, favors and praise from his master in particular and from society in general.

Castiglione associated the idea of writing *The Book of the Courtier* with his stay at the ducal court of Urbino and stated that the four books were composed "but in a few days." In 1528, at the printing of the first edition by Aldus Manutius, the dedication to Alfonso Ariosto was replaced with one to Cardinal Miguel da Silva, bishop of Vizeu. It is from this second dedicatory text, written from Spain (where Castiglione died on February 2, 1529), that one learns about Castiglione's life after the death of Urbino's duke Guidobaldo da Montefeltro and the accession of Francesco Maria della Rovere (1490-1538) to the ducal throne.

According to its author, the text had circulated prior to publication in several manuscript versions, some of which were heavily altered. Castiglione therefore decided to restore the book to its authentic state and to present it to its readers in printed form.

In his original dedication to da Silva, Castiglione explained the nature of the book, which he meant to be a realistic portrait of aristocratic life at the court of Urbino. With great modesty, he judged himself a mediocre literary portraitist and argued that he was not attempting to imitate Giovanni Boccaccio's *Decameron: O, Prencipe Galetto* (1349-1351; *The Decameron*, 1620), to which his work had been compared. In explaining the scope of *The Book of the Courtier*, Castiglione allied himself with figures from classical antiquity, such as Plato, Xenophon, and Cicero, and pleaded that "just as, according to these authors, there is the Idea of the perfect Republic, the perfect king, and the perfect Orator, so likewise there is that of the perfect Courtier."

The personages depicted in Castiglione's work were real people associated at the time with the ducal court of Urbino: Giuliano de' Medici, Cardinal Pietro Bembo, Gaspare Pallavicino, the poet Bernardo Accolti, Cardinal Bernardo (Dovizi) Bibbiena, Madonna Emilia Pia (d. 1528), and others. Most of the witty, animated conversations and activities related in the book took place on four successive evenings in 1507 (hence the partition of the work in four books), in the *Sala delle Veglie* of the ducal palace. The participants were all highly born, elegant, learned, and sophisticated. They took turns in proposing and discussing major topics of the day, including love; the dynamics of virtue and vice; the nature of human knowledge and reasoning; literature, old and new; the appropriateness of using Latin or vernacular dialects (especially Tuscan) and neologisms in writing and speaking; the relative merits of the Italian and the French of the period, and of the Greeks and the Romans of classical times; the role and social position of women; and the fine, performing, and martial arts, both ancient and modern.

One evening, Count Ludovico da Canossa is "given the task of forming in words a perfect Courtier." All the

465

CASTIGLIONE ON THE FUNCTION OF THE COURTIER

Book 1 of Baldassare Castiglione's Book of the Courtier *catalogs the features of the perfect courtier. Book 4, however, addresses the purpose of courtiers and their proper function or duty within the court. The remarks of Lord Ottaviano are excerpted below.*

For in truth, if in being noble, graceful, and charming and skilled in so many exercises, the Courtier produces no other fruit than to be such as he is for his own sake, I would not consider that to possess this perfection of Courtiership a man would be justified in expending so much study and toil as the acquisition of it demands. . . . Now in my estimation the end of the perfect Courtier . . . is to win for himself by means of the traits ascribed to him by these lords the good will and mind of the prince whom he serves, to such a point that this Courtier, without fear of danger of displeasing the prince, can tell and always does tell him the truth concerning everything proper for him to know. And if the Courtier knows that the prince's mind is bent on doing something unbecoming, he may dare to oppose the prince and in a courteous way take advantage of the favor acquired through his good traits to draw the prince away from every evil design and lead him into the path of virtue.

Source: From *The Book of the Courtier*, by Baldassare Castiglione. Translated and edited by Friench Simpson (New York: Frederick Ungar, 1959), pp. 49-50.

nets of Petrarch and the *Decameron* of Boccaccio to the writings of Poliziano (1454-1494).

The speakers praise the singing and lute playing of their own contemporary, Marco Cara (d. 1525), author of *frottole* and other songs in the vernacular and Mantuan marchioness Isabella d'Este's favorite composer. They comment on the paintings of Leonardo da Vinci, Andrea Mantegna, Michelangelo, and Raphael and invoke contemporary science and philosophy from the works of Paolo Nicola Vernia (Nicoletto Vernia, d. 1499), a professor at the University of Padua. Furthermore, recent historical events, such as the Battle of Fornovo (July 6, 1495) between the army led by Gianfrancesco Gonzaga of Mantua and that of the French king Charles VIII, also provide ammunition for the learned battle of words.

participants engage in a lively dialogue, proposing, rejecting, and refining ideas. The company share a common educational background, and they all understand the references, allusions, and implications of what is being said. Both men and women are widely read: They quote copiously from classical authors, both Greek and Latin, or paraphrase them.

The text of Castiglione's book, then, is interwoven with quotations from and paraphrases of Aristotle's *Politica* (335-323 B.C.E.; *Politics*, 1598) and *Aporemata Homerika* (335-323 B.C.E.; *Homeric Problems*, 1812); Plato's *Politeia* (388-368 B.C.E.; *Republic*, 1701) and *Phaedō* (388-368 B.C.E.; *Phaedo*, 1675); Aesop's *Aesopea* (fourth century B.C.E.; *Aesop's Fables*, 1484); Plutarch's *Bioi Paralleloi* (c. 105-115; *Parallel Lives*, 1579) and *Ethika* (after c. 100; *Moralia*, 1603); Cicero's *De oratore* (55 B.C.E.; *On Oratory*, 1742), *De officiis* (44 B.C.E.; *On Duties*, 1534), and *Tusculanae disputationes* (44 B.C.E.; *Tusculan Disputations*, 1561); Livy's *Ab urbe condita libri* (c. 26 B.C.E.; *The History of Rome*, 1600); Pliny the Elder's *Historia naturalis* (late first century; *Natural History*, 1855); Catullus's *Carmina* (mid-first century B.C.E.; English translation, 1893); Ovid's *Ars amatoria* (c. 2 B.C.E.; *Art of Love*, 1612); and other classics. Early Renaissance poetry and prose provide material for debate as well, from the son-

The profile of the perfect courtier begins to emerge as the company gradually arrive at the conclusion that he must be noble of birth and countenance, physically beautiful, and, quite important, graceful. Grace is defined as the quality that makes everything appear to have been done with great ease, regardless of the effort actually spent in accomplishing the task. By extension, definitions of art, too, include the criteria of nonchalance and ease, for Castiglione's characters believe that true artworks must also give the impression of having been created with no effort at all.

The courtier is expected to be an excellent, wise, and prudent warrior, physically fit and ready to fight. Furthermore, he should be well-read and able to manipulate language—both written and spoken—with ease, elegance, and eloquence; be conversant with both Latin and Greek; and apply discernment in his choice of subject and vocabulary. It is further agreed, against those maintaining that music making is a feminine occupation, that he must be able to read music, play an instrument or two, sing acceptably well, and be a graceful dancer. In addition, he must have a decent knowledge of drawing and painting. Finally, his moral standing should be such as to inspire and encourage his master, too, toward welcoming virtue and repulsing vices, among which ignorance and self-conceit are seen as the most serious.

The literary and artistic achievements of the ideal court lady for Castiglione are similar to those of a man. Physical strength and fitness, however, are not considered desirable attributes, although a lady can play tennis, ride, and hunt in moderation—something that many women of the Renaissance actually did. Her morals must be impeccable, and she should be discreet, of demure manners, and a gracious entertainer.

SIGNIFICANCE

In addition to being a manual of ideal Renaissance courtly manners, *The Book of the Courtier* is a mirror of the actual aristocratic lifestyle practiced at the small court of Urbino—and, by extension, at Italian courts in general—in the early sixteenth century. The book has become an invaluable source of information for historians of Renaissance dance, music, painting, sports, and other forms of entertainment and for those who study the reception and propagation of such forms and of philosophical trends in Italy in the early sixteenth century.

In its own time, the book was quite popular as well, both on the Continent and in the British Isles, which Castiglione himself had visited from November of 1506 to January, 1507, as the ambassador of Duke Guidobaldo da Montefeltro to the court of King Henry VII. *The Book of the Courtier* was translated into English by Sir Thomas Hoby (1530-1566), a Cambridge-educated diplomat, and his translation had both an immediate and a lasting effect on high society, on manners and conduct, and on higher education in England, as well as influencing William Shakespeare and Sir Philip Sidney.

—*Luminita Florea*

FURTHER READING

Berger, Harry. *The Absence of Grace: Sprezzatura and Suspicion in Two Renaissance Courtesy Books.* Stanford, Calif.: Stanford University Press, 2000. The chapters devoted to *The Book of the Courtier* examine the topics of grace and nonchalance (*sprezzatura*) in arts and social behavior, the status of women around 1500, and the reliability of the narrator.

Burke, Peter. *The Fortunes of the Courtier: The European Reception of Castiglione's Cortegiano.* University Park: Pennsylvania State University Press, 1996. Detailed examination of the book's reception in its own time, in Italy and elsewhere. Discusses its translators and imitators. Includes appendices with the book's editions and the names of its readers before 1700.

Kennedy, Teresa. *Elyot, Castiglione, and the Problem of Style.* New York: P. Lang, 1996. A study of Castiglione's influence on Sir Thomas Elyot's *The Boke Named the Governour*, written in 1531 and dedicated to King Henry VIII.

Raffini, Christine. *Marsilio Ficino, Pietro Bembo, Baldassare Castiglione: Philosophical, Aesthetic, and Political Approaches in Renaissance Platonism.* New York: P. Lang, 1998. Includes biographies of all three writers; discusses their works from the perspective of their inclusion of Neoplatonic philosophical concepts.

Rebhom, Wayne A. *Courtly Performances: Masking and Festivity in Castiglione's "Book of the Courtier."* Detroit: Wayne State University Press, 1978. A study of *The Book of the Courtier* as a specific literary genre.

Wiggins, Peter DeSa. *Donne, Castiglione, and the Poetry of Courtliness.* Bloomington: Indiana University Press, 2000. Parallel readings of five satires by John Donne and Castiglione's *Book of the Courtier.* Donne's work is seen as a poetic metamorphosis of Castiglione's prose.

SEE ALSO: 1490's: Aldus Manutius Founds the Aldine Press; Sept., 1494-Oct., 1495: Charles VIII of France Invades Italy.

RELATED ARTICLES in *Great Lives from History: The Renaissance & Early Modern Era, 1454-1600:* Baldassare Castiglione; Vittoria Colonna; Charles VIII; Henry VII; Isabella d'Este; Aldus Manutius; Raphael.

1520's

1528-1536
NARVÁEZ'S AND CABEZA DE VACA'S EXPEDITIONS

After claiming Florida for Spain, Spanish explorers faced attacks by North American Indians and lost hundreds of crew members to hunger, disease, and weather. A report by the expeditions' four survivors is the first European document to describe a hurricane, the buffalo and the opossum, local geography, and the interaction of Europeans and indigenous peoples in North America.

LOCALE: Florida, the Gulf coast, southwestern United States, and northern Mexico

CATEGORIES: Exploration and discovery; colonization; expansion and land acquisition

KEY FIGURES

Pánfilo de Narváez (c. 1478-1528), commander of the expedition to Florida

Álvar Núñez Cabeza de Vaca (c. 1490-c. 1560), second in command of the expedition to Florida

Andrés Dorantes de Carranza (c. 1500-c. 1550), Spanish conqueror

Alonso del Castillo Maldonado (fl. sixteenth century), Spanish conqueror

Estevanico (Esteván; d. 1539), Moorish slave

Antonio de Mendoza (c. 1490-1552), first viceroy of New Spain and later viceroy of Peru

Francisco Vásquez de Coronado (1510-1554), Spanish expedition leader

SUMMARY OF EVENT

Spain had expanded its empire from a few islands to include Mexico, or New Spain, after the conquest of the Aztecs in 1521 by Hernán Cortés. Operating from bases in the Caribbean, Juan Ponce de León and other Spanish explorers had also explored and established a short-lived colony in Florida. These expeditions fueled the imagination of other Spaniards, and after the conquest of Mexico, Florida acquired important strategic value. In 1527, the Spanish crown approved another expedition to Florida, to be commanded by Pánfilo de Narváez, a veteran of the conquests of Cuba and Mexico. The treasurer and second in command of the expedition was Álvar Núñez Cabeza de Vaca.

Although he had not been to America, Cabeza de Vaca had an impressive military background and pedigree. His mother's surname, which means "head of the cow," was an honorary title her family had received when an ancestor marked a mountain pass with a cow's skull that en-

abled the Christians to surprise the Muslims in a crucial battle. His paternal grandfather, Pedro de Vera, was the conqueror of Gran Canaria (Grand Canary), and Cabeza de Vaca grew up with indigenous Guanche slaves from the Canary Islands and his grandfather's stories of conquest and adventure. Born around 1490, Cabeza de Vaca reached adulthood during Spain's imperial expansion and chose a military career. Before his assignment to the Narváez expedition, he had already served the Crown in Italy, Navarre, and Spain.

Commander Narváez already had an ill-starred career. During the conquest of Cuba, he oversaw the slaughter of thousands of indigenous peoples. When he was sent to arrest Hernán Cortés, Narváez lost his men to the conqueror of Mexico and he lost an eye in the process. The Florida expedition also started off badly when 140 men deserted shortly after arriving in Santo Domingo. On their way to Florida, the fleet was scattered by a hurricane off Cuba, several ships ran aground, and 60 men and 20 horses were lost.

The expedition finally reached Florida on April 12, 1528. After claiming the land in the name of the king of Spain and trading with the North American Indians for food, the expedition moved inland in search of Apalachen, a province purportedly rich in gold. Despite the objections of Cabeza de Vaca to separating the ships from the land force, Narváez ordered the ships to sail on to a port, leaving three hundred people on shore. It was the last time they would see their ships.

The Spaniards encountered a fierce resistance from indigenous archers whose arrows could penetrate trees and Spanish armor. When they reached Apalachen, it was a disappointing village of forty thatched huts inhabited by women and children, and they were constantly under attack. Suffering from wounds, hunger, and disease, they tried to locate a harbor where they might find the ships. Failing that, they decided to build barges to escape to Pánuco, Mexico, by sailing along the Gulf coast. After consuming their horses, the 242 survivors embarked in five leaky and overcrowded barges. Narváez and his men, separating from the slower barges, disappeared, never to be seen again.

After almost two months at sea, Cabeza de Vaca and his troops crashed on Galveston Island, off what is now Texas. Although they were befriended by local tribes, they had little food. All but sixteen of the ninety Spaniards died from disease and hunger, while their hosts were dying from a disease they blamed on the Spaniards. Gradually, all but four of the Spaniards perished, some resorting to cannibalism before dying or being killed by shocked Indians.

The four survivors, Cabeza de Vaca, Captains Andrés Dorantes de Carranza and Alonso del Castillo Maldonado, and Estevanico (sometimes called Estevéan), a Moorish slave, spent the next seven years wandering among the indigenous tribes of what is now the southwestern United States. Although initially worshiped for their medical powers, they were reduced to slaves and forced to work under harsh masters. After he escaped from his group, Cabeza de Vaca took up trade and became a successful merchant who could travel freely between hostile tribes. Despite his new status, he was naked and barely survived on the roots or plants he could scavenge.

When the four survivors were reunited, they became medicine men, praying over their patients, who experienced miraculous recoveries. Considered to have magical powers, they became famous, and their fame as healers spread. They were followed by hordes of believers and were welcomed and showered with presents in every village they visited. Although they developed an appreciation for their hosts and the indigenous cultures, they never abandoned their Christian faith and viewed their own survival and medical cures as divinely inspired.

When they arrived in Mexico in the spring of 1536, eight years after landing in Florida, their reports of their experiences stimulated interest in further exploration.

Seeking to preempt any competitors, the Spanish viceroy of New Spain, Antonio de Mendoza, dispatched Fray Marcos and Estevanico on a reconnaissance mission to northern Mexico. When Estevanico disappeared, apparently killed by resentful Mexican Indians, Fray Marcos returned with reports of seven fabulous cities, rumored to be the Seven Cities of Cíbola founded by seven legendary bishops who had fled Portugal centuries earlier.

Acting on this news, Mendoza authorized Francisco Vásquez de Coronado to explore northern Mexico. With three hundred soldiers, seven Franciscans, and a thousand indigenous allies, Coronado searched as far as Kansas without locating any fabulous riches, and returned to Mexico a broken man. Nevertheless, his expedition had initiated the Spanish conquest of Texas and New Mexico and the introduction of horses and cattle into these territories.

SIGNIFICANCE

In 1537, Cabeza de Vaca returned to Spain and presented his official report to Charles I, king of Spain and Holy Roman Emperor. This document, along with a joint report prepared by Cabeza de Vaca, Castillo, and Dorantes, described the disastrous Florida expedition and is an important source of information on the explorers' experiences and the indigenous cultures they encountered from Florida to Mexico, many of which were soon extinct.

Although Cabeza de Vaca considered Florida to have great potential as a colony and believed in other fabulous

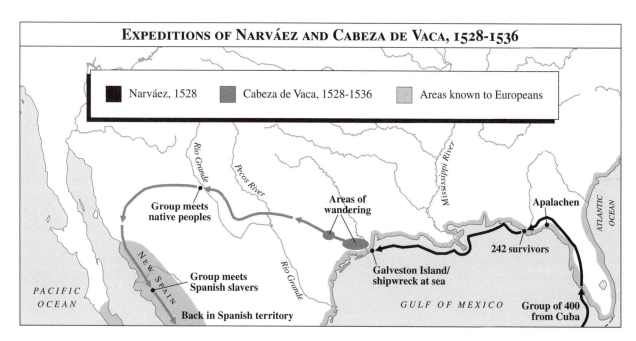

EXPEDITIONS OF NARVÁEZ AND CABEZA DE VACA, 1528-1536

Narváez, 1528 — Cabeza de Vaca, 1528-1536 — Areas known to Europeans

Rio Grande
Pecos River
Mississippi River

Group meets native peoples
Areas of wandering
Apalachen
242 survivors
Galveston Island/ shipwreck at sea
Group meets Spanish slavers
Rio Grande
NEW SPAIN
PACIFIC OCEAN
Back in Spanish territory
GULF OF MEXICO
ATLANTIC OCEAN
Group of 400 from Cuba

civilizations in North America, he refused to offer his services as second in command of Hernando de Soto's ill-fated expedition to Florida. In 1540, Cabeza de Vaca sailed to South America in command of an expedition to relieve a struggling Spanish settlement in Paraguay and marched 1,000 miles overland to Asunción. He was overthrown because of his efforts to protect the indigenous from enslavement and was sent back to Spain in chains. Although he was deprived of his titles and banished from the Indies, he also was pardoned and given a pension by the king just before his death around 1560.

—*D. Anthony White*

FURTHER READING

Adorno, Rolena, and Patrick Charles Pautz. *Alvar Núñez Cabeza de Vaca: His Account, His Life, and the Expedition of Pánfilo de Narváez.* 3 vols. Lincoln: University of Nebraska Press, 1999. Volume 1 contains Cabeza de Vaca's own narrative of his adventures. Volumes 2 and 3 provide close readings and interpretations of the narrative together with analyses of its place in literary history and in the history of Spanish exploration in the Americas.

Bishop, Morris. *The Odyssey of Cabeza de Vaca.* Westport, Conn.: Greenwood Press, 1991. The best full-length biography of Cabeza de Vaca. Describes the conqueror's early life but has been challenged for the accuracy of Cabeza de Vaca's itinerary.

Cabeza de Vaca, Álvar Núñez. *The Narrative of Cabeza de Vaca.* Translated and edited by Rolena Adorno and Patrick Charles Pautz. Lincoln: University of Nebraska Press, 2003. A stand-alone edition of Adorno and Pautz's critically praised translation of Cabeza de Vaca's narrative.

Chipman, Donald E. "Álvar Núñez Cabeza de Vaca." In *The New Handbook of Texas,* edited by Ron Tyler et al. Vol. 4. Austin: Texas State Historical Association, 1996. The best brief biography of Cabeza de Vaca, with a good review of the issue of his route to Mexico and his place in history.

_____. "In Search of Cabeza de Vaca's Route Across Texas: An Historiographical Survey." *Southwestern Historical Quarterly* 91 (October, 1987): 127-148. A survey of the literature on Cabeza de Vaca's route through Texas and New Mexico.

González-Casanovas, Roberto J. *Imperial Histories from Alfonso X to Inca Garcilaso: Revisionist Myths of Reconquest and Conquest.* Potomac, Md.: Scripta Humanistica, 1997. Examines the political and ideological functions of official historiographies of Spanish conquest in America and reconquest in Iberia. Includes a reading of Cabeza de Vaca's narrative and the ways it authorizes Spanish colonialism.

Hallenbeck, Cleve. *Álvar Núñez Cabeza de Vaca: The Journey and Route of the First European to Cross the Continent of North America, 1534-1536.* Glendale, Calif.: Arthur H. Clark, 1940. A still-valuable reconstruction of the itinerary of Cabeza de Vaca through Texas across the Rio Grande into Northern Mexico.

Hedrick, Basil C., and Carroll L. Riley, eds. and trans. *The Journey of the Vaca Party: The Account of the Narváez Expedition, 1528-1536, as Related by Gonzalo Fernández de Oviedo y Valdés.* Carbondale: University Museum, Southern Illinois University, 1964. Translation from the sixteenth century Spanish chronicler's general history of the Indies. Includes the joint report of Cabeza de Vaca, Castillo, and Dorantes, written in Mexico in 1536.

Howard, David A. *Conquistador in Chains: Cabeza de Vaca and the Indians of the Americas.* Tuscaloosa: University of Alabama Press, 1997. A biography of Cabeza de Vaca that sees his Texas experience as a key influence in his change from exploiter to protector of the American Indians in the Rio de la Plata province.

Sauer, Carl O. *Sixteenth Century North America: The Land and the Peoples as Seen by the Europeans.* Berkeley: University of California Press, 1971. An analysis of sixteenth century European descriptions of North America by a well-known scholar of cultural geography.

SEE ALSO: 1493-1521: Ponce de León's Voyages; 1495-1510: West Indian Uprisings; Apr., 1519-Aug., 1521: Cortés Conquers Aztecs in Mexico; May 28, 1539-Sept. 10, 1543: De Soto's North American Expedition; Feb. 23, 1540-Oct., 1542: Coronado's Southwest Expedition; 1542-1543: The New Laws of Spain; Sept., 1565: St. Augustine Is Founded.

RELATED ARTICLES in *Great Lives from History: The Renaissance & Early Modern Era, 1454-1600:* Álvar Núñez Cabeza de Vaca; Charles V; Francisco Vásquez de Coronado; Hernán Cortés; Pedro Menéndez de Avilés; Juan Ponce de León; Hernando de Soto.

1529-1574
NORTH AFRICA RECOGNIZES OTTOMAN SUZERAINTY

The individual independent states of the North African coast found themselves unable to resist Christian encroachments in the region. Gradually, they looked to the Ottoman Turks for defense, becoming nominal vassals of the Ottoman Empire.

LOCALE: North African coast, from Tripolitania to Algiers (now in Libya, Tunisia, and Algeria)

CATEGORIES: Diplomacy and international relations; expansion and land acquisition

KEY FIGURES

Süleyman the Magnificent (1494/1495-1566), sultan of the Ottoman Empire, r. 1520-1566

Charles V (1500-1558), Holy Roman Emperor, r. 1519-1556, and king of Spain as Charles I, r. 1516-1556

Barbarossa (Khayr al-Dīn; d. 1546), Ottoman military leader and admiral of the Ottoman fleet, 1533-1546

SUMMARY OF EVENT

From the rise of Islam in the seventh century until the sixteenth century, North Africa came under various levels of political control either by distant imperial regimes or by locally initiated dynasties. Often at question was the religious legitimacy of those who claimed, if not direct political rule, some form of suzerainty. During the heyday of the ʿAbbāsid Caliphate in Baghdad (751-1258), the Fāṭimids of Syria migrated to the Aurès Mountains (in modern Algeria) and fostered an anti-Caliphate based on Shīʿite principles. By the mid-tenth century, however, Fāṭimid control in North Africa, which at its height ran from modern Tunisia to western Algeria, had been reduced when the dynasty returned eastward and made a new capital at Cairo.

The next major period of religious and political consolidation in North Africa was associated with the Berber Almohad Dynasty, with its capital in Marrakech. As the Almohads extended their claims to an actual empire, they also utilized the banner of Islam, again in opposition to what were by then only the remnants of ʿAbbāsid caliphal authority in Baghdad. To do this, the Almohads needed to extract some acknowledgment of their governing legitimacy from the many different tribal groupings living in hinterland areas. In more settled areas, in particular wherever coastal port conditions could sustain trade

(either with other Islamic ports or with European merchants), more formal governmental authority was installed. Thus, port cities like Mahdia, Tunis, and Bona (Annaba) were assumed (in theory if not in practice) to fall under the control of appointees of distant Almohad "rulers." As Almohad imperial power declined after about 1225, this situation inevitably led to claims by local dynasts to govern extensive regions in their own name. This process created three significant North African successor states that survived into the sixteenth century: the Ḥafṣids, the Zayyānids in Algeria, and the Marīnids in Morocco.

In the centuries when major Islamic empires like the Fāṭimids and the Almohads held sway and then lost control over North Africa, Christian powers in Europe could not really affect developments one way or the other. After about 1400, however, the situation changed, as the various successor states that replaced the Almohads showed signs of weakness. The fall of Constantinople to Ottoman sultan Mehmed II in 1453 was followed by wider clashes with the Holy Roman Empire. These clashes intensified during the reigns of two famous sovereigns: Sultan Süleyman the Magnificent and the Habsburg Holy Roman Emperor Charles V, who also ruled Spain as Charles I. Muslim-Christian conflict over North African territory began in a context separate from Ottoman-Habsburg rivalries, but it eventually came to affect both empires directly.

When the Spanish Reconquista defeated the Naṣrid kingdom of Granada in 1492, a series of Spanish outposts, both for trade and for possible continuation of a crusade, grew up along the African coast. Small states like the Ḥafṣids were not able to muster sufficient military strength to stop Spanish incursions. By the time Sultan Selim I's forces invaded Syria and Egypt and took the holy city of Mecca in 1517, however, there were unofficial naval forces crossing the Mediterranean to confront Christians in North Africa.

Although the term "Barbary corsair" is usually associated with pirate attacks on European and American shipping early in the nineteenth century, the danger of privateer raids to both Christian and Muslim shipping was a fact of life by 1500. Attacks by Barbarossa and his brother ʿArūj were apparently aimed at gaining footholds in small port areas in Muslim-held territory. In the context of the Spanish incursions, the relationship of Barbarossa and ʿArūj to the Ḥafṣids was complex. While the brothers attacked Christian raiders and no doubt indirectly defended the coast from European influence, they also gained control of the port of Halq al-Wadi, right next to Tunis. The control of this strategically vital port by unpredictable corsairs left the Ḥafṣids more vulnerable than ever to Spanish attack. The Ḥafṣids ultimately entered into protectorate alliances with the Spaniards, forcing corsairs to look elsewhere for safe havens.

By the 1520's and 1530's, several developments would lead to overlaps between these specifically North African conditions and the larger Muslim-Christian rivalry between the Ottomans and the Holy Roman Empire. A key issue, beyond Süleyman's increasingly aggressive military campaigns, was the fact that the thrones of Spain and the Holy Roman Empire were united under Charles V. When Süleyman marched his forces to the gates of the empire's capital of Vienna in 1529, therefore, they succeeded in provoking two empires at once. Charles sought out weaknesses in the Ottoman Empire, and he struck back with both his imperial forces and Spain's renowned armada.

Concern for different types of Christian claims on Mediterranean territory, whether along the North African shore or islands held since the era of the Crusades, had already begun to increase when the Ottomans took Rhodes in 1522. From that point on, maritime clashes between the Ottoman navy and a Christian coalition, led symbolically by the Papacy and militarily by Charles V, became a common feature of Ottoman-Christian hostility. In the Mediterranean naval arena, several major struggles would be fought, beginning with the Battle of Préveza (won by the Ottomans in 1538), including Süleyman's failed bid to capture Malta in 1565, and ending with the defeat of the Ottomans at Lepanto in 1571. At each stage of naval conflict in the Aegean or central Mediterranean, both sides must have weighed the importance of having safe havens in North Africa for their respective fleets.

This need for secure naval bases induced Süleyman to grant Barbarossa military titles and reinforcements in return for his pledge of fealty to the Ottoman Empire. With this aid, Barbarossa was able to add Algiers to the empire in 1529. Four years later, Süleyman made Barbarossa admiral of the Ottoman navy, and in 1534, the new admiral retook Ḥafṣid Tunis, temporarily dethroning the Ḥafṣids. However, neither this de facto alliance of Ottoman and corsair forces nor a promise from Charles's enemy Francis I of France to support the Ottomans was enough to hold Tunis for more than a year. Charles V came to Ḥafṣid aid in 1535, and he retook Tunis on the condition

that the Ḥafṣids align themselves with the Habsburgs, forming a Muslim-Christian alliance.

Thus began a series of efforts by both the Ottoman and the Holy Roman Empires to hold the key ports of North Africa running west from Tunis. Charles V sent an expedition to Algiers in 1541 to try to dislodge Barbarossa's successors from what had become the major base of Ottoman operations against both Christian and Muslim resistance. Primary among resistors were the Ḥafṣids, but also the fiercely independent Moroccan Saʿdīan sultanate. The latter ultimately became the last holdouts against Ottoman suzerainty in North Africa. Unlike Tripolitania, Tunis, and Algiers, Morocco never transferred its loyalty to Istanbul.

What the Ottomans did to establish their suzerainty in stages was to make Barbarossa the first so-called *beylerbey* ("Bey of the Beys"), representing formal imperial ties between Istanbul and Algiers. If Algiers could impose its will on lesser ports and hinterland areas like Bona or Oran, then its status as an Ottoman regency would in effect cover a whole province. Barbarossa died in 1546, but the Ottomans conquered Tripoli in 1551, wresting its control from the Knights of Saint John of Malta.

As the struggle between Christians and Muslims reached a zenith in 1571 at Lepanto and then receded, Süleyman's successor, Selim II, was finally able to conquer Tunis decisively in 1574. With that victory, Ottoman suzerainty appeared to extend to the entire North African coast east of Morocco. In actuality, however, the nearly autonomous local regimes that soon emerged in Tripoli, Tunis, and Algiers were never completely loyal to Istanbul, and the region was never fully integrated under central Ottoman control.

SIGNIFICANCE

The later history of Ottoman North Africa illustrates the difficulties the Ottomans had in maintaining their vast empire. By 1574, Algiers, Tunis, and Tripoli were all vassal states of the empire. All three were governed by Ottoman governors, sent from Istanbul for that purpose, and policed or at least inhabited by Ottoman troops. In all three states, the Ottoman troops eventually rebelled against the governor of their province and took control of the state, beginning their own dynasties. Tunis was the site of the first of these rebellions in 1591, while Algiers followed suit in 1689. In 1711, the commander of Tripoli's cavalry established himself as the ruler of a new dynasty as well. In the long term, then, the recognition or nonrecognition of Ottoman suzerainty in North Africa was less important than the quartering of Ottoman troops that took place there, as it was these troops, rather than the sultan of the empire, that ultimately shaped the political fates of the region's nations.

—*Byron Cannon*

FURTHER READING
Goodwin, Jason. *Lords of the Horizons: The Ottomans.* New York: Holt, 1999. A general history that places North African events in the broader context of Ottoman imperial history.
Heers, Jacques. *The Barbary Corsairs: Warfare in the Mediterranean, 1480-1580.* Translated by Jonathan North. Greenhill, Pa.: Stackpole, 2003. Translated version of a French history of corsair operations that contributed to, but did not end with, extension of Ottoman control to North Africa.
Wolf, John. *The Barbary Coast and Algiers Under the Turks.* New York: Norton, 1979. A popular history of the peculiar relationship that developed between the North African "regencies" and the presumed central imperial authority of Istanbul.

SEE ALSO: May, 1485-Apr. 13, 1517: Mamlūk-Ottoman Wars; Beginning 1504: Decline of the Ḥafṣid Dynasty; 1510-1578: Saʿdī Sharifs Come to Power in Morocco; 1512-1520: Reign of Selim I; June 28, 1519: Charles V Is Elected Holy Roman Emperor; 1520-1566: Reign of Süleyman; 1525-1600: Ottoman-Ruled Egypt Sends Expeditions South and East; Sept. 27-28, 1538: Battle of Préveza; Oct. 20-27, 1541: Holy Roman Empire Attacks Ottomans in Algiers; 1552: Struggle for the Strait of Hormuz; 1566-1574: Reign of Selim II; Aug. 4, 1578: Battle of Ksar el-Kebir; 1593-1606: Ottoman-Austrian War.

RELATED ARTICLES in *Great Lives from History: The Renaissance & Early Modern Era, 1454-1600:* Barbarossa; Charles V; Francis I; Mehmed II; Süleyman the Magnificent.

March 7, 1529
BATTLE OF SHIMBRA-KURE

The Muslim leader of Adal, Aḥmad Grāñ, defeated the army of Emperor Lebna Dengel and ended the hegemony of the Christian kingdom of Ethiopia over northeast Africa.

LOCALE: Shimbra-Kure, Shewan Plateau, Ethiopian Empire (now in Ethiopia)
CATEGORIES: Wars, uprisings, and civil unrest; government and politics; religion; expansion and land acquisition

KEY FIGURES
Aḥmad Grāñ (Aḥmad ibn Ibrāhim al-Ghāzī; 1506-1543), leader of a militant Muslim movement in Adal, r. 1529-1543
Lebna Dengel (d. 1540), Ethiopian emperor, r. 1508-1540
Christóvão da Gama (d. 1542), commander of Portuguese troops sent to aid the Christian kingdom of Ethiopia
Galawdewos (d. 1559), Ethiopian emperor, r. 1540-1559

SUMMARY OF EVENT
By the end of the fifteenth century, the Christian kingdom of Ethiopia, which had dominated the northeast African political scene for the preceding two centuries, came under increasing pressure from its Muslim vassal territories in the east. Weakened by dynastic squabbles and internecine warfare, the Christian polity was unable effectively to counter the Muslim insurgency, which continued to spread across the length and breadth of the Horn of Africa.

Adal, a Muslim sultanate located farther to the east, out of reach of the Ethiopian army, served as the rallying point for the growing Muslim resistance. Adal's strategic location allowed it to control the trade routes leading to and from the port of Zeila on the Gulf of Aden. This port served as the single most important outlet for the commerce of the Ethiopian hinterland and the lowland areas of the Horn of Africa. Adal's proximity to the coastline also allowed it to maintain close relations and to receive support from Arabia and other Muslim powers. By the beginning of the sixteenth century, Adal's resistance was preventing any further Christian expansion toward the east.

The Islamic threat to Ethiopia assumed a new dimension with the rise to power of a gifted leader called Aḥmad Grāñ. Preaching a fiery brand of Islam, the young and charismatic imam, who had risen through the ranks of the army of Adal, set out to build up a strong power base for an eventual *jihad* against Christian Ethiopia.

Grāñ initiated his spectacular military career by first carrying out a series of campaigns against his fellow Afar and Somali tribesmen to create internal unity and order within the Islamic community. Once pacified, these desert warrior tribes became important sources of manpower for Grāñ's growing army. The ecological stress aggravated by population pressure in the lowlands appears to have made the Muslim pastoral communities more responsive to Grāñ's call for a *jihad* against the rich areas of the Christian highlands.

Grāñ's consolidation of power over the Horn of Africa coincided with the expansion of Ottoman power in Egypt, the Red Sea, and Yemen. The entry of the Turks into the region provided an additional moral and material boost to Grāñ's projected *jihad*. Grāñ's army was the first in the region to be equipped with firearms. The new weapons and the few hundred Turkish matchlock men he received from the sultan played a role in tilting the balance of power in northeast Africa against the Christian forces.

In 1527, Aḥmad Grāñ officially declared the *jihad* he had been preparing against the Christian kingdom. He invaded the border provinces of Yifat, Dawaro, Fatagar, Hadiyya, and Bali. The predominantly Muslim inhabitants of these provinces welcomed Grāñ as their liberator. Demoralized Christian garrisons abandoned the frontier defenses, allowing Grāñ's army to penetrate deep into the core areas of the kingdom. The emperor of Ethiopia, Lebna Dengel, commanded a much larger army than Grāñ's, composed of recruits from all over the empire. However, he was slow to recognize the magnitude of the threat Grāñ posed and made no effort to meet him at the frontier. Instead, Dengel waited to engage Grāñ until he reached Shewa, the center of the empire.

In Shewa, the imperial army and the forces of Adal finally engaged one another in a series of battles. The war's decisive conflict was fought at Shimbra-Kure on March 7, 1529. Despite losing more than five thousand men, Grāñ's Muslim forces won a resounding victory. The bulk of the Christian military and political elite was destroyed by the smaller Muslim force. Emperor Lebna Dengel became a fugitive in his own kingdom, taking refuge in various mountain fortresses but fleeing each whenever it seemed he might be discovered. What was left of his army engaged in haphazard guerrilla strikes, but they remained more a nuisance than a threat to Aḥmad Grāñ.

SIGNIFICANCE

In the wake of his victory at Shimbra-Kure, Aḥmad Grāñ pushed inexorably toward the densely populated Christian provinces of Amhara and Lasta, reaching as far north as Tigray. Whole regions of the empire were laid waste, and much of the intellectual and artistic heritage of the land was destroyed. Thousands of ancient churches and monasteries, including the Cathedral of Axum, the rock churches of Lalibela, and the famous monastery of Debre Libanos, were burnt, together with invaluable illuminated manuscripts and art objects.

Despite his spectacular military victories, however, Grāñ was unable to stamp out Christian resistance completely. With thinly spread out forces and overstretched supply lines, Grāñ found it increasingly difficult to consolidate his control over the rugged terrain of the Ethiopian plateau.

The arrival, in 1541, of some four hundred Portuguese musketeers, sent in response to Lebna Dengel's appeal to Christian Europe, galvanized the resistance against the Muslim occupation. About half of this small Portuguese force were killed, together with their commander, Christóvão da Gama (son of the famous explorer Vasco da Gama), during their first engagement with Grāñ. However, the remaining troops managed to join forces with Emperor Galawdewos, who had succeeded Lebna Dengel upon the latter's death in 1540. Galawedos was already rallying his Christian subjects to revive the struggle against the Muslim occupation when the Portuguese arrived. The newly energized Christian force under Galawdewos fought and killed Grāñ at the Battle of Woina Dega on February 22, 1543. The Muslim army disintegrated following the death of the imam.

The Muslim explosion into the Christian kingdom in the sixteenth century was a major turning point in the history of northeast Africa. The destruction that accompanied the conquests of Aḥmad Grāñ left Ethiopia in disarray. The rich material and spiritual culture achieved by medieval Ethiopia, and the mighty political and military power built by a succession of able Solomonic leaders, were almost completely destroyed. The Muslim side did not fare any better. The wars they waged on the Christian kingdom and their subsequent defeat left them politically weakened and severely depopulated. By the end of the Christian-Muslim conflict, both sides were exhausted and possessed few resources with which to defend their respective territories from the new intruders who exploited the political and military vacuum to overrun the fertile Christian and Muslim regions. By the end of the sixteenth century, the Kingdom of Adal was reduced to the single walled city of Harar, and the once mighty Ethiopian empire had shrunk to a few provinces in the northern highland.

—*Shumet Sishagne*

FURTHER READING

Crummey, Donald. *Land and Society in the Christian Kingdom of Ethiopia, from the Thirteenth to the Twentieth Century.* Urbana-Champaign: University of Illinois, 2000. A political and social history of Ethiopia, with helpful discussion on the economic basis of political domination.

Henze, Paul B. *Layers of Time: A History of Ethiopia.* New York: Palgrave, 2000. A readable general work that is especially useful in tracing the history of the Christian kingdom's expansion southward during medieval times under the leadership of the Solomonic rulers. It also includes interesting information on daily life, art, architecture, religion, culture, and customs.

Marcus, Harold. *History of Ethiopia.* Berkeley: University of California Press, 1994. A general survey of Ethiopian history from ancient times to the present.

Shihab ad-Din Ahmad bin Abd al-Qader bin Salem bin Utman. *Futuh al-Habasha/The Conquest of Abyssinia.* Translated by Paul Lester Stenhouse. Hollywood, Calif.: Tsehai, 2003. An invaluable account of the sixteenth century *jihad* in Ethiopia by a Yemeni author who witnessed several of the battles he describes.

Tadesse Tamrat. *Church and State in Ethiopia, 1270-1527.* Oxford, England: Clarendon Press, 1972. An authoritative work on the history of medieval Ethiopia, especially useful for understanding the background to the decline of the Solomonic Dynasty.

_____. "The Horn of Africa: The Solomonids in Ethiopia and the States of the Horn of Africa." In *Africa from the Twelfth to the Sixteenth Century.* Vol. 4 in *General History of Africa.* Berkeley: University of California Press, 1984. A succinct account of the political conditions in the Horn of Africa in the fifteenth and sixteenth centuries.

Trimingham, J. S. *Islam in Ethiopia.* New York: Clarendon Press, 1952. A valuable work on the history of Muslim-Christian interaction in Ethiopia.

SEE ALSO: 1460-1600: Rise of the Akan Kingdoms; c. 1464-1591: Songhai Empire Dominates the Western Sudan; Late 15th cent.: Mombasa, Malindi, and Kilwa Reach Their Height; May, 1485-Apr. 13, 1517: Mamlūk-Ottoman Wars; 1491-1545: Christianity Is Established in the Kingdom of Kongo; Jan., 1498: Portuguese Reach the Swahili Coast; 1510-1578: Saʿdī Sharifs Come to Power in Morocco; 1525-1600: Ottoman-Ruled Egypt Sends Expeditions South and East; 1527-1543: Ethiopia's Early Solomonic Period Ends; 1529-1574: North Africa Recognizes Ottoman Suzerainty; 1591: Fall of the Songhai Empire.

RELATED ARTICLE in *Great Lives from History: The Renaissance & Early Modern Era, 1454-1600:* Vasco da Gama.

September 27-October 16, 1529
SIEGE OF VIENNA

Outnumbered Viennese defenders held off a superior Ottoman force, establishing the westward limit of Ottoman expansion in Europe.

LOCALE: Vienna, Austria

CATEGORIES: Wars, uprisings, and civil unrest; expansion and land acquisition

KEY FIGURES

Süleyman the Magnificent (1494/1495-1566), Ottoman sultan, r. 1520-1566

Ferdinand I (1503-1564), archduke of Austria, r. 1521-1564, king of Bohemia, r. 1526-1564, and Holy Roman Emperor, r. 1558-1564

John I (John Zápolya, 1487-1540), king of Hungary, r. 1526-1540

Louis II (1506-1526), king of Hungary, r. 1516-1526, and king of Bohemia, r. 1509-1526

Niklas Graf Salm (1459-1530), leader of Vienna's defense

SUMMARY OF EVENT

When Süleyman the Magnificent became the sultan of the Ottoman Empire in 1520, he inherited a vast realm stretching from the Danube River to the Red Sea and from the Caspian Sea to beyond the Nile. It included Greece, the Balkans, Anatolia, Syria, Egypt, and most of Arabia. Protector of the holy cities of Mecca and Medina, Süleyman was the military leader of the Muslim world. Although tolerant of Christians and Jews, Süleyman planned to continue the expansion of Islam into the territory of European infidels. His disciplined infantry, the

Janissaries, was the only regular standing army in the sixteenth century, and Ottoman siege artillery was the most powerful in the world.

In 1521, Süleyman captured the Hungarian fortress of Belgrade, opening the way to the upper Danube. In 1522, he successfully ejected the militant Knights of St. John from the island of Rhodes, giving the Ottoman navy control of the eastern Mediterranean. Süleyman invaded Hungary in 1526 and destroyed the Hungarian army at the Battle of Mohács. King Louis II, two archbishops, five bishops, four thousand knights, and possibly twenty thousand soldiers died. Ottoman troops sacked and burned the Hungarian capital of Buda.

Archduke Ferdinand I of Austria attempted to claim the vacant thrones of Bohemia and Hungary, and the Bohemians elected him king. The majority of the Hungarian nobility, however, did not want a member of the imperial Habsburg family as king. Instead, they elected a Transylvanian prince, John Zápolya, as their leader. A minority of Hungarians chose Ferdinand. Both claimants were crowned king of Hungary and sent missions to Süleyman in 1527 seeking recognition. Ferdinand's envoy irritated

the Turks by demanding return of parts of Hungary conquered by the Ottomans, including Belgrade. The grand vizier sarcastically inquired why he did not ask for Constantinople as well. Süleyman recognized Zápolya as King John I of Hungary, promising him military assistance as a vassal of the Ottomans.

When Ferdinand sent an army into Hungary in 1528 and captured Buda, Süleyman decided to fulfill his pledge to aid John while also attacking Ferdinand's capital, Vienna. The Ottoman army assembled in the spring of 1529. Süleyman had some eighty thousand combat troops and five hundred cannons, including two hundred huge siege guns. On May 10, the expedition marched north. The spring rains were exceptionally heavy, however; rivers overflowed, sweeping away bridges, and roads became quagmires.

It took the Ottoman army two months to reach Belgrade. Oxen could not move the heavy siege guns over the rutted, muddy roads. Süleyman had to leave his big guns behind and depend on three hundred light cannons. When the Ottomans reached Mohács, John joined them with a troop of six thousand Hungarian Christians. The

Vienna, with an impressive cathedral spire in the background, before the siege. (Hulton|Archive by Getty Images)

Janissaries easily took Pest, terrorizing their enemies by massacring the garrison and many of the inhabitants of the city. A full month behind schedule, the main body of the army finally camped outside Vienna on September 27. The terrified defenders trembled at the sight of the huge army, convinced that their attackers numbered more than 300,000.

When Ferdinand heard that Süleyman was moving north, he frantically appealed to his Christian fellow monarchs for help. He received very little assistance. His brother, Holy Roman Emperor Charles V, was fully engaged in Italy, battling Francis I of France, and could not spare any troops. Charles did exert pressure on the Protestant princes of Germany to send aid against the Muslims, but few troops arrived. The most useful help came with the arrival of Niklas Graf Salm, a seventy-year-old professional soldier. He brought with him one thousand German pikemen, experts at handling twelve-foot spears, and seven hundred Spaniards equipped with the latest faster-firing wheel-lock muskets.

Ferdinand went to Linz, 100 miles (161 kilometers) west of Vienna. Although a higher-ranking aristocrat was nominally in command, Salm effectively took charge of the defense. He directed a force of twenty-three thousand infantry, two thousand cavalry, and seventy-five cannons. During the respite provided by the slow progress of the Ottoman army, Salm strengthened Vienna's fortifications. He repaired as much as he could of the decrepit city wall and had earthen bastions and wooden palisades erected behind the first wall. Three of the four city gates were sealed; only one was left operable to serve as a sally port for the cavalry. Buildings outside the walls were demolished, providing a clear field of fire for artillery.

When the Viennese refused Süleyman's surrender ultimatum, he ordered his three hundred cannons to bombard the city. The siege artillery he had been forced to abandon on the road would have cracked open the city walls, but the light field guns he brought with him did little harm. When the cannon mouths were elevated, however, the projectiles curved over the walls and damaged

A contemporary depiction of the Siege of Vienna. (Hulton\Archive by Getty Images)

many houses. The Viennese retaliated with a cavalry sortie that destroyed two gun emplacements, followed by a night raid on Ottoman tents. Ottoman sources record annihilating an Austrian attack and erecting a pyramid of five hundred heads for the sultan.

Unable to breach the wall with his artillery, Süleyman ordered miners to tunnel under it, planning to explode powder kegs and break the barrier. When a miner of Christian parentage defected and informed Salm of the plans, however, Salm organized counter-miners to head off the Ottoman tunnels, leading to bizarre underground battles between the two groups of miners. On October 5, mines exploded under Vienna's Salt Gate, opening a breach in the city's defenses. The Janissaries rushed to exploit the breach, only to be repulsed with heavy losses: Their scimitars proved ineffective against twelve-foot pikes and Spanish muskets. A few days later, a breach at the city's Carinthian Gate resulted in a similar defeat. The weather grew colder and food supplies were running low. Süleyman decided to try one final assault. The Janissaries launched several attacks on October 14, failing each time to widen an opening in the wall. Two days later, as it began to snow, the Ottomans broke camp and began their retreat to Istanbul.

Süleyman saved face as best he could regarding his defeat, claiming that he had never intended to seize Vienna, but had only sought to find and defeat Ferdinand I. Once it became clear that Ferdinand had fled and would not fight, Süleyman said, he had magnanimously lifted the siege to spare the Viennese people further bloodshed; therefore, the battle was really an Ottoman victory. When he reached Buda, his courtiers and King John congratulated Süleyman on his "victorious" campaign.

The Viennese, meanwhile, celebrated the Turkish withdrawal and claimed their successful defense had saved Europe from Muslim conquest. They asserted that, if Süleyman had captured Vienna, he would have wintered his army in Austria, attacked Germany in the spring, and established garrisons along the Rhine before year's end.

SIGNIFICANCE

The Viennese do deserve credit for their valiant defense. The main barriers to Turkish expansion into Europe, however, were the severe Balkan climate and the long distance between Europe and Istanbul, rather than the military prowess of the Europeans. Rainfall levels were high in the early sixteenth century, and winter came early. The viable campaign season lasted little more than six months. Süleyman, however, needed to return to Istanbul each year, because he also faced warfare with Persia that might compel him to suspend European operations and march his army eastward. In 1529, Süleyman's siege of Vienna lasted only twenty days.

Ottoman logistical problems were formidable. The army's advance guard regularly destroyed crops and settlements in areas under attack, denying food and other supplies to the enemy, but also preventing the Ottomans from living off the land. The farther the army penetrated, the more difficult it became for pack horses, wagons, and camels to move enough food, gunpowder, and missiles along the rutted, muddy roads created by the massive Ottoman army. After a successful siege, Süleyman might have left a garrison to hold Vienna, but the sultan and the main army would have needed to return to Istanbul through a ravaged countryside.

Süleyman invaded Austria again in 1532 but was held up for a month reducing the border fortress of Güns and never reached Vienna. In 1566, Süleyman died while besieging the Hungarian citadel of Szeged. The Ottomans besieged Vienna a second time more than a century later, in 1683, again failing to capture the city. Vienna became the high-water mark of Ottoman expansion into Europe.

An indirect but significant effect of Süleyman's campaigns upon European history was their aid to the survival of Lutheranism. Resources devoted by the Catholic Habsburgs to fighting the Ottoman menace could not be used against the German reformers, who might well have been overwhelmed by the full force of Habsburg military might.

—*Milton Berman*

FURTHER READING

Clot, André. *Suleiman the Magnificent*. Translated by Matthew J. Reisz. New York: New Amsterdam Books, 1992. Contains a brief description of the siege from the Ottoman point of view.

Fichtner, Paula Sutter. *Ferdinand I of Austria: The Politics of Dynasticism in the Age of the Reformation*. New York: Columbia University Press, 1982. Favorable account of Ferdinand's struggle with the Ottomans.

Godwin, John. "Siege of the Moles." *Military History* 18 (2001): 46-53. Detailed account of the defense of Vienna.

Goffman, Daniel. *The Ottoman Empire and Early Modern Europe*. Cambridge, England: Cambridge University Press, 2002. Places the Ottoman state and its military activity within the context of the sixteenth century European political system.

Maltby, William. *The Reign of Charles V*. New York: Palgrave, 2002. A concise explanation of Charles V's policies regarding Ottoman expansionism.

SEE ALSO: June 12, 1477-Aug. 17, 1487: Hungarian War with the Holy Roman Empire; 1520-1566: Reign of Süleyman; June 28, 1522-Dec. 27, 1522: Siege and Fall of Rhodes; 1526-1547: Hungarian Civil Wars; Aug. 29, 1526: Battle of Mohács; Sept. 27-28, 1538: Battle of Préveza; 1552: Struggle for the Strait of Hormuz; 1559-1561: Süleyman's Sons Wage Civil War; May 18-Sept. 8, 1565: Siege of Malta; 1589: Second Janissary Revolt in Constantinople; 1593-1606: Ottoman-Austrian War.

RELATED ARTICLES in *Great Lives from History: The Renaissance & Early Modern Era, 1454-1600*: Charles V; İbrahim Paşa; Süleyman the Magnificent.

1530's-1540's
PARACELSUS PRESENTS HIS THEORY OF DISEASE

Paracelsus rejected the dominant medical and scientific thinking of his day, arguing that disease was locatable within the body and was caused by external factors that disrupted body chemistry. He also argued against medicine's reliance on the work of ancient physicians and instead for methods of direct observation. He advocated concepts such as the mind-body connection, the power of suggestion, and the therapeutic presence of the physician.

LOCALE: Basel, Switzerland

CATEGORIES: Health and medicine; biology; science and technology

KEY FIGURE

Paracelsus (1493-1541), German physician

SUMMARY OF EVENT

Paracelsus made contributions to modern medicine that can be appreciated only when one understands the times in which he lived. The Middle Ages was an era ravaged by wars and widespread social and economic chaos. Health was precarious, and poverty, ignorance, and poor sanitation and hygiene contributed to epidemics that raged throughout Europe. God was considered the source of almost everything that happened: Disease was believed to be God's punishment for sin, and epidemics were blamed on demons or, in some cases, Jews.

Occultism, mysticism, superstition, and astrology dominated medical practice; magical potions, herbs, bloodletting, charms, and prayers—the treatments of the day—were administered according to the position of the planets. Wounds were packed with moss, and suppuration (the development of infection) was considered essential to wound healing. Even though the Renaissance had begun at the end of the fourteenth century, it had little impact on science initially. Dogmatism was entrenched, knowledge was stagnant, and observation and experimentation were discouraged. Medical education consisted of studying ancient texts by Galen (129-199) and Avicenna (980-1037), who were regarded as almost infallible. After the Roman Empire collapsed and the Middle Ages began in Europe, ancient Greco-Roman classical manuscripts were preserved by the Arab world. Avicenna's writings on Greco-Arabian medicine were translated from Arabic into Latin in the sixteenth century and dominated medical education for six centuries after his death.

Galen, the chief source of ancient medical writings, was scientific in many ways, but he also was superstitious; he worshiped Aesculapius, the Greco-Roman god of medicine, and believed in dreams, prophecies, and what would now be considered absurd folk remedies. The Hippocratic concept of disease was central to his teaching. According to Hippocrates (c. 460-c. 370 B.C.E.), disease was caused by an imbalance in the four humors, or body fluids—blood, phlegm, black bile, and yellow bile—which Galen related to the classical doctrine of the four elements—earth, air, fire, and water. (The Greco-Roman element "earth" was later expanded to include new elements—mercury, salt, and sulfur.) Each humor was associated with a different emotion: sanguine (blood), phlegmatic (phlegm), melancholy (black bile), and choleric (yellow bile). Treatment required restoring the natural balance in these humors. Paracelsus was the first to challenge the humoral theory of disease entrenched in medical education.

Paracelsus was given the name Philippus Theophrastus Bombast von Hohenheim when he was born in 1493. Because Humanists of the day often Latinized their names, Hohenheim later called himself Aureolus, from the Latin "golden" (crown), and Paracelsus, which may be a Latinization of Hohenheim or may mean "surpassing Celsus," a famous first century Roman physician. His father, Wilhelm of Hohenheim, was a physician to the poor in Einsiedeln, where Paracelsus was born.

After his mother died, the young Paracelsus and his father moved to Villach, a lead-mining community in Tirol, where his father practiced alchemy and taught in a school for mining and metallurgy. Paracelsus studied the basics of chemical analysis at the mining school and learned medicine, astrology, and alchemy from his father. (Alchemy, the study of secrets hidden in metals by nature, was the chemistry of the day. Its intent was to refine metal into purer states, with the goal of transforming base materials into gold.) In Tirol, Paracelsus became interested also in miner's disease (silicosis).

The young Paracelsus attended several universities in Europe but did not earn a degree, a possible cause of resentment by the medical establishment. He gained practical experience as a barber-surgeon in the army of the Spanish king Charles I (later Holy Roman Emperor Charles V) in 1515, and in the German Peasants' War in 1525 in Salzburg, where he later lectured to barber-surgeons. In his surgical practice throughout Europe, he insisted that wounds be kept clean and drained and denied the need for suppuration in wound healing. Physicians of his day had little respect for the new barber-surgeons, but Paracelsus's growing reputation for "miraculous cures" led to his appointment in 1526 or 1527 as town physician of Basel, where he was appointed to the faculty of medicine at the university.

Contrary to the current practice of relying on the ancients and lecturing in Latin, he offended the authorities by lecturing in the vernacular Swiss-German dialect. He publicly demonstrated his contempt for classical medicine by burning the works of Avicenna and Galen. His colleagues hated his innovations and forced him to flee Basel in 1528, not long after his appointment. He never gained another academic post and wandered throughout Switzerland, Austria, and Bavaria for many years, studying diseases and preaching his theories. He wrote numerous works on medicine, science, and philosophy during this time.

Paracelsus taught that disease essentially was related to chemical malfunctions in the body arising from external causes rather than to an imbalance of body humors.

He stressed the specificity of disease: Every disease was a different entity with a specific location in the body, a specific external cause, and a specific remedy. In contrast to his contemporaries, who valued the logic of ancient physicians, Paracelsus valued observation. He was the first to recognize the connection between goiter (thyroid enlargement) and cretinism (the congenital thyroid deficiency that results in deformity and mental deficiency), and his clinical descriptions of miner's disease, syphilis, and hospital gangrene are brilliant.

His experience with alchemy convinced him that minerals had specific healing properties, and he introduced many new mineral remedies (such as calomel) and advocated mineral baths. His treatment of syphilis with internal doses of mercury compounds foreshadowed therapy with the drug Salvarsan, which became the standard treatment for syphilis in the early 1900's, and he was the first to make tincture of opium (laudanum). He proposed classifying diseases according to the drugs that cured them.

Alchemy, astronomy, philosophy, and ethics were the pillars of his new medicine. His thinking, a curious mixture of modern experimentalism and old ideas—the occult, superstitions, alchemy, and astronomy—represented all the contradictions of his era. He never was able to separate magic from science. His colossal conceit, violent temper, and utter contempt for his fellow physicians made many enemies and won him few converts in his day, but after his death, his disciples, who came to be known as Paracelsians, spread his ideas throughout Europe and gained wide acceptance.

SIGNIFICANCE

Although unable to influence his own generation, Paracelsus had a significant impact on the next generation and on the future of medicine. His acceptance of the folk belief that "what makes a man ill also cures him," or "like cures like," persists into the twenty-first century in homeopathic medicine. He bridged the gap between medicine and surgery, advocating conservative treatment of wounds and chronic ulcers. His rejection of traditional medicine reduced the hold of Galenic medicine and opened the way to inquiry and experimentation in medicine.

Engraving of an alchemist and his work space. (Frederick Ungar Publishing Co.)

Engraving of an alchemist's busy, chaotic laboratory. (Frederick Ungar Publishing Co.)

His understanding of the importance of chemistry in nature and medicine advanced the application of chemistry in therapeutics. He contributed to the modern understanding that human beings are made of the same elements as the universe—salts, sulfur, and mercury—and relate to the universe as microcosm to macrocosm.

The influence of Paracelsus continues through the current "quiet revolution" in health care, in which many are questioning conventional therapy and turning to alternative practitioners and alternative medicines and therapies. Swiss psychologist and psychiatrist Carl Jung (1875-1961) was profoundly influenced by his writings as well and wrote an influential biographical sketch of his life and work.

—*Edna B. Quinn*

FURTHER READING

Debus, Allen G. *The Chemical Philosophy: Paracelsian Science and Medicine in the Sixteenth and Seventeenth Centuries*. Rev. ed. Mineola, N.Y.: Dover, 2002. Scholarly research describing the impact of Paracelsus's philosophy and work. Copious footnotes, no index.

Jacobi, Yolande, ed., and Norbert Guterman, trans. *Paracelsus: Selected Writings*. Princeton, N.J.: Princeton University Press, 1995. Useful anthology of direct quotations from Paracelsus's works. Illustrated with 148 woodcuts.

Jung, Carl G. "Paracelsus" and "Paracelsus the Physician." In *The Spirit in Man, Art, and Literature*. Translated by R. F. C. Hull. New York: Pantheon Books, 1966. Jung's insights into the essence of Paracelsus remain valuable. The second, longer essay is one of the best short introductions in English to Paracelsus's thought.

Paracelsus and Franz Hartmann. *The Prophecies of Paracelsus: Occult Symbols and Magic Figures with Esoteric Explanations* and *The Life and Teachings of Paracelsus*. Blauvelt, N.Y.: Rudolf Steiner, 1973. A comprehensive, two-books-in-one account (the second "book" was first published by Hartmann in 1887) of the life and thought of Paracelsus, highlighting his mysticism and occult leanings.

Stillwell, John Maxson. *Paracelsus: His Personality and Influence as Physician, Chemist, and Reformer.* Belle-Fourche, S.Dak.: Kessinger, 1997. An overview of Paracelsus's early life and medical theories and ethics.

Weeks, Andrew. *Paracelsus: Speculative Theory and the Crisis of the Early Reformation.* New York: State University of New York Press, 1997. Explores myths regarding Paracelsus's view of nature and scientific orientation.

Williams, Gerhild Scholz, and Charles D. Gunnoe, Jr., eds. *Paracelsian Moments: Science, Medicine, and Astrology in Early Modern Europe.* Kirksville, Mo.:

Truman State University Press, 2002. A wide-ranging anthology that includes an essay about his biography as written by his detractors, the role of gender in Paracelsus's model of truth, and a study of Renaissance representations of magic and demonology. Illustrations, bibliographic references, and index.

SEE ALSO: 1543: Vesalius Publishes *On the Fabric of the Human Body*; 1553: Servetus Describes the Circulatory System.

RELATED ARTICLES in *Great Lives from History: The Renaissance & Early Modern Era, 1454-1600:* Georgius Agricola; Andrea Cesalpino; Girolamo Fracastoro; Leonhard Fuchs; William Gilbert; Nostradamus; Paracelsus; Michael Servetus; Andreas Vesalius.

December 30, 1530
HUMĀYŪN INHERITS THE THRONE IN INDIA

Mughal emperor Humāyūn faced multiple political and military crises that demonstrated the precarious nature of the Mughal possessions in Transoxiana and Hindustan. He also bequeathed a culturally vibrant and politically secure kingdom that was unified by his son and successor Akbar.

LOCALE: North-central Asia and north and east India
CATEGORY: Government and politics

KEY FIGURES

Humāyūn (1508-1556), emperor of Hindustan, r. 1530-1540 and 1555-1556
Shēr Shāh Sūr (1486?-1545), sultan-i-ʿĀdil (king) of Hindustan, r. 1540-1545
Bahādur (d. 1537), sultan of Gujarat, r. 1526-1535 and 1536-1537
Ṭahmāsp I (1514-1576), shah of Persia, r. 1524-1576, and conqueror of the Uzbeks
Bābur (1483-1530), king of Kabul and Ghazni, r. 1504-1526, king of India, r. 1526-1530

SUMMARY OF EVENT

Humāyūn was born in Kabul to Bābur, the founder of the Mughal Empire of India, and Maham Begum, daughter of a distinguished Shīʿite saint. At Bābur's death in 1530, the Mughal Empire comprised part of north and north-central Asia, including parts of what are now Uzbekistan, Tajikistan, and Afghanistan.

During Bābur's terminal illness, Humāyūn's *wazir* (prime minister) hatched a plot at Āgra to get the dying emperor's brother-in-law, captain of a division of the Mughal army, declared successor. Luckily for Humāyūn, the *wazir* changed his mind at the last moment and had the heir presumptive proclaimed on December 30, 1530, four days after Bābur's death.

For the twenty-three-year old emperor, the throne of Hindustan was far from secure because of the machinations of his three ambitious and unruly brothers—Kamran, Askari, and Hindal—on one hand, and the dangers posed by the indomitable Rājputs, the Afghan adventurer Shēr Shāh Sūr of Bengal and Bihar, and Bahādur of Gujarat. The young emperor's habits and hobbies—some lamentable and some laudable—such as opium, art, and books, did not help him cope with the political and military exigencies plaguing his reign, which was made up of a series of military campaigns interspersed with short intervals of respite.

Humāyūn not only maintained his father's arrangements but even added the Punjab and Multan to Kamran's jurisdiction, giving the province of Sambhal to Askari, and Alwar to Hindal. Provincial administration, as devised by Bābur, consisted of a governor, a *diwan*, a *sikdar*, and a *kotwal*, supported by the local *jagirdars* (feudal landlords). The Hindus and the Muslims had accepted the Mughal supremacy as a matter of course.

The emperor's brothers and kinsmen, especially the

Mirzas of Herāt, all coveted the throne of Hindustan and conspired against him, though the softhearted Humāyūn dealt with most of them with unusual and dangerous leniency. Then, the Afghans, who had lost their hegemony in Hindustan to the newcomers from north-central Asia, remained resentful and mindful of any opportunity to overwhelm the new masters. Especially in the regions of Bihar and Bengal, they began consolidating their hold and preparations for attacking the Mughal headquarters at Āgra and Delhi. Moreover, the redoubtable Rājputs were yet to be subdued. Lastly, Bahādur, sultan of the prosperous region of Gujarat and an avowed enemy of the Mughals, was aiming to conquer the whole of Rājputana, lying dangerously close to the western borders of Mughal territory in northern India.

Humāyūn was successful in his first campaign against the Afghan ruler of Bihar and Bengal, Shēr Shāh Sūr. In the Battle of Dourah in October, 1532, he defeated the Afghans, and he besieged the fort of Chunar in November. Humāyūn, however, had to abandon his eastern campaign and move west, where he was triumphant as well.

Following his victories in the west, the emperor installed (1536) his brother Askari as the ruler of Gujarat and passed a considerable period of time at Mandu feasting and frolicking in celebration of his military victory. The appointment of Askari as the governor of Gujarat proved to be unwise because the heedless royal sibling was emboldened to make a bid for the imperial throne, though he was restrained by his elder brother and pardoned subsequently. Meanwhile, the people of Gujarat had risen in support of their former king Bahādur, who soon recovered his territories lost to the Mughals. Humāyūn submitted to the fait accompli and returned to Āgra in March, 1537.

The emperor lost not just Gujarat; he almost lost his empire in India when he confronted the rising Afghan power in the east. Since 1536, Shēr Shāh had been gathering strength in the east. An astute administrator and military commander, he recovered his territories in Bengal and Bihar. Humāyūn, along with his brothers Askari and Hindal, attacked the Afghan headquarters at Chunar in November of 1537 and captured the fort there in March of 1538. He was decisively defeated by Shēr Shāh at the Battle of Chausa, however, in 1539. While retreating to Āgra, the emperor was pursued by the Afghans and was beaten by them again, at Kannauj, in 1540. Humāyūn fled to Amarkot (Sind), and Shēr Shāh assumed the title of sultan-i-ʿĀdil, king of Hindustan. From Sind, the fugitive emperor wandered for three years seeking help from his brothers Kamran and Askari to retrieve

his throne, but to little effect. He moved farther west and sought shelter under the Ṣafavid emperor of Persia, Ṭahmāsp I, on December 28, 1543.

Shēr Shāh died in 1545 and was followed by his son Islām Shāh Sūr, who ruled until 1553. The Sūri Dynasty disintegrated after Islām Shāh Sūr's death. Meanwhile, Humāyūn had strengthened his position with Persian help, and between 1545 and 1555, he conquered Kandahar and Kabul, marched to Peshawar, and occupied Lahore. On May 29, 1555, he defeated the last Sūri usurper, Sikandar Sur, at the Battle of Sirhind. On July 4 of the same year, Humāyūn ascended the imperial throne of Delhi. Unfortunately, he did not live long enough to enjoy his hard-won restoration and died after an accidental fall on January 24, 1556.

Emperor Humāyūn was neither a great military strategist nor an astute statesman, but personally he was magnanimous, generous, and benevolent. He was well educated in Arabic, Persian, and Turkic languages and composed *ghazals*, *masnavis*, and *rubaisa*. He was an aesthete who admired the Ṣafavid school of painting and invited a number of Persian painters to Hindustan, who then laid the foundation of the Mughal style. Similarly, he was fond of Persian poetry and appointed a number of Persian scholars and poets to his court. A pious Muslim, Humāyūn constructed a citadel named Din Panah (refuge of religion) in Delhi.

SIGNIFICANCE

Humāyūn's reign demonstrated the volatile political situation of northern, western, and eastern India that the Mughal rulers had to confront while seeking to consolidate their hold over what were to them a strange land and strange people. Yet Humāyūn regained Hindustan for the Mughals, facilitated the triumph of Mughal cultural influence in Hindustan, and facilitated its political unification under Akbar.

—*Narasingha P. Sil*

FURTHER READING

Banerji, Sukumar. *Humāyūn Badshah*. Oxford, England: Oxford University Press, 1938. A scholarly study that examines Humāyūn's confrontation with Shēr Shāh in 1540.

Begum, Gul-Badan. *Humāyūn-nama (The History of Humāyūn)*. Translated by Annette S. Beveridge. Lahore, Pakistan: Sang-e-Meel, 1974. An important contemporary history by Humāyūn's sister.

Eraly, Abraham. *The Last Spring: The Lives and Times of the Great Mughals*. New Delhi, India: Viking Press,

1997. A long narrative of the lives and times of India's Mughal emperors, including Humāyūn.

Jauhar. *The Tezkereh al Vakiat: Or, Private Memoirs of the Mughal Emperor Humāyūn.* Translated by Charles Stewart. Reprint. New York: Augustus M. Kelley, 1969. An account by an intimate servant of Humāyūn. A major primary source.

Ray, Sukumar. *Humāyūn in Persia.* Kolkata: Royal Asiatic Society of Bengal, 1948. An authoritative account of a little known but significant phase in Humāyūn's life.

Wolpert, Stanley. *A New History of India.* New York: Oxford University Press, 2000. This readily accessible

and well-written text examines Mughal India and Humāyūn's reign.

SEE ALSO: 1451-1526: Lodī Kings Dominate Northern India; Early 16th cent.: Fuzuli Writes Poetry in Three Languages; Apr. 21, 1526: First Battle of Panipat; Mar. 17, 1527: Battle of Khānua; 1540-1545: Shēr Shāh Sūr Becomes Emperor of Delhi; 1556-1605: Reign of Akbar; Feb. 23, 1568: Fall of Chitor; Feb., 1586: Annexation of Kashmir.

RELATED ARTICLES in *Great Lives from History: The Renaissance & Early Modern Era, 1454-1600:* Akbar; Bābur; Humāyūn; Ibrāhīm Lodī; Krishnadevaraya.

1531-1540
CROMWELL REFORMS BRITISH GOVERNMENT

Thomas Cromwell came to power rapidly in England during the early 1530's. He helped Henry VIII seize control of the church from Rome and move it slowly toward a reformed Protestantism.

LOCALE: London, England
CATEGORIES: Government and politics; religion

KEY FIGURES
Thomas Cromwell (1485?-1540), chief minister of Henry VIII, 1531-1540
Henry VIII (1491-1547), king of England, r. 1509-1547
Cardinal Thomas Wolsey (1471/1472-1530), English religious leader and politician
Thomas Cranmer (1489-1556), archbishop of Canterbury, 1533-1556
Sir Thomas More (1478-1535), Lord Chancellor of England, 1529-1532
Catherine of Aragon (1485-1536), queen of England, r. 1509-1533
Anne Boleyn (c. 1500/1501-1536), queen of England, r. 1533-1536
Jane Seymour (c. 1509-1537), queen consort of England, r. 1536-1537
Anne of Cleves (1515-1557), queen consort of England, r. 1540

SUMMARY OF EVENT
Thomas Cromwell played a dominant role in English politics during the 1530's. When Cardinal Thomas Wolsey fell from power (1529-1530) as a result of his failure to negotiate an annulment of Henry VIII's mar-

riage to Catherine of Aragon, Thomas Cromwell, Wolsey's former servant and Collector of Revenues (1514-1530), emerged as the king's principal adviser. Cromwell, who was appointed a member of the Privy Council in 1531, advanced Henry VIII's interests and, for the most part, cooperated with the new religious leader, Thomas Cranmer, who was named archbishop of Canterbury.

Cromwell assisted Henry in securing his annulment from Queen Catherine, and he facilitated the arrangements for Henry's 1533 marriage to Anne Boleyn. He was also instrumental in formulating and implementing the Henrician strategy of utilizing Parliament as an instrument of the Crown. During 1533 and 1534, Cromwell managed to persuade Parliament to pass a series of enactments that provided essential support for Henry VIII's break with Roman Catholicism. That break was intrinsically linked to his marriage plans, which Henry justified based on his need for a male heir. In 1533, Parliament passed the Act of Annates, which suspended payments by the bishops to the pope. The Act in Restraint of Appeals, passed the same year, authorized the end of Henry VIII's marriage to Catherine of Aragon and permitted him to marry Anne Boleyn.

In the following year, Cromwell guided through Parliament the Act of Succession, which detailed England's official line of succession. The act proclaimed that the children of Henry VIII and Anne Boleyn would be the heirs to the throne, because their marriage was legal and legitimate. Mary, Henry's daughter with Catherine of Aragon, was declared illegitimate. Cromwell added a provision to the Act of Succession stating that all En-

Thomas Cromwell aided England's king Henry VIII in drafting the Act of Supremacy, which made Henry the head of the Church of England, and he helped rid the country of noncompliant Catholics, many of whom were beheaded. This illustration shows the beheading of John Fisher, the bishop of Rochester, in 1535. (Frederick Ungar Publishing Co.)

glishmen could be required to take an oath in its support. Anyone who refused would be declared a traitor. Also in 1534, Cromwell managed the Act of Supremacy through the Parliament. The Supremacy Act declared the monarch to be the supreme head of the Church in England and thus formalized the break with the Roman pope. In 1536, with the condemnation and subsequent execution of Anne Boleyn on charges of adultery (the equivalent of treason when the king was the victim), Cromwell managed a second Act of Succession declaring that the children of Henry VIII and the new queen, Jane Seymour, would succeed to the throne. Like her half sister Mary before her, Elizabeth, Queen Anne's daughter by Henry, lost her legal claim to succession.

Cromwell was instrumental in formulating the internal policy that led to the imprisonment and eventual execution of Sir Thomas More in 1535; More's removal provided Cromwell with further opportunities for ad-

vancement. In response to resistance from Catholic loyalists and some Catholic noble unrest in northern England in 1535-1536, Henry VIII's government suppressed the opposition to the king's policies; the pro-Catholic effort was led by Robert Aske and assisted by Reginald Pole (later cardinal and adviser to Mary Tudor).

The Catholic suppression was followed by two other significant religious developments in 1536: the dissolution of the smaller monasteries and the announcement of the Ten Articles of Faith. Cromwell was deeply involved in the seizure of the many monasteries that were operating throughout England. Henry VIII denounced these Catholic institutions as dangerous, seized their buildings and land, and either sold or gave away the land to his loyal supporters. In 1539, the larger monasteries were seized in a second wave of antimonasticism, and abbots lost the right to have seats in Parliament. The sale of monastery lands greatly replenished the king's treasury.

The Ten Articles of Faith were primarily the work of Archbishop Cranmer and a group of bishops, but Cromwell, as Henry VIII's key adviser, was involved in their composition. By this time Cromwell, in addition to serving on the Privy Council, had acquired the titles of the king's principal secretary, master of the rolls, and Lord Privy Seal; in these capacities there was very little that was not within his jurisdiction. The Ten Articles of Faith constituted an attempt to move England theologically toward the reformed Protestant positions. While the English church had formally eschewed Rome's authority and declared King Henry to be its supreme head, there had as yet been no substantive shift within the church away from Catholic doctrines. Writing the Ten Articles of Faith was a cautious first step, by omission, toward a mildly Lutheran form of Protestantism. No identifiably Protestant concepts were evident in the document. Rather, some essential Catholic doctrines—on the sacraments and the Catholic view of the Eucharist (transubstantiation)—were not mentioned.

Cromwell, representing Henry VIII, supported Cranmer in his efforts to move the country toward Protestantism. Henry and his court were largely theologically conservative, but they recognized that those who supported Catholicism were usually the friends of France and enemies of England, and, conversely, those political entities that were Lutheran were usually pro-English. The English breech with Rome, motivated by Henry's desire for a divorce rather than any ambition toward comprehensive reform, nonetheless unavoidably identified England as a Protestant nation. Because this identification was a result of circumstances as much as of ideology, however, the Crown's gestures toward true reform were somewhat halfhearted. When mounting opposition to the Ten Articles of Faith manifested itself during the next few years, Henry VIII and Cromwell withdrew their support from Cranmer. Instead, the Crown issued the Six Articles of Faith (1539), which supported traditional Catholic theology.

Cromwell's ascendancy in power continued in 1539, when he was named Lord Great Chamberlain of England. His sudden fall came the very next year, however, precipitated by Henry's short-lived marriage (January-June, 1540) to the German princess, Anne of Cleves. Cromwell initiated the plan for the marriage, anticipating that it would result in an English alliance with north German Lutheran states. When Anne arrived for the wedding, however, Henry was not pleased with her physical appearance. Once they were married, the status of their sexual relationship was also a source of dissatisfaction.

Henry was aware, moreover, of Cromwell's unpopularity at court and of accusations that Cromwell was a Protestant. Blaming Cromwell, whom he had recently named the earl of Essex, for his unhappiness, he turned on his loyal aide and ordered his execution in the Tower of London without trial.

SIGNIFICANCE

Throughout the period from 1531 to 1540, Thomas Cromwell reformed and developed the bureaucracy that came to serve as the backbone of the English political system. He sought to increase the efficiency of the bureaucracy and the accuracy and timeliness of information imparted to the king. This increase in bureaucratic efficiency served in turn to increase Henry VIII's control over his nation. Cromwell also enhanced Henry's power through an effective partnership with Parliament. The government became more centralized, finances were improved after the dissolution of the monasteries in 1536, and the king was able to survive the turbulence associated with his multiple marriages, turbulence that might well have doomed a less ably supported monarch. Historians have recognized Cromwell's efforts and have concluded that his policies and procedures constituted a genuine revolution in government that survived the chaos of the sixteenth century and served as the foundation of the modern English system of governance.

—*William T. Walker*

FURTHER READING

Beckingsale, B. W. *Thomas Cromwell: Tudor Minister.* Totowa, N.J.: Rowman and Littlefield, 1978. Still the best biography of Thomas Cromwell, Beckingdale's highly readable study portrays Cromwell as an effective and loyal servant of Henry VIII who, at times, was the victim of his own zealousness.

Bernard, G. W. "Elton's Cromwell." In *Power and Politics in Tudor England: Essays.* Burlington, Vt.: Ashgate, 2000. Reexamination and critique of G. R. Elton's biography of Cromwell. Includes bibliographic references and index.

Elton, G. R. *Policy and Police: The Enforcement of the Reformation in the Age of Thomas Cromwell.* Cambridge, England: Cambridge University Press, 1972. An important study by one of the most important Tudor historians of the past half century, based on extensive use of archives. Cromwell emerges as the dedicated enforcer of Henry VIII's policies.

Graves, Michael A. R. *Henry VIII: A Study in Kingship.* London: Pearson Longman, 2003. In this biography of Henry VIII, Cromwell is viewed as a talented but not too perceptive agent of the king, an individual who overextended his political reach and fell victim to his own overreaching.

Weir, Alison. *Henry VIII: The King and His Court*. New York: Ballantine Books, 2001. A well-written study that addresses the complex political and religious shifts that dominated Henry VIII's court throughout his reign; the focus on Thomas Cromwell during the 1530's portrays an ambitious and talented adviser who came to assume too much.

Wilson, Derek A. *In the Lion's Court: Power, Ambition, and Sudden Death in the Court of Henry VIII*. New York: St. Martin's Press, 2002. Wilson's study advances an interpretation of Cromwell as one of the disposable figures in the Henrician era; Henry VIII was always in command and discarded those who came under his broad interpretation of "treason."

SEE ALSO: Beginning 1485: The Tudors Rule England; Aug. 22, 1513-July 6, 1560: Anglo-Scottish Wars; 1515-1529: Wolsey Serves as Lord Chancellor and Cardinal; Oct. 31, 1517: Luther Posts His Ninety-five Theses; Apr.-May, 1521: Luther Appears Before the Diet of Worms; July, 1535-Mar., 1540: Henry VIII Dissolves the Monasteries; Oct., 1536-June, 1537: Pilgrimage of Grace; May, 1539: Six Articles of Henry VIII; July, 1553: Coronation of Mary Tudor; 1558-1603: Reign of Elizabeth I.

RELATED ARTICLES in *Great Lives from History: The Reinaissance & Early Modern Era, 1454-1600:* Anne of Cleves; Anne Boleyn; Catherine of Aragon; Thomas Cranmer; Thomas Cromwell; Elizabeth I; Henry VIII; Sir Thomas More; Jane Seymour; Cardinal Thomas Wolsey.

1531-1585
ANTWERP BECOMES THE COMMERCIAL CAPITAL OF EUROPE

The city of Antwerp became northern Europe's most important commercial, financial, and cultural center, taking over from the prominent port town of Bruges, whose Zwin River became ineffective as a trade route because of silt buildup.

LOCALE: Flanders and Brabant, Belgium
CATEGORIES: Economics; trade and commerce; cultural and intellectual history

KEY FIGURES
Maximilian I (1459-1519), Holy Roman Emperor, r. 1493-1519
Alessandro Farnese (1545-1592), duke of Parma, governor of the Spanish Netherlands
Jan Moretus (1543-1610), printer
Christophe Plantin (c. 1520-1589), printer

SUMMARY OF EVENT
Situated in the heart of Western Europe, the plains of Flanders lay at the crossroads of the trade routes that linked France, the Holy Roman Empire, and the North Sea. A buffer state against the Vikings, the county of Flanders was created in 864 after one of many divisions of Holy Roman Emperor Charlemagne's old empire. As French vassals, the counts of Flanders ruled Europe's most valuable, and perhaps most difficult to govern, fiefdom.

The most important, though not most populous, Flemish town was Bruges, at the time northern Europe's busiest harbor. Called the Venice of the North because of its many canals, Bruges was accessible to the North Sea after the great Dunkerque Floods of 1134 profoundly altered the coastline. The Zwin River, mostly an estuary, stretched to Damme, where the River Reie then connected the North Sea to Bruges two miles inland. Nearby Ghent's population was second only to that of Paris in northern Europe. Elsewhere, market towns, monasteries, and castles dotted the countryside.

Europe's economic functioning had changed fundamentally by the late Middle Ages. An interdependent economy arose with the advent of product specialization and the development of new trade routes. Integration meant that imports could offset local scarcities. Such dependence, however, could also easily spread one area's misfortune to another. For example, Flemish cloth, woven from local and English wool, was exported throughout Europe. Production was controlled by merchant guilds, composed of the city's elite traders, while highly disciplined, often militant craft guilds served as unions for virtually all urban occupations. Bruges, Ghent, Ypres, and other towns were able to win charters and rights from the counts.

Medieval commerce was based on a system of grand fairs and local markets. Linking northern and southern

Europe, a highly organized cycle of six grand fairs emerged in the French county of Champagne in the late 1100's. Visiting several markets on their way to fairs, traveling merchants journeyed considerable distances, employing couriers to ride ahead and advertise their goods. In the thirteenth century, the fairs declined with the development of Atlantic shipping and the rise of Bruges and other towns as permanent trade centers engaging in year-round commerce. The Hanseatic League, a powerful trade alliance of northern cities, extended from Holland to Novgorod in Russia and linked Britain and Flanders in the west with Asia's Silk Road in the east. Textiles, salt, wine, fish, furs, hemp, honey, oats, amber, timber, and pitch entered what was increasingly a world market. One of the most important Hanseatic League offices was in Bruges.

The existence of a cash economy and respect for contracts encouraged Flemish economic activity. Temporary joint companies became the norm for long-distance trade. Several merchants would lease ships to spread both their cargos and their risks. Italian bankers provided loans to merchants and nobles to finance both trade and war. Europe's most important bankers, the Medici family of Florence and the Fugger family of Augsburg, opened branches in Bruges and Antwerp, respectively. Amid the fourteenth century's constant inflation, speculation, and coinage debasement, bankers cooperated with broker-hoteliers to provide accounts, loans, investments, and even banknotes for local use to traders. Later bills of exchange were developed to transfer money. Courier services between the major commercial centers of northern Europe and Italy ensured that documents arrived safely and on time. Flanders became the hub of a "paper" economy unknown in much of Europe at the time. The financial services of Bruges were focused around the warehouses of Genoese, Florentine, and Venetian traders,

The port of Antwerp in a drawing by Albrecht Dürer. (Frederick Ungar Publishing Co.)

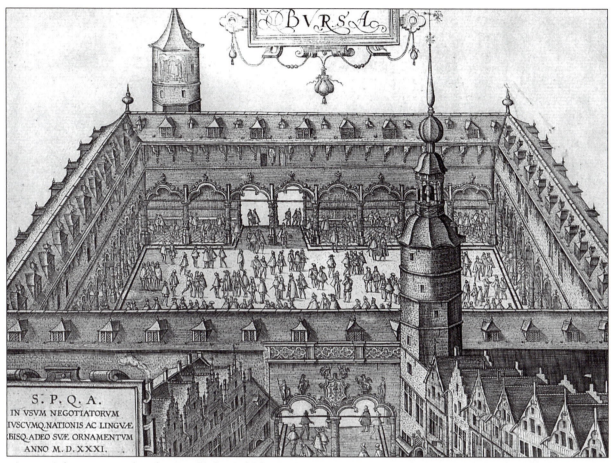

Antwerp's bourse, or stock exchange, was the model for stock exchanges throughout Europe. (Hulton|Archive by Getty Images)

where the Van der Beurse family ran an inn noted as a venue for transactions. In 1302, their inn developed into the world's first securities market and the family's name metamorphosed to "bourse" or "burse," the term for "stock exchange" in several languages.

However, Flanders had a rebellious reputation. In 1302, Bruges successfully challenged French domination. Ghent also rebelled frequently, most seriously under rich burgher Jacob van Artevelde, who made a treaty with England in the 1330's. Infighting within and among towns, however, sparked a long decline. When markets began to shrink after 1350, many merchants began to bypass the guilds by manufacturing their own products at lower costs. Rulers and traders alike began looking to Antwerp, the eastern neighbor of Flanders.

Arising from a Gallo-Roman settlement on the River Scheldt, Antwerp was a modest local-market town with a fairly important port by the seventh century. Rebuilt following Norse raids in 836, it became a margravate (bor-

der province) of the Holy Roman Empire in the late 900's. Chartered in 1291, the city was known for its abbey and later its vast cathedral, one of the largest religious buildings north of the Alps. In the thirteenth and early fourteenth centuries, the dukes of Brabant ruled the city and favored it with numerous commercial and political privileges. However, the duchy of Brabant was annexed by Flanders in 1356, and Bruges and Ghent rebounded. In 1446, the English Merchant Adventurers and other traders moved their operations from Bruges to Antwerp. By then, Bruges was in rapid decline as the silt-clogged Zwin became unnavigable, marking Antwerp's accession as the commercial capital of northern Europe.

The marriage in 1477 of Holy Roman Emperor Frederick III's oldest son, Maximilian I, to Mary of Burgundy, the only child of Duke Charles the Bold, led to Habsburg control over the Low Countries (modern Netherlands, Belgium, and Luxembourg). Unaccustomed to the region's deeply rooted civic traditions, Maximilian

489

ignored the rights of rebellious Flanders and offered inducements to foreigners settling in Antwerp and other Brabantine communities along the Scheldt and Dender, where support for him was strong. Eventually, the Burgundian inheritance passed on to Maximilian's grandson and heir, Charles V.

Known as the Burgundian city of the North, Antwerp became northern Europe's hub of commerce, shipping, finance, and culture. Influenced by Italian and Iberian merchants, it diversified beyond the traditional textile trade. Established in the 1400's, Antwerp's diamond industry expanded considerably after the arrival of Jewish artisans who were expelled from Spain and Portugal in the 1490's. In 1531, the city opened its bourse, the model for future stock exchanges.

Antwerp became also a center of northern Humanism. The city's printing presses produced some of the most important works of the age, including the first printed announcement of a major world event, Thierry Maertens's Latin translation of Christopher Columbus's 1492 letter announcing his New World discoveries. The era's most important printer was Christophe Plantin, whose masterpiece was the Antwerp Polyglot Bible. He and Jan Moretus, his son-in-law and successor, brought fortune to the city with a monopoly on the production of devotional books throughout Spain's vast empire. Artists Albrecht Dürer, Quentin Massys, Hieronymus Bosch, and Pieter Bruegel, the Elder, worked there. Thomas More wrote parts of his *Utopia* in Antwerp, where humanist philosopher Desiderius Erasmus and cartographers Gerardus Mercator and Abraham Oertel all spent time.

Antwerp, however, became the focus of conflicts between Protestant Holland and Catholic Spain. In August, 1566, radical Calvinists vandalized its cathedral and numerous other churches. Hatred of Spanish domination flared with the atrocious rule of the duke of Alva. In 1576, Spanish troops sacked the city, killing six thousand of its inhabitants. In 1584-1585, the Spanish, under Alessandro Farnese, captured Antwerp after a fourteen-month siege. The city lost more than half its population, including most of its commercial elite. The vital wool trade with England was disrupted. The Protestant Netherlands to the north closed off the Scheldt.

Economically devastated, the city nevertheless continued to flourish culturally until the mid-1600's, with painters Anthony van Dyck, Jacob Jordaens, Adriaen Brouwer, and David Teniers; anatomist Andreas Vesalius; and mathematician Simon Stevin. Musicians and composers, such as German-born George Frideric Handel (1685-1759) and England's Peter Philips (1561-1628) and John Bull (c. 1562-1628), played instruments made by Antwerp's Ruckers family. Among these notables, Antwerp's most distinguished citizen was painter and diplomat Peter Paul Rubens.

SIGNIFICANCE

After the Peace of Westphalia in 1648, the Scheldt was formally closed to navigation. Amsterdam's status rose, while Antwerp's dwindled to that of a provincial town. In 1863, the Dutch ended shipping restrictions on the Scheldt. Since then, apart from the interruptions of two world wars, Antwerp has experienced steady growth. During the twentieth century, it became the world's second busiest port, the world's most important diamond center, and a European "City of Culture" in 1993. Its cultural prominence has continued, too. Dutch artist Vincent van Gogh (1853-1890), French architect Le Corbusier (1887-1965), and Flemish novelist Hendrik Conscience (1812-1883) worked and studied there.

Meanwhile, Bruges, with its thousands of medieval buildings, has reemerged as a major tourist destination. More important, the histories of these cities reveal the origins of the world economy, capitalism, socialism, labor unions, banking, securities trading, industrialization, mass politics, mass production, and mass media.

—*Randall Fegley*

FURTHER READING

Bindhoff, S. T. "The Greatness of Antwerp." In *The New Cambridge Modern History*. Cambridge, England: Cambridge University Press, 1958. This chapter in volume 2 provides a good description of sixteenth century Antwerp.

Blom, J. C. H., and E. Lamberts, eds. *History of the Low Countries*. Translated by James C. Kennedy. New York: Berghahn Books, 1999. An excellent history of Belgium, the Netherlands, and Luxembourg, with much on Bruges and Antwerp.

Fegley, R. *The Golden Spurs of Kortrijk*. Jefferson, N.C.: MacFarland, 2002. Describes the significance of Bruges and other Flemish cities since late medieval times.

Nicholas, David. *Medieval Flanders*. London: Longman, 1992. This history covering late antiquity to Charles V's time is particularly good on Flemish economic and urban affairs.

Van der Wee, H. *The Growth of the Antwerp Market and European Economy*. The Hague, the Netherlands: 1963. A description of Antwerp's economic significance.

SEE ALSO: Early 1460's: Labor Shortages Alter Europe's Social Structure; 1490's: Decline of the Silk Road; c. 1500: Netherlandish School of Painting; July 26, 1581: The United Provinces Declare Independence from Spain.

RELATED ARTICLES in *Great Lives from History: The Renaissance & Early Modern Era, 1454-1600:* Hieronymus Bosch; Charles V; Albrecht Dürer; Desiderius Erasmus; Alessandro Farnese; Mary of Burgundy; Maximilian I; Gerardus Mercator; Sir Thomas More.

February 27, 1531
FORMATION OF THE SCHMALKALDIC LEAGUE

The Schmalkaldic League created a defensive military alliance among Protestant German states, whose rulers had adopted Lutheranism. The alliance was formed to defend against Holy Roman Emperor Charles V's demands that the states conform to the Catholic faith. The League, through the 1555 Peace of Augsburg with Charles, helped expand Lutheranism throughout Northern Europe.

LOCALE: Schmalkald (now in Germany)

CATEGORIES: Religion; organizations and institutions; diplomacy and international relations

KEY FIGURES

Philip the Magnanimous (1504-1567), leader of the Schmalkaldic League and Lutheran prince

Charles V (1500-1558), Holy Roman Emperor, r. 1519-1556

Elizabeth, duchess of Brunswick (Elizabeth von Brandenburg Hohenzollern; 1510-1558), protector of Martin Luther

John (1468-1532), elector of Saxony, 1525-1532

Ferdinand I (1503-1564), archduke of Austria, younger brother of Charles, and Holy Roman Emperor, r. 1558-1564

Francis I (1494-1547), king of France, r. 1515-1547

John Frederick (1503-1554), elector of Saxony, 1532-1547

Martin Luther (1483-1546), German Protestant leader

Maurice (1521-1554), duke of Saxony and son-in-law of Philip the Magnanimous

SUMMARY OF EVENT

Although the Diet of Worms had officially condemned Lutheranism, the movement developed strong support among princes and in the towns. Holy Roman Emperor Charles V, busy with other problems throughout Europe, could not take effective action against the Lutherans, although he had every intention of doing so when he could.

The unsuccessful Peasants' War in 1525 strengthened the Catholics by arousing anti-Lutheran feelings among the conservatives who blamed the new religion for the upheaval, and also among the radicals who believed that Martin Luther had betrayed the peasants. Taking advantage of the situation, the Catholic princes of northern Germany formed an alliance in 1525.

At the Diet of Speyer in June of 1526, however, the Lutheran princes also formed a solid front, and they were supported by some Catholics. The Archduke Ferdinand I, acting for his brother, Holy Roman Emperor Charles V, was forced to grant temporary concessions. Each prince was to be responsible for the religious settlement of his own territory "until a general council of the whole Church could be summoned." Various attempts were later made to modify this "Recess" of 1526, and for a long time it was regarded as merely a temporary agreement, but ultimately it was the settlement that prevailed in Germany.

On February 1, 1529, Charles V summoned another Diet at Speyer. Again, he did not attend himself, but he demanded that the concessions of 1526 be revoked and the Edict of Worms put into effect. Most members of the Diet were Catholics and voted to accept the emperor's demands. The substantial Protestant minority, however, protested the decision and insisted that the Recess of 1526 was a solemn agreement that could not be unilaterally revoked.

The Protestant princes were by that time under the unofficial leadership of Prince Philip the Magnanimous, who in the fall of 1529 sponsored the Marburg Colloquy, a gathering of Protestant theologians who met to create a common creed that would permit a united front against the Catholics. At the Marburg Colloquy, there was some animosity between Martin Luther and Huldrych Zwingli, the Swiss reformer who held different interpretations of the Eucharist. Luther believed in some form of Christ's bodily presence, while Zwingli considered the Eucharist to be merely a sign. When the northern German princes officially adopted the Lutheran position,

Lutheran prince Philip the Magnanimous, the principal organizer of the Protestant Schmalkaldic League, was imprisoned by Holy Roman Emperor Charles V after the league's forces were defeated by the Catholics of the Holy Roman Empire at a battle in 1547. (Hulton Archive by Getty Images)

most of the south German and Swiss Protestants withdrew.

At the Diet of Augsburg on June 20, 1530, the papal legates put strong pressure on Charles to enforce the Edict of Worms. At the same time, Philipp Melanchthon, Luther's close associate, worked hard to effect a theological compromise with the Catholics, a compromise to which Luther was strongly opposed. When Charles solemnly demanded that all Protestants conform to the Catholic Church by April 15, 1531, the Diet broke up and Protestant leaders began preparing for armed resistance.

At Schmalkald, on February 27, 1531, Protestant leaders formed a Protestant League, with Philip the Magnanimous as its unofficial head. Other members included Luther's patron John, the elector of Saxony, the brother of and successor to Frederick the Wise, and several other princes together with the cities of Bremen, Strasbourg, and Constance. The Zwinglians were excluded, but the

Strasbourg reformer Martin Bucer was able to persuade Luther to accept other south German Protestants whose theology was less radical than Zwingli's.

At the Diet of Nuremberg in the summer of 1532, the league was so strong that Charles was forced to agree to a truce that continued the toleration of Lutheranism indefinitely. Philip then took the offensive and defeated the imperial troops in 1534, restoring the Lutheran duke Ulrich to the territory of Württemberg. In north Germany, more princes and towns became Lutheran, including Ducal Saxony (distinct from Electoral Saxony), which had been a bulwark of Catholicism.

Philip hopelessly compromised himself in 1540, however, when he married a second time without divorcing his first wife. Other Protestant princes condemned him for embarrassing the cause. Philip was now at the mercy of the emperor for having violated a fundamental civil and moral law. Charles forced him to restrain the Schmalkaldic League, which became sharply divided between militant and moderate factions.

Lutheranism, in general, aided the creation of stronger states by ending the Catholic Church's dominance of laws, courts, and tax collections while providing popular support for government. Thus, Lutheranism was favored by many wealthy Protestant princes, some of whom provided protection and security from Catholic persecutions. Sometimes these protectors included women, such as Elizabeth, duchess of Brunswick, whose support was vital to the continued existence of Lutheranism.

The Protestant forces were still strong, however, and at another Diet of Speyer, in 1544, the emperor promised that all religious questions would be solved in the future by a German church council in which the Lutherans would be given a full voice. In 1545, another theological meeting was held at Regensburg, but when Catholics and Protestants failed to agree, relations between the two groups worsened.

The Diet of Regensburg of 1546 was boycotted by members of the Schmalkaldic League, and Charles finally withdrew his earlier concessions. He won over Philip the Magnanimous's son-in-law, the Protestant Maurice, duke of Saxony, and declared war on the league. At first, the Protestants were successful, but in April of 1547, Charles captured the Saxon elector John Frederick, son of the deceased John. A short time later, Charles also took Philip, under promise of good treatment. He forced several recently converted Protestants, including the archbishop of Cologne, to return to the Catholic Church, and he compelled other Protestant states to accept his authority.

At the Diet of Augsburg in 1548, Charles issued the Augsburg Interim, which granted concessions to the Protestants, including clerical marriage, subject to papal approval. Most of the Protestant leaders were forced to accept the document, but they considered it unsatisfactory.

The Augsburg Interim was largely ignored in the next few years, as resentment against Charles slowly built. In 1551, Maurice, angry at the continued imprisonment of his father-in-law, organized a new Protestant League with French support. The league was successful, and Charles was forced to release Philip and John Frederick and issue another recess. Disgusted with the German situation, Charles left for the Netherlands and gave Archduke Ferdinand the authority to conclude a settlement.

SIGNIFICANCE

The Schmalkaldic League's lasting significance was the settlement concluded by Ferdinand known as the Peace of Augsburg, signed in September of 1555. The German princes were permitted to choose between Lutheranism and Catholicism for their state churches. In addition, Catholic properties captured before 1552 were retained by their Lutheran conquerors. No concessions were made to other Protestant groups, such as the Calvinists and Zwinglians.

The League's formation, and its success with the Peace of Augsburg, helped to solidify the Protestant faith, generally, and to spread Lutheranism, specifically, in Northern Europe.

—*James F. Hitchcock, updated by Leslie V. Tischauser*

FURTHER READING

Armstrong, Edward. *The Emperor, Charles V.* Reprint. London: Macmillan, 1929. An older study that remains the standard biography of Charles. Armstrong provides a detailed, richly drawn portrait of the defender of Catholicism.

Brady, Thomas A., Jr. *Communities, Politics, and Reformation in Early Modern Europe.* Boston: Brill, 1998. This study of Reformation Europe includes both an account of the Schmalkaldic League's seizure of Brunswick-Wolfenbuttel in the 1540's and an overall assessment of the importance and effects of the league from a present-day point of view.

Cahill, Richard Andrew. *Philip of Hesse and the Reformation.* Mainz, Germany: P. von Zabern, 2001. Study of Philip the Magnanimous's rule and his effects upon both the Reformation in particular and Protestantism in general.

Grimm, Harold J. *The Reformation Era, 1500-1650.* 2d ed. New York: Macmillan, 1973. Grimm's work remains the standard text and contains an excellent general history of the period.

Holborn, Hajo. *The Reformation.* Vol. 1 in *A History of Modern Germany.* 1959. Reprint. Princeton, N.J.: Princeton University Press, 1982. An older interpretation of the Reformation period that emphasizes politics rather than religion as the motivating force in the formation of the Schmalkaldic League.

Hsia, R. Po-chin. *The German People and the Reformation.* Ithaca, N.Y.: Cornell University Press, 1988. Describes social conditions in central Europe at the time of the Reformation, including a brief description of the formation of the Schmalkaldic League.

Jedin, Hubert. *A History of the Council of Trent.* Translated by Ernest Graf. 2 vols. London: Thomas Nelson and Sons, 1961. Contains an excellent account of Charles's policies concerning the Lutherans and their effect on his attitude toward Church reform.

McEntegart, Rory. *Henry VIII, the League of Schmalkalden, and the English Reformation.* Rochester, N.Y.: Boydell Press, 2002. Study of Henry's alliance and consultation with the Schmalkaldic League, analyzing his partial incorporation of German religious ideology into his own theology and the nascent Church of England. Looks at both the evolution of Henry's religious thought and the wider political implications of that evolution.

Marty, Martin. *Martin Luther.* New York: Viking Penguin, 2004. Subtle and balanced portrayal of Luther's theology and its cultural context, explaining the importance of the debates in which he intervened as well as tracing the ultimate results of that intervention. Luther's character receives an equally nuanced treatment.

_____. *The Two Reformations: The Journey from the Last Days to the New World.* Edited by Donald Weinstein. New Haven, Conn.: Yale University Press, 2003. Posthumous collection of essays by one of the foremost Reformation scholars of the twentieth century. Revisits debates on Luther's anti-Semitism. Argues that medieval religious thought was essential to both Calvin's and Luther's understandings of Christianity.

Ozment, Stephen B. *Protestants: The Birth of a Revolution.* New York: Doubleday, 1992. The best up-to-date interpretation of the Reformation and the religious wars of the period.

SEE ALSO: Oct. 31, 1517: Luther Posts His Ninety-five Theses; 1523: Gustav I Vasa Becomes King of Sweden; 1555-1556: Charles V Abdicates; Sept. 25, 1555: Peace of Augsburg.

RELATED ARTICLES in *Great Lives from History: The Renaissance & Early Modern Era, 1454-1600:* Martin Bucer; John Calvin; Charles V; Gustav I Vasa; Balthasar Hubmaier; Martin Luther; Maximilian I; Philipp Melanchthon; Menno Simons; Philip the Magnanimous; Huldrych Zwingli.

1532
HOLBEIN SETTLES IN LONDON

Holbein was a major force in art and design during the sixteenth century. As court painter to Henry VIII, he produced portraits and book illustrations, as well as decorative objects for the royal household and for state occasions, that had far-reaching political implications.

LOCALE: London, England
CATEGORY: Art

KEY FIGURES

Hans Holbein, the Younger (1497/1498-1543), major artist of the northern Renaissance
Henry VIII (1491-1547), king of England, r. 1509-1547
Sir Thomas More (1478-1535), chief minister to Henry VIII, 1515-1530
Thomas Cromwell (1485?-1540), chief minister to Henry VIII, 1531-1540
Jane Seymour (c. 1509-1537), queen consort of England, r. 1536-1537
Anne of Cleves (1515-1557), queen consort of England, r. 1540

SUMMARY OF EVENT

The son of an important painter from Augsburg, Germany, Hans Holbein, the Younger, received commissions for religious images and stained-glass windows early in his career. His woodcuts were popular as well, especially the tongue-in-cheek *Dance of Death* series (pb. 1538), in which the skeletal figure of Death surprises people of all social ranks. Around 1515, he moved to Basle, where he became friendly with leading Humanists, including Desiderius Erasmus. Holbein drew the margin illustrations for Erasmus's *Moriæ Encomium* (1511; *The Praise of Folly,* 1549). The work's Latin title played on the name of Thomas More, Erasmus's closest friend, at whose house in London the book was written— the same house where Holbein was welcomed in 1526.

More was, at that time, a prestigious member of King Henry VIII's inner circle. In addition to making portraits of More and his family, Holbein painted, among other court luminaries, Nicholas Kratzer, the king's astronomer; William Warham, archbishop of Canterbury; and Sir Henry Guildford, comptroller of the royal household. Clues about each sitter's character, occupation, and taste were revealed symbolically through minute details such as flowers, ornate settings of jewels, and emblems of state, as well as accessories such as hatpins and buttons, which Holbein later would design as part of his duties as court painter. His portraits had the quality of icons: bodies set against backdrops of lush fabric, as in More's portrait, or an ethereally blue sky, as in the portrait of Mary Wotton, Lady Guildford, both done in 1527. It was this combination of naturalism and iconicity that made Holbein's art ideally suited for representing the grandeur of the Tudor court.

Holbein went back to Basle in 1528 to bring Erasmus the sketch of More's family, and while there he bought a house for his wife and children. It was also during this visit on the continent that he worked on the woodcuts for Martin Luther's translation of the Bible, and he painted a miniature of Luther's right-hand man, the conciliatory Philipp Melanchthon. With religious art under attack at the height of the Reformation in central Europe, however, Holbein decided to return to England, even though many of his former patrons were gone, casualties of the changing policies of Henry VIII.

Holbein settled back in London in 1532, and he quickly found work painting portraits of visiting dignitaries. These pictures abound in humanistic wit. For example, *The Ambassadors* contains numerous emblems of vanity, including an anamorphic trick image which, when viewed at an extreme angle, brings a death's head into focus. This "hallow bone" is also a sly pun on Holbein's name, *hohle Bein.* Such clever compositions were welcomed by members of the German community in

London, like Georg Gisze of Danzig, a Hanseatic merchant Holbein painted surrounded by objects of his trade, signs of his prosperity, and the motto "No Pleasure Without Regret." Holbein also worked on *The Triumph of Riches and of Poverty* for the German Steelyard's Great Hall in Blackfriars: The series consists of allegorical reminders of the virtues of hard work and company loyalty. This commission exemplified the propagandistic role played by artists of the day and, for Holbein, foreshadowed greater things to come at court.

Indeed, it was during his first year back in London that Holbein met and painted Sir Bryan Tuke, governor of the king's post, as well as secretary and treasurer of the royal household. The following year, 1533, he painted Thomas Cromwell, at whose prompting Henry VIII had made himself head of the Church of England so that he could, against the pope's decree, divorce Catherine of Aragon. The result was an extension of the king's prerogative beyond anything previously conceived, and it was Holbein who gave an image to that power, serving officially now as "the King's Painter." In 1535 he depicted Henry as King Solomon receiving homage from the queen of Sheba, symbolizing the Church's new subservience to the Crown. Also that same year, his title page for the Coverdale Bible shows Henry, not God, handing the Bible to the bishops.

Further expressions of the king's extended sovereignty can be seen in portraits of the royal family for Whitehall, as well as in the portrait of Jane Seymour, Henry's third wife, whom he married shortly after Anne Boleyn's execution for infidelity. It was for Jane Seymour that Holbein designed a magnificent golden cup set with pearls and diamonds, bearing the apt motto "Bound to Obey and Serve" and an intricately designed love knot entwining the initials "H" and "J." Jane Seymour died from childbirth complications in 1537. In short order, Holbein painted the long-awaited male heir, the future King Edward VI, his right hand raised in a gesture of blessing reminiscent of the baby Jesus in Italian Renaissance

Part of Hans Holbein, the Younger's, Dance of Death *series of drawings, in which the skeletal figure of Death surprises people of all social ranks and all ages, in this case the merchant, street vendor, infant or child, and the old man.* (Frederick Ungar Publishing Co.)

paintings, and, in his left, a golden rattle that unmistakably resembled a scepter.

Henry then speedily sent Holbein abroad to make portraits of prospective brides. This was a delicate matter for the painter and a potentially humiliating event for the sitter. Christiana of Denmark, for example, in 1538, would sit for only three hours. This incident sheds light on Holbein's remarkable skill at being able to sketch quickly for future reference. During this circuit he visited the duke of Cleves, who had two sisters, Amelia and Anne. Thomas Cromwell long had been urging Henry to ally himself with the Protestant nobility in the Rhine area, and so, in 1540, when Holbein returned with the portraits, Henry wed Anne. Six months later the marriage was annulled, ostensibly because Henry found her unattractive, calling her a "fat Flanders mare."

Holbein died during the London plague of 1543. At the time, he was working on a huge painting for the Company of Barber Surgeons (founded by Henry in 1540), showing the king, sitting in state amid a sea of faces, handing down a charter. This last, unfinished work continued Holbein's career-long tendency to mix the myth and the man for the betterment of the king's image. His work for the Tudor dynasty recast the terms in which art and history thereafter were to be conceived by court culture and played out on the world stage.

SIGNIFICANCE

Hans Holbein, the Younger, set the standard for future court painters, both in England and abroad. He played a preeminent role in advancing the conception of the artist as an integral part of a monarch's political arsenal, used to create a totalizing view of absolute sovereignty and dynastic security. A gifted draftsman and master manip-

King Henry VIII in a commanding portrait by his court painter, Hans Holbein, the Younger. (Royal Library, Windsor Castle)

ulator of symbols of power, Holbein was entrusted to design robes and seals of court, presentation swords, and emblems of state—all of which contributed to the overall aura of majesty while providing a sense of aesthetic continuity.

Although artists long had been commissioned to aggrandize dukes, popes, potentates, and kings, Holbein's place in the history of courtly image-making was both groundbreaking and unique. His representations of the king have remarkable staying power, and, in fact, continue to this day to characterize the image of sovereignty in general and Henry VIII in particular. Henry is best remembered as Holbein portrayed him, as a robust and healthy man, feet firmly planted, knees locked, hands defiantly on hip-belt and dagger, shooting a cool glance at the viewer. The power of Holbein's portraits does not come from blatant compositional manipulation, making the king tower over the other figures or loom far above the viewer. Such techniques were favored in continental courts, especially in Habsburg Spain and Austria. Holbein instead imparted Henry with power in less obvious and more effective ways, stemming from the artist's subtle use of tint, texture, and design to make the kingly image stand out, shimmering, as it were, with an inner splendor that cannot be contained by the body, no matter how strong, or absorbed by its costume, no matter how sumptuous.

—*William E. Engel*

FURTHER READING

Bätschmann, Oskar, and Pascal Griener. *Hans Holbein.* Translated by Cecilia Hurley and Pascal Griener. Princeton, N.J.: Princeton University Press, 1997. Important analysis of Holbein's entire corpus, ranging from general insights into the artist's place in political and artistic history to close readings of paintings to diverting anecdotes about specific incidents in Holbein's career. Includes illustrations, bibliographic references, and index.

Brooke, Xanthe, and David Crombie. *Henry VIII Revealed: Holbein's Portrait and Its Legacy.* London: Paul Holberton, 2003. Extremely detailed study of Holbein's portrait of Henry VIII, incorporating hightech analysis of the physical paintings, historical research on Henry's court and the artist's workshop, and surveys of the effects of the painting, both on Holbein's contemporary culture and on subsequent portrayals of Henry in literature, film, and television. Includes illustrations, map, bibliographic references, index.

Buck, Stephanie, and Jochen Sander. *Hans Holbein the*

Younger: Painter at the Court of Henry VIII. London: Thames & Hudson, 2004. Includes essays on Holbein as portraitist and on Erasmus's importance in his career. Useful glossary of key figures and ideas; 180 illustrations.

Langdon, Helen. *Holbein*. 1976. Reprint. London: Phaidon Press, 1998. Notes by James Malpas accompany forty-eight color illustrations in this representative survey of Holbein's lifework.

Lloyd, Christopher, and Simon Thurley. *Henry VIII: Images of a Tudor King*. 1990. Reprint. London: Phaidon Press, 1995. Monarch's biography told in terms of the works he commissioned to reflect and project his power as head of English church and state.

Warnicke, Retha M. *The Marrying of Anne of Cleves: Royal Protocol in Early Modern England*. New York: Cambridge University Press, 2000. Addresses ceremonial and diplomatic issues of foreign brides, as well as implications of this match and its dissolution.

Weir, Alison. *Henry VIII: King and Court*. London: Pimlico Press, 2002. Richly details the minutiae of daily life at court.

Zwingenberger, Jeanette. *The Shadow of Death in the Work of Hans Holbein the Younger*. London: Parkstone Press, 1999. Studies witty uses of "image and text" in Holbein's paintings, with special emphasis on emblems of vanity.

SEE ALSO: June 5-24, 1520: Field of Cloth of Gold; 1531-1540: Cromwell Reforms British Government; July, 1535-Mar., 1540: Henry VIII Dissolves the Monasteries; May, 1539: Six Articles of Henry VIII; 1558-1603: Reign of Elizabeth I.

RELATED ARTICLES in *Great Lives from History: The Renaissance & Early Modern Era, 1454-1600:* Anne of Cleves; Thomas Cromwell; Edward VI; Desiderius Erasmus; Henry VIII; Hans Holbein, the Younger; Sir Thomas More; Jane Seymour.

1532-1536
TEMMON HOKKE REBELLION

The Temmon Hokke Rebellion began with the armed takeover of the capital of Japan by Nichiren Buddhist militants in 1532. Kyōto, already partly devastated by earlier sectarian conflict, was largely destroyed by fighting in 1536, when the combined forces of other sects and the civil authorities put down this rebellion.

LOCALE: Kyōto, Japan
CATEGORIES: Wars, uprisings, and civil unrest; religion

KEY FIGURES
Hosokawa Harumoto (1514-1563), an adviser to the shogun
Rokkaku Sadayori (1495-1552), a warrior and the lord of Omi
Keō-bō no sō (fl. mid-sixteenth century), a priest who came to Kyōto to deliver Tendai sermons
Matsumoto Shinzaemon (fl. mid-sixteenth century), an affluent lay follower of the Hokke sect

SUMMARY OF EVENT
The Temmon Hokke Rebellion had its origins in a series of conflicts among the members of three Buddhist religious sects in the Kyōto area. The Tendai sect in Kyōto had a history going back to the eighth century, as old as

the capital itself, and a long tradition of defending its own interests, by force if necessary. The Jōdo Shinshū sect had originally been established in the Kyōto area in the thirteenth century, but its founder, Shinran (1173-1262), had been banished from the capital, and Jōdo Shinshū believers throughout Japan had become militant in the face of continued intolerance. The Nichiren sect, also known as the Hokke sect, was founded in the thirteenth century by Nichiren (1222-1282) and had been a militant organization from the outset. Each of these three sects was antagonistic to the other two in varying degrees, and each was centered on a main temple as its Kyōto power base.

The Enryakuji, the Tendai power base on Mount Hiei, had a garrison of warrior monks, or *sōhei*, trained in martial arts, who occasionally came down to Kyōto in force to assert temple interests. The Jōdo Shinshū clergy, whose main temple was the Honganji, were married rather than celibate, and their protective forces were made up of militant secular believers. Nevertheless, their temple was attacked and destroyed by the Tendai warrior monks in 1465. The number of Jōdo Shinshū converts continued to grow regardless of this, and they rebuilt the Honganji temple in 1481.

The Nichiren, or Hokke, sect succeeded in gaining many converts among the merchants and artisans in

Kyōto, where the sect established its main temple, the Honpōji, in 1436. Despite persecution and the destruction of the Honpōji by the Ashikaga shogunate in 1440, the Hokke faith in the capital continued to gain converts. A number of neighborhood temples were established, and the Honpōji was finally rebuilt in 1487.

The Jōdo Shinshū and Hokke sects were both winning an increasing number of converts and found themselves in a situation of mutual competition and antagonism. The well-established Tendai clergy and their conservative followers wished to preserve their traditional practices and privileges, and they opposed the expansion of both the Shinshū and Hokke sects in the capital. Various factions among the civil authorities in the capital also attempted to manipulate the struggles among the sects to further their own schemes and ambitions.

The Hokke followers in the capital included many merchants and local officials, concentrated in the southern third of the city. They were called *machi-shū*, "townsfolk," and formed associations for mutual defense, centering on their neighborhood temples, which they fortified. On the other hand, members of the Jōdo Shinshū sect in the capital were still recovering from their earlier expulsion by the Tendai warrior monks. Many Jōdo Shinshū believers in the countryside, however, were peasants who formed militant groups to assert their rights, and in some cases their demonstrations turned into successful rebellions.

Fearing that Jōdo Shinshū followers in Kyōto would ally with countryside militants, the Hokke *machi-shū* launched an attack on them in the summer of 1532. The *machi-shū* were supported by some of the aristocracy in Kyōto, as well as by some of the lords of domains surrounding the capital, who felt threatened by Jōdo Shinshū militants in the countryside. The aristocratic forces in Kyōto were led by Hosokawa Harumoto, the power behind the Ashikaga shogun. The forces in the countryside were led by Rokkaku Sadayori, the lord of Omi, who brought troops into Kyōto to assist the Hokke militants. Just as the Tendai warrior monks had done in 1465, they burned down the Honganji once more and drove away the Jōdo Shinshū followers. The aristocratic forces also joined the Hokke militants in attacking Jōdo Shinshū enclaves in the surrounding countryside. This coup by the Hokke forces, aided by the aristocracy, was known as the Hokke Uprising (*Hokke ikki*). The Hokke *machi-shū* remained in effective control of most of the capital for the next four years.

Since the Hokke militants in the capital had broad support among the local merchants, their Hokke regime managed to govern the city. Nevertheless, significant friction developed with the Tendai followers and with the aristocrats as well. The presence of the Hokke regime in the capital was a symbolic challenge both to the authority of the shogunate and the imperial court in northern Kyōto and to the traditional power of the Tendai establishment on Mount Hiei. These discords gradually united all these elements in mutual hostility toward the Hokke regime.

In the spring of 1536, when a Tendai priest from Mount Hiei, known only as the Keō Cloister Priest (*Keō-bō no sō*), came to the city to deliver sermons attacking Hokke doctrines, he was challenged by a Hokke lay preacher, Matsumoto Shinzaemon. Matsumoto overcame the Tendai priest in debate, intimidated him, and caused him to withdraw. The Tendai clergy on Mount Hiei were deeply offended, and tensions began to build. The same aristocrats who four years earlier had supported the Hokke militants against the Jōdo Shinshū followers now joined forces with the Tendai warrior monks to drive the Hokke forces out of the city.

At dawn on July 22, the Hokke forces launched a preemptive strike that put the Tendai forces temporarily on the defensive, but on July 27 Lord Rokkaku of Omi brought his troops into the city, attacking the Hokke temples and setting fire to them. All twenty-one temples were destroyed, and tens of thousands of Hokke followers were either killed or driven out of the city. The victors also took possession of large quantities of food, clothing, and other goods that had belonged to the Hokke merchants. The southern third of the city, which had been the Hokke power base, was almost entirely destroyed. The remnants of the Kyōto Hokke followers took refuge in the Ōsaka area, until hostility against them eased enough for them to begin returning to the capital six years later. The Nichiren sect was never again capable of wielding significant power in the capital, however.

SIGNIFICANCE

As a result of the Temmon Hokke Rebellion in 1532 and its suppression in 1536, the Nichiren faith was never again able to achieve the influence it had briefly imposed upon the aristocracy and the merchant class in Kyōto. The Jōdo Shinshū faith gradually regained popularity in the capital and even was favored by the military overlord Oda Nobunaga, who ended the power of both the aristocratic elements and the Tendai forces in the capital. In 1571, Nobunaga destroyed the entire Mount Hiei complex and killed many of the Tendai clergy there.

Under the Tokugawa shogunate, starting in 1603, the Tendai sect regained much of its traditional position in

Kyōto, and the various Buddhist sects and their temples became institutionalized under state supervision. The result was the end of most sectarian strife among Buddhist sects.

—*Michael McCaskey*

FURTHER READING

Berry, Mary Elizabeth. *The Culture of Civil War in Kyōto*. Berkeley: University of California Press, 1994. An in-depth account and analysis of the culture of constant tension created by a century of social and religious upheaval and constant strife in Kyōto, during the Sengoku Jidai, or Warring States period (1477-1600).

McMullin, Neil. *Buddhism and the State in Sixteenth-Century Japan*. Princeton, N.J.: Princeton University Press, 1984. A scholarly study of the political relationships among the various Buddhist sects in pre-Tokugawa Japan, and their mutual interactions with civil and military state power.

Plutschow, Herbert E. *Historical Kyōto: With Illustrations and Guide Maps*. Tokyo: Japan Times, 1983. A semipopular account of Japan's ancient capital, useful for placing historical events in their geographical context.

Richie, Donald. *The Temples of Kyōto*. Tokyo: Charles E. Tuttle, 1995. An illustrated cultural and historical guide to the major Buddhist temples of Kyōto.

Turnbull, Stephen. *Japanese Warrior Monks AD 949-1603*. Oxford, England: Osprey, 2003. A popular study of the role that armed Buddhist monks, or *sōhei*, played in pre-Tokugawa Japan.

SEE ALSO: 1457-1480's: Spread of Jōdo Shinshū Buddhism; 1467-1477: Ōnin War; 1477-1600: Japan's "Age of the Country at War"; Mar. 5, 1488: Composition of the *Renga* Masterpiece *Minase sangin hyakuin*; Beginning 1513: Kanō School Flourishes; 1549-1552: Father Xavier Introduces Christianity to Japan; 1550's-1567: Japanese Pirates Pillage the Chinese Coast; 1550-1593: Japanese Wars of Unification; Sept., 1553: First Battle of Kawanakajima; June 12, 1560: Battle of Okehazama; 1568: Oda Nobunaga Seizes Kyōto; 1587: Toyotomi Hideyoshi Hosts a Ten-Day Tea Ceremony; 1590: Odawara Campaign; 1592-1599: Japan Invades Korea; 1594-1595: Taikō Kenchi Survey; Oct., 1596-Feb., 1597: *San Felipe* Incident; Oct. 21, 1600: Battle of Sekigahara.

RELATED ARTICLES in *Great Lives from History: The Renaissance & Early Modern Era, 1454-1600:* Hōjō Ujimasa; Hosokawa Gracia; Oda Nobunaga; Ōgimachi; Oichi; Sesshū; Toyotomi Hideyoshi.

1530's

1532-1537
PIZARRO CONQUERS THE INCAS IN PERU

Pizarro's conquering of the Incas extended Spanish colonial control in the New World and brought an end to the vast Inca Empire.

LOCALE: Peru
CATEGORIES: Expansion and land acquisition; wars, uprisings, and civil unrest; colonization

KEY FIGURES

Francisco Pizarro (c. 1478-1541), Spanish conquistador
Atahualpa (c. 1502-1533), last Inca king, r. 1532-1533, and half brother of Huáscar
Huáscar (c. 1495-1532), Inca king, r. 1525-1532, and half brother of Atahualpa
Diego de Almagro (1475-1538), Pizarro's partner and enemy
Hernando de Soto (c. 1496-1542), one of Pizarro's lieutenants

SUMMARY OF EVENT

Spanish conquistadores marauding through Central America to the Pacific received reports of Birú, a rich, powerful indigenous culture to the south. Among those captivated by the rumor was one of Governor Pedro Arias d'Ávila's chief lieutenants, Francisco Pizarro. He formed a partnership with Diego de Almagro, a business associate, and a priest, Hernando de Luque. The three were to share equally in the costs and profits of the endeavor to seize the wealth of Birú, or Peru.

While Almagro gathered more men and supplies, Pizarro sailed in November, 1524. He reached the San Juan River, plundered gold and silver artifacts, and then returned to Panama. He set sail again in 1526 and, despite great hardship, reached Tumbes, an Incan coastal city near what is now the Peru-Ecuador border. Its wealth and splendor convinced Pizarro the rumors and reports about Peru were correct, and he returned to Panama to organize an expedition of conquest. First, however, he went to Spain and secured a charter from Emperor Charles V, authorizing him to undertake the expedition and granting him, Pizarro, most of the rewards, if it proved successful. He also discussed with Hernán Cortés the conquest of Mexico and the Aztecs (1519-1521). Accompanied by several of his half brothers, Pizarro returned to Panama. Convinced Pizarro had cheated him when obtaining the charter, Almagro could do little except cooperate and contemplate revenge.

In late 1530, Pizarro set out for Peru with 180 men and 30 horses. They plundered the coast of Ecuador before reaching Tumbes in February, 1532. The Spaniards discovered the city partially destroyed in a civil war among the Incas. Huayna Capac, the last great Inca ruler (r. 1493-1525), had died in 1525, probably from small-pox that spread from the Caribbean and devastated the Andean peoples. Two of his sons, half brothers Huáscar and Atahualpa, fought to succeed their father. They represented rival factions: Huáscar's power centered in Cuzco, the traditional Inca capital, while Atahualpa's power base was Quito, recently added to Tahuantinsuyu (four quarters), as the Incas called their empire. Furthermore, the Incas had created Tahuantinsuyu through conquest, and many of the recently subjugated people were restless. Pizarro was ready to exploit the dissension.

With reinforcements from Panama, Pizarro departed Tumbes in May of 1532, moving into the mountains toward Atahualpa's army. Having defeated and captured Huáscar, Atahualpa knew the strangers' movements and might have destroyed Pizarro's men in a mountainous ambush. Perhaps overconfident, he allowed them to reach Cajamarca, where he was encamped. Pizarro sent two squads, headed by Hernando de Soto and Hernando Pizarro, to the South American Indian camp. Using as translators South American Indians seized during Pizarro's second expedition, the emissaries conversed with Atahualpa, who agreed to visit the Spaniards in Cajamarca.

The following afternoon, May 16, Atahualpa traveled into the town, carried on a litter and accompanied by several thousand bodyguards. Pizarro sent out Father Diego de Valverde, who explained through a translator to Atahualpa the requirement (a legalism that asserted Spain's sovereignty over the New World by way of papal donation). When Atahualpa haughtily rejected Valverde's demands, Spaniards stormed out of buildings around the square where they had been hidden. They captured Atahualpa and slaughtered his men.

Through his captive, Pizarro wielded great influence in the Inca Empire. Atahualpa's own faction grudgingly obeyed the captive's orders, fearful for his safety. To

Francisco Pizarro and his troops, before conquering the Inca of Peru. (R. S. Peale and J. A. Hill)

them he was not only the supreme ruler of a highly centralized regime but also divine. Worried the Spaniards might ally with his defeated half brother, Atahualpa secretly ordered Huáscar's execution. Eager to take revenge on Atahualpa, Huáscar's supporters assisted the Spaniards.

Away from Cajamarca, Atahualpa's lieutenants struggled to maintain control over the Inca Empire. Hoping to buy his own freedom, Atahualpa offered to fill a room once with gold and again with silver. While llama trains brought treasure to Cajamarca, the Spaniards reconnoitered. In early 1533, Hernando Pizarro looted the great religious shrine at Pachacámac, near modern-day Lima. Another contingent went to Cuzco, the Inca capital. By June, Atahualpa had amassed the promised ransom, making rich men out of all the Spaniards present

Atahualpa, after his capture, kneels before Francisco Pizarro. (Hulton|Archive by Getty Images)

at his capture, but Pizarro refused to free him. Accusing Atahualpa of murdering Huáscar and organizing a rebellion, Pizarro executed his prisoner on July 26, 1533. Sentenced to be burned alive, the Inca converted to Catholicism and was instead strangled. Hernando Pizarro left for Spain to pay the king's fifth of the treasure and to inform Charles V of their exploits.

Reinforced by 150 men under Almagro, the Spaniards set out for Cuzco. At Jauja Atahualpa's supporters attacked, but Spanish horsemen overwhelmed them. In open terrain, Andean soldiers armed primarily with clubs and slingshots were no match for horses and Spanish steel swords and body armor. At Vilcaconga on November 8, the advance guard commanded by Hernando de Soto was ambushed, but then saved by the arrival of Almagro. They fought another battle outside Cuzco before Pizarro's forces entered the city on November 15, 1533.

The Spanish held Cuzco but had not pacified Tahuantinsuyu. They installed Manco Inca as puppet ruler in December, 1533. Drawn from Panama by the fabulous reports, more Spaniard reinforcements arrived, including those led by Pedro de Alvarado, a captain under Hernán Cortés during the conquest of Mexico. During the first half of 1534, Sebastián Benalcázar conquered Quito. On January 6, 1535, Pizarro founded the City of the Kings, or Lima, on the coast for easier communication with Pan-

ama. He and Almagro tried to resolve their differences. Pizarro assigned his partner the uncharted lands south of Cuzco, and in July of 1535, Almagro led a disappointing expedition into Chile.

Meanwhile, Manco Inca grew tired of Spanish abuse and exploitation. Slipping out of Cuzco, he organized a massive army in 1536 and laid siege to Cuzco, held by two hundred Spaniards. From Lima, Pizarro sent several relief expeditions, but they were ambushed before reaching Cuzco. The native Indians attacked Lima itself but could not take it. Neither could they capture Cuzco, despite their overwhelming numbers. The fighting grew more and more bitter, the atrocities of each side denying the essential humanity of the other. After several months' siege Manco's army withdrew. Ethnic rivalries among the indigenous peoples weakened Manco's Great Rebellion, and, indeed, some of them remained firm Spanish allies.

SIGNIFICANCE

The failure of Manco's Great Rebellion sealed the Spanish conquest of Peru, although it did not bring peace to the Andes.

Almagro seized Cuzco from the Pizarros in 1537 but was defeated at Las Salinas and executed on July 8, 1538. In retaliation, Almagro's men murdered Francisco Pizarro in 1541.

Manco Inca launched another rebellion in 1539. He then retreated into the mountains north of Cuzco and set up an independent kingdom at Vilcapampa, which survived until destroyed by the Spaniards in 1572.

To assert royal control over the Andes, Charles V sent Blasco Núñez de Vela to Peru as viceroy with orders to limit the conquistadors' exploitation of indigenous peoples. His arrival in 1544 touched off a rebellion against the Crown. The viceroy died in the rebellion. Only in the mid-1550's did royal authority over Peru become more secure.

—*Kendall W. Brown*

FURTHER READING

Abercrombie, Thomas A. *Pathways of Memory and Power: Ethnography and History Among an Andean People.* Madison: University of Wisconsin Press, 1998. A groundbreaking historical and anthropological study detailing the social memory and inherited rituals—hybrids of indigenous and European custom—of the Andean people. Discusses Pizarro's conquest of the region. Illustrations, maps, bibliographic references, glossary, and index.

Adams, Charles. "How Cortés and Pizarro Found That Taxes Were the Chink in the Armor of the Aztec and Inca Rulers." In *For Good and Evil: The Impact of Taxes on the Course of Civilization.* 2d ed. Lanham, Md.: Madison Books, 1999. Study of one of the factors that enabled Pizarro to defeat the Incas and take control of their civilization. Includes bibliographic references and index.

Beardsell, Peter. *Europe and Latin America: Returning the Gaze.* New York: Manchester University Press, 2000. Collection of indigenous Latin American reactions to encounters with Europe, including Inca perspectives on Pizarro. Includes illustrations, bibliographic references, and index.

Davies, Nigel. *The Incas.* Niwot: University of Colorado Press, 1995. A readable and rigorous study of the Inca Empire from its legend-shrouded origins to its catastrophic collapse.

Guilmartin, John F., Jr. "The Cutting Edge: An Analysis of the Spanish Invasion and Overthrow of the Inca Empire, 1532-1539." In *Transatlantic Encounters: Europeans and Andeans in the Sixteenth Century,* edited by Kenneth J. Andrien and Rolena Adorno. Berkeley: University of California Press, 1991. Argues that although the Incas were adaptive and re-sourceful, Spanish technological superiority proved decisive to the military outcome.

Hemming, John. "Atahualpa and Pizarro." In *The Peru Reader: History, Culture, and Politics,* edited by Orin Starn, Carlos Iván Degregori, and Robin Kirk. Durham, N.C.: Duke University Press, 1995. Account of the meeting between Pizarro and Atahualpa at Cajamarca, attempting to evaluate the success or failure of attempts at communication and mutual understanding. Illustrations, map, bibliographic references, index.

_____. *The Conquest of the Incas.* New York: Harcourt Brace Jovanovich, 1970. Reprint. San Diego, Calif.: Harvest Books, 2003. The best narrative account in English of the conquest, based on Spanish chronicles and archival sources.

Prescott, William H. *The Conquest of Peru.* Rev. ed. New York: New American Library, 1961. A classic narrative, first published in 1847, that still makes rewarding reading, especially on the Spanish side of the conquest. Early chapters on Inca culture are more outdated.

Spalding, Karen. *Huarochirá: An Andean Society Under Inca and Spanish Rule.* Stanford, Calif.: Stanford University Press, 1984. Places the conquest in ethnohistorical context by explaining the nature of Andean culture prior to the rise of Inca power, the changes imposed by the Incas, and the consequences of Spanish victory.

Varón Gabai, Rafael. *Francisco Pizarro and His Brothers: The Illusion of Power in Sixteenth Century Peru.* Translated by Javier Flores Espinoza. Norman: University of Oklahoma Press, 1997. Study of the short-lived dominance of Pizarro and his family in Peru. Interprets the Pizarros' project as essentially a private business enterprise and examines the relationship of the business both to the government and public funds of Spain and to indigenous groups in South America. Includes illustrations, bibliography, and index.

SEE ALSO: 1471-1493: Reign of Topa Inca; 1493-1525: Reign of Huayna Capac; 1500-1530's: Portugal Begins to Colonize Brazil; 1525-1532: Huáscar and Atahualpa Share Inca Rule.

RELATED ARTICLES in *Great Lives from History: The Renaissance & Early Modern Era, 1454-1600:* José de Acosta; Atahualpa; Huáscar; Pachacuti; Francisco Pizarro; Hernando de Soto.